Hopewell Village

*The Dynamics of
a Nineteenth Century
Iron-Making Community*

Hopewell Village

*The Dynamics of
a Nineteenth Century
Iron-Making Community*

JOSEPH E. WALKER

Philadelphia
University of Pennsylvania Press

To
Rachael

Library of Congress Catalogue Card Number: 64–24506

First Pennsylvania Paperback edition 1974

ISBN: 0-8122-1072-7

Printed in the United States of America

Acknowledgments

ONE OF THE PLEASURES OF RESEARCH IS THE DISCOVERY OF the large number of persons who will give many hours of their valuable time for no apparent reason except that they are kind, generous and helpful to aspiring writers.

The author is deeply grateful for the detailed and valuable suggestions made by Dr. Harry M. Tinkcom and Dr. John M. Mickelson in the development of this study. He is particularly indebted to Dr. James A. Barnes for the constant guidance and help and the many hours of constructive criticism which he gave during the weekend visits to his home.

The writer is also debtor to the personnel of the Hopewell Village National Historical Site for their assistance with the research work. Mr. Robert Ronsheim and Mr. Joseph Prentice first suggested a history of Hopewell Furnace; Superintendent Benjamin Zerbey, Mrs. Charlotte Fairbairn and Mr. Leland Abel gave valuable aid at several critical points; and Mr. Earl Heydinger generously shared the product of his own research and worked almost daily to fill in needed areas of background. Mr. Ronald Lee and Mr. Frank Barnes of the Philadelphia Regional Office of the National Park Service were also most cooperative.

Valued help on certain technical matters was supplied by Dr. C. M. Myers, Dr. and Mrs. V. A. Champa, Dr. David Voigt, Mr. William Caulwell, Mr. Henry Kauffman, Col. Wayne Homan, Mrs. Freas Downing, Mr. Richard Murr, Mr. Edward Smuck, Mrs. Esther Turner and Mrs. Betty Meyers. Much assistance was also received from the persons who are responsible for the records and manuscripts at the Berks County Historical Society, Berks County Court House, Chester County Historical Society, Historical Society of Pennsylvania, Lancaster County Historical Society, Lancaster County Law Library and Millersville State College Library. All photographs unless otherwise specified are reproduced through the courtesy of the National Park Service.

Finally the author is under obligation to his wife Rachael and sons Bob, Sam and Wally for absorbing his frustrations and sharing his enthusiasms and particularly to Sam for his help with tabulating the statistical data and to Rachael for her suggestions for improvements on style and form.

Millersville State College
Millersville, Pa.

J.E.W.

Contents

PART SIX : THE SOCIAL VILLAGE

Tables

9

Introduction

A TRAVELER DRIVING ALONG UNITED STATES HIGHWAY 22 IN THE Lehigh Valley of Southeastern Pennsylvania is impressed with the miles of buildings, furnaces and yards of the Bethlehem Steel Company. Thousands of persons are employed at these works and support the businesses of prosperous cities and towns. If this same traveler crosses into the Schuylkill Valley, a few miles to the south, he may find his way to quite a different kind of iron works. At the Hopewell Village restoration of the National Park Service is the single stack of a small iron smelting furnace with its cast house, ironmaster's mansion and workers' homes. Here a few furnace men produced about a thousand tons of cast iron per year and helped to support several hundred workers and families in auxiliary occupations.

The visitor may see little resemblance between the two industrial sites. But until after the middle of the nineteenth century, Hopewell Furnace, in Southern Berks County, was one of several hundred similar works scattered through the forests of Pennsylvania from the Delaware to the Ohio, representing a major share of America's primary iron producing industry. From these hearths flowed the molten metal to be shaped into pigs and hundreds of cast iron products for homes and industries of the new nation.

Hopewell had no particular eminence among the many similar smelting works. It missed by more than half a century the right to claim the distinction which Colebrookdale bears as the first Pennsylvania furnace. Warwick Furnace had a larger capacity and a longer history. Joanna Furnace was in

11

operation after Hopewell's last blast had ended. Hopewell records make no note of such distinguished visitors as George Washington and Benjamin Franklin, who were reported to have accepted the hospitality of nearby Warwick Furnace. Hopewell had its periods of prosperity and its bankruptcies. So did many other furnaces. Hopewell made good iron and attracted users in distant markets. So did its neighbors.

Nor is it possible at this time to assert that Hopewell was typical of Pennsylvania furnaces of its period. Until a number of studies have been made of other furnaces, no such judgment can be made. It is also not possible to write a full history of the Pennsylvania iron industry in the nineteenth century until the records of other furnaces and forges have been researched. Comparisons have been made in this book with other furnaces and forges in a few instances where it seemed that the Hopewell story was made more meaningful by so doing. But no comparative research in depth was attempted.

Perhaps the greatest advantage in selecting Hopewell as the subject for research of an iron–making community was the opportunity to use the extremely valuable collection of documents and microfilm available to students and scholars at the Hopewell Village National Historic Site. Journals, ledgers, time books, molders' books, transportation books, letters and business papers are in this collection which has been compiled by the professional staff members of the National Park Service. Facilities for its use are made available through the employees on duty at the site to the fullest extent compatible with their other responsibilities.

This book is not a technical study of iron manufacturing. A study of that nature can be made from the Hopewell records and in a number of the works listed in the bibliography. Since the original edition of *Hopewell Village* was published in 1966, two graduate theses have been written by Donald Crownover (Washington: Government Printing Office, 1970) and Jay Leary (unpublished, Millersville State College, 1971) on stove casting at Hopewell Furnace. More research on related topics may be done by scholars. However, chief emphasis in this work has been directed not to iron but to people—the men, women and children of the community where iron was made.

The furnace was a dominating influence in the life of these people of the village. The flare from the stack cast a dim light over the village at night. The roar of the blast, the squeak of the water wheel, the peal of the cast house bell, the rumble of wagon wheels were comforting sounds of production and prosperity. Quiet in the furnace area was a sign of hard times. But the furnace operation was only the backdrop against which the life of people was enacted.

The title chosen is Hopewell Village rather than Hopewell Furnace. In part this choice was made because the National Park Service has given meaning to the former term for the more than two million persons who have visited the site. But, more important, the term "village" emphasizes social and economic factors rather than industrial ones. "Village" is used in a somewhat unaccustomed way, however, as meaning the much wider community of all those who were tied together by their common interest in and concern for the prosperity of Hopewell Furnace. Not only the residents of the ironmaster's mansion and the tenant houses along the road to Warwick, but also the woodcutters and colliers in their forest cabins, the miners at several miles distance, the local farmers who provided a part–time labor force and sold provisions at the Furnace, the storekeepers in Birdsboro or Morgantown, and even the merchants in distant cities became at times a part of this wider Hopewell community.

The book is divided into different sections to call attention to several aspects of the interassociation of the people concerned with Hopewell. Chief emphasis is placed upon the first half of the nineteenth century because it was at this time that the Furnace reached its peak of prosperity and also because the records are more complete for this era. The end of stove casting at Hopewell in 1844 began a period of decline which culminated in the final blast–out in 1883. The Civil War and the growth of the railroads created demands for iron which postponed, but could not prevent, the demise of the charcoal furnaces. Hopewell history began before 1800 and continued after 1850. These earlier and later periods are included in the historical sketches and in some references in the social and economic studies, but a principal part of the material is taken from the half century of concentration.

In the era of charcoal iron the furnace plantation was a strange hybrid of agriculture and industry. The voracious consumption of fuel tied the furnace to the proximity of extensive forests. Food for the workers provided an outlet for farm products. While forest and farm offered employment to many workers, their economy was tied to the prosperity of the furnace. The author has attempted to recreate the interrelationships among these different kinds of workers through the scattered bits of information which are buried in the business records, the letters and the recorded reminiscences of people who once lived at Hopewell.

A brief history of the Hopewell Furnace is given in three chapters, each chapter devoted to a fairly distinct era. The economy of the community is examined through the furnace product, the. market, management and labor relations, the operation of the store and the product of farm and forest. Social life of the community is investigated with particular attention given to the black population, women, children, education, religion, and the influence of the outside world upon the furnace enclave.

Restoration and research continue at Hopewell Village by the National Park Service personnel. Since 1966 extensive archeological digs have established the original site of the schoolhouse and added to the knowledge of furnace products. The cast house has been rebuilt. Several workers' homes have been restored and furnished with authentic household items from the 1830's. During the summer months visitors to the Village may observe craftsmen engaged in many activities typical of a nineteenth century iron–making community: metal casting, blacksmithing, candle making, spinning, weaving, charcoal burning and the baking of bread.

Some illustrations in this edition show the recent changes and additions in picture provided through the cooperation of Superintendent Wallace B. Elms and Historian Earl J. Heydinger of the Park Site staff. Continuing research by Heydinger has revealed new evidence of cannon casting at Hopewell Furnace during the American Revolution. It now appears certain that cannon barrels were cast here as well as being tested against the side of the nearby hill.

In this book the reader discovers how several hundred people lived and loved and worked in a closely coordinated community to produce pig iron and iron castings for a growing nation in the eighteenth and nineteenth centuries.

Part One
The Historical Village

I   An Uncertain Youth,
1771-1800

MARK BIRD BUILT HIS NEW FURNACE ON THE EDGE OF A
meadow where French Creek flows between Mount Pleasure
and Brushy Hill in Union Township, Berks County, Pennsylvania, close to the Chester County line. Proof that the location
was a good one was demonstrated by the production of iron
on this site for more than a century. But there must have
been times when Bird and his successors wondered whether a
successful business was possible here. The first half century
of the history of Hopewell Furnace was replete with crises—
financial, legal and physical. It was shut down and reopened.
The stack was rebuilt and extensively repaired. The sheriff
was a frequent visitor. There were disputes over land ownership. Partnerships were formed and dissolved. Water was too
abundant or in too short supply. However, despite all of the
troubles, there were always those individuals who believed
that Hopewell Furnace could be made to produce iron profit-
ably.

The French Creek Valley offered many advantages to the
person who hoped to make iron in a charcoal furnace. Some
specific ingredients for this business in the eighteenth century

were four natural resources: iron ore near the surface of the ground, abundant woodland to supply the fuel, fast-flowing water to provide power to the blast bellows at the furnace and a quantity of limestone to serve as the "flux" in the smelting process.[1] It was also desirable to have a hill against which to anchor the charging bridge, an available supply of common labor, housing for the workers and capital for building on the site.[2]

Hopewell Furnace had one serious fault in its location: the meadow in front of it was marshy.[3] Because water around the foundation interfered with proper operation of the furnace, the area had to be dry. This problem was controlled at Hopewell by placing the structure higher than the bank of the creek and by digging ditches along the side of the road which passed by the workers' houses. Eventually, too, the slag piles built up a porous plateau around the furnace.

The other needs of the furnace also were met by the energetic Bird. On August 23, 1770 he was granted rights to a little more than 157 acres in "Eastnantmill Township," Chester County,[4] upon which he developed the Old Hopewell Mine, also called Birdtown. Three and a half years later he recorded a deed for nearly 40 acres known as the Jones Good Luck mine tract.[5] These two areas would provide for much of the ore needs of the furnace although later owners secured mining rights in the Warwick mine holes.

The land upon which the furnace and nearby homes were built was included in a purchase of 33 acres from Owen Hugh in 1769 for £76 10s. and subject to a quitrent due to the

[1] Edna M. Handwork, "First in Iron-Berks County's Iron Industry, 1716 to 1815," *Historical Review of Berks County,* XXV, 4 (Fall 1960), p. 121.
[2] E. N. Hartley, *Ironworks on the Saugus* (Norman: University Press, 1957), p. 100.
[3] Leland Abel, "Archeological Report of Hopewell Furnace Site" (unpublished study, 1962). Hopewell Village Library.
[4] *Berks County Deed Book,* AA, Vol. 11, p. 140. Berks County Court House.
[5] *Ibid.,* B. Vol. 2, p. 530.

provincial proprietors of a half penny sterling per acre.[6] Apparently the quitrent payment did not prove burdensome, for Bird's name seldom appeared on the list of those who paid this fee.[7]

Reports existed that Mark Bird was a sharp dealer in acquiring title to lands. He was said to have ejected Clement Hughes from a house he had built earlier on the furnace plot.[8] Peter Cox testified under oath in 1811 that he, also, had been forced off a piece of land upon which he had a house partially built.[9]

Charcoal for the furnace came from forest lands, valued at almost £13,000, which had been inherited by Bird from his father William Bird who died in 1761.[10] Mark was in possession of 8,050 acres of land in Union Township in 1763,[11] and he had added to these holdings by the time the furnace was built.[12]

Despite its location Hopewell Furnace did not at first use the water of French Creek for its power supply. Instead water was brought from springs on the mountain side in an east headrace one mile long and a west headrace twice that length. The west ditch crossed land which did not belong to the Furnace, a circumstance which was later the cause of an eviction suit and the building of a dam on the creek not far from the iron works.[13]

Limestone was available locally. The Furnace records over

[6] *Ibid.*, A. Vol. 6, p. 237.
[7] Charles B. Montgomery, "Report on Hopewell Furnace in Berks County, Pa." (unpublished report, 1941). Hopewell Village Library.
[8] Albert Painter Interview, 1950. Hopewell Village Library.
[9] *Berks County Court Continuance Dockets, 1800–1820. Penn Lessee v. Kahler,* tried 1810, and *Buckley et al v. Kahler,* tried Jan. 16, 1811, Berks County Court House.
[10] *Alden's Appeal Record,* 93, Pennsylvania 182, Philadelphia, 1878, p. 119.
[11] *Union Township Assessment Records* for 1763. Microfilm, Hopewell Village Library.
[12] The nature of some of Bird's land titles were to plague his successors with suits at law. See chapter 2 for discussion of these.
[13] Harker A. Long, *A Short History of the Hopewell Furnace Estate in Union Township, Berks County* (Reading: Reading Eagle Press, undated).

a number of years show that lime was bought from neighbors or hauled from furnace land.

The availability of laborers and housing for them will be discussed in later chapters.

The capital for Hopewell came from several sources. One was the paternal inheritance already mentioned. When in 1764 Mark Bird transferred Berkshire Furnace to his mother and her new husband John Patton,[14] he may have secured additional funds for investment. Apparently the inheritances of a sister and two brothers were used by Mark for on November 18, 1772 he gave a mortgage to Mary Bird, William Bird and James Bird for their shares in their father's estate.[15] The mention of Hopewell Furnace in this mortgage was one of the earliest specific references to it found in any extant document.

The absence of early Furnace business records caused a long controversy over the date of the founding of the works at this site. Morton L. Montgomery, historian of Berks County, wrote that Hopewell Furnace was built in 1759 by William Bird;[16] but later in the same volume he said it was erected about 1765.[17] Since this latter date was after the death of William Bird, the furnace could not have been built in that year by him. Other writers followed Montgomery in giving the 1759 date.[18] In support of an earlier date a diary left by a visitor to Hopewell in 1837 recorded that Manager Clement Brooke told the writer that the furnace had been in operation for 80 years.[19] If taken literally, that statement would have dated the founding in 1757; but Brooke was certainly mistaken. Much evidence exists to support a later date.

[14] *Alden's Appeal Record, op. cit.,* p. 119.

[15] *Berks County Court Pleadings,* 1770–1785, November 18, 1772. Berks County Court House.

[16] Morton L. Montgomery, *Historical and Biographical Annals of Berks County, Pennsylvania* (2 Vols.; Chicago: J. M. Beers and Company, 1909), I, p. 27.

[17] *Ibid.,* pp. 309 and 326.

[18] For example: *Industrial Berks County,* 1748–1948 (Reading: Textile Machine Works, 1948), p. 6.

[19] Otis Cary, *Diary of A Trip from New York to Pennsylvania in 1837* (unpublished, Berks County Historical Society), Feb. 17, 1837.

An inventory of the estate of William Bird did not mention Hopewell Furnace.[20] Since it was unlikely that so valuable a possession would have been overlooked, it is probable that there was no such establishment in his possession at the time of his death in 1761. In sworn testimony a witness in a suit tried in 1811 stated that he had cut wood on land next to the furnace tract in 1770. He thought that the furnace had been erected a year or two earlier.[21] In 1787 an advertisement for the sale of the furnace noted that it had been operating for seventeen years[22] Evidence in another law suit noted that Mark Bird was in possession of the furnace tract in January 1770, and that he had had it surveyed during April and May of that year.[23]

On more direct evidence the tax records show that Mark Bird's property tax in Union Township increased sharply for the year 1768 and took another jump in 1770. It then remained the same through 1773. In the absence of a general tax increase, which did not appear for other tax payers, it seems probable that Bird's valuation was increasing in those years. The furnace itself witnesses to a later founding date. A stone at the edge of the cast arch has the date 1771 cut into its face.[24] The oldest known product of Hopewell Furnace is a stove, owned by the Birdsboro Y.M.C.A., bearing on its surface the name of the Furnace and the date 1772. It seems probable, therefore, that Mark Bird built the furnace in 1771 on land he had recently acquired.

Specific events at Hopewell in the next thirteen years are not too clear because of the absence of Furnace books and records. Stoves were cast with the inscriptions "Hopewell

[20] *Hopewell Furnace Papers* (uncatalogued documents at Hopewell Village National Historical Site).

[21] Evan Lewis in Ejectment Suit of *Buckley et al. v. Kahler, op. cit.*

[22] *Pennsylvania Gazette*, April 11, 1787.

[23] *Peregrin Pickle Les. of Penn and Richard Penn Esq. v. Mathew Brooke, Pleadings and Miscellaneous Old Papers, 1752–1843* (Prothonatory's Office, Berks County, Reading, Pennsylvania), Case tried March 5–8, 1811.

[24] Photographed in 1962 by Archeologist Leland Abel.

Six-Plate Stove Made in 1772, Oldest Known Product of Hopewell
Furnace

Furnace" or "Mark Bird." One patriotic model appeared with
the motto, "Be Liberty Thine."[25]

Hopewell, like many of its neighboring furnaces, was used
to help with arming the American military forces in the
Revolutionary War. Surviving papers contain one specific
reference to munitions at Hopewell and considerable support
for the contention that cannons were made here. Sam Hodg-
don, Commissary General of Military Stores, left a record of
"the Shot and Shell at the Several Furnaces." The document,

[25] Committee on Historical Research, *Forges and Furnaces in the
Province of Pennsylvania* (Philadelphia: Pennsylvania Society of the
Colonial Dames of America, 1914), p. 154.

undated but bundled with others for 1781, listed "Hopewell (Mark Bird) 10 Inch Shells 517."[26] The importance of this contribution to the war effort was emphasized in the following action of the Continental Congress:

> The Board of War reported June 23 : "That eleven workmen employed by Colonel Mark Bird at his Cannon and Nail Rod works in Berks County, Pennsylvania, be discharged from the Militia into which they are drafted, as Congress are of opinion they are of more extensive uses to the continent in their employment as artificers, as it is represented that the works must stand still if these workmen march out with the Militia."
>
> Tuesday, June 24, 1777.
>
> The Board of War having recommended, that eleven workmen employed by Colonel Mark Bird in the cannon foundry and nail works . . . carried on by him for the use of the United States, be discharged from the militia into which they are now drafted,
>
> Ordered, That this matter be referred to the Supreme executive council of the State of Pennsylvania.[27]

The *Journals of the Continental Congress* contained a number of references to Bird's cannon. He was advanced $2,000 on August 22, 1776 because of his contract ". . . to cast cannon for the United States."[28] Twice he was issued powder ". . . to prove the cannon he has made. . . ."[29] In 1778 he was allowed ten pounds Pennsylvania currency per ton more than the original contract for his cannon ". . . in consideration of his loss sustained by the additional quantity of powder required to be used in the proof of the said cannon. . . ."[30]

On April 8, 1780, payment was authorized to Mark Bird in the amount of $125,691.60 ". . . for sundry quantities of

[26] *Knox Papers* (Colonial National Park, Yorktown, Virginia). Photocopy at Hopewell Village.
[27] *Journal of the Continental Congress* (34 Volumes; Philadelphia: Government Printing Office, 1904–1937), VIII, pp. 495–496.
[28] *Ibid.*, V, p. 695.
[29] *Ibid.*, IV, p. 355 and VI, p. 860.
[30] *Ibid.*, XI, p. 473–474.

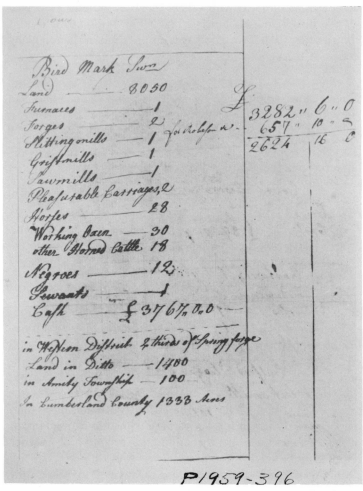

Mark Bird's Property as Listed in the Berks County Tax Book for 1779

military stores . . . the . . . contracts have been compleated, and the stores proved and accepted. . . ."[31] But Bird must have had some cannon on hand when the war ended; for on

[31] *Ibid.,* XVI, p. 338–339.

August 12, 1784 he sold to John Pasmore "2 great guns wt. 2T : 8C : @ £5–12/6 = £13–10."[32]

There was no mention in these journals of Hopewell Furnace in connection with the manufacture of cannon for the Continental Army. But the old Hopewell residents were familiar with a story that cannon were buried near the furnace after the Battle of Brandywine when the British Army advanced up the Schuylkill Valley.[33] In 1858 Hopewell Furnace sold six old cannon weighing 18,600 pounds to the railroad for scrap iron at twenty-four dollars per ton.[34] The Furnace journal did not report when these cannon were cast, but it might have been during the Revolution. The museum at Hopewell Furnace now contains a part of an old cannon which, according to tradition, was uncovered at Hopewell during the Civil War. In 1935 a cannon ball was recovered from the slag pile, and three more were found in excavations in the furnace area in 1962.[35]

If Hopewell Furnace worked for the American cause in obscurity, its owner was frequently mentioned for his activities. He was probably not in active management at the Furnace during this time, for as early as 1772 he was listed as a citizen of the county of Philadelphia.[36] He rented his furnace to William Hays sometime in the 1770's, and Hays was probably the manager during the Revolutionary period.[37]

Before the outbreak of the war Mark Bird served on the Committee on Observation and the Committee of Correspondence and was chosen to the Provincial Conference of 1775.

[32] *Hopewell Furnace Day Book, 1784–1794*, p. 70. There are 76 volumes of Hopewell Furnace Ledgers and Journals available for use. They have been named by the historians at Hopewell Village as source material, and each one has been assigned a number. They are referred to as SM 1, etc. The above named book is SM 41. Subsequent references to these books will be by the SM numbers.

[33] For example, the Thomas Hoffman Interview, November 22, 1940.

[34] SM 60, p. 69.

[35] Appleman, *op. cit.*, p. 8; Report of Archeologist Leland Abel.

[36] Arthur Cecil Bining, *Pennsylvania Iron Manufacture in the 18th Century* (Harrisburg : Pennsylvania Historical Commission, 1938), p. 194.

[37] Ejectment Suit of *Buckley et al. v. Kahler, op. cit.*

When the war came, he was Lieutenant Colonel of the Second Battalion of Berks County militia and later became its Colonel. He was credited with providing uniforms, tents and provisions for three hundred men at his own expense.[38] He was a member of the Pennsylvania Assembly;[39] chairman of the General Committee of Berks County which selected eight members, including himself, to serve in the Provincial Convention of 1776;[40] and judge of the Berks County Court.[41]

Perhaps the most important services that Mark Bird performed for the American cause were those executed while he was deputy quartermaster general. He may have advanced some of his own money to obtain supplies, for Congress voted on February 8, 1776, that he be paid $5.80 for necessities provided for several prisoners. The next month he was granted $50,000 for which he was accountable.[42] In February of 1778 he took advantage of high water on the Schuylkill River to ship 1000 barrels of flour to Washington's army at Valley Forge.[43] Earl J. Heydinger wrote of this action, "The timely shipment . . . was only the minimum for four or five days requirements, but those four or five days . . . enabled Washington's army to survive. . . . "[44]

The end of the war found Mark Bird a creditor of the government of the United States. On September 15, 1783 he requested that he be given the chain ". . . which was prepared to throw across Hudson River. . . ."[45] But this request was denied ". . . as the memorialist being a creditor of the United States may obtain a settlement of his accounts in common

[38] Montgomery, op. cit., I, p. 326.
[39] Bining, "Early Ironmasters of Pennsylvania," reprint from Pennsylvania History, XVIII, 2 (April 1951), p. 12.
[40] James E. Gibson, "The Pennsylvania Provincial Conference of 1776," The Pennsylvania Magazine of History and Biography, LVIII, 4 (October 1934), p. 326.
[41] Reading Eagle, July 27, 1930. Article by C. M. Montgomery.
[42] Journals of the Continental Congress, IV, pp. 119, 243–244.
[43] Ibid., X, p. 189.
[44] Earl J. Heydinger, "The Schuykill, Lifeline to Valley Forge," Bulletin of the Historical Society of Montgomery County, Pennsylvania, IX, 3 (October 1954), p. 161.
[45] Journals of the Continental Congress, XXV, p. 585.

with others under similar circumstances, it is unnecessary to give any particular order in his behalf."[46]

Bird at this time was 44 years of age,[47] brother-in-law to two signers of the Declaration of Independence, George Ross and James Wilson;[48] and a businessman with broadly scattered interests. Beside owning Hopewell Furnace and Birdsboro Forge, Slitting Mill and Steel Furnace, he was partner in a number of other iron works: Gibraltar Forge[49] and Spring Forge[50] in Berks County and the Delaware Falls Iron Works near Trenton. In this last business he had James Wilson as his partner.[51]

That he was willing to invest in hazardous ventures was indicated by his presence among the owners of the *United States,* which was one of the first ships to leave this country to trade with China. There were six other owners, including James Wilson. This investment was probably no success, because the ship and cargo were seized upon their return to Philadelphia by the creditors of some of the partners.[52]

However, failure in the China trade was not the only sign of financial difficulty for the Bird enterprises. In 1784 he appealed for a reduction in his taxes on Hopewell Furnace property on the plea that his iron works had not operated for some time. The tax records showed that his taxes already had been sharply reduced in the preceding two years.[53] Apparently he was caught in the post-Revolution depression and inflation. A letter from Mark Bird to an unknown creditor on October 14, 1785 said ". . . as my misfortune has been, as it now is, I

[46] *Ibid.,* XXV, p. 626

[47] *St. Gabriels Episcopal Church Records,* Douglasville, Pennsylvania, lists his baptism on February 4, 1739, p. 103. Berks County Historical Society.

[48] *Ibid.,* p. 70.

[49] Bining, *Pennsylvania Iron Manufacture in the 18th Century, op. cit.,* p. 189.

[50] Committee on Historical Research, *op. cit.,* p. 158.

[51] Bining, *op. cit.,* p. 109.

[52] Samuel W. Woodhouse, "Log and Journal of the Ship *United States* on a voyage to China in 1784," *The Pennsylvania Magazine of History and Biography,* LV, 3 (July 1931), p. 226–227.

[53] *Union Township Tax Records,* 1782–1784. Berks County Historical Society.

have no money otherwise would have paid you Long since but if I was to a Been Crusified I could get none. . . ."[54]

Post-war business for the ironmasters was slow with imports creating a surplus of bar iron. The Pennsylvania Assembly, when asked to adopt an import tax to protect the industry in this state,[55] voted against a bill which would have imposed a forty shilling per ton tariff on bar iron.[56]

Nature also conspired to complicate Bird's problems when floods did extensive damage in southeastern Pennsylvania in the fall of 1786.[57] Both Hopewell and the Birdsboro properties suffered,[58] and a fire at Birdsboro caused further loss.[59]

Mark Bird and James Wilson were in partnership in the Delaware Falls iron works. They had built rolling and slitting mills, a forge, a grist mill and a saw mill. But by 1785 their capital was exhausted, and in a final attempt to recover, Wilson tried unsuccessfully to borrow 500,000 florins in Holland.[60] One reason why the partners found it difficult to borrow was that they had already overextended their credit. On March 29, 1785, they had given to John Nixon, a Philadelphia merchant, a mortgage on about 8000 acres of Hopewell and Birdsboro land in Berks and Chester Counties and on the Delaware Falls property in Bucks County. In return they received from Nixon "200,000 fine Spanish milled Silver Dollars."[61] Another debt to the Bank of North America was of concern to the directors of that institution as shown by at least six separate entries in the minutes of their meetings from 1784 to 1789. Possibly more forceful action to collect was

[54] *Montgomery Manuscripts*, book 3, p. 1. Hopewell Village Library.
[55] *Pennsylvania Gazette*, February 1, 1786.
[56] *Ibid.*, April 21, 1787.
[57] *Ibid.*, November 22, 1786.
[58] Appleman, *op. cit.*, p. 8.
[59] Jackson Kemper, III, "The Making of Charcoal," *The Historical Review of Berks County,,* II, 4 (July 1937), n. p.
[60] *James Wilson Papers*, Vol. 3, p. 24, Historical Society of Pennsylvania. Letter dated July 16, 1785.
[61] *Berks County Surveyor. General Draughts and Miscellaneous Old Papers, 1700 to Early 1800* (Prothonotory's Office, Berks County Court House, Reading), March 29, 1785.

long since I have heard from Penn[a] and my lims are
-d, that I am under the Necessity of moveing on Cruches,
annot ride on Horseback, so I think, I shall never see
any more, when I was last there by the Best observations
d make, you and your sister Mrs. Buckley, shewed the
riendly countnance to me, and seem[d] to feel the most
y, for my situation, then any others I met with in the
-I wrote to Mr. Coleman [probably Robert Coleman of
all Furnace] two years ago or near it, but he has never
red, I shall not think well of the Iron masters, when
ome to know my Situation, if they do not fall on some
in some measure, to relieve me, either by lone, or other
they know I was Ruined, by the Warr, it was not,
enness, Idleness, or want of Industry, that I was ruined,
abour, cannot be had, in this Country, or I should have
very well, small as my Capital was, but I have been
unate, whether, for want of sence or what, I cannot
ith all that, if I had had, 10 or 12 Negres to have kept
the Business, I should have done well—Can I prevale
u to spend a little time for me by going to the Iron
rs, who is now, I am told grown Verry welthy, in general
me a poor Cripple along and not be quite reduced to
ry—The person I expect will hand you this is a neighbor
e . . . who will bring your answer. . . .[71]

was no indication what reply was made to this letter.
rd died in 1816 and was buried in the cemetery of the
Baptist Church near Bostic, North Carolina.[72] The
ily connection with Hopewell was revived very briefly
ark's son George Bird visited the Furnace on June 9,
d was presented with $25.[73]

well Furnace should have enjoyed prosperity in the
ears after its sale to Morris and Old. This was a
us period for the iron industry. Many old furnaces
ng reopened and new ones erected.[74] Hopewell, with

e Family Papers, Historical Society of Berks County, Mark Bird
w Brooke, June 1, 1807.
er Papers, Genealogical Notes. Hopewell Village Library.
1, p. 34.
r S. Clark, History of Manufactures in the United States, 1607–
. I; New York, Peter Smith, 1949), p. 500.

accounts, to settle the same immediately, with either of them,
otherwise they will be proceeded against as the law directs.
  JACOB PAUL, Abington,   ⎰ Assignees.
¶ CORNELIUS COMEGYS Philadelphia, ⎱

To be Sold by Public Auction,

On MONDAY, the 15th day of May next, and the succeeding
    days, till the whole shall be sold,
SEVEN tracts of Land in Union and Robinson townships, in
 the county of Berks; they contain from 150 to 200 acres
each, six of them have fronts on the river Schuylkill, on one of
them is the Birdsborough house, with the numerous and valuable
improvements around it, on four others are houses, barns, orchards
and other improvements, the remaining two consist chiefly of
woodland; the soil is good, and there is a great proportion of watered meadow.
  The vendue will be held on the premises, and the terms will
be made known at the time of sale. It is probable that three o-
ther Tracts, adjoining the foregoing seven, will be exposed to
sale at the same time.

To be Sold by Private Sale,

Hopewell Furnace, the Birdsborough Forges, and Spring Forge,
all in the county of Berks. To Hopewell Furnace will be allotted 4000 acres of land, to the Birdsborough Forges 1500 acres, all
well timbered, and extending three miles on Hay Creek, to
Spring Forge 800 acres. Along with the Furnace will be sold
3 banks of good iron ore, all within a reasonable distance. It will
be a term of the sale of the Furnace to supply, during four years,
all the foregoing Forges with a certain quantity of pig iron at a
stipulated price. Bar iron and castings will be received in payment for the whole iron work estate.
  To any person inclining to purchase, the lands, lines and works
will be shewn, from the 8th to the 15th day of May, by the sub-
scriber, who will attend at Birdsborough for that purpose. The
Furnace will be in blast, with a provision of five thousand cords
of wood, and eight hundred loads of ore. Two thousand cords of
wood are cut for the Birdsborough Forges, and two thousand and
two hundred for Spring Forge. Five teams compleat may be purchased along with the Furnace.   MARK BIRD.

Cumberland county, State of New-Jersey, April 17, 1786.
THE Creditors of David Joslin and Jonas Mullica, debtors,
 confined in the goal of said county, are requested to appear

Hopewell Furnace Offered for Sale in the *Pennsylvania Gazette* for
April 26, 1786

not taken because Wilson had been a member of the board of directors from 1781 to 1784.[62]

Bird tried to sell part of the property in an effort to save the rest. A public sale was advertised of Hopewell Furnace with 4000 acres of land, 5,000 cords of wood and 800 loads of ore. Birdsboro and Spring Forges were also offered for sale at the same time.[63] Perhaps the bids were insufficient, for no sale was consummated. Nixon insisted on payment; and on August 16, 1786 he received from Mark Bird and James Wilson a release of "all rights to the Equity of Redemption."[64] This in effect was a quitclaim deed to permit Nixon to sell the properties named in his mortgage at public or private sale to recover the amount of his note.

In 1788 Nixon brought suit for recovery of his money. This was apparently a preliminary action to a forced sale; and in April of that year a sheriff's sale was held of "Hopewell plantation."[65] The furnance and 5163 acres of land were purchased by Cadwallader Morris with one third interest and James Old with two-thirds interest.[66]

With this sale Mark Bird temporarily passed out of the picture of Hopewell Furnace history. Financial problems continued to plague him. He left Pennsylvania for North Carolina and in 1790 appealed to the legislature of that state for bankruptcy relief. On November 17, 1790 the House of Commons of the North Carolina Legislature heard the following report:

> The committee of propositions and grievances to whom we referred the petition of Mark Bird, report—On information before the committee, it appears that the said Mark Bird became bankrupt when a citizen of the state of Pennsylvania—that he has since that time become an inhabitant of this State,

[62] *Minutes and Letter Book of the Bank of North America.* November 2, 1781, to January 21, 1792, *Montgomery Manuscripts,* Book 3, p. 92.
[63] *Pennsylvania Gazette,* April 26, 1786.
[64] Box on Iron Industry, *Miscellaneous Manuscripts,* Mortgage Book G, p. 299. Historical Society of Pennsylvania.
[65] *Berks County Pleadings, op. cit.,* 1788.
[66] Morton L. Montgomery, *History of Berks County in Pennsylvania* (Philadelphia: Evorts, Peck and Richards, 1886), p. 89.

and wishes the legislature to subst
—your committee having duly co
are of opinion that the legislature
business, therefore reject the pet

In 1796 James Wilson paid all the
Bird and Wilson to the Bank of
satisfactory to the Directors."[68] Thi
some of the pressure on Bird, beca
County in 1796[69] for a short stay.
from Rutherford County, North (
revealed much of his life and posit
written to Dr. Benjamin Rush of
a hope of recovering his fortune. I

> . . . I was Bankrupt by the Vi
> has been Able to get anything of
> There is no doubt my principle
> Depreciation . . . I had three N
> the other Two I was obliged to s
> Value, but the land would nc
> Value, so I thought it most prude
> would not dye. If all my frienc
> send as much, as will buy three
> land, I can get along, the Laybo
> there is no getting a long with th
> a number of welthy acquaintance
> that I have been a friendly Man, a
> by the Warr, they will give me

Dr. Rush wrote on the back of the
relief for him as all his friends of 17

The second letter was addressec
was by this time one of the partr
pleading:

[67] *Colonial and State Records of Nort*
ment of Archives and History, Raleigh,
Photocopy at Hopewell Village Library.
[68] *Montgomery Manuscripts,* book 1, p.
[69] *Berks County Deed Books* 15, pp. 21
[70] *Dr. Benjamin Rush Collection,* Vol. E
Pennsylvania.

It
so F
and
Penn
I co
most
sensi
state
Corr
answ
they
mod
wise
Dru
and
don
unfc
say,
a lo
on y
Mas
to g
Begg
of m

The
Mark
Conco
Bird fa
when
1847,

Hop
twelve
prospe
were b

[71] Bro
to Math
[72] Ke
[73] SM
[74] Vic
1860 (V

post-war production costs about the same as those at Warwick Furnace and only a little higher than costs at Cornwall Furnace,[75] was the second largest of the fourteen Pennsylvania furnaces in 1789 with a listed capacity of 700 tons annually.[76] But this was an uncertain period for the Furnace, and the number of changes of owners indicated business troubles. Absentee ownership may have been one of the problems.

In 1790 Cadwallader Morris sold his share in the furnace to his brother Benjamin. A year later Benjamin Morris bought the share of James Old to become the sole owner of Hopewell Furnace.[77] But James Old had not lost interest in Hopewell, for two years later he bought it from Benjamin Morris for £14,000 in gold or silver money of Pennsylvania. Payment was to have been made in four annual installments.[78] As this price was more than $37,000, Hopewell was a valuable property despite its problems.

Old may not have intended to operate the furnace, for two months later he sold it to James Wilson for £2,000 down payment and a mortgage in the amount of £11,901 9s. 6d.[79] Since Wilson also acquired the Birdsboro Forge in the same year,[80] his chief interest in Hopewell was as a source of pig iron for his forges. Not intending to manage these properties personally, he entered into an agreement with three men, John Lewis Barde of Berks County, John René Barde of Philadelphia and Paul Henry Mallet Prevost of New Jersey, to

[75] Samuel Gustof Hamerlin, *Report About the Mines in the United States, 1783* (Philadelphia: John Morton Memorial Museum, 1931), p. 67.

[76] John B. Pearse, *A Concise History of the Iron Manufacture of the American Colonies up to the Revolution and of Pennsylvania Until the Present Time* (Philadelphia: Allen, Lane and Scott, 1876), p. 88.

[77] *Hopewell Village Cataloged Documents,* 8730407, "Brief of Title of Hopewell Property." (The catalogued collections of some 8000 documents at Hopewell Village are identified by number which represents the date on the document. The above number means 1873, April 7. Subsequent references to these documents will use this numbering system.)

[78] *Montgomery Manuscripts,* "Indenture for sale of Hopewell Furnace," December 1, 1793.

[79] *Brooke Family Papers,* Mortgage from Wilson to Old, February 3, 1794. Berks County Historical Society.

[80] John C. Wetzel, *200th Anniversary of Birdsboro, Pennsylvania* (Birdsboro: The Executive Committee, 1940), p. 77.

lease ". . . All . . . the said James Wilson's Works called Hopewell Furnace, Birdsborough Forges and Gibraltar Forges and
the Messuages, Mills, Plantations or Tracts or Pieces of land
thereunto belonging. . . ." Wilson reserved for his own use a
house and thirty acres of land. The lessees agreed to furnish
at least eight hundred tons of cast iron from the furnace each
year which Wilson contracted to buy at a price of six pounds
per ton of pig iron, £9 10s. per ton for "country and forge
castings" and £14 per ton for "hollow ware or flask work." If
Wilson should default, the partners were free to sell iron at the
market price.[81]

Once again floods ravaged Birdsboro Forge in the periodic
overflow of Hay Creek in 1795. Hopewell Furnace escaped at
this time, but the damage to the forge property weakened
Wilson's financial position.[82] In 1796 he sold the forges and
2,200 acres of land to John Lewis Barde.[83] Later that year the
following advertisement appeared in a Reading newspaper :

Sheriffs Sale
. . . Sale by *Public Vendue,* . . . on Monday the Seventh
Day of November next, at Two o'Clock in the Afternoon, at
the House of George Flieger Innkeeper in the Borough of
Reading and the County of Berks, viz.
All those Tenements, Messuages, and Furnace for casting
of Iron commonly called or known by the Name of Hopewell
Furnace, with the lands appertinent thereto, situate in the
Townships of Union and Caernarvon, in the County aforesaid,
containing About Four Thousand Acres . . . seized and taken
in the Execution as Late the Estate of James Wilson Esqr.[84]

Wilson did not long survive the failure of his businesses.
He moved to New Jersey in 1797 to avoid arrest for debt, and
early the next year moved to Edenton, North Carolina where

[81] HV 7950501A, Lease Agreement.
[82] *Gratz Collection, American Clergy,* Case 9, Box 23, Historical Society
of Pennsylvania. Letter from Bird Wilson in Birdsboro to William Wilson
in Philadelphia, n. d.
[83] Montgomery, *History of Berks County,* op. cit., p. 894.
[84] *The Weekly Advertiser,* (Reading, Pennsylvania), October 15, 1796.

he died on August 21, 1798.[85] His wife wrote concerning his last days, ". . . his mind had been in such a state for the last six months, harassed and perplexed, that it was more than he could possibly bear, and brought on a violent nervous fever. . . ."[86]

James Old purchased Hopewell Furnace for a third time, and again it was involved in a financial failure. A notice appeared in December 1799 that Sheriff Nicholas Dick would sell on January 6, 1800, "that well known Estate called Hopewell Furnace with the Mine and Lands appurtenant containing upwards of Three Thousand Acres of Land . . . the property of James Old."[87]

During the time between these two sheriff's sales, Hopewell was under the active management of John Bishop[88] and Mathew Brooke.[89] At the sale in 1800 the Hopewell Furnace property was purchased by Benjamin Morris once more.[90] Later in the year Morris sold it to a partnership consisting of Daniel Buckley of Lancaster County and his two brothers-in-law Thomas Brooke of Montgomery County and Mathew Brooke, Junior of Berks County.[91]

Now after so many changes of ownership, several sheriff's sales and the financial ruin of at least three of its owners, Hopewell had come into the possession of the Buckley and Brooke families who would nourish it through many lean years and at last reap a rich reward from its prosperous period of production. Hopewell remained in the possession of descendants of these men until the property was sold to the United States Government in the 1930's.

[85] *Dictionary of American Biography,* "James Wilson" (Volume XX; New York: Scribners, 1936), pp. 326–330.
[86] *James Wilson Papers,* Business Correspondence, Historical Society of Pennsylvania, Volume 6, p. 12.
[87] *Brooke Family Papers,* Copy of Notice of Sheriff's Sale.
[88] HV 7980603, Farm Agreement.
[89] *Montgomery Manuscripts,* book 3, p. 46.
[90] Berks County Prothonotory Office, *Old Book* 2, p. 162.
[91] *Berks County Deed Book* 17, p. 219.

2   Growth to Prosperity, 1800-1845

THE NEW PARTNERSHIP OF DANIEL BUCKLEY, THOMAS Brooke and Mathew Brooke, Junior, provided active and personal management for Hopewell Furnace. Except for a few years during the first decade of their ownership, a member of one of these families was manager in residence at the "Big House," overseeing Furnace operation for more than half a century. Thomas Brooke's son Clement held this place for forty years, and it was he who finally proved that Hopewell could be made a profitable enterprise.

Success was not immediate for the new owners. They were plagued by debt, general business conditions and legal contest to protect title to the land they had bought. During one period of more than seven years the furnace hearth was cold, and little more than maintenance work was conducted at Hopewell. When the furnace was put back in blast, it was hampered by the business panic beginning in 1819. One law suit was contested for a quarter of a century before the courts affirmed the Buckley-Brooke title. Prosperity followed these troubled times, and for twenty years Hopewell Furnace played its part in the rapid expansion of the charcoal iron industry of

Daniel Buckley, Hopewell Partner 1800–1828

Pennsylvania. Then a new threat came from technological advances in iron-making.

The deed from Benjamin Morris and his wife Francis to Buckley and Brooke listed seven different tracts of land with a total area of about 5,360 acres. Among these were the Birdstown and Jones Good Luck mines. The deed mentioned that possession was given, in addition to land, to ". . . all houses— outhouses — buildings — improvements — mines — minerals, quarries—woods—waters—watercourses—   rights,   liberties, etc."[1] The purchase price was £10,000.

The new owners made extensive alterations in the furnace area. Beside rebuilding the hearth walls, they changed the direction of the original north-south water wheel to one running east-west. The west headrace was built to bring water from French Creek and thus supplement the older east headrace. A new "colehaus" for the storage of charcoal was constructed. This was the earliest mention in the furnace books of such a structure at Hopewell although possibly an older one was being replaced.[2]

In order that the purchasers might have a definite record of what they had bought beside land and buildings, an appraisement of movable property was made by Robert May, Thomas Bull and John Buckley. It was also possible that these items belonged to John Bishop, manager under James Old, and were bought from him in a separate transaction. Among the items listed were the following :

One Bay hors and gairs combleat
1 Rone fifth hors
1 Bay hind hors
1 Sarl mare
One Wagon and Body all Readey to hidch in to hale mine
Black Backer Team
Foylan Team

[1] *Berks County Deed Book* 17, p. 219 ff.
[2] Richard P. Donahoe, "The Charcoal House and Shed, Hopewell Village National Historic Site" (unpublished study, 1956). Hopewell Village Library.

accounts, to fettle the fame immediately, with either of them, otherwife they will be proceeded againft as the law directs.

JACOB PAUL, Abington,   )
¶ CORNELIUS COMEGYS Philadelphia,) Affignees.

To be Sold by Public Auction,

On MONDAY, the 15th day f May next, and the fucceeding days, till the whole fhall be fold,

SEVEN tracts of Land in Union and Robinfon townfhips, in the county of Berks; they contain from 150 to 200 acres each, fix of them have fronts on the river Schuylkill, on one of them is the Birdfborough houfe, with the numerous and valuable improvements around it, on four others are houfes, barns, orchards and other improvements, the remaining two confift chiefly of woodland; the foil is good, and there is a great proportion of watered meadow.

The vendue will be held on the premifes, and the terms will be made known at the time of fale. It is probable that three other Tracts, adjoining the foregoing feven, will be expofed to fale at the fame time.

To be Sold by Private Sale,

Hopewell Furnace, the Birdfborough Forges, and Spring Forge, all in the county of Berks. To Hopewell Furnace will be allotted 4000 acres of land, to the Birdfborough Forges 1500 acres, all well timbered, and extending three miles on Hay Creek, to Spring Forge 800 acres. Along with the Furnace will be fold 3 banks of good iron ore, all within a reafonable diftance. It will be a term of the fale of the Furnace to fupply, during four years, all the foregoing Forges with a certain quantity of pig iron at a ftipulated price. Bar iron and caftings will be received in payment for the whole iron work eftate.

To any perfon inclining to purchafe, the lands, lines and works will be fhewn, from the 8th to the 15th day of May, by the fubfcriber, who will attend at Birdfborough for that purpofe. The Furnace will be in blaft, with a provifion of five thoufand cords of wood, and eight hundred loads of ore. Two thoufand cords of wood are cut for the Birdfborough Forges, and two thoufand and two hundred for Spring Forge. Five teams compleat may be purchafed along with the Furnace.   MARK BIRD.

Cumberland county, State of New-Jerfey, April 17, 1786.

THE Creditors of David Joflin and Jonas Mullica, debtors, confined in the goal of faid county, are requefted to appear

Hopewell Furnace Offered for Sale in the *Pennsylvania Gazette* for
April 26, 1786

not taken because Wilson had been a member of the board of directors from 1781 to 1784.[62]

Bird tried to sell part of the property in an effort to save the rest. A public sale was advertised of Hopewell Furnace with 4000 acres of land, 5,000 cords of wood and 800 loads of ore. Birdsboro and Spring Forges were also offered for sale at the same time.[63] Perhaps the bids were insufficient, for no sale was consummated. Nixon insisted on payment; and on August 16, 1786 he received from Mark Bird and James Wilson a release of "all rights to the Equity of Redemption."[64] This in effect was a quitclaim deed to permit Nixon to sell the properties named in his mortgage at public or private sale to recover the amount of his note.

In 1788 Nixon brought suit for recovery of his money. This was apparently a preliminary action to a forced sale; and in April of that year a sheriff's sale was held of "Hopewell plantation."[65] The furnance and 5163 acres of land were purchased by Cadwallader Morris with one third interest and James Old with two-thirds interest.[66]

With this sale Mark Bird temporarily passed out of the picture of Hopewell Furnace history. Financial problems continued to plague him. He left Pennsylvania for North Carolina and in 1790 appealed to the legislature of that state for bankruptcy relief. On November 17, 1790 the House of Commons of the North Carolina Legislature heard the following report:

> The committee of propositions and grievances to whom we referred the petition of Mark Bird, report—On information before the committee, it appears that the said Mark Bird became bankrupt when a citizen of the state of Pennsylvania— that he has since that time become an inhabitant of this State,

[62] *Minutes and Letter Book of the Bank of North America.* November 2, 1781, to January 21, 1792, *Montgomery Manuscripts,* Book 3, p. 92.

[63] *Pennsylvania Gazette,* April 26, 1786.

[64] Box on Iron Industry, *Miscellaneous Manuscripts,* Mortgage Book G, p. 299. Historical Society of Pennsylvania.

[65] *Berks County Pleadings, op. cit.,* 1788.

[66] Morton L. Montgomery, *History of Berks County in Pennsylvania* (Philadelphia: Evorts, Peck and Richards, 1886), p. 89.

and wishes the legislature to substantiate the said bankruptcy,
—your committee having duly considered the circumstances,
are of opinion that the legislature have nothing to do in the
business, therefore reject the petition.[67]

In 1796 James Wilson paid all the debts owed by the firm of
Bird and Wilson to the Bank of North America "in notes
satisfactory to the Directors."[68] This action may have relieved
some of the pressure on Bird, because he was back in Berks
County in 1796[69] for a short stay. Two letters written by him
from Rutherford County, North Carolina on June 1, 1807,
revealed much of his life and position in the South. One was
written to Dr. Benjamin Rush of Philadelphia and indicated
a hope of recovering his fortune. In it he asserted:

> . . . I was Bankrupt by the Vile unnatural war, and never
> has been Able to get anything of Acct. in my hands since . . .
> There is no doubt my principle ruin, was by the Warr and
> Depretiation . . . I had three Nagroes, one of which Died,
> the other Two I was obliged to sell . . . They brought there
> Value, but the land would not bring a quarter of the
> Value, so I thought it most prudent, to sell them, as the Land
> would not dye. If all my friends and acquaintance would
> send as much, as will buy three Nagroes, as I still hold my
> land, I can get along, the Laybourers here will do Nothing,
> there is no getting a long with them . . . You have I expect
> a number of welthy acquaintance . . . If they are Informed
> that I have been a friendly Man, and a good Whig, and ruined
> by the Warr, they will give me a lift.

Dr. Rush wrote on the back of the letter: "declined soliciting
relief for him as all his friends of 1776 were dead or reduced."[70]

The second letter was addressed to Mathew Brooke, who
was by this time one of the partners at Hopewell Furnace,
pleading:

[67] *Colonial and State Records of North Carolina* (Vol. XXI; Department of Archives and History, Raleigh, North Carolina), pp. 933–934.
Photocopy at Hopewell Village Library.
[68] *Montgomery Manuscripts,* book 1, p. 80.
[69] *Berks County Deed Books* 15, pp. 216, 382; 20, p. 139.
[70] *Dr. Benjamin Rush Collection,* Vol. B2–2, p. 10. Historical Society of
Pennsylvania.

It is long since I have heard from Penn^a and my lims are so Faled, that I am under the Necessity of moveing on Cruches, and Cannot ride on Horseback, so I think, I shall never see Penn^a any more, when I was last there by the Best observations I could make, you and your sister Mrs. Buckley, shewed the most friendly countnance to me, and seem^d to feel the most sensibly, for my situation, then any others I met with in the state—I wrote to Mr. Coleman [probably Robert Coleman of Cornwall Furnace] two years ago or near it, but he has never answered, I shall not think well of the Iron masters, when they come to know my Situation, if they do not fall on some mode, in some measure, to relieve me, either by lone, or other wise, they know I was Ruined, by the Warr, it was not, Drunkenness, Idleness, or want of Industry, that I was ruined, and Labour, cannot be had, in this Country, or I should have done very well, small as my Capital was, but I have been unfortunate, whether, for want of sence or what, I cannot say, with all that, if I had had, 10 or 12 Negres to have kept a long the Business, I should have done well—Can I prevale on you to spend a little time for me by going to the Iron Masters, who is now, I am told grown Verry welthy, in general to get me a poor Cripple along and not be quite reduced to Beggery—The person I expect will hand you this is a neighbor of mine . . . who will bring your answer. . . .[71]

There was no indication what reply was made to this letter. Mark Bird died in 1816 and was buried in the cemetery of the Concord Baptist Church near Bostic, North Carolina.[72] The Bird family connection with Hopewell was revived very briefly when Mark's son George Bird visited the Furnace on June 9, 1847, and was presented with $25.[73]

Hopewell Furnace should have enjoyed prosperity in the twelve years after its sale to Morris and Old. This was a prosperous period for the iron industry. Many old furnaces were being reopened and new ones erected.[74] Hopewell, with

[71] *Brooke Family Papers*, Historical Society of Berks County, Mark Bird to Mathew Brooke, June 1, 1807.
[72] *Kemper Papers*, Genealogical Notes. Hopewell Village Library.
[73] SM 31, p. 34.
[74] Victor S. Clark, *History of Manufactures in the United States, 1607–1860* (Vol. I; New York, Peter Smith, 1949), p. 500.

post-war production costs about the same as those at Warwick Furnace and only a little higher than costs at Cornwall Furnace,[75] was the second largest of the fourteen Pennsylvania furnaces in 1789 with a listed capacity of 700 tons annually.[76] But this was an uncertain period for the Furnace, and the number of changes of owners indicated business troubles. Absentee ownership may have been one of the problems.

In 1790 Cadwallader Morris sold his share in the furnace to his brother Benjamin. A year later Benjamin Morris bought the share of James Old to become the sole owner of Hopewell Furnace.[77] But James Old had not lost interest in Hopewell, for two years later he bought it from Benjamin Morris for £14,000 in gold or silver money of Pennsylvania. Payment was to have been made in four annual installments.[78] As this price was more than $37,000, Hopewell was a valuable property despite its problems.

Old may not have intended to operate the furnace, for two months later he sold it to James Wilson for £2,000 down payment and a mortgage in the amount of £11,901 9s. 6d.[79] Since Wilson also acquired the Birdsboro Forge in the same year,[80] his chief interest in Hopewell was as a source of pig iron for his forges. Not intending to manage these properties personally, he entered into an agreement with three men, John Lewis Barde of Berks County, John René Barde of Philadelphia and Paul Henry Mallet Prevost of New Jersey, to

[75] Samuel Gustof Hamerlin, *Report About the Mines in the United States, 1783* (Philadelphia: John Morton Memorial Museum, 1931), p. 67.

[76] John B. Pearse, *A Concise History of the Iron Manufacture of the American Colonies up to the Revolution and of Pennsylvania Until the Present Time* (Philadelphia: Allen, Lane and Scott, 1876), p. 88.

[77] *Hopewell Village Cataloged Documents,* 8730407, "Brief of Title of Hopewell Property." (The catalogued collections of some 8000 documents at Hopewell Village are identified by number which represents the date on the document. The above number means 1873, April 7. Subsequent references to these documents will use this numbering system.)

[78] *Montgomery Manuscripts,* "Indenture for sale of Hopewell Furnace," December 1, 1793.

[79] *Brooke Family Papers,* Mortgage from Wilson to Old, February 3, 1794. Berks County Historical Society.

[80] John C. Wetzel, *200th Anniversary of Birdsboro, Pennsylvania* (Birdsboro: The Executive Committee, 1940), p. 77.

lease ". . . All . . . the said James Wilson's Works called Hopewell Furnace, Birdsborough Forges and Gibraltar Forges and the Messuages, Mills, Plantations or Tracts or Pieces of land thereunto belonging. . . ." Wilson reserved for his own use a house and thirty acres of land. The lessees agreed to furnish at least eight hundred tons of cast iron from the furnace each year which Wilson contracted to buy at a price of six pounds per ton of pig iron, £9 10s. per ton for "country and forge castings" and £14 per ton for "hollow ware or flask work." If Wilson should default, the partners were free to sell iron at the market price.[81]

Once again floods ravaged Birdsboro Forge in the periodic overflow of Hay Creek in 1795. Hopewell Furnace escaped at this time, but the damage to the forge property weakened Wilson's financial position.[82] In 1796 he sold the forges and 2,200 acres of land to John Lewis Barde.[83] Later that year the following advertisement appeared in a Reading newspaper:

Sheriffs Sale
. . . Sale by *Public Vendue,* . . . on Monday the Seventh Day of November next, at Two o'Clock in the Afternoon, at the House of George Flieger Innkeeper in the Borough of Reading and the County of Berks, viz.

All those Tenements, Messuages, and Furnace for casting of Iron commonly called or known by the Name of Hopewell Furnace, with the lands appertinent thereto, situate in the Townships of Union and Caernarvon, in the County aforesaid, containing About Four Thousand Acres . . . seized and taken in the Execution as Late the Estate of James Wilson Esqr.[84]

Wilson did not long survive the failure of his businesses. He moved to New Jersey in 1797 to avoid arrest for debt, and early the next year moved to Edenton, North Carolina where

---

[81] HV 7950501A, Lease Agreement.
[82] *Gratz Collection, American Clergy,* Case 9, Box 23, Historical Society of Pennsylvania. Letter from Bird Wilson in Birdsboro to William Wilson in Philadelphia, n. d.
[83] Montgomery, *History of Berks County,* op. cit., p. 894.
[84] *The Weekly Advertiser,* (Reading, Pennsylvania), October 15, 1796.

he died on August 21, 1798.[85] His wife wrote concerning his last days, ". . . his mind had been in such a state for the last six months, harassed and perplexed, that it was more than he could possibly bear, and brought on a violent nervous fever. . . ."[86]

James Old purchased Hopewell Furnace for a third time, and again it was involved in a financial failure. A notice appeared in December 1799 that Sheriff Nicholas Dick would sell on January 6, 1800, "that well known Estate called Hopewell Furnace with the Mine and Lands appurtenant containing upwards of Three Thousand Acres of Land . . . the property of James Old."[87]

During the time between these two sheriff's sales, Hopewell was under the active management of John Bishop[88] and Mathew Brooke.[89] At the sale in 1800 the Hopewell Furnace property was purchased by Benjamin Morris once more.[90] Later in the year Morris sold it to a partnership consisting of Daniel Buckley of Lancaster County and his two brothers-in-law Thomas Brooke of Montgomery County and Mathew Brooke, Junior of Berks County.[91]

Now after so many changes of ownership, several sheriff's sales and the financial ruin of at least three of its owners, Hopewell had come into the possession of the Buckley and Brooke families who would nourish it through many lean years and at last reap a rich reward from its prosperous period of production. Hopewell remained in the possession of descendants of these men until the property was sold to the United States Government in the 1930's.

[85] *Dictionary of American Biography,* "James Wilson" (Volume XX; New York: Scribners, 1936), pp. 326–330.
[86] *James Wilson Papers,* Business Correspondence, Historical Society of Pennsylvania, Volume 6, p. 12.
[87] *Brooke Family Papers,* Copy of Notice of Sheriff's Sale.
[88] HV 7980603, Farm Agreement.
[89] *Montgomery Manuscripts,* book 3, p. 46.
[90] Berks County Prothonotory Office, *Old Book* 2, p. 162.
[91] *Berks County Deed Book* 17, p. 219.

2 Growth to Prosperity, 1800-1845

THE NEW PARTNERSHIP OF DANIEL BUCKLEY, THOMAS Brooke and Mathew Brooke, Junior, provided active and personal management for Hopewell Furnace. Except for a few years during the first decade of their ownership, a member of one of these families was manager in residence at the "Big House," overseeing Furnace operation for more than half a century. Thomas Brooke's son Clement held this place for forty years, and it was he who finally proved that Hopewell could be made a profitable enterprise.

Success was not immediate for the new owners. They were plagued by debt, general business conditions and legal contest to protect title to the land they had bought. During one period of more than seven years the furnace hearth was cold, and little more than maintenance work was conducted at Hopewell. When the furnace was put back in blast, it was hampered by the business panic beginning in 1819. One law suit was contested for a quarter of a century before the courts affirmed the Buckley-Brooke title. Prosperity followed these troubled times, and for twenty years Hopewell Furnace played its part in the rapid expansion of the charcoal iron industry of

Daniel Buckley, Hopewell Partner 1800–1828

Pennsylvania. Then a new threat came from technological advances in iron-making.

The deed from Benjamin Morris and his wife Francis to Buckley and Brooke listed seven different tracts of land with a total area of about 5,360 acres. Among these were the Birdstown and Jones Good Luck mines. The deed mentioned that possession was given, in addition to land, to ". . . all houses— outhouses — buildings — improvements — mines — minerals, quarries—woods—waters—watercourses— rights, liberties, etc."[1] The purchase price was £10,000.

The new owners made extensive alterations in the furnace area. Beside rebuilding the hearth walls, they changed the direction of the original north-south water wheel to one running east-west. The west headrace was built to bring water from French Creek and thus supplement the older east headrace. A new "colehaus" for the storage of charcoal was constructed. This was the earliest mention in the furnace books of such a structure at Hopewell although possibly an older one was being replaced.[2]

In order that the purchasers might have a definite record of what they had bought beside land and buildings, an appraisement of movable property was made by Robert May, Thomas Bull and John Buckley. It was also possible that these items belonged to John Bishop, manager under James Old, and were bought from him in a separate transaction. Among the items listed were the following:

One Bay hors and gairs combleat
1 Rone fifth hors
1 Bay hind hors
1 Sarl mare
One Wagon and Body all Readey to hidch in to hale mine
Black Backer Team
Foylan Team

[1] *Berks County Deed Book* 17, p. 219 ff.
[2] Richard P. Donahoe, "The Charcoal House and Shed, Hopewell Village National Historic Site" (unpublished study, 1956). Hopewell Village Library.

Paid on Jan. 10, 1816	8,500.00
Balance Due	12,641.16
Paid on Feb. 2, 1816	8,000.00[7]

Finances were a worry to the partners and a threat to the continued operation of the furnace. In the spring of 1802 Daniel Buckley wrote to Mathew Brooke.

> Mathew Davis[8] has been here and has let me know his Situation at the furnace Respecting Money it is Bad but not at all different from mine here [Brooke Forge in Lancaster County] it is with the utmost Difficulty I can get as much money as will keep off the Constable . . .
>
> Whether the furnace Blows or not altogether Depends upon you and Thomas as you have there all the former Produce of it . . .[9]

A month later Buckley wrote again to report on a trip to Lancaster where he had proposed a partnership to "Mr. Grubb," who it was hoped would put some cash into the business. He had also made a similar proposal to William Coleman. He cautioned Brooke to keep these negotiations very quiet as Grubb and Coleman were bitter rivals.[10] Nothing came of these hopes. A year later the same Coleman refused to give Buckley and Brooke any more pig iron from Cornwall Furnace until they paid for what they had already received.[11]

The Furnace was probably losing money at this time. A study of labor costs for the years 1805–1807 shows that the total value of the iron produced in two blasts was less then $1,000 more than wages and salaries paid. Other expenses would certainly have netted an operating loss.[12]

Notations by the Clerk in 1803 indicated trouble at the

[7] HV 8160110A, 8160110B, 8160110C, 8160110D. 8160205.
[8] Davis was employed to manage the Furnace after Thomas Brooke had been manager in 1800–1801.
[9] HV 8020418.
[10] HV 8020520. "Mr. Grubb" was probably ironmaster Henry B. Grubb.
[11] *Brooke Family Papers*, Wm. Coleman to Buckley and Brooke, July 22, 1803.
[12] See Appendix B.

furnace and probably with the founder as well: "August 12
. . . This day at 2 o'clock quit Putting mine on the Furnace
working bad." The blast was back in after a new hearth was
installed. Seventeen days were lost. In the interim Frederick
Meck agreed to blow the furnace,[13] replacing William Templin
as founder. A possible explanation for the change was this
observation, "This day Wᴹ Templer [sic] went hoam not fit
to work."[14] This wording was often used in the clerk's books
when a workman came on the job drunk. Meck had been
founder at nearby Changewater Furnace.[15] In August of 1804
the furnace had to be stopped again for one week because of
malfunction.[16]

The dam was a source of difficulty in 1807 when it was
broken by a flood on April 29. Repairs were begun, but another break took place on July 27. Two months later lightning
struck the dam wall and knocked it to the bottom.[17]

The partners maintained a faith in the eventual success of
Hopewell through this discouraging period. In 1803 they built
a log house[18] and in 1806 a stone tenant house and a spring
house.[19]

An air of excitement and expectancy surrounded the beginning of a blast. Final repairs were rushed to get back into
operation as soon as possible. Men were taken from other jobs
to facilitate the work. Here was the sequence of events which
led to the beginning of the blast of 1805:

April 23—Millwright began work on the wheel in the
          afternoon.
          C. Remley reported to dress the bellows.
May   4—The millwright finished the furnace wheel.
May   5—Put fire to the Furnace about 7 o'clock and 40
          Minnets in the Evening.

[13] SM 1, p. 36.
[14] *Ibid.*, p. 37.
[15] *Ibid.*, p. 39.
[16] *Ibid.*, p. 59.
[17] SM 45, under dates April 29, May 22, July 27, September 14, 1807.
[18] SM 2, p. 104.
[19] SM 4, p. 127.

May   7—Put Mine on the Furnace about 9 O'clock in the
          Morning in expectation of a prosperous Blast.
          Wind east SE.
May   9—This Morning about 6 O'clock and 40 Minnets
          Blew.[20]

The Furnace business continued but in a most precarious
condition in 1807 and 1808. There were numerous letters to
the partners demanding money for unpaid bills and some
threats of suits to collect.[21] Daniel Buckley wrote to Mathew
Brooke on December 22, 1808 that he had discussed with
". . . Mr. Tench Cox the possibility of entering a bid for
making cannon balls from 4 lb. to 32 lb." Buckley suggested
that they place a bid; and if they were to get a contract,
". . . it might answer to make another Blast at hopewell if not
we may be no worse."[22]

This attempt must have failed because Hopewell Furnace
was out of blast from 1808 to 1816. Activity at the village was
sharply reduced. Peter Turner, a Negro teamster, drew his
wages for hauling and for farm work. Mathew Brooke,
manager, and Frederisk Meck, founder, were paid their wages
to date. Meck later did some wood-cutting and hauling of
mine.[23] Wages from 1809 forward were usually for work
which was essentially maintenance. The Birdsboro Forge books
showed that some Hopewell men were given employment elsewhere by the Buckley and Brooke Company, included were :
Adam Johnston, Thomas Cuthbert, Thomas Rutherford,
George North, George Moyers, Henry Jacobs, John Richards,
Samuel Richards, Philip Shaffer and Henry Minker. Among
these were several miners, a molder and a blacksmith. Henry
Jacobs was a Negro laborer.[24] With Hopewell out of blast, the
forge found it necessary to turn to other sources for its pig iron.
One supplier was William Coleman at Cornwall and Elizabeth

[20] SM 1, May 4–9, 1805.
[21] *Brooke Family Papers* for these years.
[22] *Brooke Family Papers.*
[23] SM 5, p. 78–109; SM 4, p. 235.
[24] *Birdsboro Forge Time Book,* 1809–1810. Hopewell Village Library.

M. Brooke Buckley, Hopewell Partner 1827–1853

Furnaces.[25] Mt. Vernon Furnace exchanged pig iron for nails.[26]

The furnace store closed out its business in food and cloth early in 1809. The last normal day of activity at the store was December 16, 1808. In January, February, and March of 1809 there were only 45 purchases noted and nothing more after that except some cast iron items. The smith shop also stopped its active business of horse-shoeing and farm-machine repairing.[27]

The shutdown of the furnace left many workers with wages due them. These were settled in many ways. Some got cash or store goods from Hampton Forge, another Buckley-Brooke operation. Nicholas Hunter, Robert Gilmore and John Benson, all of them miners, settled their accounts by living in houses at the mines and paying no rent until their accounts were evened.[28] Thomas Wynn sued to collect his account and was paid his wages plus court costs by Hampton Forge on May 12, 1812.[29]

Laverty and McFarland, wholesalers, had a balance due to them when the store closed in the amount of £381 15s. This debt was also paid by Hampton Forge in three installments over the next three years.[30] Hampton Forge accounts paid many Hopewell bills, including taxes and interest on bonds in an apparent effort of the partners to prevent loss of Hopewell by sheriff's sale. The Hopewell ledger for these years closed with the note for November 9, 1812, that Hopewell Furnace owed Hampton Forge $25,507.35.[31]

Hampton Forge received in return some iron from the only industrial activity which continued at Hopewell Furnace, the operation of a stamping mill. This machine was erected in

[25] *Brooke Family Papers,* Wm. Coleman to Buckley and Brooke, 1810, Several Letters.
[26] *Ibid.,* H. B. Grubb to Buckley and Brooke, October 13, 1809.
[27] SM 4, pp. 251–254.
[28] SM 5, pp. 68, 84, 92.
[29] SM 5, p. 56.
[30] SM 5, p. 95.
[31] SM 5, p. 133.

Clement Brooke, Hopewell Manager 1816–1848, Partner 1827–1861

1805 at a cost of a little more than $100[32] to crush pieces of slag in order that beads of iron might be recovered. Clement Brooke was given the job of running the stamping mill for at least the period from 1809 to 1814.[33] Good iron was obtained from the stamping mill, according to Daniel Buckley, who wrote Mathew Brooke on February 23, 1808, "Pray have the stamping mill repaired and let it go on with Spirit, as that stamt stuff would Impove the Quality of the Iron . . . I would be glad to have some of it . . . and when it can be got with so little trouble why is it neglected?"[34] The price received for the

[32] SM 2, July 22, 1805.
[33] *Hopewell Papers,* Buckley and Brooke a/c with Clement Brooke, 1809–1814. Hopewell Village Library.
[34] HV 8080223.

stamped iron varied from $10 per ton to $20 per ton, with Hampton Forge buying most of it at $18 per ton.[35] As late as 1816 Edward Hughes was paid for running the stamping mill.[36]

Why did Hopewell Furnace close its business? Why was it not making iron during the War of 1812 when the demand was great? The general business conditions, financial problems and technical difficulties were certainly a part of the cause. But perhaps the most compelling reason was the one recorded in a notation made by a lawyer for the Buckley and Brooke Company. He placed the blame for the Furnace's problems on the law suits in which the partners had tried to defend their land titles. He declared that:

> The ejectment . . . claim was not terminated after repeated tryals till 1815. The defendants during the term from the fall of 1808 to which time, was prevented from the use of the furnace for want of sufficient wood, and were oblidged to expend large sums of money to defend and carry on the tryals against the Penn Claim.
>
> During which time the works etc. went into decay and after the Decision of the cause Cost near $8000 to repair before the furnace could be of any use.[37]

The Penn Claim case referred to in this note was one of a great many suits at law which involved the Hopewell partners for years after they assumed ownership. Some were minor actions to recover wages, to collect tavern or grocery bills, and for trespass or damage suits. The court records do not disclose the nature of many of these suits.[38] There were, however, three cases which dragged on for many years and involved major claims against Hopewell property.

In the April,1801, term of the Berks County Court Matthias

[35] HV 8097227; 8140321; SM 4, p. 241; 8160416.
[36] SM 9, p. 137.
[37] *Brooke Family Papers.* "Memorandum: Points to be made and proven at the Reading Court, April, 1818."
[38] *Berks County Court Appearances Dockets,* April, 1800–April, 1811.

Edward S. Buckley, Hopewell Partner 1853–1895

Kahler challenged the title of a part of the Hopewell lands and received a verdict to eject Buckley and Brooke from 50 acres of arable and 300 acres of wood land in Union Township.[39] The defendants appealed the case. In 1806 Kahler asked for arbitrators.[40] Four years later the matter was adjudged by five men in favor of Kahler, and again Mathew Brooke appealed.[41] The final verdict awarded Kahler 239 acres of woodland.[42]

Daniel Buckley's reaction to the outcome of the Kahler action was noted in a letter to Mathew Brooke while this final appeal was still pending:

> I observe you have not suceeded in Kellers [sic] Suit and I think it very proper to Renew the Suit . . . God only knows what [wil]l be the Consequences . . . I am endeavoring to reconcile myself to the most Disastrous Consequences . . . my Business ever since I have been concerned in Berks County has been going Backwards and unless someting meraculous turns up I fear I shall be Ruined . . . My mind has almost sunk under my Trouble. . . .[43]

A complex suit called *Leasee of John Penn and Richard Penn Esqr v. Mathew Brooke* ("Penn Claims Case") tied up the use of woodland and was blamed for the inability of Hopewell Furnace to operate until title was cleared, as noted earlier in this chapter. This claim was entered on behalf of Warwick Furnace owners for "one house, one barn, and one thousand acres of land with the appurtenances situate in Union Township . . ."[44] The argument involved the disputed wording of an old grant from the Penns to Reading Furnace on September 14, 1742. A jury decided in favor of the defendant in 1809, and the judge upheld this decision on appeal in 1811. But further appeals delayed settlement until 1815.[45]

[39] *Berks County Court Pleadings,* August, 1800–September, 1801.
[40] *Ibid.,* January, 1806, Number 74.
[41] *Berks County Court Records,* Term of January, 1806–July, 1810.
[42] *Berks County Court Pleadings,* January, 1810–May, 1813.
[43] HV 8110206.
[44] *Berks County Court Pleadings and Miscellaneous Old Papers,* 1752–1800.
[45] *Ibid.,* 1802–1817.

The case with the record for continuance was one referred to as the *Bishop-Smith Case*. John Bishop had been manager of Hopewell Furnance before its purchase by Buckley and Brooke, and John Smith was the manager of Dale and Joanna Furnaces. They probably wished to get control of Hopewell Furnance, and certainly they wanted a large tract of woodland for the use of Joanna Furnace. The first intimation of trouble from this quarter appeared in a letter from Daniel Buckley to Mathew Brooke in May, 1802:

> . . . Mr. Morris and those who hold our Bonds have sold them to a Company of whom Bull Smith at Joanna and Smith the Cashier of the Bank of Pennsylvania and Frazier the Lawyer of Phila^d are some of them and that Mr. Morris has turned against us to favor them and keep the land not sold at Sherrifs sale. Should these things be true I think that the Idea of Just Dealings is Departed from him, and that we must Imediately take some measures to counteract their Intentions . . .[46]

On the same day this letter was written, Bishop and Smith purchased Hopewell bonds from Benjamin Morris. Smith then ordered Hopewell workers to avoid trespassing on land claimed by Joanna Furnace, and Mathew Brooke assumed responsibility for any of his workmen who cut wood or dug for ore in the disputed area.[47] Bishop and Smith announced the sale of 1876 acres of land which had been part of the Hopewell Furnace property and then bid it in for themselves on June 18, 1802. Buckley and Brooke gave public notice at the sale of their claim to the land and offered to pay all money owed to Bishop and Smith ". . . Provided Bishop and Smith would convey all the lands to which the[y] pretended claim and complete our title."[48] Three days later Bishop and Smith sent the sheriff to Hopewell to levy on personal property of Buckley and Brooke, but Sheriff Nicholas Dick refused to

---

[46] HV 8020510.
[47] *Brooke Family Papers*, Draft of Papers Relating to Jones Mine Hole.
[48] *Ibid.*, Memorandum: Points to be made and proven at the Reading Court, April, 1818.

make the levy until Mathew Brooke had a chance to talk to him.[49] However, on June 23 he seized 50 tons of pig iron, 4 teams with wagons, 10 head of "Horned cattle" and 3,000 cords of wood. The total value was £2,535.[50]

In the autumn the dispute moved into court with a suit in ejectment from 1876 acres in Union, Robeson and Caernarvon Townships of Berks County. Mathew Brooke was ordered to appear before the court and present any claims he had to the property.[51] No settlement was reached at this time. In 1805 Buckley wrote to Mathew Brooke:

> . . . I have had several Conversations with Mr. Frazier on the Hopewell Business. . . . He offers to Extinguish the Claim of Bishop Smith and Co to the part of the Estate put in Dispute Provided that the money Remaining due, which he says by his Calculating amounts to $10,440—or something more, be paid in three Equal parts . . . within the next year.[52]

A month later Buckley wrote that he was convinced that the object of Bishop and Smith was to get control of the Hopewell property. He urged his partner to raise all the money he could to pay off the bonds.[53] Some payment was evidently made, as it was noted on January 1, 1807, "Paid Bishop and Smith at sundry times £2743–2/6."[54]

Soon after this, all payment on the bonds was suspended until settlement was reached on the title to the disputed land. In 1815 Buckley and Brooke were trying for some kind of decision so they could reopen the Furnace. Smith and Bishop had both died recently, and there was apparently more hope of a settlement with the heirs. Buckley wrote on September 15, 1815:

[49] *Ibid.,* William Brown to Mathew Brooke, June 21, 1802.
[50] *Ibid.,* Sheriff's Levy, June 23, 1802.
[51] *Hopewell Papers,* Notice of Suit in Berks County Court.
[52] *Brooke Family Papers,* Daniel Buckley to Mathew Brooke, February 18, 1805.
[53] *Ibid.,* March 20, 1805.
[54] SM 4, p. 132.

". . . As the tryal of the Dispute about the Hopewell property will I suppose soon come on I have sent Clement over to make Inquiry of Thomas Smith what mesures he is likely to take to have the Business terminated. Clement is not much engaged at this time I wish that he might Employ himself in Endeavouring to Descover which of the tracts have not been patented . . . Any other Business which you may think Clement can be of service at . . . you will Inform him of and he will attend to it.[55]

There were numerous references to this action in the Berks County Court in the years 1816–1818. In November of the latter year a jury ruled in favor of Buckley and Brooke.[56] The case was appealed, and the courts ruled again for them in an application for a writ of mandamus in 1820.[57] Another appeal was tried in the Pennsylvania Supreme Court sitting in Lancaster in May 1824. James Buchanan was the lawyer for the Bishop and Smith Estates and the firm of Baird and Hopkins represented Buckley and Brooke.[58]

The summary of the evidence presented to the Supreme Court gave a review of the entire dispute. It showed that the title given by Benjamin Morris to part of the land was disputed by Matthias Keller (sic) and others. In 1806 Buckley and Brooke brought an action of ejectment against Keller and lost. They then refused to pay the bonds, representing a mortgage on the property, held by John Bishop and John Smith until there should have been an adjustment in the purchase price by Morris. The basis of this action was that Morris had not given a valid title to all of the lands. Morris, acting for the executors of Bishop and Smith, brought action against Buckley and Brooke to collect the principal and interest on the bonds. But the Supreme Court upheld the decision of the Berks County Court in favor of Buckley and Brooke.[59]

[55] *Brooke Family Papers*. Daniel Buckley to Mathew Brooke.

[56] *Berks County Court Appearance Docket*, 1815–1817.

[57] *Hopewell Papers*, Sam Barde to Daniel Buckley, May 21, 1820.

[58] Thomas Sergant and William Rawle (Editors), *Reports of Cases Adjudged in the Supreme Court of Pennsylvania* (Volume VIII; Philadelphia: Abraham Small, 1824), p. 211–214.

[59] *Ibid.*, Volume IX, pp. 168–176.

The *Bishop-Smith Case* was apparently closed for all time by this action, but a curious revival came seventy years later. Edward S. Buckley planned to sell his interest in Hopewell in 1895 and discovered that there was an unsatisfied mortgage for £9,000 standing on record against Hopewell Estates for the purchase money in 1800. He had the record cleared by the county court.[60]

On March 20, 1816, business began again at Hopewell, at least in the store. It is not clear exactly when the furnace was put back in blast. But in July a letter from a customer stated, "Mr. Buckley was to let us know whether he could not supply our whole quantity now he has the furnace in blast . . ."[61] And in September Amos H. Slaymaker of Columbia wrote that he had Hopewell stoves in his store.[62] A new bookkeeping series began with Journal A, and the first two entries on March 20, 1816 read :

Paid for two a/c Books	4.00
Paid M. Richards Collector for Lisence	15.00

There followed then a number of entries for the sale of store goods.[63]

The postwar market for iron was good. In 1815 charcoal pig iron sold for an average price of $53.75.[64] This price may have been one of the biggest inducements for putting the furnace in operation. Some hope for expanded molding at Hopewell was indicated by the construction in 1816 or early in 1817 of a cupola to make use of pig or scrap iron for molding.[65] There were a number of references to the cupola for several years, and then mention of it ceased. So it was probably not a great success.[66]

[60] HV 8950223, E. S. Buckley to Maria T. Clingan.
[61] *Brooke Family Papers,* Whitestone Manufacturing Company to Matthew Brooke, Esq., July 24, 1816.
[62] HV 8160906.
[63] SM 8, p. 1.
[64] Birkinbine, *Manufacture of Pig Iron in Pennsylvania, op. cit.,* p. 37.
[65] SM 7 and SM 8, *passim.*
[66] *Ibid.*

Furnace business was not very firmly established when the severe business depression of 1819 struck. In the two blasts extending from 1818 into 1820 the Furnace may have shown a small profit. The iron produced was worth about $5,000 more than the wages and salaries paid.[67] Because the journals for the depression years have disappeared, the full effects of the depression cannot be assessed; but the Furnace weathered the panic and emerged into a period of great prosperity. In the blasts of 1825–1827 the value of iron produced over labor costs was more than $36,000. For the period 1835–1837 it was about $83,000.[68] Another evidence of growth was an inventory of stock on hand at Hopewell in 1820 giving a total valuation of $27,009.34. Included in this total were furnishings for the ironmaster's home to the value of $550, store goods of $387, beef and pork of $480, thirteen horses worth $925 and eleven milch cows valued at $220.[69]

Under the shrewd management of Clement Brooke, Hopewell Furnace found new markets for its products, took advantage of the improvements in transportation and profited from the demands for new products of iron. Stoves became the largest item of Furnace produce and the source of its greatest profit.[70] New mine property and forest lands were purchased as they came on the market. Five tracts were bought at sheriff's sales in 1825 and two in 1826. Additional woodland was bought at private sales in 1832 and 1833.[71]

The death of members of the firm forced several changes in the partnership organization. The reorganized company in 1816 was known as Daniel Buckley and Company. Until the time of his death some twelve years later Daniel Buckley drew profits from the firm to the amount of $31,301.40.[72] Part of this was in pig iron sent to the Brooke Forge in Lancaster

[67] See Appendix B.
[68] *Ibid.*
[69] HV 8200307A and 8200307B.
[70] These items will be discussed in detail in subsequent chapters.
[71] SM 46, p. 64; SM 12, pp. 13, 125; SM 6, pp. 6, 36.
[72] HV 8270517.

County which was operated by his sons Clement and M. B. Buckley. On May 15, 1827, these two men were included in the Hopewell partnership, owning with their father a one-half share. The other half was shared by Clement Brooke, his brother Charles and his sisters Tacy and Ann. The firm name was then changed to Buckley and Brooke.[73] The women had a share worth $3,000 each and drew interest on that amount but probably were not regarded as active partners.[74]

The company was reorganized once more in 1831. M. Brooke Buckley paid $40,000 to the estate of his father for the half interest the Buckleys owned. Then he sold to Clement and Charles Brooke one third of the Buckley interest for $13,333.33. Each of these men now owned one third of a firm known as Clement Brooke and Company. An appraisal of the stock at the Furnace at this time placed its value at $13,562.93$\frac{1}{2}$, not including real estate.[75]

A survey of the iron industry made in 1829–1830 gave these statistics for Hopewell Furnace : "Employees—168; wood used—15,000 cords; produced—1,000 tons of pig iron and 700 tons of castings over past three years."[76] The Louis McLane report to the national House of Representatives in 1832 listed for Hopewell :

Men employed—168
Supposed No. of dependants—800
No. of Horses—84
Pig Metal—1,000 Tons
Castings—700 Tons[77]

The most prosperous period for Hopewell was from 1830 to 1838. In one blast from January 3, 1836, to April 10, 1837, the furnace operated continuously for 445 days and

[73] *Ibid.*
[74] SM 17, p. 2.
[75] HV 8310111.
[76] Pearse, *op. cit.*, p. 155.
[77] *Hazard's Register of Pennsylvania,* XIV, 18 (November 1, 1834), p. 350.

produced 1,169 tons of mixed castings.[78] But trouble was not far ahead in the forms of technical improvements in the iron business and another severe business depression beginning in 1837. Clement Brooke was full of confidence when he wrote in 1836:

> . . . if you wish us to furnish you with castings the next year, be Punctial in meeting us in Philad[a] on Tuesday the 3rd Jany. next, as it will be necessary for us by that time to know who we may Contract with, the supposed Price of stove Castings will be from $100 to $110 per ton . . . We presume castings will be very scarce in the marked next season, Pig Iron is now selling on the Furnace Banks from $50 to $60 per ton and a Supply cannot be got at any Price, we intend making a winter Blast and must know who we are to supply . . ."[79]

Four years later the Furnace was making castings for which it had no contract and was offering to fill orders immediately.[80]

In 1836 the Pennsylvania legislature authorized the formation of corporations to make iron with coke and in 1838 added anthracite coal.[81] The coal-operated furnaces proved to be advantageous, and their expansion began the period of decline for the charcoal furnaces. The end of an era took place at Hopewell when stove-casting was halted in 1844. Some small castings were made after that date, but the Furnace operated then primarily to produce pig iron. It survived on this basis for almost forty years.

[78] Dennis C. Kurjack, *Hopewell Village National Historical Site* (Washington: National Park Service Handbook Series, Hamberg, 1950), p. 28.
[79] HV 8361207A.
[80] HV 8400309.
[81] Pearse, *op. cit.*, p. 272.

3 Decline, Shutdown and Survivals, 1845-1963

THE END OF STOVE-MAKING AT HOPEWELL BROUGHT MANY changes in the business. The skilled, well-paid molders left for employment elsewhere. The Furnace was dependent upon the sale of pig iron for its operation, but the expansion of the country and the Civil War created so great a demand for iron that Hopewell Furnace continued to operate at a profit for many years.

Most of the iron communities had been formed in the eighteenth century. Many of them continued well into the nineteenth, but by the middle of the latter century they were feeling the effects of the competition from larger iron works which were located nearer the centers of population. The large capitalistic enterprises and consolidations after the Civil War made it impossible for these small local iron works to continue.[1] Charcoal iron was better suited for agricultural castings, blacksmiths' bars and nails than was anthracite iron. But anthracite and coke iron were preferred by the roller-mills producing iron for the railroads and industry.[2]

[1] Bining, *Pennsylvania Iron Manufacture in the 18th Century, op. cit.*, p. 29.
[2] Harold F. Williamson (Editor), *The Growth of the American Economy* (New York : Prentice-Hall, 1946), p. 216.

There were other factors unfavorable to the small charcoal furnaces: the depletion of forests and ore deposits in the East, the development of the hot blast, the new iron ore mines in the midwest, and the movement of the center of population west of the mountains.[3] At midcentury, however, charcoal furnaces still outnumbered anthracite furnaces in Eastern Pennsylvania by 103 to 100.[4]

Hopewell, like many of its competitors of Berks and Chester Counties, gave up its attempt to compete in the market for finished products. It sold its stove patterns to a small foundry at Parkersford, and many of the Hopewell molders moved there to find employment. Others went to furnaces which were still making castings. For some years former Hopewell molders worked at Rock Furnace in Lancaster County.[5]

The Triennial Assessment in 1846 gave a view of Hopewell in this period of transition:

> Owner—Clement Brooke and Company
> Seated Acres—3,800
> Valuation—$66,000
> 12 Horses—$600
> 6 Cattle—$72
> 1 Pleasure Carriage—$150
> Occupation—Ironmaster
> Occupation Tax valuation—$200
> Yearly income above $200 @ 1% Tax. Ironmaster $500
> Public Loan or Stock Owned $240
> 1 Gold Watch $75
> 14 Tenants on C. Brooke Property.
>   [8 others may have been Brooke tenants and 5 single men gave Hopewell as their place of residence].[6]

Hopewell suffered a great loss from the decision of Clement Brooke to retire from active management in 1848. He re-

[3] Gemmell, *op. cit.,* p. 116.
[4] Victor S. Clark, *History of Manufactures in the United States* (Volume I; New York: Peter Smith, 1949), p. 329.
[5] Long, *op. cit.,* p. 9–10.
[6] *Triennial Assessment Book,* Berks County, Union Township, 1846. Berks County Court House.

Doctor Charles M. Clingan, Hopewell Manager 1849–1859

mained as a partner until his death in 1861, but after 1849 he was living in his home in Pottstown. For one year Hopewell was managed by John Church, nephew of Clement Brooke's wife, who had been the clerk under Brooke. After Church's short tenure active management was taken over by Charles M. Clingan who had married Maria Brooke six years before.[7]

In 1852 the partnership of Clement and Charles Brooke and Mathew Brooke Buckley was formally dissolved by the Court of Common Pleas of Berks County upon the petition of Clement Brooke. The reason for this action was apparently to remove Charles Brooke from the company. The Furnace valua-

[7] SM 32, *passim*.

tion was placed at $87,833.00, and Clement agreed to pay one third of that amount to each of the others. The Furnace lands were listed in various tracts which totaled 3958 acres and 123 perches.[8] Clement resold a half interest to Mathew Brooke Buckley for $43,916.50.[9] The latter died in 1853 bequeathing his share of Hopewell Furnace to his son Edward S. Buckley.[10]

Charles M. Clingan was the manager for ten years, after which he entered the banking and provision businesses in Philadelphia. He made frequent visits to Hopewell until his death in 1875, but he entrusted the supervision to hired managers.[11] Two of these last managers were John R. Shafer[12] and Harker A. Long.[13]

Clement Brooke was too good an ironmaster not to recognize the advantages of the new anthracite fuel for his furnaces. Overman, writing in 1849, asserted, ". . . good anthracite is undoubtedly the most perfect of all fuels for the manufacture of iron. Its application is simple; its hardness prevents it from falling into slack; and the small amount of hydrogen it contains makes it advantageous for the blast furnace operation."[14] The saving on labor over charcoal iron was phenomenal. In 1848 it cost $12.35 per ton for labor to produce charcoal iron,[15] but the labor cost for anthracite iron was only $2.50 per ton.[16] For the blast periods from 1851 to 1853 the labor cost at Hopewell was $15.44 per ton of pig iron.[17]

Clement Brooke had had experience with an anthracite

---

[8] *Berks County Deed Book* 59, p. 529.

[9] *Stokes Collection, Hopewell Papers,* Deed of Sale, December 6, 1853. Hopewell Village Library.

[10] *Berks County Deed Book* 76, p. 64.

[11] *Reading Eagle,* February 11, 1917. Article by Cyrus Fox.

[12] H. F. Bridgens and A. R. Witmer; *Atlas of Chester County, Pennsylvania* (Safe Harbor, Pennsylvania; A. R. Witmer, 1873), p. 55.

[13] HV 8761110.

[14] Frederick Overman, *The Manufacture of Iron* (Philadelphia: Henry C. Baird, 1854), p. 99.

[15] *Documents Relating to the Manufacture of Iron in Pennsylvania* (Philadelphia: Published by the General Committee of the Convention of Iron Masters, 1850), p. 90.

[16] Overman, *op. cit.,* p. 183.

[17] See Appendix B.

operation at Robesonia Furnace which he purchased in 1841 and where he helped to erect an anthracite furnace in 1845. This experience, plus the discovery in 1846 or 1847 of a large body of sulphur ore at the old Hopewell Mines, may have been the reason for the decision to build an anthracite furnace at Hopewell. Possibly Charles Brooke opposed this venture and thus precipitated the dissolution of the partnership in 1852. At any rate the new partnership built an anthracite furnace at Hopewell in 1853.[18]

The anthracite operation at Hopewell was very brief. The new ore was not usable unless mixed with other ore which was not available at Hopewell,[19] and the cost of hauling the coal from the Schuylkill Canal to the Furnace and the iron back to the canal was too great. After less than four years the furnace machinery was moved from Hopewell to Monocacy on the canal, where smelting operations began in 1857.[20] Hopewell records show that ore was hauled from 1857 to 1859 to what was at first called "the new furnace" and later "the Teresa Furnace."[21] In the latter year this furnace was sold to another firm and was then operated as the Monocacy Furnace.[22]

With this upstart rival removed, the old Hopewell charcoal furnace resumed its place as the center of industrial activity for the community. In 1850 it was listed among the cold blast charcoal furnaces with this data :

Post Office—Douglasville
Owner—Clement, Brooke and Co.
Kind of Ore used—Magnetic
Largest Product—1,150 tons
Actual Make in 1849—1,000 tons
No. of men and boys employed—80
   ,,   ,, Oxen, horses and mules—50

[18] Benjamin J. Zerbey and Earl J. Heydinger, "Anthracite Furnace, Hopewell National Historic Site" (unpublished study, 1962). Hopewell Village Library.
[19] Wilmer W. MacElree, *Around the Boundaries of Chester County* (West Chester, Pennsylvania : Published by the Author, 1934), p. 556.
[20] Zerbey and Heydinger, *op. cit.*
[21] *Kemper Manuscripts,* "Book of Ore Hauling."
[22] *Montgomery Manuscripts,* Book I, p. 108.

Blast—Cold
Tuyeres—1
Pressure—3/4 lb
Stack—Bosh—6½ feet
        Height—30 feet
Kind of Power—Water
Kind of Metal Made—No. 1
Market for Sales—Philadelphia
Capacity—1,150 tons[23]

There was evidence that the owners continued to have faith in the old furnace in the purchase of additional tracts of land in 1849 and 1857.[24] They also may have found a new source of income in the sale of charcoal, for in 1851 Edward Gault was paid $555.45 "for hauling charcoal to the canal."[25]

The Civil War brought new activity to the charcoal-iron industry. The price of pig iron rose so rapidly that cost of production was no longer a worry. Iron which in normal times had sold for $30 per ton was bringing $80 in 1864[26] and touched $99 before it began its decline.[27] Prices remained high after the war largely because of the demands of the expanding railroads. Most Hopewell iron was purchased at this time by a Philadelphia manufacturer of railroad car wheels.[28] Because of the strain placed upon them and the need for reliability, a special quality of iron was used in casting car wheels. Uniformity of contraction was obtained by slow cooling for several days in modified annealing furnaces.[29] This casting and annealing were not done at Hopewell, however, but in Philadelphia. This new business encouraged extensive repairs to the furnace in 1869 according to this report by the clerk:

[23] *Documents Relating to the Manufacture of Iron in Pennsylvania,* op. cit.
[24] SM 31, p. 89 and SM 65, August 19, 1857.
[25] SM 32, p. 119.
[26] HV 8640629.
[27] Long, *op. cit.,* p. 12.
[28] "Hopewell Village," *International Molders and Foundry Workers' Journal,* 94, 10 (October 1958), p. 6.
[29] Clark, *op. cit.,* p. 504.

Repaired old Stack and put in new inwals the inwalls of new fire brick—Started on an iron ring Seven feet wide with a regular taper to the top which is twenty two inches—the new inwall was 9 inch brick backed by 12 inches of fire brick bats, and a Space of four inches between them and the Stone Wall which was filled with Sand.[30]

Another new customer was the Reading Railroad Company which agreed to try 10 tons of Hopewell iron in 1876 at $33 per ton.[31] More orders came from the railroad after this initial trial.[32]

But there were signs of approaching death for the Furnace. The Hopewell Mines were leased by the Patterson Iron Company.[33] The furnace was out of blast in 1874[34] and again in 1877–1878. In 1877 the mules were sold. But a rise in the price of iron postponed the decease and encouraged the owners to make the necessary repairs to resume operations in 1880.[35] E. S. Buckley wrote to Long:

. . . Get all the wood cut off the property that it is possible to get out by paying as much wages as any one else in the neighborhood; and blow the furnace *as early in the Spring as it may be possible to get coal made from our own wood, say by 1st of May* and keep her going until all our own coal is consumed and then blow out. Proceed steadily with this view in mind, and do not think of any project, as I have never entertained any others, and will not. In relation to wood choppers do the best you can, *but keep the men at work.* Do not let a man leave who is doing good work.[36]

During the next winter a severe cold spell froze the water wheel and forced the furnace to shut down for lack of a blast. To insure against a recurrence of this mishap, a boiler was

[30] SM 60, p. 7.
[31] HV 8760201. Edward S. Buckley to Chas. M. Clingan.
[32] SM 60, p. 201.
[33] *Jeffersonian*, West Chester, Pennsylvania, March 30, 1872.
[34] *Daily Local News*, West Chester, Pennsylvania, November 22, 1874.
[35] Long, *op. cit.*, p. 13.
[36] HV 8800214A.

installed to run a steam engine as auxiliary power to the water wheel. Water was heated in the boiler by the hot gas from the furnace stack.[37] Another technical improvement, installed in 1882, was an ore roaster to remove impurities and improve the texture of the ore for use in the furnace.[38] Buckley had opposed spending money for these improvements. "Hopewell is about 'played out,' and next years blast is probably the last she will ever make, and there is no use of spending any more money on her," he wrote.[39]

The company did not operate a store at Hopewell for some years before the furnace closed. Sally Care Boone said that she and her husband came to Hopewell in 1875 and opened a store in one of the tenant houses. Business was good so long as the furnace was in operation, but after the shutdown the villagers could not pay their bills. The Boone store closed in 1891.[40]

The last blast at the Hopewell Furnace ended on June 15, 1883. After this no more iron was produced.[41] In the year the operation ceased, the Union Township tax collector raised the assessment on the property from $58,000 to $84,600.[42] As recently as 1877 the assessment had been $32,369.[43] Buckley expressed the view that this increase was outrageous and that he intended to protest.[44]

While there might have been reason to sympathize with Mr. Buckley for an assessment which almost tripled in six years and was levied on an inactive business, the future records show that there was still much value in the Hopewell property; and

[37] Harker A. Long Interview, August 13, 1936.
[38] Franklin Kemper, "J. Lincoln Palsgrove" (unpublished study, n.d.), p. 6. Hopewell Village Library.
[39] *Kemper Manuscripts,* Edward S. Buckley to Harker A. Long, November 8, 1880.
[40] Sally Boone Interview, March 22, 1941.
[41] SM 61, p. 206.
[42] *Hopewell Papers,* Edward S. Buckley to Maria T. Clingan, April 25, 1883.
[43] SM 34, April 1, 1877.
[44] *Hopewell Papers,* Edward S. Buckley to Maria T. Clingan, April 25, 1883.

several sources of income were derived from it. As late as 1886 there were 360 tons of pig iron on hand. On September 14 of that year the Reading Railroad bought 100 tons of this at $26 per ton.[45] The Furnace books were kept until March 23, 1896. During this period there were records of the sale of pig iron, ore and wood; payments of freight bills; farm operations; rental of houses; and royalty on stone quarried on the property. The last pig iron was sold in 1888;[46] the horses and mules had gone a year earlier.[47]

At the time the furnace closed, it was owned in equal shares by Edward S. Buckley as the heir of M. Brooke Buckley and Maria T. Clingan, daughter of Clement Brooke and widow of Charles Clingan. Buckley frequently expressed a lack of hope for income from Hopewell in letters to his partner. In 1886 he said he had been spending his own money on taxes and repairs and proposed that they divide the remaining pig iron between them to realize what they could on it.[48]

Five years later he wrote of his disappointment in failing to lease ground for a stone quarry. He was not at all hopeful that a buyer of the property could be found,[49] and the next year he said he would take $25,000 for his half interest if anyone would make an offer[50] In 1894 Mrs. Clingan proposed to trade her share in two store buildings on Front Street in Philadelphia for Buckley's half of Hopewell.[51] Buckley agreed to the trade, and his part of the partnership was transferred to Mrs. Clingan's children Charles B. Clingan, Alan Hunter Clingan and A. Louise Clingan Brooke.[52]

The Clingans found a number of uses for Hopewell. The old mansion house served as a summer home until 1915. The rear wing, however, was occupied by Harker A. Long and later by

[45] *Hopewell Papers*, Record book of Maria T. Clingan.
[46] SM 61, pp. 206–241.
[47] HV 8870314.
[48] HV 8860710.
[49] HV 8911008.
[50] HV 8920219.
[51] HV 8941124.
[52] *Berks County Deed Book* 209, p. 22.

Remains of Anthracite Furnace at Hopewell Village

Nathan Care, who acted as caretakers.[53] Fence posts and rails were cut from the woodland under the direction of the Clingan sons and sold in carload lots. The records indicate that this was a major operation.[54] Charcoal was again a Hopewell product, but this time it was sold instead of being used for furnace fuel.[55]

In 1894 Richard Humphreys signed an agreement to quarry stone on Hopewell property.[56] There was no record of the extent of this quarrying. But in 1906 A. Louise C. Brooke and

[53] *Hopewell Papers*, File H 3019.
[54] HV 8980817.
[55] HV 9030928.
[56] *Hopewell Papers*, "Agreement between E. S. Brooke and Maria T. Clingan with Richard Humphreys, Jr."

her husband Edward Brooke sold quarrying rights on 3,000 acres, of which 2,829 acres were Hopewell Furnace property, to the Schuylkill Stone Company for $157,000.[57] This transaction alone justified the faith of the Clingans. In another kind of "quarrying" the Pottstown Iron Company was continuing to mine iron ore from the old Hopewell Mine. As late as 1913 a carload per day was going to the Eastern Steel Company at Pottstown.[58]

Most of the activity described involved the land and not the buildings at Hopewell Furnace. Repairs were neglected. One of the tenants described the house in which he lived as in a bad state of disrepair—fences rotting, porch falling off and roof leaking.[59] The furnace was deteriorating. Some of the machinery installed there was thought to have historical value, and Mrs. Brooke offered it to the Franklin Institute in Philadelphia. They accepted the gift, dismantled the wooden working parts and in 1930 built a shed to house them pending removal to Philadelphia. They were still at Hopewell when the National Park Service decided to restore the old furnace, and the Franklin Institute gave permission for the machinery to be reinstalled in its original place.[60]

Renewed activity came to Hopewell Village in 1935 and thereafter. The United States Government purchased about 6,000 acres of land from A. Louise Brooke and others. Mrs. Brooke received $86,970.82 for the main tract of 3,781.34 acres[61] and $11,301.62 for an additional 458.95 acres. John T. Dyer Quarry Company sold 1,217 acres for $17,211.60. There were also other smaller purchases.[62]

In 1935 two Civilian Conservation Corps camps were located in the area with a total of about 400 men. They did

[57] *Berks County Deed Book* 330, p. 449.
[58] *West Chester* (Pennsylvania) *Star*, November 20, 1913.
[59] HV 8990418, H. A. Care to Hunter Clingan.
[60] Roy Edgar Appleman, "Historical Report, French Creek Area" (unpublished study, n. d.). Hopewell Village Library.
[61] *Berks County Deed Book* 768, p. 642.
[62] *Hopewell Papers,* Abstract of Deeds to Hopewell Property, February 11, 1938.

repair work at Hopewell Village and constructed some road-
ways. A Works Progress Administration program was also
engaged in restoration work from 1935 to 1939.[63]

The original reasons for the government purchase of this
property were given as:

> . . . the lands are being acquired for use as a public park
> and recreational area, for the restoration of structures of
> historic interest, the conservation of natural resources, the
> preservation of scenic beauty, forestation and reforestation and
> for use in connection with the construction of certain improve-
> ments necessary and appropriate to provide public facilities
> for the purposes of the project.[64]

In 1938 a new purpose was stated for the Hopewell Furnace area:

> *Whereas* certain lands and structures in Hopewell Village,
> Pennsylvania, including the old furnace, mansion house,
> blacksmith shop, etc., by reason of their relationship to the
> colonial history of the United States, have been declared by
> the Advisory Board of National Parks, Historic Sites, Build-
> ings, and Monuments to be a historic site of National signifi-
> cance . . . *Now, therefore*, I, E. K. Burlew, Acting Secretary
> of the Interior . . . do hereby designate the following
> described lands, with the structures standing thereon, to be a
> national historic site, having the name "Hopewell Village
> National Historic Site. August 3, 1938."[65]

In 1947 the national government deeded to the Commonwealth of Pennsylvania about 5,000 acres of the land purchased and retained 848 acres for the Hopewell Village site.[66]
On this area the National Park Service has been engaged at
restoration work aimed at making the life of an old iron plan-

---

[63] Roy Edgar Appleman, "Memorandum Respecting the Historical and
Archeological Importance of the French Creek Recreational Demonstra-
tion Area, Pennsylvania, and the Proposal that it be made a National
Monument" (unpublished study, 1939). Hopewell Village Library.

[64] *Hopewell Papers*, Abstract of Deeds to Hopewell Property, *op. cit.*

[65] *Ibid.*

[66] *Birdsboro* (Pennsylvania) *Dispatch*, June 13, 1952.

tation come alive. In 1963 alone more than 100,000 visitors came to look and listen to the story of charcoal iron and of the people who made it. The target date for completion of the restoration is 1966.

Part Two

The Physical Village

4 The Ironmaster's Mansion

In the heyday of charcoal iron the successful operator of one or more furnaces and forges was a man of affluence and power. He lived well in the mansion, or "big house," which he built close enough to the iron works that he could supervise the industrial activity of his establishment. His house may have lacked something of the advantage of setting enjoyed by the Philadelphia merchant at his country seat or the Southern planter in the midst of his cotton fields, but it did not suffer by comparison in size or elegance of appointment with the homes of other entrepreneurs of the era. A number of the homes of the ironmasters, including the one at Hopewell Village, survive to our day as evidence of the scale of living their occupants enjoyed.

There are differences of opinion about the quality of the architectural style of the Hopewell mansion house. One observer called it one of the "three best examples of country homes of the Revolutionary period in existence in Pennsylvania."[1] Another said, "The mansion house at Hopewell is of a not very interesting colonial style."[2] It is large, and probably it was utilitarian in the day it was built.

Parts of this house were constructed at three different times.

[1] Cyrus Fox in the *Reading Eagle,* February 25, 1917.
[2] Appleman, "Historical Report," *op. cit.,* p. 28.

Front View of Hopewell Mansion

Northeast Corner of Hopewell Mansion, Basement Dining Area and
Bake Ovens

North Side of Hopewell Mansion, Bathroom in Frame Addition in Center

South Side of Hopewell Mansion

The northwest wing of the T-shaped house may have been built about 1771 when the furnace was constructed. The east-wing corner was probably added next, and the southwest corner last. It was possibly completed essentially in its present form by 1830, but the porches were certainly added much later.[3] The east wing may have been built in 1802 when Thomas Lloyd sold "40 logs for raising the kitchen."[4] Architect Gustavus Mang thought the rear wing was built about 1820.[5]

As it stands today, the mansion is a four-storied stone house built against the side of a hill. The door from the front porch opens into the second-floor entry hall. The rear court has direct access to the first floor. This ground floor includes three cellars, a dining room and a kitchen; the second contains four large rooms; the third consists of six bedrooms, a bath and a hallway; the fourth has two non-communicating suites of two rooms each. The building's three chimneys served seven fireplaces which are still visible and possibly two more which are no longer open on the top floor. From the entry hall a broad stairway leads to the third floor. Steep, narrow stairs join all the floors at the rear of the house. Separate service stairs also lead from the first to the second and from the third to the fourth floors at the front of the house.[6]

The original part of the house is separated from the later additions by a stone wall two feet thick extending from the basement floor to the roof. A wide, open area around the east wing lies lower than the basement floor. Its purpose was apparently to facilitate the admission of light to the basement kitchen and dining room where the molders and some other

[3] Information from National Park Service architect Norman Souder.
[4] SM 2, p. 26; SM 1, p. 13.
[5] *Kemper Manuscripts,* Report of Gustavus Mang, April, 1935. Harker Long thought this last section of the house was completed in 1849. In 1964 Archeologist Leland Abel reported to the National Park Service that physical evidence within the house indicates that it was built in three sections between 1820 and 1846. He said it could have replaced an older house on the same site.
[6] Parts of the first and second floor are open to visitors.

Bathroom Appointments in Hopewell Mansion

workmen ate. A ten-foot wide veranda was built across the entire west side of the house, and porches were added on each side of the rear wing.[7] A bathroom was installed in a frame addition above the north rear veranda in 1870. Probably at the same time the windows of the first story in the west wing were extended to the floor. The overall dimensions of the house

[7] Mang, *op. cit.*

are : main wing 53 feet 10 inches long by 28 feet wide and the stem of the "T," 35 feet 2 inches long and 22 feet 1 inch wide.[8]

Water was brought into the house at an early period. The earliest known date is a record for December 23, 1816, that "the Repairs acount paid John Hagen $30.70 for 168′ pipe bored and pump from spring house to house."[9] That this amount was charged to "repairs" may have indicated that there was a pipe from the spring house to the mansion earlier. The spring house was built in 1806.[10] It enclosed what one of its users declared was "one of the finest springs that ever came out of the earth."[11] At some later, but unknown, date a wooden pipeline was run from the house to a large spring about 2,000 feet away. This conduit was made by boring holes approximately two inches in diameter through the length of 16 foot to 18 foot logs, each about ten inches in diameter. A section of this old pipe was uncovered by Civilian Conservation Corps workers in the 1930's.[12] Perhaps some modernization of the water system was made in 1850 when the Furnace paid $43.80 to install "Hidraulic Ram, pipes, Etc."[13]

How were the rooms furnished? Unfortunately little information is available. Alterations would have been made with changing style, obsolescence and the taste of the several mistresses of the mansion. Violet Care remembered the southwest room as containing a large pedestal table surrounded by eight cane-seated chairs; a large chest for storage of linens, silver, and china; a large tier table; a drop-leaf table; a tall whatnot; a corner cupboard made in two parts and the parts used separately; a piano and a rocking horse which had belonged to the Clingan children.[14]

When the National Park Service was beginning its work of

[8] *Ibid.*
[9] SM 7, December 23, 1816, n. p.
[10] SM 4, December 20, 1806, n.p.
[11] *Kemper Manuscripts,* H. A. Long's Notes on Hopewell.
[12] Appleman, "Historical Report," *op. cit.,* p. 28.
[13] SM 31, p. 18.
[14] Violet Care Interview, January 15, 1941.

Bedroom Furnishings in Hopewell Mansion

restoration, J. C. Fisher Motz took advantage of an offer from
the Brooke Family to purchase a large collection of furniture
and furnishings which were identified by the family as having
been associated with Hopewell. No government money was
available; so Motz put up the necessary sum from his own
funds to prevent this collection from being dispersed at public
sale. He was later reimbursed by the government. Francis
Brinton, an antique dealer from West Chester, established the
approximate dates for the various items listed. The inventory
of the Motz purchase contained the following:

Four Poster Bed	Mahogany	1860's
Double Wardrobe	,,	1850
Serving Stand	,,	?
Arrow Back Chair	Pine	1840
Wash Stand—2 Faucets	,,	1870
Double Sleigh Bed	Possibly Walnut	1850
Urn-Back Rocker	Painted	1830
Wash Stand—Faucets and 4 Drawers	Walnut	1870
Sofa—Red Plush	Mahogany	1840
Four Poster Bed	,,	1850
Sewing Stand	,,	1830's
Four Poster Bed	,,	1830's
Wardrobe	,,	1830's
Armchair	Walnut	1850's
Tilt-Top Table	Possibly Mahogany	1860's
2 Matching Wardrobes	Mahogany	1830's
Single Sleigh Bed	Possibly Walnut	1830
Spool Bed	Soft Wood	1850's
6 Chairs—Red Plush Seats	Mahogany Veneered	1830
Drop-Leaf Table	Mahogany	1815
8 Chairs—Red Plush Seats	Mahogany Veneered	?
Sideboard	Mahogany With Marble Top	?
2 Matching Sofas— Red Silk	Rosewood	1850
Whatnot	Mahogany	1850
Chest of Drawers Chippendale	Walnut	1770
Upholstered Armchair— Red Silk	Rosewood	1850
2 Matching Sofas— Ribbed Red Plush	Walnut	1840's
Mirror in Gilt Frame		1830
Whatnot—with Drawer	Mahogany	1840
Desk—with Book Cupboard	Mahogany Veneered	1840
Cradle	Mahogany	?
Cradle	Pine	?
Serving Stand—Marble Top	Mahogany	?

Sitting Room of Hopewell Mansion

Wash Stand—Marble
   Top   ,,   ?
Five Oil Paintings:
   Charles Brooke, Jr.
   Charles Brooke
   Dr. Charles Clingan
   Clement Clingan
   Mrs. Charles Clingan[15]

[15] *Hopewell Papers,* Furniture Cataloguing, D6215.

It was not possible to determine whether all of these items had been used at Hopewell. The dates indicated purchases spanning a century of occupation. By searching the Furnace record books, the following purchases of furniture for the mansion were discovered, but details were usually lacking or were too incomplete to make possible positive identification with articles on the Motz list:

August 14, 1802	6 Winser Chairs @ 11/3. Made by William Bird.	
December 5, 1802	1 Spinning Wheel £1-2/6	
August 20, 1803	A Breakfast Table £1-17/6	
November 19, 1803	1 Cupboard 60/	
November 20, 1817	1 doz Chairs received last spring	$19.50
July 17, 1819	2 bed cords	$ 1.00
July 28, 1819	A spinning Wheel	$ 4.50
March 7, 1820	Furniture for Big House valued at $550.00 in furnace inventory of this date.	
October 31, 1822	Pair Andirons	$ 5.00
	Pair Tongs and Shovel	$ 3.50
	2 Candlesticks	$ 1.00
August 28, 1828	A Clock Case	$25.00
	Bureau	$12.00
April 26, 1830	Large Looking Glass	$44.00
April 27, 1830	12 Fancy Cane seat Chairs from Philadelphia	$46.00
? 1831	A Bureau	$14.00
April 23, 1832	looking glass	?
? 1835	Dining Room Table	$ 9.00
	Ward robe	$30.00
April 30, 1835	2 pair of beadsteads	$20.00
	1 doughtrough	4.00
August 12, 1841	cleaning the clock	$ 1.00
November 29, 1847	Parlor rocking chair from Philadelphia	?
March 3, 1853	Bench Table	$3.58
November 4, 1854	Sideboard	$20.00[16]

[16] Items collected from the journals and cash books for these dates.

More frequent mention was made of purchases for the dining table and of bedroom china at the Big House:

July 11, 1803	2 Qt. Decanter	8/8	
	Large White pitcher	2/9	
	$\frac{1}{2}$ doz. Knives and forks	8/3	
October 6, 1803	1 doz Knives and forks	17/0	
February 10, 1806	$\frac{1}{2}$ doz tea spoons	1/10$\frac{1}{2}$	
	$\frac{1}{2}$,, knifs and forks	10/6	
January 31, 1820	Plates tumblers and Snuffers	$1.75[17]	

Mrs. Brooke must have acquired a new set of dishes in October 1822. A bill from Patrick Ryan of Philadelphia listed the following purchases by Clement Brooke:

1 Doz handled Grecian Teas	1.50
3/4 ,, blue print plates	1.05
$\frac{1}{2}$ Doz blue print Twifflers	.62$\frac{1}{2}$
$\frac{1}{2}$,, ,, ,, Muffins	.55
1 Pitcher ,, $\frac{1}{2}$ gallon	.50
2 Blue print Bakers	.80
2 egd ,, ,,	.50
3 blue ,, Bowls	.56$\frac{1}{2}$
1 egd dish	.33
$\frac{1}{2}$ doz Tumblers Ground bottoms	.75
1 C C Chamber	.31$\frac{1}{4}$
1 Decanter	.50
Box etc.	.31$\frac{1}{4}$
	8.29\frac{1}{2}$[18]

"Blue print" ware was mentioned in many of these items, and in 1825 two small pitchers were added.[19] In an archeological dig made under the direction of Archeologist Leland Abel in 1962 many pieces of Chinese-made "blue willow" patterned dinnerware were found. Perhaps these broken bits identified the "blue print" dishes bought in 1822.

Purchases continued from time to time of dishes, pottery and eating utensils:

[17] *Ibid.*
[18] HV 8221031.
[19] HV 8250615A.

March 18, 1825	6 knives and 6 forks	$2.50
May 19, 1825	Silver Spoons in City	?
May 29, 1827	1 8/11 Damask Table Cloth	$4.50
	1 ,, (Nail Holes)	$2.50
	¼ Doz Napkins	1.37½

Bought of John Reed and Co., Philadelphia[20]

April 13, 1831 Bought of R. Tyndale, Philadelphia

	1 Chamber Sett	$3.00
	1 Cut Cellery	1.50
	1 Doz Cut Tumblers	2.00
	1 pr. sma. Dishes	1.00
	2 ,, Muffins	5.00
	1 pr. fruit baskets	3.00
	1 sma. Ireg.	1.00
	1 Doz cup plates	.37½
	1 pr. sma. dishes on foot	1.25
	1 horsradish	.25[21]

Bought of Carey and Preston, Philadelphia

	1 Doz Silver Desart	$25.00
	1 Pair [————?] and	
	Silver B. Knives	5.00
December 4, 1823	Table Linen	$3.75
	½ Doz Tea sps	5.00

June 27, 1838 from R. Tyndale, Philadelphia

	1 Doz Canton Cups and	
	saucers	$4.50
	1 ,, ,, Plates	1.75
	1 ,, tumblers	1.75
	1 Pr. glass dishes	3.00
	1 ,, Butter Dishes	1.00
	1 ,, China Cake plates	.20[22]
January 6, 1841	China Ware	$80.87
? 1841	1 Sett Bratania ware	14.00
January 29, 1850	China Ware	11.25
	Spice Box	1.25
April 29, 1850	Table linen	6.75
October 21, 1851	Table Linen	16.47[23]

[20] HV 8270529.
[21] HV 8310413A.
[22] HV 8380627.
[23] Unless otherwise identified the items are from the journals of the appropriate date.

Fireplace in Hopewell Mansion

Family Dining Room in Hopewell Mansion

Heat and light were items of cost and concern in a house as large as this one. The seven or nine fireplaces constituted the means of heating the house for much of its history. Probably when stoves became a principal article for sale by the company, one or more of these would have been installed in the mansion. Stove purchases probably did not appear on the earlier Furnace books because no cash payment was made for them. Just about the time stove-casting ended at Hopewell, a new kind of heating system must have been installed somewhere in the house. Clement Brooke bought from Francis McIlvain, Philadelphia, "Mfg. of Warm Air Furnaces,"

One 11 in. Cast Radiator and Urn	$18.00
piece of Line	1.50
2 Elbows and 2 joints of Russia Pipe	1.75[24]

Ten years later "1 Hathaway Stove" was purchased for $12.84.[25] Mrs. Clingan had heat in her bedroom radiated from a large drum through which passed the smoke pipe from a stove in the first floor dining room.[26]

Lights of many kinds were used in the house. In the southwest room a candelabra held eight candles and could be lowered to make lighting easier. The front-hall light was made of wrought iron, the sides covered with red glass. It had a small tin oil fount to hold the fuel.[27] In 1802 the Furnace purchased "3 large lantrens."[28] These might have been used for work around the furnace or barn rather than in the house. More decorative lighting appliances were bought in 1831 : "1 Astral Lamp" at $11.00, "1 Entry Lamp" at $3.50[29] and "A Lamp" $16.00.[30] The lamp purchased in 1838 for twelve and one half cents[31] and the "Kitchen Lamp, Lamp

[24] HV 8430925.
[25] SM 32, p. 140.
[26] Sally Boone Interview, March 22, 1941.
[27] Violet Care Interview, February 13, 1941.
[28] SM 2, p. 67.
[29] HV 8310413E.
[30] SM 28, p. 65.
[31] HV 8380627.

Kitchen in Hopewell Mansion

wicks and Chimneys" bought for eighty cents in 1850[32] were probably of a strictly utilitarian nature.

Since whale oil was regularly available at the village store, it was doubtless the fuel used in the lamps before the 1850's. But the march of progress was shown when the Furnace bought:

November 11, 1858	1 Carasene Lamp	$2.75
	Oil, Bottle Wicks, etc	1.42
	One Shade	.50[33]

[32] SM 31, p. 120.
[33] SM 65, November 11, 1858, n. p.

A startling circumstance about this purchase was that it dated from the year before Colonel Edwin Drake drilled his famous pioneer oil well at Titusville.

All rooms at the Big House were papered and most were carpeted, according to the memory of one resident of the village.[34] This recollection was supported by two items for the purchase of wall paper in the 1840's and two bills for "Painting and Papering the House."[35] In the late years of Furnace operation the paper in the hallway showed English hunting scenes.[36] There were many purchases of carpet, and sometimes carpet was made for the mansion. Maria Brooke wrote to a Mr. Davis in Morgantown, "I have sent you more yarn to finish the carpet I left with you some time ago—Please weave 34 yds. full yard wide (for room) and $9\frac{1}{4}$ yds. to be $1\frac{1}{4}$ yds wide (for Entry) the same pattern that you wove for us some time ago. . . ."[37]

The windows, at least after 1830, were fitted with window shades[38] and covered with curtains.[39] The most costly of decorative touches in the house were two marble mantels. In 1829 the Furnace "paid Magers for Marble Mantle $75.00, paid for hauling and putting up $6.00."[40] Eight years later Clement Brooke reimbursed Charles W. Warnick $78.75 for a marble mantel.[41]

The Big House was not all for show or even for living quarters for the ironmaster's family. It had its part to play in the iron business as well. There was a reason, too, for its size; it was home for a considerable number of workers. There were often relatives of the family in residence, as Ann and John Church spent much of their early lives at Hopewell mansion. Maids and apprentices lived there. It is possible that the

[34] Sally Boone Interview, March 22, 1941.
[35] SM 28, pp. 18, 154; SM 31, pp. 88, 106.
[36] Violet Care Interview, February 13, 1941.
[37] HV 8321129.
[38] SM 14, p. 89 and SM 31, p. 105.
[39] SM 65, December 3, 1858, n. p.
[40] Cash Book, July 17, 1829, Berks County Historical Society.
[41] SM 21, p. 195.

Cook Stove in Hopewell Mansion

divided attic, reached by separate stairways, was used for quarters by servants of both sexes.

The censuses showed sizable groups in residence under the name of the ironmaster. In 1810 Clement Brooke was listed as having had a household of two males and four females.[42] Since at that time he was a bridegroom of two years,[43] it is unlikely that these persons were all members of his family. The population in the mansion may have reached a peak in 1830 when Brooke enumerated nine males and six females in his household. Four of the females were Negroes[44] who were doubtless maids or cooks.

The basement of the mansion served as a dining area for the single men of the community. They slept in one of the tenant houses set aside for them.[45] The molders also took their meals in the basement dining room, perhaps because it was close to their work at the cast house. They slept elsewhere. Beds were kept in the wheelwright shop for single molders or for any of them who needed a place to rest while they waited for the founder to begin casting. Some molders were married and lived at home.[46]

A rumor persisted in the village to recent times that the dirt floor of the cellar had served as the burial place of an employee who died in the winter when the ground outside was frozen too hard to dig and the roads were impassable.[47]

The food served to the workmen in this basement dining area was reported to have been very good; one molder said that the meals were the equal of "the best that could be gotten at the best Hotels."[48] If this report were the general opinion of the boarders, it was in contrast with reports from other furnaces

[42] *United States Census of 1810*, Berks County, Union Township, p. 679.

[43] *St. Mary's Episcopal Church Record*, p. 185. March 4, 1808. Berks County Historical Society.

[44] *Census of 1830*, p. 515. See Appendix B for more census reports on residents of the Hopewell mansion.

[45] *Kemper Manuscripts*, H. A. Long Interview, November 9, 1936.

[46] H. A. Long Interview, December, 1935.

[47] Grace Styer Interview, June 1, 1941.

[48] *Kemper Manuscripts*, Notes on Hopewell.

Outdoor Bake Ovens, Front View

Outdoor Bake Ovens, South Side

of beans, bacon and fried mush as the regular fare.[49] Martha
Furnace in New Jersey had several food riots in its dining
room in protest against the meals.[50] However, food delivered to
the Hopewell mansion indicated that someone ate, and drank,
well; but the journals did not reveal what food was served in
the basement to the workers and what was on the table in the
upstairs dining room where the family and their guests were
eating.

The outdoor bake oven produced bread and pastries and
was also used to dry apples, peaches and corn.[51] Hams, flitches
and shoulders came from the smoke house.[52] Oysters and cran-
berries were bought at Christmas time in sufficient quantities
to indicate that they were for many people.[53] Sweet potatoes
were frequently mentioned in the journals as having been
purchased from outsiders. Large quantities of Irish potatoes
were raised on the farm, and more were purchased from
neighbors. In the fall melons were brought to the village and
become the basis for feasts for everyone. Cabbage was a
regular purchase; turnips and beets were sometimes bought
and were probably raised also on the plantation. Pork, beef,
veal and fowls were produced on the farm and bought from
neighbors. The amount used indicated that everyone ate meat
with regularity.[54] In 1831 the furnace purchased a keg each of
brandy and Lisbon wine and an unspecified quantity of "A
Very Superior old real Cognac."[55]

The store ledgers and journals showed no purchases of food
by the manager or the clerk. Nor did these men pay for boarding, as did the people who ate in the basement. Free room and
meals would appear to have been a fringe benefit of the
management class at the Furnace.

[49] Rowe, *op. cit.*, p. 19.
[50] *Martha Furnace Diary*, Microfilm in Hopewell Village Library,
passim.
[51] Sally Boone Interview, March 22, 1941.
[52] SM 35, p. 74.
[53] SM 31, p. 136.
[54] *Passim* in store journals.
[55] HV 8310601A.

Spring House at Hopewell Village

Outside of the mansion there were several utility buildings and a garden. The spring house, the smoke house and the bake oven have been mentioned previously in this chapter. In addition to supplying water the spring house cooled milk and butter, and a fireplace in the south end heated water for laundering and butchering. Milk pails and equipment were also cleaned here.[56] The smoke house, to the east of the Big House, was 30 feet square and built of stone below and logs above.[57] This building could have provided for a large supply of meat. The bake oven was behind the kitchen.

On terraces to the north of the house was the garden, within which stood a building with a multiple purpose. Above ground

[56] Violet Care Interview, February 13, 1941.
[57] Appleman, "Proposed Restoration Plan," *op. cit.*

it was an open summer house, shielded with lattice-work and topped by an eight-gabled roof. A wide path led from the house[58] to this shaded area where the summer breezes made life more pleasant, and possibly a courting couple could have found welcome seclusion. Beneath the floor of the summer house was the ice house. During the winter ice was cut from a nearby pond and placed in the underground storage area. This space, 15 feet square and 20 feet deep, was insulated with a lining of rye straw.[59] A supply of ice was thereby insured with which to cool drinks and preserve food during the summer months. Ice was cut from January to March when it had frozen thick enough to make good blocks.[60]

A most important auxiliary building was the latrine, dating from about 1876, at the east end of the garden area. It was about six by eight feet and partitioned in the middle. A path ran from the front of the house to the north half of the privy which was used by the ironmaster's family. Another path ran from the rear of the house to the south, or servant, portion of the outhouse.[61] A lattice-work screen covered with trumpet vine concealed the family door.[62]

A greenhouse was built about 1829 to the north and east of the mansion where its remains are still visible. It was about 80 feet long, and more than half of its space was used to grow grapes.[63] It was also used to start plants for spring transfer to outdoor beds.[64]

The terraces north of the Big House were occupied by the garden. It was useful for producing asparagus, strawberries and raspberries in beds[65] and grapes on an arbor.[66] Rosemary, migonette, sage and thyme were grown for their fragrance or

[58] *Ibid.*
[59] *Ibid.*
[60] SM 32, p. 84 and SM 35, pp. 97–98.
[61] *Kemper Manuscripts,* H. A. Long's Notes on Hopewell, *op. cit.*
[62] *Hopewell Papers,* H3015, Map of the Garden by M. A. Krewson.
[63] *Kemper Manuscripts,* H. A. Long's Notes on Hopewell, *op. cit.*
[64] SM 67, December 12, 1808, n.p. and SM 31, p. 113.
[65] *Kemper Manuscripts,* H. A. Long's Notes on Hopewell, *op. cit.*
[66] H. A. Long Interview, August 13, 1936.

flavor. Bee hives rested near the summer house to provide honey for the mansion tables. But the chief purpose for the garden must have been decorative.[67]

There were two terraces with a stone wall separating them. Areas on each terrace were marked with rows of boxwoods.[68] At the east end were daffodils, poppies, foxgloves, yellow roses, red and pink ramblers, violets, blue bells and hyacinths in their individual beds. Snow ball, lilac, orange blossom and rose of sharon bushes shared the guardian duties with boxwoods.[69] Pinks, lilies and hollyhocks added their heads to the colorful array.[70] Pavilions and benches lined the paths for any who desired to rest and enjoy the flowers.[71]

Somewhere about the house or garden there must have been some bird boxes; for in the 1830's Ann Brooke wrote, ". . . I am writing to you by [sic] side the window on my Music book, interrupted occasionally by the chattering of the Martins above my head, harbingers of spring."[72]

The attractions of Hopewell may have been greater in the summer than in the winter. Letters made many references to the ironmasters' families having gone to Philadelphia for the winter months.[73]

The Hopewell mansion was the center of bustling activity for more than a century. Within its walls occurred marriages, births and deaths. The ironmaster and his family, often the clerk and always a number of servants made it their home. Buyers and guests were entertained. Relatives visited. Parties were given for the families of other ironmasters who sometimes came from a distance and stayed for days. Sometimes, too, the

[67] *Hopewell Papers,* H3015, Map of the Garden, *op. cit.*
[68] Appleman, "Proposed Restoration Plan," op. cit.
[69] Map of the Garden, *op. cit.*
[70] Franklin Kemper, *op. cit.,* p. 5.
[71] Samuel Westey Freese Interview, September 21, 1959.
[72] *Stokes Collection,* Ann Brooke to Sarah R. Brooke, May 2, year not given.
[73] For example see *Brooke Family Papers,* John Springer to Edward Brooke, January 11, 1833.

families of the Village were invited to special festivities at the Big House.[74]

For the people of Hopewell Village, then, the ironmaster's mansion served many purposes as residence, dining room, seat of authority and center of social life.

[74] More details on the entertainments at the mansion will be given in Chapter 20.

5 Homes for the Workers

THE OPERATION OF A CHARCOAL FURNACE DEMANDED THE services of a fairly large force of workmen who would usually have been required to live in an area remote from towns. Hopewell Furnace was about five miles from Birdsboro or Douglasville and eight from Morgantown. These villages had stores which furnished Hopewell workers with many things not stocked by the company store. But they were too far away to provide homes for many of the workers. Some of the Furnace employees were needed near the furnace; others worked at the mines, the coaling pits or the wood lots. Since some of these areas were several miles from the furnace, it was more convenient for these men to live near their work than close to the stack. Besides the regular employees the Furnace had need of many part-time workers, especially wood cutters during the winter months. It was helpful to have neighboring farmers and their sons available to lend a hand for such work.

All of these workmen needed places to live. Some were married and required a house for a family; others were single and wanted a place to eat and sleep. The Furnace management had to make certain that living quarters were available to all of their workmen. Lodgings at Hopewell took many forms. They were neither luxurious nor pretentious. In some cases they were decidedly makeshift; other dwellings were solidly built. Purchases of furnishings indicate that at least a part of the families lived well above the level described by Arthur C. Bining and other historians of the eighteenth century iron villages.

Some workers lived in homes they owned; others rented houses from the Furnace or local landlords. They were scattered over many square miles in Union, Robeson and Caernarvon Townships of Berks County and East Nantmeal, West Nantmeal and Warwick Townships of Chester County. Even this area may not have encompassed the entire population. When one writer stated that 200 people lived in the village,[1] the immediate area of the furnace could scarcely have been considered "the village." The largest number of company-owned tenant houses in the Union Township tax records before the end of the Civil War was 14 in 1855.[2] In other representative years the tax records showed the numbers to have been 10 in 1837, 11 in 1840 and 1843, 12 in 1852, 10 in 1864,[3] 10 single and one double in 1867, 10 in 1873,[4] 9 in 1877[5] and 5 in 1883.[6] Harker Long remembered 14 tenant houses "near the furnace" when it was closed in 1883,[7] although at another time he said there had been15.[8] He reported that the molders' families lived elsewhere and that the tenant houses near the furnace were occupied by laborers who worked around the furnace.[9] In 1936 three tenant houses survived in the furnace area and three others in the immediate vicinity.[10] The restoration area under the National Park Service includes two double and two single tenant houses.

[1] Committee on Historical Research of the Colonial Dames of America, *op. cit,* .p. 155.
[2] *Tax Records,* Berks County, Union Township.
[3] *Ibid.*
[4] *Triennial Assessments,* Berks County, Union Township.
[5] SM 34, tax evaluation for April 1, 1877, n. p.
[6] *Hopewell Papers,* Assessment, April 25, 1883.
[7] Long, *Historical Sketch, op. cit.,* p. 17.
[8] H. A. Long Interview, August 13, 1936.
[9] Long, *Historical Sketch, op. cit.,* p. 17.
[10] H. A. Long Interview, August 13, 1936.

View of Four Surviving Tenant Houses in Hopewell Village

Group of Tenant Houses about 1940

The Furnace also owned some homes in the neighborhood of the mines. In 1866 Haskebiah Clemons rented three company-owned houses at Hopewell Mine. The office house at the Jones Mine was rented as late as 1872.[11] An atlas for 1873 showed five buildings at the "Hopewell Iron Mines" belonging to Dr. Charles M. Clingan, a building of Clingan and Buckley along the creek near the Baptist Church in Warwick Township and two buildings listed as belonging to Dr. Chas. M. Clingan along the county line about two miles west of the furnace.[12] Presumably other homes occupied by the workers belonged to owners other than Hopewell Furnace.

Appleman believed that the surviving tenant houses dated from the Revolutionary Period,[13] but this seems rather improbable considering the changes in the number of houses which existed in different years. In 1941 an old resident visited Hopewell and identified 23 buildings or sites of buildings which he claimed had been used at some time as tenant houses. They ranged from the brick structure originally built as a kiln to the respectable duplex, the "boarding house," the Nathan Care House and the Houck House, all of which are still standing. It is not known how many of the 23 houses were occupied at any one time. Some may have burned or have been torn down before others were built. Several were built after 1883. The area covered was from beyond the lake on the west to beyond the public highway on the east.[14]

The Furnace records show payments for new tenant houses in 1803[15] and 1826. At least the latter one had an excavated cellar.[16] In 1878 John Roberts paid rental on the brick kiln for a residence at the rate of one dollar per month.[17] If this appears to be an insignificant rental by present standards, we should

[11] SM 34, p. 200.
[12] Bridgans and Witman, *op. cit.,* p. 55.
[13] Appleman, "Proposed Restoration Plan," *op. cit.,* p. 11.
[14] Reginald Smith Interview, March 16, 1941.
[15] SM 2, p. 148.
[16] SM 59, p. 5.
[17] SM 34, May 5, 1878, n.p.

Tenant House Number 1

note that the same amount was paid for quite respectable houses.

There is now no way of knowing whether the houses presently surviving were typical of all the tenant homes. Perhaps they survived because they were better houses in original construction. But the best idea of the workers' housing is to be gained by examining the ones which still stand.

The house nearest the furnace is called for identification purposes by the National Park Service Tenant House Number 1. It is built of native stone and currently contains four rooms. Its outside dimensions are 28 feet by 18 feet plus a stone shed built against the south wall measuring 13 feet by 10 feet. The large fireplace in the southwest corner of the lower floor of the main structure was the principal source of heat when the house was built. The two upper floor bedrooms are reached by a steep circular staircase.

Tenant House Number 2 is very similar to its next-door neighbor. It has a porch along its east side and a two-part shed, one of stone and one of frame. The next house in line is the duplex previously mentioned. It is 26 feet by 30 feet with a 6-foot porch running the entire length of the east side. There is a divided cellar under the entire house. Each apartment has a front and a rear door, two rooms on the first floor, two on the second and one on the third. Each side also has its stairway near the center of the house from the cellar to the third floor and a chimney serving a first floor fireplace. This structure was sometimes called the Shaffer House.

Last of the houses along this "street" is the Nathan Care House. Care was one of the founders and probably built this home for himself and his family. It is not then properly a tenant house, but it is an example of a worker's domicile. This residence is built of stone and measures 29 feet by 22 feet and has an 8-foot porch running across the front of the house. There is a single room cellar under the entire house. Above it are two rooms on the first floor, three on the second and one on the third. The stairway connecting all floors is located in

Tenant House Number 2

the southwest corner. A first floor fireplace is served by a chimney on the west end of the house. A well in the front yard provided water which was drawn by a bucket and windlass.

Across the Warwick Road from the tenant houses already described is a structure called by the old inhabitants "the boarding house." It is stone and measures 50 feet by 20 feet plus a stone shed built against the west end of the south section of the house. The other section has a small frame porch at the west entrance. The front of the house has two entrances, and there are separate stairways connecting the first and second floors which would have made possible the use of this dwelling as a duplex. The west end was built about

Interior of Tenant House

Interior of Restored Worker's Home

Duplex Tenant House One Mile from Village

1830, and the east end was added about a decade later. The older section has two rooms on each floor and a central chimney for the first floor fireplace. The newer part of the house has but a single room on each of the two floors and a first floor fireplace on the east side. Between the house and the road is a well with an old wooden pump. This was the source of water for the families in the tenant houses.[18]

Behind the duplex house is a stone barn 20 feet by 14 feet with a frame shed 20 feet by 20 feet. This is the only surviving tenant barn; but probably the other houses also

[18] Details for descriptions of the houses come in part from J. C. F. Motz, "Historical Base Map," (unpublished study, 1941). Hopewell Village Library.

Nathan Care House and Barn

had had some kind of shelter for pigs, poultry, cows and horses. Outside each house was formerly a yard and garden surrounded by a picket fence which served the purpose of keeping cows and chickens from the flowers and vegetables. The children had the job of whitewashing the fence.[19]

The animals and children enjoyed playing in the water in a ditch which ran along the west side of the Warwick Road carrying water from springs on Mount Pleasant. Each house on this side of the road had a little foot bridge across the ditch and a path to the front door.[20]

[19] Albert Painter Interview, May 9, 1958. The picket fences probably were of a comparatively recent date.
[20] David Care Interview, March 22, 1941.

How large were the families which lived in these houses? Unfortunately it is not possible to tell which specific worker resided in any one of these tenant houses at any definite time. The houses identified by the clerk with particular families were usually those away from the furnace where a descriptive association seemed more necessary. Some who were listed as renting houses in this area were checked in the census reports to obtain some idea of family sizes. John Mills, who rented in 1807,[21] had a family of ten members by 1810.[22] Jacob Cramp had a family of four in 1810[23] and eight by 1820.[24] David Hart in 1830 had a family of seven.[25] A boarding housekeeper, although it was not certain that he lived in "the boarding house," was John Wert with a family of three in 1830.[26]

Purchases of furniture and home furnishings by workers indicate that their houses were provided with normal pieces and in some cases a luxury or two. Tables and chairs, and doubtless many other items such as beds and cupboards were usually home made.[27] Mattresses were made from ticking purchased at the store and filled with straw or feathers. It must have required eight yards of material for a mattress, for that specific quantity was frequently sold. In 1818 it cost $62\frac{1}{2}$¢ per yard.[28] Random items selected from the journals show purchases of mirrors, bedsteads, "doughtroughs," chests, "beaurows," desks, dishes, chairs, trunks, rugs, cradles, tubs, clocks, cupboards, tables, stoves, coverlets, comforters and sheets.[29]

There were many notes on purchases of tableware and

[21] SM 4, p. 39.
[22] *Census of 1810,* p. 682.
[23] *Ibid.*
[24] *Census of 1820,* p. 98.
[25] *Census of 1830,* p. 515.
[26] *Ibid.*
[27] H. A. Long Interview, December, 1935.
[28] SM 9, p. 116.
[29] See Appendix B for more purchases for their homes by Hopewell workers.

Windlass and Bucket at Nathan Care Well

cooking utensils. Some idea of the kind of furnishings needed
in the home can be gained from examining an order placed
in 1844 by Jacob Winings at the Eli Keen Store in nearby
Warwick. This purchase may have represented the outfitting
of a newly married couple who were setting up housekeeping
or one that had just moved into the community. Here is the
list of their needs:

1 Tea Canister	.12½	½ doz. plates	.28
1 Sald Celler	.10	2 small ,,	.08
1 Pepper Box	.08	I Large Tin Bucket	.62½
1 Sugar Bowl	.15	1 ,, ,,	.50
½ doz. spoons large	.31	2 Candle Sticks	.25
½ ,, ,, small	.16	3½ yds. Crash	.31½

1 Cream jog	.15	4 ,, Table diaper	.60
2 round deep dishes	.48	2 Bowls	.14
1 long dish	.14	1 Butcher Knife	.20
2 ,, ,,	.32	$\frac{1}{2}$ lb. Pepper	.10
1 Pitcher	.28	Small Deep dish	.09
1 Doz. cups and saucers	.40	1 White Wash Brush	.31$\frac{1}{4}$
$\frac{1}{2}$,, knives and forks	.87$\frac{1}{2}$	1 Coffee Mill	$1.25
1 Hand Brush	.12$\frac{1}{2}$	Pair Snuffers	.12$\frac{1}{2}$[30]
$\frac{1}{2}$ doz. plate	.31		

Since the workers bought relatively little food from the company store, they must have raised much of what they ate. There were records of sales of melons, potatoes, turnips, turkeys, much pork, veal and beef and a little mutton; shad, herring and mackerel; pickles, peaches, sweet potatoes, beans, cherries and cabbage. Corn meal was a regular item of store purchase before 1808 and seldom appeared after that. Rye and wheat flour were the more common bases for baked items in later years. Sugar, tea, coffee, chocolate, salt, pepper and spices were kept in regular stock at the store.[31]

Preserving of meat was a problem before freezing was available. The workers used the smoke house at the mansion, or they might have had their own. Pickling meat in a salt brine was another method used. A formula for that process read : "10 gal water, 15 lb. of salt, 5 lb. of sugar and 5 oz. salt petre. Boil until no more scum appears."[32] Spoilage was a not uncommon occurrence. A large loss was recorded by the clerk in 1817 : "Note : there was 13 shoulders weighed 146 lbs. which was intirely Spoiled which can not be allowed for —we agreed with David Hart to take them for $7. in case he could make any use of them and if not he was to have them for nothing."[33]

[30] *Eli Keen's Storebook,* 1844–1845, pp. 9, 10. 25.

[31] Appendix C gives complete purchases at the company store for twenty-six accounts covering a period of fifteen months. Much detail on items purchased and quantities consumed may be obtained from this source.

[32] James L. Morris, *Diary or Daily Notes,* December 17, 1841. Berks County Historical Society, Reading, Pennsylvania.

[33] SM 7, August 22, 1817, n. p.

Boarding House

The fireplace began to give way to the stove in the homes of Hopewell workers at a fairly early period. In 1784 several workmen bought ten-plate stoves at £5 5s. each.[34] This style was a cook stove which probably was first introduced to America about 1765 at the Mary Ann Furnace. The sale of stoves to workers continued during the entire period of stove making at Hopewell Furnace. The usual fuel was wood, and the journals showed many purchases of cordwood from the Furnace. There were also instances of agreements for rental of Furnace houses which included either wood or the right to cut wood on Furnace property as a part of the contract.[35]

Homes were lighted partly by the open fire from the fire-

[34] SM 41, p. 20.
[35] Examples will be noted later in this chapter .

place; but candles were sold at the store, even as late as 1850 the sale was good.[36] Doubtless many housewives made their own candles. "Lanthorns" were stocked at the Hopewell store as early as 1803,[37] and lamps were on sale before the middle of the century.[38]

Homes required maintenance and repair. In 1803 the Furnace paid John McGowan £5 1s. 6d. for work he had done on the house in which he lived.[39] There were payments for plastering, painting and whitewashing in or on Furnace-owned houses at various times.

Housecleaning was a semi-annual disruption of household routine. One husband wrote this account of the autumn cleaning at his house in 1842:

> Things are torn upside down, furniture displaced, beds and bedding thrown out of the house, closets and wardrobes turned inside out and not a nook or cranny or hiding place on or in premises, but what has to give up its secrets and its contents. . . . Order has fled from the house and happy is the man who has had the good fortune or good sense to fly with them . . . dirty handkerchiefed turbaned heads, slip shod shoes, smutty faces, angry looks and pinned up petticoats are the marks of the house cleaning woman . . .
>
> The very victuals, the only stay and support of the animal economy under such great affliction, is grudgingly doled out to you with complaints of the loss of time in making them ready. The coffee looks the very impersonification of the sloppy water under your feet, the beefsteak is done black on one side and not done at all on the other and your cake, if not all dough is pretty near it. And even these are served up to you . . . most likely on the bare dough trough in the kitchen corner. . . .[40]

Fires were a threat and a calamity in all rural areas. On July 12, 1803, the clerk recorded, "This night J. McColasters

[36] SM 31, p. 130.
[37] SM 2, p. 154.
[38] SM 31, p. 130.
[39] SM 2, p. 148.
[40] Morris Diary, op. cit., pp. 237–239.

Barn Behind Tenant House

Restored Church House Now a Home

Hous Burnt."[41] One of the tenant houses burned in the 1870's.[42] Chimney fires were frequent and often dangerous because of wind-borne sparks. In the 1840's steps were built at the south end of the mansion house to enable workers to climb to the chimney quickly when it caught on fire.[43]

Not all houses had their own wells, because drilling a well was expensive. To reduce the risk of drilling without finding water, many people hired an expert to locate an underground stream before they began drilling. James Morris wrote on October 4, 1842:

> Today father had the famous old Dutch water smeller from near Adamstown searching for water round about his new house. The old man uses no rod or witch hazle as the other "water smellers" do, but depends entirely on a peculiar sensitiveness in his legs—a slight twitching of the muscles which he feels on passing over the underground course of a spring or stream of water. . . . He charged $1 for locating water at 30-35 feet.[44]

Rent for Furnace houses was usually from $12 to $25 per year. In 1840 John Miller paid $45 per year for a "house and lot at Hopewell Mines," and others were paying from $25 to $35 for houses at Hopewell Mines and Jones Mineholes.[45] The Furnace rented two houses at the Jones Mineholes from Daniel Uble in 1819 and used them to house miners. The owner received $67.[46]

Renting a house to a workman must have been a condition of employment in some instances. Two examples are quoted below to show rental terms:

> Rented to Isaac Danfield the house in which Isaac Hoffman now resides adjoining land of John Fries for One year to Commence the first of April next . . . for the sum of twelve

[41] SM 1, p. 33.
[42] Charles Sheridan Painter Interview, February 16, 1957.
[43] Rose Sands and Catherine Rhodes Interview, May 13, 1941.
[44] *Morris Diary, op. cit.,* pp. 233–234.
[45] SM 32, p. 103.
[46] SM 9, p. 6.

South End of Main Wing of Hopewell Mansion Showing Step Roofline
(Courtesy of William Caulwell)

dollars per year for house and fire wood. Danfield is to cut no thriving timber but old decayed timber, he is likewise to assist in haymaking and harvest if Called upon, he is likewise to take care of the pruning and see that there is no hoop poles, rails or any timber taken of the land by people that has no Authority so to do.

Hopewell, January 26th, 1824[47]

Rented to Samuel Steel the house at Joneses Mineholes now occupied by Mary Phillips for One year from 1st April next insuing for the sum of Ten dollars. Saml Steel is to raise or wash ore during the time that the rest of the hands are employed and to get the customary wages—Steel is to be Constant at the work except two weeks in harvest and he is to find his own fire wood. Hopewell January 22*nd* 1825[48]

Single men and molders made arrangements for sleeping quarters as best they could. Sometimes several men rented a house and hired a woman to care for them;[49] sometimes they stayed in the home of a married worker. Bunks were provided in a plastered room in the attic of the wheelright shop for the use of the molders when off duty or while waiting for the next run of iron from the furnace. The founder had the bell on the cast house rung when he was ready to run off the iron.[50]

Because no taverns or ordinaries were near enough to furnish meals, providing food for the men without families was an extensive business throughout the history of the Furnace. In the preceding chapter it was related that some of these men ate in the basement dining room of the mansion. Sometimes they left this arrangement and "went to housekeeping" or "left the house and went to board himself."[51] Charges for boarding at the mansion varied from $4 to $6 per month.[52] In 1800 a board bill stated that the charge was 2s. per day "with liquor."[53] Later accounts did not mention liquor with the

[47] SM 46, page not readable.
[48] *Ibid.*
[49] Hunter Care Interview, January 26, 1941.
[50] David Boone Interview, March 22, 1941.
[51] SM 1, p. 37.
[52] Furnace journals from 1802 to 1851.
[53] HV 8000116.

meals. Meals may not have been served on Sundays. At least when the clerk calculated the meals eaten, there was no count for Sundays until about 1851 when the month was 30 days. All meals were charged at the same rate per meal.[54]

At times the Furnace paid someone else to board its hands. This could have been when the work was at a distance from the furnace—for example at the mines[55]—or when someone was hired to do special work such as rebuilding the hearth at the furnace.[56] In the 1850's when Ann Parliman was running a boarding house, the Furnace paid her to board Alexander Church, the company clerk.[57] A strange entry in 1851 showed that the Furnace also paid Mrs. Parliman for boarding her own son Edward Parliman.[58] Apparently at that time boarding was a part of the wage or the cost of boarding was withheld from the wage and paid to the keeper of the boarding house.

Another manager of a boarding house was John Wert who was also a keeper at the Furnace. One of his boarders was his father-in-law Thomas Care, founder and molder. Wert had married Rebecca Care,[59] and her father came to board with them soon after. Care may have helped the young couple when finances were low, for he bought food and was later repaid by Wert.[60] At Wert's death in 1832, Care paid for a coffin in which to bury him.[61] When Doctor Clingan was Furnace manager, more workers were boarded in private homes; and few men ate in the basement of the mansion.

How did prices at Hopewell compare with boarding charges at other furnaces? William Sullivan said that there was not much change from furnace to furnace between 1800 and 1840 with the usual charge for boarding having been $1 to $2 per week.[62] Hopewell was within that range.

[54] For example see SM 46 for 1822.
[55] SM 12, p. 136.
[56] SM 59, p. 19.
[57] SM 32, p. 122.
[58] SM 32, p. 113.
[59] St. Marys Episcopal Church Record, op. cit., p. 195.
[60] SM 59, p. 25.
[61] SM 21, p. 25.
[62] Sullivan, op. cit., pp. 61–62.

Housing at Hopewell Furnace varied widely from the luxury of the ironmaster's mansion to the makeshift accommodations of John Roberts in the brick kiln. Available evidence, however, does not show squalor or starvation. Food was plentiful and reasonably varied. Homes were provided with essential furniture and furnishings, and some had mirrors, clocks, silver spoons and stoves to show that living was above the subsistence level.

6 The Farm and Forest

A CHARCOAL FURNACE IN PRODUCTION NEEDED LARGE QUAN-
tities of food and fuel for man, beast and furnace hearth; and
these requirements necessitated the ownership of large areas of
land for farm crops, gardens, orchards and forests. In 1833 a
report was submitted to the national House of Representatives
on the cost of producing cast and bar iron. One interesting
section of this study showed the consumption of farm products
and depreciation of animals per ton of metal produced to have
been: 20 bushels of wheat and rye, 57 pounds of pork, 43
pounds of beef, 10 pounds of butter, 2 bushels of potatoes, $\frac{1}{2}$
ton of hay, $1.00 in fruits and vegetables and $1.43 depreciation on the purchase value of horses. The total cost of farm
produce and live stock was $27.35 per ton of castings or bars.
The same report noted that the mortality among horses
averaged one of seven per year.[1]

No similar estimates were given for the agricultural costs
of producing pig iron; so it was not possible to make an
exact application of these figures to Hopewell Furnace. But
there were years when Hopewell was making over 700 tons
of castings plus a quantity of pig iron; and, therefore, some
idea of the consumption of food could be obtained from the
general figures quoted for the industry.

[1] *Hazard's Register of Pennsylvania*, XI, 7 (February 16, 1833), p. 103.

The operators of Hopewell Furnace owned farm land close
to the furnace and at a distance from it. Rental agreements
mentioned several different farms. But not all of the needs
of the people of the village were supplied by the partner-
owned farms; for the records showed many neighboring farmers were trading grain, fruits, vegetables, meats, dairy
products and animals for store goods, castings or the services
of the blacksmith and wheelright. Grain, flour and feed were
purchased at grist mills a number of miles distant from the
furnace. It was not possible to determine the acreage of land
cultivated for Hopewell Village consumption, but the area
would necessarily have been large.

Two writers reported that in New Jersey a charcoal furnace
required 20,000 acres of timber land to furnish wood for
charcoal. A common practice was to divide the forest into
tracts of 1,000 acres each with one tract being cut each year.
At the end of twenty years the first section would have grown
enough to cut again, and thus a continuous supply of wood
was provided.[2]

Forest lands in southeastern Pennsylvania must have been
more productive than those in New Jersey, because none of
the furnaces in the former region possessed a domain approaching 20,000 acres. Representative furnaces in the Hopewell area were listed as owning in the eighteenth century the
following estates, in acres: Elizabeth 10,124; Cornwall 9,669,
Reading 5,600 and Warwick 1,796.[3] The land associated with
Hopewell Furnace varied in different periods from about 3,900
to about 8,000 acres. All of these figures included both farm
and forest lands with the greater amount devoted to producing
wood for charcoal.

The history of the Hopewell farms showed several different
kinds of agreements between proprietor and farmer. In 1814

[2] Robert J. Sims and Harry B. Weiss, *Charcoal-Burning in New Jersey
from Early Times to the Present* (Trenton: New Jersey Agricultural
Society, 1955), p. 11.
[3] *Pennsylvania Archives*, Third Series (Volume XII; Harrisburg: Wm.
Stanley Ray, 1897), pp. 65, 295; *Aliens Appeal Record, op. cit.*, p. 189.

Buckley and Brooke agreed to pay Matthew Foy $65 per year and to provide him a house, in return for which Foy agreed to do the farming and other work as required of him.[4] Ten years later Clement Brooke preferred a straight cash rental basis on two of his farms. Henry Shick rented the farm which was "formerly William Thomas' " for $135 for 1824. The next year the payment was $150 and remained the same through 1830.[5] James Reperts paid Clement Brooke $212 in 1832 "For 1 year Rent of Farm and Tenant House in East Nantmeal Township . . ."[6]

The more common arrangement between farm owner and tenant was a formal share-crop agreement. John Bishop and Samuel Cox signed a contract in 1798 which required Cox to clear a field, fence, plow and sow it "upon his own expense;" and he was to have "two thirds of the corn above the furnace race and half below, and half the buckwheat, or any other kind of summer grain, . . . the winter grain [was] to be sowd and seed found by Cox—for which he [was] to have two thirds in the shock." . . ." Cox was also to be permitted to mow the meadow "to the Haves."[7] Later a farmer paid $50 in cash for the use of the meadow.[8]

The specific obligations of both parties were detailed in this farm contract between Clement Brooke and Isaac Hayer in 1829 :

> ". . . Said Hayer is to sow thirty acres of winter grain and Sumer grain in proportion according to the rules of farming and deliver Said Brooke the one half of all the grain in the bushel to Birdsborough Mill and likewise to make and repair all the fences and make all the rails at his own expense, the rails to be made on the wood land belonging to the premises and he is to haul six hundred bushels lime . . . and spread it on the land in a farmer like maner and likewise to find all the clover seed that may be wanted—Said Brooke is to pay

[4] *Hopewell Papers,* Agreement, January 4, 1814.
[5] SM 12, p. 136; SM 59, p. 22; SM 14, pp. 53, 92.
[6] SM 21, p. 25.
[7] HV 7980603.
[8] HV 8361228B.

for the lime and be at the expense of the one half of all the seed grain—Said Hayer is to have one half acre of ground for Potatoes and one half acre for flax to sell no hay or straw of the premises—Said Hayer is to have firewood for the use of the mansion house but no fire wood for the tenant house and to pay the road tax for said Farm."[9]

When the time of year came to renew or cancel the rental agreements, there must have been some anxiety on the part of the farmer. Note the tenor of this letter:

Sir this is to let you now that you did not let me now according to promise you promised to let me now between Chrismus and New Year before witness and I am resolve to stay anther year and I will make you satisfaction as good as anny man and you may cum down and let me now how it is wether I can stay or now and your grain is all thraght . . ."[10]

One of the farmers recorded the way he and his two sons had used their time during a part of the year. It may have been that Mathew Brooke was to pay them extra for some kinds of work done beyond the usual farming activities. A sampling of the jobs listed tells something of the work of a farm family in 1804:

May	1	Sowd the front lot with flax
May	2	Hauld dung in garding
May	30	Hauld Brush out young orchard
June	11	Plowed petatoes in garding
July	4	Hauld clover out the orchard
July	18	Hauld his part of the wheat to the Barn
July	28	Sowed Buckwheat
August	2	Cross plowed Barn lot
August	4	Sowd flax lot and Barn lot with turnip seed and sowd meadow grond with turnip seed
August	6	Hauld a load Brush and wood from Young Orchard to Big House
August	13	Hauld a load of oats

[9] HV 8290112A.
[10] *Brooke Family Papers,* John Bohn to Mathias Brooke, January 1, 1803.

August	27	Moad clover in Young Orchard
August	31	Hauld a load of hay
September	10	Hauld a load flour from Stichters to Big House
September	18	Threshed 15 bushels
September	25	Hauld sill for sider press
September	26	Hauld Beam post—1 Sill Sweep
September	29	3/4 of a day thrasht and John helped to clean 6 Bushels
October	3	Hauld load Corn from Bishops Mill to Big House
October	11	Hauld Rails to fence turnip ground
October	13	Laid the worm for the fence and hauled Stone for Trunnels
October	16	Made fence
October	18	killd 2 Beefs at twise Black and Red Cows
October	23	hauld 1 load from Bishops Mill to Hopewell and 1 load of Stoves back
October	27	hauld 1 load Stoves to Reading and a load flour and feed . . . back. killed Beef Cut up and Salted
October	28-29	to 2 days Riding of a hors when Jack Run away
November	30	to 1 day Cleand Ditch
December	13	hauld fire wood to Big House half a day Self and Mark
December	17	killed hoggs and Cut and Salted
December	21	hauld wood for . . . forgemen
December	22	hauled hoggshears from hofmans
December	17	hauld load feed and pork from Reading[11]

The usual grain crops of wheat, corn, oats, buckwheat and rye were sold directly from the farm to people of the village or were taken to the mill to be ground into flour, meal or feed The miller took his pay in a percentage of the grain ground. An important byproduct of the grain crops was straw which was sold in bundles at $5 per hundred bundles.[12] Straw had uses as bedding for animals, possibly as a cover for dirt floors

[11] *Brooke Family Papers,* Account Pages, Mathew Brooke to Elishu Bard, 1804.
[12] SM 4, p. 224. This was in 1808.

and certainly as filler for mattresses. Potatoes, turnips, Indian corn and hay were other products of the Furnace farms.

Before 1820 farming was a hand-tool operation for the most part. A hoe, rake, axe, scythe, sickle, flail and plow, costing from $15 to $20, put a family in the farming business.[13] But the next forty years brought inventions of expensive farm machines such as drills, planters, reapers, mowers, horse rakes, threshers, feed grinders and plows of many kinds.[14] These new tools provided Hopewell with new markets for its iron[15] and lightened the work of the farmers. Among the new machines put into operation on the Hopewell farms were: A horse-drawn rake in 1819; a winnowing mill, improved plow and a "revolving rake" in 1827; a threshing machine by 1849. An inventory of farm tools at Hopewell in 1876 listed a mowing machine, a grain drill, a roller, single and double "Hoca plows," spike and hoe harrows, a fodder cutter and a portable engine.[16]

The farmers of the nineteenth century had their troubles with nature when unusual numbers of locusts and grasshoppers appeared and cutworms destroyed the young corn stalks. The Hessian fly damaged the wheat; smut and mildew took their toll both in wheat and in rye. Potatoes rotted in the ground when the weather was too wet to harvest them.[17]

Hopewell owners were conscious of the necessity of maintaining the fertility of their lands and wrote into their farm agreements specific requirements upon the tenants for good farm practices. James Wilson demanded that not less than 1,000 bushels of lime be put on the arable Furnace lands each year and that clover be planted.[18] Daniel Buckley and Company bought clover seed which was presumably sown on

[13] Williamson, *op. cit.*, p. 136.
[14] *Ibid.*, p. 117.
[15] See chapter 7.
[16] HV 8760401.
[17] *Morris Diary, op. cit.* Many references to the problems of area farmers.
[18] *Hopewell Papers,* Rental Agreement, May 1, 1795.

their farms.[19] Ground plaster and manure were used for ferti-
lizers.[20]

Before the introduction of tractors and other power
machinery, farming required work animals. Horses, mules and
oxen were used around the furnace and for transportation to
the distant markets. Poultry, cows, hogs and sheep were kept
to provide meat, eggs, milk, leather and wool. Dogs were
used in farm work as well as in providing companionship to
the isolated rural families. The animals were in turn consumers
of much that the farm produced, and they returned a portion
to the soil in nitrogen-rich manure. Providing for the needs
of the animals was costly in labor and money to build shelter
and fences, to feed and water, to milk and butcher and to
care for them when they were ill.

Hopewell had its animal population in profusion of numbers and of kinds. Mark Bird reported to the Union Township tax collector in 1779 that he was the possessor of 16
horses, 21 cows and 46 sheep.[21] He may have possessed other
animals as well, but these were the only kinds which were
included in the tax return. In 1832 Hopewell Furnace was
reported to have had 84 horses,[22] and in 1850 the draft animals
at the Furnace were 50 oxen, horses and mules.[23] The business
records of the company contained many references to the
purchase or sale of animals or to some other expense or income from the possession of beasts and fowls.

There were at least two buildings in the immediate area of
the furnace for the sheltering of the nonhuman population.
Below and to the south of the mansion was a large barn which
contained 6 sets of stalls, each capable of holding 6 horses,
mules, cows or steers. Above the stalls were three haymows

[19] Examples are found in HV 8210409B and 8260323B.

[20] *Hopewell Papers,* Farm Rental Agreement, May 20, 1805.

[21] *Pennsylvania Archives,* Third Series, XVIII, Berks County, Union
Township Tax Return for 1779.

[22] McLane Report in *Hazard's Register,* XIV, 18 (November 1, 1834),
p. 350.

[23] *Documents Relating to the Manufacture of Iron in Pennsylvania,*
op. cit., "Table on Cold Blast Charcoal Furnaces."

North Side of Restored Hopewell Village Barn

which, among them, could hold enough hay to feed 36 horses or mules for a year.[24] Obviously this barn alone was not sufficient to shelter all the draft animals when the Furnace owned 84 or even 50. Some livestock may have been kept at other farms, or teamsters may have cared for their own teams. In the late years of Furnace operation the east end of

[24] H. A. Long Interview, August 13, 1936.

West Side of Restored Hopewell Village Barn

the barn was used for cattle and the west end for horses and mules.[25]

East of the barn was a large pen, about 40 feet square, used to house hogs and chickens. It had two separate sections for its different kinds of denizens.[26]

The price of horses remained remarkably stable in the first

[25] Violet Care Interview, February 13, 1941.
[26] *Kemper Manuscripts,* H. A. Long's Notes on Hopewell.

half of the nineteenth century. A good sound horse in the prime ages was never very far from $100 in price. There were many sales at that exact price and numerous others at a range from $90 to $120 each. Animals lost rapidly in value when they were past their best work years or when they were impaired in some way. "An old horse" brought only $20 in 1807,[27] and a blind mare was sold for the same price in 1818.[28] Horses were priced much higher when there was a special reason for their value, as in 1820 the Furnace received "$150 in part for the Stud horse."[29] The total price was not reported. When horses were bought or sold, they were usually identified in the records by color. Other means of identification included names of the animals or of the teamster who had driven them.

Horses involved their owners in other kinds of expense beside purchase and shelter. Horseshoes at the blacksmith shop were priced at about 20¢ to 30¢ each, and there was an additional charge of 10¢ for removing the old shoe. In 1827 the Furnace purchased from a harnessmaker for $13 : 5 horse collars, 6 blind bridles, 1 back band and 1 creeper.[30] Thomas Care, the founder, paid $15.00 "for keeping horse,"[31] but the record did not report whether he was paying for feed in addition to shelter.

Oxen seldom appeared in the Hopewell records, but that they were used was verified by the purchase of a pair in the summer of 1818 for $20.[32] Cattle for milk and meat, however, were often mentioned. As proof that many of the village families had their own cows, frequently the purchase price of "a cow" or "a milch cow" was charged against the account of a workman. Prices varied widely for the cows which changed hands. In 1808 the going price was about $16.00,[33] in 1818

[27] SM 4, p. 198.
[28] SM 9, p. 18.
[29] SM 10, p. 51.
[30] SM 59, p. 22.
[31] SM 54, p. 117.
[32] SM 9, p. 145 and SM 6, p. 24.
[33] SM 4, p. 250.

from $17.00 to $32.75,[34] in 1825 about $16.00,[35] through the
1830's about $15.00 and in 1850 about $20.00.[36] Age again
was a factor in price, for in 1852 Henry Ammon bought "1
old cow" from the Furnace for only $6.[37]

Cattle were purchased for butchering by the Furnace and
by individuals. Through the 1840's there were many references
to "store cattle" and to "fat cattle." Store cattle were bought
for $17 each in 1845,[38] for $27 each in 1847[39] and the same in
1850. This last purchase was made from Timothy Parker, a
drover, who spent the night at the Furnace and paid $1.50 for
pasturing his herd in the meadow. The Furnace also sold him
eleven "Fat cattle at $40 per head."[40]

About 20 steers were butchered each autumn to provide
beef for the employees and their families.[41] South of the Furnace office was an iron ring fastened to a large rock and called
by the old Hopewell residents "the bull ring." A steer for
butchering was tied here so that its head could be drawn down
into a position where it was easy to hit the forehead with a
sledge hammer to stun the animal before its throat was cut.[42]

Butter making at the Furnace was indicated by the purchase in 1846 of a set of "milch pans and bowls."[43] These
containers were used to hold the milk while the cream
gathered at the top to be skimmed and placed in the churn.
Women of the village also made butter to sell to the company
store.

Hogs were raised by both the Furnace and the Village
families to furnish the large quantities of pork sold at the store
and in private sales. Probably most of the tenant houses had

[34] SM 10, pp. 14–40.
[35] SM 14, pp. 67–70.
[36] SM 32, p. 97.
[37] SM 32, p. 120.
[38] SM 28, p. 162.
[39] SM 31, p. 41.
[40] SM 31, p. 132.
[41] Charles Sheridan Care Interview, February 24, 1941.
[42] Charles E. Stevenson Interview, September 23, 1940.
[43] SM 31, p. 10.

pigpens on the premises. On at least one occasion the Furnace provided shelter and food for a hog belonging to one of the workmen when David Griffith paid three dollars "for keeping and fattening his hog from last Spring."[44] The price of pigs depended upon their size. "Little pigs" sold for 75¢ each,[45] but "Shoats" brought $4 each.[46]

Sheep were seldom mentioned in the office records of the Furnace. They were reported among Mark Bird's assets for most years for which the tax records were available.[47] A note in 1834 stated that the Furnace had sold 20 head of sheep to Charles Brooke, Senior.[48] Although mutton appeared at rare intervals among the meats sold by the store, sheepskins were frequently recorded among the sales.[49]

The value of animals made the breeding of livestock an important part of rural life. One clerk made note of the dates when a mare was "Put . . . to Horse," and when he "Put the Pony to Wallys Black Horse." The foaling of colts also received official report.[50] In the same period of the 1850's the record of the breeding of dogs[51] was one of the few references to pets at Hopewell, although several years earlier a "puppy" had been sold for two dollars.[52]

Most families kept some fowls for eggs and meat. The store did not often sell these items; but scattered references, mostly from the 1850's, mentioned the presence at the Furnace of chickens, turkeys, ducks and geese. The clerk of this era was again the source for much of the surviving information about the animals and birds around the Furnace grounds. In his detailed record for 1857 and 1858 appeared evidences that these four varieties of fowls were a part of the picture of the

[44] SM 7, December 7, 1816.
[45] SM 31, p. 121.
[46] SM 59, p. 17.
[47] *Pennsylvania Archives, op. cit.,* XVIII.
[48] SM 21, p. 104.
[49] For example in 1830 Thomas Care paid $7.47½ for one. SM 14, p. 89.
[50] SM 35, pp. 80–82.
[51] SM 38, pp. 126–127.
[52] SM 31, p. 110.

life of Hopewell Village. Judging from the following notes, some of them must have had freedom from confinement : "Set a turkey in the Spring House," "two hens with Duck Eggs in Carage and under hog house," "Set a hen in Coal House," "Set a Hen in Chicken House 13 Eggs," "Set a hen Sunday 21st," "Set 2 hens in Chick House," "Set a Goose," "Set a Hen with 7 duck Eggs," "Set a duck at Window," "Set a hen 6 turkey Eggs," "Set a duck in Calf Stabel," "Set a Hen Turkey Eggs in Spring House Loft."[53]

Confining animals to the areas where they belonged and paying costs when they did not remain there were sometimes the causes of expenses for the owners. Rails and fence posts were cut in each year for which the labor study was made from 1805 to 1853. In 1832 Samuel Peirce was paid $91.20 "for cutting . . . and Putting up 420 Panniels five rail fence on the Property that Roberts now lives on."[54] Clement Brooke paid 50¢ to a man who had caught and kept a horse which had run away at the mineholes.[55] Jacob Felman was credited with $7 for damage done his corn by a neighbor's cattle.[56] And a reward was paid in 1828 by the Furnace for "giving information of our Black Horse when stolen last fall."[57]

Veterinary expenses appeared in the record after 1828. Several journal items showed that $5 was paid "for Doctoring Horses." Several other payments were made for "altering Swine" and for medicine for ailing horses.[58]

Farming at Hopewell included vegetable gardens and orchards as well as the previously mentioned field crops. Two sizable garden plots were remembered by Harker Long. One, about a quarter of an acre in area, was located to the west of the barnyard. Stray animals were kept out of the beans and cabbage by a whitewashed picket fence. Another half acre

[53] SM 35, pp. 108–128
[54] HV 8321117A.
[55] SM 44, August 21, 1806.
[56] *Lewis Evans Ledger, 1801–1840,* November 27, 1826. Hopewell Village Library.
[57] SM 14, p. 67.
[58] See for example SM 28, pp. 107–109.

plot near the brick kiln was used for vegetables.[59] This space grew potatoes in 1857, and in the same year potatoes were raised "in Back field."[60] Other vegetables common in gardens of the Village area were onions, beets, radishes, lettuce, cauliflower, tomatoes, salsify, peas, cucumbers, squash and egg plant.[61]

Most of the fruit used in Hopewell Village also was produced in local orchards. The company store was a market for orchard products for the neighborhood, although it is not clear whether purchases were made because the Furnace orchards did not produce enough or because a kind of barter was carried on for store goods. Quantity purchases were made of apples, plums and prunes, quinces, peaches, cherries, cider and vinegar. Dried apples and peaches were bought by the bushel as well as being dried in the outdoor oven at the Big House. One customer requested that his payment be a barrel of rye whiskey or a barrel of "apple whiskey."[62]

There was at least one peach orchard at Hopewell, because a notation in 1835 stated that wood was being hauled "from old peach orchard."[63] Apple orchards were planted at several different times in Furnace history, but these may have been replacements for overage trees rather than the opening of new ground. The advertisements for the sale of Hopewell Furnace in 1787[64] and also in 1788[65] mentioned an excellent young orchard of 250 apple trees. In 1804 Elishu Bard reported that he had "Hauld Brush out Young Orchard."[66] The Furnace bought 160 apple trees in 1829 at 10¢ each[67] and two years

[59] H. A. Long Interview, December, 1935.
[60] SM 35, p. 108.
[61] Morris Diary, op. cit., passim.
[62] Brooke Family Papers, Lewis Wohr to Mathew Brooke, November 5, 1810.
[63] SM 21, p. 127.
[64] Pennsylvania Gazette, April 11, 1787.
[65] Pennsylvania Packet and Daily Advertiser, March 22, 1788.
[66] Brooke Family Papers, Account Pages. Mathew Brooke to Elishu Bard.
[67] Cash Book for 1828–1830, April 10, 1829, n. p. Berks County Historical Society.

later paid Samuel Peirce "for Triming the young orchard."[68] An additional 304 young apple trees were purchased in 1834 at 12½¢ each.[69] Another "Young Orchard" was mentioned in 1844.[70]

What kind of apples were grown in the orchard? The journals just called them apples without further identification. Hopewell Historian Robert D. Ronsheim made inquiry of S. W. Fletcher, author of *Pennsylvania Agriculture and Country Life, 1840–1940,* about the varieties of apples grown in Pennsylvania in the first half of the nineteenth century. Fletcher replied that about half of the orchard was probably in three kinds of apples: Baldwin, Northern Spy and Rhode Island Greening.[71] In 1916 Cyrus Fox saw trees in the Hopewell orchard producing Baldwins and Northern Spies.[72] Other varieties grown nearby were: Rusty Coats, Rambos, Pippins and Grindstones.[73]

Fletcher also said there was little or no pruning of the orchards, but at Hopewell payments were made in both 1807 and 1827 for trimming the apple trees.[74]

The Furnace paid for 1,289 grafts in the young orchard in 1844.[75] During the same spring James Morris of Morgantown had had eighty grafts made to his fruit trees. Possibly the same persons did the work in both orchards, for the price to each customer was 4¢ per graft. Morris reported that he had gotten grafts of Pound, Eollowalter, Bellflower, Black Apple, Smokehouse, Jones Apple and Summer Iwen.[76] Perhaps these same kinds of apples grew at Hopewell.

One other kind of fruit which was certainly grown at Hope-

[68] SM 15, p. 59.
[69] *Hopewell Papers,* Bill from Isaac Hambleton to Clement Brooke, 1834.
[70] SM 58, June 10, 1844.
[71] *Hopewell Papers,* Fletcher to Ronsheim, March 19, 1958.
[72] *Reading Eagle,* February 25, 1917.
[73] *Morris Diary, op. cit.,* p. 161.
[74] SM 4, p. 137 and SM 59, p. 19.
[75] SM 58, June 10, 1844, n. p.
[76] *Morris Diary, op. cit.,* p. 115.

well was grapes. Twice in 1832 and once in 1857 the journals showed payments for dressing the vineyard."

A great part of the land was used for growing wood for the production of charcoal for the furnace. The furnace manager who failed to take care of his wood supply did not stay in business very long. England had stopped making charcoal iron by 1775 "except for a few isolated furnaces, mainly in remote regions" because of the scarcity of wood." Salford Forge ceased to operate in 1810 because of the depletion of its timber, and Green Lane Forge was inactive for twenty years after 1813 while a new stand of timber grew in its area." An acre of land in Southeastern Pennsylvania grew cn an average about a cord of wood per year." Matthew Cary reported in 1837 that Clement Brooke had told him that Hopewell Furnace burned 6,000 cords of wood per year, "and the growth of his land is 4,000 cords per year."" But the furnace did not depend entirely upon company owned land for its wood supply. Wood "leave" or "leif" was bought to permit wood cutting on the land owned by neighbors. The usual fee was from 70¢ to $1 per cord. Some men cut wood on their own land and sold it to the Furnace, but apparently most of the wood came from Hopewell property.

As was evidenced by several memoranda, the Hopewell managers were aware of the importance of protecting their own growing timber. The word "sprouts" used in the following excerpts meant the new growth in a cut-over area of wood-land :

1836 Henry Sheets was paid $9.75 "for Sundry work and saving sprouts.""

" SM 17, pp. 16, 27 and SM 65, April 17, 1857, n. p.
" H. R. Schubert, *History of the British Iron and Steel Industry* (London: Routledge and Kegan Paul, 1957), p. IX.
" Gemmell, *op. cit.,* p. 99.
" *Ibid.,* p. 109.
" *Cary Diary, op. cit.,* February 17, 1837, n. p.
" SM 21, p. 184.

1851 A fence was built "around the Sprouts near
      Geigertown."[83]
1863 "Levi Keller and J: Bland have been getting Stone
      off our land and done considerable damage to Sprouts."
      A note beside this said, "paid."[84]

The thousands of acres of land associated with Hopewell
Furnace served many purposes in providing food and fuel. Although land was used generally for auxiliary production to
facilitate the making of iron, possibly some grain was sold off
the premises, and in the last years of the Furnace's history
charcoal and cordwood were marketed in Pottstown and
Philadelphia.

[83] SM 32, p. 119.
[84] *Kemper Manuscripts,* C. W. Clingan Pocket Note Book, n. p.

Part Three
The Industrial Village

7   The Furnace Product

THE CENTER OF ACTIVITY AND THE RAISON D'ETRE FOR
Hopewell Village was the little stone furnace in which iron was
smelted. While relatively few people worked right at the
furnace, the entire labor force was engaged in service to its
needs and was subject to its whims. The old charcoal furnace
was called a fickle mistress by those who served her and who
were dependent upon her operation for their economic well-
being. Many of the villagers were constantly aware of the
evidences of furnace operation, for as Bining wrote:

> The intermittent roar of the forced blast could be heard a
> long distance away. From the top of the furnace stack a stream
> of sparks was occasionally emitted as the flames rose and fell.
> At night the almost smokeless flames cast a lurid glare upon
> the sky, visible for miles around which illuminated the sur-
> rounding buildings.[1]

The furnace operation required a coal shed where the coal
was kept until all danger of fire from it was past and a coal
house where 30,000 bushels of charcoal were stored. To put
hot coal into the coal house too soon would endanger the
entire supply on hand. Between the coal house and the furnace

---

[1] Bining, *Pennsylvania Iron Manufacture in the 18th Century, op. cit.,*
p. 33.

Hopewell Furnace Group in 1887

Hopewell Furnace and Bridgehouse After Shutdown

stack was the bridge house upon which were stored the
ingredients for charging the furnace for the next few hours and
from which the fillers dumped the fuel, ore and flux into the
charging hole. On a lower level was the casting house into
which the molten iron flowed through its trenches of sand.
Nearby, too, were the blacksmith shop and the cleaning shed.
Around the furnace were the piles of ore and limestone and
the slag heaps of furnace waste. This was the industrial heart
of Hopewell Village. To it came the wagon loads of raw
materials; and from it went the wagon loads of pig iron, gate
metal and cast products which constituted the source of
income to pay the wages of the several hundred men and
women who worked for the owners of Hopewell Furnace.

About 25 men were employed on each of two shifts at the
furnace.[2] This did not include the blacksmith, the wheelwright
or their helpers. It did include a founder, a keeper, fillers,
guttermen, and molders as well as men who did the jobs
described as "putting in the mine," "putting in the night
stock" or "stocking coal." In later years there was also a
"banksman."[3]

The furnace was charged about every half hour with 15
bushels of charcoal, 400 to 500 pounds of ore and 30 to 40
pounds of limestone. In the two year period from May 1,
1880, to May 17, 1882, Hopewell Furnace consumed 352,365
bushels of charcoal in 23,491 charges.[4] The consumption of
charcoal was always higher in the first week of the blast, perhaps 50 to 100 charges more than in the second week,[5] because
of the necessity of heating the inwalls before the charge was
put in. In normal operations it required about 160 bushels of
charcoal to make a ton of iron.[6] The annual requirements for
charcoal at Hopewell consumed 5,000 to 6,000 cords of wood.[7]

[2] Atwood Lacey Interview, October 17, 1940.
[3] For the various classifications of furnace workers see Appendix B.
[4] SM 34, p. 175.
[5] SM 60, *passim*.
[6] Overman, *op. cit.*, p. 168.
[7] *Morris Diary, op. cit.*, p. 4

Abandoned Hopewell Furnace

The iron ore for Hopewell Furnace came from three mines owned in whole or in part by the furnace proprietors. In addition there was a reciprocal arrangement in 1802 with Changewater Furnace by which Hopewell obtained ore and Changewater received castings.[8] The earliest source of ore was the mine called Hopewell, or sometimes Birdtown, opened about 1770.[9] Ore from this mine was reported in 1883 to contain 37.85 per cent metallic iron, but it may have produced richer ore at an earlier period of its operation. It contained

[8] *Changewater Furnace Account Books,* 1802. Microfilm at Hopewell Village Library.
[9] Charles William Heathcote, "The Iron Industry of Northern Chester County" (*Bulletin of the Chester County Historical Society,* 1936), p. 50.

Water Wheel and Blast Machinery from Top of Furnace Bank Looking South

two veins each about 7 feet thick at the top and as much as 25 feet at a lower level.[10]

Jones Mine was operated for more than one hundred years in Robeson and Caernarvon Townships of Berks County not far from Morgantown. Hopewell owned a section of this mining land. The metallic content of the Jones ore was apparently fairly high, for in 1824 Hopewell used about 4,500 pounds of ore per ton of iron produced.[11] An additional source of income was derived from the Jones Mine after 1843 when an English company leased the right to the copper at ten dollars per ton raised.[12]

As early as 1821 Hopewell was receiving some of its ore from the Warwick mines near St. Mary's Episcopal Church in Chester County. This mine was opened before 1760 and had numerous veins varying in thickness from 1 to 17 feet. It averaged about 45 per cent metallic iron.[13] Royalty was paid on the ore used, based on the tonnage of iron produced by the furnace, at rates ranging from $.87½ to $1.12½ per ton of iron.[14] In 1829 Hopewell became part owner of Warwick by the purchase of 1/11 of 1/8 of the mines from Miss Martha Rutter for a price of $350, and 5/11 of 1/8 from John P. Rutter for $800.[15] For the very profitable blast of 1837 the royalty on ore from Warwick Mine amounted to $1,268.76, of which $1,182.23 was paid to other partners, the remainder being the Hopewell share.[16]

About 1840 Hopewell Furnace joined a new kind of partnership called the Warwick Furnace Reserve. Anyone who owned a share could search for ore anywhere in the 20,000 acre reserve in Chester and Berks Counties. Any iron found

[10] *Second Pennsylvania Geological Survey*, 1883, Chester County, pp. 176, 236. (Microfilm.)
[11] HV 8240725.
[12] *Morris Diary, op. cit.*, p. 88.
[13] *Second Pennsylvania Geological Survey, op. cit.*, p. 240.
[14] SM 12, p. 124.
[15] *Cash Book* for 1828–1830, November 20, 1829; SM 14, p. 72.
[16] SM 21, Blast of January 3, 1836, to April 10, 1837.

Another View of Blowing Machinery

Partial Restoration of Furnace Group

could be removed and paid for at the rate of 50¢ per ton, less
the proportionate share of the reserve owned.[17]

The limestone for the flux was sometimes obtained from
quarries on Hopewell land. More of it was apparently bought
from the Christian Mast quarry east of Morgantown. The
price paid Mast in 1851 was 50¢ per load for the 169 loads
used during the year.[18]

No charcoal furnace could operate continuously. The intense heat, friction and draft gradually wore away the inwalls
and hearth, and eventually the furnace had to shut down for
repairs. It often happened, too, that the supply of charcoal on
hand in the fall was not sufficient to keep the furnace in blast

[17] Long, *Short History of Hopewell Furnace, op. cit.*, p. 7.
[18] SM 37, p. 106.

Partial Restoration of Stack, Front View

over the winter when no new supply of fuel was arriving.[19] When the charcoal was exhausted, the operation ceased until the colliers resumed their work in the spring. During this period of inactivity the necessary repairs were made on the stack and hearth in order to have it in good operating order when the new supplies of charcoal arrived. Probably some repair work would have been necessary about once a year even if there had been no other reason to shut down.

The frequency with which the repair work was done during the winter led one observer to conclude that ". . . they meant to go out of blast every fall, and if they did not there was some extraordinary reason for it. . . ."[20] Many iron men were aware that their furnaces worked better in the clear, dry air of winter than in the moist, humid air of summer. Henry Huse Campbell explained the greater efficiency of winter operation in terms of fuel needs, "On a moist summer day the air holds about 6 grains of water per cu. ft. On a cold winter day it holds 1.7 grains or less. The average for the year is about 3.6 grains."[21] To reduce one pound of water to H^2 and O^2 absorbed the heat produced by burning 0.8 pounds of coke. Thus the moisture in the air on a humid day used fuel not necessary on a dry, cold day[22]

Hopewell Furnace made iron during the winter months when it could do so. A letter in 1823 spoke of an intention to continue the blast all winter.[23] The longest blast in Hopewell history lasted through most of two winters from January 3, 1836 to April 10, 1837.[24] In 1859 the furnace was blown until April 8 before it was shut down "For want of coal" and was back in blast three weeks later.[25] The average blast of

[19] For the problems of charcoal-making see Chapter 11.
[20] *Allens Appeal Record, op. cit.*, p. 96.
[21] Harry Huse Campbell, *The Manufacture and Properties of Iron and Steel* (New York: Hill Publishing Company, 1907), p. 74.
[22] *Ibid.*, p. 48.
[23] HV 8231118A.
[24] SM 21, p. 206.
[25] SM 60, p. 5.

Partial Restoration of Bridge House

Hopewell furnace was eleven and one-half months from 1820 to 1840 and ten and one-half months after 1840.[26] The winter of 1881 presented some unusual difficulties according to a newspaper report:

> Owing to the severity of the weather during the present winter the proprietors of Joanna and Hopewell Furnaces have been unable to get their usual quantity of wood cut for burning charcoal for these establishments, and fears are entertained that they will have to close their works in the spring for want of fuel.[27]

[26] Kurjack's Chart of Furnace Operation. Hopewell Village Library.
[27] *Daily Local News*, West Chester, Pennsylvania, February 1, 1881.

Restored Furnace Group

The end of a blast was a period of hilarity for the furnace crew at whatever time of year it took place. The clerk at Martha Furnace made note of several of these occasions: "Blew the Furnace out at 8 o'clock P. M. All Hands drunk," and again, "All in very high glee." He also chronicled many fights during these celebrations.[28] That Martha was not the only furnace where drinking marked this event was proved by this entry about a Hopewell founder: John Painter was

[28] *Martha Furnace Diary, op. cit.,* January 7, 1809, and January 16, 1811.

charged for ". . . 2 quts. whiskey . . . between you and Jacob when Furnace blowd out."[29]

The purpose of all furnace activity was to get a supply of iron extracted from the ore in a usable form. The product of the furnace was cast iron, but there were many variations of the form and shape it assumed when it cooled. One of the most important jobs at the furnace was to mold the iron into useful articles of commerce. For the first three-quarters of a century the most important finished product of Hopewell Furnace was stoves, but there were many other cast items made. Throughout its history Hopewell also sold pig iron and gate metal to forges where it was further treated to produce yet other commodities of iron.

Pig iron was a raw material for further refinement and was sold wholesale to other iron establishments. One pig now in the Hopewell museum is 48 inches long and about $5\frac{1}{2}$ inches by 2 inches on an end. These pigs were formed by running molten iron into sand trenches to cool. The pieces were broken into convenient size for handling. Pig iron, by chemical definition, was ". . . a granular crystalline compound of iron with carbon, silicon, sulphur, phosphorus, and Manganese, with oftentimes also smaller quantities of other metals. . . ."[30] It contained from 2 per cent. to 4 per cent. of carbon which was either in compound or in mixture with the iron. Quantities of the two forms and the presence of other foreign elements determined the different varieties of pig iron: black, gray, white and mottled. Each kind had special uses.[31]

Gate metal was waste from the casting process. Although it was as good metal as the pig iron, it was not as convenient to handle; so it usually sold for about $2 per ton less than the price of pigs.

During its early history Hopewell sold most of its pig iron to forges owned by partners in the furnace company. Mark

[29] *Lewis Evans Journal, op. cit.,* January 16, 1805.
[30] William Henry Greenwood, *Steel and Iron* (London: Cassell and Company, 1900), p. 62.
[31] Overman, *op. cit.,* p. 140.

Restored Water Wheel at the Furnace

Bird, James Wilson and Buckley and Brooke used it at Birdsboro Forge, and Charles Brooke took most of his share of
Hopewell profits in pig iron for his Hibernia Forge. But after
the halt of stove-making the production of pig iron was great
enough to interest other customers. From 1852 to 1875 the

names of 27 different forges, located from Lancaster County to Philadelphia, appeared on the Hopewell records as customers.[32]

Prices for pig iron from Hopewell Furnace ranged from a low of $24 per ton in 1802[33] to a reported $99 in 1865. Charles M. Clingan listed an actual sale September 3, 1864, at $93 per ton to Douglassville.[34] For most of the period of furnace operation the price seemed to have been fairly stable at within a few dollars of $30 per ton.

More profit from the furnace iron was available when the fluid metal was poured into molds instead of the pig beds and marketable finished articles were manufactured. Until about the middle of the nineteenth century Hopewell produced and sold a variety of molded products. Although the kind of articles changed with the demands of a changing economy, some idea of the variety can be obtained from listings of castings, other than stoves which were always of first importance, made in several decades for which records were available. The following kinds of castings were representative:

For the 1780's: Foundry castings, hammers, anvils, forge castings, potts.

For the 1800's: Dutch ovens, hallow ware, riddles, pots [in many sizes], skillets, kettles, lids, bake plates, flat irons, wheelbarrow wheels, French kettles, sash weights, wagon boxes, mill screws, apple mill nuts, tea kettles, and irons, clock weights, forge castings, anvils.

For the 1810's: Backs and jambs, clock weights, sash weights, street grates, stew pans, cambooses, pots, mold boards, mortars, handware, mill gudgeons, bake plates, windmill irons, waffle irons, hollow ware, fire places, mandrels, wagon irons, skillets, anvils.

For the 1820's: Grindstone wheels, mortars and pestals, wing gudgeons, friction wheels, corn-plow machines, mold boards, turning lathe, apple drying kiln, plaster mill, windmill irons,

[32] *Hopewell Papers*, 42215.
[33] SM 1, June 1, 1802, page unreadable.
[34] *C. M. Clingan Pocket Note Book, op. cit.*, n. p.

sash weights, small wheels, tires, shear wings, coulter lays, land sides, scalleped iron, country iron, finery bottoms, anvils, rolling mill castings.

For the 1830's : Furnace grates, sash weights, plow castings, rough castings, mold boards, windmill irons, oil troughs, bake plates, anvils, mesheinery, threshing machines, griddles, shelling machines, land sides, sifter grates, wagon boxes.

For the 1850's : Cinder hole plates, plow castings, mold boards, iron blocks, sand sides, plow handle pieces, beams.

The above tally shows that the invention of farm machinery brought a demand for new kinds of castings after 1820. Sometimes the market for Hopewell products was quite distant, as in 1836 when the furnace had a rush order for a large supply of sash weights to be shipped to New Orleans. Speed was necessary to get the weights on board a ship about to sail from Philadelphia.[35]

A letter to Clement Brooke in 1825 mentioned the possibility of a new customer and resulted in the sale of a large amount of Hopewell iron during the next three years. It reported :

> I rec^d a letter from my father the other day stating that proposals are to be made to the Commissioners for erecting the City Prison for a considerable quantity of Castings and bar iron . . . I have business in town and will go tomorrow . . . If I can do any thing for you on the subject please inform me by letter . . .[36]

It was apparent that this approach was followed up. In November the Furnace was paid $1,000 for materials sold for the erection of the "New State Penitentiary."[37] During 1826 and 1827 the molders were making door frames in two sizes, "peepholes," cones and racks. The price was $65.00 per ton which was the same as that charged for stoves.[38] Over $3,500

[35] HV 8360109A.
[36] HV 8250411. C. A. Buckley to Clement Brooke.
[37] SM 12, p. 82.
[38] SM 59, p. 11.

Franklin Stove Molded at Hopewell Furnace in the Eighteenth Century

Franklin Fireplace Cast by Buckley and Brooke at Hopewell Furnace

was received for this work in five different payments from June 1, 1826, to April 4, 1827.[39]

A very valuable part of the Furnace product from its founding until 1844 was the stoves molded at Hopewell. Mark Bird was doubtless familiar with casting stoves at his father's iron works. William Bird was making stoves at Berkshire Furnace as early as 1756,[40] and Mark probably continued this work after he became the manager of the Bird enterprises. The number made at Hopewell Furnace must have been relatively small before 1824. The only year before that for which records are available in which Hopewell produced more than one hundred tons of castings was 1783 when cannon and shot were still accounting for a part of the castings total. In 1821 the total weight of castings was sixty-nine tons. Records are not available for the next two years; then in 1824 there were $323\frac{1}{2}$ tons of castings poured. Castings production reached its peak in the celebrated "long blast" of 1836–1837 when $720\frac{1}{2}$ tons of castings were made.[41] Not all of this iron was used for stoves, as we have already noted a variety of castings from this period; but an examination of the labor records showed that the molders were paid for more stoves than for any other kind of castings. To take two examples, in January of 1826 Henry Care was paid for molding $43\frac{1}{4}$ tons of stoves or stove parts and a little more than $7\frac{1}{2}$ tons of all other kinds of castings.[42] Ten years later he was credited with $26\frac{1}{4}$ tons of stoves and less than two tons of other castings.[43] In 1846 the entire weight of cast products was $2\frac{1}{2}$ tons.[44] This last figure demonstrated how little importance castings played after stoves were no longer made.

For most of its history Hopewell did not actually make stoves. It cast the separate plates and shipped them to stove

[39] SM 59, pp. 1, 9, 11, 14, 21.
[40] *Montgomery Manuscripts,* Book I, p. 93.
[41] Kurjack's Chart of Furnace Operation, *op. cit.*
[42] SM 12, p. 108.
[43] SM 21, p. 158.
[44] Kurjack's Chart of Furnace Operation, *op. cit.*

Hopewell Ten-Plate Cooking Stove

Group of Stoves in Hopewell Museum. Note Teakettle in its own base

dealers who supplied the connecting rods, bolts and sheet iron parts. The merchant also did the fine finishing which gave the outside surface its polished look.[45] But a few stoves were finished at Hopewell. The store made retail sales to its customers; and in 1836 this note appeared in the clerk's journal, ". . . stoves are now made on Furnace Bank and not sent off."[46]

As molders were paid during the 1830's from six to twelve dollars per ton for castings made, it was of great importance to have an exact record of what each man had done. Loose papers found in the *Moulders Book for 1832* appear to be

[45] Clark, *op. cit.,* p. 503.
[46] SM 21, p. 159.

daily and monthly records of molding done by each man. The record of weight and kind of casting was later transferred to the *Moulders Book*. Castings were presumably made for orders already received in most cases, for the molders' books also contained the names of the customers for whom the casting was being done.[47] Even with this record at hand it is not possible to determine what a good molder could do in a day. The records seem to have been for a period rather than the day of the dated entry. It is unlikely that George North made 22 stoves on April 2, 1833, as the record credited him with doing.[48]

The work sheet for the molder sometimes noted that he was paid for a number of "half-price stoves." This did not mean the price at which it was sold to a customer but rather that the molder was paid only half of his usual rate because the stove was in some way defective. When these stoves were sold to the customer, the price was about two-thirds of the regular price for a perfect stove.[49]

Stove styles, designs and uses changed over the years, and different names were assigned from time to time. It is a complex task to assemble even a partial list of the Hopewell stoves. Henry C. Mercer described what must have been one of the earliest models as a six-plate stove with a flower design and a ribbon across the top with the inscription, "Mark Bird Hopewell Furnace 1772."[50] Ten-plate stoves in at least three sizes were sold in the early 1800's and also a "Rittenhouse Stove."[51]

When the furnace was reopened in 1816 after seven years of inactivity, it offered more variety along with some more imaginative names for its stoves. The patriotic fervor of the postwar period was evident in such names as New Orleans Victory Stove, Perry Victory Stove, Don't Give Up the Ship

[47] SM 22 and SM 49, *passim*.
[48] SM 22, p. 15.
[49] SM 4, p. 203.
[50] Henry C. Mercer, *The Bible in Iron* (Doylestown, Pa.: Bucks County Historical Society, 1914), p.104.
[51] SM 4, pp. 112, 189–190.

Stove, Ship Stove, Peace Stove, Decatur Flat Front Stove and William Penn Stove.[52] By the 1820's the war motif had been replaced, although the Hulls Victory Stove and the Ship Stove were still being sold in 1827.[53] The new patterns included the Flower Pot, Hornet and Peacock, Shepherd, and Fox Chase.[54]

Ownership pride reappeared, also, when in 1823 stoves were being identified as "Hopewell Stoves" or "D. Buckley Stoves." Many stoves were marked with the name of the merchant who sold them instead of the furnace which molded them. Some of Hopewell's larger customers furnished the molds for the kinds of stoves they found sold most readily.[55] At least one Hopewell customer had a pattern upon which a patent had been issued.[56]

For the late years of stove-making the names given were often descriptive of the shapes or uses for the stoves. A memorandum of the kinds of stoves made in the blasts of 1831 and 1832 showed that the amazing total of 98 different patterns had been molded, distributed as follows:

29 Circular	8 Cabbin
13 Oval	5 Franklin
10 Cannon	8 John J. Hess
2 Square	6 Cornell Cunningham and
9 Cooke	Company
2 Coal grate	2 Henry J. Fougeray
	4 Jacob F. Pliess[57]

The *Moulders Book for 1839* listed the kinds of stoves made in that year and showed several varieties on the same model: Canon Stove No. 1, Cooking Stove No. 8, Cannon Stove No. 1—Back Circular, Cabbin Stove No. 1—New Top, Cabbin Stove No. 1—Plain Top, Franklin Stove No. 4, Circular Stove

[52] SM 8, pp. 14, 56, 59, 62 and HV 8170122.
[53] HV 8270810.
[54] HV 8201006 and HV 8201012B.
[55] HV 8230822 and HV 8270810.
[56] William John Keep, "A History of Stove Making by a man who engaged in the trade for 5 Years," p. 69. Typescript of a manuscript in the Harvard College Library.
[57] *Kemper Manuscripts,* Memorandum of the Weight and Length of Furnace Stoves of Different Patterns.

No. 3—Plain, Cannon Stove No. 1—Bare Cylinder, Cannon Stove No. 1—One Story, Circular Stove No. 3, F. L. Cannon Stove, Premium Stove, Six-Plate Stove, Square Coal Stove, Pagoda Stove, Summer Cook Stove, W. and V. Small Cook Stove, W. and V. Small Heater, J. V. Large Size Stove, Warwick Cook Stove, Radiator Stove and John Volkman Large Stove.[58]

Hopewell stoves must have had a reputation for quality in the region where they were sold, for a firm in West Chester identified for their customers a shipment from this furnace in an advertisement:

> Stoves—The subscribers have just received from Hopewell Furnace an assortment of well finished stoves, which they offer for sale on reasonable terms. November 12.
>
> Baily and Valintine[59]

Customers for Hopewell stoves were located in an area extending west to York and Harrisburg, south to Baltimore, north to Albany and east to Portsmouth, New Hampshire. Clients of the Furnace in May 1831 numbered 40, ranging from retail buyers of a single stove to large purchasers of hundreds of units.[60] For 1832 orders included one to John J. Hess, Philadelphia, for 543 stoves of 25 different varieties; and on the same day Cornell and Cunningham, New York, ordered 260 stoves in four of their own patterns.[61] A single statement of the account of Morrison and Willard of Portsmouth showed shipments to them of $126\frac{1}{2}$ tons of stoves worth \$8,729.63.[62]

Occasionally a stove was ordered for a particular purpose or for a special person. Doctor Joseph Shippen of Philadelphia asked for a "steam stove" to be built for him, and he probably provided the design for the kind he wanted.[63] The Reverend

---

[58] SM 49, pp. 5–19.

[59] *Chester and Delaware Federalist,* West Chester, Pennsylvania, November 12, 1817.

[60] SM 15, pp. 48–49.

[61] SM 47, May 9, 1832, n. p.

[62] HV 8331218B.

[63] Kurjack, *Hopewell Furnace, op. cit.,* p. 28. This was in 1817.

Mister Samuel Bell of Newark, Delaware, ordered two stoves for his church of the ". . . Largest Square Paterns that one with the Lead Mouldings and Sun on front plate. . . ."[64] The Chester County Courthouse also wanted two stoves; and partner Charles Brooke wrote, ". . . the large Square end and Strate Sides is the kind I think will be best for the place. . . ."[65] The school at Churchtown ordered a stove in September 1825 with the request that it be rushed because it would soon be needed.[66]

One special order must have created a bit of excitement at the furnace, for Hopewell was to serve royalty—even though his royal personage had been unemployed in government for a few years. Daniel Buckley wrote from Philadelphia in 1822,

> . . . old Mr. Fougeray told me a few Days ago he is Coming to the furnace with some patterns for King Joseph Boneparte the price is No object he says, only to have them done well and soon, you will if there is Extra Expense in flasks Put it on the Castings. . . .[67]

The great merchant, himself, was coming to Hopewell to see that this order was handled properly.

Most sales of Hopewell stoves were at wholesale, and prices were quoted by the ton. Some representative prices were: 1806—$50, 1816—$90, 1822—$70, 1831—$65, 1836—$70 to $90, 1837—$110, 1842—$62.50. The number of units per ton varied with the weight of the kind of stoves ordered. In 1806 the ten-plate stoves varied from 200 to 300 pounds each.[68] Twenty years later stoves were being molded which ranged in weight from a small coal-grate stove weighing 97 pounds to a giant "H A Stove" containing

[64] HV 8221106A.
[65] *Hopewell Papers.* Charles Brooke to Clement Brooke, October 16, 1823.
[66] HV 8220906.
[67] HV 8221010B.
[68] SM 4, p. 113.

691 pounds of iron.[69] Prices quoted usually meant the stoves would be delivered in Philadelphia for that amount. When the merchant sent his own team to pick up his order, he was reimbursed for the cost of hauling.[70] Customers beyond Philadelphia paid the freight from that city. Prices were sometimes quoted to customers in other areas at the Philadelphia rate, as was this one in 1817 to Steinman and Cottrell of Lancaster who were to receive the quantity of stoves they required ". . . not to exceed ten ton of such as are made at Hopewell Furnace at ninety dollars per ton or the phil[a] price . . ."[71] When one customer tried to get a lower price by saying that other furnaces were selling for less, the clerk replied that this was the price from Clement Brooke and Company, and they ". . . did not enquire what others were charging."[72]

An occasional retail sale of a stove at the Furnace gave information on the prices of individual pieces. In 1807 one tenplate stove sold for $14.[73] In 1816 the plain models sold for $11.50–$16, but the patriotic items ranged from $25 for the Don't Give up the Ship to $30 for a Perry Victory.[74] In 1827 a small oval cost $6 and a large circular $12.[75]

Complaints of two kinds came to the Furnace about stoves, defective work and slow delivery. For one letter of the latter kind in 1816 Daniel Buckley noted on the bottom that the stoves were all cast, but he was waiting until he could find a team to go to Wilmington.[76] The demand for stoves was very good in 1836 as indicated by a letter from James H. Deas in Philadelphia, ". . . there is 4 or 5 housekeepers who are harrasing me continually every day and one lady in particular who

[69] SM 12, pp. 108–111.
[70] For examples see SM 21, p. 206.
[71] HV 8170612.
[72] HV 8310222B.
[73] SM 4, p. 189.
[74] SM 8, pp. 40, 59, 62.
[75] SM 59, p. 11.
[76] HV 8161129.

. . . cannot positively have a particle of heat in her house until you send me a cylinder. . . ."[77]

Parts for the stoves were packed in boxes for shipment, and the customer was charged for the box. This item was added to the bill and not included in the prices quoted.[78]

Clement Brooke was still soliciting orders for stoves in 1843,[79] and stoves were sold to nine customers in Philadelphia and one in Quakertown, New Jersey in 1844.[80] But the decision to end stove-making in this latter year was probably forced upon the partners by competition from the new anthracite and hot-blast furnaces. The stove patterns were sold to Isaac Buckwalter for $100.[81] Hopewell would henceforth depend almost completely upon the sale of pig iron for its income from the furnace.

Hopewell Furnace had its golden age to help meet the demand for home heaters and cook stoves in the first half of the nineteenth century. It brought prosperity to its owners for the three decades it was able to compete for its share of the stove market. For forty years longer it showed a profit on pig iron in the years when prices were high.

[77] HV 8361020.
[78] SM 21, pp. 160–164.
[79] HV 8430301.
[80] SM 72, *passim.*
[81] SM 31, p. 42.

8 Management and Business Methods

IF WE WERE TO CONTINUE THE METAPHOR OF THE CHARCOAL furnace as a fickle mistress, we would note that she responded best when the ironmaster was present and in actual control. A firm hand, a wide knowledge and an owner's interest in her success brought a greater reward than the administration of hirelings. At least the history of Hopewell Furnace showed that its periods of prosperity coincided with the active management of one of the owners.

The manager of an iron furnace in the first half of the nineteenth century had a complex and exacting job; he needed an almost impossible combination of talents and skills to find the answer to all the problems which faced him day by day. He was of necessity a technician, a production expert, a personnel director, a transportation control agent, a salesman, an expediter, an economist, a market analyst, a currency expert, a credit manager, a bill collector, a purchasing agent, an investment counselor and a bookkeeper. He had some technical and administrative help from the founder and the clerk, but the final decisions were those of the ironmaster.

The ironmaster was a special breed, and relatively few men

165

met all of the requirements of the position. Those who succeeded were richly rewarded by the profits a little furnace yielded in the day when charcoal iron was meeting the demands of an expanding nation. Those who made a wrong guess on the market, quality of ore, transportation costs or any one of many problems lost all they had. The roll of bankrupt ironmasters was long and included such names as Mark Bird, James Wilson, Matthias Slaugh, James Old, Frederick Delaplank, John Truckenmiller, Henry William Stiegel and Charles Read. Eastern Pennsylvania furnaces sold by the sheriff in 1847 numbered 15, in 1848—20, in 1849—30 and in the first four months of 1850—15. The Walker Tariff of 1846 might have caused an unusually larger number at this time.[1] The ironmasters, themselves, described their business as a most hazardous one. They related :

There has been no employment in this State that has met with so many revulsions, ruined so many fortunes, impoverished so many families, and in which so few fortunes have been made . . . as in the manufacture of Pig Iron. . . .[2]

Our business . . . is . . . a species of adventure, looked upon by the capitalists as more hazardous than any shipping or commercial speculation however wild; for in any particular enterprise in commerce, even if there should be a loss, there remains a balance in cash But to make Iron, there must be invested in buildings and machinery, a capital greater than many of our merchants employ in their whole business. . . .[3]

[The ironmaster's expenses include a large sum for the] necessary preparation of stock for blast . . . heavy amounts in stock in horses, teams and fixtures. These fixtures are almost valueless to anyone but the iron master. His stock has to be in course of preparation 20 months before it is used; and he lays out of the money invested in this way before it is turned into Pig Iron, at least an average of 10 months. A years stock is

[1] *Documents Relating to the Iron Industry in Pennsylvania, op. cit.*, pp. 109–110.
[2] *Ibid.*, p. 48.
[3] *Ibid.*, p. 25.

worth $25 to $35,000. It is evident how he would lose if he had prepared stock under one situation of affairs, and before that stock is brought even into a useful shape, an entire change has come over the market, and he may find himself obliged to work this stock up, with loss staring him in the face.[4]

Most of the men who had to face these multiple difficulties had had little opportunity to receive training for their jobs. Most ironmasters before 1850 directed both production and sales; but because they did not understand well either techniques or business, they were poorly prepared to introduce advantageous changes.[5] Overman wrote, ". . . we all well know how difficult it is to eradicate an established prejudice, or even an opinion, among workmen at the iron manufacturing establishments."[6] More improvements in furnaces were brought about by accident than by scientific investigation. For example, the opening at the top of the stack was widened after a furnace in England had had the top give way and was then found to produce more iron of a better quality than before.[7] The first chemical analysis of blast-furnace operation was not made until 1838, and this did not become a common practice in America until after 1860.[8] Obsolete equipment and methods were retained after they were no longer economically advantageous. No clear business records were kept of the exact cost of any part of the process.[9]

What has so far been said about the iron industry in general applied also to Hopewell. Attempts to find information about the cost of labor or of raw materials necessitated sorting the individual payments from the journals and ledgers. Even this was not always possible with complete accuracy because the clerk often lumped many separate payments together and

[4] *Ibid.*, p. 49.
[5] W. Paul Stressman, *Risks and Technological Innovations: American Manufacturing Methods during the Nineteenth Century* (Ithaca: Cornell University Press, 1959), p. 59.
[6] Overman, *op. cit.*, p. 169. This was written about 1850.
[7] Scrivenor, *op. cit.*, p. 248.
[8] Stressmann, *op. cit.*, p. 52.
[9] *Ibid.*, pp. 23, 48.

recorded them as "sundries." No system of maintaining a profit or loss balance for either the furnace or the store was discovered in the extant records.

Some application of science to the iron ore was begun in 1846 when a payment of $15 was made to Thomas Ridgway "for 3 days Geological Surveying at the old Mineholes."[10] Four years later an "analysis of ore" cost ten dollars.[11] Perhaps Charles M. Clingan brought a respect for a scientific approach to the Furnace in the period of these activities. As a medical doctor he would have had training in science before he became an ironmaster.

The ironmaster did not account for his time or the jobs he did, but a little pocket notebook carried by Dr. Clingan contained notes about work done by, and sums of cash paid to, workers. The clerk was doubtless informed of these data to be included in the permanent records. There were lists of hardware items needed and to be purchased when Clingan next went to town. One page had an item concerning labor relations, "To meet choppers on Williams Hill on Thursday Morning."[12] Sally Care Boone said that the manager had to be an expert on the furnace. She remembered several times when her father was recalled hastily from a trip to correct some difficulty with the operation. Usually some "expert tinkering with the tuyere" would bring the furnace back to proper functioning.[13]

One document found among the Hopewell papers, undated but with notations for the tax of 1829, appeared to be an estimate of the operating cost of the furnace for a year. Because it was the only such record which was found, it is quoted below to show the expected operating costs for a year—perhaps 1830:

[10] SM 31, p. 19.
[11] SM 32, p. 111.
[12] *Kemper Manuscripts,* C. M. Clingan pocket note book, n. p.
[13] Sally Boone Interview, March 22, 1941.

5000 Cords Wood @ $1.20	6000.00
Coaling	1500.00
Hauling Wood	500.00
Leaves and Dust	150.00
Hauling Coal	1875.00
[Cost of Charcoal]	10025.00

hauling 1200 loads Mine @ 10/	1600.00
Washing 1200 ,, ,, @ 1.50	1800.00
	3400.00
Mine Leaf	800.00
[Cost of Ore]	4200.00

Lime Stone	250.00
Workmen [At furnace?]	666.00
Founder	800.00
Repairs, etc.	300.00
[Cost of furnace operation]	2016.00
	42.00.00
	10025.00
[Total Cost]	16241.00[14]

Note that there were no items for depreciation or capital costs. These expenses did not appear except as principal and interest paid on bonds and then never as an operating cost. But if these were the operating figures for 1830, the Furnace should have realized a good profit from the 430 tons of pig iron and 357 tons of castings produced in that year,[15] as the value of this iron would have been about $36,000. By general report Hopewell was averaging about $17,000 per year profit for several years before the blast of 1836–1837. In this blast it

[14] *Hopewell Papers,* H 2215.
[15] Kurjack's Chart of Furnace Operation, *op. cit.*

was reported to have made over $40,000 "clear of all expenses."[16] In 1842 Clement Brooke wrote to Charles Brooke, a partner, that he expected the profit for that blast would be $9,000.[17] This was during a depression, and 1842 was considered a poor year in the iron business generally. Hopewell profits were down, but the furnace was still making money for its owners.

Hopewell was owned during most of its history as a partnership. Mark Bird built it and hired a "Mr. Markey" as manager; later a "Mr. Lewis" and William Hayes were managers for Bird. Hayes rented the furnace from Bird during the Revolutionary War.[18] From 1787 to 1800 the furnace had a rapid succession of owners and several changes of managers; only James Old was his own manager. After 1800 ownership was a partnership of the Brooke and Buckley families as long as the furnace operated. Thomas Brooke was the first manager for this partnership in the years 1800–1801.[19] Matthew Davis was hired to run the Furnace for two years[20] and was succeeded by Daniel Knabb who served until 1807 when Mathew M. Brooke became ironmaster.[21] When the Furnace reopened in 1816, the partners made Clement Brooke the manager; and he remained in that position for thirty-two years.

The financial arrangments between the partners is not very clear from the records. Clement Brooke was paid a salary, usually about $600 per year, for managing the Furnace. But the distribution of profits did not seem to have had any regular pattern. In the 1840's there were several notations of cash drawn by Clement Brooke in the sums of $5,563, $2,964, $3,945, $7,800, $7,200 and $6,199.95½ "paid at Sundry times as per his memorandum."[22] Settlement was apparently

[16] *Morris Diary, op. cit.,* May 20, 1837, p. 19.
[17] HV 8421112.
[18] *Montgomery Manuscripts,* Book III, p. 39.
[19] SM 4, p. 251.
[20] SM 1, p. 322.
[21] *Brooke Family Papers,* Mathew M. Brooke to Mathew Brooke, April 23, 1808.
[22] SM 28, pp. 45, 72, 125; SM 31, pp. 9, 31.

balanced among the partners in some way, because in 1842 Clement informed Charles Brooke that his share of the profits would entitle him to receive 100 tons of pig iron.[23]

A few items in the Furnace papers indicate that relations were not always smooth among the partners. This note by the clerk in 1817 was one:

> . . . D. Buckley said he received the Balance in full from Ober and Kline Some time last winter the amount of the Balance was $393.74 cts and Charles Brooke received from D. Buckley at Pequea in February last $240 and the remainder $153.74 cts has never Been paid or Received at the Furnace . . ."[24]

Possibly that incident represented only an oversight, but the following letter shows some hostility in the company:

> . . . in reply to yours concerning Charles Brooke's reflection, must say that he has not sent any money or Note since his return to Hib.[ernia Forge] nor do I expect any under the circumstances, the bad humour he was in when he left, merely because I asked him to do what was Equal Justice to the parties concerned. I tried to reason the matter with him, but his replies were curses and harsh Epithets such as no Gentleman would use . . . he says there is a conspiracy formed against him . . . I mentioned to him what I had written to you when I wrote for your note and also your reply that what ever time you had extended you to charge you interest. I told him I would have to charge him in like manner [for pig iron secured from Hopewell].
>
> He said to Hell with the interest and that you were a rich man that I might do with your account as I pleased . . . He is a very unpleasant man to do business with or for—the thing might of been better arranged had Mr. Clement Brooke of been here. He stands in his own light by avoiding Chas. Brooke. I think there is but little prospect of their ever settling their business unless they meet each other face to face. . . . I understand he has no coal to drive on his forge—if he wanted Pig Iron he would most likely of made a payment . . ."[25]

[23] HV 8421112.
[24] SM 7, August 23, 1817, n. p.
[25] *Kemper Manuscripts,* 1851 letter to M. B. Buckley, unsigned but probably from Charles M. Clingan.

During the next year this partnership was dissolved in a court suit to partition Hopewell assets, and Charles Brooke was paid his share of the valuation put upon the property.[26]

Hopewell's period of greatest prosperity was reached under the management of Clement Brooke, son of Thomas Brooke. Clement was an outstanding example of the men who made a success of the iron business—"the shrewd, calculating and trained businessmen who emerged in the first part of the nineteenth century."[27] This assessment by a recent historian was similar to the view of a man who, wanting Clement for a partner in a new furnace, wrote, ". . . I consider you one of the best Iron Masters in Pa.. . . ."[28]

Clement Brooke's success as ironmaster was due in part to his early training in furnace operation and business. He resided at Hopewell as early as 1800 when he was assisting the clerk.[29] A little later Clement secured cash by selling some of his used clothing to four men for a total of £3 5s. $4\frac{1}{2}$d.[30] Two journal entries in 1803 showed that he was paid as a substitute keeper at the furnace.[31] This was a very responsible job for a young man who had not reached his majority, for the keeper was in charge of furnace operation during the night shift. He must certainly have had previous experience around the furnace before being given so much responsibility.

A new relationship between Clement Brooke and Hopewell Furnace apparently began on February 19, 1804, when the clerk recorded, "This day Clement Brooke came to the Furnace."[32] That may even have been his own public notice that he had assumed a new position, for during the next five years the jobs he was doing indicated that he had become the

[26] *Berks County Deed Book* 59, p. 529.
[27] Bining, *Early Ironmasters of Pennsylvania, op. cit.,* p. 13.
[28] HV 8361205, John J. Hess to Clement Brooke.
[29] Clement Brooke was born May 10, 1784. Brooke Family Geneological Record, *Hopewell Papers,* H 18 General; SM 43, p. 350 and SM 1, pp. 73, 172, 255.
[30] SM 2, p. 77.
[31] SM 1, p. 31; SM 2, p. 107.
[32] SM 1, p. 47.

company clerk. His expenses were paid "when going to Dowlins, Red Lion, Potsgrove and Sundry other Places;" he went several times to Birdsboro Forge to "post the books;" he both made and received cash payments for the company.[33] These were duties and activities which were usually the work of the clerk. It is not clear what salary Brooke was paid during this time. In a little more than four years there were two payments credited to his account. On May 28, 1804, he received £32½ "for his Time at this place to the 1st of April last."[34] For about six weeks work this was a respectable wage of $58 per month. But four years later the journal contained a curious item which read, "Note Clement Brooke commenced Business 17th of February 1804 and charges to amount of his debt to the 1st April 1808 which is £236-7-3½." He was then credited with that sum to pay off his accumulated debts.[35] One year later he was paid $300 for his work for the preceding year.[36]

When the furnace was out of blast from 1808 to 1816, Clement gained more experience of value to an ironmaster by running the stamping mill and by serving as caretaker at Hopewell. In these jobs he had employees under him, and so he gained experience with personnel problems.[37]

When the furnace reopened, Brooke had had a training period which included both the technical and the business aspects of the work. He was prepared to assume wide responsibilities. He and his family lived well as was indicated by the improvements made at the mansion[38] and by such records as that for November 4, 1825, showing that he had paid $200 and his old "Gigg" for a new one. An apparently related item on the same day said that the Furnace had pur-

[33] SM 44, November 17, 1804, September 16, and October 7, 1805, n. p.

[34] SM 43, p. 370.

[35] SM 5, p. 58.

[36] SM 4, p. 256.

[37] *Hopewell Papers,* Account of Daniel Buckley and Co. with Clement Brooke.

[38] See Chapter 4.

chased for $145 "a cream coloured Gigg horse of Henry High inn keeper in Philadelphia."[39] Clement's salary was $600 per year plus $70 for his wife's services as housekeeper. The use of the mansion house was rent free, and he received food for himself and family at Furnace expense.

Clement Brooke became a man of influence in the business world of Pennsylvania. He owned a share in other iron works beside Hopewell—Black Rock Furnace in Lancaster County, Marion Furnace in Mifflin County, Berlin Iron Works in Union County and Reading Furnace and Robesonia Iron Company in Berks County. At the last-named place he helped to start an anthracite furnace in 1845.[40] He owned shares in the Wilmington and Northern Railroad and in the "New Castle and F. Town Rail Road."[41] He purchased coal land in Schuylkill County,[42] and in 1846 received $13,046.50 in cash and notes of the Bank of Pennsylvania from his son-in-law William R. White as his balance on stocks purchased.[43]

The feeling of the people who worked for him, or perhaps the desire to court his favor, was reflected in the number of Hopewell Village families who named sons for Clement Brooke. The census of 1850 for the nearby townships showed the following names: Clement Hughes, Clement Care, Clement Rutter, Clement Squibb, Clement Russell, Clement Painter, Clement B. Clingan and Clement B. Kephart.

Clement Brooke retired from active management of Hopewell Furnace in 1848. Late in 1849 or early in 1850 he moved into a new house in Pottstown,[44] where he lived until 1859; then he moved to Philadelphia and died there in 1861.[45] His will made special bequests to his wife and son and provided

[39] SM 12, p. 88.
[40] *One Hundred and Twenty-Five Years of The Robesonia Iron Company, op. cit.,* p. 2.
[41] *Hopewell Papers,* Notes on Stock Purchases, December 8, 1838 and September 6, 1841.
[42] HV 8300407A.
[43] HV 8460218.
[44] SM 32, p. 82.
[45] *Richards Scrap Books,* Vol. S, p. 95. Berks County Historical Society.

that the residue of his estate should go to his daughter Maria Clingan and the children of his deceased daughter Ann White.[46] John Church received half of the Berlin Iron Works on condition he pay $100 to Alexander Church.[47]

John Church succeeded Clement Brooke as Hopewell manager for one year before the job was assumed by Dr. Charles M. Clingan. Clingan was twenty-nine years of age and had been the husband of Maria Teresa Brooke for six years when he was given the position of manager by his father-in-law. He had attended West Chester Academy and was graduated from Jefferson Medical College in Philadelphia in 1840. He seemed to have preferred the iron business which his father had followed to his own profession of medicine and had leased Rock Furnace before his marriage.[48]

Clingan continued as manager at Hopewell for ten years, and then he moved his family to Philadelphia where he engaged in the banking and provision businesses. Until his death in 1876 he retained an interest in Hopewell Furnace and came back frequently. The Hopewell records gave no reason for the departure of the Clingan family from the village in 1859, but a heavy loss from the unfortunate experiment with an anthracite furnace at Hopewell[49] could have been one reason. Boredom bred by Hopewell's isolation and limited social activities may have been another cause. But the family still liked food from the farm after they moved to the city. The housekeeper at Hopewell received instructions to send a weekly box of food to Philadelphia containing such delicacies as sauerkraut, doughnuts, smoked meats and fresh eggs.[50] At Clingan's death his estate was valued at $27,483.20 of which $10,000 was the valuation put upon his share of Clingan and Buckley Company, the owners of Hopewell Furnace.

Clingan was remembered by two surviving Hopewell

[46] HV 8620404.
[47] *Hopewell Papers*, H 18 General, Will of Clement Brooke.
[48] *Reading Eagle*, February 11, 1917.
[49] See Chapter 3.
[50] Sally Boone Interview, March 22, 1941.

residents as a good-looking man who was quite popular with the ladies of the community, but "a good and just man" who was "possibly a bit hen pecked" by his wife.[51]

Clingan's departure ended the experience with owner-management at Hopewell. The last twenty-four years of Furnace operation saw hired managers in charge. Nathan Care, John R. Shafer and Harker Long were the managers during this period.[52]

The business assistant to the ironmaster was the clerk who, if capable, could relieve the ironmaster of many of the details of management. Sometimes there was a storekeeper, as in the early 1800's and in the 1830's; but usually the clerk was in charge of the store. He ordered supplies, made the sales and kept track of the store's accounts with the workers.

But this was only a part of the complex job of the clerk; he was also paymaster in a quite complex system. Furnace workers and general laborers had their wages recorded in the journal monthly or quarterly; colliers and molders were paid over longer units of time, sometimes annually or at the end of a blast. Some casual workers were paid in cash, and records of these payments were kept on loose papers and then transferred to the cash book. A daily record was kept of the work done by each molder, but these were grouped into larger units for posting.[53]

The clerk kept track of orders for pig iron and castings, determined the priority for filling orders and took the abuse of customers when orders were delayed.[54] He collected on some of the customers' accounts.[55] He was held responsible when he extended credit to a worker who was already too far in debt to the company.[56]

Money was usually not paid out for wages. The clerk

[51] Rose Sands and Catherine Rhoads Interview, May 13, 1941.
[52] HV 8761110 and Birdgens and Witmer *Atlas, op. cit.,* p. 55.
[53] *Hopewell Papers,* pages of clerks notes on work by molders.
[54] HV 8321103C, HV 8330423A and HV 8320818.
[55] HV 8281016.
[56] SM 2, p. 90.

recorded earnings in the journal and ledger, and the worker drew against this for credit at the store and for the settlement of accounts. The clerk paid for goods bought in other stores and for transactions among the workers or with outsiders. Sometimes such business could become rather complex, for example this notation in 1806 : Frederick Meck was charged $1.50 in favor of Robert Gilmore "for a Debt owed by Adam Johnston and Meck bot a cow from Johnston and is charged with ten dollars on acct. the cow Meck has give Johnston Cr. for $5½ and $1½ is what Johnston owed Gilmore."[57]

The clerk made payments, and usually these were made with mutual trust. But once in a while there was a record of a witness to a payment, as this one : "Peter Geiger Paid him in full on Williams Hill after his wood was taken up in the presence of M. Walters."[58]

The clerk had to be able to differentiate among workers who were credited or debited in the books. Similarity of names was a possible cause of confusion. One John Painter was always identified as "founder" long after he had ceased to work at that job. Others, too, were matched with their occupation. Negroes were identified as such. Juniors and seniors were common, and now present a perplexing problem to the researcher who tries to follow several generations of the same family at Hopewell. The clerk in 1843 did not find any of these usual methods suitable to distinguish between two workers named Joseph Quinter; so he called the one "Black Head" and the other "Red Head."[59]

Most of the clerks were probably of limited training and experience as bookkeepers. It is not too surprising, therefore, to find that they had made errors. Some of these were never corrected, but in the journal for 1818 there were four pages devoted to correcting "errors in journalizing."[60] The prize error

[57] SM 44, November 6, 1806, n. p.
[58] SM 31, p. 7.
[59] Index to SM 29.
[60] SM 8, p. 158 ff.

probably was the £2592 13s. 6d. misplaced by the clerk in 1805.[61]

For all of his multitudinous duties and extensive responsibilities, the clerk was paid a salary ranging from $60 per year paid to Samuel Heister in 1804[62] to $300 per year paid to Thomas Foster in 1837.[63] The most common rate was $200. Most of the clerks had free room and meals at the mansion house, which added considerably to the monetary emolument.

Both the manager and the clerk did considerable traveling on company business and had their expenses paid from company funds. A long list of travel expenses for the years 1818–1820 ranged from 0.37\frac{1}{2}$ for a trip to Reading to $16.57 "for D. Buckley to Baltimore." In addition there are payments for trips to Lancaster, York, Philadelphia, Marietta, Churchtown, West Chester, the Swamp, Columbia, Manheim, Wilmington, Downingtown, Hamburg, Orwigsburg, Evansburg, Conowingo, Harrisburg and "to sundry places." Usually the journal did not say who had done the traveling, but both Daniel Buckley and Clement Brooke as well as Valentine Hoffman, a carter, were named for some of these journeys.[64] Distant customers were not neglected; for the furnace paid a tavern bill for two at Portsmouth, New Hampshire in 1838.[65] Although travel expenses were usually not itemized, a tavern bill in 1834 from the Golden Swan in Philadelphia listed these expenses for "Mr. Brooke" :

To	9 Days Board	9.00
	Horse	4.50
	Washing	.25
2 Lemonades		.25
	Postage	.12
		$14.12[66]

[61] SM 44, June 18, 1805, n. p.
[62] SM 1, p. 322.
[63] SM 21, p. 200.
[64] SM 10, pp. 2–60.
[65] HV 8380529.
[66] HV 8340107.

Most business was conducted on credit. One customer wrote that it would not be profitable for him to buy for cash and sell on credit; so he would not buy iron if he could not get it on credit.[67] On one occasion a reduced price was offered by the clerk for payment in twenty days.[68] The more usual payment was in the form of a note to run for 60 days to six months. These notes were often discounted for cash or passed on to someone else in payment for Furnace bills. The Office of Discount and Deposit in Reading was used extensively by Hopewell Furnace to convert its time payments into cash.[69] At the end of the year, however, the company had often received only a small percentage of payment for the castings sold. The ledger on December 31, 1832, showed that ten customers had bought $19,375.56 worth of castings for which the company had received at that date $8,300.[70]

Another method of collecting was to pay Furnace bills by issuing drafts against a customer.[71] The S. V. Anderson Company in Philadelphia which sold storegoods to Hopewell also acted as Furnace agent to receive accounts in the city. Hopewell paid a small fee for this service,[72] but one customer refused to pay a man sent to collect from him because there was no written authorization presented.[73] Drafts were not always honored and were then returned by the person to whom they had been given for some other kind of payment.[74]

Keeping account of the notes the company held, the dates due, by whom issued and whether or not discounted was an important job for the clerk. Several different systems were devised by different clerks to do this as accurately and thoroughly as possible. In 1826 it was done by a separate

[67] HV 8161101A.
[68] *Hopewell Papers,* undated letter to J. and A. Morrison, Portsmouth, N. H.
[69] For example see SM 10, p. 17.
[70] HV 8330227B.
[71] HV 8361018.
[72] SM 21, p. 160 and HV 8260927.
[73] HV 8281028A.
[74] HV 8200512.

account in the regular ledger,[75] and in 1854 a "Bill Book" was begun to record notes both given and received. All notes issued by Hopewell were reported in this record as paid through 1863, but several of those owed to Hopewell were marked "protested and returned" or written off as uncollectable. Beside one of the latter the clerk had penciled "Bad Eggs."[76]

Occasionally barter was conducted—"Pig Mettal on accunt of the Horse."[77] pig iron for castings[78] or whiskey for iron.[79]

Some kinds of castings were made only when an order was on hand, and an advance payment was required on orders of pots and kettles at the time the order was placed.[80]

The price Hopewell Furnace charged for its castings was usually the same regardless of the size of the order. In 1836, John J. Hess wanted $2.50 per ton reduction because he was placing a large order. Smaller customers, however, complained about the competition when they had to pay a higher price.[81]

Under the system of bookkeeping used at the Furnace, payments were often overlooked and were recorded years after the work was done or the obligation incurred. Perhaps the prize delayed payment for labor was the case of Peter Fox who built a chimney in 1808, and payment was recorded in 1822.[82] The Furnace was also on the receiving end of delayed payments. David Hart did not pay his rent for five years between 1832 and 1837.[83]

Although some workers were in debt to the Furnace, a study of the accounts of 14 workers over a period of about twenty-five years showed only four of them were consistently

[75] SM 12, p. 144.
[76] *Kemper Manuscripts,* Clingan and Buckley Bill Book, 1854–1863.
[77] HV 8200526A.
[78] HV 8221219.
[79] SM 1, p. 87.
[80] SM 44, December 8, 1806 and SM 9, p. 97.
[81] HV 8360105 and HV 8360108.
[82] SM 4, p. 262.
[83] SM 21, p. 200.

in debt, and no one of these was never out of debt. The other 10 were on the credit side of the ledger for most of the time.[84] The Furnace carried a quite large balance for some workers as indicated by the withdrawal of $1300 at one time in 1836 by Thomas Care.[85] No interest was paid on these balances, but neither was interest charged on arrears unless an account was unpaid for several years after the worker left employment at Hopewell.

Hopewell never had a payroll, and almost all business at the store was a book transaction. In all probability little money was kept in the office or the store, but what money was used constituted a problem to the managers. In 1784 they were accepting "Doubleoons" and "Johannas"[86] as well as Pennsylvania currency and doubtless that of other States. Even after the United States created a national monetary system, there were often periods of scarcity of species and uncertainty about the currency. In 1817 the editor of a Reading newspaper made a plea for persons who possessed small coins to take them to a bank for notes because of the difficulty of doing business without coins.[87] Coins were again scarce during the depression of 1837. "Shin plasters," or fractional currency, were substituted for scarce coins.[88]

Depreciated bank notes and counterfeit notes were a frequent problem to the Hopewell clerk. A general rule followed was to charge a larger discount on banks located at a great distance. In 1816 "Western paper" was discounted at 10 per cent, but the rate was 8 per cent on paper from banks on "this Side the mountains."[89] There were many references in the next year or two to discount rates on various kinds of paper money ranging from 2 per cent to 10 per cent. The clerk was careful to note the kind of money received and the

---

[84] A summary of this study is found in Appendix B.
[85] SM 21, p. 161.
[86] SM 41, p. 39.
[87] *Berks and Schuylkill Journal,* March 1, 1817.
[88] *Morris Diary, op. cit.,* pp. 59, 102.
[89] SM 8, p. 45.

bank of issue, apparently in case of future question. In one case he even recorded the serial number and date of issue of a $10 note of the Franklin Bank of New York City.[90] One customer included an apology with money sent saying, "I believe the money is all equal to Philadelphia but one 3 dollar note which I would not send if I had other enough. . . ."[91] The furnace also specified that payment for stoves was to be ". . . in York or Lancaster Paper or Good Bank Paper of Maryland or Pennsylvania."[92] Several entries from 1818 to 1823 noted that counterfeit bills had been received and returned to the sender.[93]

Payments by check, frequently posted in the records after 1846, indicated the use of more bank services.[94] The opening of Western mines was probably responsible for the references in 1854 to payments made "in Gold."[95]

A successful ironmaster needed to be a man of many talents and broad experience. Clement Brooke met the requirements because of his background and training for the job, but he was also favored by a generally rising economy while he was manager at Hopewell Furnace. He made a sizable fortune and retired while profits were still being made from charcoal iron. No other Hopewell manager did so well either before or after him.

[90] SM 46, March 10, 1823, n. p.

[91] HV 8160925.

[92] *Hopewell Papers,* Agreement with George Small and Morriss of York. Undated, but probably about 1820.

[93] Examples are: HV 8180210, HV 8181212, SM 9, p. 126.

[94] SM 31, p. 2 ff.

[95] SM 65, p. 1 ff.

Part Four
The Commercial Village

9   The Store

Beside the administrative duties mentioned in the previous chapter, the clerk had complete responsibility for the village store during most of the history of Hopewell Furnace. However, for a few years a storekeeper was employed in addition to the clerk.

The multiple tasks performed by the clerk were conveniently grouped in a single building between the Big House and the furnace in which were located both the company office and the store. This structure had a basement, a main floor, an attic and a lean-to shed on the east side in which bulk grain and feed were stored. The main section was built of stone and the shed of tongue and groove boards. Norman M. Souder, National Park Service architect, found an earlier building concealed by a more recent one. He believed the earlier one dated from the late 1700's, and the more recent alterations appeared to have been made in the 1860's.[1]

In the later building the basement had two rooms, and some crude attempt at insulation with mud and straw indicated that they were used to store perishable goods. A fireplace provided heat to the west end. The packed earth floor in both rooms showed evidence that flood waters of French Creek

[1] Norman M. Souder, "The Office and Store Building" (unpublished study, 1960). Hopewell Village Library.

Office-Store Before Restoration

General View of Village Showing Office-Store, Ironmaster's House and West End of the Barn. Looking Northeast.

had reached this height. On the main floor were also two rooms with the west one having been used as the office and the other as the store. The walls were plastered directly over the stone. Two fireplaces had been a part of the original construction. But surely when stoves were the chief furnace product, one would have been used to advertise its superior heating ability to customers and visitors to the store. At some time an iron safe had been set into the space where one fireplace had been.[2]

The attic was used as a bedroom for some of the clerks. For a time after the store closed, this building was rented for a residence.[3] Some alterations may have been made in this period.

Although a store was a necessity for the isolated charcoal furnaces, it was often regarded by the owners as more than a convenience to the workers. In fact it was sometimes the only source of profit to the ironmaster.[4] According to a British writer, the system of paying wages in credit at the store ". . . was obviously open to grave abuse; and there is abundant evidence that it was often used as a means of surreptitiously reducing earnings and of increasing profits by exploitation."[5] This study of the Hopewell Furnace store presents evidence upon which it will be possible to arrive at some conclusions as to whether these charges can be applied to this business.

The legal basis for store operation was a state license system for which a fee was paid to the county treasurer. In 1830 the following notation appeared in the treasurer's records of Berks County concerning the Hopewell store:

Clement Brooke Has paid to me for the use of the Commonwealth Six dolls. 67 cts. which entitles him to wholesale or retail Foreign merchandise and Liquors, as a wholesale dealer or a retailer of the Eighth Class, within the County of

[2] *Ibid.*
[3] Charles Sheridan Care Interview, February 24, 1941.
[4] Scrivinor, *op. cit.,* p. 299.
[5] Thomas Southcliffe Ashton, *Iron and Steel in the Industrial Revolution* (Manchester: Manchester University Press, 1951), p. 189.

Rear of Office-Store Restored with Charcoal House in Background

Front of Office-Store Partially Restored

Berks, for Eight months, from the first of September, one thousand eight hundred and thirty.[6]

Annual fees for other years ranged from a low of $7.00 to a high of $10.75.

It is possible that the store was run for a time in the early 1800's by a man who was in private business for himself as well as operating the company merchandising. John Brower was the storekeeper from December 1, 1807 to April 27, 1809 —and perhaps also earlier than this—but at no time in almost a year and a half was there any indication that he was being paid a salary. He received a small sum from the Furnace and "sundries" which could have included some salary. But neither the amount nor the time of payment seem to indicate this. He was also paid by some of the employees with no reason given for the payment. He bought hollow ware and stoves from the Furnace which he apparently sold on his own.[7] If this represented a different kind of arrangement, it was the only time the store was not run by a salaried employee of the Furnace.

The source of supply for goods to be sold was changed from time to time. Until 1807 the chief wholesaler was Samuel Laverty and Company of which Mathew Brooke was one of the partners. He received about $6600 when the partnership was dissolved.[8] For some succeeding years storegoods were supplied through the Buckley and Brooke store in Birdsboro; then in the autumn of 1821 a long association began between the Hopewell store and Samuel V. Anderson and Company in Philadelphia.[9] Thirty years later wholesale purchases were being made from George Lippincott and Company, McFarland Evans and Company, Levick Brothers and Company and Bowlby and Brenner. These wholesalers also were located in Philadelphia.[10] Purchases at times were made locally from

[6] HV 8301126.
[7] SM 5, pp. 87, 119.
[8] SM 44, January 20, 1807, n. p.
[9] SM 6, p. 372.
[10] SM 32, p. 108.

Clerk's Desk in Office-Store

farmers, millers and neighbors. A journal entry in 1819 said the Furnace had purchased "linen at oction."[11]

The clerk kept records of his sales on scraps of paper and later recorded them in the day book, and from this to regular posting in the journal and ledger.[12] Shortage of coins was a problem when the storekeeper had money payments to make. In 1848 Henry Sheets drew his account in full to the amount of 29.23\frac{1}{2}$, but the clerk had no coins. He gave Sheets $30 with the understanding that 76$\frac{1}{2}$¢ would be returned, which a later notation showed was done.[13]

The Hopewell store did not try to encourage quantity

[11] SM 10, p. 30.
[12] HV 8350331B.
[13] SM 31, p. 62.

buying, for no reduction in price was given with the purchase of large quantities. For example the price on 100 "segars" was 25¢, and it was also $6\frac{1}{4}$¢ for 25.[14]

Interest was not normally charged when purchases ran ahead of a worker's earnings, but as well as being charged on accounts which were not settled for some time after the workers left the employment of the Furnace,[15] interest was also collected on a purchase by a non-worker when the account was not paid within a year after the transaction.[16]

The store acted as agent for villagers in the purchase of goods from other stores. For example John Painter was debited for six yards of chintz for which the Furnace paid cash to a city store, possibly through the services of a teamster going to Philadelphia.[17] The Hopewell store also purchased shad and mackerel by the barrel on behalf of several of the workers. Cash was sent by the Furnace teamster to make the purchase.[18]

Considerable informality marked the business done with neighbors and employees. The journals contained many instances of goods charged to a workman but "delivered" to someone else. Often the person named as having received the goods was a son, daughter or wife; not infrequently it was a housekeeper or neighbor. Apparently women often picked up orders at the store for men at work when they were making purchases for their own families. Sometimes the clerk noted that sales were made "per your order" or "by your written order," but often there was no indication of anything other than verbal authorization.

The company lost some money on unpaid accounts. A list of debtors at the beginning of 1820 included 33 customers who owed a total of over $4,300. Apparently these were not a cause of worry, however, for an additional listing was desig-

[14] SM 9, p. 87.
[15] Some examples are found in SM 12, pp. 123, 138.
[16] SM 12, p. 122.
[17] SM 12, p. 113.
[18] SM 9, p. 28 and SM 12, p. 91.

nated "Bad Debts" to the amount of $346 owed by 41 accounts.[19]

The volume of sales at the store never gave evidence of a large operation. Including some payments for blacksmith services and making no attempt to allow for changes in the value of the dollar, the following were the total and average monthly sales for the periods indicated:

Inclusive Dates	Total Sales	Monthly Average
October 1, 1805–September 30, 1806	$ 2,888.19	$240.68
September 1, 1831–August 1, 1832	4,911.25	446.66
March 21, 1853–September 20, 1856	12,018.93	386.16
January 1, 1865–January 1, 1875	17,895.40	135.67[20]

No balance sheet of store profits was found to show what the company made from these sales.

On the next page are shown the per cent markups on some goods sold. The usual range on most common items was 20 per cent to 40 per cent, based upon wholesale prices which did not include the cost of transportation, salary of clerk or storekeeper, or heat and light for the store.

Price Markup at Hopewell Furnace Store

		1802		
Item	*Unit*	*Wholesale Price*	*Retail Price*	*Per Cent Markup*
Shoes	pr.	$1.00	$1.33	33%
Sugar	lb.	.067	.13½	100
Whiskey	gal.	.60	1.00	67
Coffee	lb.	.24	.267	9
		1817		
Coffee	lb.	.21	.25	19%
Fur Hats	each	3.00	4.00	33
Flour	bbl.	4.125	4.00	–3

[19] *Hopewell Papers,* List of Store Accounts, January 1, 1820.
[20] SM 4, pp. 1–27; SM 21, pp. 4–38; SM 36, *passim;* SM 37, *passim.*

1827

Shoes	pr.	1.25	1.50	20%
Tea	lb.	1.00	1.24	24
Flour	bbl.	3.125	3.24	3
Sugar	lb.	.0975	.125	29

December, 1831—March, 1833

Sugar	lb.	.07$\frac{1}{4}$ –.0834	.125	30–58
Coffee	lb.	.13$\frac{1}{2}$ –.15	.16–.17	19–13
Soap	lb.	.06 –.05$\frac{1}{2}$	.10	67–75
Molasses	gal.	.48	.56	17
Rice	lb.	.03 3/4	.05	33
Mackerel, No. 1	bbl.	5.00	7.00	40
„ *No. 2*	bbl.	4.00	5.50	37$\frac{1}{2}$
S. H. Molasses	gal.	.53	.64	21
Salt Petre	lb.	.11	.24	118
Chocolate	lb.	.12$\frac{1}{2}$	.20	60
Ground Salt	lb.	.48	.64	33
Oil	gal.	.40	.48–.50	20–25
Potatoes	bu.	.33	.37–.40	12–21
Cheese	lb.	.08	.09–.12$\frac{1}{2}$	12$\frac{1}{2}$–56
Tea	lb.	.85	1.25	47
Epsom Salts	oz.	.05	.06$\frac{1}{2}$	30

Note : Wholesale prices did not include the cost of transporting the goods from Philadelphia.

Based upon these figures, the profit from the store operation would not appear to have been a major factor in the total profit from Furnace operation. Perhaps the store was primarily a convenience for the workers and a medium for purchases of goods used at the Furnace and in the mansion rather than a source of profit to the partners.

Further evidence that the store was not operated on a professional merchandising basis is found in the table of retail price trends at the Hopewell store given on the next page. In the period from 1802 to 1841 for which the prices of a selected group of items were traced, there was a rather remarkable uniformity despite two definite cycles of general American business in this period. The prices on imported goods—such as sugar, molasses, chocolate and coffee—were rather high in the early 1800's. All prices were relatively high in the period following the War of 1812. They dropped in the depression of 1819 and following but seemed little influenced by the depression of 1837 and following:

Retail Price Trends on Selected Items
Hopewell Furnace Store—1802–1841

(All prices in cents per pound except molasses which is per quart.)

Year	Sugar	Molasses	Rye Flour	Choco- late	Pork	Beef	Coffee
1802	13.3c	20c	3c		12c	5.5c	26.7c
1803	13.3	20	2	31c	7	9.3	26.7
1805		20	2.2		5.5	5.5	
1806		20	3	31	7.7	5.5	
1807		19	2.4		6	7.7	35
1808		19	2.4		6.6		33
1809			2		6.7	6.7	
1816	22	31	3		10	9	31
1817	20	22.5	3.5	25		8	25
1818	16	25	2.7		8	8	30
1819	18	22.5	2.7	30	12.5	8	38
1824	12.5	10	1.8	25	10		25
1825	12.5	10	1.8		4.5	4	25
1826	12.5	12.5	1.8	20	8*	5	25
1827	12.5	12.5	2.1	20	4	4	20
1828	12.5	15	1.8				20
1829	12.5	15	3.5	15			20
1830	12.5	15	3.5	20	4		20
1831	12.5	14	2.1	20	5	4.3	16
1832	12.5	14	1.8	20	8	8	16
1833	12.5	16	2.1	20	5	8	17
1834	12.5	16	2.1				17
1835		18			7	5	13
1836	12.5	18	2.1		7	4.8	13.5
1837	13	18	3.5	20	15*	14	17
1838	12.5	17	3	20		10	15
1839	12.5	16	3	20	15*		15
1840	12.5	18	2.3	20	12*		16
1841	12.5	18	2.1			7	16

* Bacon. Others in that column are for "pork."

Note : All prices were taken from as close to January 1 of the year as they could be found in order to eliminate as much as possible the fluctuation during the year.

Note : Missing years have no store journals available to obtain prices. Missing prices indicate the store was not selling the item in that year, or no unit price could be determined.

How did Hopewell store prices compare with those of other furnace stores or of general stores in the neighborhood? A comparison of prices from the *Hopewell Journals* was made with the journals of several other stores where prices of similar goods were found for the same period of time. There was a common difficulty that the clerk often did not give a unit price for the articles sold. For this reason the results of the study are not too conclusive. But Hopewell's prices were not out of line with any of those from the other stores; they were lower in more instances than they were higher. There was not a great amount of difference in price on most items, and in a fair number of cases the price was identical in the two stores being compared. It is also apparent that the furnace stores observed did not charge prices which were noticeably higher than the neighboring general store. That Hopewell workers traded in both stores would have been one guarantee of a fairly uniform pricing at both places. The results of this study are summarized in the following table :

Price Comparison Between Hopewell Furnace Store and
Other Stores of the General Area.

Year	*Item*	*Unit*	*Hopewell Price*	*Other Store Price*
				Changewater *Furnace Store*
1802	Molasses	qt.	.20	.20
,,	Sugar	lb.	.13	.14½
,,	Shoes	pr.	1.20–1.33	1.13–2.00
,,	Tobacco	lb.	.20	.27
,,	Whiskey	qt.	.20	.20
,,	Potatoes	bu.	.43	.52

,,	Corn	bu.	.67	.67
,,	Rye	bu.	.80	.87
,,	Beef	lb.	.05$\frac{1}{2}$	.05$\frac{1}{2}$

				Mt. Hope
				Furnace Store
1806	Shoes	pr.	1.13–1.50	1.50–2.13
,,	Salt	bu.	.73	.80
,,	Nails	lb.	.11–.12	.15

				Mary Ann
				Furnace Store
1837	Coffee	lb.	.17	.19
,,	Flour	lb.	.035	.04
,,	Salt	lb.	.04	.04
,,	Tea	lb.	1.60	1.36

				Lewis Evans
				Store
1827	Coffee	lb.	.20	.25
1828	Sugar	lb.	.125	.125
,,	Molasses	qt.	.15	.14
1832	Coffee	lb.	.16	.18
1833	,,	lb.	.17	.18
,,	Molasses	qt.	.17	.125

Note : Changewater Furnace was a close neighbor; the other two furnaces were farther inland. Lewis Evans operated a store about four miles from Hopewell and sold goods to many Hopewell workers.

The size of the store room and the storage space precluded a large inventory of storegoods at any one time. The kinds of goods carried varied greatly from one period to another. In 1805 sales implied that relatively few articles were carried in stock with flour, beef, "mushmeal," whiskey, nails and salt comprising most of the sales. On October 31 of that year molasses sales resumed after a long lapse. Sales of this item were brisk in the next few days; so probably a new barrel had arrived.[21] There were many other instances when sales

[21] SM 4, pp. 1–9.

records denoted that commodities were sold at the time the store had received a supply rather than from goods kept on hand at all times. The store was also handling the retail sale of stoves for the furnace in 1805 as was shown by the many transactions in which a single stove was purchased.[22] An inventory made in 1820 set the value of goods on hand, except meat, at $387 and of beef and pork at $480.[23]

As the Furnace production increased its tempo in the 1820's and 1830's, the business at the store increased and so did the kinds of merchandise kept in stock. A small booklet in the Hopewell papers enumerates the items sold in 1832. This record appears to have been a memorandum the clerk was keeping for new stock needed rather than an inventory of supplies on hand. A summary of the tabulation with the clerk's descriptions and notations concerning them is listed below :

Memorandum for Storegoods
Nov 5th 1832

Red flannel
Yellow flannel
2 pieces lowpriced Sattinette
1 Ps Sattinett (Steel Mixd) of
    a good quality
Buckskin Mitts
Buckskin Gloves
6 lb Black Pattent thread N 30
White Cotton Balls N 24
Gilt Coat buttons of a good
    quality
Gilt Vest Buttons of a good
    quality (and Plain)
Black bone Suspender buttons
Black do Vest   do
    of different Sizes
Silk flag hdkf of a good quality
Winter Schawls

Russia Sheeting
Apron Tapes
low priced Calicos
dark Calicoes
1 ps Mourning Chince Do
1 doz prs Germantown hose
Ticking
a few pieces Cotton flannels
5 yds dark drab Cloth (Double
    milled)
2 yds Green Cloth (dark) about
    $3 p yd
Horse Rasps
large Files
3 in Butt hinges & Screws
Thumb Latches
2 Blade Buckhorn Handled
    Pocket knives

[22] SM 4, pp. 10, 22.
[23] HV 8200307A.

a Piece of blue worsted Stuff for Ladies Cloaks
Means Seal Skin Caps
Boys   ditto   do
a few Pieces Worsted binding of different colors
Shoe Blacking
Writing Paper
Letter   do
Wrapping do
Quills
Black Sand
Brimstone

1 blade   ditto   do
Barlow knives
Curry Combs
Flat bottomed Candle Sticks
1 Paper 12 oz Tacks
1 Paper 6 oz Tacks
Table Spoons
Butcher Knives
Putty
Salt Petre
Wafers[24]

In an effort to discover what the customers of the Hopewell store bought, a study was made of the purchases of 26 regular customers for a period of fifteen months from December 1831 through February 1833. The period chosen was one of Furnace prosperity and also one in which James Benson as clerk made detailed records of sales. The customers included persons with incomes ranging from a maid earning 75¢ per week to the manager-owner with an annual income of thousands of dollars. Because of the bulk of this study the results were placed in Appendix C. These records show the quantity and price of each purchase by each of these customers over the fifteen months, a summary of the various kinds of goods bought and the total amount spent at the store.

It will be noted by an examination of these accounts that some customers bought little or no food. They were the people who boarded at the Big House and had food provided as a part of their pay, or they paid the Furnace a monthly rate for boarding. Men with large families spent a high percentage of their total for food. Bulk purchases of flour, beef, pork and bacon were common. Molasses was the usual sweetening agent, with both West India and "sugar house" (maple syrup) varieties on sale. Sugar was a luxury at a price per pound of about one fourth of a day's wage for a laboring man. Choc-

[24] HV 8321105.

olate was a delicacy usually kept in stock, as also were some spices.

Home clothing fabrication accounted for extensive sales of cloth and notions. Many kinds of cloth were sold with quality ranging widely from the inexpensive buckram, calico, check, flannel, muslin, nankeen and quilting to a type called "blue cloth" which sold at $5 per yard. This latter may have been material for a coat as its sale was usually associated with the purchase of lining, padding and buttons. Needles, thread, scissors, buttons in many varieties, ribbons, tape and patterns were available to the wife, seamstress and tailor who made the Village clothing.

Although some purchases of ready-made clothing were recorded, these were usually stockings, handkerchiefs, suspenders, belts, shoes, cravats, gloves, hats, shawls and similar accessories. Articles for personal care included razors and strops, shaving soap and brushes, medicines and combs. That last commodity included useful pocket combs, decorative side combs for the ladies, and utilitarian fine-toothed combs for combatting head lice.

The purchase of bulk feed was an indication of ownership of one or more domestic animals, probably a horse or a cow. Perhaps there was some social status represented as possession of a horse set one on a higher social level, if the horse served for riding or driving and not just as a work animal.

Pocket knives had a good sale in Barlow, pen and double-bladed varieties. A demand for window glass and putty showed that windows had progressed from the oiled paper stage of the early frontier. Nails, paper, oil, almanacs and plowshares were kept in stock.

The amount of meat mentioned in the records signified that this was a very important part of the diet of the villagers. Steers and hogs were raised on the Furnace farm and by individual families to be butchered for their meat supply. Neighboring farmers sold meat in the Village. For example in

1827 Thomas Care bought 1,269 pounds of pork at 4¢ per pound from Frederick Landis.[25] In addition to such sources the Furnace in 1834–1835 bought the following amount of dressed meat:

Beef	3,576	pounds
Pork	14,480	,,
Bacon	1,447	,,
Shoulder	1,576	,, [26]

Some of the dressed meat was not in the best of condition as was shown by this notation concerning some pork bought from Charles Brooke of Hibernia Forge, "We took off 2 lbs. per cwt. for green rot."[27] Because brine was one of the commonest preservatives for meat, the sale of salt at the Hopewell store was always high in the autumn months when many people were butchering.

Mackerel by the piece or by the barrel were bought for immediate or long-range use. Shad were less commonly available. In 1839 they were selling at 31¢ each; and they were ". . . very high and very scarce at the fishery," according to the Morgantown storekeeper.[28] Tobacco was stocked regularly and was sold in papers and rolls, by the pound or half pound; and after 1818 "segars" were vended.[29]

Some barter was conducted when the villagers or their wives brought butter, cheese, cabbage, "winager," eggs, dried apples and dried peaches, cherries, mutton, potatoes, "cyder," beets, watermelons, homespun linen, beans, cucumbers and chickens to trade for storegoods. Such transactions were usually not recorded in the journal except for any balance remaining; and, therefore, there was seldom a price mentioned.[30] The store rarely resold any of these wares which probably meant that they were used in the Big House.

[25] SM 59, p. 14.
[26] SM 12, *passim.*
[27] HV 8331212B. Charles Brooke was a Hopewell partner.
[28] *Morris Diary, op. cit.,* April 18, 1839, p. 76.
[29] SM 9, p. 85.
[30] *Hopewell Journals,* 1819–1836, *passim.*

The modern housewife would have missed greengoods, baked products and milk. Modern children would probably not have been happy with a choice of confections limited to "liquorice balls and hoarhound candy."[31]

Something of the history of fashions can be learned by a study of the clothing sold over a period of a half century.[32] In the first decade of the nineteenth century men were wearing both wool and fur hats, and a fancy "white hat" cost Frederick Hart $5.[33] Judging from the quantity of "Red Coating" the store was selling,[34] this color was much in style. William Taylor was probably a bit of a dandy about the furnace in his velvet trousers.[35] But velvet was still good ten years later; and equally expensive, at about $2.00–$2.50 per yard, were "sattennett" and "Coburg Cassimer."[36] Charles Brooke paid $37 for four yards of "Blue Cloth" for his best coat.[37] The Furnace was selling some ready-made "great coats" for men at eight dollars each.[38] The most popular item for either men or women was a shawl. Most were a conservative black, but John Keller had "1 red shall."[39] "Perl buttons" were sold at 25¢ for a set of eight to those who wanted such a decoration.[40]

During the 1820's the distinctive new article of dress was the "Roran hat" which was wool on the outside and lined with fur. Prices started at three dollars each in the summer of 1825, but by fall had increased by a half-dollar and then held firmly at that figure.[41] "Blue Cloth" was still fashionable

[31] *Morris Diary, op. cit.,* December 6, 1844, p. 75.
[32] Men's clothing only was considered as women's apparel will be discussed in Chapter 16.
[33] SM 44, November 29, 1806, n. p.
[34] SM 2, p. 60.
[35] SM 2, p. 122.
[36] SM 9, pp. 97–119.
[37] SM 9, p. 171.
[38] SM 8, p. 71.
[39] SM 9, p. 92.
[40] SM 9, p. 97.
[41] SM 12, *passim.*

at $6.50 per yard.[42] Fancy vests were popular with the trimmings selling for 82¢ per set.[43]

In the 1830's the young executive, James Benson, invested $2.50 in "a black silk velvet stock;"[44] and his superior, Clement Brooke, wore a fur collar on his coat.[45] The furnace expected at least five of its customers in 1837 to be interested in silk hats @ $2.75 plus the store profit and also offered to sell "1 white Russia" to someone for more than $3.00.[46] Pantaloons and "Bangup" coats were tailored by George Wert for Hopewell men.[47]

In the 1840's men were wearing wide stripes and very large plaids. Long, single-breasted vests were made to match the pantaloons in figures and colors. Neck stocks were being replaced by "kravats and scarves." The well-dressed man used a buckled waistband instead of suspenders, preferred his shoes to be square toed and had his "pants to button up before and without a fall."[48]

Most children's clothing must have been made at home and probably was handed down from older to younger. There were very few references in the store books to ready-made clothing for children with the exception of shoes.

The storekeeper had to be alert to check new cloth purchases for damage. In 1833 the invoice from Potts, Reynolds and Company was reduced by $7.40 "For a deduction on Sattinett for moth holes, etc."[49]

Furnace workers and farmers needed tools. The Village store supplied them with axes, shovels, copper kettles, mold boards, empty barrels, chisels, rakes, scythes, files, whetstones, screws and screw plates, hinges, steel traps, curry combs, wood saws,

[42] SM 12, p. 103.
[43] SM 12, p. 60.
[44] SM 17, p. 4.
[45] SM 21, p. 152.
[46] SM 21, p. 199.
[47] SM 21, p. 165.
[48] *Morris Diary, op. cit.,* November 12, 1844, p. 169.
[49] SM 21, p. 58.

horse rasps, bellows and casks. For household use there were snuffers, combs, blacking, lamps, cork screws, "Britania table spoons," iron spoons, tea spoons, locks and mouse traps.[50] Whale oil was sold for the lamps.[51]

The store probably did not keep pocket watches in stock but sometimes arranged to purchase one for a villager. These were real luxury items and must have earned their possessors a degree of distinction to warrant a cost which equaled the wages for a working man for more than a month of labor. Philip Shafer, Junior, paid the equivalent of one and one-half months of his 1807 blacksmith's wages for a silver watch;[52] and George Kephart in 1823 paid $20 for a silver watch out of his income of $122.40 for filling the furnace that year.[53] Henry Care was more conservative when he purchased a watch in Reading for 58¢.[54] Others who owned silver watches were: Peter Yocum, woodcutter; Alexander Church, miner; Anthony Steward, stove finisher; Jonathan Jones, teamster; Charles Smith, stove finisher; Joseph McKewen, molder; John Benson, clerk; John Church, manager. The following partners in the firm bought gold watches:

Charles Brooke	1819	$160	
Daniel Buckley	1819	129.37\frac{1}{2}$ for 2 watches.	
Daniel Buckley	1825	$ 60	for watch, seal and key.
Clement Brooke	1828	$144	for watch, seal, key and chain.
Clement Brooke	1830	$134.50[55]	

Most sales at the store were recorded against the income earned by the worker with no money changing hands. But the cash books did show a few cash sales; most frequently these

[50] Most of these items were on an invoice for hardware bought in 1828, HV 8281104A.
[51] SM 21, p. 143.
[52] SM 4, p. 195.
[53] SM 11, p. 144.
[54] SM 12, p. 84.
[55] SM 9, p. 137; SM 12, p. 135; SM 14, p. 27; *Cash Book* for 1828–1830, March 8, 1830, n. p.

were for products of the molders such as kettles, pots, mold boards or clock weights. In 1818 there were 7 such sales in March, 4 in April, 5 in May, 1 in each of the next months through August and 2 each in September and October.[56]

Hopewell workers were not required to make all of their purchases at the company store. There were frequent references in the journals to bills paid for goods purchased at stores in Morgantown, Reading, Birdsboro and Philadelphia. The store book of the Eli Keen Store, near the St. Mary's Episcopal Church, for the years 1844–1845 showed many Hopewell people were trading there—among the regular customers were Doctor and Mrs. Charles Clingan. For many Hopewell workers this store was closer to their homes than the Furnace store. Keen carried many items that were not ordinarily obtainable at Hopewell : figs, canned peaches, Indian vegetable pills, turpentine, camphor, Swain's Vermifuge, paregoric, curtain paper, matches, tacks, rope, eggs, saleratus, nutmegs, cloves, mintsticks, sulphur, Scots pills, tin basins, sand paper, pie dishes, tooth powder, rosin and cinnamon.[57]

A trip to the store might have been a relief from monotony for the women and children of the village. Its crowded shelves and bins held the produce of the outside world; it smelled of far places. The small volume of trade betokened an absence of rush or hurry in selecting merchandise to be purchased and gave a chance for a little social visiting if several customers happened to be at the store at the same time. The Boone store in the village in the 1870's and 1880's was the loafing place for the men in the evenings,[58] but no evidence was found showing a similar use for the company operated store.

The Hopewell store served a useful purpose in providing a convenient place to secure some of the necessities of life. Its prices were in line with other stores in the area, and the mark-

[56] SM 10, pp. 1–15.
[57] *Eli Keen Store Book, 1844–1845*, Hopewell Village Library.
[58] Sally Boone Interview, March 22, 1941.

up over wholesale prices was moderate. Probably it was not a source of very great profit to the owners. Trading at the store was easy because credit was already established through the record of the workers' wages on the company books, but it was not necessary for the worker to do his buying there. The clerk would even make payment for the goods bought by a Hopewell worker at another store in the neighborhood or in Philadelphia.

10 Transportation and Sales

A CHARCOAL-IRON FURNACE WAS LOCATED IN A FORESTED AREA to avoid long hauls of the fuel necessary for its operation, but the solution to this transportation problem created other problems of access to markets and sources of supply. As we have seen, the village store was necessary to supply the needs of workers who had to live in locations remote from towns; so storegoods had to be hauled to the furnace site. But of equal necessity were the transportation facilities to take the furnace products to the customers who had use for pig iron and cast items. Transportation costs were a critical factor in determining the success or failure of any furnace and were, in combination with technological improvements, the principal causes for the eventual demise of the charcoal-iron industry. The selection of a site for a new furnace must have taken into consideration the availability of existing transportation facilities and the cost of connecting the furnace with these roads, waterways or railroads. Markets changed as new means of shipping goods were developed. Hopewell Furnace changed its marketing pattern several times in its history because of the opening of roads, canals and railroads.

Mark Bird chose a location for his furnace which was conveniently near an already existing public road; and other roads, public and private, were added during the history of Hopewell Furnace. It never had immediate access to any other means of transportation and was, therefore, always dependent upon wagons to reach its markets or to connect with points on the river, canal or railroad.

In 1758 a public road had been opened from Scarlet's Mill in Berks County to Coventry Forge in Chester County. Hopewell Furnace was built about two hundred yards from that road and was joined with it by a private road. Another private road was built to the Hopewell mines; but a year after operation at the Furnace began, a new public road was opened from the Jones mines to the Schuylkill River. It passed conveniently near to Hopewell and added a new transportation facility. In 1804 a road from Birdsboro to Warwick Furnace passed within a few feet of Hopewell Furnace and formed a street for some of the nearby tenant houses. Five years later a new road was opened to the Jones mines, and a new access road to the Schuylkill River was built from the Birdsboro Road. Connecting roads near Hopewell were built to the Schuylkill Canal in 1827 and 1856.[1] The last one was convenient for reaching the new anthracite furnace at Monocacy, about four and one half miles away.[2]

The road built in 1827 was built in response to a petition to Robert Porter, Judge of the Berks County Court, which presented the necessity of a good road "from Hopewell to Douglass Ford" now that the new canal was going into operation. The petition requested the appointment of a jury to view the old road, declared barely passable for loaded wagons, or to propose a better route for a new road.[3]

In addition to the routes to the river on the north, Hopewell was favored by the opening of roads on the south which connected the Furnace with the best markets in the state. Four

[1] Russel A. Apple, "The Public Roads Serving Hopewell Furnace" (unpublished study, 1955). Hopewell Village Library.
[2] Long, *Historical Sketch, op. cit.,* p. 5.
[3] *Hopewell Papers,* Petition to Honorable Robert Porter, 1824.

miles away was the road from Lancaster to Valley Forge, now Pennsylvania Route 23. The opening of the Philadelphia-to-Lancaster Turnpike in 1794 probably did not aid Hopewell Furnace directly because of its distance, but two connections with it helped to open new markets for Hopewell products. Local iron men were influential in securing a new turnpike which was surveyed from the Lancaster Turnpike "near the Warren tavern, to the base of the Welsh Mountain, near Morgantown; thence to Blue Ball, and thence to Lancaster via New Holland." This road was a failure as a turnpike but was maintained as a public road.[4] In 1819 a public road from Downingtown through Ephrata to Harrisburg was completed.[5] These two roads helped to open markets to the west. Another main route of travel for Hopewell villagers was the river road through Pottstown to Philadelphia. This route was made more favorable about the middle of the century when the Schuylkill was bridged at Monocacy.[6]

The condition of the roads was a matter of great concern to the Furnace manager. Customers could be supplied only when the roads were passable. One of them wrote in 1831, "You will please send me [hollow ware] as Soon as the State of Roads will admit . . ."[7] There were frequent references to Furnace men and teams working at repair of the road, using Furnace slag to fill holes or soft spots. Wages and hauling costs for these repairs were deducted from the road tax owed by the company to the township.[8] Hopewell Village men also worked on the roads to pay for their road tax in lieu of money payments.

To meet the need for wagons and teams for furnace hauling, the manager used three different systems. From 1815 to 1825

[4] *Reading Eagle,* February 18, 1917.

[5] James A. Barnes, *Wealth of the American People* (New York: Prentice-Hall, 1949), p. 158.

[6] *Hopewell Papers,* H. A. Long to Roy Edgar Appleman, August 5, 1935.

[7] HV 8310302C.

[8] SM 46, August 28, 1824, n. p.

it was common to contract for some of the hauling with Village men who owned teams. Examples of these pacts were found in the Furnace records :

> Agreed with William Thomas for his team by the day from last Monday Morning Being the 16 instant [September,] 1816 @ $2 per day we are to find the horses in feed and Board the Carter Thomas is to pay for shoeing the horses and the Carter his wages.[9]

> Agreed with David Shafer February 7th 1823 to haul the wood on Millers hill above the old orchard Computed to be about 2000 c when done Chopping @ 10 cts per cord, and he is to have a collar, one pair traces and back band etc. and to have his horses shod gradis during the time he is employed in hauling the above wood.[10]

> Agreed with Fredrick Landis to haul 20 loads sand from near Manor Meeting house at $2 per load and 20 loads Mettal to Hibernia Forge each load to be one and a half tons @ $3 per Load.[11]

A second kind of transportation agreement was to have the customer haul his own castings. Sometimes the Furnace set its price for stoves delivered and then credited the cost of transportation to the customer who hauled his own. In 1818 pig iron prices were set at $33 per ton at Hopewell and $43 in Philadelphia.[12] Later the usual cost for a load of a ton and a half to the city was $7.50.[13] In the 1850's the Furnace charged customers 35¢ per ton to haul pig iron to the "Exit Roads" and one dollar per ton to the railroad. From these points it became the responsibility of the buyer.[14]

The third kind of transportation in and out of Hopewell Furnace was by Furnace teams driven by teamsters who were

[9] SM 7, September 18, 1816, n. p.
[10] SM 46, February 7, 1823.
[11] *Ibid.*, p. 58.
[12] SM 8, p. 149.
[13] SM 14, p. 71 was an example.
[14] SM 32, p. 107.

paid a regular monthly salary. Wages for teamsters ranked above those for ordinary labor but not as high as the skilled molders and colliers. There were other kinds of costs on the trips made by the teamster beside his wages. The expenses of the driver and his team and road or bridge tolls were sometimes more than wages. In 1816 and 1817 typical expenses for trips were listed as Lancaster $3, Wilmington $5, Philadelphia $6, "To the mountain for Stone Coal" $10.[15] Sometimes the driver wanted some cash of his own in addition to Furnace money given him for expenses.[16] When he stayed over night, there were tavern charges. The following bill was submitted from a Unionville tavern for a Negro driver, Samson Coggins, in 1818 :

Hay	.25
1 Bushel Oats	.50
Supper	.25
1 Pint Sider	.06½
1 gill Biters	.06
[Unexplained but probably bed and stable]	2.50
	———
	3.62½[17]

Accidents or bad weather added to the costs. In 1804 a bill for 14s. 3d. was presented to Mathew Brooke for food for a driver and team when a wagon was stuck in the snow on returning from Cornwall.[18] During the same year a Hopewell wagon broke an axle on the outskirts of Philadelphia and had to wait for its repair.[19]

The teamster was apparently alone on his trips most of the time, but an exception was made in 1825 when several journal

[15] SM 7, *passim.*
[16] *Ibid.*, October 4, 1817, n. p.
[17] HV 8181108A.
[18] *Brooke Family Papers,* Michael Valentine to Mathew Brooke, March 5, 1804.
[19] *Ibid.*, Davis and Brooke to Buckley and Brooke, April 20, 1804.

entries stated that the teams hauling stoves had "2 hands with wagon."[20] It would have been natural, too, that once in a while a wife, son, daughter or neighbor would have made a trip to the city or to visit a relative along the way. Hopewell records were silent on this point, but the *Martha Furnace Diary* had a number of such citations.

Turnpike and bridge tolls also added to the cost of travel. In 1806 Birdsboro Forge paid 9¢ for ". . . going Through Ye gate twice."[21] Later the custom was to pay for travel over a period of time on the roads commonly used. In 1817 Hopewell Furnace paid $13.77 for "Passing and Repassing [at] Gate No. 3 on Turnpike" for a period of a little more than three months. Charges were based on the number of horses and the size of the wagon wheels. Hopewell teams consisted of five horses on these trips.[22] Valentine Hofman paid 62¢ for turnpike "tole at Churchtown" for a trip in 1820.[23] On one occasion a customer advanced a Hopewell carter two dollars because he had not been given enough money to pay the tolls.[24]

Use of the turnpikes made possible a form of communication for the Furnace when there was no regular mail delivery. Daniel Buckley wrote to his partner a letter ". . . to be forwarded by Jesse McKnight and to be left at the turnpike gate at Brandywine Meeting House."[25]

The Schuylkill Bridge was a convenience to Hopewell but one which also cost money from 1835 onward. In that year a receipt acknowledged payment of $6.25 "to entitle Brooke and Famelly to pass over the Schuylkill Bridge between the Black and White Horse Taverns one year from the first of January last."[26] In 1855 the Furnace paid $15.00 in advance for the

[20] SM 46, p. 57.
[21] *Birdsborough Forge Cash Book,* December 15, 1806. Hopewell Village Library.
[22] HV 8170426.
[23] SM 10, p. 62.
[24] *Brooke Family Papers,* Whitestone Manfacty Co. to Mathew Brooke July 24, 1816.
[25] *Ibid.,* Daniel Buckley to Mathew Brooke, July 25, 1809.
[26] HV 8350606A.

privilege of crossing the bridge at Douglassville for the year.[27]

The teamsters often performed services for the Furnace and the villagers when they made business trips. They bought articles in the city for which the Furnace made payment and then charged the workers' accounts.[28] Store goods were brought back from the city whenever possible in order to assure a pay load in both directions. At other times the drivers made some purchases on their own and sold them in the Village; for example in 1826 Jacob Mock brought cheese and oysters, and George Marquet sold shad both to the Furnace and to individuals.[29] In 1831 such varied items as oil, tar, sweet potatoes and candlewick were retailed in these private enterprise operations.[30]

Neighbors were accommodated on the trips to Philadelphia. The clerk at Warwick Furnace wrote in 1822 to ask, ". . . Please let me know whether any team load from you to Philad[a] this week—the name of the Carters and where they stop. . . ."[31]

Teamsters carried money in both directions to pay bills, and there were at times considerable sums entrusted to their care— $100, $81.50, $160 and $50 were amounts picked at random from the Hopewell records. The only instance found of any money going awry was this notation in 1817:

> Note Gave David Hart an order on Bullock and Peters to Draw $100 the 25th March last the said David Hart Received from them as per his Receipt $49—and brought or gave up but 40 dollars when he came home.[32]

The incident was closed by charging Hart's account for the missing nine dollars. Hart continued to work at the Furnace for many years.

[27] SM 65, January 3, 1855.
[28] For example see SM 12, p. 82.
[29] SM 59, p. 9; SM 12, p. 140.
[30] SM 15, pp. 35–36.
[31] HV 8220729.
[32] SM 7, August 26, 1817, n. p.

The life of Hopewell Furnace depended upon transportation, and transportation depended upon a supply of animals to pull the wagons. Naturally, then, much attention was given to the problem of obtaining good animals. Purchases of both work and riding horses were frequently entered in the Furnace records, and the prices proved that the Furnace wanted horses in their prime. Sometimes a man wrote to offer horses he had for sale; this letter was an example:

> . . . I understand that Mr. Brooke wishes to purchase a good family Horse, I have two for sale, and will give him the choise a black and a bay both young and well broke to either the saddle or harnes, both handsome and gay and the price low.[33]

But voluntary overtures did not meet the need for animals, and the next year a customer wrote that he regretted that his stoves had not been delivered because the Furnace was short of teams.[34] Twenty years later the Furnace found it necessary to pay a commission to a man who undertook to buy horses.[35]

Horses were bought from employees, neighboring farmers and distant markets. The management seemed to favor purchases when the animals were from four to seven years of age, but even at this last age the price was declining by $10 or $20 from the peak.[36] Almost never did they sell a horse in its prime. There were many recorded sales of old horses or blind horses, but the only example seen of the sale of a superior animal was "a yellow horse" sold in 1851 for $140.00—a very good price.[37] When horses died their hides were sold to the leather dealer, and on one occasion the Furnace paid 25¢ to have a horse killed.[38]

Horse trading was another source for Furnace animals. In almost every transaction the Furnace paid "boot money," an

[33] HV 8240914A.
[34] HV 8250815.
[35] SM 31, p. 14.
[36] For examples see SM 28, p. 124 and SM 31, p. 11.
[37] SM 31, p. 146.
[38] SM 21, p. 93.

indication that the manager was trying to upgrade his teams.[39] A guarantee of soundness was a part of some deals, and in 1844 the Furnace demanded the refunding of $50 "boot money" when the "Horse was not sound and Returned."[40] The purchase of stud horses in 1803, 1817 and 1818 proved that the Furnace was breeding some of its own animals.[41]

Horses were the beasts most used to pull the wagons to and from the Furnace, but oxen and mules had their place at the Furnace also. One pair of oxen was purchased in 1802 at a price of $93.45.[42] Perhaps William Welsh had charge of this yoke, because he appears on the record as a "Bool driver."[43] Oxen again appeared on the inventory of purchases in 1830, 1848 and 1849.[44]

The later managers, beginning with Dr. Clingan, preferred mules; or perhaps they were easier to find than horses. In 1848 a mule was bought for use "at the mineholes,"[45] and mules were frequently mentioned after this date. One six-mule team was purchased in 1850 for $810 plus $83.75 paid for mule harness and the cost of delivering the team to the Furnace.[46] Harker Long bought and sold many mules during his term as manager.[47] He said that in 1864 Dr. Clingan had paid $2700 for nine unbroken mules, which was a quite high price; but of course the Civil War was influencing the market. Long said that six mules were used for heavy hauling and were hitched in three pairs known as the tongue, middle and lead teams. The teamster had a saddle on the left-rear animal; but when the load was heavy, he walked beside this mule and controlled the team with a single "jerk line" attached to the bridle of the left mule of the lead team.[48]

[39] Examples may be found at SM 28, pp. 126, 135, 138.
[40] SM 28, p. 138.
[41] SM 1, p. 25 and SM 8, pp. 144, 156.
[42] SM 1, p. 1.
[43] *Ibid.*, p. 28.
[44] SM 14, p. 86 and SM 31, pp. 104, 130.
[45] SM 31, p. 61.
[46] *Ibid.*, pp. 128, 129.
[47] See HV 8810311.
[48] H. A. Long Interviews, *passim.*

Charcoal Wagon of Late Period

Rear of Charcoal Wagon Showing Rings Used to Draw Bottom Boards
in Unloading

The usual hitch for horses had apparently been four horses, as several references were found to pay based on a four-horse wagon load.[49] There was another kind of hauling, however, which required a quite different hitch. Wood was hauled from the cutting tract to the hearth on a sled drawn by a single horse, mule or ox.[50]

Several different kinds of wagons were used for the hauling done by the Furnace. Among those mentioned were "Broad wheel," "Narrow wheel," "high wagon," "dearbourne wagon," "one horse wagon" and "road wagon." Charcoal wagons were built in several different sizes varying in capacity from one hundred to three hundred bushels. They had high sides and were built with bottom boards which would pull out for quick unloading. The lead team was unhitched, brought to the rear of the wagon and used to pull out the bottom boards.[51] To load the charcoal a plank was placed with one end against iron bars along the side of the wagon and the other end on the ground. The teamster, carrying baskets of charcoal on his head or shoulders, walked up the plank and filled his wagon bed. A short plank projecting from the left side of the wagon was called the "lazy board" because the driver sometimes rode on it instead of walking. In front of the bed was a tool box in which were kept the supplies necessary to make emergency repairs—and, according to report, a quart of whiskey was some times concealed among the tools.[52]

Not all of the wheeled vehicles at the Furnace were of the commercial variety. The manager had his carriage for travel by himself and his family. A space was reserved for carriages between the mows on the second floor of the barn until Dr. Clingan built a carriage shed.[53] Carriage operation had some aspects which resembled modern family transportation—a

[49] HV 8340122A.
[50] Kemper, "The Making of Charcoal," op. cit., n. p.
[51] Ibid.
[52] John Sparr Interview, October 18, 1940.
[53] Nathan Care, Junior, Interview, February 13, 1941.

No.

This is to certify, That *Matthew Brooke*, of the
Township of *Union* the county of *Berks*
in the ninth collection district of Pennsylvania, has paid the duty of
two dollars for the year to end on the thirty first of
December next, for and upon a *two* wheel Carriage, called a *Chaise*
owned by *him* and the harness used therefor.

THIS Certificate to be of no avail any longer than the aforesaid carriage
shall be owned by the said *Matthew Brooke*, unless said certificate
shall be produced to a collector and an entry be made thereon specifying the
name of the then owner of said carriage, and the time when he or she became
possessed thereof.

GIVEN in conformity with the laws of the United States, this *first*
day of *February* 1817.

Matthias Richards. **Collector**
of the Revenue of the ninth collection district
of Pennsylvania.

Receipt of Tax Paid on Matthew Brooke's Carriage

license fee was required, and repairs and remodelling were
needed. In 1817 the tax on a chaise was $2 per year.[54]
Clement Brooke received the following bill for work on his
carriage a few years later:

Varnishing Body and Carage	$ 5.00
Lether work	2.00
Hedlining	7.00
Carpet and Shaft	1.75
New Front Bow	1.25
Molding on Top	1.25
Stufing Cushings	.75
	$19.00[55]

[54] *Brooke Family Papers,* Tax receipt, February 1, 1817.
[55] HV 8290827B.

Accessories included a whip @ $1.25.[56] The cost of a carriage could have cut deeply into a family income, judging from the $356 which Clement Brooke paid for one in 1829.[57] This was more than half of his salary as furnace manager, but he had other sources of income.

While transportation in and out of Hopewell was dependent upon teams for the entire history of the Furnace operations, the development of water travel and the railroad had an influence on the distance the wagons needed to travel and upon the direction of commerce. Markets for Furnace products were changed as new transportation connections became available.

The nearness to the Schuylkill River was an inducement to try cheap water transportation to the towns down the river. Even before Hopewell was built, Bird iron had gone down the river; for example, Samuel High transported three tons of pig iron from Reading *in a canoe*.[58] In 1773 Mark Bird was appointed one of twelve commissioners instructed by act of the Pennsylvania Assembly to investigate means "for making the River Schuylkill navigable."[59]

Early in the nineteenth century there were many tons of iron carried for Buckley and Brooke on a boat operated by Mordicai Millard. He hauled bar iron, stoves and hollow ware to Sweedsford, Phoenixville and Valley Forge.[60] The risks involved in river travel were demonstrated by an incident in 1803 of the stranding of a boat carrying 1800 pounds of Hopewell hollow ware destined for Philadelphia. The boat ran aground near Pottsgrove where a man named "Shance" rescued the iron and undertook to sell it for Buckley and Brooke. He had sold part of it but still had some on hand when he died. Thomas Brooke made a trip to Pottsgrove to

[56] SM 31, p. 68.
[57] *Cash Book* for 1828–1830, May 27, 1829, n. p.
[58] *Montgomery Manuscripts*, Book I, p. 106. William Bird Ledger.
[59] *Pennsylvania Gazette*, April 28, 1773. William Bird had served on a similar commission in 1760.
[60] SM 2, pp. 131, 199, 320; HV 8221100.

reclaim what pieces remained.[61] James Rogers was hauling flour for Mathew Brooke on a river boat in 1817.[62] Wages paid to Birdsboro Forge employees for "Boading to Philadelphia" in 1822 were $7.50 to Rogers for steering and $5.50 to each of four other men listed as "a hand."[63]

The Delaware River also was used for the shipment of goods, especially to dealers in Wilmington. Instructions were written to Hopewell by Delaware merchants to deliver iron or stoves to sloops leaving regularly from Philadelphia. Thomas Garrett operated his own boat, the *Sloop Mary Ann,* to haul his purchases from Philadelphia to his Wilmington store.[64]

But later transportation for Hopewell products had its principal expansion with the opening of the Schuylkill Canal. A charter was issued to the Schuylkill Navigation Company on March 15, 1815, with permission to issue 10,000 shares of stock at $50 per share. Work was begun in 1816; a short section was opened during 1818, and traffic was moving from Reading to Philadelphia by 1825. Eventually the canal was extended west to Mount Carbon. Dividends on stock were first paid in 1829 and increased during the next decade to reach a peak of 19 per cent in 1839. The best year for tolls was 1841 when well over a half-million dollars was collected, but the next year the tolls were cut almost in half because the Reading Railroad was taking business from the canal.[65]

Apparently Hopewell Furnace partners were interested in the canal quite early, for Mathew Brooke was assessed $5 per share for his 20 shares of Schuylkill Navigation Company stock in 1817.[66] The switch from wagons to canal boats is shown by

[61] SM 2, p. 104.

[62] HV 8170501A.

[63] *Birdsborough Forge Book, 1821–1823,* p. 20.

[64] HV 8260315A.

[65] James W. Livingood, "The Heyday of the Schuylkill Navigation Company," *The Historical Review of Berks County,* IV, 1 (October 1938), p. 11–14.

Robert McCullough and Walter Leuba, *The Pennsylvania Main Line Canal* (Martinsburg, Pennsylvania: Morrisons Cove Herald, 1962), pp. 11–12.

[66] HV 8170912.

the following tally for stoves shipped by wagon and by water over a period of five years after the canal opened:

	May 1826– May 1827	May– December 1827	May– December 1828	1830
Wagon	1451	326	326	683
Canal	1090	1488	2128	3007[67]

By 1836 most of the finished goods from the Furnace was moving on the canal with the major part of it going to customers in Philadelphia, New York, Boston and Portsmouth.[68] Robert Cunningham of New York wrote to request that all of his stoves be sent by canal, because they "come so much quicker and I believe safer . . ."[69] Probably the New York shipments were also using the New Brunswick Canal across New Jersey.[70]

But the canals created some problems too. A customer requested the Furnace to rush to him all the stoves possible "before navigation closes" for the winter.[71] Another wrote, ". . . Send me a load By waggon as I understand the canal is frozen and the Canal Boats not able to descend the River."[72] The canal boats caused delays because they were not always ready to take on freight immediately, resulting in this instruction from John J. Hess of Philadelphia:

> . . . I have received the Castings in the Waggons as soon as those arrived by the Canal now I wish you not to delay in waiting for the Boats but to prokure Waggons and furnish me with Castings as fast as you possibly can. . . ."[73]

Another merchant offered to pay the difference in cost between the canal and a wagon to insure quicker delivery.[74]

Another modification in the transportation of stoves came

[67] SM 14 and SM 50, *passim.*
[68] SM 51, pp. 1–37. This was a Canal Book kept at the Furnace.
[69] HV 8361001A.
[70] HV 8360910B.
[71] HV 8321112.
[72] HV 8311206.
[73] HV 8311104.
[74] HV 8311109A.

with the opening of sections of the Reading Railroad to Philadelphia. The change in the relative importance of three methods of hauling was shown in the shipments of stoves for three years:

	1839	1840	1841
Wagon	268	77	54
Canal	3669	3512	1675
Railroad	41	852	1804[75]

The canal assumed a new importance to the Furnace, however, after it no longer carried stoves to the city markets. Coal fields with access to the canals were shipping fuel to the Furnace in sufficient quantity to warrant the erection of a coal house at the canal in 1847.[76] This coal house may have been in Lebanon County. Canal tolls of $205.45 and boat fees of $264 were paid on eleven boat loads of coal delivered during that year from Big Dam on the Union Canal in Lebanon County.[77] Charcoal was shipped by canal in 1851.[78] When the anthracite furnace was operating at Monocacy, at least a part of its iron ore came by canal as indicated in this memorandum by Dr. Clingan:

> George Hoofman has undertaken to boat the Cornwall ore from Lebanon to our furnace at $1.48 per ton—he paying toll on said ore—and he is also to unload the boat or pay any hands that we may give him to help. The hands get at Birdsboro 15 cents per hour for helping.

> Whole Cost of Cornwall Ore at the Furnace:
> Ore mined at the hill and put in the Cars $1.25
> Delivered from the hill to Lebanon   .50
> Freight and Toll on canal   1.48
> ——————
> $3.23[79]

[75] SM 39, *passim.*
[76] SM 31, p. 44.
[77] SM 32, p. 31.
[78] SM 32, p. 119.
[79] *Kemper Manuscripts,* C. M. Clingan Pocket Note Book. This note was undated. The nearest date to it was July 2, 1857.

A comparison of costs from Philadelphia to Hopewell showed that a wagon load of supplies weighing about three thousand pounds had cost $7.50 in the 1830's. But in 1851 "merchandize" from Philadelphia was billed, for canal charges, at the rate of 12¢ per hundredweight with an additional charge of $1 per ton for hauling from the canal to the furnace.[80] Thus freighting costs via the canal totalled $5.10 for a load, representing a 32 per cent saving from the expense for wagoning. As late as 1860 the furnace sent 130 tons of pig iron on the canal and paid a toll of $52 on the shipment.[81]

Railroading in the Schuylkill Valley had a beginning late in 1837 when a section of the track out of Reading was opened to travel. James Morris recorded in his diary on December 6, 1837, "The first cars started on the Reading and Philadephia at Reading."[82] Several years later its trains had reached Philadelphia. Freight charges were a little higher than those on the canal: in 1851 a wagon load of storegoods from Philadelphia to Douglassville cost $3.75 by rail or $3.60 by water.[83] But the trains were much faster than the boats. The railroad also attracted passenger business from the village at a rate of $3.50 "from the City to Douglassville up and down."[84]

Changes in transportation brought alterations in the market for Hopewell Furnace products. It is possible to trace this effect by checking the locations of customers and the sources of Furnace supplies over the years of our principal interest. In the period 1802–1808 shipments and purchases involved customers at Red Lion, Strasburg, Reading, West Chester, Lancaster, Birdsboro, Conestoga, Philadelphia, Bulls Mill, Warwick, New Holland, Pine Grove Forge, Spring Forge and

---

[80] SM 32, p. 116.
[81] SM 65, October 15, 1860, n. p.
[82] *Morris Diary, op. cit.,* p. 34.
[83] SM 31, p. 150.
[84] SM 31, p. 49. The date for this rate was 1848.

Coventry. These places were generally local or near the east-west turnpike.[85]

Ten years later the market to the west was still of great importance, and a York dealer was given an exclusive marketing agency for as many Hopewell stoves as he could sell.[86] Other towns to the west mentioned in this period are Marietta, Morgantown, Harrisburg, Lancaster, Middletown, Pequea, Columbia, Lititz, Leacock, Elizabethtown and Ephrata. Wilmington and Baltimore were of interest to the south.[87] In the 1820's the bulk of sales shifted to the east, with Philadephia the major center. More distant markets were opened in 1821 when John W. Jenkins of Hudson, New York ordered plow castings.[88]

After the canal had been opened a few years, there was relatively little concern with sales in the towns to the west. Almost all shipments of molded articles were to or through Philadelphia while pig iron was sold to local forges. Although Lancaster, Columbia and Ephrata were still receiving some stoves, goods were no longer moving to the west in their former quantity. For the period from 1837 to 1845 68 dealers in Hopewell stoves were recorded in the Blast Book. Of these Philadelphia addresses were given for 48. There were four for whom no addresses were given; and, therefore, they may have been in the city. An additional nine were located in towns where transshipment from Philadelphia was probable. Pig iron was still being sold to nearby forges.[89]

How were these customers contacted to place orders? The chief responsibility for sales rested upon the manager, members of the partnership and the clerk. Much of the extensive travel for which the Furnace paid expenses must have been for calling upon new and old customers. In 1816 the Furnace

[85] SM 2 and SM 3, *passim.*
[86] *Hopewell Papers,* undated but apparently about 1817, agreement with George Small and Morris of York, Pennsylvania.
[87] SM 6 and SM 9, *passim.*
[88] HV 8210308A.
[89] SM 39, *passim.*

paid $17.75 for advertising furnace castings in two news-papers,[90] the only recorded instance of advertising of products by Hopewell Furnace. In a four-year period after this date there were scattered references to eight individuals or com-panies which were selling Hopewell stoves on a commission basis.[91] A customer mentioned a call by one of the Buckley boys as the reason for placing an order.[92] Several dealers ordered stoves because they had heard about Hopewell products and service from another merchant.[93]

Abundant evidence survives, however, to prove that not all the buyers were happy all of the time with either product or service. Complaints about slow delivery predominated, especially as there was a certain season when stoves sold well. John Getz of Lancaster seems to have been a little bitter when he wrote:

> I received your stoves but it is 9 or 10 Days after the time so . . . that people that I had engaged stoves to had to supply themselves elseware on act of the whether setting in so cold and the town being over stocked with Phila stoves It will be hard for m[e to] sell them now but whatever I do not I shall consider to your disadvantage . . .[94]

Other customers complained that stove parts were missing or broken in transit, parts were poorly cast or did not fit properly, or the holes were not large enough for the bolts. Hopewell iron was said to have been too hard to drill; so the merchants wanted the molders to be instructed to mold properly. None of these complaints seemed to have been serious enough to cause dealers to cancel orders, although they sometimes threatened to do so. The letter usually concluded with a plea to send more stoves and soon.[95] One buyer of

[90] SM 7, July 6, 1816, n. p. Bills paid but newspapers not named.
[91] SM 8, p. 52; SM 9, pp. 62, 134, 135, 153; HV 8200902A.
[92] HV 8160907.
[93] For example see HV 8160926.
[94] HV 8161112.
[95] Many such letters were found. Examples are HV 8310806A and HV 8330501A.

plow parts complained that Hopewell was making mold boards which were too heavy by as much as 25 per cent. This was a serious matter because moldings were sold by the ton, and the heavier the piece the fewer there would have been per ton.[96] Another complaint was of articles lost or stolen in transit. A pig iron buyer wrote:

> . . . if I buy some again, I will take it away at once, as you sent it over, for I believe that some is carried off, if it lays there at the tavern, the last load we brought away fell short 130 lbs, it laid there about a week before I could get it hauled.[97]

No doubt the manager made some of his calls to try to answer the complaints and find out about the kinds of moldings which were selling well or badly. The alert Furnace manager had to be aware of many trends in product sales. He needed to be prepared to take advantages of new changes and new markets opened by new means of transportation. In the first half of the nineteenth century, the Hopewell managers must have used the changing conditions to their advantage, for the furnace owner who failed to keep his lines of transportation open and at reasonable cost did not stay in business long. Iron-making was highly competitive.

[96] HV 8200225.
[97] *Kemper Manuscripts,* David G. Hertzog to Clingan and Buckley, 1865.

Part Five

The Vocational Village

11 The Worker and His Job

THE OPERATION OF A FURNACE REQUIRED MANY HANDS TRAINED
to do a variety of tasks. Some were highly skilled and some
were easily learned. Some provided full-time employment and
some were seasonal. Some paid a high wage and some were
marginal. In an effort to discover the employment needs and
labor use at Hopewell Furnace, the author made a study of
all classes of employees during five periods of two blasts each
between 1805 and 1853. Thirty-three different job classifications were identified in work records kept by the clerks. Not
all of these were used in any one of the blast periods, and four
of them appeared only once. There may have been other
kinds of jobs concealed in such generalizations as "sundries"
and "labour."

In Appendix B two tables summarize some of the results
of this labor study. The first one shows the number of different
persons who were employed at each of the jobs, and the second
one shows the approximate man-days of work for which wages
were paid for each kind of employment. It is apparent that
the most men and the most days were devoted to cutting
wood, making charcoal, mining, operating the furnace and
driving the teams. Many other jobs were incidental to the
production of iron but of importance in maintenance or in

229

caring for the needs of the other workers and their families. The total number of employees varied from 170 in the 1818–1820 period to 246 in the 1835–1837 blasts. Man-days expended had their extremes in the same two periods and ranged from 28,368 to 49,086.

A comparison of the two tables shows clearly that not all the workers could have been full-time employees. For example in 1851–1853 the average woodcutter had about one hundred days of work in twenty-seven months. The reason for this was that almost all wood was cut during the winter months, and the man working with his axe during the cold weather may have been a farmer the rest of the year or a worker at some other job for the Furnace. The tables on the next page show the extent of part-time employment. If we assume that $100 per year represented a minimum wage for full-time employment, most of the employees worked part-time. The second table shows that a fair percentage of the workers did find employment at more than one task at the Furnace, proving that this number did not work all the time at any one job. There were many specialists, however; and the percentage of these was highest in the years when the Furnace was at its productive peak. These data probably show that valuable employees were retained by giving them whatever jobs were available while the furnace was not in blast.

Wage Distribution :
Number of Workers Who Earned Specified Amounts of Wages
in the Blast Periods Indicated

Wages Paid	1805–1807	1818–1820	1825–1827	1835–1837	1851–1853
Less than $1.00	10	5	6	3	1
$1.00 to $9.99	34	33	38	47	52
$10.00 to $24.99	34	29	44	49	56
$25.00 to $49.99	27	21	28	34	38

$50.00 to $99.99	17	24	19	30	17
$100.00 to $149.99	15	13	15	18	14
$150.00 to $199.99	11	11	6	10	10
$200.00 to $299.99	14	12	16	15	11
$300.00 to $399.99	14	6	9	8	11
$400.00 to $499.99	2	6	6	4	4
$500.00 to $999.99	2	7	17	22	3
$1000.00 and over	2	3	4	6	8
Unknown	4	2	5	0	0
Total	186	170	213	246	225

Job Specialization:
Number of Persons Paid for One or More Than One Job
in the Blast Periods Indicated

	1805–1807	1818–1820	1825–1827	1835–1837	1851–1853
One Job	127	120	153	189	158
Two Jobs	34	34	30	37	41
Three Jobs	14	13	18	13	9
Four Jobs	7	2	9	4	11
Five Jobs	3	1	3	2	5
Six Jobs	1	0	0	1	1

In previous chapters the duties and responsibilities of manager, clerk, molders and teamsters have been examined. Similar attention is deserved by those who worked at the furnace and those who were responsible for keeping the furnace men supplied with raw materials.

The success of the operation of the furnace was dependent upon the knowledge and skill of the founder. The manager was expected to know how a furnace was run and to be able to solve difficult problems, but the founder was on hand for the hour-by-hour supervision of operations. It was he who would have been responsible for preventing too many crises from arising; a good founder left the manager more freedom to attend to the other duties of his office. He needed skills which it was believed could be learned only by working at a furnace. E. S. Cook wrote:

> . . . no one was competent to manage the practical end of blast furnace work unless he was "born in a tuyere arch." This expression was meant to imply that the mysteries could only be solved and handled by a man starting as a laborer and working up through the various positions pertaining to the stock-house and cast-house—first helper, keeper, and finally founder—involving an experience of five or ten years or more. The founders were men separated by the forces of natural selection from their fellow workmen, possessing more than ordinary natural intelligence and good judgment, quick to meet emergencies, of some mechanical skill and close observers of blast furnace phenomena.[1]

Success in furnace operation was not assured, however, even when the founder had had that kind of background. The human factors were also important, according to John Lewis Barde in a letter to his manager at Hopewell Furnace in the 1790's:

> . . . I must . . . give you a Caution that is Thomas Hogsett has never pushed her to what she could or has been pushed before he is in general over cautious of loading her . . . I give you this hint that he may know it. He ought to average at least 20 [tons] per week when everything is in order . . . what has been done should be done again and if one's method through obstinacy or other wise will not do I would not be unwilling to try another.[2]

---

[1] E. S. Cook, "Management of Blast Furnaces – Transition from 'Rule of Thumb' to Application of Scientific Methods," *Schools of Mines Quarterly,* XIX, 3 (April 1898), pp. 227–248.

[2] *Daniel Miller Papers,* J. L. B. to M. Brooke, Jr. Undated. Microfilm at Hopewell Village Library.

Trade secrets were valuable possessions of the founder which were kept hidden from visitors and even from fellow employees. Methods of making good iron and economical furnace management were passed from father to son. "Technology was more in the heads and hands of skilled iron-workers than in technical works in print."[3] The Care family showed this consanguineous influence by providing founders for about sixty-five years of Hopewell operation.

The founder had many things to watch if his job was done well. He adjusted the blast to the condition of the burden in the furnace, prepared trenches for the sows, set the molds and decided when the furnace was ready to tap.[4] He looked through a space between the nozzles of the bellows to judge the state of the smelting from the color of the molten mass. He wanted bright drops of iron and slag to show a good separation of the two. Another method to observe the iron was to insert a long iron implement called a "ringer" and examine the iron and slag which clung to it when it was withdrawn. He had to recognize signs of danger such as the building of a "scaffold" against the inside of the stack.[5] The founder assumed the duty of tapping the furnace to release the slag and iron; casting was usually at six o'clock in the morning and the same time in the evening so that each twelve hour tour would have the iron from a cast.[6]

The founder watched the flame and gases emerging from the stack, as they could tell him much about the state of the interior. According to Overman :

A heavy, dark top flame indicates that the furnace is cold, and that the burden is too heavy. A bright smoky flame, which throws off white fumes, indicates a too liquid cinder; that too much limestone is present; or that the burden is too light. . . . An almost invisible, lively flame at the top is significant of a

[3] Hartley, *op. cit.*, p. 12.
[4] *Ibid.*, p. 150.
[5] H. R. Schubert, *History of the British Iron and Steel Industry* (London: Routledge and Kegan Paul, 1957), p. 238.
[6] Overman, *op. cit.*, p. 201.

healthy state of the furnace. . . . Where the flame wavers, that is, where it is sometimes large and sometimes small, there is, without doubt, scaffolding in the lining.[7]

Frederick Meck was the Hopewell founder for about five years before the shutdown in 1808. Judging from the number of lawsuits in which he engaged, he was a controversial figure. He was deeply in debt to the Furnace, leaving an indebtedness of £133 19s. 9½d. when he departed at the end of 1808.[8] When the furnace reopened in 1816, John Painter was the founder at a wage of $62.50 per month.[9] Although the Painters were among the most permanent and most numerous residents of Hopewell Village, and this John Painter was long associated with the Furnace, he must have had a short tenure as founder, for on January 1, 1819, Thomas Care was paid "for blowing the furnace."[10] Care continued in this position until December 19, 1835, when he was succeeded by his son Henry.[11] Fifteen years later Nathan Care was the founder, continuing in that position until the end of iron-production in 1883. Apparently he also served for a time as manager.[12] Both Henry and Nathan had had experience as keepers and molders in preparation for the job of founder.

The founder was one of the highest-paid men in the Village in keeping with his responsibilities. In about nineteen years at this position Thomas Care averaged more than $1,000 per year income from the Furnace.[13] Not all of that was pay for blowing the furnace, however, as he was also listed as a molder. Pay for the founder was sometimes based on the output of the furnace during the blast; for example, in 1831 Care was paid $982.12 calculated at $2 per ton of molders' iron, 5s. per ton for pig iron and 50¢ per ton for gate metal.[14] He

[7] *Ibid.*, p. 205.
[8] SM 5, p. 101.
[9] SM 7, January 17, 1817, n. p.
[10] SM 6, p. 75.
[11] SM 21, pp. 161, 206; SM 19, pp. 264, 460.
[12] SM 32, p. 120.
[13] See Appendix B.
[14] SM 15, p. 53.

Molding Pig Iron with Cross Section View of Blast Furnace in
Operation

paid some wages to other furnace workers on a basis which is
not clear from the records, for the Furnace paid some of these
wages too. In 1825 Thomas Care paid the keeper; and in
1876 Nathan Care paid a keeper, two fillers and a man who
put in the ore.[15]

One keeper and one filler were employed on each twelve
hour tour with a gutterman to assist on the daylight one. The
latter wheeled all the cinder to the slag heap from both tap-
pings of the furnace but was able to do it all in the twelve
hours he worked.[16] Some of the time there was also a workman,
or more than one, who was hired for "putting in the ore,"
"putting in the night stock" or "stocking coal." Fillers in 1858

[15] SM 12, p. 32 and SM 61, p. 16.
[16] Long, *Historical Sketch, op. cit.*, p. 19.

were responsible for "puting up their night stock;"[17] so there was not always a separate person hired to do this work.

The keeper was assistant to the founder and would have been expected to operate the furnace when the founder was not present, especially during the night tour. The founder was usually not far away and was called when any emergency arose. In the early days of Hopewell operation the filler needed to be a highly skilled man. His "practiced eye" was the only means of determining the correct amount of the ingredients of the charge which went into the furnace.[18] Scales were installed in the bridgehouse in 1847 to assure more exact loading of the furnace, and then less skill was required on the part of the fillers. Filling must have been a fairly hazardous job with its many opportunities for accidents or burns. It would have been somewhat unpleasant in cold weather to move rhythmically from the open-sided bridge to the heat of the stack. Fillers had a larger amount of absenteeism than other workers, and often it was noted that they were sick or hurt.[19] Wages for a filler were usually above those for common labor but not as high as those for the most skilled jobs.

The ore was brought from the banks to the bridgehouse in wheelbarrows during the day for the use of the workers on the day turn and enough stocked ahead to last through the night.[20] Many references were also made to "putting in the night stock" and "stocking coal," showing that other ingredients beside the ore were placed on the bridge or in the bridgehouse for the use of the night workers. Charcoal was brought from the coal house in baskets or in "coal barrows."[21] Many wheelbarrows were mentioned among the purchases at the furnace.[22]

Usually Hopewell Furnace did only rough casting of stove

[17] SM 35, p. 135.
[18] Miller, *op. cit.*, p. 104.
[19] For example see SM 46, pp. 66–68.
[20] *Martha Furnace Diary, op. cit.*, August 9, 1811 and SM 44, December 15, 1807, n. p.
[21] HVX 8000320.
[22] See for example SM 15, p. 38.

Interior of Hopewell Blacksmith Shop

plates with the merchant assuming the responsibility for finishing and assembling. At one period from 1817 to 1819 the Furnace experimented with hiring its own stove finishers. First Anthony Stewart and then Charles Smith of Philadelphia were hired to assemble stoves and put the hinges and latches on the doors.[23] It is not clear whether the Furnace was wholesaling finished stoves at this time or just preparing stoves for the retail trade at the Furnace store.

Another necessary skilled worker at Hopewell throughout its history was the blacksmith. The blacksmith shop apparently dated from the early years of Furnace operation, possibly as early as 1775.[24] This shop was a social center for the men and

[23] SM 8, p. 148; SM 6, p. 144; SM 9, pp. 114, 115, 176.
[24] J. C. Fisher Motz, "Field Notes—Archeological Investigation of Black Smith Shop" (unpublished study, 1940), p. 5. Hopewell Village Library.

boys of the village. Here the blacksmith made wagon-wheel tires and farm, mine and furnace tools; repaired machinery for the Furnace and neighboring farmers; shod horses, mules and oxen; made hardware items such as hinges, latches, bolts, locks and lock plates; sharpened harrow teeth, coulters and hoes; steeled axes; made his own tools and, when nothing else was to be done, made horseshoe nails out of old horseshoes.[25] Cold feet was one of the discomforts of the smith, partially relieved by placing planks and boards on the dirt floor in front of the forge and anvil, where he spent most of his time.[26]

The Furnace depended upon a regular supply of its raw materials from the woodcutters, colliers and miners who worked in the forest, often several miles from the stack and store. Many of these men lived near their work and were seldom seen at the furnace. Others lived nearby and went out to their cutting, pit or minehole each morning.

The most numerous of all the Hopewell employees were the woodcutters. In the blast periods of 1851–1853 there were 225 persons who were paid wages for all kinds of work, and of these 116 were paid for cutting cordwood.[27] Many choppers were men who added a little to their regular income by cutting a few cords of wood during the winter months. Several cut only 12 cords and earned less than $4. At the other extreme Fred Lindeman earned $504.22 for 325½ cords, Jonah Knauer realized $784 from 560 cords, and Edward C. Gault was paid $882.60 for 1993½ cords.[28] Wages varied from 25¢ per cord for cutting on Brushy Hill near the furnace to 35¢ for some locations on Bear Hill. The pay scale was based on distance from the furnace and condition of the timber tract, with higher pay on rocky slopes or where the timber was scattered.[29]

If the cutter worked on woodlots he owned, he was paid

[25] SM 4, *passim;* C. W. Straley Interview, August 14, 1940.
[26] *Ibid.*
[27] See Appendix B.
[28] SM 32, *passim.*
[29] See for example SM 4, p. 89.

about one dollar per cord for the wood plus the price for the cutting. He could also earn an additional amount if he had a team and hauled the wood to the pit where a collier was to make charcoal. Some of the pay Edward C. Gault earned was for "wood in the rank," hauled to the coaling pit at $1.50 per cord. Other pay for "delivering in the ring" was as high as $1.75 per cord.[30]

How much wood could be cut in a day? James Morris reported, "John Diehm sawed, split and piled up a cord of hickory wood today in 3 hours . . ."[31] But this was a feat about which Diehm was boasting in the Morgantown store. The average was probably near two cord per day.[32] Note that Diehm was using a saw. Hopewell cutters apparently were axe men; seldom was there any mention of saws among their purchases. Each man was responsible for purchasing his own axe and keeping it sharpened; occasionally he had to take it to the blacksmith to have a thin strip of steel welded to the edge—"steeling the axe."[33]

Since the worker was paid by the cord, he cut his pieces in four foot lengths to facilitate measuring of a cord pile which was 4 feet by 4 feet by 8 feet. He ranked his own wood and was credited for it after the rank was measured. Some workers tried to deceive the measurement by piling wood over rocks or stumps, piling loosely or cutting billets too short. Such practices could reduce the wood by 30 per cent of volume if not detected.[34] Numerous references to dockage against cutters was evidence that the manager was watching for such tactics and found them at least a part of the time.[35] A man could also lose credit for wood he had cut for reasons which were not necessarily his fault. In 1830 David Hoffman lost $7\frac{1}{2}$ cords of wood "Being Burnt by D.

[30] SM 32, *passim.*
[31] *Morris Diary, op. cit.,* p. 2, January 10, 1837.
[32] Overman, *op. cit.,* p. 84.
[33] Schubert, *op. cit.,* p. 322.
[34] Overman, *op. cit.,* p. 84.
[35] Many references to dockage in SM 1 and SM 46.

Evans tenants,"[36] and Thomas Kurt lost much of his winter's labor in 1802 when 422 cords of his wood burned.[37]

When a woodcutter was working at a distance from home, he sometimes built a shelter near his work and stayed there for a week. Food was taken to him from his home with the boys of the family providing the delivery service.[38]

The Furnace cut about 4,000 cords per year from its own land and bought another 3,000 from woodland owners within a radius of four to five miles from the furnace, according to H. A. Long who was familiar with the last years of Furnace operation.[39] Clement B. Grubb reported in 1839 that Mount Hope Furnace used 4.66 cords of wood to produce the charcoal needed for making one ton of pig iron.[40] An acre of woodland produced from 30 to 40 cords, depending upon the quality of the timber.[41]

The experts were not in agreement about what kind of wood made the best charcoal. Elm and hickory each had its supporters. White oak, black oak, Chestnut, ash, pine and beech were considered acceptable. In America first-growth timber was considered best for coaling,[42] while the English ironmasters preferred charcoal from young trees.[43] Hopewell avoided participation in any such arguments by cutting a tract clean and using all the live wood growing there, then permitting that area to resprout and grow for thirty years before it was recut.[44]

The collier was a very important workman, controlling to some degree the quality and quantity of the furnace product. The ironmaster required a strong, compact, heavy charcoal:

[36] SM 14, p. 78.
[37] SM 1, p. 5.
[38] Thomas Hoffman Interview, November 22, 1940.
[39] H. A. Long Interview, August 13, 1936.
[40] *Mount Hope Letters,* Clement B. Grubb to Edward B. Grubb, November 7, 1839.
[41] Overman, *op. cit.,* p. 85.
[42] *Allens Appeal Record, op.* cit., pp. 182–184.
[43] Schubert, *op. cit.,* p. 222.
[44] H. A. Long Interviews, *passim.*

Collier's Hut in the Woods

Charcoal Making: Building the Chimney

If the charring is pushed too fast, or if, from the kindling of the wood, it is too lively, the coal will be small, light, and the yield will be meagre. If on the Contrary, charring proceeds slowly, the Coal will be light and friable; though the yield, if the cover has been kept tight, will be good.[45]

Charcoal was made by the destructive distillation of wood. By burning a part of the wood, enough heat was produced to expel the tar, "pyroligneous acid" and moisture, leaving the charred remains of the rest of the wood. Charcoal from the common woods varied in weight from 9.8 pounds per bushel for white pine to 18.95 pounds per bushel for sugar maple.[46]

The master collier and his helpers lived in rude huts in the woods while the coaling was going on. Wood was piled in mounds, covered with leaves and dirt and then set afire in the center. Care and skill were needed by a good collier:

> From the time the pit was first "fired" until the very last piece of charcoal was hauled away by the teamster with his large swaying wagon, . . . the pit had to be constantly tended and watched. A master collier and one or two helpers "coaled" together, working as many as eight or nine pits at a time.[47]

> Each hearth was located about the distance of a city block from one another throughout the various charcoal tracts, and the collier's hut was placed, therefore, as conveniently as possible to the group of pits then being coaled.[48]

About twenty-five to fifty cords of wood were used by Hopewell colliers in each pit measuring 30 to 40 feet in diameter.[49] A pit of this size needed from ten days to two weeks to "come to post," and as much as sixteen days was not unusual.[50]

[45] Overman, *op. cit.*, p. 115.

[46] Charles Herman Fulton, *Principles of Metallurgy* (New York: McGraw-Hill Book Company, 1910), pp. 352–353).

[47] Margaret Piersol, whose family were Hopewell colliers, said three men worked three pits at a time.

[48] Kemper, "The Making of Charcoal," *op. cit.*, n. p.

[49] *Ibid.*

[50] Fred W. Shearer, "A Bygone Industry" *Service Letter, The Pennsylvania Department of Forests and Waters,* 7, 11 (March 12, 1936), pp. 1–3.

Charcoal Making: Setting Cordwood Against the Chimney

Charcoal Making: Putting on the Second Tier of Cordwood

Charcoal Making: Cordwood in Place

Charcoal Making: Covering Cordwood with Lapwood, Dirt and Leaves

During this time the pit must never be neglected; so the collier had no work-day or work-week. He was on constant duty, eating and sleeping when the condition of the work permitted him to do so.

Coaling was not done in the winter in the Hopewell area, because "wind, rain, fog, temperature, etc., had a marked effect on the rate of burning."[51] A heavy snow could have flooded the pit area, and excessive moisture made the charcoal unfit to use in the furnace.[52] The end of the coaling season came at different times: Martha Furnace reported the convocation at " the finishing jug" on January 24, 1811; Mount Hope on December 25, 1839, and Hopewell on November 12, 1842.[53]

A good collier was one who could get the highest yield of good-quality charcoal from the wood he used. A good yield was 35 to 40 bushels of charcoal per cord of wood.[54] In 1825 the clerk noted that the wood coaled by Henry Houck "averaged 39 bu. to the cord and some over." Daniel Frye, another Hopewell master collier, averaged 38 bushels per cord during the same year.[55] The conditions for the coaling had been set down in an agreement signed with Frye:

> Agreed with Daniel Frye February 28th 1824 to coal all the wood cut at Hopewell mineholes and the wood bought of Isaac Whitaker and the wood cut on Nathaniel Kerbys land at Thirty Cents per Cord and the waggons to be heaped from end to end and not more than three Baskets brands to each load, the Coal to be drawed a sufficient time before the waggons come so that there be no fire in the Coal, he is to make as much yield out of this wood as David Hoffman will make out of the same number cords. . . .[56]

David Hoffman was apparently considered a good collier, as he was being used for a standard; but Hoffman was work-

---

[51] *Ibid.*

[52] *Allens Appeal Record, op. cit.,* p. 78.

[53] *Martha Furnace Diary, op. cit.;* HV 8391225B and HV 8421112.

[54] *Allens Appeal Record, op. cit.,* p. 19.

[55] SM 12, pp. 103–105.

[56] SM 46, for date given.

Charcoal Making: Lighting the Pile

Charcoal Making: Collier Working on Top of the Burning Pile

Charcoal Making: Uncovering the Finished Product

ing on a different kind of contract. In 1825 he bought 2,048 cords of wood from the furnace for $682.67 and coaled it at a rate of $2.25 per load. He obtained 642 loads, paid five men a total of $396.70½ wages, and received $1,421.43½ from the Furnace for his charcoal. His wages and profits for the season were $342.06.[57]

The collier was charged for Furnace wood which he permitted to burn through his neglect. In 1822 a fire consumed 108 cords of the wood assigned to David Hoffman.[58] Neglect of the coaling pit could cause too much burning and a low yield of

[57] SM 12, p. 105.
[58] SM 46, pp. 6–19.

Charcoal Making: Raking Charcoal from the Pile

charcoal. Another kind of fire which was especially costly was one on a wagon load of coal on its way from the pit to the furnace. A wagon might have been lost as well as several hundred bushels of good furnace fuel. In 1802 and 1803 the clerk noted fires in wagons driven by Samuel York and J. Simmons as well as two other fires in which the colliers rather than the drivers were named. In two of these four fires the driver was able to save a part of the load, possibly by pulling the bottom boards and scattering the coal on the road. The collier was fined for loading the wagons before the fire was out of the charcoal.[59] Two others kinds of dockage were made from the colliers' pay: when loads were too small and when there were too many uncharred faggots.[60]

Harmony did not always prevail around the coaling pits. Many of the colliers were Irish of both Catholic and Protestant faiths, resulting in "frequent reenactments of the Battle of Boyne in the woods" of Berks County.[61]

Another necessity for the successful operation of an iron furnace was a dependable supply of high-grade iron ore located within reasonable hauling distance from the furnace site. Competition would ruin a company which had to pay more than $7 or $8 at the Furnace for sufficient ore to make one ton of iron.[62]

Hopewell was fortunate in having access to three good ore fields within about five miles of the furnace. Early mining was open pit and bell pit mining with limits upon the depths to which digging could safely go. Ore near the surface was therefore a necessity. Daniel Udree tried a shaft at Oley Furnace before 1800 but found it was too expensive and too dangerous to operate.[63] The usual mining consisted of one man in the pit digging loose the ore and placing it in a bucket or basket and

[59] SM 1, April 24, 1802; May 18, 1803; July 1, 1803; October 24, 1803; n. p.
[60] SM 1 and SM 46, *passim.*
[61] *Reading Eagle,* April 8, 1917.
[62] Overman, *op. cit.,* p. 51.
[63] Handwork, *op. cit.,* p. 123.

Restored Hopewell Coal House and Cooling Shed

another man on the surface drawing up the loaded container on a rope. In the 1780's one such pair of workers supplied the needs of Hopewell Furnace.[64] In the early 1800's seven men were paid for full-time work, and several others apparently were doing some part-time mining.[65] By 1819 there were eight regular miners..[66] Seven years later the Furnace was no longer paying wages to miners but instead bought ore by the load from those who were doing the mining,[67] and from this developed the mining partnerships which hired their own

[64] Bining, *Iron Manufacture in Pennsylvania in the 18th Century, op. cit.,* p. 71.
[65] SM 3 and SM 4, *passim.*
[66] SM 6 and SM 9, *passim.*
[67] SM 59, *passim.*

Washing Iron Ore at Hopewell Mine

workers and delivered ore to the Furnace for a contracted price.[68] Still another system was used in the 1850's when eight or more men were paid wages by the furnace, but a separate bookkeeping account was maintained for the "Mine Holes." Mining expenses including wages were debited and the value of the ore delivered was credited to this account.[69] Miners' wages were relatively high, placing them in the category of skilled workers.

After the ore was on the surface, it was cleaned of its extraneous dirt by washing in a sluice. The miners were docked for dirt in the ore delivered at the furnace.[70] Washing

[68] SM 19 and SM 21, *passim.*
[69] SM 38 and SM 32, *passim.*
[70] SM 46, p. 254.

the ore sometimes created problems with the neighbors, as this letter shows:

> Martha McCormick complains and says that the water running from where the hands are washing mine flows over her meadow lot below and is doing great damage to it, she is willing the water may run through her meadow provided they clean the ditch and keep it from running over and spoiling the meadow, She also says Geo. Simmers is willing to help clean the ditch and Peter Moyers swears he will not put a shovel to it, you will be so obliging to give them some directions about it. . . .[71]

Another extra job was necessary in preparing the ore for furnace use in the 1830's. This was known as "roasting" or "burning mine" and consisted of heating the ore in ovens, piles or pits to remove volatile matter, especially sulphur, before the ore went into the furnace.[72] In the two blasts of 1835–1837 the Furnace paid four men a total of $125.03 for this work at a rate of $7 to $10 per month.[73] Further evidence that mining was becoming more complex at this time was found in payments for "90 yards tunneling at the old mineholes" and for "Sinking Shafts."[74]

The Furnace must have bought at least part of the equipment the miners used, for Peter Moyers and William Clark were reimbursed for tools they had purchased in 1829.[75] Special and heavy equipment was also purchased by the Furnace. In 1806 a "new Screw pump for Hopewell Furnace mineholes" cost £60.[76] In 1849 six "oil cloth coats for miners" were purchased at $1.75 each.[77]

This last purchase was one evidence that a new kind of mining was beginning about this time. There were many references in the journal for this year to timbering, drifting and

[71] HV 8290422, Evan Evans to Charles Brooke.
[72] Overman, *op. cit.,* pp. 39–48.
[73] SM 19 and SM 21, *passim.*
[74] SM 15, p. 32.
[75] SM 14, p. 50.
[76] SM 4, p. 110.
[77] SM 31, p. 96.

tunneling at the old Hopewell Mine; and also in this year an engine house was built,[78] evidence that mechanical power was being used. Drift cars and mules were purchased for the mines in 1848. Tin lamps were used in 1850, and "coal for Engine" indicates the use of steam power.[79] A derrick, two coal buckets and two upright posts on the list of purchases in 1857 point to power lifting of the ore. Powder and safety fuses were purchased in that year also.[80]

The need for more ore was shown by a number of payments for "searching for ore" or discovering new ore beds in the mine fields. At least one man was paid for trying to find a new area for mine operations "on Bear Hill."[81]

Rivalry among the miners for the best veins of ore resulted in many fights in the mine fields. When one group tried to get into a good vein another pair was already working, the owners would settle the dispute by drawing lines for each pair of miners.[82]

The skilled workers have been considered in the preceding pages. Relatively little could be discovered about the unskilled labor, even though in every period of the labor study made there were numerous payments "for labour." There were also workers who appeared in the time books regularly as "labourers" whose wages were considerably below those of the skilled classifications. But sometimes the clerk used this term to generalize for a variety of jobs done, and the wages paid indicate a more highly skilled task had been performed. It seems apparent that the Furnace needed and used some men at unskilled jobs with enough regularity to keep several workers for such assignment. There were also specialized workers who came to the Furnace to perform their tasks as needed. Among these were the weaver, the tailor, the shoemaker, the cabinetmaker, the carpenter, the mason, the

[78] SM 31, p. 87
[79] SM 31, pp. 61, 125, 128.
[80] SM 65, May 16, 1857 and July 24, 1857, n.p.
[81] SM 31, p. 97.
[82] *Allens Appeal Record, op. cit.,* p. 178.

plasterer, the chimney sweep, the tinsmith, the wheelwright and others. Occasionally some of these workers were employed full-time, but usually they were hired when needed or made periodic visits to the furnace.

The operation of a charcoal furnace involved the labor of many people possessing many kinds of skills and earning a wide range of wages. Some were required for full-time employment; others were used during certain seasons or when special kinds of jobs needed to be done. The furnace manager had important responsibilities as a personnel director of his labor force as will appear in the next chapter.

12 The Worker and His Boss

THE WORKER AT A CHARCOAL IRON FURNACE HAD A VERY personal relationship with his employer. The isolated location and the relatively small size of the community made it possible for the ironmaster to know each worker, his wife and children. Family problems and needs were common knowledge and received the sympathetic attention of most of the owners of furnaces. "The living conditions on the iron plantation were good, fair, or bad, according to the character of the iron-master."[1] But there was also a matter of self-interest involved. Good iron workers were not always easy to find, and good labor-management relations made it possible to retain workers or find replacements more readily.

There were rarely evidences of labor discontent which resulted in strikes or other concerted action of workers. Employers handled their labor problems on an individual basis, except in a few instances when concerted action by employers on matters of setting wages or blacklisting an employee were worked on the basis of family interrelationships and friendships. A considerable uniformity of wages and working conditions existed among the furnaces of Eastern Pennsylvania in the first half of the nineteenth century. Harold F. Williamson

---

[1] Handwork, *op. cit.*, p. 127.

255

believed that there was little consciousness of "management" as a separate job in the first half of the nineteenth century. There was no "managerial hierarchy" in the mill or foundry.[2]

The ironmaster performed a variety of services for his workers of both a business and a welfare nature. Mixed motives may have induced his doing so, ranging from self-interest in keeping an employee to a genuine sympathy for community needs. Perhaps foremost among the reasons was the almost total absence of commercial establishments which could have provided the people of the Furnace community with goods and services. Working conditions on the iron plantations would have horrified a present-day labor union leader or social worker. But little question was raised about them in the period before the Civil War. They were not worse than those found in other lines of employment and were better than in many factories.

Sullivan was unable to find any strikes among furnace workers in the years 1800–1840.[3] He contended that there was no protest or organized discontent among the wage earners largely because of the nature of the relationship between the owner and his employees.[4] England, on the other hand, had a number of strikes at the furnaces and mines. Several at the Dowlais mine were so serious that troops were called to quell the riots.[5]

Hopewell and its neighboring furnaces were neither as peaceful in labor relations as Sullivan believed nor as violent as their English contemporaries. Changewater Furnace had a dining-room riot in 1803 when James Gold objected to the kind of food being served.[6] More organized labor trouble developed in August of the same year. The clerk reported:

[2] Williamson, *op. cit.*, p. 310.
[3] Sullivan, *op. cit.*, pp. 221–230.
[4] *Ibid.*, p. 62.
[5] Madeleine Elsas (Editor), *Iron in the Making, Dowlais Iron Company Letters, 1782–1860* (London: Glamorgan County Council, 1960), pp. 33–64.
[6] *Changewater Account Book*, p. 39.

A number of Men came to work at the Laid-out Road from Mill to Forge with Jno Todd (Township Orator) at their head, actuated by his presence and plenty of our whiskey became Revolut[ionary] and Determined not to work upon said Road . . . In the Evening most of them u[nable] to stand.[7]

Hopewell had a strike at the Jones Mine in 1838 when William McIlwain wrote to Clement Brooke that, "A part of our hands turned out last friday for higher wages etc and it is agreed [sic] proposed by a part of the Company to have a special meeting next Monday."[8] Unionization of iron workers began with a molders' union formed in Philadelphia in 1855 with some men bearing names familiar at Hopewell among the early pioneers: Edward Parlaman, David Thomas and Edward Buckley.[9] At least sixty years earlier the ironmasters had organized a kind of loose association which could act on affairs of mutual interest. Berks County ironmasters held a meeting in 1794 to discuss their position on the tariff.[10] Several letters in the Hopewell collection of manuscripts show that there was an expected cooperation among the employers. A letter in 1821 had a hint of blacklisting:

If you have any influence with Wm Long Esq. be so good as to prevent the employment of John Gordon and Sons at the Canall if you can—this in Confidence— . . ."[11]

In 1838 Clement Brooke asked Robert L. Potts to discharge employees for unsatisfactory work:

. . . we think it now Proper to Give you this notice that unless those Persons you have engaged to Wash Mine by the Ton do not deliver ore Clear of Sand . . . that we will not Receive Any ore from them washed after this date and will

---

[7] *Ibid.* p, p. 40.
[8] HV 8380621.
[9] Barford, *op. cit.,* pp. 10–11.
[10] Bining, *The Iron Manufacture in Pennsylvania in the 18th Century, op. cit.,* p. 145.
[11] HV 8210519A. Signature partly destroyed, but apparently Lewis Evans to Clement Brooke.

not be Accountable for Any Part of their Labour and as far as this place is interested we demand of you to discharge them.[12]

The clearest case of proposed collusion was contained in a letter written to Hopewell in the depression year of 1842:

. . . owing to the low price for Iron and no prospects of iron getting much better for some time we consider it to our advantage and to sustain our selves in our business to reduce the rates of our workingmen the 1st day of next month which we have notified them to that effect—and want your opinion as well as Whites [probably William R. at Warwick] on the subject—which you will please give . . . all the iron works that are of any standing are agoing to do so. And the sooner this is done with, us all will be the better if we intend going on to make iron at the presence prices—moulding $8 per ton keeping $18 per month fillers $18 all other hands at $15 and $16 and board themselves—Carters at $9 single—married $16—the Coleman works Cornwall are agoing to stop for the purpose of reducing the rates—they think it cannot be done without stopping for one month—but we think we can reduce the rates without stopping; and if not—will not stop moulding more than one week or two—for several of our moulders are in debt and they must go on; others perhaps will strike for a few days—but owing to the large quantities of Protested paper we have received from customers—(stove men) we think it not advisable to make all castings—on account of the cost being more than pigs—and if some of our moulders does strike it will be no disappointment to us—Grubbs intend stoping 2 of their furnaces we have received letters from their hands for employment as it is generally understood that Hopewell and Warwick will also follow us in Lancaster County and if that be the case all will and can be done without any difficulty— and we hope you will notify your moulders at once—for now is the time when stove men will not pay and the great risk in sending stoves to men that have not paid for last years stoves; David Care we suppose will endeavour to get all the information he can about what stand you are going to take at Hopewell—give him no satisfaction except you are a agoing to lower rates and stop—and that Rock will do the same—we have

[12] HV 8380815.

told our moulders that Hopewell and Warwick will or had done so and we must follow—keep Dave in the dark—so as he will bring gloomy noose home."[13]

Two months before that letter was written the Phoenix Iron Company of Phoenixville had informed its workers that their wages would be reduced by 20 per cent, and Joanna Furnace cut the wages of all of its "monthly hands" by $1 per month.[14] Another wage reduction came after the Civil War as announced in a curious news item which is quoted here in full:

> Protecting Labor—We learn that the wages of the hands employed at the Hopewell mines and Furnace, Berks County, have been reduced to one dollar a day.[15]

The work-day and the work-week were long and varied with different kinds of jobs. Once started, the furnace and the coaling pits could not be stopped day or night or for weekends. They required constant attendance. The usual organization at the furnace was to have two groups of workers who each worked a 12-hour shift, changing at six in the morning and six in the evening.[16] William Darling of Joanna Furnace replied to a United States Treasury questionnaire in 1832 that he employed 95 men who worked all the year on a 10-hour day.[17] He did not explain how his furnace was supervised during the remaining hours.

For some Hopewell workers the day was more than twelve hours long. When a teamster drove a charcoal wagon from Birdsboro to the Furnace, he left at two o'clock in the morning and returned after his children were in bed.[18] In 1825 George

[13] HV 8420610, Brooke Coheen and Company at Rock Furnace to Clement Brooke.
[14] *Village Record,* West Chester, Pennsylvania, April 12, 1842, and *Joanna Furnace Time Book,* 1842–1843, n.p. Hopewell Village Library.
[15] *Jeffersonian,* West Chester, Pennsylvania, July 3, 1867.
[16] SM 35, p. 3.
[17] *McLane Report on Manufacture, op. cit.,* p. 227.
[18] Mary L. Cramp Interview, November 6, 1961.

Painter quit work several times at six o'clock and was paid for only three-fourths of a day. However, on another day under similar circumstances he received a full wage for the day.[19] In 1854 James Friar was paid extra for working $15\frac{1}{2}$ hours; and numerous entries were found showing workers paid for $1\frac{1}{4}$, $1\frac{1}{2}$ or even two days for the same date. These extra-length tours were paid at the normal hourly wage.

For most workers, other than employees at the furnace and coaling pits, the work-week was six full days, Monday through Saturday. The time books show that many workers quit early on Saturday and received credit for only half or three-fourths of a day.[20] Maids and housekeepers were employed by the week and would have had some duties on Sunday in serving meals and routine housework.[21] Workers who were employed by the month had their wages calculated on the basis of 26 days in January of 1834 and were credited with one month and one day; but in February there were only 24 working days, and they were paid for just that number.[22] A working month, evidently, was 26 days rather than a calendar month.

Most of the cost of making iron was represented in the wages paid to the workers.[23] The furnace owner kept his wages from varying widely during the period 1800–1850. Earnings were different because of the number of days worked, but the basic wage rate changed little in good times or in depressions. The table on the next page shows the wages paid for sixteen job classifications in five different periods. The greatest fluctuations were in the managerial class of founder, clerk and manager. The range was not as much as may appear on the surface, because the high and low were often indications of pay with or without boarding rather than differences in scale. Extremely low wages, as with the carpenters, were for a son helping his father.

[19] SM 46, pp. 59–60.
[20] For example see SM 1 and SM 35, *passim.*
[21] SM 65, April 2, 1857, n. p.
[22] HV 8340501C and SM 21, p. 154.
[23] Overman, *op. cit.,* p. 49.

Wages Paid for Different Job Classifications
for Five Periods of Two Blasts Each

	1805–1807	1818–1820	1825–1827	1835–1837	1851–1853
Carpenter per day					
	.73	.75–$1.20	.60–.65	.35–.87½	.31–.65
Clerk per year					
	$300		$135	250–$300	$150
Collier per month					
	$8.62–$20.62	$16–$23	$13.50–$18	$13.50–$18	$17.50–$24
Farm Worker per day					
	.50–.73	.25–.50	.40–.50	.50–$1	.23–.54
Filler per month					
	$10–$18	$12–$18	$9–$14	$15–$16	$14–$18
Founder per year					
	$640	$480	$970	$540–$600	$480
Houseworker per week					
	.67–.80	$1	.80	.50–$1	.75–$1.50
Keeper per month					
	$20	$12–$20	$17–$20	$18	$18
Laborer per month					
	$7.50–$10	$6–$13	$8–$13.75	$6–$14	$6–$15
Manager per year					
	$325	$541	$652	$600	$650
Miner per month					
	$12–$15	$11–$19.50	$11.33–$21	$9.50–$18	$13–$32
Molder per ton					
		$12	$8–$10	$6–$10	
Putting in Mine per month					
		$12	$10	$7–$16	$20–$24
Smith per month					
	$14–$16	$17	$9–$13	$8–$20	$15
Teamster per month					
	$10–$14.66	$10–$12	$9–$14	$8–$14	$8–$14
Woodcutter per cord					
	.35–.45	.35–.40	.25–.30	.27–.40	.20–.35

The ironmasters considered their pay scale sufficient to feed, clothe and lodge a worker and "to enable the prudent to make some savings for sickness, reverses and old age."[24] It was true

[24] *Documents Relating to the Manufacture of Iron in Pennsylvania, op. cit.*, p. 9.

that the money wage did not tell the whole story of workers' income. Employees often were given a house at very low rent, wood, pasture land, vegetables grown on Hopewell farms and other domestic commodities in addition to their wages.[25]

How did Hopewell wages compare with other kinds of workers or with other furnaces at the same time? Workers on the canals were being paid $14–$15 per month "and found" in the 1820's. Some contractors offered as high as a dollar a day on the Pennsylvania Canal in 1837, but work was not very steady.[26] Women textile workers in Pennsylvania in 1829 were paid $1.50 per week for working from sunrise to ten or eleven o'clock at night.[27] Hopewell's wages for maids compared favorably because they also included room and board.

Comparisons with wages paid at other furnaces may be made from the following scales for some of the same years as the table for Hopewell wages:

> *Mount Hope Furnace—1806*
> Carpenter—$16 per month
> Clerk—$158.50 per year
> Farm Worker—   .50 per day
> Housework—   .85 per week
> Laborer—$7–$9 per month.[28]

> *Dale Forge—1827*
> Carpenter—$14 per month
> Collier—$17 per month
> Farm Worker—   .40 per day
> Housework—   .75 per day
> Mason—   .70 per day.[29]

> *Manada Furnace—1837*
> Carpenter—$1 per day
> Collier—$20 per month
> Farm Worker—   .50–62½ per day

[25] Thomas N. Care Interview, February 10, 1941.
[26] Sullivan, *op. cit.*, pp. 29–42.
[27] Barnes, *op. cit.*, p. 289.
[28] *Mount Hope Furnace Journal, 1800–1819, passim*. Microfilm at Hopewell Village Library.
[29] Gemmell, *op. cit.*, pp. 94–95.

Housework— .75 per week
 Laborer—$4–$7 per month
 Mason—$1–$1.12½ per day
 Teamster—$11 per month
 Woodcutter— .30–.45 per cord.[30]

Amounts earned by fourteen Hopewell workers over a period of many years as well as the ways they used their income can be seen on the charts in Appendix B.

There never was a payday at Hopewell because the amount earned was simply credited to the worker's account with the Furnace. This credit could be used to make purchases at the store, to pay bills to the Furnace, to pay for purchases made elsewhere or to make payments for goods delivered at their homes. Unlike the situation at many other furnaces, Hopewell workers seemed always to have been able to draw cash against their credit on company books. Cash books and cash pages in the journals show that money was obtained even in years when business was slow. Most payments were made at the store or office, but numerous entries prove that a worker could meet the manager or clerk almost anywhere and get money from his pocket. A list of such honored requests included payments "at his house," "at D. High's," "at Barny Tavern," "in Reading," "in the city,' "at the mineholes," "at the township meeting," "in Birdsborough," "at Mount Airy" (sixteen men were paid here at the same time), "at Beards Tavern," "in the wood cutting," "at his church," "at the election," "at Golden Swan Hotel," "in Potts Grove," "at the canal" and "at court."[31] The greatest demand for cash was at the end of a blast or of the coaling season. At Mount Hope Furnace $1,500 lasted only a few days against the demands for cash by the colliers at the close of their coaling.[32]

A worker was paid for the time he was actually on the job whether he was a day laborer or a salaried employee. If he

[30] *Manada Furnace Journal, 1837,* August–December, 1837.
[31] These items were taken from the cash records covering many years.
[32] HV 8391225B.

Labor Record from Hopewell Journal for 1836

missed work for any reason, his pay was docked for the time he was away from the job. There were no paid vacations, no paid holidays and no excused absences.

In 1822 there was a full complement of workers on Independence Day, but the next year none was listed as working on either Christmas or January 1. Workers were not paid for these days either.[33] According to reports of residents of Hopewell Village, the workers and their families were invited to

[33] See SM 46 for appropriate dates.

parties at the Big House on these last two holidays. It is probable that the furnace group had to work to avoid a costly holiday closing of this operation, but this supposition could not be checked because their work was not recorded in the time book.

At the Martha Furnace the molders took an informal vacation when all of them decided to go to the shore for a weekend.[34] Hopewell had a similar incident when some of the molders refused to do their work because they wanted to go hunting. The clerk reported these circumstances:

> The Casting of Pigs left out Monday Morning September 5, 1825 before day weighed 626.1.14
>
> Note. The above castings of Pigs was left out owing to Joseph McKewen, George North and Henry Care Neglecting to mold up last Saturday Sept. 3rd 1825 as it was their duty to have moulded up. Thomas Care told them on Saturday to lade immediately after breakfast and they refused. he presed them to lade at 9 oclock and could not get them to do it until 11 oclock. The Iron all that time was running out of the furnace. McKewen and North was out hunting with their guns.
>
> B. The above Casting was the second casting left out from Saturday.[35]

There was no punishment of these three molders for this neglect except the loss of their earnings for that period. All of them remained with the Furnace, and Henry Care eventually became founder.

There were many records of absenteeism from jobs for a variety of reasons such as sickness, doing farm work, attending a vendue, going to visit relatives, going to Philadelphia, attending a funeral or taking a vacation. In 1803 the clerk lost 21 days "when his Brother died" and two other periods of seven days each without any explanation except that he was "at Mr. Vanleers." He lost pay for these days from his

[34] *Martha Furnace Diary, op. cit.,* July 28–August 1, 1809.
[35] SM 46, p. 62.

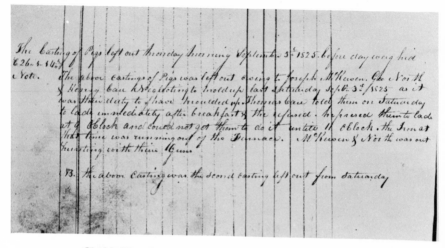

Clerk's Notation of Men Neglecting Work to Go Hunting

annual salary of $300.[36] Drinking was a frequent cause of
loss of time; for example, George Harn lost time at the Birdsboro Forge because he was "Drunk frolicken and Idle all this
week."[37] The record of time lost was usually accompanied with
the name of the person who substituted for the absent worker.
Sometimes the turn was shared by two men who each worked
one half day. Occasionally a search had to be made to find a
man to do the work, and he would not begin until after the
tour had started.[38]

Loss of time was not always the only punishment for a man
who missed work. Martha Furnace had a collier sign a contract which provided for a fine of $5 for missing one day of
work.[39] Fines were also used at Hopewell Furnace, especially
when there was a loss in addition to the time not worked.
Samuel York had $1 deducted from his earnings "for getting

[36] SM 2, p. 143. There was a Vanleer Tavern.
[37] *Birdsborough Ledger*, 1810, *op. cit.*, p. 7.
[38] For example see SM 35, p. 148.
[39] *Martha Furnace Diary*, *op. cit.*, October 9, 1809.

intoxesitated with liquer and neglecting hauling 3 loads wash Dird at Joneses."[40] Thomas Johnson lost the same amount "for Neglecting Sending 1 load Coal in—was laying Drunk in ye Cabin."[41] Keeping a team out "all day and part of the night without feed" cost a teamster $2 in 1830.[42] Other kinds of neglect or carelessness which brought fines against Hopewell workers included "neglecting his work and let his pitts burn," wood burned, teams standing idle, failure to bring in loads, failure to load the wagons, small loads, "loosing 2/3 of a load of coal," wood left on the hills which should have been hauled to the coaling areas, coal burned on the road and "Cutting high stumps in the lot of wood cut by him."[43]

Harker Long said that men did not work very hard at Hopewell Village and were never in a hurry but that it was very rare for a man to be discharged for not doing enough.[44] This observation was supported by a search of the Furnace records which showed that many workers quit but few were discharged. Discharging an employee was difficult when he was a friend of a partner, as shown by this letter from Daniel Buckley to Mathew Brooke:

At your advice and desire I took your friend Mathew Davis into partnership who has during three years acted offen very Improperly, and now at the close seems to shew a very Extraordinary disposition so much so that I fear we shall not part without laying the foundation of much trouble in consequence of your recommendation he came, therefore think you are under some kind or tipe of obligation to get us seperated, I wish you to come over tomorrow and advise what is best to do . . . should you not come I will . . . seize his Property till I get security for the Rent or Paid.

I have at no time been in such a straight if he was not some way a Conection I would think little of putting the Business

[40] SM 44, March 13, 1808, n. p.
[41] SM 2, p. 39.
[42] SM 14, p. 77.
[43] Examples are taken from journals and time books covering the first half of the nineteenth century.
[44] Long, *Historical Sketch, op. cit.,* p. 17.

Perfectly straight and Easey but under the circumstances that are I am lothe your friendship will be considered an obligation.[45]

Another kind of problem which developed between labor and management was the loss or stealing of Furnace property. Tools were stolen in 1816,[46] and a teamster was charged for a log chain he lost in 1852.[47] The most frequent and costly loss, however, was fuel. One man was paid for cutting wood for Hopewell, but later it was discovered that he had hauled 16 cords of it to the canal and sold it in Manayunk.[48] Edward C. Gault, a contract collier, paid $12 in 1851 for charcoal which had been stolen, but there is no certainty whether he was accused of stealing it or having had it stolen from his coaling operation.[49]

The Furnace assessed fines for neglect, but it less frequently gave rewards for diligence. Henry Sheets was paid $9.75 in 1836 "for Sundry work and saving sprouts."[50] No information was given on what was threatening the sprouts or what he did to save them, but he was rewarded with cash for some effort he made. More explicit was this 1847 note, "Furnace Paid for a silver watch and made it a present to Joseph Hart for his perseverance in discovering the new body of mine near old mineholes." The cost of the watch was $14.50.[51]

The Furnace apparently had no rules against a man holding more than one job at the same time. For example in 1803 Edward Hughs received pay for filling, putting up the night stock, putting in the mine, cutting wood and cleaning castings.[52] Possibly some of this work was done by sons who were too young to collect their own wages. David Struck combined woodcutting with shoe making; these could have been seasonal

[45] *Brooke Family Papers,* April 2, 1808.
[46] SM 7, November 17, 1816, n. p.
[47] SM 32, p. 126.
[48] SM 21, p. 170.
[49] SM 32, p. 119.
[50] SM 21, p. 184.
[51] SM 31, p. 26.
[52] SM 2, pp. 173–177.

alternations, however.[53] Perhaps the clearest case of double jobs was that of Thomas Care who was paid for both molding and founding over a period of many years.[54] It was not possible to determine whether his job as founder permitted him sufficient free time to mold some stoves or whether he worked part of the night tour. His wages were high because of his dual services.

The association between employer and employee at Hopewell Village showed a considerable character of paternalism in the many services the management performed for the workers. One such case was in dealing with suits at law on behalf of workers. Many references were found to payments of judgments, costs, fines, debts, bills, interest and constable charges against Hopewell workers. The Furnace paid for a pardon for a Negro teamster in 1803,[55] but the record failed to say for what he was being pardoned. Several times the Furnace provided bail money.[56] Notes given by workers and protested by banks were paid by the Furnace and collected from the worker. In one such case in 1832 the Furnace had difficulty recovering the amount of such a note.[57] Philip Shafer, a blacksmith, spent part of 1806 in jail and had his jail costs of $16.50 paid by Hampton Forge.[58]

On at least two occasions the Furnace resorted to jail to punish workers. In 1809 the account of George Proudfoot, a teamster, was charged $1.45 in favor of Mathew Brooke with this notation "per order in favour Michael Westly for Putting Proudfoot in Jaol." There was no statement of the charge preferred, but Proudfoot had owed Hopewell Furnace a debt with no payment on it for more than three years. If this had been the reason for the jailing, the results were not favorable; for his indebtedness was simply increased by the amount of

[53] SM 6, p. 29. This was in 1821.
[54] SM 9, p. 128 was one example.
[55] SM 2, p. 120.
[56] See examples in SM 1, p. 43; SM 4, p. 93.
[57] SM 17, pp. 16, 22.
[58] SM 4, p. 236.

the costs. No payment was made to reduce the debt.[59] In 1816 Samuel Coggins, a Negro servant, was jailed by Mathew Brooke. Again there was no record of the reason, but Coggins was still driving a team for Brooke several years later.[60]

Public sales were popular places to purchase goods and also served as rural social occasions. Men who wanted to make purchases at the vendue sometimes asked for cash, if they could find the boss, or charged the goods to their accounts at the Furnace. The prize example of a public sale transaction must surely have been the purchase of a farm for a worker who did not even know he was bidding. According to a Hopewell tradition, David Shaffer told Clement Brooke he wished he had enough money to buy a farm offered for sale. A few days later Brooke handed Shaffer a deed for the farm. Shaffer protested that he owned no farm. Brooke said he did now, for he had bid in the farm for $1,200 and paid for it out of money Shaffer had standing on the Hopewell books. Shaffer was surprised to discover that he had possessed any such sum of money.[61]

It was an advantage to workers to be able to say that a bill would be paid by Hopewell Furnace. All kinds of persons sold goods and services to employees and were assured that they need only present their bills to the clerk to receive payment. Peddlers and distant merchants; milliners, tailors and shoemakers; doctors and lawyers; carpenters, masons and cabinetmakers all received payments on bills they presented. The tax collector accepted a bulk payment for the money due from a long list of Hopewell employees. Administrators of estates collected the balances due to the deceased at the time of death less bills paid. In some cases the Furnace continued to act as banker for a widow who let her husband's balance stand on the Furnace books.[62] Many workers borrowed money from the

[59] SM 4, p. 253; SM 5, p. 96.
[60] HV 8161128A and HV 8180221.
[61] Albert Painter Interview, January 8, 1959.
[62] For example see *Cash Book* for 1828–1830, *op. cit.*, May 3, 1830.

Furnace when their accounts did not cover needs. For some reason a payment to William Gott in 1826 was recorded as a loan despite the record which showed he had credit on his account for more than the twenty dollar loan.[63] One man rented a stove and paid $2.56 rental, but the clerk did not record the length of time for which it was rented.[64]

The Furnace manager was entrusted with the most delicate missions of social life, although no instance was found to match that of the manager of Martha Furnace who ". . . went with Josh Townsend to settle his business with a lady."[65] In case of illness the mistress of the Big House was the first person called or consulted.[66] On at least two occasions Hopewell Furnace paid the cost of taking an aged resident of the Village to the county poorhouse.[67]

The following letter disclosed that real friendship must have existed between some workers and the owners' families:

> Do you remember the blacksmith, Israel and his wife Julia, they are both here now on a visit, they look very well, Charley and Tom are as fond of them as when they lived here . . .[68]

Labor relations at Hopewell Furnace in the first half of the nineteenth century were relatively stable. Wages changed little but probably represented the basis of as high a scale of living as was available to similar classifications of workmen in other industries and occupations. There were few strikes or walkouts and little evidence of a trend toward labor unionism despite some instances of united action by furnace owners. Workers were kept in line by a system of fines. No evidence was found of any use of corporal punishment, and few workers were discharged for either negligence or dishonesty. Paternalism and self-interest combined to induce the owners to provide a wide variety of services and aids to their workers.

[63] SM 12, p. 130 and SM 11, p. 315.
[64] SM 12, p. 48.
[65] *Martha Furnace Diary, op. cit.,* June 19, 1809, n. p.
[66] Kemper, *American Charcoal Making, op. cit.,* p. 5.
[67] SM 28, pp. 99, 166.
[68] *Brooke Family Papers,* Ann Brooke to George W. Brooke, August 3, 1831.

13   Labor Recruitment, Training and Tenure

THE SUPPLY OF TRAINED, SKILLED FURNACE WORKERS WAS inadequate to meet the demand when the charcoal-iron industry was prosperous. Even common laborers were not always easy to find in the comparative isolation of the furnace sites. Good relations between workers and boss resulted from the difficulty in replacing the dissatisfied workers who went to another furnace; but, on the other hand, the relative uniformity of wages among the furnaces served as a check on much labor migration. Turnover was greatest in the lowest paid and least skilled jobs and rather light in the highly skilled tasks. This must certainly have reflected the attention the manager gave to keeping his founder, miners, molders and colliers contented in their work. When a furnace closed its operations, the workers usually found employment with other ironmasters.

Hopewell Furnace recruited its workers in many places and used many means to induce persons to take employment. This area of Berks and Chester Counties had been a center of iron-making for more than half a century before Hopewell was built; so many of the families living nearby were in possession of the required skills. Local recruitment provided many of the men needed. This source of labor supply was continually cultivated throughout the history of Hopewell Furnace by giving employment to the children of workers and neighboring farmers. Apprentices, indentured servants and probably slaves appeared among the laborers; on-the-job training passed on skills to the new generations maturing in the village. But recruitment programs of several kinds were used to attract workers from greater distances. The large number of Negroes who appeared on the Hopewell books showed that black laborers formed an important element in the work force.[1]

The similarity between European and American methods of furnace and coaling procedures was noted by many writers. The reason was fairly clear : American iron was first produced by men who brought their skills across the Atlantic. England made an effort to guard its industrial secrets by the passage of an Act of Parliament in 1765 to prohibit the emigration of skilled workmen.[2] Regardless of the effectiveness of the enforcement of this law, it did not serve its purpose of preventing competition for English iron-making. For one reason it came too late. America already had a number of ironmasters who had come here from the British Isles and also from several countries on the continent. Places of origin of some Eastern Pennsylvania Furnace men before 1800 were :

England :	Thomas Rutter, Samuel Nutt, William Branson, John Ross, William Bird, Mathew Brooke.
Wales :	Thomas Potts, James Morgan, James Old.
Germany :	Henry William Stiegel, John Lester, Gerrard Etter.
Hanover :	Valentine Eckert.
Alsace :	George Anshertz.
Scotland :	William Keith, Samuel McCall, James Wilson.
Ireland :	Robert Grace, Robert Coleman, George Taylor.
France :	William Dewees, Daniel Udree.[3]

[1] The Negro workers will be given special attention in Chapter 15.
[2] Williamson, *op. cit.*, p. 50.
[3] Most of these were identified by Bining, *Pennsylvania Iron Manufacture in the 18th Century, op. cit.*, p. 131.

Union Township was settled by Swedes, English, Welsh, Palatine Germans, New Englanders, New Yorkers, Jerseyites, Dutch, and French Huguenots.[4] Charles B. Montgomery, Berks County historian, checked the family names in the early Hopewell record books and identified the following by point of European origin :

Swedes :   Likens, Boon, Jones, Hulings.
Welsh :   Morgan, Cadwalader, Reese, Jones, Roberts, Hughs, Edwards.
Germans :   Rhoades, Colver, Redcay, Custar.
Scotch-Irish : Richards, Campbell, Murphy, Robison, Armstrong.[5]

The census of the United States began in 1850 to list the place of birth of each person. A check of this census report for Berks and Chester Counties showed that most of the Hopewell people reported that they had been born in Pennsylvania. Among those of foreign birth the Irish and Germans were numerous; and England, Wales, France and Scotland were listed as the birthplaces of one or more.[6] It is possible that at least a part of these immigrants came to the Furnace for employment because they were familiar with the processes of smelting.

Another possible source of foreign workers at the Furnace was soldiers who decided not to return to their homelands at the end of the Revolutionary War. On April 29, 1779, the Continental Congress passed a resolution offering free land and farm animals to any foreign soldiers who deserted from the British Army. One paragraph in the resolution was aimed particularly at skilled industrial workers :

Such of you as are skilled in manufactures, over and above these lands and other articles, will find riches in prosecuting

[4] *Montgomery Manuscripts,* Origin of Union Township.
[5] *Hopewell Letters,* Charles B. Montgomery to Lemuel Garrison, December 18, 1940.
[6] *Census of 1850* for Berks and Chester Counties, Pennsylvania.

your occupations, the necessities of life being very cheap in proportion to the price of manufactures, and the demand for them is so great, that every mechanic will find full employment. . . .[7]

It is not known now whether any foreign troops came to Hopewell in response to this invitation, but it is certain that two former British soldiers came to the Furnace. John Lewis Barde, who leased the furnace from James Wilson in 1794, was a British officer stationed in Florida before he came north to engage in the iron business.[8] Joseph Whitaker deserted from the British Army some time prior to 1781 and took over a tract of land about a mile from Hopewell. For a half century he appeared on the Hopewell books as a weaver, and several of his sons were employed at the Furnace.[9]

Hopewell Furnace counted upon permanent residents of the village to furnish a considerable share of its work force. Many families provided laborers for several generations; sons grew up to follow their fathers as Furnace employees. The Union Township tax returns for 1779 included the names of many men, and one woman, whose families would be associated with the Furnace for much of its history: Edward Dehaven, Evan Evans, John Gray, Thomas Hughs, Edward Hughs, Geo. Kirst, Stanley Kirby, Cath. Kramp, Evan Lewis, Joseph Millard, Mordecai Millard, Thomas Millard, James Roberts, John Sands, John Umstead, Peter Wampser, William Wampser, William Williams and Martin Wirt.[10] The Hopewell Journal for 1784–1792 contained many more names of families which remained for a long period in the village: John Hart, David Mee, John Rice, William Roads, John Painter, Nicholas Hunter, Ezekiel Thomas, Abram Sink, William Philips, Jacob Meese, Thomas Cuthbert, David Jenkins, Thomas Simes, Peter Moyer, Adam Kephart, John Haws,

[7] *Journals of the Continental Congress*, X, p. 408.
[8] *Brooke Family Papers*, Genealogical Data.
[9] Dennis C. Kurjack, "Joseph Whitaker of Hopewell Furnace," *The Historical Review of Berks County*, XIV, 3 (April 1949), pp. 66–73.
[10] *Berks County Tax Record for 1779*, Union Township, pp. 80–81.

William Merwin, Jacob Yocum and Charles Cramp were some of them.[11]

The Furnace also drew the sons of families living a short distance outside the village area. For example Micajah, Henry, Jessie and William Posey came from the Brandywine region of Chester County. Micajah began work at Hopewell at the age of fifteen, became a molder in 1831 and continued for the most prosperous period of stove-making until 1841. He married a daughter of a Hopewell woodcutter.[12]

Many a Hopewell father brought his son or sons to assist him at his job and thus introduced them to Furnace employment. In 1803 Edward Hughs paid his son David to assist at "Washing mine," and David remained as a long-time worker.[13] Three years later Edward Hughs was being paid for several sons' work, including Isaac as the gutterman.[14] In 1866 Nathan Care signed a contract for himself and his son John to provide the services of both founder and keeper.[15] There were many similar references to a son's doing work and his wages being paid to his father before the son was old enough to collect his own wages.

Another source of workers was the employees of other furnaces. The similarity of names in the records available for other furnaces revealed many who apparently left to come to Hopewell. The original staff for Hopewell must have been drawn largely from Warwick Furnace, for the Warwick ledger in the three years before Hopewell was built contained the names of at least 19 men who were a part of the Hopewell work force in the oldest records extant.[16] The Changewater Furnace account books for 1802 and 1803 listed as employees the following men who shortly after became Hopewell skilled

[11] SM 41, pp. 1–4.
[12] *Posey Family History* (unpublished typescript). Hopewell Village Library.
[13] SM 2, p. 143.
[14] SM 44, December 17, 1806, n. p.
[15] SM 60, April 17, 1866. Recorded on front cover of book.
[16] *Warwick Furnace Ledger*, 1767–1770. Historical Society of Pennsylvania.

workers: Frederick Meck, founder; Samuel Meck, keeper; Samuel and Peter Cox, teamsters; James Benson, miner; David Hart, filler; Philip Shafer, Senior and Philip Shafer, Junior, blacksmiths; Adam Johnston, keeper and miner. In 1821 Hopewell hired James T. Johnson after he had worked as molder and flask maker "at the Valley Works."[17] The Joanna Furnace records show that many workers moved back and forth between these two neighboring furnaces. A none too exhaustive survey of the Joanna journals and ledgers for the period 1810–1812 revealed 107 names that were the same as those of people who either had formerly worked at Hopewell or would later be employed there.[18] Of course one reason for so great a number was that Hopewell had ceased operation in 1808. This circumstance also accounted for the appearance in the *Martha Furnace Diary* of Hopewell names in 1808–1810. Philip Shafer, Peter Cox, James Hughs and William Williams were working at this New Jersey furnace during some part of those years.[19] Mary Ann Forge in York County was employing at least seven men with Hopewell names in this period.[20] Three other men left Hopewell Village to go to Orwigsburg in 1809 to help to build a new furnace.[21] Another major migration of workers from Hopewell took place in the 1840's when stove-making was ended, and at least half of the Hopewell molders went to Black Rock Furnace in Lancaster County.[22]

Not all of the workers were free to seek employment elsewhere if conditions did not suit them. It is not certain that slave labor was used at Hopewell, although the fact that Mark Bird owned slaves made it highly probable that some worked there in its early history.[23] But if doubt remains about the use

[17] SM 6, inside front cover, also August 8 and 20, 1816.
[18] *Joanna Furnace Journals* for 1810, 1811 and *Ledgers* for 1811, 1812, *op. cit.*
[19] *Martha Furnace Diary, op. cit., passim.*
[20] *Mary Ann Forge Ledger, 1810–1811, op. cit., passim.*
[21] SM 67, *passim.*
[22] *Black Rock Furnace Ledger,* 1845–1851. Hopewell Village Library.
[23] The account of Negroes at Hopewell is discussed in Chapter 15.

of slaves, there is none about the employment of indentured and apprenticed workers.

In 1773 Mark Bird offered a reward of three pounds for the return of a Dutch servant by the name of Christian Metz who was described as a miller by trade and "a good Scholar in the German language."[24] A few years later Hopewell Furnace paid fourteen pounds and eight shillings for "indenture payments for time of servitude" to each of the following: Patrick Fee, Joseph Somerset, Arthur Money, Edward Riley and Michael Riley.[25] No indication was given as to how or why these men had entered into "servitude;" but the indenture agreement of Jacob Hampf on May 16, 1804, gave these circumstances:

> This Indenture witnesseth, That Jacob Hampf of his own free Will hath bound himself Servant to Mathew Brooke, for the Consideration of Seventy Dollars paid Captn John Green for his Passage from Hamberg . . . during the full Term of Three Years . . . and the said Mathew Brooke . . . during the said Term shall find and provide for the said Servant sufficient Meat, Drink, Apparel, Washing and Lodging and at the Expiration of his Term, the said servant shall have two complete Suits of Cloaths one whereof to be New.[26]

Two of the Hopewell partners were concerned with the problem of how best to use another servant. One wrote:

> I also [wish] to see you on the Subject of my Black fellow Tobe as Mathew Davis [Hopewell manager] wishes him not to work for him and I am unwilling to Dispose of his time he is a stout good workman and only wants steady Employ.[27]

Indentures were still a problem in 1816 when the furnace paid William Duane of the *Country Aurora* $2 for advertising a reward of $30 for the return of a runaway servant.[28] In

---

[24] *Pennsylvania Gazette,* April 21, 1773.

[25] SM 41, p. 84. This payment was in 1784.

[26] *Brooke Family Papers,* indenture Hampf to Brooke.

[27] HV 8060405, Daniel Buckley to Mathew Brooke.

[28] HV 8160304A. It is possible that this runaway servant incident was associated with the jailing of Sampson Coggins mentioned in Chapter 12.

1818 payment was made for two pairs of shoes soled "for Sampson and Jack."[29] "Sampson" was quite probably the Negro teamster Sampson Coggins. "Jack" was James Jack who received some schooling at Furnace expense and so probably was an apprentice boy.

The use of indentured labor received a sharp setback in Pennsylvania in 1833 when the General Assembly enacted a law against imprisonment for debt. Evidence of involuntary servitude could still be found for a number of years longer, however.[30] The use of apprentice children would also continue for many years. The census of 1860 showed that a number of skilled craftsmen in Union Township had one or more apprentices listed as members of their households. George Montan, wheelwright, had a boy of 17; Levi Keller, blacksmith, two of 20 and 19; Charles Klink, shoemaker, two of 19 and 16; Jacob Hense, carpenter, two of 19 and 19; Samuel Boyer, one of 15; Franklin James, miller, one of 22.[31]

Boys apparently learned most of the jobs at the Furnace by observation, by instruction from their father or another relative, or simply by taking a job and learning while they worked. Two exceptions were noted of examples of more formal instruction for a job. Lewis Evans received $5 from Samuel Templin for "Teaching Jas. Roberts Bookeeping."[32] But the only job at the Furnace for which there was a fairly regular system of vocational training was molding. Boys were not apprenticed to the ironmaster to learn this skill but, instead, paid a journeyman molder to teach them. The boys were paid for any molding they did at the same rate as the adult molders, but they gave a percentage of their earnings to their teachers. In 1819 William Thomas had two pupils. Ezekiel Thomas earned $219.75 and paid one half of it to William. William Rickets also paid William Thomas half of his income of $155.26. Rickets had been a woodcutter but

[29] HV 8180302.
[30] Sullivan, op. cit., p. 211 (footnote).
[31] Apprenticeship at Hopewell will be considered in Chapter 17.
[32] Lewis Evans Journal, op. cit., September 16, 1819, p. 122.

became a Hopewell molder after this instruction, as did Ezekiel Thomas. John Sheeler collected $76.20 for teaching the molders' skills to Joseph McKewen, another woodcutter who became a Hopewell molder.[33] Samuel Williams, a teamster, paid William Rickets $84.23½ out of molding earnings of $182.19½ in 1832. Probably this payment was for teaching molding to a ward, for Williams collected the molder's earnings of Joseph Elliott from 1832 to the beginning of 1837.[34]

Workmen sometimes were recommended to the Furnace by letter of application or reference. A few such letters have survived. J. Hamill applied for the job of manager in 1801 in this manner:

> Being informed by Mr. Fincher that you will want some person at Hopewell next Spring to manage if you do and your brother should leave there if you and I could agree I would have no objection to go there. . . .[35]

He did not get the job, nor did Justin Smith who offered to "do writing" or any other of the clerk's duties.[36]

A letter might have come from a person who could recommend the worker. William Linderman was recommended for a job as collier by a relative who wrote that "he is a sober and industerous man."[37] Impediments were sometimes placed in the way of employing men as indicated in this caution that "if his Intended *Lady* is satisfied perhaps you may get him" to work.[38]

On at least two occasions Furnace employees were paid for bringing girls to work as maids at the Big House. The record is not clear, however, whether the payment was for expenses or a reward for helping to recruit a new employee.[39] But near

[33] SM 9, p. 126; SM 6, pp. 37, 98, 127, 128.
[34] SM 19, p. 268; SM 21 ,pp. 158, 190, 205.
[35] *Brooke Family Papers,* J. Hamill to Mathew Brooke, February 10, 1810.
[36] *Ibid.,* Justin Smith to Mathew Brooke, January 13, 1810.
[37] HV 8321216, F. Linderman to Clement Brooke.
[38] HV 8120301, Daniel Buckley to Mathew Brooke.
[39] SM 2, p. 101; SM 31, p. 123.

the middle of the century the services of an employment agency were used to find maids. There were several fees of 25¢ to $1 paid to the Intelligence Office in Philadelphia for securing girls to work at Hopewell. Railroad fare for their passage to Douglassville was an additional expense. Once Mrs. Clingan went to Philadelphia to bring her new maid back, and on another occasion her sister Mrs. William R. White put the girl on the coach and paid her fare.[40]

Workers were given some inducements to take employment at the Furnace; the most common ones found were advancements to pay debts and provide housing for the new employee. Samuel Steel offered his services on the condition that the company would "let him have twenty-five dollars to pay some debts."[41] The employer sometimes lost on this kind of a deal. In 1847 the Furnace advanced Julia Garey $5 for housework she promised to do, but she did not do the work and returned only $1 of the advancement.[42] Daniel Buckley wrote to Mathew Brooke about the necessity to provide a workman with a house as a condition of employment:

John Funk, the father of Abraham who you have agreed with, has an Inclination to moove into your part of the country, if he can be provided with a house. Should it be convenient for you to let him have one, you will find him and his family Industrious sober and Honest people, and if it was in my power to furnish him with a house that would suit him I would be much Pleased if he would remain in this part of the Country.[43]

The Furnace often gave assistance to the new employee by providing a wagon to move his household goods. Usually the cost was charged to the worker's account, but there were cases in which moving costs were paid by the Furnace as a condition of employment.[44] The usual charges were $2 to $4 for

[40] SM 31, pp. 91, 122, 139, 147, 156.
[41] HV 8400227, Charles Brooke, Junior, to Clement Brooke.
[42] SM 31, p. 46.
[43] HV 8201230A.
[44] Examples are SM 32, pp. 26, 40 and SM 7, April 5, 1817, n. p.

moving from a nearby community. But in 1849 the Furnace must have been recruiting workers at a distance; for William Ellet was paid $25 "to bring his Family," and James Walls drew $50.50 cash for the same reason.[45]

A final kind of attraction for workers to take employment at a furnace was the opportunity which existed there for an ambitious man to rise in power and riches. Many ironmasters began as common laborers at a furnace.[46] Harker Long came to Hopewell as a messenger and office boy and remained to become Furnace manager.[47] Thomas Foster came as teacher and became the company clerk.[48] John Benson began as a miner, advanced to clerk at Hopewell and left in 1835 to become manager of the Oak Grove Furnace in Perry County at a salary of $1200 per year.[49] Two of Joseph Whitaker's sons began to work as laborers at Hopewell and went on to found the Wheeling Steel Company and earn large fortunes.[50]

Clement Brooke gave encouragement and help to at least one of his employees to leave for a better job, as this letter of recommendation proves:

> The Bearer of this is John Care who has Moulded at this place and done other work at the Furnace from his Boy hood up to the Present time he is Anxious to be imployed by you as Founder at the Furnace you intend Building in Maryland the ensuing Summer. his father Thomas Care has Blowed Hopewell for the last twenty years lately his son Henry has taken his place, I can Safely Recomend John as Capable of Blowing Furnace — is otherwise Sober Moral and upright in his Conduct in Case you and him agree his Father Says he would be willing to assist his Son at your Furnace as long as his Services Should be thought Necessary.[51]

For all the advantages of furnace employment it still re-

[45] SM 31, p. 104.
[46] Bining, "Iron Plantations," *op. cit.,* p. 20.
[47] *Reading Eagle,* February 11, 1917.
[48] HV 8361207A.
[49] HV 8351216.
[50] Kurjack, "Joseph Whitaker," *op. cit.*
[51] HV 8360000B.

mained true that life in the isolated villages was not very lively, the work was hard, and the hours were long. It was difficult to secure workers and often more difficult to retain them, especially those in the lower-paid categories. Housemaids, guttermen and fillers were hard to keep, and turnover was especially high in these jobs. Many different people worked as woodcutters, also, but these were largely local and part-time workers. The city girls who came to work at the Big House in the Clingan era were of especially short tenure. They probably found the forest setting too different from their city ways.

But judging from the following note, incentive pay was used successfully to hold employees:

> Hired this day Henry Henry to do our smithing for one year from the time he is free we are to give him $19.00 per month and if he does his work well we are to give him a pair of coarse boots.[52]

The next year the contract was renewed, and the boots were to be given with no condition imposed.[53] He must have done his work well.

---

[52] *Kemper Manuscripts,* Charles M. Clingan Pocket Note Book, *op. cit.,* March 13, 1858, n. p.
[53] *Ibid.,* February 18, 1859.

Part Six

The Social Village

14 The Worker and His Associates

THE ECONOMIC CENTER FOR THE COMMUNITY DEPENDING UPON Hopewell Furnace for its industrial income was the company office and store. No similar social center existed for the families of the scattered Hopewell employees. Their associations tended to converge in several rather distinct social groups.

The residents near the furnace did much of their buying at the company store, attended the Bethesda Baptist Church, sent their children to the tutors engaged by the ironmaster and later to the Hopewell schoolhouse, and looked to Birdsboro and Douglassville for their wider community associations. The Pine Swamp dwellers and miners at the Warwick Mines traded at the stores in Warwick, attended the St. Mary's Episcopal Church and sent their children to Lewis Evans' school. The Jones Mine families went to Morgantown to trade at the Morris and Morgan stores; to attend the Episcopal, Methodist or Presbyterian churches; and to enroll their children in the village school. Another group of workers gravitated toward Geigertown. The colored residents of this area built an African Methodist Church, about three miles from the furnace, in 1856.

Community orientation was not this simple, however, for

there were many exceptions. Some Furnace-area people preferred an Episcopal service to the Baptist and, therefore, held membership in a church in Warwick or Douglassville. The Furnace store did not carry sufficient stock to supply all needs, and orders were sent to other stores. Credit established at the company store and ore wagons making regular trips between the furnace and mines made it convenient for mine families to buy goods at Hopewell. Pine Swamp boys crossed the mountain to court girls who lived near the furnace. Workers became acquainted on their jobs, and it was natural for some of their families to form friendships. Members of the same families lived and worked in each of the centers and visited in each others' homes. Then the annual Christmas and New Year's Day parties at the Big House brought together all of the families of employees.[1]

In a sense, then, the Hopewell community had several centers of social life within the general area encompassed by the Furnace business activities. Intermarriage among the families created many family ties in the village. There were both close friendships and animosities. The necessities of rural life developed many interrelationships among the workers and their families: They helped each other in time of need, cooperated on large projects, provided for the necessities of life, sold each other goods and services, occasionally stole from each other, got into fights, took their differences to court and gave aid and comfort to the sick and bereaved.

Hopewell Furnace provided no retirement plan, no health or accident insurance and no unemployment compensation for its workers. These hazards of life were the responsibility of the individual and his family, but in some cases the community or neighborhood provided a kind of welfare program for the unfortunate residents. One rather common means of giving aid was to pass around a "subscription paper" upon which those who desired to do so could pledge to contribute a specified sum to the person whose name appeared at the

[1] These interrelationships will be discussed in subsequent chapters.

top. This paper was then sent to the clerk who debited the accounts of all the donors and credited the account of the recipient. The amounts were not large, and the number of signers indicated that only close friends or immediate neighbors were solicited. Clement Brooke was always among those who gave during his time as manager, but he did not contribute noticeably larger amounts than some of his employees. On several such collections he gave $1, the same amount as one or more of the others.[2] In 1848 he gave $5 on one such collection.[3] John Church contributed one dollar out of his clerk's pay to a collection for James McCormick in 1845; but he was matched by James Mock, and Enoch Squibb gave half as much.[4]

Another kind of help came in the form of mutual aid to a fellow. For example in 1805 Peter Cox and John Boyers each took off one half day, and lost their pay for that time, to go "to John Hart's choping in the Afternoon." Cox was also credited, along with his son Samuel, for helping with "Richards moving" in the same year—an act of charity which cost each of them a day's pay.[5] Such assistance was not altogether in the spirit of altruism, however; for these events were made social occasions, and whiskey was supplied to all who came.

Widows were often left with little or no inheritance from their husbands to provide for themselves and their children. The Furnace record books contain many entries of goods delivered to a widow and paid for by someone else. The clerk did not usually distinguish between gifts and payments for goods or services; so it is not possible to know whether these were examples of welfare or of business transactions. The Furnace made payment in 1806 for goods ordered from Samuel Laverty and Company for "Widow Kephart."[6] In 1819 John

[2] For example see SM 10, p. 30.
[3] SM 31, p. 69.
[4] SM 28, p. 153.
[5] SM 1, pp. 73, 74, 76.
[6] SM 4, p. 114.

Anderson paid for "one quarter of flour for Widow Adams,"[7] and Founder Thomas Care gave a verbal order at the store for "the Widow Roger" to receive the following goods:

10 yards Calico	@	2/6
15 yards Cotton Plaid	@	2/6
2 lb Coffee	@	.37
2 lb Sugar	@	.18
Total		$9.43[8]

Funeral expenses were another form of welfare contribution. Clement Brooke paid the carpenter $8 "for Mrs. Hudson coffin." Before her death he had bought some coffee for her.[9]

Partnerships of several kinds existed among the workers. David Hughs and George Painter made a joint purchase of a barrel of mackerel at $7.50 and divided the fish between them.[10] They saved a little money over the cost of each buying what he needed separately. In 1817 David Hughs, Samuel Richard and Montgomery Hughs operated an equal partnership known as David Hughs and Company to carry on coaling operations for the Furnace. In January of that year each was paid $279.48 as his share of what had been earned.[11] Two decades later Jacob and Peter Hartenstine were listed as partners, but the nature of their enterprise was not given.[12]

Because no one was paid wages and the clerk or manager was not always available to make a cash payment against credit on the company books, employees sometimes found themselves in need of coins or currency; so they borrowed from a friend or acquaintance. Most of these transactions doubtless took place with no notice in the business records, but there were times when the repayment involved a journal entry. George Painter took a note from Jacob Wolf when he lent him £5 9s. in 1809. Both of them had been casual workers for

[7] SM 9, p. 144.
[8] *Ibid.,* p. 172.
[9] SM 17, p. 9; SM 9, p. 81.
[10] SM 14, p. 60. This was in 1829.
[11] SM 7, January 18, 1817, n. p.
[12] SM 21, p. 164.

the Furnace.[13] In 1827 Joseph McKewen received $2 from the wages of David Hart to repay a loan which had run for some time without payment.[14] John Sheeler repaid a loan of 25¢ made by his son William from Thomas Forster.[15]

Private homes served the purposes now assumed by some commercial establishments or institutions, as can be seen by the following bill paid by Isaac Hughes to David Hughes:

```
1 Year, 8 mo. 12 days washing and
                     mending          @   .75    15.33
             8  „  29  „   boarding    @  $5.00   44.82
For making 4 shirts                    @   .25     1.00
  „     „    4 pairs pantaloons        @   .25     1.00
  „     „    1 jacket                                .25
  „   footing 2 pairs stockings                     .50
  „   soaling 1 pair shoes                          .50
  „   Attendance when laying sick at my house      5.00[16]
```

Protecting the interests of orphans in their inheritance was another kind of service performed by neighbors. The same Isaac Hughes mentioned above had received money the previous year from George Lloyd, administrator of the estate of Mary Hughes. Lloyd had had a trustee appointed for Isaac at a legal cost of $28.50. Two payments in cash to the heir amounted to $185.00.[17] The settlement of an estate sometimes involved holding a public sale of the assets of the deceased, and the Furnace records became involved by paying for purchases by workers or by the Furnace.[18]

The Hopewell community provided many services for its residents by means of work performed for one another. A wide variety of skilled workmen were available in the neighborhood of whom some worked for the Furnace, and some were occupied full time at their trades. The journal for a few

[13] SM 4, pp. 245, 249, 253.
[14] SM 59, p. 24.
[15] SM 28, p. 84. The date was in 1842.
[16] SM 12, p. 146. This was paid in 1826.
[17] SM 12, p. 86.
[18] For example see SM 28, p. 93.

months in 1830 showed that the following men received pay for the vocation indicated : William McKinty, tailor; Robert Gilmore, weaver; Abraham Dehaven, furniture maker; David Rogers, shoemaker; John Seabold, tailor; Henry Shick, weaver; Henry McKinty, tailor; Joseph Whitaker, weaver; Thomas Kirkpatrick, furniture maker; Thomas Lambert, shoemaker; Jacob Hartenstine, shoemaker; James Everhart, tanner; Samuel Haws, tailor; David Smith, shoemaker; Henry Landis, weaver; Andrew McMichael, shoemaker; George Goheen, shoemaker; Christian Rice, weaver; George Wert, tailor; Samuel Whitman, shoemaker; William Patton, wagonmaker; Jesse Kineday, shoemaker and Thomas Lloyd, shoemaker.[19] It is evident that shoemakers, tailors and weavers were in demand in this period when relatively little ready-made clothing was available. Secondhand clothing was sometimes sold in private transactions between villagers.[20]

A man with a horse and plow could earn some money in the spring by plowing the garden plots of his neighbors. In 1849 Isaac Cadwalader and Sam Wamsher were both plowing gardens and were paid for each plot from 50¢ to $2.50.[21] Gardens also entered into the relationships among families when excess products were sold to neighbors. Potatoes, cabbage, turnips and beets were mentioned among such sales.[22] Orchards, too, produced a surplus of apples and cider to be sold.[23]

As the following note to the clerk demonstrated, trust of one neighbor for another existed to a remarkable degree :

> Please to Let John Himes have goods to any Amount that May Suit him and return to me the Amount. Thos. Lloyd.[24]

There were many similar notes preserved in the store records

[19] From SM 19, *passim*.
[20] SM 14, p. 64 and SM 21, p. 168.
[21] SM 31, p. 99 and SM 32, p. 60.
[22] SM 21, p. 137; SM 21, p. 2.
[23] SM 14, p. 53.
[24] *Hopewell Papers,* uncatalogued, May 22, 1824.

with the exception that most of them specified a limit to the guarantee extended.

It was not unusual that among so many people the spirit of honesty and amity would not always prevail. A charge of $8.55 was made against the account of David Hart with this explanation, "for $\frac{1}{2}$ ton hay fed of William Thomas. W. Thomas got $\frac{1}{2}$ ton of our hay that was at John Richards in Lieu of his $\frac{1}{2}$ ton fed by you."[25] Most disputes among people of the village were doubtless settled by those involved or by the mediation of the ironmaster, but sometimes they went to law. Three kinds of lawsuits predominated among those recorded in the Furnace books as involving workers. Storekeepers brought suit to secure payment of overdue bills.[26] Worker sued worker in numerous actions of which the only cause recorded in the journals was for debt and costs.[27] Among the suits for which no reason was given doubtlessly some were for damages or trespass. Other frequent suits resulted from charges brought by constables—possibly the aftermath of fights or violations of the law.[28]

One of the greatest needs for social interdependence was the care of the ill, the injured and the dead. No reference to hospital care was found in the Hopewell Furnace records. Each family had most of the responsibility for providing for the incapacitated and incompetent, but the community assumed a share of the work when there was no family to provide the sick room care. John Roberts died in 1843 at the age of 86 or 87 years after his last days had been eased by neighborhood attention, given under difficult circumstances. James Morris reported :

His habits and manner of living, which were filthy in the extreme, precluded that attendance upon his last days and hours, which would otherwise have been given. Nevertheless,

[25] SM 7, November 1, 1817, n. p.
[26] Examples are SM 4, p. 92 and SM 7, November 25, 1817, n. p.
[27] See SM 28, p. 82; SM 9, p. 15; SM 4, pp. 59, 125; SM 44, August 9, 1806, n. p.
[28] SM 44, August 9, 1806, n. p. and SM 10, pp. 38, 40, 41, 46.

he was not left to suffer alone and unaided and unattended. The neighborhood, amongst whom Miss Ann Clymer was the most kind and attentive, rendered every assistance that could, under the circumstances, be given.[29]

Those who could afford to pay for help did not depend entirely on charitable impulses but still drew upon the community for the assistance they needed, as can be seen in this letter :

> I am concerned about Mother I could wish you to have every attention paid her and if her feet have got no better you must procure some person to wait on her perhaps one of Brother Thomas' Daughters could be had. Anne Davis is of the same oppinion. Say she should not be left alone. No expence should be spared.[30]

In the absence of expert medical diagnosis the determination of the nature of illnesses was lacking in thorough credibility. The lay opinions of the community, however, listed a wide variety of ailments. The yellow fever epidemic of 1798 may not have reached so far west as Hopewell, but it did hit customers of the Furnace products. A letter from Wilmington, Delaware asked that no more iron be sent and requested an extension of time on payments because :

> . . . our little place exhibits a melancholy appearance the yellow fever or some fever which brings great mortality sweeping away our citizens—it appears likely 8 or 10 are or will be buried this day . . . the Tobacconists we believe are all gone as are great part of the inhabitants—and it is likely three or four days will have the place almost desolate . . .[31]

Children's diseases were accepted with a degree of fatalism which in the following instance seems almost callous :

[29] *Morris Diary, op. cit.,* II, p. 74.
[30] *Brooke Family Papers,* George Brooke to Mathew Brooke, no date except 1805.
[31] *Ibid.,* Ferris and Gilpin to Mathew Brooke, September 20, 1798.

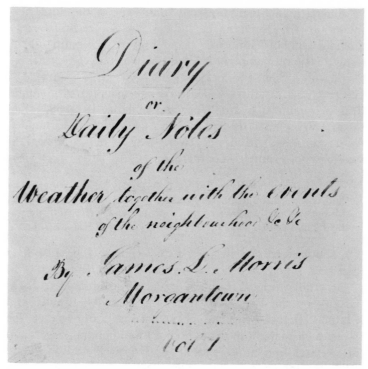

Title Page of the Diary of James Morris, Storekeeper in Morgantown

The dysentery has been prevailing, to some extent, throughout the neighborhood for a few weeks past, but as it has confined itself to children it has as yet excited little alarm. Two children have died of it within the week.[32]

As the writer was a sensitive man with children of his own, he was probably only reflecting the general reaction to childhood diseases. Fatalities among children were noted from typhus, scarlet fever, measles, and "putrid sore throat." Other common childhood diseases were rash, "Bilious pleurisy," whooping cough and "cholera infantum."[33]

[32] *Morris Diary, op. cit.,* September 30, 1843, p. 69.
[33] *Ibid., passim.*

Among adults many suffered from some of the same sicknesses as the children, but other illnesses recorded were "bilious typhoid," influenza, "consumption or bleeding at the lungs," "bowel complaints," "violent pains in the stomach," "sick with a Bile" and lockjaw.[34]

Preventive measures which were taken indicated common fear of smallpox, hydrophobia and malaria. In 1838 James Morris wrote that he had had his son William vaccinated with cow pox.[35] Mad dogs were feared and destroyed, if possible. For example note this case :

> A great hubbub raised in town yesterday by the appearance and transit through of a mad dog. A great crowd armed with bludgeons etc. followed him, but he was protected by his drunken master. . . .[36]

On another occasion five or six dogs were shot because they had been bitten by a dog suspected of being mad.[37]

According to local tradition, malaria was brought to Berks County by the Irish workers on the Schuylkill Canal, and Mathew Brooke was one of its victims. Support for the presence of malaria in the period of canal building was found in the large number of sales at the Hopewell store in 1825–1826 of quinine pills, "Peruvian bark," "yellow bark" and "barks."[38]

Accidents were the causes of disabilities and deaths of many Furnace workers. The Changewater Furnace books listed time lost by laborers for such reasons as "foot cut," "finger cut," "sore foot," "kicked by horse," "Burnt his shoulder badly" and "Fell against wagon and hurt shoulder." One man was killed when the bank wall collapsed and fell on him.[39] Fillers suffered many burns and injuries to hands, feet

[34] *Ibid.;* SM 46, p. 38.
[35] *Morris Diary, op. cit.,* p. 53.
[36] *Ibid.,* p. 71.
[37] *Ibid.,* p. 47.
[38] SM 12, pp. 17, 89, 93, *Hopewell Papers,* Receipt from Joseph Reakert, date destroyed except 1825.
[39] *Changewater Furnace Time Book, op. cit.,* pp. 2–46.

and backs. Broken bones and cuts caused loss of time.[40] Harriet Finger died when her clothing caught fire and "burned off her back."[41]

Travel accidents also caused injury and death to some men of the village. Clement Brooke had expenses of $63 to pay doctor bills and tavern expenses "when laying at Reading Hurt by the upsetting of the Stage some time ago."[42] Samuel Yocum was killed by being "Crushed to death between two cars on the railroad," and Robert Wynn "drowned in the Canal."[43]

The census records showed that many persons suffering from mental diseases were kept in their homes. In 1860 one household in Caernarvon Township was listed as consisting of :

Margaret Wilson	age 49	Housekeeper[44]
Ann Irions	age 73	Insane
Jane Irions	age 47	Idiot
Samuel Irions	age 42	Idiot

Medical help was available to the people of the community from doctors in the nearby towns who were consulted in their offices or who would come to the homes. Like so many other people who worked for the villagers, the doctor received his pay from the Furnace. Occasionally he would take part of his fee in storegoods or iron instead of cash. Perhaps the Hopewell people got more medical service than was customary among rural people because the doctor was more sure of payment, and collection was easy. The Furnace books show many instances of doctors having been paid sizeable sums which were taken from the accounts of workers. The doctor often treated a number of patients on the same trip to the

[40] *Birdsborough Forge Time Book, op. cit.,* pp. 27, 33.

[41] *Morris Diary, op. cit.,* II, p. 12.

[42] *Hopewell Papers.* Memorandum of Expenses. Undated but probably in the 1840's.

[43] St. Gabriel's Episcopal Church, record of burials, March 28, 1847, and November 8, 1861. Berks County Historical Society.

[44] *United States Census of 1860,* Berks County, p. 152.

Furnace. The doctor sometimes performed services that were not medical in nature, as demonstrated by Doctor Isaac L. Vansant who delivered an order of store goods when he came to a woodcutter's home.[45]

Dr. Vansant was not the only doctor listed as receiving payments in 1817 and 1818, and in subsequent years the names of many doctors were listed on the Furnace books: Doctor Jacob Leaser in 1818 and 1819, Doctor James B. Chevington and "Doctor Mitchner" in 1819–1842, "Doctor Evans" in 1821, Doctor Robert May in 1826–1851, Doctor William Happersett in 1826–1829, Doctor David E. Gordon in 1838, Doctor H. Weiman in 1841–1847, "Doctor Meredith" in 1847, "Doctor Jones" in 1848-1849, "Doctor Gross" in 1847 and Doctor Levi Rooke in 1849-1851.[46] The fee most frequently paid was $2, but there were some for $1 and many for higher amounts. The clerk often noted that the payment was for "medicine and attendance."[47] A member of the Clement Brooke family must have undergone surgery in the 1830's, for a receipt from Doctor Joseph Parrish of Philadelphia acknowledged payment of $35 "for Medical and Surgical Services to this date."[48] The only instance found of a payment for nursing service was $2 "paid a Nurse" by John Hoofman in 1850.[49]

Probably the doctor was called only when serious illness was suspected. Patent medicines and home remedies were used for lesser ailments. In addition to malaria cures and many entries for undifferentiated "medicine," the store carried or ordered from Philadelphia many patent medicines and cures for a variety of ills: Epsom salts, calomel, worm oil and worm syrup, "physicks" and "pukes," quick silver and brimstone, "worm tea," paregoric, castor oil, "Ear Oil and

---

[45] SM 9, p. 44.
[46] From the Journals of the dates listed. Some first names were not given by the clerks.
[47] For example see SM 21, p. 97.
[48] HV 8350110.
[49] SM 31, p. 126.

syringe," "embrocation lotion," eye salve, salve, "bolsom of wild cherry," vermifuge for worms, "worm medicine," "asso-foldida" and carminative for gas pains.[50]

The villagers seemed to have been much troubled by worms. A bottle obtained in an archeological dig at the site of the Big House privy had this legend: "Bumstead's Worm Syrup— . —One Bottle has killed 100 worms— . —Children cry for more— . —Just Try It— . —Philada."[51]

The Eli Keen Store at Warwick sold Indian Vegetable Pills, essence of Peppermint, camphor, Swains Vermifuge, saleratus, Scots Pills and tooth powder.[52] Another neighboring storekeeper wrote of the changing demands of his customers for medicines:

> Purchased some "Wright Indian Vegetable Pills," have been keeping them for sale this Year past. They have nearly superseded "Brandreth's," which were all the rage a few years since. Before them I sold the "Dutch," "Keyser," or "Blood Pills,"—they succeeded the "Lees Antibilious" and years ago the "Scots" or "Andderson's" were almost the only ones in use.[53]

Jeremiah Dougherty, Elizabeth Mervine, Henry Care, Levi Care and Clement Brooke bought eye glasses at a cost which increased from 50¢ in 1816 to $3.50 in 1825.[54] Mrs. Mervine was a seamstress for many Hopewell families, and Clement Brooke and Henry Care subscribed to newspapers; so it is possible that these people used their eyes in ways which required the aid of lenses. Samuel Williams and Samuel Witman apparently suffered from hernias as they purchased trusses at prices ranging from 75¢ to $2.50.[55]

[50] From the Journals for many years of store operation.
[51] Leland J. Abel, "Excavation of a Privy at the Ironmaster's House, Hopewell Village, 1962" (unpublished manuscript, 1962). Hopewell Village Library.
[52] *Eli Keen Store Book, op. cit.,* 1844–1845.
[53] *Morris Diary, op.* cit., p. 210. This was in 1842.
[54] SM 8, p. 52; SM 12, p. 45; SM 28, p. 80; SM 31, pp. 54, 66.
[55] *Cash Book* for 1828–1830, *op. cit.,* March 8, 1830, n. p.; SM 31, pp. 16, 112.

Doctors had their problems of diagnosis and treatment in an age when diagnostic aids were few and laboratories nonexistent. A trip to the seashore, perhaps to Cape May, was considered a possible cure; but it did not always bring results.[56] If the doctor knew the cause of a sickness he was treating, he often failed to enlighten the family. Daniel Buckley showed his anxiety in the following letter :

> Sally still continues confined to her room is some better and other times worse but I think gets weaker. I am much at a loss to know whether she will recover or not as the season is now so Inclement that she cannot be Expected to leave the room, and it [is] the doctors particular directions that [she] use no Exercise whatever, and be most particular in her diet, which we find Extremely difficult, what she may take that does not make her worse.[57]

On the other hand some persons untrained in medicine were quite sure of the cure for other people's illnesses. Daniel Buckley wrote to Mathew Brooke, ". . . you ought to take physick as I am told you have a head ach, it proceeds from a disordered stomach. . . . "[58] Castor oil was regarded as a cure for many of life's troubles, and wild turnips were also used by Hopewell people as a cathartic. An area near the lake was known as the "turnip patch" because this herb grew there in such profusion.[59]

Hex doctors or powwow cures also were available in the community. A farmer claimed to be able to stop hemorrhage from a wound by smearing three wooden wedges with the blood and then driving the wedges into some place where they would remain dry. He also claimed to be able to stop bleeding "by saying some words," and did not even need "to see the person or animal bleeding."[60]

[56] *Brooke Family Papers,* Daniel Buckley to Clement Brooke, August 24, 1821.
[57] HV 8201230. Daniel Buckley to Mathew Brooke.
[58] HV 8080223.
[59] Interview with Albert Painter, January 16, 1956.
[60] *Morris Diary, op. cit.,* II, p. 169.

Ann F. Brooke included some health hints in her letters to her brother George while he was attending West Chester Academy in 1832–1833 :

> I am glad you go to the gymnasium it will be such good exercise for your limbs . . . do . . . not eat much meat — it makes you dull — only take a little ham to strengthen you.[61]

> . . . do not eat much fruit before going to bathe, I believe you often get fruit on your way to the creek, you had better eat it after bathing — the cholera is expected again this summer by almost every one — you particularly ought to avoid the hot sun and eating immoderately of any thing which disagrees with you — you know — in warm weather you are subject to spells of choleramorbus.[62]

> It is well you had your teeth examined by the dentist . . . all you have to do to preserve them is to brush them every morning with water, use no tooth powder.[63]

Sanitation was probably not regarded as a major problem for the Furnace, but there were some provisions made. Homemade soap was boiled for the Furnace[64] and perhaps was used at the catch basin where running water gave the workmen a chance to wash their hands on the way to the dining room in the basement of the mansion.[65] Since Alexander McCarraher was paid $3 for "mason work at Bath house,"[66] it is apparent that provision was made for bathing somewhere in the Furnace area. Close by the office-store was a privy used by the workers in and near the Furnace.[67] Control of pests was attempted by the use of rat poison, roach poison, fly poison and mouse traps.[68]

[61] *Brooke Family Papers,* April 15, 1833.
[62] *Ibid.,* May 1833.
[63] *Ibid.,* February 29, 1832.
[64] SM 28, p. 148.
[65] Interview with Mrs. Sally Boone, March 22, 1941.
[66] SM 21, p. 35.
[67] Earl J. Heydinger, "Orientation Report for Archeology in Lower Working Level at Hopewell Village NHS" (unpublished report, 1962). Hopewell Village Library.
[68] SM 28, p. 124; SM 31, p. 115; SM 65, August 14, 1858, n. p.

Some of the men at the Furnace evidently were vain or interested in good grooming; for in the bottles recovered from the mansion privy were several marked "Batchelor's Liquid Hair Dye No. 1," "Boyle's Electric Hair Dye, Boston, No. 2" and "Bear's Oil."[69]

The final service rendered to its members by any community was to provide a decent burial. The workers at Hopewell were usually laid to rest in a plain wooden box made by the carpenter or cabinetmaker. The normal expenses were $2 for digging the grave and $8 to $10 for a coffin. For a child these prices were 75¢ and $2 respectively. The costs were usually paid from the estate of the deceased or by a member of the family,[70] but in at least one instance the Furnace paid for the coffin of the wife of one of the workmen.[71]

In a few cases the records show a more elaborate preparation for burial. Patrick Clemens sent an order to the store saying:

> . . . please to Let the Bearer have the things [several words unreadable] musling for winding Sheet and Shraud two pound of Cofy two pound Shuger one yard of Black Crape one pair Black Stockings one paire of Black Gloves.[72]

A funeral director's charges were included for the funeral of Samuel Downing in 1821 when these expenses were incurred:

> . . . Clothes for Saml Downing Jr minor to attend his
> fathers funeral $18.79
> For the Coffin, David Finger   12.00
> For digging the grave, John Gordon   1.50
> For the funeral, Robt. Laverty   30.00[73]

Deaths in the wealthy Clingan family brought greater expenses. The funeral of Sarah Clingan, mother of Ironmaster

---

[69] Abel, *op. cit.*
[70] SM 31, pp. 8, 37, 55; SM 28, pp. 42, 72, 179; SM 65, p. 5.
[71] SM 2, p. 28. This was in 1802.
[72] HV 8260910.
[73] *Lewis Evans Ledger, op. cit.*, p. 173.

Charles M. Clingan, cost $229.75. This charge included $108 for the casket and furnishings; and the remainder was for attendants, grave digger, carriers, hire of hearse and carriages, flowers, ribbon for the door and use of the ice cooler. Later other payments were made, including $150 for a grave stone and $25 to the minister.[74] For Dr. Clingan, himself, the funeral cost $422.12, including $125 for 25 carriages and $226.40 for the coffin and case.[75]

Hopewell Village found many ways and reasons for co-operation among its residents. Like most rural communities of the nineteenth century, it would have had difficulty surviving without much mutual interaction within its group.

[74] HV 8720109 and HV 8750208A.
[75] HV 8750510.

15 The Colored Population

NEGRO WORKERS WERE A PART OF HOPEWELL VILLAGE during the entire history of the Furnace operation. A survey of the records provided a list of 107 Negroes employed by the Furnace, but this number was not necessarily complete. The clerk noted beside some names in his ledgers the words "colored man," "negro," "black man" or "a man of color." From other sources some persons were known to have been Negroes, but not all of these were identified as such in the ledgers. For example Ben Hill was placed on the list because his estate was assigned to Wilkinson Hill who was colored. Since Ben was not designated as Negro by the clerk, possibly others were similarly missed. Some persons were listed because they were called by such names at "Negro Bendigo," "Black Frank," "Black Boy," "Black Cook" or "Little Negro." Duplication was possible because some of these later acquired last names, as "Black Bill" and "Black William" became William Jacobs. These repetitions were eliminated when it was definite that the same person was intended, but both names were included when doubt remained. Whatever the exact total should be, Negroes formed a respectable proportion of the entire work force.

Hopewell Furnace was in no way unique in its employment of Negroes, for the iron industry used many colored workers in both the North and the South. Slave-owners of the South sometimes collected wages of $200 per year for permitting an ironmaster to use a slave.[1] A British traveler in 1796 reported that "all the furnaces and forges in Maryland were worked by blacks."[2] Israel Acrelius observed many Negro slaves working at the Pennsylvania furnaces during his travels in the 1750's. He thought they were better treated here than anywhere else in America.[3]

Cornwall Furnace had about 24 slaves when Pennsylvania abolished slavery in 1780. Some of these were house servants; but others were listed as furnace men, wood cutters and colliers.[4] At the same time George Ege owned 10 slaves at Charming Forge.[5]

No positive proof was found that slaves were used at Hope-- well, but the records were clear that Mark Bird possessed slaves during the time he was the owner of the Furnace. When slaves were registered according to the Pennsylvania act of emancipation, Mark Bird was the largest slave-owner in Berks County. He listed 10 adult males, 4 adult females, 3 boys and 1 girl.[6] Several times he advertised for runaway slaves. Cuff Dix, a skilled hammerman, escaped in 1774 and again in 1775; in the latter year he was apprehended in Delaware but disappeared from the New Castle jail before he could be returned to Bird.[7] Another escapee was a man of accomplishments, judging from the description given in the advertisement in which a $200 reward was offered for the return of:

[1] Cheesman A. Herrick, *History of Commerce and Industry* (New York: The Macmillan Company, 1918), p. 492.
[2] Victor A. Clark, *History of Manufactures in the United States,* 1607–1860 (Volume I; New York: Peter Smith, 1949), p. 399.
[3] *Allen's Appeal Record, op. cit.,* p. 131.
[4] Hiram H. Shenk, *A History of the Lebanon Valley in Pennsylvania* (Harrisburg: The National Historical Association, 1930), p. 298.
[5] Montgomery, *History of Berks County, op. cit.,* p. 93.
[6] Paul N. Shaeffer, "Slavery in Berks County," *The Historical Review of Berks County,* VI, 4 (July 1941), p. 112.
[7] *Pennsylvania Gazette,* December 7, 1774, June 7, 1775, October 11, 1775, October 16, 1775. The name "Cuff" was used for slaves who were troublemakers.

. . . A Negroe man named Jack, about 30 years of age . . . he plays on the violin and other instruments of music, speaks the English and French languages . . . he is a cunning designing fellow, and it is likely he may forge a pass, and travel the country as a freeman.[8]

As shown by a bill of sale, at least one of Mark Bird's slaves was sold in his bankruptcy on July 9, 1787:

Know all men by these Presents that I Peter Filbert, Esquire Sheriff of Berks County. In consideration of the sum of thirty-three pounds in [one word unreadable] to me in hand paid by William Hays . . . Have sold . . . unto the said William Hays: A certain female negro slave named Matty. Aged nine years, or thereabouts; late the property of Mark Bird, Esq., seized and taken in execution by me at the suit of John Bishop. . . .[9]

Hays wrote in his will that Mattie was to be freed when she was twenty-two years old, but she was only sixteen when he died. Her remaining time was sold to James Biddle of Philadelphia for $60.[10]

Slavery declined rapidly in Berks County after 1780. The Census of 1800 showed only 19 slaves in the county, and of these only one was in Union Township where Hopewell Furnace was located.[11] At the same time East Nantmeal Township, nearest area of Chester County, had no slaves.[12] Caernarvon Township in Berks County listed 3 slaves and West Nantmeal in Chester County 2 in the Census of 1820.[13]

The wooded area of Southeastern Pennsylvania gained a reputation as a refuge for slaves escaping from the South. George Washington wrote to a friend on November 20, 1786, that it was almost impossible to recover a Negro who made his way to this area because there were so many people who

---

[8] *Ibid.*, November 24, 1779.
[9] *Louis Richards Collection*, Berks County Historical Society.
[10] *Ibid.*
[11] *United States Census for 1800.* Berks County, p. 694.
[12] *Ibid.*, Chester County.
[13] *Census of 1820.*

would "facilitate the escape."[14] Elizabeth Pownall Scarlett
gave shelter to escaping slaves at her home "The Forest" near
Scarlett's Mill, a short distance from Hopewell, from 1826 to
1839. After her death her son Joseph and son-in-law Thomas
Lewis continued the work for several more years.[15]

Hopewell's neighbor, Joanna Furnace, was reported to have
given shelter and work to escaping slaves. The forested hills
and the remote huts of the colliers and wood cutters made
ideal hiding places until the search ended and it was safe to
move on north. While they were hiding, the Negroes could
earn their food and some money.[16]

Were the Negroes who worked at Hopewell escaped
slaves? Many of them were residents of the area over a long
period of time, and several generations of some families
worked at the Furnace. These may have been the descendants
of slaves freed by Pennsylvania law. On the other hand there
were circumstances which indicate that Negroes from the
South worked here. Most of the 107 names collected from the
Hopewell books appeared very briefly, often only one entry, to
suggest the possibility of persons passing through. The census
for the townships near the Furnace showed a small Negro
population for every counting from 1800 to 1870, and those
mentioned by names as fairly permanent residents seldom
matched the names on the Furnace books. The totals of non-
whites in Union Township for 1810 was 4, for 1820—7, for
1830—39, for 1840—8, for 1850—31, for 1860—62, for
1870—40.[17] The fluctuation and increase in the later years
disclosed that Negroes were coming into the area at the time
of abolition agitation.

In 1850 the census began to report the place of birth of all

[14] Wayne Homan, "The Underground Railroad," *The Historical
Review of Berks County*, XXIII, 4 (Fall 1958), p. 112.

[15] John E. Eshelman, "Berks County's Station on The Underground
Railroad," *The Historical Review of Berks County*, VI, 4 (July 1941)
p. 107–109.

[16] Wayne Homan, "Pennsylvania Heritage, Our Refuge for Runaway
Slaves," *Sunday Today, The Philadelphia Inquirer*, September 24, 1961,
p. 26.

[17] Census Reports for the years given.

persons and listed all Furnace-area Negroes as born in Pennsylvania except one in Delaware, a slave area, and two "unknown."[18] The next census recorded no Union Township colored persons as having been born out of Pennsylvania.[19] In 1870 it was reported that Samuel Curtis, Robert Miller and James Miller had been born in Virginia and Isaac Cole and Charles Ruth in Maryland.[20] Of these Isaac Cole had stated in 1860 that Pennsylvania was his place of birth.

The Hopewell books and papers were unrevealing about the source of its colored laborers. The only indication of anti-slavery feeling by the management was the discovery among the Furnace papers of a pamphlet with the names of Iron-master Clement Brooke and Clerk John Church on the flyleaf. The contents and viewpoint were revealed in this brief quotation :

> Let then every Christian minister, and every religious associ-ation, and each individual member of a religious society endeavor to eradicate the stain of slavery from our land, by the effectual operation of the lenient principles of Christianity . . . let the fiat of universal emancipation be issued from every Conference, Synod, and General Assembly throughout the Country. . . .[21]

But Abolition sentiment was not universal in Berks County. James Morris noted that a Presbyterian minister named McKim had delivered Abolition addresses at the Harmony Meeting House on March 11 and 13, 1837. Morris was not converted to the cause of abolition. He wrote :

> A mission truly for the Rev'd gentleman — though not of peace and charity, I take it — or at least the Abolition course pursued by J. Q. Adams in the H. R. at Washington did not

[18] *Census of 1850*, Berks County.
[19] *Census of 1860*, Berks County.
[20] *Census of 1870*, Berks County.
[21] The pamphlet was by Evan Lewis under the title *An Address to Christians* [some destroyed] *inations* [some destroyed] *of Admitting Slave-holders to Communion and Church Membership* (Philadelphia : S. C. Atkinson, 1831), p. 19.

appear to produce peace but its contrary and whatever charity abolition may bear for the blacks—which even admits of strong doubts—it is surely not charity to the Southerners to force them into measures repugnant to them and their idea—of worse than evil tendency—or measures fraught with evil not only to the South, but to the whole Union.

The next day the lecturer came to Morgantown and brought this comment from the diarist: "The house was full. This is the first lecture delivered in this place on this subject—may it be the last."[22] In 1844 he reported, ". . . there is not a single abolition vote in the District" for James G. Birney for president.[23]

Mathew Brooke used several Negro boys as indentured servants. In 1812 he obtained from Reubin Moore of Philadelphia the remaining seven years of the indenture of John Petres, a Negro boy. Seven years earlier Moore had paid $20 to Marian Dick, "negress and next friend of John Peter."[24] In 1816 Brooke inserted this advertisement in four issues of a Reading newspaper:

> For Sale, The unexpired time of a Negroe Man, he has upwards of seven years to serve—he has been brought up to farming business, is a good carter and is a serviceable hand at all sort of labor. . . ."[25]

The early Hopewell records contained a number of workers who used no family names, as in the *Day Book* for 1784–1792 appeared Negro Robin, Negro Cruse, Negro Moriah, Black Majer, Peter Negroe and Negro Samuel. These people were apparently free laborers, however, as they had their own accounts, were paid their own wages and made purchases at the Furnace store. Other Negroes received full names in the

[22] *Morris Diary, op. cit.,* II, pp. 9–10.
[23] *Ibid.,* p. 166.
[24] *Brooke Family Papers,* Indenture, June 9, 1812.
[25] *Berks and Schuylkill Journal,* December 21, 1816, and the three following issues.

same book, as witness James Hooper, Sam Kellar, Anthony Lewis, John Sebass, Isaac Williams and Charles Cox;[26] but most of these were long time employees. James Hooper appeared in the Furnace records as late as 1822.[27]

It is apparent that not all the Negroes were completely free agents, for in 1806 John Hulbey received the wages earned by Negro Levi.[28] Several workers in this period were at the Furnace for a brief time and then disappeared. "Black Frank" worked for 15 days in the autumn of 1802 and was not heard from again.[29] "Black Dine" came on June 22, 1803, and on July 14 "went away" after collecting her wages "as made 3 weeks and 2 day @ 6/ per week."[30] In 1809 "Black Luce" served as maid for 10 weeks.[31]

The company valued its colored workers and gave encouragement to them to come to work. In 1810 James Carmich was lent the following articles to set up housekeeping: "1 bed 2 blankets 1 rug 1 iron pot 2 tins 2 spoons 1 pewter plate 1 erthen dish 2 knives Ironbale Bucket 1 bred Basket."[32] Judging from the purchase of a "a Silver Broach" by Peter Major,[33] life for some colored workers was above the subsistence level. Another Negro paid cash for a large ten-plate stove. The price was identical to that paid by a white customer on the same day and only a few shillings higher than dealers were charged for wholesale quantities of stoves.[34] Homes in the Furnace area were rented to colored families—evidence that segregation in housing was not practiced.[35] Two of these families scandalized the village, however, in the 1870's when Sam England and

[26] SM 41, *passim.*
[27] SM 5, p. 19.
[28] SM 4, p. 129.
[29] SM 1, October 1, November 2, 1802, n. p.
[30] SM 1, pp. 31, 33; SM 2, p. 207.
[31] SM 5, p. 123.
[32] *Birdsborough Store Journal,* 1810, *op. cit.,* p. 8.
[33] SM 41, p. 8.
[34] SM 4, p. 247.
[35] HV 8320203C and Interview with Reginald Smith, March 16, 1941.

George Toogood traded wives without the aid of the law or the clergy.[36]

In the first half of the nineteenth century the colored people of the area participated in the religious activities of several of the Episcopal churches. Between 1808 and 1822 the records of the St. Mary's Episcopal Church at Warwick included the baptisms of the following Negroes: Hester, "a black Woman;" Quash, Kuba, Benjamin and John, "black people;" Draper,[37] "a black man;" Elizabeth Morgan, "a colored woman;" Dorethea, "a black woman;" "Hannah, Wife of Quash (colored)" and "Andrew, (colored) born December 23, 1820, son of Phillis." Quash and Catherine were recorded as communicants in 1814. The marriage register for 1812 listed Stephen Brown to Hester Charms and Quash to Catherine and for 1816 Joseph Cagers to Susan Robeson.[38] Most of these people had no family names given; although if the "Hesters" were the same person, she acquired a second name between her baptism and her marriage. The St. Gabriel's Episcopal Church at Douglassville listed three Ford and two Dunlap children baptized on October 8, 1830, and four colored men buried in their churchyard from 1818 to 1850.[39]

The demise of Negro James Green at Hopewell in 1834 was attended by the same kind of care as for a white person. He had received the medical services of Doctor Robert May, and his account was debited 9.65\frac{1}{2}$ for a coffin and the digging of his grave.[40] These were nearly normal costs for any adult.

An increase in the colored population in the townships near the Furnace about the middle of the century probably accounted for the building of a Negro church about three miles from the Furnace. Near the peak of the roof a stone was set upon which was carved this inscription:

[36] Interview with Hunter Care, January 26, 1941.
[37] There was a Draper Nixon at Hopewell.
[38] St. Mary's Episcopal Church Records, op. cit., pp. 166, 170, 186, 188, 203.
[39] St. Gabriel's Episcopal Church Records, op. cit., pp. 191, 305, 309, 317.
[40] SM 21, p. 97.

THE
A M E
MOUNT FRISBY
CHURCH
FOUNDED IN
AD 1856[41]

Wayne Homan said this church was founded by escaped slaves and was also known as the Six Penny Colored Church and the Mt. Zion Church.[42] An area map drawn in 1860 showed this church and nine homes surrounding it which were identified as the residences of P. Jones, J. Watson, J. Nixon, C. Butler, I. Dehart, D. R. Wamsher, S. Wamsher, I. Coal, Bodley and G. Woolf.[43] The census of 1860 identified Peter Jones, John Watson, Jehu Nixon, Charles Butler, Catherine Bodly and Isaac Coal as heads of Negro households in Union Township. A John Dehart was registered as living with Charles Butler; so the Deharts may have been colored.[44] The other three families were presumably white, but a Negro colony centered around the new church.

The Mount Frisby Church was still being used for religious services as late as 1886.[45] A picture taken in 1936 shows an entrance on the north side covered with a shed roof. There were no windows in this end, but a tablet of some kind was set into the wall.[46] This wall has since been removed to make a garage of the other three sides. The present remains of the old church are of a building 24 feet by 30 feet. There are two windows on the east, two more and evidence of an old door on the south, and one window and evidence of another on the west. The remaining walls are of brown field stone. A hole, apparently for a stove pipe, had gone through the wall; but

[41] Reading obtained from a pencil rubbing taken in December 1962 by Earl Heydinger and the author.
[42] Homan, "The Underground Railroad," *op. cit.*, p. 114.
[43] D. J. Lake and N. S. Beers, "Map of Vicinity of Philadelphia and Reading," Based on Actual Surveys, Philadelphia, 1860.
[44] *Census of 1860*, Berks County, pp. 887 ff.
[45] Montgomery, *History of Berks County, op. cit.*, p. 1187.
[46] Photo Collection at Hopewell Village.

no chimney remains. South of the building is a cemetery where among the graves are those of James Jackson and Isaac Cole, veterans of the Union Army.[47]

In 1888 the Bethesda Baptist Church, near the Furnace, accepted for baptism and membership five "colored Brethren" and two months later dismissed them to form a new Baptist congregation at Sancanock in Chester County.[48]

Work was not very steady for some of the Negro workers. The following time report showed an employment record which would have applied also to other short-term workers. James Thomas began work as a laborer on Friday, August 22, 1823, and was credited with one-half day. He appeared on the time sheets for every working day through September 23, but on the next day he was on the job only one-half day and none on any of the next four work days. On September 30 he worked three-fourths of a day and continued in full employment until the first Saturday in November. The next week he worked six full days, but on Monday, November 10, he was absent. The clerk noted, "James Thomas was drunk." He managed a half-day on Tuesday and then eleven full days in succession. He missed five days at the end of November, and worked five and one-half in the first week of December. On Saturday, December 6, he got a hat and $7.93 in cash and then disappeared from the record. He had earned a total of $23.79 in a little more than three months.[49]

Examples such as James Thomas' irregular employment and the large number of Negroes who came to Hopewell and left after working for only a few weeks could have meant that the work pattern of "last hired and first fired" applied to colored employees at the Furnace. But in contrast to these transient laborers there were other Negroes who held highly skilled jobs, who were trusted with large sums of money, who worked for long periods of time, who secured the status

[47] Information from observation on a visit in December 1962.
[48] *Bethesda Church Minute Book*, September 30, 1888, and November 25, 1888, n. p. Hopewell Village Library.
[49] SM 46, pp. 36, 37, 38, 39, 40; SM 11, p. 213.

symbols of modest affluence, and who were the recipients of neighborly charity from their white colleagues. The following examples were selected to illustrate these points.

Joab Lee was a skilled worker and a respected member of the Furnace family from 1806 to 1809. His wages as filler were 135s. per month—among the highest paid to any of the employees—and he boarded with the white Furnace men at the Big House. He hired white men to work for him when he took time off. His purchases of bulk feed indicate that he owned some kind of livestock. When he left the village in 1809, he borrowed $50 from Buckley and Brooke[50] and found immediate employment at Joanna Furnace.[51]

The Negro longest in the employment of the Furnace was William Jacobs with a record of sixty years in Hopewell Village. In his later years he was unable to work and received care from another elderly man who had been assigned the task by the Furnace management. Jacobs claimed that in his boyhood he had attended school in "Lloyd's Baptist Church" (Bethesda).[52]

Several Negro teamsters for the furnace were at times entrusted with large sums of money. In 1818 Robert Coleman acknowledged receipt of $497.75 "per Negro Peter" (probably Peter Jones) and $500 delivered by "Negro Sampson" (Coggins).[53] Edward Ford owned his own team and was paid by the Furnace for hauling goods to and from Philadelphia.[54]

Another Negro who worked for the Furnace for a long period of time was Wilkinson Hill, a laborer on monthly salary from 1827 to at least 1846.[55] He rented a house in the Village from John Care at $12 per year. The rental agreement provided for Care to furnish rails to fence the lot and "to put

[50] SM 4, pp. 74, 194; 205; SM 5, p. 60; SM 44, November 20, 1806, n. p.
[51] Joanna Furnace Journal, op. cit., passim.
[52] Long, Historical Sketch, op. cit., pp. 10–11.
[53] HV 8180501 and HV 8181208.
[54] SM 8, p. 56. This was in 1816.
[55] SMR 19, p. 2; SM 28, pp. 108, 122, 136.

on a new upper floor and a new six Light window sash and glass." Hill agreed to give a week of labor to the building of a chimney for which Care would provide the materials.[56] In 1843 Hill paid $20 in cash for a cow.[57] Possibly he had some education, for in 1844 he paid postage on letters "sent to his Brother." At least two of his children were educated in the subscription school.[58]

Wilkinson Hill apparently was related to several other Hopewell employees who bore that family name. Benjamin Hill was apprenticed to the Furnace, or to Clement Brooke, in the late 1820's and early 1830's. Educated in the Village school at Furnace expense from 1830 to 1834,[59] he worked for two years as hostler for $6 per month until a general wage increase in 1836 raised his pay to $7. When he died in 1841, his balance on the Furnace books, the sum of twenty dollars, was paid to Wilkinson Hill.[60] In 1850 Charles Clingan employed Eliza Hill, a thirty-three-year-old Negress, as a maid in the Big House at $1.25 per week.[61]

Moses Morton came to the Furnace in 1829, worked as a laborer at $8 per month and later put up the night stock at $12,[62] on which he supported a wife, two boys and two girls. The children were all under ten years of age in 1830.[63] The next year he bought a cow for $14 and pastured her on Samuel Lloyd's land at 18¢ per week.[64] He bought goods at the store and even hired the Village seamstress to do some sewing for the family.[65] There was every appearance of normal life for the Morton family until the middle of April, 1832, when the

[56] HV 8320203C.
[57] SM 28, p. 104.
[58] *Ibid.*, pp. 61, 128, 134.
[59] *Cash Book* for 1828–1830, January 25, 1830, n. p.; SM 15, p. 39; SM 21, pp. 32, 101.
[60] SM 21, *passim.*
[61] *Census of 1850*, Berks County, pp. 569 ff. and SM 32, p. 96.
[62] SM 14, p. 95. His wage was the same as that paid to white workers who did the same work.
[63] *Census of 1830*, Berks County, pp. 515–521.
[64] SM 15, p. 64; SM 21, p. 31.
[65] SM 14, pp. 68, 74, 76.

worst tragedy in Hopewell history befell them. This account appeared in a Norristown newspaper:

> A most distressing accident happened near Hopewell Furnace, Berks County, the week before last, which adds another to the many warnings to mothers already published. A home occupied by a colored man in the service of Mr. Brooks of Hopewell, was destroyed by fire, together with three of his children. It appears that the mother, having occasion to visit some neighbor, locked up the children in the house, and when she returned the house was a pile of ruins, and her children victims of the devouring elements. The cries of the children were heard soon after the mother had left home, but nothing unusual was to be seen about the house, the flames having not yet burnt out, their cries were unheeded.[66]

The newspaper account did not mention Moses Morton by name, but events at the furnace in the next few weeks identified him with the tragedy. The community rallied to his support with "a subscription paper" which raised $18.75. Clement Brooke gave $2 and 12 others gave $1 each—most of the molders and the clerk were in this group. Polly Kid, a maid, gave half of her week's salary of $1; and another maid gave 25¢. In all, 26 persons made contributions.[67] On May 19 Morton sold his cow to David Smith for $12, paid his bill at the Furnace store and disappeared from the Furnace accounts.[68]

Negro workers were an important part of the labor force at Hopewell Furnace; and while they never reached any managerial positions, they were used in skilled jobs and sometimes attained a measure of prosperity. The records, understandably, contain no reference to the hiring of escaping slaves; but the census records on place of birth and the large number of nameless Negroes who appeared briefly on the Furnace books suggest that a traveler from the South might have found aid at the Furnace. Negro families lived in amity among their

---

[66] *Norristown* (Pennsylvania) *Free Press*, April 25, 1832.
[67] SM 21, p. 33.
[68] SM 21, pp. 31, 32; SM 19, p. 245.

white neighbors, attended the churches of the area, went to school with the white children and received the same wages as white workers engaged in the same jobs. But most of the colored workers were kept in the least skilled and lowest paid jobs, and many of their families apprenticed their children for years of service. The community response to the Morton fire showed that misfortune elicited compassion regardless of the color of the victims.

16   The Women

THERE WAS A SAYING THAT HOPEWELL "WAS HEAVEN FOR horses but hell for women" because horses were given the best of care, and the women had to look out for themselves.[1] The historians of the iron plantations have had little to say about the place of women and have dismissed the subject with such statements as, "Women had little or no part in the production of iron,"[2] or, "Women in Berks County did not work in mine, forge or furnaces." They were credited with doing house and farm work and little else.[3]

The women of Hopewell Village concentrated largely upon the traditional women's jobs of the care of the home and the rearing of children, and many of them worked on the farm. But they also entered into the economic life of the community in an amazing number of ways, not all of which were in keeping with the tradition of retiring home-bodies of the nineteenth century.

Women of the Village found a number of ways to add to the family income without going from their homes to work. Men without homes needed food and were willing to pay for the

[1] Reginald and Emlen Smith Interview, August 4, 1940.
[2] Bining, *Pennsylvania Iron Manufacture in the 18th Century, op. cit.,* p. 115.
[3] Handwork, *op. cit.,* p. 127.

privilege of eating where a housewife was preparing meals for
her own family. Eight cents per meal did not add up to riches,
but it helped to put meat on the table for the family.[4] Homes
with spinning wheels afforded the wife a chance at income
through the sale of thread. She sometimes used her needle
at "footing a stocking."[5] Foods were prepared to sell, such as
butter, pickles and baked goods.[6] Home-dipped candles and
home-boiled soap found a market along with eggs and
chickens from the family coop.[7]

Men's clothing needed a woman's care, providing a source
of income for a large number of Village women who were
paid for washing and mending. Rebecca Richard furnished
this service for a number of the single men in 1816 and
received her pay in the form of storegoods charged to the
accounts of the men for whom she had worked. Since she was
also good with the needle, she made clothing for William
Thomas and was paid 33¢ by Clement Brooke "for Making
Eliza a frock."[8] William Jacobs, Negro, had his washing done
by Rebecca Williams, who had been a maid at the mansion
before she married Samuel Williams.[9] The Furnace paid many
women and girls for laundering at the Big House. A Yankee
inventor came into the area in 1843 demonstrating a washing
machine which he guaranteed to get the clothes clean without
injuring the garments,[10] but no record was found to indicate
that any Hopewell housewives invested in this labor-saving
device.

The majority of women supporting themselves or adding to
family income did not do their work at home. Instead, they
found a variety of jobs they could perform throughout the
community, even though most still sought the traditional
women's jobs. The only occupation on a professional level was

[4] See SM 32, p. 104.
[5] SM 17, p. 10.
[6] SM 7, June 4 and November 4, 1817; SM 28, pp. 68, 77.
[7] SM 7, November 7, 1817; SM 31, pp. 51, 89, 127.
[8] SM 7, November 8, 1816.
[9] SM 17, p. 6; SM 31, pp. 39, 83.
[10] *Morris Diary, op. cit.,* II, p. 85.

teaching. There were several women teachers in the Hopewell public schools, but just one among the private tutors[11] More women worked as maids, cooks or seamstresses than at any other occupation except housewife.

The operation of the mansion for the ironmaster's family, the clerk, guests and downstairs boarders required a staff of maids, cooks and housekeepers. In the early part of the nineteenth century the girls who worked at the Big House were evidently drawn from the locality as their names were of familiar Village families—Painter, Griffith, Wynn, Williams, Sheeler, North, Rhoads and Ford. Mary Youst, Rebecca Elliot and Eliza Cook married Furnace men[12] Older women, both married and widowed, worked at these jobs, too.[13] Some like Polly Kid worked for a long period of time as maids.[14] But by the middle of the century a fast turnover of employees was indicated by the numerous journal entries for girls hired and quitting, and the names were seldom those of Furnace families. Mrs. Clingan brought some of her maids from Philadelphia; and the names Murray, Brady and Lafsley suggest that some were Irish immigrants.[15]

Wages were never very high for housework, ranging from 50¢ to $1.50 for a seven-day week. But most of the maids' needs were supplied, and wages were sometimes not touched for several years. Some of the maids bought goods at the store and found themselves in debt. For example Mary Youst owed money to the Furnace and to John Sheeler in 1818. She evened her store account with her maid's wages and possibly her debt to Sheeler by marrying him.[16] Purchases at the store were most often shoes, clothing accessories, cloth and food. In 1819 Clement Brooke executed an order in Phila-

[11] The censuses of 1850, 1860 and 1870 contained many listings of women as "teacher in the Common School."
[12] St. Mary's Church Records.
[13] SM 1, p. 81.
[14] SM 28, p. 14.
[15] SM 31, p. 134; SM 32, pp. 54, 66.
[16] SM 6, p. 36 and St. Mary's Church Record, p. 190.

delphia to purchase "a silk shall" for $5 and have a bonnet repaired @ $1.25 for Caty Wynn." Wages sometimes increased as the services of the worker improved, as verified by the record of Susan Munshower whose compensation rose from 50¢ per week in 1847 to three times that in 1851.[18] House-cleaning was more highly paid than normal housework. Susan Griffith received $1 for three days of cleaning in 1830 when the normal wage for maids was that amount per week[19]

The scarcity of good maids brought an exasperated comment from the Morgantown diarist:

> Was out nearly all day in search of that tease and torment of married life or housekeeping — that necessary evil — a maid of all work and without success.

> Of all the ills of married life this one thing of maidhunting and maidkeeping is the worst.

> Husbands may expect to hear a continual tale from their wives of faults and shortcomings . . . until his soul is fairly sickened at the sins of the maid-kind.[20]

When women looked for sources of income, another normal feminine pursuit was sewing, for which there was a considerable demand at Hopewell Furnace. Married women did most of the sewing for their families, but there were men without wives and special sewing jobs which demanded the services of an expert seamstress. Many instances appear in the Furnace records of women who did sewing for the Furnace or for employees on a casual basis, and other examples of those who made it a regular business. Margaret Benson was paid a weekly wage for sewing and "making carpet and quilting for the furnace" over a period of six years. However, she did not have steady work and earned additional income by selling butter and dried peaches.[21] In 1829 Margaret Cook was

[17] SM 9, p. 167.
[18] SM 32, pp. 33, 100, 106.
[19] SM 15, p. 14.
[20] *Morris Diary, op. cit.*, p. 233.
[21] SM 12, p. 137; SM 17, pp. 19, 22, 24.

sewing for a group of Furnace men. Four of them paid for
her boarding over a period of time during which she ate
$11.50 worth of food. The time was not given, but this charge
for boarding would have covered meals for several months.
She continued to earn money with her needles for the next
four years.[22] Widow Elizabeth Merwine rented a house from
Clement Brooke and sewed for the Furnace and individuals
in the 1820's and 1830's. She was apparently skilled in all
kinds of sewing and tailoring.[23] Eliza Hudson had a specialty
of making stockings to sell in wholesale lots to the Furnace
store.[24] The store sold large quantities of cloth of many
varieties, buttons, trimmings, needles, pins, thimbles, scissors,
dye and patterns to the amateur and professional seamstresses
of the community.

These normal female occupations did not fill all the needs
of women to add to the family incomes in Hopewell Village.
Contrary to the common view of their limited opportunities
for employment in the iron plantations, there were women
who found jobs in many of the areas of vocational activity
of farm, furnace and forest.

Recruiting women and children was the normal method
of securing most of the seasonal workers needed on the farms.
Harvest time required many extra hands, but even some of
the regular needs were filled by the women and children.
A search of the farm time books for 1811–1814 revealed these
different tasks being done by them: hoeing corn, binding
grain, hauling grain, pulling flax, shearing sheep, harvesting
oats, mowing, haymaking, picking apples, sorting apples,
dressing corn, spreading flax, picking potatoes, planting corn,
loading dung, reaping, cradling, killing caterpillars, cutting
buckwheat, cutting apples, pulling corn and pulling turnips.
Women were used on all of these except mowing and loading
dung where boys were employed. In later years women were

[22] *Cash Book* for 1828–1830, July 17, 1829, and February 2, 1830;
SM 12, p. 4; SM 17, pp. 13, 34, 39.
[23] SM 59, pp. 2, 15; SM 14, pp. 44, 46.
[24] SM 28, p. 78.

also employed at whitewashing fences and buildings, milking, butchering, rendering lard, raking oats, setting up cornfodder and picking stones. The pay for this work was most commonly 25¢ per day with a top of 30¢ in 1816.[25]

Less common than farm work for women were jobs about the furnace, at the mines or in the wood lots; but women worked in all of these places. Two widows, Margaret Painter and Elizabeth Mervine, were paid for "cleaning castings" in 1831 and 1832. This was heavy work tipping the stove plates and other cast items to remove the molders' sand clinging to the surface. The compensation was 75¢ per ton paid by the molder.[26] In this same period of Furnace history Mary Beavens, Elizabeth Mauger and Eliza Painter were paid for ore mined; and Henry Painter collected for more than 13 loads of "mine" sent to the Furnace by his daughter.[27] Over a period of more than thirty years six women were credited with cutting wood for the furnace, and in 1829 Eve Jones was paid for hauling wood "bought of her in 1827."[28] Elizabeth Mock earned over $90 in two years cutting wood and spent all of that plus an additional $28.19 at the Furnace store.[29] Elizabeth Hughs was paid for cutting 41 cords in 1836 which would represent about twenty days of work for a good male chopper.[30]

It is possible that all of this heavy work was done by teenage sons whose wages were collected by widowed mothers. But the clerks were usually quite careful to record the information that the work was done by someone other than the person who received the wages. Since no such record was found in the instances given, it is presumed that the work was done by the women.

Among Hopewell Village women there were some who

---

[25] SM 7, September 3, 1816, n. p.
[26] SM 15, pp. 23, 24, 52; SM 21, pp. 11, 12, 32.
[27] SM 14, p. 27; *Cash Book* for 1828–1830, July 11, 1829, and October 17, 1829, n. p.; SM 21, p. 164.
[28] SM 14, p. 145.
[29] SM 6, p. 84.
[30] SM 21, p. 182.

conducted their own businesses. Operating a farm and handling the details of the sale of crops was fairly common for Village women. Indian corn, feathers, cows, pork, pigs, potatoes, veal and grain were among the wares sold to the Furnace by women farmers. In a number of instances the purveyors were listed as widows, indicating that they were carrying on the work after their husbands had died.[31] Stoves with a price of more than $20 each were sold to several women with payments made in cash or services.[32] Barbara Thomas, Elizabeth Lloyd and Phoebe Shaner owned woodland and sold "wood leave" or cord wood to the Furnace.[33]

Even the iron business itself was not beyond the competence of nineteenth century women. "Widow" Lynch, Rebecca Lukens and Rachel L. Smith were regular buyers of Hopewell furnace castings. The size of their orders implied a considerable retail business. Mrs. Smith sold Hopewell products on commission from her Philadelphia store.[34] Sarah Loeser bought pig iron in 1825 to process at Dale Forge which she was operating.[35] Sarah Gilmore was listed as a merchant in Caernarvon Township of Berks County, and the census of 1850 placed a valuation of $28,000 on her real estate. Eliza Mast at the age of 34 owned real estate worth $20,000 according to the same source. Two other women of some means were Margaret Amon and Rebecca Wynn, each of whom held Furnace notes amounting to more than $800.[36]

When a woman had a husband, he could collect her wages. Numerous notations in the records show that husbands received pay for sewing, washing, farm work, spinning and butter-making. Men also were credited with work done by their mothers, and Hugh Welsh was compensated for spinning

[31] For example see SM 5, p. 38.
[32] SM 6, p. 168; SM 10, p. 33.
[33] SM 14, pp. 28, 55; SM 31, p. 60; SM 32, p. 120.
[34] SM 19, pp. 107, 126; SM 6, p. 166; SM 15, p. 35; SM 21, pp. 14, 17, 26, 35, 40.
[35] HV 8250501A.
[36] SM 9, p. 135; SM 12, p. 25; SM 10, pp. 17, 25, 28.

done by his mother-in-law.[37] But on the other hand wives
bought at the Village store or even ordered goods from more
distant merchants and charged the amounts to their husbands' accounts. It was also possible for a wife to secure cash
against the credit balance of a husband as many, many entries
in the cash books attested. Acording to one such entry Mrs.
Charles Smith was paid $10 in Philadelphia. Smith at that
time in 1818 was working at Hopewell as a stove finisher, and
apparently the Furnace was advancing his wife money for
living expenses in the city.[38] Women were also paid considerable sums for work done by their children.[39]

Not all women paid their bills or had a man who could
be held accountable for what they spent. In 1818 Hannah
Whitaker owed a debt to Buckley and Brooke of $14.25. She
managed to pay only $1 of it in the next thirteen years, and
the remainder was written off as a bad debt.[40]

One of the most frequent ways in which women were
recorded in the Furnace books was as the recipients of payments from men. Usually no reason was given for the payment, but often it can be surmised that it was for sewing
or washing. More difficult to account for was such a blanket
endorsement as this one :

> Sir please to let Mary Simins have what goods She wants
> at this time and charg it to my Acc Please to Send abill and
> ablig yours and
> April 15, 1823   John McGowan[41]

Possibly the lady was a housekeeper for McGowan and was
trusted to buy only what was needed. But more intriguing
was an item in the *Lewis Evans Journal* which gave a long
list of articles as an "acct of Goods gave delivered [Note the
word "gave" was crossed out] Hetty Filman." Among the com-

[37] SM 4, p. 39.
[38] SM 10, p. 19.
[39] SM 41, p. 110; SM 6, p. 254; SM 11, p. 92; SM 14, p. 50.
[40] SM 6, p. 9; SM 11, p. 5; SM 54, p. 3.
[41] Hopewell Papers at Berks County Historical Society.

modities were: "Bed and bedding, rose Blanketts, bed quilt
$7.50, looking glass, Coverlid $5.00, ½ doz. chairs, queens
ware" and 2 cows at $13 each. At the end was this note,
"The above amt. of goods is carried to page 151 in the
day book under conditions there stated." Unfortunately the
day book is not available to check the conditions. No record
of payment was noted in the journal.[42] Apparently someone
was setting up housekeeping at well above the subsistence
level, but who was paying the bill and why?

In many respects other than economic the women of Hopewell Village showed interests like those of any other community or in any other time. They were interested in clothes,
shopping, men and marriage. They gossiped and visited. Most
were reasonably moral, and some were not.

Ready-made dresses and coats were not kept in stock at
the store. There was no record of purchases of lingerie. The
store carried the raw materials, and most women must have
made their own. Some dresses were made by the seamstresses
at rates ranging from 50¢ to 62¢ for labor.[43] The materials
would have been extra. Although the store sold a wide
variety of kinds of cloth, the girls did not always find what
they wanted and placed orders in Morgantown, Reading or
Philadelphia.[44] The store journals recorded kinds of cloth and
sometimes colors but seldom any information about designs.
But for 1844 in Morgantown James Morris reported, "The
fashionable apparel for both men and women is now very
gay—even gaudy. Stripes and plaids of worsted material, . . .
of the most brilliant colours are much worn by the ladies."[45]

The articles of clothing most frequently bought were shoes
and hats. Shoes were sold at the store and also custom-made
by the shoemakers. Most women's shoes or slippers sold for
about $1.25 to $1.50 per pair, but some were bought as low
as one dollar and as high as $2.12½. The latter price was paid

[42] *Lewis Evans Journal, op. cit.,* May 10, 1822–February 11, 1825, p. 32.
[43] SM 10, p. 18; SM 31, p. 52; SM 13, p. 107.
[44] For example see SM 9, p. 45; SM 10, p. 66.
[45] *Morris Diary, op. cit.,* II, p. 168.

in 1820 by Rebecca Elliot for a pair she bought in Reading
while she was working as a maid at $1 per week.[46] "Bonnetts"
were rather expensive with prices ranging from $1 to a sum
of $10 which George Kephart paid Mrs. Clingan "for a
Bonnett and to go to Reading."[47] Normally travel expenses
to Reading were not more than $1. In general the single girls
paid more for their bonnets than did the married women.
Rebecca Elliot put more than a month's salary into her $4.50
hat in 1819.[48] Perhaps she wore it and her Reading shoes the
next winter when she married Samuel Williams. Hats, judging
from the frequency with which they were repaired, must have
been meant to last more than one season.

Shawls were in fashion for much of the nineteenth century
and were available in a wide range of materials at many
prices. Polly Kid paid $2.25 for a silk hood in 1832.[49] Gloves,
"mits," stockings and umbrellas were purchased; but there
were few references to ornamentation except side combs.
However, Blacksmith David Jenkins spent 10¢ for "beeds" in
1827.[50] Whatever cosmetics and grooming materials that were
used must have been produced at home as none were seen
among purchases except "A Bottle Hare Tonick" for which
Ann Church paid 50¢[51]

Possibly because they were not tied to a very rigid time
schedule, the women did much of the marketing at the Village
store. Those who came from some distance often had lists
for a number of men or families and charged the items to the
persons for whom they were shopping. The miners regularly
sent one of the women to make their purchases.[52] Mrs. Clingan
made frequent trips to Reading or Philadelphia; and on many
occasions she took money entrusted to her to buy articles of

[46] SM 10, p. 54; SM 31, p. 10; SM 4, p. 134; SM 9, p. 129.
[47] SM 31, p. 104.
[48] SM 10, p. 41.
[49] SM 17, p. 25.
[50] SM 13, p. 98.
[51] SM 28, p. 20.
[52] SM 9, pp. 26, 29, 34, 42, 52, 53.

clothing for women of the community, especially the maids.[53]

Women were honored by being selected to preside at the ceremony of putting fire in the furnace for the beginning of a new blast. Most frequently, however, this privilege was reserved for the wife of the ironmaster and, therefore, did not become the basis for a popularity contest among the Village belles.[54]

Young women's interests as revealed in their letters to each other were of clothes, travel, parties, visits, family health and gossip about their friends. Matchmaking was a favorite topic of speculation.[55] Sarah Brooke asked her brother:

> Have you heard any talk of our Cousin Clements [possibly C. B. Buckley] going to be married? report says he is engaged to Miss Sarah Penrose . . . one of those young ladies who spent a day at Hibernia last Summer. . . . She is very pretty and quite young, not more than half his age, the old capitain is doing very well for himself, I hope he will not get disappointed this time, if he does I think he will take it hard; . . . he is now in the city and appears to be very attentive to her.[56]

But girls were not the only ones who were interested in gossip or in trying to get each other married, since a male letter reported that John Birkenbine ". . . is . . . flying around with the girls at a great rate. . . ." and that "Jane Barde has got a Beau already he had her out Sleighing yesterday."[57] The most avowed matchmaker was also a man who wrote to a bachelor friend:

> . . . I have often enquired after thee and from all Information I could get concured in pronouncing they determination to gog on through time with the title of batchelor. I know not what charms that name can produce to thee but I can

[53] SM 31, *passim.*
[54] SM 6, pp. 5, 6, 7.
[55] See *Sharpe-Marshall Letters* and *Brooke Family Papers.*
[56] *Brooke Family Papers,* Sarah Brooke to Edward Brooke, May 16, 1833.
[57] *Ibid.,* John Springer to Edward Brooke, January 11, 1833.

say since I have tryed both that I greatly prefer the Married
state and I believe if thee would condescend to honour us
with a visit thee would be convinced that my Ideas are
no delusion for besides an agreable wife I have a lovely
Daughter turned of 2 years old . . . I saw Dan*l* Buckley at
Phila. about two years ago and he promised me to Inform
thee of a Charming young Lady living in our Neighbourhood
of about 3000 pound portion and such natural perfections
that I believed that all that was wanting was thy seeing her
to be in love with her—but I kept her as long as I could for
thee she was married about two weeks since but . . . we have
several others of euquel Charms if not quite as much money.[58]

What did a young Hopewell lass want out of life? One of
them gave her ambitions under the title "What are your most
anxious wishes:"

1. To be independent
2. To be admired
3. To receive and offer
4. To be joined in matrimony
6. To set the fashions
7. To be happy
8. To go to Europe
9. To see the one you love
10. Reign in all things
11. To be an ornament in society
12. To be envied
13. To be virtuous
14. To meet the esteem of all
15. To get a convert
16. To be always visiting
17. To keep a carriage
18. To have patience
19. To do as you should
20. To be as you should
21. To be alone
22. To inherit a title
23. To be in love
24. To be wealthy[59]

It was perhaps not significant that virtue came far behind
admiration, or that it made the list ahead of the possession of
a carriage or a title. A proposal and marriage came early.

Courting on horseback, with the girls riding sidesaddles,
was a common practice among the young people at Hopewell.[60] Winning the ironmaster's daughter required something
more formal, including a very flowery request of her parents.

[58] *Ibid.*, Israel Lancaster to Mathew Brooke, Junior, March 18, 1806.
[59] *Hopewell Papers,* undated and unsigned. Found among school sums
and penmanship practices.
[60] Albert Lloyd Interview, September 1962.

Charles M. Clingan wrote this letter to Mr. and Mrs. Clement Brooke :

> Dear Sir and Madam;
> The object of this communication, in propriety should have been made long ago.
> But as I hoped, the nature and intentions of my visiting your family were neither unknown nor misunderstood; the immediate necessity of the avowal and request I am about to make did not appear to me necessary.
> In soliciting to become a member of your Family, I have nothing to urge why you should grant the favour; but the kindness and attention you have both invariably treated me with, and the firm attachment I have for your daughter.
> To support my claims I can neither urge the influence of family conexions, nor the aid of wealth; in lieu of which all I offer is the steady exertion to acquire and support a character which gives me a pasport into good society, and a Profession which I purport to follow, with Industry and attention . . .
> I now with the permission of your daughter, and under the influence, of the serious importance of the step, request that you will give me the pleasure, of admitting me into your family, by permitting her to unite her destiny with mine.
> . . . .[61]

June was not the month of brides at Hopewell Village. Of 118 marriages involving Hopewell family names taken from the St. Mary's Episcopal Church records from 1808 to 1846, only four took place in June. January was most popular with nineteen, closely followed by December with eighteen. Christmas season, even Christmas Day, was the time for many weddings. July was least popular with two weddings, and August was next with three.[62] Although most Hopewell girls married men from the immediate neighborhood, there were examples of weddings involving men from Philadelphia and one from as far away as Erie, Pennsylvania.[63]

Weddings were high social occasions in the Furnace com-

[61] HV 8420930.
[62] *St. Mary's Episcopal Church Records, passim.*
[63] *Ibid.*

munity. In 1803 Matthew Dunkings and Christian Heverly
"went to the weding the Evening before and were Sick the
next Day."[64] Early in the century it was customary for wedding parties among the Amish to last for several days for
everyone invited. By the 1840's this practice was largely
abandoned; but an Amish wedding was still "quite a party"
with "the young Homish folks . . . invited by the dozens," and
"cakes and wine were provided in abundance."[65] Guests at
rural weddings reacted differently to the solemn occasion.
Some ". . . had a great time ended of kissing the Bride and
. . . taking gates of the hinges and throwing them in the woods
and some . . . quarreling."[66] The married couples and the
wedding attendants were each expected to give a large party
for the newlyweds. For one marriage in Morgantown on
January 13, 1842, there had been four parties given for the
couple within the next nine days.[67]

Childbirth was seldom attended by the doctor in the iron
plantations. The women of the community looked after one
another and did what was necessary for mother, child and
family. For special needs the midwife or "granny" was on
hand. Births were happy events with the proud father standing treat for drinks for all his friends.[68]

Not all marriages of the nineteenth century were endlessly
happy or free from discord. Men got drunk and abused their
wives and children.[69] One "put his wife out of doors and told
her to seek Lodgings."[70] Another man hanged himself, and
". . . Some of the neighbors say he could not live agreeable
with his wife."[71] According to report even the ironmaster's
family had domestic difficulties. On one occasion Dr. Clingan
had apparently been abusing a mule and was reprimanded by

[64] SM 1, p. 23.
[65] *Morris Diary, op. cit.*, II, p. 73.
[66] *Martha Furnace Diary, op .cit.*, July 30, 1814.
[67] *Morris Diary, op. cit.*, p. 179–180.
[68] *Martha Furnace Diary, op. cit., passim.*
[69] *Ibid., July* 5–6, 1813.
[70] *Ibid.,* January 29, 1811.
[71] HV 8400306A.

Mrs. Clingan, who reminded him that her money had bought the mule. The doctor's reported reply was, "Well, damn it, your money bought me, too."[72]

Chastity for the unmarried and fidelity to the marriage bed were not universal practices although the iron community may have been neither better nor worse than other groups of people in this respect. Hopewell history did not contain very many instances of illicit activities, but there were some. The Reverend Mister Levi Bull of St. Mary's Episcopal Church did not record that a child baptized was a bastard, as the rector of St. Gabriel's Church did. Mr. Bull just enrolled the mother's name without the usual entry of a father or the identification of widows.[73] The Pennsylvania General Assembly passed an act in 1828 to legitimize Marie Eve Snyder as the daughter of Daniel Udree and to give her rights of inheritance in his property.[74]

Although the following reference is no longer clear, it is apparent that even the highest Furnace families were not immune from the tongues of gossips:

> Mrs. Cabeen on Tuesday last made you an uncle by presenting me with a fine daughter, which I think will be apt to put the noses of the Cats out of Joint completely.[75]

Many of the old residents of Hopewell Village recalled Dr. Clingan as having been "extremely popular among the female sex throughout the section."[76] He was quite handsome, was reported to have had affairs with several village women[77] and was suspected of being the father of two of the children of a Mrs. Strock who lived across French Creek from the mansion. A Hopewell story related that the doctor was dumped from a foot log into the creek while returning at night from

[72] Morris Lyman Care Interview, February 6, 1941.
[73] *St. Mary's Church Record*, pp. 165–184.
[74] *Pamphlet Laws of Pennsylvania*, P. L. 1828, p. 28.
[75] HV 8420610, Rob B. Cabeen to Clement Brooke.
[76] Morris Lyman Care Interview, February 6, 1941.
[77] Albert Painter Interview, December 12, 1947.

a visit to Mrs. Strock. Lief Houck and several other furnace workers were supposed to have been responsible for the "ducking."[78]

Hopewell had its "bad girls" of whom Mary Ann Marks and Sally Hampton had the most lasting notoriety for ill-repute.[79] Sally worked in the woods cutting timber with the men, sharing their hard work and difficulties. Some aspersions were cast that difficulties were not the only things she shared with the men. She was reputed to have had several children by both white and Negro fathers.[80] Sally's conduct became a matter of record in an agreement between the Furnace management and John Hampton for the rental of a house in 1881. The clerk recorded:

> Agreed . . . that he could have the house formerly occupied by the family . . . The understanding is that they must keep a decent and respectable house. If Sarah's conduct is as it used to be, it will be sufficient at any time to remove them. Must not abuse or disturb any of their neighbors.[81]

Life was difficult and often lonesome for the women who lived in the remote homes on the wooded hillsides of Hopewell Village. Beside the normal activities of home and family care, many of them found ways to add to the family income through jobs requiring normal feminine skills and also from tasks usually reserved for the men. But on the whole they worked hard, lived fairly orderly lives and retained quite normal interest.

[78] Reginald Smith Interview, August 24, 1941.
[79] Mary Krewson Interview, June 29, 1941.
[80] Hunter Care Interview, January 26, 1941.
[81] SM 34, p. 232.

17   The Children

According to a respected authority on iron-making in the eighteenth century, "Child labor found small place in iron manufacture."[1] The situation must have changed by the nineteenth century, or Hopewell was an exception; for many children were employed, and they were found in almost every type and kind of occupation around the Furnace except administrative positions. Many bound or apprenticed children lived and worked at Hopewell Furnace, but also many parents put their children to work and collected their wages.

In 1824 the General Assembly of Pennsylvania placed upon the Directors of the Poor for Berks County the responsibility:

> . . . to bind out as apprentices to any art, mystery or occupation, so that such apprenticeship may expire, if males, at or before the age of 21 years; if females, at or before the age of eighteen years, such poor children as shall come under their notice, or as may now be bound apprentices by the overseers of the poor, but no such apprentices shall be bound to any person or persons whose religious persuasion shall be different from that which the parents of such apprentices may have last professed, or to persons that are not of good repute, if others of good repute and of the same persuasion may or can be found. . . .[2]

[1] Bining, *Pennsylvania Iron Manufacture in the 18th Century, op. cit.*, p. 111.
[2] *Pamphlet Laws of Pennsylvania*, P. L. 1824, p. 201.

This law must have legitimized a practice which had long been followed or clarified the responsibilities of the stated officials in the matter, because indentured or apprenticed children were working at Hopewell Furnace at a much earlier date. Clement Brooke had at least two children bound to him in 1816 and then hired their services to the Furnace. On two dates he received payment, the first "for 6½ months work done from the first of april last to the 17th of Octor by his Black Boy James @ $9 per month," and the second for $31.29 as wages for 39 weeks of work "by Mary."[3] The year after the new law was passed, the Furnace paid a shoemaker $9 "for making and mending shoes for Bound girls and Boy."[4] The number of girls was not given, but the size of the bill indicated several as shoes at this time were about $1.50 per pair. The expense for mending was not specified. In 1830 Clement Brooke had in his household four female Negroes, one under ten years of age, another under 24, and two between that age and 36.[5] Five years later Brooke paid a tailor $4.50 for "Making Suit for Black Boy."[6]

Children could be had from the county poorhouse for apprenticing at a quite young age—one girl was taken at the age of 8 to become a house servant.[7] But some agreements for even younger children were made directly with the parents. David Johnston must have been less than five when his mother placed him with the Brooke family in this agreement:

This Indenture witnesseth that David Johnston of the Township of Union in the County of Berks Son of Sarah Johnston by and with the Consent of his Mother . . . both put himself and by These Presents doth voluntary and of his own free will and accord put himself Apprentice to Clement and Maria Brooke their heirs and Asignes of the Same Place to learn his art Trade and mystery; and after the manner of an apprentice to Serve them from the day

[3] SM 7, December 23, 1816, and February 24, 1817, n. p.
[4] SM 12, p. 103.
[5] *Census of 1830*, Berks County, pp. 515–521.
[6] HV 8350407A.
[7] *Morris Diary, op. cit.*, II, p. 146.

of the date hereof; for and during the full end and term of Sixteen years and one month Next ensuing. During all which term the apprentice his said Master faithfully shall serve, his Secrets keep; his lawfull commands every where gladly obey. He shall do no damage to his said master nor see it done by others; without letting or giving notice thereof to his said master. He shall not waste his said Masters goods nor lend them unlawfully to any. With his own goods nor the goods of them; without license from his said Master he shall neither buy nor sell. He shall not Absent himself day nor night from his said Masters Service; without Leave, nor haunt ale-houses, Taverns; or Play houses; but in all things behave himself as a faithfull, Apprentice ought to do; during the said Term. And the said Master Shall use the utmost of his Endeavours to teach, or cause to be taught or instructed; the said apprentice in the trade or mystery of husbandry and procure for him sufficient meat; and drink; apparel; Lodging and washing, fitting for an apprentice, during the said term of sixteen years and one month and give him within the said term one years Schooling. And when he is free to give him one suit of Cloths to be Entirely new and all his old cloths. . . .[8]

Thomas Lloyd took Mary Young when she was only six to live at his farm until she was eighteen years of age. During her apprenticeship she was to receive eighteen months of schooling "one half of which after she attains the age of fourteen years." Mary was to be given religious instruction and to be confirmed by a minister "of her own choosing." At the end of her service she was to receive the usual two changes of clothing, and Lloyd also promised to give her "a bed and bed Stead worth seventy dollars, and a Chest or Spining wheel whichever She may Choose."[9]

The tax records in the years before the public school system was founded contained the names of "poor children" who were eligible for aid in schooling. In Union Township the number was 14 in 1829, 16 in 1830, 18 in 1831, 13 in 1833, 20 in 1834 and 19 in 1835. The ages ranged from 5 to 11,

[8] HV 8300212A.
[9] *Brooke Family Papers,* Indenture of Poor Girl, 1846.

inclusive.[10] These names were not of bound children whose education was provided by their masters but of the children of parents who could not afford to educate them.

The records show that the Furnace met its obligations to educate its bound children. Tutor Andrew Collins was paid by the company for teaching "A. Church, Benj. Hill and D. Johnston in 1834."[11] Ann Church, who lived at the mansion, was a niece of Mrs. Brooke; D. Johnston was apparently the apprentice whose terms of service were related above; and Ben Hill was a Negro apprentice and later a hostler for several years. All three of these names appeared in other years for schooling; Ben Hill attended school during parts of six years. There were also memoranda of clothing provided for these children.[12]

If Mary Monshour was at all typical, bound girls must have had time to give to plans for their lives after they reached freedom age. She apparently attracted the attention of Blacksmith Samuel Henderson while she was an apprentice at the Big House and married him when she gained her freedom. Mary was the daughter of Jacob Monshour who cut wood for the Furnace. In 1846 the Furnace bought for her a pair of shoes costing $1; and the next year paid for her a $15 doctor bill, 75¢ for repairing a bonnet and $2.09½ which she owed a peddler.[13] During this time Henderson was paying for boarding and to have his washing done—signs of bachelorhood. On March 22, 1848, Mary collected $20 for her "Freedom Money," and a month later the Furnace paid $13.80 "per Mary Munshour freedom Clothes in Philadelphia." On the same day Samuel Henderson "Paid for Sundries in Philadelphia got by Mary Munshour" to the amount of $10.65. Henderson began paying bills for storegoods on January 1, 1849, and the following year he was a householder providing

---

[10] *Berks County Tax Records,* Union Township.
[11] SM 21, p. 101.
[12] For example see SM 21, p. 32.
[13] SM 31, pp. 12, 29, 33, 41, 54, 58.

boarding for his brother George.[14] All of this seems to add up to romance and marriage; which is further confirmed by the census of 1850 which included a Furnace household of Samuel Henderson, age 26, occupation smith; Mary, age 19, and William, age 2.[15] The ages of mother and son possibly disclose that Mary had gained her freedom before she was eighteen and William had been born early.

Furnace employees, other than the manager, had apprentice children who were employed by the company. Edward Hughes collected wages for James Lacey over a considerable period of time, and Esabella Ewens had an income from the work of Esram Haselip.[16] Perhaps the outstanding success story of a "poor child" at Hopewell was that of Joseph Elliot. He was included among the pauper children in the tax records of 1823 when his age was given as seven years.[17] In 1832 at the age of sixteen he was a molder; but his wages were being paid to Samuel Williams, teamster.[18] Williams paid for a coat "for J. Elliot" in 1837,[19] and in May of that year the boy came of age and began to draw his own wages.[20] In 1840 he was married and the father of a little girl under five years of age.[21]

Why did Samuel Williams collect wages earned by Elliot? Williams had worked at the Furnace in 1802 when his father died while Samuel was a minor. The boy began boarding at the mansion two days after his father's death;[22] he even collected the wages of his younger brother Jesse.[23] He was, therefore, a man of maturity when he married Rebecca Elliot on January 1, 1820.[24] Rebecca had been a maid for Clement

[14] SM 32, pp. 64, 93.
[15] *Census of 1850*, Berks County, p. 569.
[16] SM 9, pp. 137, 152.
[17] *Berks County Tax Records*, Union Township, 1823.
[18] SM 21, p. 190.
[19] *Ibid.*, p. 193.
[20] SM 19, p. 184.
[21] *Census of 1840*, Berks County, p. 397.
[22] SM 1, p. 15.
[23] SM 2, p. 177.
[24] *St. Mary's Episcopal Church Records, op. cit.*

Brooke before the marriage. Joseph Elliot must have been a relative of hers, perhaps a brother or son. Elliot worked as a molder at Hopewell Furnace until molding ended and afterwards continued to reside in the village. In 1846 he had a child in the Hopewell school.[25]

Children of Hopewell Village were to be found working at almost every kind of job the company offered. The Furnace, itself, provided work for many boys before they reached their majorities. The job of gutterman was handled regularly by a boy. From Samuel Williams in 1802 to Robert Wampsher in 1851 many boys did this work and had their wages paid to parents or guardians.[26] Isaac and John Hughes were the guttermen from 1817 to 1825 with their wages going to Edward Hughes and Mary Hughes.[27] The next most frequent Furnace jobs done by minors were putting in the mine and stocking coal. Frederick Meck, David Hart and John Painter provided sons who did this work from 1808 to 1831.[28] Samuel McCollister, minor, was entrusted with substitute work as filler in 1803,[29] and several boys earned money cleaning castings for the molders.[30] The height of success for a family was to have a son who could become a molder and earn the high wages paid to these skilled workers. Thomas Care trained several of his sons for this work and at one time was collecting molding pay, based on production, for sons David and Thomas in addition to his own salary as founder and molder. His income was high at that time.[31] John Care, John Painter, Joseph Hart and Joseph Elliot also began molding before they were old enough to collect their own wages.[32]

Providing iron ore for the furnace also furnished work for

[25] SM 31, p. 20.
[26] SM 2, November 2, 1802, n. p.; SM 32, p. 120.
[27] SM 6, p. 254; SM 11, p. 92; SM 7, January 31, 1817, n.p.; SM 9, p. 137.
[28] SM 4, p. 249; SM 5, p. 101; SM 9, p. 142; SM 15, p. 50.
[29] SM 1, p. 217.
[30] SM 9, p. 129; SM 8, pp. 63, 66.
[31] SM 12, p. 144.
[32] SM 59, p. 12; SM 21, pp. 69, 70, 88; SM 12, p. 108; SM 14, p. 59.

many boys and young men, with several instances where a father and son formed a mining team. Jonathan McKewen and Thomas Ray both appeared in the time record as miners in 1818. But their wages were added to those of their fathers who were miners also.[33] William Philips was paid for his own work at raising ore and also for the same work done by his son Nugent in 1818 and 1819. In 1817, however, Nugent Philips' wages had been credited to the account of William Adams with no reason recorded. Two years later Adams was paid for mine work by his son William.[34] Robert Gilmore had several boys working at mining and loading ore into the wagons in 1816–1819.[35] Esram Haselip worked for William Adams and Company, mining contractors, from 1818 to 1820 as the bound boy of Esabella Ewens. He must have been a good workman because his employment was steady, and his wage of 75¢ per day was higher than that of several of the adults working "at the mineholes." Haselip apparently became of age about April 10, 1820, when the clerk opened an account in his name into which wages were credited until the end of 1821.[36] Some boys earned the same wages as their fathers for mining; others were paid less—possibly these latter ones were learning the business.[37]

The work of a collier would seem to have been another good opportunity for a father-son partnership, but little evidence was found that such was the case. Henry Houck was a master collier and received wages for coaling done by his son Samuel. However, Samuel worked with Daniel Frey's coaling team and not with his father.[38] Jacob Cramp, David Ireson, Henry Wampser and Jacob Woolf's son worked at the colliers' pits before they were old enough to collect their wages; and Edward Hughes was paid $19 per month in 1818

[33] SM 9, p. 121; SM 6, p. 13.
[34] SM 9, pp. 124, 142, 151, 192; SM 8, p. 138.
[35] SM 7, December 24, 1816, n. p.; SM 9, p. 135.
[36] SM 9, pp. 120, 140, 151, 152; SM 4, pp. 265, 357.
[37] SM 32, pp. 109, 113.
[38] SM 21, p. 5; SMR 19, p. 13.

for coaling by his bound boy James Lacey. Lacey's rate was a little under the $23 per month paid some other colliers.[39]

Several of the skilled crafts were open to boys as workers or apprentices. When Henry Frye quit as blacksmith in 1807, his partner Philip Shafer brought Philip, Junior, to the shop. The son began work at 60s. per month, compared with his father's 110s. The boy must have proved a good worker, however, as his wage jumped to $97\frac{1}{2}$s. after only four months of employment.[40] The next year Shafer began to use another son, Abraham, at a starting wage of 45s. per month. Within the year he, too, earned a pay boost to $83\frac{1}{2}$s.[41]

In the last half of the nineteenth century the Hopewell Village blacksmith shop employed several apprentices. In 1855 Henry Henry began a training period of three years during which he was to recieve $25 worth of "cloaths" each year and a freedom suit at the end of his term.[42] The same conditions were offered to Davis Painter six years later.[43] Henry Care was promised more in 1862. He was to receive, in addition, a pair of boots; and the Furnace was to pay Nathan Care $75 per year to board his son.[44] Lincoln Palsgrove said he began to work at the blacksmith shop with his father at a very young age. He remembered making frequent trips to check the sundial in front of the shop to find how much longer the work day would last.[45]

Several father-son carpenter teams appeared in the Hopewell Furnace records. Jacob Keim, John Crosby and George Painter each collected wages for himself and a son. Keim was paid $1.25 per day and his son only 50¢.[46] But at about the same time John Sands earned at the very good rate of

---

[39] SM 2, pp. 53, 63; SM 4, p. 208; SM 14, p. 50; SM 9, p. 113.
[40] SM 4, pp. 167, 193.
[41] *Ibid.*, pp. 221, 235, 244.
[42] SM 35, p. 56.
[43] *Kemper Manuscripts,* C. M. Clingan Pocket Note Book, May 21, 1861.
[44] *Ibid.*, June 27, 1862.
[45] J. Lincoln Palsgrove Interview, October 13, 1940.
[46] SM 9, p. 125.

$1 per day which was paid to his father.[47] George Painter collected wages in 1835 for both himself and David and then asked the clerk to credit $119 to David's account.[48] Joseph Thomas was paid $4\frac{1}{2}$s. per day for mending flasks "by his Prentise."[49]

According to an old resident, about 1821 a 16-year-old boy named Wortz came to Hopewell as an apprentice wheelwright under Master Henry Houck. They made ox yokes, plow beams, wagon wheels and wagon tongues. After Houck died, Wortz stayed on as Hopewell's last resident wheelwright.[50]

The less skilled tasks in the community naturally offered opportunity for boys, and even girls, to earn some money for their families. Cutting wood was probably available to older boys most of the time because of the constant demand and also because the pay was on a piecework basis. There were a number of specific references to wood cut by boys[51] and possibly others where payment was made for wood without a concern for which member of the family did the work. Boys also found a source of income in picking pieces of iron from the slag heaps. The Furnace paid 1¢ per pound for this iron in the 1870's.[52]

Both boys and girls worked on the farms when there was a need for extra help, especially at reaping and harvesting. Day-rate pay for farm work held steady at 25¢ during the first half of the nineteenth century; but compensation for some farm jobs was on a piecework basis—for example, picking up potatoes. In almost all cases earnings were credited to the parents, but an exception was made in 1806

[47] SM 7, July 25, 1817, n. p.
[48] SM 21, p. 160.
[49] SM 44, June 15, 1805, n. p.
[50] Reginald Smith Interview, March 16, 1941. There was no record of such an employee in 1825 although John Wert and Peter Wert were teamsters. Henry Houck was a collier at that time.
[51] Some examples are SM 1, pp. 238, 267; SM 59, p. 18; SM 15, p. 27; SM 31, p. 29.
[52] Thomas Hoffman Interview, November 22, 1940.

when the clerk noted that cash payments had been made to "Cramp Girls" and "Hughes boys" for making hay. "John Harts Daug" also received cash for eggs which she sold to the Furnace.[53] On another occasion James Simmons was paid for haymaking done by his daughter, and two days later the daughter drew the same amount in cash from her father's account.[54]

Girls had fewer choices of kinds of work available to them than did the boys. Aside from farm work the girls were most frequently employed as maids and housekeepers. References to "Little Negro" and "Little dutch girl" indicated that they began service at the mansion at a young age.[55] In 1784 Mary Paine, seamstress, was collecting the wages for two daughters who were working as housekeepers.[56] "A Boadley girl" went to Philadelphia to do housework in 1830.[57] Since some of the Boadleys were Negroes, this girl may have been colored.

Much of the work done by children was not specifically identified as to the kind of job. The only reference found in many cases was the clerk's statement in the books that an adult was receiving payment "for work done" by a son, daughter or ward. Sometimes, but not always, the name of the child was included. Another source of income for a few fathers was a payment to sons for attending "the Batallion."[58]

Having a child working for the Furnace and collecting his pay was not all profit for a parent, however; for there were expenses which had to be met. Clothing represented the greatest cash outlay. Hats, trousers, jackets and shirts were sometimes purchased; and shoes were the cause of regular cash expenditures. In addition to shoes bought at the company store, several shoemakers made regular calls at the Fur-

[53] SM 4, pp. 88, 93.
[54] SM 1, p. 198.
[55] SM 35, pp. 66, 70.
[56] SM 41, p. 110.
[57] *Brooke Family Papers,* Probably Sarah Brooke to Edward Brooke, December 5, 1830.
[58] SM 10, p. 33. The reference was to militia duty.

nace and took orders. Jacob Hartenstine submitted an accounting for three years work done for Clement Brooke showing shoes bought or repaired at Brooke's expense in that time : "For Margaret 7 pairs, Miss Ann 1, Mr. Brooke 2, Charoline 10, Mariah 8, Church 8, Ben 5, Charles 7, Adoline 3, Eliza 4, Clement 3 and Mrs. Brooke 2." These people include members of the family and also children working at the Big House[59]

Grown children entered the record in relation to parents in a number of ways. So long as they were unmarried, they continued to live at home and paid for boarding, washing and sewing.[60] Joseph Hart employed his father to clean castings as additional income. David Hart had a large family and probably needed the extra money he could earn in this way.[61] David Hart, Junior, settled the account at the store after his father's death by a payment of 76.36\frac{1}{2}$.[62] Daniel Buckley sent his daughter Mary to the Furnace to collect cash in the amount of $1,060 owed to him, a small fortune by 1827 values.[63]

Children were prohibited from playing in the area around the cast house because of the danger of burns from the hot metal. They were not welcome anywhere that their presence would interfere with the work being done. But the attraction of the glowing stream of molten iron drawn from the furnace and flowing into the sand beds was too great for the children. When no one noticed, they would at least find a vantage point near a window to watch the casting. The ore roaster was also out of bounds to children when the fire was burning. Accidents were frequent around a furnace, and many children were injured in falls on the flight of stone steps near the office.[64]

[59] HV 8290228.
[60] SM 14, pp. 38, 69; SM 21, pp. 160, 161.
[61] SM 14, pp. 61, 78, 79.
[62] SM 38, p. 95.
[63] SM 59, p. 7.
[64] Samuel March Interview, January 22, 1941.

Lincoln Palsgrove recalled a gang fight between the boys who lived near the furnace and those who lived at the Pine Swamp. Fighting erupted in the area near the furnace over the attention paid to Hopewell girls by the boys from across the mountain.[65]

Some of the Furnace books had blank pages after the accounts ended, and the school children used these pages to practice their school sums and penmanship. On several pages the signatures of a long list of children appeared. Most of them were Cares, but scattered among them were several Coles. Since the Cares were white and the Coles were black, it would appear that integrated play was practiced in the Village.[66]

The Hopewell records show that the children worked from an early age and made a contribution to the family income. Boys were employed at most of the jobs at the furnace, and many girls found employment on the farms and in the homes. Orphans and the children in poorer families were sometimes bound or apprenticed under formal contracts which specified the conditions of their service and the obligations of the guardians. Except in the wealthier families the carefree period of childhood was of short duration, although many of the young people did not work full-time until their late teens.

[65] J. Lincoln Palsgrove Interview, October 13, 1940.
[66] SM 5.

18   Education

HAVING THE FURNACE OWNER LIVING IN CLOSE PROXIMITY TO his workers and remote from others of his class was an aid to the promotion of education among the children of the Hopewell community. The Brookes and Buckleys had children of their own to educate; so they found a teacher and permitted the other families to share the cost by paying tuition for sending their children. The Furnace was too far from other furnaces or from the towns to send the children to a central school or for a school to operate for ironmasters' children alone. The Hopewell Village child attended the one of several schools which was closest to his home. A school was located each year near the furnace with others at Warwick, Morgantown and the Jones Mine.

Until 1836 teaching was on a subscription or tuition basis. After that a public school for Union Township was located at the Furnace, although for some time longer a subscription school was conducted during the summer months. Ordinarily the instruction did not go beyond the elementary grades. The ironmasters sent their children to boarding school for secondary education, and most other children did not go any further with formal schooling. There were, however, other means to improve the mind for older children and adults such as newspapers, magazines, books and lectures.

346

The school at the Furnace had a number of men and at least one woman teacher from the beginning of the nineteenth century until the establishment of the public school. The earliest one was John Mullan (or McMullen) who gave Clement Brooke some of the last formal education he was to receive.[1] James Sands and Abraham Corb taught Hopewell children in the period from 1804 until the Furnace ceased operation in 1808. The number of pupils was not large, and they were for the most part from the families of higher incomes. Matthew Davis, manager; the two blacksmith Shafers; Edward Hughes, filler and job contractor; and Hugh Welsh, teamster, each sent one or more children.[2] Corb allowed his pay for 1808 to stand on the books until 1822 when it was transferred to Hampton Forge.[3] Perhaps he had taught at the Forge in the meanwhile.

William Brown, Robert Rankin, Ralph McClintock and William McGillivoray were paid for tuition in the period from 1817 to 1820.[4] McGillivoray was listed as a resident of East Nantmeal and was paid only by Clement Brooke; so he may not have been teaching at the Furnace. Lewis Evans taught the children of the Warwick area in the same period.[5] Rankin earned $57.82 in tuition for two quarters in 1819. Of this he drew $45.60½ in cash when he left in 1820.[6] Two payments for Rankin's tuition were made to Merchant R. Laverty of Morgantown and apparently were for storegoods.[7]

In the next fifteen years the following four masters and one mistress presided over the school sessions of the Hopewell subscription school: Christian Halderman, Andrew Collins, Thomas Foster, Robert D. Powell and Susan Brown. Collins was a minister who opened a school at least as early as 1825

[1] SM 2, p. 5.
[2] SM 1, p. 320; SM 4, p. 235; SM 5, p. 70; SM 67, May 6, 1807, n. p.
[3] SM 5, p. 70.
[4] SM 6, pp. 190, 216; SM 10, p. 18; HV 8170800; HV 8180710.
[5] Lewis Evans Journal, op. cit., pp. 30, 164.
[6] SM 6, p. 190.
[7] SM 10, p. 61.

when he proposed teaching in a house which, he was notified, was too far from the Furnace and in too bad condition for winter classes. He was informed that he might hold summer school there, however.[8] He was still teaching at Hopewell as late as 1837,[9] but there were several others who taught one or more terms during this period.

Teaching was not a full-time occupation for some of these men. Collins performed religious duties and Foster did a variety of jobs about the Furnace and became the clerk in 1836.[10]

While the higher-income families predominated among the pupils in this era, there were children from every economic level in the school. Many more of the children were receiving an education, including some who were apprenticed to the Furnace and the children of Wilkinson Hill, a Negro laborer.

The cost of sending a child to the subscription school was based on days of attendance with a flat rate for the quarter for those who attended regularly. In 1830 Foster assessed $1.75 per pupil per quarter, and Collins was charging the same the following year. The latter collected $2\frac{1}{2}c$ per day for a pupil who did not attend the entire quarter.[11] Clement Brooke paid full tuition for four unnamed children, and the Furnace paid "for E. North and B. Hill" at these rates.[12] Gilmore and Miss Brown received several payments of $3.00; so perhaps this was their fee per quarter.[13] It is possible that summer school had a different rate, for in 1833 Collins received payments ranging from 25c to $1.75 with only two being the same amount at $1.62\frac{1}{2}$.[14] Or maybe the quarterly payment was the same, but pupils were more difficult to hold

[8] *Hopewell Papers,* Note to Rev*d* Andrew Collins, unsigned and undated but notes on reverse of the paper were dated October 22, 1825.
[9] SM 21, p. 201.
[10] SM 15, p. 39; SM 21, p. 200. His name was also spelled Forster.
[11] SM 15, pp. 39, 61.
[12] *Cash Books* for 1828–1830, *op. cit.,* January 25, 1830, n. p.
[13] SM 59, p. 20; SM 14, p. 45.
[14] SM 21, p. 75.

to regular attendance when the weather was pleasant. By 1835 the tuition was raised to 3¢ per day.[15]

Subscription teaching continued at Hopewell after a public school had been established near the Furnace. In one quarter of 1840–1841 Daniel Jones had 21 pupils in attendance, including 4 Negroes. The tuition had dropped to $1.15 per quarter.[16] Another woman teacher must have served in 1846, for several persons made payments to "the School Mrs."[17]

Agreements with the teacher sometimes took the form of a contract, as this one in 1830 with Thomas Foster :

> We the subscribers do hereby Engage Thomas Foster to teach an English School Viz Spelling, Reading, Writing and Arithmetic for the term of three months to Commence on the first day of Dec 1830 for which we do agree to pay him one Dollar and Seventy five cts per quarter for Each Scholar Including firewood the School to be taught in the house lately occupied by Peter Wert.[18]

Although most of the education at the local school was on the lower level of elementary courses, there was at least one effort to teach some secondary subjects. Note in the following contract that prices were considerably higher for these classes, but the results were guaranteed :

> We the undersigned promise to pay Robert D. Powell for the tuition of our children the following prices, viz for instruction in the Latin Language five dollars per quarter, for English Grammar, Geography, or any of the higher branches of an english education three dollars per quarter, and for Reading writing and arithmetic two dollars and twenty five cents per quarter—with this understanding that if any subscriber should be dissatisfied to the price, at the expiration of one month he shall have the prevelege of withdrawing his subscription. The quarter shall consist of thirteen weeks. Those

[15] SM 21, pp. 124, 135.
[16] SM 28, pp. 61, 62.
[17] SM 31, pp. 19, 20.
[18] *Hopewell Papers,* Copy of agreement with Thomas Foster, uncatalogued.

who subscribe for a quarter and should exceed that time will be charged in the ratio as above stated—those who do not subscribe for a quarter, and should send by the day will be charged 4 cents per day.[19]

Under the public school system the county superintendent of schools made an effort to maintain standards for the teachers under him by means of examinations in the subjects to be taught. The following letter shows the struggle he faced :

> Have raised the standard and Warwick must come up to a higher mark in qualification or lose the state appropriation. They are disposed to employ teachers of too low qualification. This year I rejected 2 Employed last year, who made no improvement whatever. I will do this in an emergency : If the School Board of Warwick are disposed to employ you, they must request me to endorse your Certificate or Examine. This must be done in writing and signed by at least 3 Members of the S. B. They had better have 4.
>
> I cannot promise you a certificate, if Examined, for my standard has been raised and as you barely received one before, and have been off for one year, the probabilities are you cannot reach it. But, if you are conscious of having improved since then in any of the branches, I would try to secure better marks. . . .[20]

Sending a child to school involved expenses other than tuition. Writing materials were costly as "1 led Pencell" sold at the Hopewell store in 1817 for $12\frac{1}{2}$¢, one-half-day's pay for work on the farm.[21] Quills cost $\frac{1}{2}$¢ each, ink powder $12\frac{1}{2}$¢ per packet [22] and paper 1¢ per sheet. The children often used pages spoiled by the clerk for their arithmetic and penmanship practices. Spelling, grammar and arithmetic books were purchased by parents from the Hopewell store, from stores in Reading or West Chester, from the teacher or from another

[19] *Ibid.,* Contract between Parents and Teacher. Undated but Powell taught at Hopewell in 1835–1836. See SM 21, p. 165.
[20] HV 8750731. HFP on letterhead of Superintendent of Common Schools of Chester County to "Friend Long." This may have been Harker Long, sometime manager of Hopewell Furnace.
[21] SM 8, p. 79.
[22] *Ibid.,* p. 136; SM 40, p. 234.

parent. "Lewis' Arithmetic" sold for $37\frac{1}{2}$¢ and "Kirkham's Grammer" at $87\frac{1}{2}$¢. Spelling books cost 25¢ new and 11¢ on the secondhand market.[23] Mathematics students sometimes compiled a kind of textbook of their own by copying rules and problems on folded ledger paper and working out the solutions on the bottom of the sheets.[24]

Pupils came from all classes of Hopewell society, from apprentices who were sent to fulfill the requirements of their apprenticeship agreement and poor children who received some help from the township to the children of the ironmaster's family. They began at less than five years of age[25] and continued as long as the parents could afford to send them or until they were old enough for jobs. Apparently by 1830 most of the Hopewell people were able to sign their own names. In that year a subscription for the Bethesda Baptist Church contained 32 signatures. The handwriting differed for each name and was clearly not all done by the same person.[26] On the other hand the official collector of militia fines for Union Township in 1820 signed his receipts with "his mark" and had them witnessed. He was not a Furnace employee, however.[27]

The public school system brought a new kind of financing of education for Union Township. School taxes were collected in 1844 in the amount of $53.45 for the Furnace property. The clerk also paid the collector for the individual tax of 23 workers in amounts ranging from 10¢ to $2.70.[28] State appropriations now provided another source of educational income. Union Township forfeited its state allotment in 1835, because it had no public school in operation. It began collecting its appropriation in 1836 and continued regularly thereafter. For

[23] SM 9, pp. 181–183; SM 10, pp. 37, 38; SM 28, p. 16; *Cash Book for 1828–1830*, November 10, 1829, and January 8, 1830, n. p.
[24] *Hopewell Papers, Stokes Collection.*
[25] *Mount Hope Journal, 1800–1819,* memorandum page.
[26] HV 8300111.
[27] HV 8200609A.
[28] SM 28, pp. 130, 131.

1839 the amount was $155.38.[29] Caernarvon Township received $189 for 1838.[30]

The early school sessions were held in vacant houses in the Village, in the "boarding house" and at the Bethesda Baptist Church, which was located about three-fourths of a mile from the Furnace.[31] In 1836 the company paid to have a schoolhouse built near the center of furnace operations. Thomas Knaur received $34.80 for the mason work and an additional $1 for building a chimney at the new school. The Union Township School District reimbursed Clement Brooke and Company the sum of $425 "for building a new schoolhouse etc." An additional payment of $20.25 was made for "3 Tons of Stone coal del. to schoolhouse."[32] There were later payments for both coal and wood used for fuel.[33]

From the descriptions given by old Hopewell residents this building was 28 feet by 35 feet, one story, built of stone with a shingle roof. The single door opened inward to a partitioned entry extending the length of the building and used to store wood and supplies. The building was heated by a stove placed in the center of the room. A "disciplinary bench" was placed between the teacher's desk and the stove. The desks and backless benches occupied by the pupils were ordered along three sides. The pupils sat with their faces to the wall and their backs to the teacher. Boys sat on the north side, girls on the south and the excess of each on the west. The teacher's desk was on a raised platform on the east side of the room. Books and papers had to be kept on the tops of the study tables because there were no drawers or under-desk compartments.[34]

There must have been an earlier movement to build a

[29] *Berks and Schuylkill Journal,* January 20, 1838.
[30] *Morris Diary, op. cit.,* p. 53.
[31] Long, *Historical Sketch, op. cit.,* p. 10.
[32] SM 21, pp. 194, 195.
[33] SM 28, p. 120; SM 32, p. 39.
[34] Sally Boone Interview, March 22, 1941, and Katherine Rhoads and Rose Sands Interview, March 4, 1941. Mrs. Rhoads taught at Hopewell in 1871.

school at Hopewell, for in 1832 David Shaffer paid his tuition for two children and gave an additional 25¢ as "so much paid subscription to school house."[35] Another building, constructed about 1870 a half mile from the furnace along the road to the Jones mine, served the educational needs of Hopewell children until after the Furnace closed in 1883.[36]

The public school law received criticism from the Village people, with particular opposition to the system of State appropriations from one writer who declared:

> It is time that this humbuggery on the part of the state in the matter of common school appropriations should cease. Let the people in each school district elect directors as they now do and let these directors have power . . . to raise by taxation, a sum sufficient to keep the schools of the district open as they now are. . . . In any case the state should cease her appropriations for educational purposes, even if the whole common school system should fall to the ground. She ought to be honest before being liberal.[37]

Mrs. Catherine Rhoads, who taught at Hopewell in 1871, said she had 25 pupils ranging in age from 6 to 20. The school term at this time was six months, and in addition a summer subscription school of two months was held. Although most parents paid for the summer school, Dr. Clingan paid for some whose parents could not afford it. Mrs. Rhoads was of the opinion that summer school was scheduled whenever Dr. Clingan was annoyed by the number of children playing around the Furnace. He would say, "There are too damn many youngsters about; we'd better open a summer school."[38]

In its earliest period the free school had a five-month term beginning in August and was sometimes followed by a subscription term in the spring.[39] The schoolmaster summoned the pupils for each session by the ringing of a small hand bell.

[35] SM 21, p. 32.
[36] H. A. Long Interview, August 13, 1936.
[37] *Morris Diary, op. cit.,* II, p. 103. Written in 1844.
[38] Catherine Rhoads Interview, May 13, 1941.
[39] *Morris Diary, op. cit.,* pp. 84, 115.

Hopewell Schoolhouse Built About 1870

1870 Schoolhouse, Side View

On the last day of school teacher and pupils brought lunches and walked to a grove on the northwest slope of Mount Pleasant for a picnic.[40]

Conduct of pupils was not always exemplary. Ann Church wrote on her penmanship practice sheet, "Nathan Care is a very bad Boy he . . . has threatened the girls very bad."[41] Later the bigger boys persuaded a pupil to start a fight with a woman teacher, but she won and administered a good whipping.[42] Lincoln Palsgrove recalled a quick exit through a window to escape a switching.[43] Physical punishment was evidently severe at the boarding schools, also. Ann Brooke wrote to her brother Edward :

> I heard in the city of Mr. Fuller having chastised George in the most brutal manner . . . I heard that for some slight provocation (throwing a chesnut shell) Mr. Fuller had whiped and then *kicked* George, such treatment as that no man shall ever inflict on a brother of mine while he is at school. . . .[44]

The ironmaster's children, and occasionally others, went to boarding school after attending the Hopewell school. George Brooke progressed from Mr. Buck's School in Lititz to Mr. Fuller's in West Chester and finished with Samuel Gummere in Burlington, New Jersey.[45] The girls studied at Mr. Price's School in West Chester and then went to Mr. Hamilton's in Philadelphia and possibly to Bristol College or Mr. Gummere's, both in Burlington.[46]

Tuition in the boarding schools was $30 to $40 per quarter in the 1830's. Master Gummere announced that for 1835 he

[40] Sally Boone Interview, March 22, 1941.

[41] *Hopewell Papers,* Penmanship practice sheets. The date March 25, 1831, appeared.

[42] Charles Sheridan Painter Interview, April 12, 1958. The teacher was the Mrs. Rhoades previously mentioned.

[43] J. Lincoln Palsgrove Interview, November 26, 1948.

[44] *Brooke Family Papers,* probably March, 1832, as George entered Mr. Fuller's School at West Chester in 1831.

[45] *Ibid.,* September 3, 1831; HV 8351228B.

[46] SM 12, p. 107; HV 8320420; *Hopewell Papers, Stokes Collection,* Elizabeth Barde to Sarah A. Brooke, February 12, 1837; HV 8351228B.

was raising his fee from $35 to $40 per quarter; but he also stated that he was striking out the charge formerly made for fuel, candles, pens, ink and slate pencils.[47] Other expenses added considerably to the cost of education. In 1825 Clement Brooke paid one bill of $388.21 "for schooling received in City."[48] Caroline and Marie Brooke had a total of $5 for spending money for a quarter at West Chester, but they were not intrusted with this sum at one time. It was left with Philip Price to be advanced to them.[49] The kinds of expenses a child at school incurred are shown in the following accounting for Caroline and Maria for 1831 and 1832 at the Price School :

For Stationery etc . .   for 2 qrs. Viz
Blank Books 89 Knife $37\frac{1}{2}$ India Rubber $12\frac{1}{2}$ 1.39
Woodbridge's Geog. and Atlas 1.00
        Willard's Geog. and At. 50   1.50
Lead Pencils 49 Paper 51 B. Bks 2 17   3.17
Ruler $6\frac{1}{4}$ Slate 25 Knives $50\frac{1}{4}$ Paper 76 $1.63\frac{1}{4}$
Willard's Atlas $37\frac{1}{2}$ Quills etc for each 1 qr 1.00 $1.37\frac{1}{2}$
Paper 94 2 Gummere's Geog 50 Gramr $37\frac{1}{2}$ $1.81\frac{1}{2}$
India Rubber 6 Pencil 4 Blank bks 1.153/4 $1.25\frac{3}{4}$
1 Sheet of Transparent ppr. 50 ppr $12\frac{1}{2}$ $.62\frac{1}{2}$
Wafers $6\frac{1}{4}$ Arith 25 Quills etc 1.00 $1.31\frac{1}{2}$
Board and Tuition of each 1 qr.   60.00
1 Course of Lessons in Painting   5.00

Extras Furnished
Cash for glass etc $93\frac{3}{4}$ Cutting hair and tooth
        brush 25 $1.18\frac{3}{4}$
1 Pr of Booties 1.44 lacings 8 Hooks 6 Tape 5   1.63
Comb 20 Mending shoes 25 Trunk $1.12\frac{1}{2}$ $1.57\frac{1}{2}$
Shoes for M. $1.12\frac{1}{2}$ Comb, Brush Cup and Soap
        for C. $62\frac{1}{2}$ 1.75
Cup and Comb for M. $31\frac{1}{4}$ Boots for do. $1.37\frac{1}{2}$ $1.68\frac{3}{4}$
Medicine $1.00 Shoes for Caroline $1.37\frac{1}{2}$ 2 Bags $37\frac{1}{2}$ 2.75
Vaccination (for 2) 50 Filing teeth 50 Carmine 25   1.25
Medical Attendance of Marie 5.25   5.25
Carmine $43\frac{1}{4}$ Lacings 8 2 prs. of Gloves 1.50 $2.01\frac{3}{4}$

[47] HV 8351228B.
[48] SM 12, p. 44.
[49] SM 15, p. 24.

Bristol Board 40 Postage 1.75 Mending Shoes 12½	2.27½
Show 40 Pins 10 Print Box 3.00 Buttons 10	3.60
Allowance of .25 per wk for C and M 24 Wks	6.00
Repairing Clothes 1.14 Cash 23½ Ribband 1.06	2.43½

Total Amount $112.49[50]

The expenses of a young man at boarding school are disclosed in this accounting for John Church:

TO 1 Olneys Gography and Atlas $1.00   1 Slate .25 1
     Arith .31¼
   1 Gummals Surveying $1.62½ Box Instruments $5.25
   1 Blank Book .81¼ 1 Bonnycastle Mensuration .87½
   18½ weeks Board and Tuition @ $30 per 12 weeks
   Light $1.15½ Medicine .12½
   8 sheets paper .08 Quills .10 Ink .12½ Pencils .02
   Hickman and Mercers shoe acct. $2.12½
                                   $60.10½[51]

Boarding schools had their financial problems and sometimes were forced to close. Elizabeth Barde wrote in 1837:

> . . . I suppose you have heard long ere this that Bristol
> Colege was very much involved in debt; for the last two weeks
> the studants had but one meal a day, the butchers and baker
> were not willing to trust and of course they were obliged to
> eat food of the coarest kind . . . College closes Wednesday
> and if they can collect funds sufficiently to go on they will
> commence again. . . .[52]

In addition to the common school subjects young ladies learned dancing, riding, French and Latin.[53] Young gentlemen learned natural philosophy, Latin, French, Greek and surveying.[54] Apparently both boys and girls found difficulty in keep-

[50] HV 8320420.
[51] HV 8340109A.
[52] *Hopewell Papers, Stokes* Collection, Elizabeth Barde to Sarah R. Brooke, February 12, 1837.
[53] *Brooke Family* Papers, Sarah Brooke to Edward Brooke, January 14, 1835; Ann F. Brooke to George W. Brooke, April 15, 1833.
[54] *Ibid.,* G. B. R. to Edward Brooke, January 28, 1833.

ing their minds on their work. A young man announced he was "... banishing from my mind the gravity of . . . hard study, the girls, and a thousand other ills that flesh is heir to. . . ."[55] A young lady complained of Professor Cleveland's long lessons. But she spent "very little time in committing them to memory."[56]

George Brooke gave some impressions of his school at Burlington in the following letter to his brother:

> We have but 16 or 18 schollars, 5 of which are old ones and 4 preachers or rather learners to be preachers. One of the latter is 41 years old another about 30 and the remainder over 21. We have a Chapter of the Bible read and a prayer every morning before school commences besides grace said before every meal. . . . The man I spoke of as being 41 years old rents a little house by our dwelling house, to live in; he cooks for himself and makes his own bed and does everything for himself but washing. He lives on bread and milk and studies in his own room but recites in the school house. . . ."[57]

Any consideration of education in the Village would be incomplete without some attention to the reading matter available and non-institutional means of education. The wide interests of the ironmaster and a part of the workers was reflected in the number and variety of newspapers which came to the Furnace in the nineteenth century. The market for Furnace products created an interest in events in nearby communities and the large cities.

Berks County news was obtained from the *Berks and Schuylkill Journal* for which a subscription appeared as a Furnace expense as early as 1816 and as late as 1859. This newspaper was a weekly published in Reading and sold at $2 per year for most of the span of time mentioned.[58] Interest in the Lancaster area market accounted for subscriptions over many

[55] *Ibid.*
[56] *Ibid.*, Sarah to Edward Brooke, January 14, 1835.
[57] *Ibid.*, G. W. Brooke to Edward Brooke, May 8, 1834.
[58] HV 8160806A; SM 65, January 29, 1859, n. p.

years to the *Lancaster Journal* at as much as $5 per year.[59] The Furnace paid $12.25 "for newspapers at Harrisburg," but the clerk did not name the publications.[60]

Politics as well as business entered into Clement Brooke's interest in the *Chester County Whig* in 1834 when he ordered subscriptions for himself, John Care and James Roberts. He added, "Probably I may get more Subscribers in the Course of this Month." He obtained at least one more, for later in the year David Care was listed with this group.[61] Chester County news was also secured from the *Village Record* of West Chester and possibly from the *Chronicle of the Times*—no place of publication was given for this newspaper.[62]

City newspapers were common at the Furnace with chief emphasis on the Philadelphia publications. In 1809 Mathew Brooke subscribed to William Duane's *Aurora*. He received the country edition which was published three times per week at $5 per year. The city editions appeared daily at $9. The *Aurora* was continued for a number of years among Furnace expenses.[63] Many names of newspapers appeared only once; or possibly the same newspaper was intended by similar but not identical names, for example: *Pennsylvania Enquirer, Inquirer and Gazette, United States Gazette, United States Post, United States Saturday Post and Chronicle* and *Saturday Chronicle*. The Furnace had subscribed for many years to the *National Gazette* and continued through several mergers in the 1840 which brought the *Pennsylvania Inquirer* and *United States Gazette* into the same publication. In 1859 this combination became *The Philadelphia Inquirer*.[64] The *New York Ledger* and a newspaper called the *Repertory* of unknown origin also were among the publications read at Hope-

---

[59] HV 8190501A.
[60] SM 28, p. 84.
[61] HV 8340422A and HV 8341213E.
[62] SM 65, April 2, 1857, n. p.; SM 17, p. 8.
[63] *Brooke Family Papers,* Bill from William Duane, February 1, 1809, and HV 8181020A.
[64] *The Philadelphia Inquirer,* Supplement, September 16, 1962; HV 8350107A; HV 8390103A; HV 8400103B.

well.[65] Special interests and vocational concern accounted for subscriptions to *The Episcopal Recorder, The Temperance Advocate, The Tariffite and Guard* and *The Miners Journal.*

In addition to the ironmaster there were workers who had their own subscriptions to newspapers. Specific mention was made of subscription or postage charges for newspapers bought by John Lloyd, J. B. Wickel, Hashabiah Clemens, John Wamsher, John Richards, Henry Care, Joseph Hart, David Smith and Thomas Care. These included not only a founder and several molders but also a shoemaker, a farm worker and two woodcutters.

For the magazine readers the *Saturday Evening Post* came to the Furnace during a number of years. The price was $2 per year in the 1840's but dropped to $1 in the 1850's.[66] Magazine tie-in sales evidently were not unknown early in the nineteenth century when this offer appeared:

> For $10 sent postage free to C. Alexander, Athenian Building, Franklin Place, Phila., he furnishes 5 Copies of the Weekly Messenger and 5 of the Silk Growers and Farmers Manual and a premium Copy of the Popular Magazine or 1000 Nights Entertainment.[67]

Books were present in the homes of quite a few Hopewell families. On several occasions the Furnace purchased a number of books, but there was no indication whether they were for sale or as managerial reading matter.[68] For several years the Furnace also paid a $5 subscription to "the Select Circulating Library,"[69] and in 1847 bought a map of the United States for $6.[70] Many purchases of books were probably school texts for the use of children in the family, but the house-to-house book salesman made visits to the Village to sell books

---

[65] SM 12, p. 95; SM 65, February 19, 1859, n. p.
[66] SM 31, pp. 4, 108, 137; SM 65, January 9, 1855, n. p.
[67] *Morris Diary, op. cit.,* p. 67.
[68] SM 21, p. 151; SM 28, pp. 59, 136, 142.
[69] SM 17, p. 31; HV 8350106B.
[70] SM 31, p. 45.

for more general reading. In 1833 seven of the molders paid
$2.75 each for copies of *The Family Encyclopaedia*.[71] In the
next decade Isaac Eaby sold books to eight village families at
prices ranging from 25¢ to $2.[72] The almanac was stocked
annually at the Furnace store.

Traveling lecturers brought a different kind of educational
opportunity to the people of the Village in the middle decades
of the nineteenth century. A handbill announcing a series of
lectures by Alex. A. Young was circulated at Hopewell to
ascertain interest and promote ticket sales. According to the
handbill, the speaker proposed to deliver:

> A course of Lectures, on Ancient and Modern History,
> Geography, and miscellaneous subjects of Natural Philosophy,
> etc.
>   The main object of these Lectures being, to cultivate the
> understanding, by rendering the exercises both interesting and
> instructive, he will make it his principal aim, to deliver his
> illustrations, in an easy and familiar style. . . .[73]

The weekly series cost $1, or $1.50 for a "gentleman and
lady." Children under twelve years of age could hear all
addresses for 50¢. Admission for a single lecture was 25¢ for
adults and half that amount for children. Twelve Hopewell
men signed the handbill to signify an interest; but, when it
came to making payment, eight lost their enthusiasm. However, seven adults and three children paid $10.50 for twelve
admissions. Benjamin Hill, Negro hostler, paid $2 from his
weekly pay of six dollars.[74]

The handbill did not say where the lectures were to be held,
but the next January this man gave his talks at Morgantown.
The response of one customer was not effusive:

[71] SM 17, p. 47.
[72] SM 31, p. 17.
[73] *Hopewell Papers*. Handbill of Lectures by Alex. A. Young, probably
1836.
[74] *Ibid*.

attended a lecture by Alex. E. Young on ancient history, illustrated by the magic lanthorn. He exhibited Adam and Eve leaving the garden, the building of the Tower of Babel, Moses striking the Rock, the Feast of Balshazaar, the gathering of the Manna, etc. — Lecture poor.[75]

Other lectures in the series considered Egypt, Carthage and "Phrenology with a mapped head."[76] The evident versatility of the speaker, however, did not prevent him from certain indiscretions. The sheriff came looking for him to answer charges that he had used "some hard names as scoundrel, villian, swindler" in reference to General George M. Keim, the "Democratic-Van Buren-Loco Foco-Radical-Hard Money Candidate" for Congress.[77]

Morgantown was also treated, over a period of several years, to lectures on astronomy, phrenology by another expert on "the science of bumps on the craniums" and education. The last was a free address by "a Mr. Warren," who was seeking scholars for an academy which he had recently opened in Strasburg.[78]

An interest in science led James Morris to visit Reading to see "an electro-magnetic machine exhibiting at the public buildings."[79] He also experimented personally in science by spending a day making a camera obscura and "succeeded tolerably well."[80]

The people of Hopewell Village showed an interest in education for their children in their support of subscription schools until the public school act encouraged the building of a school at the Furnace. Even after this a subscription school found support for at least summer terms. In the early Furnace history education was largely for the children of the better-paid employees, but by the 1820's the children of the

[75] *Morris Diary, op. cit.,* p. 3.
[76] *Ibid.,* pp. 5, 10.
[77] *Ibid.,* pp. 12, 44.
[78] *Ibid.,* I, p. 100; II, pp. 26, 116.
[79] *Ibid.,* p. 52.
[80] *Ibid.,* p. 222.

lower-paid workers also were receiving some instruction. Many people of the Village kept informed by reading newspapers, books and magazines and by attending public lectures and exhibits.

19   Religion

ACCORDING TO TRADITION THE IRON COMMUNITIES WERE rough and irreligious. George Whitefield, the celebrated Methodist evangelist, was reported to have been saved from bodily harm at Coventry Forge only by the intervention of Rebecca Grace, wife of ironmaster Robert Grace.[1] Support for a claim of lack of religious zeal at Hopewell Furnace was found on a Berks County map for 1820 which showed no church in Union Township, location of the Furnace.[2] But an examination of Hopewell records showed much religious activity among its people from ironmaster to laborer.

In 1806 young Clement Brooke made a contribution of £7½ for "the Subscription Money in Behalf of the New Church."[3] No identification of the church was given, but it was probably the St. Mary's Episcopal Church at Warwick. In the same year Daniel Buckley wrote to Mathew Brooke that he would like to see him about a business matter to be settled with the firm of Laverty and Jenkins. He suggested:

I will be at the meeting . . . at Warwick mine holes, about

[1] MacElree, *op. cit.*, pp. 510–511. Doubt about this incident, however, arises from the failure of Whitefield to mention Coventry in his journal.
[2] "Map of Berks County in 1820," Berks County Historical Society, F10HC.
[3] SM 44, November 20, 1806, n. p.

Noon to lay the foundation of the New Church . . . Mr.
Laverty will be there and perhaps Mr. Jenkins also.[4]

Clement Brooke later made contributions of money to assist
a church in Morgantown and one in Potts Grove.[5] In 1833
he received a letter thanking him for a gift of a stove for a
church in Junerville.[6]

The interest of the ironmaster in churches was a pattern
followed also by many of the workers. The Bethesda Baptist
Church, also known as Lloyd's Church, was located about
three-fourths of a mile from the Furnace and was supported
by Hopewell Village people. The African Methodist Episcopal
Mount Frisby Church was about three miles away. Many
villagers also attended St. Mary's Episcopal Church at Warwick, the Evangelical Association Church along the road from
the Furnace to Warwick, St. Gabriel's Episcopal Church in
Douglasville, St. Thomas' Episcopal Church or the Methodist
and Presbyterian Churches in Morgantown, and the Plow
Lutheran Church in Robeson Township.

An early interest in regular religious instruction in Berks
County was shown in a letter signed by a number of settlers,
including William Bird, and sent in 1760 "To the Venerable
Society for Propagating the Gospel in Foreign Parts." The
Society in London was requested to send a missionary to reside in Reading, and the signers promised to pay him £60
in Pennsylvania money above whatever the Society allowed
him. The petitioners regretted that the children were not being
instructed in the Episcopal faith and lamented that "various
sorts of Sectaries, and which is still worse the Roman Cathalic
priests are making converts among us."[7]

The absence of a church at the Furnace compound did not
mean that religious services were not held there. The

[4] HV 8060404.
[5] SM 12, p. 60; *Cash Book* for 1828–1830, August 13, 1829, n. p.
[6] HV 8331119.
[7] Quoted in William DuHamel, "Historical Sketch of Willam Bird,
Founder of Birdsboro, Pa." (Unpublished typescript, 1928), Hopewell
Village Library.

Reverend Mister Levi Bull, who served the St. Mary's Church for about half of the nineteenth century, recorded in his diaries a number of times that he had preached at Hopewell. He mentioned services in the private homes of the Buckleys, Bensons and Wynns and at the "Union S. H.," which indicated meetings were held in the East Nantmeal schoolhouse. In the period from 1838 to 1847 he listed services at Hopewell with regularity in the winter months during some of these years. He seemed to think that the Psalms were the most valuable sources of texts for sermons to the Furnace-area residents. He also held services at the Hopewell Mineholes.[8]

St. Gabriel's Episcopal Church at Douglasville was the earliest regular center for the worship of Furnace people. The building had been used first by a Swedish Lutheran congregation, but it became Episcopal in 1753.[9] William Bird's marriage to Brigitte Hulings was published there in 1735, and also his widow's remarriage to John Patton in 1762.[10] William was one of the first two trustees chosen for the St. Gabriel's congregation, and his son Mark served several terms as vestryman in the 1760's.[11] Maria Church, who became Mrs. Clement Brooke, was confirmed in this church two years before her marriage in 1808.[12] Mathew Brooke took Elizabeth Barde as his bride there some five years before he received the sacrament of adult baptism in 1815.[13]

Many other Hopewell families were among the communicants and officers of St. Gabriel's Church in the nineteenth century. Prominent among them were Umstead, Kirlin, Jones, Sands, Trago, Millard, Yocom, Bannan, McKinty, Donehower, Bunn, Wamsher, Dehaven, Chestnutwood, Pierce and Evans. The Reverend Mister Levi Bull served as rector of this church, as well as St. Mary's and St. Thomas', until about

---

[8] *Levi Bull Diaries, passim* pages, Chester County Historical Society.
[9] Montgomery, *History of Berks County, op. cit.,* p. 949.
[10] *St. Gabriel's Church Records,* Berks County Historical Society, pp. 65, 70.
[11] *Ibid.,* pp. 62, 103.
[12] *Ibid.,* p. 113.
[13] *Ibid.,* pp. 275, 343.

1830 when "Rev. Mentzer" began his pastorate at Douglasville.[14]

Levi Bull was a celebrated minister who made Warwick the center of his activities for more than fifty years. He covered a large parish and was frequently invited to preach at more distant churches. He was the son of Colonel Thomas Bull of Revolutionary War fame and a celebrated ironmaster.[15] Levi was a businessman as well as preacher; he must have needed the additional income to support his household of 19 persons in 1830.[16] At St. Mary's many Hopewell families were communicants: Ubel, Goheen, Chestnutwood, Painter, Richards, Mervine, Danahower, Yocum, Templin, Kaler, Filman, Pawling, Millard, Thomas, Bingaman, Hare, Dampman, Mengel, Lloyd, Mee, Care, Sheeler, Landis, Palsgrove, Wamsher, Dehaven, Hartenstine, Gilmore, Kephart and North were among them. Both the Mathew and Clement Brookes families were members there.[17] Clement Brooke was baptized in 1813 as were his six children over the years from 1809 to 1825.[18]

In 1843 St. Mary's church was closed in order that a new building could be erected on the same site. During the construction Mr. Bull served full time at Morgantown at a salary of $200 per year. Since this was an increase over the amount St. Thomas' had been paying, the congregation found it necessary to raise the pew rents by 40 per cent to 50 per cent.[19] The cornerstone of the new Warwick church was laid before a large crowd on June 14, 1843; and the building was consecrated the following December 22.[20]

The St. Thomas' Episcopal Church was opened at Morgantown in 1825. Support for the religious program was obtained

[14] *Ibid.,* pp. 6, 397.
[15] *Reading Eagle,* February 18, 1917.
[16] *Census of 1830,* Chester County, East Nantmeal Township, p. 198 ff.
[17] *St. Mary's Episcopal Church Records,* Berks County Historical Society.
[18] *Ibid.,* pp. 167–179.
[19] *Morris Diary, op. cit.,* II, p. 30.
[20] *Ibid.,* pp. 59–60.

Bethesda Baptist Church and Churchyard

by renting the pews at annual fees ranging from $3 to $8. Some pews were shared by two families who divided the expenses. Hopewell names among the first pew renters were Henry Mengel, Robert Laverty, Jacob Kurtz, Daniel Ubil and Edward Goheen. All paid $6 rental except Merchant Laverty who paid a dollar more.[21] Women were much more numerous than men in the early work of this church. The membership roll for 1828 included 85 women, 41 men and 5 names which could not be identified by sex.[22]

The Plow Lutheran Church in Robeson Township was founded in 1810 when a lottery was held to raise money to build a church and school. Five thousand tickets were sold

[21] *St. Thomas Episcopal Church Records,* Berks County Historical Society, p. 114.
[22] *Ibid.,* p. 120.

at $3 each. Everyone with a ticket was to receive a prize
ranging from a top of $600 to a low of $2. There were 4,723
of the latter amount. Twenty per cent was deducted from
each prize for the church-school fund. Many ticket-holders
did not draw their prizes but gave the entire amount to the
church. Hopewell names among the communicants at Plow
Church included : Segfred, Fries, Ammon, Westley, Wirt,
Donahauer, Wamsher, Mengel, Ehrgood, Kramp, Roads,
Handwart, Handwork, Hartenstine, Hottenstein and Pals-
grof.[23]

The church most closely identified with the Furnace was
the Bethesda Baptist Church, located in Chester County but
less than a mile from the Big House. Tradition claims this
area as a place of worship as early as 1780, and on a collar-
beam in the attic of the present building someone wrote with
charcoal, "Built 1782 By T. Lloyd." In 1962 the earliest
readable date on a tombstone in the cemetery was May 10,
1807, but several crude stones were undated and could have
been earlier. The will of Thomas Lloyd, dated July 27, 1819,
contained this provision :

> . . . I do . . . convey all that certain lot of three quarters
> of an acre of land whereon the meeting house and grave yards
> stands on my land for the use it was intended.[24]

The Lloyd family identified this lot as the one on which the
Bethesda Church was located. Transfer of title to the land
appears not to have been made, however, as this ground
was mentioned in several subsequent transfers of the Lloyd
titles. It was always stated that this lot was to be reserved
for church use.[25]

From the evidence presented above it is apparent that a
building which had been used for worship services stood at

[23] History of Plow Church, Robeson Township, Berks County, Pennsylvania (unpublished typescript, 1874), Berks County Historical Society.
[24] *Hopewell Papers,* Will of Thomas Lloyd, H–18 General.
[25] Russell A. Apple, "Bethesda Baptist Church Lot of $\frac{3}{4}$ Acre" (unpublished typescript, 1956), Hopewell Village Library.

that place prior to 1819. But the formal organization of the Baptist congregation took place on December 8, 1827. Simeon Seigfried, Senior, assisted with the organization and served for some years as the pastor.[26] Another early minister was Andrew Collins who also acted as schoolmaster for Hopewell children and taught classes at the church.[27] The 1827 founding date was confirmed by a service held in the church on December 8, 1877, to mark the fiftieth anniversary of the congregation.[28] Baptisms were held in the nearby stream, which gave it the name Baptizing Creek.[29]

In 1848 when a fund was solicited by David Lloyd to do some work at the graveyard, $22 was collected from Hopewell families.[30] A charter of incorporation was issued to the Bethesda Baptist Church on August 20, 1888, with the name of H. A. Long appearing as one of the ten petitioners.[31] As of 1963 services are still being held in this church with The Reverend Mister J. W. Sandiford as the minister. Like at least one of his predecessors he is a schoolteacher.

Support for services at the Bethesda Church was by pledges from its members rather than the more aristocratic pew rental. In 1830 the list of subscribers included 32 names, almost all of them Hopewell employees:

Thomas Lloyd	$ 8.00	William Hartman	$ 3.00
David High	8.00	Thomas S. Sharp	4.00
Nathaniel Sands	6.00	George Painter	2.00
George Lloyd	3.00	David High	1.00
David Lloyd	3.00	John Sheeler	3.00
Martin Richards	2.00	Susana Beavens	1.50
David Smith	2.50	Jonah John	2.00
Levi Bolls	2.00	John Hartenstine	1.00
David Smith	2.50	Samuel Richards	1.00
Sarah Matthias	2.00	Jacob Hartenstine	1.00

[26] *Daily Local News,* West Chester, Pennsylvania, August 24, 1929.
[27] *Bethesda Minute Book, op. cit.,* p. 6.
[28] *Ibid.*
[29] H. A. Long Interview, August 13, 1936.
[30] SM 31, pp. 72, 77, 81.
[31] *Bethesda Minute Book, op. cit.*

John Sands	2.00	John Richards	1.00
E. R. Sands	2.00	Henry Hartenstine	1.00
Samuel Hill	2.00	Andrew Keene	1.00
Samuel Lloyd	3.00	Frederick Miers	1.00
Isaac Kaplin	3.00	Lewis Evans	2.00
Nathaniel Kirby	3.00	Margaret Cook	1.00[32]

Activity at the church fluctuated, probably with the vigor of the pastors. In some years there were a number of accessions and then long periods when there were none.[33] The arrival of John J. Eberle as pastor in 1864 began a period of cleansing of the church roll and a check on the conduct of members. A committee of five men was appointed to call on "Delinquent Members," and 22 persons were named as worthy of the attention of the committee. The checkers reported back that two of those listed had joined another church. The remainder wanted to be continued on the Bethesda roll, but Henry Hartenstine "gave a very poor excuse for himself."[34]

At the same time a committee consisting of Sisters Parlaman and Smith was directed to call upon Sister Hannah Pearson and instruct her to be present at the next church meeting where her case would be considered. On February 4, 1865, the clerk recorded that "Sister H. Pearson Case was to lie over till the next meeting." But the wayward member never was able to answer whatever charges were made against her. Death came before trial.[35]

According to the minutes, Clerk Edward Parlaman resigned in 1865 and asked for his church letter:

> On account of Misconduct in the Church on the part of some evil disposed persons, he believing it his duty with others to prosecute the offenders, there being a difference of opinion in regards to it, in not taking legal process—he felt it his duty to offer his resignation and ask for his Letter. . . .

[32] *Brooke Family Papers,* List of subscribers to support Baptist Services at Bethesda Meeting House, January 11, 1830.
[33] *Bethesda Minute Book, op. cit.*
[34] *Ibid.,* December 10 and 31, 1864.
[35] *Ibid.*

He was persuaded to remain with the promise that "hereafter any violation of good order in the Church should be dealt with According to Law."[36]

This high resolve prompted action against additional members in the following year when the records stated :

> Moved . . . that John H. Miller be Excluded from the Church after hearing testamony of Several witteness and considerable talk he was Excluded for Neglecting the Church and drunkeness. Brother Eberle was appointed a committee to wait on John Houck, Hannah Houck his wife, Julia Keims to Say to them that the church has brought a charge against them of profanity and unless they doe appear at Church and give an Account of themselves they will be excluded.

These cases ended with the report that the accused persons had joined another church.[37]

Religion entered the Hopewell Furnace account books most frequently when the clerk made a payment of a pledge or pew rent for one of the employees. Many such payments were made to St. Mary's Church. Clement Brooke paid $5.33 in each of several years.[38] Jacob Mock had a better seat at an annual rent of $6,[39] but Henry Care could have listened to the same sermons from his $1.10 seat.[40] James Morris gave $5 for a pew which he shared with Samuel Jones in the Morgantown church.[41]

At a fashionable church in the city the cost of pew rental ran considerably higher. The estate of Charles M. Clingan in 1875 paid $51 for six months rent on "Pew Number 45" at the Church of the Holy Trinity in Philadelphia.[42] However, pew rights in this church were valuable assets. In the appraisement of the Clingan estate the pew right was valued at $900;

[36] *Ibid.*, February 4, 1865.
[37] *Ibid.*, March 18, 1866.
[38] SM 12, p. 131; SM 17, p. 17.
[39] SM 31, p. 9.
[40] SM 28, p. 98.
[41] *Morris Diary, op. cit.*, p. 12.
[42] HV 8750401B.

and, proving that this was not assessed too high, it sold soon afterwards for $1200.[43]

Men were expected to dress properly when they attended church services in the first half of the nineteenth century. But sometimes meteorological conditions dictated that less attention be paid to decorum than to comfort. In the intense heat of summer, coats and stocks were discarded.[44]

Judging from this Hopewell letter, the ministers' sermons had their critics:

> . . . this morning we attended church — the Rev gave us one of his *declamatory* sermons — addressed particularly to Parents — his style of preaching does not suit me — tho it may be the best adapted for the majority of his audience — there's nothing soothing or composing in his manner or language — mildness and persuasion forms the smallest part of his discourse. . . .[45]

Funerals were social occasions for the gathering of many people. James Morris noted that:

> The burial of Christian Hertzler at 10 A.M. was very numerously attended.
>
> As usual, with the Germans especially, a general and pressing invitation was given out for *all* to stay and dine. The number that set down to dinner is differently estimated at from 150 to 200.
>
> The preparations for this meal had been immense. Two whole quarters of beef had been provided, some 30 odd fowls and other things in proportion.[46]

Funeral plans were sometimes subject to change because of weather conditions. Henry A. Muhlenberg of Reading died on August 11, 1844, while he was campaigning for governor of Pennsylvania. The funeral was set for August 14, but "owing to Mr. Muhlenberg's retaining his freshness of appear-

[43] HV 8750508; HV 8751207.

[44] *Morris Diary, op. cit.,* p. 157.

[45] *Hopewell Papers, Stokes Collection,* Anna [no last name given] to Ann T. Brooke, February 16. No year given but probably 1835.

[46] *Morris Diary, op. cit.,* p. 229.

ance, the family on yesterday postponed his burial until today."[47]

In addition to the regular church services on Sundays, the people of Hopewell Village also attended prayer meetings, camp meetings and "protracted meetings." Prayer meetings were held either on weekdays or Sundays and were not always in the church.[48] Camp meetings were a popular summer activity and attracted a varied gathering of Furnace people. Clement Brooke attended in 1820 and May Hoyle, a maid, in 1849.[49] Miners, molders, founders, blacksmiths, keepers, teamsters and ordinary laborers drew cash in amounts from 22¢ to $10 to take with them when they went to the camp meeting.[50]

James Morris reported a Baptist protracted meeting in his diary:

August 9, 1844 Friday
This afternoon the Baptists commenced holding a protracted meeting out at the Rock School House near Jones' Mine holes. They have prepared a stand and seats and a large congregation. Very few attended this afternoon. . . .

August 11, 1844 Sunday
A large congregation assembled in the woods. Revᵈ. Mr. Nichols preached. . . .

August 18, 1844 Sunday
The Baptist meeting is still going on in Col. Jacob's woods. There were 5 persons baptized in the pool at the mine holes. A great number of people were present—some 2000 perhaps. . . .

August 25, 1844 Sunday
The Baptists immersed 6 or 7 men and women at the mine holes this forenoon. . . .

September 1, 1844 Sunday
The Baptists are still holding their protracted meeting in the woods by day and in the neighboring houses by night. . . .

[47] *Ibid.*, II, p. 148. August 15, 1844.
[48] *Ibid.*, II, p. 8.
[49] SM 10, p. 61; SM 31, August 6–16, 1849, n. p.
[50] Examples are SM 31, p. 153; SM 10, p. 39.

Revd. Mr. Bull [Episcopalian] took occasion this afternoon to preach a sermon on Baptism, in which he advocated infant baptism and sprinkling. . . .

September 4, 1844 Wednesday

The Baptists, whose meeting still continues, baptized nine persons this afternoon at Jones' Mine holes. They likewise organized a Society and have made some arrangements towards building a Church on land of David Potts, who has given them a free grant of ¾ of an acre, near the mine holes. The Society has 23 names on its lists.[51]

The Episcopalians of the Village area held their Associations and the Methodists their Quarterly Meetings "to make new converts" and "to rally the spirits of the old ones." Ministers combined their efforts, and people attended from distant towns at these fall or winter gatherings which lasted ten days to two weeks.[52]

Sunday School picnics were the high points of summer religious activity. July 3, 1841, was an especially lively day in and around Morgantown. According to one observer:

A celebration of the various Presbyterian and Episcopal Sunday Schools within some miles around takes place today at Waynesburg. The Episcopal S. School of this place [Morgantown] attends there. The Methodist Schools of the Circuit meet also today at Springfield for the same purpose.

From 8 to 10 o'clock A.M. the town was quite thronged with neatly dressed children with their teachers. A procession of the Episcopal School was got up. Several banners were aloft by the children bearing appropriate mottoes. A hymn was sung and the young folks with their teachers and parents shortly after moved off in wagons, dearborns, carriages, etc. to the number of about sixty.

The Methodist S. School got up no procession, being few in numbers, but moved off towards Springfield in a two horse wagon, dearborn, etc. Cakes in profusion were carried along with each party.[53]

[51] *Morris Diary, op. cit.,* II. Items taken from dates given.
[52] *Morris Diary, op. cit.,* pp. 240, 241, 248, 249; *Brooke Family Papers,* Ann to George W, September 3, 1831.
[53] *Morris Diary, op. cit.,* p. 155.

The Methodists must have picked up considerable strength in the next two years, for in 1843 they were reported to have had more than 2,000 in attendance at their Sunday School "Celebration" at the foot of Welsh Mountain.[54] The Episcopalian children carried a banner that year which read, "Morgantown Sunday School," on one side and on the other, "We have seen thy star and have come to worship thee." Cakes for the occasion consumed 150 pounds of flour. It was a successful affair except "that a couple of drunken men knocked up a fight towards evening."[55]

Religious reading matter at the furnace included family Bibles and regular issues of the *Episcopal Recorder*. Thomas Lloyd paid $5.00 for a Bible in 1819,[56] and a number of families had Bibles costing from $2.50 to $3.00 each.[57] Clement Brooke possessed a "Quarto Bible No. 4" for which he paid $2.25 in 1843.[58] Thomas Lloyd and John Painter bought testaments at 30¢ and 37½¢ each.[59]

The religious ferment in the nation in the 1840's brought some agitation to the people of Hopewell Village. A Mormon preacher was locked out of the Morgantown schoolhouse when he proposed preaching there in 1842. A "considerable congregation" had come to hear him.[60] A few months later two itinerant ministers of the Church of God were permitted to use the schoolhouse to proclaim the necessity of immersion to salvation and the damnation of all Mormons.[61] The Methodists were greatly alarmed in 1843 by a report that the Roman Catholics were collecting arms to massacre Protestants. This was a time when anti-Catholic feeling was strong in Philadelphia and elsewhere in the East.[62]

[54] *Ibid.,* II, p. 58.
[55] *Ibid.,* II, pp. 65, 66.
[56] SM 10, p. 38.
[57] SM 31, pp. 10, 12, 20.
[58] HV 8430503C.
[59] SM 6, p. 226; *Cash Book* for 1828–1830, March 3, 1830, n. p.
[60] *Morris Diary, op. cit.,* p. 181.
[61] *Ibid.,* p. 208.
[62] *Ibid.,* II, p. 26.

William Miller's Adventist movement won some Village people to watch for the end of the world. The Millerite newspaper, *Midnight Cry,* was read in the area; but interest declined after the foretold date passed without heavenly visitation.[63]

Some people in the Hopewell area still held a belief in witchcraft as late as the middle of the nineteenth century. Educated people, however, did not believe or were "ashamed to say so" if they did. Witchcraft was credited with being the cause of the following series of events in 1842 :

> The dinner pot of a family which had been used a couple of days before, was found to contain three small balls of silvery lustre. These balls were a token of witchcraft, especially as some of the family had been very restless at night and unable to sleep. It was plain that they were bewitched, so the balls were taken and according to the regular method in such cases, were fired from a gun into a tree—a white oak and shortly after a woman in the immediate neighborhood complained sadly of a sore leg. The case was now plainer than ever. It was undoubtedly one of witchcraft and the woman with the sore leg was the witch that had bewitched the family and that was shot by the silver bullets. So the witches are not all dead yet.[64]

David Mast, Junior, shocked the community in 1839 by hauling his grain from the fields on Sunday. Farmers did not work in the fields on the Lord's Day.[65] But, of course, everyone was aware that furnace workers and colliers kept their fires burning seven days a week.

Religious holidays were observed or ignored according to the strength of traditions, superstitions clinging to the day or nationalities. The Germans, in general, were holding onto the old traditions more firmly than others; and they were most likely to associate weather conditions with certain days. The

[63] *Ibid.,* II, pp. 1, 11. This was in 1843 and 1844.
[64] *Ibid.,* p. 225. Morris was relating this with tongue in cheek. He was not a believer.
[65] *Ibid.,* p. 82.

new year was welcomed by "watch meetings" in most churches.[66] Sunshine on Candlemas Day caused the ground-hog to see its shadow and was believed to frighten it into returning to its burrow for forty days more of cold weather.[67] Whitsun Monday was a day for Amish visiting dressed in their best clothes, but rain on Whit Sunday meant seven wet Sundays in succession.[68] To the Germans, also, July second was the day "Mary goes over the mountain;" and whatever weather prevailed on that day would continue for the next six weeks.[69] The Irish took time from work to celebrate "Sent Pattrick Day" and honor their homeland.[70] By the 1830's few except the Amish considered Good Friday a holy day, but some "Germans and Catholics observed Easter Monday."[71] Many farm children hid eggs for a month or more before Easter and brought them to the house on Good Friday to be boiled and colored.[72]

Thanksgiving Day received political as well as religious sanction on December 21, 1843, when Governor David R. Porter proclaimed its observance for Pennsylvania. Most of the people of the Hopewell community seemed uncertain about the proper commemoration of the new holiday. Church services were held with few worshipers attending. Both of the stores in Morgantown were officially closed for the day but sold goods to people who came and asked at the door.[73]

Christmas was the most generally observed of the religious days; but, it was said, "Some few keep it strict as a *holy* day while with the vast majority it is only kept for pleasure, visit-ing feasting, etc."[74] Religious service, held on Christmas and sometimes the day after, was like the Sabbath service but dealt

[66] *Ibid.*, II, p. 90.
[67] *Ibid.*, p. 97.
[68] *Ibid.*, pp. 202, 203.
[69] *Ibid.*, p. 81.
[70] *Changewater Account Books, op. cit.*, II, p. 4.
[71] *Morris Diary, op. cit.*, pp. 11, 12, 104.
[72] *Lewis Rishards Scrapbook, op. cit.*, Vol. D., p. 340.
[73] *Morris Diary, op. cit.*, II, p. 88.
[74] *Ibid.*, p. 250.

with the birth of Christ. Christmas night was spent quietly at home, and the next day was used for visiting among the country people.

"Belsnickling" was practiced in Berks County, with people dressing in grotesque uniforms and frightful masks to visit the homes. They carried switches to hit the children who stooped to pick up nuts dropped on the floor.

Children received as gifts molasses and sugar cakes molded into horses, riders, hearts, birds and other shapes. Few gifts were given, and stores were seldom decorated or stocked with special Christmas goods. A large family did not spend more than $2 for Christmas. But still a belief in Saint Nicholas or Santa Claus persisted among the children.[75] Sales at the Hopewell store did not show any large increase in the weeks before Christmas except for some luxury foods such as sugar, tea, coffee, oysters and cranberries.

Irreligious persons, doubtless, were numbered among the people of Hopewell Village; but religion played an important part in the lives of many families in the community. Perhaps the religious interest of the ironmasters set the pattern for the community.

[75] *Lewis Richards Scrapbook, op. cit.*, Vol. 9, p. 245. This description of Christmas was for about 1835 and came from the recollections of an old minister after fifty years.

20 Amusements and Recreation

"SOCIAL LIFE [AT THE FURNACES] CONSISTED OF SUCH AFFAIRS as corn huskings, barn dances, quilting and apple-butter bees and . . . visits to fairs."[1] Thus did one writer describe the amusements and recreation of the people of the iron plantations. This picture of rural, and essentially frontier, social life was similarly presented in several other articles on the iron furnaces.[2] Hopewell Village had all of the activities named above, but the lives of the workers and their families were enriched with a much greater variety of amusements. And the ironmasters' families drew upon the resources of the outside world for a more sophisticated social fare. Philadelphia, New York and even more distant places were available to amuse or divert those who could afford to travel.

Organized sports played little part in the lives of the children of the village, although they may have been familiar with town ball, predecessor of baseball. Small children found much to attract their attention in the working world of the furnace community. They liked to play on the high cinder piles[3] and found the casting house fascinating. When the molders caught

[1] Victoria Lyles, "Forges and Furnaces of York County," *Papers of the Historical Society of York County*, New Series, No. 4, n. d.
[2] Gemmell, *op. cit.*, p. 88; Handwork, *op. cit.*, p. 125.
[3] Sally Boone Interview, March 22, 1941.

a child, they put him in the tub of water used to cool the tools after the furnace was tapped—to the huge delight of everyone concerned.[4] In warm weather the waters of French Creek and the Furnace pond were available for swimming or bathing.[5] Spelling bees filled a need for competition in the schools. Sometimes teams from one school competed against the representatives of a neighboring school.[6]

"Frolicking" was a common amusement for the Furnace men. Frequently these were combinations of work and amuse-ment as when Joseph Ogal entertained at a "Chopping Frolick" during the winter of 1803.[7] Frolics sometimes lasted for days. John Cummings at Martha Furnace, beginning one on July 31, 1808, did not return to the furnace until August 5; and even then he was "not yet able to work."[8] The frolics usually lasted as long as the whiskey held out, for it was the practice to treat all who came to work.[9] But some change in this custom was apparently taking place in the 1840's when James Morris reported :

> John Gillespie was engaged with a number of hands this afternoon, in raising "old Johnny's House" from one story to two, by means of logs. No liquor—and as a consequence very little noise, no drunkenness and no wounds or accidents. Twenty years ago—aye even ten—and such a thing as a "raising" without liquor, would have been a perfect anomaly. I even doubt whether *any* persons would have touched a tim-ber. Now *very few* indeed expect or think of any drink being offered on such occasions.[10]

Apparently many furnace men were gamblers, for instances of card-playing were mentioned throughout the nineteenth century. Matthew Davis, Hopewell manager, purchased cards

[4] *Ibid.,* February 25, 1941.
[5] *Brooke Family Letters,* Ann Brooke to George W. Brooke, May 1833.
[6] *Reading Eagle,* February 4, 1917.
[7] SM 1, p. 23.
[8] *Martha Furnace Diary, op. cit.,* see dates mentioned.
[9] *Changewater Account Books, op. cit.,* III, pp. 14, 19, 35.
[10] *Morris Diary, op. cit.,* II, p. 105.

in 1803.[11] Near the end of the century the workmen gathered
to play poker in the evening, at Boone's Store—"Hopewell's
den of iniquity."[12] At neighboring Changewater Furnace
Henry Conner was fined one half day's pay for "playing cards
with Jane Stratten." The clerk failed to note whether the
objection was to the cards, to Miss Stratten's company, or to
playing during working hours.[13] The latter reason was probably the correct one, because there were other references to
gambling with no penalty. Quarts of whiskey were often the
forfeit of the loser at card games, "drawing cuts" or "tossing."[14] A few Furnace employees bet on horse races.[15]

A more respectable form of gambling was the purchase of
lottery tickets, the sale of which was a recognized means of
raising money for a church, a school or a public work. The
Hopewell record books contained many references to accounts
debited for the amount of a lottery ticket, especially in the
period from 1825 to 1827. Clement Brooke invested $63.50
in a lottery in 1826 which also was patronized by Clerk James
Benson, Founder Thomas Care and two molders.[16] Tickets
in this same lottery were shared by some who could not afford
a whole ticket or who did not want to risk so much. Seven men
were each charged $1 for one-fourth of a ticket.[17] Henry Care
purchased one and sold one-third of it to Joseph McKewen
and the same to John Care.[18]

Since Furnace people were outdoor folk, it was natural that
much of their amusement came from outdoor activities. In
the winter skating and sleighing were popular sports. Matthew
Davis hired "Kerby's four horse slay" in January 1804 and
took all of the hands for a ride.[19] But many individuals owned

[11] SM 2, p. 152.
[12] Reginald and Emlen Smith Interview, August 4, 1940.
[13] *Changewater Furnace Account Books, op. cit.,* II, p. 39.
[14] *Ibid.,* pp. 23, 24, 33.
[15] *Ibid.,* pp. 4, 60.
[16] SM 12, p. 107.
[17] *Ibid.,* p. 122.
[18] SM 59, p. 22.
[19] SM 2, p. 297.

one- or two-horse sleighs; so, when snow was on the roads, there was "a perpetual jingle of bells all day."[20] Not everyone, however, was enthusiastic about the sport. A few disliked the resulting "blue noses and cold fingers,"[21] and Sarah Brooke pitied the horses which, she said, were "completely worn down" from pulling the sleighs.[22]

Men and boys of the Village enjoyed hunting and fishing. Trout were taken from the streams with a seine, and eels were found in the pool under the Warwick Road bridge.[23] When mill ponds were drained, people gathered to catch the fish stranded in the low water.[24] Many Furnace men owned guns for hunting foxes, rabbits, "pheasants," partridges, wild geese and deer. But hunting was curtailed somewhat in 1844 when the Pennsylvania General Assembly adopted a law prohibiting the shooting of "pheasants" from January 1 to August 1.[25]

A flock of wild geese landed on the mill pond at Morgantown on April 4, 1838; and an army of hunters surrounded the pond. The slaughter continued until dark and was resumed at daylight the next morning. Not one member of that flock escaped. One observer remarked, "They were strangers and the sportsmen took 'em in. They'll learn better next time they come along here. . . ."[26]

Hunting dogs were purchased by the Furnace and by the ironmasters; for example, Charles Clingan paid $10 "for a pup" in 1863.[27] Possibly this animal was a foxhound, for fox

[20] *Morris Diary, op. cit.,* p. 42.

[21] *Ibid.,* p. 43.

[22] *Brooke Family Letters,* Sarah Brooke to Edward Brooke, January 14, 1835.

[23] Reginald Smith Interview, August 24, 1941; David Boone Interview, March 22, 1941.

[24] *Morris Diary, op. cit.,* p. 24.

[25] *Ibid.,* II, p. 177. Morris probably meant grouse when he used the word pheasant.

[26] *Ibid.,* p. 49. Morris was a lover of wild life and something of an amateur naturalist.

[27] SM 69, p. 9; *Kemper Manuscripts,* C. M. Clingan Pocket Note Book, *op. cit.,* n. p.

hunting was popular in the village in the nineteenth century. Even as late as the 1880's John Care was noted for possessing the best foxhounds in the area.[28] James Morris described a fox hunt in 1843 :

> The letting of a "bag fox" . . . was made the occasion of a great gathering of men, horses and hounds, much to the profit of the landlord at whose tavern the fox was let off. Then followed the confusion of starting — the neighing of horses, the yelping of hounds, the cheering of hunters and then the pell mell hurry of the chase — the hounds are on the track and give "mouth" — horsemen hurry off by the roads while numerous footmen pursue the route the fox has taken.[29]

The wooded hillsides provided an opportunity to combine pleasure and profit in the gathering of wild fruits. Native black mulberries came into season about the middle of June. Early the next month the red sour cherries, esteemed for pies, attracted "parties of from two up to a half dozen, going out, armed with baskets, kettles, buckets, etc."[30] Later in July, blackberries enticed those pickers who were convinced the fruit was worth the annoyance from the bite of ticks.[31] Chestnuts drew the Furnace people into the woods in the autumn when the prickly burs opened to drop their fruit.[32]

For those who could afford a trip to the shore Cape May, New Jersey was a popular summer resort. A memorandum found among the Hopewell Papers, in Clement Brooke's handwriting, listed these expenses:

At Cape May	$82.50
Passage	36.00
Stage Fair and expenses	3.00
Porters at different times	1.50
Expenses at Cape for wriding, etc.	6.00[33]

[28] John Henry Interview, January 23, 1941.
[29] *Morris Diary, op. cit.,* II, p. 85.
[30] *Ibid.,* II, pp. 51, 133.
[31] *Ibid.,* p. 218.
[32] *Brooke Family Letters,* Ann to Edward, October 15, 1828.
[33] *Hopewell Papers,* uncatalogued and undated but apparently the 1830's.

Elizabeth Brooke received an invitation to join a group of relatives going to Cape May in July, 1845. She was advised to bring a riding habit, as "a ride upon the Beach with an agreeable Companion is esteemed Bliss by the young ladies."[34]

Quilting bees for the women were sometimes combined with harvesting or "raisings" for the men, and the mixed parties produced "great hilarity."[35] Among the Hopewell Village people another very popular heterosexual affair was the "apple-butter boiling."[36] A kind of social calendar was established in the autumn, because several boilings were scheduled each week over a period of six or eight weeks. The young men came to "see home" the girls after the kettles were emptied, and the elders enjoyed a chance to visit and gossip.

Three to 5 barrels of cider were used with 12 to 15 bushels of apples pared and sliced into "schnitz." Cooking was done over an outdoor fire or in a summer kitchen. The container—often several were used—was a huge copper kettle, owned by the family or rented at 25¢ per day.

Activity began for the host family at about 3.00 A. M., and the finished butter was in crocks by midnight. The cider was boiled for an hour before dawn when the first pailful of 'schnitz" was added. From this time on the stirring with a long-handled wooden paddle was never stopped for fear that the butter would burn on the bottom of the kettle and spoil the flavor—possibly, also, ruin the kettle. As the volume of liquid in the kettle was reduced by evaporation, more cider, more 'schnitz," sugar and spices were added.

Father and mother may have taken a nap during the morning when the larger children were on hand to keep the stirring going. Perhaps a few neighbors dropped in during the day for a glass of cider. There was never a limit to the amount of cider they could have, but in return for the hospitality they would customarily stir for fifteen or twenty minutes.

[34] *Hopewell Papers, Elizabeth Brooke Letters,* M. G. B. to Elizabeth Brooke, July 7, 1845. Hopewell Village Library.
[35] *Martha Furnace Diary, op. cit.,* July 6, 1811, n. p.
[36] For examples see SM 35, pp. 134, 135, 136.

The real fun began about six o'clock in the evening when the neighbors started to arrive. They came and went until midnight, with the largest influx between eight and nine o'clock. No one was specifically invited; everyone was welcome. Each guest was expected to stir the apple butter for a few minutes. If a young man and a young lady grasped the wooden handle together, it was a public announcement of their engagement; so a close watch was kept on that handle.

Outdoor games were played during the evening, but all activity ceased when the time came to unhook the kettles. The contents were cooled a little and then dipped into crocks. Everyone tested the taste quality by scraping a little from the kettle with his fingers. Sometimes the young people ended with their faces well smeared with apple butter. The whole crowd left together with the young men escorting the young ladies along the dark roads and paths through the woods.[37]

A few holidays or special days provided amusement for the Hopewell community. In the early part of the nineteenth century New Year's Eve was the occasion for calls upon the scattered homes by groups of the young men. James Morris remembered the custom and left this description :

> . . . a troop of 30, 40 or even 50 jovial young fellows would join in a band, equipped with powder, wadding and shooting irons and after having appointed a captain to guide and direct them and a musician to blow music out of a conch shell or on some particular occasions, scrape it out of an old Cremona—the line of march would be taken up for the nearest farm house, where a salute would be given, executed with a grand running fire precision, followed by a most hearty "wish you a happy New Year" from the throats and open mouths of the grand troupe. . . .
>
> After all this the party is invited into the house where all manner of good cheer is set before them. . . . Full justice having been rendered to the collation, . . . the party takes its leave, to make another call at the next neighbors where the same [procedure] is repeated, to be again renewed until every

[37] This account was based upon *Lewis Richards Scrapbooks, op. cit.,* Vol. H, p. 93.

farm house shall have received a call and greeting, thus oftentimes consuming the whole night. . . ."[38]

This custom had about died out by 1843 when Morris was
writing. One reason was that careless shooting by revelers
who had enjoyed too many "collations" had resulted in the
wounding and even death of several men.[39] On New Year's
Day the children received cakes, sweetmeats and toys as
presents.[40]

The day to express patriotism was July 4. One village resident observed :

> This day as usual will be celebrated by all sorts of societies
> — military, political, temperance, literary, benevolent and
> Sunday School — in all sorts of ways — too many in a way to
> beget drunken men and drunken habits and too many in a
> manner to beget evil feelings and animosities. Nevertheless, it
> is a good thing to celebrate, in a becoming way the Declara-
> tion of our Independence. . . ."[41]

But Independence Day in Philadelphia was not very enjoy-
able for Polly Grubb in 1833 when she was attending school
there. She wrote :

> The 4th of July passed a little duller than any I ever
> remember spending, almost all the gentlemen had gone to
> public dinners, and the ladies were too much occupied with
> their own concerns to attend to my amusement : we had no
> precession, but a few companies were out; it is said there was
> a grand music at the Adelphi in 5 street, but I did not hear
> it. . . ."[42]

October 31 was a night for mischief for the boys of the
Hopewell area. One report stated :

[38] *Morris Diary, op. cit.,* p. 252.
[39] *Ibid.,* II, p. 181.
[40] *Ibid.,* p. 176.
[41] *Ibid.,* p. 211.
[42] *Hopewell Papers, Stokes Collection,* Polly Grubb to Ann F. Brooke,
July 6, 1833.

. . . it was . . . the rule on this night [for] our boys to steal folks cabbage and then thump their doors with it, while children of larger growth would remove and change gates — fence up roads — post up plows and harrows . . . on stacks, etc.[43]

Dances were held at the Big House on Christmas and New Year's Day, and the entire Village was invited. Of course some men had to work at the furnace on these days, but perhaps they came to the party after their tour was over. Lincoln Palsgrove claimed to have been the best jig dancer at Hopewell in his youth. He also recalled that his mother "used to dance on a pewter plate." A Negro shoemaker and a Negro woodcutter played their fiddles for the dances.[44] Henry F. Care may have been another fiddler for these occasions; for in 1929 he was one of the featured performers at the Chester-Lancaster Old Fiddlers Association reunion where he played tunes from his younger days, such as "Bummers' Reel," "Devils Dream," "Turkey in the Straw," and "Fishers Hornpipe."[45]

Fairs of several kinds were popular in the first half of the nineteenth century. The semi-annual fairs in nearby boroughs drew the Furnace families until drinking and gambling caused many towns to abandon them—York, Lancaster and Harrisburg in 1816. Mechanical and agricultural fairs generally replaced the borough fairs.[46] Some Hopewell people were probably in Reading on June 5, 1806, when, according to Bennett Nolan, this scene would have greeted them :

The square was lined with booths and festooned with bunting. Around the central court-house and under the arcades of the brick marketplace which flanked it, swirled an eddying throng of merrymakers. Venders cried their wares; jugglers and sword-swallowers amused the spectators. The taverns were doing a thriving business and some tipsy revelers had hoisted

[43] *Morris Diary, op. cit.,* p. 32.
[44] J. Lincoln Palsgrove Interview, October 13, 1940, and Hunter Care Interview, January 20, 1941.
[45] *Reading Eagle,* August 14, 1929.
[46] Bining, "Iron Plantations," *op. cit.,* pp. 12–13.

a wagon upon the roof of the markethouse for the discomfiture of the village constable.[47]

In that same year bachelor Clement Brooke drew $1 in cash "when he went to the "water millen" fair."[48] And Helen Brooke visited her relatives, the William R. Whites, in Philadelphia in 1864 to attend a fair in the city.[49]

Since leisure time was not a plentiful commodity in the Hopewell community, it is not surprising that hobbies received little mention. The storekeeper in Morgantown was a coin collector who noted that he had "put away . . . a collection of cents beginning at 1793 and from thence to 1841 inclusive excepting only those of 1804 and 1815."[50] A modern numismatist would value that collection, and he would know that few cents were made in 1804 and none in 1815.

Traveling entertainers were welcomed on their infrequent visits to the Furnace. "Mr. Skelline" gave a demonstration "on ventriloquism and vocal illusion" and was so popular he returned for a repeat performance.[51] The organ grinder played his tunes and asked for a donation at each house as he walked through the Village.[52] A more elaborate show was provided in 1837 with the arrival of a "Cosmorama" on wheels. A room, built on a wagon thirty feet long and seven or eight wide, contained pictures of "battles, harbours, towns, etc." Sixty to 70 people could get into it at the same time.[53] Animal shows were fairly common; but they always attracted attention, whether the *pièce de résistance* was "the learned Goat" or "the Exhibition of Wild Beasts."[54] An especially large ani-

[47] J. Bennett Nolan, *Play at Reading Town* (Reading, Pennsylvania: The Feroe Press, 1935), n. p., identified as Plate IV.
[48] SM 44, August 26, 1806, n. p.
[49] HV 8640621. William R. White to C. M. Clingan.
[50] *Morris Diary, op. cit.,* p. 223.
[51] *Ibid.,* II, pp. 73, 83. The year was 1843.
[52] *Ibid.,* p. 20
[53] *Ibid.,* p. 28.
[54] *Martha Furnace Diary, op. cit.,* October 11, 1809; *Morris Diary, op. cit.,* II, p. 42.

mal show was in the area in 1844 and passed through Morgantown on November 7. A resident of the town reported :

> The town was thrown into a great stir and commotion this forenoon by the passage through it of a caravan of animals. First came four enormous elephants with their keepers on horseback. The appearance of these, coming on us by surprize, completely aroused the attention of the goodly citizens . . . and caused them to throng men, women and children to the upper end of town. The elephants were next followed by a train of some 20 or more wagons ,containing the lions, etc. of the exhibition, Behind these came a camel and two shetland ponies. There were about 70 horses. They came from Reading and were going to Waynesburg for their next show.[55]

Balloon ascensions drew Furnace people to Reading in 1835 and again in 1838.[56] But in 1841 the people at the Jones Mine had a balloon land among them. An observer wrote :

> A great stir was made at about $4\frac{1}{2}$ o'clock P.M. by the sight of a balloon to the N. East. It remained but a very little time in sight and then disappeared as though it had descended. In the evening we learned that the balloon had descended at Jones' mine holes and that Wise the aeronaut had landed in safety having left Danville in Columbia County some $2\frac{1}{2}$ hours previous.[57]

Two occasions of civic significance which never failed to attract Hopewell Village people were election day and militia training day. Elections, combining civic duty with a holiday, were the cause of much absenteeism from jobs for part or all of the day. Many workers asked for cash to spend "at the election," because the voting place was usually a tavern.[58] Battalion Day for militia drills was observed in Pennsylvania from soon after the Revolution until the Civil War. Berks

[55] *Ibid.*, pp. 167–168.

[56] *Ibid.*, p. 65; *Lewis Evans Ledger, op. cit.*, p. 211.

[57] *Morris Diary, op. cit.*, p. 152. This was probably John Wise.

[58] Examples are to be found in SM 67, October 13, 1807; October 11, 1808; SM 7, October 15, 1817; SM 10, p. 53; SM 17, p. 24; SM 31, pp. 74, 157; SM 35, pp. 19–20; SM 65, p. 3.

County had six battalions, each of which held its own review days. But Battalion Day was much more than a military parade. Personal grudges were settled in bare-fisted fights; dances were held in the tavern; tables were set up in the streets to sell cakes, confections and mead. Dancing began after dinner and lasted until late at night. One man in a set paid the fiddler and another bought the drinks, whiskey at 3¢ with a free cigar for the men and cream beer for the women.

The militia were supposed to drill about two hours before dinner and the same in the afternoon;[59] but, judging from the following description, the military aspect of Battalion Day was of questionable quality:

> Today our Battalion of Militia trains at the White Bear [Tavern], which will be made the occasion of a vast meeting of half uniformed officers without science or knowledge of what they pretend to teach—of citizen soldiers whose arms and accoutrements consist of a cornstalk perhaps, or at farthest nothing more dangerous than an umbrella or a goodly cudgel and whose knowledge of the art of war is equivalent to the "little end of nothing whittled down." These with a numerous band of lookers on in the shape of young boys . . . of cripples—of old men "out of the muster rolls" years agone—old women and young ones—married and single—with and without babies—black, blue and brown, "from snowy white to sooty"—comely and plain, trigged out in finery—some neat and others tawdry, ill-looking and well-looking—well behaved and ill behaved. These with a sprinkling of old huckster women, drunken men, fiddlers, dancers, fights and squabbles make up the grand rare show of a training in Battalion.[60]

Officers were generally disobeyed or even made to appear ridiculous by the privates who were more interested in the drinking, dancing, fighting and gambling.[61]

Many Furnace people attended the annual Battalion Days and drew cash to finance the fun. In 1801 the following

[59] *Lewis Richards Scrapbooks, op. cit.,* Vol. H, p. 63.
[60] *Morris Diary, op. cit.,* p. 200. The year was 1842.
[61] *Ibid.,* p. 147.

Hopewell men were on the muster roll of Captain Will Witman when the call was issued for a training day at the White Horse Tavern on May 2 : Mathew Brooke, Samuel Umstead, Matthew Davis, Thomas Kerby, James Sands, Peter Huttenstein and Amos Lewis.[62] Men were paid to attend the muster and fined for failure to report. The number of fines collected from Hopewell employees indicated that there was less enthusiasm for Battalion Day among those with military duties than among the revelers.[63]

Visiting among friends and relatives occupied much of the time of the ironmasters' families. The big mansions were filled with visitors who came and stayed for days and then moved on to another house. Ann Brooke wrote, "You will go to Hopewell I expect and to Birdsborough during your vacation perhaps to Lititz with Elizabeth Mary. . . ."[64] The group often was quite large: "Uncle Charles and Cousin Brooke Buckley are here . . . We expect Aunt Tacy and Aunt Anna and Aunt Sarah and her 2 children up tomorrow."[65]

The young ladies planned parties and dances for their visitors. Ann instructed her brother, "When you come here . . . bring your new black clothes . . . [Sarah] is quite *fidgety* for fear the boys will not bring their *Sunday Clothes*."[66] But they spent much time on the move, as Ann later reported :

> . . . Cousin Eliza Buckley was here [Morgantown] the week before last and I went with her to Hopewell and spent a few days there. I had not been home more than a day or two when Sarah and Louisa Anderson came up in the stage to Morgantown we sent the barouche over for them and the next day Ann C. Brooke and Charles came for us in their handsome new carriage so we all accompanied them home and staid there [Hopewell] a week, we went to Birdsborough

[62] *Brooke Family Papers,* Muster Roll.
[63] For examples see SM 10, pp. 16, 20; HV 8200609A; SM 12, p. 72; HV 8271004A; SM 28, pp. 18, 59, 155.
[64] *Brooke Family Papers,* Ann to Edward, July, 1829.
[65] *Hopewell Papers,* Unsigned and undated, possibly Ann Brooke to Elizabeth Brooke about 1830.
[66] *Brooke Family Papers,* Ann to Edward, July 1829.

and staid over night, from there we returned home. . . . I
have just received a letter from Louisa Anderson in which
she says she and Ann are going with Cousin Clemment to
Mauchunk next Thursday and I must go to Hopewell tomorrow to go with [them].[67]

Ann Brooke seems to have felt there was a kind of obligation upon the ironmaster's family to create diversion for the
people of the neighborhood when she wrote to her cousin :

Well Sally the time is rapidly progressing when I shall
expect your Ladyship here — then I shall insist upon the
Grubbs coming over and invite Mrs. Jenny Hopkins — Ann
Hopkins — and have a little turn out — something of the kind
is necessary to set them a going in this neighborhood.[68]

The ironmasters' families also spent time traveling. In 1834
Sarah and George Brooke went to Niagara Falls,[69] and the
young people often visited Philadelphia and New York. Life
in the cities must have been gay for the children of wealthy
iron families. From January to June of 1840 Ann C. Brooke
was advanced $6,961.78 in cash for her stay in Philadelphia.[70]
It was a good investment, however; for in June she married
William R. White, a promising young Philadelphia banker.

Sally Brooke wrote to her cousin Elizabeth Brooke about
her trip to New York in 1844 with three other girls and Edward Brooke. They stayed at the Astor House and found the
food prepared by the new French chef not to their liking.
They toured the town "in a cab" but missed "the Croton
Water Works and the Theological Seminary" which Sally
had especially wanted to see. Edward promised to take them
to the opera but failed to do so. However, they had a good
time at the weekly dance sponsored by the hotel for its guests

[67] *Brooke Family Papers*, Ann to Edward, August 4, 1829.
[68] *Hopewell Papers, Stokes Collection*, Ann Brooke to Sarah R. Brooke.
Dated May 3, no year but probably in the 1830's.
[69] *Brooke Family Letters*, G. W. Brooke to Edward Brooke, May 8, 1834.
[70] *Kemper Manuscripts*, Memorandum of Cash paid by Clement
Brooke for Ann C. Brooke, January–June, 1840.

where they danced until midnight with partners they had never seen before. The girls shopped for clothes and found the dresses were gayer than those offered by the stores in Philadelphia.[71]

Despite all the apparent activity the following letter shows that there were dull moments in the mansions:

> . . . I wish you to bring me Irving's Alhambra — Swallow Barn — or any new publication, you can get in West Chester — I am dreadfully at a loss for something to read our old books I have read—and reread some of them—they are getting stale to me, and require a *tale* to freshen them up.[72]

Cultural opportunities or interests were limited among these people in the first half of the nineteenth century. Ann Brooke attended a performance of *Hamlet* in 1832, and Elizabeth Brooke heard Jenny Lind sing in Philadelphia in 1850.[73] George Brooke played the flute and possessed a collection of music for that instrument.[74] For the workmen's families the winter singing school filled a cultural void.[75]

Long working hours left little time for recreation among the Hopewell villagers, but they found a surprisingly large number of opportunities for entertainment and social and cultural enrichment.

---

[71] *Hopewell Papers,* Cousin Sallie to Elizabeth Brooke, April 24, 1844.
[72] *Brooke Family Papers,* Ann to Edward, probably 1829 but no date given except July.
[73] *Ibid.,* Ann to George W., February 29, 1832; *Hopewell Papers,* Fanny Crutcher to Elizabeth Brooke, January 19, 1851.
[74] *Ibid.,* R. D. Powell to Clement Brooke, undated but probably 1835.
[75] *Morris Diary, op. cit.,* pp. 35, 172, 182; *Lewis Evans Ledger,* p. 179.

21   Hopewell and the Outside World

HOPEWELL FURNACE WAS IN A WOODED REGION OF HILLS AND narrow valleys, distant from cities and not located on any of the main routes of transportation. Was it therefore an isolated and self-contained community? Earlier chapters have demonstrated the influence of changing transportation upon the Furnace market and the dependence upon the surrounding cities and towns for supplies and cultural outlets. In the following pages the Village will be considered as a part of the economic, political and social growth of the wider community of nineteenth century America. How did it reach into Hopewell Village? What reaction did it evoke from the people?

Since Hopewell was an industrial unit with a product to sell to an outside market, it was naturally linked with the state of business in general. Iron sold well on a lively market and poorly on a dull market. The ironmaster had to consider the probable demands for his pig iron and cast items when he was writing contracts to make charcoal or when he was setting a selling price to his customers for future deliveries. Errors in predicting the influence of business cycles caused many bankruptcies. The iron manufacturer needed large financial resources to see him through an unprofitable season. As Victor S. Clark wrote, "The dependence of the iron industry upon special skills and an organized personnel, and therefore upon continuous operation, was greater than that of most other manufactures."[1]

The iron industry, suffering from foreign competition since the end of the Napoleonic wars, began a decline in 1816. By 1819 the Pittsburgh iron works were shut down, a condition which lasted until 1821. Then a slow recovery began and continued until 1826 when Pittsburgh iron production had returned to the 1815 level.[2]

Hopewell encountered less difficulty from the national depression which began in 1819 than did the Pittsburgh furnaces, but there were anxious moments for the partners in 1820 and 1821. Daniel Buckley wrote on May 23, 1820:

> . . . I have not been able to sell any iron of Consequence in Lancaster or Columbia . . . at Columbia business is so Dull that no . . . man seems Inclined to take Iron only for Lumber which would not suit us to Deal for. . . .[3]

Customers were reluctant to place orders. One wrote, "The Iron appears to be of a good quality but would not wish you to send any more at this time. . . ."[4] Another said, "I have been in Philadelphia . . . and I found that Iron was much more duller sale then wen you ware in town. . . . I think you must com down with your Pigs according to Market. . . ."[5]

Even when iron was sold, collections were difficult: ". . . you state in your letter," wrote Lewis Morgan, "that you stand in grait need of money . . . [I shall] youse every exertion in my power to accomodant [sic] you with some against Saterday two weeks. . . ."[6] Two other merchants were apolo-

---

[1] Clark, *op. cit.,* p. 384.
[2] Richard C. Wade, *The Urban Frontier: The Rise of Western Cities, 1790–1830* (Cambridge: Harvard University Press, 1959), p. 168.
[3] *Hopewell Papers,* uncatalogued. Daniel Buckley to Clement Brooke.
[4] HV 8201024, H. F. Slaymaker to D. Buckley and Company.
[5] HV 8201215, J. S. Spang to Daniel Buckley and Company.
[6] HV 8201221, Lewis Morgan to Mathew Brooke.

getic: "It is almost more then I can ask but I must beg a little time yet. . . ."[7] and, ". . . I have been Last week down in Maryland after money but find it is not to be had. . . ."[8] Respected customers found it impossible to continue in business, and Hopewell learned that some who owed the Furnace money were being subjected to sheriff's sales "unexpectedly to almost everybody. . . ."[9]

Hopewell apparently made most of its iron into pigs in the emergency.[10] Stoves were in little demand; some customers expressed the belief that "they will come Lower" in price.[11] The income of the molders was much below normal for the blast of 1820, and William Ricketts was employed at coaling instead of molding. But in the next blast Ricketts was again molding, and three other molders more than doubled their incomes over the previous year.[12]

Even in the midst of the depression Hopewell's credit was considered the equivalent of cash by people in the neighborhood. A weaver informed a customer, "You may call for your Blanketing any time. Please to Bring the cash or an order from Hopewell we dont Intend weaving any more on Trust. . . ."[13]

Business improved by the spring of 1822. Two customers wrote that they wished to order stoves as word had reached them that Hopewell Furnace would be back in production about March 1, 1822.[14] Stove prices moved up during the year from $65.00 per ton to $75.00.[15] Stove dealers, wrote Daniel Buckley, "seem to want castings much," and one offered to

[7] HV 8201031A, William Hamill to Mathew Brooke.
[8] HV 8201030, William Walker to D. Buckley and Company.
[9] HV 8211024B.
[10] HV 8210409C.
[11] HV 8210409A.
[12] SM 6, *passim.*
[13] HV 8201228.
[14] HV 8220221A; HV 8220308A. These letters indicate the furnace had been shut down. They may have meant merely the normal period of repairs between blasts. If there had been any cessation because of business condition, it must have been quite short.
[15] HV 8220508A; HV 8221010B.

pay cash for quick delivery.[16] Men who had wanted no stoves the previous year were now complaining that they were not having their orders filled fast enough.[17] William Walker in Wilmington feared he had been forgotten because he had received no stoves for so long, and he hoped he would be sent a wagon load before the end of the blast.[18]

The backlog of orders seemingly had been filled by the autumn of 1824, when a Philadelphia dealer wrote on September 30:

> You will please be careful not to send us any more stoves this season we have so many on hand and the sales appear so dull that we are afraid we shall not be able to get them off.[19]

After 1824 business in general improved throughout the country.[20] Hopewell Furnaces benefited from the enlarged demand for iron and cast products and entered into a period of about fifteen years of the greatest prosperity it ever knew.

Two factors combined to bring an end to the "boom" times of the 1830's: The Jacksonian money supply and the increases in productive capacity in the iron industry. Since these two did not coincide, there was a short recession in 1837 followed by a brief revival and then a prolonged depression.[21] Hopewell had its most productive blast in 1836-1837, but already there were signs of coming trouble. One of the largest buyers of Hopewell stoves wrote in 1836, ". . . the price appears so high we shall not want so many castings as we should if they came at a lower rate. . . ."[22] The same customer said he was finding payments difficult because of the money shortage:

[16] HV 82201010B; HV 8221022A.
[17] HV 8221106; HV 8221108.
[18] HV 8221125.
[19] HV 8240930.
[20] Sullivan, *op. cit.*, pp. 51–57.
[21] Douglas C. North, *The Economic Growth of the United States* (Englewood Cliffs: Prentice Hall, Inc., 1961), p. 13.
[22] HV 8361212A. G. P. Willard Company of Portsmouth, New Hampshire.

Such is the unprecedented scarcity of money and the facilities of raising it being entirely cut off, we have thought best to say that we do not wish you to draw on us for any part of your a/c. it has always before afforded us pleasure and have a source of pride that we could anticipate all our demands before they become due but from a man of 20 to 30,000 dollars the best of paper which before has always commanded cash at our Bank; we are unable to raise one dollar. . . .[23]

By the late Spring of 1837 the depression was becoming severe. James Morris had much to say of business conditions in his diary entries for these months:

April 28. A universal complaint of a scarcity of money— many failures. . . .

May 9. One nowadays hears of nothing else but hard-times, failures, scarcity of money and what is worse bread-stuffs. The ironmasters are beginning to feel the pressure. Pig-iron has fell from $50 to $20[24] per ton—for Casting there is no sale—some of the forges have stopped and several of the furnaces intend discharging their moulders. . . .

May 12. Report that Reading banks had suspended species payment. . . .

May 17. It is rumored that the shin plasters—ie—small notes . . . are about to be inflicted upon us.[25]

Three days after this rumor on fractional currency, Morris reported seeing the first one—a ten cent note of the city of Philadelphia. They were promptly named "Hickory leaves" by the Whigs, a designation "much disliked by the Jackson men."[26]

[23] HV 8361128.
[24] This was certainly an exaggeration, at least in so far as Hopewell is concerned. But the price did fall below $30 per ton for pig iron. Stove casting dropped in price from $110 per ton in 1837 to $60 in 1844. HV 8440605.
[25] *Morris Diary, op. cit.*, pp. 15–18.
[26] *Ibid.*, p. 25.

Letters from customers show that Hopewell was having trouble making collections for its iron in 1839. One said :

> Frequent and continued disappointment in the receipt of money funds from the South, long since due us, and the necessity of taking up lately large amts of the protested paper of correspondents, will make it impossible for me to meat our note to you. . . ."[27]

Another apologized :

> I am very sorry to inform you that I cannot let you have that money according to promise I have Been out trying to Collect it for you and I could not get a cent. . . ."[28]

Business conditions were still bad in 1842 when a Philadelphia dealer wrote, ". . . Times are no better, rather worse, Girard Bank is broke, One other is Strongly suspected of going next."[29] Discounts were charged on paper money. Store keepers refused to take it on "book accounts" and would not give coins in change.[30] However, by May 1843 paper money had recovered most of its value with discounts as low as 5 per cent and even less.[31] Pig iron prices rose to $28 per ton. By 1844 Clement Brooke was offering Hopewell pig iron at $30 per ton. "We have a quantity . . . on hand at Present," he wrote on June 17. "Not selling any for sometime owing to no regular price being established," he added.[32] Casting of stoves ended at Hopewell before the close of the year.

The depression hastened the adoption of such new technical improvements in iron-manufacturing as the hot-blast and the anthracite furnaces. From 1839 to 1850 there were 27 sheriff's sales of the 60 cold-blast charcoal furnaces in Eastern

[27] HV 8391113. From New Castle, Delaware.
[28] HV 8391102. From New Holland, Pennsylvania.
[29] *Hopewell Papers,* Uncatalogued, James H. Deas to Clement Brooke and Company.
[30] *Morris Diary, op. cit.,* p. 189.
[31] *Ibid.,* II, p. 37.
[32] HV 8440617A.

Pennsylvania. Of these 27 only seven were in blast in 1850. Thirteen of those which had not been sold were also out of blast.[33] Hopewell Furnace was one which survived and continued to produce iron for many more years although business conditions troubled the management again in 1854, 1857 and on several occasions in the 1870's.[34] While Hopewell Furnace managed to survive the serious depressions of the first half of the nineteenth century and for thirty-three years longer, its production and profits were seriously curtailed. The Depression of 1837 was undoubtedly influential in the decision of the partners to discontinue stove-casting.

Defending the American market for their products, according to William Sullivan, made the ironmasters of Pennsylvania "The most zealous partisans of the protective tariff."[35] The first session of Congress placed a tariff on slit and rolled iron, iron castings, nails and unwrought steel.[36] Further provisions for protection against imports of iron were made in the revenue acts of 1791, 1792 and 1794.[37] The tariff acts of the first half of the nineteenth century also retained provisions for protecting the iron manufacture. In 1816 a duty on cast iron was set at 20 per cent *ad valorum,* and this was changed in 1818 to 50¢ per hundredweight. The latter rate was raised to $62\frac{1}{2}$¢ in 1828. The tariff of 1832 put a 50¢ rate on each hundredweight of pig iron, changed to $9 per ton in 1842 and set at 30 per cent *ad valorum* in the Walker Tariff of 1846.[38] The ironmasters blamed the depression of 1819 on the inadequacies of the tariff of 1816, but they considered the

[33] *Documents Relating to the Manufacture of Iron in Pennsylvania, op. cit.,* "Table on Cold Blast Charcoal Furnaces."

[34] HV 8541216; *Kemper Manuscripts,* protest of note September 26, 1857; *Ibid.,* Edward S. Buckley to Harker A. Long, November 17, 1876.

[35] Sullivan, *op. cit.,* p. 9.

[36] Harold F. Williamson, *The Growth of the American Economy* (New York: Prentice-Hall, 1946), p. 229.

[37] Barnes, *op. cit.,* p. 155.

[38] Harry Scrivenor, *History of the Iron Trade from the Earliest Records to the Present Time* (London: Longman, Brown, Green, and Longmans, 1854), pp. 210, 223, 236, 238.

Tariff of 1828 "a triumph of protection."[39] The reduction in
rates under the Walker Tariff permitted the English to flood
the American market with iron which they could not sell on
the European market. But the settlement of California and
the restoration of the English market on the continent revived
the prosperity of the American furnaces.[40]

The ironmasters' convention of 1850 noted that in the previous year 20 per cent of the iron used in the United States
was imported.[41] They did not mention, however, the rise in
exports of American iron which increased from 85,000 tons
in 1839 to over 500,000 tons in 1852.[42] The convention went
on record as approving the following resolution :

> Resolved, That a crisis has arisen in the iron business which
> calls for the immediate revision of the revenue laws, so far as
> that article is concerned, and that the number of establish-
> ments which have already been forced to suspend by the influx
> of foreign iron, proves that without such a change, the business
> cannot permanently sustain itself in its rightful position, as
> a great branch of our national industry.[43]

Charles M. Clingan represented Hopewell at the Philadelphia convention where the above resolution was adopted. He
did not oppose the action. But the manager at Hopewell
probably would have been in agreement with the views expressed in 1832 by William Darling, manager of Joanna Furnace. In reply to a Congressional inquiry on the need for a
tariff on iron, he wrote :

> I am satisfied that furnaces would not be materially injured;
> but, of the twenty-seven forges, nearly two thirds of them
> would be compelled to stop [if protection were removed]; and,
> when you take into consideration the thousands of men,

[39] Arthur Cecil Bining, "The Rise of Iron Manufacturing in Western
Pennsylvania," Reprint from *The Western Pennsylvania Historical
Magazine,* 16, 4 (November 1933), pp. 235–256.
[40] *Ibid.*
[41] *Documents Relating to the Manufacture of Iron, op. cit.,* p. 2.
[42] Scrivenor, *op. cit.,* p. 318.
[43] *Documents Relating to the Manufacture of Iron, op. cit.,* p. 19.

women, and children, who derive their support from these works, it is obvious that such an event would produce great distress. As far as I am interested in iron works, I feel but little interest in the fate of the tariff; but as a matter which is to affect so large a portion of my fellow-citizens, I feel a deep interest in it.[44]

As Mr. Darling pointed out, the furnaces had less foreign competition for their pig iron and rough castings than had the forges for their more expensive bar iron and finished products.

The influence of tariffs upon the iron industry naturally led to participation in politics by the ironmasters. Among Hopewell owners Mark Bird, James Wilson and James Old combined furnace management with public office; and Daniel Buckley served two terms as the Lancaster County representative to the Pennsylvania legislature before he became a Hopewell partner.[45] After 1800 the managers were not public office holders, except for Charles M. Clingan's service on the Union Township School Board.[46] But politics was a matter of great interest to the people of Hopewell Village in the nineteenth century.

In the midst of the financial problems which troubled him in 1807, Mathew Brooke was urged to take a greater part in the politics of the day. A Berks County political leader wrote:

We all know Sir that you are a firm and stedfast Repub —but we must sensure you for being so inactive these fiew years past, there is now a glorious field for triumph Open, the Quids and Federalists are now divided, we have no longer to fear their United force, if we will but exert ourselves. . . .[47]

The specific reason for this letter was a campaign for the election of another ironmaker, Colonel Daniel Udree, to the office of Brigadier General.

[44] *McLane Report on Manufacture, op. cit.,* p. 227.
[45] *Reading Eagle,* February 4, 1917.
[46] HV 8590318.
[47] *Brooke Family Papers,* Gabl Heister to Mathew Brooke, August 27, 1807.

Buckley-Brooke correspondence sometimes revealed a depth of political feeling on one side or the other. In 1823 Clement A. Buckley wrote to Clement Brooke from Brooke Forge in Lancaster County:

> We have had a complete triumph over the Shultsites in our township, after the greatest exertions made by his friends we have a majority of 48 votes. . . . If you know anything about the results in your adjacent townships let me know. The demos are most sanguine of success.[48]

A stove dealer included in an order for stoves a wrong guess about the outcome of the election of 1828, "What do you think of the Election now Adams will Be Presadent."[49] Berks County, however, voted 4,583 for Jackson and 894 for Adams.[50] George W. Buckley was pessimistic about the outcome of the election for governor in 1829:

> Lanc[aster] Co. gave Ritner a majority of 1600 votes—But tis my Opinion that the wolves will be hard on the sheep in the end.[51]

The Anti-Masonic movement reached into the Hopewell community. Clement Brooke was a member of the lodge at Morgantown, but he withdrew because of the political furor against the Masonic Order.[52] His political leadership in the area was attested by a letter containing political "tickets" which he was asked to distribute among his "neighbors and hands" in 1832.[53]

Another letter to Brooke commented on the national political scene in 1836:

[48] HV 8231015.
[49] HV 8281028A, Ephr Bailey to C. Brooke.
[50] Sullivan, *op. cit.*, p. 231.
[51] *Hopewell Papers*, Uncatalogued, George W. Buckley to Clement Brooke, 1829.
[52] *Ibid.*, H. A. Long to A. Clingan, November 20, 1904.
[53] HV 8321001A, Henry Betz to Clement Brooke.

I regret very much to see that the opposition in Va. have nominated Judge White — I think if they had waited for the action of Pennsylvania upon that subject they would have taken up Harrison — and the Key-Stone State and the Old Dominion shoulder to shoulder would have borne him triumphantly through — But the Va politicians have been so much accustomed to lead that they have not *yet* learned the lesson of following. . . .[54]

Whig sentiment was strong in Morgantown, and James Morris left no doubt about his political beliefs:

Monday next being the day for the Whig Convention of young men of Pennsylvania at Reading, everybody almost is talking of it and talking of going.

Sunday . . . convention delegates are passing through here on their way to Reading in sulkies, gigs, dearborns. . . .

All Morgantown appeared to be astir by 4 o'clock [this] morning getting ready for a start. In company with B. Jones I got off about 5. When we neared Reading the roads were full of people. . . . The Loco foco also had a convention — a County one, and again it was "fair" day. All these produced a jam unexampled in old Reading.

I remained in Reading over last night Attended Convention and listened with pleasure to a speech by Ed. McCoy Morris of Philadelphia and one by Mr. Pennepacker of W. Chester. 1700 delegates are in attendance.[55]

To the diarist political parties were black or white. The Democrats were despicable people—at least when engaged in political activities:

Yesterday was the great Loco foco Porter State Convention at Reading and today some 10 or 12 of the Chester County delegation passed through here . . . with pink banners flying with the inscription "Chester County delegation Porter and Democracy" . . . which inscription ought to have read . . . "Porter and Drunkenness" for to say the truth some of them were not a little the "wus for licker," and looked Loco-foco-ism.[56]

[54] *Hopewell Papers,* Uncatalogued, R. D. Powell to Clement Brooke, no date.
[55] *Morris Diary, op. cit.,* June 2–5, 1838, p. 52.
[56] *Ibid.,* p. 59.

Again in reference to a Democratic convention to pick a slate of officers, he wrote:

> Today . . . the hearts of some hundreds of office hunters, beat high with hope—and fear—for today their destiny will be fixed, and what the leaders say, the Convention will do and what they do, will be agreed to by the "dear people," who follow their "dimmykratik" leaders like a herd of sheep follows the old bell whether of the flock.[57]

The elections of 1840 and 1844 produced much excitement in the Hopewell Village area. A gigantic rally for William Henry Harrison drew many Furnace people to Morgantown on August 17, 1840. Morris, again, was the reporter:

> A Whig meeting had been advertized to be held here today and to be addressed by [John W.] Baer, the celebrated Buckeye Blacksmith. In the morning early David Morgan had the Stars and Stripes flying from his sign post. The Committee of escort had met and gone out to meet Baer and the Reading people and another had gone to meet the Chester County delegation and log cabin. About 10 the people began to come in on foot, on horseback and in vehicles of every description. At 11 o'clock the Reading and Forest folks, under escort came in—there was quite a throng. Shortly after the Chester County delegation, about a mile long, appeared carrying several beautiful banners, being accompanied with a band, a neat Log Cabin, and about a dozen Miner's Carts filled with folks from Jones' Mine holes. There was also a 6 horse wagon along filled with delegates. There was said to be about 650 people in that single arrival. . . .
>
> About 1 o'clock, the people went to Kurtz's Woods where seats and a stand had been prepared . . . and after organizing by appointing John M. Keim of Reading as Chairman . . . Mr. Hazlehurst of Phila. was called and gave us a short speech after which the Buckeye was listened to with great interest and attention for the course of an hour or two. . . .
>
> The number of people present was very differently estimated —some saying 1000, 1500, 2000, 2500 and one man computed them at above 3000. . . .

[57] *Ibid.,* p. 86.

In the evening there was a good deal of drunkenness, Much noise and a little squabbling — not very much blood was shed however.[58]

After all the excitement was over, Morgantown gave Harrison a disappointing majority of only 25 votes when the Whigs had expected as many as 40.[59] Berks County gave its usual two-to-one majority to the Democratic candidate, Martin Van Buren. In most elections Union Township, like Morgantown, supported the Whig candidates. Later this area favored the Republicans.[60] In their politics the area residents were usually found voting the same ticket as the Hopewell ironmasters. Support of the latter for the Whig ticket in 1844 was shown by contributions of $100 each by Clement Brooke, Charles Brooke and M. Brooke Buckley to "the Whig Committee of Philad[a] for Election purposes."[61] The tariff issue was undoubtedly influential in this support of Whig candidates. No record was found to show whether or not the Hopewell ironmasters used pressure to get their workers to vote the "right ticket."

Much excitement again prevailed at Hopewell over this election of 1844. Rallies for Henry Clay were held near the Furnace and at Morgantown, Birdsboro and Mt. Airy.[62] Undoubtedly many Furnace people attended these meetings in their neighborhood. They would have heard Thaddeus Stevens give the main address at Morgantown on September 24.[63] Some of the speeches were in both English and German.[64]

Charles M. Clingan continued the interest in politics which had been shown by his predecessors as Hopewell ironmasters. In 1852 he received an invitation to join a group going to a Whig mass meeting at Pottsville. Two passenger cars were

[58] *Ibid.*, pp. 113–114.
[59] *Ibid.*, p. 122.
[60] *Lewis Richards Scrapbooks,* Volume G, pp. 1–24.
[61] SM 28, p. 136.
[62] *Morris Diary, op. cit., passim* in Volume II.
[63] *Ibid.*, p. 156.
[64] *Ibid.*, p. 157.

reserved by the Reading Railroad to take the delegates and the Birdsboro Band.[65] In the 1860's Clingan had a page in his pocket notebook headed "Political Expenses." He gave no indication about who was running for what office, but the page listed payments in amounts from $1 to $200 and totaled $500.[66] Union township gave a strong vote to A. G. Curtin, the Republican candidate for governor in 1860.[67] The outcome might have been influenced by the presence on the ticket of a neighbor, Ironmaster Levi Smith of Joanna Furnace, who made an unsuccessful campaign for Congress on the Republican slate.

From time to time other matters of national import attracted attention or influenced actions at Hopewell Village. The Brooke family had an interest in the attempts of the United States Government to reach a settlement on the French Spoliation Claims. Clement Brooke wrote to his Congressman about this matter:

> I am informed that there is a bill now before Congress for the settlement of claims held by our citizens for Spoliation committed by the French Government prior to the year 1800 — I have taken the liberty of addressing you on this subject and hope you will be among those favorable to the adjustment of these claims — I have not a large interest myself but several of my relations have, one of whom is a widow now . . . with several children and stands greatly in need of any means she could receive . . . in payment of those claims.[68]

Wars had their influences in two ways upon the iron furnaces: Demand for iron and drain upon manpower. Hopewell Furnace was closed during all of the War of 1812; so there was no prosperity from an increased demand for pig iron. On the contrary Birdsboro Forge, owned by Buckley and Brooke, found itself overstocked with pig iron bought at war prices when the war ended sooner than expected.[69] A number of

[65] HV 8520922.
[66] *Kemper Manuscripts,* C. M. Clingan Pocket Note Book.
[67] *Lewis Richards Scrapbooks,* Volume G, p. 21.
[68] *Hopewell Papers,* Clement Brooke to John Ritter, June 29, 1846.
[69] HV 8150401B.

Hopewell Village men served in the army during this war:
Thomas May, John Linderman, Captain Jonathan Jones,
Sergeant Thomas Church, Philip Filman, Daniel Stubblebein,
Henry Minker, Matthew M. Brooke, Robert May, Samuel
Barde, Abraham Seifert and William Dewees.[70]

A gap in the existing Furnace books made it difficult to
trace an influence at Hopewell of the Mexican War. But the
Civil War revived the prosperity of the company when the
price of pig iron rose from its normal $30 to almost $100 per
ton. John Rutter Brooke of the Birdsboro branch of the family
raised a volunteer company and attained the rank of major
general in the Union Army before the end of the war.[71] Henry
Houck and Frederick Mosteller also served in the Union
Army,[72] and several Hopewell men were among the casualties
of the war. Henry F. Care was taken prisoner and held in
both the Andersonville and the Libby prisons;[73] Daniel
Buckley, Linderman Britton and Henry Wamback died of
wounds; and Daniel Hunsberger "Died of disease contracted
in the Army."[74]

Hopewell-area people were among those attracted by the
cheap land in the West, and some of them became a part of
the "westward movement." David Evans moved to Morgan
County, Illinois, in 1829 in time to break ground for spring
planting.[75] Two families from the Morgantown area, the
David Buckwalters and the James Flemings, left for Daven-
port, Iowa, on June 3, 1840. Buckwalter took with him " a 2
horse wagon complete, bed and all, one or two ploughs,
harness of all descriptions, tools of almost every kind, two
tables, one bureau, Queensware and a quantity of clothing
and clothing stuff." He went by the canal from Columbia.[76]

[70] *Lewis Richards Scrapbooks*, Volume G, pp. 239–240.
[71] Witzel, *op. cit.*, p. 83.
[72] Bethesda Baptist Church Cemetery.
[73] *Reading Eagle*, August 14, 1929.
[74] *St. Gabriel's Church Records, op. cit.*, Record of Burials.
[75] *Brooke Family Letters*, Ann to Edward, April 12, 1829.
[76] *Morris Diary, op. cit.*, p. 106.

A few days earlier neighbors had raised $50 on a subscription for a family moving west; possibly it was one of these two families who received the help.[77] Two years later Benjamin W. Gehman and his wife Elizabeth Morris Gehman started for Ohio. They sent their goods ahead by canal.[78] In 1880 the Bethesda Baptist Church near the Furnace dismissed Brother John Stoneback and Sister Sarah Stoneback to a Baptist church in an unspecified town in Kansas.[79]

One regular source of contact with the outside world for Furnace families was by means of letters, packages and newspapers delivered by the United States mails. It is not clear how mail reached Hopewell. In 1816 the Furnace paid postage of 16¢ for two letters "at the Reading Post Office."[80] Several references indicated that mail was left at the tollgate on the turnpikes to be picked up by the teamsters returning to Hopewell. After 1823 a carrier delivered mail to the Furnace and was paid his total bill quarterly or annually. Perhaps the mailman left letters at the company store and received his pay from the clerk, for many workers' accounts were debited for postage on personal letters. The charge in the first half of the nineteenth century usually ranged from 5¢ to 10¢ per letter. Among those paid for carrying mail to Hopewell were Rees Evans, David Morgan, "Lewis," Abraham Dehaven, "Doctor Ludwig" and "Spatz."[81]

On April 22, 1852, the Furnace purchased "30 Letter Stamps" at 3¢ each,[82] but for several years more they paid "Doctor Ludwig" and L. B. Holloway lump sums for mail service over a period of time.[83] In 1859 Hopewell was listed as a post office.[84]

[77] *Ibid.*, p. 103.
[78] *Ibid.*, p. 224.
[79] *Bethesda Baptist Church Minutebook, op. cit.,* April 11, 1880.
[80] SM 7, November 2, 1816, n. p.
[81] *Passim* in Furnace journals.
[82] SM 32, p. 126.
[83] SM 65, November 5, 1854, January 9, 1855, July 21, 1857, February 19, 1859.
[84] J. P. Lesley, *The Iron Manufacturers Guide to Furnaces, Forges and Rolling Mills of the United States* (New York: John Wiley, 1859), p. 40.

The outside world also came to the Furnace area in the form of business people who had goods or services to sell to the villagers : The tinker, drover, salesman, "foot peddler" and "wagon peddler," shoemaker, tailor, tinsmith, hatter, saddler, chimney sweep, spinner, weaver, clock repairer, gunsmith, candlemaker, basketmaker, pumpmaker, whipmaker, coppersmith, cabinetmaker and fishmonger served many of the people's needs. They brought with them scythes, kettles, worm syrup, brushes, books, pins, needles, tapes, thread, mirrors, cutlery, cigars, chewing tobacco, snuff, paper, hats, coffee mills, fish nets, shovels, baskets, powder, confections, drugs, whetstones, whips, crackers, rope, boots and shoes, axes, cotton yarn, and garden seed. One basketmaker had a small wagon to which he hitched a team of dogs. He thus attracted attention and increased his sale of baskets.[85]

Did the humanitarian and reform movements of the first half of the nineteenth century reach into Hopewell Village for adherents? It has already been noted that there was support for Abolition and public education and opposition to the compulsory military drills. Labor organization and labor reforms made little headway among the Furnace employees. One observer thought there was general opposition to the abolishing of debtor prisons in 1842. He argued :

> Rich and poor are alike loud in their denunciations — the former because it takes off a means of enforcing payments from their debtors and the latter because it takes away their credit.[86]

In the same year the movement against capital punishment was attacked from the Episcopal pulpit by the Reverend Mister Levi Bull.[87]

The reform movement with the greatest support in the Hopewell area, however, was temperance. Perhaps because of

---

[85] *Morris Diary, op. cit.*, II, pp. 33, 43, 44.
[86] *Ibid.*, pp. 222–223.
[87] *Ibid.*, p. 190.

the danger from accidents, the ironmasters had made early attempts to control the sale of intoxicants near the Pennsylvania furnaces and forges. In 1726 the colonial legislature prohibited the sale of liquor within two miles of a furnace except with the permission of the ironmaster. Ten years later the distance was made three miles.[88] But of course intoxicants were not barred at the company stores, and were sold at most of them. Whiskey was regularly stocked at the Hopewell store in its early history. Seldom were sales of other intoxicants mentioned; but the store purchased, apparently for use in the Big House, brandy, fine wines, beer, rum, "peach whiskey" and cognac.

Whiskey sales appeared in the store journals until November 8, 1816. The last recorded sale on that day was one quart bought by Daniel Buckley "for the molders to make plates."[89] Sales then ceased until 1822. Whiskey was sold to workers as late as 1826,[90] but after this was no longer stocked by the store. Manager Clement Brooke and Clerk John Benson were both regular subscribers to a publication called the *Temperance Advocate*,[91] and Hopewell workers were fined for having whiskey on the job.[92] Someone at Hopewell wrote a letter to the legislature requesting support for a bill relating to "Temperance Taverns." A local judge had recently declared that such taverns were illegal. The writer of the letter thought the legislature should legalize taverns which did not serve intoxicants.[93]

In the community generally the temperance movement made progress. James Morris discontinued at his store the sale of any "ardent spirits but Brandy, which is often wanted for medicinal purposes."[94] Temperance meetings were held under

[88] Bining, "Iron Plantations," *op. cit.*, p. 11.
[89] SM 7, November 8, 1806, n. p.
[90] SM 12, *passim*.
[91] HV 8340414A.
[92] SM 46, October 24, 1822, n. p.
[93] *Hopewell Papers*, Uncatalogued, unsigned and undated but reference to Marion Furnace places it as probably in the 1840's.
[94] *Morris Diary, op. cit.*, p. 30. The date was September 25, 1837.

the auspices of "The Sunday School Beneficial Society Temperence Men" or "The Sons of Temperence."[95] The Methodist Church in Morgantown was the location for many of the rallies held in the 1840's. In 1843 a mass meeting assembled in the woods south of the Jones mine holes about which one participant reported :

> The Morgantown Band went out to play for it. Many people were present and among the rest, the very celebrated "Razor Strop Man" who sold perhaps a hundred of his strops at 25 cents each . . . The speakers were Wm. Darling, Esq., the "Razor Strop Man" and a gentleman from Pottsgrove.[96]

The program of the temperance movement included an attempt to induce people to "sign the pledge" against use of intoxicants and a demand for the closing of "all unlicensed drinking houses, and the bars of all taverns, on the Sabbath."[97] The activity of the societies failed to generate enough support, however. Prohibition was submitted to a popular vote in Pennsylvania in 1854 and lost by 5,178 ballots. Berks County voted against the proposed law.[98]

Hopewell Village obviously was influenced by and participated in many of the same activities as engaged Americans generally. The Village was not isolated from the world of ideas and movements.

---

[95] *Ibid.,* p. 155; *Lewis Richards Scrapbooks,* Volume G, p. 126.
[96] *Morris Diary, op. cit.,* II, p. 63.
[97] *Lewis Richards Scrapbooks,* Volume G, p. 37.
[98] Louis Hartz, *Economic Policy and Democratic Thought: Pennsylvania, 1776–1860* (Cambridge : Harvard University Press, 1948), p. 211.

22   Conclusion

Needing iron for weapons, for tools and for household utensils and conveniences, colonial Americans defied the British legal restrictions on the fabrication of iron products in the colonies.[1] Perhaps because of their long experience in flouting English laws, the ironmasters were numerous and active in the fight for independence.

Hopewell Furnace, born during the controversy over the Townshend taxes, helped to provide the arms and ammunition for the Continental Army in the Revolutionary War. Mark Bird, founder of the Furnace, was an early and energetic worker in the cause of separation from the mother country.

The end of the war in 1783 reduced the demand for iron and brought the American iron industry into competition with the British. A business recession in the postwar period forced bankruptcy upon many ironmasters, including Mark Bird. During the Federalist period Hopewell Furnace was bought and sold by a succession of business men and speculators who tried to make a profit from its operation. In 1800 the Furnace was purchased by a partnership consisting of members of the Buckley and Brooke families. After a legal struggle to establish

[1] For a discussion of British restrictions on colonial iron see Arthur Cecil Bining, *British Regulation of the Colonial Iron Industry* (Philadelphia: University of Pennsylvania Press, 1933).

their land titles, the partnership profited from a long period of prosperity at Hopewell.

Success for the owners of the Furnace was the result of a fortunate combination of circumstances: the effective management of the business by Clement Brooke; the growing demand in America for all kinds of iron products; and the opening near Hopewell of highways, canals and railroads leading to the markets in and beyond Philadelphia. Brooke made a decision in the 1820's to convert most of the iron from the Furnace into stoves. In the next twenty years tens of thousands of Hopewell stoves in more than a hundred patterns were sold to heat homes and public buildings from Baltimore to Portsmouth, New Hampshire.

Except for a brief and costly experiment with an anthracite furnace in the 1850's, Hopewell was always a cold-blast, charcoal furnace. The peculiar needs of this kind of operation created a distinctive community to serve it and to share its periods of prosperity or depression. The making of charcoal consumed the wood grown on thousands of acres of forest land and gave employment to many men who worked at a distance from the furnace. Miners also lived several miles from the furnace stack.

A charcoal furnace was not the center of an urban community. The people who worked for the furnace were living a rural life. Most Hopewell families did some farming. Some of them were primarily farmers, becoming Furnace employees only during the winter months. Therefore, they were never so dependent upon their employer as city industrial workers were. They showed little interest in the labor unions which were struggling for recognition in the cities.

In Hopewell Village the ironmaster and his clerk were the management. From the front door of the mansion the owner could have seen almost all that was transpiring in his little industrial empire. The activity at the furnace and cast house, the wagons coming and going, and even the work on his nearest farm were all under his immediate gaze. Many of his workers lived in houses within sight. Their wives came to the store, only a few steps below the mansion; and their children played around the grounds. Both women and children were also a part of the work force.

The owner was almost solely responsible for the success of his furnace. He provided the working capital, he purchased land and raw materials, he found the market for his products, he set his prices on the basis of competition with rival furnaces, he hired his laborers and tried to keep them content on their jobs.

The relationship between the ironmaster and his workers was much more than that of employer-employee. He operated a store largely for their convenience. He performed many services for them in the distant cities or in nearby towns. He, or his wife, gave medical and legal advice and entertained the Village families in the mansion. From the clerk the manager could obtain a financial statement for any employee, and often he provided advice and help in money matters.

The Hopewell managers, especially Clement Brooke, gave community leadership in religion and education. They hired tutors before 1836 and in that year constructed a building at the furnace to house a public school. They bought books, magazines, newspapers, trade journals and religious publications. They gave employment in their homes and in the furnace operation to large numbers of Negroes, some of whom may have been escaped slaves. The use of intoxicants was discouraged, and the temperance movement received support from the Hopewell management.

The managers displayed patience with their workers for neglect of duty and even dishonesty. The usual form of punishment was a fine assessed against the earnings of the worker. Seldom was an employee discharged. The skilled workers, particularly, formed a stable work force. Wages were competitive with other furnaces and with other jobs and remained remarkably uniform for the same tasks over long periods of time. Fringe benefits sometimes provided low rental in company houses, free moving by Furnace teams, free fuel and a plot of ground for a garden.

By his business acumen Clement Brooke became a man of wealth and influence in the world of industry and politics. He owned several other furnaces and forges as well as stock in railroads, canals and coal mines. The income of his workers did not improve as rapidly as the wealth he gained from the Furnace.

Hopewell families lived in plain but usually substantial houses, furnished them with necessities and some luxuries, ate well and dressed adequately. Most of them stayed out of debt and paid their bills to the Furnace and others. The Village was not a slum area. The people cooperated on jobs which needed the labor of many hands and in support of the sick and unfortunate among their members. There was a high value placed upon the ability to read and write. Parents sent their children to the tutor even when the tuition represented a considerable sacrifice. They also participated extensively in the religious activities of the surrounding communities.

Next to management the skilled workers at the Furnace formed the upper level of Village society. The founder, the keeper and the molders had incomes several times as great as those of the unskilled workers. They were able to afford a higher scale of living and sometimes owned a riding or driving horse. Skilled jobs were often handed down from father to son. But there was no rigid caste system. A boy with skill and industry could learn the mysteries of the molders' trade, and some attained this position before they reached adulthood. Some Hopewell workers left to become managers or even owners of their own iron works.

Negro and white, skilled and unskilled, intermingled in vocations and residences, sent their children to school and attended the parties at the ironmaster's mansion. The iron-master's children usually married within their own class, but woodchoppers' daughters sometimes married molders and blacksmiths.

Hopewell workers had six or seven long workdays per week. They sometimes took time from the job, with or without permission, and seldom suffered any penalty other than loss of wages for the time not worked. They enjoyed no paid vacations or sick leave. But they apparently considered it worth a day's pay to attend a fair, a battalion day, an election, a camp meeting, a political rally, a house raising, an apple-butter boiling or a "frolic."

The character of Hopewell Village began to change before the middle of the nineteenth century. The introduction of hot-blast, coke furnaces reduced the labor cost of producing iron and permitted large concentrations of furnaces in urban centers where transportation facilities were available. The cold-blast, charcoal furnaces could no longer compete. Stove-casting ended at Hopewell in 1844. The expansion of the rail-roads and the Civil War created a high demand for iron and permitted another forty years of Furnace operation for the production of pig iron. But this was only a reprieve. In 1883 the last blast ended at Hopewell Furnace.

Hopewell Furnace, with its single stack producing a thousand tons of iron annually by the efforts of a hundred or more workers, may appear to have had little in common with today's gigantic iron and steel plants. But only a century and a quarter ago this furnace and several hundred others much like it were the American iron industry.

Glossary

Blast—The period the furnace was in operation before it closed to rebuild the hearth. In Blast was the time the furnace was making iron. *OUT* of Blast was any period when the furnace was not operating.

Burning Mine—Heating the ore to remove impurities, especially sulphur, which would interfere with the production of good iron.

Coaling—The destructive distillation of wood to produce charcoal.

Collier—The workman who made charcoal.

Filler—The workman who fed the raw materials into the furnace stack.

Flasks—Wooden frames used in making cast products. They held the sand into which the molten iron was poured.

Founder—The highly skilled manager of furnace operation. His experience and knowledge were important factors in determining the quality of the iron the furnace produced.

Gatemetal—Scraps of iron left from the molding process.

GUTTERMAN—Unskilled workman at the furnace whose principal duty was to remove the slag, or cinder, to the slag piles.

HOLLOW WARE—Molded cooking utensils such as pots, kettles and skillets.

IRONMASTER—The general manager of the furnace enterprise. He was usually the owner or a partner of the company.

KEEPER—Principal assistant to the founder. Directed the furnace work when the founder was not present.

MINE HOLES—Site of open pit mining for iron ore.

PUTTING IN THE MINE—Wheeling ore from the banks to the bridge house where it would be available to the filler to feed into the furnace.

PUTTING UP THE NIGHT STOCK—Placing in the bridge house the quantities of ore, limestone and charcoal which would be needed to keep the furnace supplied during the night.

STEELING AN AXE—Welding a thin strip of steel to the cutting edge of an iron axe to improve its ability to hold its sharp edge.

TUYERE—The opening into the furnace through which the air blast was carried. The founder used this opening to observe the interior of the furnace to determine how the smelting was proceeding.

WASHING MINE—Removing dirt from the ore by means of a stream of water running through a trough.

Appendix A

Year			
1771	Mark Bird		
1785	John Nixon		
1788	Cadwallader Morris ($\frac{1}{3}$)		James Old ($\frac{2}{3}$)
1790	Benjamin Morris ($\frac{1}{3}$)		James Old ($\frac{2}{3}$)
1791	Benjamin Morris		
1793	James Old		
1794	James Wilson		
1796	James Old		
1800	Benjamin Morris		
1800	Daniel Buckley ($\frac{1}{3}$)	Mathew Brooke ($\frac{1}{3}$)	Thomas Brooke ($\frac{1}{3}$)
1824	Daniel Buckley ($\frac{1}{2}$)		Thomas Brooke ($\frac{1}{2}$)
1827	Daniel Buckley ($\frac{1}{6}$) Clement Buckley ($\frac{1}{6}$) M. Brooke Buckley (($\frac{1}{6}$)		Charles Brooke ($\frac{1}{6}$) Clement Brooke ($\frac{1}{6}$) Ann and Tacy Brooke ($\frac{1}{6}$)
1831	M. Brooke Buckley ($\frac{1}{3}$)	Charles Brooke ($\frac{1}{3}$)	Clement Brooke ($\frac{1}{3}$)
1852	Clement Brooke		
1852	M. Brooke Buckley ($\frac{1}{2}$)		Clement Brooke ($\frac{1}{2}$)
1856	Edward Buckley ($\frac{1}{2}$)		Clement Brooke ($\frac{1}{2}$)
1859	Edward Buckley ($\frac{1}{2}$)		Maria Brooke Clingan ($\frac{1}{2}$)
1895	Charles Clingan ($\frac{1}{6}$) Louise C. Brooke ($\frac{1}{6}$) Alan Clingan ($\frac{1}{6}$)		Maria Brooke Clingan ($\frac{1}{2}$)

Appendix B

TABLE I

RESIDENTS AT THE IRONMASTER'S MANSION,
CENSUS OF 1850

Name	Age	Occupation
Charles M. Clingan	30	Manufacturer
Maria T. Clingan	29	. .
Clement B. Clingan	7	. .
William W. Clingan	5	. .
Andrew Bust	25	Gardner
Eliza Hill	33	Negro
Sarah Bendigo	28	Mulatto
Susanna Bendigo	5	Mulatto
Anna Maria Wilson	23	Negro
William Jacobs	50	Negro
Anna Keller	22	. .

RESIDENTS AT THE IRONMASTER'S MANSION,
CENSUS OF 1860

Name	Age	Occupation
Charles Clingan	40	. .
Maria Clingan	39	. .
Clement B. Clingan	16	. .
Charles B. Clingan	9	. .
David D. Clingan	6	. .
Alan H. Clingan	3	. .
John Shafer	36	Clerk
Lidgu Chafer (Female)	22	. .
Rebecca Graham	17	Servant
William Jacobs	55	Negro
Ellen Dickerson	14	Mulatto
Letitia Watson	15	Negro
Samuel Everhart	27	Clerk

TABLE II

HOUSEHOLD ARTICLES PURCHASED BY WORKERS

Date	Article	Price
April 28, 1785	Looking Glass	£1-2/6
December 2, 1802	1 Beadstead	£1-5/0
. .	1 Chest	£1-0/0
. .	1 Doughtrough	10/9
. .	2 Coffins	£4-2/6
February 2, 1803	A Beaurow	£7-10/0
March 3, 1803	Desk	£7-10/0
June 15, 1805	A Beaurow	£5-12/6
April 5, 1805	Bed and Bedding	$9.50
. .	Puter Dish	1.05
. .	6 puter plates	1.10
. .	2 Winsor Chairs	1.20
. .	Bed and bed stead	9.50
. .	4 Winsor Chairs	1.20
. .	Bed and Bedstead	6.10
. .	Large Chest	1.60
May 4, 1807	Clothes Chest	£3-0/0
July 24, 1819	Chest	$3.00
September 28, 1819	A Trunk	4.00
February 22, 1826	A Rug	.50
March 22, 1828	A pair bedsteads	3.50
September 1, 1829	A half doz. chairs	7.25
November 16, 1829	A tub	1.18½
June 1, 1830	A Pair Bedsteads	3.00
. .	Cradle	2.00

April 4, 1832	A Clock	10.00
December 6, 1832	A Shaving Cup	.18½
November 26, 1832	A clock	10.00
February 28, 1833	A Clock	10.00
December 12, 1832	A bureau	20.00
April 30, 1835	1 pair of bedsteads	3.00
. .	,, ,,	5.00
. .	,, ,,	3.00
. .	1 Rocking Cradle	2.50
. .	Bedsteads and Breakfast Table	9.50
October 26, 1835	30″ circular stove	9.12½
April 6, 1843	A Coverlet	7.00
February 6, 1849	Carpet	3.03
June 10, 1848	A cupboard	9.50
November 16, 1849	Chairs	10.00
May 5, 1851	Washing Tubs	2.75
April 7, 1857	Comforters and Sheets	5.00

TABLE III

FURNACE PRODUCTION AND LABOR USED IN FIVE SELECTED PERIODS OF TWO BLASTS EACH

	1805– 1807	1818– 1820	1825– 1827	1835– 1837	1851– 1853
Duration of Blasts	2 years	2 years	2 years	2 years 2 mo.	2 years, 3 mo.
Pig Iron (Tons)	448	618	752	355	1,904
Gate Metal (Tons)	...	...	143	315	...
Cast Iron (Tons)	118	123	565	1,144	...
Value of Iron (Approx.)	$20,000	$28,700	$67,700	$126,500	$61,000
Total Persons Employed	186	170	213	246	225
Wages Paid	$19,070	$23,410	$31,020	$43,760	$29,500
Man-days Worked	30,580	28,370	42,860	49,090	41,580

Table IV

NUMBER OF PERSONS EMPLOYED IN DIFFERENT JOB
CLASSIFICATIONS FOR FIVE PERIODS OF
TWO BLASTS EACH

	1805–1807	1818–1820	1825–1827	1835–1837	1851–1853
Banksman	...	...	...	...	2
Burning Mine	...	...	...	4	...
Cabinet Maker	...	...	...	2	...
Carpenter	2	2	3	6	3
Clerk	2	...	1	3	2
Collier	27	21	20	18	14
Commission Sales	...	1	...	...	...
Farm Worker	12	11	21	11	15
Filler	5	3	5	2	6
Founder	1	1	1	2	1
Gardner	...	...	...	2	3
Hostler	...	...	...	2	1
Houseworker	4	6	10	3	16
Keeper	3	4	6	2	3
Laborer	35	19	31	18	27
Maker of Boxes and Baskets	2	6	12	3	...
Manager	1	1	1	2	1
Mason	3	1	4	3	2
Miner	18	23	20	18	35
Misc. Furnace Repair	5	6	5	3	5
Misc. Work by Outsiders	10	10	17	6	7
Misc. Work for Employees	...	...	7	10	...
Molder	6	8	13	19	...
Molder's Helper	1	4	7	10	...
Patternmaker	1	2	2	3	...
Putting in Mine	...	2	3	6	2
Smith	7	1	2	5	1
Stocking Coal	3	3	...	1	3
Teamster for Furnace	11	5	7	9	10
Teamster, Indep.	31	35	49	27	10
Tutor	1	4	2	3	...
Wheelwright	1	3	4	2	1
Woodcutter, Cord.	70	52	60	112	116

Woodcutter, Posts and Rails	13	4	3	3	21
Total Persons Employed	186	170	213	246	225

TABLE V

MAN-DAYS OF LABOR USED IN DIFFERENT JOB CLASSIFICATIONS FOR FIVE PERIODS OF TWO BLASTS EACH

	1805–1807	1818–1820	1825–1827	1835–1837	1851–1853
Banksman	...	...	...	...	93
Burning Mine	...	...	...	375	...
Cabinet Maker	...	...	...	55	...
Carpenter	28	284	1,033	1,419	397
Clerk	624	...	624	1,300	703
Collier	4,843	4,134	5,300	4,787	4,484
Commission Sales	...	9	...	...	...
Farm Worker	61	112	116	51	1,310
Filler	1,690	787	1,147	1,321	1,337
Founder	624	624	624	762	672
Gardner	...	...	...	371	283
Gutterman	...	453	486	637	524
Hostler	...	...	...	731	62
Houseworker	322	1,281	1,366	2,216	1,967
Keeper	316	737	769	644	679
Laborer	353	1,523	1,994	2,602	1,193
Maker of Boxes and Baskets	299	132	123	237	...
Manager	624	624	624	1,248	1,404
Mason	108	20	681	153	6
Miner	5,035	3,695	4,541	6,528	8,514
Misc. Furnace Repair	184	179	39	148	73
Misc. Work by Outsiders	130	703	393	272	399
Misc. Work for Employees	...	...	72	216	...
Molder	1,687	3,636	3,402	5,797	...
Molder's Helper	3	139	406	663	...
Patternmaker	3	77	71	346	...
Putting in Mine	...	566	1,065	598	668
Smith	870	613	444	1,210	768
Stocking Coal	96	3	...	364	378

Teamster, 　Furnace　1,467	1,552	1,840	1,901	2,281
Teamster, 　Independent　322	936	1,880	2,996	1,490
Tutor　　　　　50	300	100	200	...
Wheelwright　205	158	519	185	102
Woodcutter, 　Cordwood　9,973	5,082	13,193	8,698	11,711
Woodcutter, 　Posts, etc.　124	7	8	58	85
Total　　30,583	28,368	42,858	49,086	41,581

Note: Fractions of days were rounded.

TABLE VI

SUMMARY OF INCOME AND EXPENDITURES FOR 14 WORKERS, 1818–1842

	John Benson	*Thomas Boyer*	*Thomas Care*
Occupation	Miner–Clerk	Teamster	Founder–Moulder
Years Covered	1818–1830	1818–1836	1818–1841
Total Income	$608.22	$1,193.51	$21,350.93
Cash Drawn	93.63	173.00	6,089.57
Storegoods Bought	130.69	676.91	3,411.51
Storegoods and Cash	...	...	801.62
Furnace Products 　and Services	5.65	13.81	575.93
Paid to Outsiders	331.39	210.18	9,154.21*
Sundries	89.07	59.19	1,703.28
Unaccounted for	−41.21	+41.21	−384.21

	David Evans	*Robert Gilmore*	*David Hart*
Occupation	Woodcutter	Miner	Teamster
Years Covered	1818–1837	1818–1836	1818–1840
Total Income	$1,252.93	$954.41	$5,690.37
Cash Drawn	926.85	591.98	553.52
Storegoods Bought	304.82	231.45	4,248.05
Storegoods and Cash	5.43	2.30	48.68
Furnace Products 　and Services	8.70	32.62	203.22
Paid to Outsiders	80.31	113.09	600.30
Sundries	4.43	...	87.39
Unaccounted for	−77.59	−17.03	−50.77

* Includes some labor at the furnace for which the founder paid the wages.

	Henry Houck	George Kephart	Thomas Lloyd
Occupation	Collier	Filler–Keeper	Farmer
Years Covered	1818–1842	1819–1842	1818–1842
Total Income	$3,685.78	$3,483.61	$2,570.89
Cash Drawn	1,947.38	506.69	1,293.41
Storegoods Bought	515.20	2,364.19	726.69
Storegoods and Cash	25.68	51.28	39.79
Furnace Products and Services	19.25	4.27	128.98
Paid to Outsiders	688.16*	378.49	325.87
Sundries	250.61	80.21	126.00
Unaccounted for	+239.50	+98.48	−69.85

	George North	William Pierce	Samuel Williams
Occupation	Moulder	Woodcutter	Teamster
Years Covered	1818–1841	1819–1829	1819–1842
Total Income	$5,303.77	$511.01	$4,696.54
Cash Drawn	693.98	31.82	295.75
Storegoods Bought	3,259.05	268.84	3,254.91
Storegoods and Cash	235.90	...	39.05
Furnace Products and Services	71.88	22.11	2.21
Paid to Outsiders	735.29	24.23	802.34
Sundries	280.63	116.31	266.39
Unaccounted for	+27.02	+47.71	+35.89

	Solomon Williams	Thomas Wynn
Occupation	Woodcutter	Farmer–Miner
Years Covered	1818–1839	1818–1841
Total Income	$344.38	$2,135.44
Cash Drawn	83.42	1,039.87
Storegoods Bought	172.57	45.14
Storegoods and Cash	10.48	...
Furnace Products and Services	9.45	2.25
Paid to Outsiders	29.97	464.62
Sundries	27.90	...
Unaccounted for	+10.59	+593.56

Note: Fractions of a cent were rounded.
Note: The "unaccounted for" item is due in part to the absence of journals for some years.

Appendix C

A RECORD OF THE PURCHASES AT THE HOPEWELL FURNACE store by 26 customers during the period from December 1831 to February 1833. The information was taken from the Hopewell record book referred to as SM 20. The period used was one in which the operation of the Furnace was prosperous. The accounts were for a variety of classifications of wages and skills. Purchases have been grouped by the kind of goods bought. Examination of the record book would show the chronology of the transactions.

JOHN BENSON, CLERK

Cloth	Prices	Quantity	Amount of Purchase
Cord	No Price	None given	$1.00
Calico	$0.21, .25, .30 yard	30 yards	7.53
Buckram	.16 ,,	1¼ ,,	.20
Padding	.40 ,,	1¼ ,,	.50
"Cloth"	2.37½, 2.40 ,,	7 ,,	16.67½
Holland, B	.22 ,,	4 ,,	.88
Muslin	.12½, .14, .18½ ,,	16 ,,	2.70
Nankeen, Blue	.16½ ,,	8 ,,	1.32
		2 pieces	3.00
		Total	$33.80½

Clothing			
Cravat, Jaconete	.30, .40 each	3	1.00
Gloves	.70 pair	1	.70
Handkerchief	.44 each	2	.88
Shoes	1.50 pair	1	1.50
Suspenders	.20 pair	1	.20
		Total	$4.28

Miscellaneous			
Saltpetre	.20 pound	1 lb.	.20
Knives	.20, .40 each	2	.60
Nails	.09 pound	2 lb.	.18
Shoe Polish	.10 box	2	.20
Storegoods to Charity	...	...	34½
		Total	$1.52½

429

Notions			
Buttons	.06, .12½, .25 doz.	50	1.18½*
Cord	.06 piece	1	.06
Pattern, Vest	.75 each	1	.75
Thread, Silk	.06¼ skein	17	1.05¾
		Total	$3.05¼
Personal Items			
Tobacco	.03 roll	1	.03
		Total Spent	$42.69¼

Note: Lived at Big House and bought no food. Family of three in 1830.

* Totals so marked are incorrect, but they are given as the clerk listed them in his records.

CLEMENT BROOKE, MANAGER

Cloth	*Prices*		*Quantity*		*Amount*
Bobinette	$0.70, .80, 1.00	yard	3 15/16	yards	$ 3.25
Buckram	.16	,,	2½	,,	.40
Padding	.30, .40	,,	2¼	,,	.75
Calico	.12½, .13, .15, .18, .20, .22, .25, .27, .31	,,	131	,,	27.76
Cashmere	.30	,,	3¼	,,	.97½
Casinete	1.25	,,	1 lot and 3½	,,	6.03½
Check	.22	,,	1¼	,,	.22*
Cloth, Blue	5.00	,,	3¼	,,	15.00*
Drilling	.20, .22, .25, .50	,,	11⅜	,,	3.33½
Flannel Cotton	.16, .20, .24, .35, .44, .53	,,			
Yellow	.30	,,	22¼	,,	7.57
Holland, Brown	.20, .25	,,	2¾	,,	.58½
Jaconete	.35, .62é	,,	1⅛	,,	.68
Lace	.18	,,	2½	,,	.45
Lace Bobinete	.18½, .80	,,	1¾	,,	.78½
Linen, Irish	.58	,,	66	,,	38.28
Marino	.41, .44	,,	26	,,	10.73
Marino, Black	.56	,,	2	,,	1.12
Millinete	No price given		?		?
Millinete and wire	.20	,,	½	,,	.10
Muslin	.12½, .14, .15, .18, .18½, .30 .31, .40, .60, .65, .75	,,			
Black	.10, .14	,,			
Brown	.12½	,,			
Book	.44, .75	,,			
Mull	.60, .67	,,			

Jaconete	.60	,,	117⅜ ,,	28.74
Nankeen	.14	,,	1 piece and	
			¾ ,,	1.35½
Pittsburgh Cord	.37½	,,	¾ ,,	.28
Quilting	.12½, .15, .18¢	,,	8¾ ,,	1.33¢
Satinette	1.40	,,	3¼ ,,	4.55
Vesting	1.12	,,	½ ,,	.56
Waist Ribbon	.15 each		3 ,,	.45
			Total	$155.29½

Clothing	Prices	Quantity	Amount
Belt	$0.20 each	1	$0.20
Handkerchief	.20, .35, .50, .62½, .87½, 1.00 each	15	8.27
Stockings	.20, .22, .25, .27, .37½, .40, .44, .46 pair	38 pair	14.13¢
Suspenders	18½ pair	1	18½
		Total	$22.79

Miscellaneous			
Paper	.20 quire	1½	.30

Notions			
Buttons	.20 dozen		
Gilt	.15 ,,		
Bone	.06 ,,		
Small gilt	.18½ ,,		
Pearl	.18 ,,		
Molds	.03 ,,	9 purchases	
Patterns	.25, .65, .75, .87½ each	4	2.52½
Ribbon, Black	.12½ yard		
Green	.04, .10, .12½, .25 yard		
Belt	.12, .20 yard	20½ yards	2.52
Scissors	.18¾ pair	2	.37½
Tape	?	3 pieces	.16
Thread, Silk	.06¼ skein	6 purchases	1.76¾
		Total	$9.13¾

Personal Items			
Comb, Pocket	.12½ each		
Fine toothed	,,		
Side	.05, .25 each	6	.97½
Soap	.03 cake	2	.06
		Total	$1.03½
		Total Spent	$188.54¾

Note: Lived at Big House and bought no food. A household of 15 in 1830.

JOHN CARE, MOULDER

Bulk Items	Prices		Quantity	Amount
Corn, Shelled	$0.56 bushel			
Ear	.37 ,,		$3\frac{1}{2}$ bu.	$1.77
Feed	.01 pound or		52 lb. and	
	.60, .62 bushel		$8\frac{1}{4}$ bu.	5.63$\frac{1}{2}$
Rye Seed	?		$2\frac{3}{4}$,,	?
			Total	7.40\frac{1}{2}$

Cloth				
Bobinette	1.00	yard	$\frac{5}{8}$ yards	.62$\frac{1}{2}$
Calico	.10, .12$\frac{1}{2}$, .15,			
	.16, .17,.18			
	.18$\frac{1}{2}$, .20, .21			
	.23, .25	,,	62$\frac{3}{8}$,,	11.47$\frac{1}{2}$
Casinette	.56, .67	,,	5$\frac{3}{4}$,,	3.43$\frac{1}{2}$
Check	.16, .18$\frac{1}{4}$, .20,			
	.22	,,	8$\frac{1}{4}$,,	1.10*
Drilling	.33	,,	3$\frac{1}{2}$,,	1.15$\frac{1}{4}$
Flannel	.24, .50 .56	,,	10 ,,	3.57
Gingham	.37$\frac{1}{2}$	,,	1$\frac{1}{4}$,,	.47$\frac{1}{2}$
Jaconete	.40, .67	,,	$\frac{5}{8}$,,	.35$\frac{1}{2}$
Millinette	.16	,,	$\frac{1}{2}$,,	.08
Muslin	.10, .12$\frac{1}{2}$, .13,			
	.14, .18$\frac{1}{2}$	,,		
Plain	.18	,,		
Book	.68	,,		
Cotton	.28, .40	,,	65 ,,	6.76*
Pittsburgh Cord	.22	,,	10 ,,	2.20
Plaid	.18, .18$\frac{3}{4}$	,,	4 ,,	.73$\frac{1}{2}$
			Total	31.96\frac{1}{2}$

Clothing		Quantity	Amount
Cravat	.62$\frac{1}{2}$ each	1	.62$\frac{1}{2}$
Gloves, Buckskin	.75 pair	1	.75
Mitts	.50 ,,	1	.50
Handkerchiefs,			
Cotton	.15, .23, .25, .28 each	6	1.31
Silk	1.12$\frac{1}{2}$ each	1	1.12$\frac{1}{2}$
Hat, Palm leaf	.37 each	1	.37
Fur	3.50 each	1	3.50
Cap—boy's	1.00 each	1	1.00
Shoes	1.25, 1.50 pair	3	4.25
Stockings	.32 pair	1	.32
		Total	$13.75

Food	Prices	Quantity	Amount
Bacon	$0.10 pound	62$\frac{1}{2}$ lb.	$6.25
Beef	.05 ,,	9$\frac{3}{4}$,,	.49
Cheese	.12$\frac{1}{2}$	4$\frac{3}{8}$,,	.54
Coffee	.16, .17 pound	57 ,,	10.53*

Flour	.60 quarter (28 lb.)	4 quarters	2.40
„ , Wheat	.03 pound	11 lb.	.33
Mackeral	5.50 Barrel	2 bbl.	11.00
Molasses	.14, .16 quart	37 qts.	5.47
Pork	.04½ pound	303 lb. (1 Hog)	13.63½
Potatoes	.34, .40, .50 bushel	11¼ bu.	4.47
Salt, Coarse	.03 quart		
Fine	.04 „ or .85,		
	1.00 bu.	4¾ „	2.17½*
Spices, Pepper	.40 pound	¼ lb.	.10
Saltpeter	.24 „	¼ „	.06
Sugar	.12½ „	70 „	8.75
Tea	.31, .31¼, .32 per	3 „	3.42½
	¼ lb.		
		Total	$69.62½

Miscellaneous

Almanac	.08 each	1	.08
Blacksmith work	…	2 jobs	.40
Hardware, Building	…	7 purchases	.85
File	.10	1	.10
Glass	.05 each	11 panes	.55
Putty	.05 pound	1 lb.	.05
Coffee Mill	1.00 each	1	1.00
Starch	.16 pound	¼ lb.	.04
Nails	.09, .11, .12 pound	26 „	4.19*
Nails, Ceiling	.11, .12½ „	21 „	2.32½
Spikes	.08 pound	4¼ „	.34
Jar	.10 each	1	.10
Oil	.12, .12½ quart	3 qt.	.37
Packing Box	.10, .75 each	2	.85
Fish net	1.12½ each	1	1.12½
Horse Collar	2.00 „	1	2.00
Fish Barrel	.37½ each	1	.37½
Black Lead	.24 pound	¼ lb.	.06
Paper	.01 sheet	5	.05
Pasteboard	.06 each	1	.06
		Total	$14.91½

Notions

Braid	.03 yard	5 yd.	.15
Buttons	.06, .19 dozen	20 purchases	.92½
Cotton Balls	.02 each	19	.38
Cord	.04 piece	1 piece	.04
Patterns, vest	0.87½ each	1	0.87½
Pins	.12½ sheet	3 sheets	.37½
Ribbon	.03½, .04, .15 yd.	2¾ yds.	.12
Black	.05, .15 yard	3 „	.35
Tape	?	2 pieces	.12¼
Thread, Spool	.03 spool	2	.06
Skein	.01 skein	12	.12
Silk	.06¼ „	8	.50
Others	?	?	.51
		Total	$4.52¾

Personal Items

Comb, Large	.31 each	1	.31
Pocket	.15	1	.15
Fine Toothed	.15, .17, .25,		
	.31 each	4	.88
Medicine, Magnesia	.18½ ounce	1 oz.	.18½
Castor Oil	.12½ ,,	2 ,,	.25
Razor	.63½ each	1	.63½
Shaving Soap	.05 cake	2 cakes	.10
Tobacco, Rolls	.03 each	46	1.38
Papers	.05, .10	3	.25
Half Pounds	.20, .28 pound	2 ½-lb.	.24

Total $.4.38

Total Spent $146.56¾

Note: No family record identified in census of 1830.

ALEXANDER CHURCH, MINER

Bulk Items	*Prices*	*Quantity*	*Amount*
Corn, ear	$0.74 bushel	¼ bu.	$0.18½
Feed	.61 ,,	1⅛ bu.	.67
		Total $0.85½	
Cloth			
Calico	.14, .16½, .18, .25 yd.	32½ yards	6.02
Check	.16, .20, .22 ,,	3¾ ,,	.68
Muslin	.10, .12½, .13, .15 ,,	51 ,,	6.44½
Plaid	.12½, .13, .17 ,,	24 ,,	3.12½
Russia Sheeting	.31 ,,	¾ ,,	.22½
		Total $16.49½	
Clothing			
Handkerchief	.16 each	1	.16
Hat, Fur	3.00 ,,	1	3.00
Palm Leaf	.37½ ,,	1	.37½
Mitts, Buckskin	.50	1	.50
Shawl	.25	1	.25
		Total $4.28½	
Food			
Bacon	.10 pound	10 lb.	1.00
Chocolate	.20 ,,	1 ,,	.20
Coffee	.16, .17 pound	35 ,,	6.04
Flour	.60 quarter (28 lbs.)	53 qr.	30.60*
Mackeral	.05 each	6	.30
Molasses	.14, .16 quart	13 quarts	1.97
Pork	.05 pound	230 lb. (1 hog)	11.50
Potatoes	.37, .40 bushel	10 bu.	3.94½
Salt	.04 quart	6½ qt.	.26
Spices, Saltpetre	.48 pound	¼ lb.	.06
Pepper	.40, .48 pound	⅝ ,,	.32
Sugar	.12½ pound	23 ,,	2.87½
Tea	.31, .31¼ per ¼ pound	2¾ ,,	3.73½
		Total $62.80½	

Miscellaneous

Glass	.05 each	4 panes	.20
Putty	.10 pound	$\frac{1}{2}$ lb.	.05
Knives and Forks	1.00 dozen	1 doz.	1.00
Paper and Tape	.06 lot	1 lot	.06
		Total $1.31	

Notions	*Prices*	*Quantity*	*Amount*
Braid, pins and thread		1 lot	$0.12
Buttons	$0.01 per $\frac{1}{4}$ dozen	9	.03
Cotton Balls	.02 each	16	.32
Pins, Row	.01 row	1	.01
Sheet	.12 sheet	$\frac{1}{2}$	.06
Ribbon, Black	.20 yard	1 yd.	.20
Tape w Paper	.06 lot	1 lot	.06
Tape w Thread	.22$\frac{1}{4}$ lot	1 ,,	.22$\frac{1}{4}$
Thread, Skein	.01		
Spool	.03	9 purchases	1.08
		Total 2.10\frac{1}{4}$	

Personal Items

Comb, Fine Tooth	.12, .12$\frac{1}{2}$, .40 each		
Side	.04 pair	6	.97$\frac{1}{2}$
Medicine, Salts	.03 ounce	2 oz.	.06
Tobacco	.03 roll	1 roll	.03
Tobacco	.20 pound	3$\frac{1}{2}$ lb.	.70
Soap	.10 ,,	14$\frac{1}{2}$,,	1.45
		Total 3.21\frac{1}{2}$	
		Total Spent 91.06\frac{3}{4}$	

Note: Supporting a household of nine persons in 1830.

PHILIP FILMAN, COMMERCIAL TEAMSTER

Cloth	*Prices*	*Quantity*	*Amount*
Bobinete	0.87\frac{1}{2}$ yard	1 yd.	0.87\frac{1}{2}$
Buckram	.16 ,,	$\frac{1}{4}$ yd.	.04
Calico	.18, .20, .22 yard	21 ,,	4.27
Casinete	.80, 1.50 ,,	5$\frac{3}{4}$,,	6.70
Check	.20 ,,	2$\frac{1}{2}$,,	.50
Drill	.37$\frac{1}{2}$,,	4$\frac{1}{2}$,,	1.68$\frac{1}{2}$
Muslin	.12$\frac{1}{2}$, .14, .15 ,,	8 ,,	1.06
Velvet	.67 ,,	2$\frac{1}{4}$,,	1.51
Vesting, Silk	1.31 ,,	1 ,,	1.31
		Total $17.95	

Clothing			
Gloves, Buckskin	.37$\frac{1}{2}$, .75 pair	2	1.12$\frac{1}{2}$
Hat, Palm leaf	.37$\frac{1}{2}$ each	1	.37$\frac{1}{2}$
Cap, boys'	1.00 ,,	1	1.00
Stockings	.35 pair	1	.35
		Total $2.85	

Food			
Coffee	.16 pound	24 lb.	5.76*
Cheese	.09, .12½ pound	5 ,,	.53½
Chocolate	.20 ,,	1 ,,	.20
Lard	.09 ,,	1 keg of 53 lb.	4.77
Sugar	.12½ ,,	9 lb.	1.12½
Tea	.31 per ¼ ,,	¾ lb.	.93
		Total $13.32	
Miscellaneous			
Blacksmithing	...	1 job	.07
Candlestick	.15	1	.15
Knives and Forks	2.75	½ doz.	1.37½
		Total $1.59½	
Notions			
Buttons and Thread	...	...	.22½
Pattern, Vest	.87½ each	1	.87½
Thread	.03 spool		
Thread Silk	.06¼ ,,	7	.45½*
		Total $1.55½	
		Total Spent $37.27	

Note: Supporting family of five in 1830.

BARNEY HART, KEEPER

Bulk Items	*Prices*	*Quantity*	*Amount*
Corn, Eear	$0.25, .38 bushel	2½ bu.	$0.81
Feed	.60, 62½ ,,	3¼ ,,	2.00
	1.24 per 100 pounds	28 lb.	.31
Wheat	1.10 bushel	2 bu.	2.20
		Total $5.32	
Cloth			
Brown Holland	.25 yard	2 yards	.50
Buckram	.16 ,,	⅝ ,,	.10
Padding	.40 ,,	⅝ ,,	.25
Calico	.10, .12½, .16, .17, .20 yard	12 ,,	1.54½
Casinete	.67, 1.06 yard	3¾	3.68
Check	.16, .20, .22 yard	12¾ ,,	2.32
"Cloth"	4.25 ,,	2 ,,	8.50
Drilling	.23 ,,	3 ,,	.69
Flannel	.24, .56 ,,	5¾ ,,	1.62
Muslin	.09, .10, .13, .14, .15 yard	20 ,,	2.85½
Pittsburg Cord	.24 ,,	3 ,,	.72
Plaid	.18½ ,,	12 ,,	2.22
Russia Sheeting	.15, .22 yard	10½ ,,	2.06½
Ticking	.33 ,,	2½ ,,	.82
		Total $27.88½	

Clothing

Cravat, Jaconete	.44 each	1	.44
Mitts, Buckskin	.50 pair	1	.50
Handkerchief	.25 each	1	.25
Hat	.87½ ,,	1	.87½
Shoes	1.25, 1.50 pair	5	6.95
Stockings	.31 pair	1	.31
Suspenders	.15 ,,	1	.15
		Total	$ 9.47½

Food

Bacon	.08, .10 pound	143 lb.	13.72
Beef	.08 ,,	76¼ ,,	5.90*
,, Side	.04¼ ,,	231 ,,	10.39½
,,	.05 ,,	11¼ ,,	.56
Cheese	.12 ,,	3¾ ,,	.47½*
Coffee	.17 ,,	44 ,,	7.48
Flour	.60 quarter (28 lbs.)	37 qr.	22.20
,,	.03 pound	12 lb.	.36
Lard	.10 ,,	22⅞ ,,	2.28½
Mackerel	7.00 barrel	½ bbl.	3.50

Food—Continued	*Prices*	*Quantity*	*Amount*
Molasses	$0 14, .16 quart	32 qt.	$4.91
Pork, Spare ribs	.03 lb.	28 lb.	.84
,, Pickeled	.09 ,,	6¼ ,,	.56½
,, Hog	.04½ ,,	250 ,,	11.25
Potatoes	.30, .32, .40, 1.00 bu.	12 bu.	4.56½
Rice	.05 pound	1 lb.	.05
Salt	.04 quart	26 qt.	1.04
,,	.85, .88, 1.00 bushel	1⅛ bu.	1.05
Spices, Pepper	.40 pound	½ lb.	.20
Sugar	.12½ ,,	27 ,,	3.37½
Tea	.31 per ¼ pound	2¼ ,,	2.48*
		Total	$ 97.20

Miscellaneous

Barter, Wool and Pigs for Storegoods		...	2.25
Charity, Storegoods	...	...	1.87½
Almanac	.08 each	1	.08
Bedcord	.45 ,,	1	.45
Broom	.12½ ,,	1	.12½
Fish Net	1.12 ,,	1	1.12
Knives, Pen	.33 ,,	1	.33
,, Butcher	.20 ,,	1	.20
Oil	.12½ quart	7 qt.	.87¼
Pasteboard	.05 each	2	.10
Whetstone	.09	1	.09
Plaister	.74 bushel	¼ bu.	.18½
		Total	$ 7.68

Notions

Buttons	.06 dozen		
,, Pearl	.01 each		
,, Giltcoat	.62½ dozen		
,, Giltvest	.20 ,,	?	.89½

Cord	.24 yard	1 yd.	.24
Cotton Balls	.02 each	8	.16
Pattern	.45 each	1	.45
Tape	...	4 pieces	.21½
Thread	.01 skein		
,, Silk	.06¼ spool	?	.56
		Total $2.52	

Personal Items	*Prices*	*Quantity*	*Amount*
Comb, Fine toothed	$ .18 each	2	$0.36
Medicine, Salts	.06¼ dose	1	.06¼
Soap	.10 lb.	6¾ lb.	.67
Tobacco, Roll	.03 each	97	
,, Paper	.10 ,,	10	
,, Pound	.20	1	3.94*
		Total $5.03¼	
		Total Spent $155.11¼	

Note: Supporting a family of six in 1830.

DAVID HART, COLLIER

Bulk Items	*Prices*	*Quantity*	*Amount*
Corn	$0.50, .56 bushel	29 bu.	$14.68
,, Ear	.37½ ,,	14 ,,	4.85*
Feed	.60, .62 ,,	7 ,,	4.21
Oats	.37, .40 ,,	2½ ,,	.94*
Plaister	.75 ,,	2 ,,	1.50
Wheat	1.10, .25 ,,	30½ ,,	22.85*
		Total $49.03	

Cloth			
Calico	.12½, .15 yard	3½ yd.	.45
Cashmere	.22½, .37½, 2.87½ yard	10¾ ,,	10.91½
Casinette	.50, .80 ,,	6½ ,,	4.45
Check	.16, .18½, .20, .22 ,,	5⅛ ,,	1.16*
Cord, Velvet	.67 ,,	3½ ,,	2.34½
Flannel, Cotton	.17, .24 ,,	5 ,,	1.13
Muslin	.12 .13¼, .14, .15, .22, .22½ ,,	74½ ,,	
,, Domestic	.13 ,,	and	
,, Black	.17 ,,	1 lot	11.42½
Buckram	.16 ,,	⅞ yd.	.14
Padding	.42 ,,	½ ,,	.21
Pittsburgh Cord	.22, .28 ,,	6¾ ,,	1.53
Plaid	.18½ ,,	7 ,,	1.30
Russian Sheeting	.22½ ,,	¾ ,,	.16½
Stripe	.18, .37½ ,,	3 ,,	.93
		Total $36.15	

Clothing	*Prices*	*Quantity*	*Amount*
Cap, Men's	$1.25 each	1	$ 1.25
Mitts, Buckskin	.50 pair	1	.50
Hat, Boys' Wool	.62½ each	1	.62½
,, ,,	.80 ,,	1	.80
,, Fur	3.50 ,,	1	3.50
Handkerchiefs	.18, .23, .25,.28 , .30,	2 silk	1.55
	.31½, .65, .90 each	6 cotton	1.55½
Shoes	1.25, 1.37½, 1.50 pair	7	9.87½
Stock	.67 each	1	.67
Stockings	.50, .56 pair	2	1.06
Suspenders	.15 ,,	2	.30
		Total	$21.68½
Food			
Bacon	.10 pound	357½ lb.	35.39½*
Beef	.08 ,,	9 ,,	
,, Offal	.50 each	1 ,,	
,, Side	.04½ pound	256 ,,	12.33½
Cheese	.12, .12½ pound	17¼ ,,	2.12½
Chocolate	.20	1½ ,,	.30
Coffee	.16, .17 ,,	72 ,,	12.21
Fats, Lard and Tallow	.10 ,,	20¾ ,,	2.04*
Flour	.50, .60 qtr. (28 lb.)	45 qr.	25.50
,, Wheat	.03, .04 pound	17 lb.	.59
Mackerel	5.75, 6.00, 7.00 barrel	2 bbl.	12.25
Molasses	.14, .15 quart	57½ qt.	8.06½
Pork	.03, .05 pound	11¾ lb.	.45
,, Hog	.04½ ,,	196¼ ,,	8.30
Potatoes	...	...	3.59½
Rice	.05 ,,	2 ,,	.10
Salt	.03, .04 quart	?	
	.85, .88 bushel		2.10
Spices, Pepper	.37, .40 pound	1¼ ,,	.48½
,, Alspice	.40 ,,	¼ ,,	.10
Storegoods	...	1 lot	.12
Sugar	.12½ ..	27 lb.	3.37½
Tea	.31 per ¼ ,,	3¼ ,,	4.03
		Total	$133.36½
Miscellaneous			
Blacksmith work	...	7 jobs	1.82
Firewood	.50 load	1	.50
Boiler	.40 each	1	.40
Tools, Collier's			
Hoe	.50 ,,	1	.50
Pitch fork	.37½ ,,	1	.37½
File	.12½ ,,	1	.12½
Curry comb	.27 ,,	1	.27
Knives, Pen	.18½, .33 each	2	.51½
,, Barlow	.12½ ,,	1	.12½
,, Butcher	.20	1	.20
Shoeblacking	.10 box	2	.20
		Total	$ 5.03

Notions			
Buttons	.01, .01½ each, .06 dozen		
„ Bone	.00½ each		
„ Pearl	.05, .10, .12½ dozen		
„ Yankee	.12½ „		
„ Gilt vest	.25 „	14 purchases	1.83
Cotton Balls	.02 each	8	.16
Braid	.01, .03 yard	4 yards	.05
Patterns	.45, .87½, 1.00 each	3	2.32½
Pins	.01 row	4 rows	.04
Tape	.01, .02 yard	5 yd., 1 piece	.12
Thread	.01, .01½ skein		
„ Silk	.06¼ „	28 sk., 12 lts.	1.92
		Total	$ 6.45½

Personal Items			
Combs	.08, .12½, .15, .17 ea.	4	.54½*
Soap	.10 pound	4⅝ lb.	.49½*
Tobacco	.03 roll, .20 lb., .10 paper		12.13
		Total	$13.17
		Total Spent	$264.88½

Note: A household of seven in 1830.

WILKINSON HILL, NEGRO LABORER

Bulk Items	*Prices*	*Quantity*	*Amount*
Corn	$0.50, .56 bushel	9 bu.	$ 4.56
Feed	.62½ „	1 „	.62½
Oats	.33 „	1 „	.33
Wheat	.56, 1.10 „	2¼ „	2.34
		Total	$ 7.85½

Cloth	*Prices*	*Quantity*	*Amount*
Calico	.10, .12½, .16, .25, .31 yard	49½ yd.	6.90½
Cap Stuff	.42 „	½ „	.21
Casinette	.45 „	½ „	.22½
Check	.16, .18½ „	6⅜ „	1.18
Flannel	.40 „		
„ Cotton	.12, .18½, .24 „		
„ Red	.33 „	14¾ „	3.52½
Jaconete	.67 „	⅛ „	.08½
Muslin	.10, .12½, .13, .14 yd.	31¼ „	3.58
Pittsburg Cord	.22 „	7 „	1.54
Ticking	.20 „	11½ „	2.30
		Total	$ 19.55

Clothing

Handkerchief	.12½ each	2	.25
Hat, cotton	.25	1	.25
Mitts, Buckskin	.50 pair	1	.50
		Total $ 1.00	

Food

Bacon	.10 pound	45¾ lb.	4.57½
Beef	.08 ,,	16½ ,,	1.32
	.04½ ,,	129 ,,	5.80½
,, offal	.50 each	1	.50
Cheese	.12 pound	1¼ ,,	.18½*
Coffee	.17 ,,	18 ,,	3.06
Fat, lard	.10 ,,	2¾ ,,	.26½*
Flour	.60 quarter (28 lb.)	15 qr.	9.00
Mackerel	.05, .07½ each, 6.75 bbl.	9 and ½ bbl.	3.87½
Molasses	.15, .16 quart	3 qt.	.47
Salt	.03 quart, .21½, .25 peck	2 pk. & 6 qt.	.63½
Spices, Pepper	.40 pound	¼ lb	.10
Sugar	.12½ ,,	52	6.50
Tea	.31, .31¼ per ¼ pd.	½ ,,	.62¼
		Total $ 36.91¼	

Miscellaneous

Sugar Bowl	.18½ each	1	.18½
Dutch Oven w. Lid	.62½ ,,	1	.62½
Starch	.20 pound	¼ lb.	.05
Oil Barrel, empty	.37½ each	1	.37½
Oil	.12½ quart	6 qt.	.75
		Total $ 1.98½	

Notions	*Prices*	*Quantity*	*Amount*
Buttons	$0.10 dozen	6	$0.05
Cotton Balls	.02 each	9	.18
Tape	...	2 pieces	.08
Thread, Patent	.12½ each		
Thread	.03 each, .01 skein	10 purchases	.36
		Total $ .67	

Personal Items

Soap	.10 pound	9½ bl.	.91
Tobacco	.10 paper	4 papers	.40
		Total $ 1.31	
		Total Spent $ 69.28¼	

Note: No report on family identified in census of 1830.

ISAAC HUGHES, GUTTERMAN

Cloth	*Prices*	*Quantity*	*Amount*
Cloth, Blue	$1.00 yard	$\frac{1}{4}$ yard	$0.25
Flannel, Red	.56 ,,		
,, Yellow	.50 ,,	$12\frac{1}{2}$,,	
,, Cotton, Red	.24 ,,		5.44
Linen, Tow	.25 ,,	2 ,,	.50
Muslin	.14 ,,	1 ,,	.14
Pittsburg Cord	.22, .24 yard	6 ,,	1.38
		Total $ 7.71	

Clothing			
Handkerchief	.23 each	1	.23
Hat, Wool	.80 ,,	1	.80
Shoes	1.25 pair	1	1.25
Stockings,			
Germantown	2.00 .,	1	2.00
		Total $ 4.28	

Food			
Pork	.04$\frac{1}{2}$ pound	444 lb.	21.05*

Miscellaneous			
Knives, Pen	.16 each		
,, Pocket	.45 ,,	4	.93

Notions			
Thread	.05 hank	3	.15

Personal Items			
Shaving Soap	.05 cake	1	.05
Soap	.10 pound	$1\frac{1}{8}$ lb.	.11$\frac{1}{2}$
		Total $	.16$\frac{1}{2}$
		Total Spent	$ 34.28$\frac{1}{2}$

Note : Probably lived with relatives.

WILLIAM JACOBS, NEGRO TEAMSTER

Cloth	*Prices*	*Quantity*	*Amount*
Baize	$1.00 yard	$\frac{3}{4}$ yd.	$0.75
Buckram	.16 ,,	$\frac{1}{2}$,,	.08
Padding	.40 ,,	$\frac{1}{4}$,,	.10
Calico	.12$\frac{1}{2}$, .17, .18, .23,		
	,27 yard	23 ,,	4.52$\frac{1}{2}$
Casinette	.70, .80, 1.06 ,,		
	1.12$\frac{1}{2}$,,	4$\frac{1}{4}$,,	5.87*
Check	.21, .22 ,,	5 ,,	1.06$\frac{1}{2}$
Flannel	.24, .50, .56 ,,	17$\frac{1}{8}$,,	6.82
Jaconete	.40, .67 ,,	1 ,,	.47
Muslin	.12, .12$\frac{1}{2}$, .13, .14 yd.	12$\frac{1}{2}$,,	1.68$\frac{1}{8}$

Pittsburg Cord	.24 yard	8¼ ,,	2.15½*
Tear-not Cloth	1.25 ..	4½ ,,	5.62½
Ticking	.33 ,,	3 ,,	.99
Velvet	.37½ ,,	½ ,,	.18
		Total $ 30.31½	
Clothing			
Gloves	.75 pair	1	.75
Mitts, Buckskin	.45, .50 pair	3	1.45
Hat, Wool	.75 each	1	.75
,, Fur	2.75, 3.50 each	2	6.25
Handkerchief	.12½, .20, .29, .44,	5	1.39
	.65, .99 each	3 silk	2.45
Shoes	1.50, 1.75 pair	2	3.25
Stockings	.37½, .56, 1.00 pair	6	3.87
Suspenders	.37½ pair	1	.37½
		Total $ 20.53½	
Food			
Cheese	.12 pound	2 lb.	.24
Coffee (given to others)	.17 ,,	?	.54½
Molasses	.15 quart	2	.30
Sugar	.12½ pound	2	.25
Tea	.31 per ¼ pound	¼ lb.	.31
		Total $ 1.64½	
Miscellaneous			
Barter	...	1 lot	.37½
Knives, Barlow	.10 each		
Double Bladed	.30 ,,		
Pocket	.45 ,,	3	.95*
Storegoods, Charity	...	...	2.62½
		Total $ 3.95	
Notions			
Braid	.03 yard	4½ yd.	.13
Binding	.03 ,,	3 ,,	.09
Buttons	.04, .06 dozen		
Pearl	.18 ,,		
Gilt	.01 each		
Yankee	.01 ,,	14 purchases	1.33
Cotton Balls	.02 ,,	2	.04
Pattern	.50 ,,	1	.50
Ribbon	.15 yard	¾ yd.	.11½
Tape	.01½ ..	2 yd. and 2 pieces	.15
Thread, Silk	.06¼ skein	11 sk.	.78*
		Total $ 3.13½	
		Total Spent $ 59.58	

Note: May have lived at Big House. He was listed there in later censuses when each person was named.

POLLY KIDD, HIRED GIRL

Cloth	*Prices*	*Quantity*	*Amount*
Calico	$0.12½, .23 yard	16 yd.	$2.84
Muslin	.20	2 ,,	.40
		Total	$ 3.24
Clothing			
Shawl	.20 each	1	.20
Notions			
Thread, Silk	.06 skein	1 sk.	.06
		Total Spent	$ 3.50

Note: Undoubtedly lived at the Big House.

THOMAS LLOYD, NEIGHBORING FARMER

Cloth	*Prices*	*Quantity*	*Amount*
Bobonete	$1.00 yard	⅝ yd.	$0.62½
Calico	.18½ ,,	1¼ ,,	.23
Cashmere	.22, .23 yard	9 ,,	2.04
Casinete	1.06 ,,	2¾ ,,	2.91½
Check	.20, .22 ,,	2½ ,,	.52
Drilling	.20 ,,	9 ,,	1.80
Jaconete	.75 ,,	⅝ ,,	.46½
Muslin	.12, .13, .14, .15, .18, .22, .24 yard	48 ,,	7.97½
Quilting	.18½ ,,	9 ,,	1.68½*
Velvet	.56 ,,	2¾ ,,	1.54
		Total	$ 19.79½
Clothing			
Gloves	.31 pair	1	.31
Handkerchief	.15, .20 each	3	.50
Hat, Palm leaf	.31, .37½ ,,	2	.68½
		Total	$ 1.49½
Food			
Cheese	.12 pound	2¾ lb.	.33*
Coffee	.17 ,,	34 ,,	5.78
Molasses	.14, .16 quart	29 qt.	4.50
Salt	.04 quart, 1.00 bu.	4 qt., ¾ bu.	.83½*
Spices, Pepper	.37, .40 pound	1½ lb.	.58½
,, Saltpetre	.25 ,,	½ ,,	.12½
Sugar	.12½ ,,	29 ,,	3.62½
Tea	.31 per ¼ pound	¾ ,,	.93¼*
		Total	$ 16.71¼

Miscellaneous	Prices	Quantity	Amount
Black Lead	$0.25 pound	$\frac{1}{2}$ lb	0.12\frac{1}{2}$
Blacksmith Work	...	12 jobs	1.17$\frac{1}{2}$
Calf Skins	.10 ,,	53 lb.	5.30
Glass	.05 pane	6 panes	.30
Putty	.10 pound	$\frac{1}{2}$lb.	.05
Knife, Barlow	.10 each	1	.10
,, Pen	.16 .,	1	.16
Nails	.09 pound	1 ,,	.09
Oil	.12 quart	$\frac{1}{2}$ qt.	.06
Paper	.01 sheet	26 sh.	.26
Plowshares	.37$\frac{1}{2}$ each	3	1.12$\frac{1}{2}$
		Total $ 8.67$\frac{1}{2}$	

Notions	Prices	Quantity	Amount
Buttons, Gilt	.20 dozen		
,, Pearl	.01$\frac{1}{2}$ each	3 purchases	.49
Braid, Black	.03 yard	2$\frac{1}{2}$ yards	.07$\frac{1}{2}$
Tape	...	2 pieces	.10
Pins	.12$\frac{1}{2}$ sheet	1 sh.	.12$\frac{1}{2}$
,,	.01 row	2 row	.02
Cotton Balls	.02 each	2	.04
Hooks and Eyes	.12$\frac{1}{2}$ box	1 box	.12$\frac{1}{2}$
Scissors	.25 pair	2	.50
Thread, Silk	.06$\frac{1}{4}$ skein	6 sk.	.43$\frac{1}{3}$*
,, Others	...	12 purchases	.80$\frac{1}{4}$
		Total $ 2.71$\frac{1}{4}$	

Personal Items	Prices	Quantity	Amount
Combs, Dressing	.12$\frac{1}{2}$ each	1	.12$\frac{1}{2}$
,, Fine toothed	.06 ,,	1	.06
Soap	.10 pound	5 lb.	.50
Tobacco, Rolls	.03 each	4	.12
,, Pound	.20 pound	6 lb.	1.20
		Total $ 2.00$\frac{1}{2}$	
		Total Spent $ 49.90$\frac{1}{2}$	

Note: Supporting a household of seven persons in 1830.

MOSES MORTEN, NEGRO LABORER-TEAMSTER

Bulk Items	Prices	Quantity	Amount
Feed	$0.01 pound	10 lb.	$0.10
Wheat	1.10 bushel	1$\frac{1}{4}$ bu.	1.65
Corn, Ear	.37 ,,	$\frac{1}{2}$,,	.18$\frac{1}{2}$
		Total $ 1.93$\frac{1}{2}$	

Cloth	Prices	Quantity	Amount
Calico	0.18\frac{1}{2}$, .20 yard	20 yd.	$3.85
Check	.18$\frac{1}{2}$, .22 ,,	2$\frac{3}{8}$ yd.	.48$\frac{1}{2}$
Flannel	.33 ,,	1 ,,	.33
Jaconete	.40, .67 ,,	$\frac{7}{8}$,,	.41$\frac{1}{2}$

Muslin	.12½, .13, .14, .15 yd.		
„ Black	.25 yard	35¼ „	4.60½
Pittsburg Cord	.22, .24 yard	11 „	2.48
Ticking	.20 „	12 „	2.40
		Total $ 14.56	

Clothing

Handkerchief	.12½, .37½ each	2	.50
Hat, Wool	.87½ each	1	.87½
Shoes	1.50 pair	2	3.00
Stockings	.37½ „	1	.37½
		Total $ 4.75	

Food

Bacon	.10 pound	8¾ lb.	.85*
Cheese	.12½ „	1½ „	.18½
Chocolate	.20 „	½ „	.10
Coffee	.17 „	5½ „	.93½
Flour	.60 quarter (28 lb.)	11½ qr.	6.90
„ Wheat	.05 pound	9½ lb.	.47½
Mackerel	.05 each	18	.90
Molasses	.12½, .14 quart	26 qt.	3.42
Pork, Hog	.05 pound	308 lb.	15.40
Potatoes	1.75 row	1½ row	2.62½
Salt	.04, .05 quart	12 qt.	.46*
Spices, Pepper	.40 pound	¼ lb.	.10
„ Alspice	.48 pound	⅛ „	.06
Sugar	.12½ „	1 „	.12½
Tea	.31 per ¼ pound	1 „	1.71¼
Goose	.40 each	1⅜ „	.40
		Total $34.64¾	

Miscellaneous

Blanket	3.75 pair	1 pr.	3.75
Comforter	1.44 each	1	1.44
Black Lead	.24 pound	¼ lb.	.06
Oil	.12½ quart	4 qt.	.50
		Total $ 5.75	

Notions	*Prices*	*Quantity*	*Amount*
Buttons w. thread	…	2 lots	$0.32½
Thread	.01 skein	6 sk.	.06
Cotton Balls	.02 each	3	.06
		Total $ .44½	

Personal Items

Combs	.12½ each	2	.25
Medicine, Salts	.03 ounce	3 oz.	.09
„ Caster Oil	.12½ „	1 „	12½
Razor	.62½ each	1	.62½
Strop and Box	.45	1	.45
Shaving Brush	.10 „	1	.10
Soap	.10 pound	4⅝ lb.	.46½

Tobacco, Roll	.03 each	18	.54
,, Paper	.10 each	3	.30
,, Pound	.20 pound	1	.20
		Total $ 3.14½	
		Total Spent $65.23¾	

Note: A family of six in 1830.

ELIZABETH MOYERS, HIRED GIRL
(Salary—$.75 per week)

Cloth

Calico	$0.12½, .23, .27, .31,		
	.40 yard	29 yards	$6.54½
Check	.20, .21, .22, .25 yard	7½ ,,	1.61
Chince	.32 yard	8 ,,	2.56
Flannel	.44 ,,	1¼ ,,	.55
Muslin	.12½, .14, .15,.17 ,,	8½ ,,	1.14
		Total $12.40½	

Clothing

Handkerchief	.30, .44 each	2	.74
Hood, Silk	1.50 ,,	1	1.50
Shoes, Monroes	1.75 pair	1	1.75
		Total $ 3.99	

Food

Coffee	.17 pound	2 lb. and 1 lot .46½	
Sugar	.12½ ,,	1 ,,	.12½
		Total $ .59	

Miscellaneous

Pasteboard	$0.06 per sheet	1	$0.06
Storegoods	. . .	1 lot	.12½
		Total $ 0.18½	

Notions

Tape, Buttons and Thread	. . .	1 lot	.10
Buttons	.01 each	6	.06
Braid, Black	.03 yard	1 yard	.03
Tape	.01 ,,	2 ,, and 2 pieces	.18
Braid and Thread	. . .	1 lot	.07
Cotton Balls	.02 each	3	.06
Hooks and Eyes	.10 box	1 box	.10
Pattern	.25 each	1	.25
Thread	. . .	6 purchases	.34
		Total $ 1.19	

Personal Items

Comb, large, Side	.20 pair	1 pair	.20
,,	.12½ each	1	.12½
		Total $ 0.32½	
		Total Spent $18.68½	

Note: Undoubtedly lived at the Big House.

FREDERICK PAINTER, BEGINNING MOULDER

Bulk Items	*Prices*	*Quantity*	*Amount*
Wheat	$1.10 bushel	2 bu.	$2.20
Cloth			
Calico	.21 yard	7½ yd.	1.52*
Linen, Tow	.17 ,,	⅝ ,,	.10½
Muslin	.12½, .15 yard	12 ,,	1.75
Sheeting	.31 ,,	7 ,,	2.17
		Total $ 5.54½	
Clothing	*Prices*	*Quantity*	*Amount*
Cravat, Jaconete	$0.62½ each	1	$0.62½
Handkerchief	.15 ,,	1	.15
Shoes	1.50 pair	1	1.50
Stock	.67 each	1	.67
		Total $ 2.94½	
Food			
Bacon	.10 pound	108¾ lb	10.87
Chocolate	.20 ,,	2 ,,	.40
Coffee	.17 ,,	1 ,,	.17
Flour	.60 quarter (28 lb.)	1 qr.	.60
Molasses	.14, .16 quart	13 qt.	1.98
Pork, 1 Hog	.04½ pound	256 lb.	11.92½*
Salt	.03 quart, .84 bushel	12 qt.	.33½
Tea	.31 per ¼ pound	1 lb.	1.24¼*
Sugar	.12½ pound	16 ,,	1.99¾*
Spices, Pepper	.40 pound	¼ ,,	.10
,, Saltpetre	.32 ,,	1 oz.	.02
		Total $29.61	
Notions			
Thread	...	3 lots	.15
Personal Items			
Comb	.31 each	1	.31
Tobacco	.03 roll	39 rolls	
,,	.20 pound	½ lb.	1.30
		Total $ 1.61	
		Total Spent $42.06	

Note: May have been living with parents at this time.

JOHN PAINTER, FILLER

Bulk Items	*Prices*	*Quantity*	*Amount*
Corn, Ear	$0.37, .50 bushel	6¼ bu.	$3.18½*
Feed	.60, .61 ,,	3 ,,	1.81½
Mushmeal	.01½ pound	13 lb.	.20
Wheat	1.10 bushel	6 bu.	6.60
		Total $11.80	

Cloth	*Prices*	*Quantity*	*Amount*
Baize, Green	$1.00 yard	½ yd.	$0.50
Calico	.12½, .20, .28		
,, Blue	.21 yard	23¾ ,,	4.38
Casinete	.67, 1.12½, 1.87½ yd.	8¾ ,,	9.92½
Check	.16, .20 .22 ,,	5¼ ,,	1.00½
Flannel, Cotton	.24, .33 ,,		
,, Green	.24 ,,		
,,	.50 ,,	16⅝ ,,	5.08¼
Drill	.33, .37½, .50 ,,		
,, Check	.21, .27 ,,	12 ,,	4.59
Millente	.15 ,,	1 ,,	.15
Muslin	.12, .12½, .13, .14 ,,		
,,	.15, .18, .22 ,,		
,, Domestic	.10 ,,	73 ,,	9.93½
Patron	.32 ,,	1¾ ,,	.57*
Pittsburg Cord	.24 ,,	8½ ,,	2.04
Plaid	.18½ ,,	12 ,,	2.24*
Russian Sheeting	.31 ,,	2½ ,,	.78
Stripe	.18 ,,	4 ,,	.72
Ticking	.33 ,,	3 ,,	.99
		Total $42.90¾	

Clothing			
Belt	.27 each	1	.27
Gloves	.37½, .75 pair	2	1.12½
Mitts, Buckskin	.50 ,,	2	1.00
Handkerchief	.10, .25 each		
,, Cotton	.20, .23 ,,		
,, Cravat	.62½ ,,		
,, Silk	.90, 1.66 ,,	7	3.33
Hat, Fur	2.50 ,,	1	2.50
,, Wool	.75 ,,	1	.75
,,	3.50 ,,	1	3.50
Shoes	1.50 pair	3	4.50
Stockings	.27, .67 pair		
,, Cotton	.27 ,,	3	1.21
Suspenders	.15 ,,	2	.30
		Total $18.48½	

Food			
Bacon	.10 pound	374 lb.	37.36¾*
Beef, Side	.04½ ,,	266 ,,	11.97
Butter	.13 ,,	4 ,, and 1 lot	.53

Cheese	.12½ ,,	19⅛ ,,	2.48
Chocolate	.20 ,,	1 ,,	.20
Coffee	.16, .17 pound	125 ,,	19.49
Fats, Lard	.10 ,,	8 ,,	.80
Flour	.50, .60 quarter (28 lb.)	?	48.95
Mackerel	.05 each, 10.70 barrel	10 and ½ bbl.	5.85
Molasses	.14, .16 quart	125 qt.	18.70
Pork, Spare Ribs	.03 pound	?	.50½
,, Hog	.04½ ,,	506 lb.	22.67
Rice	.05 ,,	3 ,,	.15
Salt	.03, .04 quart	74 qt.	2.44½
Spices, Pepper	.40 pound	1⅛ lb.	.45
,, Allspice	.40 ,,	¼ ,,	.10
,, Irespec	?	?	.05
Sugar	.12½ ,,	49 ,,	6.37½
Tea	.30, .31, .31¼ per ¼ lb.	2⅞ ,,	3.72½
Veal	.04 pound	14 ,,	.56
		Total	$183.36¾

Miscellaneous
Store Goods Bartered for butter—Amount not Recorded

Almanac	.08 each	1	.08
Bedcord	.45 ,,	1	.45
Building Hardware			.04½
,, Glass	.05 pane	1	.05
Knives, Pen	.33		
,, Double Blade	.45 each	3	1.13*
Pasteboard	.06 sheet	1	.06
Starch	.32 pound	½ lb.	.16
		Total	$ 1.97½

Notions

Braid	.03 yard	8½ yards	.25½
Braiding	.01 ,,	5 ,,	.05
Buttons	.01, .01½, .02 each		
,,	.25 dozen		
,, Yankee	.13 ,,	11 purchases	1.14
Cotton Balls	.02 each	24	.48
Pins	.01 row	8 rows	.08
Tape	...	2 pieces	.24
Thread	.01 skein		
,, Silk	.06, .06¼, .06½ skein	?	1.66¼
		Total	$ 3.90¾

Personal Items

Combs, Fine Tooth	.15 each		
,, Side	.20 ,,		
	.06 pair	3	.41
Soap	.10 pound	5½ lb.	.55
Tobacco	.03, .05, .10, .20	?	10.86
		Total	$11.82
		Total Spent	$274.26¼

Note: Supporting a household of six in 1830.

MARGARET PAINTER, WIDOW

Bulk Items	Prices	Quantity	Amount
Plaister	$0.75 bushel	1½ bu.	$1.12½

Cloth	Prices	Quantity	Amount
Flannel, Cotton	.16 yard	2⅞ yd.	.49*
Linen, Figured	.75 ,,	½ ,,	.37½
Muslin	.14 yard	9 ,,	1.26
		Total $ 2.12½	

Clothing	Prices	Quantity	Amount
Shawl	.20 each	1	.20
Shoes	1.50 pair	1	1.50
		Total $ 1.70	

Food	Prices	Quantity	Amount
Bacon	.10 pound	13½ lb.	1.32*
Coffee	.17 ,,	3 ,,	.51
Molasses	.15 quart	3 qt.	.45
Sugar	.12½ pound	3 lb.	.37½
Tea	.30¼, .31 per ¼ lb.	⅜ ,,	.46
		Total $ 3.11½	

Miscellaneous	Prices	Quantity	Amount
Knife	.45 each	1	.45
Nails	.09 pound	2 lb.	.18
		Total $ 0.63	

Notions	Prices	Quantity	Amount
Tape	...	1 piece	.06
Thread	.02 skein	6 sk.	.12
,,	...	1 lot	.06
		Total $ 0.24	

Personal Items	Prices	Quantity	Amount
Soap	.10 pound	2⅛ lb.	.21½
		Total Spent	$ 9.15

Note: Supporting a household of eight in 1830.

POLLY PARLIMENT, HIRED GIRL

Cloth	Prices	Quantity	Amount
Calico	$0.12½, .20, .28 yard	10½ yd.	$1.60
Check	.18½, .25 ,,	2¾ ,,	.43½
Flannel, Yellow	.37½ ,,	1½ ,,	.56
Muslin	.13, .50 ,,	1¼ ,,	.43¾
		Total $ 3.03¼	

Clothing	Prices	Quantity	Amount
Handkerchief, Crepe	.44 each	2	.88
Stockings, Cotton	.50 pair	1	.50
		Total $ 1.38	

Food

Chocolate	.20 pound	½ lb.	.10
Coffee	.17 ,,	3½ ,,	.59
Cheese	.12½ ,,	1⅞ ,,	.23½
Fats, Lard	.10 ,,	2 ,,	.20
Potatoes	.40 bushel	1 bu.	.40
Spices, Pepper	.40 pound	⅛ lb.	.05
Sugar	.12½ ,,	4	.49*
Tea	.31 per ¼ pound	½ of ¼ lb.	.15½

Total $ 2.22

Notions

Cotton Ball	.02 each	1	.02
Ribbon	.20 yard	1 yd.	.20
Tape	.01 ,,	5 ,, and 1 piece	.09
Thread	...	1 lot	.08

Total $ 0.39

Personal Items

| Tobacco, Rolls | .03 each | 2 | .06 |

Total Spent $ 7.08¼

Note : Probably lived at the Big House.

MICAJAH POSEY, MOULDER

Bulk Items	Prices	Quantity	Amount
Corn, Ear	$0..25 bushel	2 bu.	$0.50
Feed	.60, .62 bushel	1 ,,	.61
Wheat	1.10 ,,	10 ,,	11.00

Total $12.11

Cloth

Calico	.20 yard	7 yd.	1.40
Casinete	.50, 1.50 yard	5¾ ,,	5.62½
Flannel, White	.17, .18 ,,	11 ,,	2.97*
Satinette	.67 ,,	3¼ ,,	2.18

Total $12.17½

Clothing

Gloves and Fur Hat	...	...	3.94
Handkerchief, Silk	.87½	1	.87½
,, Cotton	.25	1	.25
Stockings	.50 pair	1 pr.	.50
Suspenders	.15 ,,	1 ,,	.15

Total $ 5.71½

Food

Bacon	.10 pound	76¾ lb.	7.67¼
Beef	.08, .09 pound	49 ,,	4.06
Cheese	.12½ ,,	11⅜ ,,	1.50¼
Chocolate	.20 ,,	½ ,,	.10
Coffee	.17 ,,	23 ,,	3.91

Fats, Lard	.10 ,,	3$\frac{2}{8}$,,	.33*
Flour	.60 quarter (28 lb.)	15 qr.	9.00
Mackerel, No. 1	7.00 barrel	$\frac{1}{2}$ bbl.	3.50
Molasses	.14, .16 quart	38 qt.	5.90
Pork, Chine	.03 pound	6$\frac{1}{2}$ lb.	.19
,, Spare Ribs	.03 ,,	22$\frac{1}{4}$,,	.66
,, Hog	.04$\frac{1}{2}$,,	513 ,,	23.08$\frac{1}{2}$
,, Pickled	.10 ,,	4 ,,	.40
Potatoes	.30, .37$\frac{1}{2}$ bushel	5 bu.	1.80
Salt	.90, 1.00 ,,	$\frac{3}{4}$,,	.47$\frac{1}{2}$*
Sugar	.12$\frac{1}{2}$ pound	65 lb.	8.12$\frac{1}{2}$
Spices, Pepper	.40 ,,	$\frac{1}{2}$,,	.20
,, Saltpetre	.12 ,,	$\frac{1}{4}$,,	.03
Tea	.31 per $\frac{1}{4}$ pound	3$\frac{1}{8}$,,	3.87$\frac{1}{4}$
		Total 74.81\frac{1}{2}$	

Miscellaneous

Almanac	.08 each	1	.08
Blacking	.10 box	1	.10
Black Lead	.25 pound	$\frac{1}{4}$ lb.	.06$\frac{1}{4}$
Glass	.05 pane	2	.10
Knives, Barlow	.12$\frac{1}{2}$ each	1	
,, Pocket	.18$\frac{1}{2}$,,	1	.31
Oil	.12$\frac{1}{2}$ quart	2 qt.	.25
Pot, Four-Gallon	1.31 each	1	1.31
Soap	.10 pound	2$\frac{1}{4}$ lb.	.22$\frac{1}{2}$
Storegoods	. . .	2 lots	.80
Tablespoons	1.50 dozen	$\frac{1}{2}$ doz.	.75
		Total $ 3.98$\frac{3}{4}$	

Notions

Braid	.03 yard	1 yd.	.03
Buttons	.04, .06 dozen	5 purchases	.08
Scissors	.40 pair	1	.40
Thread, Silk	.06 skein	5 ,,	.45
		Total $ 0.96	

Personal Items

Comb	.37$\frac{1}{2}$ each	1	.37$\frac{1}{2}$
Medicine, Salts	.03 ounce	3 oz.	.09
,, Castor Oil	.12$\frac{1}{2}$,,	1	.12$\frac{1}{2}$
Razor Strop	.25 cach	1	.25
Tobacco, Roll	.03	97	
,, Paper	.05	2	
,, ,,	.10	3	
,, Pound	.20	1	3.51
		Total $ 4.35	
		Total Spent 113.04\frac{3}{4}$	

Note: No family record identified in census of 1830.

DAVID SHAFFER, COLLIER

Bulk Items	*Prices*	*Quantity*	*Amount*
Buckwheat Meal	$0.03 pound	11¼ lb.	$0.33
Corn, Ear	.56, .37 bushel	1¼ bu.	.65
Feed	.60, .62, .67 ,,	6¼ ,,	3.87
Oats	.40 ,,	½ ,,	.20
Wheat	1.10 ,,	7 ,,	7.70
		Total $12.75	
Cloth			
Calico	.10, .16, .18, .18½ .32 yard	15¼ yd.	2.25
Casinete	1.12½ ,,	½ ,,	.56
Flannel, Cotton	.20, .21 yard		
,, Red	.67 ,,	14½ ,,	4.10½
Muslin	.11, .12½, .13, .14,		
,,	.15, .18, .25 yard		
,, Figured Book	.67 ,,		
,, Cotton	.50 ,,	53⅜ yd.	7.29
Pittsburgh Cord	.22 ,,	2 ,,	.44
Russia Sheeting	.22 ,,	2 ,,	.44
Ticking	.20 ,,	2½ ,,	.50
		Total $15.58½	
Clothing			
Buckskin Mitts	.50 pair	2 pr.	1.00
Food			
Bacon	.10 pound	190 lb.	19.00
Beef	.08 ,,	16¼ ,,	1.30
Cheese	.12½ ,,	10¾ ,,	1.34
Chocolate	.20 ,,	1½ ,,	.30
Coffee	.17 ,,	49 ,,	8.55*
Fats, Lard	.10 ,,	21¾ ,,	2.17
Flour, Wheat	.04 ,,	51½ ,,	2.06
,,	.60 quarter (28 lb.)	43 qr.	22.80*
Mackerel, No. 1	8.75 barrel	½ bbl.	4.37½
,, ,, 2	7.00 ,,	½ ,,	3.50
,,	.05 each	6	.30
Molasses	.14, .16 quart	38 qt.	5.66½
Pork, Hog	.04½ pound	210 lb.	9.45
Potatoes	.27½, .40 bushel	1½ bu.	.57½
Salt	.04 quart, 1.00 bushel	4 qt., 2½ bu.	2.22*
Spices, Allspice	.40 pound	¼ lb.	.10
,, Pepper	.40, .44 pound	⅜ ,,	.15½
Sugar	.12½ ,,	13 ,,	1.62½
Tea	.31 per ¼ pound	1½ ,,	1.86
		Total $87.34½	
Miscellaneous			
Barter for sewing	...	1 lot	.44
Bed Cord	.45 each	1	.45

		$\frac{1}{4}$ lb.	
Black Lead	.24 pound	$\frac{1}{4}$ lb.	.06
Glass	.05 pane	5	.60*
Horse Rasp	.40 each	1	.40
Knives	...	5	1.30
Nails and Spikes	.09, .10, .12$\frac{1}{2}$ pound	12$\frac{3}{4}$,,	1.16
Paper	.01 sheet	2	.02
Storegoods, Charity	...	3 lots	5.02$\frac{1}{4}$
Teaspoons	.40 dozen	$\frac{1}{2}$ doz.	.20

Total $ 9.65$\frac{1}{2}$

Notions	Prices	Quantity	Amount
Braid	$0.03 yard	1$\frac{1}{2}$ yd.	0.04\frac{1}{2}$
Buttons	.03, .06, .12$\frac{1}{2}$ dozen		
,, Pearl	.12$\frac{1}{2}$,,	5 purchases	.48$\frac{1}{8}$
Cotton Balls	.02 each	27	.54
Knitting Needle	.01 ,,	4	.04
Pins	.01 row	4 rows	.04
Thread	.01 skein		
,, Patent	no price		
,, Cotton	.06 hank	6 purchases	.37$\frac{1}{4}$

Total $ 1.52$\frac{1}{2}$

Personal Items			
Comb, Horn	.08$\frac{1}{2}$, .12$\frac{1}{2}$ each		
,, Fine Tooth	.15, .16 ,,	4	.51$\frac{1}{2}$
Medicine, Salts	.04 ounce	1 oz.	.04
Soap	.10 pound	10$\frac{5}{8}$ lb.	1.06
Tobacco, Pound	.20 ..	11 ,,	
,, Roll	.03 each	5 rolls	2.39*

Total $ 4.00$\frac{1}{2}$
Total Spent 131.86\frac{1}{2}$

Note: No family record identified in census of 1830.

JOHN SHEELER, MOULDER

Bulk Items	Prices	Quantity	Amount
Corn, Ear	0.37\frac{1}{2}$ Bushel		
,, Shelled	.50 ,,	16 bu.	$7.55
Feed	.37, .50 ,,	1$\frac{1}{2}$,.	.60
Oats	.40 ,,	6 ,,	2.40
Wheat	1.10 ,,	9 ,,	9.90

Total $20.45

Cloth			
Bobinette	no price	4 pieces	.14
Buckram	.16 yard	$\frac{5}{8}$ yd.	.10
,, Padding	.25 ,,	$\frac{5}{8}$,,	.25*
Calico	.18$\frac{1}{2}$, .21, .23, .27,		
	.31 yard	25$\frac{1}{4}$,,	6.31$\frac{1}{2}$
Cap Stuff	.44, .67 yard	1$\frac{1}{2}$,,	.89
Cashmere	.37$\frac{1}{2}$,,	7 ,,	2.62$\frac{1}{4}$
Check	.18$\frac{1}{2}$, .20, .22 yard	8$\frac{7}{8}$,,	1.78

Flannel, Red	.67 yard		
,, Yellow	.40 ,,		
,,	.44 ,,	$3\frac{3}{4}$ yd.	$1.86\frac{1}{4}$
Holland, Brown	.22 ,,	$2\frac{1}{4}$,,	$.49\frac{1}{2}$
Jaconete	.40 ,,	2 ,,	.80
Muslin	.13, .14, .25 yd.		
,, Figured	.44 ,,		
,, Book	.40, .70 ,,	$31\frac{1}{4}$,,	$4.85\frac{1}{2}$
Plaid	.18 ,,	6 ,,	1.08
Ticking	.20, .40 ,,	2 ,,	.50
		Total	$21.69\frac{1}{2}$

Clothing

Gloves	$.37\frac{1}{2}$ pair	1	$.37\frac{1}{2}$
Handkerchief	.20, .23, $.37\frac{1}{2}$ each		
,, Black Gauze	.44 ,,		
,, Flag Silk	1.12 ,,	5	$2.36\frac{1}{4}$
Hat, Boy's Wool	$.62\frac{1}{2}$,,	2	1.25
,, Man's	$.87\frac{1}{2}$,,	1	$.87\frac{1}{2}$
,, Palm Leaf	.31 ,,	1	.31
Stockings	.35 pair	2 pr.	.70
		Total	$ 5.87\frac{1}{2}$

Food

Cheese	$.12\frac{1}{2}$ pound	$9\frac{3}{4}$ lb.	1.19
Chocolate	.20 ,,	2 ,,	.40
Coffee	.17 ,,	$34\frac{1}{2}$,,	$5.86\frac{1}{2}$
Fats, Lard	.10 ,,	$35\frac{3}{8}$,,	$3.53\frac{1}{2}$
Flour	.60 quarter (28 lb.)	9 qr.	5.40
,, Wheat	.03 pound	17 lb.	.50*
Mackerel, No. 1	7.00 barrel	1 bbl.	7.00
Molasses	.14, .16 quart	41 qt.	6.21
Rice	.05 pound	3 lb.	.15
Salt, Fine	.04 quart		
,, Coarse	.03 ,,	28 qt.	$.85\frac{1}{2}$
Spices, Pepper	.40 pound	$\frac{1}{4}$ lb.	.10
,, Saltpetre	.20 ,,	$\frac{5}{8}$,,	$.12\frac{1}{2}$
Sugar	$.12\frac{1}{2}$,,	$44\frac{1}{2}$,,	$5.42\frac{1}{2}$
Tea	.31 per $\frac{1}{4}$ pound	3 ,,	3.72
		Total	$40.47\frac{1}{2}$

Miscellaneous

Almanac	.08 each	1	.08
Blacking	.10 box	1	.10
Blacksmithing	...	12 visits	3.13
Fish Net	2.24 each	$\frac{1}{2}$	1.12
Hame Strap	.06 ,,	1	.06
Kettle, 20 gal.	$3.62\frac{1}{2}$,,	1	$3.62\frac{1}{2}$
Knives	$.12\frac{1}{2}$, .20, .31	3	$.63\frac{1}{2}$
Moulds	.06 dozen	1 doz.	.06
Nails	.09 pound	4 lb.	.36
Paper	.01 sheet, $.12\frac{1}{2}$ quire	12 sh. and $1\frac{1}{2}$ qr.	.24*
Storegoods, Undesignated	.	...	.60
Tar	.10 quart	1 qt.	.10
		Total	$10.11

Notions

Braid	.01, .03, .12 yard	4¼ yd.	.27½
Buttons, vest	.06, .12 dozen		
„ Bone	.06, .06¾ „		
„ Plain	.12½ „		
„ Coat	.25 „	80 buttons	.74
Cotton Ball	.02 each	3	.06
Pins	.01 row	24 rows, 1 lot	.48
Tape		9 pieces	.44
Thread	01 skein		
„ Silk	.06 „	15 purchases	2.10¼
		Total $ 4.09¾	

Personal Items

Comb, Side	.08 each		
„ Dressing	.12½ „	3	.28½
Soap	.10 pound	9 lb.	.90
Tobacco	.20 „	½ lb.	.10
		Total $ 1.28½	
		Total Spent $103.98¾	

Note: Supporting a family of seven in 1830.

JOHN WERT, DIED APRIL 1832

Bulk Items	Prices	Quantity	Amount
Mushmeal	$0.01 pound	6 lb.	$0.06

Cloth

Bobonete	.87 yard	½ yd.	.44
Flannel	.30 „	¼ „	.07½
Muslin	.37½ ‚ ‚	5 ‥	1.87½
		Total $ 2.39	

Clothing

Gloves	.37½ pair	1	0.37½
Handkerchief, Blue Silk	.65 each	1	.65
		Total $ 1.02½	

Food

Coffee	.16, .17 pound	4 lb.	.66
Molasses	.14 quart	7 qt.	.98
Salt	1.50 bushel	¼ bu.	.37½
Sugar	.12½ pound	5 lb.	.62½
Tea	.31 per ¼ pound	¼ „	
		Total $ 2.95	

Personal Items

Castor Oil	.12½ ounce	1 oz.	.12½
		Total Spent $ 6.55	

Note: A family of three in 1830.

REBECCA WERT, WIDOW OF JOHN

Cloth	Prices	Quantity	Amount
Jaconete	$0.75 yard	$\frac{1}{8}$ yd.	0.09\frac{1}{2}$
Food			
Cheese	.12$\frac{1}{2}$ pound	3$\frac{3}{4}$ lb.	.46
Chocolate	.20 ,,	$\frac{1}{2}$,,	.10
Coffee	.17 ,,	17 ,,	2.89
Eggs	.06$\frac{1}{2}$ dozen	2 doz.	.12$\frac{1}{2}$*
Flour	.60 quarter (28 lb.)	2 qr.	1.20
Mackerel	.05 each	2	.10
Molasses	.14, .15 quart	24 qt.	3.35
Potatoes	1.75 row	1 row	1.75
,,	.40 bushel	1 bu.	.40
Sugar	.12$\frac{1}{4}$ pound	9 lb.	1.12$\frac{1}{2}$
Tea	.30 per $\frac{1}{4}$ pound	$\frac{3}{8}$,,	.46
		Total $11.96	

Notions

Tape and Thread	...	2 lots	.12$\frac{1}{4}$

Personal Items

Castor Oil	.12$\frac{1}{4}$ ounce	1 oz.	0.12$\frac{1}{2}$
Soap	.10 pound	5$\frac{5}{8}$ lb.	.56
		Total $ 0.68$\frac{1}{2}$	
		Total Spent 12.86\frac{1}{4}$	

Note: This account began after husband's death.

JOSEPH WHITAKER, WOODCUTTER, FARMER AND WEAVER

Clothing	Prices	Quantity	Amount
Handkerchief, Cotton	$0.22 each	1	$0.22
Shoes, Monroes	1.62$\frac{1}{2}$ pair	1	1.62$\frac{1}{2}$
		Total $ 1.84$\frac{1}{2}$	
Food			
Bacon, Pickled	.08 pound	16 lb.	1.28
Flour	.60 quarter (28 lb.)	2 qr.	1.20
Potatoes	.30 bushel	$\frac{1}{2}$ bu.	.15
Sugar	.12$\frac{1}{2}$ pound	4$\frac{1}{2}$ lb.	.56
Tea	.31 per $\frac{1}{4}$ pound	$\frac{1}{2}$,,	.62
		Total $ 3.81	
Miscellaneous			
Oil	.12$\frac{1}{2}$ quart	1$\frac{1}{2}$ qt.	.19$\frac{1}{2}$
Personal Items			
Tobacco, Rolls	.03 each	2	.06
,, Paper	.10 ,,	1	.10
		Total $ 0.16	
		Total Spent $ 6.01	

Note: A family of three in 1830.

SAMUEL WILLIAMS, TEAMSTER

Bulk Items	*Prices*	*Quantity*	*Amount*
Buckwheat	$0.50 bushel	2 bu.	$ 1.00
Corn	.50 "	2 "	1.00
" Ear	.25, .27 bushel	26¼ "	6.68½
Feed		5 "	3.51*
"	1.20 per hundred wt.	1 qr.	.30
Wheat	1.10 bushel	6 bu.	6.60
		Total	$19.09½
Cloth			
Baize, Green	1.00 yard		
"	.10 "	1⅛ yd.	.56
Calico	.20, .23 yard	12 "	2.67
Cashmere	.37½ "	6 "	2.25
Casinete	.62, .67, .80 yard	11½ "	6.61
Check	.16, .22 "	2½ "	.46
Flannel	.21 "		
" Cotton	.24 "		
" Green	.24 "	13 "	2.83
Linen, Tow	.17 "	2 "	.51*
Muslin	.10, .11 .12, .12½ .13, .14, .15 yard	74$\frac{15}{16}$ "	9.86
Pittsburg Cord	.22¼, .24 "	3¼ "	.75
Plaid	.15, .18, .18½ "	20¼ "	3.54½
Ticking	.20, .22 "	5 "	1.03
		Total	$31.07½
Clothing			
Handkerchief	.18½, .25, .28 each	3	.71½
Hat, Wool	.80 "	2	1.60
" Palm Leaf	.37½ "	1	.37½
" Man's Cap	1.25 "	1	1.25
Mitts, Buckskin	.33, .40 pair		
"	.50 "	3	1.30
Shoes	1.25, 1.50, 1.75 pair	5	7.25
		Total	$12.49
Food			
Bacon	.10 pound	100 lb.	10.00
Beef	.08 "	49⅝ "	3.61*
" Side	.04½ "	247 "	11.11½
" Offal	.50 lot	1 lot	.50
Butter	.13 pound	13 lb.	1.70½
Cheese	.12½ "	11⅜ "	1.40½
Chocolate	.20 "	2 "	.40
Coffee	.17 "	62 "	10.87*
Fats, Lard	.10 pound		
" Tallow	.10 "	13 lb.	1.30½
Flour, Wheat	.04 "	19¼ "	.77
"	.50, .60 quarter (28 lb.)	42½ qr.	23.15

Molasses	.14, .16 quart	70 qt.	10.64
Pork, Spare Ribs	.03 pound	4½ lb.	.13½
„ Hogs	.04½ „	492 „	22.14
Potatoes	1.75 row	2 rows	3.50
„	.40 bushel	1½ bu.	.60
Salt	.03, .04 quart	7 qt.	
	.85, 1.00 bushel	2 bu.	2.24½
Spices, Pepper	.40 pound	1¾ lb.	.70
„ Saltpetre	.20, .25 pound	½ „	.11½
Sugar	.12½ „	15 „	1.87½
Tea	.31, .31¼ per ¼ pound	2¼ „	3.75*
Turkey	.50 each	1	.50
Veal	.03½ pound	25 „	.87½
		Total	$111.90½

Miscellaneous

Broom	.10 each	1	.10
Knives, Pen	.16, .18 each		
„ Barlow	.12½ „		
„ Two Bladed	.40 „	5	.99
Oil	.12½ quart	7 qt.	.87½
Paper	.01 sheet		
Pasteboard	.06 „	3 purchases	.17
Soap	.10 „	4½ lb.	.41*
Starch	.12 „	½ lb.	.06
Storegoods, Undefined	...	1 lot	1.45
		Total	$ 4.06

Notions

Braid	.01½ yard		
„ Black	.04 „	4 yd.	.06½
Buttons	.04, .06 dozen		
„ Gilt, Vest	.12½ „	6 lots	.59
Cord	...	1 „	.12
Cotton Balls	.02 each	7	.14
Pattern	.25 „	1	.25
Pins	.01 row	1 row	.01
„ Paper	.06 paper	1 paper	.06
Tape	...	8 pieces	.44
Thread	.01 skein, .00½ hank		
„ Silk	.06¼ „	6 purchases	.41½
		Total	$ 2.09

Personal Items

Medicine, Salts	.03, .06½ ounce	?	.15½
Shaving Soap	.05 cake	1	.05
Tobacco	.03 roll, .20 pound	20 rolls, 8½ lb.	2.28
		Total	$ 2.48½
		Total Spent	$183.20

Note: A family of six in 1830.

DAVID WYNN, TEAMSTER

Bulk Items	Prices	Quantity	Amount
Corn, Ear	$0.25 bushel	1 bu.	$0.25
Feed	.60 ,,	$\frac{1}{2}$,,	.30
Oats	.33 ,,	$\frac{1}{2}$,,	.16$\frac{1}{2}$
Wheat	1.10 ,,	4 ,,	4.40
		Total	$ 5.11$\frac{1}{2}$

Cloth			
Calico	.10, .16, .18, .20, .23, .27 yard	24 yd.	4.26$\frac{1}{2}$
Cambric	.28 ,,	$\frac{1}{2}$,,	.28*
Cap Stuff	.40 ,,	$\frac{1}{4}$,,	.10
Casinette	.45, .56, .62$\frac{1}{2}$, .67 yard	7 ,,	4.22$\frac{1}{2}$
Check	.16, .20 ,,	2$\frac{5}{8}$,,	.46$\frac{1}{2}$
Flannel, Red and Cotton	.24 ,,	7$\frac{1}{2}$,,	1.80
Gingham	.27$\frac{1}{2}$,,	$\frac{1}{2}$,,	.18$\frac{1}{4}$
Jaconete	.40, .67. .75 yard	$\frac{7}{8}$,,	.37$\frac{1}{4}$
Muslin	.10, .13, .14, .15 yard	41$\frac{1}{4}$,,	5.45$\frac{1}{4}$
Pittsburg Cord	.24 yard	3 ,,	.72
Ticking	.30 ,,	9 ,,	2.70
Velvet Cord	.67 ,,	3$\frac{1}{4}$,,	2.18*
		Total	$22.75

Clothing			
Gloves	.75 pair	1	.75
Handkerchief	.12$\frac{1}{2}$, .23, .37$\frac{1}{2}$ .56 each	4	1.29
Hat, Wool	.75 ,,	1	.75
Shoes	1.50 pair	3	4.50
		Total	$ 7.29

Food			
Bacon	.10 pound	130$\frac{3}{4}$ lb.	14.07$\frac{1}{4}$*
Beef	.08 ,,	18 ,,	2.15*
,, Quarter	.04$\frac{1}{2}$,,	138 ,,	6.21
Cheese	.12$\frac{1}{2}$,,	6 ,,	.73$\frac{1}{2}$
Chocolate	.20 ,,	$\frac{1}{2}$,,	.10
Fats, Lard	.10 ,,	11 ,,	1.10$\frac{1}{4}$
Flour, Wheat	.03 ,,	9$\frac{1}{2}$,,	.29
	.60 quarter (28 lb.)	27$\frac{1}{2}$ qr.	16.50
,, Mackerel	5.75 barrel	1$\frac{1}{2}$ bbl.	8.62$\frac{1}{2}$
Molasses	.14, .16 quart	54 qt.	8.17
Pork, Chine and Spare Ribs	.03 pound	20 lb.	.60
,, Hog	.04$\frac{1}{2}$,,	531 ,,	23.89
Potatoes	.30, .40 bushel	4 bu.	3.52$\frac{1}{4}$*
Salt	.02, .05 quart	4 qt.	
	.84 bushel	1$\frac{1}{4}$ bu.	1.30$\frac{1}{2}$

Spices, Pepper	.40 pound	$1\frac{3}{8}$ lb.	.50
,, Allspice	.40 ,,	$\frac{1}{8}$,,	.05
,, Saltpetre	.24 ,,	$\frac{1}{8}$,,	.03
Sugar	$.12\frac{1}{2}$,,	$22\frac{1}{2}$,,	2.68
Tea	.30, .31 per $\frac{1}{4}$ pound	2 ,,	2.76
		Total $93.30	

Miscellaneous

Black Lead	.12 pound	$\frac{1}{4}$ lb.	.03
Oil	$.12\frac{1}{2}$ quart	4 qt.	$.62\frac{1}{2}$*
		Total $ 0.65$\frac{1}{2}$	

Notions

Buttons	.03, .04, .06,		
	.08 dozen	6 purchases	$.21\frac{1}{2}$
Cord	.20 yard	$2\frac{1}{2}$ yd.	.50
Cotton Balls	.02 each	16	.32
Knitting Needle	$.01\frac{1}{2}$,,	1	$.01\frac{1}{2}$
Pins	.01 row	3 rows	.03
Thread	.01, .03, $.06\frac{1}{4}$ skein	12 purchases	$.52\frac{1}{4}$
		Total $ 1.60$\frac{1}{4}$	

Personal Items

Comb	$.12\frac{1}{2}$ each	1	$.12\frac{1}{2}$
Soap	.10 pound	$10\frac{1}{4}$ lb.	$1.08\frac{1}{2}$*
Tobacco, Rolls	.02, .03 each	57	1.54
,, Pound	.20 pound	1 ,,	.20
		Total $ 2.95	

Total Spent 133.66\frac{1}{4}$

Note: In 1840 he had six children all except one old enough to have been living in this period. Others may have left home in the decade.

SUMMARY OF STORE PURCHASES BY 26 WORKERS
DECEMBER, 1831–FEBUARY, 1833

	John Benson	*Clement Brook*	*John Care*
Bulk Items	...	...	$ 7.41
Cloth	$33.81	$155.29	31.97
Clothing	4.28	22.79	13.75
Food	...	...	69.63
Miscellaneous	1.53	.30	14.91
Notions	3.05	9.14	4.53
Personal Items	.03	1.03	4.38
Total Spent	42.70	188.55	146.58

	Alexander Church	Philip Filman	Barney Hart
Bulk Items	$ 0.85	...	$ 5.32
Cloth	16.49	$ 17.95	27.89
Clothing	4.29	2.85	9.47
Food	62.81	13.32	97.20
Miscellaneous	1.31	1.59	7.68
Notions	2.10	1.55	2.52
Personal Items	3.21	...	5.03
Total Spent	96.06	37.26	155.11

	David Hart	Wilkinson Hill	Isaac Hughes
Bulk Items	$ 49.03	$ 7.85	...
Cloth	36.15	19.55	$ 7.71
Clothing	21.69	1.00	4.28
Food	133.37	36.91	21.05
Miscellaneous	5.03	1.99	.93
Notions	6.45	.67	.15
Personal Items	13.17	1.31	.17
Total Spent	264.89	69.28	34.29

	William Jacobs	Polly Kidd	Thomas Lloyd
Bulk Items	...	...	...
Cloth	6 30.31	$ 3.24	$ 19.79
Clothing	20.53	.20	1.49
Food	1.65	...	16.71
Miscellaneous	3.95	...	8.67
Notions	3.13	.06	2.71
Personal Items	...	...	2.01
Total Spent	59.57	3.50	49.88

	Moses Morten	Eliz. Moyers	Fred. Painter
Bulk Items	$ 1.93	...	$ 2.20
Cloth	14.57	$12.41	5.55
Clothing	4.75	3.99	2.95
Food	34.65	.59	29.61
Miscellaneous	5.75	.18	...
Notions	.45	1.19	.15
Personal Items	3.15	.33	1.61
Total Spent	65.25	18.69	42.07

	Marg. Painter	John Painter	Polly Parliment
Bulk Items	$ 1.13	$11.80	...
Cloth	2.13	42.91	$ 3.03
Clothing	1.70	18.49	1.38
Food	3.11	183.37	2.22
Miscellaneous	.63	1.97	...
Notions	.24	3.91	.39
Personal Items	.21	11.82	.06
Total Spent	9.15	274.27	7.08

	Mica. Posey	David Shaffer	John Sheeler
Bulk Items	$12.17	$12.75	$20.45
Cloth	12.17	15.59	21.69
Clothing	5.71	1.00	5.87
Food	74.81	87.35	40.47
Miscellaneous	3.99	9.65	10.11
Notion	.96	1.53	4.10
Personal Items	4.35	4.01	1.29
Total Spent	113.06	131.88	103.98

	John Wert	Rebecca Wert	Joseph Whitaker
Bulk Items	$ 0.06	...	...
Cloth	2.39	$ 0.10	...
Clothing	1.03	...	$ 1.85
Food	2.95	11.96	3.81
Miscellaneous	...	...	.20
Notions	...	.12	...
Personal Items	.13	.69	.16
Total Spent	6.56	12.87	6.02

	Samuel Williams	David Wynn
Bulk Items	$ 19.09	$ 5.11
Cloth	31.07	22.75
Clothing	12.49	7.29
Food	111,91	93.30
Miscellaneous	4.06	.65
Notions	2.09	1.60
Personal Items	2.49	2.95
Total Spent	183.20	133.65

Note: Fractions of a cent were rounded. The largest error resulting was 0.02\frac{1}{2}$.

Bibliographic Essay

IN ONE SENSE THERE IS AN EXTENSIVE LITERATURE ON Hopewell Village, but in another sense it is very restricted. Since the remains of the old furnace and surrounding buildings became the property of the National Park Service in 1938, there have been many pamphlets and articles in magazines and newspapers giving the historical background of the present tourist attraction. The bibliography lists some of these. For the most part the material in them appears to have been drawn from two published pamphlets: Harker A. Long's *A Short History of the Hopewell Furnace Estate*[1] or Dennis C. Kurjack's *Hopewell Village National Historical Site*.[2] Long was the last manager of Hopewell Furnace, and Doctor Kurjack was for several years the historian at Hopewell for the National Park Service.

In addition to Kurjack there have been a number of other professional staff members at the Hopewell project who have written historical or archeological articles based upon their research. Most of these, prepared as guides for the restoration work at the Village, are unpublished and exist only at type-

[1] Harker A. Long, *A Short History of the Hopewell Furnace Estate* (Reading: Reading Eagle Press, no date given).
[2] Dennis C. Kurjack, *Hopewell Village National Historical Site* (Washington: National Park Service Handbook Series, Number 8, 1950).

scripts in the files of the National Park Service. This author is most grateful for having had the opportunity to read them. In none of these papers was any attempt made to write a connected account of the life of the community. The social history has received very little attention.

A somewhat similar condition exists when the literature of the charcoal-iron communities in general is surveyed. The best account of a single furnace is E. N. Hartley's *Ironworks on the Saugus.*[3] Dr. Hartley has directed the restoration of the pioneer iron furnace of Massachusetts. In his book he has a valuable account of the seventeenth century iron industry of the British Colonies in America, but he made no attempt to discuss the life of the workers at Saugus.

No similar booklength account of any Pennsylvania furnace was found. There were regional and statewide studies[4] and a few pamphlet length studies of a single iron works.[5] The story of Pennsylvania's charcoal-iron communities, therefore, remains rather generalized. Arthur Cecil Bining died before he was able to carry his account into the nineteenth century, but his book on the eighteenth century has been most influential since it was published.[6]

Three characteristics of the iron-making villages appear with considerable frequency in the literature written about the charcoal-iron industry: These communities resembled medieval, feudal manors; they were essentially self-sufficient; they resembled Southern tobacco or cotton plantations. Bining

[3] E. N. Hartley, *Ironworks on the Saugus, op. cit.*
[4] For examples see: Committee on Historical Research, *Forges and Furnaces in the Province of Pennsylvania, op. cit.*
    Alfred Gemmell, *The Charcoal Iron Industry in the Perkiomen Valley* (Norristown: Hartenstine Printing House, 1949).
[5] Some examples are: *Geigertown* (Reading: Leon D. Evans, 1959). *One Hundred and Twenty-Five Years of Pig Iron Manufacture at Robesonia, Pennsylvania* (Philadelphia: The Robesonia Iron Company, 1918). John C. Wetzel, *200th Anniversary of Birdsboro, Pennsylvania* (Birdsboro: The Executive Committee, 1940). Dean Freiday, "Tinton Manor: the Iron Works," *Proceedings of the New Jersey Historical Society,* LXX, 4 (October 1952), p. 250.
[6] Bining, *Pennsylvania Iron Manufacture in the 18th Century, op. cit.*

was one of the first to compare the iron villages with small feudal manors of medieval Europe.[7] Evarts B. Greene called the iron plantation "a quasifeudal community."[8] Each of the above writers had reference to the eighteenth century; but Dean Freiday said that through the first half of the nineteenth century, also, the iron communities were "semi-feudal" in organization, labor relations and economics. He said that they were isolated and self-contained establishments.[9]

Alvin P. Stauffer and Charles W. Porter spoke of "a compact semifeudal industrial village,"[10] and Kurjack said Hopewell was "feudalike."[11] Jackson Kemper went all the way and called it "a little feudal village."[12]

The idea of a feudal community was coupled with isolation and self-sufficiency by these and other writers. Bining used this idea also when he wrote that the furnaces "made up an almost self-sufficient community."[13] Frederick K. Miller was more specific about the degree of independence with his statement that with a very few exceptions the necessities of life were produced on the plantation.[14] Raymond E. and Marion F. Murphy called the iron plantations independent, self-supporting communities.[15] John Birkenbine asserted, "Each aggregation of houses about the iron works . . . was a settlement independent of others, often reached by long and tedious

[7] *Ibid.*, p. 30.
[8] Evarts Boutell Greene, *The Revolutionary Generation, 1763–1790* (New York: The Macmillan Company, 1943), p. 62.
[9] Freiday, *op. cit.*, p. 250.
[10] Alvin P. Stauffer and Charles W. Porter, "The National Park Service Program of Conservation," *Mississippi Valley Historical Review*, XXX, 1 (June 1943). Typescript, p. 7. Hopewell Village Library.
[11] Kurjack, *op. cit.*, p. 6.
[12] Jackson Kemper, 3rd, *American Charcoal-Making, op. cit.*, p. 1.
[13] Bining, "The Rise of Iron Manufacture in Western Pennsylvania," *op. cit.*, p. 238.
[14] Frederick K. Miller, *The Rise of an Iron Community,* published in three parts by the Lebanon County (Pennsylvania) Historical Society, 1950–1952, p. 88.
[15] Raymond E. and Marion F. Murphy, *Pennsylvania Landscapes* (State College: Penns Valley Publishers, Inc., 1954), p. 41.

journeys."[16] Kemper described the company store as supplying every need of the people from food to clothing.[17]

The analogy of the iron-making community with a Southern plantation occurred to several writers. One used the reference only in the sense of the importance of the iron industry to early American life.[18] Others saw a more specific similarity. Bining believed the iron plantations could be compared in *many* respects with the Virginia tobacco plantations.[19] Douglas A. Fisher thought that the only difference between an iron plantation and a cotton plantation was that the product was different.[20] Stevenson Whitcomb Fletcher was emphatic that the iron furnaces of central Pennsylvania were similarly organized to the great plantations of the Old South.[21]

Most of the more general accounts of charcoal-iron communities did not go beyond these stereotypes. A few supplied more details.

How large was the community? Frank H. Rowe said that a typical furnace in Scioto County, Ohio, in the 1830's employed from 100 to 250 workers.[22] Fisher thought that Hopewell Village at one time had 1,000 inhabitants.[23]

Feeding the workers and their families was an important part of the work of the furnace management. Rowe wrote that beans, bacon and fried mush were the menu on almost every table.[24] Gemmell thought the Pennsylvania workers ate better than that. He said that the furnace owner produced on his farm and sold through the company store, meat, eggs, dairy

---

[16] Birkinbine, "Changes in the Manufacture of Pig Iron," *op. cit.*, p. 225.

[17] Kemper, "The Making of Charcoal," *op. cit.*, no pages given.

[18] "Hopewell Village," *International Moulders' and Foundry Workers' Journal*, 94, 10 (October 1958), p. 3.

[19] Bining, *British Regulation of the Colonial Iron Industry*, *op. cit.*, p. 19.

[20] Douglas A. Fisher, *Steel Making in America* (United States Steel Corporation, 1949), p. 19.

[21] Fletcher, *op. cit.*, p. 336.

[22] Frank H. Rowe, *History of the Iron and Steel Industry in Scioto County, Ohio* (Columbus: State Archeological and Histroical Society, 1938), p. 10.

[23] Fisher, *op. cit.*, p. 19.

[24] Rowe, *op. cit.*, p. 19.

products, fruit and grain. He imported sugar and molasses. Neighborhood growers sold parsnips, beans, onions, cucumbers and cabbage. The workers put meat on the table by hunting and fishing.[25]

Bining said the farms produced wheat, buckwheat, corn, rye, oats, barley, flax and hemp. He thought the farms were poorly operated with an absence of crop rotation and use of fertilizer.[26]

Gemmell pointed out the numerous influences of the furnace upon the neighboring farmers. They bought iron tools and utensils and sold some of their produce at the furnace; used the roads built for furnace transportation; found off-season employment at the furnace, mine or woodlot; sold timber and iron ore; and benefited from reduced taxes because of the heavy assessments on furnace property. But the furnace was not an unmixed blessing to its neighbors. Roads were cut up by heavily laden wagons, mines ruined farm land, cut-over timber land eroded, and the furnace and coaling pits produced unpleasant gases.[27]

Birkinbine placed the work year for the furnace at eight to ten months, and he said it would be blown out early in the year when the fuel was exhausted. The furnace was relined each winter. While the repairs were going on, those miners or furnace men not engaged in the restoration work were sent into the woods to cut cordwood for coaling.[28] He said that coaling for the next blast usually began in April or May, depending upon the weather.[29] Harry Scrivenor pointed out that a furnace operated better in cold weather than in hot and thought the furnace was operated as long as possible in the winter.[30]

[25] Gemmell, *op. cit.*, p. 84.
[26] Bining, "The Iron Plantations," *op. cit.*, pp. 7–8.
[27] Gemmell, *op. cit.*, pp. 115–116.
[28] Birkinbine, *op. cit.*, p. 226.
[29] John Birkinbine, *The Manufacture of Pig Iron in Pennsylvania* (Washington: Department of Internal Affairs—Statistics, Official Document Number 10, 1894), p. 26.
[30] Scrivenor, *op. cit.*, p. 259.

Several writers noted a wide contrast between the mansions of the ironmasters and the cottages of the workers. Bining described the mansions as containing many large rooms heated by wide fireplaces and furnished with oak or mahogany furniture. The tables were set on damask cloths with pewter plates, china cups and saucers and imported Delft ware. The families slept in curtained beds. Outside, the gardens grew lilies, violets, hollyhocks, phlox and other old-fashioned flowers.[31]

Victoria Lyles said that life for the workers followed a simple pattern. The small houses were heated by a single fireplace which also served for cooking. The walls were whitewashed, and the floors were sanded. The people ate with iron knives and forks and dressed in clothing made of flannel, camblet or calico.[32] Bining wrote that the bedrooms were nearly empty and seldom contained mirrors, tables, wardrobes, drawers or even chairs.[33] Lighting was provided by tallow candles, and water was carried from a spring or well.[34] Smaller houses had two rooms with a loft above. The better homes had one or two more rooms.[35]

The store was an important feature of the iron-making village, but the authorities were not in agreement about the relationship between the store and the workers. Arthur D. Pierce said that the workers were usually in debt long before pay day.[36] According to Birkinbine, ". . . most of the pay . . . was expected to be expended at the store. . . . Some old managers would reduce the balance due a workman at the

[31] Bining, "The Iron Plantations," *op. cit.*, pp. 3–4.
[32] Victoria Lyles, "Forges and Furnaces of York County," *Papers of the Historical Society of York County* (Pennsylvania), New Series, Number 4, no date given, p. 4.
[33] Bining, "The Iron Plantations," *op. cit.*, p. 5.
[34] *Ibid.*, p. 20.
[35] Bining, *The Pennsylvania Iron Manufacture in the 18th Century*, *op. cit.*, p. 32.
[36] Arthur D. Pierce, *Iron in the Pines* (New Brunswick: Rutgers University Press, 1957), p. 17.

end of the year if it was believed that he had 'saved too much;' or rather 'traded too little.'"[37]

Other writers saw the store as more of a service than a profitable business. Gemmell believed the ironmasters were more interested in keeping their workers happy than in profiteering on prices at the store and that prices were generally cheaper than in nearby stores.[38] Borchers also found that goods were sold to employees at reasonable prices.[39]

How did the workers get along with the boss? William A. Sullivan found no evidence of union activity among the iron workers before 1840 nor any interest in the democratic forces of the Jacksonian era. He believed that many workers were close to a state of peonage.[40] Gemmell saw the worker-manager relationship as the product of the interaction of the workers' loyalty and a benevolent attitude by the ironmaster.[41]

Borchers found the wages to have been considerably below today's standards but that commodity prices were relatively still lower, producing for the iron workers a much higher standard of living than any working group in Europe.[42] Bining also thought the wages of skilled workers were higher than those paid in European countries.[43] In addition to his money wage the worker often was furnished a house, a garden, pasture for his animals and fuel for his fireplace or stove.[44]

The picture of village life on the furnace plantations presented in the literature cited was not very clear because the writers were not in agreement on most points. Such differences of view can be attributed to several circumstances: The authors were not all writing about the same communites, they were writing about different periods, they did not have the

[37] Birkinbine, *American Blast-Furnace Progress, op. cit.,* p. 292.
[38] Gemmell, *op. cit.,* p. 87.
[39] Sam Borchers, "America's Iron Industry in Colonial Times," *Forgings,* 7, 2 (March 1945), p. 7.
[40] Sullivan, *op. cit.,* p. 70.
[41] Gemmell, *op. cit.,* p. 88.
[42] Borchers, *op. cit.,* p. 7.
[43] Bining, *The Pennsylvania Iron Manufacture in the 18th Century, op. cit.,* p. 8.
[44] Sullivan, *op. cit.,* p. 59.

same data from which to draw their conclusions, some were writing from a biased view, and there was a wide difference in the competence as historians among the writers cited. Bining, Hartley, Sullivan, Miller and Kurjack were trained in historical method and in addition were able to pursue extensive research. Some of the others used only secondary sources or had little training in historical method. Harker A. Long had most personal information about Hopewell Furnace, but he erred because he relied too much upon his memory after many years had elapsed.

Bibliography

SOURCE MATERIAL

Unpublished

ABSTRACT OF DEEDS FOR HOPEWELL PROPERTY AND Correspondence Covering Acquisition by the Government of the United States, Hopewell Village Library.

Abstract of Title of the Warwick Ore Reserve Located in Berks and Chester Counties, Pennsylvania, 1790–1936; Hopewell Village Library.

American Clergy Collection, Vol. VII, Historical Society of Pennsylvania.

Archeological Reports of Work at Hopewell Village, Hopewell Village Library.

Autograph Collection, Historical Society of Pennsylvania.

Bank of North America, Minutes and Letter Book, November 2, 1781–January 21, 1792, Historical Society of Pennsylvania.

Berks and Montgomery County Papers, Historical Society of Pennsylvania.

Berks County Assessment Records, 1763–1815 (some years missing); Berks County Historical Society.

473

Berks County Constables' Returns of People—Estates—
Servants—Stock, etc., 1756 and Miscellaneous Old Papers;
Prothonotary's Office, Berks County Court House.

Berks County Court Appearance Dockets, 1800–1820;
Prothonotary's Office, Berks County Court House.

Berks County Court Continuance Dockets, 1800–1820;
Prothonotary's Office, Berks County Court House.

Berks County Court Pleadings and Miscellaneous Old Papers,
1752–1843; Prothonotary's Office, Berks County Court
House.

Berks County Court Records Of Cases, Prothonotary's Office,
Berks County Court House.

Berks County Deed Books, Office of Recorder of Deeds, Berks
County Court House.

Berks County Mortgages, 1762–1888; Prothonotary's Office,
Berks County Court House.

Berks County Surveyor-General's Draughts and Miscellaneous
Old Papers, 1700–1800; Prothonotary's Office, Berks
County Court House.

Berks County Tax Duplicates, 1829–1840; Berks County
Historical Society.

Berks County Tax Lists, 1809–1819; Berks County Historical
Society.

Berks County Tax Records, 1760–1864; Berks County
Historical Society.

Berks County Triennial Assessments, 1846–1873; Office of the
County Commissioners, Berks County Court House.

Bethesda Baptist Church, Cemetery Gravestones.

Bethesda Baptist Church Charter of Incorporation, Hopewell
Village Library.

Bethesda Baptist Church Minute Book, Hopewell Village
Library.

Bird, Mark, Petition in Bankruptcy, Historical Society of
Pennsylvania.

Bird, William, Ledgers, 1744–1761, 3 volumes; Historical
Society of Pennsylvania.

Bird, William, Papers, Berks County Historical Society.

Birdsborough Forge Book, 1821–1825; Hopewell Village Library.

Birdsborough Forge Cash Book, 1806; Hopewell Village Library.

Birdsborough Forge Journal, 1821–1824; Berks County Historical Society.

Birdsborough Forge Ledger, 1829–1831; Hopewell Village Library.

Birdsborough Forge Time Book, 1789–1810; Hopewell Village Library.

Birdsborough Store Journal, 1810, Hopewell Village Library.

Box on Iron Industry, Historical Society of Pennsylvania.

Brooke Family Letters, Hopewell Village Library.

Brooke Family Papers, Berks County Historical Society.

Buckley and Brooke, Cash Books, 1807–1810, 1829–1833, 3 volumes; Berks County Historical Society.

Buckley and Brooke, Journal Account with Clement Brooke, 1809–1814; Hopewell Village Library.

Bull, Levi, Diaries, 1806–1859, Chester County Historical Society.

Cary, Otis, Diary of a trip from New York to Pennsylvania in 1837, Microfilm at Hopewell Village Library.

Changewater Furnace Account Books, microfilm at Hopewell Village Library.

Chester County Deed Books, Office of Recorder of Deeds, Chester County Court House.

Clingan, Maria T., List of Assets, 1880, Hopewell Village Library.

Eckert and Brothers, Henry Clay Furnace Sales Book, 1867–1884; Hopewell Village Library.

Eckert and Brothers, Record of Land Purchases, 1845–1882; Hopewell Village Library.

Ege, George, Manuscripts of Mary Ann Furnace, Kemper Papers, Hopewell Furnace.

Evans, Lewis, Ledgers, 1801–1840; Hopewell Village Library.

Farmers Bank of Reading, Pennsylvania, Letter Books, 1815–1833; Hopewell Village Library.

"History of Plow Church, Robeson Township, Berks County, Pennsylvania" (unpublished, 1874) Berks County Historical Society.

Hopewell Cash Book, 1828–1830; Berks County Historical Society.

Hopewell Forge Journal, 1803–1817; Historical Society of Pennsylvania.

Hopewell Furnace and Area, Collection of old photographs, Hopewell Village Library.

Hopewell Furnace Books, 76 Volumes, some on microfilm, Hopewell Village Library. These volumes are identified as Source Material and assigned a number. They are identified in the footnotes as SM1, SM 2, etc. The originals of most of the volumes are at Hopewell. Others are at Berks County Historical Society, Chester County Historical Society and Historical Society of Pennsylvania.

Hopewell Furnace Documents, Berks County Historical Society.

Hopewell Furnace Farm Time Books, 5 volumes, Hopewell Village Library.

Hopewell Village Documents. About 8,000 loose papers on business and life at Hopewell Furnace. Some have been catalogued and assigned numbers derived from the date; *i.e.* 8161125 would mean the document was dated November 25, 1816. A letter after the number means more than one document exists for that day. Some documents were undated and some were not yet catalogued in 1962. These are identified in the footnotes by description.

Iron Masters Association, *Statistics of Iron Manufacture in Pennsylvania*. Published for the 1850 Convention of the Iron Masters Association held in Philadelphia.

James, Mrs. T. P., Manuscript Collections of Papers Relating to the Ironworks of the Potts Family, Historical Society of Pennsylvania.

Joanna Furnace Journals and Ledgers, 22 volumes, Hopewell Village Library.

Jones Keim and Company, Journals of Windsor and Schuylkill Furnaces, 1841–1845; microfilm, Hopewell Village Library.

Keen, Eli, Storebook, 1844–1845; Hopewell Village Library.

Keep, William John, "A History of Stove Making by a man who engaged in the trade for 50 years," Typescript in Hopewell Village Library.

Kemper Manuscripts on Hopewell Furnace, Hopewell Village Library.

Knox Papers, photocopy of pages in Hopewell Village Library.

Kurtz Family Bible, Berks County Historical Society.

Lake, D. J. and N. S. Beers, "Map of Vicinity of Philadelphia and Reading," Based on Actual Surveys. Philadelphia: 1860.

Lancaster County Record of County Tax and Exempt Fines, 1808; Lancaster County Historical Society.

Lightfoot Papers, Field Book, 1744–1771; Historical Society of Pennsylvania.

Lloyd Family Papers, private collection in possession of Dorothy Lloyd Collender, Pottstown, R. D., Pennsylvania.

Ledger of J. W. Patton Store, Shippensburg, Pennsylvania; private collection in possession of Henry Kauffman, Millersville, Pennsylvania.

Manada Furnace Journal, 1837–1841; microfilm at Hopewell Village Library.

Martha Furnace Diary (New Jersey), 1808–1815; microfilm at Hopewell Village Library.

Mary Ann Forge Ledger, 1810–1811; microfilm at Hopewell Village Library.

Mary Ann Furnace Journals and Ledgers, 1762–1838 (not complete for these years.) 8 volumes; microfilm at Hopewell Village Library.

McCaa, James, Pig, Coal and Cordwood Book, 1850–1868; Lancaster County Historical Society.

Miller, Daniel, Collection of Letters and Papers, Hopewell Village Library.

Miscellaneous Papers of Bucks County, Historical Society of Pennsylvania.

Montgomery Manuscripts, Hopewell Village Library.

Montgomery Manuscripts Relating to the Iron Industry in the Schuylkill Valley, Berks County Historical Society.

Morris, James L., Diary or Daily Notes of the Weather, Together with the Events of the Neighborhood, 1837–1844, 2 volumes; microfilm at Hopewell Village Library.

Mount Frisby AME Church and Cemetery.

Mount Hope Letters, microfilm at Hopewell Village Library.

Mt. Hope Furnace Ledgers and Journals, 1797–1819; microfilm at Hopewell Village Library.

Mt Hope Furnace Provision Book, 1809–1824; microfilm at Hopewell Village Library.

Mt. Hope Furnace Time Book, 1820–1822; microfilm at Hopewell Village Library.

New Pine Forge Day Book, 1759; microfilm at Hopewell Village Library.

Parsons, William, Collection, Historical Society of Pennsylvania.

Peale Papers, typescript, Historical Society of Pennsylvania.

Pennsylvania, *Proceedings of the Provincial Conference,* June 18—June 25, 1776; Historical Society of Pennsylvania.

"Posey Family History," typescript at Hopewell Village Library.

Potts and Francis, Store Ledger, 1851–1854; Hopewell Village Library.

Potts Manuscripts, 1799–1825; Historical Society of Pennsylvania.

Reber, Ira J. J., Collection, microfilm at Hopewell Village Library.

Richards, Henry M., "Map of Berks County, 1820; Con-

structed by Virtue of an Act of the Legislature of Pennsylvania, 19th March, 1816;" microfilm at Hopewell Village
Library.

Richards, Louis, Scrapbooks, Historical Society of Berks
County.

Rush Collection, Historical Society of Pennsylvania.

Rush, Dr. Benjamin, Collection of Manuscripts, Ridgeway
Branch Library, Philadelphia.

Sharpe-Marshall Collection of Letters, 1830–1840; microfilm
at Hopewell Village Library.

St. Gabriel's Episcopal Church Records, 1753–1901; Berks
County Historical Society.

St. Marks Episcopal Church Records, 1836–1902; Berks
County Historical Society.

St. Mary's Episcopal Church Records, 1806–1846; Berks
County Historical Society.

St. Thomas' Episcopal Church Records, 1825–1901; Berks
County Historical Society.

Stiegel Family Record Book, microfilm at Hopewell Village
Library.

Stokes Collection of Documents, Hopewell Village Library.

United States Government, Census Population Schedules,
Pennsylvania, Berks and Chester Counties, 1800–1870;
microfilm at Hopewell Village Library.

Warwick Furnace Journals and Ledgers, 1745–1770; Historical Society of Pennsylvania.

Wilson, James, Papers, Historical Society of Pennsylvania.

Young, Alex A., "Public Lectures," handbill at Hopewell
Village Library.

Ziemers, John, Day Book, 1822–1823; Lancaster County
Historical Society.

Published

Aldens Appeal Record. Robert Coleman and George Dawson
vs. Clement B. Brooke and Henry P. Robinson, Robert W.

Coleman and William Coleman, July Term, 1856. Equity. Reported 93 Pennsylvania 182. Philadelphia, 1878.

Barford, Joseph A., "Reminiscences of the Early Days of Stove Plate Molding and the Union," *International Molders' and Foundry Workers' Journal*, 94, 7 (July 1958), p. 8-11. Reprint from the March 1902 issue of the *Iron Molders' Journal*.

Bridgens, H. F. and A. R. Witmer, *Atlas of Chester County, Pennsylvania*. Safe Harbor, Pennsylvania : A. R. Witmer, 1873.

Colonial and State Records of North Carolina, Volume XXI. Raleigh; Department of Archives and History. Photocopy of pages on Mark Bird.

Combination Atlas Map of Lancaster County, Pennsylvania. Philadelphia : Everts and Stewart, 1875.

Documents Relating to the Manufacture of Iron in Pennsylvania. Philadelphia : General Committee of the Convention of Iron Masters, 1850.

Dudley, Dud, *Mettallum Martis*. West Bromwich, England: J. N. Bagnall, 1851.

Elsas, Madeleine (Editor), *Iron in the Making Dowlais Iron Company Letters, 1782–1860*. London: Glamorgan County Council, 1960.

Gruner, M. L., *Studies of Blast Furnace Phenomena*. Philadelphia : Henry Carey Baird, 1874.

Hemerlin, Samuel Gustof, *Report about the Mines in the United States, 1783*. Philadelphia : John Morton Memorial Museum, 1931.

Long, Harker A., *A Short History of the Hopewell Furnace Estate in Union Township, Berks County*. Reading : Reading Eagle Press, no date given.

Nicholson, John, *The Operative Mechanic*, Volume I. Philadelphia : H. C. Carey and I. Lea, 1826.

Overman, Frederick, *The Manufacture of Iron*. Philadelphia : Henry C. Baird, 1854.

Pennsylvania Archives, Third Series, Volumes XI, XII, XVIII. Harrisburg : Wm. Stanley Ray, 1897.

Pennsylvania, *Index to Local Legislation in Pennsylvania from 1700 to 1892.* Compiled to Giles D. Price. Philadephia : T. and J. W. Johnson and Company, 1894.

Pennsylvania, *Laws of the Commonwealth of Pennsylvania.* Compiled by Thomas McLean Thompson. Octarora: Francis Bailey, 1804.

Pennsylvania, *Laws of the General Assembly of the Commonwealth of Pennsylvania Passed at the Session of 1842.* Known as the Pamphlet Laws of Pennsylvania. Harrisburg: Published by Authority, 1842.

Pennsylvania, *Reports of Cases Adjudged in the Supreme Court of Pennsylvania.* Edited by Thomas Sergant and Wm. Rawle, Volume VIII. Philadelphia : Abraham Small, 1824. Volume XI, Philadelphia : M'Carty and Davis, 1826.

Pennsylvania, *Shepard's Pennsylvania Table of Cases.* New York : The Frank Shepard Company, 1925.

Pennsylvania, *Vale's Pennsylvania Digest,* Volume 44. St. Paul : West Publishing Company, 1950.

Sisco, Anneliese Grumbaldt (Editor), *Réaumier's Memoirs on Steel and Iron.* Chicago : University of Chicago Press, 1956.

United States, *Congress of the United States, Hearings Before the Joint Economic Committee, April 7–10, 1959. Historical and Comparative Rates of Production, Productivity, and Prices.* Washington : Government Printing Office, 1959.

United States, *Journals of the Continental Congress,* 34 volumes. Washingtcn : Government Printing Office, 1904–1937.

United States House of Representatives, *House Documents,* 22nd Congress, First Session, Volume 7, Part 1. "Report of Louis McLane, Secretary of the Treasury, 1933, on Manufacturing."

Interviews With Former Hopewell Residents

(Typescripts of these Interviews are
in Hopewell Village Library.)

Boone, David, Interviewed March 22, 1941.

Boone, Sally, March 22, 1941, and February 25, 1941.

Care, Charles Sheridan, February 24, 1941.

Care, Elizabeth A., January 30, 1941.

Care, Hunter, January 26, 1941, and March 14, 1948.

Care, Morris Lyman, February 6, 1941.

Care, Nathan, Junior, January 15, 1941, and February 13,
1941.

Care, Thomas Noble, February 10, 1941.

Care, Violet, January 15, 1941, and February 13, 1941.

Freese, Samuel Wesley, September 21, 1959.

Henry, John, January 23, 1941.

Hoffman, Thomas, November 22, 1940.

House, Harry, December 10, 1940.

Huston, H. H., June 29, 1941.

Krewson, Mary, June 29, 1941.

Lacey, Charles Atwood, October 17, 1940.

Lloyd, Albert, September 15, 1962.

Long, Harker A., August 7, 8, 13, 1936, and December, 1935.

March, Mrs. Samuel, January 22, 1941.

Painter, Albert, December 12, 1947; September 24, 1950;
January 16, 1956; May 9, 1958; January 8, 1959.

Painter, Charles Sheridan, April 15, 1953; February 16,
1957; April 17, 1958.

Painter, William, July 24, 1949.

Palsgrove, J. Lincoln, October 13, 1940.

Piersol, Margaret, June 6, 1961.

Rhodes, Catherine, March 4, 1941; May 13, 1941.

Sands, Rose, March 4, 1941; May 13, 1941.

Seidel, Sally Addison, January 30, 1941.

Smith, E. O., August 4, 1940.

Smith, Reginald, September 15, 1940; March 16, 1941;
August 24, 1941.
Sparr, John, October 8, 1940.
Stroley, C. W., August 14, 1940.
Styer, Grace, June 1, 1941.

Newspapers

Berks and Schuylkill Journal, Reading, Pennsylvania, 1816–
1910.
Birdsboro Dispatch, Birdsboro, Pennsylvania, 1947, 1948,
1952.
Chester and Delaware Federalist, West Chester, Pennsylvania,
1817.
The Christian Science Monitor, Boston, 1950.
Daily Local News, West Chester, Pennsylvania, 1874, 1881,
1929.
Evening Bulletin, Philadelphia, 1935–1937.
Hazard's Register of Pennsylvania, 1833–1835.
Jeffersonian, West Chester, Pennsylvania, 1867,1872.
Lancaster (Pennsylvania) *Sunday News,* 1962.
New York Times, 1937.
Norristown (Pennsylvania) *Free Press,* 1832.
Pennsylvania Gazette, Philadelphia, 1773, 1783, 1786–1787.
Pennsylvania Packet, Philadelphia, 1788.
Philadelphia Inquirer, 1932.
Reading (Pennsylvania) *Eagle,* 1915–1937.
Readinger (Pennsylvania) *Zeitung,* 1790–1791.
Village Record, West Chester, Pennsylvania, 1842.
Weekly Advertiser, Reading, Pennsylvania, 1797–1799.
West Chester (Pennsylvania) *Star,* 1913.

SECONDARY MATERIAL

Books

Agricola, Georgius, *De Re Metallica,* Translation by Herbert

Clark Hoover and Lou Henry Hoover. New York: Dover Publications, Inc., 1950.

Ashton, Thomas Southcliffe, *Iron and Steel in the Industrial Revolution*. Manchester: Manchester University Press, 1951.

Ballard, Lloyd V., *Social Institutions*. New York: D. Appleton-Century Company, 1936.

Barnes, James A., *Wealth of the American People*. New York: Prentice-Hall, 1949.

Bell, I. Lowthian, *Chemical Phenomena of Iron Smelting*. New York: D. Van Nostrand, 1872.

Bezanson, Anne, Robert D. Gray and Miriam Hussey, *Wholesale Prices in Philadelphia, 1784–1861*, 2 volumes. Philadelphia: University of Pennsylvania Press, 1937.

Bining, Arthur Cecil, *British Regulation of the Colonial Iron Industry*. Philadelphia: University of Pennsylvania Press, 1933.

Bining, Arthur Cecil, *Pennsylvania Iron Manufacture in the Eighteenth Century*. Harrisburg: Pennsylvania Historical Commission, 1938.

Bining, Arthur Cecil, *The Rise of American Economic Life*. New York: Charles Scribner's Sons, 1943.

Bogardus, Emory S., *Development of Social Thought*. New York: Longmans, Green and Company, 1940.

Bolland, Simpson, *The Art of Casting in Iron*. New York: John Wiley and Sons, 1893.

Bowen, Eli, *The Pictorial Sketch-Book of Pennsylvania*. Philadelphia: William Bromwell, 1853.

Boyer, Charles S., *Early Forges and Furnaces in New Jersey*. Philadelphia: University of Pennsylvania Press, 1931.

Brunhouse, Robert L., *The Counter-Revolution in Pennsylvania, 1776–1790*. Harrisburg: Pennsylvania Historical Commission, 1942.

Buckmaster, Henrietta, *Let My People Go*. New York: Harper and Brothers, 1941.

Burlingame, Roger *March of the Iron Men*. New York: Charles Scribner's Sons, 1940.

Campbell, Harry Huse, *The Manufacture and Properties of Iron and Steel*. New York: Hill Publishing Company, 1907.

Clark, Victor S., *History of Manufactures in the United States*, volume I, 1607–1860. New York: Peter Smith, 1949.

Committee on Historical Research, *Forges and Furnaces in the Province of Pennsylvania*. Philadelphia: Pennsylvania Society of the Colonial Dames of America, 1914.

Dictionary of American Biography, "James Wilson," Volume 20. New York: Scribners, 1936.

Diderot, Denis, *A Diderat Pictorial Encyclopedia of Trades and Industry*, Edited by Charles Caulston Gillispie. New York: Dover Publications, Inc., 1959.

Dornbusch, Charles H., *Pennsylvania German Barns*. Allentown: The Pennsylvania German Folklore Society, 1958.

Dunaway, Wayland F., *A History of Pennsylvania*. New York: Prentice Hall, Inc., 1950.

Faulkner, Harold Underwood, *American Economic History*. New York: Harper and Brothers Publishers, 1949.

Faulkner, Harold Underwod, *American Political and Social History*. New York: Appleton-Century-Crofts, 1957.

Fish, Carl Russell, *The Rise of the Common Man*. New York: The Macmillan Company, 1950.

Fisher, Douglas A., *Steel Making in America*. New York: United States Steel Corporation, 1949.

Fletcher, Stevenson Whitcomb, *Pennsylvania Agriculture and Country Life, 1640–1840*. Harrisburg: Pennsylvania Historical and Museum Commission, 1950.

Fulton, Charles Herman, *Principles of Metallurgy*. New York: McGraw-Hill Book Company, 1910.

Geigertown. Reading: Leon D. Evans, 1959.

Gemmell, Alfred, *The Charcoal Iron Industry in the Perkiomen Valley*. Morristown: Hartenstine Printing House, 1949.

Goodwin, Maud Wilder and Sidney G. Fisher, *Dutch and Quakers*. New Haven : Yale University Press, 1919.

Greeley, Horace and Others, *The Great Industries of the United States*. Hartford : J. B. Burr and Hyde, 1872.

Greene, Evarts Boutell, *The Revolutionary Generation, 1763–1790*. New York : The Macmillan Company, 1943.

Greenwood, William Henry, *Steel and Iron*. London : Cassell and Company, 1900.

Hartley, E. N., *Ironworks on the Saugus*, Norman : University of Oklahoma Press, 1957.

Hartz, Louis, *Economic Policy and Democratic Thought: Pennsylvania, 1776–1860*. Cambridge : Harvard University Press, 1948.

Herrick, Cheesman A., *History of Commerce and Industry*. New York; The Macmillan Company, 1918.

Industrial Berks County, 1748–1948. Reading : Textile Machine Works, 1948.

International Library of Technology. Scranton : International Textbook Company, 1903.

Jensen, Merrill, *The New Nation*. New York : Alfred A. Knopf, 1950.

Knollenberg, Bernhard, *Origins of the American Revolution, 1759–1766*. New York : The Macmillan Company, 1960.

Kraut, John Allen and Dixon Ryan Fox, *The Completion of Independence—1790–1830*. New York : The Macmillan Company, 1958.

Kurtz, Stephen G., *The Presidency of John Adams*. Philadelphia : The University of Pennsylvania Press, 1957.

Langdon, William Chauncy, *Everyday Things in American Life, 1607–1776*. New York : Charles Scribner's Sons, 1937.

Lesley, J. P., *A Geological Hand Atlas of the Sixy-Seven Counties of Pennsylvania*. Harrisburg : Board of Commissioners for the Second Geological Survey, 1885.

Lesley, J. P., *The Iron Manufacturers' Guide to the Furnaces, Forges and Rolling Mills of the United States*. New York : John Wiley, 1859.

MacDonald, William, *Jacksonian Democracy—1829–1837*. New York: Harper and Brothers, 1906. *American Nation Series.*

MacElree, Wilmer W., *Around the Boundaries of Chester County*. West Chester, Pennsylvania: The Author, 1934.

Martin, Robert F., *National Income in the United States, 1799–1938*. New York: National Industrial Conference Board, 1939.

Mathews, Mitford M. (Editor), *A Dictionary of Americanisms on Historical Principles*. Chicago: University of Chicago Press 1956.

McCullough, Robert and Walter Leuba, *The Pennsylvania Main Line Canal*. Martinsburg, Pennsylvania: Morrisons Cove Herald, 1962.

Mercer, Henry C., *Ancient Carpenters' Tools*. Doylestown: The Bucks County Historical Society, 1951.

Mercer, Henry C., *The Bible in Iron*. Doylestown: Bucks County Historical Society, 1914.

Montgomery, Morton L., *Historical and Biographical Annals of Berks County, Pennsylvania*, 2 volumes. Chicago, J. H. Beers and Company, 1909.

Montgomery, Morton L., *History of Berks County in Pennsylvania*. Philadelphia: Everts, Peck and Richards, 1886.

Murphy, Raymond E. and Marion Murphy, *Pennsylvania— A Regional Geography*. Harrisburg: Pennsylvania Book Service, 1937.

Murphy, Raymond E. and Marion F. Murphy, *Pennsylvania Landscapes*. State College, Pennsylvania: Penns Valley Publishers, Inc., 1954.

Nolan, J. Bennett, *Play at Reading Town*. Reading, Pennsylvania: The Feroe Press, 1935.

North, Douglas C., *The Economic Growth of the United States*. Englewood Cliffs, Prentice Hall, Inc., 1961.

One Hundred and Twenty-Five Years of Pig Iron Manufacture at Robesonia, Pennsylvania. Philadelphia: The Robesonia Iron Company, 1918.

488   HOPEWELL VILLAGE

Pearse, John B., *A Concise History of the Iron Manufacture of the American Colonies up to the Revolution and of Pennsylvania until the Present Time*. Philadelphia: Allen, Lane and Scott, 1876.

Pierce, Arthur D., *Iron in the Pines*. New Brunswick: Rutgers University Press, 1957.

The Picture Story of Steel. New York: American Iron and Steel Institute, 1952.

Porter, Burton P., *Old Canal Days*. Columbus: Herr Printing Company, 1942.

Riegel, Robert E., *Young America, 1830–1840*. Norman: University of Oklahoma Press, 1949.

Rowe, Frank H., *History of the Iron and Steel Industry in Scioto County, Ohio*. Columbus: State Archaeological and Historical Society, 1938.

Schlesinger, Arthur M., Jr., *The Age of Jackson*. Boston: Little, Brown and Company, 1945.

Schubert, H. R., *History of the British Iron and Steel Industry*. London: Routledge and Kegan Paul, 1957.

Scrivenor, Harry, *History of the Iron Trade from the Earliest Records to the Present Period*. London: Longman, Brown, Green, and Longmans, 1854.

Selsam, J. Paul, *The Pennsylvania Constitution of 1776*. Philadelphia: University of Pennsylvania Press, 1936.

Shenk, Hiram H., *A History of the Lebanon Valley in Pennsylvania*. Harrisburg: The National Historical Association, Inc., 1930.

Sim, Robert J. and Harry B. Weiss, *Charcoal-Burning in New Jersey from Early Times to the Present*. Trenton: New Jersey Agricultural Society, 1955.

Singer, Charles and Others, *A History of Technology*, volume IV. New York: Oxford University Press, 1958.

Smedley, R. C., *History of the Underground Railroad in Chester and Neighboring Counties of Pennsylvania*. Lancaster: The Journal, 1883.

Smith, Cyril Stanley, *A History of Metallography*. Chicago : University of Chicago Press, 1960.

Smith, Timothy L., *Revivalism and Social Reform in Mid-Nineteenth Century America*. New York : Abingdon Press, 1957.

Stoughton, Bradley, *The Metallurgy of Iron and Steel*. New York : Hill Publishing Company, 1908.

Strassmann, W. Paul, *Risk and Technological Innovation : American Manufacturing Methods during the Nineteenth Century*. Ithaca : Cornell University Press, 1959.

Sullivan, William A., *The Industrial Worker in Pennsylvania, 1800–1840*. Harrisburg : Pennsylvania Historical and Museum Commission, 1955.

Swank, J. M., *History of the Manufacture of Iron in all Ages and Particularly in the United States from Colonial Times to 1891*. Philadelphia : Allen, Lane and Scott, 1892.

Swank, J. M., *Introduction to a History of Ironmaking and Coal Mining in Pennsylvania*. Philadelphia : Allen, Lane and Scott, 1878.

Taylor, George Rogers, *Jackson Versus Biddle*. Boston : D. C. Heath and Company, 1949.

Transactions of the American Institute of Mining Engineers, volumes XIV and XV. New York : Published by the Institute, 1886 and 1887.

Transactions of the Historical Society of Berks County, volume III. Reading Eagle Press, 1923.

Turner, Frederick Jackson, *The United States, 1830–1850*. New York, Peter Smith, 1950.

Tyler, A. F., *Freedom's Ferment : Phases of American Social History*. Minneapolis : University of Minnesota Press, 1944.

Van Wagenen, Jaud, Jr., *The Golden Age of Homespun*. Ithaca : Cornell University Press, 1954.

Wade, Richard C., *The Urban Frontier, The Rise of Western Cities, 1790–1830*. Cambridge : Harvard University Press, 1959.

Wetzel, John C. (Editor), *200th Anniversay of Birdsboro,*

Pennsylvania. Birdsboro: The Executive Committee, 1940.

White, Mortong, *Social Thought in America*. New York: Viking Press, 1949.

Williamson, Harold F. (Editor), *The Growth of the American Economy*. New York: Prentice-Hall, 1946.

Woodward, Carl Raymond, *Ploughs and Politics : Charles Read of New Jersey and his Notes on Agriculture, 1715– 1774*. New Brunswick: Rutgers University Press, 1941.

Pamphlets

Beck, Herbert H., *Common Hill and the Hessian Ditch with Personal Reminiscences of the Furnace Hills*. Lancaster: Lancaster County Historical Society, 1940.

Bining, Arthur C., *Early Ironmasters of Pennsylvania*. Reprint from Pennsylvania History, XVIII, 2 (April 1951).

Birkinbine, John, *American Blast-Furnace Progress*. Washington: Government Printing Office, 1885.

Birkinbine, John, *The Manufacture of Pig Iron in Pennsylvania*. Washington: Department of Internal Affairs— Statistics, Official Document Number 10, 1894.

Brooke, G. Clymer, *Birdsboro Company with a Past Built to Last*. New York: The Newcomen Society in North America, 1959.

Croll, P. C., *The Tulpehocken Bi-Centennial*. Womelsdorf: Executive Committee, 1923.

Cummings, Hubertis, *The Pennsylvania Canals*. Harrisburg: Pennsylvania Historical and Museum Commission, 1949.

Hopewell Village National Historic Site Pennsylvania. Washington: United States Department of the Interior, National Park Service, 1940.

Jones, Louis C., *The Farmers' Museum*. Cooperstown: New York State Historical Association, 1948.

Kemper, Jackson, III, *American Charcoal Making in the Era of the Cold-Blast Furnace*. Washington: United States Department of the Interior, 1941.

BIBLIOGRAPHY

Kurjack, Dennis C., *Hopewell Village National Historic Site*. Washington : National Park Service Handbook Series, number 8, 1950.

Miller, Frederick K., *The Rise of an Iron Community*, 3 parts. Lebanon, Pennsylvania : Lebanon County Historical Society, 1950–1952.

Schultz, George W., *Antique Iron Works and Machines of the Water Power Age*. Bowers, Pennsylvania : The Author, 1927.

Spargo, John, *Iron Mining and Smelting in Bennington, Vermont—1786–1842*. Bennington : Historical Museum, 1958.

Steel Serves the Farmer. New York : American Iron and Steel Institute, 1954.

Periodicals

Bining, Arthur Cecil, "The Early Iron Industry in Pennsylvania," *The General Magazine and Historical Chronicle, University of Pennsylvania*, XXXIV, 1 (October 1931), 51–55.

Bining, Arthur Cecil, "The Iron Plantations of Early Pennsylvania," *The Pennsylvania Magazine of History and Biography*, LVII, 2 (April 1933), 7–8.

"Bird, Barde, Brooke and Boro," *Time, The Weekly Magazine*, XXX, 1 (July 5, 1937), 48.

Birkinbine, John, "Changes in the Manufacture of Pig Iron as Illustrated by the Development of the American Blast Furnace," *Proceedings of the Engineers' Club of Philadelphia*, XIX, 3 (July 1902), 223–240.

Birkinbine, John, "The Distribution and Proportions of American Blast Furnaces," *Transactions of the American Institute of Mining Engineers*, XIV (June 1885 to May 1886), 561–575.

Borchers, Sam, "American Iron Industry in Colonial Times," *Forgings*, 7, 2 (March 1945), 6–7.

Borchers, S. J., "Forge Men of Quaker State Foremost in Revolutionary Arms Production," *Forgings*, 6, 5 (September 1944), 10–11.

"Cast Iron and Early Stoves," *International Molders' and Foundry Workers' Journal*, 94, 6 (June 1958), 9–13.

Cochran, Hamilton, "Hopewell Village—Last of the Iron Plantations," *Philadelphia Magazine*, XXXVII, 7 (July 1950), 16–18, 34.

Cook, E. S., "Management of Blast Furnaces—Transition from 'Rule of Thumb' to Application of Scientific Methods," *School of Mines Quarterly*, XIX, 3 (April 1898), 227–248.

Crockard, Frank Hearne, "Modern Iron Blast-Furnace Practice," *The Engineering Magazine* (January 1, 1902), 493–513.

D'Invilliers, E. V., "The Cornwall Iron-Ore Mines; Lebanon County, Pa.," *Transaction of the American Institute of Mining Engineers, XIV* (June 1885 to May 1886), 873–904.

"Early Iron Furnaces," *U S Steel News*, 7, 1 (January 1942), 4–15.

Eshelman, John E., "Berks County's Station on the Underground Railroad," *The Historical Review of Berks County*, VI, 4 (July 1941), 107–109.

Eshleman, H. Frank, "The Great Conestoga Road," *Papers Read Before the Lancaster County Historical Society*, XII, 6 (June 5, 1908), 215–232.

Frackenthal, B. F., Junior, "Tuyeres in the Iron Blast-Furnace," *Transactions of the American Institute of Mining Engineers*, XXVIII (1903), 673.

Freiday, Dean, "Tinton Manor: The Iron Works," *Proceedings of the New Jersey Historical Society*, LXX, 4, (October 1952), 250–261.

Garrison, L. A., "Hopewell Village Site Now Open," *Reading Automobile Club Magazine*, 18, 5 (July 1940), 7–8, 25.

Gemmell, Alfred, "On the Trail of America's First Cook

Stove," *The Historical Review of Berks County,* XV, 1 (October 1949), 142–144.

Gibson, James E., "The Pennsylvania Provincial Conference of 1776," *The Pennsylvania Magazine of History and Biography,* LVIII, 4 (October 1934), 312–341.

Handwork, Edna M., "First in Iron—Berks County's Iron Industry, 1716–1815," *The Historical Review of Berks County,* XXV, 4 (Fall 1960), 120–127.

Heathcote, Charles William, "The Iron Industries of Northern Chester County," *Bulletin of the Chester County Historical Society,* (1936), 38–50.

Heydinger, Earl J., "The Schuylkill, Lifeline to Valley Forge," *Bulletin of the Historical Society of Montgomery County, Pennsylvania,* IX, 3 (October 1954), 159–170.

Homan, Wayne E., "Pennsylvania Heritage, Our Refuge for Runaway Slaves," *Sunday Today, The Philadelphia Inquirer Magazine* (September 24, 1961), 26.

Homan, Wayne E., "The Underground Railroad," *The Historical Review of Berks County,* XXIII, 4 (Fall 1958), 112–118.

"Hopewell Village," *International Molders' and Foundry Workers' Journal,* 94, 10 (October 1958), 3–7.

"Hopewell—Where the Story of Ironmaking in Early America Comes Alive," *Lancaster Motorist,* LII, 8 (August 1962), 2, 24.

Hudson, J. Paul, "Iron Manufacturing During the Eighteenth Century," *The Iron Worker,* XXI, 4 (Autumn 1957), 9–13.

Hudson, J. Paul, "The Story of Iron at Jamestown, Virginia —Where Iron Objects Were Wrought by Englishmen almost 350 Years Ago," *The Iron Worker,* XX, 3 (Summer 1956), 2–14.

Hunter, Louis C., "Financial Problems of the Early Pittsburgh Iron Manufacturers," *Journal of Economic and Business History,* II, 3 (Mal 1930), 520–544.

Hunter, Louis C., "Influence of the Market upon Techniques in the Iron Industry in Western Pennsylvania up to 1860,"

Journal of Economic and Business History, I, 2 (February 1929), 241–281.

Hyde, Frederic G., "Built to Last," *The Philadelphia Inquirer Magazine* (May 14, 1950).

"James Wilson at Hopewell National Park," *The Historical Review of Berks County,* IV, 1 (October 1938), 16–17.

Kemper Jackson, 3rd, "American Charcoal Making in the Era of the Cold-Blast Furnace," *The Regional Review,* V, 1 (July 1940), 3–15.

Kemper Jackson, III, "The Making of Charcoal," *The Historical Review of Berks County,* II, 4 (July 1937), 98–103.

Kendig, John D., "Charcoal Burning in Hopewell," *American Forests,* 65, 10 (October 1959), 41, 59.

Kurjack, Dennis C., "Joseph Whitaker of Hopewell Furnace," second of two parts, *The Historical Review of Berks County,* XIV, 3 (April 1949), 66–73.

Livingood, James W., "The Heyday of the Schuylkill Navigation Company," *The Historical Review of Berks County,* IV, 1 (October 1938), 11–14.

Lyles, Victoria, "Forges and Furnaces of York County," *Papers of the Historical Society of York County,* New Series, number 4 (no date).

"Metals and Ancient Heating Methods," *International Molders' and Foundry Workers' Journal,* 94, 5 (May 1958), 31–33.

Montgomery, Morton L., "Early Furnaces and Forges of Berks County, Pennsylvania," *The Pennsylvania Magazine of History and Biography,* VIII, 1 (March 1884), 56–81.

Peirce, Patricia, "Iron and Copper Mining in Caernarvon Township," *The Historical Review of Berks County,* XVI, 1 (October-December 1950, 12–15, 25–31.

Rice, William S., "Mount Hope Furnace, An Early Landmark," *The American-German Review,* XVII, 5 (June 1951), 28–29.

Ruffner, Margaret C., "Hopewell Cradle of American Industry," *The Rotarian,* LXXVIII, 3 (March 1951), 21.

Sandford, Joseph E., "Charcoal Burning," *The Historian,* I, 5 (Winter 1960–1961), 25–27.

Schaeffer, Paul N., "Slavery in Berks County," *The Historical Review of Berks County,* VI, 4 (July 1941), 110–115.

Shearer, Fred W., "A Bygone Industry," *Service Letter The Pennsylvania Department of Forests and Waters,* series 7, number 11 (March 12, 1936), 1–3.

Starratt, F. Weston, "Visiting Hopewell Furnace," *Journal of Metals,* 14, 7 (July 1962), 484–485.

Stauffer, Alvin P. and Charles W. Porter, "The National Park Service Program of Conservation for Areas and Structures of National Historical Significance," *Mississipi Valley Historical Review,* XXX, 1 (June 1943). Typescript at Hopewell Village.

Thomas, Earl A., "Hopewell Iron Plantation," *The Highway Magazine* (August 1949), 171–175.

"When Charcoal Iron Industry Held Sway," *Steel* (August 3, 1942), 80 and (August 10, 1942), 78.

Whitely, Henry C., "The Principio Company," *The Pennsylvania Magazine of History and Biography,* XI, 1 (April 1887), 63.

Woodhouse, Samuel W., "Log and Journal of the Ship *United States* on a voyage to China in 1784," *"The Pennsylvania Magazine of History and Biography,* LV, 3 (July 1931), 225–258.

Unpublished Studies

Abel, Leland, "Archeological Report of Hopewell Furnace Site," typescript, 1962, Hopewell Village Library.

Apple, Russell A., "The Public Roads Serving Hopewell Furnace," typescript, 1953, Hopewell Village Library.

Apple, Russell A., "Historical Documentary Report on the

Bridge and Wheel House, Hopewell Furnace," typescript, 1956, Hopewell Village, Library.

Apple, Russel A., "The Public Serving Hopewell Furnace," typescript, 1953, Hopewell Village Library.

Appleman, Roy Edgar, "Historical Report French Creek Area," typescript, no date, Hopewell Village Library.

Appleman, Roy Edgar, "Memorandum Respecting the Historical and Archeological Importance of the French Creek Recreational Demonstration Area, Pennsylvania, and the Proposal that it Be Made a National Monument," typescript, 1939, Hopewell Village Library.

Appleman, Roy Edgar, "Proposed Restoration Plan for Old Iron Making Village," typescript, 1936, Hopewell Village Library.

Cowan, John P., "Notes on an Inventory of Buildings and Contents Hopewell, French Creek, Pennsylvania," type script, 1938, Hopewell Village Library.

Donohoe, Richard P., "The Charcoal House and Shed, Hopewell Village National Historic Site," typescript, 1956. Hopewell Village Library.

Du Hamel, William, "Historical Sketch of William Bird. Founder of Birdsboro, Pa.," typescript, 1928, Hopewell Village Library.

Fox, Cyrus T., "William Bird, Pioneer Founder of Birdsboro," typescript, no date, Hopewell Village Library.

Gale, Howard, "Report on the Furnishings and Equipment and Methods Used in the Blacksmith Shop," typescript. 1941, Hopewell Village Library.

Heydinger, Earl J., "History of French Creek Mine, 1846-1928," typescript, no date, Hopewell Village Library.

Heydinger, Earl J., "Orientation Report for Archeology in Lower Working Level at Hopewell Village NHS," typescript, 1962, Hopewell Village Library.

Heydinger, Earl J., "The Office-Store," typescript, 1959, Hopewell Village Library.

Kemper, Franklin, "J. Lincoln Palsgrove," typescript, no date, Hopewell Village Library.

Kemper, Jackson, "The Making of Charcoal as Followed by the Colliers of the Schuylkill Valley," typescript, no date, Hopewell Village Library.

Kurjack, Dennis C., "Chart of Furnace Operation, 1783–1883," typescript, no date, Hopewell Village Library.

Montgomery, Charles B., "Report on Hopewell Furnace in Berks County, Pa.," typescript, probably 1941, Hopewell Village Library.

Motz, J. C. Fisher, "The Big House," typescript, 1941, Hopewell Village Library.

Motz, J. C. Fisher, "Field Notes—Archeological Investigation of Blacksmith Shop," typescript, 1940, Hopewell Village Library.

Motz, J. C. Fisher, "Historical Base Map," typescript, 1941, Hopewell Village Library.

Motz, J. C. Fisher, "Report on Archeological Investigation of the Blacksmith Shop," typescript, 1940, Hopewell Village Library.

Motz, J. C. Fisher, "Restoration of Houck House," typescript, 1940, Hopewell Village Library.

"Restoration of Tenant Barn," typescript, 1940, Hopewell Village Library.

Ronsheim, Robert D., "Charcoal House and Charcoal Shed, Hopewell Village National Historical Site," typescript, 1957, Hopewell Village Library.

Ronsheim, Robert D., "Survey Report, Tenant House 3," typescript, 1958, Hopewell Village Library.

Ronsheim, Robert D., and Earl J. Heydinger, "Village Barn," typescript, 1961, Hopewell Village Library.

Schumacher, Paul J. F., "Archeological Exploration at the Furnace Group—1935–1951," typescript, 1951, Hopewell Village Library.

Souder, Norman M., "The Office and Store Building," typescript, 1960, Hopewell Village Library.

Sylvester, Arthur C., and Jackson Kemper, 3rd, "The Making of Charcoal as Followed by the Colliers of the Schuylkill Valley," typescript, 1937, Hopewell Village Library.

Zerbey, Benjamin J. and Earl J. Heydinger, "Anthracite Furnace, Hopewell Village National Historical Site," typescript, 1962, Hopewell Village Library.

Index

F. Scott Fitzgerald

In Scott Fitzgerald, as in every writer of genius, there was something of the seer. He gave a name to an age – the Jazz Age – lived through that age, and saw it burn itself out. As a *New York Times* editorial stated after his death: 'He was better than he knew, for in fact and in the literary sense he invented a "generation" . . . he might have interpreted them and even guided them, as in their middle years they saw a different and nobler freedom threatened with destruction.'

F. Scott Fitzgerald was born in St Paul, Minnesota; even as a schoolboy in St Paul he was writing, and later at Princeton. In 1917, he left Princeton for the army – but didn't get to France – and wrote in his spare moments. Then came *This Side of Paradise*, the first of his novels, followed by two volumes of short stories, and at last *The Great Gatsby*, which alone would assure Scott Fitzgerald's place among our writers of major stature. He died in 1940.

Besides *The Great Gatsby* and *This Side of Paradise*, he wrote three other novels, *The Beautiful and Damned*, *Tender is the Night* and *The Last Tycoon* (his last and unfinished work); four volumes of short stories; and *The Crack-Up*, a selection of his autobiographical pieces and stories.

THE COLLECTED SHORT STORIES
OF
F. SCOTT FITZGERALD

Penguin Books

Penguin Books Ltd, Harmondsworth, Middlesex, England
Viking Penguin Inc., 40 West 23rd Street, New York, New York 10010, U.S.A.
Penguin Books Australia Ltd, Ringwood, Victoria, Australia
Penguin Books Canada Limited, 2801 John Street, Markham, Ontario, Canada L3R 1B4
Penguin Books (N.Z.) Ltd, 182–190 Wairau Road, Auckland 10, New Zealand

This collection first published 1986

Scanned and phototypeset by
Datasolve, London
Made and printed in Great Britain by
Cox & Wyman Ltd, Reading
Set in Photina

CONTENTS

PUBLISHER'S NOTE

Most of the stories in this collection were published together originally in *The Bodley Head Scott Fitzgerald*, 6 vols. (1958–63).

The complete Pat Hobby sequence of seventeen stories was first published by Charles Scribner's Sons, New York, in 1962. It comprised thirteen previously uncollected stories, which had been published first in *Esquire* between 1939 and 1941, and four stories ('Boil Some Water – Lots of It', 'Teamed with Genius', 'A Patriotic Short' and 'Two Old-Timers') that were reproduced by permission of The Bodley Head Ltd. A revised version of 'A Patriotic Short', which arrived too late to be published in the December 1940 issue of *Esquire*, was also included in that volume.

THE CUT-GLASS BOWL

I

There was a rough stone age and a smooth stone age and a bronze age, and many years afterward a cut-glass age. In the cut-glass age, when young ladies had persuaded young men with long, curly moustaches to marry them, they sat down several months afterward and wrote thank-you notes for all sorts of cut-glass presents – punch-bowls, finger-bowls dinner-glasses, wine-glasses, ice-cream dishes, bonbon dishes, decanters, and cases – for, though cut glass was nothing new in the nineties, it was then especially busy reflecting the dazzling light of fashion from the Back Bay to the fastnesses of the Middle West.

After the wedding the punch-bowls were arranged on the sideboard with the big bowl in the centre; the glasses were set up in the china-closet; the candlesticks were put at both ends of things – and then the struggle for existence began. The bonbon dish lost its little handle and became a pin-tray upstairs; a promenading cat knocked the little bowl off the sideboard, and the hired girl chipped the middle-sized one with the sugar-dish; then the wine-glasses succumbed to leg fractures, and even the dinner-glasses disappeared one by one like the ten little niggers, the last one ending up, scarred and maimed, as a toothbrush holder among other shabby genteels on the bathroom shelf. But by the time all this had happened the cut-glass age was over, anyway.

It was well past its first glory on the day the curious Mrs Roger Fairboalt came to see the beautiful Mrs Harold Piper.

'My *dear*,' said the curious Mrs Roger Fairboalt, 'I *love* your house. I think it's *quite* artistic.'

'I'm *so* glad,' said the beautiful Mrs Harold Piper, lights appearing in her young, dark eyes; 'and you must come often. I'm almost *always* alone in the afternoon.'

Mrs Fairboalt would have liked to remark that she didn't believe this at all and couldn't see how she'd be expected to – it was all over town that Mr Freddy Gedney had been dropping in on Mrs Piper five afternoons a week for the past six months. Mrs Fairboalt was at that ripe age where she distrusted all beautiful women –

'I love the dining-room *most*,' she said, 'all that *marvellous* china, and that huge cut-glass bowl.'

Mrs Piper laughed, so prettily that Mrs Fairboalt's lingering reservations about the Freddy Gedney story quite vanished.

'Oh, that big bowl!' Mrs Piper's mouth forming the words was a vivid rose petal. 'There's a story about that bowl –'

'Oh –'

'You remember young Carleton Canby? Well, he was very attentive at one time, and the night I told him I was going to marry Harold, seven years ago, in ninety-two, he drew himself way up and said: "Evylyn, I'm going to give a present that's as hard as you are and as beautiful and as empty and as easy to see through." He frightened me a little – his eyes were so black. I thought he was going to deed me a haunted house or something that would explode when you opened it. That bowl came, and of course it's beautiful. Its diameter or circumference or something is two and a half feet – or perhaps it's three and a half. Anyway, the sideboard is really too small for it; it sticks way out.'

'My *dear*, wasn't that *odd*! And he left town about then, didn't he?' Mrs Fairboalt was scribbling italicized notes on her memory – 'hard, beautiful, empty, and easy to see through.'

'Yes, he went West – or South – or somewhere,' answered Mrs Piper, radiating that divine vagueness that helps to lift beauty out of time.

Mrs Fairboalt drew on her gloves, approving the effect of largeness given by the open sweep from the spacious music-room through the library, disclosing a part of the dining-room beyond. It was really the nicest smaller house in town, and Mrs Piper had talked of moving to a larger one on Devereaux Avenue. Harold Piper must be *coining* money.

As she turned into the sidewalk under the gathering autumn dusk she assumed that disapproving, faintly unpleasant expression that almost all successful women of forty wear on the street.

If *I* were Harold Piper, she thought, I'd spend a *little* less time on business, and a *little* more time at home. Some *friend* should speak to him.

But if Mrs Fairboalt had considered it a successful afternoon she would have named it a triumph had she waited two minutes longer. For while she was still a black receding figure a hundred yards down the street, a very good-looking distraught young man turned up the walk to the

Piper house. Mrs Piper answered the door-bell herself, and with a rather dismayed expression led him quickly into the library.

'I had to see you,' he began wildly; 'your note played the devil with me. Did Harold frighten you into this?'

She shook her head.

'I'm through, Fred,' she said slowly, and her lips had never looked to him so much like tearings from a rose. 'He came home last night sick with it. Jessie Piper's sense of duty was too much for her, so she went down to his office and told him. He was hurt and – oh, I can't help seeing it his way, Fred. He says we've been club gossip all summer and he didn't know it, and now he understands snatches of conversation he's caught and veiled hints people have dropped about me. He's mighty angry, Fred, and he loves me and I love him – rather.'

Gedney nodded slowly and half closed his eyes.

'Yes,' he said, 'yes, my trouble's like yours. I can see other people's points of view too plainly.' His grey eyes met her dark ones frankly. 'The blessed thing's over. My God, Evylyn, I've been sitting down at the office all day looking at the outside of your letter, and looking at it and looking at it –'

'You've got to go, Fred,' she said steadily, and the slight emphasis of hurry in her voice was a new thrust for him. 'I gave him my word of honour I wouldn't see you. I know just how far I can go with Harold, and being here with you this evening is one of the things I can't do.'

They were still standing, and as she spoke she made a little movement toward the door. Gedney looked at her miserably, trying, here at the end, to treasure up a last picture of her – and then suddenly both of them were stiffened into marble at the sound of steps on the walk outside. Instantly her arm reached out grasping the lapel of his coat – half urged, half swung him through the big door into the dark dining-room.

'I'll make him go upstairs,' she whispered close to his ear. 'Don't move till you hear him on the stairs. Then go out the front way.'

Then he was alone listening as she greeted her husband in the hall.

Harold Piper was thirty-six, nine years older than his wife. He was handsome – with marginal notes: these being eyes that were too close together, and a certain woodenness when his face was in repose. His attitude toward this Gedney matter was typical of all his attitudes. He had told Evylyn that he considered the subject closed and would never reproach her nor allude to it in any form; and he told himself that this was rather a big way of looking at it – that she was not a little impressed.

Yet, like all men who are preoccupied with their own broadness, he was exceptionally narrow.

He greeted Evylyn with emphasized cordiality this evening.

'You'll have to hurry and dress, Harold,' she said eagerly. 'We're going to the Bronsons'.'

He nodded.

'It doesn't take me long to dress, dear,' and, his words trailing off, he walked on into the library. Evylyn's heart clattered loudly.

'Harold –' she began, with a little catch in her voice, and followed him in. He was lighting a cigarette. 'You'll have to hurry, Harold,' she finished, standing in the doorway.

'Why?' he asked, a trifle impatiently. 'You're not dressed yourself yet, Evie.'

He stretched out in a Morris chair and unfolded a newspaper. With a sinking sensation Evylyn saw that this meant at least ten minutes – and Gedney was standing breathless in the next room. Supposing Harold decided that before he went upstairs he wanted a drink from the decanter on the sideboard. Then it occurred to her to forestall this contingency by bringing him the decanter and a glass. She dreaded calling his attention to the dining-room in any way, but she couldn't risk the other chance.

But at the same moment Harold rose and, throwing his paper down, came toward her.

'Evie, dear,' he said, bending and putting his arms about her, 'I hope you're not thinking about last night –' She moved close to him, trembling. 'I know,' he continued, 'it was just an imprudent friendship on your part. We all make mistakes.'

Evylyn hardly heard him. She was wondering if by sheer clinging to him she could draw him out and up the stairs. She thought of playing sick, asking to be carried up – unfortunately, she knew he would lay her on the couch and bring her whisky.

Suddenly her nervous tension moved up a last impossible notch. She had heard a very faint but quite unmistakable creak from the floor of the dining-room. Fred was trying to get out the back way.

Then her heart took a flying leap as a hollow ringing note like a gong echoed and re-echoed through the house. Gedney's arm had struck the big cut-glass bowl.

'What's that!' cried Harold. 'Who's there?'

She clung to him but he broke away, and the room seemed to crash about her ears. She heard the pantry-door swing open, a scuffle, the rattle of a tin pan, and in wild despair she rushed into the kitchen and pulled up the gas. Her husband's arm slowly unwound from Gedney's neck, and he stood there very still, first in amazement, then with pain dawning in his face.

'My golly!' he said in bewilderment, and then repeated: 'My *golly*!'

He turned as if to jump again at Gedney, stopped, his muscles visibly relaxed, and he gave a bitter little laugh.

'You people – you people –' Evylyn's arms were around him and her eyes were pleading with him frantically, but he pushed her away and sank dazed into a kitchen chair, his face like porcelain. 'You've been doing things to me, Evylyn. Why, you little devil! You little *devil*!'

She had never felt so sorry for him; she had never loved him so much.

'It wasn't her fault,' said Gedney rather humbly. 'I just came.' But Piper shook his head, and his expression when he stared up was as if some physical accident had jarred his mind into a temporary inability to function. His eyes, grown suddenly pitiful, struck a deep, unsounded chord in Evylyn – and simultaneously a furious anger surged in her. She felt her eyelids burning; she stamped her foot violently; her hands scurried nervously over the table as if searching for a weapon, and then she flung herself wildly at Gedney.

'Get out!' she screamed, dark eyes blazing, little fists beating helplessly on his outstretched arm. 'You did this! Get out of here – get out – get *out*! *Get out*!'

II

Concerning Mrs Harold Piper at thirty-five, opinion was divided – women said she was still handsome; men said she was pretty no longer. And this was probably because the qualities in her beauty that women had feared and men had followed had vanished. Her eyes were still as large and as dark and as sad, but the mystery had departed; their sadness was no longer eternal, only human, and she had developed a habit, when she was startled or annoyed, of twitching her brows together and blinking several times. Her mouth also had lost: the red had receded and the faint down-turning of its corners when she smiled, that had added to the sadness of the eyes and been vaguely mocking and beautiful, was quite gone. When she smiled now the corners of her lips turned up. Back in the days when she revelled in her own beauty Evylyn had enjoyed that smile of hers – she had accentuated it. When she stopped accentuating it, it faded out and the last of her mystery with it.

Evylyn had ceased accentuating her smile within a month after the Freddy Gedney affair. Externally things had gone on very much as they had before. But in those few minutes during which she had discovered how much she loved her husband, Evylyn had realized how indelibly she had hurt him. For a month she struggled against aching silences, wild reproaches, and accusations – she pled with him, made quiet, pitiful little love to him, and he laughed at her bitterly – and then she, too, slipped gradually into silence and a shadowy impenetrable barrier dropped between them. The surge of love that had risen in her she lavished on Donald, her little boy, realizing him almost wonderingly as a part of her life.

The next year a piling up of mutual interests and responsibilities and some stray flicker from the past brought husband and wife together again – but after a rather pathetic flood of passion Evylyn realized that her great opportunity was gone. There simply wasn't anything left. She might have been youth and love for both – but that time of silence had slowly dried up the springs of affection and her own desire to drink again of them was dead.

She began for the first time to seek women friends, to prefer books she had read before, to sew a little where she could watch her two children to whom she was devoted. She worried about little things – if she saw crumbs on the dinner-table her mind drifted off the conversation: she was receding gradually into middle age.

Her thirty-fifth birthday had been an exceptionally busy one, for they were entertaining on short notice that night, and as she stood in her bedroom window in the late afternoon she discovered that she was quite tired. Ten years before she would have lain down and slept, but now she had a feeling that things needed watching: maids were cleaning downstairs, bric-à-brac was all over the floor, and there were sure to be grocery-men that had to be talked to imperatively – and then there was a letter to write Donald, who was fourteen and in his first year away at school.

She had nearly decided to lie down, nevertheless, when she heard a sudden familiar signal from little Julie downstairs. She compressed her lips, her brows twitched together, and she blinked.

'Julie!' she called.

'Ah-h-h-ow!' prolonged Julie plaintively. Then the voice of Hilda, the second maid, floated up the stairs.

'She cut herself a little, Mis' Piper.'

Evylyn flew to her sewing-basket, rummaged until she found a torn handkerchief, and hurried downstairs. In a moment Julie was crying in her arms as she searched for the cut, faint, disparaging evidences of which appeared on Julie's dress!

'My *thu*-mb!' explained Julie. 'Oh-h-h-h, t'urts.'

'It was the bowl here, the he one,' said Hilda apologetically. 'It was waitin' on the floor while I polished the sideboard, and Julie come along an' went to foolin' with it. She yust scratch herself.'

Evylyn frowned heavily at Hilda. and twisting Julie decisively in her lap, began tearing strips off the handkerchief.

'Now – let's see it, dear.'

Julie held it up and Evylyn pounced.

'There!'

Julie surveyed her swatched thumb doubtfully. She crooked it; it waggled. A pleased, interested look appeared in her tear-stained face. She sniffled and waggled it again.

'You *precious*!' cried Evylyn and kissed her, but before she left the room she levelled another frown at Hilda. Careless! Servants all that way nowadays. If she could get a good Irishwoman – but you couldn't any more – and these Swedes –

At five o'clock Harold arrived and, coming up to her room, threatened in a suspiciously jovial tone to kiss her thirty-five times for her birthday. Evylyn resisted.

'You've been drinking,' she said shortly, and then added qualitatively, 'a little. You know I loathe the smell of it.'

'Evie,' he said, after a pause, seating himself in a chair by the window, 'I can tell you something now. I guess you've known things haven't been going quite right down-town.'

She was standing at the window combing her hair, but at these words she turned and looked at him.

'How do you mean? You've always said there was room for more than one wholesale hardware house in town.' Her voice expressed some alarm.

'There *was*,' said Harold significantly, 'but this Clarence Ahearn is a smart man.'

'I was surprised when you said he was coming to dinner.'

'Evie,' he went on, with another slap at his knee, 'after January first "The Clarence Ahearn Company" becomes "The Ahearn, Piper Company" – and "Piper Brothers" as a company ceases to exist.'

Evylyn was startled. The sound of his name in second place was somehow hostile to her; still he appeared jubilant.

'I don't understand, Harold.'

'Well, Evie, Ahearn had been fooling around with Marx. If those two had combined we'd have been the little fellow, struggling along, picking up smaller orders, handing back on risks. It's a question of capital, Evie, and "Ahearn and Marx" would have had the business just like "Ahearn and Piper" is going to now.' He paused and coughed and a little cloud of whisky floated up to her nostrils. 'Tell you the truth, Evie, I've suspected that Ahearn's wife had something to do with it. Ambitious little lady, I'm told. Guess she knew the Marxes couldn't help her much here.'

'Is she – common?' asked Evie.

'Never met her, I'm sure – but I don't doubt it. Clarence Ahearn's name's been up at the Country Club five months – no action taken.' He waved his hand disparagingly. 'Ahearn and I had lunch together today and just about clinched it, so I thought it'd be nice to have him and his wife up tonight – just have nine, mostly family. After all, it's a big thing for me, and of course we'll have to see something of them, Evie.'

'Yes,' said Evie thoughtfully, 'I suppose we will.'

Evylyn was not disturbed over the social end of it – but the idea of 'Piper Brothers' becoming 'The Ahearn, Piper Company' startled her. It seemed like going down in the world.

Half an hour later, as she began to dress for dinner, she heard his voice from downstairs.

'Oh, Evie, come down!'

She went out into the hall and called over the banister: 'What is it?'

'I want you to help me make some of that punch before dinner.'

Hurriedly rehooking her dress, she descended the stairs and found him grouping the essentials on the dining-room table. She went to the sideboard and, lifting one of the bowls, carried it over.

'Oh, no,' he protested, 'let's use the big one. There'll be Ahearn and his wife and you and I and Milton, that's five, and Tom and Jessie, that's seven, and your sister and Joe Ambler, that's nine. You don't know how quick that stuff goes when *you* make it.'

'We'll use this bowl,' she insisted. 'It'll hold plenty. You know how Tom is.'

Tom Lowrie, husband to Jessie, Harold's first cousin, was rather inclined to finish anything in a liquid way that he began.

Harold shook his head.

'Don't be foolish. That one holds only about three quarts and there's nine of us, and the servants'll want some – and it isn't very strong punch. It's so much more cheerful to have a lot, Evie; we don't have to drink all of it.'

'I say the small one.'

Again he shook his head obstinately.

'No; be reasonable.'

'I *am* reasonable,' she said shortly. 'I don't want any drunken men in the house.'

'Who said you did?'

'Then use the small bowl.'

'Now, Evie –'

He grasped the smaller bowl to lift it back. Instantly her hands were on it, holding it down. There was a momentary struggle, and then, with a little exasperated grunt, he raised his side, slipped it from her fingers, and carried it to the sideboard.

She looked at him and tried to make her expression contemptuous, but he only laughed. Acknowledging her defeat but disclaiming all future interest in the punch, she left the room.

III

At seven-thirty, her cheeks glowing and her high-piled hair gleaming with a suspicion of brilliantine, Evylyn descended the stairs. Mrs Ahearn, a little woman concealing a slight nervousness under red hair and an extreme Empire gown, greeted her volubly. Evylyn disliked her on the spot, but the husband she rather approved of. He had keen blue eyes and a natural gift of pleasing people that might have made him, socially, had he not so obviously committed the blunder of marrying too early in his career.

'I'm glad to know Piper's wife,' he said simply. 'It looks as though your husband and I are going to see a lot of each other in the future.'

She bowed, smiled graciously, and turned to greet the others: Milton Piper, Harold's quiet, unassertive younger brother; the two Lowries, Jessie and Tom; Irene, her own unmarried sister; and finally Joe Ambler, a confirmed bachelor and Irene's perennial beau.

Harold led the way into dinner.

'We're having a punch evening,' he announced jovially – Evylyn saw that he had already sampled his concoction – 'so there won't be any cocktails except the punch. It's m' wife's greatest achievement, Mrs Ahearn; she'll give you the recipe if you want it; but owing to a slight' – he caught his wife's eye and paused – 'to a slight indisposition, I'm responsible for this batch. Here's how!'

All through dinner there was punch, and Evylyn, noticing that Ahearn and Milton Piper and all the women were shaking their heads negatively at the maid, knew she had been right about the bowl; it was still half full. She resolved to caution Harold directly afterward, but when the women left the table Mrs Ahearn cornered her, and she found herself talking cities and dressmakers with a polite show of interest.

'We've moved around a lot,' chatted Mrs Ahearn, her red hair nodding violently. 'Oh, yes, we've never stayed so long in a town before – but I do hope we're here for good. I like it here; don't you?'

'Well, you see, I've always lived here, so, naturally –'

'Oh, that's true,' said Mrs Ahearn and laughed. 'Clarence always used to tell me he had to have a wife he could come home to and say: "Well, we're going to Chicago tomorrow to live, so pack up." I got so I never expected to live *any*where.' She laughed her little laugh again; Evylyn suspected that it was her society laugh.

'Your husband is a very able man, I imagine.'

'Oh, yes,' Mrs Ahearn assured her eagerly. 'He's brainy, Clarence is. Ideas and enthusiasm, you know. Finds out what he wants and then goes and gets it.'

Evylyn nodded. She was wondering if the men were still drinking punch back in the dining-room. Mrs Ahearn's history kept unfolding jerkily, but Evylyn had ceased to listen. The first odour of massed cigars began to drift in. It wasn't really a large house, she reflected; on an evening like this the library sometimes grew blue with smoke, and next day one had to leave the windows open for hours to air the heavy staleness out of the curtains. Perhaps this partnership might . . . she began to speculate on a new house . . .

Mrs Ahearn's voice drifted in on her:

'I really would like the recipe if you have it written down some-where –'

Then there was a sound of chairs in the dining-room and the men strolled in. Evylyn saw at once that her worst fears were realized. Harold's face was flushed and his words ran together at the ends of sentences, while Tom Lowrie lurched when he walked and narrowly missed Irene's lap when he tried to sink on to the couch beside her. He sat there blinking dazedly at the company. Evylyn found herself blinking back at him, but she saw no humour in it. Joe Ambler was smiling contentedly and purring on his cigar. Only Ahearn and Milton Piper seemed unaffected.

'It's a pretty fine town, Ahearn,' said Ambler, 'you'll find that.'

'I've found it so,' said Ahearn pleasantly.

'You find it more, Ahearn,' said Harold, nodding emphatically, ' 'f I've an'thin' do 'th it.'

He soared into a eulogy of the city, and Evylyn wondered uncomfortably if it bored everyone as it bored her. Apparently not. They were all listening attentively. Evylyn broke in at the first gap.

'Where've you been living, Mr Ahearn?' she asked interestedly. Then she remembered that Mrs Ahearn had told her, but it didn't matter. Harold mustn't talk so much. He was such an *ass* when he'd been drinking. But he plopped directly back in.

'Tell you, Ahearn. Firs' you wanna get a house up here on the hill. Get Stearne house or Ridgeway house. Wanna have it so people say: "There's Ahearn house." Solid, you know, tha's effec' it gives.'

Evylyn flushed. This didn't sound right at all. Still Ahearn didn't seem to notice anything amiss, only nodded gravely.

'Have you been looking –' But her words trailed off unheard as Harold's voice boomed on.

'Get house – tha's start. Then you get know people. Snobbish town first toward outsider, but not long – not after know you. People like you' – he indicated Ahearn and his wife with a sweeping gesture – 'all right. Cordial as an'thin' once get by first barrer-bar-barrer –' He swallowed, and then said 'barrier', repeated it masterfully.

Evylyn looked appealingly at her brother-in-law, but before he could intercede a thick mumble had come crowding out of Tom Lowrie, hindered by the dead cigar which he gripped firmly with his teeth.

'Huma uma ho huma ahdy um –'

'What?' demanded Harold earnestly.

Resignedly and with difficulty Tom removed the cigar – that is, he removed part of it, and then blew the remainder with a *whut* sound across the room, where it landed liquidly and limply in Mrs Ahearn's lap.

'Beg pardon,' he mumbled, and rose with the vague intention of going after it. Milton's hand on his coat collapsed him in time, and Mrs Ahearn not ungracefully flounced the tobacco from her skirt to the floor, never once looking at it.

'I was sayin',' continued Tom thickly, ' 'fore 'at happened' – he waved his hand apologetically toward Mrs Ahearn – 'I was sayin' I heard all truth that Country Club matter.'

Milton leaned and whispered something to him.

'Lemme 'lone,' he said petulantly, 'know what I'm doin'. 'At's what they came for.'

Evylyn sat there in a panic, trying to make her mouth form words. She saw her sister's sardonic expression and Mrs Ahearn's face turning a vivid red. Ahearn was looking down at his watch-chain, fingering it.

'I heard who's been keepin' y' out an' he's not a bit better'n you. I can fix whole damn thing up. Would've before, but I didn't know you. Harol' tol' me you felt bad about the thing –'

Milton Piper rose suddenly and awkwardly to his feet. In a second everyone was standing tensely and Milton was saying something very hurriedly about having to go early, and the Ahearns were listening with eager intentness. Then Mrs Ahearn swallowed and turned with a forced smile toward Jessie. Evylyn saw Tom lurch forward and put his hand on Ahearn's shoulder – and suddenly she was listening to a new, anxious voice at her elbow, and, turning, found Hilda, the second maid.

'Please, Mis' Piper, I tank Yulie got her hand poisoned. It's all swole up and her cheeks is hot and she's moanin' an' groanin' –'

'Julie is?' Evylyn asked sharply. The party suddenly receded. She turned quickly, sought with her eyes for Mrs Ahearn, slipped toward her.

'If you'll excuse me, Mrs –' She had momentarily forgotten the name, but she went right on: 'My little girl's been taken sick. I'll be down when I can.' She turned and ran quickly up the stairs, retaining a confused picture of rays of cigar smoke and a loud discussion in the centre of the room that seemed to be developing into an argument.

Switching on the light in the nursery, she found Julie tossing feverishly and giving out odd little cries. She put her hand against the cheeks. They were burning. With an exclamation she followed the arm down under the cover until she found the hand. Hilda was right. The whole thumb was swollen to the wrist and in the centre was a little inflamed sore. Blood-poisoning! her mind cried in terror. The bandage had come off the cut and she'd gotten something in it. She'd cut it at three o'clock – it was now nearly eleven. Eight hours. Blood-poisoning couldn't possibly develop so soon. She rushed to the phone.

Dr Martin across the street was out. Dr Foulke, their family physician, didn't answer. She racked her brains and in desperation called her throat specialist, and bit her lip furiously while he looked up the numbers of two physicians. During that interminable moment she thought she heard loud voices downstairs – but she seemed to be in another world now. After fifteen minutes she located a physician who sounded angry and sulky at being called out of bed. She ran back to the nursery and, looking at the hand, found it was somewhat more swollen.

'Oh, God!' she cried, and kneeling beside the bed began smoothing back Julie's hair over and over. With a vague idea of getting some hot water, she rose and started toward the door, but the lace of her dress caught in the bed-rail and she fell forward on her hands and knees. She struggled up and jerked frantically at the lace. The bed moved and Julie groaned. Then more quietly but with suddenly fumbling fingers she found the pleat in front, tore the whole pannier completely off, and rushed from the room.

Out in the hall she heard a single loud, insistent voice, but as she reached the head of the stairs it ceased and an outer door banged.

The music-room came into view. Only Harold and Milton were there, the former leaning against a chair, his face very pale, his collar open, and his mouth moving loosely.

'What's the matter?'

Milton looked at her anxiously.

'There was a little trouble –'

Then Harold saw her and, straightening up with an effort, began to speak.

' 'Sult m'own cousin m'own house. God damn common nouveau rish. 'Sult m'own cousin –'

'Tom had trouble with Ahearn and Harold interfered,' said Milton.

'My Lord, Milton,' cried Evylyn, 'couldn't you have done something?'

'I tried; I –'

'Julie's sick,' she interrupted; 'she's poisoned herself. Get him to bed if you can.'

Harold looked up.

'Julie sick?'

Paying no attention, Evylyn brushed by through the dining-room, catching sight, with a burst of horror, of the big punch-bowl still on the table, the liquid from melted ice in its bottom. She heard steps on the front stairs – it was Milton helping Harold up – and then a mumble: 'Why, Julie's a'righ'.'

'Don't let him go into the nursery!' she shouted.

The hours blurred into a nightmare. The doctor arrived just before midnight and within a half-hour had lanced the wound. He left at two after giving her the addresses of two nurses to call up and promising a return at half-past six. It was blood-poisoning.

At four, leaving Hilda by the bedside, she went to her room, and slipping with a shudder out of her evening dress, kicked it into a corner. She put on a house dress and returned to the nursery while Hilda went to make coffee.

Not until noon could she bring herself to look into Harold's room, but when she did it was to find him awake and staring very miserably at the ceiling. He turned blood-shot hollow eyes upon her. For a minute she hated him, couldn't speak. A husky voice came from the bed.

'What time is it?'

'Noon.'

'I made a damn fool –'

'It doesn't matter,' she said sharply. 'Julie's got blood-poisoning. They may' – she choked over the words – 'they think she'll have to lose her hand.'

'What?'

'She cut herself on that – that bowl.'

'Last night?'

'Oh, what does it matter?' she cried. 'She's got blood-poisoning. Can't you hear?'

He looked at her bewildered – sat half-way up in bed.

'I'll get dressed,' he said.

Her anger subsided and a great wave of weariness and pity for him rolled over her. After all, it was his trouble, too.

'Yes,' she answered listlessly, 'I suppose you'd better.'

IV

If Evylyn's beauty had hesitated in her early thirties it came to an abrupt decision just afterward and completely left her. A tentative outlay of wrinkles on her face suddenly deepened and flesh collected rapidly on her legs and hips and arms. Her mannerism of drawing her brows together had become an expression – it was habitual when she was reading or speaking and even while she slept. She was forty-six.

As in most families whose fortunes have gone down rather than up, she and Harold had drifted into a colourless antagonism. In repose they looked at each other with the toleration they might have felt for broken old chairs; Evylyn worried a little when he was sick and did her best to be cheerful under the wearying depression of living with a disappointed man.

Family bridge was over for the evening and she sighed with relief. She had made more mistakes than usual this evening and she didn't care. Irene shouldn't have made that remark about the infantry being particularly dangerous. There had been no letter for three weeks now, and, while this was nothing out of the ordinary, it never failed to make her nervous; naturally she hadn't known how many clubs were out.

Harold had gone upstairs, so she stepped out on the porch for a breath of fresh air. There was a bright glamour of moonlight diffusing on the sidewalks and lawns, and with a little half yawn, half laugh, she remembered one long moonlight affair of her youth. It was astonishing to think that life had once been the sum of her current love-affairs. It was now the sum of her current problems.

There was the problem of Julie – Julie was thirteen, and lately she was growing more and more sensitive about her deformity and preferred to stay always in her room reading. A few years before she had been frightened at the idea of going to school, and Evylyn could not bring herself to send her, so she grew up in her mother's shadow, a pitiful little figure with the artificial hand that she made no attempt to use but kept forlornly in her pocket. Lately she had been taking lessons in using it because Evylyn had feared she would cease to lift the arm altogether, but after the lessons, unless she made a move with it in listless obedience to her mother, the little hand would creep back to the pocket of her dress. For a while her dresses were made without pockets, but Julie had moped around the house so miserably at a loss all one month that Evylyn weakened and never tried the experiment again.

The problem of Donald had been different from the start. She had attempted vainly to keep him near her as she had tried to teach Julie to lean less on her – lately the problem of Donald had been snatched out of her hands; his division had been abroad for three months.

She yawned again – life was a thing for youth. What a happy youth she must have had! She remembered her pony, Bijou, and the trip to Europe with her mother when she was eighteen –

'Very, very complicated,' she said aloud and severely to the moon, and, stepping inside, was about to close the door when she heard a noise in the library and started.

It was Martha, the middle-aged servant: they kept only one now.

'Why, Martha!' she said in surprise.

Martha turned quickly.

'Oh, I thought you was upstairs. I was jist –'

'Is anything the matter?'

Martha hesitated.

'No; I –' She stood there fidgeting. 'It was a letter, Mrs Piper, that I put somewhere.'

'A letter? Your own letter?' asked Evylyn, switching on the light.

'No, it was to you. 'Twas this afternoon, Mrs Piper, in the last mail. The postman give it to me and then the back door-bell rang. I had it in my hand, so I must have stuck it somewhere. I thought I'd just slip in and find it.'

'What sort of a letter? From Mr Donald?'

'No, it was an advertisement, maybe, or a business letter. It was a long, narrow one, I remember.'

They began a search through the music-room, looking on trays and mantelpieces, and then through the library, feeling on the tops of rows of books. Martha paused in despair.

'I can't think where. I went straight to the kitchen. The dining-room, maybe.' She started hopefully for the dining-room, but turned suddenly at the sound of a gasp behind her. Evylyn had sat down heavily in a Morris chair, her brows drawn very close together, eyes blinking furiously.

'Are you sick?'

For a minute there was no answer. Evylyn sat there very still and Martha could see the very quick rise and fall of her bosom.

'Are you sick?' she repeated.

'No,' said Evylyn slowly, 'but I know where the letter is. Go 'way, Martha. I know.'

Wonderingly, Martha withdrew, and still Evylyn sat there, only the muscles around her eyes moving – contracting and relaxing and contracting again. She knew now where the letter was – she knew as well as if she had put it there herself. And she felt instinctively and unquestionably what the letter was. It was long and narrow like an advertisement, but up in the corner in large letters it said 'War Department' and, in smaller letters below, 'Official Business'. She knew it lay there in the big bowl with her name in ink on the outside and her soul's death within.

Rising uncertainly, she walked toward the dining-room, feeling her way along the bookcases and through the doorway. After a moment she found the light and switched it on.

There was the bowl, reflecting the electric light in crimson squares edged with black and yellow squares edged with blue, ponderous and glittering, grotesquely and triumphantly ominous. She took a step forward and paused again; another step and she would see over the top and into the inside – another step and she would see an edge of white – another step – her hands fell on the rough, cold surface –

In a moment she was tearing it open, fumbling with an obstinate fold, holding it before her while the typewritten page glared out and struck at her. Then it fluttered like a bird to the floor. The house that had seemed whirring, buzzing a moment since, was suddenly very quiet; a breath of air crept in through the open front door carrying the noise of a passing motor; she heard faint sounds from upstairs and then a grinding racket in the pipe behind the bookcases – her husband turning off a water-tap –

And in that instant it was as if this were not, after all, Donald's hour except in so far as he was a marker in the insidious contest that had gone on in sudden surges and long, listless interludes between Evylyn and this cold, malignant thing of beauty, a gift of enmity from a man whose face she had long since forgotten. With its massive, brooding passivity it lay there in the centre of her house as it had lain for years, throwing out the ice-like beams of a thousand eyes, perverse glitterings merging each into each, never ageing, never changing.

Evylyn sat down on the edge of the table and stared at it fascinated. It seemed to be smiling now, a very cruel smile, as if to say:

'You see, this time I didn't have to hurt you directly. I didn't bother. You know it was I who took your son away. You know how cold I am and how hard and how beautiful, because once you were just as cold and hard and beautiful.'

The bowl seemed suddenly to turn itself over and then to distend and swell until it became a great canopy that glittered and trembled over the room, over the house, and, as the walls melted slowly into mist, Evylyn saw that it was still moving out, out and far away from her, shutting off far horizons and suns and moons and stars except as inky blots seen faintly through it. And under it walked all the people, and the light that came through to them was refracted and twisted until shadow seemed light and light seemed shadow – until the whole panorama of the world became changed and distorted under the twinkling heaven of the bowl.

Then there came a far-away, booming voice like a low, clear bell. It came from the centre of the bowl and down the great sides to the ground and then bounced toward her eagerly.

'You see, I am fate,' it shouted, 'and stronger than your puny plans;

and I am how-things-turn-out and I am different from your little dreams, and I am the flight of time and the end of beauty and unfulfilled desire; all the accidents and imperceptions and the little minutes that shape the crucial hours are mine. I am the exception that proves no rules, the limits of your control, the condiment in the dish of life.'

The booming sound stopped; the echoes rolled away over the wide land to the edge of the bowl that bounded the world and up the great sides and back to the centre where they hummed for a moment and died. Then the great walls began slowly to bear down upon her, growing smaller and smaller, coming closer and closer as if to crush her; and as she clinched her hands and waited for the swift bruise of the cold glass the bowl gave a sudden wrench and turned over – and lay there on the sideboard, shining and inscrutable, reflecting in a hundred prisms myriad, many-coloured glints and gleams and crossings and interlacings of light.

The cold wind blew in again through the front door, and with a desperate, frantic energy Evylyn stretched both her arms around the bowl. She must be quick – she must be strong. She tightened her arms until they ached, tauted the thin strips of muscle under her soft flesh, and with a mighty effort raised it and held it. She felt the wind blow cold on her back where her dress had come apart from the strain of her effort, and as she felt it she turned toward it and staggered under the great weight out through the library and on toward the front door. She must be quick – she must be strong. The blood in her arms throbbed dully and her knees kept giving way under her, but the feel of the cool glass was good.

Out the front door she tottered and over to the stone steps, and there, summoning every fibre of her soul and body for a last effort, swung herself half around – for a second, as she tried to loose her hold, her numb fingers clung to the rough surface, and in that second she slipped and, losing balance, toppled forward with a despairing cry, her arms still around the bowl . . . down . . .

Over the way lights went on; far down the block the crash was heard, and pedestrians rushed up wonderingly; upstairs a tired man awoke from the edge of sleep and a little girl whimpered in a haunted doze. And all over the moonlit sidewalk around the still, black form, hundreds of prisms and cubes and splinters of glass reflected the light in little gleams of blue, and black edged with yellow, and yellow, and crimson edged with black.

MAY DAY

There had been a war fought and won and the great city of the conquering people was crossed with triumphal arches and vivid with thrown flowers of white, red, and rose. All through the long spring days the returning soldiers marched up the chief highway behind the strump of drums and the joyous, resonant wind of the brasses, while merchants and clerks left their bickerings and figurings and, crowding to the windows, turned their white-bunched faces gravely upon the passing battalions.

Never had there been such splendour in the great city, for the victorious war had brought plenty in its train, and the merchants had flocked thither from the South and West with their households to taste of all the luscious feasts and witness the lavish entertainments prepared – and to buy for their women furs against the next winter and bags of golden mesh and varicoloured slippers of silk and silver and rose satin and cloth of gold.

So gaily and noisily were the peace and prosperity impending hymned by the scribes and poets of the conquering people that more and more spenders had gathered from the provinces to drink the wine of excitement, and faster and faster did the merchants dispose of their trinkets and slippers until they sent up a mighty cry for more trinkets and more slippers in order that they might give in barter what was demanded of them. Some even of them flung up their hands helplessly, shouting:

'Alas! I have no more slippers! and alas! I have no more trinkets! May Heaven help me, for I know not what I shall do!'

But no one listened to their great outcry, for the throngs were far too busy – day by day, the foot-soldiers trod jauntily the highway and all exulted because the young men returning were pure and brave, sound of tooth and pink of cheek, and the young women of the land were virgins and comely both of face and of figure.

So during all this time there were many adventures that happened in the great city, and, of these, several – or perhaps one – are here set down.

I

At nine o'clock on the morning of the first of May 1919, a young man spoke to the room clerk at the Biltmore Hotel, asking if Mr Philip Dean were registered there, and if so, could he be connected with Mr Dean's rooms. The inquirer was dressed in a well-cut shabby suit. He was small, slender, and darkly handsome; his eyes were framed above with unusually long eyelashes and below with the blue semicircle of ill health, this latter effect heightened by an unnatural glow which coloured his face like a low, incessant fever.

Mr Dean was staying there. The young man was directed to a telephone at the side.

After a second his connexion was made; a sleepy voice hello'd from somewhere above.

'Mr Dean?' – this very eagerly – 'it's Gordon, Phil. It's Gordon Sterrett. I'm downstairs. I heard you were in New York and I had a hunch you'd be here.'

The sleepy voice became gradually enthusiastic. Well, how was Gordy, old boy! Well, he certainly was surprised and tickled! Would Gordy come right up, for Pete's sake!

A few minutes later Philip Dean, dressed in blue silk pyjamas, opened his door and the two young men greeted each other with a half-embarrassed exuberance. They were both about twenty-four, Yale graduates of the year before the war; but there the resemblance stopped abruptly. Dean was blond, ruddy, and rugged under his thin pyjamas. Everything about him radiated fitness and bodily comfort. He smiled frequently, showing large and prominent teeth.

'I was going to look you up,' he cried enthusiastically. 'I'm taking a couple of weeks off. If you'll sit down a sec I'll be right with you. Going to take a shower.'

As he vanished into the bathroom his visitor's dark eyes roved nervously around the room, resting for a moment on a great English travelling bag in the corner and on a family of thick silk shirts littered on the chairs amid impressive neckties and soft woollen socks.

Gordon rose and, picking up one of the shirts, gave it a minute examination. It was of very heavy silk, yellow with a pale blue stripe –

and there were nearly a dozen of them. He stared involuntarily at his own shirt-cuffs – they were ragged and linty at the edges and soiled to a faint grey. Dropping the silk shirt, he held his coat-sleeves down and worked the frayed shirt-cuffs up till they were out of sight. Then he went to the mirror and looked at himself with listless, unhappy interest. His tie, of former glory, was faded and thumb-creased – it served no longer to hide the jagged buttonholes of his collar. He thought, quite without amusement, that only three years before he had received a scattering vote in the senior elections at college for being the best-dressed man in his class.

Dean emerged from the bathroom polishing his body.

'Saw an old friend of yours last night,' he remarked. 'Passed her in the lobby and couldn't think of her name to save my neck. That girl you brought up to New Haven senior year.'

Gordon started.

'Edith Bradin? That whom you mean?'

' 'At's the one. Damn good looking. She's still sort of a pretty doll – you know what I mean: as if you touched her she'd smear.'

He surveyed his shining self complacently in the mirror, smiled faintly, exposing a section of teeth.

'She must be twenty-three anyway,' he continued.

'Twenty-two last month,' said Gordon absently.

'What? Oh, last month. Well, I imagine she's down for the Gamma Psi dance. Did you know we're having a Yale Gamma Psi dance tonight at Delmonico's? You better come up, Gordy. Half of New Haven'll probably be there. I can get you an invitation.'

Draping himself reluctantly in fresh underwear, Dean lit a cigarette and sat down by the open window, inspecting his calves and knees under the morning sunshine which poured into the room.

'Sit down, Gordy,' he suggested, 'and tell me all about what you've been doing and what you're doing now and everything.'

Gordon collapsed unexpectedly upon the bed; lay there inert and spiritless. His mouth, which habitually dropped a little open when his face was in repose, became suddenly helpless and pathetic.

'What's the matter?' asked Dean quickly.

'Oh, God!'

'What's the matter?'

'Every God damn thing in the world,' he said miserably. 'I've absolutely gone to pieces, Phil. I'm all in.'

'Huh?'

'I'm all in.' His voice was shaking.

Dean scrutinized him more closely with appraising blue eyes.

'You certainly look all shot.'

'I am. I've made a hell of mess of everything.' He paused. 'I'd better start at the beginning – or will it bore you?'

'Not at all; go on.' There was, however, a hesitant note in Dean's voice. This trip East had been planned for a holiday – to find Gordon Sterrett in trouble exasperated him a little.

'Go on,' he repeated, and then added half under his breath, 'Get it over with.'

'Well,' began Gordon unsteadily, 'I got back from France in February, went home to Harrisburg for a month, and then came down to New York to get a job – one with an export company. They fired me yesterday.'

'Fired you?'

'I'm coming to that, Phil. I want to tell you frankly. You're about the only man I can turn to in a matter like this. You won't mind if I just tell you frankly, will you, Phil?'

Dean stiffened a bit more. The pats he was bestowing on his knees grew perfunctory. He felt vaguely that he was being unfairly saddled with responsibility; he was not even sure he wanted to be told. Though never surprised at finding Gordon Sterrett in mild difficulty, there was something in this present misery that repelled him and hardened him, even though it excited his curiosity.

'Go on.'

'It's a girl.'

'Hm.' Dean resolved that nothing was going to spoil his trip. If Gordon was going to be depressing, then he'd have to see less of Gordon.

'Her name is Jewel Hudson,' went on the distressed voice from the bed. 'She used to be "pure", I guess, up to about a year ago. Lived here in New York – poor family. Her people are dead now and she lives with an old aunt. You see it was just about the time I met her that everybody began to come back from France in droves – and all I did was to welcome the newly arrived and go on parties with 'em. That's the way it started, Phil, just from being glad to see everybody and having them glad to see me.'

'You ought to've had more sense.'

'I know.' Gordon paused, and then continued listlessly. 'I'm on my own now, you know, and Phil, I can't stand being poor. Then came this darn girl. She sort of fell in love with me for a while and, though I never intended to get so involved, I'd always seem to run into her somewhere.

You can imagine the sort of work I was doing for those exporting people – of course, I always intended to draw; do illustrating magazines; there's a pile of money in it.'

'Why didn't you? You've got to buckle down if you want to make good,' suggested Dean with cold formalism.

'I tried, a little, but my stuff's crude. I've got talent, Phil; I can draw – but I just don't know how. I ought to go to art school and I can't afford it. Well, things came to a crisis about a week ago. Just as I was down to about my last dollar this girl began bothering me. She wants some money; claims she can make trouble for me if she doesn't get it.'

'Can she?'

'I'm afraid she can. That's one reason I lost my job – she kept calling up the office all the time, and that was sort of the last straw down there. She's got a letter all written to send to my family. Oh, she's got me, all right. I've got to have some money for her.'

There was an awkward pause. Gordon lay very still, his hands clenched by his side.

'I'm all in,' he continued, his voice trembling. 'I'm half crazy, Phil. If I hadn't known you were coming East, I think I'd have killed myself. I want you to lend me three hundred dollars.'

Dean's hands, which had been patting his bare ankles, were suddenly quiet – and the curious uncertainty playing between the two became taut and strained.

After a second Gordon continued:

'I've bled the family until I'm ashamed to ask for another nickel.'

Still Dean made no answer.

'Jewel says she's got to have two hundred dollars.'

'Tell her where she can go.'

'Yes, that sounds easy, but she's got a couple of drunken letters I wrote her. Unfortunately she's not at all the flabby sort of person you'd expect.'

Dean made an expression of distaste.

'I can't stand that sort of woman. You ought to have kept away.'

'I know,' admitted Gordon wearily.

'You've got to look at things as they are. If you haven't got money you've got to work and stay away from women.'

'That's easy for you to say,' began Gordon, his eyes narrowing. 'You've got all the money in the world.'

'I most certainly have not. My family keep darn close tabs on what I spend. Just because I have a little leeway I have to be extra careful not to abuse it.'

He raised the blind and let in a further flood of sunshine.

'I'm no prig, Lord knows,' he went on deliberately. 'I like pleasure – and I like a lot of it on a vacation like this, you you're – you're in awful shape. I never heard you talk just this way before. You seem to be sort of bankrupt – morally as well as financially.'

'Don't they usually go together?'

Dean shook his head impatiently.

'There's a regular aura about you that I don't understand. It's a sort of evil.'

'It's an air of worry and poverty and sleepless nights,' said Gordon, rather defiantly.

'I don't know.'

'Oh, I admit I'm depressing. I depress myself. But, my God, Phil, a week's rest and a new suit and some ready money and I'd be like – like I was. Phil, I can draw like a streak, and you know it. But half the time I haven't had the money to buy decent drawing materials – and I can't draw when I'm tired and discouraged and all in. With a little ready money I can take a few weeks off and get started.'

'How do I know you wouldn't use it on some other woman?'

'Why rub it in?' said Gordon quietly.

'I'm not rubbing it in. I hate to see you this way.'

'Will you lend me the money, Phil?'

'I can't decide right off. That's a lot of money and it'll be darn inconvenient for me.'

'It'll be hell for me if you can't – I know I'm whining, and it's all my own fault but – that doesn't change it.'

'When could you pay it back?'

This was encouraging, Gordon considered. It was probably wisest to be frank.

'Of course, I could promise to send it back next month, but – I'd better say three months. Just as soon as I start to sell drawings.'

'How do I know you'll sell any drawings?'

A new hardness in Dean's voice sent a faint chill of doubt over Gordon. Was it possible that he wouldn't get the money?

'I supposed you had a little confidence in me.'

'I did have – but when I see you like this I begin to wonder.'

'Do you suppose if I wasn't at the end of my rope I'd come to you like this? Do you think I'm enjoying it?' He broke off and bit his lip, feeling that he had better subdue the rising anger in his voice. After all, he was the suppliant.

'You seem to manage it pretty easily,' said Dean angrily. 'You put me in the position where, if I don't lend it to you, I'm a sucker – oh, yes, you do. And let me tell you it's no easy thing for me to get hold of three hundred dollars. My income isn't so big but that a slice like that won't play the deuce with it.'

He left his chair and began to dress, choosing his clothes carefully. Gordon stretched out his arms and clenched the edges of the bed, fighting back a desire to cry out. His head was splitting and whirring, his mouth was dry and bitter and he could feel the fever in his blood resolving itself into innumerable regular counts like a slow dripping from a roof.

Dean tied his tie precisely, brushed his eyebrows, and removed a piece of tobacco from his teeth with solemnity. Next he filled his cigarette case, tossed the empty box thoughtfully into the waste basket, and settled the case in his vest pocket.

'Had breakfast?' he demanded.

'No; I don't eat it any more.'

'Well, we'll go out and have some. We'll decide about that money later. I'm sick of the subject. I came East to have a good time.

'Let's go over to the Yale Club,' he continued moodily, and then added with an implied reproof: 'You've given up your job. You've got nothing else to do.'

'I'd have a lot to do if I had a little money,' said Gordon pointedly.

'Oh, for Heaven's sake drop the subject for a while! No point in glooming on my whole trip. Here, here's some money.'

He took a five-dollar bill from his wallet and tossed it over to Gordon, who folded it carefully and put it in his pocket. There was an added spot of colour in his cheeks, an added glow that was not fever. For an instant before they turned to go out their eyes met and in that instant each found something that made him lower his own glance quickly. For in that instant they quite suddenly and definitely hated each other.

II

Fifth Avenue and 44th Street swarmed with the noon crowd. The wealthy, happy sun glittered in transient gold through the thick windows of the smart shops, lighting upon mesh bags and purses and strings of pearls in grey velvet cases; upon gaudy feather fans of many colours;

upon the laces and silks of expensive dresses; upon the bad paintings and the fine period furniture in the elaborate showrooms of interior decorators.

Working-girls, in pairs and groups and swarms, loitered by the windows, choosing their future boudoirs from some resplendent display which included even a man's silk pyjamas laid domestically across the bed. They stood in front of the jewellery stores and picked out their engagement rings, and their wedding rings and their platinum wrist-watches, and then drifted on to inspect the feather fans and opera cloaks; meanwhile digesting the sandwiches and sundaes they had eaten for lunch.

All through the crowd were men in uniform, sailors from the great fleet anchored in the Hudson, soldiers with divisional insignia from Massachusetts to California wanting fearfully to be noticed, and finding the great city thoroughly fed up with soldiers unless they were nicely massed into pretty formations and uncomfortable under the weight of a pack and rifle.

Through this medley Dean and Gordon wandered; the former interested, made alert by the display of humanity at its frothiest and gaudiest; the latter reminded of how often he had been one of the crowd, tired, casually fed, over-worked, and dissipated. To Dean the struggle was significant, young, cheerful; to Gordon it was dismal, meaningless, endless.

In the Yale Club they met a group of their former classmates who greeted the visiting Dean vociferously. Sitting in a semicircle of lounges and great chairs, they had a highball all around.

Gordon found the conversation tiresome and interminable. They lunched together *en masse*, warmed with liquor as the afternoon began. They were all going to the Gamma Psi dance that night – it promised to be the best party since the war.

'Edith Bradin's coming,' said someone to Gordon. 'Didn't she used to be an old flame of yours? Aren't you both from Harrisburg?'

'Yes.' He tried to change the subject. 'I see her brother occasionally. He's sort of a socialistic nut. Runs a paper or something here in New York.'

'Not like his gay sister, eh?' continued his eager informant. 'Well, she's coming tonight with a junior named Peter Himmell.'

Gordon was to meet Jewel Hudson at eight o'clock – he had promised to have some money for her. Several times he glanced nervously at his wrist-watch. At four to his relief, Dean rose and announced that he was going over to Rivers Brothers to buy some collars and ties. But as they left the Club another of the party joined them, to Gordon's great dismay. Dean was in a jovial mood now, happy, expectant of the evening's party, faintly hilarious. Over in Rivers he chose a dozen neckties, selecting each one after long consultations with the other man. Did he think narrow ties were coming back? And wasn't it a shame that Rivers couldn't get any more Welsh Margotson collars? There never was a collar like the 'Covington'.

Gordon was in something of a panic. He wanted the money immediately. And he was now inspired also with a vague idea of attending the Gamma Psi dance. He wanted to see Edith – Edith whom he hadn't met since one romantic night at the Harrisburg Country Club just before he went to France. The affair had died, drowned in the turmoil of the war and quite forgotten in the arabesque of these three months, but a picture of her, poignant, debonair, immersed in her own inconsequential chatter, recurred to him unexpectedly and brought a hundred memories with it. It was Edith's face that he had cherished through college with a sort of detached yet affectionate admiration. He had loved to draw her – around his room had been a dozen sketches of her – playing golf, swimming – he could draw her pert, arresting profile with his eyes shut.

They left Rivers at five-thirty and paused for a moment on the sidewalk.

'Well,' said Dean genially, 'I'm all set now. Think I'll go back to the hotel and get a shave, haircut and massage.'

'Good enough,' said the other man, 'I think I'll join you.'

Gordon wondered if he was to be beaten after all. With difficulty he restrained himself from turning to the man and snarling out, 'Go on away, damn you!' In despair he suspected that perhaps Dean had spoken to him, was keeping him along in order to avoid a dispute about the money.

They went into the Biltmore – a Biltmore alive with girls – mostly from the West and South, the stellar débutantes of many cities gathered for the dance of a famous fraternity of a famous university. But to Gordon they were faces in a dream. He gathered together his forces for a last appeal, was about to come out with he knew not what, when Dean suddenly excused himself to the other man and taking Gordon's arm led him aside.

'Gordy,' he said quickly, 'I've thought the whole thing over carefully and I've decided that I can't lend you that money. I'd like to oblige you, but I don't feel I ought to – it'd put a crimp in me for a month.'

Gordon, watching him dully, wondered why he had never before noticed how much those upper teeth projected.

'– I'm mighty sorry, Gordon,' continued Dean, 'but that's the way it is.'

He took out his wallet and deliberately counted out seventy-five dollars in bills.

'Here,' he said, holding them out, 'here's seventy-five; that makes eighty altogether. That's all the actual cash I have with me, besides what I'll actually spend on the trip.'

Gordon raised his clenched hand automatically, opened it as though it were a tongs he was holding, and clenched it again on the money.

'I'll see you at the dance,' continued Dean. 'I've got to get along to the barber shop.'

'So long,' said Gordon in a strained and husky voice.

'So long.'

Dean began to smile, but seemed to change his mind. He nodded briskly and disappeared.

But Gordon stood there, his handsome face awry with distress, the roll of bills clenched tightly in his hand. Then, blinded by sudden tears, he stumbled clumsily down the Biltmore steps.

III

About nine o'clock of the same night two human beings came out of a cheap restaurant in Sixth Avenue. They were ugly, ill-nourished, devoid of all except the very lowest form of intelligence, and without even that animal exuberance that in itself brings colour into life; they were lately vermin-ridden, cold, and hungry in a dirty town of a strange land; they were poor, friendless; tossed as driftwood from their births, they would be tossed as driftwood to their deaths. They were dressed in the uniform of the United States Army, and on the shoulder of each was the insignia of a drafted division from New Jersey, landed three days before.

The taller of the two was named Carrol Key, a name hinting that in his veins, however thinly diluted by generations of degeneration, ran blood of some potentiality. But one could stare endlesssly at the long, chinless face, the dull, watery eyes, and high cheek-bones, without finding a suggestion of either ancestral worth or native resourcefulness.

His companion was swart and bandy-legged, with rat-eyes and a much-broken hooked nose. His defiant air was obviously a pretence, a weapon of protection borrowed from that world of snarl and snap, of physical bluff and physical menace in which he had always lived. His name was Gus Rose.

Leaving the café they sauntered down Sixth Avenue, wielding toothpicks with great gusto and complete detachment.

'Where to?' asked Rose, in a tone which implied that he would not be surprised if Key suggested the South Sea Islands.

'What you say we see if we can getta holda some liquor?' Prohibition was not yet. The ginger in the suggestion was caused by the law forbidding the selling of liquor to soldiers.

Rose agreed enthusiastically.

'I got an idea,' continued Key, after a moment's thought, 'I got a brother somewhere.'

'In New York?'

'Yeah. He's an old fella.' He meant that he was an elder brother. 'He's a waiter in a hash joint.'

'Maybe he can get us some.'

'I'll say he can!'

'B'lieve me, I'm goin' to get this darn uniform off me tomorra. Never get me in it again, neither. I'm goin' to get me some regular clothes.'

'Say, maybe I'm not.'

As their combined finances were something less than five dollars, this intention can be taken largely as a pleasant game of words, harmless and consoling. It seemed to please both of them, however, for they reinforced it with chuckling and mention of personages high in biblical circles, adding such further emphasis as 'Oh, boy!' 'You know!' and 'I'll say so!' repeated many times over.

The entire mental pabulum of these two men consisted of an offended nasal comment extended through the years upon the institution – army, business, or poorhouse – which kept them alive, and toward their immediate superior in that institution. Until that very morning the institution had been the 'government' and the immediate superior had been the 'Cap'n' – from these two they had glided out and were now in the vaguely uncomfortable state before they should adopt their next bondage. They were uncertain, resentful, and somewhat ill at ease. This they hid by pretending an elaborate relief at being out of the army, and by assuring each other that military discipline should never again rule their stubborn, liberty-loving wills. Yet, as a matter of fact, they would have felt more at home in a prison than in this new-found and unquestionable freedom.

Suddenly Key increased his gait. Rose, looking up and following his glance, discovered a crowd that was collecting fifty yards down the street. Key chuckled and began to run in the direction of the crowd; Rose thereupon also chuckled and his short bandy legs twinkled beside the long, awkward strides of his companion.

Reaching the outskirts of the crowd they immediately became an indistinguishable part of it. It was composed of ragged civilians somewhat the worse for liquor, and of soldiers representing many divisions and many stages of sobriety, all clustered around a gesticulating little Jew with long black whiskers, who was waving his arms and delivering an excited but succinct harangue. Key and Rose, having wedged themselves into the approximate parquet, scrutinized him with acute suspicion, as his words penetrated their common consciousness.

'– What have you got outa the war?' he was crying fiercely. 'Look arounja, look arounja! Are you rich? Have you got a lot of money offered you? – no; you're lucky if you're alive and got both your legs; you're lucky if you came back an' find your wife ain't gone off with some other fella that had the money to buy himself out of the war! That's when you're lucky! Who got anything out of it except J. P. Morgan an' John D. Rockerfeller?'

At this point the little Jew's oration was interrupted by the hostile impact of a fist upon the point of his bearded chin and he toppled backward to a sprawl on the pavement.

'God damn Bolsheviki!' cried the big soldier-blacksmith who had delivered the blow. There was a rumble of approval, the crowd closed in nearer.

The Jew staggered to his feet, and immediately went down again before a half-dozen reaching-in fists. This time he stayed down, breathing heavily, blood oozing from his lip where it was cut within and without.

There was a riot of voices, and in a minute Rose and Key found themselves flowing with the jumbled crowd down Sixth Avenue under the leadership of a thin civilian in a slouch hat and the brawny soldier who had summarily ended the oration. The crowd had marvellously swollen to formidable proportions and a stream of more non-committal citizens followed it along the sidewalks lending their moral support by intermittent huzzas.

'Where we goin'?' yelled Key to the man nearest him. His neighbour pointed up to the leader in the slouch hat.

'That guy knows where there's a lot of 'em! We're goin' to show 'em!'

'We're goin' to show 'em!' whispered Key delightedly to Rose, who repeated the phrase rapturously to a man on the other side.

Down Sixth Avenue swept the procession, joined here and there by soldiers and marines, and now and then by civilians, who came up with the inevitable cry that they were just out of the army themselves, as if presenting it as a card of admission to a newly formed Sporting and Amusement Club.

Then the procession swerved down a cross street and headed for Fifth Avenue and the word filtered here and there that they were bound for a Red meeting at Tolliver Hall.

'Where is it?'

The question went up the line and a moment later the answer floated back. Tolliver Hall was down on 10th Street. There was a bunch of other sojers who was goin' to break it up and was down there now!

But 10th Street had a faraway sound and at the word a general groan went up and a score of the procession dropped out. Among these were Rose and Key, who slowed down to a saunter and let the more enthusiastic sweep on by.

'I'd rather get some liquor,' said Key, as they halted and made their way to the sidewalk amid cries of 'Shell hole!' and 'Quitters!'

'Does your brother work around here?' asked Rose, assuming the air of one passing from the superficial to the eternal.

'He oughta,' replied Key. 'I ain't seen him for a coupla years. I been out to Pennsylvania since. Maybe he don't work at night anyhow. It's right along here. He can get us some o'right if he ain't gone.'

They found the place after a few minutes' patrol of the street – a shoddy tablecloth restaurant between Fifth Avenue and Broadway. Here Key went inside to inquire for his brother, George, while Rose waited on the sidewalk.

'He ain't here no more,' said Key emerging. 'He's a waiter up to Delmonico's.'

Rose nodded wisely, as if he'd expected as much. One should not be surprised at a capable man changing jobs occasionally. He knew a waiter once – there ensued a long conversation as they walked as to whether waiters made more in actual wages than in tips – it was decided that it depended on the social tone of the joint wherein the waiter laboured. After having given each other vivid pictures of millionaires dining at Delmonico's and throwing away fifty-dollar bills after their first quart of champagne, both men thought privately of becoming waiters. In fact, Key's narrow brow was secreting a resolution to ask his brother to get him a job.

'A waiter can drink up all the champagne those fellas leave in bottles,' suggested Rose with some relish, and then added as an afterthought, 'Oh, boy!'

By the time they reached Delmonico's it was half-past ten, and they were surprised to see a stream of taxis driving up to the door one after the other and emitting marvellous, hatless young ladies, each one attended by a stiff young gentleman in evening clothes.

'It's a party,' said Rose with some awe. 'Maybe we better not go in. He'll be busy.'

'No, he won't. He'll be o'right.'

After some hesitation they entered what appeared to them to be the least elaborate door and, indecision falling upon them immediately, stationed themselves nervously in an inconspicuous corner of the small dining-room in which they found themselves. They took off their caps and held them in their hands. A cloud of gloom fell upon them and both started when a door at one end of the room crashed open, emitting a comet-like waiter who streaked across the floor and vanished through another door on the other side.

There had been three of these lightning passages before the seekers mustered the acumen to hail a waiter. He turned, looked at them suspiciously, and then approached with soft, catlike steps, as if prepared at any moment to turn and flee.

'Say,' began Key, 'say, do you know my brother? He's a waiter here.'

'His name is Key,' annotated Rose.

Yes, the waiter knew Key. He was upstairs, he thought. There was a big dance going on in the main ballroom. He'd tell him.

Ten minutes later George Key appeared and greeted his brother with the utmost suspicion; his first and most natural thought being that he was going to be asked for money.

George was tall and weak chinned, but there his resemblance to his brother ceased. The waiter's eyes were not dull, they were alert and twinkling, and his manner was suave, indoor, and faintly superior. They exchanged formalities. George was married and had three children. He seemed fairly interested, but not impressed by the news that Carrol had been abroad in the army. This disappointed Carrol.

'George,' said the younger brother, these amenities having been disposed of, 'we want to get some booze, and they won't sell us none. Can you get us some?'

George considered.

'Sure. Maybe I can. It may be half an hour, though.'

'All right,' agreed Carrol, 'we'll wait.'

At this Rose started to sit down in a convenient chair, but was hailed to his feet by the indignant George.

'Hey! Watch out, you! Can't sit down here! This room's all set for a twelve o'clock banquet.'

'I ain't going to hurt it,' said Rose resentfully. 'I been through the delouser.'

'Never mind,' said George sternly, 'if the head waiter seen me here talkin' he'd romp all over me.'

'Oh.'

The mention of the head waiter was full explanation to the other two; they fingered their overseas caps nervously and waited for a suggestion.

'I tell you,' said George, after a pause, 'I got a place you can wait; you just come here with me.'

They followed him out the far door, through a deserted pantry and up a pair of dark winding stairs, emerging finally into a small room chiefly furnished by piles of pails and stacks of scrubbing brushes, and illuminated by a single dim electric light. There he left them, after soliciting two dollars and agreeing to return in half an hour with a quart of whisky.

'George is makin' money, I bet,' said Key gloomily as he seated himself on an inverted pail. 'I bet he's making fifty dollars a week.'

Rose nodded his head and spat.

'I bet he is too.'

'What'd he say the dance was of?'

'A lot of college fellas. Yale College.'

They both nodded solemnly at each other.

'Wonder where that crowda sojers is now?'

'I don't know. I know that's too damn long to walk for me.'

'Me too. You don't catch me walkin' that far.'

Ten minutes later restlessness seized them.

'I'm goin' to see what's out here,' said Rose, stepping cautiously towards the other door.

It was a swinging door of green baize and he pushed it open a cautious inch.

'See anything?'

For answer Rose drew in his breath sharply.

'Doggone! Here's some liquor I'll say!'

'Liquor?'

Key joined Rose at the door, and looked eagerly.

'I'll tell the world that's liquor,' he said, after a moment of concentrated gazing.

It was a room about twice as large as the one they were in – and in it was prepared a radiant feast of spirits. There were long walls of alternating bottles set along two white covered tables; whisky, gin, brandy, French and Italian vermouths, and orange juice, not to mention an array of syphons and two great empty punch-bowls. The room was as yet uninhabited.

'It's for this dance they're just starting,' whispered Key; 'hear the violins playin'? Say, boy, I wouldn't mind havin' a dance.'

They closed the door softly and exchanged a glance of mutual comprehension. There was no need of feeling each other out.

'I'd like to get my hands on a coupla those bottles,' said Rose emphatically.

'Me too.'

'Do you suppose we'd get seen?'

Key considered.

'Maybe we better wait till they start drinkin' 'em. They got 'em all laid out now, and they know how many of them there are.'

They debated this point for several minutes. Rose was all for getting his hands on a bottle now and tucking it under his coat before anyone came into the room. Key, however, advocated caution. He was afraid he might get his brother in trouble. If they waited till some of the bottles were opened it'd be all right to take one, and everybody'd think it was one of the college fellas.

While they were still engaged in argument George Key hurried through the room and, barely grunting at them, disappeared by way of the green-baize door. A minute later they heard several corks pop, and then the sound of crackling ice and splashing liquid. George was mixing the punch.

The soldiers exchanged delighted grins.

'Oh, boy!' whispered Rose.

George reappeared.

'Just keep low, boys,' he said quickly. 'I'll have your stuff for you in five minutes.'

He disappeared through the door by which he had come.

As soon as his footsteps receded down the stairs, Rose, after a cautious look, darted into the room of delights and reappeared with a bottle in his hand.

'Here's what I say,' he said, as they sat radiantly digesting their first drink. 'We'll wait till he comes up, and we'll ask him if we can't just stay here and drink what he brings us – see. We'll tell him we haven't got any place to drink it – see. Then we can sneak in there whenever there ain't nobody in that there room and tuck a bottle under our coats. We'll have enough to last us a coupla days – see?'

'Sure,' agreed Rose enthusiastically. 'Oh, boy! And if we want to we can sell it to sojers any time we want to.'

They were silent for a moment thinking rosily of this idea. Then Key reached up and unhooked the collar of his O.D. coat.

'It's hot in here, ain't it?'

Rose agreed earnestly.

'Hot as hell.'

IV

She was still quite angry when she came out of the dressing-room and crossed the intervening parlour of politeness that opened on to the hall – angry not so much at the actual happening which was, after all, the merest commonplace of her social existence, but because it had occurred on this particular night. She had no quarrel with herself. She had acted with that correct mixture of dignity and reticent pity which she always employed. She had succinctly and deftly snubbed him.

It had happened when their taxi was leaving the Biltmore – hadn't gone half a block. He had lifted his right arm awkwardly – she was on his right side – and attempted to settle it snugly around the crimson fur-trimmed opera cloak she wore. This in itself had been a mistake. It was inevitably more graceful for a young man attempting to embrace a young lady of whose acquiescence he was not certain, to first put his far arm around her. It avoided that awkward movement of raising the near arm.

His second *faux pas* was unconscious. She had spent the afternoon at the hairdresser's; the idea of any calamity overtaking her hair was extremely repugnant – yet as Peter made his unfortunate attempt the point of his elbow had just faintly brushed it. That was his second *faux pas*. Two were quite enough.

He had begun to murmur. At the first murmur she had decided that he was nothing but a college boy – Edith was twenty-two, and anyhow, this dance, first of its kind since the war, was reminding her, with the accelerating rhythm of its associations, of something else – of another dance and another man, a man for whom her feelings had been little more than a sad-eyed, adolescent mooniness. Edith Bradin was falling in love with her recollection of Gordon Sterrett.

So she came out of the dressing-room at Delmonico's and stood for a second in the doorway looking over the shoulders of a black dress in front of her at the groups of Yale men who flitted like dignified black moths around the head of the stairs. From the room she had left drifted out the heavy fragrance left by the passage to and fro of many scented young beauties – rich perfumes and the fragile memory-laden dust of fragrant powders. This odour drifting out acquired the tang of cigarette smoke in the hall, and then settled sensuously down the stairs and permeated the ballroom where the Gamma Psi dance was to be held. It was an odour she knew well, exciting, stimulating, restlessly sweet – the odour of a fashionable dance.

She thought of her own appearance. Her bare arms and shoulders were powdered to a creamy white. She knew they looked very soft and would gleam like milk against the black backs that were to silhouette them tonight. The hairdressing had been a success; her reddish mass of hair was piled and crushed and creased to an arrogant marvel of mobile curves. Her lips were finely made of deep carmine; the irises of her eyes were delicate, breakable blue, like china eyes. She was a complete, infinitely delicate, quite perfect thing of beauty, flowing in an even line from a complex coiffure to two small slim feet.

She thought of what she would say tonight at this revel, faintly presaged already by the sounds of high and low laughter and slippered footsteps, and movements of couples up and down the stairs. She would talk the language she had talked for many years – her line – made up of the current expressions, bits of journalese and college slang-strung together into an intrinsic whole, careless, faintly provocative, delicately sentimental. She smiled faintly as she heard a girl sitting on the stairs near her say: 'You don't know the half of it, dearie!'

And as she smiled her anger melted for a moment, and closing her eyes she drew in a deep breath of pleasure. She dropped her arms to her sides, until they were faintly touching the sleek sheath that covered and suggested her figure. She had never felt her own softness so much nor so enjoyed the whiteness of her own arms.

'I smell sweet,' she said to herself simply, and then came another thought – 'I'm made for love.'

She liked the sound of this and thought it again; then in inevitable succession came her new-born riot of dreams about Gordon. The twist of her imagination which, two months before, had disclosed to her her unguessed desire to see him again, seemed now to have been leading up to this dance, this hour.

For all her sleek beauty, Edith was a grave, slow-thinking girl. There was a streak in her of that same desire to ponder, of that adolescent idealism that had turned her brother socialist and pacifist. Henry Bradin had left Cornell, where he had been an instructor in economics, and had come to New York to pour the latest cures for incurable evils into the columns of a radical weekly newspaper.

Edith, less fatuously, would have been content to cure Gordon Sterrett. There was a quality of weakness in Gordon that she wanted to take care of; there was a helplessness in him that she wanted to protect. And she wanted someone she had known a long while, someone who had loved her a long while. She was a little tired; she wanted to get married. Out of a pile of letters, half a dozen pictures and as many memories, and this weariness, she had decided that next time she saw Gordon their relations were going to be changed. She would say something that would change them. There was this evening. This was her evening. All evenings were her evenings.

Then her thoughts were interrupted by a solemn undergraduate with a hurt look and an air of strained formality who presented himself before her and bowed unusually low. It was the man she had come with, Peter Himmel. He was tall and humorous, with horn-rimmed glasses and an air of attractive whimsicality. She suddenly rather disliked him – probably because he had not succeeded in kissing her.

'Well,' she began, 'are you still furious at me?'

'Not at all.'

She stepped forward and took his arm.

'I'm sorry,' she said softly. 'I don't know why I snapped out that way. I'm in a bum humour tonight for some strange reason. I'm sorry.'

'S'all right,' he mumbled, 'don't mention it.'

He felt disagreeably embarrassed. Was she rubbing in the fact of his late failure?

'It was a mistake,' she continued, on the same consciously gentle key. 'We'll both forget it.' For this he hated her.

A few minutes later they drifted out on the floor while the dozen swaying, sighing members of the specially hired jazz orchestra informed the crowded ballroom that 'if a saxophone and me are left alone why then two is compan-ee!'

A man with a moustache cut in.

'Hello,' he began reprovingly. 'You don't remember me.

'I can't just think of your name,' she said lightly – 'and I know you so well.'

'I met you up at –' His voice trailed disconsolately off as a man with very fair hair cut in. Edith murmured a conventional 'Thanks, loads – cut in later,' to the *inconnu*.

The very fair man insisted on shaking hands enthusiastically. She placed him as one of the numerous Jims of her acquaintance – last name a mystery. She remembered even that he had a peculiar rhythm in dancing and found as they started that she was right.

'Going to be here long?' he breathed confidentially.

She leaned back and looked up at him.

'Couple of weeks.'

'Where are you?'

'Biltmore. Call me up some day.'

'I mean it,' he assured her. 'I will. We'll go to tea.'

'So do I – Do.'

A dark man cut in with intense formality.

'You don't remember me, do you?' he said gravely.

'I should say I do. Your name's Harlan.'

'No-ope. Barlow.'

'Well, I knew there were two syllables anyway. You're the boy that played the ukulele so well up at Howard Marshall's house party.'

'I played – but not –'

A man with prominent teeth cut in. Edith inhaled a slight cloud of whisky. She liked men to have had something to drink; they were so much more cheerful, and appreciative, and complimentary – much easier to talk to.

'My name's Dean, Philip Dean,' he said cheerfully. 'You don't remember me, I know, but you used to come up to New Haven with a fellow I roomed with senior year, Gordon Sterrett.'

Edith looked up quickly.

'Yes, I went up with him twice – to the Pump and Slipper and the Junior prom.'

'You've seen him, of course,' said Dean carelessly. 'He's here tonight. I saw him just a minute ago.'

Edith started. Yet she had felt quite sure he would be here.

'Why no, I haven't –'

A fat man with red hair cut in.

'Hello, Edith,' he began.

'Why – hello there –'

She slipped, stumbled lightly.

'I'm sorry, dear,' she murmured mechanically.

She had seen Gordon – Gordon very white and listless, leaning against the side of a doorway, smoking and looking into the ballroom. Edith could see that his face was thin and wan – that the hand he raised to his lips with a cigarette was trembling. They were dancing quite close to him now.

'– They invite so darn many extra fellas that you –' the short man was saying.

'Hello, Gordon,' called Edith over her partner's shoulder. Her heart was pounding wildly.

His large dark eyes were fixed on her. He took a step in her direction. Her partner turned her away – she heard his voice bleating –

'– but half the stags get lit and leave before long, so –'

Then a low tone at her side.

'May I, please?'

She was dancing suddenly with Gordon; one of his arms was around her; she felt it tighten spasmodically; felt his hand on her back with the fingers spread. Her hand holding the little lace handkerchief was crushed in his.

'Why Gordon,' she began breathlessly.

'Hello, Edith.'

She slipped again – was tossed forward by her recovery until her face touched the black cloth of his dinner coat. She loved him – she knew she loved him – then for a minute there was silence while a strange feeling of uneasiness crept over her. Something was wrong.

Of a sudden her heart wrenched, and turned over as she realized what it was. He was pitiful and wretched, a little drunk, and miserably tired.

'Oh –' she cried involuntarily.

His eyes looked down at her. She saw suddenly that they were blood-streaked and rolling uncontrollably.

'Gordon,' she murmured, 'we'll sit down, I want to sit down.'

They were nearly in mid-floor, but she had seen two men start toward her from opposite sides of the room, so she halted, seized Gordon's limp hand and led him bumping through the crowd, her mouth tight shut, her face a little pale under her rouge, her eyes trembling with tears.

She found a place high up on the soft-carpeted stairs, and he sat down heavily beside her.

'Well,' he began, staring at her unsteadily, 'I certainly am glad to see you, Edith.'

She looked at him without answering. The effect of this on her was immeasurable. For years she had seen men in various stages of intoxication from uncles all the way down to chauffeurs, and her feelings had varied from amusement to disgust, but here for the first time she was seized with a new feeling – an unutterable horror.

'Gordon,' she said accusingly and almost crying, 'you look like the devil.'

He nodded. 'I've had trouble, Edith.'

'Trouble?'

'All sorts of trouble. Don't you say anything to the family, but I'm all gone to pieces. I'm a mess, Edith.'

His lower lip was sagging. He seemed scarcely to see her.

'Can't you – can't you,' she hesitated, 'can't you tell me about it, Gordon? You know I'm always interested in you.'

She bit her lip – she had intended to say something stronger, but found at the end that she couldn't bring it out.

Gordon shook his head dully. 'I can't tell you. You're a good woman. I can't tell a good woman the story.'

'Rot,' she said defiantly. 'I think it's a perfect insult to call anyone a good woman in that way. It's a slam. You've been drinking, Gordon.'

'Thanks.' He inclined his head gravely. 'Thanks for the information.'

'Why do you drink?'

'Because I'm so damn miserable.'

'Do you think drinking's going to make it any better?'

'What you doing – trying to reform me?'

'No; I'm trying to help you, Gordon. Can't you tell me about it?'

'I'm in an awful mess. Best thing you can do is to pretend not to know me.'

'Why, Gordon?'

'I'm sorry I cut in on you – it's unfair to you. You're a pure woman – and all that sort of thing. Here, I'll get someone else to dance with you.'

He rose clumsily to his feet, but she reached up and pulled him down beside her on the stairs.

'Here, Gordon. You're ridiculous. You're hurting me. You're acting like a – like a crazy man –'

'I admit it. I'm a little crazy. Something's wrong with me, Edith. There's something left me. It doesn't matter.'

'It does, tell me.'

'Just that. I was always queer – little bit different from other boys. All right in college, but now it's all wrong. Things have been snapping inside me for four months like little hooks on a dress, and it's about to come off when a few more hooks go. I'm very gradually going loony.'

He turned his eyes full on her and began to laugh, and she shrank away from him.

'What *is* the matter?'

'Just me,' he repeated. 'I'm going loony. This whole place is like a dream to me – this Delmonico's –'

As he talked she saw he had changed utterly. He wasn't at all light and gay and careless – a great lethargy and discouragement had come over him. Revulsion seized her, followed by a faint, surprising boredom. His voice seemed to come out of a great void.

'Edith,' he said, 'I used to think I was clever, talented, an artist. Now I know I'm nothing. Can't draw, Edith. Don't know why I'm telling you this.'

She nodded absently.

'I can't draw, I can't do anything. I'm poor as a church mouse.' He laughed, bitterly and rather too loud. 'I've become a damn beggar, a leech on my friends. I'm a failure. I'm poor as hell.'

Her distaste was growing. She barely nodded this time, waiting for her first possible cue to rise.

Suddenly Gordon's eyes filled with tears.

'Edith,' he said, turning to her with what was evidently a strong effort at self-control, 'I can't tell you what it means to me to know there's one person left who's interested in me.'

He reached out and patted her hand, and involuntarily she drew it away.

'It's mighty fine of you,' he repeated.

'Well,' she said slowly, looking him in the eye, 'anyone's always glad to see an old friend – but I'm sorry to see you like this, Gordon.'

There was a pause while they looked at each other and the momentary eagerness in his eyes wavered. She rose and stood looking at him, her face quite expressionless.

'Shall we dance?' she suggested, coolly.

– Love is fragile – she was thinking – but perhaps the pieces are saved, the things that hovered on lips, that might have been said. The new love-words, the tenderness learned, and treasured up for the next lover.

V

Peter Himmel, escort to the lovely Edith, was unaccustomed to being snubbed; having been snubbed, he was hurt and embarrassed, and ashamed of himself. For a matter of two months he had been on special delivery terms with Edith Bradin and knowing that the one excuse and explanation of the special delivery letter is its value in sentimental correspondence, he had believed himself quite sure of his ground. He searched in vain for any reason why she should have taken this attitude in the matter of a simple kiss.

Therefore when he was cut in on by the man with the moustache he went out into the hall and, making up a sentence, said it over to himself several times. Considerably deleted, this was it:

'Well, if any girl ever led a man on and then jolted him, she did – and she has no kick coming if I go out and get beautifully boiled.'

So he walked through the supper room into a small room adjoining it, which he had located earlier in the evening. It was a room in which there were several large bowls of punch flanked by many bottles. He took a seat beside the table which held the bottles.

At the second highball, boredom, disgust, the monotony of time, the turbidity of events, sank into a vague background before which glittering cobwebs formed. Things became reconciled to themselves, things lay quietly on their shelves; the troubles of the day arranged themselves in trim formation and at his curt wish of dismissal, marched off and disappeared. And with the departure of worry came brilliant, permeating symbolism. Edith became a flighty, negligible girl, not to be worried over; rather to be laughed at. She fitted like a figure of his own dream into the surface world forming about him. He himself became in a measure symbolic, a type of the continent bacchanal, the brilliant dreamer at play.

Then the symbolic mood faded and as he sipped his third highball his imagination yielded to the warm glow and he lapsed into a state similar to floating on his back in pleasant water. It was at this point that he noticed that a green baize door near him was open about two inches, and that through the aperture a pair of eyes were watching him intently.

'Hm,' murmured Peter calmly.

The green door closed – and then opened again – a bare half-inch this time.

'Peek-a-boo,' murmured Peter.

The door remained stationary and then he became aware of a series of tense intermittent whispers.

'One guy.'

'What's he doin'?'

'He's sittin' lookin'.'

'He better beat it off. We gotta get another li'l' bottle.'

Peter listened while the words filtered into his consciousness.

'Now this,' he thought, 'is most remarkable.'

He was excited. He was jubilant. He felt that he had stumbled upon a mystery. Affecting an elaborate carelessness he arose and walked around the table – then, turning quickly, pulled open the green door, precipitating Private Rose into the room.

Peter bowed.

'How do you do?' he said.

Private Rose set one foot slightly in front of the other, poised for fight, flight, or compromise.

'How do you do?' repeated Peter politely.

'I'm o'right.'

'Can I offer you a drink?'

Private Rose looked at him searchingly, suspecting possible sarcasm.

'O'right,' he said finally.

Peter indicated a chair.

'Sit down.'

'I got a friend,' said Rose, 'I got a friend in there.' He pointed to the green door.

'By all means let's have him in.'

Peter crossed over, opened the door and welcomed in Private Key, very suspicious and uncertain and guilty. Chairs were found and the three took their seats around the punch-bowl. Peter gave them each a highball and offered them a cigarette from his case. They accepted both with some diffidence.

'Now,' continued Peter easily, 'may I ask why you gentlemen prefer to lounge away your leisure hours in a room which is chiefly furnished, as far as I can see, with scrubbing brushes. And when the human race has progressed to the stage where seventeen thousand chairs are manufactured on every day except Sunday –' he paused. Rose and Key regarded him vacantly. 'Will you tell me,' went on Peter, 'why you choose to rest yourselves on articles intended for the transportation of water from one place to another?'

At this point Rose contributed a grunt to the conversation.

'And lastly,' finished Peter, 'will you tell me why, when you are in a building beautifully hung with enormous candelabra, you prefer to spend these evening hours under one anaemic electric light?'

Rose looked at Key; Key looked at Rose. They laughed; they laughed uproariously; they found it was impossible to look at each other without laughing. But they were not laughing with this man – they were laughing at him. To them a man who talked after this fashion was either raving drunk or raving crazy.

'You are Yale men, I presume,' said Peter, finishing his highball and preparing another.

They laughed again.

'Na-ah.'

'So? I thought perhaps you might be members of that lowly section of the university known as the Sheffield Scientific School.'

'Na-ah.'

'Hm. Well, that's too bad. No doubt you are Harvard men, anxious to preserve your incognito in this – this paradise of violet blue, as the newspapers say.'

'Na-ah,' said Key scornfully, 'we was just waitin' for somebody.'

'Ah,' exclaimed Peter rising and filling their glasses, 'very interestin'. Had a date with a scrublady, eh?'

They both denied this indignantly.

'It's all right,' Peter reasssured them, 'don't apologize. A scrublady's as good as any lady in the world. Kipling says "Any lady and Judy O'Grady under the skin." '

'Sure,' said Key, winking broadly at Rose.

'My case, for instance,' continued Peter, finishing his glass. 'I got a girl up there that's spoiled. Spoildest darn girl I ever saw. Refused to kiss me; no reason whatsoever. Led me on deliberately to think sure I want to kiss you and then plunk! Threw me over! What's the younger generation comin' to?'

'Say tha's hard luck,' said Key – 'that's awful hard luck.'

'Oh boy!' said Rose.

'Have another?' said Peter.

'We got in a sort of fight for a while,' said Key after a pause, 'but it was too far away.'

'A fight? – tha's stuff!' said Peter, seating himself unsteadily. 'Fight 'em all! I was in the army.'

'This was a Bolshevik fella.'

'Tha's stuff!' exclaimed Peter, enthusiastic. 'That's what I say! Kill the Bolshevik! Exterminate 'em!'

'We're Americuns,' said Rose, implying a sturdy, defiant patriotism.

'Sure,' said Peter. 'Greatest race in the world! We're all Americuns! Have another.'

They had another.

VI

At one o'clock a special orchestra, special even in a day of special orchestras, arrived at Delmonico's, and its members, seating themselves arrogantly around the piano, took up the burden of providing music for the Gamma Psi Fraternity. They were headed by a famous flute-player, distinguished throughout New York for his feat of standing on his head and shimmying with his shoulders while he played the latest jazz on his flute. During his performance the lights were extinguished except for the spotlight on the flute-player and another roving beam that threw flickering shadows and changing kaleidoscopic colours over the massed dancers.

Edith had danced herself into that tired, dreamy state habitual only with débutantes, a state equivalent to the glow of a noble soul after several long highballs. Her mind floated vaguely on the bosom of her music; her partners changed with the unreality of phantoms under the colourful shifting dusk, and to her present coma it seemed as if days had passed since the dance began. She had talked on many fragmentary subjects with many men. She had been kissed once and made love to six times. Earlier in the evening different undergraduates had danced with her, but now, like all the more popular girls there, she had her own entourage – that is, half a dozen gallants had singled her out or were alternating her charms with those of some other chosen beauty; they cut in on her in regular, inevitable succession.

Several times she had seen Gordon – he had been sitting a long time on the stairway with his palm to his head, his dull eyes fixed at an infinite speck on the floor before him, very depressed, he looked, and quite drunk – but Edith each time had averted her glance, hurriedly. All that seemed long ago; her mind was passive now, her senses were lulled to trance-like sleep; only her feet danced and her voice talked on in hazy sentimental banter.

But Edith was not nearly so tired as to be incapable of moral indignation when Peter Himmel cut in on her, sublimely and happily drunk. She gasped and looked up at him.

'Why, *Peter!*'

'I'm a li'l stewed, Edith.'

'Why, Peter, you're a *peach*, you are! Don't you think it's a bum way of doing – when you're with me?'

Then she smiled unwillingly for he was looking at her with owlish sentimentality varied with a silly spasmodic smile.

'Darlin' Edith,' he began earnestly, 'you know I love you, don't you?'

'You tell it well.'

'I love you – and I merely wanted you to kiss me,' he added sadly.

His embarrassment, his shame, were both gone. She was a 'mos' beautiful girl in whole worl'. Mos' beautiful eyes, like stars above. He wanted to 'pologize – firs', for presuming to try to kiss her; second, for drinking – but he'd been so discouraged 'cause he had thought she was mad at him –'

The red-fat man cut in, and looking up at Edith smiled radiantly.

'Did you bring anyone?' she asked.

No. The red-fat man was a stag.

'Well, would you mind – would it be an awful bother for you to – to take me home tonight?' (this extreme diffidence was a charming affectation on Edith's part – she knew that the red-fat man would immediately dissolve into a paroxysm of delight).

'Bother? Why, good Lord, I'd be darn glad to! You know I'd be darn glad to.'

'Thanks *loads*! You're awfully sweet.'

She glanced at her wrist-watch. It was half past one. And, as she said 'half past one' to herself, it floated vaguely into her mind that her brother had told her at luncheon that he worked in the office of his newspaper until after one-thirty every evening.

Edith turned suddenly to her current partner.

'What street is Delmonico's on, anyway?'

'Street? Oh, why Fifth Avenue, of course.'

'I mean, what cross street?'

'Why – let's see – it's on 44th Street.'

This verified what she had thought. Henry's office must be across the street and just around the corner, and it occurred to her immediately that she might slip over for a moment and surprise him, float in on him, a shimmering marvel in her new crimson opera cloak and 'cheer him up'. It was exactly the sort of thing Edith revelled in doing – an unconventional, jaunty thing. The idea reached out and gripped at her imagination – after an instant's hesitation she had decided.

'My hair is just about to tumble entirely down,' she said pleasantly to her partner; 'would you mind if I go and fix it?'

'Not at all.'

'You're a peach.'

A few minutes later, wrapped in her crimson opera cloak, she flitted down a side-stairs, her cheeks glowing with excitement at her little adventure. She ran by a couple who stood at the door – a weak-chinned waiter and an over-rouged young lady, in hot dispute – and opening the outer door stepped into the warm May night.

VII

The over-rouged young lady followed her with a brief, bitter glance – then turned again to the weak-chinned waiter and took up her argument.

'You better go up and tell him I'm here,' she said defiantly, 'or I'll go up myself.'

'No, you don't!' said George sternly.

The girl smiled sardonically.

'Oh, I don't, don't I? Well, let me tell you I know more college fellas and more of 'em know me, and are glad to take me out on a party, than you ever saw in your whole life.'

'Maybe so –'

'Maybe so,' she interrupted. 'Oh, it's all right for any of 'em like that one that just ran out – God knows where *she* went – it's all right for them that are asked here to come or go as they like – but when I want to see a friend they have some cheap, ham-slinging, bring-me-a-doughnut waiter to stand here and keep me out.'

'See here,' said the elder Key indignantly, 'I can't lose my job. Maybe this fella you're talking about doesn't want to see you.'

'Oh, he wants to see me all right.'

'Anyway, how could I find him in all that crowd?'

'Oh, he'll be there,' she asserted confidently. 'You just ask anybody for Gordon Sterrett and they'll point him out to you. They all know each other, those fellas.'

She produced a mesh bag, and taking out a dollar bill handed it to George.

'Here,' she said, 'here's a bribe. You find him and give him my message. You tell him if he isn't here in five minutes I'm coming up.'

George shook his head pessimistically, considered the question for a moment, wavered violently, and then withdrew.

In less than the allotted time Gordon came downstairs. He was drunker than he had been earlier in the evening and in a different way. The liquor seemed to have hardened on him like a crust. He was heavy and lurching – almost incoherent when he talked.

' 'Lo, Jewel,' he said thickly. 'Came right away. Jewel, I couldn't get that money. Tried my best.'

'Money nothing!' she snapped. 'You haven't been near me for ten days. What's the matter?'

He shook his head slowly.

'Been very low, Jewel. Been sick.'

'Why didn't you tell me if you were sick. I don't care about the money that bad. I didn't start bothering you about it at all until you began neglecting me.'

Again he shook his head.

'Haven't been neglecting you. Not at all.'

'Haven't! You haven't been near me for three weeks, unless you been so drunk you didn't know what you were doing.'

'Been sick, Jewel,' he repeated, turning his eyes upon her wearily.

'You're well enough to come and play with your society friends here all right. You told me you'd meet me for dinner, and you said you'd have some money for me. You didn't even bother to ring me up.'

'I couldn't get any money.'

'Haven't I just been saying that doesn't matter? I wanted to see *you*, Gordon, but you seem to prefer your somebody else.'

He denied this bitterly.

'Then get your hat and come along,' she suggested.

Gordon hesitated – and she came suddenly close to him and slipped her arms around his neck.

'Come on with me, Gordon,' she said in a half whisper. 'We'll go over to Devineries' and have a drink, and then we can go up to my apartment.'

'I can't, Jewel –'

'You can,' she said intensely.

'I'm sick as a dog!'

'Well, then, you oughtn't to stay here and dance.'

With a glance around him in which relief and despair were mingled, Gordon hesitated; then she suddenly pulled him to her and kissed him with soft pulpy lips.

'All right,' he said heavily. 'I'll get my hat.'

VIII

When Edith came out into the clear blue of the May night she found the Avenue deserted. The windows of the big shops were dark; over their doors were drawn great iron masks until they were only shadowy tombs of the late day's splendour. Glancing down towards 42nd Street she saw a commingled blur of lights from the all-night restaurants. Over on Sixth Avenue the elevated, a flare of fire, roared across the street between the glimmering parallels of light at the station and streaked along into the crisp dark. But at 44th Street it was very quiet.

Pulling her cloak close about her Edith darted across the Avenue. She started nervously as a solitary man passed her and said in a hoarse whisper – 'Where bound, kiddo?' She was reminded of a night in her childhood when she had walked around the block in her pyjamas and a dog had howled at her from a mystery-big back yard.

In a minute she had reached her destination, a two-storey, comparatively old building on 44th in the upper windows of which she thankfully detected a wisp of light. It was bright enough outside for her to make out the sign beside the window – the *New York Trumpet*. She stepped inside a dark hall and after a second saw the stairs in the corner.

Then she was in a long, low room furnished with many desks and hung on all sides with file copies of newspapers. There were only two occupants. They were sitting at different ends of the room, each wearing a green eye-shade and writing by a solitary desk light.

For a moment she stood uncertainly in the doorway, and then both men turned around simultaneously and she recognized her brother.

'Why, Edith!' He rose quickly and approached her in surprise, removing his eye-shade. He was tall, lean, and dark, with black, piercing eyes under very thick glasses. They were far-away eyes that seemed always fixed just over the head of the person to whom he was talking.

He put his hands on her arms and kissed her cheek.

'What is it?' he repeated in some alarm.

'I was at a dance across at Delmonico's, Henry,' she said excitedly, 'and I couldn't resist tearing over to see you.'

'I'm glad you did.' His alertness gave way quickly to a habitual vagueness. 'You oughtn't to be out alone at night though, ought you?'

The man at the other end of the room had been looking at them curiously, but at Henry's beckoning gesture he approached. He was loosely fat with little twinkling eyes, and, having removed his collar and tie, he gave the impression of a Middle-Western farmer on a Sunday afternoon.

'This is my sister,' said Henry. 'She dropped in to see me.'

'How do you do?' said the fat man, smiling. 'My name's Bartholomew, Miss Bradin. I know your brother has forgotten it long ago.'

Edith laughed politely.

'Well,' he continued, 'not exactly gorgeous quarters we have here, are they?'

Edith looked around the room.

'They seem very nice,' she replied. 'Where do you keep the bombs?'

'The bombs?' repeated Bartholomew, laughing. 'That's pretty good – the bombs. Did you hear her, Henry? She wants to know where we keep the bombs. Say, that's pretty good.'

Edith swung herself around on to a vacant desk and sat dangling her feet over the edge. Her brother took a seat beside her.

'Well,' he asked, absentmindedly, 'how do you like New York this trip?'

'Not bad. I'll be over at the Biltmore with the Hoyts until Sunday. Can't you come to luncheon tomorrow?'

He thought a moment.

'I'm especially busy,' he objected 'and I hate women in groups.'

'All right,' she agreed, unruffled. 'Let's you and me have luncheon together.'

'Very well.'

'I'll call for you at twelve.'

Bartholomew was obviously anxious to return to his desk, but apparently considered that it would be rude to leave without some parting pleasantry.

'Well' – he began awkwardly.

They both turned to him.

'Well, we – we had an exciting time earlier in the evening.'

The two men exchanged glances.

'You should have come earlier,' continued Bartholomew, somewhat encouraged. 'We had a regular vaudeville.'

'Did you really?'

'A serenade,' said Henry. 'A lot of soldiers gathered down there in the street and began to yell at the sign.'

'Why ?' she demanded.

'Just a crowd,' said Henry, abstractedly. 'All crowds have to howl. They didn't have anybody with much initiative in the lead, or they'd probably have forced their way in here and smashed things up.'

'Yes,' said Bartholomew, turning again to Edith, 'you should have been here.'

He seemed to consider this a sufficient cue for withdrawal, for he turned abruptly and went back to his desk.

'Are the soldiers all set against the Socialists?' demanded Edith of her brother. 'I mean do they attack you violently and all that?'

Henry replaced his eye-shade and yawned.

'The human race has come a long way,' he said casually, 'but most of us are throw-backs; the soldiers don't know what they want, or what they hate, or what they like. They're used to acting in large bodies, and they seem to have to make demonstrations. So it happens to be against us. There've been riots all over the city tonight. It's May Day, you see.'

'Was the disturbance here pretty serious?'

'Not a bit,' he said scornfully. 'About twenty-five of them stopped in the street about nine o'clock, and began to bellow at the moon.'

'Oh –' She changed the subject. 'You're glad to see me, Henry?'

'Why, sure.'

'You don't seem to be.'

'I am.'

'I suppose you think I'm a – a waster. Sort of the World's Worst Butterfly.'

Henry laughed.

'Not at all. Have a good time while you're young. Why? Do I seem like the priggish and earnest youth?'

'No –' She paused, '– but somehow I began thinking how absolutely different the party I'm on is from – from all your purposes. It seems sort of – of incongruous, doesn't it? – me being at a party like that, and you over here working for a thing that'll make that sort of party impossible ever any more, if your ideas work.'

'I don't think of it that way. You're young, and you're acting just as you were brought up to act. Go ahead – have a good time.'

Her feet, which had been idly swinging, stopped and her voice dropped a note.

'I wish you'd – you'd come back to Harrisburg and have a good time. Do you feel sure that you're on the right track –'

'You're wearing beautiful stockings,' he interrupted. 'What on earth are they?'

'They're embroidered,' she replied, glancing down. 'Aren't they cunning?' She raised her skirts and uncovered slim, silk-sheathed calves. 'Or do you disapprove of silk stockings?'

He seemed slightly exasperated, bent his dark eyes on her piercingly.

'Are you trying to make me out as criticizing you in any way, Edith?'

'Not at all –'

She paused. Bartholomew had uttered a grunt. She turned and saw that he had left his desk and was standing at the window.

'What is it?' demanded Henry.

'People,' said Bartholomew, and then after an instant: 'Whole jam of them. They're coming from Sixth Avenue.'

'People.'

The fat man pressed his nose to the pane.

'Soldiers, by God!' he said emphatically. 'I had an idea they'd come back.'

Edith jumped to her feet, and running over joined Bartholomew at the window.

'There's a lot of them!' she cried excitedly. 'Come here, Henry!'

Henry readjusted his shade, but kept his seat.

'Hadn't we better turn out the lights?' suggested Bartholomew.

'No. They'll go away in a minute.'

'They're not,' said Edith, peering from the window. 'They're not even thinking of going away. There's more of them coming. Look – there's a whole crowd turning the corner of Sixth Avenue.'

By the yellow glow and blue shadows of the street lamp she could see that the sidewalk was crowded with men. They were mostly in uniform, some sober, some enthusiastically drunk, and over the whole swept an incoherent clamour and shouting.

Henry rose, and going to the window exposed himself as a long silhouette against the office lights. Immediately the shouting became a steady yell, and a rattling fusillade of small missiles, corners of tobacco plugs, cigarette-boxes, and even pennies beat against the window. The sounds of the racket now began floating up the stairs as the folding doors revolved.

'They're coming up!' cried Bartholomew.

Edith turned anxiously to Henry.

'They're coming up, Henry.'

From downstairs in the lower hall their cries were now quite audible.

'– God damn Socialists!'

'Pro-Germans! Boche-lovers!'

'Second floor, front! Come on.'

'We'll get the sons –'

The next five minutes passed in a dream. Edith was conscious that the clamour burst suddenly upon the three of them like a cloud of rain, that there was a thunder of many feet on the stairs, that Henry had seized her arm and drawn her back towards the rear of the office. Then the door opened and an overflow of men were forced into the room – not the leaders, but simply those who happened to be in front.

'Hello, Bo!'

'Up late, ain't you?'

'You an' your girl. Damn *you*!'

She noticed that two very drunken soldiers had been forced to the front, where they wobbled fatuously – one of them was short and dark, the other was tall and weak of chin.

Henry stepped forward and raised his hand.

'Friends!' he said.

The clamour faded into a momentary stillness, punctuated with mutterings.

'Friends!' he repeated, his far-away eyes fixed over the heads of the crowd, 'you're injuring no one but yourselves by breaking in here tonight. Do we look like rich men? Do we look like Germans? I ask you in all fairness –'

'Pipe down!'

'I'll say you do!'

'Say, who's your lady friend, buddy?'

A man in civilian clothes, who had been pawing over a table, suddenly held up a newspaper.

'Here it is!' he shouted. 'They wanted the Germans to win the war!'

A new overflow from the stairs was shouldered in and of a sudden the room was full of men all closing around the pale little group at the back. Edith saw that the tall soldier with the weak chin was still in front. The short dark one had disappeared.

She edged sightly backward, stood close to the open window, through which came a clear breath of cool night air.

Then the room was a riot. She realized that the soldiers were surging forward, glimpsed the fat man swinging a chair over his head – instantly the lights went out, and she felt the push of warm bodies under rough cloth, and her ears were full of shouting and trampling and hard breathing.

A figure flashed by her out of nowhere, tottered, was edged sideways, and of a sudden disappeared helplessly out through the open window with a frightened, fragmentary cry that died staccato on the bosom of the clamour. By the faint light streaming from the building backing on the area Edith had a quick impression that it had been the tall soldier with the weak chin.

Anger rose astonishingly in her. She swung her arms wildly, edged blindly towards the thickest of the scuffling. She heard grunts, curses, the muffled impacts of fists.

'Henry!' she called frantically, 'Henry!'

Then, it was minutes later, she felt suddenly that there were other figures in the room. She heard a voice, deep, bullying, authoritative; she saw yellow rays of light sweeping here and there in the fracas. The cries became more scattered. The scuffling increased and then stopped.

Suddenly the lights were on and the room was full of policemen, clubbing left and right. The deep voice boomed out:

'Here now! Here now! Here now!'

And then:

'Quiet down and get out! Here now!'

The room seemed to empty like a wash-bowl. A policeman fast-grappled in the corner released his hold on his soldier antagonist and started him with a shove towards the door. The deep voice continued. Edith perceived now that it came from a bull-necked police captain standing near the door.

'Here now! This is no way! One of your own sojers got shoved out of the back window an' killed hisself!'

'Henry!' called Edith, 'Henry!'

She beat wildly with her fists on the back of the man in front of her; she brushed between two others; fought, shrieked, and beat her way to a very pale figure sitting on the floor close to a desk.

'Henry,' she cried passionately, 'what's the matter? What's the matter? Did they hurt you?'

His eyes were shut. He groaned and then looking up said disgustedly –

'They broke my leg. My God, the fools!'

'Here now!' called the police captain. 'Here now! Here now!'

IX

'Childs', 59th Street', at eight o'clock of any morning differs from its sisters by less than the width of their marble tables or the degree of polish on the frying-pans. You will see there a crowd of poor people with sleep in the corners of their eyes, trying to look straight before them at their food so as not to see the other poor people. But Childs', 59th, four hours earlier is quite unlike any Childs' restaurant from Portland, Oregon, to Portland, Maine. Within its pale but sanitary walls one finds a noisy medley of chorus girls, college boys, débutantes, rakes, *filles de joie* – a not unrepresentative mixture of the gayest of Broadway, and even of Fifth Avenue.

In the early morning of May the second it was unusually full. Over the marble-topped tables were bent the excited faces of flappers whose fathers owned individual villages. They were eating buckwheat cakes and scrambled eggs with relish and gusto, an accomplishment that it would have been utterly impossible for them to repeat in the same place four hours later.

Almost the entire crowd were from the Gamma Psi dance at Delmonico's except for several chorus girls from a midnight revue who sat at a side table and wished they'd taken off a little more make-up after the show. Here and there a drab, mouse-like figure, desperately out of place, watched the butterflies with a weary puzzled curiosity. But the drab figure was the exception. This was the morning after May Day, and celebration was still in the air.

Gus Rose, sober but a little dazed, must be classed as one of the drab figures. How he had got himself from 44th Street to 59th Street after the riot was only a hazy half-memory. He had seen the body of Carrol Key put in an ambulance and driven off, and then he had started uptown with two or three soldiers. Somewhere between 44th Street and 59th Street the other soldiers had met some women and disappeared. Rose had wandered to Columbus Circle and chosen the gleaming lights of Childs' to minister to his craving for coffee and doughnuts. He walked in and sat down.

All around him floated airy, inconsequential chatter and high-pitched laughter. At first he failed to understand, but after a puzzled five minutes he realized that this was the aftermath of some gay party. Here and there a restless, hilarious young man wandered fraternally and familiarly between the tables, shaking hands indiscriminately and pausing occasionally for a facetious chat, while excited waiters, bearing cakes and eggs aloft, swore at him silently, and bumped him out of the way. To Rose, seated at the most inconspicuous and least crowded table, the whole scene was a colourful circus of beauty and riotous pleasure.

He became gradually aware, after a few moments, that the couple seated diagonally across from him, with their backs to the crowd, were not the least interesting pair in the room. The man was drunk. He wore a dinner coat with a dishevelled tie and shirt swollen by spillings of water and wine. His eyes, dim and bloodshot, roved unnaturally from side to side. His breath came short between his lips.

'He's been on a spree!' thought Rose.

The woman was almost if not quite sober. She was pretty, with dark eyes and feverish high colour, and she kept her active eyes fixed on her companion with the alertness of a hawk. From time to time she would lean and whisper intently to him, and he would answer by inclining his head heavily or by a particularly ghoulish and repellent wink.

Rose scrutinized them dumbly for some minutes, until the woman gave him a quick, resentful look; then he shifted his gaze to two of the most conspicuously hilarious of the promenaders who were on a protracted circuit of the tables. To his surprise he recognized in one of them the young man by whom he had been so ludicrously entertained at Delmonico's. This started him thinking of Key with a vague sentimentality, not unmixed with awe. Key was dead. He had fallen thirty-five feet and split his skull like a cracked coconut.

'He was a darn good guy,' thought Rose mournfully. 'He was a darn good guy, o'right. That was awful hard luck about him.'

The two promenaders approached and started down between Rose's table and the next, addressing friends and strangers alike with jovial familiarity. Suddenly Rose saw the fair-haired one with the prominent teeth stop, look unsteadily at the man and girl opposite, and then begin to move his head disapprovingly from side to side.

The man with the blood-shot eyes looked up.

'Gordy,' said the promenader with the prominent teeth, 'Gordy.'

Prominent Teeth shook his fingers pessimistically at the pair, giving the woman a glance of aloof condemnation.

'What'd I tell you Gordy?'

Gordon stirred in his seat.

'Go to hell!' he said.

Dean continued to stand there shaking his finger. The woman began to get angry.

'You go away!' she cried fiercely. 'You're drunk, that's what you are!'

'So's he,' suggested Dean, staying the motion of his finger and pointing it at Gordon.

Peter Himmel ambled up, owlish now and oratorically inclined.

'Here now,' he began, as if called upon to deal with some petty dispute between children. 'Wha's all trouble?'

'You take your friend away,' said Jewel tartly. 'He's bothering us.'

'What's 'at?'

'You heard me!' she said shrilly. 'I said to take your drunken friend away.'

Her rising voice rang out above the clatter of the restaurant and a waiter came hurrying up.

'You gotta be more quiet!'

'That fella's drunk,' she cried. 'He's insulting us.'

'Ah-ha, Gordy,' persisted the accused. 'What'd I tell you.' He turned to the waiter. 'Gordy an' I friends. Been tryin' help him, haven't I, Gordy?'

Gordy looked up.

'Help me? Hell, no!'

Jewel rose suddenly, and seizing Gordon's arm assisted him to his feet.

'Come on, Gordy!' she said, leaning towards him and speaking in a half whisper. 'Let's get out of here. This fella's got a mean drunk on.'

Gordon allowed himself to be urged to his feet and started towards the door. Jewel turned for a second and addressed the provoker of their flight.

'I know all about you!' she said fiercely. 'Nice friend, you are, I'll say. He told me about you.'

Then she seized Gordon's arm, and together they made their way through the curious crowd, paid their check, and went out.

'You'll have to sit down,' said the waiter to Peter after they had gone.

'What's 'at? Sit down?'

'Yes – or get out.'

Peter turned to Dean.

'Come on,' he suggested. 'Let's beat up this waiter.'

'All right.'

They advanced towards him, their faces grown stern. The waiter retreated.

Peter suddenly reached over to a plate on the table beside him and picking up a handful of hash tossed it into the air. It descended as a languid parabola in snowflake effect on the heads of those near by.

'Hey! Ease up!'

'Put him out!'

'Sit down, Peter!'

'Cut out that stuff!'

Peter laughed and bowed.

'Thank you for your kind applause, ladies and gents. If someone will lend me some more hash and a tall hat we will go on with the act.'

The bouncer hustled up.

'You've gotta get out!' he said to Peter.

'Hell, no!'

'He's my friend!' put in Dean indignantly.

A crowd of waiters were gathering. 'Put him out!'

'Better go, Peter.'

There was a short struggle and the two were edged and pushed towards the door.

'I got a hat and coat here!' cried Peter.

'Well, go get 'em and be spry about it!'

The bouncer released his hold on Peter, who, adopting a ludicrous air of extreme cunning, rushed immediately around to the other table, where he burst into derisive laughter and thumbed his nose at the exasperated waiters.

'Think I just better wait a l'il' longer,' he announced.

The chase began. Four waiters were sent around one way and four another. Dean caught hold of two of them by the coat, and another struggle took place before the pursuit of Peter could be resumed; he was finally pinioned after overturning a sugar-bowl and several cups of coffee. A fresh argument ensued at the cashier's desk, where Peter attempted to buy another dish of hash to take with him and throw at policemen.

But the commotion upon his exit proper was dwarfed by another phenomenon which drew admiring glances and a prolonged involuntary 'Oh-h-h!' from every person in the restaurant.

The great plate-glass front had turned to a deep creamy blue, the colour of a Maxfield Parrish moonlight – a blue that seemed to press close upon the pane as if to crowd its way into the restaurant. Dawn had come up in Columbus Circle, magical, breathless dawn, silhouetting the great statue of the immortal Christopher, and mingling in a curious and uncanny manner with the fading yellow electric light inside.

X

Mr In and Mr Out are not listed by the census-taker. You will search for them in vain through the social register or the births, marriages, and deaths, or the grocer's credit list. Oblivion has swallowed them and the testimony that they ever existed at all is vague and shadowy, and inadmissible in a court of law. Yet I have it upon the best authority that for a brief space Mr In and Mr Out lived, breathed, answered to their names, and radiated vivid personalities of their own.

During the brief span of their lives they walked in their native garments down the great highway of a great nation; were laughed at, sworn at, chased, and fled from. Then they passed and were heard of no more.

They were already taking form dimly, when a taxicab with the top open breezed down Broadway in the faintest glimmer of May dawn. In this car sat the souls of Mr In and Mr Out discussing with amazement the blue light that had so precipitately coloured the sky behind the statue of Christopher Columbus, discussing with bewilderment the old, grey faces of the early risers which skimmed palely along the street like blown bits of paper on a grey lake. They were agreed on all things, from the absurdity of the bouncer in Childs' to the absurdity of the business of life. They were dizzy with the extreme maudlin happiness that the morning had awakened in their glowing souls. Indeed, so fresh and vigorous was their pleasure in living that they felt it should be expressed by loud cries.

'Ye-ow-ow!' hooted Peter, making a megaphone with his hands – and Dean joined in with a call that, though equally significant and symbolic, derived its resonance from its very inarticulateness.

'Yo-ho! Yea! Yoho! Yo-buba!'

53rd Street was a bus with a dark, bobbed-hair beauty atop; 52nd was a street cleaner who dodged, escaped, and sent up a yell of, 'Look where you're aimin'!' in a pained and grieved voice. At 50th Street a group of men on a very white sidewalk in front of a very white building turned to stare after them, and shouted:

'Some party, boys!'

At 49th Street Peter turned to Dean. 'Beautiful morning,' he said gravely, squinting up his owlish eyes.

'Probably is.'

'Go get some breakfast, hey?'

Dean agreed – with additions.

'Breakfast and liquor.'

'Breakfast and liquor,' repeated Peter, and they looked at each other, nodding. 'That's logical.'

Then they both burst into loud laughter.

'Breakfast and liquor! Oh, gosh!'

'No such thing,' announced Peter.

'Don't serve it? Ne'mind. We force 'em serve it. Bring pressure bear.'

'Bring logic bear.'

The taxi cut suddenly off Broadway, sailed along a cross street, and stopped in front of a heavy tomb-like building in Fifth Avenue.

'What's idea?'

The taxi-driver informed them that this was Delmonico's.

This was somewhat puzzling. They were forced to devote several minutes to intense concentration, for if such an order had been given there must have been a reason for it.

'Somep'm 'bouta coat,' suggested the taxi-man.

That was it. Peter's overcoat and hat. He had left them at Delmonico's. Having decided this, they disembarked from the taxi and strolled towards the entrance arm in arm.

'Hey!' said the taxi-driver.

'Huh?'

'You better pay me.'

They shook their heads in shocked negation.

'Later, not now – we give orders, you wait.'

The taxi-driver objected; he wanted his money now. With a scornful condescension of men exercising tremendous self-control they paid him.

Inside Peter groped in vain through a dim, deserted check-room in search of his coat and derby.

'Gone, I guess. Somebody stole it.'

'Some Sheff student.'

'All probability.'

'Never mind,' said Dean, nobly. 'I'll leave mine here too – then we'll both be dressed the same.'

He removed his overcoat and hat and was hanging them up when his roving glance was caught and held magnetically by two large squares of cardboard tacked to the two coat-room doors. The one on the left-hand bore the word 'In' in big black letters, and the one on the right-hand door flaunted the equally emphatic word 'Out'.

'Look!' he exclaimed happily –

Peter's eyes followed his pointing finger.

'What?'

'Look at the signs. Let's take 'em.'

'Good idea.'

'Probably pair very rare an' valuable signs. Probably come in handy.'

Peter removed the left-hand sign from the door and endeavoured to conceal it about his person. The sign being of considerable proportions, this was a matter of some difficulty. An idea flung itself at him, and with an air of dignified mystery he turned his back. After an instant he wheeled dramatically around, and stretching out his arms displayed himself to the admiring Dean. He had inserted the sign in his vest, completely covering his shirt front. In effect, the word 'In' had been painted upon his shirt in large black letters.

'Yoho!' cheered Dean. 'Mister In.'

He inserted his own sign in like manner.

'Mister Out!' he announced triumphantly. 'Mr In meet Mr Out.'

They advanced and shook hands. Again laughter overcame them and they rocked in a shaken spasm of mirth.

'Yoho!'

'We probably get a flock of breakfast.'

'We'll go – go to the Commodore.'

Arm in arm they sallied out the door, and turning east in 44th Street set out for the Commodore.

As they came out a short dark soldier, very pale and tired, who had been wandering listlessly along the sidewalk, turned to look at them.

He started over as though to address them, but as they immediately bent on him glances of withering unrecognition, he waited until they had started unsteadily down the street, and then followed at about forty paces, chuckling to himself and saying, 'Oh, boy!' over and over under his breath, in delighted, anticipatory tones.

Mr In and Mr Out were meanwhile exchanging pleasantries concerning their future plans.

'We want liquor; we want breakfast. Neither without the other. One and indivisible.'

'We want both 'em!'

'Both 'em!'

It was quite light now, and passers-by began to bend curious eyes on the pair. Obviously they were engaged in a discussion which afforded each of them intense amusement, for occasionally a fit of laughter would seize upon them so violently that, still with their arms interlocked, they would bend nearly double.

Reaching the Commodore, they exchanged a few spicy epigrams

with the sleepy-eyed doorman, navigated the revolving door with some difficulty, and then made their way through a thinly populated but startled lobby to the dining-room, where a puzzled waiter showed them an obscure table in a corner. They studied the bill of fare helplessly, telling over the items to each other in puzzled mumbles.

'Don't see any liquor here,' said Peter reproachfully.

The waiter became audible but unintelligible.

'Repeat,' continued Peter, with patient tolerance, 'that there seems to be unexplained and quite distasteful lack of liquor upon bill of fare.'

'Here!' said Dean confidently, 'let me handle him.' He turned to the waiter – 'Bring us – bring us –' he scanned the bill of fare anxiously. 'Bring us a quart of champagne and a – a – probably ham sandwich.'

The waiter looked doubtful.

'Bring it!' roared Mr In and Mr Out in chorus.

The waiter coughed and disappeared. There was a short wait during which they were subjected without their knowledge to a careful scrutiny by the head waiter. Then the champagne arrived, and at the sight of it Mr In and Mr Out became jubilant.

'Imagine their objecting to us having champagne for breakfast – jus' imagine.'

They both concentrated upon the vision of such an awesome possibility, but the feat was too much for them. It was impossible for their joint imaginations to conjure up a world where anyone might object to anyone else having champagne for breakfast. The waiter drew the cork with an enormous *pop* – and their glasses immediately foamed with pale yellow froth.

'Here's health, Mr In.'

'Here's the same to you, Mr Out.'

The waiter withdrew; the minutes passed; the champagne became low in the bottle.

'It's – it's mortifying,' said Dean suddenly.

'Wha's mortifying?'

'The idea their objecting us having champagne breakfast.'

'Mortifying?' Peter considered. 'Yes, tha's word – mortifying.'

Again they collapsed into laughter, howled, swayed, rocked back and forth in their chairs, repeating the word 'mortifying' over and over to each other – each repetition seeming to make it only more brilliantly absurd.

After a few more gorgeous minutes they decided on another quart. Their anxious waiter consulted his immediate superior, and this discreet person gave implicit instructions that no more champagne should be served. Their check was brought.

Five minutes later, arm in arm, they left the Commodore and made their way through a curious, staring crowd along 42nd Street, and up Vanderbilt Avenue to the Biltmore. There, with sudden cunning, they rose to the occasion and traversed the lobby, walking fast and standing unnaturally erect.

Once in the dining-room they repeated their performance. They were torn between intermittent convulsive laughter and sudden spasmodic discussions of politics, college, and the sunny state of their dispositions. Their watches told them it was now nine o'clock, and a dim idea was born in them that they were on a memorable party, something that they would remember always. They lingered over the second bottle. Either of them had only to mention the word 'mortifying' to send them both into riotous gasps. The dining-room was whirring and shifting now; a curious lightness permeated and rarefied the heavy air.

They paid their check and walked out into the lobby.

It was at this moment that the exterior doors revolved for the thousandth time that morning, and admitted into the lobby a very pale young beauty with dark circles under her eyes, attired in a much-rumpled evening dress. She was accompanied by a plain stout man, obviously not an appropriate escort.

At the top of the stairs this couple encountered Mr In and Mr Out.

'Edith,' began Mr In, stepping towards her hilariously and making a sweeping bow, 'darling, good morning.'

The stout man glanced questioningly at Edith, as if merely asking her permission to throw this man summarily out of the way.

' 'Scuse familiarity,' added Peter, as an afterthought. 'Edith, good morning.'

He seized Dean's elbow and impelled him into the foreground.

'Meet Mr Out, Edith, my bes' frien'. Inseparable. Mr In and Mr Out.'

Mr Out advanced and bowed; in fact he advanced so far and bowed so low that he tipped slightly forward and only kept his balance by placing a hand lightly on Edith's shoulder.

'I'm Mr Out, Edith,' he mumbled pleasantly, 'S'misterin Misterout.'

' 'Smisterinanout,' said Peter proudly.

But Edith stared straight by them, her eyes fixed on some infinite speck in the gallery above her. She nodded slightly to the stout man, who advanced bull-like and with a sturdy brisk gesture pushed Mr In and Mr Out to either side. Through this alley he and Edith walked.

But ten paces farther on Edith stopped again – stopped and pointed to a short, dark soldier who was eyeing the crowd in general, and the tableau of Mr In and Mr Out in particular, with a sort of puzzled, spell-bound awe.

'There,' cried Edith. 'See there!'

Her voice rose, became somewhat shrill. Her pointing finger shook slightly.

'There's the soldier who broke my brother's leg.'

There were a dozen exclamations; a man in a cutaway coat left his place near the desk and advanced alertly; the stout person made a sort of lightning-like spring towards the short dark soldier, and then the lobby closed around the little group and blotted them from the sight of Mr In and Mr Out.

But to Mr In and Mr Out this event was merely a particoloured iridescent segment of a whirring, spinning world.

They heard loud voices; they saw the stout man spring; the picture suddenly blurred.

Then they were in an elevator bound skyward.

'What floor, please?' said the elevator man.

'Any floor,' said Mr In.

'Top floor,' said Mr Out.

'This is the top floor,' said the elevator man.

'Have another floor put on,' said Mr Out.

'Higher,' said Mr In.

'Heaven,' said Mr Out.

XI

In a bedroom of a small hotel just off Sixth Avenue Gordon Sterrett awoke with a pain in the back of his head and a sick throbbing in all his veins. He looked at the dusky grey shadows in the corners of the room and at a raw place on a large leather chair in the corner where it had long been in use. He saw clothes dishevelled, rumpled clothes on the floor and he smelt stale cigarette smoke and stale liquor. The windows were tight shut. Outside the bright sunlight had thrown a dust-filled beam across the siil – a beam broken by the head of the wide wooden bed in which he had slept. He lay very quiet – comatose, drugged, his eyes wide, his mind clicking wildly like an unoiled machine.

It must have been thirty seconds after he perceived the sunbeam with the dust on it and the rip on the large leather chair that he had the sense of life close beside him, and it was another thirty seconds after that before he realized he was irrevocably married to Jewel Hudson.

He went out half an hour later and bought a revolver at a sporting goods store. Then he took a taxi to the room where he had been living on East 27th Street, and, leaning across the table that held his drawing materials, fired a cartridge into his head just behind the temple.

THE DIAMOND
AS BIG AS THE RITZ

I

John T. Unger came from a family that had been well known in Hades –
a small town on the Mississippi River – for several generations. John's
father had held the amateur golf championship through many a heated
contest; Mrs Unger was known 'from hot-box to hot-bed', as the local
phrase went, for her political addresses; and young John T. Unger, who
had just turned sixteen, had danced all the latest dances from New York
before he put on long trousers. And now, for a certain time, he was to
be away from home. That respect for a New England education which
is the bane of all provincial places, which drains them yearly of their
most promising young men, had seized upon his parents. Nothing would
suit them but that he should go to St Midas's School near Boston –
Hades was too small to hold their darling and gifted son.

Now in Hades – as you know if you ever have been there – the names
of the more fashionable preparatory schools and colleges mean very
little. The inhabitants have been so long out of the world that, though
they make a show of keeping up to date in dress and manners and
literature, they depend to a great extent on hearsay, and a function that
in Hades would be considered elaborate would doubtless be hailed by a
Chicago beef-princess as 'perhaps a little tacky'.

John T. Unger was on the eve of departure. Mrs Unger, with maternal
fatuity, packed his trunks full of linen suits and electric fans, and Mr
Unger presented his son with an asbestos pocket-book stuffed with
money.

'Remember, you are always welcome here,' he said. 'You can be sure,
boy, that we'll keep the home fires burning.'

'I know,' answered John huskily.

'Don't forget who you are and where you come from,' continued his
father proudly, 'and you can do nothing to harm you. You are an
Unger – from Hades.'

So the old man and the young shook hands and John walked away

with tears streaming from his eyes. Ten minutes later he had passed
outside the city limits, and he stopped to glance back for the last time.
Over the gates the old-fashioned Victorian motto seemed strangely
attractive to him. His father had tried time and time again to have it
changed to something with a little more push and verve about it, such
as 'Hades – Your Opportunity', or else a plain 'Welcome' sign set over
a hearty handshake pricked out in electric lights. The old motto was a
little depressing, Mr Unger had thought – but now . . .

So John took his look and then set his face resolutely towards his
destination. And, as he turned away, the lights of Hades against the sky
seemed full of a warm and passionate beauty.

St Midas's School is half an hour from Boston in a Rolls-Pierce motor-
car. The actual distance will never be known, for no one, except John
T. Unger, had ever arrived there save in a Rolls-Pierce and probably no
one ever will again. St Midas's is the most expensive and the most
exclusive boys' preparatory school in the world.

John's first two years there passed pleasantly. The fathers of all
the boys were money-kings and John spent his summers visiting at
fashionable resorts. While he was very fond of all the boys he visited,
their fathers struck him as being much of a piece, and in his boyish way
he often wondered at their exceeding sameness. When he told them
where his home was they would ask jovially, 'Pretty hot down there?'
and John would muster a faint smile and answer, 'It certainly is.' His
response would have been heartier had they not all made this joke – at
best varying it with, 'Is it hot enough for you down there?' which he
hated just as much.

In the middle of his second year at school, a quiet, handsome boy
named Percy Washington had been put in John's form. The newcomer
was pleasant in his manner and exceedingly well dressed even for St
Midas's, but for some reason he kept aloof from the other boys. The only
person with whom he was intimate was John T. Unger, but even to John
he was entirely uncommunicative concerning his home or his family.
That he was wealthy went without saying, but beyond a few such
deductions John knew little of his friend, so it promised rich confectionery
for his curiosity when Percy invited him to spend the summer at his
home 'in the West'. He accepted, without hesitation.

It was only when they were in the train that Percy became, for the
first time, rather communicative. One day while they were eating lunch
in the dining-car and discussing the imperfect characters of several of

the boys at school, Percy suddenly changed his tone and made an abrupt remark.

'My father,' he said, 'is by far the richest man in the world.'

'Oh,' said John, politely. He could think of no answer to make to this confidence. He considered 'That's very nice', but it sounded hollow and was on the point of saying 'Really?' but refrained since it would seem to question Percy's statement. And such an astounding statement could scarcely be questioned.

'By far the richest,' repeated Percy.

'I was reading in the *World Almanack*,' began John, 'that there was one man in America with an income of over five million a year and four men with incomes of over three million a year, and –'

'Oh, they're nothing,' Percy's mouth was a half-moon of scorn. 'Catch-penny capitalists, financial small-fry, petty merchants, and money-lenders. My father could buy them out and not know he'd done it.'

'But how does he –'

'Why haven't they put down *his* income tax? Because he doesn't pay any. At least he pays a little one – but he doesn't pay any on his *real* income.'

'He must be very rich,' said John simply. 'I'm glad. I like very rich people.'

'The richer a fella is, the better I like him.' There was a look of passionate frankness upon his dark face. 'I visited the Schnlitzer-Murphys last Easter. Vivian Schnlitzer-Murphy had rubies as big as hen's eggs, and sapphires that were like globes with lights inside them –'

'I love jewels,' agreed Percy enthusiastically. 'Of course I wouldn't want anyone at school to know about it, but I've got quite a collection myself. I used to collect them instead of stamps.'

'And diamonds,' continued John eagerly. 'The Schnlitzer-Murphys had diamonds as big as walnuts –'

'That's nothing.' Percy had leaned forward and dropped his voice to a low whisper. 'That's nothing at all. My father has a diamond bigger than the Ritz-Carlton Hotel.'

II

The Montana sunset lay between two mountains like a gigantic bruise from which dark arteries spread themselves over a poisoned sky. An immense distance under the sky crouched the village of Fish, minute, dismal, and forgotten. There were twelve men, so it was said, in the village of Fish, twelve sombre and inexplicable souls who sucked a lean milk from the almost literally bare rock upon which a mysterious populatory force had begotten them. They had become a race apart, these twelve men of Fish, like some species developed by an early whim of nature, which on second thought had abandoned them to struggle and extermination.

Out of the blue-black bruise in the distance crept a long line of moving lights upon the desolation of the land, and the twelve men of Fish gathered like ghosts at the shanty depot to watch the passing of the seven o'clock train, the Transcontinental Express from Chicago. Six times or so a year the Transcontinental Express, through some inconceivable jurisdiction, stopped at the village of Fish, and when this occurred a figure or so would disembark, mount into a buggy that always appeared from out of the dusk, and drive off towards the bruised sunset. The observation of this pointless and preposterous phenomenon had become a sort of cult among the men of Fish. To observe, that was all; there remained in them none of the vital quality of illusion which would make them wonder or speculate, else a religion might have grown up around these mysterious visitations. But the men of Fish were beyond all religion – the barest and most savage tenets of even Christianity could gain no foothold on that barren rock – so there was no altar, no priest, no sacrifice; only each night at seven the silent concourse by the shanty depot, a congregation who lifted up a prayer of dim, anaemic wonder.

On this June night, the Great Brakeman, whom, had they deified anyone, they might well have chosen as their celestial protagonist, had ordained that the seven o'clock train should leave its human (or inhuman) deposit at Fish. At two minutes after seven Percy Washington and John T. Unger disembarked, hurried past the spellbound, the agape, the fearsome eyes of the twelve men of Fish, mounted into a buggy which had obviously appeared from nowhere, and drove away.

After half an hour, when the twilight had coagulated into dark, the silent Negro who was driving the buggy hailed an opaque body somewhere ahead of them in the gloom. In response to his cry, it turned upon them a luminous disk which regarded them like a malignant eye out of the unfathomable night. As they came closer, John saw that it was the tail-light of an immense automobile, larger and more magnificent than any he had ever seen. Its body was of gleaming metal richer than nickel and lighter than silver, and the hubs of the wheels were studded with iridescent geometric figures of green and yellow – John did not dare to guess whether they were glass or jewel.

Two Negroes, dressed in glittering livery such as one sees in pictures of royal processions in London, were standing at attention beside the car and as the two young men dismounted from the buggy they were greeted in some language which the guest could not understand, but which seemed to be an extreme form of the Southern Negro's dialect.

'Get in,' said Percy to his friend, as their trunks were tossed to the ebony roof of the limousine. 'Sorry we had to bring you this far in that buggy, but of course it wouldn't do for the people on the train or those Godforsaken fellas in Fish to see this automobile.'

'Gosh! What a car!' This ejaculation was provoked by its interior. John saw that the upholstery consisted of a thousand minute and exquisite tapestries of silk woven with jewels and embroideries, and set upon a background of cloth of gold. The two armchair seats in which the boys luxuriated were covered with stuff that resembled duvetyn, but seemed woven in numberless colours of the ends of ostrich feathers.

'What a car!' cried John again, in amazement.

'This thing?' Percy laughed. 'Why, it's just an old junk we use for a station wagon.'

By this time they were gliding along through the darkness towards the break between the two mountains.

'We'll be there in an hour and a half,' said Percy, looking at the clock. 'I may as well tell you it's not going to be like anything you ever saw before.'

If the car was any indication of what John would see, he was prepared to be astonished indeed. The simple piety prevalent in Hades has the earnest worship of and respect for riches as the first article of its creed – had John felt otherwise than radiantly humble before them, his parents would have turned away in horror at the blasphemy.

They had now reached and were entering the break between the two mountains and almost immediately the way became much rougher.

'If the moon shone down here, you'd see that we're in a big gulch,' said Percy, trying to peer out of the window. He spoke a few words into the mouthpiece and immediately the footman turned on a searchlight and swept the hillsides with an immense beam.

'Rocky, you see. An ordinary car would be knocked to pieces in half an hour. In fact it'd take a tank to navigate it unless you knew the way. You notice we're going uphill now.'

They were obviously ascending, and within a few minutes the car was crossing a high rise, where they caught a glimpse of a pale moon newly risen in the distance. The car stopped suddenly and several figures took shape out of the dark beside it – these were Negroes also. Again the two young men were saluted in the same dimly recognizable dialect; then the Negroes set to work and four immense cables dangling from overhead were attached with hooks to the hubs of the great jewelled wheels. At a resounding 'Hey-yah!' John felt the car being lifted slowly from the ground – up and up – clear of the tallest rocks on both sides – then higher, until he could see a wavy, moonlit valley stretched out before him in sharp contrast to the quagmire of rocks that they had just left. Only on one side was there still rock – and then suddenly there was no rock beside them or anywhere around.

It was apparent that they had surmounted some immense knife-blade of stone, projecting perpendicularly into the air. In a moment they were going down again, and finally with a soft bump they were landed upon the smooth earth.

'The worst is over,' said Percy, squinting out the window. 'It's only five miles from here, and our own road – tapestry brick – all the way. This belongs to us. This is where the United States ends, father says.'

'Are we in Canada?'

'We are not. We're in the middle of the Montana Rockies. But you are now on the only five square miles of land in the country that's never been surveyed.'

'Why hasn't it? Did they forget it?'

'No,' said Percy, grinning, 'they tried to do it three times. The first time my grandfather corrupted a whole department of the State survey; the second time he had the official maps of the United States tinkered with – that held them for fifteen years. The last time was harder. My father fixed it so that their compasses were in the strongest magnetic field ever artificially set up. He had a whole set of surveying instruments made with a slight defection that would allow for this territory not to appear, and he substituted them for the ones that were to be used. Then he had a river deflected and he had what looked like a village built up on its banks – so that they'd see it, and think it was a town ten miles farther up the valley. There's only one thing my father's afraid of,' he concluded, 'only one thing in the world that could be used to find us out.'

'What's that?'

Percy sank his voice to a whisper.

'Aeroplanes,' he breathed. 'We've got half-a-dozen anti-aircraft guns and we've arranged it so far – but there've been a few deaths and a great many prisoners. Not that we mind *that*, you know, father and I, but it upsets mother and the girls, and there's always the chance that some time we won't be able to arrange it.'

Shreds and tatters of chinchilla, courtesy clouds in the green moon's heaven, were passing the green moon like precious Eastern stuffs paraded for the inspection of some Tartar Khan. It seemed to John that it was day, and that he was looking at some lads sailing above him in the air, showering down tracts and patent-medicine circulars, with their messages of hope for despairing, rockbound hamlets. It seemed to him that he could see them look down out of the clouds and stare – and stare at whatever there was to stare at in this place whither he was bound – What then? Were they induced to land by some insidious device there to be immured far from patent medicines and from tracts until the judgement day – or, should they fail to fall into the trap, did a quick puff of smoke and the sharp round of a splitting shell bring them drooping to earth – and 'upset' Percy's mother and sisters. John shook his head and the wraith of a hollow laugh issued silently from his parted lips. What desperate transaction lay hidden here? What amoral expedient of a bizarre Croesus? What terrible and golden mystery? . . .

The chinchilla clouds had drifted past now and outside the Montana night was bright as day. The tapestry brick of the road was smooth to the tread of the great tyres as they rounded a still, moonlit lake; they passed into darkness for a moment, a pine grove, pungent and cool, then they came out into a broad avenue of lawn and John's exclamation of pleasure was simultaneous with Percy's taciturn 'We're home'.

Full in the light of the stars, an exquisite château rose from the borders of the lake, climbed in marble radiance half the height of an adjoining mountain, then melted in grace, in perfect symmetry, in translucent feminine languor, into the massed darkness of a forest of pine. The many towers, the slender tracery of the sloping parapets, the chiselled wonder of a thousand yellow windows with their oblongs and hectagons and triangles of golden light, the shattered softness of the intersecting planes of star-shine and blue shade, all trembled on John's spirit like a chord of music. On one of the towers, the tallest, the blackest at its base, an arrangement of exterior lights at the top made a sort of floating fairy-land – and as John gazed up in warm enchantment the faint *acciaccare* sound of violins drifted down in a rococo harmony that was like nothing he had ever heard before. Then in a moment the car stopped before wide, high marble steps around which the night air was fragrant with a host of flowers. At the top of the steps two great doors swung silently open and amber light flooded out upon the darknesss, silhouetting the figure of an exquisite lady with black, high-piled hair, who held out her arms towards them.

'Mother,' Percy was saying, 'this is my friend, John Unger, from Hades.'

Afterwards John remembered that first night as a daze of many colours, of quick sensory impressions, of music soft as a voice in love, and of the beauty of things, lights and shadows, and motions and faces. There was a white-haired man who stood drinking a many-hued cordial from a crystal thimble set on a golden stem. There was a girl with a flowery face, dressed like Titania with braided sapphires in her hair. There was a room where the solid, soft gold of the walls yielded to the pressure of his hand, and a room that was like a platonic conception of the ultimate prison – ceiling, floor, and all, it was lined with an unbroken mass of diamonds, diamonds of every size and shape, until, lit with tall violet lamps in the corners, it dazzled the eyes with a whiteness that could be compared only with itself, beyond human wish or dream.

Through a maze of these rooms the two boys wandered. Sometimes the floor under their feet would flame in brilliant patterns from lighting below, patterns of barbaric clashing colours, of pastel delicacy, of sheer whiteness, or of subtle and intricate mosaic, surely from some mosque on the Adriatic Sea. Sometimes beneath layers of thick crystal he would see blue or green water swirling, inhabited by vivid fish and growths of rainbow foliage. Then they would be treading on furs of every texture and colour or along corridors of palest ivory, unbroken as though carved complete from the gigantic tusks of dinosaurs extinct before the age of man . . .

Then a hazily remembered transition, and they were at dinner – where each plate was of two almost imperceptible layers of solid diamond between which was curiously worked a filigree of emerald design, a shaving sliced from green air. Music, plangent and unobtrusive, drifted down through far corridors – his chair, feathered and curved insidiously to his back, seemed to engulf and overpower him as he drank his first glass of port. He tried drowsily to answer a question that had been asked him, but the honeyed luxury that clasped his body added to the illusion of sleep – jewels, fabrics, wines, and metals blurred before his eyes into a sweet mist . . .

'Yes,' he replied with a polite effort, 'it certainly is hot enough for me down there.'

He managed to add a ghostly laugh; then, without movement, without resistance, he seemed to float off and away, leaving an iced dessert that was pink as a dream . . . He fell asleep.

When he awoke he knew that several hours had passed. He was in a great quiet room with ebony walls and a dull illumination that was too faint, too subtle, to be called a light. His young host was standing over him.

'You fell asleep at dinner,' Percy was saying. 'I nearly did, too – it was such a treat to be comfortable again after this year of school. Servants undressed and bathed you while you were sleeping.'

'Is this a bed or a cloud?' sighed John. 'Percy, Percy – before you go, I want to apologize.'

'For what?'

'For doubting you when you said you had a diamond as big as the Ritz-Carlton Hotel.'

Percy smiled.

'I thought you didn't believe me. It's that mountain, you know.'

'What mountain?'

'The mountain the château rests on. It's not very big for a mountain. But except about fifty feet of sod and gravel on top it's solid diamond. *One* diamond, one cubic mile without a flaw. Aren't you listening? Say –'

But John T. Unger had again fallen asleep.

III

Morning. As he awoke he perceived drowsily that the room had at the same moment become dense with sunlight. The ebony panels of one wall had slid aside on a sort of track, leaving his chamber half open to the day. A large Negro in a white uniform stood beside his bed.

'Good evening,' muttered John, summoning his brains from the wild places.

'Good morning, sir. Are you ready for your bath, sir? Oh, don't get up – I'll put you in, if you'll just unbutton your pyjamas – there. Thank you, sir.'

John lay quietly as his pyjamas were removed – he was amused and delighted; he expected to be lifted like a child by this black Gargantua who was tending him, but nothing of the sort happened; instead he felt the bed tilt up slowly on its side – he began to roll, startled at first, in the direction of the wall, but when he reached the wall its drapery gave way, and sliding two yards farther down a fleecy incline he plumped gently into water the same temperature as his body.

He looked about him. The runway or rollway on which he had arrived had folded gently back into place. He had been projected into another chamber and was sitting in a sunken bath with his head just above the level of the floor. All about him, lining the walls of the room and the sides and bottom of the bath itself, was a blue aquarium, and gazing through the crystal surface on which he sat, he could see fish swimming among amber lights and even gliding without curiosity past his out-stretched toes, which were separated from them only by the thickness of the crystal. From overhead, sunlight came down through sea-green glass.

'I suppose, sir, that you'd like hot rosewater and soapsuds this morning, sir – and perhaps cold salt water to finish.'

The Negro was standing beside him.

'Yes,' agreed John smiling inanely, 'as you please.' Any idea of ordering this bath according to his own meagre standards of living would have been priggish and not a little wicked.

The Negro pressed a button and a warm rain began to fall, apparently from overhead, but really, so John discovered after a moment, from a fountain arrangement near by. The water turned to a pale rose colour and jets of liquid soap spurted into it from four miniature walrus heads at the corners of the bath. In a moment a dozen little paddle-wheels, fixed to the sides, had churned the mixture into a radiant rainbow of pink foam which enveloped him softly with its delicious lightness, and burst in shining, rosy bubbles here and there about him.

'Shall I turn on the moving-picture machine, sir?' suggested the Negro deferentially. 'There's a good one-reel comedy in this machine today, or I can put in a serious piece in a moment, if you prefer it.'

'No, thanks,' answered John, politely but firmly. He was enjoying his bath too much to desire any distraction. But distraction came. In a moment he was listening intently to the sound of flutes from just outside, flutes dripping a melody that was like a waterfall, cool and green as the room itself, accompanying a frothy piccolo, in play more fragile than the lace of suds that covered and charmed him.

After a cold salt-water bracer and a cold fresh finish, he stepped out and into a fleecy robe, and upon a couch covered with the same material he was rubbed with oil, alcohol, and spice. Later he sat in a voluptuous chair while he was shaved and his hair was trimmed.

'Mr Percy is waiting in your sitting-room,' said the Negro, when these operations were finished. 'My name is Gygsum, Mr Unger, sir. I am to see Mr Unger every morning.'

John walked out into the brisk sunshine of his living-room, where he found breakfast waiting for him and Percy, gorgeous in white-kid knickerbockers, smoking in an easy chair.

IV

This is a story of the Washington family as Percy sketched it for John during breakfast.

The father of the present Mr Washington had been a Virginian, a direct descendant of George Washington, and Lord Baltimore. At the close of the Civil War he was a twenty-five-year-old Colonel with a played-out plantation and about a thousand dollars in gold.

Fitz-Norman Culpepper Washington, for that was the young Colonel's name, decided to present the Virginia estate to his younger brother and go West. He selected two dozen of the most faithful blacks, who, of course, worshipped him, and bought twenty-five tickets to the West, where he intended to take out land in their names and start a sheep and cattle ranch.

When he had been in Montana for less than a month and things were going very poorly indeed, he stumbled on his great discovery. He had lost his way when riding in the hills, and after a day without food he began to grow hungry. As he was without his rifle, he was forced to pursue a squirrel, and in the course of the pursuit he noticed that it was carrying something shiny in its mouth. Just before it vanished into its hole – for Providence did not intend that this squirrel should alleviate his hunger – it dropped its burden. Sitting down to consider the situation Fitz-Norman's eye was caught by a gleam in the grass beside him. In ten seconds he had completely lost his appetite and gained one hundred thousand dollars. The squirrel which had refused with annoying persistence to become food, had made him a present of a large and perfect diamond.

Late that night he found his way to camp and twelve hours later all the males among his darkies were back by the squirrel hole digging furiously at the side of the mountain. He told them he had discovered a rhinestone mine, and, as only one or two of them had ever seen even a small diamond before, they believed him without question. When the magnitude of his discovery became apparent to him, he found himself in a quandary. The mountain was *a* diamond – it was literally nothing else but solid diamond. He filled four saddle bags full of glittering samples and started on horseback for St Paul. There he managed to dispose of half a dozen small stones – when he tried a larger one a storekeeper fainted and Fitz-Norman was arrested as a public disturber. He escaped from jail and caught the train for New York, where he sold a few medium-sized diamonds and received in exchange about two hundred thousand dollars in gold. But he did not dare to produce any exceptional gems – in fact, he left New York just in time. Tremendous excitement had been created in jewellery circles, not so much by the size of his diamonds as by their appearance in the city from mysterious sources. Wild rumours became current that a diamond mine had been discovered in the Catskills, on the Jersey coast, on Long Isand, beneath Washington Square. Excursion trains, packed with men carrying picks and shovels, began to leave New York hourly, bound for various neighbouring El Dorados. But by that time young Fitz-Norman was on his way back to Montana.

By the end of a fortnight he had estimated that the diamond in the mountain was approximately equal in quantity to all the rest of the diamonds known to exist in the world. There was no valuing it by any regular computation however, for it was *one solid diamond* – and if it were offered for sale not only would the bottom fall out of the market, but also, if the value should vary with its size in the usual arithmetical progression, there would not be enough gold in the world to buy a tenth part of it. And what could anyone do with a diamond that size?

It was an amazing predicament. He was, in one sense, the richest man that ever lived – and yet was he worth anything at all? If his secret should transpire there was no telling to what measures the Government might resort in order to prevent a panic, in gold as well as in jewels. They might take over the claim immediately and institute a monopoly.

There was no alternative – he must market his mountain in secret. He sent South for his younger brother and put him in charge of his coloured following – darkies who had never realized that slavery was abolished. To make sure of this, he read them a proclamation that he had composed, which announced that General Forrest had reorganized the shattered Southern armies and defeated the North in one pitched battle. The Negroes believed him implicitly. They passed a vote declaring it a good thing and held revival services immediately.

Fitz-Norman himself set out for foreign parts with one hundred thousand dollars and two trunks filled with rough diamonds of all sizes. He sailed for Russia in a Chinese junk and six months after his departure from Montana he was in St Petersburg. He took obscure lodgings and called immediately upon the court jeweller, announcing that he had a diamond for the Czar. He remained in St Petersburg for two weeks, in constant danger of being murdered, living from lodging to lodging, and afraid to visit his trunks more than three or four times during the whole fortnight.

On his promise to return in a year with larger and finer stones, he was allowed to leave for India. Before he left, however, the Court Treasurers had deposited to his credit, in American banks, the sum of fifteen million dollars – under four different aliases.

He returned to America in 1868, having been gone a little over two years. He had visited the capitals of twenty-two countries and talked with five emperors, eleven kings, three princes, a shah, a khan, and a sultan. At that time, Fitz-Norman estimated his own wealth at one billion dollars. One fact worked consistently against the disclosure of his secret. No one of his larger diamonds remained in the public eye for a week before being invested with a history of enough fatalities, amours, revolutions, and wars to have occupied it from the days of the first Babylonian Empire.

From 1870 until his death in 1900, the history of Fitz-Norman Washington was a long epic in gold. There were side issues, of course – he evaded the surveys, he married a Virginia lady, by whom he had a single son, and he was compelled, due to a series of unfortunate complications, to murder his brother whose unfortunate habit of drinking himself into an indiscreet stupor had several times endangered their safety. But very few other murders stained these happy years of progress and expansion.

Just before he died he changed his policy, and with all but a few million dollars of his outside wealth bought up rare minerals in bulk, which he deposited in the safety vaults of banks all over the world, marked as bric-à-brac. His son, Braddock Tarleton Washington, followed this policy on an even more intensive scale. The minerals were converted into the rarest of all elements – radium – so that the equivalent of a billion dollars in gold could be placed in a receptacle no bigger than a cigar box.

When Fitz-Norman had been dead three years his son, Braddock, decided that the business had gone far enough. The amount of wealth that he and his father had taken out of the mountain was beyond all exact computation. He kept a notebook in cipher in which he set down the approximate quantity of radium in each of the thousand banks he patronized, and recorded the alias under which it was held. Then he did a very simple thing – he sealed up the mine.

He sealed up the mine. What had been taken out of it would support all the Washingtons yet to be born in unparalleled luxury for generations. His one care must be the protection of his secret, lest in the possible panic attendant on its discovery he should be reduced with all the property-holders in the world to utter poverty.

This was the family among whom John T. Unger was staying. This was the story he heard in his silver-walled living-room the morning after his arrival.

V

After breakfast, John found his way out the great marble entrance, and looked curiously at the scene before him. The whole valley, from the diamond mountain to the steep granite cliff five miles away, still gave off a breath of golden haze which hovered idly above the fine sweep of lawns and lakes and gardens. Here and there clusters of elms made delicate groves of shade, contrasting strangely with the tough masses of pine forest that held the hills in a grip of dark-blue green. Even as John looked he saw three fawns in single file patter out from one clump about a half-mile away and disappear with awkward gaiety into the black-ribbed half-light of another. John would not have been surprised to see a goat foot-piping his way among the trees or to catch a glimpse of pink nymph-skin and flying yellow hair between the greenest of the green leaves.

In some such cool hope he descended the marble steps, disturbing the sleep of two silky Russian wolfhounds at the bottom, and set off along a walk of white and blue brick that seemed to lead in no particular direction.

He was enjoying himself as much as he was able. It is youth's felicity as well as its insufficiency that it can never live in the present, but must always be measuring up the day against its own radiantly imagined future – flowers and gold, girls and stars, they are only pre-figurations and prophecies of that incomparable, unattainable young dream.

John rounded a soft corner where the massed rose-bushes filled the air with heavy scent, and struck off across a park towards a patch of moss under some trees. He had never lain upon moss, and he wanted to see whether it was really soft enough to justify the use of its name as an adjective. Then he saw a girl coming towards him over the grass. She was the most beautiful person he had ever seen.

She was dressed in a white little gown that came just below her knees, and a wreath of mignonettes clasped with blue slices of sapphire bound up her hair. Her pink bare feet scattered the dew before them as she came. She was younger than John – not more than sixteen.

'Hello,' she cried softly, 'I'm Kismine.'

She was much more than that to John already. He advanced towards her, scarcely moving as he drew near lest he should tread on her bare toes.

'You haven't met me,' said her soft voice. Her blue eyes added, 'Oh, but you've missed a great deal!' . . . 'You met my sister, Jasmine, last night. I was sick with lettuce poisoning,' went on her soft voice, and her eyes continued, 'and when I'm sick I'm sweet – and when I'm well.'

'You have made an enormous impression on me,' said John's eyes, 'and I'm not so slow myself' – 'How do you do?' said his voice. 'I hope you're better this morning.' 'You darling,' added his eyes tremulously.

John observed that they had been walking along the path. On her suggestion they sat down together upon the moss, the softness of which he failed to determine.

He was critical about women. A single defect – a thick ankle, a hoarse voice, a glass eye – was enough to make him utterly indifferent. And here for the first time in his life he was beside a girl who seemed to him the incarnation of physical perfection.

'Are you from the East?' asked Kismine with charming interest.

'No,' answered John simply. 'I'm from Hades.'

Either she had never heard of Hades, or she could think of no pleasant comment to make upon it, for she did not discuss it further.

'I'm going East to school this fall,' she said. 'D'you think I'll like it? I'm going to New York to Miss Bulge's. It's very strict, but you see over the week-ends I'm going to live at home with the family in our New York house, because father heard that the girls had to go walking two by two.'

'Your father wants you to be proud,' observed John.

'We are,' she answered, her eyes shining with dignity. 'None of us has ever been punished. Father said we never should be. Once when my sister Jasmine was a little girl she pushed him downstairs and he just got up and limped away.

'Mother was – well, a little startled,' continued Kismine, 'when she heard that you were from – from where you *are* from, you know. She said that when she was a young girl – but then, you see, she's a Spaniard and old-fashioned.'

'Do you spend much time out here?' asked John, to conceal the fact that he was somewhat hurt by this remark. It seemed an unkind allusion to his provincialism.

'Percy and Jasmine and I are here every summer, but next summer Jasmine is going to Newport. She's coming out in London a year from this fall. She'll be presented at Court.'

'Do you know,' began John hesitantly, 'you're much more sophisticated than I thought you were when I first saw you?'

'Oh, no, I'm not,' she exclaimed hurriedly. 'Oh, I wouldn't think of being. I think that sophisticated young people are *terribly* common, don't you? I'm not at all, really. If you say I am I'm going to cry.'

She was so distressed that her lip was trembling. John was impelled to protest:

'I didn't mean that; I only said it to tease you.'

'Because I wouldn't mind if I *were*,' she persisted, 'but I'm *not*. I'm very innocent and girlish. I never smoke, or drink, or read anything except poetry. I know scarcely any mathematics or chemistry. I dress *very* simply – in fact, I scarcely dress at all. I think sophisticated is the last thing you can say about me. I believe that girls ought to enjoy their youths in a wholesome way.'

'I do too,' said John heartily.

Kismine was cheerful again. She smiled at him, and a stillborn tear dripped from the corner of one blue eye.

'I like you,' she whispered, intimately. 'Are you going to spend all your time with Percy while you're here, or will you be nice to me? Just think – I'm absolutely fresh ground. I've never had a boy in love with me in all my life. I've never been allowed even to *see* boys alone – except Percy. I came all the way out here into this grove hoping to run into you, where the family wouldn't be around.'

Deeply flattered, John bowed from the hips as he had been taught at dancing school in Hades.

'We'd better go now,' said Kismine sweetly. 'I have to be with mother at eleven. You haven't asked me to kiss you once. I thought boys always did that nowadays.'

John drew himself up proudly.

'Some of them do,' he answered, 'but not me. Girls don't do that sort of thing – in Hades.'

Side by side they walked back towards the house.

VI

John stood facing Mr Braddock Washington in the full sunlight. The elder man was about forty with a proud, vacuous face, intelligent eyes, and a robust figure. In the mornings he smelt of horses – the best horses. He carried a plain walking-stick of grey birch with a single large opal for a grip. He and Percy were showing John around.

'The slaves' quarters are there.' His walking-stick indicated a cloister of marble on their left that ran in graceful Gothic along the side of the mountain. 'In my youth I was distracted for a while from the business of life by a period of absurd idealism. During that time they lived in luxury. For instance, I equipped every one of their rooms with a tile bath.'

'I suppose,' ventured John, with an ingratiating laugh, 'that they used the bathtubs to keep coal in. Mr Schnlitzer-Murphy told me that once he –'

'The opinions of Mr Schnlitzer-Murphy are of little importance, I should imagine,' interrupted Braddock Washington, coldly. 'My slaves did not keep coal in their bathtubs. They had orders to bathe every day, and they did. If they hadn't I might have ordered a sulphuric acid shampoo. I discontinued the baths for quite another reason. Several of them caught cold and died. Water is not good for certain races – except as a beverage.'

John laughed, and then decided to nod his head in sober agreement. Braddock Washington made him uncomfortable.

'All these Negroes are descendants of the ones my father brought North with him. There are about two hundred and fifty now. You notice that they've lived so long apart from the world that their original dialect has become an almost indistinguishable patois. We bring a few of them up to speak English – my secretary and two or three of the house servants.

'This is the golf-course,' he continued, as they strolled along the velvet winter grass. 'It's all a green, you see – no fairway, no rough, no hazards.'

He smiled pleasantly at John.

'Many men in the cage, father?' asked Percy suddenly.

Braddock Washington stumbled, and let forth an involuntary curse.

'One less than there should be,' he ejaculated darkly – and then added after a moment, 'We've had difficulties.'

'Mother was telling me,' exclaimed Percy, 'that Italian teacher –'

'A ghastly error,' said Braddock Washington angrily. 'But of course there's a good chance that we may have got him. Perhaps he fell somewhere in the woods or stumbled over a cliff. And then there's always the probability that if he did get away his story wouldn't be believed. Nevertheless, I've had two dozen men looking for him in different towns around here.'

'And no luck?'

'Some. Fourteen of them reported to my agent that they'd each killed a man answering to that description, but of course it was probably only the reward they were after –'

He broke off. They had come to a large cavity in the earth about the circumference of a merry-go-round and covered by a strong iron grating. Braddock Washington beckoned to John, and pointed his cane down through the grating. John stepped to the edge and gazed. Immediately his ears were assailed by a wlld clamour from below.

'Come on down to Hell!'

'Hello, kiddo, how's the air up there?'

'Hey! Throw us a rope!'

'Got an old doughnut, Buddy, or a couple of second-hand sandwiches?'

'Say, fella, if you'll push down that guy you're with, we'll show you a quick disappearance scene.'

'Paste him one for me, will you?'

It was too dark to see clearly into the pit below, but John could tell from the coarse optimism and rugged vitality of the remarks and voices that they proceeded from middle-class Americans of the more spirited type. Then Mr Washington put out his cane and touched a button in the grass, and the scene below sprang into light.

'These are some adventurous mariners who had the misfortune to discover El Dorado,' he remarked.

Below them there had appeared a large hollow in the earth shaped like the interior of a bowl. The sides were steep and apparently of polished glass, and on its slightly concave surface stood about two dozen men clad in the half costume, half uniform, of aviators. Their upturned faces, lit with wrath, with malice, with despair, with cynical humour, were covered by long growths of beard, but with the exception of a few who had pined perceptibly away, they seemed to be a well-fed, healthy lot.

Braddock Washington drew a garden chair to the edge of the pit and sat down.

'Well, how are you, boys?' he inquired genially.

A chorus of execration in which all joined except a few too dispirited to cry out, rose up into the sunny air, but Braddock Washington heard it with unruffled composure. When its last echo had died away he spoke again.

'Have you thought up a way out of your difficulty?'

From here and there among them a remark floated up.

'We decided to stay here for love!'

'Bring us up there and we'll find us a way!'

Braddock Washington waited until they were again quiet. Then he said:

'I've told you the situation. I don't want you here. I wish to heaven I'd never seen you. Your own curiosity got you here, and any time that you can think of a way out which protects me and my interests I'll be glad to consider it. But so long as you confine your efforts to digging tunnels – yes, I know about the new one you've started – you won't get very far. This isn't as hard on you as you make it out, with all your howling for the loved ones at home. If you were the type who worried much about the loved ones at home, you'd never have taken up aviation.'

A tall man moved apart from the others, and held up his hand to call his captor's attention to what he was about to say.

'Let me ask you a few questions!' he cried. 'You pretend to be a fair-minded man.'

'How absurd. How could a man of *my* position be fair-minded towards *you*? You might as well speak of a Spaniard being fair-minded towards a piece of steak.'

At this harsh observation the faces of the two dozen steaks fell, but the tall man continued:

'All right!' he cried. 'We've argued this out before. You're not a humanitarian and you're not fair-minded, but you're human – at least you say you are – and you ought to be able to put yourself in our place for long enough to think how – how – how –'

'How what?' demanded Washington, coldly.

'– how unnecessary –'

'Not to me.'

'Well – how cruel –'

'We've covered that. Cruelty doesn't exist where self-preservation is involved. You've been soldiers: you know that. Try another.'

'Well, then, how stupid.'

'There,' admitted Washington, 'I grant you that. But try to think of an alternative. I've offered to have all or any of you painlessly executed if you wish. I've offered to have your wives, sweethearts, children, and mothers kidnapped and brought out here. I'll enlarge your place down there and feed and clothe you the rest of your lives. If there was some method of producing permanent amnesia I'd have all of you operated on and released immediately, somewhere outside of my preserves. But that's as far as my ideas go.'

'How about trusting us not to peach on you?' cried someone.

'You don't proffer that suggestion seriously,' said Washington, with an expression of scorn. 'I did take out one man to teach my daughter Italian. Last week he got away.'

A wild yell of jubilation went up suddenly from two dozen throats and a pandemonium of joy ensued. The prisoners clog-danced and cheered and yodelled and wrestled with one another in a sudden uprush of animal spirits. They even ran up the glass sides of the bowl as far as they could, and slid back to the bottom upon the natural cushions of their bodies. The tall man started a song in which they all joined –

> 'Oh, we'll hang the kaiser
> On a sour apple tree –'

Braddock Washington sat in inscrutable silence until the song was over.

'You see,' he remarked, when he could gain a modicum of attention. 'I bear you no ill-will. I like to see you enjoying yourselves. That's why I didn't tell you the whole story at once. The man – what was his name? Critchtichiello? – was shot by some of my agents in fourteen different places.'

Not guessing that the places referred to were cities, the tumult of rejoicing subsided immediately.

'Nevertheless,' cried Washington with a touch of anger, 'he tried to run away. Do you expect me to take chances with any of you after an experience like that?'

Again a series of ejaculations went up.

'Sure!'

'Would your daughter like to learn Chinese?'

'Hey, I can speak Italian! My mother was a wop.'

'Maybe she'd like t'learna speak N'Yawk!'

'If she's the little one with the big blue eyes I can teach her a lot of things better than Italian.'

'I know some Irish songs – and I could hammer brass once't.'

Mr Washington reached forward suddenly with his cane and pushed the button in the grass so that the picture below went out instantly, and there remained only that great dark mouth covered dismally with the black teeth of the grating.

'Hey!' called a single voice from below, 'you ain't goin' away without givin' us your blessing?'

But Mr Washington, followed by the two boys, was already strolling on towards the ninth hole of the golf-course, as though the pit and its contents were no more than a hazard over which his facile iron had triumphed with ease.

VII

July under the lee of the diamond mountain was a month of blanket nights and of warm, glowing days. John and Kismine were in love. He did not know that the little gold football (inscribed with the legend *Pro deo et patria et St Mida*) which he had given her rested on a platinum chain next to her bosom. But it did. And she for her part was not aware that a large sapphire which had dropped one day from her simple coiffure was stowed away tenderly in John's jewel-box.

Late one afternoon when the ruby and ermine music room was quiet, they spent an hour there together. He held her hand and she gave him such a look that he whispered her name aloud. She bent towards him – then hesitated.

'Did you say "Kismine"?' she asked softly, 'or –'

She had wanted to be sure. She thought she might have misunderstood.

Neither of them had ever kissed before, but in the course of an hour it seemed to make little difference.

The afternoon drifted away. That night when a last breath of music drifted down from the highest tower, they each lay awake, happily dreaming over the separate minutes of the day. They had decided to be married as soon as possible.

VIII

Every day Mr Washington and the two young men went hunting or
fishing in the deep forests or played golf around the somnolent course –
games which John diplomatically allowed his host to win – or swam in
the mountain coolness of the lake. John found Mr Washington a somewhat exacting personality – utterly uninterested in any ideas or opinions
except his own. Mrs Washington was aloof and reserved at all times. She
was apparently indifferent to her two daughters, and entirely absorbed in
her son Percy, with whom she held interminable conversations in rapid
Spanish at dinner.

Jasmine, the elder daughter, resembled Kismine in appearance – except
that she was somewhat bow-legged, and terminated in large hands and
feet – but was utterly unlike her in temperament. Her favourite books
had to do with poor girls who kept house for widowed fathers. John
learned from Kismine that Jasmine had never recovered from the shock
and disappointment caused her by the termination of the World War,
just as she was about to start for Europe as a canteen expert. She had
even pined away for a time, and Braddock Washington had taken steps
to promote a new war in the Balkans – but she had seen a photograph
of some wounded Serbian soldiers and lost interest in the whole proceedings. But Percy and Kismine seemed to have inherited the arrogant
attitude in all its harsh magnificence from their father. A chaste and
consistent selfishness ran like a pattern through their every idea.

John was enchanted by the wonders of the château and the valley.
Braddock Washington, so Percy told him, had caused to be kidnapped
a landscape gardener, an architect, a designer of stage settings, and a
French decadent poet left over from the last century. He had put his
entire force of Negroes at their disposal, guaranteed to supply them with
any materials that the world could offer, and left them to work out some
ideas of their own. But one by one they had shown their uselessness.
The decadent poet had at once begun bewailing his separation from the
boulevards in spring – he made some vague remarks about spices, apes,
and ivories, but said nothing that was of any practical value. The stage
designer on his part wanted to make the whole valley a series of tricks
and sensational effects – a state of things that the Washingtons would
soon have grown tired of. And as for the architect and the landscape
gardener, they thought only in terms of convention. They must make
this like this and that like that.

But they had, at least, solved the problem of what was to be done with them – they all went mad early one morning after spending the night in a single room trying to agree upon the location of a fountain, and were now confined comfortably in an insane asylum at Westport, Connecticut.

'But,' inquired John curiously, 'who did plan all your wonderful reception rooms and halls, and approaches and bathrooms –?'

'Well,' answered Percy, 'I blush to tell you but it was a moving-picture fella. He was the only man we found who was used to playing with an unlimited amount of money, though he did tuck his napkin in his collar and couldn't read or write.'

As August drew to a close John began to regret that he must soon go back to school. He and Kismine had decided to elope the following June.

'It would be nicer to be married here,' Kismine confessed, 'but of course I could never get father's permission to marry you at all. Next to that I'd rather elope. It's terrible for wealthy people to be married in America at present – they always have to send out bulletins to the Press saying that they're going to be married in remnants, when what they mean is just a peck of old second-hand pearls and some used lace worn once by the Empress Eugénie.'

'I know,' agreed John fervently. 'When I was visiting the Schnlitzer-Murphys, the eldest daughter, Gwendolyn, married a man whose father owns half of West Virginia. She wrote home saying what a tough struggle it was carrying on on his salary as a bank clerk – and then she ended up by saying that "Thank God, I have four good maids anyhow, and that helps a little." '

'It's absurd,' commented Kismine. 'Think of the millions and millions of people in the world, labourers and all, who get along with only two maids.'

One afternoon late in August a chance remark of Kismine's changed the face of the entire situation, and threw John into a state of terror.

They were in their favourite grove, and between kisses John was indulging in some romantic forebodings which he fancied added poignancy to their relations.

'Sometimes I think we'll never marry,' he said sadly. 'You're too wealthy, too magnificent. No one as rich as you are can be like other girls. I should marry the daughter of some well-to-do wholesale hardware man from Omaha or Sioux City, and be content with her half-million.'

'I knew the daughter of a wholesale hardware man once,' remarked Kismine. 'I don't think you'd have been contented with her. She was a friend of my sister's. She visited here.'

'Oh, then you've had other guests?' exclaimed John in surprise.

Kismine seemed to regret her words.

'Oh, yes,' she said hurriedly, 'we've had a few.'

'But aren't you – wasn't your father afraid they'd talk outside?'

'Oh, to some extent, to some extent,' she answered. 'Let's talk about something pleasanter.'

But John's curiosity was aroused.

'Something pleasanter!' he demanded. 'What's unpleasant about that? Weren't they nice girls?'

To his great surprise Kismine began to weep.

'Yes – th – that's the – the whole t-trouble. I grew qu-quite attached to some of them. So did Jasmine, but she kept inv-viting them anyway. I couldn't under*stand* it.'

A dark suspicion was born in John's heart.

'Do you mean that they *told*, and your father had them – removed?'

'Worse than that,' she muttered brokenly. 'Father took no chances – and Jasmine kept writing them to come, and they had *such* a good time!'

She was overcome by a paroxysm of grief.

Stunned with the horror of this revelation, John sat there open-mouthed, feeling the nerves of his body twitter like so many sparrows perched upon his spinal column.

'Now, I've told you, and I shouldn't have,' she said, calming suddenly and drying her dark blue eyes.

'Do you mean to say that your father had them *murdered* before they left?'

She nodded.

'In August usually – or early in September. It's only natural for us to get all the pleasure out of them that we can first.'

'How abominable! How – why, I must be going crazy! Did you really admit that –'

'I did,' interrupted Kismine, shrugging her shoulders. 'We can't very well imprison them like those aviators, where they'd be a continual reproach to us every day. And it's always been made easier for Jasmine and me, because father had it done sooner than we expected. In that way we avoided any farewell scene –'

'So you murdered them! Uh!' cried John.

'It was done very nicely. They were drugged while they were asleep – and their families were always told that they died of scarlet fever in Butte.'

'But – I fail to understand why you kept on inviting them!'

'I didn't,' burst out Kismine. 'I never invited one. Jasmine did. And they always had a very good time. She'd give them the nicest presents towards the last. I shall probably have visitors too – I'll harden up to it. We can't let such an inevitable thing as death stand in the way of enjoying life while we have it. Think how lonesome it'd be out here if we never had *any* one. Why, father and mother have sacrificed some of their best friends just as we have.'

'And so,' cried John accusingly, 'and so you were letting me make love to you and pretending to return it, and talking about marriage, all the time knowing perfectly well that I'd never get out of here alive –'

'No,' she protested passionately. 'Not any more. I did at first. You were here. I couldn't help that, and I thought your last days might as well be pleasant for both of us. But then I fell in love with you, and – and I'm honestly sorry you're going to – going to be put away – though I'd rather you'd be put away than ever kiss another girl.'

'Oh, you would, would you?' cried John ferociously.

'Much rather. Besides, I've always heard that a girl can have more fun with a man whom she knows she can never marry. Oh, why did I tell you? I've probably spoiled your whole good time now, and we were really enjoying things when you didn't know it. I knew it would make things sort of depressing for you.'

'Oh, you did, did you?' John's voice trembled with anger. 'I've heard about enough of this. If you haven't any more pride and decency than to have an affair with a fellow that you know isn't much better than a corpse, I don't want to have any more to do with you!'

'You're not a corpse!' she protested in horror. 'You're not a corpse! I won't have you saying that I kissed a corpse!'

'I said nothing of the sort!'

'You did! You said I kissed a corpse!'

'I didn't!'

Their voices had risen, but upon a sudden interruption they both subsided into immediate silence. Footsteps were coming along the path in their direction, and a moment later the rose bushes were parted displaying Braddock Washington, whose intelligent eyes set in his good-looking vacuous face were peering in at them.

'Who kissed a corpse?' he demanded in obvious disapproval.

'Nobody,' answered Kismine quickly. 'We were just joking.'

'What are you two doing here, anyhow?' he demanded gruffly. 'Kismine you ought to be – to be reading or playing golf with your sister. Go read! Go play golf! Don't let me find you here when I come back!'

Then he bowed at John and went up the path.

'See?' said Kismine crossly, when he was out of hearing. 'You've spoiled it all. We can never meet any more. He won't let me meet you. He'd have you poisoned if he thought we were in love.'

'We're not, any more!' cried John fiercely, 'so he can set his mind at rest upon that. Moreover, don't fool yourself that I'm going to stay around here. Inside of six hours I'll be over those mountains, if I have to gnaw a passage through them, and on my way East.'

They had both got to their feet, and at this remark Kismine came close and put her arm through his.

'I'm going, too.'

'You must be crazy –'

'Of course I'm going,' she interrupted patiently.

'You most certainly are not. You –'

'Very well,' she said quietly, 'we'll catch up with father now and talk it over with him.'

Defeated, John mustered a sickly smile.

'Very well, dearest,' he agreed, with pale and unconvincing affection, 'we'll go together.'

His love for her returned and settled placidly on his heart. She was his – she would go with him to share his dangers. He put his arms about her and kissed her fervently. After all she loved him; she had saved him, in fact.

Discussing the matter, they walked slowly back towards the château. They decided that since Braddock Washington had seen them together they had best depart the next night. Nevertheless, John's lips were unusually dry at dinner, and he nervously emptied a great spoonful of peacock soup into his left lung. He had to be carried into the turquoise and sable card-room and pounded on the back by one of the under-butlers, which Percy considered a great joke.

IX

Long after midnight John's body gave a nervous jerk, and he sat suddenly upright, staring into the veils of somnolence that draped the room. Through the squares of blue darkness that were his open windows, he had heard a faint faraway sound that died upon a bed of wind before identifying itself on his memory, clouded with uneasy dreams. But the sharp noise that had succeeded it was nearer, was just outside the room – the click of a turned knob, a footstep, a whisper, he could not tell; a hard lump gathered in the pit of his stomach, and his whole body ached in the moment that he strained agonizingly to hear. Then one of the veils seemed to dissolve, and he saw a vague figure standing by the door, a figure only faintly limned and blocked in upon the darkness, mingled so with the folds of the drapery as to seem distorted, like a reflection seen in a dirty pane of glass.

With a sudden movement of fright or resolution John pressed the button by his bedside, and the next moment he was sitting in the green sunken bath of the adjoining room, waked into alertness by the shock of the cold water which half filled it.

He sprang out, and, his wet pyjamas scattering a heavy trickle of water behind him, ran for the aquamarine door which he knew led out on to the ivory landing of the second floor. The door opened noiselessly. A single crimson lamp burning in a great dome above lit the magnificent sweep of the carved stairways with a poignant beauty. For a moment John hesitated, appalled by the silent splendour massed about him, seeming to envelop in its gigantic folds and contours the solitary drenched little figure shivering upon the ivory landing. Then simultaneously two things happened. The door of his own sitting-room swung open, precipitating three naked Negroes into the hall – and, as John swayed in wild terror towards the stairway, another door slid back in the wall on the other side of the corridor, and John saw Braddock Washington standing in the lighted lift, wearing a fur coat and a pair of riding boots which reached to his knees and displayed, above, the glow of his rose-coloured pyjamas.

On the instant the three Negroes – John had never seen any of them before, and it flashed through his mind that they must be the professional executioners – paused in their movement towards John, and turned expectantly to the man in the lift, who burst out with an imperious command:

'Get in here! All three of you! Quick as hell!'

Then, within the instant, the three Negroes darted into the cage, the oblong of light was blotted out as the lift door slid shut, and John was again alone in the hall. He slumped weakly down against an ivory stair.

It was apparent that something portentous had occurred, something which, for the moment at least, had postponed his own petty disaster. What was it? Had the Negroes risen in revolt? Had the aviators forced aside the iron bars of the grating? Or had the men of Fish stumbled blindly through the hills and gazed with bleak, joyless eyes upon the gaudy valley? John did not know. He heard a faint whir of air as the lift whizzed up again, and then, a moment later, as it descended. It was probable that Percy was hurrying to his father's assistance, and it occurred to John that this was his opportunity to join Kismine and plan an immediate escape. He waited until the lift had been silent for several minutes; shivering a little with the night cool that whipped in through his wet pyjamas, he returned to his room and dressed himself quickly. Then he mounted a long flight of stairs and turned down the corridor carpeted with Russian sable which led to Kismine's suite.

The door of her sitting-room was open and the lamps were lighted. Kismine, in an angora kimono, stood near the window of the room in a listening attitude, and as John entered noiselessly, she turned towards him.

'Oh, it's you!' she whispered, crossing the room to him. 'Did you hear them?'

'I heard your father's slaves in my –'

'No,' she interrupted excitedly. 'Aeroplanes!'

'Aeroplanes? Perhaps that was the sound that woke me.'

'There're at least a dozen. I saw one a few moments ago dead against the moon. The guard back by the cliff fired his rifle and that's what roused father. We're going to open on them right away.'

'Are they here on purpose?'

'Yes – it's that Italian who got away –'

Simultaneously with her last word, a succession of sharp cracks tumbled in through the open window. Kismine uttered a little cry, took a penny with fumbling fingers from a box on her dresser, and ran to one of the electric lights. In an instant the entire château was in darkness – she had blown out the fuse.

'Come on!' she cried to him. 'We'll go up to the roof garden, and watch it from there!'

Drawing a cape about her, she took his hand, and they found their way out the door. It was only a step to the tower lift, and as she pressed the button that shot them upward he put his arms around her in the darkness and kissed her mouth. Romance had come to John Unger at last. A minute later they had stepped out upon the star-white platform. Above, under the misty moon, sliding in and out of the patches of cloud that eddied below it, floated a dozen dark-winged bodies in a constant circling course. From here and there in the valley flashes of fire leaped

towards them, followed by sharp detonations. Kismine clapped her hands
with pleasure, which a moment later turned to dismay as the aeroplanes
at some pre-arranged signal, began to release their bombs and the whole
of the valley became a panorama of deep reverberant sound and lurid
light.

Before long the aim of the attackers became concentrated upon the
points where the anti-aircraft guns were situated, and one of them was
almost immediately reduced to a giant cinder to lie smouldering in a
park of rose bushes.

'Kismine,' begged John, 'you'll be glad when I tell you that this attack
came on the eve of my murder. If I hadn't heard that guard shoot off
his gun back by the pass I should now be stone dead –'

'I can't hear you!' cried Kismine, intent on the scene before her.
'You'll have to talk louder!'

'I simply said,' shouted John, 'that we'd better get out before they
begin to shell the château!'

Suddenly the whole portico of the Negro quarters cracked asunder, a
geyser of flame shot up from under the colonnades, and great fragments
of jagged marble were hurled as far as the borders of the lake.

'There go fifty thousand dollars' worth of slaves,' cried Kismine, 'at
pre-war prices. So few Americans have any respect for property.'

John renewed his efforts to compel her to leave. The aim of the
aeroplanes was becoming more precise minute by minute, and only two
of the anti-aircraft guns were still retaliating. It was obvious that the
garrison, encircled with fire, could not hold out much longer.

'Come on!' cried John, pulling Kismine's arm, 'we've got to go. Do
you realize that those aviators will kill you without question if they find
you?'

She consented reluctantly.

'We'll have to wake Jasmine!' she said, as they hurried towards the
lift. Then she added in a sort of childish delight: 'We'll be poor, won't
we? Like people in books. And I'll be an orphan and utterly free. Free
and poor! What fun!' She stopped and raised her lips to him in a
delighted kiss.

'It's impossible to be both together,' said John grimly. 'People have
found that out. And I should choose to be free as preferable of the two.
As an extra caution you'd better lump the contents of your jewel-box
into your pockets.'

Ten minutes later the two girls met John in the dark corridor and
they descended to the main floor of the château. Passing for the last

time through the magnificence of the splendid halls, they stood for a moment out on the terrace, watching the burning Negro quarters and the flaming embers of two planes which had fallen on the other side of the lake. A solitary gun was still keeping up a sturdy popping, and the attackers seemed timorous about descending lower, but sent their thunderous fireworks in a circle around it, until any chance shot might annihilate its Ethiopian crew.

John and the two sisters passed down the marble steps, turned sharply to the left, and began to ascend a narrow path that wound like a garter about the diamond mountain. Kismine knew a heavily wooded spot halfway up where they could lie concealed and yet be able to observe the wild night in the valley – finally to make an escape, when it should be necessary, along a secret path laid in a rocky gully.

X

It was three o'clock when they attained their destination. The obliging and phlegmatic Jasmine fell off to sleep immediately, leaning against the trunk of a large tree, while John and Kismine sat, his arm around her, and watched the desperate ebb and flow of the dying battle among the ruins of a vista that had been a garden spot that morning. Shortly after four o'clock the last remaining gun gave out a clanging sound and went out of action in a swift tongue of red smoke. Though the moon was down, they saw that the flying bodies were circling closer to the earth. When the planes had made certain that the beleaguered possessed no further resources, they would land and the dark and glittering reign of the Washingtons would be over.

With the cessation of the firing the valley grew quiet. The embers of the two aeroplanes glowed like the eyes of some monster crouching in the glass. The château stood dark and silent, beautiful without light as it had been beautiful in the sun, while the woody rattles of Nemesis filled the air above with a growing and receding complaint. Then John perceived that Kismine, like her sister, had fallen sound asleep.

It was long after four when he became aware of footsteps along the path they had lately followed, and he waited in breathless silence until the persons to whom they belonged had passed the vantage-point he occupied. There was a faint stir in the air now that was not of human origin, and the dew was cold; he knew that the dawn would break soon. John waited until the steps had gone a safe distance up the mountain and were inaudible. Then he followed. About half-way to the steep summit the trees fell away and a hard saddle of rock spread itself over the diamond beneath. Just before he reached this point he slowed down his pace, warned by an animal sense that there was life just ahead of him. Coming to a high boulder, he lifted his head gradually above its edge. His curiosity was rewarded; this is what he saw:

Braddock Washington was standing there motionless, silhouetted against the grey sky without sound or sign of life. As the dawn came up out of the east, lending a cold green colour to the earth, it brought the solitary figure into insignificant contrast with the new day.

While John watched, his host remained for a few moments absorbed in some inscrutable contemplation; then he signalled to the two Negroes who crouched at his feet to lift the burden which lay between them. As they struggled upright, the first yellow beam of the sun struck through the innumerable prisms of an immense and exquisitely chiselled diamond – and a white radiance was kindled that glowed upon the air like a fragment of the morning star. The bearers staggered beneath its weight for a moment – then their rippling muscles caught and hardened under the wet shine of the skins and the three figures were again motionless in their defiant impotency before the heavens.

After a while the white man lifted his head and slowly raised his arms in a gesture of attention, as one who would call a great crowd to hear – but there was no crowd, only the vast silence of the mountain and the sky, broken by faint bird voices down among the trees. The figure on the saddle of rock began to speak ponderously and with an inextinguishable pride.

'You out there –' he cried in a trembling voice. 'You – there – !' He paused, his arms still uplifted, his head held attentively as though he were expecting an answer. John strained his eyes to see whether there might be men coming down the mountain, but the mountain was bare of human life. There was only sky and a mocking flute of wind along the tree-tops. Could Washington be praying? For a moment John wondered. Then the illusion passed – there was something in the man's whole attitude antithetical to prayer.

'Oh, you above there!'

The voice was become strong and confident. This was no forlorn supplication. If anything, there was in it a quality of monstrous condescension.

'You there –'

Words, too quickly uttered to be understood, flowing one into the other . . . John listened breathlessly, catching a phrase here and there, while the voice broke off, resumed, broke off again – now strong and argumentative, now coloured with a slow, puzzled impatience. Then a conviction commenced to dawn on the single listener, and as realization crept over him a spray of quick blood rushed through his arteries. Braddock Washington was offering a bribe to God!

That was it – there was no doubt. The diamond in the arms of his slaves was some advance sample, a promise of more to follow.

That, John perceived after a time, was the thread running through his sentences. Prometheus Enriched was calling to witness forgotten sacrifices, forgotten rituals, prayers obsolete before the birth of Christ. For a while his discourse took the form of reminding God of this gift or that which Divinity had deigned to accept from men – great churches if he would rescue cities from the plague, gifts of myrrh and gold, of human lives and beautiful women and captive armies, of children and queens, of beasts of the forest and field, sheep and goats, harvests and cities, whole conquered lands that had been offered up in lust or blood for His appeasal, buying a meed's worth of alleviation from the Divine wrath – and now he, Braddock Washington, Emperor of Diamonds, king and priest of the age of gold, arbiter of splendour and luxury, would offer up a treasure such as princes before him had never dreamed of, offer it up not in suppliance, but in pride.

He would give to God, he continued, getting down to specifications, the greatest diamond in the world. This diamond would be cut with many more thousand facets than there were leaves on a tree and yet the whole diamond would be shaped with the perfection of a stone no bigger than a fly. Many men would work upon it for many years. It would be set in a great dome of beaten gold, wonderfully carved and equipped with gates of opal and crusted sapphire. In the middle would be hollowed out a chapel presided over by an altar of iridescent, decomposing, ever-changing radium which would burn out the eyes of any worshipper who lifted up his head from prayer – and on this altar there would be slain for the amusement of the Divine Benefactor any victim He should choose, even though it should be the greatest and most powerful man alive.

In return he asked only a simple thing, a thing that for God would be absurdly easy – only that matters should be as they were yesterday at this hour and that they should so remain. So very simple! Let but the heavens open, swallowing these men and their aeroplanes – and then close again. Let him have his slaves once more, restored to life and well.

There was no one else with whom he had ever needed to treat or bargain.

He doubted only whether he had made his bribe big enough. God had His price, of course. God was made in man's image, so it had been said: He must have His price. And the price would be rare – no cathedral whose building consumed many years, no pyramid constructed by ten thousand workmen, would be like this cathedral, this pyramid.

He paused here. That was his proposition. Everything would be up to specifications and there was nothing vulgar in his assertion that it would be cheap at the price. He implied that Providence could take it or leave it.

As he approached the end his sentences became broken, became short and uncertain, and his body seemed tense, seemed strained to catch the slightest pressure or whisper of life in the spaces around him. His hair had turned gradually white as he talked, and now he lifted his head high to the heavens like a prophet of old – magnificently mad.

Then, as John stared in giddy fascination, it seemed to him that a curious phenomenon took place somewhere around him. It was as though the sky had darkened for an instant, as though there had been a sudden murmur in a gust of wind, a sound of far-away trumpets, a sighing like the rustle of a great silken robe – for a time the whole of nature round about partook of this darkness: the birds' song ceased; the trees were still, and far over the mountain there was a mutter of dull, menacing thunder.

That was all. The wind died along the tall grasses of the valley. The dawn and the day resumed their place in a time, and the risen sun sent hot waves of yellow mist that made its path bright before it. The leaves laughed in the sun, and their laughter shook the trees until each bough was like a girls' school in fairyland. God had refused to accept the bribe.

For another moment John watched the triumph of the day. Then, turning, he saw a flutter of brown down by the lake, then another flutter, then another, like the dance of golden angels alighting from the clouds. The aeroplanes had come to earth.

John slid off the boulder and ran down the side of the mountain to the clump of trees, where the two girls were awake and waiting for him. Kismine sprang to her feet, the jewels in her pockets jingling, a question on her parted lips, but instinct told John that there was no time for words. They must get off the mountain without losing a moment. He seized a hand of each, and in silence they threaded the tree-trunks, washed with light now and with the rising mist. Behind them from the valley came no sound at all, except the complaint of the peacocks far away and the pleasant undertone of morning.

When they had gone about a half a mile, they avoided the park land and entered a narrow path that led over the next rise of ground. At the highest point of this they paused and turned around. Their eyes rested upon the mountainside they had just left – oppressed by some dark sense of tragic impendency.

Clear against the sky a broken, white-haired man was slowly descending the steep slope, followed by two gigantic and emotionless Negroes, who carried a burden between them which still flashed and glittered in the sun. Half-way down two other figures joined them – John could see that they were Mrs Washington and her son, upon whose arm she leaned. The aviators had clambered from their machines to the sweeping lawn in front of the château, and with rifles in hand were starting up the diamond mountain in skirmishing formation.

But the little group of five which had formed farther up and was engrossing all the watchers' attention had stopped upon a ledge of rock. The Negroes stooped and pulled up what appeared to be a trap-door in the side of the mountain. Into this they all disappeared, the white-haired man first, then his wife and son, finally the two Negroes, the glittering tips of whose jewelled head-dresses caught the sun for a moment before the trap-door descended and engulfed them all.

Kismine clutched John's arm.

'Oh,' she cried wildly, 'where are they going? What are they going to do?'

'It must be some underground way of escape –'

A little scream from the two girls interrupted his sentence.

'Don't you see?' sobbed Kismine hysterically. 'The mountain is wired!'

Even as she spoke John put up his hands to shield his sight. Before their eyes the whole surface of the mountain had changed suddenly to a dazzling burning yellow, which showed up through the jacket of turf as light shows through a human hand. For a moment the intolerable glow continued, and then like an extinguished filament it disappeared, revealing a black waste from which blue smoke arose slowly, carrying off with it what remained of vegetation and of human flesh. Of the aviators there was left neither blood nor bone – they were consumed as completely as the five souls who had gone inside.

Simultaneously, and with an immense concussion, the château literally threw itself into the air, bursting into flaming fragments as it rose, and then tumbling back upon itself in a smoking pile that lay projecting half into the water of the lake. There was no fire – what smoke there was drifted off mingling with the sunshine, and for a few minutes longer a powdery dust of marble drifted from the great featureless pile that had once been the house of jewels. There was no more sound and the three people were alone in the valley.

XI

At sunset John and his two companions reached the high cliff which had marked the boundaries of the Washingtons' dominion, and looking back found the valley tranquil and lovely in the dusk. They sat down to finish the food which Jasmine had brought with her in a basket.

'There!' she said, as she spread the tablecloth and put the sandwiches in a neat pile upon it. 'Don't they look tempting? I always think that food tastes better outdoors.'

'With that remark,' remarked Kismine, 'Jasmine enters the middle class.'

'Now,' said John eagerly, 'turn out your pockets and let's see what jewels you brought along. If you made a good selection we three ought to live comfortably all the rest of our lives.'

Obediently Kismine put her hand in her pocket and tossed two handfuls of glittering stones before him.

'Not so bad,' cried John, enthusiastically. 'They aren't very big, but – Hello!' His expression changed as he held one of them up to the declining sun. 'Why, these aren't diamonds! There's something the matter!'

'By golly!' exclaimed Kismine, with a startled look. 'What an idiot I am!'

'Why, these are rhinestones!' cried John.

'I know.' She broke into a laugh. 'I opened the wrong drawer. They belonged on the dress of a girl who visited Jasmine. I got her to give them to me in exchange for diamonds. I'd never seen anything but precious stones before.'

'And this is what you brought?'

'I'm afraid so.' She fingered the brilliants wistfully. 'I think I like these better. I'm a little tired of diamonds.'

'Very well,' said John gloomily. 'We'll have to live in Hades. And you will grow old telling incredulous women that you got the wrong drawer. Unfortunately your father's bank-books were consumed with him.'

'Well, what's the matter with Hades?'

'If I come home with a wife at my age my father is just as liable as not to cut me off with a hot coal, as they say down there.'

Jasmine spoke up.

'I love washing,' she said quietly. 'I have always washed my own handkerchiefs. I'll take in laundry and support you both.'

'Do they have washwomen in Hades?' asked Kismine innocently.

'Of course,' answered John. 'It's just like anywhere else.'

'I thought – perhaps it was too hot to wear any clothes.'

John laughed.

'Just try it!' he suggested. 'They'll run you out before you're half started.'

'Will father be there?' she asked.

John turned to her in astonishment.

'Your father is dead,' he replied sombrely. 'Why should he go to Hades? You have it confused with another place that was abolished long ago.'

After supper they folded up the tablecloth and spread their blankets for the night.

'What a dream it was,' Kismine sighed, gazing up at the stars. 'How strange it seems to be here with one dress and a penniless fiancé!'

'Under the stars,' she repeated. 'I never noticed the stars before. I always thought of them as great big diamonds that belonged to someone. Now they frighten me. They make me feel that it was all a dream, all my youth.'

'It *was* a dream,' said John quietly. 'Everybody's youth is a dream, a form of chemical madness.'

'How pleasant then to be insane!'

'So I'm told,' said John gloomily. 'I don't know any longer. At any rate, let us love for a while, for a year or so, you and me. That's a form of divine drunkenness that we can all try. There are only diamonds in the whole world, diamonds and perhaps the shabby gift of disillusion. Well, I have that last and I will make the usual nothing of it.' He shivered. 'Turn up your coat collar, little girl, the night's full of chill and you'll get pneumonia. His was a great sin who first invented consciousness. Let us lose it for a few hours.'

So wrapping himself in his blanket he fell off to sleep.

THE RICH BOY

I

Begin with an individual, and before you know it you find that you have created a type; begin with a type, and you find that you have created – nothing. That is because we are all queer fish, queerer behind our faces and voices than we want anyone to know or than we know ourselves. When I hear a man proclaiming himself an 'average, honest, open fellow', I feel pretty sure that he has some definite and perhaps terrible abnormality which he has agreed to conceal – and his protestation of being average and honest and open is his way of reminding himself of his misprision.

There are no types, no plurals. There is a rich boy, and this is his and not his brothers' story. All my life I have lived among his brothers but this one has been my friend. Besides, if I wrote about his brothers I should have to begin by attacking all the lies that the poor have told about the rich and the rich have told about themselves – such a wild structure they have erected that when we pick up a book about the rich, some instinct prepares us for unreality. Even the intelligent and impassioned reporters of life have made the country of the rich as unreal as fairy-land.

Let me tell you about the very rich. They are different from you and me. They possess and enjoy early, and it does something to them, makes them soft where we are hard, and cynical where we are trustful, in a way that, unless you were born rich, it is very difficult to understand. They think, deep in their hearts, that they are better than we are because we had to discover the compensations and refuges of life for ourselves. Even when they enter deep into our world or sink below us, they still think that they are better than we are. They are different. The only way I can describe young Anson Hunter is to approach him as if he were a foreigner and cling stubbornly to my point of view. If I accept his for a moment I am lost – I have nothing to show but a preposterous movie.

II

Anson was the eldest of six children who would some day divide a fortune of fifteen million dollars, and he reached the age of reason – is it seven? – at the beginning of the century when daring young women were already gliding along Fifth Avenue in electric 'mobiles'. In those days he and his brother had an English governess who spoke the language very clearly and crisply and well, so that the two boys grew to speak as she did – their words and sentences were all crisp and clear and not run together as ours are. They didn't talk exactly like English children but acquired an accent that is peculiar to fashionable people in the city of New York.

In the summer the six children were moved from the house on 71st Street to a big estate in northern Connecticut. It was not a fashionable locality – Anson's father wanted to delay as long as possible his children's knowledge of that side of life. He was a man somewhat superior to his class, which composed New York society, and to his period, which was the snobbish and formalized vulgarity of the Gilded Age, and he wanted his sons to learn habits of concentration and have sound constitutions and grow up into right-living and successful men. He and his wife kept an eye on them as well as they were able until the two older boys went away to school, but in huge establishments this is difficult – it was much simpler in the series of small and medium-sized houses in which my own youth was spent – I was never far out of the reach of my mother's voice, of the sense of her presence, her approval or disapproval.

Anson's first sense of his superiority came to him when he realized the half-grudging American deference that was paid to him in the Connecticut village. The parents of the boys he played with always inquired after his father and mother, and were vaguely excited when their own children were asked to the Hunters' house. He accepted this as the natural state of things, and a sort of impatience with all groups of which he was not the centre – in money, in position, in authority – remained with him for the rest of his life. He disdained to struggle with other boys for precedence – he expected it to be given him freely, and when it wasn't he withdrew into his family. His family was sufficient, for in the East money is still a somewhat feudal thing, a clan-forming thing. In the snobbish West, money separates families to form 'sets'.

At eighteen, when he went to New Haven, Anson was tall and thick-set, with a clear complexion and a healthy colour from the ordered life he had led in school. His hair was yellow and grew in a funny way on his head, his nose was beaked – these two things kept him from being handsome – but he had a confident charm and a certain brusque style, and the upper-class men who passed him on the street knew without being told that he was a rich boy and had gone to one of the best schools. Nevertheless, his very superiority kept him from being a success in college – the independence was mistaken for egotism, and the refusal to accept Yale standards with the proper awe seemed to belittle all those who had. So, long before he graduated, he began to shift the centre of his life to New York.

He was at home in New York – there was his own house with 'the kind of servants you can't get any more' – and his own family, of which, because of his good humour and a certain ability to make things go, he was rapidly becoming the centre, and the débutante parties, and the correct manly world of the men's clubs, and the occasional wild spree with the gallant girls whom New Haven only knew from the fifth row. His aspirations were conventional enough – they included even the irreproachable shadow he would some day marry, but they differed from the aspirations of the majority of young men in that there was no mist over them, none of that quality which is variously known as 'idealism' or 'illusion'. Anson accepted without reservation the world of high finance and high extravagance, of divorce and dissipation, of snobbery and of privilege. Most of our lives end as a compromise – it was as a compromise that his life began.

He and I first met in the late summer of 1917 when he was just out of Yale, and, like the rest of us, was swept up into the systematized hysteria of the war. In the blue-green uniform of the naval aviation he came down to Pensacola, where the hotel orchestras played *I'm Sorry, Dear*, and we young officers danced with the girls. Everyone liked him, and though he ran with the drinkers and wasn't an especially good pilot, even the instructors treated him with a certain respect. He was always having long talks with them in his confident, logical voice – talks which ended by his getting himself, or, more frequently, another officer, out of some impending trouble. He was convivial, bawdy, robustly avid for pleasure, and we were all surprised when he fell in love with a conservative and rather proper girl.

Her name was Paula Legendre, a dark, serious beauty from somewhere in California. Her family kept a winter residence just outside of town, and in spite of her primness she was enormously popular; there is a large class of men whose egotism can't endure humour in a woman. But Anson wasn't that sort, and I couldn't understand the attraction of her 'sincerity' – that was the thing to say about her – for his keen and somewhat sardonic mind.

Nevertheless, they fell in love – and on her terms. He no longer joined the twilight gathering at the De Soto Bar, and whenever they were seen together they were engaged in a long, serious dialogue, which must have gone on several weeks. Long afterward he told me that it was not about anything in particular but was composed on both sides of immature and even meaningless statements – the emotional content that gradually came to fill it grew up not out of the words but out of its enormous seriousness. It was a sort of hypnosis. Often it was interrupted, giving way to that emasculated humour we call fun; when they were alone it was resumed again, solemn, low-keyed, and pitched so as to give each other a sense of unity in feeling and thought. They came to resent any interruptions of it, to be unresponsive to facetiousness about life, even to the mild cynicism of their contemporaries. They were only happy when the dialogue was going on, and its seriousness bathed them like the amber glow of an open fire. Toward the end there came an interruption they did not resent – it began to be interrupted by passion.

Oddly enough, Anson was as engrossed in the dialogue as she and as profoundly affected by it, yet at the same time aware that on his side much was insincere, and on hers much was merely simple. At first, too, he despised her emotional simplicity as well, but with his love her nature deepened and blossomed, and he could despise it no longer. He felt that if he could enter into Paula's warm safe life he would be happy. The long preparation of the dialogue removed any constraint – he taught her some of what he had learned from more adventurous women, and she responded with a rapt holy intensity. One evening after a dance they agreed to marry, and he wrote a long letter about her to his mother. The next day Paula told him that she was rich, that she had a personal fortune of nearly a million dollars.

III

It was exactly as if they could say 'Neither of us has anything: we shall be poor together' – just as delightful that they should be rich instead. It gave them the same communion of adventure. Yet when Anson got leave in April, and Paula and her mother accompanied him North, she was impressed with the standing of his family in New York and with the scale on which they lived. Alone with Anson for the first time in the rooms where he had played as a boy, she was filled with a comfortable emotion, as though she were pre-eminently safe and taken care of. The pictures of Anson in a skull-cap at his first school, of Anson on horseback with the sweetheart of a mysterious forgotten summer, of Anson in a gay group of ushers and bridesmaids at a wedding, made her jealous of his life apart from her in the past, and so completely did his authoritative person seem to sum up and typify these possessions of his that she was inspired with the idea of being married immediately and returning to Pensacola as his wife.

But an immediate marriage wasn't discussed – even the engagement was to be secret until after the war. When she realized that only two days of his leave remained, her dissatisfaction crystallized in the intention of making him as unwilling to wait as she was. They were driving to the country for dinner and she determined to force the issue that night.

Now a cousin of Paula's was staying with them at the Ritz, a severe, bitter girl who loved Paula but was somewhat jealous of her impressive engagement, and as Paula was late in dressing, the cousin, who wasn't going to the party, received Anson in the parlour of the suite.

Anson had met friends at five o'clock and drunk freely and indiscreetly with them for an hour. He left the Yale Club at a proper time, and his mother's chauffeur drove him to the Ritz, but his usual capacity was not in evidence, and the impact of the steam-heated sitting-room made him suddenly dizzy. He knew it, and he was both amused and sorry.

Paula's cousin was twenty-five, but she was exceptionally naïve, and at first failed to realize what was up. She had never met Anson before, and she was surprised when he mumbled strange information and nearly fell off his chair, but until Paula appeared it didn't occur to her that what she had taken for the odour of a dry-cleaned uniform was really whisky. But Paula understood as soon as she appeared; her only thought was to get Anson away before her mother saw him, and at the look in her eyes the cousin understood too.

When Paula and Anson descended to the limousine they found two men inside, both asleep; they were the men with whom he had been drinking at the Yale Club, and they were also going to the party. He had entirely forgotten their presence in the car. On the way to Hempstead they awoke and sang. Some of the songs were rough, and though Paula tried to reconcile herself to the fact that Anson had few verbal inhibitions, her lips tightened with shame and distaste.

Back at the hotel the cousin, confused and agitated, considered the incident, and then walked into Mrs Legendre's bedroom, saying: 'Isn't he funny?'

'Who is funny?'

'Why – Mr Hunter. He seemed so funny.'

Mrs Legendre looked at her sharply.

'How is he funny?'

'Why, he said he was French. I didn't know he was French.'

'That's absurd. You must have misunderstood.' She smiled: 'It was a joke.'

The cousin shook her head stubbornly.

'No. He said he was brought up in France. He said he couldn't speak any English and that's why he couldn't talk to me. And he couldn't!'

Mrs Legendre looked away with impatience just as the cousin added thoughtfully, 'Perhaps it was because he was so drunk,' and walked out of the room.

This curious report was true. Anson, finding his voice thick and uncontrollable, had taken the unusual refuge of announcing that he spoke no English. Years afterwards he used to tell that part of the story, and he invariably communicated the uproarious laughter which the memory aroused in him.

Five times in the next hour Mrs Legendre tried to get Hempstead on the phone. When she succeeded, there was a ten-minute delay before she heard Paula's voice on the wire.

'Cousin Jo told me Anson was intoxicated.'

'Oh, no . . .'

'Oh, yes. Cousin Jo says he was intoxicated. He told her he was French, and fell off his chair and behaved as if he was very intoxicated. I don't want you to come home with him.'

'Mother, he's all right! Please don't worry about –'

'But I do worry. I think it's dreadful. I want you to promise me not to come home with him.'

'I'll take care of it, Mother . . .'

'I don't want you to come home with him.'

'All right, Mother. Good-bye.'

'Be sure now, Paula. Ask someone to bring you.'

Deliberately Paula took the receiver from her ear and hung it up. Her face was flushed with helpless annoyance. Anson was stretched out asleep in a bedroom upstairs, while the dinner-party below was proceeding lamely toward conclusion.

The hour's drive had sobered him somewhat – his arrival was merely hilarious – and Paula hoped that the evening was not spoiled, after all, but two imprudent cocktails before dinner completed the disaster. He talked boisterously and somewhat offensively to the party at large for fifteen minutes, and then slid silently under the table; like a man in an old print – but, unlike an old print, it was rather horrible without being at all quaint. None of the young girls present remarked upon the incident – it seemed to merit only silence. His uncle and two other men carried him upstairs, and it was just after this that Paula was called to the phone.

An hour later Anson awoke in a fog of nervous agony, through which he perceived after a moment the figure of his Uncle Robert standing by the door.

'. . . I said are you better?'

'What?'

'Do you feel better, old man?'

'Terrible,' said Anson.

'I'm going to try you on another bromo-seltzer. If you can hold it down, it'll do you good to sleep.'

With an effort Anson slid his legs from the bed and stood up.

'I'm all right,' he said dully.

'Take it easy.'

'I thin' if you gave me a glassbrandy I could go downstairs.'

'Oh, no –'

'Yes, that's the only thin'. I'm all right now . . . I suppose I'm in Dutch dow' there.'

'They know you're a little under the weather,' said his uncle deprecatingly. 'But don't worry about it. Schuyler didn't even get here. He passed away in the locker-room over at the Links.'

Indifferent to any opinion, except Paula's, Anson was nevertheless determined to save the débris of the evening, but when after a cold bath he made his appearance most of the party had already left. Paula got up immediately to go home.

In the limousine the old serious dialogue began. She had known that he drank, she admitted, but she had never expected anything like this – it seemed to her that perhaps they were not suited to each other, after all. Their ideas about life were too different, and so forth. When she finished speaking, Anson spoke in turn, very soberly. Then Paula said she'd have to think it over; she wouldn't decide tonight; she was not angry but she was terribly sorry. Nor would she let him come into the hotel with her, but just before she got out of the car she leaned and kissed him unhappily on the cheek.

The next afternoon Anson had a long talk with Mrs Legendre while Paula sat listening in silence. It was agreed that Paula was to brood over the incident for a proper period and then, if mother and daughter thought it best, they would follow Anson to Pensacola. On his part he apologized with sincerity and dignity – that was all; with every card in her hand Mrs Legendre was unable to establish any advantage over him. He made no promises, showed no humility, only delivered a few serious comments on life which brought him off with rather a moral superiority at the end. When they came South three weeks later neither Anson in his satisfaction nor Paula in her relief at the reunion realized that the psychological moment had passed forever.

IV

He dominated and attracted her, and at the same time filled her with anxiety. Confused by his mixture of solidity and self-indulgence, of sentiment and cynicism – incongruities which her gentle mind was unable to resolve – Paula grew to think of him as two alternating personalities. When she saw him alone, or at a formal party, or with his casual inferiors, she felt a tremendous pride in his strong, attractive presence, the paternal, understanding stature of his mind. In other company she became uneasy when what had been a fine imperviousness to mere gentility showed its other face. The other face was gross, humorous, reckless of everything but pleasure. It startled her mind temporarily away from him, even led her into a short, covert experiment with an old beau, but it was no use – after four months of Anson's enveloping vitality there was an anaemic pallor in all other men.

In July he was ordered abroad, and their tenderness and desire reached a crescendo. Paula considered a last-minute marriage – decided against it only because there were always cocktails on his breath now, but the parting itself made her physically ill with grief. After his departure she wrote him long letters of regret for the days of love they had missed by waiting. In August Anson's plane slipped down into the North Sea. He was pulled on to a destroyer after a night in the water and sent to hospital with pneumonia; the armistice was signed before he was finally sent home.

Then, with every opportunity given back to them, with no material

obstacle to overcome, the secret weavings of their temperaments came
between them, drying up their kisses and their tears, making their voices
less loud to one another, muffling the intimate chatter of their hearts
until the old communication was only possible by letters, from far away.
One afternoon a society reporter waited for two hours in the Hunters'
house for a confirmation of their engagement. Anson denied it; nevertheless an early issue carried the report as a leading paragraph – they were
'constantly seen together at Southampton, Hot Springs, and Tuxedo
Park'. But the serious dialogue had turned a corner into a long-sustained
quarrel, and the affair was almost played out. Anson got drunk flagrantly
and missed an engagement with her, whereupon Paula made certain
behaviouristic demands. His despair was helpless before his pride and
his knowledge of himself: the engagement was definitely broken.

'Dearest,' said their letters now, 'Dearest, Dearest, when I wake up
in the middle of the night and realize that after all it was not to be, I
feel that I want to die. I can't go on living any more. Perhaps when we
meet this summer we may talk things over and decide differently – we
were so excited and sad that day, and I don't feel that I can live all my
life without you. You speak of other people. Don't you know there are
no other people for me, but only you . . .'

But as Paula drifted here and there around the East she would
sometimes mention her gaieties to make him wonder. Anson was too
acute to wonder. When he saw a man's name in her letters he felt more
sure of her and a little disdainful – he was always superior to such
things. But he still hoped that they would some day marry.

Meanwhile he plunged vigorously into all the movement and glitter
of post-bellum New York, entering a brokerage house, joining half a
dozen clubs, dancing late, and moving in three worlds – his own world,
the world of young Yale graduates, and that section of the half-world
which rests one end on Broadway. But there was always a thorough
and infractible eight hours devoted to his work in Wall Street, where
the combination of his influential family connexion, his sharp intelligence, and his abundance of sheer physical energy brought him almost
immediately forward. He had one of those invaluable minds with parti-
tions in it; sometimes he appeared at his office refreshed by less than an
hour's sleep, but such occurrences were rare. So early as 1920 his
income in salary and commissions exceeded twelve thousand dollars.

As the Yale tradition slipped into the past he became more and more
of a popular figure among his classmates in New York, more popular
than he had ever been in college. He lived in a great house, and had

the means of introducing young men into other great houses. Moreover, his life already seemed secure, while theirs, for the most part, had arrived again at precarious beginnings. They commenced to turn to him for amusement and escape, and Anson responded readily, taking pleasure in helping people and arranging their affairs.

There were no men in Paula's letters now, but a note of tenderness ran through them that had not been there before. From several sources he heard that she had 'a heavy beau', Lowell Thayer, a Bostonian of wealth and position, and though he was sure she still loved him, it made him uneasy to think that he might lose her, after all. Save for one unsatisfactory day she had not been in New York for almost five months, and as the rumours multiplied he became increasingly anxious to see her. In February he took his vacation and went down to Florida.

Palm Beach sprawled plump and opulent between the sparkling sapphire of Lake Worth, flawed here and there by house-boats at anchor, and the great turquoise bar of the Atlantic Ocean. The huge bulks of the Breakers and the Royal Poinciana rose as twin paunches from the bright level of the sand, and around them clustered the Dancing Glade, Bradley's House of Chance, and a dozen modistes and milliners with goods at triple prices from New York. Upon the trellised veranda of the Breakers two hundred women stepped right, stepped left, wheeled, and slid in that then celebrated calisthenic known as the double-shuffle, while in half-time to the music 2,000 bracelets clicked up and down on 200 arms.

At the Everglades Club after dark Paula and Lowell Thayer and Anson and a casual fourth played bridge with hot cards. It seemed to Anson that her kind, serious face was wan and tired – she had been around now for four, five, years. He had known her for three.

'Two spades.'

'Cigarette? .... Oh, I beg your pardon. By me.'

'By.'

'I'll double three spades.'

There were a dozen tables of bridge in the room, which was filling up with smoke. Anson's eyes met Paula's, held them persistently even when Thayer's glance fell between them . . .

'What was bid?' he asked abstractedly.

'Rose of Washington Square'

sang the young people in the corners:

'I'm withering there
In basement air –'

The smoke banked like fog, and the opening of a door filled the room with blown swirls of ectoplasm. Little Bright Eyes streaked past the tables seeking Mr Conan Doyle among the Englishmen who were posing as Englishmen about the lobby.

'You could cut it with a knife.'

'. . . cut it with a knife.'

'. . . a knife.'

At the end of the rubber Paula suddenly got up and spoke to Anson in a tense, low voice. With scarcely a glance at Lowell Thayer, they walked out the door and descended a long flight of stone steps – in a moment they were walking hand in hand along the moonlit beach.

'Darling, darling . . .' They embraced recklessly, passionately, in a shadow . . . Then Paula drew back her face to let his lips say what she wanted to hear – she could feel the words forming as they kissed again . . . Again she broke away, listening, but as he pulled her close once more she realized that he had said nothing – only *'Darling! Darling!'* in that deep, sad whisper that always made her cry. Humbly, obediently, her emotions yielded to him and the tears streamed down her face, but her heart kept on crying: 'Ask me – oh, Anson, ask me!'

'Paula . . . *Paula!'*

The words wrung her heart like hands, and Anson, feeling her tremble, knew that emotion was enough. He need say no more, commit their destinies to no practical enigma. Why should he, when he might hold her so, biding his own time, for another year – forever? He was considering them both, her more than himself. For a moment, when she said suddenly that she must go back to her hotel, he hesitated, thinking first, 'This is the moment, after all,' and then: 'No, let it wait – she is mine . . .'

He had forgotten that Paula too was worn away inside with the strain of three years. Her mood passed forever in the night.

He went back to New York next morning filled with a certain restless dissatisfaction. Late in April, without warning, he received a telegram from Bar Harbour in which Paula told him that she was engaged to Lowell Thayer, and that they would be married immediately in Boston. What he never really believed could happen had happened at last.

Anson filled himself with whisky that morning, and going to the office, carried on his work without a break – rather with a fear of what would happen if he stopped. In the evening he went out as usual, saying nothing of what had occurred; he was cordial, humorous, unabstracted. But one thing he could not help – for three days, in any place, in any company, he would suddenly bend his head into his hands and cry like a child.

V

In 1922 when Anson went abroad with the junior partner to investigate some London loans, the journey intimated that he was to be taken into the firm. He was twenty-seven now, a little heavy without being definitely stout, and with a manner older than his years. Old people and young people liked him and trusted him, and mothers felt safe when their daughters were in his charge, for he had a way, when he came into a room, of putting himself on a footing with the oldest and most conservative people there. 'You and I,' he seemed to say, 'we're solid. We understand.'

He had an instinctive and rather charitable knowledge of the weaknesses of men and women, and, like a priest, it made him the more concerned for the maintenance of outward forms. It was typical of him that every Sunday morning he taught in a fashionable Episcopal Sunday-school – even though a cold shower and a quick change into a cutaway coat were all that separated him from the wild night before.

After his father's death he was the practical head of his family, and, in effect, guided the destinies of the younger children. Through a complication his authority did not extend to his father's estate, which was administered by his Uncle Robert, who was the horsey member of the family, a good-natured, hard-drinking member of that set which centres about Wheatley Hills.

Uncle Robert and his wife, Edna, had been great friends of Anson's youth, and the former was disappointed when his nephew's superiority failed to take a horsey form. He backed him for a city club which was the most difficult in America to enter – one could only join if one's family had 'helped to build up New York' (or, in other words, were rich before 1880) – and when Anson, after his election, neglected it for the Yale Club, Uncle Robert gave him a little talk on the subject. But when on top of that Anson declined to enter Robert Hunter's own conservative and somewhat neglected brokerage house, his manner grew cooler. Like a primary teacher who has taught all he knew, he slipped out of Anson's life.

There were so many friends in Anson's life – scarcely one for whom he had not done some unusual kindness and scarcely one whom he did not occasionally embarrass by his bursts of rough conversation or his habit of getting drunk whenever and however he liked. It annoyed him when anyone else blundered in that regard – about his own lapses he was always humorous. Odd things happened to him and he told them with infectious laughter.

I was working in New York that spring, and I used to lunch with him at the Yale Club, which my university was sharing until the completion of our own. I had read of Paula's marriage, and one afternoon, when I asked him about her, something moved him to tell me the story. After that he frequently invited me to family dinners at his house and behaved as though there was a special relation between us, as though with his confidence a little of that consuming memory had passed into me.

I found that despite the trusting mothers, his attitude toward girls was not indiscriminately protective. It was up to the girl – if she showed an inclination toward looseness, she must take care of herself, even with him.

'Life,' he would explain sometimes, 'has made a cynic of me.'

By life he meant Paula. Sometimes, especially when he was drinking, it became a little twisted in his mind, and he thought that she had callously thrown him over.

This 'cynicism', or rather his realization that naturally fast girls were not worth sparing, led to his affair with Dolly Karger. It wasn't his only affair in those years, but it came nearest to touching him deeply, and it had a profound effect upon his attitude toward life.

Dolly was the daughter of a notorious 'publicist' who had married into society. She herself grew up into the Junior League, came out at the Plaza, and went to the Assembly; and only a few old families like the Hunters could question whether or not she 'belonged', for her picture was often in the papers, and she had more enviable attention than many girls who undoubtedly did. She was dark-haired, with carmine lips and a high, lovely colour, which she concealed under pinkish-grey powder all through the first year out, because high colour was unfashionable – Victorian-pale was the thing to be. She wore black, severe suits and stood with her hands in her pockets leaning a little forward, with a humorous restraint on her face. She danced exquisitely – better than anything she liked to dance – better than anything except making love. Since she was ten she had always been in love, and, usually, with some boy who didn't respond to her. Those who did – and there were many – bored her after a brief encounter, but for her failures she reserved the warmest spot in her heart. When she met them she would always try once more – sometimes she succeeded, more often she failed.

It never occurred to this gypsy of the unattainable that there was a certain resemblance in those who refused to love her – they shared a hard intuition that saw through to her weakness, not a weakness of emotion but a weakness of rudder. Anson perceived this when he first met her, less than a month after Paula's marriage. He was drinking rather heavily, and he pretended for a week that he was falling in love with her. Then he dropped her abruptly and forgot – immediately he took up the commanding position in her heart.

Like so many girls of that day Dolly was slackly and indiscreetly wild. The unconventionality of a slightly older generation had been simply one facet of a post-war movement to discredit obsolete manners – Dolly's was both older and shabbier, and she saw in Anson the two extremes which the emotionally shiftless woman seeks, an abandon to indulgence alternating with a protective strength. In his character she felt both the sybarite and the solid rock, and these two satisfied every need of her nature.

She felt that it was going to be difficult, but she mistook the reason – she thought that Anson and his family expected a more spectacular marriage, but she guessed immediately that her advantage lay in his tendency to drink.

They met at the large débutante dances, but as her infatuation increased they managed to be more and more together. Like most mothers, Mrs Karger believed that Anson was exceptionally reliable, so she allowed Dolly to go with him to distant country clubs and suburban houses without inquiring closely into their activities or questioning her explanations when they came in late. At first these explanations might have been accurate, but Dolly's worldly ideas of capturing Anson were soon engulfed in the rising sweep of her emotion. Kisses in the back of taxis and motor-cars were no longer enough; they did a curious thing:

They dropped out of their world for a while and made another world just beneath it where Anson's tippling and Dolly's irregular hours would be less noticed and commented on. It was composed, this world, of varying elements – several of Anson's Yale friends and their wives, two or three young brokers and bond salesmen, and a handful of unattached men, fresh from college, with money and a propensity to dissipation. What this world lacked in spaciousness and scale it made up for by allowing them a liberty that it scarcely permitted itself. Moreover, it centred around them and permitted Dolly the pleasure of a faint condescension – a pleasure which Anson, whose whole life was a condescension from the certitudes of his childhood, was unable to share.

He was not in love with her, and in the long feverish winter of their affair he frequently told her so. In the spring he was weary – he wanted to renew his life at some other source – moreover, he saw that either he must break with her now or accept the responsibility of a definite seduction. Her family's encouraging attitude precipitated his decision – one evening when Mr Karger knocked discreetly at the library door to announce that he had left a bottle of old brandy in the dining-room, Anson felt that life was hemming him in. That night he wrote her a short letter in which he told her that he was going on his vacation, and that in view of all the circumstances they had better meet no more.

It was June. His family had closed up the house and gone to the country, so he was living temporarily at the Yale Club. I had heard about his affair with Dolly as it developed – accounts salted with humour, for he despised unstable women, and granted them no place in the social edifice in which he believed – and when he told me that night that he was definitely breaking with her I was glad. I had seen Dolly here and there, and each time with a feeling of pity at the hopelessness of her struggle, and of shame at knowing so much about her that I had no right to know. She was what is known as 'a pretty little thing', but there was a certain recklessness which rather fascinated me. Her dedication to the goddess of waste would have been less obvious had she been less spirited – she would most certainly throw herself away, but I was glad when I heard that the sacrifice would not be consummated in my sight.

Anson was going to leave the letter of farewell at her house next morning. It was one of the few houses left open in the Fifth Avenue district, and he knew that the Kargers, acting upon erroneous information from Dolly, had forgone a trip abroad to give their daughter her chance. As he stepped out the door of the Yale Club into Madison Avenue the postman passed him, and he followed back inside. The first letter that caught his eye was in Dolly's hand.

He knew what it would be – a lonely and tragic monologue, full of the reproaches he knew, the invoked memories, and 'I wonder if's' – all the immemorial intimacies that he had communicated to Paula Legendre in what seemed another age. Thumbing over some bills, he brought it on top again and opened it. To his surprise it was a short, somewhat formal note, which said that Dolly would be unable to go to the country with him for the week-end, because Perry Hull from Chicago had unexpectedly come to town. It added that Anson had brought this on himself: '– if I felt that you loved me as I love you I would go with you at any time, any place, but Perry is *so* nice, and he so much wants me to marry him –'

Anson smiled contemptuously – he had had experience with such decoy epistles. Moreover, he knew how Dolly had laboured over this plan, probably sent for the faithful Perry and calculated the time of his arrival – even laboured over the note so that it would make him jealous without driving him away. Like most compromises, it had neither force nor vitality but only a timorous despair.

Suddenly he was angry. He sat down in the lobby and read it again. Then he went to the phone, called Dolly and told her in his clear, compelling voice that he had received her note and would call for her at five o'clock as they had previously planned. Scarcely waiting for the pretended uncertainty of her 'Perhaps I can see you for an hour', he hung up the receiver and went down to his office. On the way he tore his own letter into bits and dropped it in the street.

He was not jealous – she meant nothing to him – but at her pathetic ruse everything stubborn and self-indulgent in him came to the surface. It was a presumption from a mental inferior and it could not be overlooked. If she wanted to know to whom she belonged she would see.

He was on the door-step at quarter-past five. Dolly was dressed for the street, and he listened in silence to the paragraph of 'I can only see you for an hour', which she had begun on the phone.

'Put on your hat, Dolly,' he said, 'we'll take a walk.'

They strolled up Madison Avenue and over to Fifth while Anson's shirt dampened upon his portly body in the deep heat. He talked little, scolding her, making no love to her, but before they had walked six blocks she was his again, apologizing for the note, offering not to see Perry at all as an atonement, offering anything. She thought that he had come because he was beginning to love her.

'I'm hot,' he said when they reached 71st Street. 'This is a winter suit. If I stop by the house and change, would you mind waiting for me downstairs? I'll only be a minute.'

She was happy; the intimacy of his being hot, of any physical fact

about him, thrilled her. When they came to the iron-grated door and
Anson took out his key she experienced a sort of delight.

Downstairs it was dark, and after he ascended in the lift Dolly raised
a curtain and looked out through opaque lace at the houses over the
way. She heard the lift machinery stop, and with the notion of teasing
him pressed the button that brought it down. Then on what was more
than an impulse she got into it and sent it up to what she guessed was
his floor.

'Anson,' she called, laughing a little.

'Just a minute,' he answered from his bedroom . . . then after a brief
delay: 'Now you can come in.'

He had changed and was buttoning his vest.

'This is my room.' he said lightly. 'How do you like it?'

She caught sight of Paula's picture on the wall and stared at it in
fascination, just as Paula had stared at the pictures of Anson's childish
sweethearts five years before. She knew something about Paula – sometimes she tortured herself with fragments of the story.

Suddenly she came close to Anson, raising her arms. They embraced.
Outside the area window a soft artificial twilight already hovered, though
the sun was still bright on a back roof across the way. In half an
hour the room would be quite dark. The uncalculated opportunity
overwhelmed them, made them both breathless, and they clung more
closely. It was imminent, inevitable. Still holding one another, they
raised their heads – their eyes fell together upon Paula's picture, staring
down at them from the wall.

Suddenly Anson dropped his arms, and sitting down at his desk tried
the drawer with a bunch of keys.

'Like a drink?' he asked in a gruff voice.

'No, Anson.'

He poured himself half a tumbler of whisky, swallowed it, and then
opened the door into the hall.

'Come on,' he said.

Dolly hesitated.

'Anson – I'm going to the country with you tonight, after all. You
understand that, don't you?'

'Of course,' he answered brusquely.

In Dolly's car they rode on to Long Island, closer in their emotions
than they had ever been before. They knew what would happen – not
with Paula's face to remind them that something was lacking, but when
they were alone in the still, hot, Long Island night they did not care.

The estate in Port Washington where they were to spend the weekend belonged to a cousin of Anson's who had married a Montana copper operator. An interminable drive began at the lodge and twisted under imported poplar saplings toward a huge, pink Spanish house. Anson had often visited there before.

After dinner they danced at the Linx Club. About midnight Anson assured himself that his cousins would not leave before two – then he explained that Dolly was tired; he would take her home and return to the dance later. Trembling a little with excitement, they got into a borrowed car together and drove to Port Washington. As they reached the lodge he stopped and spoke to the night-watchman.

'When are you making a round, Carl?'

'Right away.'

'Then you'll be here till everybody's in?'

'Yes, sir.'

'All right. Listen: if any automobile, no matter whose it is, turns in at this gate, I want you to phone the house immediately.' He put a five-dollar bill into Carl's hand. 'Is that clear?'

'Yes, Mr Anson.' Being of the Old World, he neither winked nor smiled. Yet Dolly sat with her face turned slightly away.

Anson had a key. Once inside he poured a drink for both of them – Dolly left hers untouched – then he ascertained definitely the location of the phone, and found that it was within easy hearing distance of their rooms, both of which were on the first floor.

Five minutes later he knocked at the door of Dolly's room.

'Anson?' He went in, closing the door behind him. She was in bed, leaning up anxiously with elbows on the pillow; sitting beside her he took her in his arms.

'Anson, darling.'

He didn't answer.

'Anson . . . Anson! I love you . . . Say you love me. Say it now – can't you say it now? Even if you don't mean it?'

He did not listen. Over her head he perceived that the picture of Paula was hanging here upon this wall.

He got up and went close to it. The frame gleamed faintly with thrice-reflected moonlight – within was a blurred shadow of a face that he saw he did not know. Almost sobbing, he turned around and stared with abomination at the little figure on the bed.

'This is all foolishness,' he said thickly. 'I don't know what I was thinking about. I don't love you and you'd better wait for somebody that loves you. I don't love you a bit, can't you understand?'

His voice broke, and he went hurriedly out. Back in the saloon he was pouring himself a drink with uneasy fingers, when the front door opened suddenly, and his cousin came in.

'Why, Anson, I hear Dolly's sick,' she began solicitously. 'I hear she's sick . . .'

'It was nothing,' he interrupted, raising his voice so that it would carry into Dolly's room. 'She was a little tired. She went to bed.'

For a long time afterward Anson believed that a protective God sometimes interfered in human affairs. But Dolly Karger, lying awake and staring at the ceiling, never again believed in anything at all.

VI

When Dolly married during the following autumn, Anson was in London on business. Like Paula's marriage, it was sudden, but it affected him in a different way. At first he felt that it was funny, and had an inclination to laugh when he thought of it. Later it depressed him – it made him feel old.

There was something repetitive about it – why, Paula and Dolly had belonged to different generations. He had a foretaste of the sensation of a man of forty who hears that the daughter of an old flame has married. He wired congratulations and, as was not the case with Paula, they were sincere – he had never really hoped that Paula would be happy.

When he returned to New York, he was made a partner in the firm, and, as his responsibilities increased, he had less time on his hands. The refusal of a life-insurance company to issue him a policy made such an impression on him that he stopped drinking for a year, and claimed that he felt better physically, though I think he missed the convivial recounting of those Celliniesque adventures which, in his early twenties, had played such a part in his life. But he never abandoned the Yale Club. He was a figure there, a personality, and the tendency of his class, who were now seven years out of college, to drift away to more sober haunts was checked by his presence.

His day was never too full nor his mind too weary to give any sort of aid to anyone who asked it. What had been done at first through pride and superiority had become a habit and passion. And there was always something – a younger brother in trouble at New Haven, a quarrel to be patched up between a friend and his wife, a position to be found for this man, an investment for that. But his specialty was the solving of problems for young married people. Young married people fascinated him and their apartments were almost sacred to him – he knew the story of their love-affair, advised them where to live and how, and remembered their babies' names. Toward young wives his attitude was circumspect: he never abused the trust which their husbands – strangely enough in view of his unconcealed irregularities – invariably reposed in him.

He came to take a vicarious pleasure in happy marriages, and to be inspired to an almost equally pleasant melancholy by those that went astray. Not a season passed that he did not witness the collapse of an affair that perhaps he himself had fathered. When Paula was divorced and almost immediately remarried to another Bostonian, he talked about her to me all one afternoon. He would never love anyone as he had loved Paula, but he insisted that he no longer cared.

'I'll never marry,' he came to say; 'I've seen too much of it, and I know a happy marriage is a very rare thing. Besides, I'm too old.'

But he did believe in marriage. Like all men who spring from a happy and successful marriage, he believed in it passionately – nothing he had seen would change his belief, his cynicism dissolved upon it like air. But he did really believe he was too old. At twenty-eight he began to accept with equanimity the prospect of marrying without romantic love; he resolutely chose a New York girl of his own class, pretty, intelligent, congenial, above reproach – and set about falling in love with her. The things he had said to Paula with sincerity, to other girls with grace, he could no longer say at all without smiling, or with the force necessary to convince.

'When I'm forty,' he told his friends, 'I'll be ripe. I'll fall for some chorus girl like the rest.'

Nevertheless, he persisted in his attempt. His mother wanted to see him married, and he could now well afford it – he had a seat on the Stock Exchange, and his earned income came to twenty-five thousand a year. The idea was agreeable: when his friends – he spent most of his time with the set he and Dolly had evolved – closed themselves in behind domestic doors at night, he no longer rejoiced in his freedom. He even wondered if he should have married Dolly. Not even Paula had loved him more, and he was learning the rarity, in a single life, of encountering true emotion.

Just as this mood began to creep over him a disquieting story reached his ear. His Aunt Edna, a woman just this side of forty, was carrying on an open intrigue with a dissolute, hard-drinking young man named Cary Sloane. Everyone knew of it except Anson's Uncle Robert, who for fifteen years had talked long in clubs and taken his wife for granted.

Anson heard the story again and again with increasing annoyance. Something of his old feeling for his uncle came back to him, a feeling that was more than personal, a reversion towards that family solidarity on which he had based his pride. His intuition singled out the essential point of the affair, which was that his uncle shouldn't be hurt. It was his first experiment in unsolicited meddling, but with his knowledge of Edna's character he felt that he could handle the matter better than a district judge or his uncle.

His uncle was in Hot Springs. Anson traced down the sources of the scandal so that there should be no possibility of mistake and then he called Edna and asked her to lunch with him at the Plaza next day. Something in his tone must have frightened her, for she was reluctant, but he insisted, putting off the date until she had no excuse for refusing.

She met him at the appointed time in the Plaza lobby, a lovely, faded, grey-eyed blonde in a coat of Russian sable. Five great rings, cold with diamonds and emeralds, sparkled on her slender hands. It occurred to Anson that it was his father's intelligence and not his uncle's that had earned the fur and the stones, the rich brilliance that buoyed up her passing beauty.

Though Edna scented his hostility, she was unprepared for the directness of his approach.

'Edna, I'm astonished at the way you've been acting,' he said in a strong, frank voice. 'At first I couldn't believe it.'

'Believe what?' she demanded sharply.

'You needn't pretend with me, Edna. I'm talking about Cary Sloane. Aside from any other consideration, I didn't think you could treat Uncle Robert –'

'Now look here, Anson –' she began angrily, but his peremptory voice broke through hers:

'– and your children in such a way. You've been married eighteen years, and you're old enough to know better.'

'You can't talk to me like that! You –'

'Yes, I can. Uncle Robert has always been my best friend.' He was tremendously moved. He felt a real distress about his uncle, about his three young cousins.

Edna stood up, leaving her crab-flake cocktail untasted.

'This is the silliest thing –'

'Very well, if you won't listen to me I'll go to Uncle Robert and tell him the whole story – he's bound to hear it sooner or later. And afterward I'll go to old Moses Sloane.'

Edna faltered back into her chair.

'Don't talk so loud,' she begged him. Her eyes blurred with tears. 'You have no idea how your voice carries. You might have chosen a less public place to make all these crazy accusations.'

He didn't answer.

'Oh, you never liked me, I know,' she went on. 'You're just taking advantage of some silly gossip to try and break up the only interesting friendship I've ever had. What did I ever do to make you hate me so?'

Still Anson waited. There would be the appeal to his chivalry, then to his pity, finally to his superior sophistication – when he had shouldered his way through all these there would be admissions, and he could come to grips with her. By being silent, by being impervious, by returning constantly to his main weapon, which was his own true emotion, he bullied her into frantic despair as the luncheon hour slipped away. At two o'clock she took out a mirror and a handkerchief, shined away the marks of her tears and powdered the slight hollows where they had lain. She had agreed to meet him at her own house at five.

When he arrived she was stretched on a chaise-longue which was covered with cretonne for the summer, and the tears he had called up at luncheon seemed still to be standing in her eyes. Then he was aware of Cary Sloane's dark, anxious presence upon the cold hearth.

'What's this idea of yours?' broke out Sloane immediately. 'I understand you invited Edna to lunch and then threatened her on the basis of some cheap scandal.'

Anson sat down.

'I have no reason to think it's only scandal.'

'I hear you're going to take it to Robert Hunter, and to my father.'

Anson nodded.

'Either you break it off – or I will,' he said.

'What God damned business is it of yours, Hunter?'

'Don't lose your temper, Cary,' said Edna nervously. 'It's only a question of showing him how absurd –'

'For one thing, it's my name that's being handed around,' interrupted Anson. 'That's all that concerns you, Cary.'

'Edna isn't a member of your family.'

'She most certainly is!' His anger mounted. 'Why – she owes this house and the rings on her fingers to my father's brains. When Uncle Robert married her she didn't have a penny.'

They all looked at the rings as if they had a significant bearing on the situation. Edna made a gesture to take them from her hand.

'I guess they're not the only rings in the world,' said Sloane.

'Oh, this is absurd,' cried Edna. 'Anson, will you listen to me? I've found out how the silly story started. It was a maid I discharged who went right to the Chilicheffs – all these Russians pump things out of their servants and then put a false meaning on them.' She brought down her fist angrily on the table: 'And after Robert lent them the limousine for a whole month when we were South last winter –'

'Do you see?' demanded Sloane eagerly. 'This maid got hold of the wrong end of the thing. She knew that Edna and I were friends, and she carried it to the Chilicheffs. In Russia they assume that if a man and a woman –'

He enlarged the theme to a disquisition upon social relations in the Caucasus.

'If that's the case it better be explained to Uncle Robert,' said Anson dryly, 'so that when the rumours do reach him he'll know they're not true.'

Adopting the method he had followed with Edna at luncheon he let them explain it all away. He knew that they were guilty and that presently they would cross the line from explanation into justification and convict themselves more definitely than he could ever do. By seven they had taken the desperate step of telling him the truth – Robert Hunter's neglect, Edna's empty life, the casual dalliance that had flamed up into passion – but like so many true stories it had the misfortune of being old, and its enfeebled body beat helplessly against the armour of Anson's will. The threat to go to Sloane's father sealed their helplessness, for the latter, a retired cotton broker out of Alabama, was a notorious fundamentalist who controlled his son by a rigid allowance and the promise that at his next vagary the allowance would stop forever.

They dined at a small French restaurant, and the discussion continued – at one time Sloane resorted to physical threats, a little later they were both imploring him to give them time. But Anson was obdurate. He saw that Edna was breaking up, and that her spirit must not be refreshed by any renewal of their passion.

At two o'clock in a small night-club on 53rd Street, Edna's nerves suddenly collapsed, and she cried to go home. Sloane had been drinking heavily all evening, and he was faintly maudlin, leaning on the table and weeping a little with his face in his hands. Quickly Anson gave them his terms. Sloane was to leave town for six months, and he must be gone within forty-eight hours. When he returned there was to be no resumption of the affair, but at the end of a year Edna might, if she wished, tell Robert Hunter that she wanted a divorce and go about it in the usual way.

He paused, gaining confidence from their faces for his final word.

'Or there's another thing you can do,' he said slowly, 'if Edna wants to leave her children, there's nothing I can do to prevent your running off together.'

'I want to go home!' cried Edna again. 'Oh, haven't you done enough to us for one day?'

Outside it was dark, save for a blurred glow from Sixth Avenue down the street. In that light those two who had been lovers looked for the last time into each other's tragic faces, realizing that between them there was not enough youth and strength to avert their eternal parting. Sloane walked suddenly off down the street and Anson tapped a dozing taxi-driver on the arm.

It was almost four; there was a patient flow of cleaning water along the ghostly pavement of Fifth Avenue, and the shadows of two night women flitted over the dark façade of St Thomas's church. Then the desolate shrubbery of Central Park where Anson had often played as a child, and the mounting numbers, significant as names, of the marching streets. This was his city, he thought, where his name had flourished through five generations. No change could alter the permanence of its place here, for change itself was the essential substratum by which he and those of his name identified themselves with the spirit of New York. Resourcefulness and a powerful will – for his threats in weaker hands would have been less than nothing – had beaten the gathering dust from his uncle's name, from the name of his family, from even this shivering figure that sat beside him in the car.

Cary Sloane's body was found next morning on the lower shelf of a pillar of Queensboro Bridge. In the darkness and in his excitement he had thought that it was the water flowing black beneath him, but in less than a second it made no possible difference – unless he had planned to think one last thought of Edna, and call out her name as he struggled feebly in the water.

VII

Anson never blamed himself for his part in this affair – the situation which brought it about had not been of his making. But the just suffer with the unjust, and he found that his oldest and somehow his most precious friendship was over. He never knew what distorted story Edna told, but he was welcome in his uncle's house no longer.

Just before Christmas Mrs Hunter retired to a select Episcopal heaven, and Anson became the responsible head of his family. An unmarried aunt who had lived with them for years ran the house, and attempted with helpless inefficiency to chaperone the younger girls. All the children were less self-reliant than Anson, more conventional both in their virtues and in their shortcomings. Mrs Hunter's death had postponed the début of one daughter and the wedding of another. Also it had taken something deeply material from all of them, for with her passing the quiet, expensive superiority of the Hunters came to an end.

For one thing, the estate, considerably diminished by two inheritance taxes and soon to be divided among six children, was not a notable fortune any more. Anson saw a tendency in his youngest sisters to speak rather respectfully of families that hadn't 'existed' twenty years ago. His own feeling of precedence was not echoed in them – sometimes they were conventionally snobbish, that was all. For another thing, this was the last summer they would spend on the Connecticut estate; the clamour against it was too loud: 'Who wants to waste the best months of the year shut up in that dead old town?' Reluctantly he yielded – the house would go into the market in the fall, and next summer they would rent a smaller place in Westchester County. It was a step down from the expensive simplicity of his father's idea, and, while he sympathized with the revolt, it also annoyed him; during his mother's lifetime he had gone up there at least every other week-end – even in the gayest summers.

Yet he himself was part of this change, and his strong instinct for life had turned him in his twenties from the hollow obsequies of that abortive leisure class. He did not see this clearly – he still felt that there was a norm, a standard of society. But there was no norm, it was doubtful if there ever had been a true norm in New York. The few who still paid and fought to enter a particular set succeeded only to find that as a society it scarcely functioned – or, what was more alarming, that the Bohemia from which they fled sat above them at table.

At twenty-nine Anson's chief concern was his own growing loneliness.

He was sure now that he would never marry. The number of weddings at which he had officiated as best man or usher was past all counting – there was a drawer at home that bulged with the official neckties of this or that wedding-party, neckties standing for romances that had not endured a year, for couples who had passed completely from his life. Scarf-pins, gold pencils, cuff-buttons, presents from a generation of grooms had passed through his jewel-box and been lost – and with every ceremony he was less and less able to imagine himself in the groom's place. Under his hearty good-will toward all those marriages there was despair about his own.

And as he neared thirty he became not a little depressed at the inroads that marriage, especially lately, had made upon his friendships. Groups of people had a disconcerting tendency to dissolve and disappear. The men from his own college – and it was upon them he had expended the most time and affection – were the most elusive of all. Most of them were drawn deep into domesticity, two were dead, one lived abroad, one was in Hollywood writing continuities for pictures that Anson went faithfully to see.

Most of them, however, were permanent commuters with an intricate family life centring around some suburban country club, and it was from these that he felt his estrangement most keenly.

In the early days of their married life they had all needed him; he gave them advice about their slim finances, he exorcised their doubts about the advisability of bringing a baby into two rooms and a bath, especially he stood for the great world outside. But now their financial troubles were in the past and the fearfully expected child had evolved into an absorbing family. They were always glad to see old Anson, but they dressed up for him and tried to impress him with their present importance, and kept their troubles to themselves. They needed him no longer.

A few weeks before his thirtieth birthday the last of his early and intimate friends was married. Anson acted in his usual role of best man, gave his usual silver tea-service, and went down to the usual *Homeric* to say good-bye. It was a hot Friday afternoon in May, and as he walked from the pier he realized that Saturday closing had begun and he was free until Monday morning.

'Go where?' he asked himself.

The Yale Club, of course; bridge until dinner, then four or five raw cocktails in somebody's room and a pleasant confused evening. He regretted that this afternoon's groom wouldn't be along – they had always been able to cram so much into such nights: they knew how to attach women and how to get rid of them, how much consideration any girl deserved from their intelligent hedonism. A party was an adjusted thing – you took certain girls to certain places and spent just so much on their amusement; you drank a little, not much, more than you ought to drink, and at a certain time in the morning you stood up and said you were going home. You avoided college boys, sponges, future engagements, fights, sentiment, and indiscretions. That was the way it was done. All the rest was dissipation.

In the morning you were never violently sorry – you made no resolutions, but if you had overdone it and your heart was slightly out of order, you went on the wagon for a few days without saying anything about it, and waited until an accumulation of nervous boredom projected you into another party.

The lobby of the Yale Club was unpopulated. In the bar three very young alumni looked up at him, momentarily and without curiosity.

'Hello, there, Oscar,' he said to the bartender. 'Mr Cahili been around this afternoon?'

'Mr Cahill's gone to New Haven.'

'Oh . . . that so?'

'Gone to the ball game. Lot of men gone up.'

Anson looked once again into the lobby, considered for a moment, and then walked out and over to Fifth Avenue. From the broad window of one of his clubs – one that he had scarcely visited in five years – a grey man with watery eyes stared down at him. Anson looked quickly away – that figure sitting in vacant resignation, in supercilious solitude, depressed him. He stopped and, retracing his steps, started over 47th Street toward Teak Warden's apartment. Teak and his wife had once been his most familiar friends – it was a household where he and Dolly Karger had been used to go in the days of their affair. But Teak had taken to drink, and his wife had remarked publicly that Anson was a bad influence on him. The remark reached Anson in an exaggerated form – when it was finally cleared up, the delicate spell of intimacy was broken, never to be renewed.

'Is Mr Warden at home?' he inquired.

'They've gone to the country.'

The fact unexpectedly cut at him. They were gone to the country and he hadn't known. Two years before he would have known the date, the hour, come up at the last moment for a final drink, and planned his first visit to them. Now they had gone without a word.

Anson looked at his watch and considered a week-end with his family, but the only train was a local that would jolt through the aggressive heat for three hours. And tomorrow in the country, and Sunday – he was in no mood for porch-bridge with polite undergraduates, and dancing after dinner at a rural roadhouse, a diminutive of gaiety which his father had estimated too well.

'Oh, no,' he said to himself . . . 'No.'

He was a dignified, impressive young man, rather stout now, but otherwise unmarked by dissipation. He could have been cast for a pillar of something – at times you were sure it was not society, at others nothing else – for the law, for the church. He stood for a few minutes motionless on the sidewalk in front of a 47th Street apartment-house; for almost the first time in his life he had nothing whatever to do.

Then he began to walk briskly up Fifth Avenue, as if he had just been reminded of an important engagement there. The necessity of dissimulation is one of the few characteristics that we share with dogs, and I think of Anson on that day as some well-bred specimen who had been disappointed at a familiar back door. He was going to see Nick, once a fashionable bartender in demand at all private dances, and now employed in cooling non-alcoholic champagne among the labyrinthine cellars of the Plaza Hotel.

'Nick,' he said, 'what's happened to everything?'

'Dead,' Nick said.

'Make me a whisky sour.' Anson handed a pint bottle over the counter. 'Nick, the girls are different; I had a little girl in Brooklyn and she got married last week without letting me know.'

'That a fact? Ha-ha-ha,' responded Nick diplomatically. 'Slipped it over on you.'

'Absolutely,' said Anson. 'And I was out with her the night before.'

'Ha-ha-ha,' said Nick, 'ha-ha-ha!'

'Do you remember the wedding, Nick, in Hot Springs where I had the waiters and the musicians singing "God save the King"?'

'Now where was that, Mr Hunter?' Nick concentrated doubtfully. 'Seems to me that was –'

'Next time they were back for more and I began to wonder how much I'd paid them,' continued Anson.

'– seems to me that was at Mr Trenholm's wedding.'

'Don't know him,' said Anson decisively. He was offended that a strange name should intrude upon his reminiscences; Nick perceived this.

'Na – aw –' he admitted, 'I ought to know that. It was one of *your* crowd – Brakins . . . Baker –'

'Bicker Baker,' said Anson responsively. 'They put me in a hearse after it was over and covered me up with flowers and drove me away.'

'Ha-ha-ha,' said Nick. 'Ha-ha-ha.'

Nick's simulation of the old family servant paled presently and Anson went upstairs to the lobby. He looked around – his eyes met the glance of an unfamiliar clerk at the desk, then fell upon a flower from the morning's marriage hesitating in the mouth of a brass cuspidor. He went out and walked slowly toward the blood-red sun over Columbus Circle. Suddenly he turned around and, retracing his steps to the Plaza, immured himself in a telephone-booth.

Later he said that he tried to get me three times that afternoon, that he tried everyone who might be in New York – men and girls he had not seen for years, an artist's model of his college days whose faded number was still in his address book – Central told him that even the exchange existed no longer. At length his quest roved into the country, and he held brief disappointing conversations with emphatic butlers and maids. So-and-so was out, riding, swimming, playing golf, sailed to Europe last week. Who shall I say phoned?

It was intolerable that he should pass the evening alone – the private reckonings which one plans for a moment of leisure lose every charm when the solitude is enforced. There were always women of a sort, but the ones he knew had temporarily vanished, and to pass a New York evening in the hired company of a stranger never occurred to him – he would have considered that that was something shameful and secret, the diversion of a travelling salesman in a strange town.

Anson paid the telephone bill – the girl tried unsuccessfully to joke with him about its size – and for the second time that afternoon started to leave the Plaza and go he knew not where. Near the revolving door the figure of a woman, obviously with child, stood sideways to the light – a sheer beige cape fluttered at her shoulders when the door turned and, each time, she looked impatiently toward it as if she were weary of waiting. At the first sight of her a strong nervous thrill of familiarity went over him, but not until he was within five feet of her did he realize that it was Paula.

'Why, Anson Hunter!'

His heart turned over.

'Why, Paula –'

'Why, this is wonderful. I can't believe it, *Anson*!'

She took both his hands, and he saw in the freedom of the gesture that the memory of him had lost poignancy to her. But not to him – he felt that old mood that she evoked in him stealing over his brain, that gentleness with which he had always met her optimism as if afraid to mar its surface.

'We're at Rye for the summer. Pete had to come East on business – you know of course I'm Mrs Peter Hagerty now – so we brought the children and took a house. You've got to come out and see us.'

'Can I?' he asked directly. 'When?'

'When you like. Here's Pete.' The revolving door functioned, giving up a fine tall man of thirty with a tanned face and a trim moustache. His immaculate fitness made a sharp contrast with Anson's increasing bulk, which was obvious under the faintly tight cutaway coat.

'You oughtn't to be standing,' said Hagerty to his wife. 'Let's sit down here.' He indicated lobby chairs, but Paula hesitated.

'I've got to go right home,' she said. 'Anson, why don't you – why don't you come out and have dinner with us tonight? We're just getting settled, but if you can stand that –'

Hagerty confirmed the invitation cordially.

'Come out for the night.'

Their car waited in front of the hotel, and Paula with a tired gesture sank back against silk cushions in the corner. 'There's so much I want to talk to you about,' she said, 'it seems hopeless.'

'I want to hear about you.'

'Well' – she smiled at Hagerty – 'that would take a long time too. I have three children – by my first marriage. The oldest is five, then four, then three.' She smiled again. 'I didn't waste much time having them, did I?'

'Boys?'

'A boy and two girls. Then – oh, a lot of things happened, and I got a divorce in Paris a year ago and married Pete. That's all – except that I'm awfully happy.'

In Rye they drove up to a large house near the Beach Club, from which there issued presently three dark, slim children who broke from an English governess and approached them with an esoteric cry. Abstractedly and with difficulty, Paula took each one into her arms, a caress which they accepted stiffly, as they had evidently been told not to bump into Mummy. Even against their fresh faces Paula's skin showed scarcely any weariness – for all her physical languor she seemed younger than when he had last seen her at Palm Beach seven years ago.

The Rich Boy

At dinner she was preoccupied, and afterward, during the homage to the radio, she lay with closed eyes on the sofa until Anson wondered if his presence at this time were not an intrusion. But at nine o'clock, when Hagerty rose and said pleasantly that he was going to leave them by themselves for a while, she began to talk slowly about herself and the past.

'My first baby,' she said – 'the one we call Darling, the biggest little girl – I wanted to die when I knew I was going to have her, because Lowell was like a stranger to me. It didn't seem as though she could be my own. I wrote you a letter and tore it up. Oh, you were *so* bad to me, Anson.'

It was the dialogue again, rising and falling, Anson felt a sudden quickening of memory.

'Weren't you engaged once?' she asked – 'a girl named Dolly something?'

'I wasn't ever engaged. I tried to be engaged, but I never loved anybody but you, Paula.'

'Oh,' she said. Then after a moment: 'This baby is the first one I ever really wanted. You see, I'm in love now – at last.'

He didn't answer, shocked at the treachery of her remembrance. She must have seen that the 'at last' bruised him, for she continued:

'I was infatuated with you, Anson – you could make me do anything you liked. But we wouldn't have been happy. I'm not smart enough for you. I don't like things to be complicated like you do.' She paused. 'You'll never settle down,' she said.

The phrase struck at him from behind – it was an accusation that of all accusations he had never merited.

'I could settle down if women were different,' he said. 'If I didn't understand so much about them, if women didn't spoil you for other women, if they had only a little pride. If I could go to sleep for a while and wake up into a home that was really mine – why, that's what I'm made for, Paula, that's what women have seen in me and liked in me. It's only that I can't get through the preliminaries any more.'

Hagerty came in a little before eleven; after a whisky Paula stood up and announced that she was going to bed. She went over and stood by her husband.

'Where did you go, dearest?' she demanded.

'I had a drink with Ed Saunders.'

'I was worried. I thought maybe you'd run away.'

She rested her head against his coat.

'He's sweet, isn't he, Anson?' she demanded.

'Absolutely,' said Anson, laughing.

She raised her face to her husband.

'Well, I'm ready,' she said. She turned to Anson: 'Do you want to see our family gymnastic stunt?'

'Yes,' he said in an interested voice.

'All right. Here we go!'

Hagerty picked her up easily in his arms.

'This is called the family acrobatic stunt,' said Paula. 'He carries me upstairs. Isn't it sweet of him?'

'Yes,' said Anson.

Hagerty bent his head slightly until his face touched Paula's.

'And I love him,' she said. 'I've just been telling you, haven't I, Anson?'

'Yes,' he said.

'He's the dearest thing that ever lived in this world; aren't you, darling? . . . Well, good night. Here we go. Isn't he strong?'

'Yes,' Anson said.

'You'll find a pair of Pete's pyjamas laid out for you. Sweet dreams – see you at breakfast.'

'Yes,' Anson said.

VIII

The older members of the firm insisted that Anson should go abroad for the summer. He had scarcely had a vacation in seven years, they said. He was stale and needed a change. Anson resisted.

'If I go,' he declared, 'I won't come back any more.'

'That's absurd, old man. You'll be back in three months with all this depression gone. Fit as ever.'

'No.' He shook his head stubbornly. 'If I stop, I won't go back to work. If I stop, that means I've given up – I'm through.'

'We'll take a chance on that. Stay six months if you like – we're not afraid you'll leave us. Why, you'd be miserable if you didn't work.'

They arranged his passage for him. They liked Anson – everyone liked Anson – and the change that had been coming over him cast a sort of pall over the office. The enthusiasm that had invariably signalled up business, the consideration toward his equals and his inferiors, the lift of his vital presence – within the past four months his intense nervousness had melted down these qualities into the fussy pessimism of a man of forty. On every transaction in which he was involved he acted as a drag and a strain.

'If I go I'll never come back,' he said.

Three days before he sailed Paula Legendre Hagerty died in childbirth. I was with him a great deal then, for we were crossing together, but for the first time in our friendship he told me not a word of how he felt, nor did I see the slightest sign of emotion. His chief preoccupation was with the fact that he was thirty years old – he would turn the conversation to the point where he could remind you of it and then fall silent, as if he assumed that the statement would start a chain of thought sufficient to itself. Like his partners, I was amazed at the change in him, and I was glad when the *Paris* moved off into the wet space between the worlds, leaving his principality behind.

'How about a drink?' he suggested.

We walked into the bar with that defiant feeling that characterizes the day of departure and ordered four Martinis. After one cocktail a change came over him – he suddenly reached across and slapped my knee with the first joviality I had seen him exhibit for months.

'Did you see the girl in the red tam?' he demanded, 'the one with the high colour who had the two police dogs down to bid her good-bye.'

'She's pretty,' I agreed.

'I looked her up in the purser's office and found out that she's alone. I'm going down to see the steward in a few minutes. We'll have dinner with her tonight.'

After a while he left me, and within an hour he was walking up and down the deck with her, talking to her in his strong, clear voice. Her red tam was a bright spot of colour against the steel-grey sea, and from time to time she looked up with a flashing bob of her head, and smiled with amusement and interest, and anticipation. At dinner we had champagne, and were very joyous – afterward Anson ran the pool with infectious gusto, and several people who had seen me with him asked me his name. He and the girl were talking and laughing together on a lounge in the bar when I went to bed.

I saw less of him on the trip than I had hoped. He wanted to arrange a foursome, but there was no one available, so I saw him only at meals. Sometimes, though, he would have a cocktail in the bar, and he told me about the girl in the red tam, and his adventures with her, making them all bizarre and amusing, as he had a way of doing, and I was glad that he was himself again, or at least the self that I knew, and with which I felt at home. I don't think he was ever happy unless someone was in love with him, responding to him like filings to a magnet, helping him to explain himself, promising him something. What it was I do not know. Perhaps they promised that there would always be women in the world who would spend their brightest, freshest, rarest hours to nurse and protect that superiority he cherished in his heart.

AN ALCOHOLIC CASE

I

'Let – go – that – oh-h-h! Please, now, will you? *Don't* start drinking again! Come on – give me the bottle. I told you I'd stay awake givin' it to you. Come on. If you do like that a-way – then what are you going to be like when you go home. Come on – leave it with me – I'll leave half in the bottle. Pul-lease. You know what Dr Carter says – I'll stay awake and give it to you, or else fix some of it in the bottle – come on – like I told you, I'm too tired to be fightin' you all night . . . All right, drink your fool self to death.'

'Would you like some beer?' he asked.

'No, I don't want any beer. Oh, to think that I have to look at you drunk again. My God!'

'Then I'll drink the Coca Cola.'

The girl sat down panting on the bed.

'Don't you believe in anything?' she demanded.

'Nothing you believe in – please – it'll spill.'

She had no business there, she thought, no business trying to help him. Again they struggled, but after this time he sat with his head in his hands awhile, before he turned around once more.

'Once more you try to get it I'll throw it down,' she said quickly. 'I will – on the tiles in the bathroom.'

'Then I'll step on the broken glass – or you'll step on it.'

'Then let go – oh you promised –'

Suddenly she dropped it like a torpedo, sliding underneath her hand and slithering with a flash of red and black and the words: SIR GALAHAD, DISTILLED LOUISVILLE GIN. He took it by the neck and tossed it through the open door to the bathroom.

It was on the floor in pieces and everything was silent for a while and she read *Gone With the Wind* about things so lovely that had happened long ago. She began to worry that he would have to go into the bathroom and might cut his feet, and looked up from time to time to see if he would go in. She was very sleepy – the last time she looked up he was crying and he looked like an old Jewish man she had nursed once in California; he had had to go to the bathroom many times. On this case she was unhappy all the time but she thought:

'I guess if I hadn't liked him I wouldn't have stayed on the case.'

With a sudden resurgence of conscience she got up and put a chair in front of the bathroom door. She had wanted to sleep because he had got her up early that morning to get a paper with the story of the Yale–Dartmouth game in it and she hadn't been home all day. That afternoon a relative of his had come to see him and she had waited outside in the hall where there was a draught with no sweater to put over her uniform.

As well as she could she arranged him for sleeping, put a robe over his shoulders as he sat slumped over his writing table, and one on his knees. She sat down in the rocker but she was no longer sleepy; there was plenty to enter on the chart and treading lightly about she found a pencil and put it down:

Pulse 120
Respiration 25
Temp. 98 – 98.4 – 98.2
Remarks –
– She could make so many:
Tried to get bottle of gin. Threw it away and broke it.
She corrected it to read:
In the struggle it dropped and was broken. Patient was generally difficult.

She started to add as part of her report: *I never want to go on an alcoholic case again*, but that wasn't in the picture. She knew she could wake herself at seven and clean up everything before his niece awakened. It was all part of the game. But when she sat down in the chair she looked at his face, white and exhausted, and counted his breathing again, wondering why it had all happened. He had been so nice today, drawn her a whole strip of his cartoon just for fun and given it to her. She was going to have it framed and hang it in her room. She felt again his thin wrists wrestling against her wrist and remembered the awful things he had said, and she thought too of what the doctor had said to him yesterday:

'You're too good a man to do this to yourself.'

She was tired and didn't want to clean up the glass on the bathroom floor, because as soon as he breathed evenly she wanted to get him over to the bed. But she decided finally to clean up the glass first; on her knees, searching a last piece of it, she thought:

– This isn't what I ought to be doing. And this isn't what *he* ought to be doing.

Resentfully she stood up and regarded him. Through the thin delicate profile of his nose came a light snore, sighing, remote, inconsolable. The doctor had shaken his head in a certain way, and she knew that really it was a case that was beyond her. Besides, on her card at the agency was written, on the advice of her elders, 'No Alcoholics'.

She had done her whole duty, but all she could think of was that when she was struggling about the room with him with that gin bottle there had been a pause when he asked her if she had hurt her elbow against a door and that she had answered: 'You don't know how people talk about you, no matter how you think of yourself –' when she knew he had a long time ceased to care about such things.

The glass was all collected – as she got out a broom to make sure, she realized that the glass, in its fragments, was less than a window through which they had seen each other for a moment. He did not know about her sister, and Bill Markoe whom she had almost married, and she did not know what had brought him to this pitch, when there was a picture on his bureau of his young wife and his two sons and him, all trim and handsome as he must have been five years ago. It was so utterly senseless – as she put a bandage on her finger where she had cut it while picking up the glass she made up her mind she would never take an alcoholic case again.

II

It was early the next evening. Some Hallowe'en jokester had split the side windows of the bus and she shifted back to the Negro section in the rear for fear the glass might fall out. She had her patient's cheque but no way to cash it at this hour; there was a quarter and a penny in her purse.

Two nurses she knew were waiting in the hall of Mrs Hixson's Agency.

'What kind of case have you been on?'

'Alcoholic,' she said.

'Oh, yes – Gretta Hawks told me about it – you were on with that cartoonist who lives at the Forest Park Inn.'

'Yes, I was.'

'I hear he's pretty fresh.'

'He's never done anything to bother me,' she lied. 'You can't treat them as if they were committed –'

'Oh, don't get bothered – I just heard that around town – oh, you know – they want you to play around with them –'

'Oh, be quiet,' she said, surprised at her own rising resentment.

In a moment Mrs Hixson came out and, asking the other two to wait, signalled her into the office.

'I don't like to put young girls on such cases,' she began. 'I got your call from the hotel.'

'Oh, it wasn't bad, Mrs Hixson. He didn't know what he was doing and he didn't hurt me in any way. I was thinking much more of my reputation with you. He was really nice all day yesterday. He drew me –'

'I didn't want to send you on that case.' Mrs Hixson thumbed through the registration cards. 'You take T.B. cases, don't you? Yes, I see you do. Now here's one –'

The phone rang in a continuous chime. The nurse listened as Mrs Hixson's voice said precisely:

'I will do what I can – that is simply up to the doctor . . . That is beyond my jurisdiction . . . Oh, hello, Hattie, no, I can't now. Look, have you got any nurse that's good with alcoholics? There's somebody up at the Forest Park Inn who needs somebody. Call back will you?'

She put down the receiver. 'Suppose you wait outside. What sort of man is this anyhow? Did he act indecently?'

'He held my hand away,' she said, 'so I couldn't give him an injection.'

'Oh, an invalid he-man,' Mrs Hixson grumbled. 'They belong in sanatoria. I've got a case coming along in two minutes that you can get a little rest on. It's an old woman –'

The phone rang again. 'Oh, hello, Hattie . . . Well, how about that big Svensen girl? She ought to be able to take care of any alcoholic . . . How about Josephine Markham? Doesn't she live in your apartment house? . . . Get her to the phone.' Then after a moment, 'Joe, would you care to take the case of a well-known cartoonist, or artist, whatever they call themselves, at Forest Park Inn? . . . No, I don't know, but Dr Carter is in charge and will be around about ten o'clock.'

There was a long pause; from time to time Mrs Hixson spoke:

'I see . . . Of course, I understand your point of view. Yes, but this isn't supposed to be dangerous – just a little difficult. I never like to send girls to a hotel because I know what riff-raff you're liable to run into

. . . No, I'll find somebody. Even at this hour. Never mind and thanks. Tell Hattie I hope that the hat matches the negligée . . .'

Mrs Hixson hung up the receiver and made notations on the pad before her. She was a very efficient woman. She had been a nurse and had gone through the worst of it, had been a proud, idealistic, overworked probationer, suffered the abuse of smart internees and the insolence of her first patients, who thought that she was something to be taken into camp immediately for premature commitment to the service of old age. She swung around suddenly from the desk.

'What kind of cases do you want? I told you I have a nice old woman –'

The nurse's brown eyes were alight with a mixture of thoughts – the movie she had just seen about Pasteur and the book they had all read about Florence Nightingale when they were student nurses. And their pride, swinging across the streets in the cold weather at Philadelphia General, as proud of their new capes as débutantes in their furs going into balls at the hotels.

'I – I think I would like to try the case again,' she said amid a cacophony of telephone bells. 'I'd just as soon go back if you can't find anybody else.'

'But one minute you say you'll never go on an alcoholic case again and the next minute you say you want to go back to one.'

'I think I overestimated how difficult it was. Really, I think I could help him.'

'That's up to you. But if he tried to grab your wrists.'

'But he couldn't,' the nurse said. 'Look at my wrists: I played basketball at Waynesboro High for two years. I'm quite able to take care of him.'

Mrs Hixson looked at her for a long minute. 'Well, all right,' she said. 'But just remember that nothing they say when they're drunk is what they mean when they're sober – I've been all through that; arrange with one of the servants that you can call on him, because you never can tell – some alcoholics are pleasant and some of them are not, but all of them can be rotten.'

'I'll remember,' the nurse said.

It was an oddly clear night when she went out, with slanting particles of thin sleet making white of a blue-black sky. The bus was the same that had taken her into town, but there seemed to be more windows broken now and the bus driver was irritated and talked about what terrible things he would do if he caught any kids. She knew he was just talking about the annoyance in general, just as she had been thinking about the annoyance of an alcoholic. When she came up to the suite and found him all helpless and distraught she would despise him and be sorry for him.

Getting off the bus, she went down the long steps to the hotel, feeling a little exalted by the chill in the air. She was going to take care of him because nobody else would, and because the best people of her profession had been interested in taking care of the cases that nobody else wanted.

She knocked at his study door, knowing just what she was going to say.

He answered it himself. He was in dinner clothes even to a derby hat – but minus his studs and tie.

'Oh, hello,' he said casually. 'Glad you're back. I woke up a while ago and decided I'd go out. Did you get a night nurse?'

'I'm the night nurse too,' she said. 'I decided to stay on twenty-four-hour duty.'

He broke into a genial, indifferent smile.

'I saw you were gone, but something told me you'd come back. Please find my studs. They ought to be either in a little tortoiseshell box or –'

He shook himself a little more into his clothes, and hoisted the cuffs up inside his coat sleeves.

'I thought you had quit me,' he said casually.

'I thought I had, too.'

'If you look on that table,' he said, 'you'll find a whole strip of cartoons that I drew you.'

'Who are you going to see?' she asked.

'It's the President's secretary,' he said. 'I had an awful time trying to get ready. I was about to give up when you came in. Will you order me some sherry?'

'One glass,' she agreed wearily.

From the bathroom he called presently:

'Oh, Nurse, Nurse, Light of my Life, where is another stud?'

'I'll put it in.'

In the bathroom she saw the pallor and the fever on his face and smelled the mixed peppermint and gin on his breath.

'You'll come up soon?' she asked. 'Dr Carter's coming at ten.'

'What nonsense! You're coming down with me.'

'Me?' she exclaimed. 'In a sweater and skirt? Imagine!'

'Then I won't go.'

'All right then, go to bed. That's where you belong anyhow. Can't you see these people tomorrow?'

'No, of course not!'

She went behind him and reaching over his shoulder tied his tie – his shirt was already thumbed out of press where he had put in the studs, and she suggested:

'Won't you put on another one, if you've got to meet some people you like?'

'All right, but I want to do it myself.'

'Why can't you let me help you?' she demanded in exasperation. 'Why can't you let me help you with your clothes? What's a nurse for – what good am I doing?'

He sat down suddenly on the toilet seat.

'All right – go on.'

'Now don't grab my wrist,' she said, and then, 'excuse me.'

'Don't worry. It didn't hurt. You'll see in a minute.'

She had the coat, vest, and stiff shirt off him but before she could pull his undershirt over his head he dragged at his cigarette, delaying her.

'Now watch this,' he said. 'One – two – three.'

She pulled up the undershirt; simultaneously he thrust the crimson-grey point of the cigarette like a dagger against his heart. It crushed out against a copper plate on his left rib about the size of a silver dollar, and he said 'Ouch!' as a stray spark fluttered down against his stomach.

Now was the time to be hard-boiled, she thought. She knew there were three medals from the war in his jewel box, but she had risked many things herself: tuberculosis among them and one time something worse, though she had not known it and had never quite forgiven the doctor for not telling her.

'You've had a hard time with that, I guess,' she said lightly as she sponged him. 'Won't it ever heal?'

'Never. That's a copper plate.'

'Well, it's no excuse for what you're doing to yourself.'

He bent his great brown eyes on her, shrewd – aloof, confused. He signalled to her, in one second, his Will to Die, and for all her training and experience she knew she could never do anything constructive with him. He stood up, steadying himself on the wash-basin and fixing his eyes on some place just ahead.

'Now, if I'm going to stay here you're not going to get at that liquor,' she said.

Suddenly she knew he wasn't looking for that. He was looking at the corner where he had thrown the bottle the night before. She stared at his handsome face, weak and defiant – afraid to turn even half-way because she knew that death was in that corner where he was looking. She knew death – she had heard it, smelt its unmistakable odour, but she had never seen it before it entered into anyone, and she knew this man saw it in the corner of his bathroom; that it was standing there looking at him while he spat from a feeble cough and rubbed the result into the braid of his trousers. It shone there crackling for a moment as evidence of the last gesture he ever made.

She tried to express it next day to Mrs Hixson:

'It's not like anything you can beat – no matter how hard you try. This one could have twisted my wrists until he strained them and that wouldn't matter so much to me. It's just that you can't really help them and it's so discouraging – it's all for nothing.'

THE LEES OF HAPPINESS

I

If you should look through the files of old magazines for the first years of the present century you would find, sandwiched in between the stories of Richard Harding Davis and Frank Norris and others long since dead, the work of one Jeffrey Curtain: a novel or two, and perhaps three or four dozen short stories. You could, if you were interested, follow them along until, say, 1908, when they suddenly disappeared.

When you had read them all you would have been quite sure that here were no masterpieces – here were passably amusing stories, a bit out of date now, but doubtless the sort that would then have whiled away a dreary half-hour in a dental office. The man who did them was of good intelligence, talented, glib, probably young. In the samples of his work you found there would have been nothing to stir you to more than a faint interest in the whims of life – no deep interior laughs, no sense of futility, or hint of tragedy.

After reading them you would yawn and put the number back in the files, and perhaps, if you were in some library reading-room, you would decide that by way of variety you would look at a newspaper of the period and see whether the Japs had taken Port Arthur. But if by any chance the newspaper you had chosen was the right one and had crackled open at the theatrical page, your eyes would have been arrested and held, and for at least a minute you would have forgotten Port Arthur as quickly as you forgot Château Thierry. For you would, by this fortunate chance, be looking at the portrait of an exquisite woman.

These were the days of *Florodora* and of sextets, of pinched-in waists and blown-out sleeves, of almost bustles and absolute ballet skirts, but here, without doubt, disguised as she might be by the unaccustomed stiffness and old fashion of her costume, was a butterfly of butterflies. Here was the gaiety of the period – the soft wine of eyes, the songs that flurried hearts, the toasts and the bouquets, the dances and the dinners.

Here was a Venus of the hansom cab, the Gibson girl in her glorious prime. Here was . . .

. . . here was, you find by looking at the name beneath, one Roxanne Milbank, who had been chorus girl and understudy in *The Daisy Chain*, but who, by reason of an excellent performance when the star was indisposed, had gained a leading part.

You would look again – and wonder. Why you had never heard of her. Why did her name not linger in popular songs and vaudeville jokes and cigar bands, and the memory of that gay old uncle of yours along with Lillian Runssell and Stella Mayhew and Anna Held? Roxanne Milbank – whither had she gone? What dark trap-door had opened suddenly and swallowed her up? Her name was certainly not in last Sunday's supplement on that list of actresses married to English noblemen. No doubt she was dead – poor beautiful young lady – and quite forgotten.

I am hoping too much. I am having you stumble on Jeffrey Curtain's stories and Roxanne Milbank's picture. It would be incredible that you should find a newspaper item six months later, a single item two inches by four, which informed the public of the marriage, very quietly, of Miss Roxanne Milbank, who had been on tour with *The Daisy Chain*, to Mr Jeffrey Curtain, the popular author. 'Mrs Curtain,' it added dispassionately, 'will retire from the stage.'

It was a marriage of love. He was sufficiently spoiled to be charming; she was ingenuous enough to be irresistible. Like two floating logs they met in a head-on rush, caught, and sped along together. Yet had Jeffrey Curtain kept at scrivening for twoscore years he could not have put a quirk into one of his stories weirder than the quirk that came into his own life. Had Roxanne Milbank played three dozen parts and filled five thousand houses she could never have had a role with more happiness and more despair than were in the fate prepared for Roxanne Curtain.

For a year they lived in hotels, travelled to California, to Alaska, to Florida, to Mexico, loved and quarrelled gently, and gloried in the golden triflings of his wit with her beauty – they were young and gravely passionate; they demanded everything and then yielded everything again in ecstasies of unselfishness and pride. She loved the swift tones of his voice and his frantic, unfounded jealousy. He loved her dark radiance, the white irises of her eyes, the warm, lustrous enthusiasm of her smile.

'Don't you like her?' he would demand rather excitedly and shyly. 'Isn't she wonderful? Did you ever see –'

'Yes,' they would answer, grinning. 'She's a wonder. You're lucky.'

The year passed. They tired of hotels. They bought an old house and twenty acres near the town of Marlowe, half an hour from Chicago; bought a little car, and moved out riotously with a pioneering hallucination that would have confounded Balboa.

'Your room will be here!' they cried in turn.

– And then:

'And my room here!'

'And the nursery here when we have children.'

'And we'll build a sleeping porch – oh, next year.'

They moved out in April. In July Jeffrey's closest friend, Harry Cromwell, came to spend a week – they met him at the end of the long lawn and hurried him proudly to the house.

Harry was married also. His wife had had a baby some six months before and was still recuperating at her mother's in New York. Roxanne had gathered from Jeffrey that Harry's wife was not as attractive as Harry – Jeffrey had met her once and considered her – 'shallow'. But Harry had been married nearly two years and was apparently happy, so Jeffrey guessed that she was probably all right . . .

'I'm making biscuits,' chattered Roxanne gravely. 'Can your wife make biscuits? The cook is showing me how. I think every woman should know how to make biscuits. It sounds so utterly disarming. A woman who can make biscuits can surely do no –'

'You'll have to come out here and live,' said Jeffrey. 'Get a place out in the country like us, for you and Kitty.'

'You don't know Kitty. She hates the country. She's got to have her theatres and vaudevilles.'

'Bring her out,' repeated Jeffrey. 'We'll have a colony. There's an awfully nice crowd here already. Bring her out!'

They were at the porch steps now and Roxanne made a brisk gesture toward a dilapidated structure on the right.

'The garage,' she announced. 'It will also be Jeffrey's writing-room within the month. Meanwhile dinner is at seven. Meanwhile to that I will mix a cocktail.'

The two men ascended to the second floor – that is, they ascended half-way, for at the first landing Jeffrey dropped his guest's suitcase and in a cross between a query and a cry exclaimed:

'For God's sake, Harry, how do you like her?'

'We will go upstairs,' answered his guest, 'and we will shut the door.'

Half an hour later as they were sitting together in the library Roxanne reissued from the kitchen, bearing before her a pan of biscuits. Jeffrey and Harry rose.

'They're beautiful, dear,' said the husband, intensely.

'Exquisite,' murmured Harry.

Roxanne beamed.

'Taste one. I couldn't bear to touch them before you'd seen them all and I can't bear to take them back until I find what they taste like.'

'Like manna, darling.'

Simultaneously the two men raised the biscuits to their lips, nibbled tentatively. Simultaneously they tried to change the subject. But Roxanne, undeceived, set down the pan and seized a biscuit. After a second her comment rang out with lugubrious finality:

'Absolutely bum!'

'Really –'

'Why, I didn't notice –'

Roxanne roared.

'Oh, I'm useless,' she cried laughing. 'Turn me out, Jeffrey – I'm a parasite; I'm no good –'

Jeffrey put his arm around her.

'Darling, I'll eat your biscuits.'

'They're beautiful, anyway,' insisted Roxanne.

'They're – they're decorative,' suggested Harry.

Jeffrey took him up wildly.

'That's the word. They're decorative; they're masterpieces. We'll use them.'

He rushed to the kitchen and returned with a hammer and a handful of nails.

'We'll use them, by golly, Roxanne! We'll make a frieze out of them.'

'Don't!' wailed Roxanne. 'Our beautiful house.'

'Never mind. We're going to have the library repapered in October. Don't you remember?'

'Well –'

Bang! The first biscuit was impaled to the wall, where it quivered for a moment like a live thing.

Bang! . . .

When Roxanne returned with a second round of cocktails the biscuits were in a perpendicular row, twelve of them, like a collection of primitive spear-heads.

'Roxanne,' exclaimed Jeffrey, 'you're an artist! Cook? – nonsense! You shall illustrate my books!'

During dinner the twilight faltered into dusk, and later it was a starry dark outside, filled and permeated with the frail gorgeousness of Roxanne's white dress and her tremulous, low laugh.

– Such a little girl she is, thought Harry. Not as old as Kitty.

He compared the two. Kitty – nervous without being sensitive, temperamental without temperament, a woman who seemed to flit and never light – and Roxanne who was as young as a spring night, and summed up in her own adolescent laughter.

– A good match for Jeffrey, he thought again. Two very young people, the sort who'll stay very young until they suddenly find themselves old.

Harry thought these things between his constant thoughts about Kitty. He was depressed about Kitty. It seemed to him that she was well enough to come back to Chicago and bring his little son. He was thinking vaguely of Kitty when he said good night to his friend's wife and his friend at the foot of the stairs.

'You're our first real house guest,' called Roxanne after him. 'Aren't you thrilled and proud?'

When he was out of sight around the stair corner she turned to Jeffrey, who was standing beside her resting his hand on the end of the banister.

'Are you tired, my dearest?'

Jeffrey rubbed the centre of his forehead with his fingers.

'A little. How did you know?'

'Oh, how could I help knowing about you?'

'It's a headache,' he said moodily. 'Splitting. I'll take some aspirin.'

She reached over and snapped out the light, and with his arm tight about her waist they walked up the stairs together.

II

Harry's week passed. They drove about the dreaming lanes or idled in cheerful inanity upon lake or lawn. In the evening Roxanne, sitting inside, played to them while the ashes whitened on the glowing ends of their cigars. Then came a telegram from Kitty saying that she wanted Harry to come East and get her, so Roxanne and Jeffrey were left alone in that privacy of which they never seemed to tire.

'Alone' thrilled them again. They wandered about the house, each feelinintimately theresence of thether·; they sat   the same side of the table like honeymooners; they were intensely absorbed, intensely happy.

The town of Marlowe, though a comparatively old settlement, had only recently acquired a 'society'. Five or six years before, alarmed at the smoky swelling of Chicago, two or three young married couples, 'bungalow people', had moved out; their friends had followed. The Jeffrey Curtains found an already formed 'set' prepared to welcome them; a country club, ballroom, and golf-links yawned for them, and there were bridge parties, and poker parties, and parties where they drank beer, and parties where they drank nothing at all.

It was at a poker party that they found themselves a week after Harry's departure. There were two tables, and a good proportion of the young wives were smoking and shouting their bets, and being very daringly mannish for those days.

Roxanne had left the game early and taken to perambulation; she wandered into the pantry and found herself some grape juice – beer gave her a headache – and then passed from table to table, looking over shoulders at the hands, keeping an eye on Jeffrey and being pleasantly unexcited and content. Jeffrey, with intense concentration, was raising a pile of chips of all colours, and Roxanne knew by the deepened wrinkle between his eyes that he was interested. She liked to see him interested in small things.

She crossed over quietly and sat down on the arm of his chair.

She sat there five minutes, listening to the sharp intermittent comments of the men and the chatter of the women, which rose from the table like soft smoke – and yet scarcely hearing either. Then quite innocently she reached out her hand, intending to place it on Jeffrey's shoulder – as it touched him he started of a sudden, gave a short grunt, and, sweeping back his arm furiously, caught her a glancing blow on her elbow.

There was a general gasp. Roxanne regained her balance, gave a little cry, and rose quickly to her feet. It had been the greatest shock of her life. This, from Jeffrey, the heart of kindness, of consideration – this instinctively brutal gesture.

The gasp became a silence. A dozen eyes were turned on Jeffrey, who looked up as though seeing Roxanne for the first time. An expression of bewilderment settled on his face.

'Why – Roxanne –' he said haltingly.

Into a dozen minds entered a quick suspicion, a rumour of scandal. Could it be that behind the scenes with this couple, apparently so in love, lurked some curious antipathy? Why else this streak of fire across such a cloudless heaven?

'Jeffrey!' – Roxanne's voice was pleading – startled and horrified, she yet knew that it was a mistake. Not once did it occur to her to blame him or to resent it. Her word was a trembling supplication – 'Tell me, Jeffrey,' it said, 'tell Roxanne, your own Roxanne.'

'Why, Roxanne –' began Jeffrey again. The bewildered look changed to pain. He was clearly as startled as she. 'I didn't intend that,' he went on; 'you startled me. You – I felt as if someone were attacking me. I – how – why. how idiotic!'

'Jeffrey!' Again the word was a prayer, incense offered up to a high God through this new and unfathomable darkness.

They were both on their feet, they were saying good-bye, faltering, apologizing, explaining. There was no attempt to pass it off easily. That way lay sacrilege. Jeffrey had not been feeling well, they said. He had become nervous. Back of both their minds was the unexplained horror of that blow – the marvel that there had been for an instant something between them – his anger and her fear – and now to both a sorrow, momentary, no doubt, but to be bridged at once, at once, while there was yet time. Was that swift water lashing under their feet – the fierce glint of some unchartered chasm?

Out in their car under the harvest moon he talked brokenly. It was just – incomprehensible to him, he said. He had been thinking of the poker game – absorbed – and the touch on his shoulder had seemed like an attack. An attack! He clung to that word, flung it up as a shield. He had hated what touched him. With the impact of his hand it had gone, that – nervousness. That was all he knew.

Both their eyes filled with tears and they whispered love there under the broad night as the serene streets of Marlowe sped by. Later, when they went to bed, they were quite calm. Jeffrey was to take a week off all work – was simply to loll, and sleep, and go on long walks until this nervousness left him. When they had decided this safety settled down upon Roxanne. The pillows underhead became soft and friendly; the bed on which they lay seemed wide, and white, and sturdy beneath the radiance that streamed in at the window.

Five days later, in the first cool of late afternoon, Jeffrey picked up an oak chair and sent it crashing through his own front window. Then he lay down on the couch like a child, weeping piteously and begging to die. A blood clot the size of a marble had broken in his brain.

III

There is a sort of waking nightmare that sets in sometimes when one has missed a sleep or two, a feeling that comes with extreme fatigue and a new sun, that the quality of the life around has changed. It is a fully articulate conviction that somehow the existence one is then leading is a branch shoot of life and is related to life only as a moving picture or a mirror – that the people, and streets, and houses are only projections from a very dim and chaotic past. It was in such a state that Roxanne found herself during the first months of Jeffrey's illness. She slept only when she was utterly exhausted; she awoke under a cloud. The long, sober-voiced consultations, the faint aura of medicine in the halls, the sudden tiptoeing in a house that had echoed to many cheerful footsteps, and, most of all, Jeffrey's white face amid the pillows of the bed they had shared – these things subdued her and made her indelibly older. The doctors held out hope, but that was all. A long rest, they said, and quiet. So responsibility came to Roxanne. It was she who paid the bills, pored over his bank-book, corresponded with his publishers. She was in the kitchen constantly. She learned from the nurse how to prepare his meals and after the first month took complete charge of the sick-room. She had had to let the nurse go for reasons of economy. One of the two coloured girls left at the same time. Roxanne was realizing that they had been living from short story to short story.

The most frequent visitor was Harry Cromwell. He had been shocked and depressed by the news, and though his wife was now living with him in Chicago he found time to come out several times a month. Roxanne found his sympathy welcome – there was some quality of suffering in the man, some inherent pitifulness that made her comfortable when he was near. Roxanne's nature had suddenly deepened. She felt sometimes that with Jeffrey she was losing her children also, those children that now most of all she needed and should have had.

It was six months after Jeffrey's collapse and when the nightmare had faded, leaving not the old world but a new one, greyer and colder, that she went to see Harry's wife. Finding herself in Chicago with an extra hour before train time, she decided out of courtesy to call.

As she stepped inside the door she had an immediate impression that the apartment was very like some place she had seen before – and almost instantly she remembered a round-the-corner bakery of her childhood, a bakery full of rows and rows of pink frosted cakes – a stuffy pink, pink as a food, pink triumphant, vulgar, and odious.

And this apartment was like that. It was pink. It smelled pink!

Mrs Cromwell, attired in a wrapper of pink and black, opened the door. Her hair was yellow, heightened, Roxanne imagined, by a dash of peroxide in the rinsing water every week. Her eyes were a thin waxen blue – she was pretty and too consciously graceful. Her cordiality was strident and intimate, hostility melted so quickly to hospitality that it seemed they were both merely in the face and voice – never touching nor touched by the deep core of egotism beneath.

But to Roxanne these things were secondary; her eyes were caught and held in uncanny fascination by the wrapper. It was vilely unclean. From its lowest hem up four inches it was sheerly dirty with the blue dust of the floor; for the next three inches it was grey – then it shaded off into its natural colour, which was – pink. It was dirty at the sleeves, too, and at the collar – and when the woman turned to lead the way into the parlour, Roxanne was sure that her neck was dirty.

A one-sided rattle of conversation began, Mrs Cromwell became explicit about her likes and dislikes, her head, her stomach, her teeth, her apartment – avoiding with a sort of insolent meticulousness any inclusion of Roxanne with life, as if presuming that Roxanne, having been dealt a blow, wished life to be carefully skirted.

Roxanne smiled. That kimono! That neck!

After five minutes a little boy toddled into the parlour – a dirty little boy clad in dirty pink rompers. His face was smudgy – Roxanne wanted to take him into her lap and wipe his nose; other parts in the vicinity of his head needed attention, his tiny shoes were kicked out at the toes. Unspeakable!

'What a darling little boy!' exclaimed Roxanne, smiling radiantly. 'Come here to me.'

Mrs Cromwell looked coldly at her son.

'He *will* get dirty. Look at that face!' She held her head on one side and regarded it critically.

'Isn't he a *darling?*' repeated Roxanne.

'Look at his rompers,' frowned Mrs Cromwell.

'He needs a change, don't you, George?'

George stared at her curiously. To his mind the word rompers connotated a garment extraneously smeared, as this one.

'I tried to make him look respectable this morning,' complained Mrs Cromwell as one whose patience had been sorely tried, 'and I found he didn't have any more rompers – so rather than have him go around without any I put him back in those – and his face –'

'How many pairs has he?' Roxanne's voice was pleasantly curious. 'How many feather fans have you?' she might have asked.

'Oh –' Mrs Cromwell considered, wrinkling her pretty brow. 'Five I think. Plenty, I know.'

'You can get them for fifty cents a pair.'

Mrs Cromwell's eyes showed surprise – and the faintest superiority. The price of rompers!

'Can you really? I had no idea. He ought to have plenty, but I haven't had a minute all week to send the laundry out.' Then, dismissing the subject as irrelevant – 'I must show you some things –'

They rose and Roxanne followed her past an open bathroom door whose garment-littered floor showed indeed that the laundry hadn't been sent out for some time, into another room that was, so to speak, the quintessence of pinkness. This was Mrs Cromwell's room.

Here the hostess opened a closet door and displayed before Roxanne's eyes an amazing collection of lingerie. There were dozens of filmy marvels of lace and silk, all clean, unruffled, seemingly not yet touched. On hangers beside them were three new evening dresses.

'I have some beautiful things,' said Mrs Cromwell, 'but not much of a chance to wear them. Harry doesn't care about going out.' Spite crept into her voice. 'He's perfectly content to let me play nursemaid and housekeeper all day and loving wife in the evening.'

Roxanne smiled again.

'You've got some beautiful clothes here.'

'Yes, I have. Let me show you –'

'Beautiful,' repeated Roxanne, interrupting, 'but I'll have to run if I'm going to catch my train.'

She felt that her hands were trembling. She wanted to put them on this woman and shake her – shake her. She wanted her locked up somewhere and set to scrubbing floors.

'Beautiful,' she repeated, 'and I just came in for a moment.'

'Well, I'm sorry Harry isn't here.'

They moved toward the door.

'– and, oh,' said Roxanne with an effort – yet her voice was still gentle and her lips were smiling – 'I think it's Argile's where you can get those rompers. Good-bye.'

It was not until she had reached the station and bought her ticket to Marlowe that Roxanne realized it was the first five minutes in six months that her mind had been off Jeffrey.

IV

A week later Harry appeared at Marlowe, arrived unexpectedly at five o'clock, and coming up the walk sank into a porch chair in a state of exhaustion. Roxanne herself had had a busy day and was worn out. The doctors were coming at five-thirty, bringing a celebrated nerve specialist from New York. She was excited and thoroughly depressed, but Harry's eyes made her sit down beside him.

'What's the matter?'

'Nothing, Roxanne,' he denied. 'I came to see how Jeff was doing. Don't you bother about me.'

'Harry,' insisted Roxanne, 'there's something the matter.'

'Nothing,' he repeated. 'How's Jeff?'

Anxiety darkened her face.

'He's a little worse, Harry. Dr Jewett has come on from New York. They thought he could tell me something definite. He's going to try and find whether this paralysis has anything to do with the original blood clot.'

Harry rose.

'Oh, I'm sorry,' he said jerkily. 'I didn't know you expected a consultation. I wouldn't have come. I thought I'd just rock on your porch for an hour –'

'Sit down,' she commanded.

Harry hesitated.

'Sit down, Harry, dear boy.' Her kindness flooded out now – enveloped him. 'I know there's something the matter. You're white as a sheet. I'm going to get you a cool bottle of beer.'

All at once he collapsed into his chair and covered his face with his hands.

'I can't make her happy,' he said slowly. 'I've tried and I've tried. This morning we had some words about breakfast – I'd been getting my breakfast downtown – and – well, just after I went to the office she left the house, went East to her mother's with George and a suitcase full of lace underwear.'

'Harry!'

'And I don't know –'

There was a crunch on the gravel, a car turning into the drive. Roxanne uttered a little cry.

'It's Dr Jewett.'

'Oh, I'll –'

'You'll wait, won't you?' she interrupted abstractedly. He saw that his problem had already died on the troubled surface of her mind.

There was an embarrassing minute of vague, elided introductions, and then Harry followed the party inside and watched them disappear up the stairs. He went into the library and sat down on the big sofa.

For an hour he watched the sun creep up the patterned folds of the chintz curtains. In the deep quiet a trapped wasp buzzing on the inside of the window-pane assumed the proportions of a clamour. From time to time another buzzing drifted down from upstairs, resembling several more larger wasps caught on larger window-panes. He heard low footfalls, the clink of bottles, the clamour of pouring water.

What had he and Roxanne done that life should deal these crashing blows to them? Upstairs there was taking place a living inquest on the soul of his friend; he was sitting here in a quiet room listening to the plaint of a wasp, just as when he was a boy he had been compelled by a strict aunt to sit hour-long on a chair and atone for some misbehaviour. But who had put him here? What ferocious aunt had leaned out of the sky to make him atone for – what?

About Kitty he felt a great hopelessness. She was too expensive – that was the irremediable difficulty. Suddenly he hated her. He wanted to throw her down and kick at her – to tell her she was a cheat and a leech – that she was dirty. Moreover, she must give him his boy.

He rose and began pacing up and down the room. Simultaneously he heard someone begin walking along the hallway upstairs in exact time with him. He found himself wondering if they would walk in time until the person reached the end of the hall.

Kitty had gone to her mother. God help her, what a mother to go to! He tried to imagine the meeting: the abused wife collapsing upon the mother's breast. He could not. That Kitty was capable of any deep grief was unbelievable. He had gradually grown to think of her as something unapproachable and callous. She would get a divorce, of course, and eventually she would marry again. He began to consider this. Whom would she marry? He laughed bitterly, stopped; a picture flashed before him – of Kitty's arms around some man whose face he could not see, of Kitty's lips pressed close to other lips in what was surely passion.

'God!' he cried aloud. 'God! God! God!'

Then the pictures came thick and fast. The Kitty of this morning faded; the soiled kimono rolled up and disappeared; the pouts, and rages, and tears all were washed away. Again she was Kitty Carr – Kitty Carr with yellow hair and great baby eyes. Ah, she had loved him, she had loved him.

After a while he perceived that something was amiss with him, something that had nothing to do with Kitty or Jeff, something of a different genre. Amazingly it burst on him at last; he was hungry. Simple enough! He would go into the kitchen in a moment and ask the coloured cook for a sandwich. After that he must go back to the city.

He paused at the wall, jerked at something round, and, fingering it absently, put it to his mouth and tasted it as a baby tastes a bright toy. His teeth closed on it – Ah!

She'd left that damn kimono, that dirty pink kimono. She might have had the decency to take it with her, he thought. It would hang in the house like a corpse of their sick alliance. He would try to throw it away, but he would never be able to bring himself to move it. It would be like Kitty, soft and pliable, withal impervious. You couldn't move Kitty; you couldn't reach Kitty. There was nothing there to reach. He understood that perfectly – he had understood it all along.

He reached to the wall for another biscuit and with an effort pulled it out, nail and all. He carefully removed the nail from the centre, wondering idly if he had eaten the nail with the first biscuit. Preposterous! He would have remembered – it was a huge nail. He felt his stomach. He must be very hungry. He considered – remembered – yesterday he had had no dinner. It was the girl's day out and Kitty had lain in her room eating chocolate drops. She had said she felt 'smothery' and couldn't bear having him near her. He had given George a bath and put him to bed, and then laid down on the couch intending to rest a minute before getting his own dinner. There he had fallen asleep and awakened about eleven, to find that there was nothing in the ice-box except a spoonful of potato salad. This he had eaten, together with some chocolate drops that he found on Kitty's bureau. This morning he had breakfast hurriedly downtown before going to the office. But at noon, beginning to worry about Kitty, he had decided to go home and take her out to lunch. After that there had been the note on his pillow. The pile of lingerie in the closet was gone – and she had left instructions for sending her trunk.

He had never been so hungry, he thought.

At five o'clock, when the visiting nurse tiptoed downstairs, he was sitting on the sofa staring at the carpet.

'Mr Cromwell?'

'Yes?'

'Oh, Mrs Curtain won't be able to see you at dinner. She's not well.

She told me to tell you that the cook will fix you something and that there's a spare bedroom.'

'She's sick, you say?'

'She's lying down in her room. The consultation is just over.'

'Did they – did they decide anything?'

'Yes,' said the nurse softly. 'Dr Jewett says there's no hope. Mr Curtain may live indefinitely, but he'll never see again or move again or think. He'll just breathe.'

'Just breathe?'

'Yes.'

For the first time the nurse noted that beside the writing-desk where she remembered that she had seen a line of a dozen curious round objects she had vaguely imagined to be some exotic form of decoration, there was now only one. Where the others had been, there was now a series of little nail-holes.

Harry followed her glance dazedly and then rose to his feet.

'I don't believe I'll stay. I believe there's a train.'

She nodded. Harry picked up his hat.

'Good-bye,' she said pleasantly.

'Good-bye,' he answered, as though talking to himself and, evidently moved by some involuntary necessity, he paused on his way to the door and she saw him pluck the last object from the wall and drop it into his pocket.

Then he opened the screen door and, descending the porch steps, passed out of her sight.

V

After a while the coat of clean white paint on the Jeffrey Curtain house made a definite compromise with the suns of many Julys and showed its good faith by turning grey. It scaled – huge peelings of very brittle old paint leaned over backward like aged men practising grotesque gymnastics and finally dropped to a mouldy death in the over-grown grass beneath. The paint on the front pillars became streaky; the white ball was knocked off the left-hand door-post; the green blinds darkened, then lost all pretence of colour.

It began to be a house that was avoided by the tender-minded – some church bought a lot diagonally opposite for a graveyard, and this, combined with 'the place where Mrs Curtain stays with that living corpse', was enough to throw a ghostly aura over that quarter of the road. Not that she was left alone. Men and women came to see her, met her downtown, where she went to do her marketing, brought her home in their cars – and came in for a moment to talk and to rest, in the glamour that still played in her smile. But men who did not know her no longer followed her with admiring glances in the street; a diaphanous veil had come down over her beauty, destroying its vividness, yet bringing neither wrinkles nor fat.

She acquired a character in the village – a group of little stories were told of her: how when the country was frozen over one winter so that no wagons nor automobiles could travel, she taught herself to skate so that she could make quick time to the grocer and druggist, and not leave Jeffrey alone for long. It was said that every night since his paralysis she slept in a small bed beside his bed, holding his hand.

Jeffrey Curtain was spoken of as though he were already dead. As the years dropped by those who had known him died or moved away – there were but half a dozen of the old crowd who had drunk cocktails together, called each other's wives by their first names, and thought that Jeff was about the wittiest and most talented fellow that Marlowe had ever known. Now, to the casual visitor, he was merely the reason that Mrs Curtain excused herself sometimes and hurried upstairs; he was a groan or a sharp cry borne to the silent parlour on the heavy air of a Sunday afternoon.

He could not move; he was stone blind, dumb, and totally unconscious. All day he lay in his bed, except for a shift to his wheel-chair every morning while she straightened the room. His paralysis was creeping slowly toward his heart. At first – for the first year – Roxanne had received the faintest answering pressure sometimes when she held his hand – then it had gone, ceased one evening, and never come back, and through two nights Roxanne lay wide-eyed, staring into the dark and wondering what had gone, what fraction of his soul had taken flight, what last grain of comprehension those shattered broken nerves still carried to the brain.

After that hope died. Had it not been for her unceasing care the last spark would have gone long before. Every morning she shaved and bathed him, shifted him with her own hands from bed to chair and back to bed. She was in his room constantly, bearing medicine, straightening a pillow, talking to him almost as one talks to a nearly human dog, without hope of response or appreciation, but with the dim persuasion of habit, a prayer when faith has gone.

Not a few people, one celebrated nerve specialist among them, gave her a plain impression that it was futile to exercise so much care, that if Jeffrey had been conscious he would have wished to die, that if his spirit were hovering in some wider air it would agree to no such sacrifice from her, it would fret only for the prison of its body to give it full release.

'But you see,' she replied, shaking her head gently, 'when I married Jeffrey it was – until I ceased to love him.'

'But,' was protested, in effect, 'you can't love that.'

'I can love what it once was. What else is there for me to do?'

The specialist shrugged his shoulders and went away to say that Mrs Curtain was a remarkable woman and just about as sweet as an angel – but, he added, it was a terrible pity.

'There must be some man, or a dozen, just crazy to take care of her . . .'

Casually – there were. Here and there someone began in hope – and ended in reverence. There was no love in the woman except, strangely enough, for life, for the people in the world, from the tramp to whom she gave food she could ill afford, to the butcher who sold her a cheap cut of steak across the meaty board. The other phase was sealed up somewhere in that expressionless mummy who lay with his face turned ever toward the light as mechanically as a compass needle and waited dumbly for the last wave to wash over his heart.

After eleven years he died in the middle of a May night, when the scent of the syringa hung upon the window-sill and a breeze wafted in the shrillings of the frogs and cicadas outside. Roxanne awoke at two, and realized with a start she was alone in the house at last.

VI

After that she sat on her weather-beaten porch through many after-noons, gazing down across the fields that undulated in a slow descent to the white and green town. She was wondering what she would do with her life. She was thirty-six – handsome, strong, and free. The years had eaten up Jeffrey's insurance; she had reluctantly parted with the acres to right and left of her, and had even placed a small mortgage on the house.

With her husband's death had come a great physical restlessness. She missed having to care for him in the morning, she missed her rush to town, and the brief and therefore accentuated neighbourly meetings in the butcher's and grocer's; she missed the cooking for two, the preparation of delicate liquid food for him. One day, consumed with energy, she went out and spaded up the whole garden, a thing that had not been done for years.

And she was alone at night in the room that had seen the glory of her marriage and then the pain. To meet Jeff again she went back in spirit to that wonderful year, that intense, passionate absorption and companionship, rather than looked forward to a problematical meeting hereafter; she awoke often to lie and wish for that presence beside her – inanimate yet breathing – still Jeff.

One afternoon six months after his death she was sitting on the porch, in a black dress which took away the faintest suggestion of plumpness from her figure. It was Indian summer – golden brown all about her; a hush broken by the sighing of leaves; westward a four o'clock sun dripping streaks of red and yellow over a flaming sky. Most of the birds had gone – only a sparrow that had built itself a nest on the cornice of a pillar kept up an intermittent cheeping varied by occasional fluttering sallies overhead. Roxanne moved her chair to where she could watch him and her mind idled drowsily on the bosom of the afternoon.

Harry Cromwell was coming out from Chicago to dinner. Since his divorce over eight years before he had been a frequent visitor. They had kept up what amounted to a tradition between them: when he arrived they would go to look at Jeff; Harry would sit down on the edge of the bed and in a hearty voice ask:

'Well, Jeff, old man, how do you feel today?'

Roxanne, standing beside, would look intently at Jeff, dreaming that some shadowy recognition of this former friend had passed across that broken mind – but the head, pale, carven, would only move slowly in its sole gesture toward the light as if something behind the blind eyes were groping for another light long since gone out.

These visits stretched over eight years – at Easter, Christmas, Thanksgiving, and on many a Sunday Harry had arrived, paid his call on Jeff, and then talked for a long while with Roxanne on the porch. He was devoted to her. He made no pretence of hiding, no attempt to deepen, this relation. She was his best friend as the mass of flesh on the bed there had been his best friend. She was peace, she was rest; she was the past. Of his own tragedy she alone knew.

He had been at the funeral, but since then the company for which he worked had shifted him to the East and only a business trip had brought him to the vicinity of Chicago. Roxanne had written him to come when he could – after a night in the city he had caught a train out.

They shook hands and he helped her move two rockers together.

'How's George?'

'He's fine, Roxanne. Seems to like school.'

'Of course, it was the only thing to do, to send him.'

'Of course –'

'You miss him horribly, Harry?'

'Yes – I do miss him. He's a funny boy –'

He talked a lot about George. Roxanne was interested. Harry must bring him out on his next vacation. She had only seen him once in her life – a child in dirty rompers.

She left him with the newspaper while she prepared dinner – she had four chops tonight and some late vegetables from her own garden. She put it all on and then called him, and sitting down together they continued their talk about George.

'If I had a child –' she would say.

Afterward, Harry having given her what slender advice he could about investments, they walked through the garden, pausing here and there to recognize what had once been a cement bench or where the tennis-court had lain . . .

'Do you remember –'

Then they were off on a flood of reminiscences: the day they had taken all the snap-shots and Jeff had been photographed astride the calf; and the sketch Harry had made of Jeff and Roxanne, lying sprawled in the grass, their heads almost touching. There was to have been a covered lattice connecting the barn-studio with the house, so that Jeff could get there on wet days – the lattice had been started, but nothing remained except a broken triangular piece that still adhered to the house and resembled a battered chicken coop.

'And those mint juleps!'

'And Jeff's notebook! Do you remember how we'd laugh, Harry, when we'd get it out of his pocket and read aloud a page of material. And how frantic he used to get?'

'Wild! He was such a kid about his writing.'

They were both silent a moment, and then Harry said:

'We were to have a place out here, too. Do you remember? We were to buy the adjoining twenty acres. And the parties we were going to have!'

Again there was a pause, broken this time by a low question from Roxanne.

'Do you ever hear of her, Harry?'

'Why – yes,' he admitted placidly. 'She's in Seattle. She's married again to a man named Horton, a sort of lumber king. He's a great deal older than she is, I believe.'

'And she's behaving?'

'Yes – that is, I've heard so. She has everything, you see. Nothing much to do except dress up for this fellow at dinner-time.'

'I see.'

Without effort he changed the subject.

'Are you going to keep the house?'

'I think so,' she said, nodding. 'I've lived here so long, Harry, it'd seem terrible to move. I thought of trained nursing, but of course that'd mean leaving. I've about decided to be a boarding-house lady.'

'Live in one?'

'No. Keep one. Is there such an anomaly as a boarding-house lady? Anyway I'd have a Negress and keep about eight people in the summer and two or three, if I can get them, in the winter. Of course I'll have to have the house repainted and gone over inside.'

Harry considered.

'Roxanne, why – naturally, you know best what you can do, but it does seem a shock, Roxanne. You came here as a bride.'

'Perhaps,' she said, 'that's why I don't mind remaining here as a boarding-house lady.'

'I remember a certain batch of biscuits.'

'Oh, those biscuits,' she cried. 'Still, from all I heard about the way you devoured them, they couldn't have been so bad. I was *so* low that day, yet somehow I laughed when the nurse told me about those biscuits.'

'I noticed that the twelve nail-holes are still in the library wall where Jeff drove them.'

'Yes.'

It was getting very dark now, a crispness settled in the air; a little gust of wind sent down a last spray of leaves. Roxanne shivered slightly.

'We'd better go in.'

He looked at his watch.

'It's late. I've got to be leaving. I go East tomorrow.'

'Must you?'

They lingered for a moment just below the stoop, watching a moon that seemed full of snow float out of the distance where the lake lay. Summer was gone and now Indian summer. The grass was cold and there was no mist and no dew. After he left she would go in and light the gas and close the shutters, and he would go down the path and on to the village. To these two life had come quickly and gone, leaving not bitterness, but pity; not disillusion, but only pain. There was already enough moonlight when they shook hands for each to see the gathered kindness in the other's eyes.

GRETCHEN'S FORTY WINKS

I

The sidewalks were scratched with brittle leaves, and the bad little boy next door froze his tongue to the iron mail-box. Snow before night, sure. Autumn was over. This, of course, raised the coal question and the Christmas question; but Roger Halsey, standing on his own front porch, assured the dead suburban sky that he hadn't time for worrying about the weather. Then he let himself hurriedly into the house, and shut the subject out into the cold twilight.

The hall was dark, but from above he heard the voices of his wife and the nursemaid and the baby in one of their interminable conversations, which consisted chiefly of 'Don't!' and 'Look out, Maxy!' and 'Oh, there he *goes*!' punctuated by wild threats and vague bumpings and the recurrent sound of small, venturing feet.

Roger turned on the hall-light and walked into the living-room and turned on the red silk lamp. He put his bulging portfolio on the table, and sitting down rested his intense young face in his hand for a few minutes, shading his eyes carefully from the light. Then he lit a cigarette, squashed it out, and going to the foot of the stairs called for his wife.

'Gretchen!'

'Hello, dear.' Her voice was full of laughter. 'Come see baby.'

He swore softly.

'I can't see baby now,' he said aloud. 'How long 'fore you'll be down?'

There was a mysterious pause, and then a succession of 'Don'ts' and 'Look outs, Maxy' evidently meant to avert some threatened catastrophe.

'How long 'fore you'll be down?' repeated Roger, slightly irritated.

'Oh, I'll be right down.'

'How soon?' he shouted.

He had trouble every day at this hour in adapting his voice from the urgent key of the city to the proper casualness for a model home. But tonight he was deliberately impatient. It almost disappointed him when

Gretchen came running down the stairs, three at a time, crying 'What is it?' in a rather surprised voice.

They kissed – lingered over it some moments. They had been married three years, and they were much more in love than that implies. It was seldom that they hated each other with that violent hate of which only young couples are capable, for Roger was still actively sensitive to her beauty.

'Come in here,' he said abruptly. 'I want to talk to you.'

His wife, a bright-coloured, Titian-haired girl, vivid as a French rag doll, followed him into the living room.

'Listen, Gretchen' – he sat down at the end of the sofa – 'beginning with tonight I'm going to – What's the matter?'

'Nothing. I'm just looking for a cigarette. Go on.'

She tiptoed breathlessly back to the sofa and settled at the other end.

'Gretchen –' Again he broke off. Her hand, palm upward, was extended towards him. 'Well, what is it?' he asked wildly.

'Matches.'

'What?'

In his impatience it seemed incredible that she should ask for matches, but he fumbled automatically in his pocket.

'Thank you,' she whispered. 'I didn't mean to interrupt you. Go on.'

'Gretch —'

Scratch! The match flared. They exchanged a tense look.

Her fawn's eyes apologized mutely this time, and he laughed. After all, she had done no more than light a cigarette; but when he was in this mood her slightest positive action irritated him beyond measure.

'When you've got time to listen,' he said crossly, 'you might be interested in discussing the poorhouse question with me.'

'What poorhouse?' Her eyes were wide, startled; she sat quiet as a mouse.

'That was just to get your attention. But, beginning tonight, I start on what'll probably be the most important six weeks of my life – the six weeks that'll decide whether we're going on forever in this rotten little house in this rotten little suburban town.'

Boredom replaced alarm in Gretchen's black eyes. She was a Southern girl, and any question that had to do with getting ahead in the world always tended to give her a headache.

'Six months ago I left the New York Lithographic Company,' announced Roger, 'and went in the advertising business for myself.'

'I know,' interrupted Gretchen resentfully; 'and now instead of getting six hundred a month sure, we're living on a risky five hundred.'

'Gretchen,' said Roger sharply, 'if you'll just believe in me as hard as you can for six weeks more we'll be rich. I've got a chance now to get some of the biggest accounts in the country.' He hesitated. 'And for these six weeks we won't go out at all, and we won't have anyone here. I'm going to bring home work every night, and we'll pull down all the blinds and if anyone rings the doorbell we won't answer.'

He smiled airily as if it were a new game they were going to play. Then, as Gretchen was silent, his smile faded, and he looked at her uncertainly.

'Well, what's the matter?' she broke out finally. 'Do you expect me to jump up and sing? You do enough work as it is. If you try to do any more you'll end up with a nervous breakdown. I read about a –'

'Don't worry about me,' he interrupted; 'I'm all right. But you're going to be bored to death sitting here every evening.'

'No, I won't,' she said without conviction – 'except tonight.'

'What about tonight?'

'George Tompkins asked us to dinner.'

'Did you accept?'

'Of course I did,' she said impatiently. 'Why not? You're always talking about what a terrible neighbourhood this is, and I thought maybe you'd like to go to a nicer one for a change.'

'When I go to a nicer neighbourhood I want to go for good,' he said grimly.

'Well, can we go?'

'I suppose we'll have to if you've accepted.'

Somewhat to his annoyance the conversation abruptly ended. Gretchen jumped up and kissed him sketchily and rushed into the kitchen to light the hot water for a bath. With a sigh he carefully deposited his portfolio behind the bookcase – it contained only sketches and layouts for display advertising, but it seemed to him the first thing a burglar would look for. Then he went abstractedly upstairs, dropping into the baby's room for a casual moist kiss, and began dressing for dinner.

They had no automobile, so George Tompkins called for them at 6.30. Tompkins was a successful interior decorator, a broad, rosy man with a handsome moustache and a strong odour of jasmine. He and Roger had once roomed side by side in a boarding-house in New York, but they had met only intermittently in the past five years.

'We ought to see each other more,' he told Roger tonight. 'You ought to go out more often, old boy. Cocktail?'

'No, thanks.'

'No? Well, your fair wife will – won't you, Gretchen?'

'I love this house,' she exclaimed, taking the glass and looking admiringly at ship models, Colonial whisky bottles, and other fashionable débris of 1925.

'I like it,' said Tompkins with satisfaction. 'I did it to please myself, and I succeeded.'

Roger stared moodily around the stiff, plain room, wondering if they could have blundered into the kitchen by mistake.

'You look like the devil, Roger,' said his host. 'Have a cocktail and cheer up.'

'Have one,' urged Gretchen.

'What?' Roger turned around absently. 'Oh, no, thanks. I've got to work after I get home.'

'Work!' Tompkins smiled. 'Listen, Roger, you'll kill yourself with work. Why don't you bring a little balance into your life – work a little, then play a little?'

'That's what I tell him,' said Gretchen.

'Do you know an average business man's day?' demanded Tompkins as they went in to dinner. 'Coffee in the morning, eight hours' work interrupted by a bolted luncheon, and then home again with dyspepsia and a bad temper to give the wife a pleasant evening.'

Roger laughed shortly.

'You've been going to the movies too much,' he said dryly.

'What?' Tompkins looked at him with some irritation. 'Movies? I've hardly ever been to the movies in my life. I think the movies are atrocious. My opinions on life are drawn from my own observations. I believe in a balanced life.'

'What's that?' demanded Roger.

'Well' – he hesitated – 'probably the best way to tell you would be to describe my own day. Would that seem horribly egotistic?'

'Oh, no!' Gretchen looked at him with interest. 'I'd love to hear about it.'

'Well, in the morning I get up and go through a series of exercises. I've got one room fitted up as a little gymnasium, and I punch the bag and do shadow-boxing and weight-pulling for an hour. Then after a cold bath – There's a thing now! Do you take a daily cold bath?'

'No,' admitted Roger, 'I take a hot bath in the evening three or four times a week.'

A horrified silence fell. Tompkins and Gretchen exchanged a glance as if something obscene had been said.

'What's the matter?' broke out Roger, glancing from one to the other in some irritation. 'You know I don't take a bath every day – I haven't got the time.'

Tompkins gave a prolonged sigh.

'After my bath,' he continued, drawing a merciful veil of silence over the matter, 'I have breakfast and drive to my office in New York, where I work until four. Then I lay off, and if it's summer I hurry out here for nine holes of golf, or if it's winter I play squash for an hour at my club. Then a good snappy game of bridge until dinner. Dinner is liable to have something to do with business, but in a pleasant way. Perhaps I've just finished a house for some customer, and he wants me to be on hand for his first party to see that the lighting is soft enough and all that sort of thing. Or maybe I sit down with a good book of poetry and spend the evening alone. At any rate, I do something every night to get me out of myself.'

'It must be wonderful,' said Gretchen enthusiastically. 'I wish we lived like that.'

Tompkins bent forward earnestly over the table.

'You can,' he said impressively. 'There's no reason why you shouldn't. Look here, if Roger'll play nine holes of golf every day it'll do wonders for him. He won't know himself. He'll do his work better, never get that tired, nervous feeling – What's the matter?'

He broke off. Roger had perceptibly yawned.

'Roger,' cried Gretchen sharply, 'there's no need to be so rude. If you did what George said, you'd be a lot better off.' She turned indignantly to their host. 'The latest is that he's going to work at night for the next six weeks. He says he's going to pull down the blinds and shut us up like hermits in a cave. He's been doing it every Sunday for the last year; now he's going to do it every night for six weeks.'

Tompkins shook his head sadly.

'At the end of six weeks,' he remarked, 'he'll be starting for the sanatorium. Let me tell you, every private hospital in New York is full of cases like yours. You just strain the human nervous system a little too far, and bang! – you've broken something. And in order to save sixty hours you're laid up sixty weeks for repairs.' He broke off, changed his tone, and turned to Gretchen with a smile. 'Not to mention what happens to you. It seems to me it's the wife rather than the husband who bears the brunt of these insane periods of overwork.'

'I don't mind,' protested Gretchen loyally.

'Yes, she does,' said Roger grimly; 'she minds like the devil. She's a shortsighted little egg, and she thinks it's going to be forever until I get started and she can have some new clothes. But it can't be helped. The saddest thing about women is that, after all, their best trick is to sit down and fold their hands.'

'Your ideas on women are about twenty years out of date,' said Tompkins pityingly. 'Women won't sit down and wait any more.'

'Then they'd better marry men of forty,' insisted Roger stubbornly. 'If a girl marries a young man for love she ought to be willing to make any sacrifice within reason, so long as her husband keeps going ahead.'

'Let's not talk about it,' said Gretchen impatiently. 'Please, Roger, let's have a good time just this once.'

When Tompkins dropped them in front of their house at eleven Roger and Gretchen stood for a moment on the sidewalk looking at the winter moon. There was a fine, damp, dusty snow in the air, and Roger drew a long breath of it and put his arm around Gretchen exultantly.

'I can make more money than he can,' he said tensely. 'And I'll be doing it in just forty days.'

'Forty days,' she sighed. 'It seems such a long time – when everybody else is always having fun. If I could only sleep for forty days.'

'Why don't you, honey? Just take forty winks, and when you wake up everything'll be fine.'

She was silent for a moment.

'Roger,' she asked thoughtfully, 'do you think George meant what he said about taking me horseback riding on Sunday?'

Roger frowned.

'I don't know. Probably not – I hope to Heaven he didn't.' He hesitated. 'As a matter of fact, he made me sort of sore tonight – all that junk about his cold bath.'

With their arms about each other, they started up the walk to the house.

'I'll bet he doesn't take a cold bath every morning,' continued Roger ruminatively; 'or three times a week, either.' He fumbled in his pocket for the key and inserted it in the lock with savage precision. Then he turned around defiantly. 'I'll bet he hasn't had a bath for a month.'

II

After a fortnight of intensive work, Roger Halsey's days blurred into each other and passed by in blocks of twos and threes and fours. From eight until 5.30 he was in his office. Then a half-hour on the commuting train, where he scrawled notes on the backs of envelopes under the dull yellow light. By 7.30 his crayons, shears, and sheets of white cardboard were spread over the living-room table, and he laboured there with much grunting and sighing until midnight, while Gretchen lay on the sofa with a book, and the doorbell tinkled occasionally behind the drawn blinds. At twelve there was always an argument as to whether he would come to bed. He would agree to come after he had cleared up everything; but as he was invariably sidetracked by half a dozen new ideas, he usually found Gretchen sound asleep when he tiptoed upstairs.

Sometimes it was three o'clock before Roger squashed his last cigarette into the overloaded ash-tray, and he would undress in the dark, disembodied with fatigue, but with a sense of triumph that he had lasted out another day.

Christmas came and went and he scarcely noticed that it was gone. He remembered it afterwards as the day he completed the window-cards for Garrod's shoes. This was one of the eight large accounts for which he was pointing in January – if he got half of them he was assured a quarter of a million dollars' worth of business during the year.

But the world outside his business became a chaotic dream. He was aware that on two cool December Sundays George Tompkins had taken Gretchen horseback riding, and that another time she had gone out with him in his automobile to spend the afternoon skiing on the country-club hill. A picture of Tompkins, in an expensive frame, had appeared one morning on their bedroom wall. And one night he was shocked into a startled protest when Gretchen went to the theatre with Tompkins in town.

But his work was almost done. Daily now his layouts arrived from the printers until seven of them were piled and docketed in his office safe. He knew how good they were. Money alone couldn't buy such work; more than he realized himself, it had been a labour of love.

December tumbled like a dead leaf from the calendar. There was an agonizing week when he had to give up coffee because it made his heart pound so. If he could hold on now for four days – three days –

On Thursday afternoon H. G. Garrod was to arrive in New York. On

Wednesday evening Roger came home at seven to find Gretchen poring over the December bills with a strange expression in her eyes.

'What's the matter?'

She nodded at the bills. He ran through them, his brow wrinkling in a frown.

'Gosh!'

'I can't help it,' she burst out suddenly. 'They're terrible.'

'Well, I didn't marry you because you were a wonderful housekeeper. I'll manage about the bills some way. Don't worry your little head over it.'

She regarded him coldly.

'You talk as if I were a child.'

'I have to,' he said with sudden irritation.

'Well, at least I'm not a piece of bric-à-brac that you can just put somewhere and forget.'

He knelt down by her quickly, and took her arms in his hands.

'Gretchen, listen!' he said breathlessly. 'For God's sake, don't go to pieces now! We're both all stored up with malice and reproach, and if we had a quarrel it'd be terrible. I love you, Gretchen. Say you love me – quick !'

'You know I love you.'

The quarrel was averted, but there was an unnatural tenseness all through dinner. It came to a climax afterwards when he began to spread his working materials on the table.

'Oh, Roger,' she protested, 'I thought you didn't have to work tonight.'

'I didn't think I'd have to, but something came up.'

'I've invited George Tompkins over.'

'Oh, gosh!' he exclaimed. 'Well, I'm sorry, honey, but you'll have to phone him not to come.'

'He's left,' she said. 'He's coming straight from town. He'll be here any minute now.'

Roger groaned. It occurred to him to send them both to the movies, but somehow the suggestion stuck on his lips. He did not want her at the movies; he wanted her here, where he could look up and know she was by his side.

George Tompkins arrived breezily at eight o'clock. 'Aha!' he cried reprovingly, coming into the room. 'Still at it.'

Roger agreed coolly that he was.

'Better quit – better quit before you have to.' He sat down with a long sigh of physical comfort and lit a cigarette. 'Take it from a fellow who's

looked into the question scientifically. We can stand so much, and then –
bang!'

'If you'll excuse me' – Roger made his voice as polite as possible –
'I'm going upstairs and finish this work.'

'Just as you like, Roger.' George waved his hand carelessly. 'It isn't
that I mind. I'm the friend of the family and I'd just as soon see the
missus as the mister.' He smiled playfully. 'But if I were you, old boy,
I'd put away my work and get a good night's sleep.'

When Roger had spread out his materials on the bed upstairs he found
that he could still hear the rumble and murmur of their voices through
the thin floor. He began wondering what they found to talk about. As
he plunged deeper into his work his mind had a tendency to revert
sharply to his question, and several times he arose and paced nervously
up and down the room.

The bed was ill adapted to his work. Several times the paper slipped
from the board on which it rested, and the pencil punched through.
Everything was wrong tonight. Letters and figures blurred before his
eyes, and as an accompaniment to the beating of his temples came those
persistent murmuring voices.

At ten he realized that he had done nothing for more than an hour,
and with a sudden exclamation he gathered together his papers, replaced
them in his portfolio, and went downstairs. They were sitting together
on the sofa when he came in.

'Oh, hello!' cried Gretchen, rather unnecessarily, he thought. 'We
were just discussing you.'

'Thank you,' he answered ironically. 'What particular part of my
anatomy was under the scalpel?'

'Your health,' said Tompkins jovially.

'My health's all right,' answered Roger shortly.

'But you look at it so selfishly, old fella,' cried Tompkins. 'You only
consider yourself in the matter. Don't you think Gretchen has any
rights? If you were working on a wonderful sonnet or a – a portrait of
some madonna or something' – he glanced at Gretchen's Titian hair –
'why, then I'd say go ahead. But you're not. It's just some silly advertisement about how to sell Nobald's hair tonic, and if all the hair tonic ever
made was dumped into the ocean tomorrow the world wouldn't be one
bit the worse for it.'

'Wait a minute,' said Roger angrily; 'that's not quite fair. I'm not
kidding myself about the importance of my work – it's just as useless as

the stuff you do. But to Gretchen and me it's just about the most important thing in the world.'

'Are you implying that my work is useless?' demanded Tompkins incredulously.

'No; not if it brings happiness to some poor sucker of a pants manufacturer who doesn't know how to spend his money.'

Tompkins and Gretchen exchanged a glance.

'Oh-h-h!' exclaimed Tompkins ironically. 'I didn't realize that all these years I've just been wasting my time.'

'You're a loafer,' said Roger rudely.

'Me?' cried Tompkins angrily. 'You call me a loafer because I have a little balance in my life and find time to do interesting things? Because I play hard as well as work hard and don't let myself get to be a dull, tiresome drudge?'

Both men were angry now, and their voices had risen, though on Tompkins' face there still remained the semblance of a smile.

'What I object to,' said Roger steadily, 'is that for the last six weeks you seem to have done all your playing around here.'

'Roger!' cried Gretchen. 'What do you mean by talking like that?'

'Just what I said.'

'You've just lost your temper.' Tompkins lit a cigarette with ostentatious coolness. 'You're so nervous from overwork you don't know what you're saying. You're on the verge of a nervous break –'

'You get out of here!' cried Roger fiercely. 'You get out of here right now – before I throw you out!'

Tompkins got angrily to his feet.

'You – you throw me out?' he cried incredulously.

They were actually moving towards each other when Gretchen stepped between them, and grabbing Tompkins' arm urged him towards the door.

'He's acting like a fool, George, but you better get out,' she cried, groping in the hall for his hat.

'He insulted me!' shouted Tompkins. 'He threatened to throw me out!'

'Never mind, George,' pleaded Gretchen. 'He doesn't know what he's saying. Please go! I'll see you at ten o'clock tomorrow.'

She opened the door.

'You won't see him at ten o'clock tomorrow,' said Roger steadily. 'He's not coming to this house any more.'

Tompkins turned to Gretchen.

'It's his house,' he suggested. 'Perhaps we'd better meet at mine.'

Then he was gone, and Gretchen had shut the door behind him. Her eyes were full of angry tears.

'See what you've done!' she sobbed. 'The only friend I had, the only person in the world who liked me enough to treat me decently, is insulted by my husband in my own house.'

She threw herself on the sofa and began to cry passionately into the pillows.

'He brought it on himself,' said Roger stubbornly, 'I've stood as much as my self-respect will allow. I don't want you going out with him any more.'

'I will go out with him!' cried Gretchen wildly. 'I'll go out with him all I want! Do you think it's any fun living here with you?'

'Gretchen,' he said coldly, 'get up and put on your hat and coat and go out that door and never come back!'

Her mouth fell slightly ajar.

'But I don't want to get out,' she said dazedly.

'Well, then, behave yourself.' And he added in a gentler voice: 'I thought you were going to sleep for this forty days.'

'Oh, yes,' she cried bitterly, 'easy enough to say! But I'm tired of sleeping.' She got up, faced him defiantly. 'And what's more, I'm going riding with George Tompkins tomorrow.'

'You won't go out with him if I have to take you to New York and sit you down in my office until I get through.'

She looked at him with rage in her eyes.

'I hate you,' she said slowly. 'And I'd like to take all the work you've done and tear it up and throw it in the fire. And just to give you something to worry about tomorrow, I probably won't be here when you get back.'

She got up from the sofa, and very deliberately looked at her flushed, tear-stained face in the mirror. Then she ran upstairs and slammed herself into the bedroom.

Automatically Roger spread out his work on the living-room table. The bright colours of the designs, the vivid ladies – Gretchen had posed for one of them – holding orange ginger ale or glistening silk hosiery, dazzled his mind into a sort of coma. His restless crayon moved here and there over the pictures, shifting a block of letters half an inch to the right, trying a dozen blues for a cool blue, and eliminating the word that made a phrase anaemic and pale. Half an hour passed – he was deep in the work now; there was no sound in the room but the velvety scratch of the crayon over the glossy board.

After a long while he looked at his watch – it was after three. The wind had come up outside and was rushing by the house corners in loud, alarming swoops, like a heavy body falling through space. He stopped his work and listened. He was not tired now, but his head felt as if it was covered with bulging veins like those pictures that hang in doctors' offices showing a body stripped of decent skin. He put his hands to his head and felt it all over. It seemed to him that on his temple the veins were knotty and brittle around an old scar.

Suddenly he began to be afraid. A hundred warnings he had heard swept into his mind. People did wreck themselves with overwork, and his body and brain were of the same vulnerable and perishable stuff. For the first time he found himself envying George Tompkins' calm nerves and healthy routine. He arose and began pacing the room in a panic.

'I've got to sleep,' he whispered to himself tensely. 'Otherwise I'm going crazy.'

He rubbed his hand over his eyes, and returned to the table to put up his work, but his fingers were shaking so that he could scarcely grasp the board. The sway of a bare branch against the window made him start and cry out. He sat down on the sofa and tried to think.

'Stop! Stop! Stop!' the clock said. 'Stop! Stop! Stop!'

'I can't stop,' he answered aloud. 'I can't afford to stop.'

Listen! Why, there was the wolf at the door now! He could hear its sharp claws scrape along the varnished woodwork. He jumped up, and running to the front door flung it open; then started back with a ghastly cry. An enormous wolf was standing on the porch, glaring at him with red, malignant eyes. As he watched it the hair bristled on its neck; it gave a low growl and disappeared in the darkness. Then Roger realized with a silent, mirthless laugh that it was the police dog from over the way.

Dragging his limbs wearily into the kitchen, he brought the alarm-clock into the living-room and set it for seven. Then he wrapped himself in his overcoat, lay down on the sofa and fell immediately into a heavy, dreamless sleep.

When he awoke the light was still shining feebly, but the room was the grey colour of a winter morning. He got up, and looking anxiously at his hands found to his relief that they no longer trembled. He felt much better. Then he began to remember in detail the events of the night before, and his brow drew up again in three shallow wrinkles. There was work ahead of him, twenty-four hours of work; and Gretchen, whether she wanted to or not, must sleep for one more day.

Roger's mind glowed suddenly as if he had just thought of a new advertising idea. A few minutes later he was hurrying through the sharp morning air to Kingsley's drug-store.

'Is Mr Kingsley down yet?'

The druggist's head appeared around the corner of the prescription-room.

'I wonder if I can talk to you alone.'

At 7.30, back home again, Roger walked into his own kitchen. The general housework girl had just arrived and was taking off her hat.

'Bebé' – he was not on familiar terms with her; this was her name – 'I want you to cook Mrs Halsey's breakfast right away. I'll take it up myself.'

It struck Bebé that this was an unusual service for so busy a man to render his wife, but if she had seen his conduct when he had carried the tray from the kitchen she would have been even more surprised. For he set it down on the dining room table and put into the coffee half a teaspoonful of a white substance that was not powdered sugar. Then he mounted the stairs and opened the door of the bedroom.

Gretchen woke up with a start, glanced at the twin bed which had not been slept in, and bent on Roger a glance of astonishment, which changed to contempt when she saw the breakfast in his hand. She thought he was bringing it as a capitulation.

'I don't want any breakfast,' she said coldly, and his heart sank, 'except some coffee.'

'No breakfast?' Roger's voice expressed disappointment.

'I said I'd take some coffee.'

Roger discreetly deposited the tray on a table beside the bed and returned quickly to the kitchen.

'We're going away until tomorrow afternoon,' he told Bebé, 'and I want to close up the house right now. So you just put on your hat and go home.'

He looked at his watch. It was ten minutes to eight, and he wanted to catch the 8.10 train. He waited five minutes and then tiptoed softly upstairs and into Gretchen's room. She was sound asleep. The coffee cup was empty save for black dregs and a film of thin brown paste on the bottom. He looked at her rather anxiously, but her breathing was regular and clear.

From the closet he took a suitcase and very quickly began filling it with her shoes – street shoes, evening slippers, rubber-soled oxfords – he had not realized that she owned so many pairs. When he closed the suitcase it was bulging.

He hesitated a minute, took a pair of sewing scissors from a box, and following the telephone-wire until it went out of sight behind the dresser, severed it in one neat clip. He jumped as there was a soft knock at the door. It was the nursemaid. He had forgotten her existence.

'Mrs Halsey and I are going up to the city till tomorrow,' he said glibly. 'Take Maxy to the beach and have lunch there. Stay all day.'

Back in the room, a wave of pity passed over him. Gretchen seemed suddenly lovely and helpless, sleeping there. It was somehow terrible to rob her young life of a day. He touched her hair with his fingers, and as she murmured something in her dream he leaned over and kissed her bright cheek. Then he picked up the suitcase full of shoes, locked the door, and ran briskly down the stairs.

III

By five o'clock that afternoon the last package of cards for Garrod's shoes had been sent by messenger to H. G. Garrod at the Biltmore Hotel. He was to give a decision next morning. At 5.30 Roger's stenographer tapped him on the shoulder.

'Mr Golden, the superintendent of the building, to see you.'

Roger turned around dazedly.

'Oh, how do?'

Mr Golden came directly to the point. If Mr Halsey intended to keep the office any longer, the little oversight about the rent had better be remedied right away.

'Mr Golden,' said Roger wearily, 'everything'll be all right tomorrow. If you worry me now maybe you'll never get your money. After tomorrow nothing'll matter.'

Mr Golden looked at the tenant uneasily. Young men sometimes did away with themselves when business went wrong. Then his eye fell unpleasantly on the initialled suitcase beside the desk.

'Going on a trip?' he asked pointedly.

'What? Oh, no. That's just some clothes.'

'Clothes, eh? Well, Mr Halsey, just to prove that you mean what you say, suppose you let me keep that suitcase until tomorrow noon.'

'Help yourself.'

Mr Golden picked it up with a deprecatory gesture.

'Just a matter of form,' he remarked.

'I understand,' said Roger, swinging around to his desk. 'Good afternoon.'

Mr Golden seemed to feel that the conversation should close on a softer key.

'And don't work too hard, Mr Halsey. You don't want to have a nervous break –'

'No,' shouted Roger, 'I don't. But I will if you don't leave me alone.'

As the door closed behind Mr Golden, Roger's stenographer turned sympathetically around.

'You shouldn't have let him get away with that,' she said. 'What's in there? Clothes?'

.'No,' answered Roger absently. 'Just all my wife's shoes.'

He slept in the office that night on a sofa beside his desk. At dawn he awoke with a nervous start, rushed out into the street for coffee, and returned in ten minutes in a panic – afraid that he might have missed Mr Garrod's telephone call. It was then 6.30.

By eight o'clock his whole body seemed to be on fire. When his two artists arrived he was stretched on the couch in almost physical pain. The phone rang imperatively at 9.30, and he picked up the receiver with trembling hands.

'Hello.'

'Is this the Halsey agency?'

'Yes, this is Mr Halsey speaking.'

'This is Mr H. G. Garrod.'

Roger's heart stopped beating.

'I called up, young fellow, to say that this is wonderful work you've given us here. We want all of it and as much more as your office can do.'

'Oh, God!' cried Roger into the transmitter.

'What?' Mr H. G. Garrod was considerably startled. 'Say, wait a minute there!'

But he was talking to nobody. The phone had clattered to the floor, and Roger, stretched full length on the couch, was sobbing as if his heart would break.

IV

Three hours later, his face somewhat pale, but his eyes calm as a child's, Roger opened the door of his wife's bedroom with the morning paper under his arm. At the sound of his footsteps she started awake.

'What time is it?' she demanded.

He looked at his watch.

'Twelve o'clock.'

Suddenly she began to cry.

'Roger,' she said brokenly, 'I'm sorry I was so bad last night.'

He nodded coolly.

'Everything's all right now,' he answered. Then, after a pause: 'I've got the account – the biggest one.'

She turned towards him quickly.

'You have?' Then, after a minute's silence: 'Can I get a new dress?'

'Dress?' He laughed shortly. 'You can get a dozen. This account alone will bring us in forty thousand a year. It's one of the biggest in the West.'

She looked at him, startled.

'Forty thousand a year!'

'Yes.'

'Gosh' – and then faintly – 'I didn't know it'd really be anything like that.' Again she thought a minute. 'We can have a house like George Tompkins'.'

'I don't want an interior-decoration shop.'

'Forty thousand a year!' she repeated again, and then added softly: 'Oh, Roger –'

'Yes?'

'I'm not going out with George Tompkins.'

'I wouldn't let you, even if you wanted to,' he said shortly.

She made a show of indignation.

'Why, I've had a date with him for this Thursday for weeks.'

'It isn't Thursday.'

'It is.'

'It's Friday.'

'Why, Roger, you must be crazy! Don't you think I know what day it is?'

'It isn't Thursday,' he said stubbornly. 'Look!' And he held out the morning paper.

'Friday!' she exclaimed. 'Why, this is a mistake! This must be last week's paper. Today's Thursday.'

She closed her eyes and thought for a moment.

'Yesterday was Wednesday,' she said decisively. 'The laundress came yesterday. I guess I know.'

'Well,' he said smugly, 'look at the paper. There isn't any question about it.'

With a bewildered look on her face she got out of bed and began searching for her clothes. Roger went into the bathroom to shave. A minute later he heard the springs creak again. Gretchen was getting back into bed.

'What's the matter?' he inquired, putting his head around the corner of the bathroom.

'I'm scared,' she said in a trembling voice. 'I think my nerves are giving way. I can't find any of my shoes.'

'Your shoes? Why, the closet's full of them.'

'I know, but I can't see one.' Her face was pale with fear. 'Oh, Roger!'

Roger came to her bedside and put his arm around her.

'Oh, Roger,' she cried, 'what's the matter with me? First that newspaper, and now all my shoes. Take care of me, Roger.'

'I'll get the doctor,' he said.

He walked remorselessly to the telephone and took up the receiver.

'Phone seems to be out of order,' he remarked after a minute; 'I'll send Bebé.'

The doctor arrived in ten minutes.

'I think I'm on the verge of a collapse,' Gretchen told him in a strained voice.

Doctor Gregory sat down on the edge of the bed and took her wrist in his hand.

'It seems to be in the air this morning.'

'I got up,' said Gretchen in an awed voice, 'and I found that I'd lost a whole day. I had an engagement to go riding with George Tompkins –'

'What?' exclaimed the doctor in surprise. Then he laughed.

'George Tompkins won't go riding with anyone for many days to come.'

'Has he gone away?' asked Gretchen curiously.

'He's going West.'

'Why?' demanded Roger. 'Is he running away with somebody's wife?'

'No,' said Doctor Gregory. 'He's had a nervous breakdown.'

'What?' they exclaimed in unison.

'He just collapsed like an opera-hat in his cold shower.'

'But he was always talking about his – his balanced life,' gasped Gretchen. 'He had it on his mind.'

'I know,' said the doctor. 'He's been babbling about it all morning. I think it's driven him a little mad. He worked pretty hard at it, you know.'

'At what?' demanded Roger in bewilderment.

'At keeping his life balanced.' He turned to Gretchen. 'Now all I'll prescribe for this lady here is a good rest. If she'll just stay around the house for a few days and take forty winks of sleep she'll be as fit as ever. She's been under some strain.'

'Doctor,' exclaimed Roger hoarsely, 'don't you think I'd better have a rest or something? I've been working pretty hard lately.'

'You!' Doctor Gregory laughed, slapped him violently on the back. 'My boy, I never saw you looking better in your life.'

Roger turned away quickly to conceal his smile – winked forty times, or almost forty times, at the autographed picture of Mr George Tompkins, which hung slightly askew on the bedroom wall.

THE LAST OF THE BELLES

I

After Atlanta's elaborate and theatrical rendition of Southern charm, we all underestimated Tarleton. It was a little hotter than anywhere we'd been – a dozen rookies collapsed the first day in that Georgia sun – and when you saw herds of cows drifting through the business streets, hi-yaed by coloured drovers, a trance stole down over you out of the hot light: you wanted to move a hand or foot to be sure you were alive.

So I stayed out at camp and let Lieutenant Warren tell me about the girls. This was fifteen years ago, and I've forgotten how I felt, except that the days went along, one after another, better than they do now, and I was empty-hearted, because up North she whose legend I had loved for three years was getting married. I saw the clippings and newspaper photographs. It was 'a romantic wartime wedding', all very rich and sad. I felt vividly the dark radiance of the sky under which it took place and, as a young snob, was more envious than sorry.

A day came when I went into Tarleton for a haircut and ran into a nice fellow named Bill Knowles, who was in my time at Harvard. He'd been in the National Guard division that preceded us in camp; at the last moment he had transferred to aviation and had been left behind.

'I'm glad I met you, Andy,' he said with undue seriousness. 'I'll hand you on all my information before I start for Texas. You see, there're really only three girls here –'

I was interested; there was something mystical about there being three girls.

'– and here's one of them now.'

We were in front of a drug store and he marched me in and introduced me to a lady I promptly detested.

'The other two are Ailie Calhoun and Sally Carrol Happer.'

I guessed from the way he pronounced her name that he was interested in Ailie Calhoun. It was on his mind what she would be doing while he was gone; he wanted her to have a quiet, uninteresting time.

At my age I don't even hesitate to confess that entirely unchivalrous images of Ailie Calhoun – that lovely name – rushed into my mind. At twenty-three there is no such thing as a pre-empted beauty; though, had Bill asked me, I would doubtless have sworn in all sincerity to care for her like a sister. He didn't; he was just fretting out loud at having to go. Three days later he telephoned me that he was leaving next morning and he'd take me to her house that night.

We met at the hotel and walked uptown through the flowery, hot twilight. The four white pillars of the Calhoun house faced the street, and behind them the veranda was dark as a cave with hanging, weaving, climbing vines.

When we came up the walk a girl in a white dress tumbled out of the front door, crying, 'I'm so sorry I'm late!' and seeing us, added: 'Why, I thought I heard you come ten minutes –'

She broke off as a chair creaked and another man, an aviator from Camp Harry Lee, emerged from the obscurity of the veranda.

'Why, Canby!' she cried. 'How are you?'

He and Bill Knowles waited with the tenseness of open litigants.

'Canby, I want to whisper to you, honey,' she said, after just a second. 'You'll excuse us, Bill.'

They went aside. Presently Lieutenant Canby, immensely displeased, said in a grim voice, 'Then we'll make it Thursday, but that means sure.' Scarcely nodding to us, he went down the walk, the spurs with which he presumably urged on his aeroplane gleaming in the lamplight.

'Come in – I don't just know your name –'

There she was – the Southern type in all its purity. I would have recognized Ailie Calhoun if I'd never heard Ruth Draper or read Marse Chan. She had the adroitness sugar-coated with sweet, voluble simplicity, the suggested background of devoted fathers, brothers and admirers stretching back into the South's heroic age, the unfailing coolness acquired in the endless struggle with the heat. There were notes in her voice that ordered slaves around, that withered up Yankee captains, and then soft, wheedling notes that mingled in unfamiliar loveliness with the night.

I could scarcely see her in the darkness, but when I rose to go – it was plain that I was not to linger – she stood in the orange light from the doorway. She was small and very blonde; there was too much fever-coloured rouge on her face, accentuated by a nose dabbed clownish white, but she shone through that like a star.

'After Bill goes I'll be sitting here all alone night after night. Maybe you'll take me to the country-club dances.' The pathetic prophecy brought a laugh from Bill. 'Wait a minute,' Ailie murmured. 'Your guns are all crooked.'

She straightened my collar pin, looking up at me for a second with something more than curiosity. It was a seeking look, as if she asked, 'Could it be you?' Like Lieutenant Canby, I marched off unwillingly into the suddenly insufficient night.

Two weeks later I sat with her on the same veranda, or rather she half lay in my arms, and yet scarcely touched me – how she managed that I don't remember. I was trying unsuccessfully to kiss her, and had been trying for the best part of an hour. We had a sort of joke about my not being sincere. My theory was that if she'd let me kiss her I'd fall in love with her. Her argument was that I was obviously insincere.

In a lull between two of these struggles she told me about her brother who had died in his senior year at Yale. She showed me his picture – it was a handsome, earnest face with a Leyendecker forelock – and told me that when she met someone who measured up to him she'd marry. I found this family idealism discouraging; even my brash confidence couldn't compete with the dead.

The evening and other evenings passed like that, and ended with my going back to camp with the remembered smell of magnolia flowers and a mood of vague dissatisfaction. I never kissed her. We went to the vaudeville and to the country club on Saturday nights, where she seldom took ten consecutive steps with one man, and she took me to barbecues and rowdy watermelon parties, and never thought it was worth while to change what I felt for her into love. I see now that it wouldn't have been hard, but she was a wise nineteen and she must have seen that we were emotionally incompatible. So I became her confidant instead.

We talked about Bill Knowles. She was considering Bill; for, though she wouldn't admit it, a winter at school in New York and a prom at Yale had turned her eyes North. She said she didn't think she'd marry a Southern man. And by degrees I saw that she was consciously and voluntarily different from these other girls who sang nigger songs and shot craps in the country-club bar. That's why Bill and I and others were drawn to her. We recognized her.

June and July, while the rumours reached us faintly, ineffectually, of battle and terror overseas, Ailie's eyes roved here and there about the country-club floor, seeking for something among the tall young officers. She attached several, choosing them with unfailing perspicacity – save in the case of Lieutenant Canby, whom she claimed to despise, but, nevertheless, gave dates to 'because he was so sincere' – and we apportioned her evenings among us all summer.

One day she broke all her dates – Bill Knowles had leave and was coming. We talked of the event with scientific impersonality – would he move her to a decision? Lieutenant Canby, on the contrary, wasn't impersonal at all; made a nuisance of himself. He told her that if she married Knowles he was going to climb up six thousand feet in his aeroplane, shut off the motor and let go. He frightened her – I had to yield him my last date before Bill came.

On Saturday night she and Bill Knowles came to the country club. They were very handsome together and once more I felt envious and sad. As they danced out on the floor the three-piece orchestra was playing *After You've Gone*, in a poignant incomplete way that I can hear yet, as if each bar were trickling off a precious minute of that time. I knew then that I had grown to love Tarleton, and I glanced about half in panic to see if some face wouldn't come in for me out of that warm, singing, outer darkness that yielded up couple after couple in organdie and olive drab. It was a time of youth and war, and there was never so much love around.

When I danced with Ailie she suddenly suggested that we go outside to a car. She wanted to know why didn't people cut in on her tonight? Did they think she was already married?

'Are you going to be?'

'I don't know, Andy. Sometimes, when he treats me as if I were sacred, it thrills me.' Her voice was hushed and far away. 'And then –'

She laughed. Her body, so frail and tender, was touching mine, her face was turned up to me, and there, suddenly, with Bill Knowles ten yards off, I could have kissed her at last. Our lips just touched experimentally; then an aviation officer turned a corner of the veranda near us, peered into our darkness, and hesitated.

'Ailie.'

'Yes.'

'You heard about this afternoon?'

'What?' She leaned forward, tenseness already in her voice.

'Horace Canby crashed. He was instantly killed.'

She got up slowly and stepped out of the car.

'You mean he was killed?' she said.

'Yes. They don't know what the trouble was. His motor –'

'Oh-h-h!' Her rasping whisper came through the hands suddenly covering her face. We watched her helplessly as she put her head on the side of the car, gagging dry tears. After a minute I went for Bill, who was standing in the stag line, searching anxiously about for her, and told him she wanted to go home.

I sat on the steps outside. I had disliked Canby, but his terrible, pointless death was more real to me then than the day's toll of thousands in France. In a few minutes Ailie and Bill came out. Ailie was whimpering a little, but when she saw me her eyes flexed and she came over swiftly.

'Andy' – she spoke in a quick, low voice – 'of course you must never tell anybody what I told you about Canby yesterday. What he said, I mean.'

'Of course not.'

She looked at me a second longer as if to be quite sure. Finally she was sure. Then she sighed in such a quaint little way that I could hardly believe my ears, and her brow went up in what can only be described as mock despair.

'An-dy!'

I looked uncomfortably at the ground, aware that she was calling my attention to her involuntarily disastrous effect on men.

'Good night, Andy!' called Bill as they got into a taxi.

'Good night,' I said, and almost added: 'You poor fool.'

II

Of course I should have made one of those fine moral decisions that people make in books, and despised her. On the contrary, I don't doubt that she could still have had me by raising her hand.

A few days later she made it all right by saying wistfully, 'I know you think it was terrible of me to think of myself at a time like that, but it was such a shocking coincidence.'

At twenty-three I was entirely unconvinced about anything, except that some people were strong and attractive and could do what they wanted, and others were caught and disgraced. I hoped I was of the former. I was sure Ailie was.

I had to revise other ideas about her. In the course of a long discussion with some girl about kissing – in those days people still talked about kissing more than they kissed – I mentioned the fact that Ailie had only kissed two or three men, and only when she thought she was in love. To my considerable disconcertion the girl figuratively just lay on the floor and howled.

'But it is true,' I assured her, suddenly knowing it wasn't. 'She told me herself.'

'Ailie Calhoun! Oh, my heavens! Why, last year at the Tech spring house party –'

This was in September. We were going overseas any week now, and to bring us up to full strength a last batch of officers from the fourth training camp arrived. The fourth camp wasn't like the first three – the candidates were from the ranks; even from the drafted divisions. They had queer names without vowels in them, and save for a few young militiamen, you couldn't take it for granted that they came out of any background at all. The addition to our company was Lieutenant Earl Schoen from New Bedford, Massachusetts; as fine a physical specimen as I have ever seen. He was six-foot-three, with black hair, high colour, and glossy dark-brown eyes. He wasn't very smart and he was definitely illiterate, yet he was a good officer, high-tempered and commanding, and with that becoming touch of vanity that sits well on the military. I had an idea that New Bedford was a country town, and set down his bumptious qualities to that.

We were doubled up in living quarters and he came into my hut. Inside of a week there was a cabinet photograph of some Tarleton girl nailed brutally to the shack wall.

'She's no jane or anything like that. She's a society girl; goes with all the best people here.'

The following Sunday afternoon I met the lady at a semi-private swimming pool in the country. When Ailie and I arrived, there was Schoen's muscular body rippling out of a bathing suit at the far end of the pool.

'Hey, lieutenant!'

When I waved back at him he grinned and winked, jerking his head towards the girl at his side. Then, digging her in the ribs, he jerked his head at me. It was a form of introduction.

'Who's that with Kitty Preston?' Ailie asked, and when I told her she said he looked like a streetcar conductor, and pretended to look for her transfer.

A moment later he crawled powerfully and gracefully down the pool and pulled himself up at our side. I introduced him to Ailie.

'How do you like my girl, lieutenant?' he demanded. 'I told you she was all right, didn't I?' He jerked his head towards Ailie; this time to indicate that his girl and Ailie moved in the same circles. 'How about us all having dinner together down at the hotel some night?'

I left them in a moment, amused as I saw Ailie visibly making up her mind that here, anyhow, was not the ideal. But Lieutenant Earl Schoen was not to be dismissed so lightly. He ran his eyes cheerfully and inoffensively over her cute, slight figure, and decided that she would do even better than the other. Then minutes later I saw them in the water together, Ailie swimming away with a grim little stroke she had, and Schoen wallowing riotously around her and ahead of her, sometimes pausing and staring at her, fascinated, as a boy might look at a nautical doll.

While the afternoon passed he remained at her side. Finally Ailie came over to me and whispered, with a laugh: 'He's afollowing me around. He thinks I haven't paid my car-fare.'

She turned quickly. Miss Kitty Preston, her face curiously flustered, stood facing us.

'Ailie Calhoun, I didn't think it of you to go out and delib'ately try to take a man away from another girl.' – An expression of distress at the impending scene flitted over Ailie's face – 'I thought you considered yourself above anything like that.'

Miss Preston's voice was low, but it held that tensity that can be felt farther than it can be heard, and I saw Ailie's clear lovely eyes glance about in panic. Luckily, Earl himself was ambling cheerfully and innocently towards us.

'If you care for him you certainly oughtn't to belittle yourself in front of him,' said Ailie in a flash, her head high.

It was her acquaintance with the traditional way of behaving against Kitty Preston's naïve and fierce possessiveness, or if you prefer it, Ailie's 'breeding' against the other's 'commonness'. She turned away.

'Wait a minute kid!' cried Earl Schoen. 'How about your address? Maybe I'd like to give you a ring on the phone.'

She looked at him in a way that should have indicated to Kitty her entire lack of interest.

'I'm very busy at the Red Cross this month,' she said, her voice as cool as her slicked-back blonde hair. 'Goodbye.'

On the way home she laughed. Her air of having been unwittingly involved in a contemptible business vanished.

'She'll never hold that young man,' she said. 'He wants somebody new.'

'Apparently he wants Ailie Calhoun.'

The idea amused her.

'He could give me his ticket punch to wear, like a fraternity pin. What fun! If Mother ever saw anybody like that come in the house, she'd just lie down and die.'

And to give Ailie credit, it was fully a fortnight before he did come to her house, although he rushed her until she pretended to be annoyed at the next country-club dance.

'He's the biggest tough, Andy,' she whispered to me. 'But he's so sincere.'

She used the word 'tough' without the conviction it would have carried had he been a Southern boy. She only knew it with her mind; her ear couldn't distinguish between one Yankee voice and another. And somehow Mrs Calhoun didn't expire at his appearance on the threshold. The supposedly ineradicable prejudices of Ailie's parents were a convenient phenomenon that disappeared at her wish. It was her friends who were astonished. Ailie, always a little above Tarleton, whose beaux had been very carefully the 'nicest' men of the camp – Ailie and Lieutenant Schoen! I grew tired of assuring people that she was merely distracting herself – and indeed every week or so there was someone new – an ensign from Pensacola, an old friend from New Orleans – but always, in between times, there was Earl Schoen.

Orders arrived for an advance party of officers and sergeants to proceed to the port of embarkation and take ship to France. My name was on the list. I had been on the range for a week and when I got back to camp, Earl Schoen buttonholed me immediately.

'We're giving a little farewell party in the mess. Just you and I and Captain Craker and three girls.'

Earl and I were to call for the girls. We picked up Sally Carrol Happer and Nancy Lamar, and went on to Ailie's house; to be met at the door by the butler with the announcement that she wasn't home.

'Isn't home?' Earl repeated blankly. 'Where is she?'

'Didn't leave no information about that; just said she wasn't home.'

'But this is a darn funny thing!' he exclaimed. He walked around the familiar dusky veranda while the butler waited at the door. Something occurred to him. 'Say,' he informed me – 'say, I think she's sore.'

I waited. He said sternly to the butler, 'You tell her I've got to speak to her a minute.'

'How'm I goin' tell her that when she ain't home?'

Again Earl walked musingly around the porch. Then he nodded several times and said:

'She's sore at something that happened downtown.'

In a few words he sketched out the matter to me.

'Look here; you wait in the car,' I said. 'Maybe I can fix this.' And when he reluctantly retreated: 'Oliver, you tell Miss Ailie I want to see her alone.'

After some argument he bore this message and in a moment returned with a reply:

'Miss Ailie say she don't want to see that other gentleman about nothing never. She say come in if you like.'

She was in the library. I had expected to see a picture of cool, outraged dignity, but her face was distraught, tumultuous, despairing. Her eyes were red-rimmed, as though she had been crying slowly and painfully, for hours.

'Oh, hello, Andy,' she said brokenly. 'I haven't seen you for so long. Has he gone?'

'Now, Ailie –'

'Now, Ailie!' she cried. 'Now, Ailie! He spoke to me, you see. He lifted his hat. He stood there ten feet from me with that horrible – that horrible woman – holding her arm and talking to her, and then when he saw me he raised his hat. Andy, I didn't know what to do. I had to go in the drug store and ask for a glass of water, and I was so afraid he'd follow in after me that I asked Mr Rich to let me go out the back way. I never want to see him or hear of him again.'

I talked. I said what one says in such cases. I said it for half an hour. I could not move her. Several times she answered by murmuring something about his not being 'sincere', and for the fourth time I wondered what the word meant to her. Certainly not constancy; it was, I half suspected, some special way she wanted to be regarded.

I got up to go. And then, unbelievably, the automobile horn sounded three times impatiently outside. It was stupefying. It said as plainly as if Earl were in the room, 'All right; go to the devil then! I'm not going to wait here all night.'

Ailie looked at me aghast. And suddenly a peculiar look came into her face, spread, flickered, broke into a teary, hysterical smile.

'Isn't he awful?' she cried in helpless despair. 'Isn't he terrible?'

'Hurry up,' I said quickly. 'Get your cape. This is our last night.'

And I can still feel that last night vividly, the candlelight that flickered over the rough boards of the mess shack, over the frayed paper decorations left from the supply company's party, the sad mandolin down a company street that kept picking *My Indiana Home* out of the universal nostalgia of the departing summer. The three girls lost in this mysterious men's city felt something, too – a bewitched impermanence as though they were on a magic carpet that had lighted on the Southern country-side, and any moment the wind would lift it and waft it away. We toasted ourselves and the South. Then we left our napkins and empty glasses and a little of the past on the table, and hand in hand went out into the moonlight itself. Taps had been played; there was no sound but the far-away whinny of a horse, and a loud persistent snore at which we laughed, and the leathery snap of a sentry coming to port over by the guardhouse. Craker was on duty; we others got into a waiting car, motored into Tarleton and left Craker's girl.

Then Ailie and Earl, Sally and I, two and two in the wide back seat, each couple turned from the other, absorbed and whispering, drove away into the wide, flat darkness.

We drove through pinewoods heavy with lichen and Spanish moss, and between the fallow cotton fields along a road white as the rim of the world. We parked under the broken shadow of a mill where there was the sound of running water and restive squawky birds and over everything a brightness that tried to filter in anywhere – into the lost nigger cabins, the automobile, the fastnesses of the heart. The South sang to us – I wonder if they remember. I remember – the cool pale faces, the somnolent amorous eyes and the voices:

'Are you comfortable?'

'Yes, are you?'

'Are you sure you are?'

'Yes.'

Suddenly we knew it was late and there was nothing more. We turned home.

Our detachment started for Camp Mills next day, but I didn't go to France after all. We passed a cold month on Long Island, marched aboard a transport with steel helmets slung at our sides and then marched off again. There wasn't any more war. I had missed the war. When I came back to Tarleton I tried to get out of the Army, but I had a regular commission and it took most of the winter. But Earl Schoen was one of the first to be demobilized. He wanted to find a good job 'while the picking was good'. Ailie was non-committal, but there was an understanding between them that he'd be back.

By January the camps, which for two years had dominated the little city, were already fading. There was only the persistent incinerator smell to remind one of all that activity and bustle. What life remained centred bitterly about divisional headquarters building with the disgruntled regular officers who had also missed the war.

And now the young men of Tarleton began drifting back from the ends of the earth – some with Canadian uniforms, some with crutches or empty sleeves. A returned battalion of the National Guard paraded through the streets with open ranks for their dead, and then stepped down out of romance for ever and sold you things over the counters of local stores. Only a few uniforms mingled with the dinner coats at the country-club dance.

Just before Christmas, Bill Knowles arrived unexpectedly one day and left the next – either he gave Ailie an ultimatum or she had made up her mind at last. I saw her sometimes when she wasn't busy with returned heroes from Savannah and Augusta, but I felt like an outmoded survival – and I was. She was waiting for Earl Schoen with such a vast uncertainty that she didn't like to talk about it. Three days before I got my final discharge he came.

I first happened upon them walking down Market Street together, and I don't think I've ever been so sorry for a couple in my life; though I suppose the same situation was repeating itself in every city where there had been camps. Exteriorly Earl had about everything wrong with him that could be imagined. His hat was green, with a radical feather; his suit was slashed and braided in a grotesque fashion that national advertising and the movies have put an end to. Evidently he had been to his old barber, for his hair bloused neatly on his pink, shaved neck. It wasn't as though he had been shiny and poor, but the background of mill-town dance halls and outing clubs flamed out at you – or rather flamed out at Ailie. For she had never quite imagined the reality; in these clothes even the natural grace of that magnificent body had departed. At first he boasted of his fine job; it would get them along all right until he could 'see some easy money'. But from the moment he came back into her world on its own terms he must have known it was hopeless. I don't know what Ailie said or how much her grief weighed against her stupefaction. She acted quickly – three days after his arrival, Earl and I went North together on the train.

'Well, that's the end of that,' he said moodily. 'She's a wonderful girl, but too much of a highbrow for me. I guess she's got to marry some rich guy that'll give her a great social position. I can't see that stuck-up sort of thing.' And then, later: 'She said to come back and see her in a year, but I'll never go back. This aristocrat stuff is all right if you got the money for it, but –'

'But it wasn't real,' he meant to finish. The provincial society in which he had moved with so much satisfaction for six months already appeared to him as affected, 'dudish', and artificial.

'Say, did you see what I saw getting on the train?' he asked me after a while. 'Two wonderful janes, all alone. What do you say we mosey into the next car and ask them to lunch? I'll take the one in blue.' Halfway down the car he turned around suddenly. 'Say, Andy,' he demanded, frowning; 'one thing – how do you suppose she knew I used to command a street car? I never told her that.'

'Search me.'

III

This narrative arrives now at one of the big gaps that stared me in the face when I began. For six years, while I finished at Harvard Law and built commercial aeroplanes and backed a pavement block that went gritty under trucks, Ailie Calhoun was scarcely more than a name on a Christmas card; something that blew a little in my mind on warm nights when I remembered the magnolia flowers. Occasionally an acquaintance of Army days would ask me, 'What became of that blonde girl who was so popular?' but I didn't know. I ran into Nancy Lamar at the Montmartre in New York one evening and learned that Ailie had become engaged to a man in Cincinnati, had gone North to visit his family, and then broken it off. She was lovely as ever and there was always a heavy beau or two. But neither Bill Knowles nor Earl Schoen had ever come back.

And somewhere about that time I heard that Bill Knowles had married a girl he met on a boat. There you are – not much of a patch to mend six years with.

Oddly enough, a girl seen at twilight in a small Indiana station started me thinking about going South. The girl, in stiff pink organdie, threw her arms about a man who got off our train and hurried him to a waiting car, and I felt a sort of pang. It seemed to me that she was bearing him off into the lost midsummer world of my early twenties, where time had stood still and charming girls, dimly seen like the past itself, still loitered along the dusky streets. I suppose that poetry is a Northern man's dream of the South. But it was months later that I sent off a wire to Ailie, and immediately followed it to Tarleton.

It was July. The Jefferson Hotel seemed strangely shabby and stuffy – a boosters' club burst into intermittent song in the dining-room that my memory had long dedicated to officers and girls. I recognized the taxi-driver who took me up to Ailie's house, but his 'Sure, I do, Lieutenant,' was unconvincing. I was only one of twenty thousand.

It was a curious three days. I suppose some of Ailie's first young lustre must have gone the way of such mortal shining, but I can't bear witness to it. She was still so physically appealing that you wanted to touch the personality that trembled on her lips. No – the change was more profound than that.

At once I saw she had a different line. The modulations of pride, the vocal hints that she knew the secrets of a brighter, finer ante-bellum day, were gone from her voice; there was no time for them now as it rambled on in the half-laughing, half-desperate banter of the newer South. And everything was swept into this banter in order to make it go on and leave no time for thinking – the present, the future, herself, me. We went to a rowdy party at the house of some young married people, and she was the nervous, glowing centre of it. After all, she wasn't eighteen, and she was as attractive in her rôle of reckless clown as she had ever been in her life.

'Have you heard anything from Earl Schoen?' I asked her the second night, on our way to the country-club dance.

'No.' She was serious for a moment. 'I often think of him. He was the –' she hesitated.

'Go on.'

'I was going to say the man I loved most, but that wouldn't be true. I never exactly loved him, or I'd have married him any old how, wouldn't I?' She looked at me questioningly. 'At least I wouldn't have treated him like that.'

'It was impossible.'

'Of course,' she agreed uncertainly. Her mood changed; she became flippant: 'How the Yankees did deceive us poor little Southern girls. Ah, me!'

When we reached the country club she melted like a chameleon into the – to me – unfamiliar crowd. There was a new generation upon the floor, with less dignity than the ones I had known, but none of them were more a part of its lazy, feverish essence than Ailie. Possibly she had perceived that in her initial longing to escape from Tarleton's provincialism she had been walking alone, following a generation which was doomed to have no successors. Just where she lost the battle, waged behind the white pillars of her veranda, I don't know. But she had guessed wrong, missed out somewhere. Her wild animation, which even now called enough men around her to rival the entourage of the youngest and freshest, was an admission of defeat.

I left her house, as I had so often left it that vanished June, in a mood of vague dissatisfaction. It was hours later, tossing about my bed in the hotel, that I realized what was the matter, what had always been the matter – I was deeply and incurably in love with her. In spite of every incompatibility, she was still, she would always be to me, the most attractive girl I had ever known. I told her so next afternoon. It was one of those hot days I knew so well, and Ailie sat beside me on a couch in the darkened library.

'Oh, no, I couldn't marry you,' she said, almost frightened; 'I don't love you that way at all . . . I never did. And you don't love me, I didn't mean to tell you now, but next month I'm going to marry another man. We're not even announcing it, because I've done that twice before.' Suddenly it occurred to her that I might be hurt: 'Andy, you just had a silly idea, didn't you? You know I couldn't ever marry a Northern man.'

'Who is he?' I demanded.

'A man from Savannah.'

'Are you in love with him?'

'Of course I am.' We both smiled. 'Of course I am! What are you trying to make me say?'

There were no doubts, as there had been with other men. She couldn't afford to let herself have doubts. I knew this because she had long ago stopped making any pretensions with me. This very naturalness, I realized, was because she didn't consider me as a suitor. Beneath her mask of an instinctive thoroughbred she had always been on to herself, and she couldn't believe that anyone not taken in to the point of uncritical worship could really love her. That was what she called being 'sincere'; she felt most security with men like Canby and Earl Schoen, who were incapable of passing judgements on the ostensibly aristocratic heart.

'All right,' I said, as if she had asked my permission to marry. 'Now, would you do something for me?'

'Anything.'

'Ride out to camp.'

'But there's nothing left there, honey.'

'I don't care.'

We walked downtown. The taxi-driver in front of the hotel repeated her objection: 'Nothing there now, Cap.'

'Never mind. Go there anyhow.'

Twenty minutes later he stopped on a wide unfamiliar plain powdered with new cotton fields and marked with isolated clumps of pine.

'Like to drive over yonder where you see the smoke?' asked the driver. 'That's the new state prison.'

'No. Just drive along this road. I want to find where I used to live.'

An old racecourse, inconspicuous in the camp's day of glory, had reared its dilapidated grandstand in the desolation. I tried in vain to orient myself.

'Go along this road past that clump of trees, and then turn right – no, turn left.'

He obeyed, with professional disgust.

'You won't find a single thing, darling,' said Ailie. 'The contractors took it all down.'

We rode slowly along the margin of the fields. It might have been here –

'All right. I want to get out,' I said suddenly.

I left Ailie sitting in the car, looking very beautiful with the warm breeze stirring her long, curly bob.

It might have been here. That would make the company streets down there and the mess shack, where we dined that night, just over the way.

The taxi-driver regarded me indulgently while I stumbled here and there in the knee-deep underbrush, looking for my youth in a clapboard or a strip of roofing or a rusty tomato can. I tried to sight on a vaguely familiar clump of trees, but it was growing darker now and I couldn't be quite sure they were the right trees.

'They're going to fix up the old racecourse,' Ailie called from the car. 'Tarleton's getting quite doggy in its old age.'

No. Upon consideration they didn't look like the right trees. All I could be sure of was this place that had once been full of life and effort was gone, as if it had never existed, and that in another month Ailie would be gone, and the South would be empty for me for ever.

BABYLON REVISITED

'And where's Mr Campbell?' Charlie asked.

'Gone to Switzerland. Mr Campbell's a pretty sick man, Mr Wales.'

'I'm sorry to hear that. And George Hardt?' Charlie inquired.

'Back in America, gone to work.'

'And where is the Snow Bird?'

'He was in here last week. Anyway, his friend, Mr Schaeffer, is in Paris.'

Two familiar names from the long list of a year and a half ago. Charlie scribbled an address in his notebook and tore out the page.

'If you see Mr Schaeffer, give him this,' he said. 'It's my brother-in-law's address. I haven't settled on a hotel yet.'

He was not really disappointed to find Paris was so empty. But the stillness in the Ritz bar was strange and portentous. It was not an American bar any more – he felt polite in it, and not as if he owned it. It had gone back into France. He felt the stillness from the moment he got out of the taxi and saw the doorman, usually in a frenzy of activity at this hour, gossiping with a *chasseur* by the servants' entrance.

Passing through the corridor, he heard only a single, bored voice in the once-clamorous women's room. When he turned into the bar he travelled the twenty feet of green carpet with his eyes fixed straight ahead by old habit; and then, with his foot firmly on the rail, he turned and surveyed the room, encountering only a single pair of eyes that fluttered up from a newspaper in the corner. Charlie asked for the head barman, Paul, who in the latter days of the bull market had come to work in his own custom-built car – disembarking, however, with due nicety at the nearest corner. But Paul was at his country house today and Alix giving him information.

'No, no more,' Charlie said, 'I'm going slow these days.'

Alix congratulated him: 'You were going pretty strong a couple of years ago.'

'I'll stick to it all right,' Charlie assured him. 'I've stuck to it for over a year and a half now.'

'How do you find conditions in America?'

'I haven't been to America for months. I'm in business in Prague, representing a couple of concerns there. They don't know about me down there.'

Alix smiled.

'Remember the night of George Hardt's bachelor dinner here?' said Charlie. 'By the way, what's become of Claude Fessenden?'

Alix lowered his voice confidentially: 'He's in Paris, but he doesn't come here any more. Paul doesn't allow it. He ran up a bill of thirty thousand francs, charging all his drinks and his lunches, and usually his dinner, for more than a year. And when Paul finally told him he had to pay, he gave him a bad cheque.'

Alix shook his head sadly.

'I don't understand it, such a dandy fellow. Now he's all bloated up –' He made a plump apple of his hands.

Charlie watched a group of strident queens installing themselves in a corner.

'Nothing affects them,' he thought. 'Stocks rise and fall, people loaf or work, but they go on forever.' The place oppressed him. He called for the dice and shook with Alix for the drink.

'Here for long, Mr Wales?'

'I'm here for four or five days to see my little girl.'

'Oh-h! You have a little girl?'

Outside, the fire-red, gas-blue, ghost-green signs shone smokily through the tranquil rain. It was late afternoon and the streets were in movement; the *bistros* gleamed. At the corner of the Boulevard des Capucines he took a taxi. The Place de la Concorde moved by in pink majesty; they crossed the logical Seine, and Charlie felt the sudden provincial quality of the Left Bank.

Charlie directed his taxi to the Avenue de l'Opéra, which was out of his way. But he wanted to see the blue hour spread over the magnificent façade, and imagine that the cab horns, playing endlessly the first few bars of Le Plus que Lent, were the trumpets of the Second Empire. They were closing the iron grill in front of Brentano's Book-store, and people were already at dinner behind the trim little bourgeois hedge of Duval's. He had never eaten at a really cheap restaurant in Paris. Five-course dinner, four francs fifty, eighteen cents, wine included. For some odd reason he wished that he had.

As they rolled on to the Left Bank and he felt its sudden provincialism, he thought, 'I spoiled this city for myself. I didn't realize it, but the days came along one after another, and then two years were gone, and everything was gone, and I was gone.'

He was thirty-five, and good to look at. The Irish mobility of his face was sobered by a deep wrinkle between his eyes. As he rang his brother-in-law's bell in the Rue Palatine, the wrinkle deepened till it pulled down his brow; he felt a cramping sensation in his belly. From behind the maid who opened the door darted a lovely little girl of nine who shrieked 'Daddy!' and flew up, struggling like a fish into his arms. She pulled his head around by one ear and set her cheek against his.

'My old pie,' he said.

'Oh, daddy, daddy, daddy, daddy, dads, dads, dads!'

She drew him into the salon, where the family waited, a boy and a girl his daughter's age, his sister-in-law and her husband. He greeted Marion with his voice pitched carefully to avoid either feigned enthusiasm or dislike, but her response was more frankly tepid, though she minimized her expression of unalterable distrust by directing her regard towards his child. The two men clasped hands in a friendly way and Lincoln Peters rested his for a moment on Charlie's shoulder.

The room was warm and comfortably American. The three children moved intimately about, playing through the yellow oblongs that led to other rooms; the cheer of six o'clock spoke in the eager smacks of the fire and the sounds of French activity in the kitchen. But Charlie did not relax; his heart sat up rigidly in his body and he drew confidence from his daughter, who from time to time came close to him, holding in her arms the doll he had brought.

'Really extremely well,' he declared in answer to Lincoln's question. 'There's a lot of business there that isn't moving at all, but we're doing even better than ever. In fact, damn well. I'm bringing my sister over from America next month to keep house for me. My income last year was bigger than it was when I had money. You see, the Czechs –'

His boasting was for a specific purpose; but after a moment, seeing a faint restiveness in Lincoln's eye, he changed the subject:

'Those are fine children of yours, well brought up, good manners.'

'We think Honoria's a great little girl too.'

Marion Peters came back from the kitchen. She was a tall woman with worried eyes, who had once possessed a fresh American loveliness. Charlie had never been sensitive to it and was always surprised when

people spoke of how pretty she had been. From the first there had been
an instinctive antipathy between them.

'Well, how do you find Honoria?' she asked.

'Wonderful. I was astonished how much she's grown in ten months.
All the children are looking well.'

'We haven't had a doctor for a year. How do you like being back in
Paris?'

'It seems very funny to see so few Americans around.'

'I'm delighted,' Marion said vehemently. 'Now at least you can go
into a store without their assuming you're a millionaire. We've suffered
like everybody, but on the whole it's a good deal pleasanter.'

'But it was nice while it lasted,' Charlie said. 'We were a sort of
royalty, almost infallible, with a sort of magic around us. In the bar this
afternoon' – he stumbled, seeing his mistake – 'there wasn't a man I
knew.'

She looked at him keenly. 'I should think you'd have had enough of
bars.'

'I only stayed a minute. I take one drink every afternoon, and no
more.'

'Don't you want a cocktail before dinner?' Lincoln asked.

'I take only one drink every afternoon, and I've had that.'

'I hope you keep to it,' said Marion.

Her dislike was evident in the coldness with which she spoke, but
Charlie only smiled; he had larger plans. Her very aggressiveness gave
him an advantage, and he knew enough to wait. He wanted them to
initiate the discussion of what they knew had brought him to Paris.

At dinner he couldn't decide whether Honoria was most like him or
her mother. Fortunate if she didn't combine the traits of both that had
brought them to disaster. A great wave of protectiveness went over him.
He thought he knew what to do for her. He believed in character; he
wanted to jump back a whole generation and trust in character again
as the eternally valuable element. Everything else wore out.

He left soon after dinner, but not to go home. He was curious to see
Paris by night with clearer and more judicious eyes than those of other
days. He bought a *strapontin* for the Casino and watched Josephine Baker
go through her chocolate arabesques.

After an hour he left and strolled towards Montmartre, up the Rue
Pigalle into the Place Blanche. The rain had stopped and there were a
few people in evening clothes disembarking from taxis in front of
cabarets, and *cocottes* prowling singly or in pairs, and many Negroes.

He passed a lighted door from which issued music, and stopped with the sense of familiarity; it was Bricktop's, where he had parted with so many hours and so much money. A few doors farther on he found another ancient rendezvous and incautiously put his head inside. Immediately an eager orchestra burst into sound, a pair of professional dancers leaped to their feet and a maitre d'hôtel swooped towards him, crying, 'Crowd just arriving, sir!' But he withdrew quickly.

'You have to be damn drunk,' he thought.

Zelli's was closed, the bleak and sinister cheap hotels surrounding it were dark; up in the Rue Blanche there was more light and a local, colloquial French crowd. The Poet's Cave had disappeared, but the two great mouths of the Café of Heaven and the Café of Hell still yawned – even devoured, as he watched, the meagre contents of a tourist bus – a German, a Japanese, and an American couple who glanced at him with frightened eyes.

So much for the effort and ingenuity of Montmartre. All the catering to vice and waste was on an utterly childish scale, and he suddenly realized the meaning of the word 'dissipate' – to dissipate into thin air; to make nothing out of something. In the little hours of the night every move from place to place was an enormous human jump, an increase of paying for the privilege of slower and slower motion.

He remembered thousand-franc notes given to an orchestra for playing a single number, hundred-franc notes tossed to a doorman for calling a cab.

But it hadn't been given for nothing.

It had been given, even the most wildly squandered sum, as an offering to destiny that he might not remember the things most worth remembering, the things that now he would always remember – his child taken from his control, his wife escaped to a grave in Vermont.

In the glare of a *brasserie* a woman spoke to him. He bought her some eggs and coffee, and then, eluding her encouraging stare, gave her a twenty-franc note and took a taxi to his hotel.

II

He woke upon a fine fall day – football weather. The depression of yesterday was gone and he liked the people on the streets. At noon he sat opposite Honoria at Le Grand Vatel, the only restaurant he could think of not reminiscent of champagne dinners and long luncheons that began at two and ended in a blurred and vague twilight.

'Now, how about vegetables? Oughtn't you to have some vegetables?'

'Well, yes.'

'Here's *épinards* and *chou-fleur* and carrots and *haricots*.'

'I'd like *chou-fleur*.'

'Wouldn't you like to have two vegetables?'

'I usually only have one at lunch.'

The waiter was pretending to be inordinately fond of children. '*Qu'elle est mignonne la petite! Elle parle exactement comme une Française.*'

'How about dessert? Shall we wait and see?'

The waiter disappeared. Honoria looked at her father expectantly.

'What are you going to do?'

'First, we're going to that toy store in the Rue Saint-Honoré and buy you anything you like. And then we're going to the vaudeville at the Empire.'

She hesitated. 'I like it about the vaudeville, but not the toy store.'

'Why not?'

'Well, you brought me this doll.' She had it with her. 'And I've got lots of things. And we're not rich any more, are we?'

'We never were. But today you are to have anything you want.'

'All right,' she agreed resignedly.

When there had been her mother and a French nurse he had been inclined to be strict; now he extended himself, reached out for a new tolerance; he must be both parents to her and not shut any of her out of communication.

'I want to get to know you,' he said gravely. 'First let me introduce myself. My name is Charles J. Wales, of Prague.'

'Oh, daddy!' her voice cracked with laughter.

'And who are you, please?' he persisted, and she accepted a rôle immediately: 'Honoria Wales, Rue Palatine, Paris.'

'Married or single?'

'No, not married. Single.'

He indicated the doll. 'But I see you have a child, madame.'

Unwilling to disinherit it, she took it to her heart and thought quickly: 'Yes, I've been married, but I'm not married now. My husband is dead.'

He went on quickly, 'And the child's name?'

'Simone. That's after my best friend at school.'

'I'm very pleased that you're doing so well at school.'

'I'm third this month,' she boasted. 'Elsie' – that was her cousin – 'is only about eighteenth, and Richard is about at the bottom.'

'You like Richard and Elsie, don't you?'

'Oh, yes. I like Richard quite well and I like her all right.'

Cautiously and casually he asked: 'And Aunt Marion and Uncle Lincoln – which do you like best?'

'Oh, Uncle Lincoln, I guess.'

He was increasingly aware of her presence. As they came in, a murmur of '. . . adorable' followed them, and now the people at the next table bent all their silences upon her, staring as if she were something no more conscious than a flower.

'Why don't I live with you?' she asked suddenly. 'Because mamma's dead?'

'You must stay here and learn more French. It would have been hard for daddy to take care of you so well.'

'I don't really need much taking care of any more. I do everything for myself.'

Going out of the restaurant, a man and a woman unexpectedly hailed him.

'Well, the old Wales!'

'Hello there, Lorraine . . . Dunc.'

Sudden ghosts out of the past: Duncan Schaeffer, a friend from college. Lorraine Quarrles, a lovely, pale blonde of thirty; one of a crowd who had helped them make months into days in the lavish times of three years ago.

'My husband couldn't come this year,' she said, in answer to his question. 'We're poor as hell. So he gave me two hundred a month and told me I could do my worst on that . . . This your little girl?'

'What about coming back and sitting down?' Duncan asked.

'Can't do it.' He was glad for an excuse. As always, he felt Lorraine's passionate, provocative attraction, but his own rhythm was different now.

'Well, how about dinner?' she asked.

'I'm not free. Give me your address and let me call you.'

'Charlie, I believe you're sober,' she said judicially. 'I honestly believe he's sober, Dunc. Pinch him and see if he's sober.'

Charlie indicated Honoria with his head. They both laughed.

'What's your address?' said Duncan sceptically.

He hesitated, unwilling to give the name of his hotel.

'I'm not settled yet. I'd better call you. We're going to see the vaudeville at the Empire.'

'There! That's what I want to do,' Lorraine said. 'I want to see some clowns and acrobats and jugglers. That's just what we'll do, Dunc.'

'We've got to do an errand first,' said Charlie. 'Perhaps we'll see you there.'

'All right, you snob . . . Good-bye, beautiful little girl.'

'Good-bye.'

Honoria bobbed politely.

Somehow, an unwelcome encounter. They liked him because he was functioning, because he was serious; they wanted to see him, because he was stronger than they were now, because they wanted to draw a certain sustenance from his strength.

At the Empire, Honoria proudly refused to sit upon her father's folded coat. She was already an individual with a code of her own, and Charlie was more and more absorbed by the desire of putting a little of himself into her before she crystallized utterly. It was hopeless to try to know her in so short a time.

Between the acts they came upon Duncan and Lorraine in the lobby where the band was playing.

'Have a drink?'

'All right, but not up at the bar. We'll take a table.'

'The perfect father.'

Listening abstractedly to Lorraine, Charlie watched Honoria's eyes leave their table, and he followed them wistfully about the room, wondering what they saw. He met her glance and she smiled. 'I liked that lemonade,' she said.

What had she said? What had he expected? Going home in a taxi afterwards, he pulled her over until her head rested against his chest.

'Darling, do you ever think about your mother?'

'Yes, sometimes,' she answered vaguely.

'I don't want you to forget her. Have you got a picture of her?'

'Yes, I think so. Anyhow, Aunt Marion has. Why don't you want me to forget her?'

'She loved you very much.'

'I loved her too.'

They were silent for a moment.

'Daddy, I want to come and live with you,' she said suddenly.

His heart leaped; he had wanted it to come like this.

'Aren't you perfectly happy?'

'Yes, but I love you better than anybody. And you love me better than anybody, don't you, now that mummy's dead?'

'Of course I do. But you won't always like me best, honey. You'll grow up and meet somebody your own age and go marry him and forget you ever had a daddy.'

'Yes, that's true,' she agreed tranquilly.

He didn't go in. He was coming back at nine o'clock and he wanted to keep himself fresh and new for the thing he must say then.

'When you're safe inside, just show yourself in that window.'

'All right. Good-bye, dads, dads, dads, dads.'

He waited in the dark street until she appeared, all warm and glowing, in the window above and kissed her fingers out into the night.

III

They were waiting. Marion sat behind the coffee service in a dignified black dinner dress that just faintly suggested mourning. Lincoln was walking up and down with the animation of one who had already been talking. They were as anxious as he was to get into the question. He opened it almost immediately:

'I suppose you know what I want to see you about – why I really came to Paris.'

Marion played with the black stars on her necklace and frowned.

'I'm awfully anxious to have a home,' he continued. 'And I'm awfully anxious to have Honoria in it. I appreciate your taking in Honoria for her mother's sake, but things have changed now' – he hesitated and then continued more forcibly – 'changed radically with me, and I want to ask you to reconsider the matter. It would be silly for me to deny that about three years ago I was acting badly –'

Marion looked up at him with hard eyes.

'– but all that's over. As I told you, I haven't had more than a drink a day for over a year, and I take that drink deliberately, so that the idea of alcohol won't get too big in my imagination. You see the idea?'

'No,' said Marion succinctly.

'It's a sort of stunt I set myself. It keeps the matter in proportion.'

'I get you,' said Lincoln. 'You don't want to admit it's got any attraction for you.'

'Something like that. Sometimes I forget and don't take it. But I try to take it. Anyhow, I couldn't afford to drink in my position. The people

I represent are more than satisfied with what I've done, and I'm bringing my sister over from Burlington to keep house for me, and I want awfully to have Honoria too. You know that even when her mother and I weren't getting along well we never let anything that happened touch Honoria. I know she's fond of me and I know I'm able to take care of her and – well, there you are. How do you feel about it?'

He knew that now he would have to take a beating. It would last an hour or two hours, and it would be difficult, but if he modulated his inevitable resentment to the chastened attitude of the reformed sinner, he might win his point in the end.

Keep your temper, he told himself. You don't want to be justified. You want Honoria.

Lincoln spoke first: 'We've been talking it over ever since we got your letter last month. We're happy to have Honoria here. She's a dear little thing, and we're glad to be able to help her, but of course that isn't the question –'

Marion interrupted suddenly. 'How long are you going to stay sober, Charlie?' she asked.

'Permanently, I hope.'

'How can anybody count on that?'

'You know I never did drink heavily until I gave up business and came over here with nothing to do. Then Helen and I began to run around with –'

'Please leave Helen out of it. I can't bear to hear you talk about her like that.'

He stared at her grimly; he had never been certain how fond of each other the sisters were in life.

'My drinking only lasted about a year and a half – from the time we came over until I – collapsed.'

'It was time enough.'

'It was time enough,' he agreed.

'My duty is entirely to Helen,' she said. 'I try to think what she would have wanted me to do. Frankly, from the night you did that terrible thing you haven't really existed for me. I can't help that. She was my sister.'

'Yes.'

'When she was dying she asked me to look out for Honoria. If you hadn't been in a sanatorium then, it might have helped matters.'

He had no answer.

'I'll never in my life be able to forget the morning when Helen knocked at my door, soaked to the skin and shivering and said you'd locked her out.'

Charlie gripped the sides of the chair. This was more difficult than he expected; he wanted to launch out into a long expostulation and explanation, but he only said: 'The night I locked her out –' and she interrupted, 'I don't feel up to going over that again.'

After a moment's silence Lincoln said: 'We're getting off the subject. You want Marion to set aside her legal guardianship and give you Honoria. I think the main point for her is whether she has confidence in you or not.'

'I don't blame Marion,' Charlie said slowly, 'but I think she can have entire confidence in me. I had a good record up to three years ago. Of course, it's within human possibilities I might go wrong any time. But if we wait much longer I'll lose Honoria's childhood and my chance for a home.' He shook his head, 'I'll simply lose her, don't you see?'

'Yes, I see,' said Lincoln.

'Why didn't you think of all this before?' Marion asked.

'I suppose I did, from time to time, but Helen and I were getting along badly. When I consented to the guardianship, I was flat on my back in a sanatorium and the market had cleaned me out. I knew I'd acted badly, and I thought if it would bring any peace to Helen, I'd agree to anything. But now it's different. I'm functioning, I'm behaving damn well, so far as –'

'Please don't swear at me,' Marion said.

He looked at her, startled. With each remark the force of her dislike became more and more apparent. She had built up all her fear of life into one wall and faced it towards him. This trivial reproof was possibly the result of some trouble with the cook several hours before. Charlie became increasingly alarmed at leaving Honoria in this atmosphere of hostility against himself; sooner or later it would come out in a word here, a shake of the head there, and some of that distrust would be irrevocably implanted in Honoria. But he pulled his temper down out of his face and shut it up inside him; he had won a point, for Lincoln realized the absurdity of Marion's remark and asked her lightly since when she had objected to the word 'damn'.

'Another thing,' Charlie said: 'I'm able to give her certain advantages now. I'm going to take a French governess to Prague with me. I've got a lease on a new apartment –'

He stopped, realizing that he was blundering. They couldn't be expected to accept with equanimity the fact that his income was again twice as large as their own.

'I suppose you can give her more luxuries than we can,' said Marion. 'When you were throwing away money we were living along watching every ten francs. . . . I suppose you'll start doing it again.'

'Oh, no,' he said. 'I've learned. I worked hard for ten years, you know – until I got lucky in the market, like so many people. Terribly lucky. It won't happen again.'

There was a long silence. All of them felt their nerves straining, and for the first time in a year Charlie wanted a drink. He was sure now that Lincoln Peters wanted him to have his child.

Marion shuddered suddenly; part of her saw that Charlie's feet were planted on the earth now, and her own maternal feeling recognized the naturalness of his desire; but she had lived for a long time with a prejudice – a prejudice founded on a curious disbelief in her sister's happiness, and which, in the shock of one terrible night, had turned to hatred for him. It had all happened at a point in her life where the discouragement of ill health and adverse circumstances made it necessary for her to believe in tangible villainy and a tangible villain.

'I can't help what I think!' she cried out suddenly. 'How much you were responsible for Helen's death, I don't know. It's something you'll have to square with your own conscience.'

An electric current of agony surged through him; for a moment he was almost on his feet, an unuttered sound echoing in his throat. He hung on to himself for a moment, another moment.

'Hold on there,' said Lincoln uncomfortably. 'I never thought you were responsible for that.'

'Helen died of heart trouble,' Charlie said dully.

'Yes, heart trouble.' Marion spoke as if the phrase had another meaning for her.

Then, in the flatness that followed her outburst, she saw him plainly and she knew he had somehow arrived at control over the situation. Glancing at her husband, she found no help from him, and as abruptly as if it were a matter of no importance, she threw up the sponge.

'Do what you like!' she cried, springing up from her chair. 'She's your child. I'm not the person to stand in your way. I think if it were my child I'd rather see her –' She managed to check herself. 'You two decide it. I can't stand this, I'm sick. I'm going to bed.'

She hurried from the room; after a moment Lincoln said:

'This has been a hard day for her. You know how strongly she feels –' His voice was almost apologetic: 'When a woman gets an idea in her head.'

'Of course.'

'It's going to be all right. I think she sees now that you – can provide for the child, and so we can't very well stand in your way or Honoria's way.'

'Thank you, Lincoln.'

'I'd better go along and see how she is.'

'I'm going.'

He was still trembling when he reached the street, but a walk down the Rue Bonaparte to the *quais* set him up, and as he crossed the Seine, fresh and new by the *quai* lamps, he felt exultant. But back in his room he couldn't sleep. The image of Helen haunted him. Helen whom he had loved so until they had senselessly begun to abuse each other's love, tear it into shreds. On that terrible February night that Marion remembered so vividly, a slow quarrel had gone on for hours. There was a scene at the Florida, and then he attempted to take her home, and then she kissed young Webb at a table; after that there was what she had hysterically said. When he arrived home alone he turned the key in the lock in wild anger. How could he know she would arrive an hour later alone, that there would be a snowstorm in which she wandered about in slippers, too confused to find a taxi? Then the aftermath, her escaping pneumonia by a miracle, and all the attendant horror. They were 'reconciled', but that was the beginning of the end, and Marion, who had seen with her own eyes and who imagined it to be one of many scenes from her sister's martyrdom, never forgot.

Going over it again brought Helen nearer, and in the white, soft light that steals upon half sleep near morning he found himself talking to her again. She said that he was perfectly right about Honoria and that she wanted Honoria to be with him. She said she was glad he was being good and doing better. She said a lot of other things – very friendly things – but she was in a swing in a white dress, and swinging faster and faster all the time, so that at the end he could not hear clearly all that she said.

IV

He woke up feeling happy. The door of the world was open again. He made plans, vistas, futures for Honoria and himself, but suddenly he grew sad, remembering all the plans he and Helen had made. She had not planned to die. The present was the thing – work to do and someone to love. But not to love too much, for he knew the injury that a father can do to a daughter or a mother to a son by attaching them too closely: afterward, out in the world, the child would seek in the marriage partner the same blind tenderness and, failing probably to find it, turn against love and life.

It was another bright, crisp day. He called Lincoln Peters at the bank where he worked and asked if he could count on taking Honoria when he left for Prague. Lincoln agreed that there was no reason for delay. One thing – the legal guardianship. Marion wanted to retain that a while longer. She was upset by the whole matter, and it would oil things if she felt that the situation was still in her control for another year. Charlie agreed, wanting only the tangible, visible child.

Then the question of a governess. Charlie sat in a gloomy agency and talked to a cross Béarnaise and to a buxom Breton peasant, neither of whom he could have endured. There were others whom he would see tomorrow.

He lunched with Lincoln Peters at Griffons, trying to keep down his exultation.

'There's nothing quite like your own child,' Lincoln said. 'But you understand how Marion feels too.'

'She's forgotten how hard I worked for seven years there,' Charlie said. 'She just remembers one night.'

'There's another thing.' Lincoln hesitated. 'While you and Helen were tearing around Europe throwing money away, we were just getting along. I didn't touch any of the prosperity because I never got ahead enough to carry anything but my insurance. I think Marion felt there was some kind of injustice in it – you not even working towards the end, and getting richer and richer.'

'It went just as quick as it came,' said Charlie.

'Yes, a lot of it stayed in the hands of *chasseurs* and saxophone players and maîtres d'hôtel – well, the big party's over now. I just said that to explain Marion's feeling about those crazy years. If you drop in about six o'clock tonight before Marion's too tired, we'll settle the details on the spot.'

Back at his hotel, Charlie found a *pneumatique* that had been re-directed from the Ritz bar where Charlie had left his address for the purpose of finding a certain man.

DEAR CHARLIE:

You were so strange when we saw you the other day that I wondered if I did something to offend you. If so, I'm not conscious of it. In fact, I have thought about you too much for the last year, and it's always been in the back of my mind that I might see you if I came over here. We *did* have such good times that crazy spring, like the night you and I stole the butcher's tricycle, and the time we tried to call on the president and you had the old derby rim and the wire cane. Everybody seems so old lately, but I don't feel old a bit. Couldn't we get together some time today for old time's sake? I've got a vile hang-over for the moment, but will be feeling better this afternoon and will look for you about five in the sweat-shop at the Ritz.

Always devotedly,
LORRAINE

His first feeling was one of awe that he had actually, in his mature years, stolen a tricycle and pedalled Lorraine all over the Etoile between the small hours and dawn. In retrospect it was a nightmare. Locking out Helen didn't fit in with any other act of his life, but the tricycle incident did – it was one of many. How many weeks or months of dissipation to arrive at that condition of utter irresponsibility?

He tried to picture how Lorraine had appeared to him then – very attractive; Helen was unhappy about it, though she said nothing. Yesterday, in the restaurant, Lorraine had seemed trite, blurred, worn away. He emphatically did not want to see her, and he was glad Alix had not given away his hotel address. It was a relief to think instead of Honoria, to think of Sundays spent with her and of saying good morning to her and of knowing she was there in his house at night, drawing her breath in the darkness.

At five he took a taxi and bought presents for all the Peters – a piquant cloth doll, a box of Roman soldiers, flowers for Marion, big linen handkerchiefs for Lincoln.

He saw, when he arrived in the apartment, that Marion had accepted the inevitable. She greeted him now as though he were a recalcitrant member of the family, rather than a menacing outsider. Honoria had been told she was going; Charlie was glad to see that her tact made her conceal her excessive happiness. Only on his lap did she whisper her delight and the question 'When?' before she slipped away with the other children.

He and Marion were alone for a minute in the room, and on an impulse he spoke out boldly:

'Family quarrels are bitter things. They don't go according to any rules. They're not like aches or wounds; they're more like splits in the skin that won't heal because there's not enough material. I wish you and I could be on better terms.'

'Some things are hard to forget,' she answered. 'It's a question of confidence.' There was no answer to this and presently she asked, 'When do you propose to take her?'

'As soon as I can get a governess. I hoped the day after tomorrow.'

'That's impossible. I've got to get her things in shape. Not before Saturday.'

He yielded. Coming back into the room, Lincoln offered him a drink.

'I'll take my daily whisky,' he said.

It was warm here, it was a home, people together by a fire. The children felt very safe and important; the mother and father were serious, watchful. They had things to do for the children more important than his visit here. A spoonful of medicine was, after all, more important than the strained relations between Marion and himself. They were not dull people, but they were very much in the grip of life and circumstances. He wondered if he couldn't do something to get Lincoln out of his rut at the bank.

A long peal at the doorbell; the *bonne à tout faire* passed through and went down the corridor. The door opened upon another long ring, and then voices, and the three in the salon looked up expectantly; Richard moved to bring the corridor within his range of vision, and Marion rose. Then the maid came back along the corridor, closely followed by the voices, which developed under the light into Duncan Schaeffer and Lorraine Quarrles.

They were gay, they were hilarious, they were roaring with laughter. For a moment Charlie was astounded; unable to understand how they ferreted out the Peters' address.

'Ah-h-h!' Duncan wagged his finger roguishly at Charlie. 'Ah-h-h!'

They both slid down another cascade of laughter. Anxious and at a loss, Charlie shook hands with them quickly and presented them to Lincoln and Marion. Marion nodded, scarcely speaking. She had drawn back a step towards the fire; her little girl stood beside her, and Marion put an arm about her shoulder.

With growing annoyance at the intrusion, Charlie waited for them to explain themselves. After some concentration Duncan said:

'We came to invite you out to dinner. Lorraine and I insist that all this shishi, cagey business 'bout your address got to stop.'

Charlie came closer to them, as if to force them backward down the corridor.

'Sorry, but I can't. Tell me where you'll be and I'll phone you in half an hour.'

This made no impression. Lorraine sat down suddenly on the side of a chair, and focusing her eyes on Richard, cried, 'Oh, what a nice little boy! Come here, little boy.' Richard glanced at his mother, but did not move. With a perceptible shrug of her shoulders, Lorraine turned back to Charlie:

'Come and dine. Sure your cousins won' mine. See you so sel'om. Or solemn.'

'I can't,' said Charlie sharply. 'You two have dinner and I'll phone you.'

Her voice became suddenly unpleasant. 'All right, we'll go. But I remember once when you hammered on my door at four A.M. I was enough of a good sport to give you a drink. Come on, Dunc.'

Still in slow motion, with blurred, angry faces, with uncertain feet, they retired along the corridor.

'Good night,' Charlie said.

'Good night!' responded Lorraine emphatically.

When he went back into the salon Marion had not moved, only now her son was standing in the circle of her other arm. Lincoln was still swinging Honoria back and forth like a pendulum from side to side.

'What an outrage!' Charlie broke out. 'What an absolute outrage!'

Neither of them answered. Charlie dropped into an armchair, picked up his drink, set it down again and said:

'People I haven't seen for two years having the colossal nerve –'

He broke off. Marion had made the sound 'Oh!' in one swift, furious breath, turned her body from him with a jerk and left the room.

Lincoln set down Honoria carefully.

'You children go in and start your soup,' he said, and when they obeyed, he said to Charlie:

'Marion's not well and she can't stand shocks. That kind of people make her really physically sick.'

'I didn't tell them to come here. They wormed your name out of somebody. They deliberately –'

'Well, it's too bad. It doesn't help matters. Excuse me a minute.'

Left alone, Charlie sat tense in his chair. In the next room he could hear the children eating, talking in monosyllables, already oblivious to the scene between their elders. He heard a murmur of conversation from a farther room and then the ticking bell of a telephone receiver picked up, and in a panic he moved to the other side of the room and out of earshot.

In a minute Lincoln came back. 'Look here, Charlie. I think we'd better call off dinner for tonight. Marion's in bad shape.'

'Is she angry with me?'

'Sort of,' he said, almost roughly. 'She's not strong and –'

'You mean she's changed her mind about Honoria?'

'She's pretty bitter right now. I don't know. You phone me at the bank tomorrow.'

'I wish you'd explain to her I never dreamed these people would come here. I'm just as sore as you are.'

'I couldn't explain anything to her now.'

Charlie got up. He took his coat and hat and started down the corridor. Then he opened the door of the dining-room and said in a strange voice, 'Good night, children.'

Honoria rose and ran around the table to hug him.

'Good night, sweetheart,' he said vaguely, and then trying to make his voice more tender, trying to conciliate something, 'Good night, dear children.'

V

Charlie went directly to the Ritz bar with the furious idea of finding Lorraine and Duncan, but they were not there, and he realized that in any case there was nothing he could do. He had not touched his drink at the Peters', and now he ordered a whisky-and-soda. Paul came over to say hello.

'It's a great change,' he said sadly. 'We do about half the business we did. So many fellows I hear about back in the States lost everything, maybe not in the first crash, but then in the second. Your friend George Hardt lost every cent, I hear. Are you back in the States?'

'No, I'm in business in Prague.'

'I heard that you lost a lot in the crash.'

'I did,' and he added grimly, 'but I lost everything I wanted in the boom.'

'Selling short.'

'Something like that.'

Again the memory of those days swept over him like a nightmare –

the people they had met travelling; then people who couldn't add a row of figures or speak a coherent sentence. The little man Helen had consented to dance with at the ship's party, who had insulted her ten feet from the table; the women and girls carried screaming with drink or drugs out of public places –

– The men who locked their wives out in the snow, because the snow of twenty-nine wasn't real snow. If you didn't want it to be snow, you just paid some money.

He went to the phone and called the Peters' apartment; Lincoln answered.

'I called up because this thing is on my mind. Has Marion said anything definite?'

'Marion's sick,' Lincoln answered shortly. 'I know this thing isn't altogether your fault, but I can't have her go to pieces about it. I'm afraid we'll have to let it slide for six months; I can't take the chance of working her up to this state again.'

'I see.'

'I'm sorry, Charlie.'

He went back to his table. His whisky glass was empty, but he shook his head when Alix looked at it questioningly. There wasn't much he could do now except send Honoria some things; he would send her a lot of things tomorrow. He thought rather angrily that this was just money – he had given so many people money. . . .

'No, no more,' he said to another waiter. 'What do I owe you?'

He would come back some day; they couldn't make him pay forever. But he wanted his child, and nothing was much good now, beside that fact. He wasn't young any more, with a lot of nice thoughts and dreams to have by himself. He was absolutely sure Helen wouldn't have wanted him to be so alone.

FINANCING FINNEGAN

I

Finnegan and I have the same literary agent to sell our writings for us, but though I'd often been in Mr Cannon's office just before and just after Finnegan's visits, I had never met him. Likewise we had the same publisher and often when I arrived there Finnegan had just departed. I gathered from a thoughtful sighing way in which they spoke of him –

'Ah – Finnegan –'

'Oh yes, Finnegan was here.'

– that the distinguished author's visit had been not uneventful. Certain remarks implied that he had taken something with him when he went – manuscripts, I supposed, one of those great successful novels of his. He had taken 'it' off for a final revision, a last draft, of which he was rumoured to make ten in order to achieve that facile flow, that ready wit, which distinguished his work. I discovered only gradually that most of Finnegan's visits had to do with money.

'I'm sorry you're leaving,' Mr Cannon would tell me, 'Finnegan will be here tomorrow.' Then after a thoughtful pause, 'I'll probably have to spend some time with him.'

I don't know what note in his voice reminded me of a talk with a nervous bank president when Dillinger was reported in the vicinity. His eyes looked out into the distance and he spoke as to himself.

'Of course he may be bringing a manuscript. He has a novel he's working on, you know. And a play too.' He spoke as though he were talking about some interesting but remote events of the cinquecento; but his eyes became more hopeful as he added: 'Or maybe a short story.'

'He's very versatile, isn't he?' I said.

'Oh yes,' Mr Cannon perked up. 'He can do anything – anything when he puts his mind to it. There's never been such a talent.'

'I haven't seen much of his work lately.'

'Oh, but he's working hard. Some of the magazines have stories of his that they're holding.'

'Holding for what?'

'Oh, for a more appropriate time – an upswing. They like to think they have something of Finnegan's.'

His was indeed a name with ingots in it. His career had started brilliantly, and if it had not kept up to its first exalted level, at least it started brilliantly all over again every few years. He was the perennial man of promise in American letters – what he could actually do with words was astounding, they glowed and coruscated – he wrote sentences, paragraphs, chapters that were masterpieces of fine weaving and spinning. It was only when I met some poor devil of a screen writer who had been trying to make a logical story out of one of his books that I realized he had his enemies.

'It's all beautiful when you read it,' this man said disgustedly, 'but when you write it down plain it's like a week in the nut-house.'

From Mr Cannon's office I went over to my publishers on Fifth Avenue, and there too I learned in no time that Finnegan was expected tomorrow. Indeed he had thrown such a long shadow before him that the luncheon where I expected to discuss my own work was largely devoted to Finnegan. Again I had the feeling that my host, Mr George Jaggers, was talking not to me but to himself.

'Finnegan's a great writer,' he said.

'Undoubtedly.'

'And he's really quite all right, you know.'

As I hadn't questioned the fact I inquired whether there was any doubt about it.

'Oh, no,' he said hurriedly. 'It's just that he's had such a run of hard luck lately –'

I shook my head sympathetically. 'I know. That diving into a half-empty pool was a tough break.'

'Oh, it wasn't half-empty. It was full of water. Full to the brim. You ought to hear Finnegan on the subject – he makes a side-splitting story of it. It seems he was in a run-down condition and just diving from the side of the pool, you know –' Mr Jaggers pointed his knife and fork at the table, 'and he saw some young girls diving from the fifteen-foot board. He says he thought of his lost youth and went up to do the same and made a beautiful swan-dive – but his shoulder broke while he was still in the air.' He looked at me rather anxiously. 'Haven't you heard of cases like that – a ball player throwing his arm out of joint?'

I couldn't think of any orthopaedic parallels at the moment.

'And then,' he continued dreamily, 'Finnegan had to write on the ceiling.'

'On the ceiling?'

'Practically. He didn't give up writing – he has plenty of guts, that fellow, though you may not believe it. He had some sort of arrangement built that was suspended from the ceiling and he lay on his back and wrote in the air.'

I had to grant that it was a courageous arrangement.

'Did it affect his work?' I inquired. 'Did you have to read his stories backward – like Chinese?'

'They were rather confused for a while,' he admitted, 'but he's all right now. I got several letters from him that sounded more like the old Finnegan – full of life and hope and plans for the future –'

The far-away look came into his face and I turned the discussion to affairs closer to my heart. Only when we were back in his office did the subject recur – and I blush as I write this because it included confessing something I seldom do – reading another man's telegram. It happened because Mr Jaggers was intercepted in the hall and when I went into his office and sat down it was stretched out open before me:

With fifty I could at least pay typist and get haircut and pencils life has become impossible and I exist on dream of good news desperately. FINNEGAN

I couldn't believe my eyes – fifty dollars, and I happened to know that Finnegan's price for short stories was somewhere around three thousand. George Jaggers found me still staring dazedly at the telegram. After he read it he stared at me with stricken eyes.

'I don't see how I can conscientiously do it,' he said.

I started and glanced around to make sure I was in the prosperous publishing office in New York. Then I understood – I had misread the telegram. Finnegan was asking for fifty thousand as an advance – a demand that would have staggered any publisher no matter who the writer was.

'Only last week,' said Mr Jaggers disconsolately, 'I sent him a hundred dollars. It puts my department in the red every season, so I don't dare tell my partners any more. I take it out of my own pocket – give up a suit and a pair of shoes.'

'You mean Finnegan's broke?'

'Broke!' He looked at me and laughed soundlessly – in fact I didn't exactly like the way that he laughed. My brother had a nervous – but that is afield from this story. After a minute he pulled himself together.

'You won't say anything about this, will you? The truth is Finnegan's been in a slump, he's had blow after blow in the past few years, but now he's snapping out of it and I know we'll get back every cent we've –' He tried to think of a word but 'given him' slipped out. This time it was he who was eager to change the subject.

Don't let me give the impression that Finnegan's affairs absorbed me during a whole week in New York – it was inevitable, though, that being much in the offices of my agent and my publisher, I happened in on a lot. For instance, two days later, using the telephone in Mr Cannon's office, I was accidentally switched in on a conversation he was having with George Jaggers. It was only partly eavesdropping, you see, because I could only hear one end of the conversation and that isn't as bad as hearing it all.

'But I got the impression he was in good health . . . he did say something about his heart a few months ago but I understood it got well . . . yes, and he talked about some operation he wanted to have – I think he said it was cancer . . . Well, I felt like telling him I had a little operation up my sleeve, too, that I'd have had by now if I could afford it . . . No, I didn't say it. He seemed in such good spirits that it seemed a shame to bring him down. He's starting a story today, he read me some of it on the phone . . .

'. . . I did give him twenty-five because he didn't have a cent in his pocket . . . oh, yes – I'm sure he'll be all right now. He sounds as if he means business.'

I understood it all now. The two men had entered into a silent conspiracy to cheer each other up about Finnegan. Their investment in him, in his future, had reached a sum so considerable that Finnegan belonged to them. They could not bear to hear a word against him – even from themselves.

II

I spoke my mind to Mr Cannon.

'If this Finnegan is a four-flusher you can't go on indefinitely giving him money. If he's through he's through and there's nothing to be done about it. It's absurd that you should put off an operation when Finnegan's out somewhere diving into half-empty swimming pools.'

'It was full,' said Mr Cannon patiently – 'full to the brim.'

'Well, full or empty the man sounds like a nuisance to me.'

'Look here,' said Cannon, 'I've got a call from Hollywood due on the wire. Meanwhile you might glance over that.' He threw a manuscript into my lap. 'Maybe it'll help you understand. He brought it in yesterday.'

It was a short story. I began it in a mood of disgust, but before I'd read five minutes I was completely immersed in it, utterly charmed, utterly convinced, and wishing to God I could write like that. When Cannon finished his phone call I kept him waiting while I finished it and when I did there were tears in these hard old professional eyes. Any magazine in the country would have run it first in any issue.

But then nobody had ever denied that Finnegan could write.

III

Months passed before I went again to New York, and then, so far as the offices of my agent and my publisher were concerned, I descended upon a quieter, more stable world. There was at last time to talk about my own conscientious if uninspired literary pursuits, to visit Mr Cannon in the country, and to kill summer evenings with George Jaggers where the vertical New York starlight falls like lingering lightning into restaurant gardens. Finnegan might have been at the North Pole – and as a matter of fact he was. He had quite a group with him, including three Bryn Mawr anthropologists, and it sounded as if he might collect a lot of material there. They were going to stay several months, and if the thing had somehow the ring of a promising little house-party about it, that was probably due to my jealous, cynical disposition.

'We're all just delighted,' said Cannon. 'It's a godsend for him. He was fed up and he needed just this – this –'

'Ice and snow,' I supplied.

'Yes, ice and snow. The last thing he said was characteristic of him. Whatever he writes is going to be pure white – it's going to have a blinding glare about it.'

'I can imagine it will. But tell me – who's financing it? Last time I was here I gathered the man was insolvent.'

'Oh, he was really very decent about that. He owed me some money and I believe he owed George Jaggers a little too.' He 'believed', the old hypocrite. He knew damn well. 'So before he left he made most of his life insurance over to us. That's in case he doesn't come back – those trips are dangerous of course.'

'I should think so,' I said, 'especially with three anthropologists.'

'So Jaggers and I are absolutely covered in case anything happens – it's as simple as that.'

'Did the life-insurance company finance the trip?'

He fidgeted perceptibly.

'Oh, no. In fact when they learned the reason for the assignments they were a little upset. George Jaggers and I felt that when he had a specific plan like this with a specific book at the end of it, we were justified in backing him a little further.'

'I don't see it,' I said flatly.

'You don't?' The old harassed look came back into his eyes. 'Well, I'll admit we hesitated. In principle I know it's wrong. I used to advance authors small sums from time to time, but lately I've made a rule against it – and kept it. It's only been waived once in the last two years and that was for a woman who was having a bad struggle – Margaret Trahill, do you know her? She was an old girl of Finnegan's by the way.'

'Remember I don't even know Finnegan.'

'That's right. You must meet him when he comes back – if he does come back. You'd like him – he's utterly charming.'

Again I departed ftom New York, to imaginative North Poles of my own, while the year rolled through summer and fall. When the first snap of November was in the air, I thought of the Finnegan expedition with a sort of shiver and any envy of the man departed. He was probably earning any loot, literary or anthropological, he might bring back. Then, when I hadn't been back in New York three days, I read in the paper that he and some other members of his party had walked off into a snowstorm when the food supply gave out, and the Arctic had claimed another sacrifice of intrepid man.

I was sorry for him, but practical enough to be glad that Cannon and Jaggers were well protected. Of course, with Finnegan scarcely cold – if such a simile is not too harrowing – they did not talk about it but I gathered that the insurance companies had waived *habeas corpus* or whatever it is in their lingo, just as if he had fallen overboard into the Atlantic, and it seemed quite sure that they would collect.

His son, a fine looking young fellow, came into George Jaggers' office while I was there and from him I could guess at Finnegan's charm – a shy frankness together with an impression of a very quiet, brave battle going on inside of him that he couldn't quite bring himself to talk about – but that showed as heat lightning in his work.

'The boy writes well too,' said George after he had gone. 'He's brought in some remarkable poems. He's not ready to step into his father's shoes, but there's a definite promise.'

'Can I see one of his things?'

'Certainly – here's one he left just as he went out.'

George took a paper from his desk, opened it and cleared his throat. Then he squinted and bent over a little in his chair.

'*Dear Mr Jaggers*,' he began, '*I didn't like to ask you this in person –*' Jaggers stopped, his eyes reading ahead rapidly.

'How much does he want?' I inquired.

He sighed.

'He gave me the impression that this was some of his work,' he said in a pained voice.

'But it is,' I consoled him. 'Of course he isn't quite ready to step into his father's shoes.'

I was sorry afterwards to have said this, for after all Finnegan had paid his debts, and it was nice to be alive now that better times were back and books were no longer rated as unnecessary luxuries. Many authors I knew who had skimped along during the depression were now making long-deferred trips or paying off mortgages or turning out the more finished kind of work that can only be done with a certain leisure and security. I had just got a thousand dollars advance for a venture in Hollywood and was going to fly out with all the verve of the old days when there was chicken feed in every pot. Going in to say good-bye to Cannon and collect the money, it was nice to find he too was profiting – wanted me to go along and see a motor-boat he was buying.

But some last-minute stuff came up to delay him and I grew impatient and decided to skip it. Getting no response to a knock on the door of his sanctum, I opened it anyhow.

The inner office seemed in some confusion. Mr Cannon was on several telephones at once and dictating something about an insurance company to a stenographer. One secretary was getting hurriedly into her hat and coat as upon an errand and another was counting bills from her purse upon a table.

'It'll be only a minute,' said Cannon, 'it's just a little office riot – you never saw us like this.'

'Is it Finnegan's insurance?' I couldn't help asking. 'Isn't it any good?'

'His insurance – oh, perfectly all right, perfectly. This is just a matter of trying to raise a few hundred in a hurry. The banks are closed and we're all contributing.'

'I've got that money you just gave me,' I said. 'I don't need all of it to get to the coast.' I peeled off a couple of hundred. 'Will this be enough?'

'That'll be fine – it just saves us. Never mind, Miss Carlsen. Mrs Mapes, you needn't go now.'

'I think I'll be running along,' I said.

'Just wait two minutes,' he urged. 'I've only got to take care of this wire. It's really splendid news. Bucks you up.'

It was a cablegram from Oslo, Norway – before I began to read I was full of a premonition.

Am miraculously safe here but detained by authorities please wire passage money for four people and two hundred extra I am bringing back plenty greetings from the dead. FINNEGAN

'Yes, that's splendid,' I agreed. 'He'll have a story to tell now.'

'Won't he though,' said Cannon. 'Miss Carlsen, will you wire the parents of those girls – and you'd better inform Mr Jaggers.'

As we walked along the street a few minutes later, I saw that Mr Cannon, as if stunned by the wonder of this news, had fallen into a brown study, and I did not disturb him, for after all I did not know Finnegan and could not whole-heartedly share his joy. His mood of silence continued until we arrived at the door of the motor-boat show. Just under the sign he stopped and stared upward, as if aware for the first time where we were going.

'Oh, my,' he said stepping back. 'There's no use going in here now. I thought we were going to get a drink.'

We did. Mr Cannon was still a little vague, a little under the spell of the vast surprise – he fumbled so long for the money to pay his round that I insisted it was on me.

I think he was in a daze during that whole time because, though he is a man of the most punctilious accuracy, the two hundred I handed him in his office has never shown to my credit in the statements he has sent me. I imagine, though, that some day I will surely get it because some day Finnegan will click again and I know that people will clamour to read what he writes. Recently I've taken it upon myself to investigate some of the stories about him and I've found that they're mostly as false as the half-empty pool. That pool was full to the brim.

So far there's only been a short story about the polar expedition, a love story. Perhaps it wasn't as big a subject as he expected. But the movies are interested in him – if they can get a good long look at him first and I have every reason to think that he will come through. He'd better.

PAT HOBBY'S
CHRISTMAS WISH

I

It was Christmas Eve in the studio. By eleven o'clock in the morning, Santa Claus had called on most of the huge population according to each one's deserts.

Sumptuous gifts from producers to stars, and from agents to producers arrived at offices and studio bungalows: on every stage one heard of the roguish gifts of casts to directors or directors to casts; champagne had gone out from publicity office to the press. And tips of fifties, tens and fives from producers, directors and writers fell like manna upon the white collar class.

In this sort of transaction there were exceptions. Pat Hobby, for example, who knew the game from twenty years' experience, had had the idea of getting rid of his secretary the day before. They were sending over a new one any minute – but she would scarcely expect a present the first day.

Waiting for her, he walked the corridor, glancing into open offices for signs of life. He stopped to chat with Joe Hopper from the scenario department.

'Not like the old days,' he mourned, 'Then there was a bottle on every desk.'

'There're a few around.'

'Not many.' Pat sighed. 'And afterwards we'd run a picture – made up out of cutting-room scraps.'

'I've heard. All the suppressed stuff,' said Hopper.

Pat nodded, his eyes glistening.

'Oh, it was juicy. You darned near ripped your guts laughing –'

He broke off as the sight of a woman, pad in hand, entering his office down the hall recalled him to the sorry present.

'Gooddorf has me working over the holiday,' he complained bitterly.

'I wouldn't do it.'

'I wouldn't either except my four weeks are up next Friday, and if I bucked him he wouldn't extend me.'

As he turned away Hopper knew that Pat was not being extended anyhow. He had been hired to script an old-fashioned horse-opera and the boys who were 'writing behind him' – that is working over his stuff – said that all of it was old and some didn't make sense.

'I'm Miss Kagle,' said Pat's new secretary.

She was about thirty-six, handsome, faded, tired, efficient. She went to the typewriter, examined it, sat down and burst into sobs.

Pat started. Self-control, from below anyhow, was the rule around here. Wasn't it bad enough to be working on Christmas Eve? Well – less bad than not working at all. He walked over and shut the door – someone might suspect him of insulting the girl.

'Cheer up,' he advised her. 'This is Christmas.'

Her burst of emotion had died away. She sat upright now, choking and wiping her eyes.

'Nothing's as bad as it seems,' he assured her unconvincingly. 'What's it, anyhow? They going to lay you off?'

She shook her head, did a sniffle to end sniffles, and opened her note book.

'Who you been working for?'

She answered between suddenly gritted teeth.

'Mr Harry Gooddorf.'

Pat widened his permanently bloodshot eyes. Now he remembered he had seen her in Harry's outer office.

'Since 1921. Eighteen years. And yesterday he sent me back to the department. He said I depressed him – I reminded him he was getting on.' Her face was grim. 'That isn't the way he talked after hours eighteen years ago.'

'Yeah, he was a skirt chaser then,' said Pat,

'I should have done something then when I had the chance.'

Pat felt righteous stirrings.

'Breach of promise? That's no angle!'

'But I had something to clinch it. Something bigger than breach of promise. I still have too. But then, you see, I thought I was in love with him.' She brooded for a moment. 'Do you want to dictate something now?'

Pat remembered his job and opened a script.

'It's an insert,' he began, 'Scene 114A.'

Pat paced the office.

'Ext. Long Shot of the Plains,' he decreed. 'Buck and Mexicans approaching the hyacenda.'

'The what?'

'The hyacenda – the ranch house,' He looked at her reproachfully, ' 114 B. Two Shot: Buck and Pedro. Buck: "The dirty son-of-a-bitch. I'll tear his guts out!" '

Miss Kagle looked up, startled.

'You want me to write that down?'

'Sure.'

'It won't get by.'

'I'm writing this. Of course, it won't get by. But if I put "you rat" the scene won't have any force.'

'But won't somebody have to change it to "you rat"?'

He glared at her – he didn't want to change secretaries every day.

'Harry Gooddorf can worry about that.'

'Are you working for Mr Gooddorf?' Miss Kagle asked in alarm.

'Until he throws me out.'

'I shouldn't have said –'

'Don't worry,' he assured her. 'He's no pal of mine anymore. Not at three-fifty a week, when I used to get two thousand . . . Where was I?'

He paced the floor again, repeating his last line aloud with relish. But now it seemed to apply not to a personage of the story but to Harry Gooddorf. Suddenly he stood still, lost in thought. 'Say, what is it you got on him? You know where the body is buried?'

'That's too true to be funny.'

'He knock somebody off?'

'Mr Hobby, I'm sorry I ever opened my mouth.'

'Just call me Pat. What's your first name?'

'Helen.'

'Married?'

'Not now.'

'Well, listen Helen: What do you say we have dinner?'

II

On the afternoon of Christmas Day he was still trying to get the secret out of her. They had the studio almost to themselves – only a skeleton staff of technical men dotted the walks and the commissary. They had exchanged Christmas presents. Pat gave her a five dollar bill, Helen bought him a white linen handkerchief. Very well he could remember the day when many dozen such handkerchiefs had been his Christmas harvest.

The script was progressing at a snail's pace but their friendship had considerably ripened. Her secret, he considered, was a very valuable asset, and he wondered how many careers had turned on just such an asset. Some, he felt sure, had been thus raised to affluence. Why, it was almost as good as being in the family, and he pictured an imaginary conversation with Harry Gooddorf.

'Harry, it's this way. I don't think my experience is being made use of. It's the young squirts who ought to do the writing – I ought to do more supervising.'

'Or –?'

'Or else,' said Pat firmly.

He was in the midst of his day dream when Harry Gooddorf unexpectedly walked in.

'Merry Christmas, Pat,' he said jovially. His smile was less robust when he saw Helen. 'Oh, hello Helen – didn't know you and Pat had got together. I sent you a remembrance over to the script department.'

'You shouldn't have done that.'

Harry turned swiftly to Pat.

'The boss is on my neck,' he said. 'I've got to have a finished script Thursday.'

'Well, here I am,' said Pat. 'You'll have it. Did I ever fail you?'

'Usually,' said Harry. 'Usually.'

He seemed about to add more when a call boy entered with an envelope and handed it to Helen Kagle – whereupon Harry turned and hurried out.

'He'd better get out!' burst forth Miss Kagle, after opening the envelope. 'Ten bucks – just *ten bucks* – from an executive – after eighteen years.'

It was Pat's chance. Sitting on her desk he told her his plan.

'It's soft jobs for you and me,' he said. 'You the head of a script department, me an associate producer. We're on the gravy train for life – no more writing – no more pounding the keys. We might even – we might even – if things go good we could get married.'

She hesitated a long time. When she put a fresh sheet in the typewriter Pat feared he had lost.

'I can write it from memory,' she said. 'This was a letter he typed *himself* on February 3rd, 1921. He sealed it and gave it to me to mail –

but there was a blonde he was interested in, and I wondered why he should be so secret about a letter.'

Helen had been typing as she talked, and now she handed Pat a note.

To Will Bronson
First National Studios
  Personal

Dear Bill:

We killed Taylor. We should have cracked down on him sooner. So why not shut up.

Yours, Harry

'Get it?' Helen said. 'On February 1st, 1921, somebody knocked off William Desmond Taylor, the director, And they've never found out who.'

III

For eighteen years she had kept the original note, envelope and all. She had sent only a copy to Bronson, tracing Harry Gooddorf's signature.

'Baby, we're set!' said Pat. 'I always thought it was a *girl* got Taylor.'

He was so elated that he opened a drawer and brought forth a half-pint of whiskey. Then, with an afterthought, he demanded:

'Is it in a safe place?'

'You bet it is. He'd never guess where.'

'Baby, we've got him!'

Cash, cars, girls, swimming pools swam in a glittering montage before Pat's eye.

He folded the note, put it in his pocket, took another drink and reached for his hat.

'You going to see him now?' Helen demanded in some alarm. 'Hey, wait till I get off the lot. *I* don't want to get murdered.'

'Don't worry! Listen I'll meet you in "the Muncherie" at Fifth and La Brea – in one hour,'

As he walked to Gooddorf's office he decided to mention no facts or names within the walls of the studio. Back in the brief period when he had headed a scenario department Pat had conceived a plan to put a dictaphone in every writer's office. Thus their loyalty to the studio executives could be checked several times a day.

The idea had been laughed at. But later, when he had been 'reduced back to a writer', he often wondered if his plan was secretly followed. Perhaps some indiscreet remark of his own was responsible for the doghouse where he had been interred for the past decade, So it was with the idea of concealed dictaphones in mind, dictaphones which could be turned on by the pressure of a toe, that he entered Harry Gooddorf's office.

'Harry –' he chose his words carefully, 'do you remember the night of February 1st, 1921?'

Somewhat flabbergasted, Gooddorf leaned back in his swivel chair.

'*What?*'

'Try and think. It's something very important to you.'

Pat's expression as he watched his friend was that of an anxious undertaker.

'February 1st, 1921.' Gooddorf mused. 'No. How could I remember? You think I keep a diary? I don't even know where I was then.'

'You were right here in Hollywood.'

'Probably. If you know, tell me.'

'You'll remember.'

'Let's see. I came out to the coast in sixteen. I was with Biograph till 1920. Was I making some comedies? That's it. I was making a piece called *Knuckleduster* – on location.'

'You weren't always on location. You were in town February 1st.'

'What is this?' Gooddorf demanded. 'The third degree?'

'No – but I've got some information about your doings on that date.'

Gooddorf's face reddened; for a moment it looked as if he were going to throw Pat out of the room – then suddenly he gasped, licked his lips and stared at his desk.

'Oh,' he said, and after a minute: 'But I don't see what business it is of yours.'

'It's the business of every decent man.'

'Since when have you been decent?'

'All my life,' said Pat. 'And, even if I haven't, I never did anything like that.'

'My foot!' said Harry contemptuously. '*You* showing up here with a halo! Anyhow, what's the evidence? You'd think you had a written confession. It's all forgotten long ago.'

'Not in the memory of decent men,' said Pat. 'And as for a written confession – I've got it.'

'I doubt you. And I doubt if it would stand in any court. You've been taken in.'

'I've seen it,' said Pat with growing confidence. 'And it's enough to hang you.'

'Well, by God, if there's any publicity I'll run you out of town.'

'You'll run *me* out of town.'

'I don't want any publicity.'

'Then I think you'd better come along with me. Without talking to anybody.'

'Where are we going?'

'I know a bar where we can be alone.'

The Muncherie was in fact deserted, save for the bartender and Helen Kagle who sat at a table, jumpy with alarm. Seeing her, Gooddorf's expression changed to one of infinite reproach.

'This is a hell of a Christmas,' he said, 'with my family expecting me home an hour ago. I want to know the idea. You say you've got something in my writing.'

Pat took the paper from his pocket and read the date aloud. Then he looked up hastily:

'This is just a copy, so don't try and snatch it.'

He knew the technique of such scenes as this. When the vogue for Westerns had temporarily subsided he had sweated over many an orgy of crime.

'To William Bronson, Dear Bill: We killed Taylor. We should have cracked down on him sooner. So why not shut up. Yours, Harry.'

Pat paused. 'You wrote this on February 3rd, 1921.'

Silence. Gooddorf turned to Helen Kagle.

'Did *you* do this? Did I dictate that to you?'

'No,' she admitted in an awed voice, 'You wrote it yourself. I opened the letter.'

'I see. Well, what do you want?'

'Plenty,' said Pat, and found himself pleased with the sound of the word.

'What exactly?'

Pat launched into the description of a career suitable to a man of forty-nine. A glowing career. It expanded rapidly in beauty and power during the time it took him to drink three large whiskeys. But one demand he returned to again and again.

He wanted to be made a producer tomorrow.

'Why tomorrow?' demanded Gooddorf, 'Can't it wait?'

There were sudden tears in Pat's eyes – real tears.

'This is Christmas,' he said. 'It's my Christmas wish. I've had a hell of a time. I've waited so long.'

Gooddorf got to his feet suddenly.

'Nope,' he said. 'I won't make you a producer. I couldn't do it in fairness to the company. I'd rather stand trial.'

Pat's mouth fell open.

'What? You won't?'

'Not a chance. I'd rather swing,'

He turned away, his face set, and started toward the door.

'All right!' Pat called after him. 'It's your last chance.'

Suddenly he was amazed to see Helen Kagle spring up and run after Gooddorf – try to throw her arms around him.

'Don't worry!' she cried. 'I'll tear it up, Harry! It was a joke Harry –'

Her voice trailed off rather abruptly. She had discovered that Gooddorf was shaking with laughter.

'What's the joke?' she demanded, growing angry again. 'Do you think I haven't got it?'

'Oh, you've got it all right,' Gooddorf howled. 'You've got it – but it isn't what you think it is.'

He came back to the table, sat down and addressed Pat.

'Do you know what I thought that date meant? I thought maybe it was the date Helen and I first fell for each other. That's what I thought. And I thought she was going to raise Cain about it. I thought she was nuts. She's been married twice since then, and so have I.'

'That doesn't explain the note,' said Pat sternly but with a sinky feeling. 'You admit you killed Taylor.'

Gooddorf nodded.

'I still think a lot of us did,' he said. 'We were a wild crowd – Taylor and Bronson and me and half the boys in the big money. So a bunch of us got together in an agreement to go slow. The country was waiting for somebody to hang. We tried to get Taylor to watch his step but he wouldn't. So instead of cracking down on him, we let him "go the pace". And some rat shot him – who did it I don't know.'

He stood up.

'Like somebody should have cracked down on *you*, Pat. But you were an amusing guy in those days, and besides we were all too busy.'

Pat sniffled suddenly.

'I've *been* cracked down on,' he said. 'Plenty.'

'But too late,' said Gooddorf, and added, 'you've probably got a new

Christmas wish by now, and I'll grant it to you. I won't say anything about this afternoon.'

When he had gone, Pat and Helen sat in silence. Presently Pat took out the note again and looked it over.

' "So why not shut up?" ' he read aloud. 'He didn't explain that.'

'Why *not* shut up?' Helen said.

A MAN IN THE WAY

I

Pat Hobby could always get on the lot. He had worked there fifteen years on and off – chiefly off during the past five – and most of the studio police knew him. If tough customers on watch asked to see his studio card he could get in by phoning Lou, the bookie. For Lou also, the studio had been home for many years.

Pat was forty-nine. He was a writer but he had never written much, nor even read all the 'originals' he worked from, because it made his head bang to read much. But the good old silent days you got somebody's plot and a smart secretary and gulped benzedrine 'structure' at her six or eight hours every week. The director took care of the gags. After talkies came he always teamed up with some man who wrote dialogue. Some young man who liked to work.

'I've got a list of credits second to none,' he told Jack Berners. 'All I need is an idea and to work with somebody who isn't all wet.'

He had buttonholed Jack outside the production office as Jack was going to lunch and they walked together in the direction of the commissary.

'You bring *me* an idea,' said Jack Berners. 'Things are tight. We can't put a man on salary unless he's got an idea.'

'How can you get ideas off salary?' Pat demanded – then he added hastily: 'Anyhow I got the germ of an idea that I could be telling you all about at lunch.'

Something might come to him at lunch. There was Baer's notion about the boy scout. But Jack said cheerfully:

'I've got a date for lunch, Pat. Write it out and send it around, eh?'

He felt cruel because he knew Pat couldn't write anything out but he was having story trouble himself. The war had just broken out and every producer on the lot wanted to end their current stories with the hero going to war. And Jack Berners felt he had thought of that first for his production.

'So write it out, eh?'

When Pat didn't answer Jack looked at him – he saw a sort of whipped misery in Pat's eye that reminded him of his own father. Pat had been in the money before Jack was out of college – with three cars and a chicken over every garage. Now his clothes looked as if he'd been standing at Hollywood and Vine for three years.

'Scout around and talk to some of the writers on the lot,' he said. 'If you can get one of them interested in your idea, bring him up to see me.'

'I hate to give an idea without money on the line,' Pat brooded pessimistically, 'These young squirts'll lift the shirt off your back.'

They had reached the commissary door.

'Good luck, Pat. Anyhow we're not in Poland.'

– Good *you're* not, said Pat under his breath. They'd slit your gizzard.

Now what to do? He went up and wandered along the cell block of writers. Almost everyone had gone to lunch and those who were in he didn't know. Always there were more and more unfamiliar faces. And he had thirty credits; he had been in the business, publicity and script-writing, for twenty years.

The last door in the line belonged to a man he didn't like. But he wanted a place to sit a minute so with a knock he pushed it open. The man wasn't there – only a very pretty, frail-looking girl sat reading a book.

'I think he's left Hollywood,' she said in answer to his question. 'They gave me his office but they forgot to put up my name.'

'You a writer?' Pat asked in surprise.

'I work at it.'

'You ought to get 'em to give you a test.'

'No – I like writing.'

'What's that you're reading.'

She showed him.

'Let me give you a tip,' he said. 'That's not the way to get the guts out of a book.'

'Oh.'

'I've been here for years – I'm Pat Hobby – and I *know*. Give the book to four of your friends to read it. Get them to tell you what stuck in their minds. Write it down and you've got a picture – see?'

The girl smiled.

'Well, that's very – very original advice, Mr Hobby.'

'Pat Hobby,' he said. 'Can I wait here a minute? Man I came to see is at lunch.'

He sat down across from her and picked up a copy of a photo magazine.

'Oh, just let me mark that,' she said quickly.

He looked at the page which she checked. It showed paintings being boxed and carted away to safety from an art gallery in Europe.

'How'll you use it?' he said.

'Well, I thought it would be dramatic if there was an old man around while they were packing the pictures. A poor old man, trying to get a job helping them. But they can't use him – he's in the way – not even good cannon fodder. They want strong young people in the world. And it turns out he's the man who painted the pictures many years ago.'

Pat considered.

'It's good but I don't get it,' he said.

'Oh, it's nothing, a short short maybe.'

'Got any good picture ideas? I'm in with all the markets here.'

'I'm under contract.'

'Use another name.'

Her phone rang.

'Yes, this is Pricilla Smith,' the girl said.

After a minute she turned to Pat.

'Will you excuse me? This is a private call.'

He got it and walked out, and along the corridor. Finding an office with no name on it he went in and fell asleep on the couch.

II

Late that afternoon he returned to Jack Berners' waiting rooms. He had an idea about a man who meets a girl in an office and he thinks she's a stenographer but she turns out to be a writer. He engages her as a stenographer, though, and they start for the South Seas. It was a beginning, it was something to tell Jack, he thought – and, picturing Pricilla Smith, he refurbished some old business he hadn't seen used for years.

He became quite excited about it – felt quite young for a moment and walked up and down the waiting room mentally rehearsing the first sequence. 'So here we have a situation like *It Happened One Night* – only *new*. I see Hedy Lamarr –'

Oh, he knew how to talk to these boys if he could get to them, with something to say.

'Mr Berners still busy?' he asked for the fifth time.

'Oh, yes, Mr Hobby. Mr Bill Costello and Mr Bach are in there.'

He thought quickly. It was half-past five. In the old days he had just busted in sometimes and sold an idea, an idea good for a couple of grand because it was just the moment when they were very tired of what they were doing at present.

He walked innocently out and to another door in the hall. He knew it led through a bathroom right in to Jack Berners' office. Drawing a quick breath he plunged . . .

'. . . So that's the notion,' he concluded after five minutes. 'It's just a flash – nothing really worked out, but you could give me an office and a girl and I could have something on paper for you in three days.'

Berners, Costello and Bach did not even have to look at each other. Berners spoke for them all as he said firmly and gently:

'That's no idea, Pat. I can't put you on salary for that.'

'Why don't you work it out further by yourself,' suggested Bill Costello. 'And then let's see it. We're looking for ideas – especially about the war.'

'A man can think better on salary,' said Pat.

There was silence. Costello and Bach had drunk with him, played poker with him, gone to the races with him. They'd honestly be glad to see him placed.

'The war, eh,' he said gloomily. 'Everything is war now, no matter how many credits a man has. Do you know what it makes me think of? It makes me think of a well-known painter in the discard. It's war time and he's useless – just a man in the way.' He warmed to his conception of himself, '– but all the time they're carting away *his own paintings* as the most valuable thing worth saving. And they won't even let me help. That's what it reminds me of.'

There was again silence for a moment.

'That isn't a bad idea,' said Bach thoughtfully. He turned to the others. 'You know? In itself?'

Bill Costello nodded

'Not bad at all. And I know where we could spot it. Right at the end of the fourth sequence. We just change old Ames to a painter.'

Presently they talked money.

'I'll give you two weeks on it,' said Berners to Pat. 'At two-fifty.'

'Two-fifty!' objected Pat. 'Say there was one time you paid me ten times that!'

'That was ten years ago,' Jack reminded him. 'Sorry. Best we can do now.'

'You make me feel like that old painter –'

'Don't oversell it,' said Jack, rising and smiling. 'You're on the payroll.'

Pat went out with a quick step and confidence in his eyes. Half a grand – that would take the pressure off for a month and you could often stretch two weeks into three – sometimes four. He left the studio proudly through the front entrance, stopping at the liquor store for a half-pint to take back to his room.

By seven o'clock things were even better. Santa Anita tomorrow, if he could get an advance. And tonight – something festive ought to be done tonight. With a sudden rush of pleasure he went down to the phone in the lower hall, called the studio and asked for Miss Pricilla Smith's number. He hadn't met anyone so pretty for years . . .

In her apartment Pricilla Smith spoke rather firmly into the phone.

'I'm awfully sorry,' she said, 'but I couldn't possibly . . . No – and I'm tied up all the rest of the week.'

As she hung up, Jack Berners spoke from the couch.

'Who was it?'

'Oh, some man who came in the office,' she laughed, 'and told me never to read the story I was working on.'

'Shall I believe you?'

'You certainly shall. I'll even think of his name in a minute. But first I want to tell you about an idea I had this morning. I was looking at a photo in a magazine where they were packing up some works of art in the Tate Gallery in London. And I thought –'

'BOIL SOME WATER –
LOTS OF IT'

Pat Hobby sat in his office in the writers' building and looked at his morning's work, just come back from the script department. He was on a 'polish job', about the only kind he ever got nowadays. He was to repair a messy sequence in a hurry, but the word 'hurry' neither frightened nor inspired him for Pat had been in Hollywood since he was thirty – now he was forty-nine. All the work he had done this morning (except a little changing around of lines so he could claim them as his own) – all he had actually invented was a single imperative sentence, spoken by a doctor.

'Boil some water – lots of it.'

It was a good line. It had sprung into his mind full grown as soon as he had read the script. In the old silent days Pat would have used it as a spoken title and ended his dialogue worries for a space, but he needed some spoken words for other people in the scene. Nothing came.

'Boil some water,' he repeated to himself. 'Lots of it.'

The word boil brought a quick glad thought of the commissary. A reverent thought too – for an old-timer like Pat, what people you sat with at lunch was more important in getting along than what you dictated in your office. This was no art, as he often said – this was an industry.

'This is no art,' he remarked to Max Leam who was leisurely drinking at a corridor water cooler. 'This is an industry.'

Max had flung him this timely bone of three weeks at three-fifty.

'Say look, Pat! Have you got anything down on paper yet?'

'Say I've got some stuff already that'll make 'em –' He named a familiar biological function with the somewhat startling assurance that it would take place in the theatre.

Max tried to gauge his sincerity.

'Want to read it to me now?' he asked.

'Not yet. But it's got the old guts if you know what I mean.'

Max was full of doubts.

'Well, go to it. And if you run into any medical snags check with the doctor over at the First Aid Station. It's got to be right.'

The spirit of Pasteur shone firmly in Pat's eyes,

'It will be.'

He felt good walking across the lot with Max – so good that he decided to glue himself to the producer and sit down with him at the Big Table. But Max foiled his intention by cooing 'See you later' and slipping into the barber shop.

Once Pat had been a familiar figure at the Big Table; often in his golden prime he had dined in the private canteens of executives. Being of the older Hollywood he understood their jokes, their vanities, their social system with its swift fluctuations. But there were too many new faces at the Big Table now – faces that looked at him with the universal Hollywood suspicion. And at the little tables where the young writers sat they seemed to take work so seriously. As for just sitting down anywhere, even with secretaries or extras – Pat would rather catch a sandwich at the corner.

Detouring to the Red Cross Station he asked for the doctor. A girl, a nurse, answered from a wall mirror where she was hastily drawing her lips, 'He's out. What is it?'

'Oh. Then I'll come back.'

She had finished, and now she turned – vivid and young and with a bright consoling smile.

'Miss Stacey will help you. I'm about to go to lunch.'

He was aware of an old, old feeling – left over from the time when he had had wives – a feeling that to invite this little beauty to lunch might cause trouble. But he remembered quickly that he didn't have any wives now – they had both given up asking for alimony.

'I'm working on a medical,' he said. 'I need some help.'

'A medical?'

'Writing it – idea about a doc. Listen – let me buy you lunch. I want to ask you some medical questions.'

The nurse hesitated.

'I don't know. It's my first day out here.'

'It's all right,' he assured her, 'studios are democratic; everybody is just "Joe" or "Mary" – from the big shots right down to the prop boys.'

He proved it magnificently on their way to lunch by greeting a male star and getting his own name back in return. And in the commissary, where they were placed hard by the Big Table, his producer, Max Leam, looked up, did a little 'takem' and winked.

The nurse – her name was Helen Earle – peered about eagerly.

'I don't see anybody,' she said. 'Except oh, there's Ronald Colman. I didn't know Ronald Colman looked like that.'

Pat pointed suddenly to the floor.

'And there's Mickey Mouse!'

She jumped and Pat laughed at his joke – but Helen Earle was already staring starry-eyed at the costume extras who filled the hall with the colours of the First Empire. Pat was piqued to see her interest go out to these nonentities,

'The big shots are at this next table,' he said solemnly, wistfully, 'directors and all except the biggest executives. They could have Ronald Colman pressing pants. I usually sit over there but they don't want ladies. At lunch, that is, they don't want ladies.'

'Oh,' said Helen Earle, polite but unimpressed. 'It must be wonderful to be a writer too. It's so very interesting.'

'It has its points,' he said . . . he had thought for years it was a dog's life.

'What is it you want to ask me about a doctor?'

Here was toil again. Something in Pat's mind snapped off when he thought of the story.

'Well, Max Leam – that man facing us – Max Leam and I have a script about a doc. You know? Like a hospital picture?'

'I know.' And she added after a moment, 'That's the reason that I went in training.'

'And we've got to have it *right* because a hundred million people would check on it. So this doctor in the script he tells them to boil some water. He says, "Boil some water – lots of it." And we were wondering what the people would do then.'

'Why – they'd probably boil it,' Helen said, and then, somewhat confused by the question, 'What people?'

'Well, somebody's daughter and the man that lived there and an attorney and the man that was hurt.'

Helen tried to digest this before answering.

'– and some other guy I'm going to cut out,' he finished.

There was a pause. The waitress set down tuna fish sandwiches.

'Well, when a doctor gives orders they're orders,' Helen decided.

'Hm.' Pat's interest had wandered to an odd little scene at the Big Table while he inquired absently, 'You married?'

'No.'

'Neither am I.'

Beside the Big Table stood an extra. A Russian Cossack with a fierce moustache. He stood resting his hand on the back of an empty chair between Director Paterson and Producer Leam.

'Is this taken?' he asked, with a thick Central European accent.

All along the Big Table faces stared suddenly at him. Until after the first look the supposition was that he must be some well-known actor. But he was not – he was dressed in one of the many-coloured uniforms that dotted the room.

Someone at the table said: 'That's taken.' But the man drew out the chair and sat down.

'Got to eat somewhere,' he remarked with a grin.

A shiver went over the near-by tables. Pat Hobby stared with his mouth ajar. It was as if someone had crayoned Donald Duck into the *Last Supper*.

'Look at that,' he advised Helen. 'What they'll do to him! Boy!'

The flabbergasted silence at the Big Table was broken by Ned Harman, the Production Manager.

'This table is reserved,' he said.

The extra looked up from a menu.

'They told me sit anywhere.'

He beckoned a waitress – who hesitated, looking for an answer in the faces of her superiors.

'Extras don't eat here,' said Max Leam, still politely.

'This is a –'

'I got to eat,' said the Cossack doggedly. 'I been standing around six hours while they shoot this stinking mess and now I got to eat.'

The silence had extended – from Pat's angle all within range seemed to be poised in mid-air.

The extra shook his head wearily.

'I dunno who cooked it up –' he said – and Max Leam sat forward in his chair – 'but it's the lousiest tripe I ever seen shot in Hollywood.'

– At his table Pat was thinking why didn't they do something? Knock him down, drag him away. If they were yellow themselves they could call the studio police.

'Who is that?' Helen Earle was following his eyes innocently. 'Somebody I ought to know?'

He was listening attentively to Max Leam's voice, raised in anger.

'Get up and get out of here, buddy, and get out quick!'

The extra frowned.

'Who's telling me?' he demanded.

'You'll see.' Max appealed to the table at large, 'Where's Cushman – where's the Personnel man?'

'You try to move me,' said the extra, lifting the hilt of his scabbard above the level of the table, 'and I'll hang this on your ear. I know my rights.'

The dozen men at the table, representing a thousand dollars an hour in salaries, sat stunned. Far down by the door one of the studio police caught wind of what was happening and started to elbow through the crowded room. And Big Jack Wilson, another director, was on his feet in an instant coming around the table.

But they were too late – Pat Hobby could stand no more. He had jumped up, seizing a big heavy tray from the serving stand nearby. In two springs he reached the scene of action – lifting the tray he brought it down upon the extra's head with all the strength of his forty-nine years. The extra, who had been in the act of rising to meet Wilson's threatened assault, got the blow full on his face and temple and as he collapsed a dozen red streaks sprang into sight through the heavy grease paint. He crashed sideways between the chairs.

Pat stood over him panting – the tray in his hand.

'The dirty rat!' he cried. 'Where does he think –'

The studio policeman pushed past; Wilson pushed past – the two aghast men from another table rushed up to survey the situation.

'It was a gag!' one of them shouted. 'That's Walter Herrick, the writer. It's his picture.'

'My God!'

'He was kidding Max Leam. It was a gag I tell you!'

'Pull him out . . . Get a doctor . . . Look out, there!'

Now Helen Earle hurried over; Walter Herrick was dragged out into a cleared space on the floor and there were yells of 'Who did it? – Who beaned him?'

Pat let the tray lapse to a chair, its sound unnoticed in the confusion.

He saw Helen Earle working swiftly at the man's head with a pile of clean napkins.

'Why did they have to do this to him?' someone shouted.

Pat caught Max Leam's eye but Max happened to look away at the moment and a sense of injustice came over Pat. He alone in this crisis, real or imaginary, had *acted*. He alone had played the man, while those stuffed shirts let themselves be insulted and abused. And now he would have to take the rap – because Walter Herrick was powerful and popular, a three thousand a week man who wrote hit shows in New York. How could anyone have guessed that it was a gag?

There was a doctor now. Pat saw him say something to the manageress and her shrill voice sent the waitresses scattering like leaves toward the kitchen.

'Boil some water! Lots of it!'

The words fell wild and unreal on Pat's burdened soul. But even though he now knew at first hand what came next, he did not think that he could go on from there.

TEAMED WITH GENIUS

I

'I took a chance in sending for you,' said Jack Berners. 'But there's a job that you just *may* be able to help out with.'

Though Pat Hobby was not offended, either as man or writer, a formal protest was called for.

'I been in the industry fifteen years, Jack. I've got more screen credits than a dog has got fleas.'

'Maybe I chose the wrong word,' said Jack. 'What I mean is, that was a long time ago. About money we'll pay you just what Republic paid you last month – three-fifty a week. Now – did you ever hear of a writer named René Wilcox?'

The name was unfamiliar. Pat had scarcely opened a book in a decade.

'She's pretty good,' he ventured.

'It's a man, an English playwright. He's only here in L.A. for his health. Well – we've had a Russian Ballet picture kicking around for a year – three bad scripts on it. So last week we signed up René Wilcox – he seemed just the person.'

Pat considered.

'You mean he's –'

'I don't know and I don't care,' interrupted Berners sharply. 'We think we can borrow Zorina, so we want to hurry things up – do a shooting script instead of just a treatment. Wilcox is inexperienced and that's where you come in. You used to be a good man for structure.'

'*Used* to be!'

'All right, maybe you still are,' Jack beamed with momentary encouragement, 'Find yourself an office and get together with René Wilcox.' As Pat started out he called him back and put a bill in his hand. 'First of all, get a new hat. You used to be quite a boy around the secretaries in the old days. Don't give up at forty-nine!'

Over in the Writers' Building Pat glanced at the directory in the hall and knocked at the door of 216. No answer, but he went in to discover a blond, willowy youth of twenty-five staring moodily out the window.

'Hello, René!' Pat said. 'I'm your partner.'

Wilcox's regard questioned even his existence, but Pat continued heartily. 'I hear we're going to lick some stuff into shape. Ever collaborate before?'

'I have never written for the cinema before.'

While this increased Pat's chance for a screen credit he badly needed, it meant that he might have to do some work. The very thought made him thirsty.

'This is different from playwriting,' he suggested, with suitable gravity.

'Yes – I read a book about it.'

Pat wanted to laugh. In 1928 he and another man had concocted such a sucker-trap, *Secrets of Film Writing*. It would have made money if pictures hadn't started to talk.

'It all seems simple enough,' said Wilcox. Suddenly he took his hat from the rack, 'I'll be running along now.'

'Don't you want to talk about the script?' demanded Pat. 'What have you done so far?'

'I've not done anything,' said Wilcox deliberately. 'That idiot, Berners, gave me some trash and told me to go on from there. But it's too dismal.' His blue eyes narrowed, 'I say, what's a boom shot?'

'A boom shot? Why, that's when the camera's on a crane.'

Pat leaned over the desk and picked up a blue-jacketed 'Treatment'. On the cover he read:

BALLET SHOES

A Treatment

by

Consuela Martin

An Original from an idea by Consuela Martin

Pat glanced at the beginning and then at the end.

'I'd like it better if we could get the war in somewhere,' he said frowning. 'Have the dancer go as a Red Cross nurse and then she could get regenerated. See what I mean?'

There was no answer. Pat turned and saw the door softly closing.

What is this? he exclaimed. What kind of collaborating can a man do if he walks out? Wilcox had not even given the legitimate excuse – the races at Santa Anita!

The door opened again, a pretty girl's face, rather frightened, showed itself momentarily, said 'Oh', and disappeared. Then it returned.

'Why it's Mr Hobby!' she exclaimed, 'I was looking for Mr Wilcox.'

He fumbled for her name but she supplied it.

'Katherine Hodge. I was your secretary when I worked here three years ago.'

Pat knew she had once worked with him, but for the moment could not remember whether there had been a deeper relation. It did not seem to him that it had been love – but looking at her now, that appeared rather too bad.

'Sit down,' said Pat. 'You assigned to Wilcox?'

'I thought so – but he hasn't give me any work yet.'

'I think he's nuts,' Pat said gloomily. 'He asked me what a boom shot was. Maybe he's sick – that's why he's out here. He'll probably start throwing up all over the office.'

'He's well now,' Katherine ventured.

'He doesn't look like it to me. Come on in my office. You can work for *me* this afternoon.'

Pat lay on his couch while Miss Katherine Hodge read the script of *Ballet Shoes* aloud to him. About midway in the second sequence he fell asleep with his new hat on his chest.

II

Except for the hat, that was the identical position in which he found René next day at eleven. And it was that way for three straight days – one was asleep or else the other – and sometimes both. On the fourth day they had several conferences in which Pat again put forward his idea about the war as a regenerating force for ballet dancers.

'Couldn't we *not* talk about the war?' suggested René. 'I have two brothers in the Guards.'

'You're lucky to be here in Hollywood.'

'That's as it may be.'

'Well, what's your idea of the start of the picture?'

'I do not like the present beginning. It gives me an almost physical nausea.'

'So then, we got to have something in its place. That's why I want to plant the war –'

'I'm late to luncheon,' said René Wilcox. 'Good-bye, Mike.'

Pat grumbled to Katherine Hodge:

'He can call me anything he likes, but somebody's got to write this picture. I'd go to Jack Berners and tell him – but I think we'd both be out on our ears,'

For two days more he camped in René's office, trying to rouse him to action, but with no avail. Desperate on the following day – when the playwright did not even come to the studio – Pat took a benzedrine tablet and attacked the story alone. Pacing his office with the treatment in his hand he dictated to Katherine – interspersing the dictation with a short, biased history of his life in Hollywood. At the day's end he had two pages of script.

The ensuing week was the toughest in his life – not even a moment to make a pass at Katherine Hodge. Gradually, with many creaks, his battered hulk got in motion. Benzedrine and great drafts of coffee woke him in the morning, whiskey anaesthetized him at night. Into his feet crept an old neuritis and as his nerves began to crackle he developed a hatred against René Wilcox, which served him as a sort of *ersatz* fuel. He was going to finish the script by himself and hand it to Berners with the statement that Wilcox had not contributed a single line.

But it was too much – Pat was too far gone. He blew up when he was half through and went on a twenty-four-hour bat – and next morning arrived back at the studio to find a message that Mr Berners wanted to see the script at four. Pat was in a sick and confused state when his door opened and René Wilcox came in with a typescript in one hand, and a copy of Berners' note in the other.

'It's all right,' said Wilcox, 'I've finished it.'

'*What?* Have you been *working?*'

'I always work at night.'

'What've you done? A treatment?'

'No, a shooting script. At first I was held back by personal worries, but once I got started it was very simple. You just get behind the camera and dream.'

Pat stood up aghast.

'But we were supposed to collaborate. Jack'll be wild.'

'I've always worked alone,' said Wilcox gently. 'I'll explain to Berners this afternoon,'

Pat sat in a daze. If Wilcox's script was good – but how could a first script be good? Wilcox should have fed it to him as he wrote; then they might have had something.

Fear started his mind working – he was struck by his first original idea since he had been on the job. He phoned to the script department for Katherine Hodge and when she came over told her what he wanted. Katherine hesitated.

'I just want to read it,' Pat said hastily. 'If Wilcox is there you can't take it, of course. But he just might be out.'

He waited nervously. In five minutes she was back with the script.

'It isn't mimeographed or even bound,' she said.

He was at the typewriter, trembling as he picked out a letter with two fingers.

'Can I help?' she asked.

'Find me a plain envelope and a used stamp and some paste.'

Pat sealed the letter himself and then gave directions:

'Listen outside Wilcox's office. If he's in, push it under his door. If he's out get a call boy to deliver it to him, wherever he is. Say it's from the mail room. Then you better go off the lot for the afternoon. So he won't catch on, see?'

As she went out Pat wished he had kept a copy of the note. He was proud of it – there was a ring of factual sincerity in it too often missing from his work.

Dear Mr Wilcox:

I am sorry to tell you your two brothers were killed in action today by a long range Tommy-gun. You are wanted at home in England right away.
John Smythe
The British Consulate, New York

But Pat realized that this was no time for self-applause.

He opened Wilcox's script.

To his vast surprise it was technically proficient – the dissolves, fades, cuts, pans and trucking shots were correctly detailed. This simplified everything. Turning back to the first page he wrote at the top:

BALLET SHOES
First Revise
From Pat Hobby and René Wilcox – presently changing this to read:
From René Wilcox and Pat Hobby.

Then, working frantically, he made several dozen small changes. He substituted the word 'Scram!' for 'Get out of my sight!', he put 'Behind the eight-ball' instead of 'In trouble', and replaced 'You'll be sorry' with the apt coinage 'Or else!' Then he phoned the script department.

'This is Pat Hobby, I've been working on a script with René Wilcox, and Mr Berners would like to have it mimeographed by half-past three.'

This would give him an hour's start on his unconscious collaborator.
'Is it an emergency?'
'I'll say.'
'We'll have to split it up between several girls.'

Pat continued to improve the script till the call boy arrived. He wanted to put in his war idea but time was short – still, he finally told the call boy to sit down, while he wrote laboriously in pencil on the last page.

CLOSE SHOT: *Boris and Rita*
Rita: What does anything matter now! I have enlisted as a trained nurse in the war.
Boris (moved): War purifies and regenerates!
(He puts his arms around her in a wild embrace as the music soars way up and we FADE OUT)

Limp and exhausted by his effort he needed a drink so he left the lot and slipped cautiously into the bar across from the studio where he ordered gin and water.

With the glow, he thought warm thoughts. He had done *almost* what he had been hired to do – though his hand had accidentally fallen upon the dialogue rather than the structure. But how could Berners tell that the structure wasn't Pat's? Katherine Hodge would say nothing, for fear of implicating herself. They were all guilty but guiltiest of all was René Wilcox for refusing to play the game. Always, according to his lights, Pat had played the game.

He had another drink, bought breath tablets and for awhile amused himself at the nickel machine in the drug-store. Louie, the studio bookie, asked if he was interested in wagers on a bigger scale.

'Not today, Louie.'
'What are they paying you, Pat?'
'Thousand a week.'
'Not so bad.'
'Oh, a lot of us old timers are coming back,' Pat prophesied. 'In silent days was where you got real training – with directors shooting off the cuff and needing a gag in a split second. Now it's a sis job. They got English teachers working in pictures! What do they know?'
'How about a little something on "Quaker Girl"?'
'No,' said Pat. 'This afternoon I got an important angle to work on. I don't want to worry about horses.'

At three-fifteen he returned to his office to find two copies of his script in bright new covers.

BALLET SHOES
from
René Wilcox and Pat Hobby
First Revise

It reassured him to see his name in type. As he waited in Jack Berners' anteroom he almost wished he had reversed the names. With the right director this might be another *It Happened One Night*, and if he got his name on something like that it meant a three or four year gravy ride. But this time he'd save his money – go to Santa Anita only once a week – get himself a girl along the type of Katherine Hodge, who wouldn't expect a mansion in Beverly Hills.

Berners' secretary interrupted his reverie, telling him to go in. As he entered he saw with gratification that a copy of the new script lay on Berners' desk.

'Did you ever –' asked Berners suddenly '– go to a psychoanalyst?'

'No,' admitted Pat. 'But I suppose I could get up on it. Is it a new assignment?'

'Not exactly. It's just that I think you've lost your grip. Even larceny requires a certain cunning. I've just talked to Wilcox on the phone.'

'Wilcox must be nuts,' said Pat, aggressively. 'I didn't steal anything from him. His name's on it, isn't it? Two weeks ago I laid out all his structure – every scene. I even wrote one whole scene – at the end about the war.'

'Oh yes, the war,' said Berners as if he was thinking of something else.

'But if you like Wilcox's ending better –'

'Yes, I like his ending better. I never saw a man pick up this work so fast.' He paused. 'Pat, you've told the truth just once since you came in this room – that you didn't steal anything from Wilcox.'

'I certainly did not. I *gave* him stuff.'

But a certain dreariness, a grey *malaise*, crept over him as Berners continued:

'I told you we had three scripts. You used an old one we discarded a year ago. Wilcox was in when your secretary arrived, and he sent one of them to you. Clever, eh?'

Pat was speechless.

'You see, he and that girl like each other. Seems she typed a play for him this summer.'

'They like each other,' said Pat incredulously. 'Why, he –'

'Hold it, Pat, You've had trouble enough today.'

'He's responsible,' Pat cried. 'He wouldn't collaborate – and all the time –'

'– he was writing a swell script. And he can write his own ticket if we can persuade him to stay here and do another.'

Pat could stand no more. He stood up.

'Anyhow thank you, Jack,' he faltered. 'Call my agent if anything turns up.' Then he bolted suddenly and surprisingly for the door.

Jack Berners signalled on the Dictograph for the President's office.

'Get a chance to read it?' he asked in a tone of eagerness.

'It's swell. Better than you said. Wilcox is with me now.'

'Have you signed him up?'

'I'm going to. Seems he wants to work with Hobby. Here you talk to him.'

Wilcox's rather high voice came over the wire.

'Must have Mike Hobby,' he said. 'Grateful to him. Had a quarrel with a certain young lady just before he came, but today Hobby brought us together. Besides, I want to write a play about him, So give him to me – you fellows don't want him any more.'

Berners picked up his secretary's phone.

'Go after Pat Hobby. He's probably in the bar across the street. We're putting him on salary again but we'll be sorry.'

He switched off, switched on again.

'Oh! Take him his hat. He forgot his hat.'

PAT HOBBY AND
ORSON WELLES

I

'Who's this Welles?' Pat asked of Louie, the studio bookie. 'Every time I pick up a paper they got about this Welles.'

'You know, he's that beard,' explained Louie.

'Sure, I know he's that beard, you couldn't miss that, But what credits's he got? What's he done to draw one hundred and fifty grand a picture?'

What indeed? Had he, like Pat, been in Hollywood over twenty years? Did he have credits that would knock your eye out, extending up to – well, up to five years ago when Pat's credits had begun to be few and far between?

'Listen – they don't last long,' said Louie consolingly, 'We've seen 'em come and we've seen 'em go. Hey, Pat?'

Yes – but meanwhile those who had toiled in the vineyard through the heat of the day were lucky to get a few weeks at three-fifty. Men who had once had wives and Filipinos and swimming pools.

'Maybe it's the beard,' said Louie. 'Maybe you and I should grow a beard. My father had a beard but it never got him off Grand Street.'

The gift of hope had remained with Pat through his misfortunes – and the valuable alloy of his hope was proximity. Above all things one must stick around, one must be there when the glazed, tired mind of the producer grappled with the question 'Who?' So presently Pat wandered out of the drug-store, and crossed the street to the lot that was home.

As he passed through the side entrance an unfamiliar studio policeman stood in his way.

'Everybody in the front entrance now.'

'I'm Hobby, the writer,' Pat said.

The Cossack was unimpressed.

'Got your card?'

'I'm between pictures. But I've got an engagement with Jack Berners.'

'Front gate.'

As he turned away Pat thought savagely: 'Lousy Keystone Cop!' In his mind he shot it out with him. Plunk! the stomach. Plunk! plunk! plunk!

At the main entrance, too, there was a new face.

'Where's Ike?' Pat demanded.

'Ike's gone.'

'Well, it's all right, I'm Pat Hobby. Ike always passes me.'

'That's why he's gone,' said the guardian blandly. 'Who's your business with?'

Pat hesitated. He hated to disturb a producer.

'Call Jack Berners' office,' he said. 'Just speak to his secretary.'

After a minute the man turned from the phone.

'What about?' he said.

'About a picture.'

He waited for an answer.

'She wants to know what picture?'

'To hell with it,' said Pat disgustedly. 'Look – call Louie Griebel. What's all this about?'

'Orders from Mr Kasper,' said the clerk, 'Last week a visitor from Chicago fell in the wind machine – Hello. Mr Louie Griebel?'

'I'll talk to him,' said Pat, taking the phone.

'I can't do nothing, Pat,' mourned Louie. 'I had trouble getting my boy in this morning. Some twirp from Chicago fell in the wind machine.'

'What's that got to do with me?' demanded Pat vehemently.

He walked, a little faster than his wont, along the studio wall to the point where it joined the back lot. There was a guard there but there were always people passing to and fro and he joined one of the groups. Once inside he would see Jack and have himself excepted from this absurd ban. Why, he had known this lot when the first shacks were rising on it, when this was considered the edge of the desert.

'Sorry mister, you with this party?'

'I'm in a hurry,' said Pat. 'I've lost my card.'

'Yeah? Well, for all I know you may be a plain clothes man.' He held open a copy of a photo magazine under Pat's nose. 'I wouldn't let you in even if you told me you was this here Orson Welles.'

II

There is an old Chaplin picture about a crowded street car where the entrance of one man at the rear forces another out in front. A similar image came into Pat's mind in the ensuing days whenever he thought of Orson Welles. Welles was in; Hobby was out. Never before had the studio been barred to Pat and though Welles was on another lot it seemed as if his large body, pushing in brashly from nowhere, had edged Pat out the gate.

'Now where do you go?' Pat thought. He had worked in the other studios but they were not his. At this studio he never felt unemployed – in recent times of stress he had eaten property food on its stages – half a cold lobster during a scene from The *Divine Miss Carstairs*; he had often slept on the sets and last winter made use of a Chesterfield overcoat from the costume department. Orson Welles had no business edging him out of this. Orson Welles belonged with the rest of the snobs back in New York.

On the third day he was frantic with gloom. He had sent note after note to Jack Berners and even asked Louie to intercede – now word came that Jack had left town. There were so few friends left. Desolate, he stood in front of the automobile gate with a crowd of staring children, feeling that he had reached the end at last.

A great limousine rolled out, in the back of which Pat recognized the great overstuffed Roman face of Harold Marcus. The car rolled toward the children and, as one of them ran in front of it, slowed down. The old man spoke into the tube and the car halted. He leaned out blinking.

'Is there no policeman here?' he asked of Pat.

'No, Mr Marcus,' said Pat quickly. 'There should be. I'm Pat Hobby, the writer – could you give me a lift down the street?'

It was unprecedented – it was an act of desperation but Pat's need was great.

Mr Marcus looked at him closely.

'Oh yes, I remember you,' he said. 'Get in.'

He might possibly have meant get up in front with the chauffeur. Pat compromised by opening one of the little seats. Mr Marcus was one of the most powerful men in the whole picture world. He did not occupy himself with production any longer. He spent most of his time rocking from coast to coast on fast trains, merging and launching, launching and merging, like a much divorced woman.

'Some day those children'll get hurt.'

'Yes, Mr Marcus,' agreed Pat heartily, 'Mr Marcus –'

'They ought to have a policeman there.'

'Yes, Mr Marcus. Mr Marcus –'

'Hm-m-m!' said Mr Marcus. 'Where do you want to be dropped?'

Pat geared himself to work fast.

'Mr Marcus, when I was your press agent –'

'I know,' said Mr Marcus. 'You wanted a ten dollar a week raise.'

'What a memory!' cried Pat in gladness. 'What a memory! But Mr Marcus, now I don't want anything at all.'

'This is a miracle.'

'I've got modest wants, see, and I've saved enough to retire.'

He thrust his shoes slightly forward under a hanging blanket, The Chesterfield coat effectively concealed the rest.

'That's what I'd like,' said Mr Marcus gloomily. 'A farm – with chickens. Maybe a little nine-hole course. Not even a stock ticker.'

'I want to retire, but different,' said Pat earnestly. 'Pictures have been my life. I want to watch them grow and grow –'

Mr Marcus groaned.

'Till they explode,' he said. 'Look at Fox! I cried for him.' He pointed to his eyes, 'Tears!'

Pat nodded very sympathetically.

'I want only one thing.' From the long familiarity he went into the foreign locution. 'I should go on the lot anytime. From nothing. Only to be there. Should bother nobody. Only help a little from nothing if any young person wants advice.'

'See Berners,' said Marcus.

'He said see you.'

'Then you did want something,' Marcus smiled. 'All right, all right by me, Where do you get off now?'

'Could you write me a pass?' Pat pleaded. 'Just a word on your card?'

'I'll look into it,' said Mr Marcus. 'Just now I've got things on my mind. I'm going to a luncheon.' He sighed profoundly. 'They want I should meet this new Orson Welles that's in Hollywood.'

Pat's heart winced. There it was again – that name, sinister and remorseless, spreading like a dark cloud over all his skies.

'Mr Marcus,' he said so sincerely that his voice trembled, 'I wouldn't be surprised if Orson Welles is the biggest menace that's come to Hollywood for years. He gets a hundred and fifty grand a picture and I wouldn't be surprised if he was so radical that you had to have all new equipment and start all over again like you did with sound in 1928.'

'Oh my God!' groaned Mr Marcus.

'And me,' said Pat, 'all I want is a pass and no money – to leave things as they are.'

Mr Marcus reached for his card case.

III

To those grouped together under the name 'talent', the atmosphere of a studio is not unfailingly bright – one fluctuates too quickly between high hope and grave apprehension. Those few who decide things are happy in their work and sure that they are worthy of their hire – the rest live in a mist of doubt as to when their vast inadequacy will be disclosed.

Pat's psychology was, oddly, that of the masters and for the most part he was unworried even though he was off salary. But there was one large fly in the ointment – for the first time in his life he began to feel a loss of identity. Due to reasons that he did not quite understand, though it might have been traced to his conversation, a number of people began to address him as 'Orson'.

Now to lose one's identity is a careless thing in any case. But to lose it to an enemy, or at least to one who has become scapegoat for our misfortunes – that is a hardship. Pat was *not* Orson. Any resemblance must be faint and far-fetched and he was aware of the fact. The final effect was to make him, in that regard, something of an eccentric.

'Pat,' said Joe the barber, 'Orson was in here today and asked me to trim his beard.'

'I hope you set fire to it,' said Pat.

'I did,' Joe winked at waiting customers over a hot towel. 'He asked for a singe so I took it all off. Now his face is as bald as yours. In fact you look a bit alike.'

This was the morning the kidding was so ubiquitous that, to avoid it, Pat lingered in Mario's bar across the street. He was not drinking – at the bar, that is, for he was down to his last thirty cents, but he refreshed himself frequently from a half-pint in his back pocket. He needed the stimulus for he had to make a touch presently and he knew that money was easier to borrow when one didn't have an air of urgent need.

His quarry, Jeff Boldini, was in an unsympathetic state of mind. He too was an artist, albeit a successful one, and a certain great lady of the screen had just burned him up by criticizing a wig he had made for her.

He told the story to Pat at length and the latter waited until it was all out before broaching his request.

'No soap,' said Jeff. 'Hell, you never paid me back what you borrowed last month.'

'But I got a job now,' lied Pat. 'This is just to tide me over. I start tomorrow.'

'If they don't give the job to Orson Welles,' said Jeff humorously.

Pat's eyes narrowed but he managed to utter a polite, borrower's laugh.

'Hold it,' said Jeff. 'You know I think you look like him?'

'Yeah.'

'Honest. Anyhow I could make you look like him. I could make you a beard that would be his double.'

'I wouldn't be his double for fifty grand.'

With his head on one side Jeff regarded Pat.

'I could,' he said. 'Come on in to my chair and let me see.'

'Like hell.'

'Come on. I'd like to try it. You haven't got anything to do. You don't work till tomorrow.'

'I don't want a beard.'

'It'll come off.'

'I don't want it.'

'It won't cost you anything. In fact I'll be paying *you* – I'll loan you the ten smackers if you'll let me make you a beard.'

Half an hour later Jeff looked at his completed work.

'It's perfect,' he said. 'Not only the beard but the eyes and everything.'

'All right. Now take it off,' said Pat moodily,

'What's the hurry? That's a fine muff. That's a work of art. We ought to put a camera on it. Too bad you're working tomorrow – they're using a dozen beards out on Sam Jones' set and one of them went to jail in a homo raid. I bet with that muff you could get the job.'

It was weeks since Pat had heard the word job and he could not himself say how he managed to exist and eat. Jeff saw the light in his eye.

'What say? Let me drive you out there just for fun,' pleaded Jeff. 'I'd like to see if Sam could tell it was a phony muff.'

'I'm a writer, not a ham.'

'Come on! Nobody would never know you back of that. And you'd draw another ten bucks.'

As they left the make-up department Jeff lingered behind a minute. On a strip of cardboard he crayoned the name Orson Welles in large block letters. And outside, without Pat's notice, he stuck it in the windshield of his car.

He did not go directly to the back lot. Instead he drove not too swiftly up the main studio street. In front of the administration building he stopped on the pretext that the engine was missing, and almost in no time a small but definitely interested crowd began to gather. But Jeff's plans did not include stopping anywhere long, so he hopped in and they started on a tour around the commissary.

'Where are we going?' demanded Pat.

He had already made one nervous attempt to tear the beard from him, but to his surprise it did not come away.

He complained of this to Jeff.

'Sure,' Jeff explained. 'That's made to last. You'll have to soak it off.'

The car paused momentarily at the door of the commissary. Pat saw blank eyes staring at him and he stared back at them blankly from the rear seat.

'You'd think I was the only beard on the lot,' he said gloomily.

'You can sympathize with Orson Welles.'

'To hell with him.'

This colloquy would have puzzled those without, to whom he was nothing less than the real McCoy.

Jeff drove on slowly up the street. Ahead of them a little group of men were walking – one of them, turning, saw the car and drew the attention of the others to it. Whereupon the most elderly member of the party threw up his arms in what appeared to be a defensive gesture, and plunged to the sidewalk as the car went past.

'My God, did you see that?' exclaimed Jeff. 'That was Mr Marcus.'

He came to a stop. An excited man ran up and put his head in the car window.

'Mr Welles, our Mr Marcus has had a heart attack. Can we use your car to get him to the infirmary?'

Pat stared. Then very quickly he opened the door on the other side and dashed from the car. Not even the beard could impede his streamlined flight. The policeman at the gate, not recognizing the incarnation, tried to have words with him but Pat shook him off with the ease of a triple-threat back and never paused till he reached Mario's bar.

Three extras with beards stood at the rail, and with relief Pat merged

himself into their corporate whiskers. With a trembling hand he took
the hard-earned ten dollar bill from his pocket.

'Set 'em up,' he cried hoarsely. 'Every muff has a drink on me.'

PAT HOBBY'S SECRET

Distress in Hollywood is endemic and always acute. Scarcely an executive but is being gnawed at by some insoluble problem and in a democratic way he will let you in on it, with no charge. The problem, be it one of health or of production, is faced courageously and with groans at from one to five thousand a week. That's how pictures are made.

'But this one has got me down,' said Mr Banizon, '– because how did the artillery shell get in the trunk of Claudette Colbert or Betty Field or whoever we decide to use? We got to explain it so the audience will believe it.'

He was in the office of Louie the studio bookie and his present audience also included Pat Hobby, venerable script-stooge of forty-nine. Mr Banizon did not expect a suggestion from either of them but he had been talking aloud to himself about the problem for a week now and was unable to stop.

'Who's your writer on it?' asked Louie.

'R. Parke Woll,' said Banizon indignantly. 'First I buy this opening from another writer, see. A grand notion but only a notion. Then I call in R. Parke Woll, the playwright, and we meet a couple of times and develop it. Then when we get the end in sight, his agent horns in and says he won't let Woll talk any more unless I give him a contract – eight weeks at $3,000! And all I need him for is one more day!'

The sum brought a glitter into Pat's old eyes. Ten years ago he had camped beatifically in range of such a salary – now he was lucky to get a few weeks at $250. His inflamed and burnt over talent had failed to produce a second growth.

'The worse part of it is that Woll told me the ending,' continued the producer.

'Then what are you waiting for?' demanded Pat. 'You don't need to pay him a cent.'

'I forgot it!' groaned Mr Banizon. 'Two phones were ringing at once in my office – one from a working director. And while I was talking Woll had to run along. Now I can't remember it and I can't get him back.'

Perversely Pat Hobby's sense of justice was with the producer, not the writer. Banizon had almost outsmarted Woll and then been cheated by a tough break. And now the playwright, with the insolence of an Eastern snob, was holding him up for twenty-four grand. What with the European market gone. What with the war.

'Now he's on a big bat,' said Banizon. 'I know because I got a man tailing him. It's enough to drive you nuts – here I got the whole story except the pay-off. What good is it to me like that?'

'If he's drunk maybe he'd spill it,' suggested Louie practically.

'Not to me,' said Mr Banizon. 'I thought of it but he would recognize my face.'

Having reached the end of his current blind alley, Mr Banizon picked a horse in the third and one in the seventh and prepared to depart.

'I got an idea,' said Pat.

Mr Banizon looked suspiciously at the red old eyes.

'I got no time to hear it now,' he said.

'I'm not selling anything,' Pat reassured him. 'I got a deal almost ready over at Paramount. But once I worked with this R. Parke Woll and maybe I could find what you want to know.'

He and Mr Banizon went out of the office together and walked slowly across the lot. An hour later, for an advance consideration of fifty dollars, Pat was employed to discover how a live artillery shell got into Claudette Colbert's trunk or Betty Field's trunk or whosoever's trunk it should be.

II

The swath which R. Parke Woll was now cutting through the City of the Angels would have attracted no special notice in the twenties; in the fearful forties it rang out like laughter in church. He was easy to follow: his absence had been requested from two hotels but he had settled down into a routine where he carried his sleeping quarters in his elbow. A small but alert band of rats and weasels were furnishing him moral support in his journey – a journey which Pat caught up with at two a.m. in Conk's Old Fashioned Bar.

Conk's Bar was haughtier than its name, boasting cigarette girls and a doorman-bouncer named Smith who had once stayed a full hour with

Tarzan White. Mr Smith was an embittered man who expressed himself by goosing the patrons on their way in and out and this was Pat's introduction. When he recovered himself he discovered R. Parke Woll in a mixed company around a table, and sauntered up with an air of surprise,

'Hello, good looking,' he said to Woll. 'Remember me – Pat Hobby?'

R. Parke Woll brought him with difficulty into focus, turning his head first on one side then on the other, letting it sink, snap up and then lash forward like a cobra taking a candid snapshot. Evidently it recorded for he said:

'Pat Hobby! Sit down and wha'll you have. Genlemen, this is Pat Hobby – best left-handed writer in Hollywood. Pat h'are you?'

Pat sat down, amid suspicious looks from a dozen predatory eyes. Was Pat an old friend sent to get the playwright home?

Pat saw this and waited until a half-hour later when he found himself alone with Woll in the washroom.

'Listen Parke, Banizon is having you followed,' he said. 'I don't know why he's doing it. Louie at the studio tipped me off.'

'You don't know why?' cried Parke. 'Well, I know why. I got something he wants – that's why!'

'You owe him money?'

'Owe him money. Why that – he owes *me* money! He owes me for three long, hard conferences – I outlined a whole damn picture for him.' His vague finger tapped his forehead in several places. 'What he wants is in here.'

An hour passed at the turbulent orgiastic table. Pat waited – and then inevitably in the slow, limited cycle of the lush, Woll's mind returned to the subject.

'The funny thing is I told him who put the shell in the trunk and why. And then the Master Mind forgot.'

Pat had an inspiration.

'But his secretary remembered.'

'She did?' Woll was flabbergasted. 'Secretary – don't remember secretary.'

'She came in,' ventured Pat uneasily.

'Well then by God he's got to pay me or I'll sue him.'

'Banizon says he's got a better idea.'

'The hell he has. My idea was a pip. Listen –'

He spoke for two minutes.

'You like it?' he demanded. He looked at Pat for applause – then he must have seen something in Pat's eye that he was not intended to see. 'Why you little skunk,' he cried. 'You've talked to Banizon – he sent you here.'

Pat rose and tore like a rabbit for the door. He would have been out into the street before Woll could overtake him had it not been for the intervention of Mr Smith, the doorman.

'Where you going?' he demanded, catching Pat by his lapels.

'Hold him!' cried Woll, coming up. He aimed a blow at Pat which missed and landed full in Mr Smith's mouth.

It has been mentioned that Mr Smith was an embittered as well as a powerful man. He dropped Pat, picked up R. Parke Woll by crotch and shoulder, held him high and then in one gigantic pound brought his body down against the floor. Three minutes later Woll was dead.

III

Except in great scandals like the Arbuckle case the industry protects its own – and the industry included Pat, however intermittently. He was let out of prison next morning without bail, wanted only as a material witness. If anything, the publicity was advantageous – for the first time in a year his name appeared in the trade journals. Moreover he was now the only living man who knew how the shell got into Claudette Colbert's (or Betty Field's) trunk.

'When can you come up and see me?' said Mr Banizon.

'After the inquest tomorrow,' said Pat enjoying himself. 'I feel kind of shaken – it gave me an earache.'

That too indicated power. Only those who were 'in' could speak of their health and be listened to.

'Woll really did tell you?' questioned Banizon.

'He told me,' said Pat. 'And it's worth more than fifty smackers. I'm going to get me a new agent and bring him to your office.'

'I tell you a better plan,' said Banizon hastily, 'I'll get you on the payroll, Four weeks at your regular price.'

'What's my price?' demanded Pat gloomily. 'I've drawn everything from four thousand to zero.' And he added ambiguously, 'As Shakespeare says, "Every man has his price." '

The attendant rodents of R. Parke Woll had vanished with their small plunder into convenient rat holes, leaving as the defendant Mr Smith, and, as witnesses, Pat and two frightened cigarette girls. Mr Smith's defence was that he had been attacked. At the inquest one cigarette girl agreed with him – one condemned him for unnecessary roughness. Pat Hobby's turn was next, but before his name was called he started as a voice spoke to him from behind.

'You talk against my husband and I'll twist your tongue out by the roots.'

A huge dinosaur of a woman, fully six feet tall and broad in proportion, was leaning forward against his chair.

'Pat Hobby, step forward please . . . now Mr Hobby tell us exactly what happened.'

The eyes of Mr Smith were fixed balefully on his and he felt the eyes of the bouncer's mate reaching in for his tongue through the back of his head. He was full of natural hesitation.

'I don't know exactly,' he said, and then with quick inspiration, 'All I know is everything went white!'

'*What?*'

'That's the way it was. I saw white. Just like some guys see red or black I saw white.'

There was some consultation among the authorities.

'Well, what happened from when you came into the restaurant – up to the time you saw white?'

'Well –' said Pat fighting for time. 'It was all kind of that way. I came and sat down and then it began to go black.'

'You mean white.'

'Black *and* white.'

There was a general titter.

'Witness dismissed. Defendant remanded for trial.'

What was a little joking to endure when the stakes were so high – all that night a mountainous Amazon pursued him through his dreams and he needed a strong drink before appearing at Mr Banizon's office next morning. He was accompanied by one of the few Hollywood agents who had not yet taken him on and shaken him off.

'A flat sum of five hundred,' offered Banizon. 'Or four weeks at two-fifty to work on another picture.'

'How bad do you want this?' asked the agent. 'My client seems to think it's worth three thousand.'

'Of my own money?' cried Banizon. 'And it isn't even *his* idea. Now that Woll is dead it's in the Public Remains.'

'Not quite,' said the agent. 'I think like you do that ideas are sort of in the air. They belong to whoever's got them at the time – like balloons.'

'Well, how much?' asked Mr Banizon fearfully. 'How do I know he's got the idea?'

The agent turned to Pat.

'Shall we let him find out – for a thousand dollars?'

After a moment Pat nodded. Something was bothering him.

'All right,' said Banizon. 'This strain is driving me nuts. One thousand.'

There was silence.

'Spill it Pat,' said the agent.

Still no word from Pat. They waited. When Pat spoke at last his voice seemed to come from afar.

'Everything's white,' he gasped.

'*What?*'

'I can't help it – everything has gone white. I can see it – white. I remember going into the joint but after that it all goes white.'

For a moment they thought he was holding out. Then the agent realized that Pat actually had drawn a psychological blank. The secret of R. Parke Woll was safe forever. Too late Pat realized that a thousand dollars was slipping away and tried desperately to recover.

'I remember, I remember! It was put in by some Nazi dictator.'

'Maybe the girl put it in the trunk herself,' said Banizon ironically. 'For her bracelet.'

For many years Mr Banizon would be somewhat gnawed by this insoluble problem. And as he glowered at Pat he wished that writers could be dispensed with altogether. If only ideas could be plucked from the inexpensive air!

PAT HOBBY,
PUTATIVE FATHER

I

Most writers look like writers whether they want to or not. It is hard to say why – for they model their exteriors whimsically on Wall Street brokers, cattle kings or English explorers – but they all turn out looking like writers, as definitely typed as 'The Public' or 'The Profiteers' in the cartoons.

Pat Hobby was the exception. He did not look like a writer. And only in one corner of the Republic could he have been identified as a member of the entertainment world. Even there the first guess would have been that he was an extra down on his luck, or a bit player who specialized in the sort of father who should *never* come home. But a writer he was: he had collaborated in over two dozen moving picture scripts, most of them, it must be admitted, prior to 1929.

A writer? He had a desk in the Writers' Building at the studio; he had pencils, paper, a secretary, paper clips, a pad for office memoranda. And he sat in an overstuffed chair, his eyes not so very bloodshot, taking in the morning's *Reporter*.

'I got to get to work,' he told Miss Raudenbush at eleven. And again at twelve:

'I got to get to work.'

At quarter to one, he began to feel hungry – up to this point every move, or rather every moment, was in the writer's tradition. Even to the faint irritation that no one had annoyed him, no one had bothered him, no one had interfered with the long empty dream which constituted his average day.

He was about to accuse his secretary of staring at him when the welcome interruption came. A studio guide tapped at his door and brought him a note from his boss, Jack Berners:

Dear Pat:

Please take some time off and show these people around the lot.

Jack

'My God!' Pat exclaimed. 'How can I be expected to get anything done and show people around the lot at the same time. Who are they?' he demanded of the guide.

'I don't know. One of them seems to be kind of coloured. He looks like the extras they had at Paramount for *Bengal Lancer*. He can't speak English. The other –'

Pat was putting on his coat to see for himself.

'Will you be wanting me this afternoon?' asked Miss Raudenbush.

He looked at her with infinite reproach and went out in front of the Writers' Building.

The visitors were there. The sultry person was tall and of a fine carriage, dressed in excellent English clothes except for a turban. The other was a youth of fifteen, quite light of hue. He also wore a turban with beautifully cut jodhpurs and riding coat.

They bowed formally.

'Hear you want to go on some sets,' said Pat, 'You friends of Jack Berners?'

'Acquaintances,' said the youth. 'May I present you to my uncle: Sir Singrim Dak Raj.'

Probably, thought Pat, the company was cooking up a Bengal Lancers, and this man would play the heavy who owned the Khyber Pass. Maybe they'd put Pat on it – at three-fifty a week. Why not? He knew how to write that stuff:

Beautiful Long Shot. The Gorge. Show Tribesman firing from behind rocks.

Medium Shot. Tribesman hit by bullet making nose dive over high rock. (use stunt man)

Medium Long Shot. The Valley. British troops wheeling out cannon.

'You going to be long in Hollywood?' he asked shrewdly.

'My uncle doesn't speak English,' said the youth in a measured voice. 'We are here only a few days. You see – I am your putative son.'

II

'– And I would very much like to see Bonita Granville,' continued the youth. 'I find she has been borrowed by your studio.'

They had been walking toward the production office and it took Pat a minute to grasp what the young man had said.

'You're my what?' he asked.

'Your putative son,' said the young man, in a sort of sing-song. 'Legally I am the son and heir of the Rajah Dak Raj Indore. But I was born John Brown Hobby.'

'Yes?' said Pat. 'Go on! What's this?'

'My mother was Delia Brown. You married her in 1926. And she divorced you in 1927 when I was a few months old. Later she took me to India, where she married my present legal father.'

'Oh,' said Pat. They had reached the production office. 'You want to see Bonita Granville.'

'Yes,' said John Hobby Indore. 'If it is convenient.'

Pat looked at the shooting schedule on the wall.

'It may be,' he said heavily. 'We can go and see.'

As they started toward Stage 4, he exploded.

'What do you mean, "my potato son"? I'm glad to see you and all that, but say, are you really the kid Delia had in 1926?'

'Putatively,' John Indore said. 'At that time you and she were legally married.'

He turned to his uncle and spoke rapidly in Hindustani, whereupon the latter bent forward, looked with cold examination upon Pat and threw up his shoulders without comment. The whole business was making Pat vaguely uncomfortable.

When he pointed out the commissary, John wanted to stop there 'to buy his uncle a hot dog'. It seemed that Sir Singrim had conceived a passion for them at the World's Fair in New York, whence they had just come. They were taking ship for Madras tomorrow.

'– whether or not,' said John, sombrely, 'I get to see Bonita Granville. I do not care if I *meet* her. I am too young for her. She is already an old woman by our standards. But I'd like to *see* her.'

It was one of those bad days for showing people around. Only one of the directors shooting today was an old timer, on whom Pat could count for a welcome – and at the door of that stage he received word that the star kept blowing up in his lines and had demanded that the set be cleared.

In desperation he took his charges out to the back lot and walked them past the false fronts of ships and cities and village streets, and medieval gates – a sight in which the boy showed a certain interest but which Sir Singrim found disappointing. Each time that Pat led them around behind to demonstrate that it was all phony Sir Singrim's expression would change to disappointment and faint contempt.

'What's he say?' Pat asked his offspring, after Sir Singrim had walked eagerly into a Fifth Avenue jewellery store, to find nothing but carpenter's rubble inside.

'He is the third richest man in India,' said John. 'He is disgusted. He says he will never enjoy an American picture again. He says he will buy one of our picture companies in India and make every set as solid as the Taj Mahal. He thinks perhaps the actresses just have a false front too, and that's why you won't let us see them.'

The first sentence had rung a sort of carillon in Pat's head. If there was anything he liked it was a good piece of money – not this miserable, uncertain two-fifty a week which purchased his freedom.

'I'll tell you,' he said with sudden decision. 'We'll try Stage 4, and peek at Bonita Granville.'

Stage 4 was double locked and barred, for the day – the director hated visitors, and it was a process stage besides. 'Process' was a generic name for trick photography in which every studio competed with other studios, and lived in terror of spies. More specifically it meant that a projecting machine threw a moving background upon a transparent screen. On the other side of the screen, a scene was played and recorded against this moving background. The projector on one side of the screen and the camera on the other were so synchronized that the result could show a star standing on his head before an indifferent crowd on 42nd Street – a *real* crowd and a *real* star – and the poor eye could only conclude that it was being deluded and never quite guess how.

Pat tried to explain this to John, but John was peering for Bonita Granville from behind the great mass of coiled ropes and pails where they hid. They had not got there by the front entrance, but by a little side door for technicians that Pat knew.

Wearied by the long jaunt over the back lot, Pat took a pint flask from his hip and offered it to Sir Singrim who declined. He did not offer it to John.

'Stunt your growth,' he said solemnly, taking a long pull.

'I do not want any,' said John with dignity.

He was suddenly alert. He had spotted an idol more glamorous than Siva not twenty feet away – her back, her profile, her voice. Then she moved off.

Watching his face, Pat was rather touched.

'We can go nearer,' he said. 'We might get to that ballroom set. They're not using it – they got covers on the furniture.'

On tip toe they started, Pat in the lead, then Sir Singrim, then John. As they moved softly forward Pat heard the word 'Lights' and stopped in his tracks. Then, as a blinding white glow struck at their eyes and the voice shouted 'Quiet! We're rolling!' Pat began to run, followed quickly through the white silence by the others.

The silence did not endure.

'*Cut!*' screamed a voice, 'What the living, blazing hell!'

From the director's angle something had happened on the screen which, for the moment, was inexplicable. Three gigantic silhouettes, two with huge Indian turbans, had danced across what was intended to be a New England harbour – they had blundered into the line of the process shot. Prince John Indore had not only seen Bonita Granville – he had acted in the same picture. His silhouetted foot seemed to pass miraculously through her blonde young head.

III

They sat for some time in the guard-room before word could be gotten to Jack Berners, who was off the lot. So there was leisure for talk. This consisted of a longish harangue from Sir Singrim to John, which the latter – modifying its tone if not its words – translated to Pat.

'My uncle says his brother wanted to do something for you. He thought perhaps if you were a great writer he might invite you to come to his kingdom and write his life.'

'I never claimed to be –'

'My uncle says you are an ignominious writer – in your own land you permitted him to be touched by those dogs of the policemen.'

'Aw – bananas,' muttered Pat uncomfortably.

'He says my mother always wished you well. But now she is a high and sacred lady and should never see you again. He says we will go to our chambers in the Ambassador Hotel and meditate and pray and let you know what we decide.'

When they were released, and the two moguls were escorted apologetically to their car by a studio yes-man, it seemed to Pat that it had been pretty well decided already. He was angry. For the sake of getting his son a peek at Miss Granville, he had quite possibly lost his job – though he didn't really think so. Or rather he was pretty sure that when his week was up he would have lost it anyhow. But though it was a pretty bad break he remembered most clearly from the afternoon that Sir Singrim was 'the third richest man in India', and after dinner at a bar on La Cienega he decided to go down to the Ambassador Hotel and find out the result of the prayer and meditation.

It was early dark of a September evening. The Ambassador was full of memories to Pat – the Coconut Grove in the great days, when directors found pretty girls in the afternoon and made stars of them by night. There was some activity in front of the door and Pat watched it idly. Such a quantity of baggage he had seldom seen, even in the train of Gloria Swanson or Joan Crawford. Then he started as he saw two or three men in turbans moving around among the baggage. So – they were running out on him.

Sir Singrim Dak Raj and his nephew Prince John, both pulling on gloves as if at a command, appeared at the door, as Pat stepped forward out of the darkness.

'Taking a powder, eh?' he said. 'Say, when you get back there, tell them that one American could lick –'

'I have left a note for you,' said Prince John, turning from his Uncle's side. 'I say, you *were* nice this afternoon and it really was too bad.'

'Yes, it was,' agreed Pat.

'But we are providing for you,' John said. 'After our prayers we decided that you will receive fifty sovereigns a month – two hundred and fifty dollars – for the rest of your natural life.'

'What will I have to do for it?' questioned Pat suspiciously.

'It will only be withdrawn in case –'

John leaned and whispered in Pat's ear, and relief crept into Pat's eyes. The condition had nothing to do with drink and blondes, really nothing to do with him at all.

John began to get in the limousine.

'Goodbye, putative father,' he said, almost with affection.

Pat stood looking after him.

'Goodbye son,' he said. He stood watching the limousine go out of sight. Then he turned away – feeling like – like Stella Dallas. There were tears in his eyes.

Potato Father – whatever that meant. After some consideration he added to himself: it's better than not being a father at all.

IV

He awoke late next afternoon with a happy hangover – the cause of which he could not determine until young John's voice seemed to spring into his ears, repeating: 'Fifty sovereigns a month, with just one condition – that it be withdrawn in case of war, when all revenues of our state will revert to the British Empire.'

With a cry Pat sprang to the door, No *Los Angeles Times* lay against it, no *Examiner* – only *Toddy's Daily Form Sheet*. He searched the orange pages frantically. Below the form sheets, the past performances, the endless oracles for endless racetracks, his eye was caught by a one-inch item:

LONDON, SEPTEMBER 3RD. ON THIS MORNING'S DECLARATION BY CHAMBER-LAIN, DOUGIE CABLES 'ENGLAND TO WIN, FRANCE TO PLACE, RUSSIA TO SHOW'.

THE HOMES OF THE STARS

Beneath a great striped umbrella at the side of a boulevard in a Hollywood heat wave, sat a man. His name was Gus Venske (no relation to the runner) and he wore magenta pants, cerise shoes and a sport article from Vine Street which resembled nothing so much as a cerulean blue pajama top.

Gus Venske was not a freak nor were his clothes at all extraordinary for his time and place. He had a profession – on a pole beside the umbrella was a placard:

VISIT THE HOMES OF THE STARS

Business was bad or Gus would not have hailed the unprosperous man who stood in the street beside a panting, steaming car, anxiously watching its efforts to cool.

'Hey fella,' said Gus, without much hope. 'Wanna visit the homes of the stars?'

The red-rimmed eyes of the watcher turned from the automobile and looked superciliously upon Gus.

'I'm *in* pictures,' said the man, 'I'm in 'em myself.'

'Actor?'

'No. Writer.'

Pat Hobby turned back to his car, which was whistling like a peanut wagon. He had told the truth – or what was once the truth. Often in the old days his name had flashed on the screen for the few seconds allotted to authorship, but for the past five years his services had been less and less in demand.

Presently Gus Venske shut up shop for lunch by putting his folders and maps into a briefcase and walking off with it under his arm. As the sun grew hotter moment by moment, Pat Hobby took refuge under the faint protection of the umbrella and inspected a soiled folder which had been dropped by Mr Venske. If Pat had not been down to his last fourteen cents he would have telephoned a garage for aid – as it was, he could only wait.

After a while a limousine with a Missouri licence drew to rest beside him. Behind the chauffeur sat a little white moustached man and a large woman with a small dog. They conversed for a moment – then, in a rather shamefaced way, the woman leaned out and addressed Pat,

'What stars' homes can you visit?' she asked.

It took a moment for this to sink in.

'I mean can we go to Robert Taylor's home and Clark Gable's and Shirley Temple's –'

'I guess you can if you can get in,' said Pat.

'Because –' continued the woman, '– if we could go to the very best homes, the most exclusive – we would be prepared to pay more than your regular price.'

Light dawned upon Pat. Here together were suckers and smackers. Here was that dearest of Hollywood dreams – the angle. If one got the right angle it meant meals at the Brown Derby, long nights with bottles and girls, a new tyre for his old car. And here was an angle fairly thrusting itself at him.

He rose and went to the side of the limousine.

'Sure. Maybe I could fix it.' As he spoke he felt a pang of doubt. 'Would you be able to pay in advance?'

The couple exchanged a look.

'Suppose we gave you five dollars now,' the woman said, 'and five dollars if we can visit Clark Gable's home or somebody like that.'

Once upon a time such a thing would have been so easy. In his salad days when Pat had twelve or fifteen writing credits a year, he could have called up many people who would have said, 'Sure, Pat, if it means anything to you.' But now he could only think of a handful who really recognized him and spoke to him around the lots – Melvyn Douglas and Robert Young and Ronald Colman and Young Doug. Those he had known best had retired or passed away.

And he did not know except vaguely where the new stars lived, but he had noticed that on the folder were typewritten several dozen names and addresses with pencilled checks after each.

'Of course you can't be sure anybody's at home,' he said, 'they might be working in the studios.'

'We understand that.' The lady glanced at Pat's car, glanced away. 'We'd better go in our motor.'

'Sure.'

Pat got up in front with the chauffeur – trying to think fast. The actor who spoke to him most pleasantly was Ronald Colman – they had never exchanged more than conventional salutations but he might pretend that he was calling to interest Colman in a story.

Better still, Colman was probably not at home and Pat might wangle his clients an inside glimpse of the house. Then the process might be repeated at Robert Young's house and Young Doug's and Melvyn Douglas'. By that time the lady would have forgotten Gable and the afternoon would be over.

He looked at Ronald Colman's address on the folder and gave the direction to the chauffeur.

'We know a woman who had her picture taken with George Brent,' said the lady as they started off, 'Mrs Horace J. Ives, Jr.'

'She's our neighbour,' said her husband. 'She lives at 372 Rose Drive in Kansas City. And we live at 327.'

'She had her picture taken with George Brent. We always wondered if she had to pay for it. Of course I don't know that I'd want to go so far as *that*. I don't know what they'd say back home.'

'I don't think we want to go as far as all that,' agreed her husband.

'Where are we going first?' asked the lady, cosily.

'Well, I had a couple calls to pay anyhow,' said Pat. 'I got to see Ronald Colman about something.'

'Oh, he's one of my favourites. Do you know him well?'

'Oh yes,' said Pat, 'I'm not in this business regularly. I'm just doing it today for a friend. I'm a writer.'

Sure in the knowledge that not so much as a trio of picture writers were known to the public he named himself as the author of several recent successes.

'That's very interesting,' said the man, 'I knew a writer once – this Upton Sinclair or Sinclair Lewis. Not a bad fellow even if he was a socialist.'

'Why aren't you writing a picture now?' asked the lady.

'Well, you see we're on strike,' Pat invented. 'We got a thing called the Screen Playwriters' Guild and we're on strike.'

'Oh.' His clients stared with suspicion at this emissary of Stalin in the front seat of their car.

'What are you striking for?' asked the man uneasily.

Pat's political development was rudimentary. He hesitated.

'Oh, better living conditions,' he said finally, 'free pencils and paper, I don't know – it's all in the Wagner Act.' After a moment he added vaguely, 'Recognize Finland.'

'I didn't know writers had unions,' said the man. 'Well, if you're on strike who writes the movies?'

'The producers,' said Pat bitterly. 'That's why they're so lousy.'

'Well, that's what I would call an odd state of things.'

They came in sight of Ronald Colman's house and Pat swallowed uneasily. A shining new roadster sat out in front.

'I better go in first,' he said. 'I mean we wouldn't want to come in on any – on any family scene or anything.'

'Does he have family scenes?' asked the lady eagerly.

'Oh, well, you know how people are,' said Pat with charity. 'I think I ought to see how things are first.'

The car stopped. Drawing a long breath Pat got out. At the same moment the door of the house opened and Ronald Colman hurried down the walk. Pat's heart missed a beat as the actor glanced in his direction.

'Hello Pat,' he said. Evidently he had no notion that Pat was a caller for he jumped into his car and the sound of his motor drowned out Pat's responses as he drove away.

'Well, he called you "Pat",' said the woman impressed.

'I guess he was in a hurry,' said Pat. 'But maybe we could see his house.'

He rehearsed a speech going up the walk. He had just spoken to his friend Mr Colman, and received permission to look around.

But the house was shut and locked and there was no answer to the bell. He would have to try Melvyn Douglas whose salutations, on second thought, were a little warmer than Ronald Colman's. At any rate his clients' faith in him was now firmly founded. The 'Hello, Pat,' rang confidently in their ears; by proxy they were already inside the charmed circle.

'Now let's try Clark Gable's,' said the lady. 'I'd like to tell Carole Lombard about her hair.'

The lese majesty made Pat's stomach wince. Once in a crowd he had met Clark Gable but he had no reason to believe that Mr Gable remembered.

'Well, we could try Melvyn Douglas' first and then Bob Young or else Young Doug. They're all on the way. You see Gable and Lombard live away out in the St Joaquin valley.'

'Oh,' said the lady, disappointed, 'I did want to run up and see their bedroom. Well then, our next choice would be Shirley Temple.' She looked at her little dog. 'I know that would be Boojie's choice too.'

'They're kind of afraid of kidnappers,' said Pat.

Ruffled, the man produced his business card and handed it to Pat.

DEERING R. ROBINSON
Vice President and Chairman
of the Board
Robdeer Food Products

'Does *that* sound as if I want to kidnap Shirley Temple?'

'They just have to be sure,' said Pat apologetically. 'After we go to Melvyn –'

'No – let's see Shirley Temple's *now*,' insisted the woman. 'Really! I told you in the first place what I wanted.'

Pat hesitated.

'First I'll have to stop in some drugstore and phone about it.'

In a drugstore he exchanged some of the five dollars for a half pint of gin and took two long swallows behind a high counter, after which he considered the situation. He could, of course, duck Mr and Mrs Robinson immediately – after all he had produced Ronald Colman, with sound, for their five smackers. On the other hand they just *might* catch Miss Temple on her way in or out – and for a pleasant day at Santa Anita tomorrow Pat needed five smackers more. In the glow of the gin his courage mounted, and returning to the limousine he gave the chauffeur the address.

But approaching the Temple house his spirit quailed as he saw that there was a tall iron fence and an electric gate. And didn't guides have to have a licence?

'Not here,' he said quickly to the chauffeur. 'I made a mistake. I think it's the next one, or two or three doors further on.'

He decided on a large mansion set in an open lawn and stopping the chauffeur got out and walked up to the door. He was temporarily licked but at least he might bring back some story to soften them – say, that Miss Temple had mumps. He could point out her sick-room from the walk.

There was no answer to his ring but he saw that the door was partly ajar. Cautiously he pushed it open. He was staring into a deserted living room on the baronial scale. He listened. There was no one about, no footsteps on the upper floor, no murmur from the kitchen. Pat took another pull at the gin. Then swiftly he hurried back to the limousine.

'She's at the studio,' he said quickly, 'But if we're quiet we can look at their living-room.'

Eagerly the Robinsons and Boojie disembarked and followed him. The living-room might have been Shirley Temple's, might have been one of many in Hollywood. Pat saw a doll in a corner and pointed at it, whereupon Mrs Robinson picked it up, looked at it reverently and showed it to Boojie who sniffed indifferently.

'Could I meet Mrs Temple?' she asked.

'Oh, she's out – nobody's home,' Pat said – unwisely.

'*Nobody*. Oh – then Boojie would so like a wee little peep at her bedroom.'

Before he could answer she had run up the stairs. Mr Robinson followed and Pat waited uneasily in the hall, ready to depart at the sound either of an arrival outside or a commotion above.

He finished the bottle, disposed of it politely under a sofa cushion and then deciding that the visit upstairs was tempting fate too far, he went after his clients. On the stairs he heard Mrs Robinson.

'But there's only *one* child's bedroom. I thought Shirley had brothers.'

A window on the winding staircase looked upon the street, and glancing out Pat saw a large car drive up to the curb. From it stepped a Hollywood celebrity who, though not one of those pursued by Mrs Robinson, was second to none in prestige and power. It was old Mr Marcus, the producer, for whom Pat Hobby had been press agent twenty years ago.

At this point Pat lost his head. In a flash he pictured an elaborate explanation as to what he was doing here. He would not be forgiven. His occasional weeks in the studio at two-fifty would now disappear altogether and another finis would be written to his almost entirely finished career. He left, impetuously and swiftly – down the stairs, through the kitchen and out the back gate, leaving the Robinsons to their destiny.

Vaguely he was sorry for them as he walked quickly along the next boulevard. He could see Mr Robinson producing his card as the head of Robdeer Food Products. He could see Mr Marcus' scepticism, the arrival of the police, the frisking of Mr and Mrs Robinson.

Probably it would stop there – except that the Robinsons would be furious at him for his imposition. They would tell the police where they had picked him up.

Suddenly he went ricketing down the street, beads of gin breaking out profusely on his forehead. He had left his car beside Gus Venske's umbrella. And now he remembered another recognizing clue and hoped that Ronald Colman didn't know his last name.

PAT HOBBY DOES HIS BIT

I

In order to borrow money gracefully one must choose the time and place. It is a difficult business, for example, when the borrower is cockeyed, or has measles, or a conspicuous shiner. One could continue indefinitely but the inauspicious occasions can be catalogued as one – it is exceedingly difficult to borrow money when one needs it.

Pat Hobby found it difficult in the case of an actor on a set during the shooting of a moving picture. It was about the stiffest chore he had ever undertaken but he was doing it to save his car. To a sordidly commercial glance the jalopy would not have seemed worth saving but, because of Hollywood's great distances, it was an indispensable tool of the writer's trade.

'The finance company –' explained Pat, but Gyp McCarthy interrupted.

'I got some business in this next take. You want me to blow up on it?'

'I only need twenty,' persisted Pat. 'I can't get jobs if I have to hang around my bedroom.'

'You'd save money that way – you don't get jobs anymore.'

This was cruelly correct. But working or not Pat liked to pass his days in or near a studio. He had reached a dolorous and precarious forty-nine with nothing else to do.

'I got a rewrite job promised for next week,' he lied.

'Oh, nuts to you,' said Gyp. 'You better get off the set before Hilliard sees you.'

Pat glanced nervously toward the group by the camera – then he played his trump card.

'Once –' he said, '– once I paid for you to have a baby.'

'Sure you did!' said Gyp wrathfully. 'That was sixteen years ago. And where is it now – it's in jail for running over an old lady without a licence.'

'Well I paid for it,' said Pat. 'Two hundred smackers.'

'That's nothing to what it cost me. Would I be stunting at my age if I had dough to lend? Would I be working at all?'

From somewhere in the darkness an assistant director issued an order: 'Ready to go!'

Pat spoke quickly.

'All right,' he said. 'Five bucks.'

'No.'

'All right then,' Pat's red-rimmed eyes tightened. 'I'm going to stand over there and put the hex on you while you say your line.'

'Oh, for God's sake!' said Gyp uneasily. 'Listen, I'll give you five. It's in my coat over there. Here, I'll get it.'

He dashed from the set and Pat heaved a sigh of relief. Maybe Louie, the studio bookie, would let him have ten more.

Again the assistant director's voice:

'Quiet! . . . We'll take it now! . . . Lights!'

The glare stabbed into Pat's eyes, blinding him. He took a step the wrong way – then back. Six other people were in the take – a gangster's hide-out – and it seemed that each was in his way.

'All right . . . Roll 'em . . . We're turning!'

In his panic Pat had stepped behind a flat which would effectually conceal him. While the actors played their scene he stood there trembling a little, his back hunched – quite unaware that it was a 'trolley shot', that the camera, moving forward on its track, was almost upon him.

'You by the window – hey you, *Gyp*! hands up.'

Like a man in a dream Pat raised his hands – only then did he realize that he was looking directly into a great black lens – in an instant it also included the English leading woman, who ran past him and jumped out the window. After an interminable second Pat heard the order 'Cut.'

Then he rushed blindly through a property door, around a corner, tripping over a cable, recovering himself and tearing for the entrance. He heard footsteps running behind him and increased his gait, but in the doorway itself he was overtaken and turned defensively.

It was the English actress.

'Hurry up!' she cried. 'That finishes my work. I'm flying home to England.'

As she scrambled into her waiting limousine she threw back a last irrelevant remark. 'I'm catching a New York plane in an hour.'

Who cares! Pat thought bitterly, as he scurried away.

He was unaware that her repatriation was to change the course of his life.

II

And he did not have the five -- he feared that this particular five was forever out of range. Other means must be found to keep the wolf from the two doors of his coupe. Pat left the lot with despair in his heart, stopping only momentarily to get gas for the car and gin for himself, possibly the last of many drinks they had had together.

Next morning he awoke with an aggravated problem. For once he did not want to go to the studio. It was not merely Gyp McCarthy he feared – it was the whole corporate might of a moving picture company, nay of an industry. Actually to have interfered with the shooting of a movie was somehow a major delinquency, compared to which expensive fumblings on the part of producers or writers went comparatively unpunished.

On the other hand zero hour for the car was the day after tomorrow and Louie, the studio bookie, seemed positively the last resource and a poor one at that.

Nerving himself with an unpalatable snack from the bottom of the bottle, he went to the studio at ten with his coat collar turned up and his hat pulled low over his ears. He knew a sort of underground railway through the make-up department and the commissary kitchen which might get him to Louie's suite unobserved.

Two studio policemen seized him as he rounded the corner by the barber shop.

'Hey, I got a pass!' he protested, 'Good for a week – signed by Jack Berners.'

'Mr Berners specially wants to see you.'

Here it was then – he would be barred from the lot.

'We could sue you!' cried Jack Berners. 'But we couldn't recover.'

'What's one take?' demanded Pat. 'You can use another.'

'No we can't – the camera jammed. And this morning Lily Keatts took a plane to England. She thought she was through.'

'Cut the scene,' suggested Pat – and then on inspiration, 'I bet I could fix it for you.'

'You fixed it, all right!' Berners assured him. 'If there was any way to fix it back I wouldn't have sent for you.'

He paused, looked speculatively at Pat. His buzzer sounded and a secretary's voice said 'Mr Hilliard'.

'Send him in,'

George Hilliard was a huge man and the glance he bent upon Pat was not kindly. But there was some other element besides anger in it and Pat squirmed doubtfully as the two men regarded him with almost impersonal curiosity – as if he were a candidate for a cannibal's frying pan.

'Well, goodbye,' he suggested uneasily.

'What do you think, George?' demanded Berners.

'Well –' said Hilliard, hesitantly, 'we could black out a couple of teeth.'

Pat rose hurriedly and took a step toward the door, but Hilliard seized him and faced him around.

'Let's hear you talk,' he said.

'You can't beat me up,' Pat clamoured. 'You knock my teeth out and I'll sue you.'

There was a pause.

'What do you think?' demanded Berners.

'He can't talk,' said Hilliard.

'You damn right I can talk!' said Pat.

'We can dub three or four lines,' continued Hilliard, 'and nobody'll know the difference. Half the guys you get to play rats can't talk. The point is this one's got the physique and the camera will pull it out of his face too.'

Berners nodded.

'All right, Pat – you're an actor. You've got to play the part this McCarthy had. Only a couple of scenes but they're important. You'll have papers to sign with the Guild and Central Casting and you can report for work this afternoon.'

'What is this!' Pat demanded. 'I'm no ham –' Remembering that Hilliard had once been a leading man he recoiled from this attitude: 'I'm a writer.'

'The character you play is called "The Rat",' continued Berners. He explained why it was necessary for Pat to continue his impromptu appearance of yesterday. The scenes which included Miss Keatts had been shot first, so that she could fulfil an English engagement. But in the filling out of the skeleton it was necessary to show how the gangsters reached their hide-out, and what they did after Miss Keatts dove from the window. Having irrevocably appeared in the shot with Miss Keatts,

Pat must appear in half a dozen other shots, to be taken in the next few days.

'What kind of jack is it?' Pat inquired.

'We were paying McCarthy fifty a day – wait a minute Pat – but I thought I'd pay you your last writing price, two-fifty for the week.'

'How about my reputation?' objected Pat.

'I won't answer that one,' said Berners. 'But if Benchley can act and Don Stewart and Lewis and Wilder and Woollcott, I guess it won't ruin you.'

Pat drew a long breath.

'Can you let me have fifty on account,' he asked, 'because really I earned that yester –'

'If you got what you earned yesterday you'd be in a hospital. And you're not going on any bat. Here's ten dollars and that's all you see for a week.'

'How about my car –'

'To hell with your car.'

III

'The Rat' was the die-hard of the gang who were engaged in sabotage for an unidentified government of N-zis. His speeches were simplicity itself – Pat had written their like many times. 'Don't finish him till the Brain comes'; 'Let's get out of here'; 'Fella, you're going out feet first.' Pat found it pleasant – mostly waiting around as in all picture work – and he hoped it might lead to other openings in this line. He was sorry that the job was so short.

His last scene was on location. He knew 'The Rat' was to touch off an explosion in which he himself was killed but Pat had watched such scenes and was certain he would be in no slightest danger. Out on the back lot he was mildly curious when they measured him around the waist and chest.

'Making a dummy?' he asked.

'Not exactly,' the prop man said. 'This thing is all made but it was for Gyp McCarthy and I want to see if it'll fit you.'

'Does it?'

'Just exactly.'

'What is it?'

'Well – it's a sort of protector.'

A slight draught of uneasiness blew in Pat's mind.

'Protector for what? Against the explosion?'

'Heck no! The explosion is phony – just a process shot. This is something else.'

'What is it?' persisted Pat. 'If I got to be protected against something I got a right to know what it is.'

Near the false front of a warehouse a battery of cameras were getting into position. George Hilliard came suddenly out of a group and toward Pat and putting his arm on his shoulder steered him toward the actors' dressing tent. Once inside he handed Pat a flask.

'Have a drink, old man.'

Pat took a long pull.

'There's a bit of business, Pat,' Hilliard said, 'needs some new costuming. I'll explain it while they dress you.'

Pat was divested of coat and vest, his trousers were loosened and in an instant a hinged iron doublet was fastened about his middle, extending from his armpits to his crotch very much like a plaster cast.

'This is the very finest strongest iron, Pat,' Hilliard assured him. 'The very best in tensile strength and resistance. It was built in Pittsburgh.'

Pat suddenly resisted the attempts of two dressers to pull his trousers up over the thing and to slip on his coat and vest.

'What's it for?' he demanded, arms flailing. 'I want to know. You're not going to shoot at me if that's what –'

'No shooting.'

'Then what *is* it? I'm no stunt man –'

'You signed a contract just like McCarthy's to do anything within reason – and our lawyers have certified this.'

'What *is* it?' Pat's mouth was dry.

'It's an automobile.'

'You're going to hit me with an automobile.'

'Give me a chance to tell you,' begged Hilliard. 'Nobody's going to hit you. The auto's going to pass over you, that's all. This case is so strong –'

'Oh no!' said Pat. 'Oh no!' He tore at the iron corselet. 'Not on your –'

George Hilliard pinioned his arms firmly.

'Pat, you almost wrecked this picture once – you're not going to do it again. Be a man.'

'That's what I'm going to be. You're not going to squash me out flat like that extra last month.'

He broke off. Behind Hilliard he saw a face he knew – a hateful and dreaded face – that of the collector for the North Hollywood Finance and Loan Company. Over in the parking lot stood his coupe, faithful pal and servant since 1934, companion of his misfortunes, his only certain home.

'Either you fill your contract,' said George Hilliard, '– or you're out of pictures for keeps.'

The man from the finance company had taken a step forward. Pat turned to Hilliard.

'Will you loan me –' he faltered, '– will you advance me twenty-five dollars?'

'Sure,' said Hilliard.

Pat spoke fiercely to the credit man:

'You hear that? You'll get your money, but if this thing breaks, my death'll be on your head.'

The next few minutes passed in a dream. He heard Hilliard's last instructions as they walked from the tent. Pat was to be lying in a shallow ditch to touch off the dynamite – and then the hero would drive the car slowly across his middle. Pat listened dimly. A picture of himself, cracked like an egg by the factory wall, lay a-thwart his mind.

He picked up the torch and lay down in the ditch. Afar off he heard the call 'Quiet', then Hilliard's voice and the noise of the car warming up.

'Action!' called someone. There was the sound of the car growing nearer – louder. And then Pat Hobby knew no more.

IV

When he awoke it was dark and quiet. For some moments he failed to recognize his whereabouts. Then he saw that stars were out in the California sky and that he was somewhere alone – no – he was held tight in someone's arms. But the arms were of iron and he realized that he was still in the metallic casing. And then it all came back to him – up to the moment when he heard the approach of the car.

As far as he could determine he was unhurt – but why out here and alone?

He struggled to get up but found it was impossible and after a horrified moment he let out a cry for help. For five minutes he called out at intervals until finally a voice came from far away; and assistance arrived in the form of a studio policeman.

'What is it fella? A drop too much?'

'Hell no,' cried Pat. 'I was in the shooting this afternoon, It was a lousy trick to go off and leave me in this ditch.'

'They must have forgot you in the excitement.'

'Forgot me! *I* was the excitement. If you don't believe me then feel what I got on!'

The cop helped him to his feet.

'They was upset,' he explained. 'A star don't break his leg every day.'

'What's that? Did something happen?'

'Well, as I heard, he was supposed to drive the car at a bump and the car turned over and broke his leg. They had to stop shooting and they're all kind of gloomy.'

'And they leave me inside this – this stove. How do I get it off tonight? How'm I going to drive my car?'

But for all his rage Pat felt a certain fierce pride. He was Something in this set-up – someone to be reckoned with after years of neglect. He had managed to hold up the picture once more.

PAT HOBBY'S PREVIEW

I

'I haven't got a job for you,' said Berners. 'We've got more writers now than we can use.'

'I didn't ask for a job,' said Pat with dignity. 'But I rate some tickets for the preview tonight – since I got a half credit.'

'Oh yes, I want to talk to you about that,' Berners frowned. 'We may have to take your name off the screen credits.'

'*What?*' exclaimed Pat. 'Why, it's already on! I saw it in the *Reporter*. "By Ward Wainwright and Pat Hobby." '

'But we may have to take it off when we release the picture. Wainwright's back from the East and raising hell. He says that you claimed lines where all you did was change "No" to "No sir" and "crimson" to "red", and stuff like that.'

'I been in this business twenty years,' said Pat. 'I know my rights. That guy laid an egg. I was called in to revise a turkey!'

'You were not,' Berners assured him. 'After Wainwright went to New York I called you in to fix one small character. If I hadn't gone fishing you wouldn't have got away with sticking your name on the script.' Jack Berners broke off, touched by Pat's dismal, red-streaked eyes. 'Still, I was glad to see you get a credit after so long.'

'I'll join the Screen Writers Guild and fight it.'

'You don't stand a chance. Anyhow, Pat, your name's on it tonight at least, and it'll remind everybody you're alive. And I'll dig you up some tickets – but keep an eye out for Wainwright. It isn't good for you to get socked if you're over fifty.'

'I'm in my forties,' said Pat, who was forty-nine.

The Dictograph buzzed. Berners switched it on.

'It's Mr Wainwright.'

'Tell him to wait.' He turned to Pat: 'That's Wainwright. Better go out the side door.'

'How about the tickets?'

'Drop by this afternoon.'

To a rising young screen poet this might have been a crushing blow but Pat was made of sterner stuff. Sterner not upon himself, but on the harsh fate that had dogged him for nearly a decade. With all his experience, and with the help of every poisonous herb that blossoms between Washington Boulevard and Ventura, between Santa Monica and Vine – he continued to slip. Sometimes he grabbed momentarily at a bush, found a few weeks' surcease upon the island of a 'patch job', but in general the slide continued at a pace that would have dizzied a lesser man.

Once safely out of Berners' office, for instance, Pat looked ahead and not behind. He visioned a drink with Louie, the studio bookie, and then a call on some old friends on the lot. Occasionally, but less often every year, some of these calls developed into jobs before you could say 'Santa Anita'. But after he had had his drink his eyes fell upon a lost girl.

She was obviously lost. She stood staring very prettily at the trucks full of extras that rolled toward the commissary. And then gazed about helpless – so helpless that a truck was almost upon her when Pat reached out and plucked her aside.

'Oh, thanks,' she said, 'thanks, I came with a party for a tour of the studio and a policeman made me leave my camera in some office. Then I went to stage five where the guide said, but it was closed.'

She was a 'Cute Little Blonde'. To Pat's liverish eye, cute little blondes seemed as much alike as a string of paper dolls. Of course they had different names.

'We'll see about it,' said Pat.

'You're very nice. I'm Eleanor Carter from Boise, Idaho.'

He told her his name and that he was a writer. She seemed first disappointed – then delighted.

'A writer? . . . Oh, of course. I knew they had to have writers but I guess I never heard about one before.'

'Writers get as much as three grand a week,' he assured her firmly. 'Writers are some of the biggest shots in Hollywood.'

'You see, I never thought of it that way.'

'Bernud Shaw was out here,' he said, '– and Einstein, but they couldn't make the grade.'

They walked to the Bulletin Board and Pat found that there was work scheduled on three stages – and one of the directors was a friend out of the past.

'What did you write?' Eleanor asked.

A great male Star loomed on the horizon and Eleanor was all eyes till he had passed. Anyhow the names of Pat's pictures would have been unfamiliar to her.

'Those were all silents,' he said.

'Oh. Well, what did you write last?'

'Well, I worked on a thing at Universal – I don't know what they called it finally –' He saw that he was not impressing her at all. He thought quickly. What did they know in Boise, Idaho? 'I wrote *Captains Courageous*,' he said boldly. 'And *Test Pilot* and *Wuthering Heights* and – and *The Awful Truth* and *Mr Smith Goes to Washington*.'

'Oh!' she exclaimed. 'Those are all my favourite pictures. And *Test Pilot* is my boy friend's favourite picture and *Dark Victory* is mine.'

'I thought *Dark Victory* stank,' he said modestly. 'Highbrow stuff,' and he added to balance the scales of truth, 'I been here twenty years.'

They came to a stage and went in. Pat sent his name to the director and they were passed. They watched while Ronald Colman rehearsed a scene.

'Did you write this?' Eleanor whispered.

'They asked me to,' Pat said, 'but I was busy.'

He felt young again, authoritative and active, with a hand in many schemes. Then he remembered something.

'I've got a picture opening tonight.'

'You *have*?'

He nodded.

'I was going to take Claudette Colbert but she's got a cold. Would you like to go?'

II

He was alarmed when she mentioned a family, relieved when she said it was only a resident aunt. It would be like old times walking with a cute little blonde past the staring crowds on the sidewalk. His car was Class of 1933 but he could say it was borrowed – one of his Jap servants had smashed his limousine. Then what? he didn't quite know, but he could put on a good act for one night.

He bought her lunch in the commissary and was so stirred that he thought of borrowing somebody's apartment for the day. There was the old line about 'getting her a test'. But Eleanor was thinking only of getting to a hair-dresser to prepare for tonight, and he escorted her reluctantly to the gate. He had another drink with Louie and went to Jack Berners' office for the tickets.

Berners' secretary had them ready in an envelope.

'We had trouble about these, Mr Hobby.'

'Trouble? Why? Can't a man go to his own preview? Is this something new?'

'It's not that, Mr Hobby,' she said. 'The picture's been talked about so much, every seat is gone.'

Unreconciled, he complained, 'And they just didn't think of me.'

'I'm sorry.' She hesitated. 'These are really Mr Wainwright's tickets. He was so angry about something that he said he wouldn't go – and threw them on my desk. I shouldn't be telling you this.'

'These are *his* seats?'

'Yes, Mr Hobby.'

Pat sucked his tongue. This was in the nature of a triumph. Wainwright had lost his temper, which was the last thing you should ever do in pictures – you could only pretend to lose it – so perhaps his applecart wasn't so steady. Perhaps Pat ought to join the Screen Writers Guild and present his case – if the Screen Writers Guild would take him in.

This problem was academic. He was calling for Eleanor at five o'clock and taking her 'somewhere for a cocktail'. He bought a two-dollar shirt, changing into it in the shop, and a four-dollar Alpine hat – thus halving his bank account which, since the Bank Holiday of 1933, he carried cautiously in his pocket.

The modest bungalow in West Hollywood yielded up Eleanor without a struggle, On his advice she was not in evening dress but she was as trim and shining as any cute little blonde out of his past. Eager too – running over with enthusiasm and gratitude. He must think of someone whose apartment he could borrow for tomorrow.

'You'd like a test?' he asked as they entered the Brown Derby bar.

'What girl wouldn't?'

'Some wouldn't – for a million dollars.' Pat had had setbacks in his love life. 'Some of them would rather go on pounding the keys or just hanging around. You'd be surprised.'

'I'd do almost anything for a test,' Eleanor said.

Looking at her two hours later he wondered honestly to himself if it couldn't be arranged. There was Harry Gooddorf – there was Jack Berners – but his credit was low on all sides. He could do *something* for her, he decided. He would try at least to get an agent interested – if all went well tomorrow.

'What are you doing tomorrow?' he asked.

'Nothing,' she answered promptly. 'Hadn't we better eat and get to the preview?'

'Sure, sure.'

He made a further inroad on his bank account to pay for his six whiskeys – you certainly had the right to celebrate before your own preview – and took her into the restaurant for dinner. They ate little. Eleanor was too excited – Pat had taken his calories in another form.

It was a long time since he had seen a picture with his name on it. Pat Hobby. As a man of the people he always appeared in the credit titles as Pat Hobby. It would be nice to see it again and though he did not expect his old friends to stand up and sing *Happy Birthday to You*, he was sure there would be back-slapping and even a little turn of attention toward him as the crowd swayed out of the theatre. That would be nice.

'I'm frightened,' said Eleanor as they walked through the alley of packed fans.

'They're looking at you,' he said confidently. 'They look at that pretty pan and try to think if you're an actress.'

A fan shoved an autograph album and pencil toward Eleanor but Pat moved her firmly along. It was late – the equivalent of 'all aboard' was being shouted around the entrance.

'Show your tickets, please sir.'

Pat opened the envelope and handed them to the doorman. Then he said to Eleanor:

'The seats are reserved – it doesn't matter that we're late.'

She pressed close to him, clinging – it was, as it turned out, the high point of her debut. Less than three steps inside the theatre a hand fell on Pat's shoulder.

'Hey Buddy, these aren't tickets for here.'

Before they knew it they were back outside the door, glared at with suspicious eyes.

'I'm Pat Hobby. I wrote this picture.'

For an instant credulity wandered to his side. Then the hard-boiled doorman sniffed at Pat and stepped in close.

'Buddy you're drunk. These are tickets to another show.'

Eleanor looked and felt uneasy but Pat was cool.

'Go inside and ask Jack Berners,' Pat said. 'He'll tell you.'

'Now listen,' said the husky guard, 'these are tickets for a burlesque down in L.A.' He was steadily edging Pat to the side.'You go to your show, you and your girl friend. And be happy.'

'You don't understand. I wrote this picture.'

'Sure. In a pipe dream.'

'Look at the programme. My name's on it. I'm Pat Hobby.'

'Can you prove it? Let's see your auto licence.'

As Pat handed it over he whispered to Eleanor, 'Don't worry!'

'This doesn't say Pat Hobby,' announced the doorman. 'This says the car's owned by the North Hollywood Finance and Loan Company. Is that you?'

For once in his life Pat could think of nothing to say – he cast one quick glance at Eleanor. Nothing in her face indicated that he was anything but what he thought he was – all alone.

III

Though the preview crowd had begun to drift away, with that vague American wonder as to why they had come at all, one little cluster found something arresting and poignant in the faces of Pat and Eleanor. They were obviously gate-crashers, outsiders like themselves, but the crowd resented the temerity of their effort to get in – a temerity which the crowd did not share. Little jeering jests were audible. Then, with Eleanor already edging away from the distasteful scene, there was a flurry by the door. A well-dressed six-footer strode out of the theatre and stood gazing till he saw Pat.

'There you are!' he shouted.

Pat recognized Ward Wainwright.

'Go in and look at it!' Wainwright roared. 'Look at it. Here's some ticket stubs! I think the prop boy directed it! Go and look!' To the doorman he said: 'It's all right! *He* wrote it. I wouldn't have my name on an inch of it.'

Trembling with frustration, Wainwright threw up his hands and strode off into the curious crowd.

Eleanor was terrified. But the same spirit that had inspired 'I'd do anything to get in the movies', kept her standing there – though she felt invisible fingers reaching forth to drag her back to Boise. She had been intending to run – hard and fast. The hard-boiled doorman and the tall stranger had crystallized her feelings that Pat was 'rather simple'.

She would never let those red-rimmed eyes come close to her – at least for any more than a doorstep kiss. She was saving herself for somebody – and it wasn't Pat. Yet she felt that the lingering crowd was a tribute to her – such as she had never exacted before. Several times she threw a glance at the crowd – a glance that now changed from wavering fear into a sort of queenliness.

She felt exactly like a star.

Pat, too, was all confidence. This was *his* preview; all had been delivered into his hands: his name would stand alone on the screen when the picture was released. There had to be *some*body's name, didn't there? – and Wainwright had withdrawn.

SCREENPLAY BY PAT HOBBY.

He seized Eleanor's elbow in a firm grasp and steered her triumphantly towards the door:

'Cheer up, baby. That's the way it is. You see?'

NO HARM TRYING

I

Pat Hobby's apartment lay athwart a delicatessen shop on Wilshire Boulevard. And there lay Pat himself, surrounded by his books – the *Motion Picture Almanac* of 1928 and *Barton's Track Guide, 1939* – by his pictures, authentically signed photographs of Mabel Normand and Barbara LaMarr (who, being deceased, had no value in the pawn shops) – and by his dogs in their cracked leather oxfords, perched on the arm of a slanting settee.

Pat was at 'the end of his resources' – though this term is too ominous to describe a fairly usual condition in his life. He was an old timer in pictures; he had once known sumptuous living, but for the past ten years jobs had been hard to hold – harder to hold than glasses.

'Think of it,' he often mourned. 'Only a writer – at forty-nine.'

All this afternoon he had turned the pages of *The Times* and *The Examiner* for an idea. Though he did not intend to compose a motion picture from this idea, he needed it to get him inside a studio. If you had nothing to submit it was increasingly difficult to pass the gate. But though these two newspapers, together with *Life*, were the sources most commonly combed for 'originals', they yielded him nothing this afternoon. There were wars, a fire in Topanga Canyon, press releases from the studios, municipal corruptions, and always the redeeming deeds of 'The Trojuns', but Pat found nothing that competed in human interest with the betting page.

– If I could get out to Santa Anita, he thought – I could maybe get an idea about the nags.

This cheering idea was interrupted by his landlord, from the delicatessen store below.

'I told you I wouldn't deliver any more messages,' said Nick, 'and *still* I won't. But Mr Carl Le Vigne is telephoning in person from the studio and wants you should go over right away.'

The prospect of a job did something to Pat. It anaesthetized the crumbled, struggling remnants of his manhood, and inoculated him instead with a bland, easy-going confidence. The set speeches and attitudes of success returned to him. His manner as he winked at a studio policeman, stopped to chat with Louie, the bookie, and presented himself to Mr Le Vigne's secretary, indicated that he had been engaged with momentous tasks in other parts of the globe. By saluting Le Vigne with a facetious 'Hel-*lo* Captain!' he behaved almost as an equal, a trusted lieutenant who had never really been away.

'Pat, your wife's in the hospital,' Le Vigne said, 'It'll probably be in the papers this afternoon.'

Pat started.

'My wife?' he said. 'What wife?'

'Estelle. She tried to cut her wrists.'

'Estelle!' Pat exclaimed, 'You mean *Estelle*? Say, I was only married to her three weeks!'

'She was the best girl you ever had,' said Le Vigne grimly.

'I haven't even heard of her for ten years.'

'You're hearing about her now. They called all the studios trying to locate you.'

'I had nothing to do with it.'

'I know – she's only been here a week. She had a run of hard luck wherever it was she lived – New Orleans? Husband died, child died, no money . . .'

Pat breathed easier. They weren't trying to hang anything on him.

'Anyhow she'll live,' Le Vigne reassured him superfluously, '– and she was the best script girl on the lot once. We'd like to take care of her. We thought the way was give you a job. Not exactly a job, because I know you're not up to it.' He glanced into Pat's red-rimmed eyes. 'More of a sinecure.'

Pat became uneasy. He didn't recognize the word, but 'sin' disturbed him and 'cure' brought a whole flood of unpleasant memories.

'You're on the payroll at two-fifty a week for three weeks,' said Le Vigne, '– but one-fifty of that goes to the hospital for your wife's bill.'

'But we're divorced!' Pat protested, 'No Mexican stuff either. I've been married since, and so has –'

'Take it or leave it. You can have an office here, and if anything you can do comes up we'll let you know.'

'I never worked for a hundred a week.'

'We're not asking you to work. If you want you can stay home.'

Pat reversed his field.

'Oh, I'll work,' he said quickly. 'You dig me up a good story and I'll show you whether I can work or not.'

Le Vigne wrote something on a slip of paper.

'All right. They'll find you an office.'

Outside Pat looked at the memorandum.

'Mrs John Devlin,' it read, 'Good Samaritan Hospital.'

The very words irritated him.

'Good Samaritan!' he exclaimed, 'Good gyp joint! One hundred and fifty bucks a week.'

II

Pat had been given many a charity job but this was the first one that made him feel ashamed. He did not mind not *earning* his salary, but not getting it was another matter. And he wondered if other people on the lot who were obviously doing nothing, were being fairly paid for it. There were, for example, a number of beautiful young ladies who walked aloof as stars, and whom Pat took for stock girls, until Eric, the callboy, told him they were imports from Vienna and Budapest, not yet cast for pictures. Did half their pay-checks go to keep husbands they had only had for three weeks?

The loveliest of these was Lizzette Starheim, a violet-eyed little blonde with an ill-concealed air of disillusion. Pat saw her alone at tea almost every afternoon in the commissary – and made her acquaintance one day by simply sliding into a chair opposite.

'Hello, Lizzette,' he said. 'I'm Pat Hobby, the writer.'

'Oh, hello!'

She flashed such a dazzling smile that for a moment he thought she must have heard of him.

'When they going to cast you?' he demanded.

'I don't know.' Her accent was faint and poignant.

'Don't let them give you the run-around. Not with a face like yours.' Her beauty roused a rusty eloquence. 'Sometimes they just keep you under contract till your teeth fall out, because you look too much like their big star.'

'Oh no,' she said distressfully.

'Oh yes!' he assured her, 'I'm telling *you*. Why don't you go to another company and get borrowed? Have you thought of that idea?'

'I think it's wonderful.'

He intended to go further into the subject but Miss Starheim looked at her watch and got up.

'I must go now, Mr –'

'Hobby, Pat Hobby.'

Pat joined Dutch Waggoner, the director, who was shooting dice with a waitress at another table.

'Between pictures, Dutch?'

'Between pictures hell!' said Dutch. 'I haven't done a picture for six months and my contract's got six months to run. I'm trying to break it. Who was the little blonde?'

Afterwards, back in his office, Pat discussed these encounters with Eric the callboy.

'All signed up and no place to go,' said Eric. 'Look at this Jeff Manfred, now – an associate producer! Sits in his office and sends notes to the big shots – and I carry back word they're in Palm Springs. It breaks my heart. Yesterday he put his head on his desk and boo-hoo'd.'

'What's the answer?' asked Pat.

'Changa management,' suggested Eric, darkly. 'Shake-up coming.'

'Who's going to the top?' Pat asked, with scarcely concealed excitement.

'Nobody knows,' said Eric. 'But wouldn't I like to land up-hill! Boy! I want a writer's job. I got three ideas so new they're wet behind the ears.'

'It's no life at all,' Pat assured him with conviction. 'I'd trade with you right now.'

In the hall next day he intercepted Jeff Manfred who walked with the unconvincing hurry of one without a destination.

'What's the rush, Jeff?' Pat demanded, falling into step.

'Reading some scripts,' Jeff panted without conviction.

Pat drew him unwillingly into his office.

'Jeff, have you heard about the shake-up?'

'Listen now, Pat –' Jeff looked nervously at the walls. 'What shake-up?' he demanded.

'I heard that this Harmon Shaver is going to be the new boss,' ventured Pat. 'Wall Street control.'

'Harmon Shaver!' Jeff scoffed. 'He doesn't know anything about pictures – he's just a money man. He wanders around like a lost soul.' Jeff sat back and considered. 'Still – if you're *right*, he'd be a man you could get to.' He turned mournful eyes on Pat. 'I haven't been able to see Le Vigne or Barnes or Bill Behrer for a month. Can't get an assignment, can't get an actor, can't get a story.' He broke off. 'I've thought of drumming up something on my own. Got any ideas?'

'Have I?' said Pat. 'I got three ideas so new they're wet behind the ears.'

'Who for?'

'Lizzette Starheim,' said Pat, 'with Dutch Waggoner directing – see?'

III

'I'm with you all a hundred per cent,' said Harmon Shaver. 'This is the most encouraging experience I've had in pictures.' He had a bright bond-salesman's chuckle. 'By God, it reminds me of a circus we got up when I was a boy.'

They had come to his office inconspicuously like conspirators – Jeff Manfred, Waggoner, Miss Starheim and Pat Hobby.

'You like the idea, Miss Starheim?' Shaver continued,

'I think it's wonderful.'

'And you, Mr Waggoner?'

'I've heard only the general line,' said Waggoner with director's caution, 'but it seems to have the old emotional socko.' He winked at Pat. 'I didn't know this old tramp had it in him.'

Pat glowed with pride. Jeff Manfred, though he was elated, was less sanguine.

'It's important nobody talks,' he said nervously. 'The Big Boys would find some way of killing it. In a week, when we've got the script done we'll go to them.'

'I agree,' said Shaver. 'They have run the studio so long that, well, I don't trust my own secretaries – I sent them to the races this afternoon.'

Back in Pat's office Eric, the callboy, was waiting. He did not know that he was the hinge upon which swung a great affair.

'You like the stuff, eh?' he asked eagerly.

'Pretty good,' said Pat with calculated indifference,

'You said you'd pay more for the next batch.'

'Have a heart!' Pat was aggrieved. 'How many callboys get seventy-five a week?'

'How many callboys can write?'

Pat considered. Out of the two hundred a week Jeff Manfred was advancing from his own pocket, he had naturally awarded himself a commission of sixty per cent.

'I'll make it a hundred,' he said. 'Now check yourself off the lot and meet me in front of Benny's bar.'

At the hospital, Estelle Hobby Devlin sat up in bed, overwhelmed by the unexpected visit.

'I'm glad you came, Pat,' she said, 'you've been very kind. Did you get my note?'

'Forget it,' Pat said gruffly. He had never liked this wife. She had loved him too much – until she found suddenly that he was a poor lover. In her presence he felt inferior.

'I got a guy outside,' he said.

'What for?'

'I thought maybe you had nothing to do and you might want to pay me back for all this jack –'

He waved his hand around the bare hospital room.

'You were a swell script girl once. Do you think if I got a typewriter you could put some good stuff into continuity?'

'Why – yes. I suppose I could.'

'It's a secret. We can't trust anybody at the studio.'

'All right,' she said.

'I'll send this kid in with the stuff. I got a conference.'

'All right – and – oh Pat – come and see me again.'

'Sure, I'll come.'

But he knew he wouldn't. He didn't like sick rooms – he lived in one himself. From now on he was done with poverty and failure. He admired strength – he was taking Lizzette Starheim to a wrestling match that night.

IV

In his private musings Harmon Shaver referred to the showdown as 'the surprise party'. He was going to confront Le Vigne with a *fait accompli* and he gathered his coterie before phoning Le Vigne to come over to his office.

'What for?' demanded Le Vigne. 'Couldn't you tell me now – I'm busy as hell.'

This arrogance irritated Shaver – who was here to watch over the interest of Eastern stockholders.

'I don't ask much,' he said sharply. 'I let you fellows laugh at me behind my back and freeze me out of things. But now I've got something and I'd like you to come over.'

'All right – all right.'

Le Vigne's eyebrows lifted as he saw the members of the new production unit but he said nothing – sprawled into an armchair with his eyes on the floor and his fingers over his mouth.

Mr Shaver came around the desk and poured forth words that had been fermenting in him for months. Simmered to its essentials, his protest was: 'You would not let me play, but I'm going to play anyhow.' Then he nodded to Jeff Manfred – who opened the script and read aloud. This took an hour, and still Le Vigne sat motionless and silent.

'There you are,' said Shaver triumphantly. 'Unless you've got any objection I think we ought to assign a budget to this proposition and get going. I'll answer to my people.'

Le Vigne spoke at last.

'You like it, Miss Starheim?'

'I think it's wonderful.'

'What language you going to play it in?'

To everyone's surprise Miss Starheim got to her feet.

'I must go now,' she said with her faint poignant accent.

'Sit down and answer me,' said Le Vigne. 'What language are you playing it in?'

Miss Starheim looked tearful.

'Wenn I gute teachers hätte konnte ich dann thees role gut spielen,' she faltered.

'But you like the script.'

She hesitated.

'I think it's wonderful.'

Le Vigne turned to the others.

'Miss Starheim has been here eight months,' he said. 'She's had three teachers. Unless things have changed in the past two weeks she can say just three sentences, She can say, "How do you do"; she can say "I think it's wonderful"; and she can say "I must go now." Miss Starheim has turned out to be a pinhead – I'm not insulting her because she doesn't know what it means. Anyhow – there's your Star.'

He turned to Dutch Waggoner, but Dutch was already on his feet.

'Now Carl –' he said defensively.

'You force me to it,' said Le Vigne. 'I've trusted drunks up to a point, but I'll be goddam if I'll trust a hophead.'

He turned to Harmon Shaver.

'Dutch has been good for exactly one week apiece on his last four pictures. He's all right now but as soon as the heat goes on he reaches for the little white powders. Now Dutch! Don't say anything you'll regret. We're carrying you in *hopes* – but you won't get on a stage till we've had a doctor's certificate for a year.'

Again he turned to Harmon.

'There's your director. Your supervisor, Jeff Manfred, is here for one reason only – because he's Behrer's wife's cousin. There's nothing against him but he belongs to silent days as much as – as much as –' His eyes fell upon a quavering broken man, '– as much as Pat Hobby.'

'What do you mean?' demanded Jeff.

'You trusted Hobby, didn't you? That tells the whole story.' He turned back to Shaver. 'Jeff's a weeper and a wisher and a dreamer. Mr Shaver, you have bought a lot of condemned building material.'

'Well, I've bought a good story,' said Shaver defiantly.

'Yes. That's right. We'll make that story.'

'Isn't that something?' demanded Shaver. 'With all this secrecy how was I to know about Mr Waggoner and Miss Starheim? But I do know a good story.'

'Yes,' said Le Vigne absently. He got up. 'Yes – it's a good story . . . Come along to my office, Pat.'

He was already at the door. Pat cast an agonized look at Mr Shaver as if for support. Then, weakly, he followed.

'Sit down, Pat.'

'That Eric's got talent, hasn't he?' said Le Vigne. 'He'll go places. How'd you come to dig him up?'

Pat felt the straps of the electric chair being adjusted.

'Oh – I just dug him up. He – came in my office.'

'We're putting him on salary,' said Le Vigne. 'We ought to have some system to give these kids a chance.'

He took a call on his Dictograph, then swung back to Pat.

'But how did you ever get mixed up with this goddam Shaver. *You*, Pat – an old timer like you.'

'Well, I thought –'

'Why doesn't he go back East?' continued Le Vigne disgustedly. 'Getting all you poops stirred up!'

Blood flowed back into Pat's veins. He recognized his signal, his dog-call.

'Well, I got you a story, didn't I?' he said, with almost a swagger. And he added, 'How'd you know about it?'

'I went down to see Estelle in the hospital. She and this kid were working on it. I walked right in on them.'

'Oh,' said Pat.

'I knew the kid by sight. Now, Pat, tell me this – did Jeff Manfred think you wrote it – or was he in on the racket?'

'Oh God,' Pat mourned. 'What do I have to answer that for?'

Le Vigne leaned forward intensely.

'Pat, you're sitting over a trap door!' he said with savage eyes. 'Do you see how the carpet's cut? I just have to press this button and drop you down to hell! Will you *talk*?'

Pat was on his feet, staring wildly at the floor.

'Sure I will!' he cried. He believed it – he believed such things.

'All right,' said Le Vigne relaxing. 'There's whiskey in the sideboard there. Talk quick and I'll give you another month at two-fifty. I kinda like having you around.'

A PATRIOTIC SHORT

Pat Hobby, the writer and the man, had his great success in Hollywood during what Irving Cobb refers to as 'the mosaic swimming-pool age – just before the era when they had to have a shinbone of St Sebastian for a clutch lever.'

Mr Cobb no doubt exaggerates, for when Pat had his pool in those fat days of silent pictures, it was entirely cement, unless you should count the cracks where the water stubbornly sought its own level through the mud.

'But it *was* a pool,' he assured himself one afternoon more than a decade later. Though he was now more than grateful for this small chore he had assigned him by producer Berners – one week at two-fifty – all the insolence of office could not take that memory away.

He had been called in to the studio to work upon an humble short. It was based on the career of General Fitzhugh Lee who fought for the Confederacy and later for the U.S.A. against Spain – so it would offend neither North nor South. And in the recent conference Pat had tried to co-operate.

'I was thinking –' he suggested to Jack Berners '– that it might be a good thing if we could give it a Jewish touch.'

'What do you mean?' demanded Jack Berners quickly.

'Well I thought – the way things are and all, it would be a sort of good thing to show that there were a number of Jews in it too.'

'In what?'

'In the Civil War.' Quickly he reviewed his meagre history. 'They were, weren't they?'

'Naturally,' said Berners, with some impatience, 'I suppose everybody was except the Quakers.'

'Well, my idea was that we could have this Fitzhugh Lee in love with a Jewish girl. He's going to be shot at curfew so she grabs a church bell –'

Jack Berners leaned forward earnestly.

'Say, Pat, you want this job, don't you? Well, I told you the story.

You got the first script. If you thought up this tripe to please me you're losing your grip.'

Was that a way to treat a man who had once owned a pool which had been talked about by –

That was how he happened to be thinking about his long lost swimming pool as he entered the shorts department. He was remembering a certain day over a decade ago in all its details, how he had arrived at the studio in his car driven by a Filipino in uniform; the deferential bow of the guard at the gate which had admitted car and all to the lot, his ascent to that long lost office which had a room for the secretary and was really a director's office . . .

His reverie was broken off by the voice of Ben Brown, head of the shorts department, who walked him into his own chambers.

'Jack Berners just phoned me,' he said. 'We don't want any new angles, Pat. We've got a good story. Fitzhugh Lee was a dashing cavalry commander. He was a nephew of Robert E. Lee and we want to show him at Appomattox, pretty bitter and all that. And then show how he became reconciled – we'll have to be careful because Virginia is swarming with Lees – and how he finally accepts a U.S. commission from President McKinley –'

Pat's mind darted back again into the past. The President – that was the magic word that had gone around that morning many years ago. The President of the United States was going to make a visit to the lot. Everyone had been agog about it – it seemed to mark a new era in pictures because a President of the United States had never visited a studio before. The executives of the company were all dressed up – from a window of his long lost Beverly Hills house Pat had seen Mr Maranda, whose mansion was next door to him, bustle down his walk in a cutaway coat at nine o'clock, and had known that something was up. He thought maybe it was clergy but when he reached the lot he had found it was the President of the United States himself who was coming . . .

'Clean up the stuff about Spain,' Ben Brown was saying. 'The guy that wrote it was a Red and he's got all the Spanish officers with ants in their pants. Fix up that.'

In the office assigned him Pat looked at the script of *True to Two Flags*. The first scene showed General Fitzhugh Lee at the head of his cavalry receiving word that Petersburg had been evacuated. In the script Lee took the blow in pantomime, but Pat was getting two-fifty a week – so, casually and without effort, he wrote in one of his favourite lines:

Lee (to his officers)
Well, what are you standing here gawking for? DO *something!*
6. *Medium Shot Officers pepping up, slapping each other on back, etc.*

Dissolve to:

To what? Pat's mind dissolved once more into the glamorous past.
On that happy day in the twenties his phone had rung at about noon,
It had been Mr Maranda.

'Pat, the President is lunching in the private dining room. Doug
Fairbanks can't come so there's a place empty and anyhow we think
there ought to be one writer there.'

His memory of the luncheon was palpitant with glamour. The Great
Man had asked some questions about pictures and had told a joke and
Pat had laughed and laughed with the others – all of them solid men
together – rich, happy and successful.

Afterwards the President was to go on some sets and see some scenes
taken and still later he was going to Mr Maranda's house to meet some
of the women stars at tea. Pat was not invited to that party but he went
home early anyhow and from his veranda saw the cortège drive up,
with Mr Maranda beside the President in the back seat. Ah he was proud
of pictures then – of his position in them – of the President of the happy
country where he was born . . .

Returning to reality Pat looked down at the script of *True to Two Flags*
and wrote slowly and thoughtfully:

*Insert: A calendar – with the years plainly marked and the sheets blowing off in a cold
wind, to show Fitzhugh Lee growing older and older.*

His labours had made him thirsty – not for water, but he knew better
than to take anything else his first day on the job. He got up and went
out into the hall and along the corridor to the water-cooler.

As he walked he slipped back into his reverie.

That had been a lovely California afternoon so Mr Maranda had taken
his exalted guest and the coterie of stars into his garden, which adjoined
Pat's garden. Pat had gone out his back door and followed a low privet
hedge keeping out of sight – and then accidentally come face to face
with the Presidential party.

The President had smiled and nodded. Mr Maranda smiled and nodded.

'You met Mr Hobby at lunch,' Mr Maranda said to the President.
'He's one of our writers.'

'Oh yes,' said the President, 'you write the pictures.'

'Yes I do,' said Pat.

The President glanced over into Pat's property.

'I suppose –' he said, '– that you get lots of inspiration sitting by the side of that fine pool.'

'Yes,' said Pat, 'yes, I do.'

. . . Pat filled his cup at the cooler. Down the hall there was a group approaching – Jack Berners, Ben Brown and several other executives and with them a girl to whom they were very attentive and deferential. He recognized her face – she was the girl of the year, the It girl, the Oomph girl, the Glamour Girl, the girl for whose services every studio was in violent competition.

Pat lingered over his drink. He had seen many phonies break in and break out again, but this girl was the real thing, someone to stir every pulse in the nation. He felt his own heart beat faster. Finally, as the procession drew near, he put down the cup, dabbed at his hair with his hand and took a step out into the corridor.

The girl looked at him – he looked at the girl. Then she took one arm of Jack Berners' and one of Ben Brown's and suddenly the party seemed to walk right through him – so that he had to take a step back against the wall.

An instant later Jack Berners turned around and said back to him, 'Hello, Pat.' And then some of the others threw half glances around but no one else spoke, so interested were they in the girl.

In his office, Pat looked at the scene where President McKinley offers a United States commission to Fitzhugh Lee. Suddenly he gritted his teeth and bore down on his pencil as he wrote:

Lee
Mr President, you can take your commission and go straight to hell.

Then he bent down over his desk, his shoulders shaking as he thought of that happy day when he had had a swimming pool.

ON THE TRAIL OF
PAT HOBBY

I

The day was dark from the outset, and a California fog crept everywhere. It had followed Pat in his headlong, hatless flight across the city. His destination, his refuge, was the studio, where he was not employed but which had been home to him for twenty years.

Was it his imagination or did the policeman at the gate give him and his pass an especially long look? It might be the lack of a hat – Hollywood was full of hatless men but Pat felt marked, especially as there had been no opportunity to part his thin grey hair.

In the Writers' Building he went into the lavatory. Then he remembered: by some inspired ukase from above, all mirrors had been removed from the Writers' Building a year ago.

Across the hall he saw Bee McIlvaine's door ajar, and discerned her plump person.

'Bee, can you loan me your compact box?' he asked.

Bee looked at him suspiciously, then frowned and dug it from her purse.

'You on the lot?' she inquired.

'Will be next week,' he prophesied. He put the compact on her desk and bent over it with his comb. 'Why won't they put mirrors back in the johnnies? Do they think writers would look at themselves all day?'

'Remember when they took out the couches?' said Bee. 'In nineteen thirty-two. And they put them back in thirty-four.'

'I worked at home,' said Pat feelingly.

Finished with her mirror he wondered if she were good for a loan – enough to buy a hat and something to eat. Bee must have seen the look in his eyes for she forestalled him.

'The Finns got all my money,' she said, 'and I'm worried about my job. Either my picture starts tomorrow or it's going to be shelved. We haven't even got a title.'

She handed him a mimeographed bulletin from the scenario department and Pat glanced at the headline.

TO ALL DEPARTMENTS
  TITLE WANTED – FIFTY DOLLARS REWARD
    SUMMARY FOLLOWS

'I could use fifty,' Pat said. 'What's it about?'

'It's written there. It's about a lot of stuff that goes on in tourist cabins.'

Pat started and looked at her wild-eyed. He had thought to be safe here behind the guarded gates but news travelled fast. This was a friendly or perhaps not so friendly warning. He must move on. He was a hunted man now, with nowhere to lay his hatless head.

'I don't know anything about that,' he mumbled and walked hastily from the room.

II

Just inside the door of the commissary Pat looked around. There was no guardian except the girl at the cigarette stand but obtaining another person's hat was subject to one complication: it was hard to judge the size by a cursory glance, while the sight of a man trying on several hats in a check room was unavoidably suspicious.

Personal taste also obtruded itself. Pat was beguiled by a green fedora with a sprightly feather but it was too readily identifiable. This was also true of a fine white Stetson for the open spaces. Finally he decided on a sturdy grey Homburg which looked as if it would give him good service. With trembling hands he put it on. It fitted. He walked out – in painful, interminable slow motion.

His confidence was partly restored in the next hour by the fact that no one he encountered made references to tourists' cabins. It had been a lean three months for Pat. He had regarded his job as night clerk for the Selecto Tourists Cabins as a mere fill-in, never to be mentioned to his friends. But when the police squad came this morning they held up the raid long enough to assure Pat, or Don Smith as he called himself, that he would be wanted as a witness. The story of his escape lies in the realm of melodrama, how he went out a side door, bought a half pint of what he so desperately needed at the corner drug-store, hitch-hiked his way across the great city, going limp at the sight of traffic cops and only breathing free when he saw the studio's high-flown sign.

After a call on Louie, the studio bookie, whose great patron he once had been, he dropped in on Jack Berners. He had no idea to submit, but he caught Jack in a hurried moment flying off to a producers' conference and was unexpectedly invited to step in and wait for his return.

The office was rich and comfortable. There were no letters worth reading on the desk, but there were a decanter and glasses in a cupboard and presently he lay down on a big soft couch and fell asleep.

He was awakened by Berners' return, in high indignation.

'Of all the damn nonsense! We get a hurry call – heads of all departments. One man is late and we wait for him. He comes in and gets a bawling out for wasting thousands of dollars worth of time. Then what do you suppose: Mr Marcus has lost his favourite hat!'

Pat failed to associate the fact with himself.

'All the department heads stop production!' continued Berners. 'Two thousand people look for a grey Homburg hat!' He sank despairingly into a chair. 'I can't talk to you today, Pat. By four o'clock, I've got to get a title to a picture about a tourist camp. Got an idea?'

'No,' said Pat. 'No.'

'Well, go up to Bee McIlvaine's office and help her figure something out. There's fifty dollars in it.'

In a daze Pat wandered to the door.

'Hey,' said Berners, 'don't forget your hat.'

III

Feeling the effects of his day outside the law, and of a tumbler full of Berners' brandy, Pat sat in Bee McIlvaine's office.

'We've got to get a title,' said Bee gloomily.

She handed Pat the mimeograph offering fifty dollars reward and put a pencil in his hand. Pat stared at the paper unseeingly.

'How about it?' she asked. 'Who's got a title?'

There was a long silence.

'*Test Pilot*'s been used, hasn't it?' he said with a vague tone.

'Wake up! This isn't about aviation.'

'Well, I was just thinking it was a good title.'

'So's *The Birth of a Nation*.'

'But not for this picture,' Pat muttered. '*Birth of a Nation* wouldn't suit this picture.'

'But not for this picture,' Pat muttered. '*Birth of a Nation* wouldn't suit this picture.'

'Are you ribbing me?' demanded Bee. 'Or are you losing your mind? This is serious.'

'Sure – I know.' Feebly he scrawled words at the bottom of the page. 'I've had a couple of drinks that's all. My head'll clear up in a minute. I'm trying to think what have been the most successful titles. The trouble is they've all been used, like *It Happened One Night*.'

Bee looked at him uneasily. He was having trouble keeping his eyes open and she did not want him to pass out in her office. After a minute she called Jack Berners.

'Could you possibly come up? I've got some title ideas.'

Jack arrived with a sheaf of suggestions sent in from here and there in the studio, but digging through them yielded no ore.

'How about it, Pat? Got anything?'

Pat braced himself to an effort.

'I like *It Happened One Morning*,' he said – then looked desperately at his scrawl on the mimeograph paper, 'or else – *Grand Motel*.'

Berners smiled.

'*Grand Motel*,' he repeated. 'By God! I think you've got something. *Grand Motel*.'

'I said *Grand Hotel*,' said Pat.

'No, you didn't. You said *Grand Motel* – and for my money it wins the fifty.'

'I've got to go lie down,' announced Pat. 'I feel sick.'

'There's an empty office across the way. That's a funny idea Pat, *Grand Motel* – or else *Motel Clerk*. How do you like that?'

As the fugitive quickened his step out the door Bee pressed the hat into his hands.

'Good work, old timer,' she said.

Pat seized Mr Marcus' hat, and stood holding it there like a bowl of soup.

'Feel – better – now,' he mumbled after a moment. 'Be back for the money.'

And carrying his burden he shambled toward the lavatory.

FUN IN AN
ARTIST'S STUDIO

I

This was back in 1938 when few people except the Germans knew that they had already won their war in Europe. People still cared about art and tried to make it out of everything from old clothes to orange peel and that was how the Princess Dignanni found Pat. She wanted to make art out of him.

'No, not you, Mr DeTinc.' she said, 'I can't paint you. You are a very standardized product, Mr DeTinc.'

Mr DeTinc, who was a power in pictures and had even been photographed with Mr Duchman, the Secret Sin specialist, stepped smoothly out of the way. He was not offended – in his whole life Mr DeTinc had never been offended – but especially not now, for the Princess did not want to paint Clark Gable or Spencer Rooney or Vivien Leigh either.

She saw Pat in the commissary and found he was a writer, and asked that he be invited to Mr DeTinc's party. The Princess was a pretty woman born in Boston, Massachusetts and Pat was forty-nine with red-rimmed eyes and a soft purr of whiskey on his breath.

'You write scenarios, Mr Hobby?'

'I help,' said Pat. 'Takes more than one person to prepare a script.'

He was flattered by this attention and not a little suspicious. It was only because his supervisor was a nervous wreck that he happened to have a job at all. His supervisor had forgotten a week ago that he had hired Pat, and when Pat was spotted in the commissary and told he was wanted at Mr DeTinc's house, the writer had passed a *mauvais quart d'heure*. It did not even look like the kind of party that Pat had known in his prosperous days. There was not so much as a drunk passed out in the downstairs toilet.

'I imagine scenario writing is very well-paid,' said the Princess.

Pat glanced around to see who was within hearing. Mr DeTinc had withdrawn his huge bulk somewhat, but one of his apparently independent eyes seemed fixed glittering on Pat.

'Very well paid,' said Pat – and he added in a lower voice, '– if you can get it.'

The Princess seemed to understand and lowered her voice too.

'You mean writers have trouble getting work?'

He nodded.

'Too many of 'em get in these unions.' He raised his voice a little for Mr DeTinc's benefit. 'They're all Reds, most of these writers.'

The Princess nodded.

'Will you turn your face a little to the light?' she said politely. 'There, that's fine. You won't mind coming to my studio tomorrow, will you? Just to pose for me an hour?'

He scrutinized her again.

'Naked?' he asked cautiously.

'Oh, no,' she averred. 'Just the head.'

Mr DeTinc moved nearer and nodded.

'You ought to go. Princess Dignanni is going to paint some of the biggest stars here. Going to paint Jack Benny and Baby Sandy and Hedy Lamarr – isn't that a fact, Princess?'

The artist didn't answer. She was a pretty good portrait painter and she knew just how good she was and just how much of it was her title. She was hesitating between her several manners – Picasso's rose period with a flash of Boldini, or straight Reginald Marsh. But she knew what she was going to call it. She was going to call it Hollywood and Vine.

II

In spite of the reassurance that he would be clothed Pat approached the rendezvous with uneasiness. In his young and impressionable years he had looked through a peep-hole into a machine where two dozen postcards slapped before his eyes in sequence. The story unfolded was *Fun in an Artist's Studio*. Even now with the strip tease a legalized municipal project, he was a little shocked at the remembrance, and when he presented himself next day at the Princess's bungalow at the Beverly Hills Hotel it would not have surprised him if she had met him in a turkish towel. He was disappointed. She wore a smock and her black hair was brushed straight back like a boy's.

Pat had stopped off for a couple of drinks on the way, but his first words: 'How'ya Duchess?' failed to set a jovial note for the occasion.

'Well, Mr Hobby,' she said coolly, 'it's nice of you to spare me an afternoon.'

'We don't work too hard in Hollywood,' he assured her. 'Everything is "Mañana" – in Spanish that means tomorrow.'

She led him forthwith into a rear apartment where an easel stood on a square of canvas by the window. There was a couch and they sat down.

'I want to get used to you for a minute,' she said. 'Did you ever pose before?'

'Do I look that way?' He winked, and when she smiled he felt better and asked: 'You haven't got a drink around, have you?'

The Princess hesitated. She had wanted him to look as if he *needed* one. Compromising, she went to the ice box and fixed him a small highball. She returned to find that he had taken off his coat and tie and lay informally upon the couch.

'That *is* better,' the Princess said. 'That shirt you're wearing. I think they make them for Hollywood – like the special prints they make for Ceylon and Guatemala. Now drink this and we'll get to work.'

'Why don't you have a drink too and make it friendly?' Pat suggested.

'I had one in the pantry,' she lied.

'Married woman?' he asked.

'I have been married. Now would you mind sitting on this stool?'

Reluctantly Pat got up, took down the highball, somewhat thwarted by the thin taste, and moved to the stool. 'Now sit very still,' she said.

He sat silent as she worked. It was three o'clock. They were running the third race at Santa Anita and he had ten bucks on the nose. That made sixty he owed Louie, the studio bookie, and Louie stood determinedly beside him at the pay window every Thursday. This dame had good legs under the easel – her red lips pleased him and the way her bare arms moved as she worked. Once upon a time he wouldn't have looked at a woman over twenty-five, unless it was a secretary right in the office with him. But the kids you saw around now were snooty – always talking about calling the police.

'Please sit still, Mr Hobby.'

'What say we knock off,' he suggested. 'This work makes you thirsty.'

The Princess had been painting half an hour. Now she stopped and stared at him a moment.

'Mr Hobby, you were loaned me by Mr DeTinc. Why don't you act just as if you were working over at the studio? I'll be through in another half-hour.'

'What do I get out of it?' he demanded, 'I'm no poser – I'm a writer.'

'Your studio salary has not stopped,' she said, resuming her work. 'What does it matter if Mr DeTinc wants you to do this?'

'It's different. You're a dame. I've got my self-respect to think of.'

'What do you expect me to do – flirt with you?'

'No – that's old stuff. But I thought we could sit around and have a drink.'

'Perhaps later,' she said, and then, 'Is this harder work than the studio? Am I so difficult to look at?'

'I don't mind looking at you but why couldn't we sit on the sofa?'

'You don't sit on the sofa at the studio.'

'Sure you do. Listen, if you tried all the doors in the Writers' Building you'd find a lot of them locked and don't you forget it.'

She stepped back and squinted at him.

'Locked? To be undisturbed?' She put down her brush. 'I'll get you a drink.'

When she returned she stopped for a moment in the doorway – Pat had removed his shirt and stood rather sheepishly in the middle of the floor holding it toward her.

'Here's that shirt,' he said. 'You can have it. I know where I can get a lot more.'

For a moment longer she regarded him; then she took the shirt and put it on the sofa.

'Sit down and let me finish,' she said. As he hesitated she added, 'Then we'll have a drink together.'

'When'll that be?'

'Fifteen minutes.'

She worked quickly – several times she was content with the lower face – several times she deliberated and started over. Something that she had seen in the commissary was missing.

'Been an artist a long time?' Pat asked.

'Many years.'

'Been around artists' studios a lot?'

'Quite a lot – I've had my own studios.'

'I guess a lot goes on around those studios. Did you ever –'

He hesitated.

'Ever what?' she queried.

'Did you ever paint a naked man?'

'Don't talk for one minute, please.' She paused with brush uplifted, seemed to listen, then made a swift stroke and looked doubtfully at the result.

'Do you know you're difficult to paint?' she said, laying down the brush.

'I don't like this posing around,' he admitted. 'Let's call it a day.' He stood up. 'Why don't you – why don't you slip into something so you'll be comfortable?'

The Princess smiled. She would tell her friends this story – it would sort of go with the picture, if the picture was any good, which she now doubted.

'You ought to revise your methods,' she said. 'Do you have much success with this approach?'

Pat lit a cigarette and sat down.

'If you were eighteen, see, I'd give you that line about being nuts about you.'

'But why any line at all?'

'Oh, come off it!' he advised her. 'You wanted to paint me, didn't you?'

'Yes.'

'Well, when a dame wants to paint a guy –' Pat reached down and undid his shoe strings, kicked his shoes onto the floor, put his stockinged feet on the couch. '– when a dame wants to see a guy about something or a guy wants to see a dame, there's a payoff, see.'

The Princess sighed. 'Well I seem to be trapped,' she said. 'But it makes it rather difficult when a dame just wants to paint a guy.'

'When a dame wants to paint a guy –' Pat half closed his eyes, nodded and flapped his hands expressively. As his thumbs went suddenly toward his suspenders, she spoke in a louder voice.

'Officer!'

There was a sound behind Pat. He turned to see a young man in khaki with shining black gloves, standing in the door.

'Officer, this man is an employee of Mr DeTinc's. Mr DeTinc lent him to me for the afternoon.'

The policeman looked at the staring image of guilt upon the couch.

'Get fresh?' he inquired.

'I don't want to prefer charges – I called the desk to be on the safe side. He was to pose for me in the nude and now he refuses.' She walked casually to her easel. 'Mr Hobby, why don't you stop this mock-modesty – you'll find a turkish towel in the bathroom.'

Pat reached stupidly for his shoes. Somehow it flashed into his mind that they were running the eighth race at Santa Anita –

'Shake it up, you,' said the cop. 'You heard what the lady said.'

Pat stood up vaguely and fixed a long poignant look on the Princess.

'You told me –' he said hoarsely, 'you wanted to paint –'

'You told me I meant something else. Hurry please. And officer, there's a drink in the pantry,'

. . . A few minutes later as Pat sat shivering in the centre of the room his memory went back to those peep-shows of his youth – though at the moment he could see little resemblance. He was grateful at least for the turkish towel, even now failing to realize that the Princess was not interested in his shattered frame but in his face.

It wore the exact expression that had wooed her in the commissary, the expression of Hollywood and Vine, the other self of Mr DeTinc – and she worked fast while there was still light enough to paint by.

TWO OLD-TIMERS

Phil Macedon, once the Star of Stars, and Pat Hobby, script writer, had collided out on Sunset near the Beverly Hills Hotel. It was five in the morning and there was liquor in the air as they argued and Sergeant Gaspar took them around to the station house. Pat Hobby, a man of forty-nine, showed fight, apparently because Phil Macedon failed to acknowledge that they were old acquaintances.

He accidentally bumped Sergeant Gaspar who was so provoked that he put him in a little barred room while they waited for the Captain to arrive.

Chronologically Phil Macedon belonged between Eugene O'Brien and Robert Taylor. He was still a handsome man in his early fifties and he had saved enough from his great days for a hacienda in the San Fernando Valley; there he rested as full of honours, as rolicksome and with the same purposes in life as Man o' War.

With Pat Hobby life had dealt otherwise. After twenty-one years in the industry, script and publicity, the accident found him driving a 1933 car which had lately become the property of the North Hollywood Finance and Loan Co. And once, back in 1928, he had reached a point of getting bids for a private swimming pool.

He glowered from his confinement, still resenting Macedon's failure to acknowledge that they had ever met before.

'I suppose you don't remember Coleman,' he said sarcastically. 'Or Connie Talmadge or Bill Corker or Allan Dwan.'

Macedon lit a cigarette with the sort of timing in which the silent screen has never been surpassed, and offered one to Sergeant Gaspar.

'Couldn't I come in tomorrow?' he asked. 'I have a horse to exercise –'

'I'm sorry, Mr Macedon,' said the cop – sincerely for the actor was an old favourite of his. 'The Captain is due here any minute. After that we won't be holding *you*.'

'It's just a formality,' said Pat, from his cell.

'Yeah, it's just a –' Sergeant Gaspar glared at Pat. 'It may not be any formality for *you*. Did you ever hear of the sobriety test?'

Macedon flicked his cigarette out the door and lit another.

'Suppose I come back in a couple of hours,' he suggested.

'No,' regretted Sergeant Gaspar, 'And since I have to detain you, Mr Macedon, I want to take the opportunity to tell you what you meant to me once. It was that picture you made, *The Final Push*, it meant a lot to every man who was in the war.'

'Oh, yes,' said Macedon, smiling.

'I used to try to tell my wife about the war – how it was, with the shells and the machine guns – I was in there seven months with the 26th New England – but she never understood. She'd point her finger at me and say "Boom! you're dead," and so I'd laugh and stop trying to make her understand.'

'Hey, can I get out of here?' demanded Pat.

'You shut up!' said Gaspar fiercely. 'You probably wasn't in the war.'

'I was in the Motion Picture Home Guard,' said Pat. 'I had bad eyes.'

'Listen to him,' said Gaspar disgustedly. 'That's what all them slackers say. Well, the war was *some*thing. And after my wife saw that picture of yours I never had to explain to her. She knew. She always spoke different about it after that – never just pointed her finger at me and said "Boom!" I'll never forget the part where you was in that shell hole. That was so real it made my hands sweat.'

'Thanks,' said Macedon graciously. He lit another cigarette. 'You see, I was in the war myself and I knew how it was. I knew how it felt.'

'Yes sir,' said Gaspar appreciatively. 'Well; I'm glad of the opportunity to tell you what you did for me. You – you explained the war to my wife.'

'What are you talking about?' demanded Pat Hobby suddenly. 'That war picture Bill Corker did in 1925?'

'There he goes again,' said Gaspar. 'Sure – *The Birth of a Nation*. Now you pipe down till the Captain comes.'

'Phil Macedon knew me then all right,' said Pat resentfully. 'I even watched him work on it one day.'

'I just don't happen to remember you, old man,' said Macedon politely, 'I can't help that.'

'You remember the day Bill Corker shot that shell hole sequence don't you? Your first day on the picture?'

There was a moment's silence.

'When will the Captain be here?' Macedon asked.

'Any minute now,' Mr Macedon.'

'Well, I remember,' said Pat, '– because I was there when he had that shell hole dug. He was out there on the back lot at nine o'clock in the morning with a gang of hunkies to dig the hole and four cameras. He called you up from a field telephone and told you to go to the costumer and get into a soldier suit. Now you remember?'

'I don't load my mind with details, old man.'

'You called up that they didn't have one to fit you and Corker told you to shut up and get into one anyhow. When you got out to the back lot you were sore as hell because your suit didn't fit.'

Macedon smiled charmingly.

'You have a most remarkable memory. Are you sure you have the right picture – and the right actor?' he asked.

'Am I!' said Pat grimly. 'I can see you right now. Only you didn't have much time to complain about the uniform because that wasn't Corker's plan. He always thought you were the toughest ham in Hollywood to get anything natural out of – and he had a scheme. He was going to get the heart of the picture shot by noon – before you even knew you were acting. He turned you around and shoved you down into that shell hole on your fanny, and yelled "Camera".'

'That's a lie,' said Phil Macedon. 'I *got* down.'

'Then why did you start yelling?' demanded Pat. 'I can still hear you: "Hey, what's the idea! Is this some — — gag? You get me out of here or I'll walk out on you!"'

'– and all the time you were trying to claw your way up the side of that pit, so damn mad you couldn't see. You'd almost get up and then you'd slide back and lie there with your face working – till finally you began to bawl and all this time Bill had four cameras on you. After about twenty minutes you gave up and just lay there, heaving. Bill took a hundred feet of that and then he had a couple of prop men pull you out.'

The police Captain had arrived in the squad car. He stood in the doorway against the first grey of dawn.

'What you got here, Sergeant? A drunk?'

Sergeant Gaspar walked over to the cell, unlocked it and beckoned Pat to come out. Pat blinked a moment – then his eyes fell on Phil Macedon and he shook his finger at him.

'So you see I *do* know you,' he said. 'Bill Corker cut that piece of film and titled it so you were supposed to be a doughboy whose pal had just been killed. You wanted to climb out and get at the Germans in revenge, but the shells bursting all around and the concussions kept knocking you back in.'

'What's it about?' demanded the Captain.

'I want to prove I know this guy,' said Pat. 'Bill said the best moment in the picture was when Phil was yelling "I've al*ready* broken my first finger nail!" Bill titled it "Ten Huns will go to hell to shine your shoes!" '

'You've got here "collision with alcohol ",' said the Captain looking at the blotter. 'Let's take these guys down to the hospital and give them the test.'

'Look here now,' said the actor, with his flashing smile, 'my name's Phil Macedon.'

The Captain was a political appointee and very young. He remembered the name and the face but he was not especially impressed because Hollywood was full of has-beens.

They all got into the squad car at the door.

After the test Macedon was held at the station house until friends could arrange bail. Pat Hobby was discharged but his car would not run, so Sergeant Gaspar offered to drive him home.

'Where do you live?' he asked as they started off.

'I don't live anywhere tonight,' said Pat. 'That's why I was driving around. When a friend of mine wakes up I'll touch him for a couple of bucks and go to a hotel.'

'Well now,' said Sergeant Gaspar, 'I got a couple of bucks that ain't working.'

The great mansions of Beverly Hills slid by and Pat waved his hand at them in salute.

'In the good old days,' he said, 'I used to be able to drop into some of those houses day or night. And Sunday mornings –'

'Is that all true you said in the station,' Gaspar asked, '– about how they put him in the hole?'

'Sure, it is,' said Pat. 'That guy needn't have been so upstage. He's just an old-timer like me.'

MIGHTIER THAN THE SWORD

I

The swarthy man, with eyes that snapped back and forward on a rubber band from the rear of his head, answered to the alias of Dick Dale. The tall, spectacled man who was put together like a camel without a hump – and you missed the hump – answered to the name of E. Brunswick Hudson. The scene was a shoeshine stand, insignificant unit of the great studio. We perceive it through the red-rimmed eyes of Pat Hobby who sat in the chair beside Director Dale.

The stand was out of doors, opposite the commissary. The voice of E. Brunswick Hudson quivered with passion but it was pitched low so as not to reach passers-by.

'I don't know what a writer like me is doing out here anyhow,' he said, with vibrations.

Pat Hobby, who was an old-timer, could have supplied the answer, but he had not the acquaintance of the other two.

'It's a funny business,' said Dick Dale, and to the shoe-shine boy, 'Use that saddle soap.'

'Funny!' thundered E., 'It's *suspect*! Here against my better judgement I write just what you tell me – and the office tells me to get out because we can't seem to agree.'

'That's polite,' explained Dick Dale. 'What do you want me to do – knock you down?'

E. Brunswick Hudson removed his glasses.

'Try it!' he suggested. 'I weigh a hundred and sixty-two and I haven't got an ounce of flesh on me.' He hesitated and redeemed himself from this extremity. 'I mean *fat* on me.'

'Oh, to hell with that!' said Dick Dale contemptuously, 'I can't mix it up with you. I got to figure this picture. You go back East and write one of your books and forget it.' Momentarily he looked at Pat Hobby, smiling as if *he* would understand, as if anyone would understand except E. Brunswick Hudson. 'I can't tell you all about pictures in three weeks.'

Hudson replaced his spectacles.

'When I *do* write a book,' he said, 'I'll make you the laughing stock of the nation.'

He withdrew, ineffectual, baffled, defeated. After a minute Pat spoke.

'Those guys can never get the idea,' he commented. 'I've never seen one get the idea and I been in this business, publicity and script, for twenty years.'

'You on the lot?' Dale asked.

Pat hesitated.

'Just finished a job,' he said.

That was five months before.

'What screen credits you got?' Dale asked.

'I got credits going all the way back to 1920.'

'Come up to my office,' Dick Dale said, 'I got something I'd like to talk over – now that bastard is gone back to his New England farm. Why do they have to get a New England farm – with the whole West not settled?'

Pat gave his second-to-last dime to the bootblack and climbed down from the stand.

II

We are in the midst of technicalities.

'The trouble is this composer Reginald de Koven didn't have any colour,' said Dick Dale. 'He wasn't deaf like Beethoven or a singing waiter or get put in jail or anything. All he did was write music and all we got for an angle is that song *O Promise Me*. We got to weave something around that – a dame promises him something and in the end he collects.'

'I want time to think it over in my mind,' said Pat. 'If Jack Berners will put me on the picture –'

'He'll put you on,' said Dick Dale. 'From now on I'm picking my own writers. What do you get – fifteen hundred?' He looked at Pat's shoes, 'Seven-fifty?'

Pat stared at him blankly for a moment; then out of thin air, produced his best piece of imaginative fiction in a decade.

'I was mixed up with a producer's wife,' he said, 'and they ganged up on me. I only get three-fifty now.'

In some ways it was the easiest job he had ever had. Director Dick

Dale was a type that, fifty years ago, could be found in any American town. Generally he was the local photographer, usually he was the originator of small mechanical contrivances and a leader in bizarre local movements, almost always he contributed verse to the local press. All the most energetic embodiments of this 'Sensation Type' had migrated to Hollywood between 1910 and 1930, and there they had achieved a psychological fulfilment inconceivable in any other time or place. At last, and on a large scale, they were able to have their way. In the weeks that Pat Hobby and Mabel Hatman, Mr Dale's script girl, sat beside him and worked on the script, not a movement, not a word went into it that was not Dick Dale's coinage. Pat would venture a suggestion, something that was 'Always good'.

'Wait a minute! Wait a minute!' Dick Dale was on his feet, his hands outspread. 'I seem to see a dog.' They would wait, tense and breathless, while he saw a dog.

'Two dogs.'

A second dog took its place beside the first in their obedient visions.

'We open on a dog on a leash – pull the camera back to show another dog – now they're snapping at each other. We pull back further – the leashes are attached to tables – the tables tip over. See it?'

Or else, out of a clear sky.

'I seem to see De Koven as a plasterer's apprentice.'

'Yes.' This hopefully.

'He goes to Santa Anita and plasters the walls, singing at his work. Take that down, Mabel.' He continued on . . .

In a month they had the requisite hundred and twenty pages. Reginald de Koven, it seemed, though not an alcoholic, was too fond of 'The Little Brown Jug'. The father of the girl he loved had died of drink, and after the wedding when she found him drinking from the Little Brown Jug, nothing would do but that she should go away, for twenty years. He became famous and she sang his songs as Maid Marian but he never knew it was the same girl.

The script, marked 'Temporary Complete. From Pat Hobby' went up to the head office. The schedule called for Dale to begin shooting in a week.

Twenty-four hours later he sat with his staff in his office, in an atmosphere of blue gloom. Pat Hobby was the least depressed. Four weeks at three-fifty, even allowing for the two hundred that had slipped away at Santa Anita, was a far cry from the twenty cents he had owned on the shoeshine stand.

'That's pictures, Dick,' he said consolingly. 'You're up – you're down – you're in, you're out. Any old-timer knows.'

'Yes,' said Dick Dale absently. 'Mabel, phone that E. Brunswick Hudson. He's on his New England farm – maybe milking bees.'

In a few minutes she reported.

'He flew into Hollywood this morning, Mr Dale. I've located him at the Beverly Wilshire Hotel.'

Dick Dale pressed his ear to the phone. His voice was bland and friendly as he said:

'Mr Hudson, there was one day here you had an idea I liked. You said you were going to write it up. It was about this De Koven stealing his music from a sheepherder up in Vermont. Remember?'

'Yes.'

'Well, Berners wants to go into production right away, or else we can't have the cast, so we're on the spot, if you know what I mean. Do you happen to have that stuff?'

'You remember when I brought it to you?' Hudson asked. 'You kept me waiting two hours – then you looked at it for two minutes. Your neck hurt you – I think it needed wringing. God, how it hurt you. That was the only nice thing about that morning.'

'In picture business –'

'I'm so glad you're stuck. I wouldn't tell you the story of *The Three Bears* for fifty grand.'

As the phones clicked Dick Dale turned to Pat.

'Goddam writers!' he said savagely. 'What do we pay you for? Millions – and you write a lot of tripe I can't photograph and get sore if we don't read your lousy stuff! How can a man make pictures when they give me two bastards like you and Hudson. How? How do you think – you old whiskey bum!'

Pat rose – took a step toward the door. He didn't know, he said.

'Get out of here!' cried Dick Dale. 'You're off the payroll, Get off the lot.'

Fate had not dealt Pat a farm in New England, but there was a café just across from the studio where bucolic dreams blossomed in bottles if you had the money. He did not like to leave the lot, which for many years had been home for him, so he came back at six and went up to his office. It was locked. He saw that they had already allotted it to another writer – the name on the door was E. Brunswick Hudson.

He spent an hour in the commissary, made another visit to the bar, and then some instinct led him to a stage where there was a bedroom set. He passed the night upon a couch occupied by Claudette Colbert in the fluffiest ruffles only that afternoon.

Morning was bleaker, but he had a little in his bottle and almost a hundred dollars in his pocket. The horses were running at Santa Anita and he might double it by night.

On his way out of the lot he hesitated beside the barber shop but he felt too nervous for a shave. Then he paused, for from the direction of the shoeshine stand he heard Dick Dale's voice.

'Miss Hatman found your other script, and it happens to be the property of the company.'

E. Brunswick Hudson stood at the foot of the stand.

'I won't have my name used,' he said.

'That's good. I'll put her name on it. Berners thinks it's great, if the De Koven family will stand for it. Hell – the sheepbreeder never would have been able to market those tunes anyhow. Ever hear of any sheepherder drawing down jack from ASCAP?'

Hudson took off his spectacles.

'I weigh a hundred and sixty-three –'

Pat moved in closer.

'Join the army,' said Dale contemptuously, 'I got no time for mixing it up. I got to make a picture.' His eyes fell on Pat. 'Hello old-timer,'

'Hello Dick,' said Pat smiling. Then knowing the advantage of the psychological moment he took his chance.

'When do we work?' he said.

'How much?' Dick Dale asked the shoeshine boy – and to Pat, 'It's all done. I promised Mabel a screen credit for a long time. Look me up some day when you got an idea.'

He hailed someone by the barber shop and hurried off. Hudson and Hobby, men of letters who had never met, regarded each other. There were tears of anger in Hudson's eyes.

'Authors get a tough break out here,' Pat said sympathetically. 'They never ought to come.'

'Who'd make up the stories – these feebs?'

'Well anyhow, not authors,' said Pat. 'They don't want authors. They want writers – like me.'

PAT HOBBY'S
COLLEGE DAYS

I

The afternoon was dark. The walls of Topanga Canyon rose sheer on either side. Get rid of it she must. The clank clank in the back seat frightened her. Evylyn did not like the business at all. It was not what she came out here to do. Then she thought of Mr Hobby. He believed in her, trusted her – and she was doing this for him.

But the mission was arduous. Evylyn Lascalles left the canyon and cruised along the inhospitable shores of Beverly Hills. Several times she turned up alleys, several times she parked beside vacant lots – but always some pedestrian or loiterer threw her into a mood of nervous anxiety. Once her heart almost stopped as she was eyed with appreciation – or was it suspicion – by a man who looked like a detective.

– He had no right to ask me this, she said to herself. Never again. I'll tell him so. Never again.

Night was fast descending. Evylyn Lascalles had never seen it come down so fast. Back to the canyon then, to the wild, free life. She drove up a paint-box corridor which gave its last pastel shades to the day. And reached a certain security at a bend overlooking plateau land far below.

Here there could be no complication. As she threw each article over the cliff it would be as far removed from her as if she were in a different state of the Union.

Miss Lascalles was from Brooklyn. She had wanted very much to come to Hollywood and be a secretary in pictures – now she wished that she had never left her home.

On with the job though – she must part with her cargo – as soon as this next car passed the bend . . .

II

. . . Meanwhile her employer, Pat Hobby, stood in front of the barber shop talking to Louie, the studio bookie. Pat's four weeks at two-fifty would be up tomorrow and he had begun to have that harassed and aghast feeling of those who live always on the edge of solvency.

'Four lousy weeks on a bad script,' he said. 'That's all I've had in six months.'

'How do you live?' asked Louie – without too much show of interest.

'I don't live. The days go by, the weeks go by. But who cares? Who cares – after twenty years.'

'You had a good time in your day,' Louie reminded him.

Pat looked after a dress extra in a shimmering lamé gown.

'Sure,' he admitted, 'I had three wives. All anybody could want.'

'You mean *that* was one of your wives?' asked Louie.

Pat peered after the disappearing figure.

'No-o. I didn't say *that* was one. But I've had plenty of them feeding out of my pocket. Not now though – a man of forty-nine is not considered human.'

'You've got a cute little secretary,' said Louie. 'Look Pat, I'll give you a tip –'

'Can't use it,' said Pat, 'I got fifty cents.'

'I don't mean that kind of tip. Listen – Jack Berners wants to make a picture about U.W.C. because he's got a kid there that plays basketball. He can't get a story. Why don't you go over and see the Athaletic Superintendent named Doolan at U.W.C.? That superintendent owes me three grand on the nags, and he could maybe give you an idea for a college picture. And then you bring it back and sell it to Berners. You're on salary, ain't you?'

'Till tomorrow,' said Pat gloomily.

'Go and see Jim Kresge that hangs out in the Campus Sport Shop. He'll introduce you to the Athaletic Superintendent. Look, Pat, I got to make a collection now. Just remember, Pat, that Doolan owes me three grand.'

III

It didn't seem hopeful to Pat but it was better than nothing. Returning for his coat to his room in the Writers' Building he was in time to pick up a plainting telephone.

'This is Evylyn,' said a fluttering voice. 'I can't get rid of it this afternoon. There's cars on every road –'

'I can't talk about it here,' said Pat quickly, 'I got to go over to U.W.C. on a notion.'

'I've tried,' she wailed, '– and *tried*! And every time, some car comes along –'

'Aw, please!' He hung up – he had enough on his mind.

For years Pat had followed the deeds of 'the Trojums' of U.S.C. and the almost as fabulous doings of 'the Roller Coasters', who represented the Univ. of the Western Coast. His interest was not so much physiological, tactical or intellectual as it was mathematical – but the Rollers had cost him plenty in their day – and thus it was with a sense of vague proprietorship that he stepped upon the half De Mille, half Aztec campus.

He located Kresge who conducted him to Superintendent Kit Doolan. Mr Doolan, a famous ex-tackle, was in excellent humour. With five coloured giants in this year's line, none of them quite old enough for pensions, but all men of experience, his team was in a fair way to conquer his section.

'Glad to be of help to your studio,' he said. 'Glad to help Mr Berners – or Louie. What can I do for you? You want to make a picture? . . . Well, we can always use publicity. Mr Hobby, I got a meeting of the Faculty Committee in just five minutes and perhaps you'd like to tell them your notion.'

'I don't know,' said Pat doubtfully. 'What I thought was maybe I could have a spiel with you. We could go somewhere and hoist one.'

'Afraid not,' said Doolan jovially. 'If those smarties smelt liquor on me – Boy! Come on over to the meeting – somebody's been getting away with watches and jewellery on the campus and we're sure it's a student.'

Mr Kresge, having played his role, got up to leave.

'Like something good for the fifth tomorrow?'

'Not me,' said Mr Doolan.

'You, Mr Hobby?'

'Not me,' said Pat.

IV

Ending their alliance with the underworld, Pat Hobby and Superintendent Doolan walked down the corridor of the Administration Building. Outside the Dean's office Doolan said:

'As soon as I can, I'll bring you in and introduce you.'

As an accredited representative neither of Jack Berners' nor of the studio, Pat waited with a certain *malaise*. He did not look forward to confronting a group of highbrows but he remembered that he bore an humble but warming piece of merchandise in his threadbare overcoat. The Dean's assistant had left her desk to take notes at the conference so he repleated his calories with a long, gagging draught.

In a moment, there was a responsive glow and he settled down in his chair, his eye fixed on the door marked:

SAMUEL K. WISKETH
DEAN OF THE STUDENT BODY

It might be a somewhat formidable encounter.

. . . but why? There were stuffed shirts – everybody knew that. They had college degrees but they could be bought. If they'd play ball with the studio they'd get a lot of good publicity for U.W.C. And that meant bigger salaries for them, didn't it, and more jack?

The door to the conference room opened and closed tentatively. No one came out but Pat sat up and readied himself. Representing the fourth biggest industry in America, or *al*most representing it, he must not let a bunch of highbrows stare him down. He was not without an inside view of higher education – in his early youth he had once been the 'Buttons' in the DKE House at the University of Pennsylvania. And with encouraging chauvinism he assured himself that Pennsylvania had it over this pioneer enterprise like a tent.

The door opened – a flustered young man with beads of sweat on his forehead came tearing out, tore through – and disappeared. Mr Doolan stood calmly in the doorway.

'All right, Mr Hobby,' he said.

Nothing to be scared of. Memories of old college days continued to flood over Pat as he walked in. And instantaneously, as the juice of confidence flowed through his system, he had his idea . . .

'. . . it's more of a realistic idea,' he was saying five minutes later. 'Understand?'

Dean Wiskith, a tall, pale man with an earphone, seemed to understand – if not exactly to approve. Pat hammered in his point again.

'It's up-to-the-minute,' he said patiently, 'what we call "a topical". You admit that young squirt who went out of here was stealing watches, don't you?'

The faculty committee, all except Doolan, exchanged glances, but no one interrupted.

'There you are,' went on Pat triumphantly. 'You turn him in to the newspapers. But here's the twist. In the Picture we make it turns out he steals the watches to support his young *brother* – and his young brother is the mainstay of the football team! He's the climax runner. We probably try to borrow Tyrone Power but we use one of *your* players as a double.'

Pat paused, trying to think of everything.

' – of course, we've got to release it in the southern states, so it's got to be one of your players that's white.'

There was an unquiet pause. Mr Doolan came to his rescue.

'Not a bad idea,' he suggested.

'It's an appalling idea,' broke out Dean Wiskith. 'It's –'

Doolan's face tightened slowly.

'Wait a minute,' he said. 'Who's telling *who* around here? You listen to *him*!'

The Dean's assistant, who had recently vanished from the room at the call of a buzzer, had reappeared and was whispering in the Dean's ear. The latter started.

'Just a minute, Mr Doolan,' he said. He turned to the other members of the committee.

'The proctor has a disciplinary case outside and he can't legally hold the offender. Can we settle it first? And then get back to this –' He glared at Mr Doolan, '– to this pre*post*erous idea?'

At his nod the assistant opened the door.

This proctor, thought Pat, ranging back to his days on the vineclad, leafy campus, looked like all proctors, an intimidated cop, a scarcely civilized beast of prey.

'Gentlemen,' the proctor said, with delicately modulated respect, 'I've got something that can't be explained away.' He shook his head, puzzled, and then continued: 'I know it's all wrong – but *I* can't seem to get to the point of it. I'd like to turn it over to *you* – I'll just show you the evidence and the offender . . . Come in, you.'

As Evylyn Lascalles entered, followed shortly by a big clinking pillow cover which the proctor deposited beside her, Pat thought once more of the elm-covered campus of the University of Pennsylvania. He wished passionately that he were there. He wished it more than anything in the world. Next to that he wished that Doolan's back, behind which he tried to hide by a shifting of his chair, were broader still.

'There you are!' she cried gratefully. 'Oh, Mr Hobby – Thank God! I couldn't get rid of them – and I couldn't take them home – my mother would kill me. So I came here to find you – and this man packed into the back seat of my car.'

'What's in that sack?' demanded Dean Wiskith. 'Bombs? What?'

Seconds before the proctor had picked up the sack and bounced it on the floor, so that it gave out a clear unmistakable sound, Pat could have told them. There were dead soldiers – pints, half-pints, quarts – the evidence of four strained weeks at two-fifty – empty bottles collected from his office drawers. Since his contract was up tomorrow he had thought it best not to leave such witnesses behind.

Seeking for escape his mind reached back for the last time to those careless days of fetch and carry at the University of Pennsylvania.

'I'll take it,' he said rising.

Slinging the sack over his shoulder, he faced the faculty committee and said surprisingly:

'Think it over.'

V

'We did,' Mr Doolan told his wife that night. 'But we never made head nor tail of it.'

'It's kind of spooky,' said Mrs Doolan. 'I hope I don't dream tonight. The poor man with that sack! I keep thinking he'll be down in purgatory – and they'll make him carve a ship in *every one* of those bottles – before he can go to heaven.'

'Don't!' said Doolan quickly. 'You'll have *me* dreaming. There were plenty bottles.'

BERNICE BOBS HER HAIR

I

After dark on Saturday night one could stand on the first tee of the golf-course and see the country-club windows as a yellow expanse over a very black and wavy ocean. The waves of this ocean, so to speak, were the heads of many curious caddies, a few of the more ingenious chauffeurs, the golf professional's deaf sister – and there were usually several stray, diffident waves who might have rolled inside had they so desired. This was the gallery.

The balcony was inside. It consisted of the circle of wicker chairs that lined the wall of the combination club-room and ballroom. At these Saturday-night dances it was largely feminine; a great babel of middle-aged ladies with sharp eyes and icy hearts behind lorgnettes and large bosoms. The main function of the balcony was critical. It occasionally showed grudging admiration, but never approval, for it is well known among ladies over thirty-five that when the younger set dance in the summer-time it is with the very worst intentions in the world, and if they are not bombarded with stony eyes stray couples will dance weird barbaric interludes in the corners, and the more popular, more dangerous, girls will sometimes be kissed in the parked limousines of unsuspecting dowagers.

But, after all, this critical circle is not close enough to the stage to see the actors' faces and catch the subtler byplay. It can only frown and lean, ask questions and make satisfactory deductions from its set of postulates, such as the one which states that every young man with a large income leads the life of a hunted partridge. It never really appreciates the drama of the shifting, semi-cruel world of adolescence. No; boxes, orchestra-circle, principals, and chorus are represented by the medley of faces and voices that sway to the plaintive African rhythm of Dyer's dance orchestra.

From sixteen-year-old Otis Ormonde, who has two more years at Hill School, to G. Reece Stoddard, over whose bureau at home hangs a

Harvard law diploma; from little Madeleine Hogue, whose hair still feels strange and uncomfortable on top of her head, to Bessie MacRae, who has been the life of the party a little too long – more than ten years – the medley is not only the centre of the stage but contains the only people capable of getting an unobstructed view of it.

With a flourish and a bang the music stops. The couples exchange artificial, effortless smiles, facetiously repeat '*la*-de-*da-da* dum-*dum*,' and then the clatter of young feminine voices soars over the burst of clapping.

A few disappointed stags caught in midfloor as they had been about to cut in subsided listlessly back to the walls, because this was not like the riotous Christmas dances – these summer hops were considered just pleasantly warm and exciting, where even the younger marrieds rose and performed ancient waltzes and terrifying fox trots to the tolerant amusement of their younger brothers and sisters.

Warren McIntyre, who casually attended Yale, being one of the unfortunate stags, felt in his dinner-coat pocket for a cigarette and strolled out onto the wide, semi-dark veranda, where couples were scattered at tables, filling the lantern-hung night with vague words and hazy laughter. He nodded here and there at the less absorbed and as he passed each couple some half-forgotten fragment of a story played in his mind, for it was not a large city and everyone was Who's Who to every one else's past. There, for example, were Jim Strain and Ethel Demorest, who had been privately engaged for three years. Everyone knew that as soon as Jim managed to hold a job for more than two months she would marry him. Yet how bored they both looked, and how wearily Ethel regarded Jim sometimes, as if she wondered why she had trained the vines of her affection on such a wind-shaken poplar.

Warren was nineteen and rather pitying with those of his friends who hadn't gone East to college. But, like most boys, he bragged tremendously about the girls of his city when he was away from it. There was Genevieve Ormonde, who regularly made the rounds of dances, house-parties, and football games at Princeton, Yale, Williams, and Cornell; there was black-eyed Roberta Dillon, who was quite as famous to her own generation as Hiram Johnson or Ty Cobb; and, of course, there was Marjorie Harvey, who besides having a fairylike face and a dazzling, bewildering tongue was already justly celebrated for having turned five cart-wheels in succession during the past pump-and-slipper dance at New Haven.

Warren, who had grown up across the street from Marjorie, had long been 'crazy about her'. Sometimes she seemed to reciprocate his feeling with a faint gratitude, but she had tried him by her infallible test and informed him gravely that she did not love him. Her test was that when she was away from him she forgot him and had affairs with other boys. Warren found this discouraging, especially as Marjorie had been making little trips all summer, and for the first two or three days after each arrival home he saw great heaps of mail on the Harveys' hall table addressed to her in various masculine handwritings. To make matters worse, all during the month of August she had been visited by her cousin Bernice from Eau Claire, and it seemed impossible to see her alone. It was always necessary to hunt round and find some one to take care of Bernice. As August waned this was becoming more and more difficult.

Much as Warren worshipped Marjorie, he had to admit that Cousin Bernice was sorta dopeless. She was pretty, with dark hair and high colour, but she was no fun on a party. Every Saturday night he danced a long arduous duty dance with her to please Marjorie, but he had never been anything but bored in her company.

'Warren' – a soft voice at his elbow broke in upon his thoughts, and he turned to see Marjorie, flushed and radiant as usual. She laid a hand on his shoulder and a glow settled almost imperceptibly over him.

'Warren,' she whispered, 'do something for me – dance with Bernice. She's been stuck with little Otis Ormonde for almost an hour.'

Warren's glow faded.

'Why – sure,' he answered half-heartedly.

'You don't mind, do you? I'll see that you don't get stuck.'

' 'Sall right.'

Marjorie smiled – that smile that was thanks enough.

'You're an angel, and I'm obliged loads.'

With a sigh the angel glanced round the veranda, but Bernice and Otis were not in sight. He wandered back inside, and there in front of the women's dressing-room he found Otis in the centre of a group of young men who were convulsed with laughter. Otis was brandishing a piece of timber he had picked up, and discoursing volubly.

'She's gone in to fix her hair,' he announced wildly. 'I'm waiting to dance another hour with her.'

Their laughter was renewed.

'Why don't some of you cut in?' cried Otis resentfully. 'She likes more variety.'

'Why, Otis,' suggested a friend, 'you've just barely got used to her.'

'Why the two-by-four, Otis?' inquired Warren, smiling.

'The two-by-four? Oh, this? This is a club. When she comes out I'll hit her on the head and knock her in again.'

Warren collapsed on a settee and howled with glee.

'Never mind, Otis,' he articulated finally. 'I'm relieving you this time.'

Otis simulated a sudden fainting attack and handed the stick to Warren.

'If you need it, old man,' he said hoarsely.

No matter how beautiful or brilliant a girl may be, the reputation of not being frequently cut in on makes her position at a dance unfortunate. Perhaps boys prefer her company to that of the butterflies with whom they dance a dozen times an evening, but youth in this jazz-nourished generation is temperamentally restless, and the idea of fox-trotting more than one full fox trot with the same girl is distasteful, not to say odious. When it comes to several dances and the intermissions between she can be quite sure that a young man, once relieved, will never tread on her wayward toes again.

Warren danced the next full dance with Bernice, and finally, thankful for the intermission, he led her to a table on the veranda. There was a moment's silence while she did unimpressive things with her fan.

'It's hotter here than in Eau Claire,' she said.

Warren stifled a sigh and nodded. It might be for all he knew or cared. He wondered idly whether she was a poor conversationalist because she got no attention or got no attention because she was a poor conversationalist.

'You going to be here much longer?' he asked, and then turned rather red. She might suspect his reasons for asking.

'Another week,' she answered, and stared at him as if to lunge at his next remark when it left his lips.

Warren fidgeted. Then with a sudden charitable impulse he decided to try part of his line on her. He turned and looked at her eyes.

'You've got an awfully kissable mouth,' he began quietly.

This was a remark that he sometimes made to girls at college proms when they were talking in just such half dark as this. Bernice distinctly jumped. She turned an ungraceful red and became clumsy with her fan. No one had ever made such a remark to her before.

'Fresh!' – the word had slipped out before she realized it, and she bit her lip. Too late she decided to be amused, and offered him a flustered smile.

Warren was annoyed. Though not accustomed to have that remark taken seriously, still it usually provoked a laugh or a paragraph of sentimental banter. And he hated to be called fresh, except in a joking way. His charitable impulse died and he switched the topic.

'Jim Strain and Ethel Demorest sitting out as usual,' he commented.

This was more in Bernice's line, but a faint regret mingled with her relief as the subject changed. Men did not talk to her about kissable mouths, but she knew that they talked in some such way to other girls.

'Oh, yes,' she said, and laughed. 'I hear they've been mooning round for years without a red penny. Isn't it silly?'

Warren's disgust increased. Jim Strain was a close friend of his brother's, and anyway he considered it bad form to sneer at people for not having money. But Bernice had had no intention of sneering. She was merely nervous.

II

When Marjorie and Bernice reached home at half after midnight they said good night at the top of the stairs. Though cousins, they were not intimates. As a matter of fact Marjorie had no female intimates – she considered girls stupid. Bernice on the contrary all through this parent-arranged visit had rather longed to exchange those confidences flavoured with giggles and tears that she considered an indispensable factor in all feminine intercourse. But in this respect she found Marjorie rather cold; felt somehow the same difficulty in talking to her that she had in talking to men. Marjorie never giggled, was never frightened, seldom embarrassed, and in fact had very few of the qualities which Bernice considered appropriately and blessedly feminine.

As Bernice busied herself with tooth-brush and paste this night she wondered for the hundredth time why she never had any attention when she was away from home. That her family were the wealthiest in Eau Claire; that her mother entertained tremendously, gave little dinners for her daughter before all dances and bought her a car of her own to drive round in, never occurred to her as factors in her home-town social success. Like most girls she had been brought up on the warm milk prepared by Annie Fellows Johnston and on novels in which the female was beloved because of certain mysterious womanly qualities, always mentioned but never displayed.

Bernice felt a vague pain that she was not at present engaged in being popular. She did not know that had it not been for Marjorie's campaigning she would have danced the entire evening with one man;

but she knew that even in Eau Claire other girls with less position and less pulchritude were given a much bigger rush. She attributed this to something subtly unscrupulous in those girls. It had never worried her, and if it had her mother would have assured her that the other girls cheapened themselves and that men really respected girls like Bernice.

She turned out the light in her bathroom, and on an impulse decided to go in and chat for a moment with her aunt Josephine whose light was still on. Her soft slippers bore her noiselessly down the carpeted hall, but hearing voices inside she stopped near the partly opened door. Then she caught her own name, and without any definite intention of eavesdropping lingered – and the thread of the conversation going on inside pierced her consciousness sharply as if it had been drawn through with a needle.

'She's absolutely hopeless!' It was Marjorie's voice. 'Oh, I know what you're going to say! So many people have told you how pretty and sweet she is, and how she can cook! What of it? She has a bum time. Men don't like her.'

'What's a little cheap popularity?'

Mrs Harvey sounded annoyed.

'It's everything when you're eighteen,' said Marjorie emphatically. 'I've done my best. I've been polite and I've made men dance with her, but they just won't stand being bored. When I think of that gorgeous colouring wasted on such a ninny, and think what Martha Carey could do with it – oh!'

'There's no courtesy these days.'

Mrs Harvey's voice implied that modern situations were too much for her. When she was a girl all young ladies who belonged to nice families had glorious times.

'Well,' said Marjorie, 'no girl can permanently bolster up a lame-duck visitor, because these days it's every girl for herself. I've even tried to drop her hints about clothes and things, and she's been furious – given me the funniest looks. She's sensitive enough to know she's not getting away with much, but I'll bet she consoles herself by thinking that she's very virtuous and that I'm too gay and fickle and will come to a bad end. All unpopular girls think that way. Sour grapes! Sarah Hopkins refers to Genevieve and Roberta and me as gardenia girls! I'll bet she'd give ten years of her life and her European education to be a gardenia girl and have three or four men in love with her and be cut in on every few feet at dances.'

'It seems to me,' interrupted Mrs Harvey rather wearily, 'that you ought to be able to do something for Bernice. I know she's not very vivacious.'

Marjorie groaned.

'Vivacious! Good grief! I've never heard her say anything to a boy except that it's hot or the floor's crowded or that she's going to school in New York next year. Sometimes she asks them what kind of car they have and tells them the kind she has. Thrilling!'

There was a short silence, and then Mrs Harvey took up her refrain:

'All I know is that other girls not half so sweet and attractive get partners. Martha Carey, for instance, is stout and loud, and her mother is distinctly common. Roberta Dillon is so thin this year that she looks as though Arizona were the place for her. She's dancing herself to death.'

'But, mother,' objected Marjorie impatiently, 'Martha is cheerful and awfully witty and an awfully slick girl, and Roberta's a marvellous dancer. She's been popular for ages!'

Mrs Harvey yawned.

'I think it's that crazy Indian blood in Bernice,' continued Marjorie. 'Maybe she's a reversion to type. Indian women all just sat round and never said anything.'

'Go to bed, you silly child,' laughed Mrs Harvey. 'I wouldn't have told you that if I'd thought you were going to remember it. And I think most of your ideas are perfectly idiotic,' she finished sleepily.

There was another silence, while Marjorie considered whether or not convincing her mother was worth the trouble. People over forty can seldom be permanently convinced of anything. At eighteen our convictions are hills from which we look; at forty-five they are caves in which we hide.

Having decided this, Marjorie said good night. When she came out into the hall it was quite empty.

III

While Marjorie was breakfasting late next day Bernice came into the room with a rather formal good morning, sat down opposite, stared intently over and slightly moistened her lips.

'What's on your mind?' inquired Marjorie, rather puzzled.

Bernice paused before she threw her hand-grenade.

'I heard what you said about me to your mother last night.'

Marjorie was startled, but she showed only a faintly heightened colour and her voice was quite even when she spoke.

'Where were you?'

'In the hall. I didn't mean to listen – at first.'

After an involuntary look of contempt Marjorie dropped her eyes and became very interested in balancing a stray corn-flake on her finger.

'I guess I'd better go back to Eau Claire – if I'm such a nuisance.' Bernice's lower lip was trembling violently and she continued on a wavering note: 'I've tried to be nice, and – and I've been first neglected and then insulted. No one ever visited me and got such treatment.'

Marjorie was silent.

'But I'm in the way, I see. I'm a drag on you. Your friends don't like me.' She paused, and then remembered another one of her grievances. 'Of course I was furious last week when you tried to hint to me that that dress was unbecoming. Don't you think I know how to dress myself?'

'No,' murmured Marjorie less than half-aloud.

'What?'

'I didn't hint anything,' said Marjorie succinctly. 'I said, as I remember, that it was better to wear a becoming dress three times straight than to alternate it with two frights.'

'Do you think that was a very nice thing to say?'

'I wasn't trying to be nice.' Then after a pause: 'When do you want to go?'

Bernice drew in her breath sharply.

'Oh!' It was a little half-cry.

Marjorie looked up in surprise.

'Didn't you say you were going?'

'Yes, but –'

'Oh, you were only bluffing!'

They stared at each other across the breakfast-table for a moment. Misty waves were passing before Bernice's eyes, while Marjorie's face wore that rather hard expression that she used when slightly intoxicated undergraduates were making love to her.

'So you were bluffing,' she repeated as if it were what she might have expected.

Bernice admitted it by bursting into tears. Marjorie's eyes showed boredom.

'You're my cousin,' sobbed Bernice. 'I'm v-v-visiting you. I was to stay a month, and if I go home my mother will know and she'll wah—wonder —'

Marjorie waited until the shower of broken words collapsed into little sniffles.

'I'll give you my month's allowance,' she said coldly, and 'you can spend this last week anywhere you want. There's a very nice hotel —'

Bernice's sobs rose to a flute note, and rising of a sudden she fled from the room.

An hour later, while Marjorie was in the library absorbed in composing one of those non-committal, marvellously elusive letters that only a young girl can write, Bernice reappeared, very red-eyed and consciously calm. She cast no glance at Marjorie but took a book at random from the shelf and sat down as if to read. Marjorie seemed absorbed in her letter and continued writing. When the clock showed noon Bernice closed her book with a snap.

'I suppose I'd better get my railroad ticket.'

This was not the beginning of the speech she had rehearsed upstairs, but as Marjorie was not getting her cues — wasn't urging her to be reasonable; it's all a mistake — it was the best opening she could muster.

'Just wait till I finish this letter,' said Marjorie without looking round. 'I want to get it off in the next mail.'

After another minute, during which her pen scratched busily, she turned round and relaxed with an air of 'at your service'. Again Bernice had to speak.

'Do you want me to go home?'

'Well,' said Marjorie, considering, 'I suppose if you're not having a good time you'd better go. No use being miserable.'

'Don't you think common kindness —'

'Oh, please don't quote "Little Women"!' cried Marjorie impatiently. 'That's out of style.'

'You think so?'

'Heavens, yes! What modern girl could live like those inane females?'

'They were the models for our mothers.'

Marjorie laughed.

'Yes, they were — not! Besides, our mothers were all very well in their way, but they know very little about their daughters' problems.'

Bernice drew herself up.

'Please don't talk about my mother.'

Marjorie laughed,

'I don't think I mentioned her.'

Bernice felt that she was being led away from her subject.

'Do you think you've treated me very well?'

'I've done my best. You're rather hard material to work with.'

The lids of Bernice's eyes reddened.

'I think you're hard and selfish, and you haven't a feminine quality in you.'

'Oh, my Lord!' cried Marjorie in desperation. 'You little nut! Girls like you are responsible for all the tiresome colourless marriages; all those ghastly inefficiencies that pass as feminine qualities. What a blow it must be when a man with imagination marries the beautiful bundle of clothes that he's been building ideals round, and finds that she's just a weak, whining, cowardly mass of affectations!'

Bernice's mouth had slipped half open.

'The womanly woman!' continued Marjorie. 'Her whole early life is occupied in whining criticisms of girls like me who really do have a good time.'

Bernice's jaw descended farther as Marjorie's voice rose.

'There's some excuse for an ugly girl whining. If I'd been irretrievably ugly I'd never have forgiven my parents for bringing me into the world. But you're starting life without any handicap –' Majorie's little fist clinched. 'If you expect me to weep with you you'll be disappointed. Go or stay, just as you like.' And picking up her letters she left the room.

Bernice claimed a headache and failed to appear at luncheon. They had a matinée date for the afternoon, but the headache persisting, Marjorie made explanations to a not very downcast boy. But when she returned late in the afternoon she found Bernice with a strangely set face waiting for her in her bedroom.

'I've decided,' began Bernice without preliminaries, 'that maybe you're right about things – possibly not. But if you'll tell me why your friends aren't – aren't interested in me, I'll see if I can do what you want me to.'

Marjorie was at the mirror shaking down her hair.

'Do you mean it?'

'Yes.'

'Without reservations? Will you do exactly what I say?'

'Well, I –'

'Well nothing! Will you do exactly as I say?'

'If they're sensible things.'

'They're not! You're no case for sensible things.'

'Are you going to make – to recommend –'

'Yes, everything. If I tell you to take boxing lessons you'll have to do it. Write home and tell your mother you're going to stay another two weeks.'

'If you'll tell me –'

'All right – I'll just give you a few examples now. First, you have no ease of manner. Why? Because you're never sure about your personal appearance. When a girl feels that she's perfectly groomed and dressed she can forget that part of her. That's charm. The more parts of yourself you can afford to forget the more charm you have.'

'Don't I look all right?'

'No; for instance, you never take care of your eyebrows. They're black and lustrous, but by leaving them straggly they're a blemish. They'd be beautiful if you'd take care of them in one-tenth of the time you take doing nothing. You're going to brush them so that they'll grow straight.'

Bernice raised the brows in question.

'Do you mean to say that men notice eyebrows?'

'Yes – subconsciously. And when you go home you ought to have your teeth straightened a little. It's almost imperceptible, still –'

'But I thought,' interrupted Bernice in bewilderment, 'that you despised little dainty feminine things like that.'

'I hate dainty minds,' answered Marjorie. 'But a girl has to be dainty in person. If she looks like a million dollars she can talk about Russia, ping-pong, or the League of Nations and get away with it.'

'What else?'

'Oh, I'm just beginning! There's your dancing.'

'Don't I dance all right?'

'No, you don't – you lean on a man; yes, you do – ever so slightly. I noticed it when we were dancing together yesterday. And you dance standing up straight instead of bending over a little. Probably some old lady on the sideline once told you that you looked so dignified that way. But except with a very small girl it's much harder on the man, and he's the one that counts.'

'Go on,' Bernice's brain was reeling.

'Well, you've got to learn to be nice to men who are sad birds. You look as if you'd been insulted whenever you're thrown with any except the most popular boys. Why, Bernice, I'm cut in on every few feet – and who does most of it? Why, those very sad birds. No girl can afford to neglect them. They're the big part of any crowd. Young boys too shy to talk are the very best conversational practice. Clumsy boys are the best dancing practice. If you can follow them and yet look graceful you can follow a baby tank across a barb-wire sky-scraper.'

Bernice sighed profoundly, but Marjorie was not through.

'If you go to a dance and really amuse, say, three sad birds that dance with you; if you talk so well to them that they forget they're stuck with you, you've done something, They'll come back next time, and gradually so many sad birds will dance with you that the attractive boys will see there's no danger of being stuck – then they'll dance with you.'

'Yes,' agreed Bernice faintly. 'I think I begin to see.'

'And finally,' concluded Marjorie, 'poise and charm will just come. You'll wake up some morning knowing you've attained it, and men will know it too.'

Bernice rose.

'It's been awfully kind of you – but nobody's ever talked to me like this before, and I feel sort of startled.'

Marjorie made no answer but gazed pensively at her own image in the mirror.

'You're a peach to help me,' continued Bernice.

Still Marjorie did not answer, and Bernice thought she had seemed too grateful.

'I know you don't like sentiment,' she said timidly.

Marjorie turned to her quickly.

'Oh, I wasn't thinking about that. I was considering whether we hadn't better bob your hair.'

Bernice collapsed backward upon the bed.

IV

On the following Wednesday evening there was a dinner-dance at the country club. When the guests strolled in Bernice found her place-card with a slight feeling of irritation. Though at her right sat G. Reece Stoddard, a most desirable and distinguished young bachelor, the all-important left held only Charley Paulson. Charley lacked height, beauty, and social shrewdness, and in her new enlightenment Bernice decided that his only qualification to be her partner was that he had never been stuck with her. But this feeling of irritation left with the last of the soup-plates, and Marjorie's specific instruction came to her. Swallowing her pride she turned to Charley Paulson and plunged.

'Do you think I ought to bob my hair, Mr Charley Paulson?'

Charley looked up in surprise.

'Why?'

'Because I'm considering it. It's such a sure and easy way of attracting attention.'

Charley smiled pleasantly, He could not know this had been rehearsed. He replied that he didn't know much about bobbed hair. But Bernice was there to tell him.

'I want to be a society vampire, you see,' she announced coolly, and went on to inform him that bobbed hair was the necessary prelude. She added that she wanted to ask his advice, because she had heard he was so critical about girls.

Charley, who knew as much about the psychology of women as he did of the mental states of Buddhist contemplatives, felt vaguely flattered.

'So I've decided,' she continued, her voice rising slightly, 'that early next week I'm going down to the Sevier Hotel barber-shop, sit in the first chair, and get my hair bobbed.' She faltered, noticing that the people near her had paused in their conversation and were listening; but after a confused second Marjorie's coaching told, and she finished her paragraph to the vicinity at large. 'Of course I'm charging admission, but if you'll all come down and encourage me I'll issue passes for the inside seats.'

There was a ripple of appreciative laughter, and under cover of it G. Reece Stoddard leaned over quickly and said to her ear: 'I'll take a box right now.'

She met his eyes and smiled as if he had said something surpassingly brilliant.

'Do you believe in bobbed hair?' asked G. Reece in the same undertone.

'I think it's unmoral,' affirmed Bernice gravely. 'But, of course, you've either got to amuse people or feed 'em or shock 'em.' Marjorie had culled this from Oscar Wilde. It was greeted with a ripple of laughter from the men and a series of quick, intent looks from the girls. And then as though she had said nothing of wit or moment Bernice turned again to Charley and spoke confidentially in his ear.

'I want to ask you your opinion of several people. I imagine you're a wonderful judge of character.'

Charley thrilled faintly – paid her a subtle compliment by overturning her water.

Two hours later, while Warren McIntyre was standing passively in the stag line abstractedly watching the dancers and wondering whither and with whom Marjorie had disappeared, an unrelated perception began to creep slowly upon him – a perception that Bernice, cousin to Marjorie, had been cut in on several times in the past five minutes. He closed his eyes, opened them and looked again. Several minutes back she had been dancing with a visiting boy, a matter easily accounted for; a visiting boy would know no better. But now she was dancing with some one else, and there was Charley Paulson headed for her with enthusiastic determination in his eye. Funny – Charley seldom danced with more than three girls an evening.

Warren was distinctly surprised when – the exchange having been effected – the man relieved proved to be none other than G. Reece Stoddard himself. And G. Reece seemed not at all jubilant at being relieved. Next time Bernice danced near, Warren regarded her intently. Yes, she was pretty, distinctly pretty; and tonight her face seemed really vivacious. She had that look that no woman, however histrionically proficient, can successfully counterfeit – she looked as if she were having a good time. He liked the way she had her hair arranged, wondering if it was brilliantine that made it glisten so. And that dress was becoming – a dark red that set off her shadowy eyes and high colouring. He remembered that he had thought her pretty when she first came to town, before he had realized that she was dull. Too bad she was dull – dull girls were unbearable – certainly pretty though.

His thoughts zigzagged back to Marjorie. This disappearance would be like other disappearances. When she reappeared he would demand where she had been – would be told emphatically that it was none of his business. What a pity she was so sure of him! She basked in the knowledge that no other girl in town interested him; she defied him to fall in love with Genevieve or Roberta.

Warren sighed. The way to Marjorie's affections was a labyrinth indeed. He looked up. Bernice was again dancing with the visiting boy. Half unconsciously he took a step out from the stag line in her direction, and hesitated. Then he said to himself that it was charity. He walked towards her – collided suddenly with G. Reece Stoddard.

'Pardon me,' said Warren.

But G. Reece had not stopped to apologize. He had again cut in on Bernice.

That night at one o'clock Marjorie, with one hand on the electric-light switch in the hall, turned to take a last look at Bernice's sparkling eyes.

'So it worked?'

'Oh, Marjorie, yes!' cried Bernice.

'I saw you were having a gay time.'

'I did! The only trouble was that about midnight I ran short of talk. I had to repeat myself – with different men of course. I hope they won't compare notes.'

'Men don't,' said Marjorie, yawning, 'and it wouldn't matter if they did – they'd think you were even trickier.'

She snapped out the light, and as they started up the stairs Bernice grasped the banister thankfully. For the first time in her life she had been danced tired.

'You see,' said Marjorie at the top of the stairs, 'one man sees another man cut in and he thinks there must be something there. Well, we'll fix up some new stuff tomorrow. Good night.'

'Good night.'

As Bernice took down her hair she passed the evening before her in review. She had followed instructions exactly. Even when Charley Paulson cut in for the eighth time she had simulated delight and had apparently been both interested and flattered. She had not talked about the weather or Eau Claire or automobiles or her school, but had confined her conversation to me, you, and us.

But a few minutes before she fell asleep a rebellious thought was churning drowsily in her brain – after all, it was she who had done it. Marjorie, to be sure, had given her her conversation, but then Marjorie got much of her conversation out of things she read. Bernice had bought the red dress, though she had never valued it highly before Marjorie dug it out of her trunk – and her own voice had said the words, her own lips had smiled, her own feet had danced. Marjorie nice girl – vain, though – nice evening – nice boys – like Warren – Warren – Warren – what's-his-name – Warren –

She fell asleep.

V

To Bernice the next week was a revelation. With the feeling that people really enjoyed looking at her and listening to her came the foundation of self-confidence. Of course there were numerous mistakes at first. She did not know, for instance, that Draycott Deyo was studying for the ministry; she was unaware that he had cut in on her because he thought she was a quiet, reserved girl. Had she known these things she would not have treated him to the line which began 'Hello, Shell Shock!' and continued with the bathtub story – 'It takes a frightful lot of energy to fix my hair in the summer – there's so much of it – so I always fix it first and powder my face and put on my hat; then I get into the bathtub, and dress afterwards. Don't you think that's the best plan?'

Though Draycott Deyo was in the throes of difficulties concerning baptism by immersion and might possibly have seen a connexion, it must be admitted that he did not. He considered feminine bathing an immoral subject, and gave her some of his ideas on the depravity of modern society.

But to offset that unfortunate occurrence Bernice had several signal successes to her credit. Little Otis Ormonde pleaded off from a trip East and elected instead to follow her with a puppy-like devotion, to the amusement of his crowd and to the irritation of G. Reece Stoddard, several of whose afternoon calls Otis completely ruined by the disgusting tenderness of the glances he bent on Bernice. He even told her the story of the two-by-four and the dressing-room to show her how frightfully mistaken he and everyone else had been in their first judgement of her. Bernice laughed off that incident with a slight sinking sensation.

Of all Bernice's conversation perhaps the best known and most universally approved was the line about the bobbing of her hair.

'Oh, Bernice, when you goin' to get the hair bobbed?'

'Day after tommorrow maybe,' she would reply, laughing. 'Will you come and see me? Because I'm counting on you, you know.'

'Will we? You know! But you better hurry up.'

Bernice, whose tonsorial intentions were strictly dishonourable, would laugh again.

'Pretty soon now. You'd be surprised.'

But perhaps the most significant symbol of her success was the grey car of the hypercritical Warren McIntyre, parked daily in front of the Harvey house. At first the parlourmaid was distinctly startled when he asked for Bernice instead of Marjorie; after a week of it she told the cook that Miss Bernice had gotta hold Miss Marjorie's best fella.

And Miss Bernice had. Perhaps it began with Warren's desire to rouse jealousy in Marjorie; perhaps it was the familiar though unrecognized strain of Marjorie in Bernice's conversation; perhaps it was both of these and something of sincere attraction besides. But somehow the collective mind of the younger set knew within a week that Marjorie's most reliable beau had made an amazing face-about and was giving an indisputable rush to Marjorie's guest. The question of the moment was how Marjorie would take it. Warren called Bernice on the phone twice a day, sent her notes, and they were frequently seen together in his roadster, obviously engrossed in one of those tense, significant conversations as to whether or not he was sincere.

Marjorie on being twitted only laughed. She said she was mighty glad that Warren had at last found someone who appreciated him. So the younger set laughed, too, and guessed that Marjorie didn't care and let it go at that.

One afternoon when there were only three days left of her visit Bernice was waiting in the hall for Warren, with whom she was going to a bridge party. She was in rather a blissful mood, and when Marjorie – also bound for the party – appeared beside her and began casually to adjust her hat in the mirror, Bernice was utterly unprepared for anything in the nature of a clash. Marjorie did her work very coldly and succinctly in three sentences.

'You may as well get Warren out of your head,' she said coldly.

'What?' Bernice was utterly astounded.

'You may as well stop making a fool of yourself over Warren McIntyre. He doesn't care a snap of his fingers about you.'

For a tense moment they regarded each other – Marjorie scornful, aloof; Bernice astounded, half-angry, half-afraid. Then two cars drove up in front of the house and there was a riotous honking. Both of them gasped faintly, turned, and side by side hurried out.

All through the bridge party Bernice strove in vain to master a rising uneasiness. She had offended Marjorie, the sphinx of sphinxes, With the most wholesome and innocent intentions in the world she had stolen Marjorie's property. She felt suddenly and horribly guilty. After the bridge game, when they sat in an informal circle and the conversation became general, the storm gradually broke. Little Otis Ormonde inadvertently precipitated it.

'When you going back to kindergarten, Otis?' some one had asked.

'Me? Day Bernice gets her hair bobbed.'

'Then your education's over,' said Marjorie quickly. 'That's only a bluff of hers. I should think you'd have realized.'

'That a fact?' demanded Otis, giving Bernice a reproachful glance.

Bernice's ears burned as she tried to think up an effectual comeback. In the face of this direct attack her imagination was paralysed.

'There's a lot of bluffs in the world,' continued Marjorie quite pleasantly. 'I should think you'd be young enough to know that, Otis.'

'Well,' said Otis, 'maybe so. But gee! With a line like Bernice's –'

'Really?' yawned Marjorie. 'What's her latest bon mot?'

No one seemed to know. In fact, Bernice, having trifled with her muse's beau, had said nothing memorable of late.

'Was that really all a line?' asked Roberta curiously.

Bernice hesitated. She felt that wit in some form was demanded of her, but under her cousin's suddenly frigid eyes she was completely incapacitated.

'I don't know,' she stalled.

'Splush!' said Marjorie. 'Admit it!'

Bernice saw that Warren's eyes had left a ukulele he had been tinkering with and were fixed on her questioningly.

'Oh, I don't know!' she repeated steadily. Her cheeks were glowing.

'Splush!' remarked Marjorie again.

'Come through, Bernice,' urged Otis. 'Tell her where to get off.'

Bernice looked round again – she seemed unable to get away from Warren's eyes,

'I like bobbed hair,' she said hurriedly, as if he had asked her a question, 'and I intend to bob mine.'

'When?' demanded Marjorie.

'Any time.'

'No time like the present,' suggested Roberta.

Otis jumped to his feet.

'Good stuff!' he cried. 'We'll have a summer bobbing party. Sevier Hotel barber-shop, I think you said.'

In an instant all were on their feet. Bernice's heart throbbed violently.

'What?' she gasped.

Out of the group came Marjorie's voice, very clear and contemptuous.

'Don't worry – she'll back out!'

'Come on, Bernice!' cried Otis, starting towards the door.

Four eyes – Warren's and Marjorie's – stared at her, challenged her, defied her. For another second she wavered wildly.

'All right,' she said swiftly, 'I don't care if I do.'

An eternity of minutes later, riding down-town through the late afternoon beside Warren, the others following in Roberta's car close behind, Bernice had all the sensations of Marie Antoinette bound for the guillotine in a tumbrel. Vaguely she wondered why she did not cry out that it was all a mistake. It was all she could do to keep from clutching her hair with both hands to protect it from the suddenly hostile world. Yet she did neither. Even the thought of her mother was no deterrent now. This was the test supreme of her sportsmanship; her right to walk unchallenged in the starry heaven of popular girls.

Warren was moodily silent, and when they came to the hotel he drew up at the kerb and nodded to Bernice to precede him out. Roberta's car emptied a laughing crowd into the shop, which presented two bold plate-glass windows to the street.

Bernice stood on the kerb and looked at the sign, Sevier Barber-Shop. It was a guillotine indeed, and the hangman was the first barber, who, attired in a white coat and smoking a cigarette, leaned nonchalantly against the first chair. He must have heard of her; he must have been waiting all week, smoking eternal cigarettes beside that portentous, too-often-mentioned first chair. Would they blindfold her? No, but they would tie a white cloth round her neck lest any of her blood – nonsense – hair – should get on her clothes.

'All right, Bernice,' said Warren quickly.

With her chin in the air she crossed the sidewalk, pushed open the swinging screen-door, and giving not a glance to the uproarious, riotous row that occupied the waiting bench, went up to the first barber.

'I want you to bob my hair.'

The first barber's mouth slid somewhat open. His cigarette dropped to the floor.

'Huh?'

'My hair – bob it!'

Refusing further preliminaries, Bernice took her seat on high. A man in the chair next to her turned on his side and gave her a glance, half lather, half amazement. One barber started and spoiled little Willy Schuneman's monthly haircut. Mr O'Reilly in the last chair grunted and swore musically in ancient Gaelic as a razor bit into his cheek. Two bootblacks became wide-eyed and rushed for her feet. No, Bernice didn't care for a shine.

Outside a passer-by stopped and stared; a couple joined him; half a dozen small boys' noses sprang into life, flattened against the glass; and snatches of conversation borne on the summer breeze drifted in through the screen-door.

'Lookada long hair on a kid!'

'Where'd yuh get 'at stuff? ' 'At's a bearded lady he just finished shavin'.'

But Bernice saw nothing, heard nothing. Her only living sense told her that this man in the white coat had removed one tortoiseshell comb and then another; that his fingers were fumbling clumsily with unfamiliar hairpins; that this hair, this wonderful hair of hers, was going – she would never again feel its long voluptuous pull as it hung in a dark-brown glory down her back. For a second she was near breaking down, and then the picture before her swam mechanically into her vision – Marjorie's mouth curling in a faint ironic smile as if to say:

'Give up and get down! You tried to buck me and I called your bluff. You see you haven't got a prayer.'

And some last energy rose up in Bernice, for she clenched her hands under the white cloth, and there was a curious narrowing of her eyes that Marjorie remarked on to someone long afterward.

Twenty minutes later the barber swung her round to face the mirror, and she flinched at the full extent of the damage that had been wrought. Her hair was not curly, and now it lay in lank lifeless blocks on both sides of her suddenly pale face. It was ugly as sin – she had known it would be ugly as sin. Her face's chief charm had been a Madonna-like simplicity. Now that was gone and she was – well, frightfully mediocre – not stagy; only ridiculous, like a Greenwich Villager who had left her spectacles at home.

As she climbed down from the chair she tried to smile – failed miserably. She saw two of the girls exchange glances; noticed Marjorie's mouth curved in attenuated mockery – and that Warren's eyes were suddenly very cold.

'You see' – her words fell into an awkward pause – 'I've done it.'

'Yes, you've – done it,' admitted Warren.

'Do you like it?'

There was a half-hearted 'Sure' from two or three voices, another awkward pause, and then Marjorie turned swiftly and with serpent-like intensity to Warren.

'Would you mind running me down to the cleaners?' she asked. 'I've simply got to get a dress there before supper. Roberta's driving right home and she can take the others.'

Warren stared abstractedly at some infinite speck out the window. Then for an instant his eyes rested coldly on Bernice before they turned to Marjorie.

'Be glad to,' he said slowly.

VI

Bernice did not fully realize the outrageous trap that had been set for her until she met her aunt's amazed glance just before dinner.

'Why, Bernice!'

'I've bobbed it, Aunt Josephine.'

'Why, child!'

'Do you like it?'

'Why, Ber-nice!'

'I suppose I've shocked you.'

'No, but what'll Mrs Deyo think tomorrow night? Bernice, you should have waited until after the Deyos' dance – you should have waited if you wanted to do that.'

'It was sudden, Aunt Josephine. Anyway, why does it matter to Mrs Deyo particularly?'

'Why, child,' cried Mrs Harvey, 'in her paper on "The Foibles of the Younger Generation" that she read at the last meeting of the Thursday Club she devoted fifteen minutes to bobbed hair. It's her pet abomination. And the dance is for you and Marjorie!'

'I'm sorry.'

'Oh, Bernice, what'll your mother say? She'll think I let you do it.'

'I'm sorry.'

Dinner was an agony. She had made a hasty attempt with a curling-iron, and burned her finger and much hair. She could see that her aunt was both worried and grieved, and her uncle kept saying, 'Well, I'll be darned!' over and over in a hurt and faintly hostile tone. And Marjorie sat very quietly, entrenched behind a faint smile, a faintly mocking smile.

Somehow she got through the evening. Three boys called; Marjorie disappeared with one of them, and Bernice made a listless unsuccessful attempt to entertain the two others – sighed thankfully as she climbed the stairs to her room at half past ten. What a day!

When she had undressed for the night the door opened and Marjorie came in.

'Bernice,' she said, 'I'm awfully sorry about the Deyo dance. I'll give you my word of honour I'd forgotten all about it.'

' 'Sall right,' said Bernice shortly. Standing before the mirror she passed her comb slowly through her short hair.

'I'll take you down-town tomorrow,' continued Marjorie, 'and the hairdresser'll fix it so you'll look slick. I didn't imagine you'd go through with it, I'm really mighty sorry.'

'Oh, 'sall right!'

'Still it's your last night, so I suppose it won't matter much.'

Then Bernice winced as Marjorie tossed her own hair over her shoulders and began to twist it slowly into two long blonde braids until in her cream-coloured négligé she looked like a delicate painting of some Saxon princess. Fascinated, Bernice watched the braids grow. Heavy and luxurious they were, moving under the supple fingers like restive snakes – and to Bernice remained this relic and the curling-iron and a tomorrow full of eyes. She could see G. Reece Stoddard, who liked her, assuming his Harvard manner and telling his dinner partner that Bernice shouldn't have been allowed to go to the movies so much; she could see Draycott Deyo exchanging glances with his mother and then being conscientiously charitable to her. But then perhaps by tomorrow Mrs Deyo would have heard the news; would send round an icy little note requesting that she fail to appear – and behind her back they would all laugh and know that Marjorie had made a fool of her; that her chance at beauty had been sacrificed to the jealous whim of a selfish girl. She sat down suddenly before the mirror, biting the inside of her cheek.

'I like it,' she said with an effort. 'I think it will be becoming.'

Marjorie smiled.

'It looks all right. For heaven's sake, don't let it worry you!'

'I won't.'

'Good night, Bernice.'

But as the door closed something snapped within Bernice. She sprang dynamically to her feet, clenching her hands, then swiftly and noiselessly crossed over to her bed and from underneath it dragged out her suitcase. Into it she tossed toilet articles and a change of clothing. Then she turned to her trunk and quickly dumped in two drawerfuls of lingerie and summer dresses. She moved quietly, but with deadly efficiency, and in three-quarters of an hour her trunk was locked and strapped and she was fully dressed in a becoming new travelling suit that Marjorie had helped her pick out.

Sitting down at her desk she wrote a short note to Mrs Harvey, in which she briefly outlined her reasons for going. She sealed it, addressed it, and laid it on her pillow. She glanced at her watch. The train left at one, and she knew that if she walked down to the Marborough Hotel two blocks away she could easily get a taxicab.

Suddenly she drew in her breath sharply and an expression flashed into her eyes that a practised character reader might have connected vaguely with the set look she had worn in the barber's chair – somehow a development of it. It was quite a new look for Bernice – and it carried consequences.

She went stealthily to the bureau, picked up an article that lay there, and turning out all the lights stood quietly until her eyes became accustomed to the darkness. Softly she pushed open the door to Marjorie's room. She heard the quiet, even breathing of an untroubled conscience asleep.

She was by the bedside now, very deliberate and calm. She acted swiftly. Bending over she found one of the braids of Marjorie's hair, followed it up with her hand to the point nearest the head, and then holding it a little slack so that the sleeper would feel no pull, she reached down with the shears and severed it. With the pigtail in her hand she held her breath. Marjorie had muttered something in her sleep. Bernice deftly amputated the other braid, paused for an instant, and then flitted swiftly and silently back to her own room.

Downstairs she opened the big front door, closed it carefully behind her, and feeling oddly happy and exuberant stepped off the porch into the moonlight, swinging her heavy grip like a shopping-bag. After a minute's brisk walk she discovered that her left hand still held the two blonde braids. She laughed unexpectedly – had to shut her mouth hard to keep from emitting an absolute peal. She was passing Warren's house now, and on the impulse she set down her baggage, and swinging the braids like pieces of rope flung them at the wooden porch, where they landed with a slight thud, She laughed again, no longer restraining herself.

'Huh!' she giggled wildly. 'Scalp the selfish thing!'

Then picking up her suitcase she set off at a half-run down the moonlit street.

WINTER DREAMS

Some of the caddies were poor as sin and lived in one-room houses with a neurasthenic cow in the front yard, but Dexter Green's father owned the second-best grocery-store in Black Bear – the best one was 'The Hub', patronized by the wealthy people from Sherry Island – and Dexter caddied only for pocket-money.

In the fall when the days became crisp and grey, and the long Minnesota winter shut down like the white lid of a box, Dexter's skis moved over the snow that hid the fairways of the golf course. At these times the country gave him a feeling of profound melancholy – it offended him that the links should lie in enforced fallowness, haunted by ragged sparrows for the long season. It was dreary, too, that on the trees where the gay colours fluttered in summer there were now only the desolate sand-boxes knee-deep in crusted ice. When he crossed the hills the wind blew cold as misery, and if the sun was out he tramped with his eyes squinted up against the hard dimensionless glare.

In April the winter ceased abruptly. The snow ran down into Black Bear Lake scarcely tarrying for the early golfers to brave the season with red and black balls. Without elation, without an interval of moist glory, the cold was gone.

Dexter knew that there was something dismal about this Northern spring, just as he knew there was something gorgeous about the fall. Fall made him clench his hands and tremble and repeat idiotic sentences to himself, and make brisk abrupt gestures of command to imaginary audiences and armies. October filled him with hope which November raised to a sort of ecstatic triumph, and in this mood the fleeting brilliant impressions of the summer at Sherry Island were ready grist to his mill. He became golf champion and defeated Mr T. A. Hedrick in a marvellous match played a hundred times over the fairways of his imagination, a match each detail of which he changed about untiringly – sometimes he won with almost laughable ease, sometimes he came up magnificently from behind. Again, stepping from a Pierce-Arrow automobile, like Mr Mortimer Jones, he strolled frigidly into the lounge of the Sherry Island Golf Club – or perhaps, surrounded by an admiring crowd, he gave an exhibition of fancy diving from the springboard of the club raft . . . Among those who watched in open-mouthed wonder was Mr Mortimer Jones.

And one day it came to pass that Mr Jones – himself and not his ghost – came up to Dexter with tears in his eyes and said that Dexter was the — best caddy in the club, and wouldn't he decide not to quit if Mr Jones made it worth his while, because every other — caddy in the club lost one ball a hole for him regularly.

'No, sir,' said Dexter decisively, 'I don't want to caddy any more.' Then, after a pause: 'I'm too old.'

'You're not more than fourteen. Why the devil did you decide just this morning that you wanted to quit? You promised that next week you'd go over to the state tournament with me.'

'I decided I was too old.'

Dexter handed in his 'A Class' badge, collected what money was due him from the caddy-master, and walked home to Black Bear Village.

'The best — caddy I ever saw,' shouted Mr Mortimer Jones over a drink that afternoon. 'Never lost a ball! Willing! Intelligent! Quiet! Honest! Grateful!'

The little girl who had done this was eleven – beautifully ugly as little girls are apt to be who are destined after a few years to be inexpressibly lovely and bring no end of misery to a great number of men. The spark however was perceptible. There was a general ungodliness in the way her lips twisted down at the corners when she smiled, and in the – Heaven help us! – in the almost passionate quality of her eyes. Vitality is born early in such women. It was utterly in evidence now, shining through her thin frame in a sort of glow.

She had come eagerly out on to the course at nine o'clock with a white linen nurse and five small new golf-clubs in a white canvas bag which the nurse was carrying. When Dexter first saw her she was standing by the caddy house, rather ill at ease and trying to conceal the fact by engaging her nurse in an obviously unnatural conversation graced by startling and irrelevant grimaces from herself.

'Well, it's certainly a nice day, Hilda,' Dexter heard her say. She drew down the corners of her mouth, smiled, and glanced furtively around, her eyes in transit falling for an instant on Dexter.

Then to the nurse:

'Well, I guess there aren't many people out here this morning, are there?'

The smile again – radiant, blatantly artificial – convincing.

'I don't know what we're supposed to do now,' said the nurse looking nowhere in particular.

'Oh, that's all right. I'll fix it up.'

Dexter stood perfectly still, his mouth slightly ajar. He knew that if he moved forward a step his stare would be in her line of vision – if he moved backward he would lose his full view of her face. For a moment he had not realized how young she was. Now he remembered having seen her several times the year before – in bloomers.

Suddenly, involuntarily, he laughed, a short abrupt laugh – then, startled by himself, he turned and began to walk quickly away.

'Boy!'

Dexter stopped.

'Boy –'

Beyond question he was addressed. Not only that, but he was treated to that absurd smile, that preposterous smile – the memory of which at least a dozen men were to carry into middle age.

'Boy, do you know where the golf teacher is?'

'He's giving a lesson.'

'Well, do you know where the caddy-master is?'

'He isn't here yet this morning.'

'Oh.' For a moment this baffled her. She stood alternately on her right and left foot.

'We'd like to get a caddy,' said the nurse. 'Mrs Mortimer Jones sent us out to play golf, and we don't know how without we get a caddy.'

Here she was stopped by an ominous glance from Miss Jones, followed immediately by the smile.

'There aren't any caddies here except me,' said Dexter to the nurse, 'and I got to stay here in charge until the caddy-master gets here.'

'Oh.'

Miss Jones and her retinue now withdrew, and at a proper distance from Dexter became involved in a heated conversation, which was concluded by Miss Jones taking one of the clubs and hitting it on the ground with violence. For further emphasis she raised it again and was about to bring it down smartly upon the nurse's bosom, when the nurse seized the club and twisted it from her hands.

'You damn little mean old thing!' cried Miss Jones wildly.

Another argument ensued. Realizing that the elements of the comedy were implied in the scene, Dexter several times began to laugh, but each time restrained the laugh before it reached audibility. He could not resist the monstrous conviction that the little girl was justified in beating the nurse.

The situation was resolved by the fortuitous appearance of the caddy-master, who was appealed to immediately by the nurse.

'Miss Jones is to have a little caddy, and this one says he can't go.'

'Mr McKenna said I was to wait here till you came,' said Dexter quickly.

'Well, he's here now.' Miss Jones smiled cheerfully at the caddy-master. Then she dropped her bag and set off at a haughty mince towards the first tee.

'Well?' The caddy-master turned to Dexter. 'What you standing there like a dummy for? Go pick up the young lady's clubs.'

'I don't think I'll go out today,' said Dexter.

'You don't –'

'I think I'll quit.'

The enormity of his decision frightened him. He was a favourite caddy, and the thirty dollars a month he earned through the summer were not to be made elsewhere around the lake. But he had received a strong emotional shock, and his perturbation required a violent and immediate outlet.

It is not so simple as that, either. As so frequently would be the case in the future, Dexter was unconsciously dictated to by his winter dreams.

II

Now, of course, the quality and the seasonability of these winter dreams varied, but the stuff of them remained. They persuaded Dexter several years later to pass up a business course at the State University – his father, prospering now, would have paid his way – for the precarious advantage of attending an older and more famous university in the East, where he was bothered by his scanty funds. But do not get the impression, because his winter dreams happened to be concerned at first with musings on the rich, that there was anything merely snobbish in the boy. He wanted not association with glittering things and glittering people – he wanted the glittering things themselves. Often he reached out for the best without knowing why he wanted it – and sometimes he ran up against the mysterious denials and prohibitions in which life indulges. It is with one of those denials and not with his career as a whole that this story deals.

He made money. It was rather amazing. After college he went to the city from which Black Bear Lake draws its wealthy patrons. When he was only twenty-three and had been there not quite two years, there were already people who liked to say: 'Now *there's* a boy –' All about him rich men's sons were peddling bonds precariously, or investing patrimonies precariously, or plodding through the two dozen volumes of the 'George Washington Commercial Course', but Dexter borrowed a thousand dollars on his college degree and his confident mouth, and bought a partnership in a laundry.

It was a small laundry when he went into it, but Dexter made a speciality of learning how the English washed fine woollen golf-stockings without shrinking them, and within a year he was catering to the trade that wore knickerbockers. Men were insisting that their Shetland hose and sweaters go to his laundry, just as they had insisted on a caddy who could find golf-balls. A little later he was doing their wives' lingerie as well – and running five branches in different parts of the city. Before he was twenty-seven he owned the largest string of laundries in his section of the country. It was then that he sold out and went to New York. But the part of his story that concerns us goes back to the days when he was making his first big success.

When he was twenty-three Mr Hart – one of the grey-haired men who like to say 'Now there's a boy' – gave him a guest card to the Sherry Island Golf Club for a weekend. So he signed his name one day on the register, and that afternoon played golf in a foursome with Mr Hart and Mr Sandwood and Mr T. A. Hedrick. He did not consider it necessary to remark that he had once carried Mr Hart's bag over this same links, and that he knew every trap and gully with his eyes shut – but he found himself glancing at the four caddies who trailed them, trying to catch a gleam or gesture that would remind him of himself, that would lessen the gap which lay between his present and his past.

It was a curious day, slashed abruptly with fleeting, familiar impressions. One minute he had the sense of being a trespasser – in the next he was impressed by the tremendous superiority he felt towards Mr T. A. Hedrick, who was a bore and not even a good golfer any more.

Then, because of a ball Mr Hart lost near the fifteenth green, an enormous thing happened. While they were searching the stiff grasses of the rough there was a clear call of 'Fore!' from behind a hill in their rear. And as they all turned abruptly from their search a bright new ball sliced abruptly over the hill and caught Mr T. A. Hedrick in the abdomen.

'By Gad!' cried Mr T. A. Hedrick, 'they ought to put some of these crazy women off the course. It's getting to be outrageous.'

A head and a voice came up together over the hill:

'Do you mind if we go through?'

'You hit me in the stomach!' declared Mr Hedrick wildly.

'Did I?' The girl approached the group of men. 'I'm sorry. I yelled "Fore!"'

Her glance fell casually on each of the men – then scanned the fairway for her ball.

'Did I bounce into the rough?'

It was impossible to determine whether this question was ingenuous or malicious. In a moment, however, she left no doubt, for as her partner came up over the hill she called cheerfully:

'Here I am! I'd have gone on the green except that I hit something.'

As she took her stance for a short mashie shot, Dexter looked at her closely. She wore a blue gingham dress, rimmed at throat and shoulders with a white edging that accentuated her tan. The quality of exaggeration, of thinness, which had made her passionate eyes and down-turning mouth absurd at eleven, was gone now. She was arrestingly beautiful. The colour in her cheeks was centred like the colour in a picture – it was not a 'high' colour, but a sort of fluctuating and feverish warmth, so shaded that it seemed at any moment it would recede and disappear. This colour and the mobility of her mouth gave a continual impression of flux, of intense life, of passionate vitality – balanced only partially by the sad luxury of her eyes.

She swung her mashie impatiently and without interest, pitching the ball into a sand-pit on the other side of the green. With a quick, insincere smile and a careless 'Thank you!' she went on after it.

'That Judy Jones!' remarked Mr Hedrick on the next tee, as they waited – some moments – for her to play on ahead. 'All she needs is to be turned up and spanked for six months and then to be married off to an old-fashioned cavalry captain.'

'My God, she's good-looking!' said Mr Sandwood, who was just over thirty.

'Good-looking!' cried Mr Hedrick contemptuously, 'she always looks as if she wanted to be kissed! Turning those big cow-eyes on every calf in town!'

It was doubtful if Mr Hedrick intended a reference to the maternal instinct.

'She'd play pretty good golf if she'd try,' said Mr Sandwood.

'She has no form,' said Mr Hedrick solemnly.

'She has a nice figure,' said Mr Sandwood.

'Better thank the Lord she doesn't drive a swifter ball,' said Mr Hart, winking at Dexter,

Later in the afternoon the sun went down with a riotous swirl of gold and varying blues and scarlets, and left the dry, rustling night of Western summer. Dexter watched from the veranda of the Golf Club, watched the even overlap of the waters in the little wind, silver molasses under the harvest-moon. Then the moon held a finger to her lips and the lake became a clear pool, pale and quiet. Dexter put on his bathing-suit and swam out to the farthest raft, where he stretched dripping on the wet canvas of the springboard.

There was a fish jumping and a star shining and the lights around the lake were gleaming. Over on a dark peninsula a piano was playing the songs of last summer and of summers before that – songs from 'Chin-Chin' and 'The Count of Luxemburg' and 'The Chocolate Soldier' – and because the sound of a piano over a stretch of water had always seemed beautiful to Dexter he lay perfectly quiet and listened.

The tune the piano was playing at that moment had been gay and new five years before when Dexter was a sophomore at college. They had played it at a prom once when he could not afford the luxury of proms, and he had stood outside the gymnasium and listened. The sound of the tune precipitated in him a sort of ecstasy and it was with that ecstasy he viewed what happened to him now. It was a mood of intense appreciation, a sense that, for once, he was magnificently attuned to life and that everything about him was radiating a brightness and a glamour he might never know again.

A low, pale oblong detached itself suddenly from the darkness of the Island, spitting forth the reverberate sound of a racing motor-boat. Two white streamers of cleft water rolled themselves out behind it and almost immediately the boat was beside him, drowning out the hot tinkle of the piano in the drone of its spray. Dexter raising himself on his arms was aware of a figure standing at the wheel, of two dark eyes regarding him over the lengthening space of water – then the boat had gone by and was sweeping in an immense and purposeless circle of spray round and round in the middle of the lake. With equal eccentricity one of the circles flattened out and headed back towards the raft.

'Who's that?' she called, shutting off her motor. She was so near now that Dexter could see her bathing-suit, which consisted apparently of pink rompers.

The nose of the boat bumped the raft, and as the latter tilted rakishly he was precipitated toward her. With different degrees of interest they recognized each other.

'Aren't you one of those men we played through this afternoon,' she demanded.

He was.

'Well, do you know how to drive a motor-boat? Because if you do I wish you'd drive this one so I can ride on the surf-board behind. My name is Judy Jones' – she favoured him with an absurd smirk – rather, what tried to be a smirk, for, twist her mouth as she might, it was not grotesque, it was merely beautiful – 'and I live in a house over there on the Island, and in that house there is a man waiting for me. When he drove up at the door I drove out of the dock because he says I'm his ideal.'

There was a fish jumping and a star shining and the lights around the lake were gleaming. Dexter sat beside Judy Jones and she explained how her boat was driven. Then she was in the water, swimming to the floating surf-board with a sinuous crawl. Watching her was without effort to the eye, watching a branch waving or a sea-gull flying. Her arms, burned to butternut, moved sinuously among the dull platinum ripples, elbow appearing first, casting the forearm back with a cadence of falling water, then reaching out and down, stabbing a path ahead.

They moved out into the lake; turning, Dexter saw that she was kneeling on the low rear of the now up-tilted surf-board.

'Go faster,' she called, 'fast as it'll go.'

Obediently he jammed the lever forward and the white spray mounted at the bow. When he looked around again the girl was standing up on the rushing board, her arms spread wide, her eyes lifted towards the moon.

'It's awful cold,' she shouted. 'What's your name?'

He told her.

'Well, why don't you come to dinner tomorrow night?'

His heart turned over like the fly-wheel of the boat, and, for the second time, her casual whim gave a new direction to his life.

III

Next evening while he waited for her to come downstairs, Dexter peopled the soft deep summer room and the sun-porch that opened from it with the men who had already loved Judy Jones. He knew the sort of men they were – the men who when he first went to college had entered from the great prep schools with graceful clothes and the deep tan of healthy summers. He had seen that, in one sense, he was better than these men. He was newer and stronger. Yet in acknowledging to himself that he wished his children to be like them he was admitting that he was but the rough, strong stuff from which they eternally sprang.

When the time had come for him to wear good clothes, he had known who were the best tailors in America, and the best tailors in America had made him the suit he wore this evening. He had acquired that particular reserve peculiar to his university, that set it off from other universities. He recognized the value to him of such a mannerism and he had adopted it; he knew that to be careless in dress and manner required more confidence than to be careful. But carelessness was for his children. His mother's name had been Krimslich. She was a Bohemian of the peasant class and she had talked broken English to the end of her days. Her son must keep to the set patterns.

At a little after seven Judy Jones came downstairs. She wore a blue silk afternoon dress, and he was disappointed at first that she had not put on something more elaborate. This feeling was accentuated when, after a brief greeting, she went to the door of a butler's pantry and pushing it open called: 'You can serve dinner, Martha.' He had rather expected that a butler would announce dinner, that there would be a cocktail. Then he put these thoughts behind him as they sat down side by side on a lounge and looked at each other.

'Father and mother won't be here,' she said thoughtfully.

He remembered the last time he had seen her father, and he was glad the parents were not to be here tonight – they might wonder who he was. He had been born in Keeble, a Minnesota village fifty miles farther north, and he always gave Keeble as his home instead of Black Bear Village. Country towns were well enough to come from if they weren't inconveniently in sight and used as foot-stools by fashionable lakes.

They talked of his university, which she had visited frequently during the past two years, and of the nearby city which supplied Sherry Island with its patrons, and whither Dexter would return next day to his .
prospering laundries.

During dinner she slipped into a moody depression which gave Dexter a feeling of uneasiness. Whatever petulance she uttered in her throaty voice worried him. Whatever she smiled at, at him, at a chicken liver, at nothing – it disturbed him that her smile could have no root in mirth, or even in amusement. When the scarlet corners of her lips turned down, it was less a smile than an invitation to a kiss.

Then, after dinner, she led him out on the dark sun-porch and deliberately changed the atmosphere.

'Do you mind if I weep a little?' she said.

'I'm afraid I'm boring you,' he responded quickly.

'You're not, I like you. But I've just had a terrible afternoon. There was a man I cared about, and this afternoon he told me out of a clear sky that he was poor as a church-mouse. He'd never even hinted it before. Does this sound horribly mundane?'

'Perhaps he was afraid to tell you.'

'Suppose he was,' she answered. 'He didn't start right. You see, if I'd thought of him as poor – well, I've been mad about loads of poor men, and fully intended to marry them all. But in this case, I hadn't thought of him that way, and my interest in him wasn't strong enough to survive the shock. As if a girl calmly informed her fiancé that she was a widow. He might not object to widows, but –'

'Let's start right,' she interrupted herself suddenly. 'Who are you, anyhow?'

For a moment Dexter hesitated. Then:

'I'm nobody,' he announced. 'My career is largely a matter of futures.'

'Are you poor?'

'No,' he said frankly, 'I'm probably making more money than any man my age in the Northwest. I know that's an obnoxious remark, but you advised me to start right.'

There was a pause. Then she smiled and the corners of her mouth drooped and an almost imperceptible sway brought her closer to him, looking up into his eyes. A lump rose in Dexter's throat, and he waited breathless for the experiment, facing the unpredictable compound that would form mysteriously from the elements of their lips. Then he saw – she communicated her excitement to him, lavishly, deeply, with kisses that were not a promise but a fulfilment. They aroused in him not hunger demanding renewal but surfeit that would demand more surfeit . . . kisses that were like charity, creating want by holding back nothing at all.

It did not take him many hours to decide that he had wanted Judy Jones ever since he was a proud, desirous little boy.

IV

It began like that – and continued, with varying shades of intensity, on such a note right up to the dénouement. Dexter surrendered a part of himself to the most direct and unprincipled personality with which he had ever come in contact. Whatever Judy wanted, she went after with the full pressure of her charm. There was no divergence of method, no jockeying for position or premeditation of effects – there was a very little mental side to any of her affairs. She simply made men conscious to the highest degree of her physical loveliness. Dexter had no desire to change her. Her deficiencies were knit up with a passionate energy that transcended and justified them.

When, as Judy's head lay against his shoulder that first night, she whispered, 'I don't know what's the matter with me. Last night I thought I was in love with a man and tonight I think I'm in love with you –', it seemed to him a beautiful and romantic thing to say. It was the exquisite excitability that for the moment he controlled and owned. But a week later he was compelled to view this same quality in a different light. She took him in her roadster to a picnic supper, and after supper she disappeared, likewise in her roadster, with another man. Dexter became enormously upset and was scarcely able to be decently civil to the other people present. When she assured him that she had not kissed the other man, he knew she was lying – yet he was glad that she had taken the trouble to lie to him.

He was, as he found before the summer ended, one of a varying dozen who circulated about her. Each of them had at one time been favoured above all others – about half of them still basked in the solace of occasional sentimental revivals. Whenever one showed signs of dropping out through long neglect, she granted him a brief honeyed hour; which encouraged him to tag along for a year or so longer. Judy made these forays upon the helpless and defeated without malice, indeed half unconscious that there was anything mischievous in what she did.

When a new man came to town everyone dropped out – dates were automatically cancelled.

The helpless part of trying to do anything about it was that she did it all herself. She was not a girl who could be 'won' in the kinetic sense –

she was proof against cleverness, she was proof against charm; if any of these assailed her too strongly she would immediately resolve the affair to a physical basis, and under the magic of her physical splendour the strong as well as the brilliant played her game and not their own. She was entertained only by the gratification of her desires and by the direct exercise of her own charm. Perhaps from so much youthful love, so many youthful lovers, she had come, in self-defence, to nourish herself wholly from within.

Succeeding Dexter's first exhilaration came restlessness and dissatisfaction. The helpless ecstasy of losing himself in her was opiate rather than tonic. It was fortunate for his work during the winter that those moments of ecstasy came infrequently. Early in their acquaintance it had seemed for a while that there was a deep and spontaneous mutual attraction – that first August, for example, three days of long evenings on her dusky veranda, of strange wan kisses through the late afternoon, in shadowy alcoves or behind the protecting trellises of the garden arbours, of mornings when she was fresh as a dream and almost shy at meeting him in the clarity of the rising day. There was all the ecstasy of an engagement about it, sharpened by his realization that there was no engagement. It was during those three days that, for the first time, he had asked her to marry him. She said 'maybe some day', she said 'kiss me', she said 'I'd like to marry you', she said 'I love you' – she said – nothing.

The three days were interrupted by the arrival of a New York man who visited at her house for half September. To Dexter's agony, rumour engaged them. The man was the son of the president of a great trust company. But at the end of a month it was reported that Judy was yawning. At a dance one night she sat all evening in a motor-boat with a local beau, while the New Yorker searched the club for her frantically. She told the local beau that she was bored with her visitor, and two days later he left. She was seen with him at the station, and it was reported that he looked very mournful indeed.

On this note the summer ended. Dexter was twenty-four, and he found himself increasingly in a position to do as he wished. He joined two clubs in the city and lived at one of them. Though he was by no means an integral part of the stag-lines at these clubs, he managed to be on hand at dances where Judy Jones was likely to appear. He could have gone out socially as much as he liked – he was an eligible young man, now, and popular with down-town fathers. His confessed devotion to Judy Jones had rather solidified his position. But he had no social aspirations and rather despised the dancing men who were always on tap for the Thursday or Saturday parties and who filled in at dinners with the younger married set. Already he was playing with the idea of going East to New York. He wanted to take Judy Jones with him. No disillusion as to the world in which she had grown up could cure his illusion as to her desirability.

Remember that – for only in the light of it can what he did for her be understood.

Eighteen months after he first met Judy Jones he became engaged to another girl. Her name was Irene Scheerer, and her father was one of the men who had always believed in Dexter. Irene was light-haired and sweet and honourable, and a little stout, and she had two suitors whom she pleasantly relinquished when Dexter formally asked her to marry him.

Summer, fall, winter, spring, another summer, another fall – so much he had given of his active life to the incorrigible lips of Judy Jones. She had treated him with interest, with encouragement, with malice, with indifference, with contempt. She had inflicted on him the innumerable little slights and indignities possible in such a case – as if in revenge for having ever cared for him at all. She had beckoned him and yawned at him and beckoned him again and he had responded often with bitterness and narrowed eyes. She had brought him ecstatic happiness and intolerable agony of spirit. She had caused him untold inconvenience and not a little trouble. She had insulted him, and she had ridden over him, and she had played his interest in her against his interest in his work – for fun. She had done everything to him except to criticize him – this she had not done – it seemed to him only because it might have sullied the utter indifference she manifested and sincerely felt towards him.

When autumn had come and gone again it occurred to him that he could not have Judy Jones. He had to beat this into his mind but he convinced himself at last. He lay awake at night for a while and argued it over. He told himself the trouble and the pain she had caused him, he enumerated her glaring deficiencies as a wife. Then he said to himself that he loved her, and after a while he fell asleep. For a week, lest he imagined her husky voice over the telephone or her eyes opposite him at lunch, he worked hard and late, and at night he went to his office and plotted out his years.

At the end of a week he went to a dance and cut in on her once. For almost the first time since they had met he did not ask her to sit out with him or tell her that she was lovely. It hurt him that she did not

miss these things – that was all. He was not jealous when he saw that
there was a new man tonight. He had been hardened against jealousy
long before.

He stayed late at the dance. He sat for an hour with Irene Scheerer
and talked about books and about music. He knew very little about
either. But he was beginning to be master of his own time now, and he
had a rather priggish notion that he – the young and already fabulously
successful Dexter Green – should know more about such things.

That was in October, when he was twenty-five. In January, Dexter
and Irene became engaged. It was to be announced in June, and they
were to be married three months later.

The Minnesota winter prolonged itself interminably, and it was almost
May when the winds came soft and the snow ran down into Black Bear
Lake at last. For the first time in over a year Dexter was enjoying a certain
tranquillity of spirit. Judy Jones had been in Florida, and afterwards in
Hot Springs, and somewhere she had been engaged, and somewhere she
had broken it off. At first, when Dexter had definitely given her up, it
had made him sad that people still linked them together and asked for
news of her, but when he began to be placed at dinner next to Irene
Scheerer people didn't ask him about her any more – they told him
about her. He ceased to be an authority on her.

May at last. Dexter walked the streets at night when the darkness
was damp as rain, wondering that so soon, with so little done, so much
of ecstasy had gone from him. May one year back had been marked by
Judy's poignant, unforgivable, yet forgiven turbulence – it had been one
of those rare times when he fancied she had grown to care for him. That
old penny's worth of happiness he had spent for this bushel of content.
He knew that Irene would be no more than a curtain spread behind
him, a hand moving among gleaming teacups, a voice calling to children
. . . fire and loveliness were gone, the magic of nights and the wonder
of the varying hours and seasons . . . slender lips, down-turning, dropping to his lips and bearing him up into a heaven of eyes . . . The thing
was deep in him. He was too strong and alive for it to die lightly.

In the middle of May when the weather balanced for a few days on
the thin bridge that led to deep summer he turned in one night at Irene's
house. Their engagement was to be announced in a week now – no one
would be surprised at it. And tonight they would sit together on the
lounge at the University Club and look on for an hour at the dancers.
It gave him a sense of solidity to go with her – she was so sturdily
popular, so intensely 'great'.

He mounted the steps of the brownstone house and stepped inside.

'Irene,' he called.

Mrs Scheerer came out of the living-room to meet him.

'Dexter,' she said, 'Irene's gone upstairs with a splitting headache. She wanted to go with you but I made her go to bed.'

'Nothing serious, I –'

'Oh, no. She's going to play golf with you in the morning. You can spare her for just one night, can't you, Dexter?'

Her smile was kind. She and Dexter liked each other. In the living-room he talked for a moment before he said good night.

Returning to the University Club, where he had rooms, he stood in the doorway for a moment and watched the dancers. He leaned against the door-post, nodded at a man or two – yawned.

'Hello, darling.'

The familiar voice at his elbow startled him. Judy Jones had left a man and crossed the room to him – Judy Jones, a slender enamelled doll in cloth of gold; gold in a band at her head, gold in two slipper points at her dress's hem. The fragile glow of her face seemed to blossom as she smiled at him. A breeze of warmth and light blew through the room. His hands in the pockets of his dinner-jacket tightened spasmodically. He was filled with a sudden excitement.

'When did you get back?' he asked casually.

'Come here and I'll tell you about it.'

She turned and he followed her. She had been away – he could have wept at the wonder of her return. She had passed through enchanted streets, doing things that were like provocative music. All mysterious happenings, all fresh and quickening hopes, had gone away with her, come back with her now.

She turned in the doorway.

'Have you a car here? If you haven't, I have.'

'I have a coupé.'

In then, with a rustle of golden cloth. He slammed the door. Into so many cars she had stepped – like this – like that – her back against the leather, so – her elbow resting on the door – waiting. She would have been soiled long since had there been anything to soil her – except herself – but this was her own self outpouring.

With an effort he forced himself to start the car and back into the street. This was nothing, he must remember. She had done this before, and he had put her behind him, as he would have crossed a bad account from his books.

He drove slowly down-town and, affecting abstraction, traversed the deserted streets of the business section, peopled here and there where a movie was giving out its crowd or where consumptive or pugilistic youth lounged in front of pool halls. The clink of glasses and the slap of hands on the bars issued from saloons, cloisters of glazed glass and dirty yellow light.

She was watching him closely and the silence was embarrassing, yet in this crisis he could find no casual word with which to profane the hour. At a convenient turning he began to zigzag back towards the University Club.

'Have you missed me?' she asked suddenly.

'Everybody missed you.'

He wondered if she knew of Irene Scheerer. She had been back only a day – her absence had been almost contemporaneous with his engagement.

'What a remark!' Judy laughed sadly – without sadness. She looked at him searchingly. He became absorbed in the dashboard.

'You're handsomer than you used to be,' she said thoughtfully. 'Dexter, you have the most rememberable eyes.'

He could have laughed at this, but he did not laugh. It was the sort of thing that was said to sophomores. Yet it stabbed at him.

'I'm awfully tired of everything, darling.' She called everyone darling, endowing the endearment with careless, individual camaraderie. 'I wish you'd marry me.'

The directness of this confused him. He should have told her now that he was going to marry another girl, but he could not tell her. He could as easily have sworn that he had never loved her.

'I think we'd get along,' she continued, on the same note, 'unless probably you've forgotten me and fallen in love with another girl.'

Her confidence was obviously enormous. She had said, in effect, that she found such a thing impossible to believe, that if it were true he had merely committed a childish indiscretion – and probably to show off. She would forgive him, because it was not a matter of any moment but rather something to be brushed aside lightly.

'Of course you could never love anybody but me,' she continued, 'I like the way you love me. Oh, Dexter, have you forgotten last year?'

'No, I haven't forgotten.'

'Neither have I!'

Was she sincerely moved – or was she carried along by the wave of her own acting?

'I wish we could be like that again,' she said, and he forced himself to answer:

'I don't think we can.'

'I suppose not . . . I hear you're giving Irene Scheerer a violent rush.'

There was not the faintest emphasis on the name, yet Dexter was suddenly ashamed.

'Oh, take me home,' cried Judy suddenly; 'I don't want to go back to that idiotic dance – with those children.'

Then, as he turned up the street that led to the residence district, Judy began to cry quietly to herself. He had never seen her cry before.

The dark street lightened, the dwellings of the rich loomed up around them, he stopped his coupé in front of the great white bulk of the Mortimer Joneses' house, somnolent, gorgeous, drenched with the splendour of the damp moonlight. Its solidity startled him. The strong walls, the steel of the girders, the breadth and beam and pomp of it were there only to bring out the contrast with the young beauty beside him. It was sturdy to accentuate her slightness – as if to show what a breeze could be generated by a butterfly's wing.

He sat perfectly quiet, his nerves in wild clamour, afraid that if he moved he would find her irresistibly in his arms. Two tears had rolled down her wet face and trembled on her upper lip.

'I'm more beautiful than anybody else,' she said brokenly, 'why can't I be happy?' Her moist eyes tore at his stability – her mouth turned slowly downwards with an exquisite sadness: 'I'd like to marry you if you'll have me, Dexter. I suppose you think I'm not worth having, but I'll be so beautiful for you, Dexter.'

A million phrases of anger, pride, passion, hatred, tenderness fought on his lips. Then a perfect wave of emotion washed over him, carrying off with it a sediment of wisdom, of convention, of doubt, of honour. This was his girl who was speaking, his own, his beautiful, his pride.

'Won't you come in?' He heard her draw in her breath sharply.

Waiting.

'All right,' his voice was trembling, 'I'll come in.'

V

It was strange that neither when it was over nor a long time afterwards did he regret that night. Looking at it from the perspective of ten years, the fact that Judy's flare for him endured just one month seemed of little importance. Nor did it matter that by his yielding he subjected himself to a deeper agony in the end and gave serious hurt to Irene Scheerer and to Irene's parents, who had befriended him. There was nothing sufficiently pictorial about Irene's grief to stamp itself on his mind.

Dexter was at bottom hard-minded. The attitude of the city on his action was of no importance to him, not because he was going to leave the city, but because any outside attitude on the situation seemed superficial. He was completely indifferent to popular opinion. Nor, when he had seen that it was no use, that he did not possess in himself the power to move fundamentally or to hold Judy Jones, did he bear any malice towards her. He loved her, and he would love her until the day he was too old for loving – but he could not have her. So he tasted the deep pain that is reserved only for the strong, just as he had tasted for a little while the deep happiness.

Even the ultimate falsity of the grounds upon which Judy terminated the engagement: that she did not want to 'take him away' from Irene – Judy who had wanted nothing else – did not revolt him. He was beyond any revulsion or any amusement.

He went East in February with the intention of selling out his laundries and settling in New York – but the war came to America in March and changed his plans. He returned to the West, handed over the management of the business to his partner, and went into the first officers' training-camp in late April. He was one of those young thousands who greeted the war with a certain amount of relief, welcoming the liberation from webs of tangled emotion.

VI

This story is not his biography, remember, although things creep into it which have nothing to do with those dreams he had when he was young. We are almost done with them and with him now. There is only one more incident to be related here, and it happens seven years farther on.

It took place in New York, where he had done well – so well that there were no barriers too high for him. He was thirty-two years old, and, except for one flying trip immediately after the war, he had not been West in seven years. A man named Devlin from Detroit came into his office to see him in a business way, and then and there this incident occurred, and closed out, so to speak, this particular side of his life.

'So you're from the Middle West,' said the man Devlin with careless
curiosity. 'That's funny – I thought men like you were probably born
and raised on Wall Street. You know – wife of one of my best friends in
Detroit came from your city. I was an usher at the wedding.'

Dexter waited with no apprehension of what was coming.

'Judy Simms,' said Devlin with no particular interest; 'Judy Jones she
was once.'

'Yes, I knew her.' A dull impatience spread over him. He had heard,
of course, that she was married – perhaps deliberately he had heard no
more.

'Awfully nice girl,' brooded Devlin meaninglessly, 'I'm sort of sorry
for her.'

'Why?' Something in Dexter was alert, receptive, at once.

'Oh, Lud Simms has gone to pieces in a way. I don't mean he ill-uses
her, but he drinks and runs around –'

'Doesn't she run around?'

'No. Stays at home with her kids.'

'Oh.'

'She's a little too old for him,' said Devlin.

'Too old!' cried Dexter. 'Why, man, she's only twenty-seven.'

He was possessed with a wild notion of rushing out into the streets
and taking a train to Detroit. He rose to his feet spasmodically.

'I guess you're busy,' Devlin apologized quickly. 'I didn't realize –'

'No, I'm not busy,' said Dexter, steadying his voice. 'I'm not busy at
all. Not busy at all. Did you say she was – twenty-seven? No, I said she
was twenty-seven.'

'Yes, you did,' agreed Devlin dryly.

'Go on, then. Go on.'

'What do you mean?'

'About Judy Jones.'

Devlin looked at him helplessly.

'Well, that's – I told you all there is to it. He treats her like the devil.
Oh, they're not going to get divorced or anything. When he's particularly
outrageous she forgives him. In fact, I'm inclined to think she loves him.
She was a pretty girl when she first came to Detroit.'

A pretty girl! The phrase struck Dexter as ludicrous.

'Isn't she – a pretty girl, any more?'

'Oh, she's all right.'

'Look here,' said Dexter, sitting down suddenly. 'I don't understand.
You say she was a "pretty girl" and now you say she's "all right". I

don't understand what you mean – Judy Jones wasn't a pretty girl, at all. She was a great beauty. Why, I knew her, I knew her. She was –'

Devlin laughed pleasantly.

'I'm not trying to start a row,' he said. 'I think Judy's a nice girl and I like her. I can't understand how a man like Lud Simms could fall madly in love with her, but he did.' Then he added: 'Most of the women like her.'

Dexter looked closely at Devlin, thinking wildly that there must be a reason for this, some insensitivity in the man or some private malice.

'Lots of women fade just like *that*,' Devlin snapped his fingers. 'You must have seen it happen. Perhaps I've forgotten how pretty she was at her wedding. I've seen her so much since then, you see. She has nice eyes.'

A sort of dullness settled down upon Dexter. For the first time in his life he felt like getting very drunk. He knew that he was laughing loudly at something Devlin had said, but he did not know what it was or why it was funny. When, in a few minutes, Devlin went he lay down on his lounge and looked out of the window at the New York sky-line into which the sun was sinking in dull lovely shades of pink and gold.

He had thought that having nothing else to lose he was invulnerable at last – but he knew that he had just lost something more, as surely as if he had married Judy Jones and seen her fade away before his eyes.

The dream was gone. Something had been taken from him. In a sort of panic he pushed the palms of his hands into his eyes and tried to bring up a picture of the waters lapping on Sherry Island and the moonlit veranda, and gingham on the golf-links and the dry sun and the gold colour of her neck's soft down. And her mouth damp to his kisses and her eyes plaintive with melancholy and her freshness like new fine linen in the morning. Why, these things were no longer in the world! They had existed and they existed no longer.

For the first time in years the tears were streaming down his face. But they were for himself now. He did not care about mouth and eyes and moving hands. He wanted to care, and he could not care. For he had gone away and he could never go back any more. The gates were closed, the sun was gone down, and there was no beauty but the grey beauty of steel that withstands all time. Even the grief he could have borne was left behind in the country of illusion, of youth, of the richness of life, where his winter dreams had flourished.

'Long ago,' he said, 'long ago, there was something in me, but now that thing is gone. Now that thing is gone, that thing is gone. I cannot cry. I cannot care. That thing will come back no more.'

'THE SENSIBLE THING'

I

At the Great American Lunch Hour young George O'Kelly straightened his desk deliberately and with an assumed air of interest. No one in the office must know that he was in a hurry, for success is a matter of atmosphere, and it is not well to advertise the fact that your mind is separated from your work by a distance of seven hundred miles.

But once out of the building he set his teeth and began to run, glancing now and then at the gay noon of early spring which filled Times Square and loitered less than twenty feet over the heads of the crowd. The crowd all looked slightly upwards and took deep March breaths, and the sun dazzled their eyes so that scarcely anyone saw anyone else but only their own reflection on the sky.

George O'Kelly, whose mind was over seven hundred miles away, thought that all outdoors was horrible. He rushed into the subway, and for ninety-five blocks bent a frenzied glance on a car-card which showed vividly how he had only one chance in five of keeping his teeth for ten years. At 137th Street he broke off his study of commercial art, left the subway, and began to run again, a tireless, anxious run that brought him this time to his home – one room in a high, horrible apartment-house in the middle of nowhere.

There it was on the bureau, the letter – in sacred ink, on blessed paper – all over the city, people, if they listened, could hear the beating of George O'Kelly's heart. He read the commas, the blots, and the thumb-smudge on the margin – then he threw himself hopelessly upon his bed.

He was in a mess, one of those terrific messes which are ordinary incidents in the life of the poor, which follow poverty like birds of prey. The poor go under or go up or go wrong or even go on, somehow, in a way the poor have – but George O'Kelly was so new to poverty that had any one denied the uniqueness of his case he would have been astounded.

Less than two years ago he had been graduated with honours from the Massachusetts Institute of Technology and had taken a position with a firm of construction engineers in southern Tennessee. All his life he had thought in terms of tunnels and skyscrapers and great squat dams and tall, three-towered bridges, that were like dancers holding hands in a row, with heads as tall as cities and skirts of cable strand. It had seemed romantic to George O'Kelly to change the sweep of rivers and the shape of mountains so that life could flourish in the old bad lands of the world where it had never taken root before. He loved steel, and there was always steel near him in his dreams, liquid steel, steel in bars, and blocks and beams and formless plastic masses, waiting for him, as paint and canvas to his hand. Steel inexhaustible, to be made lovely and austere in his imaginative fire . . .

At present he was an insurance clerk at forty dollars a week with his dream slipping fast behind him. The dark little girl who had made this mess, this terrible and intolerable mess, was waiting to be sent for in a town in Tennessee.

In fifteen minutes the woman from whom he sublet his room knocked and asked him with maddening kindness if, since he was home, he would have some lunch. He shook his head, but the interruption aroused him, and getting up from the bed he wrote a telegram.

'Letter depressed me have you lost your nerve you are foolish and just upset to think of breaking off why not marry me immediately sure we can make it all right –'

He hesitated for a wild minute, and then added in a hand that could scarcely be recognized as his own: 'In any case I will arrive tomorrow at six o'clock.'

When he finished he ran out of the apartment and down to the telegraph office near the subway stop. He possessed in this world not quite one hundred dollars, but the letter showed that she was 'nervous' and this left him no choice. He knew what 'nervous' meant – that she was emotionally depressed, that the prospect of marrying into a life of poverty and struggle was putting too much strain upon her love.

George O'Kelly reached the insurance company at his usual run, the run that had become almost second nature to him, that seemed best to express the tension under which he lived. He went straight to the manager's office.

'I want to see you, Mr Chambers,' he announced breathlessly.

'Well?' Two eyes, eyes like winter windows, glared at him with ruthless impersonality.

'I want to get four days' vacation.'

'Why, you had a vacation just two weeks ago!' said Mr Chambers in surprise.

'That's true,' admitted the distraught young man, 'but now I've got to have another.'

'Where'd you go last time? To your home?'

'No, I went to – a place in Tennessee.'

'Well, where do you want to go this time?'

'Well, this time I want to go to – a place in Tennessee.'

'You're consistent, anyhow,' said the manager dryly. 'But I didn't realize you were employed here as a travelling salesman.'

'I'm not,' cried George desperately, 'but I've got to go.'

'All right,' agreed Mr Chambers, 'but you don't have to come back. So don't!'

'I won't.' And to his own astonishment as well as Mr Chambers' George's face grew pink with pleasure. He felt happy, exultant – for the first time in six months he was absolutely free. Tears of gratitude stood in his eyes, and he seized Mr Chambers warmly by the hand.

'I want to thank you,' he said with a rush of emotion, 'I don't want to come back. I think I'd have gone crazy if you'd said that I could come back. Only I couldn't quit myself, you see, and I want to thank you for – for quitting for me.'

He waved his hand magnanimously, shouted aloud, 'You owe me three days' salary but you can keep it!' and rushed from the office. Mr Chambers rang for his stenographer to ask if O'Kelly had seemed queer lately. He had fired many men in the course of his career, and they had taken it in many different ways, but none of them had thanked him – ever before.

II

Jonquil Cary was her name, and to George O'Kelly nothing had ever looked so fresh and pale as her face when she saw him and fled to him eagerly along the station platform. Her arms were raised to him, her mouth was half parted for his kiss, when she held him off suddenly and lightly and, with a touch of embarrassment, looked around. Two boys, somewhat younger than George, were standing in the background.

'This is Mr Craddock and Mr Holt,' she announced cheerfully. 'You met them when you were here before.'

Disturbed by the transition of a kiss into an introduction and suspecting some hidden significance, George was more confused when he found that the automobile which was to carry them to Jonquil's house belonged to one of the two young men. It seemed to put him at a disadvantage. On the way Jonquil chattered between the front and back seats, and when he tried to slip his arm around her under cover of the twilight she compelled him with a quick movement to take her hand instead.

'Is this street on the way to your house?' he whispered. 'I don't recognize it.'

'It's the new boulevard. Jerry just got this car today, and he wants to show it to me before he takes us home.'

When, after twenty minutes, they were deposited at Jonquil's house, George felt that the first happiness of the meeting, the joy he had recognized so surely in her eyes back in the station, had been dissipated by the intrusion of the ride. Something that he had looked forward to had been rather casually lost, and he was brooding on this as he said good night stiffly to the two young men. Then his ill-humour faded as Jonquil drew him into a familiar embrace under the dim light of the front hall and told him in a dozen ways, of which the best was without words, how she had missed him. Her emotion reassured him, promised his anxious heart that everything would be all right.

They sat together on the sofa, overcome by each other's presence, beyond all except fragmentary endearments. At the supper hour Jonquil's father and mother appeared and were glad to see George. They liked him, and had been interested in his engineering career when he had first come to Tennessee over a year before. They had been sorry when he had given it up and gone to New York to look for something more immediately profitable, but while they deplored the curtailment of his career they sympathized with him and were ready to recognize the engagement. During dinner they asked about his progress in New York.

'Everything's going fine,' he told them with enthusiasm. 'I've been promoted – better salary.'

He was miserable as he said this – but they were all so glad.

'They must like you,' said Mrs Cary, 'that's certain – or they wouldn't let you off twice in three weeks to come down here.'

'I told them they had to,' explained George hastily; 'I told them if they didn't I wouldn't work for them any more.'

'But you ought to save your money,' Mrs Cary reproached him gently. 'Not spend it all on this expensive trip.'

Dinner was over – he and Jonquil were alone and she came back into his arms.

'So glad you're here,' she sighed. 'Wish you never were going away again, darling.'

'Do you miss me?'

'Oh, so much, so much.'

'Do you – do other men come to see you often? Like those two kids?'

The question surprised her. The dark velvet eyes stared at him.

'Why, of course they do. All the time. Why – I've told you in letters that they did, dearest.'

This was true – when he had first come to the city there had been already a dozen boys around her, responding to her picturesque fragility with adolescent worship, and a few of them perceiving that her beautiful eyes were also sane and kind.

'Do you expect me never to go anywhere' – Jonquil demanded, leaning back against the sofa-pillows until she seemed to look at him from many miles away – 'and just fold my hands and sit still – forever?'

'What do you mean?' he blurted out in a panic. 'Do you mean you think I'll never have enough money to marry you?'

'Oh, don't jump at conclusions so, George.'

'I'm not jumping at conclusions. That's what you said.'

George decided suddenly that he was on dangerous grounds. He had not intended to let anything spoil this night. He tried to take her again in his arms, but she resisted unexpectedly, saying:

'It's hot. I'm going to get the electric fan.'

When the fan was adjusted they sat down again, but he was in a supersensitive mood and involuntarily he plunged into the specific world he had intended to avoid.

'When will you marry me?'

'Are you ready for me to marry you?'

All at once his nerves gave way, and he sprang to his feet.

'Let's shut off that damned fan,' he cried, 'it drives me wild. It's like a clock ticking away all the time I'll be with you. I came here to be happy and forget everything about New York and time –'

He sank down on the sofa as suddenly as he had risen. Jonquil turned off the fan, and drawing his head down into her lap began stroking his hair.

'Let's sit like this,' she said softly, 'just sit quiet like this, and I'll put you to sleep. You're all tired and nervous and your sweetheart'll take care of you.'

'But I don't want to sit like this,' he complained, jerking up suddenly, 'I don't want to sit like this at all. I want you to kiss me. That's the only thing that makes me rest. And any ways I'm not nervous – it's you that's nervous. I'm not nervous at all.'

To prove that he wasn't nervous he left the couch and plumped himself into a rocking-chair across the room.

'Just when I'm ready to marry you you write me the most nervous letters, as if you're going to back out, and I have to come rushing down here –'

'You don't have to come if you don't want to.'

'But I *do* want to!' insisted George.

It seemed to him that he was being very cool and logical and that she was putting him deliberately in the wrong. With every word they were drawing farther and farther apart – and he was unable to stop himself or to keep worry and pain out of his voice.

But in a minute Jonquil began to cry sorrowfully and he came back to the sofa and put his arm around her. He was the comforter now, drawing her head close to his shoulder, murmuring old familiar things until she grew calmer and only trembled a little, spasmodically, in his arms. For over an hour they sat there, while the evening pianos thumped their last cadences into the street outside. George did not move, or think, or hope, lulled into numbness by the premonition of disaster. The clock would tick on, past eleven, past twelve, and then Mrs Cary would call down gently over the banister – beyond that he saw only tomorrow and despair.

III

In the heat of the next day the breaking-point came. They had each guessed the truth about the other, but of the two she was the more ready to admit the situation.

'There's no use going on,' she said miserably, 'you know you hate the insurance business, and you'll never do well in it.'

'That's not it,' he insisted stubbornly; 'I hate going on alone. If you'll marry me and come with me and take a chance with me, I can make good at anything, but not while I'm worrying about you down here.'

She was silent a long time before she answered, not thinking – for she had seen the end – but only waiting, because she knew that every word would seem more cruel than the last. Finally she spoke:

'George, I love you with all my heart, and I don't see how I can ever love anyone else but you. If you'd been ready for me two months ago I'd have married you – now I can't because it doesn't seem to be the sensible thing.'

He made wild accusations – there was someone else – she was keeping something from him!

'No, there's no one else.'

This was true. But reacting from the strain of this affair she had found relief in the company of young boys like Jerry Holt, who had the merit of meaning absolutely nothing in her life.

George didn't take the situation well, at all. He seized her in his arms and tried literally to kiss her into marrying him at once. When this failed, he broke into a long monologue of self-pity, and ceased only when he saw that he was making himself despicable in her sight. He threatened to leave when he had no intention of leaving, and refused to go when she told him that, after all, it was best that he should.

For a while she was sorry, then for another while she was merely kind.

'You'd better go now,' she cried at last, so loud that Mrs Cary came downstairs in alarm.

'Is something the matter?'

'I'm going away, Mrs Cary,' said George brokenly. Jonquil had left the room.

'Don't feel so badly, George.' Mrs Cary blinked at him in helpless sympathy – sorry and, in the same breath, glad that the little tragedy was almost done. 'If I were you I'd go home to your mother for a week or so. Perhaps after all this is the sensible thing –'

'Please don't talk,' he cried. 'Please don't say anything to me now!'

Jonquil came into the room again, her sorrow and her nervousness alike tucked under powder and rouge and hat.

'I've ordered a taxicab,' she said impersonally. 'We can drive around until your train leaves.'

She walked out on the front porch. George put on his coat and hat and stood for a minute exhausted in the hall – he had eaten scarcely a bite since he had left New York. Mrs Cary came over, drew his head down and kissed him on the cheek, and he felt very ridiculous and weak in his knowledge that the scene had been ridiculous and weak at the end. If he had only gone the night before – left her for the last time with a decent pride.

The taxi had come, and for an hour these two that had been lovers rode along the less-frequented streets, He held her hand and grew calmer in the sunshine, seeing too late that there had been nothing all along to do or say.

'I'll come back,' he told her.

'I know you will,' she answered, trying to put a cheery faith into her voice. 'And we'll write each other – sometimes.'

'No,' he said, 'we won't write. I couldn't stand that. Some day I'll come back.'

'I'll never forget you, George.'

They reached the station, and she went with him while he bought his ticket . . .

'Why, George O'Kelly and Jonquil Cary!'

It was a man and a girl whom George had known when he had worked in town, and Jonquil seemed to greet their presence with relief. For an interminable five minutes they all stood there talking; then the train roared into the station, and with ill-concealed agony in his face George held out his arms towards Jonquil. She took an uncertain step towards him, faltered, and then pressed his hand quickly as if she were taking leave of a chance friend.

'Good-bye, George,' she was saying, 'I hope you have a pleasant trip.

'Good-bye, George. Come back and see us all again.'

Dumb, almost blind with pain, he seized his suitcase, and in some dazed way got himself aboard the train.

Past clanging street-crossings, gathering speed through wide suburban spaces towards the sunset. Perhaps she too would see the sunset and pause for a moment, turning, remembering, before he faded with her sleep into the past. This night's dusk would cover up forever the sun and the trees and the flowers and laughter of his young world.

IV

On a damp afternoon in September of the following year a young man with his face burned to a deep copper glow got off a train at a city in Tennessee. He looked around anxiously, and seemed relieved when he found that there was no one in the station to meet him. He taxied to the best hotel in the city where he registered with some satisfaction as George O'Kelly, Cuzco, Peru.

Up in his room he sat for a few minutes at the window looking down into the familiar street below. Then with his hand trembling faintly he took off the telephone receiver and called a number.

'Is Miss Jonquil in?'

'This is she.'

'Oh –' His voice after overcoming a faint tendency to waver went on with friendly formality.

'This is George O'Kelly. Did you get my letter?'

'Yes. I thought you'd be in today.'

Her voice, cool and unmoved, disturbed him, but not as he had expected. This was the voice of a stranger, unexcited, pleasantly glad to see him – that was all. He wanted to put down the telephone and catch his breath.

'I haven't seen you for – a long time.' He succeeded in making this sound offhand. 'Over a year.'

He knew how long it had been – to the day.

'It'll be awfully nice to talk to you again.'

'I'll be there in about an hour.'

He hung up. For four long seasons every minute of his leisure had been crowded with anticipation of this hour, and now this hour was here. He had thought of finding her married, engaged, in love – he had not thought she would be unstirred at his return.

There would never again in his life, he felt, be another ten months like these he had just gone through. He had made an admittedly remarkable showing for a young engineer – stumbled into two unusual opportunities, one in Peru, whence he had just returned, and another consequent upon it, in New York, whither he was bound. In this short time he had risen from poverty into a position of unlimited opportunity.

He looked at himself in the dressing-table mirror. He was almost black with tan, but it was a romantic black, and in the last week, since he had had time to think it, it had given him considerable pleasure. The hardiness of his frame, too, he appraised with a sort of fascination. He had lost part of an eyebrow somewhere, and he still wore an elastic bandage on his knee, but he was too young not to realize that on the steamer many women had looked at him with unusual tributary interest.

His clothes, of course, were frightful. They had been made for him by a Greek tailor in Lima – in two days. He was young enough, too, to have explained this sartorial deficiency to Jonquil in his otherwise laconic note. The only further detail it contained was a request that he should *not* be met at the station.

George O'Kelly, of Cuzco, Peru, waited an hour and a half in the hotel, until, to be exact, the sun had reached a midway position in the sky. Then, freshly shaven and talcum-powdered towards a somewhat more Caucasian hue, for vanity at the last minute had overcome romance, he engaged a taxicab and set out for the house he knew so well.

He was breathing hard – he noticed this but he told himself that it was excitement, not emotion. He was here; she was not married – that was enough. He was not even sure what he had to say to her. But this was the moment of his life that he felt he could least easily have dispensed with. There was no triumph, after all, without a girl concerned, and if he did not lay his spoils at her feet he could at least hold them for a passing moment before her eyes.

The house loomed up suddenly beside him, and his first thought was that it had assumed a strange unreality. There was nothing changed – only everything was changed. It was smaller and it seemed shabbier than before – there was no cloud of magic hovering over its roof and issuing from the windows of the upper floor. He rang the doorbell and an unfamiliar coloured maid appeared. Miss Jonquil would be down in a moment. He wet his lips nervously and walked into the sitting-room – and the feeling of unreality increased. After all, he saw, this was only a room, and not the enchanted chamber where he had passed those poignant hours. He sat in a chair, amazed to find it a chair, realizing that his imagination had distorted and coloured all these simple familiar things.

Then the door opened and Jonquil came into the room – and it was as though everything in it suddenly blurred before his eyes. He had not remembered how beautiful she was, and he felt his face grow pale and his voice diminish to a poor sigh in his throat.

She was dressed in pale green, and a gold ribbon bound back her dark, straight hair like a crown. The familiar velvet eyes caught his as she came through the door, and a spasm of fright went through him at her beauty's power of inflicting pain.

He said 'Hello', and they each took a few steps forward and shook hands. Then they sat in chairs quite far apart and gazed at each other across the room.

'You've come back,' she said, and he answered just as tritely: 'I wanted to stop in and see you as I came through.'

He tried to neutralize the tremor in his voice by looking anywhere but at her face. The obligation to speak was on him, but, unless he immediately began to boast, it seemed that there was nothing to say. There had never been anything casual in their previous relations – it didn't seem possible that people in this position would talk about the weather.

'This is ridiculous,' he broke out in sudden embarrassment. 'I don't know exactly what to do. Does my being here bother you?'

'No.' The answer was both reticent and impersonally sad. It depressed him.

'Are you engaged?' he demanded.

'No.'

'Are you in love with someone?'

She shook her head.

'Oh.' He leaned back in his chair. Another subject seemed exhausted – the interview was not taking the course he had intended.

'Jonquil,' he began, this time on a softer key, 'after all that's happened between us, I wanted to come back and see you. Whatever I do in the future I'll never love another girl as I've loved you.'

This was one of the speeches he had rehearsed. On the steamer it had seemed to have just the right note – a reference to the tenderness he would always feel for her combined with a non-committal attitude towards his present state of mind. Here with the past around him, beside him, growing minute by minute more heavy on the air, it seemed theatrical and stale.

She made no comment, sat without moving, her eyes fixed on him with an expression that might have meant everything or nothing.

'You don't love me any more, do you?' he asked her in a level voice.

'No.'

When Mrs Cary came in a minute later, and spoke to him about his success – there had been a half-column about him in the local paper – he was a mixture of emotions. He knew now that he still wanted this girl, and he knew that the past sometimes comes back – that was all. For the rest he must be strong and watchful and he would see.

'And now,' Mrs Cary was saying, 'I want you two to go and see the lady who has the chrysanthemums. She particularly told me she wanted to see you because she'd read about you in the paper.'

They went to see the lady with the chrysanthemums. They walked along the street, and he recognized with a sort of excitement just how her shorter footsteps always fell in between his own. The lady turned out to be nice, and the chrysanthemums were enormous and extraordinarily beautiful. The lady's gardens were full of them, white and pink and yellow, so that to be among them was a trip back into the heart of summer. There were two gardens full, and a gate between them; when they strolled towards the second garden the lady went first through the gate.

And then a curious thing happened. George stepped aside to let Jonquil pass, but instead of going through she stood still and stared at him for a minute. It was not so much the look, which was not a smile, as it was the moment of silence. They saw each other's eyes, and both took a short, faintly accelerated breath, and then they went on into the second garden. That was all.

The afternoon waned. They thanked the lady and walked home slowly, thoughtfully, side by side. Through dinner, too, they were silent. George told Mr Cary something of what had happened in South America, and managed to let it be known that everything would be plain sailing for him in the future.

Then dinner was over, and he and Jonquil were alone in the room which had seen the beginning of their love affair and the end. It seemed to him long ago and inexpressibly sad. On the sofa he had felt agony and grief such as he would never feel again. He would never be so weak or so tired and miserable and poor. Yet he knew that that boy of fifteen months before had had something, a trust, a warmth that was gone forever. The sensible thing – they had done the sensible thing. He had traded his youth for strength and carved success out of despair. But with his youth, life had carried away the freshness of his love.

'You won't marry me, will you?' he said quietly.

Jonquil shook her dark head.

'I'm never going to marry,' she answered.

He nodded.

'I'm going on to Washington in the morning,' he said.

'Oh –'

'I have to go. I've got to be in New York by the first, and meanwhile I want to stop off in Washington.'

'Business!'

'No-o,' he said as if reluctantly. 'There's someone there I must see who was very kind to me when I was so – down and out.'

This was invented. There was no one in Washington for him to see – but he was watching Jonquil narrowly, and he was sure that she winced a little, that her eyes closed and then opened wide again.

'But before I go I want to tell you the things that happened to me since I saw you, and, as maybe we won't meet again, I wonder if – if just this once you'd sit in my lap like you used to. I wouldn't ask except since there's no one else – yet – perhaps it doesn't matter.'

She nodded, and in a moment was sitting in his lap as she had sat so often in that vanished spring. The feel of her head against his shoulder, of her familiar body, sent a shock of emotion over him. His arms holding her had a tendency to tighten around her, so he leaned back and began to talk thoughtfully into the air.

He told her of a despairing two weeks in New York which had terminated with an attractive if not very profitable job in a construction plant in Jersey City. When the Peru business had first presented itself it had not seemed an extraordinary opportunity. He was to be third assistant engineer on the expedition, but only ten of the American party, including eight rodmen and surveyors, had ever reached Cuzco. Ten days later the chief of the expedition was dead of yellow fever. That had been his chance, a chance for anybody but a fool, a marvellous chance –

'A chance for anybody but a fool?' she interrupted innocently.

'Even for a fool,' he continued. 'It was wonderful. Well, I wired New York –'

'And so,' she interrupted again, 'they wired that you ought to take a chance?'

'Ought to!' he exclaimed, still leaning back. 'That I *had* to. There was no time to lose –'

'Not a minute?'

'Not a minute.'

'Not even time for –' she paused.

'For what?'

'Look.'

He bent his head forward suddenly, and she drew herself to him in the same moment, her lips half open like a flower,

'Yes,' he whispered into her lips. 'There's all the time in the world . . .'

All the time in the world – his life and hers. But for an instant as he kissed her he knew that though he search through eternity he could never recapture those lost April hours. He might press her close now till the muscles knotted on his arms – she was something desirable and rare that he had fought for and made his own – but never again an intangible whisper in the dusk, or on the breeze of night . . .

Well, let it pass, he thought; April is over, April is over. There are all kinds of love in the world, but never the same love twice.

ABSOLUTION

I

There was once a priest with cold, watery eyes, who, in the still of the night, wept cold tears. He wept because the afternoons were warm and long, and he was unable to attain a complete mystical union with our Lord. Sometimes, near four o'clock, there was a rustle of Swede girls along the path by his window, and in their shrill laughter he found a terrible dissonance that made him pray aloud for the twilight to come. At twilight the laughter and the voices were quieter, but several times he had walked past Romberg's Drug Store when it was dusk and the yellow lights shone inside and the nickel taps of the soda-fountain were gleaming, and he had found the scent of cheap toilet soap desperately sweet on the air. He passed that way when he returned from hearing confessions on Saturday nights, and he grew careful to walk on the other side of the street so that the smell of the soap would float upward before it reached his nostrils as it drifted, rather like incense, towards the summer moon.

But there was no escape from the hot madness of four o'clock. From his window, as far as he could see, the Dakota wheat thronged the valley of the Red River. The wheat was terrible to look upon and the carpet pattern to which in agony he bent his eyes sent his thought brooding through grotesque labyrinths, open always to the unavoidable sun.

One afternoon when he had reached the point where the mind runs down like an old clock, his housekeeper brought into his study a beautiful, intense little boy of eleven named Rudolph Miller. The little boy sat down in a patch of sunshine, and the priest, at his walnut desk, pretended to be very busy. This was to conceal his relief that some one had come into his haunted room.

Presently he turned around and found himself staring into two enormous, staccato eyes, lit with gleaming points of cobalt light. For a moment their expression startled him – then he saw that his visitor was in a state of abject fear.

'Your mouth is trembling,' said Father Schwartz, in a haggard voice.
The little boy covered his quivering mouth with his hand.

'Are you in trouble?' asked Father Schwartz, sharply. 'Take your
hand away from your mouth and tell me what's the matter.'

The boy – Father Schwartz recognized him now as the son of a
parishioner, Mr Miller, the freight-agent – moved his hand reluctantly
off his mouth and became articulate in a despairing whisper.

'Father Schwartz – I've committed a terrible sin.'

'A sin against purity?'

'No, Father . . . worse.'

Father Schwartz's body jerked sharply.

'Have you killed somebody?'

'No – but I'm afraid –' the voice rose to a shrill whimper.

'Do you want to go to confession?'

The little boy shook his head miserably. Father Schwartz cleared his
throat so that he could make his voice soft and say some quiet, kind
thing. In this moment he should forget his own agony, and try to act
like God. He repeated to himself a devotional phrase, hoping that in
return God would help him to act correctly.

'Tell me what you've done,' said his new soft voice.

The little boy looked at him through his tears, and was reassured by
the impression of moral resiliency which the distraught priest had
created. Abandoning as much of himself as he was able to this man,
Rudolph Miller began to tell his story.

'On Saturday, three days ago, my father he said I had to go to
confession, because I hadn't been for a month, and the family they go
every week, and I hadn't been. So I just as leave go, I didn't care. So I
put it off till after supper because I was playing with a bunch of kids
and father asked me if I went, and I said "no", and he took me by the
neck and he said "You go now", so I said "All right", so I went over
to church. And he yelled after me: "Don't come back till you go" . . .'

II

'On Saturday, Three Days Ago'

The plush curtain of the confessional rearranged its dismal creases,
leaving exposed only the bottom of an old man's shoe. Behind the
curtain an immortal soul was alone with God and the Reverend Adolphus
Schwartz, priest of the parish. Sound began, a laboured whispering,

sibilant and discreet, broken at intervals by the voice of the priest in audible question.

Rudolph Miller knelt in the pew beside the confessional and waited, straining nervously to hear, and yet not to hear what was being said within. The fact that the priest was audible alarmed him. His own turn came next, and the three or four others who waited might listen unscrupulously while he admitted his violations of the Sixth and Ninth Commandments.

Rudolph had never committed adultery, nor even coveted his neighbour's wife – but it was the confession of the associate sins that was particularly hard to contemplate. In comparison he relished the less shameful fallings away – they formed a greyish background which relieved the ebony mark of sexual offences upon his soul.

He had been covering his ears with his hands, hoping that his refusal to hear would be noticed, and a like courtesy rendered to him in turn, when a sharp movement of the penitent in the confessional made him sink his face precipitately into the crook of his elbow. Fear assumed solid form, and pressed out a lodging between his heart and his lungs. He must try now with all his might to be sorry for his sins – not because he was afraid, but because he had offended God. He must convince God that he was sorry and to do so he must first convince himself. After a tense emotional struggle he achieved a tremulous self-pity, and decided that he was now ready. If, by allowing no other thought to enter his head, he could preserve this state of emotion unimpaired until he went into that large coffin set on end, he would have survived another crisis in his religious life.

For some time, however, a demoniac notion had partially possessed him. He could go home now, before his turn came, and tell his mother that he had arrived too late, and found the priest gone. This, unfortunately, involved the risk of being caught in a lie. As an alternative he could say that he *had* gone to confession, but this meant that he must avoid communion next day, for communion taken upon an uncleansed soul would turn to poison in his mouth, and he would crumple limp and damned from the altar-rail.

Again Father Schwartz's voice became audible.

'And for your –'

The words blurred to a husky mumble, and Rudolph got excitedly to his feet. He felt that it was impossible to go to confession this afternoon. He hesitated tensely. Then from the confessional came a tap, a creak, and a sustained rustle. The slide had fallen and the plush curtain trembled. Temptation had come to him too late . . .

'Bless me, Father, for I have sinned . . . I confess to Almighty God and to you, Father, that I have sinned . . . Since my last confession it has been one month and three days . . . I accuse myself of – taking the Name of the Lord in vain . . .'

This was an easy sin. His curses had been but bravado – telling of them was little less than a brag.

'. . . of being mean to an old lady.'

The wan shadow moved a little on the latticed slat.

'How, my child?'

'Old Lady Swenson,' Rudolph's murmur soared jubilantly. 'She got our baseball that we knocked in her window, and she wouldn't give it back, so we yelled "Twenty-three, Skidoo," at her all afternoon. Then about five o'clock she had a fit, and they had to have the doctor.'

'Go on, my child.'

'Of – of not believing I was the son of my parents.'

'What?' The interrogation was distinctly startled.

'Of not believing that I was the son of my parents.'

'Why not?'

'Oh, just pride,' answered the penitent airily.

'You mean you thought yourself too good to be the son of your parents?'

'Yes, Father.' On a less jubilant note.

'Go on.'

'Of being disobedient and calling my mother names. Of slandering people behind their back. Of smoking –'

Rudolph had now exhausted the minor offences, and was approaching the sins it was agony to tell. He held his fingers against his face like bars as if to press out between them the shame in his heart.

'Of dirty words and immodest thoughts and desires,' he whispered very low.

'How often?'

'I don't know.'

'Once a week? Twice a week?'

'Twice a week.'

'Did you yield to these desires?'

'No, Father.'

'Were you alone when you had them?'

'No, Father. I was with two boys and a girl.'

'Don't you know, my child, that you should avoid the occasions of sin as well as the sin itself? Evil companionship leads to evil desires and evil desires to evil actions. Where were you when this happened?'

'In a barn back of –'

'I don't want to hear any names,' interrupted the priest sharply.

'Well, it was up in the loft of this barn and this girl and – a fella, they were saying things – saying immodest things, and I stayed.'

'You should have gone – you should have told the girl to go.'

He should have gone! He could not tell Father Schwartz how his pulse had bumped in his wrist, how a strange, romantic excitement had possessed him when those curious things had been said. Perhaps, in the houses of delinquency, among the dull and hard-eyed incorrigible girls can be found those for whom has burned the whitest fire.

'Have you anything else to tell me?'

'I don't think so, Father.'

Rudolph felt a great relief. Perspiration had broken out under his tight-pressed fingers.

'Have you told any lies?'

The question startled him. Like all those who habitually and instinctively lie, he had an enormous respect and awe for the truth. Something almost exterior to himself dictated a quick, hurt answer. 'Oh no, Father, I never tell lies.'

For a moment, like the commoner in the king's chair, he tasted the pride of the situation. Then as the priest began to murmur conventional admonitions he realized that in heroically denying he had told lies, he had committed a terrible sin – he had told a lie in confession.

In automatic response to Father Schwartz's 'Make an act of contrition', he began to repeat aloud meaninglessly:

'Oh, my God, I am heartily sorry for having offended Thee . . .'

He must fix this now – it was a bad mistake – but as his teeth shut on the last words of his prayer there was a sharp sound, and the slat was closed.

A minute later when he emerged into the twilight the relief in coming from the muggy church into an open world of wheat and sky postponed the full realization of what he had done. Instead of worrying he took a deep breath of the crisp air and began to say over and over to himself the words 'Blatchford Sarnemington, Blatchford Sarnemington!'

Blatchford Sarnemington was himself, and these words were in effect a lyric. When he became Blatchford Sarnemington a suave nobility flowed from him. Blatchford Sarnemington lived in great sweeping triumphs. When Rudolph half closed his eyes it meant that Blatchford had established dominance over him and, as he went by, there were envious mutters in the air: 'Blatchford Sarnemington! There goes Blatchford Sarnemington.'

He was Blatchford now for a while as he strutted homeward along the staggering road, but when the road braced itself in macadam in order to become the main street of Ludwig, Rudolph's exhilaration faded out and his mind cooled, and he felt the horror of his lie. God, of course, already knew of it – but Rudolph reserved a corner of his mind where he was safe from God, where he prepared the subterfuges with which he often tricked God. Hiding now in this corner he considered how he could best avoid the consequences of his mis-statement.

At all costs he must avoid communion next day. The risk of angering God to such an extent was too great. He would have to drink water 'by accident' in the morning, and thus, in accordance with a church law, render himself unfit to receive communion that day. In spite of its flimsiness this subterfuge was the most feasible that occurred to him. He accepted its risks and was concentrating on how best to put it into effect, as he turned the corner by Romberg's Drug Store and came in sight of his father's house.

III

Rudolph's father, the local freight-agent, had floated with the second wave of German and Irish stock to the Minnesota–Dakota country. Theoretically, great opportunities lay ahead of a young man of energy in that day and place, but Carl Miller had been incapable of establishing either with his superiors or his subordinates the reputation for approximate immutability which is essential to success in a hierarchic industry. Somewhat gross, he was, nevertheless, insufficiently hard-headed and unable to take fundamental relationships for granted, and this inability made him suspicious, unrestful, and continually dismayed.

His two bonds with the colourful life were his faith in the Roman Catholic Church and his mystical worship of the Empire Builder, James J. Hill. Hill was the apotheosis of that quality in which Miller himself was deficient – the sense of things, the feel of things, the hint of rain in the wind on the cheek. Miller's mind worked late on the old decisions of other men, and he had never in his life felt the balance of any single thing in his hands. His weary, sprightly, undersized body was growing old in Hill's gigantic shadow. For twenty years he had lived alone with Hill's name and God.

On Sunday morning Carl Miller awoke in the dustless quiet of six o'clock. Kneeling by the side of the bed he bent his yellow-grey hair and the full dapple bangs of his moustache into the pillow, and prayed for several minutes. Then he drew off his night-shirt – like the rest of his generation he had never been able to endure pyjamas – and clothed his thin, white, hairless body in woollen underwear.

He shaved. Silence in the other bedroom where his wife lay nervously asleep. Silence from the screened-off corner of the hall where his son's cot stood, and his son slept among his Alger books, his collection of cigar-bands, his mothy pennants – 'Cornell', 'Hamlin', and 'Greetings from Pueblo, New Mexico' – and the other possessions of his private life. From outside Miller could hear the shrill birds and the whirring movement of the poultry, and, as an undertone, the low, swelling click-a-click of the six-fifteen through train for Montana and the green coast beyond. Then as the cold water dripped from the wash-rag in his hand he raised his head suddenly – he had heard a furtive sound from the kitchen below.

He dried his razor hastily, slipped his dangling suspenders to his shoulder, and listened. Some one was walking in the kitchen, and he knew by the light footfall that it was not his wife. With his mouth faintly ajar he ran quickly down the stairs and opened the kitchen door.

Standing by the sink, with one hand on the still dripping faucet and the other clutching a full glass of water, stood his son. The boy's eyes, still heavy with sleep, met his father's with a frightened, reproachful beauty. He was barefooted, and his pyjamas were rolled up at the knees and sleeves.

For a moment they both remained motionless – Carl Miller's brow went down and his son's went up, as though they were striking a balance between the extremes of emotion which filled them. Then the bangs of the parent's moustache descended portentously until they obscured his mouth, and he gave a short glance around to see if anything had been disturbed.

The kitchen was garnished with sunlight which beat on the pans and made the smooth boards of the floor and table yellow and clean as wheat. It was the centre of the house where the fire burned and the tins fitted into tins like toys, and the steam whistled all day on a thin pastel note. Nothing was moved, nothing touched – except the faucet where beads of water still formed and dripped with a white flash into the sink below.

'What are you doing?'

'I got awful thirsty, so I thought I'd just come down and get –'

'I thought you were going to communion.'

A look of vehement astonishment spread over his son's face.

'I forgot all about it.'

'Have you drunk any water?'

'No –'

As the word left his mouth Rudolph knew it was the wrong answer, but the faded indignant eyes facing him had signalled up the truth before the boy's will could act. He realized, too, that he should never have come downstairs; some vague necessity for verisimilitude had made him want to leave a wet glass as evidence by the sink; the honesty of his imagination had betrayed him.

'Pour it out,' commanded his father, 'that water!'

Rudolph despairingly inverted the tumbler.

'What's the matter with you, anyways?' demanded Miller angrily.

'Nothing.'

'Did you go to confession yesterday?'

'Yes.'

'Then why were you going to drink water?'

'I don't know – I forgot.'

'Maybe you care more about being a little thirsty than you do about your religion.'

'I forgot.' Rudolph could feel the tears straining in his eyes.

'That's no answer.'

'Well, I did.'

'You better look out!' His father held to a high, persistent inquisitory note: 'if you're so forgetful that you can't remember your religion something better be done about it.'

Rudolph filled a sharp pause with:

'I can remember it all right.'

'First you begin to neglect your religion,' cried his father, fanning his own fierceness, 'the next thing you'll begin to lie and steal, and the *next* thing is the *reform* school!'

Not even this familiar threat could deepen the abyss that Rudolph saw before him. He must either tell all now, offering his body for what he knew would be a ferocious beating or else tempt the thunderbolts by receiving the Body and Blood of Christ with sacrilege upon his soul. And of the two the former seemed more terrible – it was not so much the beating he dreaded as the savage ferocity, outlet of the ineffectual man, which would lie behind it.

'Put down that glass and go upstairs and dress!' his father ordered, 'and when we get to church, before you go to communion, you better kneel down and ask God to forgive you for your carelessness.'

Some accidental emphasis in the phrasing of this command acted like a catalytic agent on the confusion and terror of Rudolph's mind. A wild, proud anger rose in him, and he dashed the tumbler passionately into the sink.

His father uttered a strained, husky sound, and sprang for him. Rudolph dodged to the side, tipped over a chair, and tried to get beyond the kitchen table. He cried out sharply when a hand gasped his pyjama shoulder, then he felt the dull impact of a fist against the side of his head, and glancing blows on the upper part of his body. As he slipped here and there in his father's grasp, dragged or lifted when he clung instinctively to an arm, aware of sharp smarts and strains, he made no sound except that he laughed hysterically several times. Then in less than a minute the blows abruptly ceased. After a lull during which Rudolph was tightly held, and during which they both trembled violently and uttered strange, truncated words, Carl Miller half dragged, half threatened his son upstairs.

'Put on your clothes!'

Rudolph was now both hysterical and cold. His head hurt him, and there was a long, shallow scratch on his neck from his father's fingernail, and he sobbed and trembled as he dressed. He was aware of his mother standing at the doorway in a wrapper, her wrinkled face compressing and squeezing and opening out into new series of wrinkles which floated and eddied from neck to brow. Despising her nervous ineffectuality and avoiding her rudely when she tried to touch his cheek with witch-hazel, he made a hasty, choking toilet. Then he followed his father out of the house and along the road towards the Catholic church.

IV

They walked without speaking except when Carl Miller acknowledged automatically the existence of passers-by. Rudolph's uneven breathing alone ruffled the hot Sunday silence.

His father stopped decisively at the door of the church.

'I've decided you'd better go to confession again. Go and tell Father Schwartz what you did and ask God's pardon.'

'You lost your temper, too!' said Rudolph quickly.

Carl Miller took a step towards his son, who moved cautiously backward.

'All right, I'll go.'

'Are you going to do what I say?' cried his father in a hoarse whisper.

'All right.'

Rudolph walked into the church, and for the second time in two days entered the confessional and knelt down. The slat went up almost at once.

'I accuse myself of missing my morning prayers.'

'Is that all?'

'That's all.'

A maudlin exultation filled him. Not easily ever again would he be able to put an abstraction before the necessities of his ease and pride. An invisible line had been crossed, and he had become aware of his isolation – aware that it applied not only to those moments when he was Blatchford Sarnemington but that it applied to all his inner life. Hitherto such phenomena as 'crazy' ambitions and petty shames and fears had been but private reservations, unacknowledged before the throne of his official soul. Now he realized unconsciously that his private reservations were himself – and all the rest a garnished front and a conventional flag. The pressure of his environment had driven him into the lonely secret road of adolescence.

He knelt in the pew beside his father. Mass began. Rudolph knelt up – when he was alone he slumped his posterior back against the seat – and tasted the consciousness of a sharp, subtle revenge. Beside him his father prayed that God would forgive Rudolph, and asked also that his own outbreak of temper would be pardoned. He glanced sidewise at his son, and was relieved to see that the strained, wild look had gone from his face and that he had ceased sobbing. The Grace of God, inherent in the Sacrament, would do the rest, and perhaps after Mass everything would be better. He was proud of Rudolph in his heart, and beginning to be truly as well as formally sorry for what he had done.

Usually, the passing of the collection box was the significant point for Rudolph in the services. If, as was often the case, he had no money to drop in he would be furiously ashamed and bow his head and pretend not to see the box, lest Jeanne Brady in the pew behind should take notice and suspect an acute family poverty. But today he glanced coldly into it as it skimmed under his eyes, noting with casual interest the large number of pennies it contained.

When the bell rang for communion, however, he quivered. There was no reason why God should not stop his heart. During the past twelve hours he had committed a series of mortal sins increasing in gravity, and he was now to crown them all with a blasphemous sacrilege.

'*Domine, non sum dignus; ut intres sub tectum meum; sed tantum dic verbo, et sanabitur anima mea . . .*'

There was a rustle in the pews, and the communicants worked their ways into the aisle with downcast eyes and joined hands. Those of larger piety pressed together their finger-tips to form steeples. Among these latter was Carl Miller. Rudolph followed him towards the altar-rail and knelt down, automatically taking up the napkin under his chin. The bell rang sharply, and the priest turned from the altar with the white Host held above the chalice:

'*Corpus Domini nostri Jesu Christi custodiat animam tuam in vitam aeternam.*'

A cold sweat broke out on Rudolph's forehead as the communion began. Along the line Father Schwartz moved, and with gathering nausea Rudolph felt his heart-valves weakening at the will of God. It seemed to him that the church was darker and that a great quiet had fallen, broken only by the inarticulate mumble which announced the approach of the Creator of Heaven and Earth. He dropped his head down between his shoulders and waited for the blow.

Then he felt a sharp nudge in his side. His father was poking him to sit up, not to slump against the rail; the priest was only two places away.

'*Corpus Domini nostri Jesu Christi custodiat animam tuam in vitam aeternam.*'

Rudolph opened his mouth. He felt the sticky wax taste of the wafer on his tongue. He remained motionless for what seemed an interminable period of time, his head still raised, the wafer undissolved in his mouth. Then again he started at the pressure of his father's elbow, and saw that the people were falling away from the altar like leaves and turning with blind downcast eyes to their pews, alone with God.

Rudolph was alone with himself, drenched with perspiration and deep in mortal sin. As he walked back to his pew the sharp taps of his cloven hoofs were loud upon the floor, and he knew that it was a dark poison he carried in his heart.

V

'*Sagitta Volante in Dei*'

The beautiful little boy with eyes like blue stones, and lashes that sprayed open from them like flower-petals, had finished telling his sin to Father Schwartz – and the square of sunshine in which he sat had moved forward an hour into the room. Rudolph had become less frightened now; once eased of the story a reaction had set in. He knew that as long as he was in the room with this priest God would not stop his heart, so he sighed and sat quietly, waiting for the priest to speak.

Father Schwartz's cold watery eyes were fixed upon the carpet pattern on which the sun had brought out the swastikas and the flat bloomless vines and the pale echoes of flowers. The hall-clock ticked insistently towards sunset, and from the ugly room and from the afternoon outside the window arose a stiff monotony, shattered now and then by the reverberate clapping of a far-away hammer on the dry air. The priest's nerves were strung thin and the beads of his rosary were crawling and squirming like snakes upon the green felt of his table top. He could not remember now what it was he should say.

Of all the things in this lost Swede town he was most aware of this little boy's eyes – the beautiful eyes, with lashes that left them reluctantly and curved back as though to meet them once more.

For a moment longer the silence persisted while Rudolph waited, and the priest struggled to remember something that was slipping farther and farther away from him, and the clock ticked in the broken house. Then Father Schwartz stared hard at the little boy and remarked in a peculiar voice:

'When a lot of people get together in the best places things go glimmering.'

Rudolph started and looked quickly at Father Schwartz's face.

'I said –' began the priest, and paused, listening. 'Do you hear the hammer and the clock ticking and the bees? Well, that's no good. The thing is to have a lot of people in the centre of the world, wherever that happens to be. Then' – his watery eyes widened knowingly – 'things go glimmering.'

'Yes, Father,' agreed Rudolph, feeling a little frightened.

'What are you going to be when you grow up?'

'Well, I was going to be a baseball-player for a while,' answered Rudolph nervously, 'but I don't think that is a very good ambition, so I think I'll be an actor or a Navy officer.'

Again the priest stared at him.

'I see *exactly* what you mean,' he said, with a fierce air.

Rudolph had not meant anything in particular, and at the implication that he had, he became more uneasy.

'This man is crazy,' he thought, 'and I'm scared of him. He wants me to help him out some way, and I don't want to.'

'You look as if things went glimmering,' cried Father Schwartz wildly. 'Did you ever go to a party?'

'Yes, Father.'

'And did you notice that everybody was properly dressed? That's what I mean. Just as you went into the party there was a moment when everybody was properly dressed. Maybe two little girls were standing by the door and some boys were leaning over the banisters, and there were bowls around full of flowers.'

'I've been to a lot of parties,' said Rudolph, rather relieved that the conversation had taken this turn.

'Of course,' continued Father Schwartz triumphantly, 'I knew you'd agree with me. But my theory is that when a whole lot of people get together in the best places things go glimmering all the time.'

Rudolph found himself thinking of Blatchford Sarnemington.

'Please listen to me!' commanded the priest impatiently. 'Stop worrying about last Saturday. Apostasy implies an absolute damnation only on the supposition of a previous perfect faith. Does that fix it?'

Rudolph had not the faintest idea what Father Schwartz was talking about, but he nodded and the priest nodded back at him and returned to his mysterious preoccupation.

'Why,' he cried, 'they have lights now as big as stars – do you realize that? I heard of one light they had in Paris or somewhere that was as big as a star. A lot of people had it – a lot of gay people. They have all sorts of things now that you never dreamed of.'

'Look here –' He came nearer to Rudolph, but the boy drew away, so Father Schwartz went back and sat down in his chair, his eyes dried out and hot. 'Did you ever see an amusement park?'

'No, Father.'

'Well, go and see an amusement park.' The priest waved his hand vaguely. 'It's a thing like a fair, only much more glittering. Go to one at night and stand a little way off from it in a dark place – under dark trees. You'll see a big wheel made of lights turning in the air, and a long slide shooting boats down into the water. A band playing somewhere, and a smell of peanuts – and everything will twinkle. But it won't remind you of anything, you see. It will all just hang out there in the night like a coloured balloon – like a big yellow lantern on a pole.'

Father Schwartz frowned as he suddenly thought of something.

'But don't get up close,' he warned Rudolph, 'because if you do you'll only feel the heat and the sweat and the life.'

All this talking seemed particularly strange and awful to Rudolph, because this man was a priest. He sat there, half terrified, his beautiful eyes open wide and staring at Father Schwartz. But underneath his terror he felt that his own inner convictions were confirmed. There was something ineffably gorgeous somewhere that had nothing to do with God. He no longer thought that God was angry at him about the original lie, because He must have understood that Rudolph had done it to make things finer in the confessional, brightening up the dinginess of his admissions by saying a thing radiant and proud. At the moment when he had affirmed immaculate honour a silver pennon had flapped out into the breeze somewhere and there had been the crunch of leather and the shine of silver spurs and a troop of horsemen waiting for dawn on a low green hill. The sun had made stars of light on their breastplates like the picture at home of the German cuirassiers at Sedan.

But now the priest was muttering inarticulate and heart-broken words, and the boy became wildly afraid. Horror entered suddenly in at the open window, and the atmosphere of the room changed. Father Schwartz collapsed precipitously down on his knees, and let his body settle back against a chair.

'Oh, my God!' he cried out, in a strange voice, and wilted to the floor.

Then a human oppression rose from the priest's worn clothes, and mingled with the faint smell of old food in the corners. Rudolph gave a sharp cry and ran in panic from the house – while the collapsed man lay there quite still, filling his room, filling it with voices and faces until it was crowded with echolalia, and rang loud with a steady shrill note of laughter.

Outside the window the blue sirocco trembled over the wheat, and girls with yellow hair walked sensuously along roads that bounded the fields, calling innocent, exciting things to the young men who were working in the lines between the grain. Legs were shaped under starchless gingham, and rims of the necks of dresses were warm and damp. For five hours now hot fertile life had burned in the afternoon. It would be night in three hours, and all along the land there would be those blonde Northern girls and the tall young men from the farms lying out beside the wheat, under the moon.

THE BABY PARTY

When John Andros felt old he found solace in the thought of life continuing through his child. The dark trumpets of oblivion were less loud at the patter of his child's feet or at the sound of his child's voice babbling mad non sequiturs to him over the telephone. The latter incident occurred every afternoon at three when his wife called the office from the country, and he came to look forward to it as one of the vivid minutes of his day.

He was not physically old, but his life had been a series of struggles up a series of rugged hills, and here at thirty-eight having won his battles against ill-health and poverty he cherished less than the usual number of illusions. Even his feeling about his little girl was qualified. She had interrupted his rather intense love-affair with his wife, and she was the reason for their living in a suburban town, where they paid for country air with endless servant troubles and the weary merry-go-round of the commuting train.

It was little Ede as a definite piece of youth that chiefly interested him. He liked to take her on his lap and examine minutely her fragrant, downy scalp and her eyes with their irises of morning blue. Having paid this homage John was content that the nurse should take her away. After ten minutes the very vitality of the child irritated him; he was inclined to lose his temper when things were broken, and one Sunday afternoon when she had disrupted a bridge game by permanently hiding up the ace of spades, he had made a scene that had reduced his wife to tears.

This was absurd and John was ashamed of himself. It was inevitable that such things would happen, and it was impossible that little Ede should spend all her indoor hours in the nursery upstairs when she was becoming, as her mother said, more nearly a 'real person' every day.

She was two and a half, and this afternoon, for instance, she was going to a baby party. Grown-up Edith, her mother, had telephoned the information to the office, and little Ede had confirmed the business by shouting 'I yam going to a *pantry*!' into John's unsuspecting left ear.

'Drop in at the Markeys' when you get home, won't you, dear?'
resumed her mother. 'It'll be funny. Ede's going to be all dressed up in
her new pink dress –'

The conversation terminated abruptly with a squawk which indicated
that the telephone had been pulled violently to the floor. John laughed
and decided to get an early train out; the prospect of a baby party in
someone else's house amused him.

'What a peach of a mess!' he thought humorously. 'A dozen mothers,
and each one looking at nothing but her own child. All the babies
breaking things and grabbing at the cake, and each mama going home
thinking about the subtle superiority of her own child to every other
child there.'

He was in a good humour today – all the things in his life were going
better than they had ever gone before. When he got off the train at his
station he shook his head at an importunate taxi man, and began to
walk up the long hill towards his house through the crisp December
twilight. It was only six o'clock but the moon was out, shining with
proud brilliance on the thin sugary snow that lay over the lawns.

As he walked along drawing his lungs full of cold air his happiness
increased, and the idea of a baby party appealed to him more and more.
He began to wonder how Ede compared to other children of her own
age, and if the pink dress she was to wear was something radical and
mature. Increasing his gait he came in sight of his own house, where
the lights of a defunct Christmas-tree still blossomed in the window, but
he continued on past the walk. The party was at the Markeys' next
door.

As he mounted the brick step and rang the bell he became aware of
voices inside, and he was glad he was not too late. Then he raised his
head and listened – the voices were not children's voices, but they were
loud and pitched high with anger; there were at least three of them
and one, which rose as he listened to a hysterical sob, he recognized
immediately as his wife's.

'There's been some trouble,' he thought quickly.

Trying the door, he found it unlocked and pushed it open.

The baby party started at half past four, but Edith Andros, calculating
shrewdly that the new dress would stand out more sensationally against
vestments already rumpled, planned the arrival of herself and little Ede
for five. When they appeared it was already a flourishing affair. Four
baby girls and nine baby boys, each one curled and washed and dressed

with all the care of a proud and jealous heart, were dancing to the music of a phonograph. Never more than two or three were dancing at once, but as all were continually in motion running to and from their mothers for encouragement, the general effect was the same.

As Edith and her daughter entered, the music was temporarily drowned out by a sustained chorus, consisting largely of the word *cute* and directed towards little Ede, who stood looking timidly about and fingering the edges of her pink dress. She was not kissed – this is the sanitary age – but she was passed along a row of mamas each one of whom said 'cu-u-ute' to her and held her pink little hand before passing her on to the next. After some encouragement and a few mild pushes she was absorbed into the dance, and became an active member of the party.

Edith stood near the door talking to Mrs Markey, and keeping an eye on the tiny figure in the pink dress. She did not care for Mrs Markey; she considered her both snippy and common, but John and Joe Markey were congenial and went in together on the commuting train every morning, so the two women kept up an elaborate pretence of warm amity. They were always reproaching each other for 'not coming to see me', and they were always planning the kind of parties that began with 'You'll have to come to dinner with us soon, and we'll go to the theatre,' but never matured further.

'Little Ede looks perfectly darling,' said Mrs Markey, smiling and moistening her lips in a way that Edith found particularly repulsive. 'So *grown-up* – I can't *believe* it!'

Edith wondered if 'little Ede' referred to the fact that Billy Markey, though several months younger, weighed almost five pounds more. Accepting a cup of tea she took a seat with two other ladies on a divan and launched into the real business of the afternoon, which of course lay in relating the recent accomplishments and insouciances of her child.

An hour passed. Dancing palled and the babies took to sterner sport. They ran into the dining-room, rounded the big table, and essayed the kitchen door, from which they were rescued by an expeditionary force of mothers. Having been rounded up they immediately broke loose, and rushing back to the dining-room tried the familiar swinging door again. The word 'overheated' began to be used, and small white brows were dried with small white handkerchiefs. A general attempt to make the babies sit down began, but the babies squirmed off laps with peremptory cries of 'Down! Down!' and the rush into the fascinating dining-room began anew.

This phase of the party came to an end with the arrival of refreshments, a large cake with two candles, and saucers of vanilla ice-cream. Billy Markey, a stout laughing baby with red hair and legs somewhat bowed, blew out the candles, and placed an experimental thumb on the white frosting. The refreshments were distributed, and the children ate, greedily but without confusion – they had behaved remarkably well all afternoon. They were modern babies who ate and slept at regular hours, so their dispositions were good, and their faces healthy and pink – such a peaceful party would not have been possible thirty years ago.

After the refreshments a gradual exodus began. Edith glanced anxiously at her watch – it was almost six, and John had not arrived. She wanted him to see Ede with the other children – to see how dignified and polite and intelligent she was, and how the only ice-cream spot on her dress was some that had dropped from her chin when she was joggled from behind.

'You're a darling,' she whispered to her child, drawing her suddenly against her knee. 'Do you know you're a darling? Do you *know* you're a darling?'

Ede laughed. 'Bow-wow,' she said suddenly.

'Bow-wow?' Edith looked around. 'There isn't any bow-wow.'

'Bow-wow,' repeated Ede. 'I want a bow-wow.'

Edith followed the small pointing finger.

'That isn't a bow-wow, dearest, that's a teddy-bear.'

'Bear?'

'Yes, that's a teddy-bear, and it belongs to Billy Markey. You don't want Billy Markey's teddy-bear, do you?'

Ede did want it.

She broke away from her mother and approached Billy Markey, who held the toy closely in his arms. Ede stood regarding him with inscrutable eyes, and Billy laughed.

Grown-up Edith looked at her watch again, this time impatiently.

The party had dwindled until, besides Ede and Billy, there were only two babies remaining – and one of the two remained only by virtue of having hidden himself under the dining-room table. It was selfish of John not to come. It showed so little pride in the child. Other fathers had come, half a dozen of them, to call for their wives, and they had stayed for a while and looked on.

There was a sudden wail. Ede had obtained Billy's teddy-bear by pulling it forcibly from his arms, and on Billy's attempt to recover it, she had pushed him casually to the floor.

'Why, Ede!' cried her mother, repressing an inclination to laugh.

Joe Markey, a handsome, broad-shouldered man of thirty-five, picked up his son and set him on his feet. 'You're a fine fellow,' he said jovially. 'Let a girl knock you over! You're a fine fellow.'

'Did he bump his head?' Mrs Markey returned anxiously from bowing the next to last remaining mother out of the door.

'No-o-o-o,' exclaimed Markey. 'He bumped something else, didn't you, Billy? He bumped something else.'

Billy had so far forgotten the bump that he was already making an attempt to recover his property. He seized a leg of the bear which projected from Ede's enveloping arms and tugged at it but without success.

'No,' said Ede emphatically.

Suddenly, encouraged by the success of her former half-accidental manoeuvre, Ede dropped the teddy-bear, placed her hands on Billy's shoulders and pushed him backward off his feet.

This time he landed less harmlessly; his head hit the bare floor just off the rug with a dull hollow sound, whereupon he drew in his breath and delivered an agonized yell.

Immediately the room was in confusion. With an exclamation Markey hurried to his son, but his wife was first to reach the injured baby and catch him up into her arms.

'Oh, *Billy*,' she cried, 'what a terrible bump! She ought to be spanked.'

Edith, who had rushed immediately to her daughter, heard this remark, and her lips came sharply together.

'Why, Ede,' she whispered perfunctorily, 'you bad girl!'

Ede put back her little head suddenly and laughed. It was a loud laugh, a triumphant laugh with victory in it and challenge and contempt. Unfortunately it was also an infectious laugh. Before her mother realized the delicacy of the situation, she too had laughed, an audible, distinct laugh not unlike the baby's, and partaking of the same overtones.

Then, as suddenly, she stopped.

Mrs Markey's face had grown red with anger, and Markey, who had been feeling the back of the baby's head with one finger, looked at her, frowning.

'It's swollen already,' he said with a note of reproof in his voice. 'I'll get some witch-hazel.'

But Mrs Markey had lost her temper. 'I don't see anything funny about a child being hurt!' she said in a trembling voice.

Little Ede meanwhile had been looking at her mother curiously. She noted that her own laugh had produced her mother's and she wondered if the same cause would always produce the same effect. So she chose this moment to throw back her head and laugh again.

To her mother the additional mirth added the final touch of hysteria to the situation. Pressing her handkerchief to her mouth she giggled irrepressibly. It was more than nervousness – she felt that in a peculiar way she was laughing with her child – they were laughing together.

It was in a way a defiance – those two against the world.

While Markey rushed upstairs to the bathroom for ointment, his wife was walking up and down rocking the yelling boy in her arms.

'Please go home!' she broke out suddenly. 'The child's badly hurt, and if you haven't the decency to be quiet, you'd better go home.'

'Very well,' said Edith, her own temper rising. 'I've never seen anyone make such a mountain out of –'

'Get out!' cried Mrs Markey frantically. 'There's the door, get out – I never want to see you in our house again. You or your brat either!'

Edith had taken her daughter's hand and was moving quickly towards the door, but at this remark she stopped and turned around, her face contracting with indignation.

'Don't you dare call her that!'

Mrs Markey did not answer but continued walking up and down, muttering to herself and to Billy in an inaudible voice.

Edith began to cry.

'I will get out!' she sobbed. 'I've never heard anybody so rude and c-common in my life. I'm glad your baby did get pushed down – he's nothing but a f-fat little fool anyhow.'

Joe Markey reached the foot of the stairs just in time to hear this remark.

'Why, Mrs Andros,' he said sharply, 'can't you see the child's hurt. You really ought to control yourself.'

'Control m-myself!' exclaimed Edith brokenly. 'You better ask her to c-control herself. I've never heard anybody so c-common in my life.'

'She's insulting me!' Mrs Markey was now livid with rage. 'Did you hear what she said, Joe? I wish you'd put her out. If she won't go, just take her by the shoulders and put her out!'

'Don't you dare touch me!' cried Edith. 'I'm going just as quick as I can find my c-coat!'

Blind with tears she took a step towards the hall. It was just at this moment that the door opened and John Andros walked anxiously in.

'John!' cried Edith, and fled to him wildly,

'What's the matter? Why, what's the matter?'

'They're – they're putting me out!' she wailed, collapsing against him. 'He'd just started to take me by the shoulders and put me out. I want my coat!'

'That's not true,' objected Markey hurriedly. 'Nobody's going to put you out.' He turned to John. 'Nobody's going to put her out,' he repeated. 'She's –'

'What do you mean "put her out"?' demanded John abruptly. 'What's all this talk, anyhow?'

'Oh, let's go!' cried Edith. 'I want to go. They're so *common*, John!'

'Look here!' Markey's face darkened. 'You've said that about enough. You're acting sort of crazy.'

'They called Ede a brat!'

For the second time that afternoon little Ede expressed emotion at an inopportune moment. Confused and frightened at the shouting voices, she began to cry, and her tears had the effect of conveying that she felt the insult in her heart.

'What's the idea of this?' broke out John. 'Do you insult your guests in your own house?'

'It seems to me it's your wife that's done the insulting!' answered Markey crisply. 'In fact, your baby there started all the trouble.'

John gave a contemptuous snort. 'Are you calling names at a little baby?' he inquired. 'That's a fine manly business!'

'Don't talk to him, John,' insisted Edith. 'Find my coat!'

'You must be in a bad way,' went on John angrily, 'if you have to take out your temper on a helpless little baby.'

'I never heard anything so damn twisted in my life,' shouted Markey. 'If that wife of yours would shut her mouth for a minute –'

'Wait a minute! You're not talking to a woman and child now –'

There was an incidental interruption. Edith had been fumbling on a chair for her coat, and Mrs Markey had been watching her with hot, angry eyes. Suddenly she laid Billy down on the sofa, where he immediately stopped crying and pulled himself upright, and coming into the hall she quickly found Edith's coat and handed it to her without a word. Then she went back to the sofa, picked up Billy, and rocking him in her arms looked again at Edith with hot, angry eyes. The interruption had taken less than half a minute.

'Your wife comes in here and begins shouting around about how common we are!' burst out Markey violently. 'Well, if we're so damn common, you'd better stay away! And what's more, you'd better get out now!'

Again John gave a short, contemptuous laugh.

'You're not only common,' he returned, 'you're evidently an awful bully – when there's any helpless women and children around.' He felt for the knob and swung the door open. 'Come on, Edith.'

Taking up her daughter in her arms, his wife stepped outside and John, still looking contemptuously at Markey, started to follow.

'Wait a minute!' Markey took a step forward; he was trembling slightly, and two large veins on his temples were suddenly full of blood. 'You don't think you can get away with that, do you? With me?'

Without a word John walked out the door, leaving it open.

Edith, still weeping, had started for home. After following her with his eyes until she reached her own walk, John turned back towards the lighted doorway where Markey was slowly coming down the slippery steps. He took off his overcoat and hat, tossed them off the path onto the snow. Then, sliding a little on the iced walk, he took a step forward.

At the first blow, they both slipped and fell heavily to the sidewalk, half rising then, and again pulled each other to the ground. They found a better foothold in the thin snow to the side of the walk and rushed at each other, both swinging wildly and pressing out the snow into a pasty mud underfoot.

The street was deserted, and except for their short tired gasps and the padded sound as one or the other slipped down into the slushy mud, they fought in silence, clearly defined to each other by the full moonlight as well as by the amber glow that shone out of the open door. Several times they both slipped down together, and then for a while the conflict threshed about wildly on the lawn.

For ten, fifteen, twenty minutes they fought there senselessly in the moonlight. They had both taken off coats and vests at some silently agreed upon interval and now their shirts dripped from their backs in wet pulpy shreds. Both were torn and bleeding and so exhausted that they could stand only when by their position they mutually supported each other – the impact, the mere effort of a blow, would send them both to their hands and knees.

But it was not weariness that ended the business, and the very meaninglessness of the fight was a reason for not stopping. They stopped because once when they were straining at each other on the ground, they heard a man's footsteps coming along the sidewalk. They had rolled somehow into the shadow, and when they heard these footsteps they

stopped fighting, stopped moving, stopped breathing, lay huddled together like two boys playing Indian until the footsteps had passed. Then,
staggering to their feet, they looked at each other like two drunken men.

'I'll be damned if I'm going on with this thing any more,' cried Markey
thickly.

'I'm not going on any more, either,' said John Andros. 'I've had
enough of this thing.'

Again they looked at each other, sulkily this time, as if each suspected
the other of urging him to a renewal of the fight. Markey spat out a
mouthful of blood from a cut lip; then he cursed softly, and picking up
his coat and vest, shook off the snow from them in a surprised way, as
if their comparative dampness was his only worry in the world.

'Want to come in and wash up?' he asked suddenly.

'No, thanks,' said John. 'I ought to be going home – my wife'll be
worried.'

He too picked up his coat and vest and then his overcoat and hat.
Soaking wet and dripping with perspiration, it seemed absurd that less
than half an hour ago he had been wearing all these clothes.

'Well – good night,' he said hesitantly.

Suddenly they walked towards each other and shook hands. It was
no perfunctory hand-shake: John Andros's arm went around Markey's
shoulder, and he patted him softly on the back for a little while.

'No harm done,' he said brokenly.

'No – you?'

'No, no harm done.'

'Well,' said John Andros after a minute, 'I guess I'll say good night.'

Limping slightly and with his clothes over his arm, John Andros
turned away. The moonlight was still bright as he left the dark patch
of trampled ground and walked over the intervening lawn. Down at the
station, half a mile away, he could hear the rumble of the seven o'clock
train.

'But you must have been crazy,' cried Edith brokenly. 'I thought you
were going to fix it all up there and shake hands. That's why I went
away.'

'Did you want us to fix it up?'

'Of course not, I never want to see them again. But I thought of
course that was what you were going to do.' She was touching the
bruises on his neck and back with iodine as he sat placidly in a hot

bath. 'I'm going to get the doctor,' she said insistently. 'You may be hurt internally.'

He shook his head. 'Not a chance,' he answered. 'I don't want this to get all over the town.'

'I don't understand yet how it all happened.'

'Neither do I.' He smiled grimly. 'I guess these baby parties are pretty rough affairs.'

'Well, one thing –' suggested Edith hopefully, 'I'm certainly glad we have beef steak in the house for tomorrow's dinner.'

'Why?'

'For your eye, of course. Do you know I came within an ace of ordering veal? Wasn't that the luckiest thing?'

Half an hour later, dressed except that his neck would accommodate no collar, John moved his limbs experimentally before the glass. 'I believe I'll get myself in better shape,' he said thoughtfully. 'I must be getting old.'

'You mean so that next time you can beat him?'

'I did beat him,' he announced. 'At least, I beat him as much as he beat me. And there isn't going to be any next time. Don't you go calling people common any more. If you get in any trouble, you just take your coat and go home. Understand?'

'Yes, dear,' she said meekly. 'I was very foolish and now I understand.'

Out in the hall, he paused abruptly by the baby's door.

'Is she asleep?'

'Sound asleep. But you can go in and peek at her – just to say good night.'

They tiptoed in and bent together over the bed. Little Ede, her cheeks flushed with health, her pink hands clasped tight together, was sleeping soundly in the cool, dark room. John reached over the railing of the bed and passed his hand lightly over the silken hair.

'She's asleep,' he murmured in a puzzled way.

'Naturally, after such an afternoon.'

'Miz Andros,' the coloured maid's stage whisper floated in from the hall. 'Mr and Miz Markey downstairs an' want to see you. Mr Markey he's all cut up in pieces, mam'n. His face look like a roast beef. An' Miz Markey she 'pear mighty mad.'

'Why, what incomparable nerve!' exclaimed Edith. 'Just tell them we're not home. I wouldn't go down for anything in the world.'

'You most certainly will.' John's voice was hard and set.

'What?'

'You'll go down right now, and, what's more, whatever that other woman does, you'll apologize for what you said this afternoon. After that you don't ever have to see her again.'

'Why – John, I can't.'

'You've got to. And just remember that she probably hated to come over here twice as much as you hate to go downstairs.'

'Aren't you coming? Do I have to go alone?'

'I'll be down – in just a minute.'

John Andros waited until she had closed the door behind her; then he reached over into the bed, and picking up his daughter, blankets and all, sat down in the rocking-chair holding her tightly in his arms. She moved a little, and he held his breath, but she was sleeping soundly, and in a moment she was resting quietly in the hollow of his elbow. Slowly he bent his head until his cheek was against her bright hair. 'Dear little girl,' he whispered. 'Dear little girl, dear little girl.'

John Andros knew at length what it was he had fought for so savagely that evening. He had it now, he possessed it forever, and for some time he sat there rocking very slowly to and fro in the darkness.

A SHORT TRIP HOME*

I

I was near her, for I had lingered behind in order to get the short walk with her from the living-room to the front door. That was a lot, for she had flowered suddenly and I, being a man and only a year older, hadn't flowered at all, had scarcely dared to come near her in the week we'd been home. Nor was I going to say anything in that walk of ten feet, or touch her; but I had a vague hope she'd do something, give a gay little performance of some sort, personal only in so far as we were alone together.

She had bewitchment suddenly in the twinkle of short hairs on her neck, in the sure, clear confidence that at about eighteen begins to deepen and sing in attractive American girls. The lamplight shopped in the yellow strands of her hair.

Already she was sliding into another world – the world of Joe Jelke and Jim Cathcart waiting for us now in the car. In another year she would pass beyond me forever.

As I waited, feeling the others outside in the snowy night, feeling the excitement of Christmas week and the excitement of Ellen here, blooming away, filling the room with 'sex appeal' – a wretched phrase to express a quality that isn't like that at all – a maid came in from the dining-room, spoke to Ellen quietly and handed her a note. Ellen read it and her eyes faded down, as when the current grows weak on rural circuits, and smouldered off into space. Then she gave me an odd look – in which I probably didn't show – and without a word, followed the maid into the dining-room and beyond. I sat turning over the pages of a magazine for a quarter of an hour.

---

* In a moment of hasty misjudgement a whole paragaph of description was lifted out of this tale where it originated, and properly belongs, and applied to quite a different character in a novel of mine. I have ventured none the less to leave it here, even at the risk of seeming to serve warmed-over fare.–F.S.F.

Joe Jelke came in, red-faced from the cold, his white silk muffler gleaming at the neck of his fur coat. He was a senior at New Haven, I was a sophomore. He was prominent, a member of Scroll and Keys, and, in my eyes, very distinguished and handsome.

'Isn't Ellen coming?'

'I don't know,' I answered discreetly. 'She was all ready.'

'Ellen!' he called. 'Ellen!'

He had left the front door open behind him and a great cloud of frosty air rolled in from outside. He went half-way up the stairs – he was a familiar in the house – and called again, till Mrs Baker came to the banister and said that Ellen was below. Then the maid, a little excited, appeared in the dining-room door.

'Mr Jelke,' she called in a low voice.

Joe's face fell as he turned towards her, sensing bad news.

'Miss Ellen says for you to go to the party. She'll come later.'

'What's the matter?'

'She can't come now. She'll come later.'

He hesitated, confused. It was the last big dance of vacation, and he was mad about Ellen. He had tried to give her a ring for Christmas, and failing that, got her to accept a gold mesh bag that must have cost two hundred dollars. He wasn't the only one – there were three or four in the same wild condition, and all in the ten days she'd been home – but his chance came first, for he was rich and gracious and at that moment the 'desirable' boy of St Paul. To me it seemed impossible that she could prefer another, but the rumour was she'd described Joe as much too perfect. I suppose he lacked mystery for her, and when a man is up against that with a young girl who isn't thinking of the practical side of marriage yet – well –.

'No, she's not.' The maid was defiant and a little scared.

'She is.'

'She went out the back way, Mr Jelke.'

'I'm going to see.'

I followed him. The Swedish servants washing dishes looked up sideways at our approach and an interested crashing of pans marked our passage through. The storm door, unbolted, was flapping in the wind, and as we walked out into the snowy yard we saw the tail light of a car turn the corner at the end of the back alley.

'I'm going after her,' Joe said slowly. 'I don't understand this at all.'

I was too awed by the calamity to argue. We hurried to his car and drove in a fruitless, despairing zigzag all over the residence section, peering into every machine on the streets. It was half an hour before the futility of the affair began to dawn upon him – St Paul is a city of almost three hundred thousand people – and Jim Cathcart reminded him that we had another girl to stop for. Like a wounded animal he sank into a melancholy mass of fur in the corner, from which position he jerked upright every few minutes and waved himself backward and forward a little in protest and despair.

Jim's girl was ready and impatient, but after what had happened her impatience didn't seem important. She looked lovely though. That's one thing about Christmas vacation – the excitement of growth and change and adventure in foreign parts transforming the people you've known all your life. Joe Jelke was polite to her in a daze – he indulged in one burst of short, loud, harsh laughter by way of conversation – and we drove to the hotel.

The chauffeur approached it on the wrong side – the side on which the line of cars was not putting forth guests – and because of that we came suddenly upon Ellen Baker just getting out of a small coupé. Even before we came to a stop, Joe Jelke had jumped excitedly from the car.

Ellen turned towards us, a faintly distracted look – perhaps of surprise, but certainly not of alarm – in her face; in fact, she didn't seem very aware of us. Joe approached her with a stern, dignified, injured and, I thought, just exactly correct reproof in his expression. I followed.

Seated in the coupé – he had not dismounted to help Ellen out – was a hard thin-faced man of about thirty-five with an air of being scarred, and a slight sinister smile. His eyes were a sort of taunt to the whole human family – they were the eyes of an animal, sleepy and quiescent in the presence of another species. They were helpless yet brutal, unhopeful yet confident. It was as if they felt themselves powerless to originate activity, but infinitely capable of profiting by a single gesture of weakness in another.

Vaguely I placed him as one of the sort of men whom I had been conscious of from my earliest youth as 'hanging around' – leaning with one elbow on the counters of tobacco stores, watching, through heaven knows what small chink of the mind, the people who hurried in and out. Intimate to garages, where he had vague business conducted in undertones, to barber shops and to the lobbies of theatres – in such places, anyhow, I placed the type, if type it was, that he reminded me of. Sometimes his face bobbed up in one of Tad's more savage cartoons, and I had always from earliest boyhood thrown a nervous glance towards the dim borderland where he stood, and seen him watching me and despising me. Once, in a dream, he had taken a few steps towards me, jerking his head back and muttering 'Say, kid' in what was intended to be a reassuring voice, and I had broken for the door in terror. This was that sort of man.

Joe and Ellen faced each other silently; she seemed, as I have said, to be in a daze. It was cold, but she didn't notice that her coat had blown open; Joe reached out and pulled it together, and automatically she clutched it with her hand.

Suddenly the man in the coupé, who had been watching them silently, laughed. It was a bare laugh, done with the breath – just a noisy jerk of the head – but it was an insult if I had ever heard one; definite and not to be passed over. I wasn't surprised when Joe, who was quick tempered, turned to him angrily and said:

'What's your trouble?'

The man waited a moment, his eyes shifting and yet staring, and always seeing. Then he laughed again in the same way. Ellen stirred uneasily.

'Who is this – this –' Joe's voice trembled with annoyance.

'Look out now,' said the man slowly.

Joe turned to me.

'Eddie, take Ellen and Catherine in, will you?' he said quickly . . . 'Ellen, go with Eddie.'

'Look out now,' the man repeated.

Ellen made a little sound with her tongue and teeth, but she didn't resist when I took her arm and moved her towards the side door of the hotel. It struck me as odd that she should be so helpless, even to the point of acquiescing by her silence in this imminent trouble.

'Let it go, Joe!' I called back over my shoulder. 'Come inside!'

Ellen, pulling against my arm, hurried us on. As we were caught up into the swinging doors I had the impression that the man was getting out of his coupé.

Ten minutes later, as I waited for the girls outside the women's dressing-room, Joe Jelke and Jim Cathcart stepped out of the elevator. Joe was very white, his eyes were heavy and glazed, there was a trickle of dark blood on his forehead and on his white muffler. Jim had both their hats in his hand.

'He hit Joe with brass knuckles,' Jim said in a low voice. 'Joe was out cold for a minute or so. I wish you'd send a bell boy for some witch-hazel and court-plaster.'

It was late and the hall was deserted; brassy fragments of the dance below reached us as if heavy curtains were being blown aside and dropping back into place. When Ellen came out I took her directly downstairs. We avoided the receiving line and went into a dim room set with scraggly hotel palms where couples sometimes sat out during the dance; there I told her what had happened.

'It was Joe's own fault,' she said, surprisingly. 'I told him not to interfere.'

This wasn't true. She had said nothing, only uttered one curious little click of impatience.

'You ran out the back door and disappeared for almost an hour,' I protested. 'Then you turned up with a hard-looking customer who laughed in Joe's face.'

'A hard-looking customer,' she repeated, as if tasting the sound of the words.

'Well, wasn't he? Where on earth did you get hold of him, Ellen?'

'On the train,' she answered. Immediately she seemed to regret this admission. 'You'd better stay out of things that aren't your business, Eddie. You see what happened to Joe.'

Literally I gasped. To watch her, seated beside me, immaculately glowing, her body giving off wave after wave of freshness and delicacy – and to hear her talk like that.

'But that man's a thug!' I cried. 'No girl could be safe with him. He used brass knuckles on Joe – brass knuckles!'

'Is that pretty bad?'

She asked this as she might have asked such a question a few years ago. She looked at me at last and really wanted an answer; for a moment it was as if she were trying to recapture an attitude that had almost departed; then she hardened again. I say 'hardened', for I began to notice that when she was concerned with this man her eyelids fell a little, shutting other things – everything else – out of view.

That was a moment I might have said something, I suppose, but in spite of everything, I couldn't light into her. I was too much under the spell of her beauty and its success. I even began to find excuses for her – perhaps that man wasn't what he appeared to be; or perhaps – more romantically – she was involved with him against her will to shield some one else. At this point people began to drift into the room and come up to speak to us. We couldn't talk any more, so we went in and bowed to the chaperones. Then I gave her up to the bright restless sea of the dance, where she moved in an eddy of her own among the pleasant islands of coloured favours set out on tables and the south winds from the brasses moaning across the hall. After a while I saw Joe Jelke sitting in a corner with a strip of court-plaster on his forehead watching Ellen as if she herself had struck him down, but I didn't go up to him. I felt queer myself – like I feel when I wake up after sleeping through an afternoon, strange and portentous, as if something had gone on in the interval that changed the values of everything and that I didn't see.

The night slipped on through successive phases of cardboard horns, amateur tableaux and flashlights for the morning papers. Then was the grand march and supper, and about two o'clock some of the committee dressed up as revenue agents pinched the party, and a facetious newspaper was distributed, burlesquing the events of the evening. And all the time out of the corner of my eye I watched the shining orchid on Ellen's shoulder as it moved like Stuart's plume about the room. I watched it with a definite foreboding until the last sleepy groups had crowded into the elevators, and then, bundled to the eyes in great shapeless fur coats, drifted out into the clear dry Minnesota night.

II

There is a sloping mid-section of our city which lies between the residence quarter on the hill and the business district on the level of the river. It is a vague part of town, broken by its climb into triangles and odd shapes – there are names like Seven Corners – and I don't believe a dozen people could draw an accurate map of it, though every one traversed it by trolley, auto or shoe leather twice a day. And though it was a busy section, it would be hard for me to name the business that comprised its activity. There were always long lines of trolley cars waiting to start somewhere; there was a big movie theatre and many small ones with posters of Hoot Gibson and Wonder Dogs and Wonder Horses outside; there were small stores with 'Old King Brady' and 'The Liberty Boys of '76' in the windows, and marbles, cigarettes and candy inside; and – one definite place at least – a fancy costumer whom we all visited at least once a year. Some time during boyhood I became aware that on one side of a certain obscure street there were bawdy houses, and all through the district were pawnshops, cheap jewellers, small athletic clubs and gymnasiums and somewhat too blatantly run-down saloons.

The morning after the Cotillion Club party, I woke up late and lazy, with the happy feeling that for a day or two more there was no chapel, no classes – nothing to do but wait for another party tonight. It was crisp and bright – one of those days when you forget how cold it is until your cheek freezes – and the events of the evening before seemed dim and far away. After luncheon I started down-town on foot through a light, pleasant snow of small flakes that would probably fall all afternoon, and I was about half through that halfway section of town – so far as I know, there's no inclusive name for it – when suddenly whatever idle thought was in my mind blew away like a hat and I began thinking hard of Ellen Baker. I began worrying about her as I'd never worried about anything outside myself before. I began to loiter, with an instinct to go up on the hill again and find her and talk to her; then I remembered that she was at a tea, and I went on again, but still thinking of her, and harder than ever. Right then the affair opened up again.

It was snowing, I said, and it was four o'clock on a December afternoon, when there is a promise of darkness in the air and the street lamps are just going on. I passed a combination pool parlour and restaurant, with a stove loaded with hot-dogs in the window, and a few loungers hanging around the door. The lights were on inside – not bright lights but just a few pale yellow high up on the ceiling – and the glow they threw out into the frosty dusk wasn't bright enough to tempt you to stare inside. As I went past, thinking hard of Ellen all this time, I took in the quartet of loafers out of the corner of my eye. I hadn't gone half a dozen steps down the street when one of them called to me, not by name but in a way clearly intended for my ear. I thought it was a tribute to my raccoon coat and paid no attention, but a moment later whoever it was called to me again in a peremptory voice. I was annoyed and turned around. There, standing in the group not ten feet away and looking at me with the half-sneer on his face with which he'd looked at Joe Jelke, was the scarred, thin-faced man of the night before.

He had on a black fancy-cut coat, buttoned up to his neck as if he were cold. His hands were deep in his pockets and he wore a derby and high button shoes. I was startled, and for a moment I hesitated, but I was most of all angry, and knowing that I was quicker with my hands than Joe Jelke, I took a tentative step back towards him. The other men weren't looking at me – I don't think they saw me at all – but I knew that this one recognized me; there was nothing casual about his look, no mistake.

'Here I am. What are you going to do about it?' his eyes seemed to say.

I took another step towards him and he laughed soundlessly, but with active contempt, and drew back into the group. I followed. I was going to speak to him – I wasn't sure what I was going to say – but when I came up he had either changed his mind and backed off, or else he wanted me to follow him inside, for he had slipped off and the three men watched my intent approach without curiosity. They were the same kind – sporty, but, unlike him, smooth rather than truculent; I didn't find any personal malice in their collective glance.

'Did he go inside?' I asked,

They looked at one another in that cagey way; a wink passed between them, and after a perceptible pause, one said:

'Who go inside?'

'I don't know his name.'

There was another wink. Annoyed and determined, I walked past them and into the pool room. There were a few people at a lunch counter along one side and a few more playing billiards, but he was not among them.

Again I hesitated. If his idea was to lead me into any blind part of the establishment – there were some half-open doors farther back – I wanted more support. I went up to the man at the desk.

'What became of the fellow who just walked in here?'

Was he on his guard immediately, or was that my imagination?

'What fellow?'

'Thin face – derby hat.'

'How long ago?'

'Oh – a minute.'

He shook his head again. 'Didn't see him,' he said.

I waited. The three men from outside had come in and were lined up beside me at the counter. I felt that all of them were looking at me in a peculiar way. Feeling helpless and increasingly uneasy, I turned suddenly and went out. A little way down the street I turned again and took a good look at the place, so I'd know it and could find it again. On the next corner I broke impulsively into a run, found a taxicab in front of the hotel and drove back up the hill.

Ellen wasn't home. Mrs Baker came downstairs and talked to me. She seemed entirely cheerful and proud of Ellen's beauty, and ignorant of anything amiss or of anything unusual having taken place the night before. She was glad that vacation was almost over – it was a strain and Ellen wasn't very strong. Then she said something that relieved my mind enormously. She was glad that I had come in, for of course Ellen would want to see me, and the time was so short. She was going back at half past eight tonight.

'Tonight!' I exclaimed. 'I thought it was the day after tomorrow.'

'She's going to visit the Brokaws in Chicago,' Mrs Baker said. 'They want her for some party. We just decided it today. She's leaving with the Ingersoll girls tonight.'

I was so glad I could barely restrain myself from shaking her hand. Ellen was safe. It had been nothing all along but a moment of the most casual adventure. I felt like an idiot, but I realized how much I cared about Ellen and how little I could endure anything terrible happening to her.

'She'll be in soon?'

'Any minute now. She just phoned from the University Club.'

I said I'd be over later – I lived almost next door and I wanted to be alone. Outside I remembered I didn't have a key, so I started up the Bakers' driveway to take the old cut we used in childhood through the intervening yard. It was still snowing, but the flakes were bigger now against the darkness, and trying to locate the buried walk I noticed that the Bakers' back door was ajar.

I scarcely know why I turned and walked into that kitchen. There was a time when I would have known the Bakers' servants by name. That wasn't true now, but they knew me, and I was aware of a sudden suspension as I came in – not only a suspension of talk but of some mood of expectation that had filled them. They began to go to work too quickly; they made unnecessary movements and clamour – those three. The parlour maid looked at me in a frightened way and I suddenly guessed she was waiting to deliver another message. I beckoned her into the pantry.

'I know all about this,' I said. 'It's a very serious business. Shall I go to Mrs Baker now, or will you shut and lock that back door?'

'Don't tell Mrs Baker, Mr Stinson!'

'Then I don't want Miss Ellen disturbed. If she is – and if she is I'll know of it –' I delivered some outrageous threat about going to all the employment agencies and seeing she never got another job in the city. She was thoroughly intimidated when I went out; it wasn't a minute before the back door was locked and bolted behind me.

Simultaneously I heard a big car drive up in front, chains crunching on the soft snow; it was bringing Ellen home, and I went in to say good-bye.

Joe Jelke and two other boys were along, and none of the three could manage to take his eyes off her, even to say hello to me. She had one of those exquisite rose skins frequent in our part of the country, and beautiful until the little veins begin to break at about forty; now, flushed with the cold, it was a riot of lovely delicate pinks like many carnations. She and Joe had reached some sort of reconciliation, or at least he was too far gone in love to remember last night; but I saw that though she laughed a lot she wasn't really paying any attention to him or any of them. She wanted them to go, so that there'd be a message from the kitchen, but I knew that the message wasn't coming – that she was safe. There was talk of the Pump and Slipper dance at New Haven and of the Princeton Prom, and then, in various moods, we four left and separated quickly outside. I walked home with a certain depression of spirit and lay for an hour in a hot bath thinking that vacation was all over for me now that she was gone; feeling, even more deeply than I had yesterday, that she was out of my life.

And something eluded me, some one more thing to do, something that I had lost amid the events of the afternoon, promising myself to go back and pick it up, only to find that it had escaped me. I associated it vaguely with Mrs Baker, and now I seemed to recall that it had poked up its head somewhere in the stream of conversation with her. In my relief about Ellen I had forgotten to ask her a question regarding something she had said.

The Brokaws – that was it – where Ellen was to visit. I knew Bill Brokaw well; he was in my class at Yale. Then I remembered and sat bolt upright in the tub – the Brokaws weren't in Chicago this Christmas, they were at Palm Beach!

Dripping I sprang out of the tub, threw an insufficient union suit around my shoulders and sprang for the phone in my room. I got the connexion quick, but Miss Ellen had already started for the train.

Luckily our car was in, and while I squirmed, still damp, into my clothes, the chauffeur brought it around to the door. The night was cold and dry, and we made good time to the station through the hard, crusty snow. I felt queer and insecure starting out this way, but somehow more confident as the station loomed up bright and new against the dark, cold air. For fifty years my family had owned the land on which it was built and that made my temerity seem all right somehow. There was always a possibility that I was rushing in where angels feared to tread, but that sense of having a solid foothold in the past made me willing to make a fool of myself. This business was all wrong – terribly wrong.

Any idea I had entertained that it was harmless dropped away now; between Ellen and some vague overwhelming catastrophe there stood me, or else the police and a scandal. I'm no moralist – there was another element here, dark and frightening, and I didn't want Ellen to go through it alone.

There are three competing trains from St Paul to Chicago that all leave within a few minutes of half past eight. Hers was the Burlington, and as I ran across the station I saw the grating being pulled over and the light above it go out. I knew, though, that she had a drawing-room with the Ingersoll girls, because her mother had mentioned buying the ticket, so she was, literally speaking, tucked in until tomorrow.

The C., M. & St P. gate was down at the other end and I raced for it and made it. I had forgotten one thing, though, and that was enough to keep me awake and worried half the night. This train got into Chicago ten minutes after the other. Ellen had that much time to disappear into one of the largest cities in the world.

I gave the porter a wire to my family to send from Milwaukee, and at eight o'clock next morning I pushed violently by a whole line of passengers, clamouring over their bags parked in the vestibule, and shot out of the door with a sort of scramble over the porter's back. For a moment the confusion of a great station, the voluminous sounds and echoes and cross-currents of bells and smoke struck me helpless. Then I dashed for the exit and towards the only chance I knew of finding her.

I had guessed right. She was standing at the telegraph counter, sending off heaven knows what black lie to her mother, and her expression when she saw me had a sort of terror mixed up with its surprise. There was cunning in it too. She was thinking quickly – she would have liked to walk away from me as if I weren't there, and go about her own business, but she couldn't. I was too matter-of-fact a thing in her life. So we stood silently watching each other and each thinking hard.

'The Brokaws are in Florida,' I said after a minute.

'It was nice of you to take such a long trip to tell me that.'

'Since you've found it out, don't you think you'd better go on to school?'

'Please let me alone, Eddie,' she said.

'I'll go as far as New York with you. I've decided to go back early myself.'

'You'd better let me alone.' Her lovely eyes narrowed and her face took on a look of dumb-animal resistance. She made a visible effort, the cunning flickered back into it, then both were gone, and in their stead was a cheerful reassuring smile that all but convinced me.

'Eddie, you silly child, don't you think I'm old enough to take care of myself?' I didn't answer. 'I'm going to meet a man, you understand. I just want to see him today. I've got my ticket East on the five o'clock train. If you don't believe it, here it is in my bag.'

'I believe you.'

'The man isn't anybody that you know and – frankly, I think you're being awfully fresh and impossible.'

'I know who the man is.'

Again she lost control of her face. The terrible expression came back into it and she spoke with almost a snarl:

'You'd better let me alone.'

I took the blank out of her hand and wrote out an explanatory telegram to her mother. Then I turned to Ellen and said a little roughly:

'We'll take the five o'clock train East together. Meanwhile you're going to spend the day with me.'

The mere sound of my own voice saying this so emphatically encouraged me, and I think it impressed her too; at any rate, she submitted – at least temporarily – and came along without protest while I bought my ticket.

When I start to piece together the fragments of that day a sort of confusion begins, as if my memory didn't want to yield up any of it, or my consciousness let any of it pass through. There was a bright, fierce morning during which we rode about in a taxicab and went to a department store where Ellen said she wanted to buy something and then tried to slip away from me by a back way. I had the feeling, for an hour, that someone was following us along Lake Shore Drive in a taxicab, and I would try to catch them by turning quickly or looking suddenly into the chauffeur's mirror; but I could find no one, and when I turned back I could see that Ellen's face was contorted with mirthless, unnatural laughter.

All morning there was a raw, bleak wind off the lake, but when we went to the Blackstone for lunch a light snow came down past the windows and we talked almost naturally about our friends, and about casual things. Suddenly her tone changed; she grew serious and looked me in the eye, straight and sincere.

'Eddie, you're the oldest friend I have,' she said, 'and you oughtn't to find it too hard to trust me. If I promise you faithfully on my word of honour to catch that five o'clock train, will you let me alone a few hours this afternoon?'

'Why?'

'Well' – she hesitated and hung her head a little – 'I guess everybody has a right to say – good-bye.'

'You want to say good-bye to that –'

'Yes, yes,' she said hastily; 'just a few hours, Eddie, and I promise faithfully that I'll be on that train.'

'Well, I suppose no great harm could be done in two hours. If you really want to say good-bye –'

I looked up suddenly, and surprised a look of such tense cunning in her face that I winced before it. Her lip was curled up and her eyes were slits again; there wasn't the faintest touch of fairness and sincerity in her whole face.

We argued. The argument was vague on her part and somewhat hard and reticent on mine. I wasn't going to be cajoled again into any weakness or be infected with any – and there was a contagion of evil in the air. She kept trying to imply, without any convincing evidence to bring forward, that everything was all right. Yet she was too full of the thing itself – whatever it was – to build up a real story, and she wanted to catch at any credulous and acquiescent train of thought that might start in my head, and work that for all it was worth. After every reassuring suggestion she threw out, she stared at me eagerly, as if she hoped I'd launch into a comfortable moral lecture with the customary sweet at the end – which in this case would be her liberty. But I was wearing her away a little. Two or three times it needed just a touch of pressure to bring her to the point of tears – which, of course, was what I wanted – but I couldn't seem to manage it. Almost I had her – almost possessed her interior attention – then she would slip away.

I bullied her remorselessly into a taxi about four o'clock and started for the station. The wind was raw again, with a sting of snow in it, and the people in the streets, waiting for buses and street cars too small to take them all in, looked cold and disturbed and unhappy. I tried to think how lucky we were to be comfortably off and taken care of, but all the warm, respectable world I had been part of yesterday had dropped away from me. There was something we carried with us now that was the enemy and the opposite of all that; it was in the cabs beside us, the streets we passed through. With a touch of panic, I wondered if I wasn't slipping almost imperceptibly into Ellen's attitude of mind. The column of passengers waiting to go aboard the train were as remote from me as people from another world, but it was I that was drifting away and leaving them behind.

My lower was in the same car with her compartment. It was an old-fashioned car, its lights somewhat dim, its carpets and upholstery full of the dust of another generation. There were half a dozen other travellers, but they made no special impression on me, except that they shared the unreality that I was beginning to feel everywhere around me. We went into Ellen's compartment, shut the door and sat down.

Suddenly I put my arms around her and drew her over to me, just as tenderly as I knew how – as if she were a little girl – as she was. She resisted a little, but after a moment she submitted and lay tense and rigid in my arms.

'Ellen,' I said helplessly, 'you asked me to trust you. You have much more reason to trust me. Wouldn't it help to get rid of all this, if you told me a little?'

'I can't,' she said, very low – 'I mean, there's nothing to tell.'

'You met this man on the train coming home and you fell in love with him, isn't that true?'

'I don't know.'

'Tell me, Ellen. You fell in love with him?'

'I don't know. Please let me alone.'

'Call it anything you want,' I went on, 'he has some sort of hold over you. He's trying to use you; he's trying to get something from you. He's not in love with you.'

'What does that matter?' she said in a weak voice.

'It does matter. Instead of trying to fight this – this thing – you're trying to fight me. And I love you, Ellen. Do you hear? I'm telling you all of a sudden, but it isn't new with me. I love you.'

She looked at me with a sneer on her gentle face; it was an expression I had seen on men who were tight and didn't want to be taken home. But it was human. I was reaching her, faintly and from far away, but more than before.

'Ellen, I want you to answer me one question. Is he going to be on this train?'

She hesitated; then, an instant too late, she shook her head.

'Be careful, Ellen. Now I'm going to ask you one thing more, and I wish you'd try very hard to answer. Coming West, when did this man get on the train?'

'I don't know,' she said with an effort.

Just at that moment I became aware, with the unquestionable

knowledge reserved for facts, that he was just outside the door. She knew it, too; the blood left her face and that expression of low-animal perspicacity came creeping back. I lowered my face into my hands and tried to think.

We must have sat there, with scarcely a word, for well over an hour. I was conscious that the lights of Chicago, then of Englewood and of endless suburbs, were moving by, and then there were no more lights and we were out on the dark flatness of Illinois. The train seemed to draw in upon itself; it took on the air of being alone. The porter knocked at the door and asked if he could make up the berth, but I said no and he went away.

After a while I convinced myself that the struggle inevitably coming wasn't beyond what remained of my sanity, my faith in the essential all-rightness of things and people. That this person's purpose was what we call 'criminal' I took for granted, but there was no need of ascribing to him an intelligence that belonged to a higher plane of human, or inhuman endeavour. It was still as a man that I considered him, and tried to get at his essence, his self-interest – what took the place in him of a comprehensible heart – but I suppose I more than half knew what I would find when I opened the door.

When I stood up Ellen didn't seem to see me at all. She was hunched into a corner staring straight ahead with a sort of film over her eyes, as if she were in a state of suspended animation of body and mind. I lifted her and put two pillows under her head and threw my fur coat over her knees, Then I knelt beside her and kissed her two hands, opened the door and went out into the hall.

I closed the door behind me and stood with my back against it for a minute. The car was dark save for the corridor lights at each end. There was no sound except the groaning of the couplers, the even click-a-click of the rails and someone's loud sleeping breath farther down the car. I became aware after a moment that the figure of a man was standing by the water cooler just outside the men's smoking-room, his derby hat on his head, his coat collar turned up around his neck as if he were cold, his hands in his coat pockets. When I saw him, he turned and went into the smoking-room, and I followed. He was sitting in the far corner of the long leather bench; I took the single armchair beside the door.

As I went in I nodded to him and he acknowledged my presence with one of those terrible soundless laughs of his. But this time it was prolonged, it seemed to go on forever, and mostly to cut it short, I asked: 'Where are you from?' in a voice I tried to make casual.

He stopped laughing and looked at me narrowly, wondering what my game was. When he decided to answer, his voice was muffled as though he were speaking through a silk scarf, and it seemed to come from a long way off.

'I'm from St Paul, Jack.'

'Been making a trip home?'

He nodded. Then he took a long breath and spoke in a hard, menacing voice:

'You better get off at Fort Wayne, Jack.'

He was dead. He was dead as hell – he had been dead all along, but what force had flowed through him, like blood in his veins, out to St Paul and back, was leaving him now. A new outline – the outline of him dead – was coming through the palpable figure that had knocked down Joe Jelke.

He spoke again, with a sort of jerking effort:

'You get off at Fort Wayne, Jack, or I'm going to wipe you out.' He moved his hand in his coat pocket and showed me the outline of a revolver.

I shook my head. 'You can't touch me,' I answered. 'You see, I know.' His terrible eyes shifted over me quickly, trying to determine whether or not I did know. Then he gave a snarl and made as though he were going to jump to his feet.

'You climb off here or else I'm going to get you, Jack!' he cried hoarsely. The train was slowing up for Fort Wayne and his voice rang loud in the comparative quiet, but he didn't move from his chair – he was too weak, I think – and we sat staring at each other while workmen passed up and down outside the window banging the brakes and wheels, and the engine gave out loud mournful pants up ahead. No one got into our car. After a while the porter closed the vestibule door and passed back along the corridor, and we slid out of the murky yellow station light and into the long darkness.

What I remember next must have extended over a space of five or six hours, though it comes back to me as something without any existence in time – something that might have taken five minutes or a year. There began a slow, calculated assault on me, wordless and terrible. I felt what I can only call a strangeness stealing over me – akin to the strangeness I had felt all afternoon, but deeper and more intensified. It was like nothing so much as the sensation of drifting away, and I gripped the arms of the chair convulsively, as if to hang onto a piece in the living world. Sometimes I felt myself going out with a rush. There would be almost a warm relief about it, a sense of not caring; then, with a violent wrench of the will, I'd pull myself back into the room.

Suddenly I realized that from a while back I had stopped hating him, stopped feeling violently alien to him, and with the realization, I went cold and sweat broke out all over my head. He was getting around my abhorrence, as he had got around Ellen coming West on the train; and it was just that strength he drew from preying on people that had brought him up to the point of concrete violence in St Paul, and that, fading and flickering out, still kept him fighting now.

He must have seen that faltering in my heart, for he spoke at once, in a low, even, almost gentle voice: 'You better go now.'

'Oh, I'm not going,' I forced myself to say.

'Suit yourself, Jack.'

He was my friend, he implied. He knew how it was with me and he wanted to help. He pitied me. I'd better go away before it was too late. The rhythm of his attack was soothing as a song: I'd better go away — *and let him get at Ellen*. With a little cry I sat bolt upright.

'What do you want of this girl?' I said, my voice shaking. 'To make a sort of walking hell of her.'

His glance held a quality of dumb surprise, as if I were punishing an animal for a fault of which he was not conscious. For an instant I faltered; then I went on blindly:

'You've lost her; she's put her trust in me.'

His countenance went suddenly black with evil, and he cried: 'You're a liar!' in a voice that was like cold hands.

'She trusts me,' I said. 'You can't touch her. She's safe!'

He controlled himself. His face grew bland, and I felt that curious weakness and indifference begin again inside me. What was the use of all this? What was the use?

'You haven't got much time left,' I forced myself to say, and then, in a flash of intuition, I jumped at the truth. 'You died, or you were killed, not far from here!' — Then I saw what I had not seen before — that his forehead was drilled with a small round hole like a larger picture nail leaves when it's pulled from a plaster wall. 'And now you're sinking. You've only a got a few hours. The trip home is over!'

His face contorted, lost all semblance of humanity, living or dead. Simultaneously the room was full of cold air and with a noise that was something between a paroxysm of coughing and a burst of horrible laughter, he was on his feet, reeking of shame and blasphemy.

'Come and look!' he cried. 'I'll show you –'

He took a step towards me, then another and it was exactly as if a door stood open behind him, a door yawning out to an inconceivable abyss of darkness and corruption. There was a scream of mortal agony, from him or from somewhere behind, and abruptly the strength went out of him in a long husky sigh and he wilted to the floor . . .

How long I sat there, dazed with terror and exhaustion, I don't know. The next thing I remember is the sleepy porter shining shoes across the room from me, and outside the window the steel fires of Pittsburgh breaking the flat perspective of the night. There was something extended on the bench also – something too faint for a man, too heavy for a shadow. Even as I perceived it it faded off and away.

Some minutes later I opened the door of Ellen's compartment. She was asleep where I had left her. Her lovely cheeks were white and wan, but she lay naturally – her hands relaxed and her breathing regular and clear. What had possessed her had gone out of her, leaving her exhausted but her own dear self again.

I made her a little more comfortable, tucked a blanket around her, extinguished the light and went out.

III

When I came home for Easter vacation, almost my first act was to go down to the billiard parlour near Seven Corners. The man at the cash register quite naturally didn't remember my hurried visit of three months before.

'I'm trying to locate a certain party who, I think, came here a lot some time ago.'

I described the man rather accurately, and when I had finished, the cashier called to a little jockeylike fellow who was sitting near with an air of having something very important to do that he couldn't quite remember.

'Hey, Shorty, talk to this guy, will you? I think he's looking for Joe Varland.'

The little man gave me a tribal look of suspicion. I went and sat near him.

'Joe Varland's dead, fella,' he said grudgingly. 'He died last winter.'

I described him again – his overcoat, his laugh, the habitual expression of his eyes.

'That's Joe Varland you're looking for all right, but he's dead.'

'I want to find out something about him.'

'What you want to find out?'

'What did he do, for instance?'

'How should I know?'

'Look here! I'm not a policeman. I just want some kind of information about his habits. He's dead now and it can't hurt him. And it won't go beyond me.'

'Well' – he hesitated, looking me over – 'he was a great one for travelling. He got in a row in the station in Pittsburgh and a dick got him.'

I nodded. Broken pieces of the puzzle began to assemble in my head.

'Why was he a lot on trains?'

'How should I know, fella?'

'If you can use ten dollars, I'd like to know anything you may have heard on the subject.'

'Well,' said Shorty reluctantly, 'all I know is they used to say he worked the trains.'

'Worked the trains?'

'He had some racket of his own he'd never loosen up about. He used to work the girls travelling alone on the trains. Nobody ever knew much about it – he was a pretty smooth guy – but sometimes he'd turn up here with a lot of dough and he let 'em know it was the janes he got it off of.'

I thanked him and gave him the ten dollars and went out, very thoughtful, without mentioning that part of Joe Varland had made a last trip home.

Ellen wasn't West for Easter, and even if she had been I wouldn't have gone to her with the information, either – at least I've seen her almost every day this summer and we've managed to talk about everything else. Sometimes, though, she gets silent about nothing and wants to be very close to me, and I know what's in her mind.

Of course she's coming out this fall, and I have two more years at New Haven; still, things don't look so impossible as they did a few months ago. She belongs to me in a way – even if I lose her she belongs to me. Who knows? Anyhow, I'll always be there.

MAGNETISM

I

The pleasant, ostentatious boulevard was lined at prosperous intervals with New England Colonial houses – without ship models in the hall. When the inhabitants moved out here the ship models had at last been given to the children. The next street was a complete exhibit of the Spanish-bungalow phase of West Coast architecture; while two streets over, the cylindrical windows and round towers of 1897 – melancholy antiques which sheltered swamis, yogis, fortune tellers, dressmakers, dancing teachers, art academies and chiropractors – looked down now upon brisk buses and trolley cars. A little walk around the block could, if you were feeling old that day, be a discouraging affair.

On the green flanks of the modern boulevard children, with their knees marked by the red stains of the mercurochrome era, played with toys with a purpose – beams that taught engineering, soldiers that taught manliness, and dolls that taught motherhood. When the dolls were so banged up that they stopped looking like real babies and began to look like dolls, the children developed affection for them. Everything in the vicinity – even the March sunlight – was new, fresh, hopeful and thin, as you would expect in a city that had tripled its population in fifteen years.

Among the very few domestics in sight that morning was a handsome young maid sweeping the steps of the biggest house on the street. She was a large, simple Mexican girl with the large, simple ambitions of the time and the locality, and she was already conscious of being a luxury – she received one hundred dollars a month in return for her personal liberty. Sweeping, Dolores kept an eye on the stairs inside, for Mr Hannaford's car was waiting and he would soon be coming down to breakfast. The problem came first this morning, however – the problem as to whether it was a duty or a favour when she helped the English nurse down the steps with the perambulator. The English nurse always said 'Please', and 'Thanks very much', but Dolores hated her and would have liked, without any special excitement, to beat her insensible. Like most Latins under the stimulus of American life, she had irresistible impulses towards violence.

The nurse escaped, however. Her blue cape faded haughtily into the distance just as Mr Hannaford, who had come quietly downstairs, stepped into the space of the front door.

'Good morning.' He smiled at Dolores; he was young and extraordinarily handsome. Dolores tripped on the broom and fell off the stoop. George Hannaford hurried down the steps, reached her as she was getting to her feet cursing volubly in Mexican, just touched her arm with a helpful gesture and said, 'I hope you didn't hurt yourself.'

'Oh, no.'

'I'm afraid it was my fault; I'm afraid I startled you, coming out like that.'

His voice had real regret in it; his brow was knit with solicitude,

'Are you sure you're all right?'

'Aw, sure.'

'Didn't turn your ankle?'

'Aw, no.'

'I'm terribly sorry about it.'

'Aw, it wasn't your fault.'

He was still frowning as she went inside, and Dolores, who was not hurt and thought quickly, suddenly contemplated having a love affair with him. She looked at herself several times in the pantry mirror and stood close to him as she poured his coffee, but he read the paper and she saw that that was all for the morning.

Hannaford entered his car and drove to Jules Rennard's house. Jules was a French Canadian by birth, and George Hannaford's best friend; they were fond of each other and spent much time together. Both of them were simple and dignified in their tastes and in their way of thinking, instinctively gentle, and in a world of the volatile and the bizarre found in each other a certain quiet solidity.

He found Jules at breakfast.

'I want to fish for barracuda,' said George abruptly. 'When will you be free? I want to take the boat and go down to Lower California.'

Jules had dark circles under his eyes. Yesterday he had closed out the greatest problem of his life by settling with his ex-wife for two hundred thousand dollars. He had married too young, and the former slavey from the Quebec slums had taken to drugs upon her failure to rise with him. Yesterday, in the presence of lawyers, her final gesture had been to smash his finger with the base of a telephone. He was tired of women for a while and welcomed the suggestion of a fishing trip.

'How's the baby?' he asked.

'The baby's fine.'

'And Kay?'

'Kay's not herself, but I don't pay any attention. What did you do to your hand?'

'I'll tell you another time. What's the matter with Kay, George?'

'Jealous.'

'Of who?'

'Helen Avery. It's nothing. She's not herself, that's all.' He got up. 'I'm late,' he said. 'Let me know as soon as you're free. Any time after Monday will suit me.'

George left and drove out by an interminable boulevard which narrowed into a long, winding concrete road and rose into the hilly country behind. Somewhere in the vast emptiness a group of buildings appeared, a barnlike structure, a row of offices, a large but quick restaurant and half a dozen small bungalows. The chauffeur dropped Hannaford at the main entrance. He went in and passed through various enclosures, each marked off by swinging gates and inhabited by a stenographer.

'Is anybody with Mr Schroeder?' he asked, in front of a door lettered with that name.

'No, Mr Hannaford.'

Simultaneously his eye fell on a young lady who was writing at a desk aside, and he lingered a moment.

'Hello, Margaret,' he said. 'How are you, darling?'

A delicate, pale beauty looked up, frowning a little, still abstracted in her work. It was Miss Donovan, the script girl, a friend of many years.

'Hello. Oh, George, I didn't see you come in. Mr Douglas wants to work on the book sequence this afternoon.'

'All right.'

'These are the changes we decided on Thursday night.' She smiled up at him and George wondered for the thousandth time why she had never gone into pictures.

'All right,' he said. 'Will initials do?'

'Your initials look like George Harris's.'

'Very well, darling.'

As he finished, Pete Schroeder opened his door and beckoned him. 'George, come here!' he said with an air of excitement. 'I want you to listen to some one on the phone.'

Hannaford went in.

'Pick up the phone and say "Hello",' directed Schroeder. 'Don't say who you are.'

'Hello,' said Hannaford obediently.

'Who is this?' asked a girl's voice.

Hannaford put his hand over the mouthpiece. 'What am I supposed to do?'

Schroeder snickered and Hannaford hesitated, smiling and suspicious.

'Who do you want to speak to?' he temporized into the phone.

'To George Hannaford, I want to speak to. Is this him?'

'Yes.'

'Oh, George; it's me.'

'Who?'

'Me – Gwen. I had an awful time finding you. They told me –'

'Gwen who?'

'Gwen – can't you hear? From San Francisco – last Thursday night.'

'I'm sorry,' objected George. 'Must be some mistake.'

'Is this George Hannaford?'

'Yes.'

The voice grew slightly tart: 'Well, this is Gwen Becker you spent last Thursday evening with in San Francisco. There's no use pretending you don't know who I am, because you do.'

Schroeder took the apparatus from George and hung up the receiver.

'Somebody has been doubling for me up in Frisco,' said Hannaford.

'So that's where you were Thursday night!'

'Those things aren't funny to me – not since that crazy Zeller girl. You can never convince them they've been sold because the man always looks something like you. What's new, Pete?'

'Let's go over to the stage and see.'

Together they walked out a back entrance, along a muddy walk, and opening a little door in the big blank wall of the studio building entered into its half darkness.

Here and there figures spotted the dim twilight, figures that turned up white faces to George Hannaford, like souls in purgatory watching the passage of a half-god through. Here and there were whispers and soft voices and, apparently from afar, the gentle tremolo of a small organ. Turning the corner made by some flats, they came upon the white crackling glow of a stage with two people motionless upon it.

An actor in evening clothes, his shirt front, collar and cuffs tinted a brilliant pink, made as though to get chairs for them, but they shook their heads and stood watching. For a long while nothing happened on the stage – no one moved. A row of lights went off with a savage hiss, went on again. The plaintive tap of a hammer begged admission to nowhere in the distance; a blue face appeared among the blinding lights above and called something unintelligible into the upper blackness. Then the silence was broken by a low clear voice from the stage:

'If you want to know why I haven't got stockings on, look in my dressing-room. I spoiled four pairs yesterday and two already this morning . . . This dress weighs six pounds.'

A man stepped out of the group of observers and regarded the girl's brown legs; their lack of covering was scarcely distinguishable, but, in any event, her expression implied that she would do nothing about it. The lady was annoyed, and so intense was her personality that it had taken only a fractional flexing of her eyes to indicate the fact. She was a dark, pretty girl with a figure that would be full-blown sooner than she wished. She was just eighteen.

Had this been the week before, George Hannaford's heart would have stood still. Their relationship had been in just that stage. He hadn't said a word to Helen Avery that Kay could have objected to, but something had begun between them on the second day of this picture that Kay had felt in the air. Perhaps it had begun even earlier, for he had determined, when he saw Helen Avery's first release, that she should play opposite him. Helen Avery's voice and the dropping of her eyes when she finished speaking, like a sort of exercise in control, fascinated him. He had felt that they both tolerated something, that each knew half of some secret about people and life, and that if they rushed towards each other there would be a romantic communion of almost unbelievable intensity. It was this element of promise and possibility that had haunted him for a fortnight and was now dying away.

Hannaford was thirty, and he was a moving-picture actor only through a series of accidents. After a year in a small technical college he had taken a summer job with an electric company, and his first appearance in a studio was in the role of repairing a bank of Klieg lights. In an emergency he played a small part and made good, but for fully a year after that he thought of it as a purely transitory episode in his life. At first much of it had offended him – the almost hysterical egotism and excitability hidden under an extremely thin veil of elaborate good-fellowship. It was only recently, with the advent of such men as Jules Rennard into pictures, that he began to see the possibilities of a decent

and secure private life, much as his would have been as a successful
engineer. At last his success felt solid beneath his feet,

He met Kay Tomkins at the old Griffith Studios at Mamaroneck and
their marriage was a fresh, personal affair, removed from most stage
marriages. Afterwards they had possessed each other completely, had
been pointed to: 'Look, there's one couple in pictures who manage to
stay together.' It would have taken something out of many people's
lives – people who enjoyed a vicarious security in the contemplation of
their marriage – if they hadn't stayed together, and their love was
fortified by a certain effort to live up to that.

He held women off by a polite simplicity that underneath was hard
and watchful; when he felt a certain current being turned on he became
emotionally stupid. Kay expected and took much more from men, but
she, too, had a careful thermometer against her heart. Until the other
night, when she reproached him for being interested in Helen Avery,
there had been an absolute minimum of jealousy between them.

George Hannaford was still absorbed in the thought of Helen Avery
as he left the studio and walked towards his bungalow over the way.
There was in his mind, first, a horror that anyone should come between
him and Kay, and second, a regret that he no longer carried that
possibility in the forefront of his mind. It had given him a tremendous
pleasure, like the things that had happened to him during his first big
success, before he was so 'made' that there was scarcely anything better
ahead; it was something to take out and look at – a new and still
mysterious joy. It hadn't been love, for he was critical of Helen Avery
as he had never been critical of Kay. But his feeling of last week had
been sharply significant and memorable, and he was restless, now that
it had passed.

Working that afternoon, they were seldom together, but he was
conscious of her and he knew that she was conscious of him.

She stood a long time with her back to him at one point, and when
she turned at length, their eyes swept past each other's, brushing like
bird wings. Simultaneously he saw they had gone far, in their way; it
was well that he had drawn back. He was glad that someone came for
her when the work was almost over.

Dressed, he returned to the office wing, stopping in for a moment to
see Schroeder. No one answered his knock, and, turning the knob, he
went in. Helen Avery was there alone.

Hannaford shut the door and they stared at each other. Her face was
young, frightened. In a moment in which neither of them spoke, it was

decided that they would have some of this out now. Almost thankfully he felt the warm sap of emotion flow out of his heart and course through his body.

'Helen!'

She murmured 'What?' in an awed voice.

'I feel terribly about this.' His voice was shaking.

Suddenly she began to cry; painful, audible sobs shook her. 'Have you got a handkerchief?' she said.

He gave her a handkerchief. At that moment there were steps outside. George opened the door halfway just in time to keep Schroeder from entering on the spectacle of her tears.

'Nobody's in,' he said facetiously. For a moment longer he kept his shoulder against the door. Then he let it open slowly.

Outside in his limousine, he wondered how soon Jules would be ready to go fishing.

II

From the age of twelve Kay Tompkins had worn men like rings on every finger. Her face was round, young, pretty and strong; a strength accentuated by the responsive play of brows and lashes around her clear, glossy, hazel eyes. She was the daughter of a senator from a Western state and she hunted unsuccessfully for glamour through a small Western city until she was seventeen, when she ran away from home and went on the stage. She was one of those people who are famous far beyond their actual achievement.

There was that excitement about her that seemed to reflect the excitement of the world. While she was playing small parts in Ziegfeld shows she attended proms at Yale, and during a temporary venture into pictures she met George Hannaford, already a star of the new 'natural' type then just coming into vogue. In him she found what she had been seeking.

She was at present in what is known as a dangerous state. For six months she had been helpless and dependent entirely upon George, and now that her son was the property of a strict and possessive English nurse, Kay, free again, suddenly felt the need of proving herself attractive. She wanted things to be as they had been before the baby was thought of. Also she felt that lately George had taken her too much for granted; she had a strong instinct that he was interested in Helen Avery.

When George Hannaford came home that night he had minimized to himself their quarrel of the previous evening and was honestly surprised at her perfunctory greeting.

'What's the matter, Kay?' he asked after a minute. 'Is this going to be another night like last night?'

'Do you know we're going out tonight?' she said, avoiding an answer.

'Where?'

'To Katherine Davis'. I didn't know whether you'd want to go –'

'I'd like to go.'

'I didn't know whether you'd want to go. Arthur Busch said he'd stop for me.'

They dined in silence. Without any secret thoughts to dip into like a child into a jam jar, George felt restless, and at the same time was aware that the atmosphere was full of jealousy, suspicion and anger. Until recently they had preserved between them something precious that made their house one of the pleasantest in Hollywood to enter. Now suddenly it might be any house; he felt common and he felt unstable. He had come near to making something bright and precious into something cheap and unkind. With a sudden surge of emotion, he crossed the room and was about to put his arm around her when the doorbell rang. A moment later Dolores announced Mr Arthur Busch.

Busch was an ugly, popular little man, a continuity writer and lately a director. A few years ago they had been hero and heroine to him, and even now, when he was a person of some consequence in the picture world, he accepted with equanimity Kay's use of him for such purposes as tonight's. He had been in love with her for years, but, because his love seemed hopeless, it had never caused him much distress.

They went on to the party. It was a housewarming, with Hawaiian musicians in attendance, and the guests were largely of the old crowd. People who had been in the early Griffith pictures, even though they were scarcely thirty, were considered to be of the old crowd; they were different from those coming along now, and they were conscious of it. They had a dignity and straightforwardness about them from the fact that they had worked in pictures before pictures were bathed in a golden haze of success. They were still rather humble before their amazing triumph, and thus, unlike the new generation, who took it all for granted, they were constantly in touch with reality. Half a dozen or so of the women were especially aware of being unique. No one had come along to fill their places; here and there a pretty face had caught the public imagination for a year, but those of the old crowd were already legends, ageless and disembodied. With all this, they were still young enough to believe that they would go forever.

George and Kay were greeted affectionately; people moved over and made place for them. The Hawaiians performed and the Duncan sisters sang at the piano. From the moment George saw who was here he guessed that Helen Avery would be here, too, and the fact annoyed him. It was not appropriate that she should be part of this gathering through which he and Kay had moved familiarly and tranquilly for years.

He saw her first when someone opened the swinging door to the kitchen, and when, a little later, she came out and their eyes met, he knew absolutely that he didn't love her. He went up to speak to her, and at her first words he saw something had happened to her, too, that had dissipated the mood of the afternoon. She had got a big part.

'And I'm in a daze!' she cried happily. 'I didn't think there was a chance and I've thought of nothing else since I read the book a year ago.'

'It's wonderful. I'm awfully glad.'

He had the feeling, though, that he should look at her with a certain regret; one couldn't jump from such a scene as this afternoon to a plane of casual friendly interest. Suddenly she began to laugh.

'Oh, we're such actors, George – you and I.'

'What do you mean?'

'You know what I mean.'

'I don't.'

'Oh, yes, you do. You did this afternoon. It was a pity we didn't have a camera.'

Short of declaring then and there that he loved her, there was absolutely nothing more to say. He grinned acquiescently. A group formed around them and absorbed them, and George, feeling that the evening had settled something, began to think about going home. An excited and sentimental elderly lady – someone's mother – came up and began telling him how much she believed in him, and he was polite and charming to her, as only he could be, for half an hour. Then he went to Kay, who had been sitting with Arthur Busch all evening, and suggested that they go.

She looked up unwillingly. She had had several highballs and the fact was mildly apparent. She did not want to go, but she got up after a mild argument and George went upstairs for his coat. When he came down Katherine Davis told him that Kay had already gone out to the car.

The crowd had increased; to avoid a general good-night he went out through the sun-parlour door to the lawn; less than twenty feet away from him he saw the figures of Kay and Arthur Busch against a bright street lamp; they were standing close together and staring into each other's eyes. He saw that they were holding hands.

After the first start of surprise George instinctively turned about, retraced his steps, hurried through the room he had just left, and came noisily out the front door. But Kay and Arthur Busch were still standing close together, and it was lingeringly and with abstracted eyes that they turned around finally and saw him. Then both of them seemed to make an effort; they drew apart as if it was a physical ordeal. George said good-bye to Arthur Busch with special cordiality, and in a moment he and Kay were driving homeward through the clear California night.

He said nothing, Kay said nothing. He was incredulous. He suspected that Kay had kissed a man here and there, but he had never seen it happen or given it any thought. This was different; there had been an element of tenderness in it and there was something veiled and remote in Kay's eyes that he had never seen there before.

Without having spoken, they entered the house; Kay stopped by the library door and looked in.

'There's someone there,' she said, and she added without interest: 'I'm going upstairs. Good night.'

As she ran up the stairs the person in the library stepped out into the hall.

'Mr Hannaford –'

He was a pale and hard young man; his face was vaguely familiar, but George didn't remember where he had seen it before.

'Mr Hannaford?' said the young man. 'I recognize you from your pictures.' He looked at George, obviously a little awed.

'What can I do for you?'

'Well, will you come in here?'

'What is it? I don't know who you are.'

'My name is Donovan. I'm Margaret Donovan's brother.' His face toughened a little.

'Is anything the matter?'

Donovan made a motion towards the door. 'Come in here.' His voice was confident now, almost threatening.

George hesitated, then he walked into the library. Donovan followed and stood across the table from him, his legs apart, his hands in his pockets.

'Hannaford,' he said, in the tone of a man trying to whip himself up to anger, 'Margaret wants fifty thousand dollars.'

'What the devil are you talking about?' exclaimed George incredulously.

'Margaret wants fifty thousand dollars,' repeated Donovan.

'You're Margaret Donovan's brother?'

'I am.'

'I don't believe it.' But he saw the resemblance now. 'Does Margaret know you're here?'

'She sent me here. She'll hand over those two letters for fifty thousand, and no questions asked.'

'What letters?' George chuckled irresistibly. 'This is some joke of Schroeder's, isn't it?'

'This ain't a joke, Hannaford. I mean the letters you signed your name to this afternoon.'

III

An hour later George went upstairs in a daze. The clumsiness of the affair was at once outrageous and astounding. That a friend of seven years should suddenly request his signature on papers that were not what they were purported to be made all his surroundings seem diaphanous and insecure. Even now the design engrossed him more than a defence against it, and he tried to re-create the steps by which Margaret had arrived at this act of recklessness or despair.

She had served as a script girl in various studios and for various directors for ten years; earning first twenty, now a hundred dollars a week. She was lovely-looking and she was intelligent; at any moment in those years she might have asked for a screen test, but some quality of initiative or ambition had been lacking. Not a few times had her opinion made or broken incipient careers. Still she waited at directors' elbows, increasingly aware that the years were slipping away.

That she had picked George as a victim amazed him most of all. Once, during the year before his marriage, there had been a momentary warmth; he had taken her to a Mayfair ball, and he remembered that he had kissed her going home that night in the car. The flirtation trailed along hesitatingly for a week. Before it could develop into anything serious he had gone East and met Kay.

Young Donovan had shown him a carbon of the letters he had signed.

They were written on the typewriter that he kept in his bungalow at the studio, and they were carefully and convincingly worded. They purported to be love letters, asserting that he was Margaret Donovan's lover, that he wanted to marry her, and that for that reason he was about to arrange a divorce. It was incredible. Someone must have seen him sign them that morning; someone must have heard her say: 'Your initials are like Mr Harris's.'

George was tired. He was training for a screen football game to be played next week, with the Southern California varsity as extras, and he was used to regular hours. In the middle of a confused and despairing sequence of thought about Margaret Donovan and Kay, he suddenly yawned. Mechanically he went upstairs, undressed and got into bed.

Just before dawn Kay came to him in the garden. There was a river that flowed past it now, and boats faintly lit with green and yellow lights moved slowly, remotely by. A gentle starlight fell like rain upon the dark, sleeping face of the world, upon the black mysterious bosoms of the trees, the tranquil gleaming water and the farther shore.

The grass was damp, and Kay came to him on hurried feet; her thin slippers were drenched with dew. She stood upon his shoes, nestling close to him, and held up her face as one shows a book open at a page.

'Think how you love me,' she whispered. 'I don't ask you to love me always like this, but I ask you to remember.'

'You'll always be like this to me.'

'Oh no; but promise me you'll remember.' Her tears were falling. 'I'll be different, but somewhere lost inside me there'll always be the person I am tonight.'

The scene dissolved slowly but George struggled into consciousness. He sat up in bed; it was morning. In the yard outside he heard the nurse instructing his son in the niceties of behaviour for two-month-old babies. From the yard next door a small boy shouted mysteriously: 'Who let that barrier through on me?'

Still in his pyjamas, George went to the phone and called his lawyers. Then he rang for his man, and while he was being shaved a certain order evolved from the chaos of the night before. First, he must deal with Margaret Donovan; second, he must keep the matter from Kay, who in her present state might believe anything; and third, he must fix things up with Kay. The last seemed the most important of all.

As he finished dressing he heard the phone ring downstairs and, with an instinct of danger, picked up the receiver.

'Hello . . . Oh, yes.' Looking up, he saw that both his doors were closed. 'Good morning, Helen . . . It's all right, Dolores. I'm taking it up here.' He waited till he heard the receiver click downstairs,

'How are you this morning, Helen?'

'George, I called up about last night. I can't tell you how sorry I am.'

'Sorry? Why are you sorry?'

'For treating you like that. I don't know what was in me, George. I didn't sleep all night thinking how terrible I'd been.'

A new disorder established itself in George's already littered mind.

'Don't be silly,' he said. To his despair he heard his own voice run on: 'For a minute I didn't understand, Helen. Then I thought it was better so.'

'Oh, George,' came her voice after a moment, very low.

Another silence. He began to put in a cuff button.

'I had to call up,' she said after a moment. 'I couldn't leave things like that.'

The cuff button dropped to the floor; he stooped to pick it up, and then said 'Helen!' urgently into the mouthpiece to cover the fact that he had momentarily been away.

'What, George?'

At this moment the hall door opened and Kay, radiating a faint distaste, came into the room. She hesitated.

'Are you busy?'

'It's all right.' He stared into the mouthpiece for a moment.

'Well, good-bye,' he muttered abruptly and hung up the receiver. He turned to Kay: 'Good morning.'

'I didn't mean to disturb you,' she said distantly.

'You didn't disturb me.' He hesitated. 'That was Helen Avery.'

'It doesn't concern me who it was. I came to ask you if we're going to the Coconut Grove tonight.'

'Sit down, Kay.'

'I don't want to talk.'

'Sit down a minute,' he said impatiently. She sat down. 'How long are you going to keep this up?' he demanded.

'I'm not keeping up anything. We're simply through, George, and you know it as well as I do.'

'That's absurd,' he said. 'Why, a week ago —'

'It doesn't matter. We've been getting nearer to this for months, and now it's over.'

'You mean you don't love me?' He was not particularly alarmed. They had been through scenes like this before.

'I don't know. I suppose I'll always love you in a way.' Suddenly she began to sob. 'Oh, it's all so sad. He's cared for me so long.'

George stared at her. Face to face with what was apparently a real emotion, he had no words of any kind. She was not angry, not threatening or pretending, not thinking about him at all, but concerned entirely with her emotions towards another man.

'What is it?' he cried. 'Are you trying to tell me you're in love with this man?'

'I don't know,' she said helplessly.

He took a step towards her, then went to the bed and lay down on it, staring in misery at the ceiling. After a while a maid knocked to say that Mr Busch and Mr Castle, George's lawyer, were below. The fact carried no meaning to him. Kay went into her room and he got up and followed her.

'Let's send word we're out,' he said. 'We can go away somewhere and talk this over.'

'I don't want to go away.'

She was already away, growing more mysterious and remote with every minute. The things on her dressing-table were the property of a stranger.

He began to speak in a dry, hurried voice. 'If you're still thinking about Helen Avery, it's nonsense. I've never given a damn for anybody but you.'

They went downstairs and into the living-room. It was nearly noon – another bright emotionless California day. George saw that Arthur Busch's ugly face in the sunshine was wan and white; he took a step towards George and then stopped, as if he were waiting for something – a challenge, a reproach, a blow.

In a flash the scene that would presently take place ran itself off in George's mind. He saw himself moving through the scene, saw his part, an infinite choice of parts, but in every one of them Kay would be against him and with Arthur Busch. And suddenly he rejected them all.

'I hope you'll excuse me,' he said quickly to Mr Castle. 'I called you up because a script girl named Margaret Donovan wants fifty thousand dollars for some letters she claims I wrote her. Of course the whole thing is –' He broke off. It didn't matter. 'I'll come to see you tomorrow.' He walked up to Kay and Arthur, so that only they could hear.

'I don't know about you two – what you want to do. But leave me out of it; you haven't any right to inflict any of it on me, for after all it's not my fault. I'm not going to be mixed up in your emotions.'

He turned and went out. His car was before the door and he said 'Go to Santa Monica' because it was the first name that popped into his head. The car drove off into the everlasting hazeless sunlight.

He rode for three hours, past Santa Monica and then along towards Long Beach by another road. As if it were something he saw out of the corner of his eye and with but a fragment of his attention, he imagined Kay and Arthur Busch progressing through the afternoon. Kay would cry a great deal and the situation would seem harsh and unexpected to them at first, but the tender closing of the day would draw them together. They would turn inevitably towards each other and he would slip more and more into the position of the enemy outside.

Kay had wanted him to get down in the dirt and dust of a scene and scramble for her. Not he; he hated scenes. Once he stooped to compete with Arthur Busch in pulling at Kay's heart, he would never be the same to himself. He would always be a little like Arthur Busch; they would always have that in common, like a shameful secret. There was little of the theatre about George; the millions before whose eyes the moods and changes of his face had flickered during ten years had not been deceived about that. From the moment when, as a boy of twenty, his handsome eyes had gazed off into the imaginary distance of a Griffith Western, his audience had been really watching the progress of a straightforward, slow-thinking, romantic man through an accidentally glamorous life.

His fault was that he had felt safe too soon. He realized suddenly that the two Fairbankses, in sitting side by side at table, were not keeping up a pose. They were giving hostages to fate. This was perhaps the most bizarre community in the rich, wild, bored empire, and for a marriage to succeed here, you must expect nothing or you must be always together. For a moment his glance had wavered from Kay and he stumbled blindly into disaster.

As he was thinking this and wondering where he would go and what he should do, he passed an apartment house that jolted his memory. It was on the outskirts of town, a pink horror built to represent something, somewhere, so cheaply and sketchily that whatever it copied the architect must have long since forgotten. And suddenly George remembered that he had once called for Margaret Donovan here the night of a Mayfair dance.

'Stop at this apartment!' he called through the speaking-tube.

He went in. The negro elevator boy stared open-mouthed at him as they rose in the cage. Margaret Donovan herself opened the door.

When she saw him she shrank away with a little cry. As he entered and closed the door she retreated before him into the front room. George followed.

It was twilight outside and the apartment was dusky and sad. The last light fell softly on the standardized furniture and the great gallery of signed photographs of moving-picture people that covered one wall. Her face was white, and as she stared at him she began nervously wringing her hands.

'What's this nonsense, Margaret?' George said, trying to keep any reproach out of his voice. 'Do you need money that bad?'

She shook her head vaguely. Her eyes were still fixed on him with a sort of terror; George looked at the floor.

'I suppose this was your brother's idea. At least I can't believe you'd be so stupid.' He looked up, trying to preserve the brusque masterly attitude of one talking to a naughty child, but at the sight of her face every emotion except pity left him. 'I'm a little tired. Do you mind if I sit down?'

'No.'

'I'm a little confused today,' said George after a minute. 'People seem to have it in for me today.'

'Why, I thought' – her voice became ironic in mid-sentence – 'I thought everybody loved you, George.'

'They don't.'

'Only me?'

'Yes,' he said abstractedly.

'I wish it had been only me. But then, of course, you wouldn't have been you.'

Suddenly he realized that she meant what she was saying.

'That's just nonsense.'

'At least you're here,' Margaret went on. 'I suppose I ought to be glad of that. And I am. I most decidedly am. I've often thought of you sitting in that chair, just at this time when it was almost dark. I used to make up little one-act plays about what would happen then. Would you like to hear one of them? I'll have to begin by coming over and sitting on the floor at your feet.'

Annoyed and yet spellbound, George kept trying desperately to seize upon a word or mood that would turn the subject.

'I've seen you sitting there so often that you don't look a bit more real than your ghost. Except that your hat has squashed your beautiful hair down on one side and you've got dark circles or dirt under your eyes. You look white, too, George. Probably you were on a party last night.'

'I was. And I found your brother waiting for me when I got home.'

'He's a good waiter, George. He's just out of San Quentin prison, where he's been waiting the last six years.'

'Then it was his idea?'

'We cooked it up together. I was going to China on my share.'

'Why was I the victim?'

'That seemed to make it realer. Once I thought you were going to fall in love with me five years ago.'

The bravado suddenly melted out of her voice and it was still light enough to see that her mouth was quivering.

· 'I've loved you for years,' she said – 'since the first day you came West and walked into the old Realart Studio. You were so brave about people, George. Whoever it was, you walked right up to them and tore something aside as if it was in your way and began to know them. I tried to make love to you, just like the rest, but it was difficult. You drew people right up close to you and held them there, not able to move either way.'

'This is all entirely imaginary,' said George, frowning uncomfortably, 'and I can't control –'

'No, I know. You can't control charm. It's simply got to be used. You've got to keep your hand in if you have it, and go through life attaching people to you that you don't want. I don't blame you. If you only hadn't kissed me the night of the Mayfair dance. I suppose it was the champagne.'

George felt as if a band which had been playing for a long time in the distance had suddenly moved up and taken a station beneath his window. He had always been conscious that things like this were going on around him. Now that he thought of it, he had always been conscious that Margaret loved him, but the faint music of these emotions in his ear had seemed to bear no relation to actual life. They were phantoms that he had conjured up out of nothing; he had never imagined their actual incarnations. At his wish they should die inconsequently away.

'You can't imagine what it's been like,' Margaret continued after a minute. 'Things you've just said and forgotten, I've put myself asleep night after night remembering – trying to squeeze something more out of them. After that night you took me to the Mayfair other men didn't exist for me any more. And there were others, you know – lots of them. But I'd see you walking along somewhere about the lot, looking at the ground and smiling a little, as if something very amusing had just happened to you, the way you do. And I'd pass you and you'd look up and really smile: "Hello, darling!" "Hello, darling" and my heart would turn over. That would happen four times a day.'

George stood up and she, too, jumped up quickly.

'Oh, I've bored you,' she cried softly. 'I might have known I'd bore you. You want to go home. Let's see – is there anything else? Oh, yes; you might as well have those letters.'

Taking them out of a desk, she took them to a window and identified them by a rift of lamplight.

'They're really beautiful letters. They'd do you credit. I suppose it was pretty stupid, as you say, but it ought to teach you a lesson about – about signing things, or something.' She tore the letters small and threw them in the wastebasket: 'Now go on,' she said.

'Why must I go now?'

For the third time in twenty-four hours sad and uncontrollable tears confronted him.

'Please go!' she cried angrily – 'or stay if you like. I'm yours for the asking. You know it. You can have any woman you want in the world by just raising your hand. Would I amuse you?'

'Margaret –'

'Oh, go on then.' She sat down and turned her face away. 'After all you'll begin to look silly in a minute. You wouldn't like that, would you? So get out.'

George stood there helpless, trying to put himself in her place and say something that wouldn't be priggish, but nothing came.

He tried to force down his personal distress, his discomfort, his vague feeling of scorn, ignorant of the fact that she was watching him and understanding it all and loving the struggle in his face. Suddenly his own nerves gave way under the strain of the past twenty-four hours and he felt his eyes grow dim and his throat tighten. He shook his head helplessly. Then he turned away – still not knowing that she was watching him and loving him until she thought her heart would burst with it – and went out to the door.

IV

The car stopped before his house, dark save for small lights in the nursery and the lower hall. He heard the telephone ringing, but when he answered it, inside, there was no one on the line. For a few minutes he wandered about in the darkness, moving from chair to chair and going to the window to stare out into the opposite emptiness of the night.

It was strange to be alone, to feel alone. In his overwrought condition the fact was not unpleasant. As the trouble of last night had made Helen Avery infinitely remote, so his talk with Margaret had acted as a catharsis to his own personal misery. It would swing back upon him presently, he knew, but for a moment his mind was too tired to remember, to imagine or to care.

Half an hour passed. He saw Dolores issue from the kitchen, take the paper from the front steps and carry it back to the kitchen for a preliminary inspection. With a vague idea of packing his grip, he went upstairs. He opened the door of Kay's room and found her lying down.

For a moment he didn't speak, but moved around the bathroom between. Then he went into her room and switched on the lights.

'What's the matter?' he asked casually. 'Aren't you feeling well?'

'I've been trying to get some sleep,' she said. 'George, do you think that girl's gone crazy?'

'What girl?'

'Margaret Donovan. I've never heard of anything so terrible in my life.'

For a moment he thought that there had been some new development.

'Fifty thousand dollars!' she cried indignantly. 'Why, I wouldn't give it to her even if it were true. She ought to be sent to jail.'

'Oh, it's not so terrible as that,' he said. 'She has a brother who's a pretty bad egg and it was his idea.'

'She's capable of anything,' Kay said solemnly. 'And you're just a fool if you don't see it. I've never liked her. She has dirty hair.'

'Well, what of it?' he demanded impatiently, and added: 'Where's Arthur Busch?'

'He went home right after lunch. Or rather I sent him home.'

'You decided you were not in love with him?'

She looked up almost in surprise. 'In love with him? Oh, you mean this morning. I was just mad at you; you ought to have known that. I was a little sorry for him last night, but I guess it was the highballs.'

'Well, what did you mean when you –' He broke off. Wherever he turned he found a muddle, and he resolutely determined not to think.

'My heavens!' exclaimed Kay. 'Fifty thousand dollars!'

'Oh, drop it. She tore up the letters – she wrote them herself – and everything's all right.'

'George.'

'Yes.'

'Of course Douglas will fire her right away.'

'Of course he won't. He won't know anything about it.'

'You mean to say you're not going to let her go? After this?'

He jumped up. 'Do you suppose she thought that?' he cried.

'Thought what?'

'That I'd have them let her go?'

'You certainly ought to.'

He looked hastily through the phone book for her name.

'Oxford –' he called.

After an unusually long time the switchboard operator answered: 'Bourbon Apartments.'

'Miss Margaret Donovan, please.'

'Why –' The operator's voice broke off. 'If you'll just wait a minute, please.' He held the line; the minute passed, then another. Then the operator's voice: 'I couldn't talk to you then. Miss Donovan has had an accident. She's shot herself. When you called they were taking her through the lobby to St Catherine's Hospital.'

'Is she – is it serious?' George demanded frantically.

'They thought so at first, but now they think she'll be all right. They're going to probe for the bullet.'

'Thank you.'

He got up and turned to Kay.

'She's tried to kill herself,' he said in a strained voice. 'I'll have to go around to the hospital. I was pretty clumsy this afternoon and I think I'm partly responsible for this.'

'George,' said Kay suddenly.

'What?'

'Don't you think it's sort of unwise to get mixed up in this? People might say –'

'I don't give a damn what they say,' he answered roughly.

He went to his room and automatically began to prepare for going out. Catching sight of his face in the mirror, he closed his eyes with a sudden exclamation of distaste, and abandoned the intention of brushing his hair.

'George,' Kay called from the next room, 'I love you.'

'I love you too.'

'Jules Rennard called up. Something about barracuda fishing. Don't you think it would be fun to get up a party? Men and girls both?'

'Somehow the idea doesn't appeal to me. The whole idea of barracuda fishing –'

The phone rang below and he started. Dolores was answering it.

It was a lady who had already called twice today.

'Is Mr Hannaford in?'

'No,' said Dolores promptly. She stuck out her tongue and hung up the phone just as George Hannaford came downstairs. She helped him into his coat, standing as close as she could to him, opened the door and followed a little way out on the porch.

'Meester Hannaford,' she said suddenly, 'that Miss Avery she call up five-six times today. I tell her you out and say nothing to missus.'

'What?' He stared at her, wondering how much she knew about his affairs.

'She call up just now and I say you out.'

'All right,' he said absently.

'Meester Hannaford.'

'Yes, Dolores.'

'I deedn't hurt myself thees morning when I fell off the porch.'

'That's fine. Good night, Dolores.'

'Good night, Meester Hannaford.'

George smiled at her, faintly, fleetingly, tearing a veil from between them, unconsciously promising her a possible admission to the thousand delights and wonders that only he knew and could command. Then he went to his waiting car and Dolores, sitting down on the stoop, rubbed her hands together in a gesture that might have expressed either ecstasy or strangulation, and watched the rising of the thin, pale California moon.

THE ROUGH CROSSING

I

Once on the long, covered piers, you have come into a ghostly country that is no longer Here and not yet There. Especially at night. There is a hazy yellow vault full of shouting, echoing voices. There is the rumble of trucks and the clump of trunks, the strident chatter of a crane and the first salt smell of the sea. You hurry through, even though there's time. The past, the continent, is behind you; the future is that glowing mouth in the side of the ship; this dim turbulent alley is too confusedly the present.

Up the gangplank, and the vision of the world adjusts itself, narrows. One is a citizen of a commonwealth smaller than Andorra. One is no longer so sure of anything. Curiously unmoved the men at the purser's desk, cell-like the cabin, disdainful the eyes of voyagers and their friends, solemn the officer who stands on the deserted promenade deck thinking something of his own as he stares at the crowd below. A last odd idea that one didn't really have to come, then the loud, mournful whistles, and the thing – certainly not the boat, but rather a human idea, a frame of mind – pushes forth into the big dark night.

Adrian Smith, one of the celebrities on board – not a very great celebrity, but important enough to be bathed in flashlight by a photographer who had been given his name, but wasn't sure what his subject 'did' – Adrian Smith and his blonde wife, Eva, went up to the promenade deck, passed the melancholy ship's officer, and, finding a quiet aerie, put their elbows on the rail.

'We're going!' he cried presently, and they both laughed in ecstasy. 'We've escaped. They can't get us now.'

'Who?'

He waved his hand vaguely at the civic tiara.

'All those people out there. They'll come with their posses and their warrants and list of crimes we've committed, and ring the bell at our door on Park Avenue and ask for the Adrian Smiths, but what ho! the Adrian Smiths and their children and nurse are off for France.'

'You make me think we really have committed crimes.'

'They can't have you,' he said frowning. 'That's one thing they're after me about – they know I haven't got any right to a person like you, and they're furious. That's one reason I'm glad to get away.'

'Darling,' said Eva.

She was twenty-six – five years younger than he. She was something precious to everyone who knew her.

'I like this boat better than the *Majestic* or the *Aquitania*,' she remarked, unfaithful to the ships that had served their honeymoon.

'It's much smaller.'

'But it's very slick and it has all those little shops along the corridors. And I think the staterooms are bigger.'

'The people are very formal – did you notice? – as if they thought everyone else was a card sharp. And in about four days half of them will be calling the other half by their first names.'

Four of the people came by now – a quartet of young girls abreast, making a circuit of the deck. Their eight eyes swept momentarily towards Adrian and Eva, and then swept automatically back, save for one pair which lingered for an instant with a little start. They belonged to one of the girls in the middle, who was, indeed, the only passenger of the four. She was not more than eighteen – a dark little beauty with the fine crystal gloss over her that, in brunettes, takes the place of a blonde's bright glow.

'Now, who's that?' wondered Adrian. 'I've seen her before.'

'She's pretty,' said Eva.

'Yes.' He kept wondering, and Eva deferred momentarily to his distraction; then, smiling up at him, she drew him back into their privacy.

'Tell me more,' she said.

'About what?'

'About us – what a good time we'll have, and how we'll be much better and happier, and very close always.'

'How could we be any closer?' His arm pulled her to him.

'But I mean never even quarrel any more about silly things. You know, I made up my mind when you gave me my birthday present last week' – her fingers caressed the fine seed pearls at her throat – 'that I'd try never to say a mean thing to you again.'

'You never have, my precious.'

Yet even as he strained her against his side she knew that the moment of utter isolation had passed almost before it had begun. His antennae were already out, feeling over this new world.

'Most of the people look rather awful,' he said – 'little and swarthy and ugly. Americans didn't use to look like that.'

'They look dreary,' she agreed. 'Let's not get to know anybody, but just stay together.'

A gong was beating now, and stewards were shouting down the decks, 'Visitors ashore, please!' and voices rose to a strident chorus. For a while the gangplanks were thronged; then they were empty, and the jostling crowd behind the barrier waved and called unintelligible things, and kept up a grin of good will. As the stevedores began to work at the ropes a flat-faced, somewhat befuddled young man arrived in a great hurry and was assisted up the gangplank by a porter and a taxi driver. The ship having swallowed him as impassively as though he were a missionary for Beirut, a low, portentous vibration began. The pier with its faces commenced to slide by, and for a moment the boat was just a piece accidentally split off from it; then the faces became remote, voiceless, and the pier was one among many yellow blurs along the water front. Now the harbour flowed swiftly toward the sea.

On a northern parallel of latitude a hurricane was forming and moving south by southeast preceded by a strong west wind. On its course it was destined to swamp the *Peter I. Eudin* of Amsterdam, with a crew of sixty-six, to break a boom on the largest boat in the world, and to bring grief and want to the wives of several hundred seamen. This liner, leaving New York Sunday evening, would enter the zone of the storm Tuesday, and of the hurricane late Wednesday night.

II

Tuesday afternoon Adrian and Eva paid their first visit to the smoking-room. This was not in accord with their intentions – they had 'never wanted to see a cocktail again' after leaving America – but they had forgotten the staccato loneliness of ships, and all activity centred about the bar. So they went in for just a minute.

It was full. There were those who had been there since luncheon, and those who would be there until dinner, not to mention a faithful few who had been there since nine this morning. It was a prosperous assembly, taking its recreation at bridge, solitaire, detective stories, alcohol, argument and love. Up to this point you could have matched it in the club or casino life of any country, but over it all played a repressed nervous energy, a barely disguised impatience that extended to old and young alike. The cruise had begun, and they had enjoyed the beginning, but the show was not varied enough to last six days, and already they wanted it to be over.

At a table near them Adrian saw the pretty girl who had stared at him on the deck the first night. Again he was fascinated by her loveliness; there was no mist upon the brilliant gloss that gleamed through the smoky confusion of the room. He and Eva had decided from the passenger list that she was probably 'Miss Elizabeth D'Amido and maid', and he had heard her called Betsy as he walked past a deck-tennis game. Among the young people with her was the flat-nosed youth who had been 'poured on board', the night of their departure; yesterday he had walked the deck morosely, but he was apparently reviving. Miss D'Amido whispered something to him, and he looked over at the Smiths with curious eyes. Adrian was new enough at being a celebrity to turn self-consciously away.

'There's a little roll. Do you feel it?' Eva demanded.

'Perhaps we'd better split a pint of champagne.'

While he gave the order a short colloquy was taking place at the other table; presently a young man rose and came over to them.

'Isn't this Mr Adrian Smith?'

'Yes.'

'We wondered if we couldn't put you down for the deck-tennis tournament. We're going to have a deck-tennis tournament.'

'Why –' Adrian hesitated.

'My name's Stacomb,' burst out the young man. 'We all know your – your plays or whatever it is, and all that – and we wondered if you wouldn't like to come over to our table.'

Somewhat overwhelmed, Adrian laughed: Mr Stacomb, glib, soft, slouching, waited; evidently under the impression that he had delivered himself of a graceful compliment.

Adrian, understanding that, too, replied: 'Thanks, but perhaps you'd better come over here.'

'We've got a bigger table.'

'But we're older and more – more settled.'

The young man laughed kindly, as if to say, 'That's all right.'

'Put me down,' said Adrian. 'How much do I owe you?'

'One buck. Call me Stac.'

'Why?' asked Adrian, startled.

'It's shorter.'

When he had gone they smiled broadly.

'Heavens,' Eva gasped, 'I believe they are coming over.'

They were. With a great draining of glasses, calling of waiters, shuffling of chairs, three boys and two girls moved to the Smiths' table. If there was any diffidence, it was confined to the hosts; for the new additions gathered around them eagerly, eyeing Adrian with respect – too much respect – as if to say: 'This was probably a mistake and won't be amusing, but maybe we'll get something out of it to help us in our after life, like at school.'

In a moment Miss D'Amido changed seats with one of the men and placed her radiant self at Adrian's side, looking at him with manifest admiration.

'I fell in love with you the minute I saw you,' she said audibly and without self-consciousness; 'so I'll take all the blame for butting in. I've seen your play four times.'

Adrian called a waiter to take their orders.

'You see,' continued Miss D'Amido, 'we're going into a storm, and you might be prostrated the rest of the trip, so I couldn't take any chances.'

He saw that there was no undertone or innuendo in what she said, nor the need of any. The words themselves were enough, and the deference with which she neglected the young men and bent her politeness on him was somehow very touching. A little glow went over him; he was having rather more than a pleasant time.

Eva was less entertained; but the flat-nosed young man, whose name was Butterworth, knew people that she did, and that seemed to make the affair less careless and casual. She did not like meeting new people unless they had 'something to contribute', and she was often bored by the great streams of them, of all types and conditions and classes, that passed through Adrian's life. She herself 'had everything' – which is to say that she was well endowed with talents and with charm – and the mere novelty of people did not seem a sufficient reason for eternally offering everything up to them.

Half an hour later when she rose to go and see the children, she was content that the episode was over. It was colder on deck, with a damp that was almost rain, and there was a perceptible motion. Opening the door of her state-room she was surprised to find the cabin steward sitting languidly on her bed, his head slumped upon the upright pillow. He looked at her listlessly as she came in, but made no move to get up,

'When you've finished your nap you can fetch me a new pillow-case,' she said briskly.

Still the man didn't move. She perceived then that his face was green.

'You can't be seasick in here,' she announced firmly. 'You go and lie down in your own quarters.'

'It's me side,' he said faintly. He tried to rise, gave out a little rasping sound of pain and sank back again. Eva rang for the stewardess.

A steady pitch, toss, roll had begun in earnest and she felt no sympathy for the steward, but only wanted to get him out as quick as possible. It was outrageous for a member of the crew to be seasick. When the stewardess came in Eva tried to explain this, but now her own head was whirring, and throwing herself on the bed, she covered her eyes.

'It's his fault,' she groaned when the man was assisted from the room. 'I was all right and it made me sick to look at him. I wish he'd die.'

In a few minutes Adrian came in.

'Oh, but I'm sick!' she cried.

'Why, you poor baby.' He leaned over and took her in his arms. 'Why didn't you tell me?'

'I was all right upstairs, but there was a steward – Oh, I'm too sick to talk.'

'You'd better have dinner in bed.'

'Dinner! Oh, my heavens!'

He waited solicitously, but she wanted to hear his voice, to have it drown out the complaining sound of the beams.

'Where've you been?'

'Helping to sign up people for the tournament.'

'Will they have it if it's like this? Because if they do I'll just lose for you.'

He didn't answer; opening her eyes, she saw that he was frowning.

'I didn't know you were going in the doubles,' he said.

'Why, that's the only fun.'

'I told the D'Amido girl I'd play with her.'

'Oh.'

'I didn't think. You know I'd much rather play with you.'

'Why didn't you, then?' she asked coolly.

'It never occurred to me.'

She remembered that on their honeymoon they had been in the finals and won a prize. Years passed. But Adrian never frowned in this regretful way unless he felt a little guilty. He stumbled about, getting his dinner clothes out of the trunk, and she shut her eyes.

When a particular violent lurch startled her awake again he was dressed and tying his tie. He looked healthy and fresh, and his eyes were bright.

'Well, how about it?' he inquired. 'Can you make it, or no?'

'No.'

'Can I do anything for you before I go?'

'Where are you going?'

'Meeting those kids in the bar. Can I do anything for you?'

'No.'

'Darling, I hate to leave you like this.'

'Don't be silly. I just want to sleep.'

That solicitous frown – when she knew he was crazy to be out and away from the close cabin. She was glad when the door closed. The thing to do was to sleep, sleep.

Up – down – sideways. Hey there, not so far! Pull her round the corner there! Now roll her, right – left – Crea-eak! Wrench! Swoop!

Some hours later Eva was dimly conscious of Adrian bending over her. She wanted him to put his arms around her and draw her up out of this dizzy lethargy, but by the time she was fully awake the cabin was empty. He had looked in and gone. When she awoke next the cabin was dark and he was in bed.

The morning was fresh and cool, and the sea was just enough calmer to make Eva think she could get up. They breakfasted in the cabin and with Adrian's help she accomplished an unsatisfactory makeshift toilet and they went up on the boat deck. The tennis tournament had already begun and was furnishing action for a dozen amateur movie cameras, but the majority of passengers were represented by lifeless bundles in deck chairs beside untasted trays.

Adrian and Miss D'Amido played their first match. She was deft and graceful; blatantly well. There was even more warmth behind her ivory skin than there had been the day before. The strolling first officer stopped and talked to her; half a dozen men whom she couldn't have known three days ago called her Betsy. She was already the pretty girl of the voyage, the cynosure of starved ship's eyes.

But after a while Eva preferred to watch the gulls in the wireless masts and the slow slide of the roll-top sky. Most of the passengers looked silly with their movie cameras that they had all rushed to get and now didn't know what to use for, but the sailors painting the lifeboat stanchions were quiet and beaten and sympathetic, and probably wished, as she did, that the voyage was over.

Butterworth sat down on the deck beside her chair.

'They're operating on one of the stewards this morning. Must be terrible in this sea.'

'Operating? What for?' she asked listlessly.

'Appendicitis. They have to operate now because we're going into worse weather. That's why they're having the ship's party tonight.'

'Oh, the poor man!' she cried, realizing it must be her steward.

Adrian was showing off now by being very courteous and thoughtful in the game.

'Sorry. Did you hurt yourself? . . . No, it was my fault . . . You better put on your coat right away, pardner, or you'll catch cold.'

The match was over and they had won. Flushed and hearty, he came up to Eva's chair.

'How do you feel?'

'Terrible.'

'Winners are buying a drink in the bar,' he said apologetically.

'I'm coming, too,' Eva said, but an immediate dizziness made her sink back in her chair.

'You'd better stay here. I'll send you up something.'

She felt that his public manner had hardened towards her slightly.

'You'll come back?'

'Oh, right away.'

She was alone on the boat deck, save for a solitary ship's officer who slanted obliquely as he paced the bridge. When the cocktail arrived she forced herself to drink it, and felt better. Trying to distract her mind with pleasant things, she reached back to the sanguine talks that she and Adrian had had before sailing: There was the little villa in Brittany, the children learning French – that was all she could think of now – the little villa in Brittany, the children learning French – so she repeated the words over and over to herself until they became as meaningless as the wide white sky. The why of their being here had suddenly eluded her; she felt unmotivated, accidental, and she wanted Adrian to come back quick, all responsive and tender, to reassure her. It was in the hope that there was some secret of graceful living, some real compensation for the lost, careless confidence of twenty-one, that they were going to spend a year in France.

The day passed darkly, with fewer people around and a wet sky falling. Suddenly it was five o'clock, and they were all in the bar again, and Mr Butterworth was telling her about his past. She took a good deal of champagne, but she was seasick dimly through it, as if the illness was her soul trying to struggle up through some thickening incrustation of abnormal life.

'You're my idea of a Greek goddess, physically,' Butterworth was saying.

It was pleasant to be Mr Butterworth's idea of a Greek goddess physically, but where was Adrian? He and Miss D'Amido had gone out on a forward deck to feel the spray. Eva heard herself promising to get out her colours and paint the Eiffel Tower on Butterworth's shirt front for the party tonight.

When Adrian and Betsy D'Amido, soaked with spray, opened the door with difficulty against the driving wind and came into the now-covered security of the promenade deck, they stopped and turned toward each other.

'Well?' she said. But he only stood with his back to the rail, looking at her, afraid to speak. She was silent, too, because she wanted him to be first; so for a moment nothing happened. Then she made a step towards him, and he took her in his arms and kissed her forehead.

'You're just sorry for me, that's all.' She began to cry a little. 'You're just being kind.'

'I feel terribly about it.' His voice was taut and trembling.

'Then kiss me.'

The deck was empty. He bent over her swiftly.

'No, really kiss me.'

He could not remember when anything had felt so young and fresh as her lips. The rain lay, like tears shed for him, upon the softly shining porcelain cheeks. She was all new and immaculate, and her eyes were wild.

'I love you,' she whispered. 'I can't help loving you, can I? When I first saw you – oh, not on the boat, but over a year ago – Grace Heally took me to a rehearsal and suddenly you jumped up in the second row and began telling them what to do. I wrote you a letter and tore it up.'

'We've got to go.'

She was weeping as they walked along the deck. Once more, imprudently, she held up her face to him at the door of her cabin. His blood was beating through him in wild tumult as he walked on to the bar.

He was thankful that Eva scarcely seemed to notice him or to know that he had been gone. After a moment he pretended an interest in what she was doing.

'What's that?'

'She's painting the Eiffel Tower on my shirt front for tonight,' explained Butterworth.

'There,' Eva laid away her brush and wiped her hands.

'How's that?'

'A *chef-d'oeuvre*.'

Her eyes swept around the watching group, lingered casually upon Adrian.

'You're wet. Go and change.'

'You come too.'

'I want another champagne cocktail.'

'You've had enough. It's time to dress for the party.'

Unwilling she closed her paints and preceded him.

'Stacomb's got a table for nine,' he remarked as they walked along the corridor.

'The younger set,' she said with unnecessary bitterness. 'Oh, the younger set. And you just having the time of your life – with a child.'

They had a long discussion in the cabin, unpleasant on her part and evasive on his, which ended when the ship gave a sudden gigantic heave, and Eva, the edge worn off her champagne, felt ill again. There was nothing to do but to have a cocktail in the cabin, and after that they decided to go to the party – she believed him now, or she didn't care.

Adrian was ready first – he never wore fancy dress.

'I'll go on up. Don't be long.'

'Wait for me, please; it's rocking so.'

He sat down on a bed, concealing his impatience.

'You don't mind waiting, do you? I don't want to parade up there all alone.'

She was taking a tuck in an oriental costume rented from the barber.

'Ships make people feel crazy,' she said. 'I think they're awful.'

'Yes,' he muttered absently.

'When it gets very bad I pretend I'm in the top of a tree, rocking to and fro. But finally I get pretending everything, and finally I have to pretend I'm sane when I know I'm not.'

'If you get thinking that way you will go crazy.'

'Look, Adrian.' She held up the string of pearls before clasping them on. 'Aren't they lovely?'

In Adrian's impatience she seemed to move around the cabin like a figure in a slow-motion picture. After a moment he demanded:

'Are you going to be long? It's stifling in here.'

'You go on!' she fired up.

'I don't want –'

'Go on, please! You just make me nervous trying to hurry me.'

With a show of reluctance he left her. After a moment's hesitation he went down a flight to a deck below and knocked at a door.

'Betsy.'

'Just a minute.'

She came out in the corridor attired in a red pea-jacket and trousers borrowed from the elevator boy.

'Do elevator boys have fleas?' she demanded. 'I've got everything in the world on under this as a precaution.'

'I had to see you,' he said quickly.

'Careful,' she whispered. 'Mrs Worden, who's supposed to be chaperoning me, is across the way. She's sick.'

'I'm sick for you.'

They kissed suddenly, clung close together in the narrow corridor, swaying to and fro with the motion of the ship.

'Don't go away,' she murmured.

'I've got to. I've –'

Her youth seemed to flow into him, bearing him up into a delicate romantic ecstasy that transcended passion. He couldn't relinquish it; he had discovered something that he had thought was lost with his own youth forever. As he walked along the passage he knew that he had stopped thinking, no longer dared to think.

He met Eva going into the bar.

'Where've you been?' she asked with a strained smile.

'To see about the table.'

She was lovely; her cool distinction conquered the trite costume and filled him with a resurgence of approval and pride. They sat down at a table.

The gale was rising hour by hour and the mere traversing of a passage had become a rough matter. In every stateroom trunks were lashed to the washstands, and the *Vestris* disaster was being reviewed in detail by nervous ladies, tossing, ill and wretched, upon their beds. In the smoking-room a stout gentleman had been hurled backward and suffered a badly cut head; and now the lighter chairs and tables were stacked and roped against the wall.

The crowd who had donned fancy dress and were dining together had swollen to about sixteen. The only remaining qualification for membership was the ability to reach the smoking-room. They ranged from a Groton-Harvard lawyer to an ungrammatical broker they had nicknamed Gyp the Blood, but distinctions had disappeared; for the moment they were samurai, chosen from several hundred for their triumphant resistance to the storm.

The gala dinner, overhung sardonically with lanterns and streamers, was interrupted by great communal slides across the room, precipitate retirements and spilled wine, while the ship roared and complained that under the panoply of a palace it was a ship after all. Upstairs afterward a dozen couples tried to dance, shuffling and galloping here and there in a crazy fandango, thrust around fantastically by a will alien to their own. In view of the condition of tortured hundreds below, there grew to be something indecent about it like a revel in a house of mourning, and presently there was an egress of the ever-dwindling survivors towards the bar.

As the evening passed, Eva's feeling of unreality increased. Adrian had disappeared – presumably with Miss D'Amido – and her mind, distorted by illness and champagne, began to enlarge upon the fact; annoyance changed slowly to dark and brooding anger, grief to desperation. She had never tried to bind Adrian, never needed to – for they were serious people, with all sorts of mutual interests, and satisfied with each other – but this was a breach of the contract, this was cruel. How could he think that she didn't know?

It seemed several hours later that he leaned over her chair in the bar where she was giving some woman an impassioned lecture upon babies, and said:

'Eva, we'd better turn in.'

Her lip curled. 'So that you can leave me there and then come back to your eighteen-year –'

'Be quiet.'

'I won't come to bed.'

'Very well. Good night.'

More time passed and the people at the table changed. The stewards wanted to close up the room, and thinking of Adrian – her Adrian – off somewhere saying tender things to someone fresh and lovely, Eva began to cry.

'But he's gone to bed,' her last attendants assured her. 'We saw him go.'

She shook her head. She knew better. Adrian was lost. The long seven-year dream was broken. Probably she was punished for something she had done; as this thought occurred to her the shrieking timbers overhead began to mutter that she had guessed at last. This was for the selfishness to her mother, who hadn't wanted her to marry Adrian; for all the sins and omissions of her life. She stood up, saying she must go out and get some air.

The deck was dark and drenched with wind and rain. The ship pounded through valleys, fleeing from black mountains of water that roared towards it. Looking out at the night, Eva saw that there was no chance for them unless she could make atonement, propitiate the storm. It was Adrian's love that was demanded of her. Deliberately she unclasped her pearl necklace, lifted it to her lips – for she knew that with it went the freshest, fairest part of her life – and flung it out into the gale.

III

When Adrian awoke it was lunchtime, but he knew that some heavier sound than the bugle had called him up from his deep sleep. Then he realized that the trunk had broken loose from its lashings and was being thrown back and forth between a wardrobe and Eva's bed. With an exclamation he jumped up, but she was unharmed – still in costume and stretched out in deep sleep. When the steward had helped him secure the trunk, Eva opened a single eye.

'How are you?' he demanded, sitting on the side of her bed.

She closed the eye, opened it again.

'We're in a hurricane now,' he told her. 'The steward says it's the worst he's seen in twenty years.'

'My head,' she muttered. 'Hold my head.'

'How?'

'In front. My eyes are going out. I think I'm dying.'

'Nonsense. Do you want the doctor?'

She gave a funny little gasp that frightened him; he rang and sent the steward for the doctor.

The young doctor was pale and tired. There was a stubble of beard upon his face. He bowed curtly as he came in and, turning to Adrian, said with scant ceremony:

'What's the matter?'

'My wife doesn't feel well.'

'Well, what is it you want – a bromide?'

A little annoyed by his shortness, Adrian said: 'You'd better examine her and see what she needs.'

'She needs a bromide,' said the doctor. 'I've given orders that she is not to have any more to drink on this ship.'

'Why not?' demanded Adrian in astonishment.

'Don't you know what happened last night?'

'Why, no, I was asleep.'

'Mrs Smith wandered around the boat for an hour, not knowing what she was doing. A sailor was sent to follow her, and then the medical stewardess tried to get her to bed, and your wife insulted her.'

'Oh, my heavens!' cried Eva faintly.

'The nurse and I had both been up all night with Steward Carton, who died this morning.' He picked up his case. 'I'll send down a bromide for Mrs Smith. Good-bye.'

For a few minutes there was silence in the cabin. Then Adrian put his arm around her quickly.

'Never mind,' he said. 'We'll straighten it out.'

'I remember now.' Her voice was an awed whisper. 'My pearls. I threw them overboard.'

'Threw them overboard!'

'Then I began looking for you.'

'But I was here in bed.'

'I didn't believe it; I thought you were with that girl.'

'She collapsed during dinner. I was taking a nap down here.'

Frowning, he rang the bell and asked the steward for luncheon and a bottle of beer.

'Sorry, but we can't serve any beer to your cabin, sir.'

When he went out Adrian exploded: 'This is an outrage. You were simply crazy from that storm and they can't be so high-handed. I'll see the captain.'

'Isn't that awful?' Eva murmured. 'The poor man died.'

She turned over and began to sob into her pillow. There was a knock at the door.

'Can I come in?'

The assiduous Mr Butterworth, surprisingly healthy and immaculate, came into the crazily tipping cabin.

'Well, how's the mystic?' he demanded of Eva. 'Do you remember praying to the elements in the bar last night?'

'I don't want to remember anything about last night.'

They told him about the stewardess, and with the telling the situation lightened; they all laughed together.

'I'm going to get you some beer to have with your luncheon,' Butterworth said. 'You ought to get up on deck.'

'Don't go,' Eva said. 'You look so cheerful and nice.'

'Just for ten minutes.'

When he had gone, Adrian rang for two baths.

'The thing is to put on our best clothes and walk proudly three times around the deck,' he said.

'Yes.' After a moment she added abstractedly: 'I like that young man. He was awfully nice to me last night when you'd disappeared.'

The bath steward appeared with the information that bathing was too dangerous today. They were in the midst of the wildest hurricane on the North Atlantic in ten years; there were two broken arms this morning from attempts to take baths. An elderly lady had been thrown down a staircase and was not expected to live. Furthermore, they had received the SOS signal from several boats this morning.

'Will we go to help them?'

'They're all behind us, sir, so we have to leave them to the *Mauretania*. If we tried to turn in this sea the portholes would be smashed.'

This array of calamities minimized their own troubles. Having eaten a sort of luncheon and drunk the beer provided by Butterworth, they dressed and went on deck.

Despite the fact that it was only possible to progress step by step, holding on to rope or rail, more people were abroad than on the day before. Fear had driven them from their cabins, where the trunks bumped and the waves pounded the portholes, and they awaited momentarily the call to the boats. Indeed, as Adrian and Eva stood on the transverse deck above the second class, there was a bugle call, followed by a gathering of stewards and stewardesses on the deck below. But the boat was sound; it had outlasted one of its cargo – Steward James Carton was being buried at sea.

It was very British and sad. There were the rows of stiff, disciplined men and women standing in the driving rain, and there was a shape covered by the flag of the Empire that lived by the sea. The chief purser read the service, a hymn was sung, the body slid off into the hurricane. With Eva's burst of wild weeping for this humble end, some last string snapped within her. Now she really didn't care. She responded eagerly when Butterworth suggested that he get some champagne to their cabin. Her mood worried Adrian; she wasn't used to so much drinking and he wondered what he ought to do. At his suggestion that they sleep instead, she merely laughed, and the bromide the doctor had sent stood untouched on the washstand. Pretending to listen to the insipidities of several Mr Stacombs, he watched her; to his surprise and discomfort she seemed on intimate and even sentimental terms with Butterworth and he wondered if this was a form of revenge for his attention to Betsy D'Amido.

The cabin was full of smoke, the voices went on incessantly, the suspension of activity, the waiting for the storm's end, was getting on his nerves. They had been at sea only four days; it was like a year.

The two Mr Stacombs left finally, but Butterworth remained. Eva was urging him to go for another bottle of champagne.

'We've had enough,' objected Adrian. 'We ought to go to bed.'

'I won't go to bed!' she burst out. 'You must be crazy! You play around all you want, and then, when I find somebody I – I like, you want to put me to bed.'

'You're hysterical.'

'On the contrary, I've never been so sane.'

'I think you'd better leave us, Butterworth,' Adrian said. 'Eva doesn't know what she's saying.'

'He won't go, I won't let him go.' She clasped Butterworth's hand passionately. 'He's the only person that's been half decent to me.'

'You'd better go, Butterworth,' repeated Adrian.

The young man looked at him uncertainly.

'It seems to me you're being unjust to your wife,' he ventured.

'My wife isn't herself.'

'That's no reason for bullying her.'

Adrian lost his temper. 'You get out of here!' he cried.

The two men looked at each other for a moment in silence. Then Butterworth turned to Eva, said, 'I'll be back later,' and left the cabin.

'Eva, you've got to pull yourself together,' said Adrian when the door closed.

She didn't answer, looked at him from sullen, half-closed eyes.

'I'll order dinner here for us both and then we'll try to get some sleep.'

'I want to go up and send a wireless.'

'Who to?'

'Some Paris lawyer. I want a divorce.'

In spite of his annoyance, he laughed. 'Don't be silly.'

'Then I want to see the children.'

'Well, go and see them. I'll order dinner.'

He waited for her in the cabin twenty minutes. Then impatiently he opened the door across the corridor; the nurse told him that Mrs Smith had not been there.

With a sudden prescience of disaster he ran upstairs, glanced in the bar, the salons, even knocked at Butterworth's door. Then a quick round of the decks, feeling his way through the black spray and rain. A sailor stopped him at a network of ropes.

'Orders are no one goes by, sir. A wave has gone over the wireless room.'

'Have you seen a lady?'

'There was a young lady here –' He stopped and glanced around. 'Hello, she's gone.'

'She went up the stairs!' Adrian said anxiously. 'Up to the wireless room!'

The sailor ran up to the boat deck; stumbling and slipping, Adrian followed. As he cleared the protected sides of the companionway, a tremendous body struck the boat a staggering blow and, as she keeled over to an angle of forty-five degrees, he was thrown in a helpless roll down the drenched deck, to bring up dizzy and bruised against a stanchion.

'Eva!' he called. His voice was soundless in the black storm. Against the faint light of the wireless-room window he saw the sailor making his way forward.

'Eva!'

The wind blew him like a sail up against a lifeboat. Then there was another shuddering crash, and high over his head, over the very boat, he saw a gigantic, glittering white wave, and in the split second that it balanced there he became conscious of Eva, standing beside a ventilator twenty feet away. Pushing out from the stanchion, he lunged desperately toward her, just as the wave broke with a smashing roar. For a moment the rushing water was five feet deep, sweeping with enormous force towards the side, and then a human body was washed against him, and frantically he clutched it and was swept with it back towards the rail. He felt his body bump against it, but desperately he held on to his burden; then, as the ship rocked slowly back, the two of them, still joined by his fierce grip, were rolled out exhausted on the wet planks. For a moment he knew no more.

IV

Two days later, as the boat train moved tranquilly south toward Paris, Adrian tried to persuade his children to look out the window at the Norman countryside.

'It's beautiful,' he assured them. 'All the little farms like toys. Why, in heaven's name, won't you look?'

'I like the boat better,' said Estelle.

Her parents exchanged an infanticidal glance.

'The boat is still rocking for me,' Eva said with a shiver. 'Is it for you?'

'No. Somehow, it all seems a long way off. Even the passengers looked unfamiliar going through the customs.'

'Most of them hadn't appeared above ground before.'

He hesitated. 'By the way, I cashed Butterworth's cheque for him.'

'You're a fool. You'll never see the money again.'

'He must have needed it pretty badly or he would not have come to me.'

A pale and wan girl, passing along the corridor, recognized them and put her head through the doorway.

'How do you feel?'

'Awful.'

'Me, too,' agreed Miss D'Amido. 'I'm vainly hoping my fiancé will recognize me at the Gare du Nord. Do you know two waves went over the wireless room?'

'So we heard,' Adrian answered dryly.

She passed gracefully along the corridor and out of their life.

'The real truth is that none of it happened,' said Adrian after a moment. 'It was a nightmare – an incredibly awful nightmare.'

'Then, where are my pearls?'

'Darling, there are better pearls in Paris. I'll take the responsibility for those pearls. My real belief is that you saved the boat.'

'Adrian, let's never get to know anyone else, but just stay together always – just we two.'

He tucked her arm under his and they sat close. 'Who do you suppose those Adrian Smiths on the boat were?' he demanded. 'It certainly wasn't me.'

'Nor me.'

'It was two other people,' he said, nodding to himself. 'There are so many Smiths in this world.'

BASIL: THE FRESHEST BOY

I

It was a hidden Broadway restaurant in the dead of the night, and a brilliant and mysterious group of society people, diplomats and members of the underworld were there. A few minutes ago the sparkling wine had been flowing and a girl had been dancing gaily upon a table, but now the whole crowd were hushed and breathless. All eyes were fixed upon the masked but well-groomed man in the dress suit and opera hat who stood nonchalantly in the door.

'Don't move, please,' he said, in a well-bred, cultivated voice that had, nevertheless, a ring of steel in it. 'This thing in my hand might – go off.'

His glance roved from table to table – fell upon the malignant man higher up with his pale saturnine face, upon Heatherly, the suave secret agent from a foreign power, then rested a little longer, a little more softly perhaps, upon the table where the girl with dark hair and dark tragic eyes sat alone.

'Now that my purpose is accomplished, it might interest you to know who I am.' There was a gleam of expectation in every eye. The breast of the dark-eyed girl heaved faintly and a tiny burst of subtle French perfume rose into the air. 'I am none other than that elusive gentleman, Basil Lee, better known as the Shadow.'

Taking off his well-fitting opera hat, he bowed ironically from the waist. Then, like a flash, he turned and was gone into the night.

'You get up to New York only once a month,' Lewis Crum was saying, 'and then you have to take a master along.'

Slowly, Basil Lee's glazed eyes turned from the barns and billboards of the Indiana countryside to the interior of the Broadway Limited. The hypnosis of the swift telegraph poles faded and Lewis Crum's stolid face took shape against the white slipcover of the opposite bench.

'I'd just duck the master when I got to New York,' said Basil.

'Yes, you would!'

'I bet I would.'

'You try it and you'll see.'

'What do you mean saying I'll see, all the time, Lewis? What'll I see?' His very bright dark-blue eyes were at this moment fixed upon his companion with boredom and impatience. The two had nothing in common except their age, which was fifteen, and the lifelong friendship of their fathers – which is less than nothing. Also they were bound from the same Middle-Western city for Basil's first and Lewis's second year at the same Eastern school.

But, contrary to all the best traditions, Lewis the veteran was miserable and Basil the neophyte was happy. Lewis hated school. He had grown entirely dependent on the stimulus of a hearty vital mother, and as he felt her slipping farther and farther away from him, he plunged deeper into misery and homesickness. Basil, on the other hand, had lived with such intensity on so many stories of boarding-school life that, far from being homesick, he had a glad feeling of recognition and familiarity. Indeed, it was with some sense of doing the appropriate thing, having the traditional rough-house, that he had thrown Lewis's comb off the train at Milwaukee last night for no reason at all.

To Lewis, Basil's ignorant enthusiasm was distasteful – his instinctive attempt to dampen it had contributed to the mutual irritation.

'I'll tell you what you'll see,' he said ominously. 'They'll catch you smoking and put you on bounds.'

'No, they won't, because I won't be smoking. I'll be in training for football.'

'Football! Yeah! Football!'

'Honestly, Lewis, you don't like anything, do you?'

'I don't like football. I don't like to go out and get a crack in the eye.' Lewis spoke aggressively, for his mother had canonized all his timidities as common sense. Basil's answer, made with what he considered kindly intent, was the sort of remark that creates lifelong enmities.

'You'd probably be a lot more popular in school if you played football,' he suggested patronizingly.

Lewis did not consider himself unpopular. He did not think of it in that way at all. He was astounded.

'You wait!' he cried furiously. 'They'll take all that freshness out of you.'

'Clam yourself,' said Basil, coolly plucking at the creases of his first long trousers. 'Just clam yourself.'

'I guess everybody knows you were the freshest boy at the Country Day!'

'Clam yourself,' repeated Basil, but with less assurance. 'Kindly clam yourself.'

'I guess I know what they had in the school paper about you –'

Basil's own coolness was no longer perceptible.

'If you don't clam yourself,' he said darkly, 'I'm going to throw your brushes off the train too.'

The enormity of this threat was effective. Lewis sank back in his seat, snorting and muttering, but undoubtedly calmer. His reference had been to one of the most shameful passages in his companion's life. In a periodical issued by the boys of Basil's late school there had appeared under the heading Personals:

> If someone will please poison young Basil, or find some other means to stop his mouth, the school at large and myself will be much obliged.

The two boys sat there fuming wordlessly at each other. Then, resolutely, Basil tried to re-inter this unfortunate souvenir of the past. All that was behind him now. Perhaps he had been a little fresh, but he was making a new start. After a moment, the memory passed and with it the train and Lewis's dismal presence – the breath of the East came sweeping over him again with a vast nostalgia. A voice called him out of the fabled world; a man stood beside him with a hand on his sweater-clad shoulder.

'Lee!'

'Yes, sir.'

'It all depends on you now. Understand?'

'Yes, sir.'

'All right,' the coach said, 'go in and win.'

Basil tore the sweater from his stripling form and dashed out on the field. There were two minutes to play and the score was 3 to 0 for the enemy, but at the sight of young Lee, kept out of the game all year by a malicious plan of Dan Haskins, the school bully, and Weasel Weems, his toady, a thrill of hope went over the St Regis stand.

'33-12-16-22!' barked Midget Brown, the diminutive little quarterback.

It was his signal –

'Oh, gosh!' Basil spoke aloud, forgetting the late unpleasantness. 'I wish we'd get there before tomorrow.'

II

St Regis School, Eastchester,
November 18, 19—

Dear Mother:

There is not much to say today, but I thought I would write you about my allowance. All the boys have a bigger allowance than me, because there are a lot of little things I have to get, such as shoe laces, etc. School is still very nice and am having a fine time, but football is over and there is not much to do. I am going to New York this week to see a show. I do not know yet what it will be, but probably the Quacker Girl or little boy Blue as they are both very good. Dr Bacon is very nice and there's a good phycission in the village. No more now as I have to study Algebra.

Your affectionate Son,
Basil D. Lee.

As he put the letter in its envelope, a wizened little boy came into the deserted study hall where he sat and stood staring at him.

'Hello,' said Basil, frowning.

'I been looking for you,' said the little boy, slowly and judicially. 'I looked all over – up in your room and out in the gym, and they said you probably might of sneaked off in here.'

'What do you want?' Basil demanded.

'Hold your horses, Bossy.'

Basil jumped to his feet. The little boy retreated a step.

'Go on, hit me!' he chirped nervously. 'Go on, hit me, cause I'm just half your size – Bossy.'

Basil winced. 'You call me that again and I'll spank you.'

'No, you won't spank me. Brick Wales said if you ever touched any of us –'

'But I never did touch any of you.'

'Didn't you chase a lot of us one day and didn't Brick Wales –'

'Oh, what do you want?' Basil cried in desperation.

'Doctor Bacon wants you. They sent me after you and somebody said maybe you sneaked in here.'

Basil dropped his letter in his pocket and walked out – the little boy and his invective following him through the door. He traversed a long corridor, muggy with that odour best described as the smell of stale caramels that is so peculiar to boys' schools, ascended a stairs and knocked at an unexceptional but formidable door.

Doctor Bacon was at his desk. He was a handsome, redheaded

Episcopal clergyman of fifty whose original real interest in boys was now tempered by the flustered cynicism which is the fate of all headmasters and settles on them like green mould. There were certain preliminaries before Basil was asked to sit down – gold-rimmed glasses had to be hoisted up from nowhere by a black cord and fixed on Basil to be sure that he was not an impostor; great masses of paper on the desk had to be shuffled through, not in search of anything but as a man nervously shuffles a pack of cards.

'I had a letter from your mother this morning – ah – Basil.' The use of his first name had come to startle Basil. No one else in school had yet called him anything but Bossy or Lee. 'She feels that your marks have been poor. I believe you have been sent here at a certain amount of – ah – sacrifice and she expects –'

Basil's spirit writhed with shame, not at his poor marks but that his financial inadequacy should be so bluntly stated. He knew that he was one of the poorest boys in a rich boys' school.

Perhaps some dormant sensibility in Doctor Bacon became aware of his discomfort; he shuffled through the papers once more and began on a new note.

'However, that was not what I sent for you about this afternoon. You applied last week for permission to go to New York on Saturday, to a matinée. Mr Davis tells me that for almost the first time since school opened you will be off bounds tomorrow.'

'Yes, sir.'

'That is not a good record. However, I would allow you to go to New York if it could be arranged. Unfortunately, no masters are available this Saturday.'

Basil's mouth dropped ajar. 'Why, I – why, Doctor Bacon, I know two parties that are going. Couldn't I go with one of them?'

Doctor Bacon ran through all his papers very quickly. 'Unfortunately, one is composed of slightly older boys and the other group made arrangements some weeks ago.'

'How about the party that's going to the *Quaker Girl* with Mr Dunn?'

'It's that party I speak of. They feel that the arrangements are complete and they have purchased seats together.'

Suddenly Basil understood. At the look in his eye Doctor Bacon went on hurriedly.

'There's perhaps one thing I can do. Of course there must be several boys in the party so that the expenses of the master can be divided up among all. If you can find two other boys who would like to make up a party, and let me have their names by five o'clock, I'll send Mr Rooney with you.'

'Thank you,' Basil said.

Doctor Bacon hesitated. Beneath the cynical incrustations of many years an instinct stirred to look into the unusual case of this boy and find out what made him the most detested boy in school. Among boys and masters there seemed to exist an extraordinary hostility towards him, and though Doctor Bacon had dealt with many sorts of schoolboy crimes, he had neither by himself nor with the aid of trusted sixth-formers been able to lay his hands on its underlying cause. It was probably no single thing, but a combination of things; it was most probably one of those intangible questions of personality. Yet he remembered that when he first saw Basil he had considered him unusually prepossessing.

He sighed. Sometimes these things worked themselves out. He wasn't one to rush in clumsily. 'Let us have a better report to send home next month, Basil.'

'Yes, sir.'

Basil ran quickly downstairs to the recreation room. It was Wednesday and most of the boys had already gone into the village of Eastchester, whither Basil, who was still on bounds, was forbidden to follow. When he looked at those still scattered about the pool tables and piano, he saw that it was going to be difficult to get anyone to go with him at all. For Basil was quite conscious that he was the most unpopular boy at school.

It had begun almost immediately. One day, less than a fortnight after he came, a crowd of the smaller boys, perhaps urged on to it, gathered suddenly around him and began calling him Bossy. Within the next week he had two fights, and both times the crowd was vehemently and eloquently with the other boy. Soon after, when he was merely shoving indiscriminately, like everyone else, to get into the dining-room, Carver, the captain of the football team, turned about and, seizing him by the back of the neck, held him and dressed him down savagely. He joined a group innocently at the piano and was told, 'Go on away. We don't want you around.'

After a month he began to realize the full extent of his unpopularity. It shocked him. One day after a particularly bitter humiliation he went up to his room and cried. He tried to keep out of the way for a while, but it didn't help. He was accused of sneaking off here and there, as if bent on a series of nefarious errands. Puzzled and wretched, he looked at his face in the glass, trying to discover there the secret of their dislike – in the expression of his eyes, his smile.

He saw now that in certain ways he had erred at the outset – he had boasted, he had been considered yellow at football, he had pointed out people's mistakes to them, he had showed off his rather extraordinary fund of general information in class. But he had tried to do better and couldn't understand his failure to atone. It must be too late. He was queered forever.

He had, indeed, become the scapegoat, the immediate villain, the sponge which absorbed all malice and irritability abroad – just as the most frightened person in a party seems to absorb all the others' fear, seems to be afraid for them all. His situation was not helped by the fact, obvious to all, that the supreme self-confidence with which he had come to St Regis in September was thoroughly broken. Boys taunted him with impunity who would not have dared raise their voices to him several months before.

This trip to New York had come to mean everything to him – surcease from the misery of his daily life as well as a glimpse into the long-waited heaven of romance. Its postponement for week after week due to his sins – he was constantly caught reading after lights, for example, driven by his wretchedness into such vicarious escapes from reality – had deepened his longing until it was a burning hunger. It was unbearable that he should not go, and he told over the short list of those whom he might get to accompany him. The possibilities were Fat Gaspar, Treadway, and Bugs Brown. A quick journey to their rooms showed that they had all availed themselves of the Wednesday permission to go into Eastchester for the afternoon.

Basil did not hesitate. He had until five o'clock and his only chance was to go after them. It was not the first time he had broken bounds, though the last attempt had ended in disaster and an extension of his confinement. In his room, he put on a heavy sweater – an overcoat was a betrayal of intent – replaced his jacket over it and hid a cap in his back pocket. Then he went downstairs and with an elaborate careless whistle struck out across the lawn for the gymnasium. Once there, he stood for a while as if looking in the windows, first the one close to the walk, then one near the corner of the building. From here he moved quickly, but not too quickly, into a grove of lilacs. Then he dashed around the corner, down a long stretch of lawn that was blind from all windows and, parting the strands of a wire fence, crawled through and stood upon the grounds of a neighbouring estate. For the moment he was free. He put on his cap against the chilly November wind, and set out along the half-mile road to town.

Eastchester was a suburban farming community, with a small shoe factory. The institutions which pandered to the factory workers were the ones patronized by the boys – a movie house, a quick-lunch wagon on wheels known as the Dog and the Bostonian Candy Kitchen. Basil tried the Dog first and happened immediately upon a prospect.

This was Bugs Brown, a hysterical boy, subject to fits and strenuously avoided. Years later he became a brilliant lawyer, but at that time he was considered by the boys of St Regis to be a typical lunatic because of the peculiar series of sounds with which he assuaged his nervousness all day long.

He consorted with boys younger than himself, who were without the prejudices of their elders, and was in the company of several when Basil came in.

'Who-ee!' he cried. 'Ee-ee-ee!' He put his hand over his mouth and bounced it quickly, making a wah-wah-wah sound. 'It's Bossy Lee! It's Bossy Lee! It's Boss-Boss-Boss-Boss-Bossy Lee!'

'Wait a minute, Bugs,' said Basil anxiously, half afraid that Bugs would go finally crazy before he could persuade him to come to town. 'Say, Bugs, listen. Don't, Bugs – wait a minute. Can you come up to New York Saturday afternoon?'

'Whe-ee-ee!' cried Bugs to Basil's distress. 'Wee-ee-ee!'

'Honestly, Bugs, tell me, can you? We could go up together if you could go.'

'I've got to see a doctor,' said Bugs, suddenly calm. 'He wants to see how crazy I am.'

'Can't you have him see about it some other day?' said Basil without humour.

'Whee-ee-ee!' cried Bugs.

'All right then,' said Basil hastily. 'Have you seen Fat Gaspar in town?'

Bugs was lost in shrill noise, but someone had seen Fat: Basil was directed to the Bostonian Candy Kitchen.

This was a gaudy paradise of cheap sugar. Its odour, heavy and sickly and calculated to bring out a sticky sweat upon an adult's palms, hung suffocatingly over the whole vicinity and met one like a strong moral dissuasion at the door. Inside, beneath a pattern of flies, material as black point lace, a line of boys sat eating heavy dinners of banana splits,

maple nut, and chocolate marshmallow nut sundaes. Basil found Fat
Gaspar at a table on the side.

Fat Gaspar was at once Basil's most unlikely and most ambitious
quest. He was considered a nice fellow – in fact he was so pleasant that
he had been courteous to Basil and had spoken to him politely all fall.
Basil realized that he was like that to everyone, yet it was just possible
that Fat liked him, as people used to in the past, and he was driven
desperately to take a chance. But it was undoubtedly a presumption,
and as he approached the table and saw the stiffened faces which the
other two boys turned towards him, Basil's hope diminished.

'Say, Fat –' he said, and hesitated. Then he burst forth suddenly. 'I'm
on bounds, but I ran off because I had to see you. Doctor Bacon told me
I could go to New York Saturday if I could get two other boys to go. I
asked Bugs Brown and he couldn't go, and I thought I'd ask you.'

He broke off, furiously embarrassed, and waited. Suddenly the two
boys with Fat burst into a shout of laughter.

'Bugs wasn't crazy enough!'

Fat Gaspar hesitated. He couldn't go to New York Saturday and
ordinarily he would have refused without offending. He had nothing
against Basil; nor, indeed, against anybody; but boys have only a certain
resistance to public opinion and he was influenced by the contemptuous
laughter of the others.

'I don't want to go,' he said indifferently. 'Why do you want to ask
me?'

Then, half in shame, he gave a deprecatory little laugh and bent over
his ice cream.

'I just thought I'd ask you,' said Basil.

Turning quickly away, he went to the counter and in a hollow and
unfamiliar voice ordered a strawberry sundae. He ate it mechanically,
hearing occasional whispers and snickers from the table behind. Still in
a daze, he started to walk out without paying his check, but the clerk
called him back and he was conscious of more derisive laughter.

For a moment he hesitated whether to go back to the table and hit
one of those boys in the face, but he saw nothing to be gained. They
would say the truth – that he had done it because he couldn't get
anybody to go to New York. Clenching his fists with impotent rage, he
walked from the store.

He came immediately upon his third prospect, Treadway. Treadway
had entered St Regis late in the year and had been put in to room with
Basil the week before. The fact that Treadway hadn't witnessed his

humiliations of the autumn encouraged Basil to behave naturally towards him, and their relations had been, if not intimate, at least tranquil.

'Hey, Treadway,' he called, still excited from the affair in the Bostonian, 'can you come up to New York to a show Saturday afternoon?'

He stopped, realizing that Treadway was in the company of Brick Wales, a boy he had had a fight with and one of his bitterest enemies. Looking from one to the other, Basil saw a look of impatience in Treadway's face and a faraway expression in Brick Wales's, and he realized what must have been happening. Treadway, making his way into the life of the school, had just been enlightened as to the status of his room-mate. Like Fat Gaspar, rather than acknowledge himself eligible to such an intimate request, he preferred to cut their friendly relations short.

'Not on your life,' he said briefly. 'So long.' The two walked past him into the Candy Kitchen.

Had these slights, so much the bitterer for their lack of passion, been visited upon Basil in September, they would have been unbearable. But since then he had developed a shell of hardness which, while it did not add to his attractiveness, spared him certain delicacies of torture. In misery enough, and despair and self-pity, he went the other way along the street for a little distance until he could control the violent contortions of his face. Then, taking a roundabout route, he started back to school.

He reached the adjoining estate, intending to go back the way he had come. Half-way through a hedge, he heard footsteps approaching along the sidewalk and stood motionless, fearing the proximity of masters. Their voices grew nearer and louder; before he knew it he was listening with horrified fascination:

'– so, after he tried Bugs Brown, the poor nut asked Fat Gaspar to go with him and Fat said, "What do you ask me for?" It serves him right if he couldn't get anybody at all.'

It was the dismal but triumphant voice of Lewis Crum.

III

Up in his room, Basil found a package lying on his bed. He knew its contents and for a long time he had been eagerly expecting it, but such was his depression that he opened it listlessly. It was a series of eight colour reproductions of Harrison Fisher girls 'on glossy paper, without printing or advertising matter and suitable for framing'.

The pictures were named Dora, Marguerite, Babette, Lucille, Gretchen, Rose, Katherine, and Mina. Two of them – Marguerite and Rose – Basil looked at, slowly tore up, and dropped in the waste-basket, as one who disposes of the inferior pups from a litter. The other six he pinned at intervals around the room. Then he lay down on his bed and regarded them.

Dora, Lucille, and Katherine were blonde; Gretchen was medium; Babette and Mina were dark. After a few minutes, he found that he was looking oftenest at Dora and Babette and, to a lesser extent, at Gretchen, though the latter's Dutch cap seemed unromantic and precluded the element of mystery. Babette, a dark little violet-eyed beauty in a tight-fitting hat, attracted him most; his eyes came to rest on her at last.

'Babette,' he whispered to himself – 'beautiful Babette.'

The sound of the word, so melancholy and suggestive, like 'Vilia' or 'I'm happy at Maxim's' on the phonograph, softened him and, turning over on his face, he sobbed into the pillow. He took hold of the bed rails over his head and, sobbing and straining, began to talk to himself brokenly – how he hated them and whom he hated – he listed a dozen – and what he would do to them when he was great and powerful. In previous moments like these he had always rewarded Fat Gaspar for his kindness, but now he was like the rest. Basil set upon him, pummelling him unmercifully, or laughed sneeringly when he passed him blind and begging on the street.

He controlled himself as he heard Treadway come in, but did not move or speak. He listened as the other moved about the room, and after a while became conscious that there was an unusual opening of closets and bureau drawers. Basil turned over, his arm concealing his tear-stained face. Treadway had an armful of shirts in his hand.

'What are you doing?' Basil demanded.

His room-mate looked at him stonily. 'I'm moving in with Wales,' he said.

'Oh!'

Treadway went on with his packing. He carried out a suitcase full, then another, took down some pennants and dragged his trunk into the hall. Basil watched him bundle his toilet things into a towel and take one last survey about the room's new barrenness to see if there was anything forgotten.

'Good-bye,' he said to Basil, without a ripple of expression on his face.

'Good-bye.'

Treadway went out. Basil turned over once more and choked into the pillow.

'Oh, poor Babette!' he cried huskily. 'Poor little Babette! Poor little Babette!' Babette, svelte and piquante, looked down at him coquettishly from the wall.

IV

Doctor Bacon, sensing Basil's predicament and perhaps the extremity of his misery, arranged it that he should go into New York, after all. He went in the company of Mr Rooney, the football coach and history teacher. At twenty Mr Rooney had hesitated for some time between joining the police force and having his way paid through a small New England college; in fact he was a hard specimen and Doctor Bacon was planning to get rid of him at Christmas. Mr Rooney's contempt for Basil was founded on the latter's ambiguous and unreliable conduct on the football field during the past season – he had consented to take him to New York for reasons of his own.

Basil sat meekly beside him on the train, glancing past Mr Rooney's bulky body at the Sound and the fallow fields of Westchester County. Mr Rooney finished his newspaper, folded it up and sank into a moody silence. He had eaten a large breakfast and the exigencies of time had not allowed him to work it off with exercise. He remembered that Basil was a fresh boy, and it was time he did something fresh and could be called to account. This reproachless silence annoyed him.

'Lee,' he said suddenly, with a thinly assumed air of friendly interest, 'why don't you get wise to yourself?'

'What, sir?' Basil was startled from his excited trance of this morning.

'I said why don't you get wise to yourself?' said Mr Rooney in a somewhat violent tone. 'Do you want to be the butt of the school all your time here?'

'No, I don't.' Basil was chilled. Couldn't all this be left behind for just one day?

'You oughtn't to get so fresh all the time. A couple of times in history class I could just about have broken your neck.' Basil could think of no appropriate answer. 'Then out playing football,' continued Mr Rooney, '– you didn't have any nerve. You could play better than a lot of 'em when you wanted, like that day against the Pomfret seconds, but you lost your nerve.'

'I shouldn't have tried for the second team,' said Basil. 'I was too light. I should have stayed on the third.'

'You were yellow, that was all the trouble. You ought to get wise to yourself. In class, you're always thinking of something else. If you don't study, you'll never get to college.'

'I'm the youngest boy in the fifth form,' Basil said rashly.

'You think you're pretty bright, don't you?' He eyed Basil ferociously. Then something seemed to occur to him that changed his attitude and they rode for a while in silence. When the train began to run through the thickly clustered communities near New York, he spoke again in a milder voice and with an air of having considered the matter for a long time:

'Lee, I'm going to trust you.'

'Yes, sir.'

'You go and get some lunch and then go on to your show. I've got some business of my own I got to attend to, and when I've finished I'll try to get to the show. If I can't, I'll anyhow meet you outside.' Basil's heart leaped up. 'Yes, sir.'

'I don't want you to open your mouth about this at school – I mean, about me doing some business of my own.'

'No, sir.'

'We'll see if you can keep your mouth shut for once,' he said, making it fun. Then he added, on a note of moral sternness, 'And no drinks, you understand that?'

'Oh, no, sir!' The idea shocked Basil. He had never tasted a drink, nor even contemplated the possibility, save the intangible and non-alcoholic champagne of his café dreams.

On the advice of Mr Rooney he went for luncheon to the Manhattan Hotel, near the station, where he ordered a club sandwich, French fried potatoes, and a chocolate parfait. Out of the corner of his eye he watched the nonchalant, debonair, blasé New Yorkers at neighbouring tables, investing them with a romance by which these possible fellow citizens of his from the Middle West lost nothing. School had fallen from him like a burden; it was no more than an unheeded clamour, faint and far away. He even delayed opening the letter from the morning's mail which he found in his pocket, because it was addressed to him at school.

He wanted another chocolate parfait, but being reluctant to bother the busy waiter any more, he opened the letter and spread it before him instead. It was from his mother:

Dear Basil:

This is written in great haste, as I didn't want to frighten you by telegraphing. Grandfather is going abroad to take the waters and he wants you and me to come too. The idea is that you'll go to school at Grenoble or Montreux for the rest of the year and learn the language and we'll be close by. That is, if you want to. I know how you like St Regis and playing football and baseball, and of course there would be none of that; but on the other hand, it would be a nice change, even if it postponed your entering Yale by an extra year. So, as usual, I want you to do just as you like. We will be leaving home almost as soon as you get this and will come to the Waldorf in New York, where you can come in and see us for a few days, even if you decide to stay. Think it over, dear.

> With love to my dearest boy,
> Mother.

Basil got up from his chair with a dim idea of walking over to the Waldorf and having himself locked up safely until his mother came. Then, impelled to some gesture, he raised his voice and in one of his first basso notes called boomingly and without reticence for the waiter. No more St Regis! No more St Regis! He was almost strangling with happiness.

'Oh, gosh!' he cried to himself. 'Oh, golly! Oh, gosh! Oh, gosh!' No more Doctor Bacon and Mr Rooney and Brick Wales and Fat Gaspar. No more Bugs Brown and on bounds and being called Bossy. He need no longer hate them, for they were impotent shadows in the stationary world that he was sliding away from, sliding past, waving his hand. 'Good-bye!' he pitied them. 'Good-bye!'

It required the din of Forty-second Street to sober his maudlin joy. With his hand on his purse to guard against the omnipresent pickpocket, he moved cautiously towards Broadway. What a day! He would tell Mr Rooney — Why, he needn't ever go back! Or perhaps it would be better to go back and let them know what he was going to do, while they went on and on in the dismal, dreary round of school.

He found the theatre and entered the lobby with its powdery feminine atmosphere of a matinée. As he took out his ticket, his gaze was caught and held by a sculptured profile a few feet away. It was that of a well-built blond young man of about twenty with a strong chin and direct grey eyes. Basil's brain spun wildly for a moment and then came to rest upon a name — more than a name — upon a legend, a sign in the sky. What a day! He had never seen the young man before, but from a

thousand pictures he knew beyond the possibility of a doubt that it was
Ted Fay, the Yale football captain, who had almost single-handed beaten
Harvard and Princeton last fall. Basil felt a sort of exquisite pain. The
profile turned away; the crowd revolved; the hero disappeared. But Basil
would know all through the next hours that Ted Fay was here too.

In the rustling, whispering, sweet-smelling darkness of the theatre he
read the programme. It was the show of all shows that he wanted to
see, and until the curtain actually rose the programme itself had a
curious sacredness – a prototype of the thing itself. But when the curtain
rose it became waste paper to be dropped carelessly to the floor.

Act I. The Village Green of a Small Town near New York

It was too bright and blinding to comprehend all at once, and it went
so fast that from the very first Basil felt he had missed things; he would
make his mother take him again when she came – next week – tomorrow.

An hour passed. It was very sad at this point – a sort of gay sadness,
but sad. The girl – the man. What kept them apart even now? Oh, those
tragic errors, and misconceptions. So sad. Couldn't they look into each
other's eyes and *see*?

In a blaze of light and sound, of resolution, anticipation and imminent
trouble, the act was over.

He went out. He looked for Ted Fay and thought he saw him leaning
rather moodily on the plush wall at the rear of the theatre, but he could
not be sure. He bought cigarettes and lit one, but fancying at the first
puff he heard a blare of music he rushed back inside.

Act 2. The Foyer of the Hotel Astor

Yes, she was, indeed, like a song – a Beautiful Rose of the Night. The
waltz buoyed her up, brought her with it to a point of aching beauty
and then let her slide back to life across its last bars as a leaf slants to
earth across the air. The high life of New York! Who could blame her if
she was carried away by the glitter of it all, vanishing into the bright
morning of the amber window borders or into distant and entrancing
music as the door opened and closed that led to the ballroom? The toast
of the shining town.

Half an hour passed. Her true love brought her roses like herself and
she threw them scornfully at his feet. She laughed and turned to the
other, and danced – danced madly, wildly. Wait! That delicate treble
among the thin horns, the low curving note from the great strings.
There it was again, poignant and aching, sweeping like a great gust of

emotion across the stage, catching her again like a leaf helpless in the wind:

> 'Rose – Rose – Rose of the night
> When the spring moon is bright you'll be fair –'

A few minutes later, feeling oddly shaken and exalted, Basil drifted outside with the crowd. The first thing upon which his eyes fell was the almost forgotten and now curiously metamorphosed spectre of Mr Rooney.

Mr Rooney had, in fact, gone a little to pieces. He was, to begin with, wearing a different and much smaller hat than when he left Basil at noon. Secondly, his face had lost its somewhat gross aspect and turned a pure and even delicate white, and he was wearing his necktie and even portions of his shirt on the outside of his unaccountably wringing-wet overcoat. How, in the short space of four hours, Mr Rooney had got himself in such shape is explicable only by the pressure of confinement in a boys' school upon a fiery outdoor spirit. Mr Rooney was born to toil under the clear light of heaven and, perhaps half-consciously, he was headed towards his inevitable destiny.

'Lee,' he said dimly, 'you ought to get wise to y'self. I'm going to put you wise y'self.'

To avoid the ominous possibility of being put wise to himself in the lobby, Basil uneasily changed the subject.

'Aren't you coming to the show?' he asked, flattering Mr Rooney by implying that he was in any condition to come to the show. 'It's a wonderful show.'

Mr Rooney took off his hat, displaying wringing-wet matted hair. A picture of reality momentarily struggled for development in the back of his brain.

'We got to get back to school,' he said in a sombre and unconvinced voice.

'But there's another act,' protested Basil in horror. 'I've got to stay for the last act.'

Swaying, Mr Rooney looked at Basil, dimly realizing that he had put himself in the hollow of this boy's hand.

'All righ',' he admitted. 'I'm going to get somethin' to eat. I'll wait for you next door.'

He turned abruptly, reeled a dozen steps, and curved dizzily into a bar adjoining the theatre. Considerably shaken, Basil went back inside.

Act 3. The Roof Garden of Mr Van Astor's House.
Night

Half an hour passed. Everything was going to be all right, after all. The comedian was at his best now, with the glad appropriateness of laughter after tears, and there was a promise of felicity in the bright tropical sky. One lovely plaintive duet, and then abruptly the long moment of incomparable beauty was over.

Basil went into the lobby and stood in thought while the crowd passed out. His mother's letter and the show had cleared his mind of bitterness and vindictiveness – he was his old self and he wanted to do the right thing. He wondered if it was the right thing to get Mr Rooney back to school. He walked towards the saloon, slowed up as he came to it and, gingerly opening the swinging door, took a quick peer inside. He saw only that Mr Rooney was not one of those drinking at the bar. He walked down the street a little way, came back and tried again. It was as if he thought the doors were teeth to bite him, for he had the old-fashioned Middle-Western boy's horror of the saloon. The third time he was successful. Mr Rooney was sound asleep at a table in the back of the room.

Outside again Basil walked up and down, considering. He would give Mr Rooney half an hour. If, at the end of that time, he had not come out, he would go back to school. After all, Mr Rooney had laid for him ever since football season – Basil was simply washing his hands of the whole affair, as in a day or so he would wash his hands of school.

He had made several turns up and down, when glancing up an alley that ran beside the theatre his eye was caught by the sign, Stage Entrance. He could watch the actors come forth.

He waited. Women streamed by him, but those were the days before Glorification and he took these drab people for wardrobe women or something. Then suddenly a girl came out and with her a man, and Basil turned and ran a few steps up the street as if afraid they would recognize him – and ran back, breathing as if with a heart attack – for the girl, a radiant little beauty of nineteen, was Her and the young man by her side was Ted Fay.

Arm in arm, they walked past him, and irresistibly Basil followed. As they walked, she leaned towards Ted Fay in a way that gave them a fascinating air of intimacy. They crossed Broadway and turned into the Knickerbocker Hotel, and twenty feet behind them Basil followed, in time to see them go into a long room set for afternoon tea. They sat at a table for two, spoke vaguely to a waiter, and then, alone at last, bent eagerly towards each other. Basil saw that Ted Fay was holding her gloved hand.

The tea room was separated only by a hedge of potted firs from the main corridor. Basil went along this to a lounge which was almost up against their table and sat down.

Her voice was low and faltering, less certain than it had been in the play, and very sad: 'Of course I do, Ted.' For a long time, as their conversation continued, she repeated, 'Of course I do,' or 'But I do, Ted.' Ted Fay's remarks were too low for Basil to hear.

'– says next month, and he won't be put off any more . . . I do in a way, Ted. It's hard to explain, but he's done everything for mother and me . . . There's no use kidding myself. It was a foolproof part and any girl he gave it to was made right then and there . . . He's been awfully thoughtful. He's done everything for me.'

Basil's ears were sharpened by the intensity of his emotion; now he could hear Ted Fay's voice too:

'And you say you love me.'

'But don't you see I promised to marry him more than a year ago.'

'Tell him the truth – that you love me. Ask him to let you off.'

'This isn't musical comedy, Ted.'

'That was a mean one,' he said bitterly.

'I'm sorry, dear, Ted darling, but you're driving me crazy going on this way. You're making it so hard for me.'

'I'm going to leave New Haven, anyhow.'

'No, you're not. You're going to stay and play baseball this spring. Why, you're an ideal to all those boys! Why, if you –'

He laughed shortly. 'You're a fine one to talk about ideals.'

'Why not? I'm living up to my responsibility to Beltzman; you've got to make up your mind just like I have – that we can't have each other.'

'Jerry! Think what you're doing! All my life, whenever I hear that waltz –'

Basil got to his feet and hurried down the corridor, through the lobby and out of the hotel. He was in a state of wild emotional confusion. He did not understand all he had heard, but from his clandestine glimpse into the privacy of these two, with all the world that his short experience could conceive of at their feet, he had gathered that life for everybody was a struggle, sometimes magnificent from a distance, but always difficult and surprisingly simple and a little sad.

They would go on. Ted Fay would go back to Yale, put her picture in his bureau drawer and knock out home runs with the bases full this spring – at 8.30 the curtain would go up and She would miss something warm and young out of her life, something she had had this afternoon.

It was dark outside and Broadway was a blazing forest fire as Basil walked slowly along towards the point of brightest light. He looked up at the great intersecting planes of radiance with a vague sense of approval and possession. He would see it a lot now, lay his restless heart upon this greater restlessness of a nation – he would come whenever he could get off from school.

But that was all changed – he was going to Europe. Suddenly Basil realized that he wasn't going to Europe. He could not forgo the moulding of his own destiny just to alleviate a few months of pain. The conquest of the successive worlds of school, college and New York – why, that was his true dream that he had carried from boyhood into adolescence, and because of the jeers of a few boys he had been about to abandon it and run ignominiously up a back alley! He shivered violently, like a dog coming out of the water, and simultaneously he was reminded of Mr Rooney.

A few minutes later he walked into the bar, past the quizzical eyes of the bartender and up to the table where Mr Rooney still sat asleep. Basil shook him gently, then firmly. Mr Rooney stirred and perceived Basil.

'G'wise to yourself,' he muttered drowsily. 'G'wise to yourself an' let me alone.'

'I am wise to myself,' said Basil. 'Honest, I am wise to myself, Mr Rooney. You got to come with me into the washroom and get cleaned up, and then you can sleep on the train again, Mr Rooney. Come on, Mr Rooney, please –'

V

It was a long hard time. Basil got on bounds again in December and wasn't free again until March. An indulgent mother had given him no habits of work and this was almost beyond the power of anything but life itself to remedy, but he made numberless new starts and failed and tried again.

He made friends with a new boy named Maplewood after Christmas, but they had a silly quarrel; and through the winter term, when a boys' school is shut in with itself and only partly assuaged from its natural savagery by indoor sports, Basil was snubbed and slighted a good deal for his real and imaginary sins, and he was much alone. But on the other hand, there was Ted Fay, and Rose of the Night on the phonograph – 'All my life whenever I hear that waltz' – and the remembered lights of New York, and the thought of what he was going to do in football next autumn and the glamorous image of Yale and the hope of spring in the air.

Fat Gaspar and a few others were nice to him now. Once when he and Fat walked home together by accident from down-town they had a long talk about actresses – a talk that Basil was wise enough not to presume upon afterwards. The smaller boys suddenly decided that they approved of him, and a master who had hitherto disliked him put his hand on his shoulder walking to a class one day. They would all forget eventually – maybe during the summer. There would be new fresh boys in September; he would have a clean start next year.

One afternoon in February, playing basketball, a great thing happened. He and Brick Wales were at forward on the second team and in the fury of the scrimmage the gymnasium echoed with sharp slapping contacts and shrill cries.

'Here yar!'

'Bill! Bill!'

Basil had dribbled the ball down the court and Brick Wales, free, was crying for it.

'Here yar! Lee! Hey! Lee-y!'

Lee-y!

Basil flushed and made a poor pass. He had been called by a nickname. It was a poor makeshift, but it was something more than the stark bareness of his surname or a term of derision. Brick Wales went on playing, unconscious that he had done anything in particular or that he had contributed to the events by which another boy was saved from the army of the bitter, the selfish, the neurasthenic and the unhappy. It isn't given to us to know those rare moments when people are wide open and the lightest touch can wither or heal. A moment too late and we can never reach them any more in this world. They will not be cured by our most efficacious drugs or slain with our sharpest swords.

Lee-y! it could scarcely be pronounced. But Basil took it to bed with him that night, and thinking of it, holding it to him happily to the last, fell easily to sleep.

JOSEPHINE:
A WOMAN WITH A PAST

I

Driving slowly through New Haven, two of the young girls became alert. Josephine and Lillian darted soft frank glances into strolling groups of three or four undergraduates, into larger groups on corners, which swung about as one man to stare at their receding heads. Believing that they recognized an acquaintance in a solitary loiterer, they waved wildly, whereupon the youth's mouth fell open, and as they turned the next corner he made a dazed dilatory gesture with his hand. They laughed. 'We'll send him a post card when we get back to school tonight, to see if it really was him.'

Adele Craw, sitting on one of the little seats, kept on talking to Miss Chambers, the chaperon. Glancing sideways at her, Lillian winked at Josephine without batting an eye, but Josephine had gone into a reverie.

This was New Haven – city of her adolescent dreams, of glittering proms where she would move on air among men as intangible as the tunes they danced to. City sacred as Mecca, shining as Paris, hidden as Timbuktu. Twice a year the life-blood of Chicago, her home, flowed into it, and twice a year flowed back, bringing Christmas or bringing summer. Bingo, bingo, bingo, that's the lingo; love of mine, I pine for one of your glances; the darling boy on the left there; underneath the stars I wait.

Seeing it for the first time, she found herself surprisingly unmoved – the men they passed seemed young and rather bored with the possibilities of the day, glad of anything to stare at; seemed undynamic and purposeless against the background of bare elms, lakes of dirty snow and buildings crowded together under the February sky. A wisp of hope, a well-turned-out derby-crowned man, hurrying with stick and suitcase towards the station, caught her attention, but his reciprocal glance was too startled, too ingenuous. Josephine wondered at the extent of her own disillusionment.

She was exactly seventeen and she was blasé. Already she had been a sensation and a scandal; she had driven mature men to a state of disequilibrium; she had, it was said, killed her grandfather, but as he was over eighty at the time perhaps he just died. Here and there in the Middle West were discouraged little spots which upon inspection turned out to be the youths who had once looked full into her green and wistful eyes. But her love affair of last summer had ruined her faith in the all-sufficiency of men. She had grown bored with the waning September days – and it seemed as though it had happened once too often. Christmas with its provocative shortness, its travelling glee clubs, had brought no one new. There remained to her only a persistent, a physical hope; hope in her stomach that there was someone whom she would love more than he loved her.

They stopped at a sporting-goods store and Adele Craw, a pretty girl with clear honourable eyes and piano legs, purchased the sporting equipment which was the reason for their trip – they were the spring hockey committee for the school. Adele was in addition the president of the senior class and the school's ideal girl. She had lately seen a change for the better in Josephine Perry – rather as an honest citizen might guilelessly approve a speculator retired on his profits. On the other hand, Adele was simply incomprehensible to Josephine – admirable, without doubt, but a member of another species. Yet with the charming adaptability that she had hitherto reserved for men, Josephine was trying hard not to disillusion her, trying to be honestly interested in the small, neat, organized politics of the school.

Two men who had stood with their backs to them at another counter turned to leave the store, when they caught sight of Miss Chambers and Adele. Immediately they came forward. The one who spoke to Miss Chambers was thin and rigid of face. Josephine recognized him as Miss Brereton's nephew, a student at New Haven, who had spent several week-ends with his aunt at the school. The other man Josephine had never seen before. He was tall and broad, with blond curly hair and an open expression in which strength of purpose and a nice consideration were pleasantly mingled. It was not the sort of face that generally appealed to Josephine. The eyes were obviously without a secret, with a sidewise gambol, without a desperate flicker to show that they had a life of their own apart from the mouth's speech. The mouth itself was large and masculine; its smile was an act of kindness and control. It was rather with curiosity as to the sort of man who would be attentive to Adele Craw that Josephine continued to look at him, for his voice that obviously couldn't lie greeted Adele as if this meeting was the pleasant surprise of his day.

In a moment Josephine and Lillian were called over and introduced.

'This is Mr Waterbury' – that was Miss Brereton's nephew – 'and Mr Dudley Knowleton.'

Glancing at Adele, Josephine saw on her face an expression of tranquil pride, even of possession. Mr Knowleton spoke politely, but it was obvious that though he looked at the younger girls he did not quite see them. But since they were friends of Adele's he made suitable remarks, eliciting the fact that they were both coming down to New Haven to their first prom the following week. Who were their hosts? Sophomores; he knew them slightly. Josephine thought that was unnecessarily superior. Why, they were the charter members of the Loving Brothers' Association – Ridgeway Saunders and George Davey – and on the glee-club trip the girls they picked out to rush in each city considered themselves a sort of élite, second only to the girls they asked to New Haven.

'And oh, I've got some bad news for you,' Knowleton said to Adele. 'You may be leading the prom. Jack Coe went to the infirmary with appendicitis, and against my better judgement I'm the provisional chairman.' He looked apologetic. 'Being one of those stone-age dancers, the two-step king, I don't see how I ever got on the committee at all.'

When the car was on its way back to Miss Brereton's school, Josephine and Lillian bombarded Adele with questions.

'He's an old friend from Cincinnati,' she explained demurely. 'He's captain of the baseball team and he was last man for Skull and Bones.'

'You're going to the prom with him?'

'Yes. You see, I've known him all my life.'

Was there a faint implication in this remark that only those who had known Adele all her life knew her at her true worth?

'Are you engaged?' Lillian demanded.

Adele laughed. 'Mercy, I don't think of such matters! It doesn't seem to be time for that sort of thing yet, does it?' ('Yes,' interpolated Josephine silently.) 'We're just good friends. I think there can be a perfectly healthy friendship between a man and a girl without a lot of –'

'Mush,' supplied Lillian helpfully.

'Well, yes, but I don't like that word. I was going to say without a lot of sentimental romantic things that ought to come later.'

'Bravo, Adele!' said Miss Chambers somewhat perfunctorily.

But Josephine's curiosity was unappeased.

'Doesn't he say he's in love with you, and all that sort of thing?'

'Mercy, no! Dud doesn't believe in such stuff any more than I do.'

He's got enough to do at New Haven, serving on the committees and the team.'

'Oh!' said Josephine.

She was oddly interested. That two people who were attracted to each other should never even say anything about it but be content to 'not believe in such stuff', was something new in her experience. She had known girls who had no beaux, others who seemed to have no emotions, and still others who lied about what they thought and did; but here was a girl who spoke of the attentions of the last man tapped for Skull and Bones as if they were two of the limestone gargoyles that Miss Chambers had pointed out on the just completed Harkness Hall. Yet Adele seemed happy – happier than Josephine, who had always believed that boys and girls were made for nothing but each other, and as soon as possible.

In the light of his popularity and achievements, Knowleton seemed more attractive. Josephine wondered if he would remember her and dance with her at the prom, or if that depended on how well he knew her escort, Ridgeway Saunders. She tried to remember whether she had smiled at him when he was looking at her. If she had really smiled he would remember her and dance with her. She was still trying to be sure of that over her two French irregular verbs and her ten stanzas of the Ancient Mariner that night; but she was still uncertain when she fell asleep.

II

Three gay young sophomores, the founders of the Loving Brothers' Association, took a house together for Josephine, Lillian and a girl from Farmington and their three mothers. For the girls it was a first prom, and they arrived at New Haven with all the nervousness of the condemned; but a Sheffield fraternity tea in the afternoon yielded up such a plethora of boys from home, and boys who had visited there and friends of those boys, and new boys with unknown possibilities but obvious eagerness, that they were glowing with self-confidence as they poured into the glittering crowd that thronged the armoury at ten.

It was impressive; for the first time Josephine was at a function run by men upon men's standards – an outward projection of the New Haven world from which women were excluded and which went on mysteriously behind the scenes. She perceived that their three escorts, who had once seemed the very embodiments of worldliness, were modest fry in this relentless microcosm of accomplishment and success. A man's world! Looking around her at the glee-club concert, Josephine had felt a grudging admiration for the good fellowship, the good feeling. She envied Adele Craw, barely glimpsed in the dressing-room, for the position she automatically occupied by being Dudley Knowleton's girl tonight. She envied her more stepping off under the draped bunting through a gateway of hydrangeas at the head of the grand march, very demure and faintly unpowdered in a plain white dress. She was temporarily the centre of all attention, and at the sight something that had long lain dormant in Josephine awakened – her sense of a problem, a scarcely defined possibility.

'Josephine,' Ridgeway Saunders began, 'you can't realize how happy I am now that it's come true. I've looked forward to this so long, and dreamed about it –'

She smiled up at him automatically, but her mind was elsewhere, and as the dance progressed the idea continued to obsess her. She was rushed from the beginning; to the men from the tea were added a dozen new faces, a dozen confident or timid voices, until, like all the more popular girls, she had her own queue trailing her about the room. Yet all this had happened to her before, and there was something missing. One might have ten men to Adele's two, but Josephine was abruptly aware that here a girl took on the importance of the man who had brought her.

She was discomforted by the unfairness of it. A girl earned her popularity by being beautiful and charming. The more beautiful and charming she was, the more she could afford to disregard public opinion. It seemed absurd that simply because Adele had managed to attach a baseball captain, who mightn't know anything about girls at all, or be able to judge their attractions, she should be thus elevated in spite of her thick ankles, her rather too pinkish face.

Josephine was dancing with Ed Bement from Chicago. He was her earliest beau, a flame of pigtail days in dancing school when one wore white cotton stockings, lace drawers with a waist attached and ruffled dresses with the inevitable sash.

'What's the matter with me?' she asked Ed, thinking aloud. 'For months I've felt as if I were a hundred years old, and I'm just seventeen and that party was only seven years ago.'

'You've been in love a lot since then,' Ed said.

'I haven't,' she protested indignantly. 'I've had a lot of silly stories started about me, without any foundation, usually by girls who were jealous.'

'Jealous of what?'

'Don't get fresh,' she said tartly. 'Dance me near Lillian.'

Dudley Knowleton had just cut in on Lillian. Josephine spoke to her friend; then waiting until their turns would bring them face to face over a space of seconds, she smiled at Knowleton. This time she made sure that smile intersected as well as met glance, that he passed beside the circumference of her fragrant charm. If this had been named like French perfume of a later day it might have been called 'Please'. He bowed and smiled back; a minute later he cut in on her.

It was in an eddy in a corner of the room and she danced slower so that he adapted himself, and for a moment they went around in a slow circle.

'You looked so sweet leading the march with Adele,' she told him. 'You seemed so serious and kind, as if the others were a lot of children. Adele looked sweet, too.' And she added on an inspiration, 'At school I've taken her for a model.'

'You have!' She saw him conceal his sharp surprise as he said, 'I'll have to tell her that.'

He was handsomer than she had thought, and behind his cordial good manners there was a sort of authority. Though he was correctly attentive to her, she saw his eyes search the room quickly to see if all went well; he spoke quietly, in passing, to the orchestra leader, who came down deferentially to the edge of his dais. Last man for Bones. Josephine knew what that meant – her father had been Bones. Ridgeway Saunders and the rest of the Loving Brothers' Association would certainly not be Bones. She wondered, if there had been a Bones for girls, whether she would be tapped – or Adele Craw with her ankles, symbol of solidity.

> Come on o-ver here,
> Want to have you near;
> Get a wel-come heart-y.
> Come on join the part-y,

'I wonder how many boys here have taken you for a model,' she said. 'If I were a boy you'd be exactly what I'd like to be. Except I'd be terribly bothered having girls falling in love with me all the time.'

'They don't,' he said simply. 'They never have.'

'Oh yes – but they hide it because they're so impressed with you, and they're afraid of Adele.'

'Adele wouldn't object.' And he added hastily, '– if it ever happened. Adele doesn't believe in being serious about such things.'

'Are you engaged to her?'

He stiffened a little. 'I don't believe in being engaged till the right time comes.'

'Neither do I,' agreed Josephine readily. 'I'd rather have one good friend than a hundred people hanging around being mushy all the time.'

'Is that what that crowd does that keeps following you around tonight?'

'What crowd?' she asked innocently.

'The fifty per cent of the sophomore class that's rushing you.'

'A lot of parlour snakes,' she said ungratefully.

Josephine was radiantly happy now as she turned beautifully through the newly enchanted hall in the arms of the chairman of the prom committee. Even this extra time with him she owed to the awe which he inspired in her entourage; but a man cut in eventually and there was a sharp fall in her elation. The man was impressed that Dudley Knowleton had danced with her; he was more respectful, and his modulated admiration bored her. In a little while, she hoped, Dudley Knowleton would cut back, but as midnight passed, dragging on another hour with it, she wondered if after all it had only been a courtesy to a girl from Adele's school. Since then Adele had probably painted him a neat little landscape of Josephine's past. When finally he approached her she grew tense and watchful, a state which made her exteriorly pliant and tender and quiet. But instead of dancing he drew her into the edge of a row of boxes.

'Adele had an accident on the cloakroom steps. She turned her ankle a little and tore her stocking on a nail. She'd like to borrow a pair from you because you're staying near here and we're way out at the Lawn Club.'

'Of course.'

'I'll run over with you – I have a car outside.'

'But you're busy; you mustn't bother.'

'Of course I'll go with you.'

There was thaw in the air; a hint of thin and lucid spring hovered delicately around the elms and cornices of buildings whose bareness and coldness had so depressed her the week before. The night had a quality of asceticism, as if the essence of masculine struggle were seeping everywhere through the little city where men of three centuries had brought their energies and aspirations for winnowing. And Dudley

Knowleton sitting beside her, dynamic and capable, was symbolic of it all. It seemed that she had never met a man before.

'Come in, please,' she said as he went up the steps of the house with her. 'They've made it very comfortable.'

There was an open fire burning in the dark parlour. When she came downstairs with the stockings she went in and stood beside him, very still for a moment, watching it with him. Then she looked up, still silent, looked down, looked at him again.

'Did you get the stockings?' he asked, moving a little.

'Yes,' she said breathlessly. 'Kiss me for being so quick.'

He laughed as if she said something witty and moved towards the door. She was smiling and her disappointment was deeply hidden as they got into the car.

'It's been wonderful meeting you,' she told him. 'I can't tell you how many ideas I've gotten from what you said.'

'But I haven't any ideas.'

'You have. All that about not getting engaged till the proper time comes. I haven't had much opportunity to talk to a man like you. Otherwise my ideas would be different, I guess. I've just realized that I've been wrong about a lot of things. I used to want to be exciting. Now I want to help people.'

'Yes,' he agreed, 'that's very nice.'

He seemed about to say more when they arrived at the armoury. In their absence supper had begun; and crossing the great floor by his side, conscious of many eyes regarding them, Josephine wondered if people thought that they had been up to something.

'We're late,' said Knowleton when Adele went off to put on the stockings. 'The man you're with has probably given you up long ago. You'd better let me get you something here.'

'That would be too divine.'

Afterwards, back on the floor again, she moved in a sweet aura of abstraction. The followers of several departed belles merged with hers until now no girl on the floor was cut in on with such frequency. Even Miss Brereton's nephew, Ernest Waterbury, danced with her in stiff approval. Danced? With a tentative change of pace she simply swung from man to man in a sort of hands-right-and-left around the floor. She felt a sudden need to relax, and as if in answer to her mood a new man was presented, a tall, sleek Southerner with a persuasive note:

'You lovely creacha. I been strainin my eyes watchin your cameo face floatin round. You stand out above all these othuz like an Amehken Beauty Rose over a lot of field daisies.'

Dancing with him a second time, Josephine hearkened to his pleadings. 'All right. Let's go outside.'

'It wasn't outdaws I was considering,' he explained as they left the floor. 'I happen to have a mortgage on a nook right hee in the building.'

'All right.'

Book Chaffee, of Alabama, led the way through the cloak-room, through a passage to an inconspicuous door.

'This is the private apartment of my friend Sergeant Boone, instructa of the battery. He wanted to be particularly sure it'd be used as a nook tonight and not a readin room or anything like that.'

Opening the door he turned on a dim light; she came in and shut it behind her, and they faced each other.

'Mighty sweet,' he murmured. His tall face came down, his long arms wrapped around her tenderly, and very slowly so that their eyes met for quite a long time, he drew her up to him. Josephine kept thinking that she had never kissed a Southern boy before.

They started apart at the sudden sound of a key turning in the lock outside. Then there was a muffed snicker followed by retreating footsteps, and Book sprang for the door and wrenched at the handle just as Josephine noticed that this was not only Sergeant Boone's parlour; it was his bedroom as well.

'Who was it?' she demanded. 'Why did they lock us in?'

'Some funny boy. I'd like to get my hands on him.'

'Will he come back?'

Book sat down on the bed to think. 'I couldn't say. Don't even know who it was. But if somebody on the committee came along it wouldn't look too good, would it?'

Seeing her expression change, he came over and put his arm around her. 'Don't you worry, honey. We'll fix it.'

She returned his kiss, briefly but without distraction. Then she broke away and went into the next apartment, which was hung with boots, uniform coats and various military equipment.

'There's a window up here,' she said. It was high in the wall and had not been opened for a long time. Book mounted on a chair and forced it ajar.

'About ten feet down,' he reported, after a moment, 'but there's a big pile of snow just underneath. You might get a nasty fall and you'll sure soak your shoes and stockin's.'

'We've got to get out,' Josephine said sharply.

'We'd better wait and give this funny man a chance –'

'I won't wait. I want to get out. Look – throw out all the blankets from the bed and I'll jump on that: or you jump first and spread them over the pile of snow.'

After that it was merely exciting. Carefully Book Chaffee wiped the dust from the window to protect her dress; then they were struck silent by a footstep that approached – and passed the outer door. Book jumped, and she heard him kicking profanely as he waded out of the soft drift below. He spread the blankets. At the moment when Josephine swung her legs out the window, there was the sound of voices outside the door and the key turned again in the lock. She landed softly, reaching for his hand, and convulsed with laughter they ran and skidded down the half block towards the corner, and reaching the entrance to the armoury, they stood panting for a moment, breathing in the fresh night. Book was reluctant to go inside.

'Why don't you let me conduct you where you're stayin? We can sit around and sort of recuperate.'

She hesitated, drawn towards him by the community of their late predicament; but something was calling her inside, as if the fulfilment of her elation awaited her there.

'No,' she decided.

As they went in she collided with a man in a great hurry, and looked up to recognize Dudley Knowleton.

'So sorry,' he said. 'Oh hello –'

'Won't you dance me over to my box?' she begged him impulsively. 'I've torn my dress.'

As they started off he said abstractedly: 'The fact is, a little mischief has come up and the buck has been passed to me. I was going along to see about it.'

Her heart raced wildly and she felt the need of being another sort of person immediately.

'I can't tell you how much it's meant meeting you. It would be wonderful to have one friend I could be serious with without being all mushy and sentimental. Would you mind if I wrote you a letter – I mean, would Adele mind?'

'Lord, no!' His smile had become utterly unfathomable to her. As they reached the box she thought of one more thing:

'Is it true that the baseball team is training at Hot Springs during Easter?'

'Yes. You going there?'

'Yes. Good night, Mr Knowleton.'

But she was destined to see him once more. It was outside the men's coat room, where she waited among a crowd of other pale survivors and their paler mothers, whose wrinkles had doubled and tripled with the passing night. He was explaining something to Adele, and Josephine heard the phrase, 'The door was locked, and the window open –'

Suddenly it occurred to Josephine that, meeting her coming in damp and breathless, he must have guessed at the truth – and Adele would doubtless confirm his suspicion. Once again the spectre of her old enemy, the plain and jealous girl, arose before her. Shutting her mouth tight together she turned away.

But they had seen her, and Adele called to her in her cheerful ringing voice:

'Come say good night. You were so sweet about the stockings. Here's a girl you won't find doing shoddy, silly things, Dudley.' Impulsively she leaned and kissed Josephine on the cheek. 'You'll see I'm right, Dudley – next year she'll be the most respected girl in school.'

III

As things go in the interminable days of early March, what happened next happened quickly. The annual senior dance at Miss Brereton's school came on a night soaked through with spring, and all the junior girls lay awake listening to the sighing tunes from the gymnasium. Between the numbers, when boys up from New Haven and Princeton wandered about the grounds, cloistered glances looked down from dark open windows upon the vague figures.

Not Josephine, though she lay awake like the others. Such vicarious diversions had no place in the sober patterns she was spinning now from day to day; yet she might as well have been in the forefront of those who called down to the men and threw notes and entered into conversations, for destiny had suddenly turned against her and was spinning a dark web of its own.

> Lit-tle lady, don't be depressed and blue,
> After all, we're both in the same can-noo –

Dudley Knowleton was over in the gymnasium fifty yards away, but proximity to a man did not thrill her as it would have done a year ago –

not, at least, in the same way. Life, she saw now, was a serious matter, and in the modest darkness a line of a novel ceaselessly recurred to her: 'He is a man fit to be the father of my children'. What were the seductive graces, the fast lines of a hundred parlour snakes compared to such realities. One couldn't go on forever kissing comparative strangers behind half-closed doors.

Under her pillow now were two letters, answers to her letters. They spoke in a bold round hand of the beginning of baseball practice; they were glad Josephine felt as she did about things; and the writer certainly looked forward to seeing her at Easter. Of all the letters she had ever received they were the most difficult from which to squeeze a single drop of heart's blood – one couldn't even read the 'Yours' of the subscription as 'Your' – but Josephine knew them by heart. They were precious because he had taken the time to write them; they were eloquent in the very postage stamp because he used so few.

She was restless in her bed – the music had begun again in the gymnasium:

> Oh, my love, I've waited so long for you,
> Oh, my love, I'm singing this song for you –
> Oh-h-h –

From the next room there was light laughter, and then from below a male voice, and a long interchange of comic whispers. Josephine recognized Lillian's laugh and the voices of two other girls. She could imagine them as they lay across the window in their nightgowns, their heads just showing from the open window. 'Come right down,' one boy kept saying. 'Don't be formal – come just as you are.'

There was a sudden silence, then a quick crunching of footsteps on gravel, a suppressed snicker and a scurry, and the sharp, protesting groan of several beds in the next room and the banging of a door down the hall. Trouble for somebody, maybe. A few minutes later Josephine's door half opened, she caught a glimpse of Miss Kwain against the dim corridor light, and then the door closed.

The next afternoon Josephine and four other girls, all of whom denied having breathed so much as a word into the night, were placed on probation. There was absolutely nothing to do about it. Miss Kwain had recognized their faces in the window and they were all from two rooms. It was an injustice, but it was nothing compared to what happened next. One week before Easter vacation the school motored off on a one-day trip to inspect a milk farm – all save the ones on probation. Miss

Chambers, who sympathized with Josephine's misfortune, enlisted her services in entertaining Mr Ernest Waterbury, who was spending a week-end with his aunt. This was only vaguely better than nothing, for Mr Waterbury was a very dull, very priggish young man. He was so dull and so priggish that the following morning Josephine was expelled from school.

It happened like this: they had strolled in the grounds, they had sat down at a garden table and had tea. Ernest Waterbury had expressed a desire to see something in the chapel, just a few minutes before his aunt's car rolled up the drive. The chapel was reached by descending winding mock-medieval stairs; and, her shoes still wet from the garden, Josephine had slipped on the top step and fallen five feet directly into Mr Waterbury's unwilling arms, where she lay helpless, convulsed with irresistible laughter. It was in this position that Miss Brereton and the visiting trustee had found them.

'But I had nothing to do with it!' declared the ungallant Mr Waterbury. Flustered and outraged, he was packed back to New Haven, and Miss Brereton, connecting this with last week's sin, proceeded to lose her head. Josephine, humiliated and furious, lost hers, and Mr Perry, who happened to be in New York, arrived at the school the same night. At his passionate indignation, Miss Brereton collapsed and retracted, but the damage was done, and Josephine packed her trunk. Unexpectedly, monstrously, just as it had begun to mean something, her school life was over.

For the moment all her feelings were directed against Miss Brereton, and the only tears she shed at leaving were of anger and resentment. Riding with her father up to New York, she saw that while at first he had instinctively and whole-heartedly taken her part, he felt also a certain annoyance with her misfortune.

'We'll all survive,' he said. 'Unfortunately, even that old idiot Miss Brereton will survive. She ought to be running a reform school.' He brooded for a moment. 'Anyhow, your mother arrives tomorrow and you and she go down to Hot Springs as you planned.'

'Hot Springs!' Josephine cried, in a choked voice. 'Oh, no!'

'Why not?' he demanded in surprise. 'It seems the best thing to do. Give it a chance to blow over before you go back to Chicago.'

'I'd rather go to Chicago,' said Josephine breathlessly. 'Daddy, I'd much rather go to Chicago.'

'That's absurd. Your mother's started East and the arrangements are all made. At Hot Springs you can get out and ride and play golf and forget that old she-devil –'.

'Isn't there another place in the East we could go? There's people I know going to Hot Springs who'll know all about this, people that I don't want to meet – girls from school.'

'Now, Jo, you keep your chin up – this is one of those times. Sorry I said that about letting it blow over in Chicago; if we hadn't made other plans we'd go back and face every old shrew and gossip in town right away. When anybody slinks off in a corner they think you've been up to something bad. If anybody says anything to you, you tell them the truth – what I said to Miss Brereton. You tell them she said you could come back and I damn well wouldn't let you go back.'

'They won't believe it.'

There would be, at all events, four days of respite at Hot Springs before the vacations of the schools. Josephine passed this time taking golf lessons from a professional so newly arrived from Scotland that he surely knew nothing of her misadventure; she even went riding with a young man one afternoon, feeling almost at home with him after his admission that he had flunked out of Princeton in February – a confidence, however, which she did not reciprocate in kind. But in the evenings, despite the young man's importunity, she stayed with her mother, feeling nearer to her than she ever had before.

But one afternoon in the lobby Josephine saw by the desk two dozen good-looking young men waiting by a stack of hat cases and bags, and knew that what she dreaded was at hand. She ran upstairs and with an invented headache dined there that night, but after dinner she walked restlessly around their apartment. She was ashamed not only of her situation but of her reaction to it. She had never felt any pity for the unpopular girls who skulked in dressing-rooms because they could attract no partners on the floor, or for girls who were outsiders at Lake Forest, and now she was like them – hiding miserably out of life. Alarmed lest already the change was written in her face, she paused in front of the mirror, fascinated as ever by what she found there.

'The darn fools!' she said aloud. And as she said it her chin went up and the faint cloud about her eyes lifted. The phrases of the myriad love letters she had received passed before her eyes; behind her, after all, was the reassurance of a hundred lost and pleading faces, of innumerable tender and pleading voices. Her pride flooded back into her till she could see the warm blood rushing up into her cheeks.

There was a knock at the door – it was the Princeton boy.

'How about slipping downstairs?' he proposed. 'There's a dance. It's full of E-lies, the whole Yale baseball team. I'll pick up one of them and introduce you and you'll have a big time. How about it?'

'All right, but I don't want to meet anybody. You'll just have to dance with me all evening.'

'You know that suits me.'

She hurried into a new spring evening dress of the frailest fairy blue. In the excitement of seeing herself in it, it seemed as if she had shed the old skin of winter and emerged a shining chrysalis with no stain; and going downstairs her feet fell softly just off the beat of the music from below. It was a tune from a play she had seen a week ago in New York, a tune with a future – ready for gaieties as yet unthought of, lovers not yet met. Dancing off, she was certain that life had innumerable beginnings. She had hardly gone ten steps when she was cut in upon by Dudley Knowleton.

'Why, Josephine!' He had never used her first name before – he stood holding her hand. 'Why, I'm so glad to see you! I've been hoping and hoping you'd be here.'

She soared skyward on a rocket of surprise and delight. He was actually glad to see her – the expression on his face was obviously sincere. Could it be possible that he hadn't heard?

'Adele wrote me you might be here. She wasn't sure.'

– Then he knew and didn't care; he liked her anyhow.

'I'm in sackcloth and ashes,' she said.

'Well, they're very becoming to you.'

'You know what happened –' she ventured.

'I do. I wasn't going to say anything, but it's generally agreed that Waterbury behaved like a fool – and it's not going to be much help to him in the elections next month. Look – I want you to dance with some men who are just starving for a touch of beauty.'

Presently she was dancing with, it seemed to her, the entire team at once. Intermittently Dudley Knowleton cut back in, as well as the Princeton man, who was somewhat indignant at this unexpected competition. There were many girls from many schools in the room, but with an admirable team spirit the Yale men displayed a sharp prejudice in Josephine's favour; already she was pointed out from the chairs along the wall.

But interiorly she was waiting for what was coming, for the moment when she would walk with Dudley Knowleton into the warm, Southern night. It came naturally, just at the end of a number, and they strolled along an avenue of early-blooming lilacs and turned a corner and another corner . . .

'You were glad to see me, weren't you?' Josephine said.

'Of course.'

'I was afraid at first. I was sorriest about what happened at school because of you. I'd been trying so hard to be different – because of you.'

'You mustn't think of that school business any more. Everybody that matters knows you got a bad deal. Forget it and start over.'

'Yes,' she agreed tranquilly. She was happy. The breeze and the scent of lilacs – that was she, lovely and intangible; the rustic bench where they sat and the trees – that was he, rugged and strong beside her, protecting her.

'I'd thought so much of meeting you here,' she said after a minute. 'You'd been so good for me, that I thought maybe in a different way I could be good for you – I mean I know ways of having a good time that you don't know. For instance, we've certainly got to go horseback riding by moonlight some night. That'll be fun.'

He didn't answer.

'I can really be very nice when I like somebody – that's really not often,' she interpolated hastily, 'not seriously. But I mean when I do feel seriously that a boy and I are really friends I don't believe in having a whole mob of other boys hanging around taking up time. I like to be with him all the time, all day and all evening, don't you?'

He stirred a little on the bench; he leaned forward with his elbows on his knees, looking at his strong hands. Her gently modulated voice sank a note lower.

'When I like anyone I don't even like dancing. It's sweeter to be alone.'

Silence for a moment.

'Well, you know' – he hesitated, frowning – 'as a matter of fact, I'm mixed up in a lot of engagements made some time ago with some people.' He floundered about unhappily. 'In fact, I won't even be at the hotel after tomorrow. I'll be at the house of some people down the valley – a sort of house party. As a matter of fact, Adele's getting here tomorrow.'

Absorbed in her own thoughts, she hardly heard him at first, but at the name she caught her breath sharply.

'We're both to be at this house party while we're here, and I imagine it's more or less arranged what we're going to do. Of course, in the daytime I'll be here for baseball practice.'

'I see.' Her lips were quivering. 'You won't be – you'll be with Adele.'

'I think that – more or less – I will. She'll – want to see you, of course.'

Another silence while he twisted his big fingers and she helplessly imitated the gesture.

'You were just sorry for me,' she said. 'You like Adele – much better.'

'Adele and I understand each other. She's been more or less my ideal since we were children together.'

'And I'm not your kind of girl?' Josephine's voice trembled with a sort of fright. 'I suppose because I've kissed a lot of boys and got a reputation for speed and raised the deuce.'

'It isn't that.'

'Yes, it is,' she declared passionately. 'I'm just paying for things.' She stood up. 'You'd better take me back inside so I can dance with the kind of boys that like me.'

She walked quickly down the path, tears of misery streaming from her eyes. He overtook her by the steps, but she only shook her head and said, 'Excuse me for being so fresh. I'll grow up – I got what was coming to me – it's all right.'

A little later when she looked around the floor for him he had gone – and Josephine realized with a shock that for the first time in her life, she had tried for a man and failed. But, save in the very young, only love begets love, and from the moment Josephine had perceived that his interest in her was merely kindness she realized the wound was not in her heart but in her pride. She would forget him quickly, but she would never forget what she had learned from him. There were two kinds of men, those you played with and those you might marry. And as this passed through her mind, her restless eyes wandered casually over the group of stags, resting very lightly on Mr Gordon Tinsley, the current catch of Chicago, reputedly the richest young man in the Middle West. He had never paid any attention to young Josephine until tonight. Ten minutes ago he had asked her to go driving with him tomorrow.

But he did not attract her – and she decided to refuse. One mustn't run through people, and, for the sake of a romantic half-hour, trade a possibility that might develop – quite seriously – later, at the proper time. She did not know that this was the first mature thought that she had ever had in her life, but it was.

The orchestra were packing their instruments and the Princeton man was still at her ear, still imploring her to walk out with him into the night. Josephine knew without cogitation which sort of man he was – and the moon was bright even on the windows. So with a certain sense of relaxation she took his arm and they strolled out to the pleasant bower she had so lately quitted, and their faces turned towards each other, like little moons under the great white ones which hovered high over the Blue Ridge; his arm dropped softly about her yielding shoulder.

'Well?' he whispered.

'Well.'

TWO WRONGS

'Look at those shoes,' said Bill – 'twenty-eight dollars.'

Mr Brancusi looked. 'Purty.'

'Made to order.'

'I knew you were a great swell. You didn't get me up here to show me those shoes, did you?'

'I am not a great swell. Who said I was a great swell?' demanded Bill. 'Just because I've got more education than most people in show business.'

'And then, you know, you're a handsome young fellow,' said Brancusi dryly.

'Sure I am – compared to you anyhow. The girls think I must be an actor, till they find out . . . Got a cigarette? What's more, I look like a man – which is more than some of these pretty boys round Times Square do.'

'Good-looking. Gentleman. Good shoes. Shot with luck.'

'You're wrong there,' objected Bill. 'Brains. Three years – nine shows – four big hits – only one flop. Where do you see any luck in that?'

A little bored, Brancusi just gazed. What he would have seen – had he not made his eyes opaque and taken to thinking about something else – was a fresh-faced young Irishman exuding aggressiveness and self-confidence until the air of his office was thick with it. Presently, Brancusi knew, Bill would hear the sound of his own voice and be ashamed and retire into his other humour – the quietly superior, sensitive one, the patron of the arts, modelled on the intellectuals of the Theatre Guild. Bill McChesney had not quite decided between the two, such blends are seldom complete before thirty.

'Take Ames, take Hopkins, take Harris – take any of them,' Bill insisted. 'What have they got on me? What's the matter? Do you want a drink?' – seeing Brancusi's glance wander towards the cabinet on the opposite wall.

'I never drink in the morning. I just wondered who it was keeps on knocking. You ought to make it stop. I get a nervous fidgets, kind of half crazy, with that kind of thing.'

Bill went quickly to the door and threw it open.

'Nobody,' he said . . . 'Hello! What do you want?'

'Oh, I'm so sorry,' a voice answered; 'I'm terribly sorry. I got so excited and I didn't realize I had this pencil in my hand.'

'What is it you want?'

'I want to see you, and the clerk said you were busy. I have a letter for you from Alan Rogers, the playwright – and I wanted to give it to you personally.'

'I'm busy,' said Bill. 'See Mr Cadorna.'

'I did, but he wasn't very encouraging, and Mr Rogers said –'

Brancusi, edging over restlessly, took a quick look at her. She was very young, with beautiful red hair, and more character in her face than her chatter would indicate; it did not occur to Mr Brancusi that this was due to her origin in Delaney, South Carolina.

'What shall I do?' she inquired, quietly laying her future in Bill's hands. 'I had a letter to Mr Rogers, and he just gave me this one to you.'

'Well, what do you want me to do – marry you?' exploded Bill.

'I'd like to get a part in one of your plays.'

'Then sit down and wait. I'm busy . . . Where's Miss Cohalan?' He rang a bell, looked once more, crossly, at the girl and closed the door of his office. But during the interruption his other mood had come over him, and he resumed his conversation with Brancusi in the key of one who was hand in glove with Reinhardt for the artistic future of the theatre.

By 12.30 he had forgotten everything except that he was going to be the greatest producer in the world and that he had an engagement to tell Sol Lincoln about it at lunch. Emerging from his office, he looked expectantly at Miss Cohalan.

'Mr Lincoln won't be able to meet you,' she said. 'He jus' 'is minute called.'

'Just this minute,' repeated Bill, shocked. 'All right. Just cross him off that list for Thursday night.'

Miss Cohalan drew a line on a sheet of paper before her.

'Mr McChesney, now you haven't forgotten me, have you?'

He turned to the red-headed girl.

'No,' he said vaguely, and then to Miss Cohalan: 'That's all right: ask him for Thursday anyhow. To hell with him!'

He did not want to lunch alone. He did not like to do anything alone now, because contacts were too much fun when one had prominence and power.

'If you would just let me talk to you two minutes –' she began.

'Afraid I can't now.' Suddenly he realized that she was the most beautiful person he had ever seen in his life.

He stared at her.

'Mr Rogers told me –'

'Come and have a spot of lunch with me,' he said, and then, with an air of great hurry, he gave Miss Cohalan some quick and contradictory instructions and held open the door.

They stood on Forty-second Street and he breathed his pre-empted air – there is only enough air there for a few people at a time. It was November and the first exhilarating rush of the season was over, but he could look east and see the electric sign of one of his plays, and west and see another. Around the corner was the one he had put on with Brancusi – the last time he would produce anything except alone.

They went to the Bedford, where there was a to-do of waiters and captains as he came in.

'This is ver' tractive restaurant,' she said, impressed and on company behaviour.

'This is hams' paradise.' He nodded to several people. 'Hello, Jimmy – Bill . . . Hello there, Jack . . . That's Jack Dempsey . . . I don't eat here much. I usually eat up at the Harvard Club.'

'Oh, did you go to Harvard? I used to know –'

'Yes.' He hesitated; there were two versions about Harvard, and he decided suddenly on the true one. 'Yes, and they had me down for a hick there, but not any more. About a week ago I was out on Long Island at the Gouverneer Haights – very fashionable people – and a couple of Gold Coast boys that never knew I was alive up in Cambridge began pulling this "Hello, Bill, old boy" on me.'

He hesitated and suddenly decided to leave the story there.

'What do you want – a job?' he demanded. He remembered suddenly that she had holes in her stockings. Holes in stockings always moved him, softened him.

'Yes, or else I've got to go home,' she said. 'I want to be a dancer – you know, Russian Ballet. But the lessons cost so much, so I've got to get a job. I thought it'd give me stage presence anyhow.'

'Hoofer, eh?'

'Oh, no, serious.'

'Well, Pavlova's a hoofer, isn't she?'

'Oh, no.' She was shocked at this profanity, but after a moment she continued: 'I took with Miss Campbell – Georgia Berriman Campbell – back home – maybe you know her. She took from New Wayburn, and she's really wonderful. She –'

'Yeah?' he said abstractedly. 'Well, it's a tough business – casting agencies bursting with people that can all do anything, till I give them a try. How old are you?'

'Eighteen.'

'I'm twenty-six. Came here four years ago without a cent.'

'My!'

'I could quit now and be comfortable the rest of my life.'

'My!'

'Going to take a year off next year – get married . . . Ever hear of Irene Rikker?'

'I should say! She's about my favourite of all.'

'We're engaged.'

'My!'

When they went out into Times Square after a while he said carelessly, 'What are you doing now?'

'Why, I'm trying to get a job.'

'I mean right this minute.'

'Why, nothing.'

'Do you want to come up to my apartment on Forty-sixth Street and have some coffee?'

Their eyes met, and Emmy Pinkard made up her mind she could take care of herself.

It was a great bright studio apartment with a ten-foot divan, and after she had coffee and he a highball, his arm dropped round her shoulder.

'Why should I kiss you?' she demanded. 'I hardly know you, and besides, you're engaged to somebody else.'

'Oh, that! She doesn't care.'

'No, really!'

'You're a good girl.'

'Well, I'm certainly not an idiot.'

'All right, go on being a good girl.'

She stood up, but lingered a minute, very fresh and cool, and not upset at all.

'I suppose this means you won't give me a job?' she asked pleasantiy.

He was already thinking about something else – about an interview and a rehearsal – but now he looked at her again and saw that she still had holes in her stockings. He telephoned:

'Joe, this is the Fresh Boy . . . You didn't think I knew you called me that, did you? . . . It's all right . . . Say, have you got those three girls for the party scene? Well, listen; save one for a Southern kid I'm sending around today.'

He looked at her jauntily, conscious of being such a good fellow.

'Well, I don't know how to thank you. And Mr Rogers,' she added audaciously. 'Good-bye, Mr McChesney.'

II

During rehearsal he used to come around a great deal and stand watching with a wise expression, as if he knew everything in people's minds; but actually he was in a haze about his own good fortune and didn't see much and didn't for the moment care. He spent most of his weekends on Long Island with the fashionable people who had 'taken him up'. When Brancusi referred to him as the 'big social butterfly', he would answer, 'Well, what about it? Didn't I go to Harvard? You think they found me in a Grand Street apple-cart, like you?' He was well liked among his new friends for his good looks and good nature, as well as his success.

His engagement to Irene Rikker was the most unsatisfactory thing in his life; they were tired of each other but unwilling to put an end to it. Just as, often, the two richest young people in a town are drawn together by the fact, so Bill McChesney and Irene Rikker, borne side by side on waves of triumph, could not spare each other's nice appreciation of what was due such success. Nevertheless, they indulged in fiercer and more frequent quarrels, and the end was approaching. It was embodied in one Frank Llewellen, a big, fine-looking actor playing opposite Irene. Seeing the situation at once, Bill became bitterly humorous about it; from the second week of rehearsals there was tension in the air.

Meanwhile Emmy Pinkard, with enough money for crackers and milk, and a friend who took her out to dinner, was being happy. Her friend, Easton Hughes fom Delaney, was studying at Columbia to be a dentist. He sometimes brought along other lonesome young men studying to be dentists, and at the price, if it can be called that, of a few casual kisses in taxicabs, Emmy dined when hungry. One afternoon she introduced Easton to Bill McChesney at the stage door, and afterwards Bill made his facetious jealousy the basis of their relationship.

'I see that dental number has been slipping it over on me again. Well, don't let him give you any laughing gas is my advice.'

Though their encounters were few, they always looked at each other. When Bill looked at her he stared for an instant as if he had not seen her before, and then remembered suddenly that she was to be teased. When she looked at him she saw many things – a bright day outside, with great crowds of people hurrying through the streets; a very good new limousine that waited at the kerb for two people with very good new clothes, who got in and went somewhere that was just like New York, only away, and more fun there. Many times she had wished she had kissed him, but just as many times she was glad she hadn't; since, as the weeks passed, he grew less romantic, tied up, like the rest of them, to the play's laborious evolution.

They were opening in Atlantic City. A sudden moodiness, apparent to everyone, came over Bill. He was short with the director and sarcastic with the actors. This, it was rumoured, was because Irene Rikker had come down with Frank Llewellen on a different train. Sitting beside the author on the night of the dress rehearsal, he was an almost sinister figure in the twilight of the auditorium; but he said nothing until the end of the second act, when, with Llewellen and Irene Rikker on the stage alone, he suddenly called:

'We'll go over that again – and cut out the mush!'

Llewellen came down to the footlights.

'What do you mean – cut out the mush?' he inquired. 'Those are the lines, aren't they?'

'You know what I mean – stick to business.'

'I don't know what you mean.'

Bill stood up. 'I mean all that damn whispering.'

'There wasn't any whispering. I simply asked –'

'That'll do – take it over.'

Llewellen turned away furiously and was about to proceed, when Bill added audibly: 'Even a ham has got to do his stuff.'

Llewellen whipped about. 'I don't have to stand that kind of talk, Mr McChesney.'

'Why not? You're a ham, aren't you? When did you get ashamed of being a ham? I'm putting on this play and I want you to stick to your stuff.' Bill got up and walked down the aisle. 'And when you don't do it, I'm going to call you just like anybody else.'

'Well, you watch out for your tone of voice –'

'What'll you do about it?'

Llewellen jumped down into the orchestra pit.

'I'm not taking anything from you!' he shouted.

Irene Rikker called to them from the stage, 'For heaven's sake, are you two crazy?' And then Llewellen swung at him, one short, mighty blow. Bill pitched back across a row of seats, fell through one, splintering it, and lay wedged there. There was a moment's wild confusion, then people holding Llewellen, then the author, with a white face, pulling Bill up and the stage manager crying: 'Shall I kill him, chief? Shall I break his fat face?' and Llewellen panting and Irene Rikker frightened.

'Get back there!' Bill cried, holding a handkerchief to his face and teetering into the author's supporting arms. 'Everybody get back! Take that scene again, and no talk! Get back, Llewellen!'

Before they realized it they were all back on the stage, Irene pulling Llewellen's arm and talking to him fast. Someone put on the auditorium lights and then dimmed them again hurriedly. When Emmy came out presently for her scene, she saw in a quick glance that Bill was sitting with a whole mask of handkerchiefs over his bleeding face. She hated Llewellen and was afraid that presently they would break up and go back to New York. But Bill had saved the show from his own folly, since for Llewellen to take the further initiative of quitting would hurt his professional standing. The act ended and the next one began without an interval. When it was over, Bill was gone.

Next night, during the performance, he sat on a chair in the wings in view of everyone coming on or off. His face was swollen and bruised, but he neglected to seem conscious of the fact and there were no comments. Once he went around in front, and when he returned, word leaked out that two of the New York agencies were making big buys. He had a hit – they all had a hit.

At the sight of him to whom Emmy felt they all owed so much, a great wave of gratitude swept over her. She went up and thanked him.

'I'm a good picker, red-head,' he agreed grimly.

'Thank you for picking me.'

And suddenly Emmy was moved to a rash remark.

'You've hurt your face so badly!' she exclaimed. 'Oh, I think it was so brave of you not to let everything go to pieces last night.'

He looked at her hard for a moment and then an ironic smile tried unsuccessfully to settle on his swollen face.

'Do you admire me, baby?'

'Yes.'

'Even when I fell in the seats, did you admire me?'

'You got control of everything so quick.'

'That's loyalty for you. You found something to admire in that fool mess.'

And her happiness bubbled up into, 'Anyhow, you behaved just wonderfully.' She looked so fresh and young that Bill, who had had a wretched day, wanted to rest his swollen cheek against her cheek.

He took both the bruise and the desire with him to New York next morning; the bruise faded, but the desire remained. And when they opened in the city, no sooner did he see other men begin to crowd around her beauty than she became this play for him, this success, the thing that he came to see when he came to the theatre. After a good run it closed just as he was drinking too much and needed someone on the grey days of reaction. They were married suddenly in Connecticut, early in June.

III

Two men sat in the Savoy Grill in London, waiting for the Fourth of July. It was already late in May.

'Is he a nice guy?' asked Hubbel.

'Very nice,' answered Brancusi; 'very nice, very handsome, very popular.' After a moment, he added: 'I want to get him to come home.'

'That's what I don't get about him,' said Hubbel. 'Show business over here is nothing compared to home. What does he want to stay here for?'

'He goes around with a lot of dukes and ladies.'

'Oh?'

'Last week when I met him he was with three ladies – Lady this, Lady that, Lady the other thing.'

'I thought he was married.'

'Married three years,' said Brancusi, 'got a fine child, going to have another.'

He broke off as McChesney came in, his very American face staring about boldly over the collar of a box-shouldered topcoat.

'Hello, Mac; meet my friend Mr Hubbel.'

'J'doo,' said Bill. He sat down, continuing to stare around the bar to see who was present. After a few minutes Hubbel left, and Bill asked:

'Who's that bird?'

'He's only been here a month. He ain't got a title yet. You been here six months, remember.'

Bill grinned.

'You think I'm high-hat, don't you? Well, I'm not kidding myself anyhow. I like it; it gets me. I'd like to be the Marquis of McChesney.'

'Maybe you can drink yourself into it,' suggested Brancusi.

'Shut your trap. Who said I was drinking? Is that what they say now? Look here; if you can tell me any American manager in the history of the theatre who's had the success that I've had in London in less than eight months, I'll go back to America with you tomorrow. If you'll just tell me –'

'It was with your old shows. You had two flops in New York.'

Bill stood up, his face hardening.

'Who do you think you are?' he demanded. 'Did you come over here to talk to me like that?'

'Don't get sore now, Bill. I just want you to come back. I'd say anything for that. Put over three seasons like you had in '22 and '23, and you're fixed for life.'

'New York makes me sick,' said Bill moodily. 'One minute you're a king; then you have two flops, they go around saying you're on the toboggan.'

Brancusi shook his head.

'That wasn't why they said it. It was because you had that quarrel with Aronstael, your best friend.'

'Friend hell!'

'Your best friend in business anyhow. Then –'

'I don't want to talk about it.' He looked at his watch. 'Look here; Emmy's feeling bad so I'm afraid I can't have dinner with you tonight. Come around to the office before you sail.'

Five minutes later, standing by the cigar counter, Brancusi saw Bill enter the Savoy again and descend the steps that led to the tea room.

'Grown to be a great diplomat,' thought Brancusi; 'he used to just say when he had a date. Going with these dukes and ladies is polishing him up even more.'

Perhaps he was a little hurt, though it was not typical of him to be hurt. At any rate he made a decision, then and there, that McChesney

was on the down-grade; it was quite typical of him that at that point
he erased him from his mind forever.

There was no outward indication that Bill was on the down-grade; a
hit at the New Strand, a hit at the Prince of Wales, and the weekly
grosses pouring in almost as well as they had two or three years before
in New York. Certainly a man of action was justified in changing his
base. And the man who, an hour later, turned into his Hyde Park house
for dinner had all the vitality of the late twenties. Emmy, very tired and
clumsy, lay on a couch in the upstairs sitting-room. He held her for a
moment in his arms.

'Almost over now,' he said. 'You're beautiful.'

'Don't be ridiculous.'

'It's true. You're always beautiful. I don't know why. Perhaps because
you've got character, and that's always in your face, even when you're
like this.'

She was pleased; she ran her hand through his hair.

'Character is the greatest thing in the world,' he declared, 'and you've
got more than anybody I know.'

'Did you see Brancusi?'

'I did, the little louse! I decided not to bring him home to dinner.'

'What was the matter?'

'Oh, just snooty – talking about my row with Aronstael, as if it was
my fault.'

She hesitated, closed her mouth tight and then said quietly, 'You got
into that fight with Aronstael because you were drinking.'

He rose impatiently.

'Are you going to start –'

'No, Bill, but you're drinking too much now. You know you are.'

Aware that she was right, he evaded the matter and they went into
dinner. On the glow of a bottle of claret he decided he would go on the
wagon tomorrow till after the baby was born.

'I always stop when I want, don't I? I always do what I say. You
never saw me quit yet.'

'Never yet.'

They had coffee together, and afterwards he got up.

'Come back early,' said Emmy.

'Oh, sure . . . What's the matter, baby?'

'I'm just crying. Don't mind me. Oh, go on; don't just stand there like
a big idiot.'

'But I'm worried, naturally. I don't like to see you cry.'

'Oh, I don't know where you go in the evenings; I don't know who you're with. And that Lady Sybil Combrinck who kept phoning. It's all right, I suppose, but I wake up in the night and I feel so alone, Bill. Because we've always been together, haven't we, until recently?'

'But we're together still . . . What's happened to you, Emmy?'

'I know – I'm just crazy. We'd never let each other down, would we? We never have –'

'Of course not.'

'Come back early, or when you can.'

He looked in for a minute at the Prince of Wales Theatre; then he went into the hotel next door and called a number.

'I'd like to speak to her Ladyship. Mr McChesney calling.'

It was some time before Lady Sybil answered:

'This is rather a surprise. It's been several weeks since I've been lucky enough to hear from you.'

Her voice was flip as a whip and cold as automatic refrigeration, in the mode grown familiar since British ladies took to piecing themselves together out of literature. It had fascinated Bill for a while, but just for a while. He had kept his head.

'I haven't had a minute,' he explained easily. 'You're not sore, are you?'

'I could scarcely say "sore".'

'I was afraid you might be; you didn't send me an invitation to your party tonight. My idea was that after we talked it all over we agreed –'

'You talked a great deal,' she said; 'possibly a little too much.'

Suddenly, to Bill's astonishment, she hung up.

'Going British on me,' he thought. 'A little skit entitled The Daughter of a Thousand Earls.'

The snub roused him, the indifference revived his waning interest. Usually women forgave his changes of heart because of his obvious devotion to Emmy, and he was remembered by various ladies with a not unpleasant sigh. But he had detected no such sigh upon the phone.

'I'd like to clear up this mess,' he thought. Had he been wearing evening clothes, he might have dropped in at the dance and talked it over with her, still he didn't want to go home. Upon consideration it seemed important that the misunderstanding should be fixed up at once, and presently he began to entertain the idea of going as he was; Americans were excused unconventionalities of dress. In any case, it was not nearly time, and, in the company of several highballs, he considered the matter for an hour.

At midnight he walked up the steps of her Mayfair house. The coat-room attendants scrutinized his tweeds disapprovingly and a footman peered in vain for his name on the list of guests. Fortunately his friend Sir Humphrey Dunn arrived at the same time and convinced the footman it must be a mistake.

Inside, Bill immediately looked about for his hostess.

She was a very tall young woman, half American and all the more intensely English. In a sense, she had discovered Bill McChesney, vouched for his savage charms; his retirement was one of her most humiliating experiences since she had begun being bad.

She stood with her husband at the head of the receiving line – Bill had never seen them together before. He decided to choose a less formal moment for presenting himself.

As the receiving went on interminably, he became increasingly uncomfortable. He saw a few people he knew, but not many, and he was conscious that his clothes were attracting a certain attention; he was aware also that Lady Sybil saw him and could have relieved his embarrassment with a wave of her hand, but she made no sign. He was sorry he had come, but to withdraw now would be absurd, and going to a buffet table, he took a glass of champagne.

When he turned around she was alone at last, and he was about to approach her when the butler spoke to him:

'Pardon me, sir. Have you a card?'

'I'm a friend of Lady Sybil's,' said Bill impatiently. He turned away, but the butler followed.

'I'm sorry, sir, but I'll have to ask you to step aside with me and straighten this up.'

'There's no need. I'm just about to speak to Lady Sybil now.'

'My orders are different sir,' said the butler firmly.

Then, before Bill realized what was happening, his arms were pressed quietly to his sides and he was propelled into a little ante-room back of the buffet.

There he faced a man in a pince-nez in whom he recognized the Combrincks' private secretary.

The secretary nodded to the butler, saying, 'This is the man'; whereupon Bill was released.

'Mr McChesney,' said the secretary, 'you have seen fit to force your way here without a card, and His Lordship requests that you leave his house at once. Will you kindly give me the check for your coat?'

Then Bill understood, and the single word that he found applicable to

Lady Sybil sprang to his lips; whereupon the secretary gave a sign to two footmen, and in a furious struggle Bill was carried through a pantry where busy bus boys stared at the scene, down a long hall, and pushed out a door into the night. The door closed; a moment later it was opened again to let his coat billow forth and his cane clatter down the steps.

As he stood there, overwhelmed, stricken aghast, a taxi-cab stopped beside him and the driver called:

'Feeling ill, gov'nor?'

'What?'

'I know where you can get a good pick-me-up, gov'nor. Never too late.' The door of the taxi opened on a nightmare. There was a cabaret that broke the closing hours; there was being with strangers he had picked up somewhere; then there were arguments, and trying to cash a cheque, and suddenly proclaiming over and over that he was William McChesney, the producer, and convincing no one of the fact, not even himself. It seemed important to see Lady Sybil right away and call her to account; but presently nothing was important at all. He was in a taxi-cab whose driver had just shaken him awake in front of his own home.

The telephone was ringing as he went in, but he walked stonily past the maid and only heard her voice when his foot was on the stair.

'Mr McChesney, it's the hospital calling again. Mrs McChesney's there, and they've been phoning every hour.'

Still in a daze, he held the receiver up to his ear.

'We're calling from the Midland Hospital, for your wife. She was delivered of a still-born child at nine this morning.'

'Wait a minute.' His voice was dry and cracking. 'I don't understand.'

After a while he understood that Emmy's child was dead and she wanted him. His knees sagged groggily as he walked down the street, looking for a taxi.

The room was dark; Emmy looked up and saw him from a rumpled bed.

'It's you!' she cried. 'I thought you were dead! Where did you go?'

He threw himself down on his knees beside the bed, but she turned away.

'Oh, you smell awful,' she said. 'It makes me sick.'

But she kept her hand in his hair, and he knelt there motionless for a long time.

'I'm done with you,' she muttered, 'but it was awful when I thought you were dead. Everybody's dead. I wish I was dead.'

A curtain parted with the wind, and as he rose to arrange it, she saw him in the full morning light, pale and terrible, with rumpled clothes and bruises on his face. This time she hated him instead of those who had hurt him. She could feel him slipping out of her heart, feel the space he left, and all at once he was gone, and she could even forgive him and be sorry for him. All this in a minute.

She had fallen down at the door of the hospital, trying to get out of the taxi-cab alone.

IV

When Emmy was well, physically and mentally, her incessant idea was to learn to dance; the old dream inculcated by Miss Georgia Berriman Campbell of South Carolina persisted as a bright avenue leading back to first youth and days of hope in New York. To her, dancing meant that elaborate blend of tortuous attitudes and formal pirouettes that evolved out of Italy several hundred years ago and reached its apogee in Russia at the beginning of this century. She wanted to use herself on something she could believe in, and it seemed to her that the dance was woman's interpretation of music; instead of strong fingers, one had limbs with which to render Tschaikowsky and Stravinski; and feet could be as eloquent in Chopiniana as voices in 'The Ring'. At the bottom, it was something sandwiched in between the acrobats and the trained seals; at the top it was Pavlova and art.

Once they were settled in an apartment back in New York, she plunged into her work like a girl of sixteen – four hours a day at bar exercises, attitudes, sauts, arabesques, and pirouettes. It became the realest part of her life, and her only worry was whether or not she was too old. At twenty-six she had ten years to make up, but she was a natural dancer with a fine body – and that lovely face.

Bill encouraged it; when she was ready he was going to build the first real American ballet around her. There were even times when he envied her her absorption; for affairs in his own line were more difficult since they had come home. For one thing, he had made enemies in those early days of self-confidence; there were exaggerated stories of his drinking and of his being hard on actors and difficult to work with.

It was against him that he had always been unable to save money and must beg a backing for each play. Then, too, in a curious way, he was intelligent, as he was brave enough to prove in several uncommercial ventures, but he had no Theatre Guild behind him, and what money he lost was charged against him.

There were successes, too, but he worked harder for them, or it seemed so, for he had begun to pay a price for his irregular life. He always intended to take a rest or give up his incessant cigarettes, but there was so much competition now – new men coming up, with new reputations for infallibility – and besides, he wasn't used to regularity. He liked to do his work in those great spurts, inspired by black coffee, that seem so inevitable in show business, but which took so much out of a man after thirty. He had come to lean, in a way, on Emmy's fine health and vitality. They were always together, and if he felt a vague dissatisfaction that he had grown to need her more than she needed him, there was always the hope that things would break better for him next month, next season.

Coming home from ballet school one November evening, Emmy swung her little grey bag, pulled her hat far down over her still damp hair, and gave herself up to pleasant speculation. For a month she had been aware of people who had come to the studio especially to watch her – she was ready to dance. Once she had worked just as hard and for as long a time on something else – her relations with Bill – only to reach a climax and misery, but here there was nothing to fail her except herself. Yet even now she felt a little rash in thinking: 'Now it's come. I'm going to be happy.'

She hurried, for something had come up today that she must talk over with Bill.

Finding him in the living-room, she called him to come back while she dressed. She began to talk without looking around:

'Listen what happened!' Her voice was loud, to compete with the water running in the tub. 'Paul Makova wants me to dance with him at the Metropolitan this season; only it's not sure, so it's a secret – even I'm not supposed to know.'

'That's great.'

'The only thing is whether it wouldn't be far better for me to make a début abroad? Anyhow Donilof says I'm ready to appear. What do you think?'

'I don't know.'

'You don't sound very enthusiastic.'

'I've got something on my mind. I'll tell you about it later. Go on.'

'That's all, dear. If you still feel like going to Germany for a month, like you said, Donilof would arrange a début for me in Berlin, but I'd rather open here and dance with Paul Makova. Just imagine –' She broke off, feeling suddenly through the thick skin of her elation how abstracted he was. 'Tell me what you've got on your mind.'

'I went to Doctor Kearns this afternoon.'

'What did he say?' Her mind was still singing with her own happiness. Bill's intermittent attacks of hypochondria had long ceased to worry her.

'I told him about that blood this morning, and he said what he said last year – it was probably a little broken vein in my throat. But since I'd been coughing and was worried, perhaps it was safer to take an X-ray and clear the matter up. Well, we cleared it up all right. My left lung is practically gone.'

'Bill!'

'Luckily there are no spots on the other.'

She waited, horribly afraid.

'It's come at a bad time for me,' he went on steadily, 'but it's got to be faced. He thinks I ought to go to the Adirondacks or to Denver for the winter, and his idea is Denver. That way it'll probably clear up in five or six months.'

'Of course we'll have to –' she stopped suddenly.

'I wouldn't expect you to go – especially if you have this opportunity.'

'Of course I'll go,' she said quickly. 'Your health comes first. We've always gone everywhere together.'

'Oh, no.'

'Why, of course.' She made her voice strong and decisive. 'We've always been together. I couldn't stay here without you. When do you have to go?'

'As soon as possible. I went in to see Brancusi to find out if he wanted to take over the Richmond piece, but he didn't seem enthusiastic.' His face hardened. 'Of course there won't be anything else for the present, but I'll have enough, with what's owing –'

'Oh, if I was only making some money!' Emmy cried. 'You work so hard and here I've been spending two hundred dollars a week for just my dancing lessons alone – more than I'll be able to earn for years.'

'Of course in six months I'll be as well as ever – he says.'

'Sure, dearest; we'll get you well. We'll start as soon as we can.'

She put an arm around him and kissed him.

'I'm just an old parasite,' she said. 'I should have known my darling wasn't well.'

He reached automatically for a cigarette, and then stopped.

'I forgot – I've got to start cutting down smoking.' He rose to the occasion suddenly: 'No, baby, I've decided to go alone. You'd go crazy with boredom out there, and I'd just be thinking I was keeping you away from your dancing.'

'Don't think about that. The thing is to get you well.'

They discussed the matter hour after hour for the next week, each of them saying everything except the truth – that he wanted her to go with him and that she wanted passionately to stay in New York. She talked it over guardedly with Donilof, her ballet master, and found that he thought any postponement would be a terrible mistake. Seeing other girls in the ballet school making plans for the winter, she wanted to die rather than go, and Bill saw all the involuntary indications of her misery. For a while they talked of compromising on the Adirondacks, whither she would commute by aeroplane for the weekends, but he was running a little fever now and he was definitely ordered West.

Bill settled it all one gloomy Sunday night, with that rough, generous justice that had first made her admire him, that made him rather tragic in his adversity, as he had always been bearable in his overweening success:

'It's just up to me, baby. I got into this mess because I didn't have any self-control – you seem to have all of that in this family – and now it's only me that can get me out. You've worked hard at your stuff for three years and you deserve your chance – and if you came out there now you'd have it on me the rest of my life.' He grinned. 'And I couldn't stand that. Besides, it wouldn't be good for the kid.'

Eventually she gave in, ashamed of herself, miserable – and glad. For the world of her work, where she existed without Bill, was bigger to her now than the world in which they existed together. There was more room to he glad in one than to be sorry in the other.

Two days later, with his ticket bought for that afternoon at five, they passed the last hours together, talking of everything hopeful. She protested still, and sincerely; had he weakened for a moment she would have gone. But the shock had done something to him, and he showed more character under it than he had for years. Perhaps it would be good for him to work it out alone.

'In the spring!' they said.

Then in the station with little Billy, and Bill saying: 'I hate these graveside partings. You leave me here. I've got to make a phone call from the train before it goes.'

They had never spent more than a night apart in six years, save when

Emmy was in the hospital; save for the time in England they had a good record of faithfulness and of tenderness towards each other, even though she had been alarmed and often unhappy at this insecure bravado from the first. After he went through the gate alone, Emmy was glad he had a phone call to make and tried to picture him making it.

She was a good woman; she had loved him with all her heart. When she went out into Thirty-third Street, it was just as dead as dead for a while, and the apartment he paid for would be empty of him, and she was here, about to do something that would make her happy.

She stopped after a few blocks, thinking: 'Why, this is terrible – what I'm doing! I'm letting him down like the worst person I ever heard of. I'm leaving him flat and going off to dinner with Donilof and Paul Makova, whom I like for being beautiful and for having the same colour eyes and hair. Bill's on the train alone.'

She swung little Billy around suddenly as if to go back to the station. She could see him sitting in the train, with his face so pale and tired, and no Emmy.

'I can't let him down,' she cried to herself as wave after wave of sentiment washed over her. But only sentiment – hadn't he let her down – hadn't he done what he wanted in London?

'Oh, poor Bill!'

She stood irresolute, realizing for the last honest moment how quickly she would forget this and find excuses for what she was doing. She had to think hard of London, and her conscience cleared. But with Bill all alone in the train it seemed terrible to think that way. Even now she could turn and go back to the station and tell him that she was coming, but she still waited, with life very strong in her, fighting for her. The sidewalk was narrow where she stood; presently a great wave of people, pouring out of the theatre, came flooding along it, and she and little Billy were swept along with the crowd.

In the train, Bill telephoned up to the last minute, postponed going back to his state-room, because he knew it was almost certain that he would not find her there. After the train started he went back and, of course, there was nothing but his bags in the rack and some magazines on the seat.

He knew then that he had lost her. He saw the set-up without any illusions – this Paul Makova, and months of proximity, and loneliness – afterwards nothing would ever be the same. When he had thought about it all a long time, reading *Variety* and *Zit's* in between, it began to seem, each time he came back to it, as if Emmy somehow were dead.

'She was a fine girl – one of the best. She had character.' He realized perfectly that he had brought all this on himself and that there was some law of compensation involved. He saw, too, that by going away he had again become as good as she was; it was all evened up at last.

He felt beyond everything, even beyond his grief, an almost comfortable sensation of being in the hands of something bigger than himself; and grown a little tired and unconfident – two qualities he could never for a moment tolerate – it did not seem so terrible if he were going West for a definite finish. He was sure that Emmy would come at the end, no matter what she was doing or how good an engagement she had.

THE BRIDAL PARTY

I

There was the usual insincere little note saying: 'I wanted you to be the first to know.' It was a double shock to Michael, announcing, as it did, both the engagement and the imminent marriage; which, moreover, was to be held, not in New York, decently and far away, but here in Paris under his very nose, if that could be said to extend over the Protestant Episcopal Church of the Holy Trinity, Avenue Georges-Cinq. The date was two weeks off, early in June.

At first Michael was afraid and his stomach felt hollow. When he left the hotel that morning, the *femme de chambre*, who was in love with his fine, sharp profile and his pleasant buoyancy, scented the hard abstraction that had settled over him. He walked in a daze to his bank, he bought a detective story at Smith's on the Rue de Rivoli, he sympathetically stared for a while at a faded panorama of the battlefields in a tourist-office window and cursed a Greek tout who followed him with a half-displayed packet of innocuous post cards warranted to be very dirty indeed.

But the fear stayed with him, and after a while he recognized it as the fear that now he would never be happy. He had met Caroline Dandy when she was seventeen, possessed her young heart all through her first season in New York, and then lost her, slowly, tragically, uselessly, because he had no money and could make no money; because, with all the energy and good-will in the world, he could not find himself; because, loving him still, Caroline had lost faith and begun to see him as something pathetic, futile, and shabby, outside the great, shining stream of life towards which she was inevitably drawn.

Since his only support was that she loved him, he leaned weakly on that; the support broke, but still he held on to it and was carried out to sea and washed up on the French coast with its broken pieces still in his hands. He carried them around with him in the form of photographs and packets of correspondence and a liking for a maudlin popular song called 'Among My Souvenirs'. He kept clear of other girls, as if Caroline would somehow know it and reciprocate with a faithful heart. Her note informed him that he had lost her forever.

It was a fine morning. In front of the shops in the Rue de Castiglione, proprietors and patrons were on the sidewalk gazing upward, for the Graf Zeppelin, shining and glorious, symbol of escape and destruction – of escape, if necessary, through destruction – glided in the Paris sky. He heard a woman say in French that it would not astonish her if that commenced to let fall the bombs. Then he heard another voice, full of husky laughter, and the void in his stomach froze. Jerking about, he was face to face with Caroline Dandy and her fiancé.

'Why, Michael! Why, we were wondering where you were. I asked at the Guaranty Trust, and Morgan and Company, and finally sent a note to the National City –'

Why didn't they back away? Why didn't they back right up, walking backwards down the Rue de Castiglione, across the Rue de Rivoli, through the Tuileries Gardens, still walking backwards as fast as they could till they grew vague and faded out across the river?

'This is Hamilton Rutherford, my fiancé.'

'We've met before.'

'At Pat's, wasn't it?'

'And last spring in the Ritz Bar.'

'Michael, where have you been keeping yourself?'

'Around here.' This agony. Previews of Hamilton Rutherford flashed before his eyes – a quick series of pictures, sentences. He remembered hearing that he had bought a seat in 1920 for a hundred and twenty-five thousand of borrowed money, and just before the break sold it for more than half a million. Not handsome like Michael, but vitally attractive, confident, authoritative, just the right height over Caroline there – Michael had always been too short for Caroline when they danced.

Rutherford was saying: 'No, I'd like it very much if you'd come to the bachelor dinner. I'm taking the Ritz Bar from nine o'clock on. Then right after the wedding there'll be a reception and breakfast at the Hôtel Georges-Cinq.'

'And, Michael, George Packman is giving a party day after tomorrow at Chez Victor, and I want you to be sure and come. And also to tea Friday at Jebby West's; she'd want to have you if she knew where you were. Where's your hotel, so we can send you an invitation? You see, the reason we decided to have it over here is because mother has been sick in a nursing home here and the whole clan is in Paris. Then Hamilton's mother's being here too –'

The entire clan; they had always hated him, except her mother; always discouraged his courtship. What a little counter he was in this game of families and money! Under his hat his brow sweated with the humiliation of the fact that for all his misery he was worth just exactly so many invitations. Frantically he began to mumble something about going away.

Then it happened – Caroline saw deep into him, and Michael knew that she saw. She saw through to his profound woundedness, and something quivered inside her, died out along the curve of her mouth and in her eyes. He had moved her. All the unforgettable impulses of first love had surged up once more; their hearts had in some way touched across two feet of Paris sunlight. She took her fiancé's arm suddenly, as if to steady herself with the feel of it.

They parted. Michael walked quickly for a minute; then he stopped, pretending to look in a window, and saw them farther up the street, walking fast into the Place Vendôme, people with much to do.

He had things to do also – he had to get his laundry.

'Nothing will ever be the same again,' he said to himself. 'She will never be happy in her marriage and I will never be happy at all any more.'

The two vivid years of his love for Caroline moved back around him like years in Einstein's physics. Intolerable memories arose – of rides in the Long Island moonlight; of a happy time at Lake Placid with her cheeks so cold there, but warm just underneath the surface; of a despairing afternoon in a little café on Forty-eighth Street in the last sad months when their marriage had come to seem impossible.

'Come in,' he said aloud.

The concierge with a telegram; brusque, because Mr Curly's clothes were a little shabby. Mr Curly gave few tips; Mr Curly was obviously a *petit client*.

Michael read the telegram.

'An answer?' the concierge asked.

'No,' said Michael, and then, on an impulse: 'Look.'

'Too bad – too bad,' said the concierge. 'Your grandfather is dead.'

'Not too bad,' said Michael. 'It means that I come into a quarter of a million dollars.'

Too late by a single month; after the first flush of the news his misery was deeper than ever. Lying awake in bed that night, he listened endlessly to the long caravan of a circus moving through the street from one Paris fair to another.

When the last van had rumbled out of hearing and the corners of the furniture were pastel blue with the dawn, he was still thinking of the look in Caroline's eyes that morning – the look that seemed to say: 'Oh, why couldn't you have done something about it? Why couldn't you have been stronger, made me marry you? Don't you see how sad I am?'

Michael's fists clenched.

'Well, I won't give up till the last moment,' he whispered. 'I've had all the bad luck so far, and maybe it's turned at last. One takes what one can get, up to the limit of one's strength, and if I can't have her, at least she'll go into this marriage with some of me in her heart.'

II

Accordingly he went to the party at Chez Victor two days later, upstairs and into the little salon off the bar where the party was to assemble for cocktails. He was early; the only other occupant was a tall lean man of fifty. They spoke.

'You waiting for George Packman's party?'

'Yes. My name's Michael Curly.'

'My name's –'

Michael failed to catch the name. They ordered a drink, and Michael supposed that the bride and groom were having a gay time.

'Too much so,' the other agreed, frowning. 'I don't see how they stand it. We all crossed on the boat together; five days of that crazy life and then two weeks of Paris. You' – he hesitated, smiling faintly – 'you'll excuse me for saying that your generation drinks too much.'

'Not Caroline.'

'No, not Caroline. She seems to take only a cocktail and a glass of champagne, and then she's had enough, thank God. But Hamilton drinks too much and all this crowd of young people drink too much. Do you live in Paris?'

'For the moment,' said Michael.

'I don't like Paris. My wife – that is to say, my ex-wife, Hamilton's mother – lives in Paris.'

'You're Hamilton Rutherford's father?'

'I have that honour. And I'm not denying that I'm proud of what he's done; it was just a general comment.'

'Of course.'

Michael glanced up nervously as four people came in. He felt suddenly that his dinner coat was old and shiny; he had ordered a new one that morning. The people who had come in were rich and at home in their richness with one another – a dark, lovely girl with a hysterical little laugh whom he had met before; two confident men whose jokes referred invariably to last night's scandal and tonight's potentialities, as if they had important rôles in a play that extended indefinitely into the past and the future. When Caroline arrived, Michael had scarcely a moment of her, but it was enough to note that, like all the others, she was strained and tired. She was pale beneath her rouge; there were shadows under her eyes. With a mixture of relief and wounded vanity, he found himself placed far from her and at another table; he needed a moment to adjust himself to his surroundings. This was not like the immature set in which he and Caroline had moved; the men were more than thirty and had an air of sharing the best of this world's goods. Next to him was Jebby West, whom he knew; and, on the other side, a jovial man who immediately began to talk to Michael about a stunt for the bachelor dinner: They were going to hire a French girl to appear with an actual baby in her arms, crying: 'Hamilton, you can't desert me now!' The idea seemed stale and unamusing to Michael, but its originator shook with anticipatory laughter.

Farther up the table there was talk of the market – another drop today, the most appreciable since the crash; people were kidding Rutherford about it: 'Too bad, old man. You better not get married, after all.'

Michael asked the man on his left, 'Has he lost a lot?'

'Nobody knows. He's heavily involved, but he's one of the smartest young men in Wall Street. Anyhow, nobody ever tells you the truth.'

It was a champagne dinner from the start, and towards the end it reached a pleasant level of conviviality, but Michael saw that all these people were too weary to be exhilarated by any ordinary stimulant; for weeks they had drunk cocktails before meals like Americans, wines and brandies like Frenchmen, beer like Germans, whisky-and-soda like the English, and as they were no longer in the twenties, this preposterous *mélange*, that was like some gigantic cocktail in a nightmare, served only to make them temporarily less conscious of the mistakes of the night before. Which is to say that it was not really a gay party; what gaiety existed was displayed in the few who drank nothing at all.

But Michael was not tired, and the champagne stimulated him and made his misery less acute. He had been away from New York for more than eight months and most of the dance music was unfamiliar to him, but at the first bars of the 'Painted Doll' to which he and Caroline had moved through so much happiness and despair the previous summer, he crossed to Caroline's table and asked her to dance.

She was lovely in a dress of thin ethereal blue, and the proximity of her crackly yellow hair, of her cool and tender grey eyes, turned his body clumsy and rigid; he stumbled with their first step on the floor. For a moment it seemed that there was nothing to say; he wanted to tell her about his inheritance, but the idea seemed abrupt, unprepared for.

'Michael, it's so nice to be dancing with you again.'

He smiled grimly.

'I'm so happy you came,' she continued. 'I was afraid maybe you'd be silly and stay away. Now we can be just good friends and natural together. Michael, I want you and Hamilton to like each other.'

The engagement was making her stupid; he had never heard her make such a series of obvious remarks before.

'I could kill him without a qualm,' he said pleasantly, 'but he looks like a good man. He's fine. What I want to know is, what happens to people like me who aren't able to forget?'

As he said this he could not prevent his mouth from drooping suddenly, and glancing up, Caroline saw, and her heart quivered violently, as it had the other morning.

'Do you mind so much, Michael?'

'Yes.'

For a second as he said this, in a voice that seemed to have come up from his shoes, they were not dancing; they were simply clinging together. Then she leaned away from him and twisted her mouth into a lovely smile.

'I didn't know what to do at first, Michael. I told Hamilton about you – that I'd cared for you an awful lot – but it didn't worry him, and he was right. Because I'm over you now – yes, I am. And you'll wake up some sunny morning and be over me just like that.'

He shook his head stubbornly.

'Oh, yes. We weren't for each other. I'm pretty flighty, and I need somebody like Hamilton to decide things. It was that more than the question of – of –'

'Of money.' Again he was on the point of telling her what had happened, but again something told him it was not the time.

'Then how do you account for what happened when we met the

other day,' he demanded helplessly – 'what happened just now? When we just pour towards each other like we used to – as if we were one person, as if the same blood was flowing through both of us?'

'Oh, don't!' she begged him. 'You mustn't talk like that; everything's decided now. I love Hamilton with all my heart. It's just that I remember certain things in the past and I feel sorry for you – for us – for the way we were.'

Over her shoulder, Michael saw a man come towards them to cut in. In a panic he danced her away, but inevitably the man came on.

'I've got to see you alone, if only for a minute,' Michael said quickly. 'When can I?'

'I'll be at Jebby West's tea tomorrow,' she whispered as a hand fell politely upon Michael's shoulder.

But he did not talk to her at Jebby West's tea. Rutherford stood next to her, and each brought the other into all conversations. They left early. The next morning the wedding cards arrived in the first mail.

Then Michael, grown desperate with pacing up and down his room, determined on a bold stroke; he wrote to Hamilton Rutherford, asking him for a rendezvous the following afternoon. In a short telephone communication Rutherford agreed, but for a day later than Michael had asked. And the wedding was only six days away.

They were to meet in the bar of the Hôtel Jéna. Michael knew what he would say: 'See here, Rutherford, do you realize the responsibility you're taking in going through with this marriage? Do you realize the harvest of trouble and regret you're sowing in persuading a girl into something contrary to the instincts of her heart?' He would explain that the barrier between Caroline and himself had been an artificial one and was now removed, and demand that the matter be put up to Caroline frankly before it was too late.

Rutherford would be angry, conceivably there would be a scene, but Michael felt that he was fighting for his life now.

He found Rutherford in conversation with an older man, whom Michael had met at several of the wedding parties.

'I saw what happened to most of my friends,' Rutherford was saying, 'and I decided it wasn't going to happen to me. It isn't so difficult; if you take a girl with common sense, and tell her what's what, and do your stuff damn well, and play decently square with her, it's a marriage. If you stand for any nonsense at the beginning, it's one of these arrangements – within five years the man gets out, or else the girl gobbles him up and you have the usual mess.'

'Right!' agreed his companion enthusiastically. 'Hamilton, boy, you're right.'

Michael's blood boiled slowly.

'Doesn't it strike you,' he inquired coldly, 'that your attitude went out of fashion about a hundred years ago?'

'No, it didn't,' said Rutherford pleasantly, but impatiently. 'I'm as modern as anybody. I'd get married in an aeroplane next Saturday if it'd please my girl.'

'I don't mean that way of being modern. You can't take a sensitive woman –'

'Sensitive? Women aren't so darn sensitive. It's fellows like you who are sensitive; it's fellows like you that they exploit – all your devotion and kindness and all that. They read a couple of books and see a few pictures because they haven't got anything else to do, and then they say they're finer in grain than you are, and to prove it they take the bit in their teeth and tear off for a fare-you-well – just about as sensitive as a fire horse.'

'Caroline happens to be sensitive,' said Michael in a clipped voice.

At this point the other man got up to go; when the dispute about the check had been settled and they were alone, Rutherford leaned back to Michael as if a question had been asked him.

'Caroline's more than sensitive,' he said. 'She's got sense.'

His combative eyes, meeting Michael's, flickered with a grey light. 'This all sounds pretty crude to you, Mr Curly, but it seems to me that the average man nowadays just asks to be made a monkey of by some woman who doesn't even get any fun out of reducing him to that level. There are darn few men who possess their wives any more, but I am going to be one of them.'

To Michael it seemed time to bring the talk back to the actual situation: 'Do you realize the responsibility you're taking?'

'I certainly do,' interrupted Rutherford. 'I'm not afraid of responsibility. I'll make the decisions – fairly, I hope, but anyhow they'll be final.'

'What if you didn't start right?' said Michael impetuously. 'What if your marriage isn't founded on mutual love?'

'I think I see what you mean,' Rutherford said, still pleasant. 'And since you've brought it up, let me say that if you and Caroline had married, it wouldn't have lasted three years. Do you know what your affair was founded on? On sorrow. You got sorry for each other. Sorrow's a lot of fun for most women and for some men, but it seems to me that a marriage ought to be based on hope.' He looked at his watch and stood up.

'I've got to meet Caroline. Remember, you're coming to the bachelor dinner day after tomorrow.'

Michael felt the moment slipping away. 'Then Caroline's personal feelings don't count with you?' he demanded fiercely.

'Caroline's tired and upset. But she has what she wants, and that's the main thing.'

'Are you referring to yourself?' demanded Michael incredulously.

'Yes.'

'May I ask how long she's wanted you?'

'About two years.' Before Michael could answer, he was gone. During the next two days Michael floated in an abyss of helplessness. The idea haunted him that he had left something undone that would sever this knot drawn tight under his eyes. He phoned Caroline, but she insisted that it was physically impossible for her to see him until the day before the wedding, for which day she granted him a tentative rendezvous. Then he went to the bachelor dinner, partly in fear of an evening alone at his hotel, partly from a feeling that by his presence at that function he was somehow nearer to Caroline, keeping her in sight.

The Ritz Bar had been prepared for the occasion by French and American banners and by a great canvas covering one wall, against which the guests were invited to concentrate their proclivities in breaking glasses.

At the first cocktail, taken at the bar, there were many slight spillings from many trembling hands, but later, with the champagne, there was a rising tide of laughter and occasional bursts of song.

Michael was surprised to find what a difference his new dinner coat, his new silk hat, his new, proud linen made in his estimate of himself; he felt less resentment towards all these people for being so rich and assured. For the first time since he had left college he felt rich and assured himself; he felt that he was part of all this, and even entered into the scheme of Johnson, the practical joker, for the appearance of the woman betrayed, now waiting tranquilly in the room across the hall.

'We don't want to go too heavy,' Johnson said, 'because I imagine Ham's had a pretty anxious day already. Did you see Fullman Oil's sixteen points off this morning?'

'Will that matter to him?' Michael asked, trying to keep the interest out of his voice.

'Naturally. He's in heavily; he's always in everything heavily. So far he's had luck; anyhow, up to a month ago.'

The glasses were filled and emptied faster now, and men were shouting at one another across the narrow table. Against the bar a group of ushers was being photographed, and the flash light surged through the room in a stifling cloud.

'Now's the time,' Johnson said. 'You're to stand by the door, remember, and we're both to try and keep her from coming in – just till we get everybody's attention.'

He went on out into the corridor, and Michael waited obediently by the door. Several minutes passed. Then Johnson reappeared with a curious expression on his face.

'There's something funny about this.'

'Isn't the girl there?'

'She's there all right, but there's another woman there, too; and it's nobody we engaged either. She wants to see Hamilton Rutherford, and she looks as if she had something on her mind.'

They went out into the hall. Planted firmly in a chair near the door sat an American girl a little the worse for liquor, but with a determined expression on her face. She looked up at them with a jerk of her head.

'Well, j'tell him?' she demanded. 'The name is Marjorie Collins, and he'll know it. I've come a long way, and I want to see him now and quick, or there's going to be more trouble than you ever saw.' She rose unsteadily to her feet.

'You go in and tell Ham,' whispered Johnson to Michael. 'Maybe he'd better get out. I'll keep her here.'

Back at the table, Michael leaned close to Rutherford's ear and, with a certain grimness, whispered:

'A girl outside named Marjorie Collins says she wants to see you. She looks as if she wanted to make trouble.'

Hamilton Rutherford blinked and his mouth fell ajar; then slowly the lips came together in a straight line and he said in a crisp voice:

'Please keep her there. And send the head barman to me right away.'

Michael spoke to the barman, and then, without returning to the table, asked quietly for his coat and hat. Out in the hall again, he passed Johnson and the girl without speaking and went out into the Rue Cambon. Calling a cab, he gave the address of Caroline's hotel.

His place was beside her now. Not to bring bad news, but simply to be with her when her house of cards came falling around her head.

Rutherford had implied that he was soft – well, he was hard enough not to give up the girl he loved without taking advantage of every chance within the pale of honour. Should she turn away from Rutherford, she would find him there.

She was in; she was surprised when he called, but she was still dressed and would be down immediately. Presently she appeared in a dinner gown, holding two blue telegrams in her hand. They sat down in armchairs in the deserted lobby.

'But, Michael, is the dinner over?'

'I wanted to see you, so I came away.'

'I'm glad.' Her voice was friendly, but matter-of-fact. 'Because I'd just phoned your hotel that I had fittings and rehearsals all day tomorrow. Now we can have our talk after all.'

'You're tired,' he guessed. 'Perhaps I shouldn't have come.'

'No. I was waiting up for Hamilton. Telegrams that may be important. He said he might go on somewhere, and that may mean any hour, so I'm glad I have someone to talk to.'

Michael winced at the impersonality in the last phrase.

'Don't you care when he gets home?'

'Naturally,' she said, laughing, 'but I haven't got much say about it, have it?'

'Why not?'

'I couldn't start by telling him what he could and couldn't do.'

'Why not?'

'He wouldn't stand for it.'

'He seems to want merely a housekeeper,' said Michael ironically.

'Tell me about your plans, Michael,' she asked quickly.

'My plans? I can't see any future after the day after tomorrow. The only real plan I ever had was to love you.'

Their eyes brushed past each other's, and the look he knew so well was staring out at him from hers. Words flowed quickly from his heart:

'Let me tell you just once more how well I've loved you, never wavering for a moment, never thinking of another girl. And now when I think of all the years ahead without you, without any hope, I don't want to live, Caroline darling. I used to dream about our home, our children, about holding you in my arms and touching your face and hands and hair that used to belong to me, and now I just can't wake up.'

Caroline was crying softly. 'Poor Michael – poor Michael.' Her hand reached out and her fingers brushed the lapel of his dinner coat. 'I was so sorry for you the other night. You looked so thin, and as if you needed a new suit and somebody to take care of you.' She sniffled and looked more closely at his coat. 'Why, you've got a new suit! And a new silk hat! Why, Michael, how swell!' She laughed, suddenly cheerful through her tears. 'You must have come into money, Michael; I never saw you so well turned out.'

For a moment, at her reaction, he hated his new clothes.

'I have come into money,' he said. 'My grandfather left me about a quarter of a million dollars.'

'Why, Michael,' she cried, 'how perfectly swell! I can't tell you how glad I am. I've always thought you were the sort of person who ought to have money.'

'Yes, just too late to make a difference.'

The revolving door from the street groaned around and Hamilton Rutherford came into the lobby. His face was flushed, his eyes were restless and impatient.

'Hello, darling; hello, Mr Curly.' He bent and kissed Caroline. 'I broke away for a minute to find out if I had any telegrams. I see you've got them there.' Taking them from her, he remarked to Curly, 'That was an odd business there in the bar, wasn't it? Especially as I understand some of you had a joke fixed up in the same line.' He opened one of the telegrams, closed it and turned to Caroline with the divided expression of a man carrying two things in his head at once.

'A girl I haven't seen for two years turned up,' he said. 'It seemed to be some clumsy form of blackmail, for I haven't and never have had any sort of obligation towards her whatever.'

'What happened?'

'The head barman had a Sûreté Générale man there in ten minutes and it was settled in the hall. The French blackmail laws make ours look like a sweet wish, and I gather they threw a scare into her that she'll remember. But it seems wiser to tell you.'

'Are you implying that I mentioned the matter?' said Michael stiffly.

'No,' Rutherford said slowly. 'No, you were just going to be on hand. And since you're here, I'll tell you some news that will interest you even more.'

He handed Michael one telegram and opened the other.

'This is in code,' Michael said.

'So is this. But I've got to know all the words pretty well this last week. The two of them together mean I'm due to start life all over.'

Michael saw Caroline's face grow a shade paler, but she sat quiet as a mouse.

'It was a mistake and I stuck to it too long,' continued Rutherford. 'So you see I don't have all the luck, Mr Curly. By the way, they tell me you've come into money.'

'Yes,' said Michael.

'There we are, then.' Rutherford turned to Caroline. 'You understand, darling, that I'm not joking or exaggerating. I've lost almost every cent I had and I'm starting life over.'

Two pairs of eyes were regarding her – Rutherford's non-committal and unrequiring, Michael's hungry, tragic, pleading. In a minute she had raised herself from the chair and with a little cry thrown herself into Hamilton Rutherford's arms.

'Oh, darling,' she cried, 'what does it matter! It's better; I like it better, honestly I do! I want to start that way; I want to! Oh, please don't worry or be sad even for a minute!'

'All right, baby,' said Rutherford. His hand stroked her hair gently for a moment; then he took his arm from around her.

'I promised to join the party for an hour,' he said. 'So I'll say good night, and I want you to go to bed soon and get a good sleep. Good night, Mr Curly. I'm sorry to have let you in for all these financial matters.'

But Michael had already picked up his hat and cane. 'I'll go along with you,' he said.

III

It was such a fine morning. Michael's cutaway hadn't been delivered, so he felt rather uncomfortable passing before the cameras and moving-picture machines in front of the little church on the Avenue Georges-Cinq.

It was such a clean, new church that it seemed unforgivable not to be dressed properly, and Michael, white and shaky after a sleepless night, decided to stand in the rear. From there he looked at the back of Hamilton Rutherford, and the lacy, filmy back of Caroline, and the fat back of George Packman, which looked unsteady, as if it wanted to lean against the bride and groom.

The ceremony went on for a long time under the gay flags and pennons overhead, under the thick beams of June sunlight slanting down through the tall windows upon the well-dressed people.

As the procession, headed by the bride and groom, started down the aisle, Michael realized with alarm he was just where everyone would dispense with the parade stiffness, become informal and speak to him.

So it turned out. Rutherford and Caroline spoke first to him; Rutherford grim with the strain of being married, and Caroline lovelier than he had ever seen her, floating all softly down through the past and forward to the future by the sunlit door.

Michael managed to murmur, 'Beautiful, simply beautiful,' and then other people passed and spoke to him – old Mrs Dandy, straight from her sickbed and looking remarkably well, or carrying it off like the very fine old lady she was; and Rutherford's father and mother, ten years divorced, but walking side by side and looking made for each other and proud. Then all Caroline's sisters and their husbands and her little nephews in Eton suits, and then a long parade, all speaking to Michael because he was still standing paralysed just at that point where the procession broke.

He wondered what would happen now. Cards had been issued for a reception at the Georges-Cinq; an expensive enough place, heaven knew. Would Rutherford try to go through with that on top of those disastrous telegrams? Evidently, for the procession outside was streaming up there through the June morning, three by three and four by four. On the corner the long dresses of girls, five abreast, fluttered many-coloured in the wind. Girls had become gossamer again, perambulatory flora; such lovely fluttering dresses in the bright noon wind.

Michael needed a drink; he couldn't face that reception line without a drink. Diving into a side doorway of the hotel, he asked for the bar, whither a *chasseur* led him through half a kilometre of new American-looking passages.

But – how did it happen? – the bar was full. There were ten – fifteen men and two – four girls, all from the wedding, all needing a drink. There were cocktails and champagne in the bar; Rutherford's cocktails and champagne, as it turned out, for he had engaged the whole bar and the ballroom and the two great reception rooms and all the stairways leading up and down, and windows looking out over the whole square block of Paris. By and by Michael went and joined the long, slow drift of the receiving line. Through a flowery mist of 'Such a lovely wedding', 'My dear, you were simply lovely', 'You're a lucky man, Rutherford' he passed down the line. When Michael came to Caroline, she took a single step forward and kissed him on the lips, but he felt no contact in the kiss; it was unreal and he floated on away from it. Old Mrs Dandy, who had always liked him, held his hand for a minute and thanked him for the flowers he had sent when he heard she was ill.

'I'm so sorry not to have written; you know, we old ladies are grateful for –' The flowers, the fact that she had not written, the wedding – Michael saw that they all had the same relative importance to her now; she had married off five other children and seen two of the marriages go to pieces, and this scene, so poignant, so confusing to Michael, appeared to her simply a familiar charade in which she had played her part before.

A buffet luncheon with champagne was already being served at small tables and there was an orchestra playing in the empty ballroom. Michael sat down with Jebby West; he was still a little embarrassed at not wearing a morning coat, but he perceived now that he was not alone in the omission and felt better. 'Wasn't Caroline divine?' Jebby West said. 'So entirely self-possessed. I asked her this morning if she wasn't a little nervous at stepping off like this. And she said, "Why should I be? I've been after him for two years, and now I'm just happy, that's all." '

'It must be true,' said Michael gloomily.

'What?'

'What you just said.'

He had been stabbed, but, rather to his distress, he did not feel the wound.

He asked Jebby to dance. Out on the floor, Rutherford's father and mother were dancing together.

'It makes me a little sad, that,' she said. 'Those two hadn't met for years; both of them were married again and she divorced again. She went to the station to meet him when he came over for Caroline's wedding, and invited him to stay at her house in the Avenue du Bois with a whole lot of other people, perfectly proper, but he was afraid his wife would hear about it and not like it, so he went to a hotel. Don't you think that's sort of sad?'

An hour or so later Michael realized suddenly that it was afternoon. In one corner of the ballroom an arrangement of screens like a moving-picture stage had been set up and photographers were taking official pictures of the bridal party. The bridal party, still as death and pale as wax under the bright lights, appeared, to the dancers circling the modulated semi-darkness of the ballroom, like those jovial or sinister groups that one comes upon in The Old Mill at an amusement park.

After the bridal party had been photographed, there was a group of the ushers; then the bridesmaids, the families, the children. Later Caroline, active and excited, having long since abandoned the repose implicit in her flowing dress and great bouquet, came and plucked Michael off the floor.

'Now we'll have them take one of just old friends.' Her voice implied that this was best, most intimate of all. 'Come here, Jebby, George – not you, Hamilton; this is just my friends – Sally –'

A little after that, what remained of formality disappeared and the hours flowed easily down the profuse stream of champagne. In the modern fashion, Hamilton Rutherford sat at the table with his arm about an old girl of his and assured his guests, which included not a few bewildered but enthusiastic Europeans, that the party was not nearly at an end; it was to reassemble at Zelli's after midnight. Michael saw Mrs Dandy, not quite over her illness, rise to go and become caught in polite group after group, and he spoke of it to one of her daughters, who thereupon forcibly abducted her mother and called her car. Michael felt very considerate and proud of himself after having done this, and drank much more champagne.

'It's amazing,' George Packman was telling him enthusiastically. 'This show will cost Ham about five thousand dollars, and I understand they'll be just about his last. But did he countermand a bottle of champagne or a flower? Not he! He happens to have it – that young man. Do you know that T. G. Vance offered him a salary of fifty thousand dollars a year ten minutes before the wedding this morning? In another year he'll be back with the millionaires.'

The conversation was interrupted by a plan to carry Rutherford out on communal shoulders – a plan which six of them put into effect, and then stood in the four-o'clock sunshine waving good-bye to the bride and groom. But there must have been a mistake somewhere, for five minutes later Michael saw both bride and groom descending the stairway to the reception, each with a glass of champagne held defiantly on high.

'This is our way of doing things,' he thought. 'Generous and fresh and free; a sort of Virginia-plantation hospitality, but at a different pace now, nervous as a ticker tape.'

Standing unselfconsciously in the middle of the room to see which was the American ambassador, he realized with a start that he hadn't really thought of Caroline for hours. He looked about him with a sort of alarm, and then he saw her across the room, very bright and young, and radiantly happy. He saw Rutherford near her, looking at her as if he could never look long enough, and as Michael watched them they seemed to recede as he had wished them to do that day in the Rue de Castiglione – recede and fade off into joys and griefs of their own, into the years that would take the toll of Rutherford's fine pride and Caroline's young, moving beauty; fade far away, so that now he could scarcely see them, as if they were shrouded in something as misty as her white, billowing dress.

Michael was cured. The ceremonial function, with its pomp and its revelry, had stood for a sort of initiation into a life where even his regret could not follow them. All the bitterness melted out of him suddenly and the world reconstituted itself out of the youth and happiness that was all around him, profligate as the spring sunshine. He was trying to remember which one of the bridesmaids he had made a date to dine with tonight as he walked forward to bid Hamilton and Caroline Rutherford good-bye.

CRAZY SUNDAY

I

It was Sunday – not a day, but rather a gap between two other days. Behind, for all of them, lay sets and sequences, the long waits under the crane that swung the microphone, the hundred miles a day by automobiles to and fro across a county, the struggles of rival ingenuities in the conference rooms, the ceaseless compromise, the clash and strain of many personalities fighting for their lives. And now Sunday, with individual life starting up again, with a glow kindling in eyes that had been glazed with monotony the afternoon before. Slowly as the hours waned they came awake like 'Puppenfeen' in a toy shop: an intense colloquy in a corner, lovers disappearing to neck in a hall. And the feeling of 'Hurry, it's not too late, but for God's sake hurry before the blessed forty hours of leisure are over.'

Joel Coles was writing continuity. He was twenty-eight and not yet broken by Hollywood. He had had what were considered nice assignments since his arrival six months before and he submitted his scenes and sequences with enthusiasm. He referred to himself modestly as a hack but really did not think of it that way. His mother had been a successful actress; Joel had spent his childhood between London and New York trying to separate the real from the unreal, or at least to keep one guess ahead. He was a handsome man with the pleasant cow-brown eyes that in 1913 had gazed out at Broadway audiences from his mother's face.

When the invitation came it made him sure that he was getting somewhere. Ordinarily he did not go out on Sundays but stayed sober and took work home with him. Recently they had given him a Eugene O'Neill play destined for a very important lady indeed. Everything he had done so far had pleased Miles Calman, and Miles Calman was the only director on the lot who did not work under a supervisor and was responsible to the money men alone. Everything was clicking into place in Joel's career. ('This is Mr Calman's secretary. Will you come to tea from four to six Sunday – he lives in Beverly Hills, number –.')

Joel was flattered. It would be a party out of the top-drawer. It was a tribute to himself as a young man of promise. The Marion Davies crowd, the high-hats, the big currency numbers, perhaps even Dietrich and Garbo and the Marquis, people who were not seen everywhere, would probably be at Calman's.

'I won't take anything to drink,' he assured himself. Calman was audibly tired of rummies, and thought it was a pity the industry could not get along without them.

Joel agreed that writers drank too much – he did himself, but he wouldn't this afternoon. He wished Miles would be within hearing when the cocktails were passed to hear his succinct, unobtrusive, 'No, thank you.'

Miles Calman's house was built for great emotional moments – there was an air of listening, as if the far silences of its vistas hid an audience, but this afternoon it was thronged, as though people had been bidden rather than asked. Joel noted with pride that only two other writers from the studio were in the crowd, an ennobled limey and, somewhat to his surprise, Nat Keogh, who had evoked Calman's impatient comment on drunks.

Stella Calman (Stella Walker, of course) did not move on to her other guests after she spoke to Joel. She lingered – she looked at him with the sort of beautiful look that demands some sort of acknowledgment and Joel drew quickly on the dramatic adequacy inherited from his mother:

'Well, you look about sixteen! Where's your kiddy car?'

She was visibly pleased; she lingered. He felt that he should say something more, something confident and easy – he had first met her when she was struggling for bits in New York. At the moment a tray slid up and Stella put a cocktail glass into his hand.

'Everybody's afraid, aren't they?' he said, looking at it absently. 'Everybody watches for everybody else's blunders, or tries to make sure they're with people that'll do them credit. Of course that's not true in your house,' he covered himself hastily. 'I just meant generally in Hollywood.'

Stella agreed. She presented several people to Joel as if he were very important. Reassuring himself that Miles was at the other side of the room, Joel drank the cocktail.

'So you have a baby?' he said. 'That's the time to look out. After a pretty woman has had her first child, she's very vulnerable, because she wants to be reassured about her own charm. She's got to have some new man's unqualified devotion to prove to herself she hasn't lost anything.'

'I never get anybody's unqualified devotion,' Stella said rather resentfully.

'They're afraid of your husband.'

'You think that's it?' She wrinkled her brow over the idea; then the conversation was interrupted at the exact moment Joel would have chosen.

Her attentions had given him confidence. Not for him to join safe groups, to slink to refuge under the wings of such acquaintances as he saw about the room. He walked to the window and looked out towards the Pacific, colourless under its sluggish sunset. It was good here – the American Riviera and all that, if there were ever time to enjoy it. The handsome, well-dressed people in the room, the lovely girls, and the – well, the lovely girls. You couldn't have everything.

He saw Stella's fresh boyish face, with the tired eyelid that always drooped a little over one eye, moving about among her guests and he wanted to sit with her and talk a long time as if she were a girl instead of a name; he followed her to see if she paid anyone as much attention as she had paid him. He took another cocktail – not because he needed confidence but because she had given him so much of it. Then he sat down beside the director's mother.

'Your son's gotten to be a legend, Mrs Calman – Oracle and a Man of Destiny and all that. Personally, I'm against him but I'm in a minority. What do you think of him? Are you impressed? Are you surprised how far he's gone?'

'No, I'm not surprised,' she said calmly. 'We always expected a lot from Miles.'

'Well now, that's unusual,' remarked Joel. 'I always think all mothers are like Napoleon's mother. My mother didn't want me to have anything to do with the entertainment business. She wanted me to go to West Point and be safe.'

'We always had every confidence in Miles.' . . .

He stood by the built-in bar of the dining-room with the good-humoured, heavy-drinking, highly paid Nat Keogh.

'– I made a hundred grand during the year and lost forty grand gambling, so now I've hired a manager.'

'You mean an agent,' suggested Joel.

'No, I've got that too. I mean a manager. I make over everything to my wife and then he and my wife get together and hand me out the money. I pay him five thousand a year to hand me out my money.'

'You mean your agent.'

'No, I mean my manager, and I'm not the only one – a lot of other irresponsible people have him.'

'Well, if you're irresponsible why are you responsible enough to hire a manager?'

'I'm just irresponsible about gambling. Look here –'

A singer performed; Joel and Nat went forward with the others to listen.

II

The singing reached Joel vaguely; he felt happy and friendly towards all the people gathered there, people of bravery and industry, superior to bourgeoisie that outdid them in ignorance and loose living, risen to a position of the highest prominence in a nation that for a decade had wanted only to be entertained. He liked them – he loved them. Great waves of good feeling flowed through him.

As the singer finished his number and there was a drift towards the hostess to say good-bye, Joel had an idea. He would give them 'Building It Up', his own composition. It was his only parlour trick, it had amused several parties and it might please Stella Walker. Possessed by the hunch, his blood throbbing with the scarlet corpuscles of exhibitionism, he sought her.

'Of course,' she cried. 'Please! Do you need anything?'

'Someone has to be the secretary that I'm supposed to be dictating to.'

'I'll be her.'

As the word spread, the guests in the hall, already putting on their coats to leave, drifted back and Joel faced the eyes of many strangers. He had a dim foreboding, realizing that the man who had just performed was a famous radio entertainer. Then someone said 'Sh!' and he was alone with Stella, the centre of a sinister Indian-like half-circle. Stella smiled up at him expectantly – he began.

His burlesque was based upon the cultural limitations of Mr Dave Silverstein, an independent producer; Silverstein was presumed to be dictating a letter outlining a treatment of a story he had bought.

'– a story of divorce, the young generators and the Foreign Legion,' he heard his voice saying, with the intonations of Mr Silverstein. 'But we got to build it up, see?'

A sharp pang of doubt struck through him. The faces surrounding him in the gently moulded light were intent and curious, but there was no ghost of a smile anywhere; directly in front the Great Lover of the screen glared at him with an eye as keen as the eye of a potato. Only Stella Walker looked up at him with a radiant, never faltering smile.

'If we make him a Menjou type, then we get a sort of Michael Arlen only with a Honolulu atmosphere.'

Still not a ripple in front, but in the rear a rustling, a perceptible shift towards the left, towards the front door.

'– then she says she feels this sex appil for him and he burns out and says, "Oh, go on destroy yourself –" '

At some point he heard Nat Keogh snicker and here and there were a few encouraging faces, but as he finished he had the sickening realization that he had made a fool of himself in view of an important section of the picture world, upon whose favour depended his career.

For a moment he existed in the midst of a confused silence, broken by a general trek for the door. He felt the undercurrent of derision that rolled through the gossip; then – all this was in the space of ten seconds – the Great Lover, his eye hard and empty as the eye of a needle, shouted 'Boo! Boo!' voicing in an overtone what he felt was the mood of the crowd. It was the resentment of the professional towards the amateur, of the community towards the stranger, the thumbs-down of the clan.

Only Stella Walker was still standing near and thanking him as if he had been an unparalleled success, as if it hadn't occurred to her that anyone hadn't liked it. As Nat Keogh helped him into his overcoat, a great wave of self-disgust swept over him and he clung desperately to his rule of never betraying an inferior emotion until he no longer felt it.

'I was a flop,' he said lightly, to Stella. 'Never mind, it's a good number when appreciated. Thanks for your cooperation.'

The smile did not leave her face – he bowed rather drunkenly and Nat drew him towards the door . . .

The arrival of his breakfast awakened him into a broken and ruined world. Yesterday he was himself, a point of fire against an industry, today he felt that he was pitted under an enormous disadvantage, against those faces, against individual contempt and collective sneer. Worse than that, to Miles Calman he was become one of those rummies, stripped of dignity, whom Calman regretted he was compelled to use. To Stella Walker on whom he had forced a martyrdom to preserve the courtesy of her house – her opinion he did not dare to guess. His gastric juices ceased to flow and he set his poached eggs back on the telephone table. He wrote:

Dear Miles: You can imagine my profound self-disgust. I confess to a taint of exhibitionism, but at six o'clock in the afternoon, in broad daylight! Good God! My apologies to your wife.

Yours ever,
Joel Coles.

Joel emerged from his office on the lot only to slink like a malefactor to the tobacco store. So suspicious was his manner that one of the studio police asked to see his admission card. He had decided to eat lunch outside when Nat Keogh, confident and cheerful, overtook him.

'What do you mean you're in permanent retirement? What if that Three-Piece Suit did boo you?

'Why listen,' he continued, drawing Joel into the studio restaurant. 'The night of one of his premières at Grauman's, Joe Squires kicked his tail while he was bowing to the crowd. The ham said Joe'd hear from him later but when Joe called him up at eight o'clock next day and said, "I thought I was going to hear from you," he hung up the phone.'

The preposterous story cheered Joel, and he found a gloomy consolation in staring at the group at the next table, the sad, lovely Siamese twins, the mean dwarfs, the proud giant from the circus picture. But looking beyond at the yellow-stained faces of pretty women, their eyes all melancholy and startling with mascara, their ball gowns garish in full day, he saw a group who had been at Calman's and winced.

'Never again,' he exclaimed aloud, 'absolutely my last social appearance in Hollywood!'

The following morning a telegram was waiting for him at his office:

You were one of the most agreeable people at our party. Expect you at my sister June's buffet supper next Sunday.

Stella Walker Calman.

The blood rushed fast through his veins for a feverish minute. Incredulously he read the telegram over.

'Well, that's the sweetest thing I ever heard of in my life!'

III

Crazy Sunday again. Joel slept until eleven, then he read a newspaper to catch up with the past week. He lunched in his room on trout, avocado salad and a pint of California wine. Dressing for the tea, he selected a pin-check suit, a blue shirt, a burnt orange tie. There were dark circles of fatigue under his eyes. In his second-hand car he drove to the Riviera apartments. As he was introducing himself to Stella's sister, Miles and Stella arrived in riding clothes – they had been quarrelling fiercely most of the afternoon on all the dirt roads back of Beverly Hills. .

Miles Calman, tall, nervous, with a desperate humour and the unhappiest eyes Joel ever saw, was an artist from the top of his curiously shaped head to his niggerish feet. Upon these last he stood firmly – he had never made a cheap picture though he had sometimes paid heavily for the luxury of making experimental flops. In spite of his excellent company, one could not be with him long without realizing that he was not a well man.

From the moment of their entrance Joel's day bound itself up inextricably with theirs. As he joined the group around them Stella turned away from it with an impatient little tongue click – and Miles Calman said to the man who happened to be next to him:

'Go easy on Eva Goebel. There's hell to pay about her at home.' Miles turned to Joel, 'I'm sorry I missed you at the office yesterday. I spent the afternoon at the analyst's.'

'You being psychoanalysed?'

'I have been for months. First I went for claustrophobia, now I'm trying to get my whole life cleared up. They say it'll take over a year.'

'There's nothing the matter with your life,' Joel assured him.

'Oh, no? Well, Stella seems to think so. Ask anybody – they can all tell you about it,' he said bitterly.

A girl perched herself on the arm of Miles's chair; Joel crossed to Stella, who stood disconsolately by the fire.

'Thank you for your telegram,' he said. 'It was darn sweet. I can't imagine anybody as good-looking as you are being so good-humoured.'

She was a little lovelier than he had ever seen her and perhaps the unstinted admiration in his eyes prompted her to unload on him – it did not take long, for she was obviously at the emotional bursting point.

'– and Miles has been carrying on this thing for two years, and I never knew. Why, she was one of my best friends, always in the house. Finally when people began to come to me, Miles had to admit it.'

She sat down vehemently on the arm of Joel's chair. Her riding breeches were the colour of the chair and Joel saw that the mass of her hair was made up of some strands of red gold and some of pale gold, so that it could not be dyed, and that she had on no make-up. She was that good-looking –

Still quivering with the shock of her discovery, Stella found unbearable the spectacle of a new girl hovering over Miles; she led Joel into a bedroom, and seated at either end of a big bed they went on talking. People on their way to the washroom glanced in and made wisecracks, but Stella, emptying out her story, paid no attention. After a while Miles stuck his head in the door and said, 'There's no use trying to explain something to Joel in half an hour that I don't understand myself and the psychoanalyst says will take a whole year to understand.'

She talked on as if Miles were not there. She loved Miles, she said – under considerable difficulties she had always been faithful to him.

'The psychoanalyst told Miles that he had a mother complex. In his first marriage he transferred his mother complex to his wife, you see – and then his sex turned to me. But when we married the thing repeated itself – he transferred his mother complex to me and all his libido turned towards this other woman.'

Joel knew that this probably wasn't gibberish – yet it sounded like gibberish. He knew Eva Goebel; she was a motherly person, older and probably wiser than Stella, who was a golden child.

Miles now suggested impatiently that Joel come back with them since Stella had so much to say, so they drove out to the mansion in Beverly Hills. Under the high ceilings the situation seemed more dignified and tragic. It was an eerie bright night with the dark very clear outside of all the windows and Stella all rose-gold raging and crying around the room. Joel did not quite believe in picture actresses' grief. They have other preoccupations – they are beautiful rose-gold figures blown full of life by writers and directors, and after hours they sit around and talk in whispers and giggle innuendoes, and the ends of many adventures flow through them.

Sometimes he pretended to listen and instead thought how well she was got up – sleek breeches with a matched set of legs in them, an Italian-coloured sweater with a little high neck, and a short brown chamois coat. He couldn't decide whether she was an imitation of an English lady or an English lady was an imitation of her. She hovered somewhere between the realest of realities and the most blatant of impersonations.

'Miles is so jealous of me that he questions everything I do,' she cried scornfully. 'When I was in New York I wrote him that I'd been to the theatre with Eddie Baker. Miles was so jealous he phoned me ten times in one day.'

'I was wild,' Miles snuffled sharply, a habit he had in times of stress. 'The analyst couldn't get any results for a week.'

Stella shook her head despairingly. 'Did you expect me just to sit in the hotel for three weeks?'

'I don't expect anything. I admit that I'm jealous. I try not to be. I worked on that with Dr Bridgebane, but it didn't do any good. I was jealous of Joel this afternoon when you sat on the arm of his chair.'

'You were?' She started up. 'You were! Wasn't there somebody on the arm of your chair? And did you speak to me for two hours?'

'You were telling your troubles to Joel in the bedroom.'

'When I think that that woman' – she seemed to believe that to omit Eva Goebel's name would be to lessen her reality – 'used to come here –'

'All right – all right,' said Miles wearily. 'I've admitted everything and I feel as bad about it as you do.' Turning to Joel he began talking about pictures, while Stella moved restlessly along the far walls, her hands in her breeches pockets.

'They've treated Miles terribly,' she said, coming suddenly back into the conversation as if they'd never discussed her personal affairs. 'Dear, tell him about old Beltzer trying to change your picture.'

As she stood hovering protectively over Miles, her eyes flashing with indignation in his behalf, Joel realized that he was in love with her. Stifled with excitement he got up to say good night.

With Monday the week resumed its workaday rhythm, in sharp contrast to the theoretical discussions, the gossip and scandal of Sunday; there was the endless detail of script revision – 'Instead of a lousy dissolve, we can leave her voice on the sound track and cut to a medium shot of the taxi from Bell's angle or we can simply pull the camera back to include the station, hold it a minute and then pan to the row of taxis' – by Monday afternoon Joel had again forgotten that people whose business was to provide entertainment were ever privileged to be entertained. In the evening he phoned Miles's house. He asked for Miles but Stella came to the phone.

'Do things seem better?'

'Not particularly. What are you doing next Saturday evening?'

'Nothing.'

'The Perrys are giving a dinner and theatre party and Miles won't be here – he's flying to South Bend to see the Notre Dame–California game. I thought you might go with me in his place.'

After a long moment Joel said, 'Why – surely. If there's a conference I can't make dinner but I can get to the theatre.'

'Then I'll say we can come.'

Joel walked to his office. In view of the strained relations of the Calmans, would Miles be pleased, or did she intend that Miles shouldn't know of it? That would be out of the question – if Miles didn't mention it Joel would. But it was an hour or more before he could get down to work again.

Wednesday there was a four-hour wrangle in a conference room crowded with planets and nebulae of cigarette smoke. Three men and a woman paced the carpet in turn, suggesting or condemning, speaking sharply or persuasively, confidently or despairingly. At the end Joel lingered to talk to Miles.

The man was tired – not with the exaltation of fatigue but life-tired, with his lids sagging and his beard prominent over the blue shadows near his mouth.

'I hear you're flying to the Notre Dame game.'

Miles looked beyond him and shook his head.

'I've given up the idea.'

'Why?'

'On account of you.' Still he did not look at Joel.

'What the hell, Miles?'

'That's why I've given it up.' He broke into a perfunctory laugh at himself. 'I can't tell what Stella might do just out of spite – she's invited you to take her to the Perrys', hasn't she? I wouldn't enjoy the game.'

The fine instinct that moved swiftly and confidently on the set muddled so weakly and helplessly through his personal life.

'Look, Miles,' Joel said frowning. 'I've never made any passes whatsoever at Stella. If you're really seriously cancelling your trip on account of me, I won't go to the Perrys' with her. I won't see her. You can trust me absolutely.'

Miles looked at him, carefully now.

'Maybe.' He shrugged his shoulders. 'Anyhow there'd just be somebody else. I wouldn't have any fun.'

'You don't seem to have much confidence in Stella. She told me she'd always been true to you.'

'Maybe she has.' In the last few minutes several more muscles had sagged around Miles's mouth. 'But how can I ask anything of her after what's happened? How can I expect her –' He broke off and his face grew harder as he said, 'I'll tell you one thing, right or wrong and no matter what I've done, if I ever had anything on her I'd divorce her. I can't have my pride hurt – that would be the last straw.'

His tone annoyed Joel, but he said:

'Hasn't she calmed down about the Eva Goebel thing?'

'No.' Miles snuffled pessimistically. 'I can't get over it either.'

'I thought it was finished.'

'I'm trying not to see Eva again, but you know it isn't easy just to drop something like that – it isn't some girl I kissed last night in a taxi. The psychoanalyst says –'

'I know,' Joel interrupted. 'Stella told me.' This was depressing. 'Well, as far as I'm concerned if you go to the game I won't see Stella. And I'm sure Stella has nothing on her conscience about anybody.'

'Maybe not,' Miles repeated listlessly. 'Anyhow I'll stay and take her to the party. Say,' he said suddenly, 'I wish you'd come too. I've got to have somebody sympathetic to talk to. That's the trouble – I've influenced Stella in everything. Especially I've influenced her so that she likes all the men I like – it's very difficult.'

'It must be,' Joel agreed.

IV

Joel could not get to the dinner. Self-conscious in his silk hat against the unemployment, he waited for the others in front of the Hollywood Theatre and watched the evening parade: obscure replicas of bright, particular picture stars, spavined men in polo coats, a stomping dervish with the beard and staff of an apostle, a pair of chic Filipinos in collegiate clothes, reminder that this corner of the Republic opened to the seven seas, a long fantastic carnival of young shouts which proved to be a fraternity initiation. The line split to pass two smart limousines that stopped at the kerb.

There she was, in a dress like ice-water, made in a thousand pale-blue pieces, with icicles trickling at the throat. He started forward.

'So you like my dress?'

'Where's Miles?'

'He flew to the game after all. He left yesterday morning – at least I think –' She broke off. 'I just got a telegram from South Bend saying that he's starting back. I forgot – you know all these people?'

The party of eight moved into the theatre.

Miles had gone after all and Joel wondered if he should have come. But during the performance, with Stella a profile under the pure grain of light hair, he thought no more about Miles. Once he turned and looked at her and she looked back at him, smiling and meeting his eyes for as long as he wanted. Between the acts they smoked in the lobby and she whispered:

'They're all going to the opening of Jack Johnson's night club – I don't want to go, do you?'

'Do we have to?'

'I suppose not.' She hesitated. 'I'd like to talk to you. I suppose we could go to our house – if I were only sure –'

Again she hesitated and Joel asked:

'Sure of what?'

'Sure that – oh, I'm haywire I know, but how can I be sure Miles went to the game?'

'You mean you think he's with Eva Goebel?'

'No, not so much that – but supposing he was here watching everything I do. You know Miles does odd things sometimes. Once he wanted a man with a long beard to drink tea with him and he sent down to the casting agency for one, and drank tea with him all afternoon.'

'That's different. He sent you a wire from South Bend – that proves he's at the game.'

After the play they said good night to the others at the kerb and were answered by looks of amusement. They slid off along the golden garish thoroughfare through the crowd that had gathered around Stella.

'You see he could arrange the telegrams,' Stella said, 'very easily.'

That was true. And with the idea that perhaps her uneasiness was justified, Joel grew angry: if Miles had trained a camera on them he felt no obligations towards Miles. Aloud he said:

'That's nonsense.'

There were Christmas trees already in the shop windows and the full moon over the boulevard was only a prop, as scenic as the giant boudoir lamps of the corners. On into the dark foliage of Beverly Hills that flamed as eucalyptus by day, Joel saw only the flash of a white face under his own, the arc of her shoulder. She pulled away suddenly and looked up at him.

'Your eyes are like your mother's,' she said. 'I used to have a scrap book full of pictures of her.'

'Your eyes are like your own and not a bit like any other eyes,' he answered.

Something made Joel look out into the grounds as they went into the house, as if Miles were lurking in the shubbery. A telegram waited on the hall table. She read aloud:

Chicago.

'Home tomorrow night. Thinking of you. Love.

Miles.'

'You see,' she said, throwing the slip back on the table, 'he could easily have faked that.' She asked the butler for drinks and sandwiches and ran upstairs, while Joel walked into the empty reception rooms. Strolling about he wandered to the piano where he had stood in disgrace two Sundays before.

'Then we could put over,' he said aloud, 'a story of divorce, the younger generation and the Foreign Legion.'

His thoughts jumped to another telegram.

'You were one of the most agreeable people at our party –'

An idea occurred to him. If Stella's telegram had been purely a gesture of courtesy then it was likely that Miles had inspired it, for it was Miles who had invited him. Probably Miles had said:

'Send him a wire – he's miserable – he thinks he's queered himself.'

It fitted in with 'I've influenced Stella in everything. Especially I've influenced her so that she likes all the men I like.' A woman would do a thing like that because she felt sympathetic – only a man would do it because he felt responsible.

When Stella came back into the room he took both her hands. 'I have a strange feeling that I'm a sort of pawn in a spite game you're playing against Miles,' he said.

'Help yourself to a drink.'

'And the odd thing is that I'm in love with you anyhow.'

The telephone rang and she freed herself to answer it.

'Another wire from Miles,' she announced. 'He dropped it, or it says he dropped it, from the aeroplane at Kansas City.'

'I suppose he asked to be remembered to me.'

'No, he just said he loved me. I believe he does. He's so very weak.'

'Come sit beside me,' Joel urged her.

It was early. And it was still a few minutes short of midnight a half-hour later, when Joel walked to the cold hearth, and said tersely:

'Meaning that you haven't any curiosity about me?'

'Not at all. You attract me a lot and you know it. The point is that I suppose I really do love Miles.'

'Obviously.'

'And tonight I feel uneasy about everything.'

He wasn't angry – he was even faintly relieved that a possible entanglement was avoided. Still as he looked at her, the warmth and softness of her body thawing her cold blue costume, he knew she was one of the things he would always regret.

'I've got to go,' he said. 'I'll phone a taxi.'

'Nonsense – there's a chauffeur on duty.'

He winced at her readiness to have him go, and seeing this she kissed him lightly and said, 'You're sweet, Joel.' Then suddenly three things happened: he took down his drink at a gulp, the phone rang loud through the house and a clock in the hall struck in trumpet notes.

Nine – ten – eleven – twelve –

V

It was Sunday again. Joel realized that he had come to the theatre this evening with the work of the week still hanging about him like cerements. He had made love to Stella as he might attack some matter to be cleaned up hurriedly before the day's end. But this was Sunday – the lovely, lazy perspective of the next twenty-four hours unrolled before him – every minute was something to be approached with lulling indirection, every moment held the germ of innumerable possibilities. Nothing was impossible – everything was just beginning. He poured himself another drink.

With a sharp moan, Stella slipped forward inertly by the telephone. Joel picked her up and laid her on the sofa. He squirted soda-water on a handkerchief and slapped it over her face. The telephone mouthpiece was still grinding and he put it to his ear.

'– the plane fell just this side of Kansas City. The body of Miles Calman has been identified and –'

He hung up the receiver.

'Lie still,' he said, stalling, as Stella opened her eyes. 'Oh, what's happened?' she whispered. 'Call them back. Oh, what's happened?'

'I'll call them right away. What's your doctor's name?'

'Did they say Miles was dead?'

'Lie quiet – is there a servant still up?'

'Hold me – I'm frightened.'

He put his arm around her.

'I want the name of your doctor,' he said sternly. 'It may be a mistake but I want someone here.'

'It's Doctor – Oh, God, is Miles dead?'

Joel ran upstairs and searched through strange medicine cabinets for spirits of ammonia. When he came down Stella cried:

'He isn't dead – I know he isn't. This is part of his scheme. He's torturing me. I know he's alive. I can feel he's alive.'

'I want to get hold of some close friend of yours, Stella. You can't stay here alone tonight.'

'Oh, no,' she cried. 'I can't see anybody. You stay, I haven't got any friend.' She got up, tears streaming down her face. 'Oh, Miles is my only friend. He's not dead – he can't be dead. I'm going there right away and see. Get a train. You'll have to come with me.'

'You can't. There's nothing to do tonight. I want you to tell me the name of some woman I can call: Lois? Joan? Carmel? Isn't there somebody?'

Stella stared at him blindly.

'Eva Goebel was my best friend,' she said.

Joel thought of Miles, his sad and desperate face in the office two days before. In the awful silence of his death all was clear about him. He was the only American-born director with both an interesting temperament and an artistic conscience. Meshed in an industry, he had paid with his ruined nerves for having no resilience, no healthy cynicism, no refuge – only a pitiful and precarious escape.

There was a sound at the outer door – it opened suddenly, and there were footsteps in the hall.

'Miles!' Stella screamed. 'Is it you, Miles? Oh, it's Miles.'

A telegraph boy appeared in the doorway.

'I couldn't find the bell. I heard you talking inside.'

The telegram was a duplicate of the one that had been phoned. While Stella read it over and over, as though it were a black lie, Joel telephoned. It was still early and he had difficulty getting anyone; when finally he succeeded in finding some friends he made Stella take a stiff drink.

'You'll stay here, Joel,' she whispered, as though she were half-asleep. 'You won't go away. Miles liked you – he said you –' She shivered violently, 'Oh, my God, you don't know how alone I feel!' Her eyes closed. 'Put your arms around me. Miles had a suit like that.' She started bolt upright. 'Think of what he must have felt. He was afraid of almost everything, anyhow.'

She shook her head dazedly. Suddenly she seized Joel's face and held it close to hers.

'You won't go. You like me – you love me, don't you? Don't call up anybody. Tomorrow's time enough. You stay here with me tonight.'

He stared at her, at first incredulously, and then with shocked understanding. In her dark groping Stella was trying to keep Miles alive by sustaining a situation in which he had figured – as if Miles's mind could not die so long as the possibilities that had worried him still existed. It was a distraught and tortured effort to stave off the realization that he was dead.

Resolutely Joel went to the phone and called a doctor.

'Don't, oh, don't call anybody!' Stella cried. 'Come back here and put your arms around me.'

'Is Doctor Bales in?'

'Joel,' Stella cried. 'I thought I could count on you. Miles liked you. He was jealous of you – Joel, come here.'

Ah then – if he betrayed Miles she would be keeping him alive – for if he were really dead how could he be betrayed?

'– has just had a very severe shock. Can you come at once, and get hold of a nurse?'

'Joel!'

Now the door-bell and the telephone began to ring intermittently, and automobiles were stopping in front of the door.

'But you're not going,' Stella begged him. 'You're going to stay, aren't you?'

'No,' he answered. 'But I'll be back, if you need me.'

Standing on the steps of the house which now hummed and palpitated with the life that flutters around death like protective leaves, he began to sob a little in his throat.

'Everything he touched he did something magical to,' he thought. 'He even brought that little gamine alive and made her a sort of masterpiece.'

And then:

'What a hell of a hole he leaves in this damn wilderness – already!'

And then with a certain bitterness, 'Oh, yes, I'll be back – I'll be back!'

THREE HOURS
BETWEEN PLANES

It was a wild chance but Donald was in the mood, healthy and bored, with a sense of tiresome duty done. He was now rewarding himself. Maybe.

When the plane landed he stepped out into a mid-western summer night and headed for the isolated pueblo airport, conventionalized as an old red 'railway depot'. He did not know whether she was alive, or living in this town, or what was her present name. With mounting excitement he looked through the phone book for her father who might be dead too, somewhere in these twenty years.

No. Judge Harmon Holmes – Hillside 3194.

A woman's amused voice answered his inquiry for Miss Nancy Holmes. 'Nancy is Mrs Walter Gifford now. Who is this?'

But Donald hung up without answering. He had found out what he wanted to know and had only three hours. He did not remember any Walter Gifford and there was another suspended moment while he scanned the phone book. She might have married out of town.

No. Walter Gifford – Hillside 1191. Blood flowed back into his fingertips.

'Hello?'

'Hello. Is Mrs Gifford there – this is an old friend of hers.'

'This is Mrs Gifford.'

He remembered, or thought he remembered, the funny magic in the voice.

'This is Donald Plant. I haven't seen you since I was twelve years old.'

'Oh-h-h!' The note was utterly surprised, very polite, but he could distinguish in it neither joy nor certain recognition.

'– *Don*ald!' added the voice. This time there was something more in it than struggling memory.

'. . . when did you come back to town?' Then cordially, 'Where *are* you?'

'I'm out at the airport – for just a few hours.'

'Well, come up and see me.'

'Sure you're not just going to bed?'

'Heavens, no!' she exclaimed. 'I was sitting here – having a highball by myself. Just tell your taxi man . . .'

On his way Donald analysed the conversation. His words 'at the airport' established that he had retained his position in the upper bourgeoisie. Nancy's aloneness might indicate that she had matured into an unattractive woman without friends. Her husband might be either away or in bed. And – because she was always ten years old in his dreams – the highball shocked him. But he adjusted himself with a smile – she was very close to thirty.

At the end of a curved drive he saw a dark-haired little beauty standing against the lighted door, a glass in her hand. Startled by her final materialization, Donald got out of the cab, saying:

'Mrs Gifford?'

She turned on the porch light and stared at him, wide-eyed and tentative. A smile broke through the puzzled expression.

'Donald – it is you – we all change so. Oh, this is remarkable!'

As they walked inside, their voices jingled the words 'all these years', and Donald felt a sinking in his stomach. This derived in part from a vision of their last meeting – when she rode past him on a bicycle, cutting him dead – and in part from fear lest they have nothing to say. It was like a college reunion – but there the failure to find the past was disguised by the hurried boisterous occasion. Aghast, he realized that this might be a long and empty hour. He plunged in desperately.

'You always were a lovely person. But I'm a little shocked to find you as beautiful as you are.'

It worked. The immediate recognition of their changed state, the bold compliment, made them interesting strangers instead of fumbling childhood friends.

'Have a highball?' she asked. 'No? Please don't think I've become a secret drinker, but this was a blue night. I expected my husband but he wired he'd be two days longer. He's very nice, Donald, and very attract-ive. Rather your type and colouring.' She hesitated, '– and I think he's interested in someone in New York – and I don't know.'

'After seeing you it sounds impossible,' he assured her. 'I was married for six years, and there was a time I tortured myself that way. Then one day I just put jealousy out of my life forever. After my wife died I was very glad of that. It left a very rich memory – nothing marred or spoiled or hard to think over.'

She looked at him attentively, then sympathetically as he spoke.

'I'm very sorry,' she said. And after a proper moment, 'You've changed a lot. Turn your head. I remember father saying, "That boy has a brain." '

'You probably argued against it.'

'I was impressed. Up to then I thought everybody had a brain. That's why it sticks in my mind.'

'What else sticks in your mind?' he asked smiling.

Suddenly Nancy got up and walked quickly a little away.

'Ah, now,' she reproached him. 'That isn't fair! I suppose I was a naughty girl.'

'You were not,' he said stoutly. 'And I *will* have a drink now.'

As she poured it, her face still turned from him, he continued:

'Do you think you were the only little girl who was ever kissed?'

'Do you like the subject?' she demanded. Her momentary irritation melted and she said: 'What the hell! We *did* have fun. Like in the song.'

'On the sleigh ride.'

'Yes – and somebody's picnic – Trudy James's. And at Frontenac that – those summers.'

It was the sleigh ride he remembered most and kissing her cool cheeks in the straw in one corner while she laughed up at the cold white stars. The couple next to them had their backs turned and he kissed her little neck and her ears and never her lips.

'And the Macks' party where they played post office and I couldn't go because I had the mumps,' he said.

'I don't remember that.'

'Oh, you were there. And you were kissed and I was crazy with jealousy like I never have been since.'

'Funny I don't remember. Maybe I wanted to forget.'

'But why?' he asked in amusement. 'We were two perfectly innocent kids. Nancy, whenever I talked to my wife about the past, I told her you were the girl I loved almost as much as I loved her. But I think I really loved you just as much. When we moved out of town I carried you like a cannon ball in my insides.'

'Were you *that* much – stirred up?'

'My God, yes! I –' He suddenly realized that they were standing just two feet from each other, that he was talking as if he loved her in the present, that she was looking up at him with her lips half-parted and a clouded look in her eyes.

'Go on,' she said, 'I'm ashamed to say – I like it. I didn't know you were so upset *then*. I thought it was *me* who was upset.'

'You!' he exclaimed. 'Don't you remember throwing me over at the drugstore.' He laughed. 'You stuck out your tongue at me.'

'I don't remember at all. It seemed to me you did the throwing over.' Her hand fell lightly, almost consolingly on his arm. 'I've got a photograph book upstairs I haven't looked at for years. I'll dig it out.'

Donald sat for five minutes with two thoughts – first the hopeless impossibility of reconciling what different people remembered about the same event – and secondly that in a frightening way Nancy moved him as a woman as she had moved him as a child. Half an hour had developed an emotion that he had not known since the death of his wife – that he had never hoped to know again.

Side by side on a couch they opened the book between them. Nancy looked at him, smiling and very happy.

'Oh, this is *such* fun,' she said. 'Such fun that you're so nice, that you remember me so – beautifully. Let me tell you – I wish I'd known it then! After you'd gone I hated you.'

'What a pity,' he said gently.

'But not now,' she reassured him, and then impulsively, 'Kiss and make up –'

'. . . that isn't being a good wife,' she said after a minute. 'I really don't think I've kissed two men since I was married.'

He was excited – but most of all confused. Had he kissed Nancy? or a memory? or this lovely trembly stranger who looked away from him quickly and turned a page of the book?

'Wait!' he said. 'I don't think I could *see* a picture for a few seconds.'

'We won't do it again. I don't feel so very calm myself.'

Donald said one of those trivial things that cover so much ground.

'Wouldn't it be awful if we fell in love again?'

'Stop it!' She laughed, but very breathlessly. 'It's all over. It was a moment. A moment I'll have to forget.'

'Don't tell your husband.'

'Why not? Usually I tell him everything.'

'It'll hurt him. Don't ever tell a man such things.'

'All right I won't.'

'Kiss me once more,' he said inconsistently, but Nancy had turned a page and was pointing eagerly at a picture.

'Here's you,' she cried. 'Right away!'

He looked. It was a little boy in shorts standing on a pier with a sailboat in the background.

'I remember –' she laughed triumphantly, '– the very day it was taken. Kitty took it and I stole it from her.'

For a moment Donald failed to recognize himself in the photo – then, bending closer – he failed utterly to recognize himself.

'That's not me,' he said.

'Oh yes. It was at Frontenac – the summer we – we used to go to the cave.'

'What cave? I was only three days in Frontenac.' Again he strained his eyes at the slightly yellowed picture. 'And that isn't me. That's Donald Bowers. We did look rather alike.'

Now she was staring at him – leaning back, seeming to lift away from him.

'But you're Donald Bowers!' she exclaimed; her voice rose a little. 'No, you're not. You're Donald *Plant*.'

'I told you on the phone.'

She was on her feet – her face faintly horrified.

'Plant! Bowers! I must be crazy. Or it was that drink? I was mixed up a little when I first saw you. Look here! What have I told you?'

He tried for a monkish calm as he turned a page of the book.

'Nothing at all,' he said. Pictures that did not include him formed and re-formed before his eyes – Frontenac – a cave – Donald Bowers – 'You threw *me* over!'

Nancy spoke from the other side of the room.

'You'll never tell this story,' she said. 'Stories have a way of getting around.'

'There isn't any story,' he hesitated. But he thought: So she was a bad little girl.

And now suddenly he was filled with wild raging jealousy of little Donald Bowers – he who had banished jealousy from his life forever. In the five steps he took across the room he crushed out twenty years and the existence of Walter Gifford with his stride.

'Kiss me again, Nancy,' he said, sinking to one knee beside her chair, putting his hand upon her shoulder. But Nancy strained away.

'You said you had to catch a plane.'

'It's nothing. I can miss it. It's of no importance.'

'Please go,' she said in a cool voice. 'And please try to imagine how I feel.'

'But you act as if you don't remember me,' he cried, '– as if you don't remember Donald *Plant*!'

'I do. I remember you too . . . But it was all so long ago.' Her voice grew hard again. 'The taxi number is Crestwood 8484.'

On his way to the airport Donald shook his head from side to side. He was completely himself now but he could not digest the experience. Only as the plane roared up into the dark sky and its passengers became a different entity from the corporate world below did he draw a parallel from the fact of its flight. For five blinding minutes he had lived like a madman in two worlds at once. He had been a boy of twelve and a man of thirty-two, indissolubly and helplessly commingled.

Donald had lost a good deal, too, in those hours between the planes – but since the second half of life is a long process of getting rid of things, that part of the experience probably didn't matter.

THE LOST DECADE

All sorts of people came into the offices of the newsweekly and Orrison Brown had all sorts of relations with them. Outside of office hours he was 'one of the editors' – during work time he was simply a curly-haired man who a year before had edited the Dartmouth *Jack-O-Lantern* and was now only too glad to take the undesirable assignments around the office, from straightening out illegible copy to playing call boy without the title.

He had seen this visitor go into the editor's office – a pale, tall man of forty with blond statuesque hair and a manner that was neither shy nor timid, nor otherworldly like a monk, but something of all three. The name on his card, Louis Trimble, evoked some vague memory, but having nothing to start on, Orrison did not puzzle over it – until a buzzer sounded on his desk, and previous experience warned him that Mr Trimble was to be his first course at lunch.

'Mr Trimble – Mr Brown,' said the Source of all luncheon money. 'Orrison – Mr Trimble's been away a long time. Or he *feels* it's a long time – almost twelve years. Some people would consider themselves lucky to've missed the last decade.'

'That's so,' said Orrison.

'I can't lunch today,' continued his chief. 'Take him to Voisin or 21 or anywhere he'd like. Mr Trimble feels there're lots of things he hasn't seen.'

Trimble demurred politely.

'Oh, I can get around.'

'I know it, old boy. Nobody knew this place like you did once – and if Brown tries to explain the horseless carriage just send him back here to me. And you'll be back yourself by four, won't you?'

Orrison got his hat.

'You've been away ten years?' he asked while they went down in the elevator.

'They'd begun the Empire State Building,' said Trimble. 'What does that add up to?'

'About 1928. But as the chief said, you've been lucky to miss a lot.' As a feeler he added, 'Probably had more interesting things to look at.'

'Can't say I have.'

They reached the street and the way Trimble's face tightened at the roar of traffic made Orrison take one more guess.

'You've been out of civilization?'

'In a sense.' The words were spoken in such a measured way that Orrison concluded this man wouldn't talk unless he wanted to – and simultaneously wondered if he could have possibly spent the thirties in a prison or an insane asylum.

'This is the famous 21,' he said. 'Do you think you'd rather eat somewhere else?'

Trimble paused, looking carefully at the brownstone house.

'I can remember when the name 21 got to be famous,' he said, 'about the same year as Moriarty's.' Then he continued almost apologetically, 'I thought we might walk up Fifth Avenue about five minutes and eat wherever we happened to be. Some place with young people to look at.'

Orrison gave him a quick glance and once again thought of bars and grey walls and bars; he wondered if his duties included introducing Mr Trimble to complaisant girls. But Mr Trimble didn't look as if that was in his mind – the dominant expression was of absolute and deep-seated curiosity and Orrison attempted to connect the name with Admiral Byrd's hideout at the South Pole or flyers lost in Brazilian jungles. He was, or he had been, quite a fellow – that was obvious. But the only definite clue to his environment – and to Orrison the clue that led nowhere – was his countryman's obedience to the traffic lights and his predilection for walking on the side next to the shops and not the street. Once he stopped and gazed into a haberdasher's window.

'Crêpe ties,' he said. 'I haven't seen one since I left college.'

'Where'd you go?'

'Massachusetts Tech.'

'Great place.'

'I'm going to take a look at it next week. Let's eat somewhere along here –' They were in the upper Fifties '– you choose.'

There was a good restaurant with a little awning just around the corner.

'What do you want to see most?' Orrison asked, as they sat down.

Trimble considered.

'Well – the back of people's heads,' he suggested. 'Their necks – how their heads are joined to their bodies. I'd like to hear what those two little girls are saying to their father. Not exactly what they're saying but whether the words float or submerge, how their mouths shut when they've finished speaking. Just a matter of rhythm – Cole Porter came back to the States in 1928 because he felt that there were new rhythms around.'

Orrison was sure he had his clue now, and with nice delicacy did not pursue it by a millimetre – even suppressing a sudden desire to say there was a fine concert in Carnegie Hall tonight.

'The weight of spoons,' said Trimble, 'so light. A little bowl with a stick attached. The cast in that waiter's eye. I knew him once but he wouldn't remember me.'

But as they left the restaurant the same waiter looked at Trimble rather puzzled as if he almost knew him. When they were outside Orrison laughed:

'After ten years people will forget.'

'Oh, I had dinner there last May –' He broke off in an abrupt manner.

It was all kind of nutsy, Orrison decided – and changed himself suddenly into a guide.

'From here you get a good candid focus on Rockefeller Centre,' he pointed out with spirit '– and the Chrysler Building and the Armistead Building, the daddy of all the new ones.'

'The Armistead Building,' Trimble rubber-necked obediently. 'Yes – I designed it.'

Orrison shook his head cheerfully – he was used to going out with all kinds of people. But that stuff about having been in the restaurant last May . . .

He paused by the brass entablature in the cornerstone of the building. 'Erected 1928,' it said.

Trimble nodded.

'But I was taken drunk that year – every-which-way drunk. So I never saw it before now.'

'Oh.' Orrison hesitated. 'Like to go in now?'

'I've been in it – lots of times. But I've never seen it. And now it isn't what I want to see. I wouldn't ever be able to see it now. I simply want to see how people walk and what their clothes and shoes and hats are made of. And their eyes and hands. Would you mind shaking hands with me?'

'Not at all, sir.'

'Thanks. Thanks. That's very kind. I suppose it looks strange – but people will think we're saying good-bye. I'm going to walk up the avenue for a while, so we *will* say good-bye. Tell your office I'll be in at four.'

Orrison looked after him when he started out, half expecting him to turn into a bar. But there was nothing about him that suggested or ever had suggested drink.

'Jesus!' he said to himself. 'Drunk for ten years.'

He felt suddenly of the texture of his own coat and then he reached out and pressed his thumb against the granite of the building by his side.

MORE ABOUT PENGUINS, PELICANS
AND PUFFINS

For further information about books available from Penguins please write to Dept EP, Penguin Books Ltd, Harmondsworth, Middlesex UB7 0DA.

In the U.S.A.: For a complete list of books available from Penguins in the United States write to Dept DG, Penguin Books, 299 Murray Hill Parkway, East Rutherford, New Jersey 07073.

In Canada: For a complete list of books available from Penguins in Canada write to Penguin Books Canada Limited, 2801 John Street, Markham, Ontario L3R 1B4.

In Australia: For a complete list of books available from Penguins in Australia write to the Marketing Department, Penguin Books Australia Ltd, P.O. Box 257, Ringwood, Victoria 3134.

In New Zealand: For a complete list of books available from Penguins in New Zealand write to the Marketing Department, Penguin Books (N.Z.) Ltd, Private Bag, Takapuna, Auckland 9.

In India: For a complete list of books available from Penguins in India write to Penguin Overseas Ltd, 706 Eros Apartments, 56 Nehru Place, New Delhi 110019.

F. SCOTT FITZGERALD IN PENGUINS

THIS SIDE OF PARADISE

In a series of brilliant literary cameos on the adolescence and youth of Amory Blaine, Scott Fitzgerald was to define the Jazz Age for a whole generation of readers.

TENDER IS THE NIGHT

Fitzgerald's most complete novel; a penetrating indictment of the twenties.

THE LAST TYCOON

His unfinished novel is a description of the Hollywood of the 1930s.

THE GREAT GATSBY

The story of a mysterious and magnetic figure, the Great Gatsby, duped by his own fanatic illusion of unrequited yet discarded love.

THE BEAUTIFUL AND THE DAMNED

Scott Fitzgerald's novel about two people 'damned' because of their dedication to false ideals.

Scott Fitzgerald's short stories are also published in five individual volumes by Penguins, as well as *Bits of Paradise*, a collection of short pieces by Scott and Zelda Fitzgerald.

AND

THE LETTERS OF F. SCOTT FITZGERALD.

PENGUIN OMNIBUSES

☐ *Life with Jeeves* **P. G. Wodehouse**   £3.95

Containing *Right Ho, Jeeves, The Inimitable Jeeves* and *Very Good, Jeeves!* in which Wodehouse lures us, once again, into the evergreen world of Bertie Wooster, his terrifying Aunt Agatha, his man Jeeves and other eggs, good and bad.

☐ *The Penguin Book of Ghost Stories*   £4.95

An anthology to set the spine tingling, including stories by Zola, Kleist, Sir Walter Scott, M. R. James, Elizabeth Bowen and A. S. Byatt.

☐ *The Penguin Book of Horror Stories*   £4.95

Including stories by Maupassant, Poe, Gautier, Conan Doyle, L. P. Hartley and Ray Bradbury, in a selection of the most horrifying horror from the eighteenth century to the present day.

☐ *The Penguin Complete Novels of Jane Austen*   £5.95

Containing the seven great novels: *Sense and Sensibility, Pride and Prejudice, Mansfield Park, Emma, Northanger Abbey, Persuasion* and *Lady Susan*.

☐ *Perfick, Perfick!* **H. E. Bates**   £4.95

The adventures of the irrepressible Larkin family, in four novels: *The Darling Buds of May, A Breath of French Air, When the Green Woods Laugh* and *Oh! To Be in England*.

☐ *Famous Trials*
   Harry Hodge and James H. Hodge   £3.95

From Madeleine Smith to Dr Crippen and Lord Haw-Haw, this volume contains the most sensational murder and treason trials, selected by John Mortimer from the classic Penguin Famous Trials series.

A CHOICE OF PENGUINS

☐ *Small World* **David Lodge** £2.50

A jet-propelled academic romance, sequel to *Changing Places*. 'A new comic débâcle on every page' – *The Times*. 'Here is everything one expects from Lodge but three times as entertaining as anything he has written before' – *Sunday Telegraph*

☐ *The Neverending Story* **Michael Ende** £3.95

The international bestseller, now a major film: 'A tale of magical adventure, pursuit and delay, danger, suspense, triumph' – *The Times Literary Supplement*

☐ *The Sword of Honour Trilogy* **Evelyn Waugh** £3.95

Containing *Men at Arms, Officers and Gentlemen* and *Unconditional Surrender*, the trilogy described by Cyril Connolly as 'unquestionably the finest novels to have come out of the war'.

☐ *The Honorary Consul* **Graham Greene** £2.50

In a provincial Argentinian town, a group of revolutionaries kidnap the wrong man . . . 'The tension never relaxes and one reads hungrily from page to page, dreading the moment it will all end' – Auberon Waugh in the *Evening Standard*

☐ *The First Rumpole Omnibus* **John Mortimer** £4.95

Containing *Rumpole of the Bailey*, *The Trials of Rumpole* and *Rumpole's Return*. 'A fruity, foxy masterpiece, defender of our wilting faith in mankind' – *Sunday Times*

☐ *Scandal* **A. N. Wilson** £2.25

Sexual peccadillos, treason and blackmail are all ingredients on the boil in A. N. Wilson's new, *cordon noir* comedy. 'Drily witty, deliciously nasty' – *Sunday Telegraph*

A CHOICE OF PENGUINS

☐ *Stanley and the Women* **Kingsley Amis** £2.50

'Very good, very powerful . . . beautifully written . . . This is Amis *père* at his best' – Anthony Burgess in the *Observer*. 'Everybody should read it' – *Daily Mail*

☐ *The Mysterious Mr Ripley* **Patricia Highsmith** £4.95

Containing *The Talented Mr Ripley, Ripley Underground* and *Ripley's Game.* 'Patricia Highsmith is the poet of apprehension' – Graham Greene. 'The Ripley books are marvellously, insanely readable' – *The Times*

☐ *Earthly Powers* **Anthony Burgess** £4.95

'Crowded, crammed, bursting with manic erudition, garlicky puns, omnilingual jokes . . . (a novel) which meshes the real and personalized history of the twentieth century' – Martin Amis

☐ *Life & Times of Michael K* **J. M. Coetzee** £2.95

The Booker Prize-winning novel: 'It is hard to convey . . . just what Coetzee's special quality is. His writing gives off whiffs of Conrad, of Nabokov, of Golding, of the Paul Theroux of *The Mosquito Coast*. But he is none of these, he is a harsh, compelling new voice' – Victoria Glendinning

☐ *The Stories of William Trevor* £5.95

'Trevor packs into each separate five or six thousand words more richness, more laughter, more ache, more multifarious human-ness than many good writers manage to get into a whole novel' – *Punch*

☐ *The Book of Laughter and Forgetting*
Milan Kundera £3.95

'A whirling dance of a book . . . a masterpiece full of angels, terror, ostriches and love . . . No question about it. The most important novel published in Britain this year' – Salman Rushdie

A CHOICE OF PENGUINS

☐ *Further Chronicles of Fairacre* 'Miss Read' £3.95

Full of humour, warmth and charm, these four novels – *Miss Clare Remembers, Over the Gate, The Fairacre Festival* and *Emily Davis* – make up an unforgettable picture of English village life.

☐ *Callanish* **William Horwood** £1.95

From the acclaimed author of *Duncton Wood*, this is the haunting story of Creggan, the captured golden eagle, and his struggle to be free.

☐ *Act of Darkness* **Francis King** £2.50

Anglo-India in the 1930s, where a peculiarly vicious murder triggers 'A terrific mystery story . . . a darkly luminous parable about innocence and evil' – *The New York Times*. 'Brilliantly successful' – *Daily Mail*. 'Unputdownable' – *Standard*

☐ *Death in Cyprus* **M. M. Kaye** £1.95

Holidaying on Aphrodite's beautiful island, Amanda finds herself caught up in a murder mystery in which no one, not even the attractive painter Steven Howard, is quite what they seem . . .

☐ *Lace* **Shirley Conran** £2.95

Lace is, quite simply, a publishing sensation: the story of Judy, Kate, Pagan and Maxine; the bestselling novel that teaches men about women, and women about themselves. 'Riches, bitches, sex and jetsetters' locations – they're all there' – *Sunday Express*

A CHOICE OF PENGUINS

☐ **West of Sunset** Dirk Bogarde £1.95

'His virtues as a writer are precisely those which make him the most compelling screen actor of his generation,' is what *The Times* said about Bogarde's savage, funny, romantic novel set in the gaudy wastes of Los Angeles.

☐ **The Riverside Villas Murder** Kingsley Amis £1.95

Marital duplicity, sexual discovery and murder with a thirties backcloth: 'Amis in top form' – *The Times*. 'Delectable from page to page . . . effortlessly witty' – C. P. Snow in the *Financial Times*

☐ **A Dark and Distant Shore** Reay Tannahill £3.95

Vilia is the unforgettable heroine, Kinveil Castle is her destiny, in this full-blooded saga spanning a century of Victoriana, empire, hatreds and love affairs. 'A marvellous blend of *Gone with the Wind* and *The Thorn Birds*. You will enjoy every page' – *Daily Mirror*

☐ **Kingsley's Touch** John Collee £1.95

'Gripping . . . I recommend this chilling and elegantly written medical thriller' – *Daily Express*. 'An absolutely outstanding storyteller' – *Daily Telegraph*

☐ **The Far Pavilions** M. M. Kaye £4.95

Holding all the romance and high adventure of nineteenth-century India, M. M. Kaye's magnificent, now famous, novel has at its heart the passionate love of an Englishman for Juli, his Indian princess. 'Wildly exciting' – *Daily Telegraph*

ENGLISH AND AMERICAN
LITERATURE IN PENGUINS

☐ *Emma* **Jane Austen** £1.25

'I am going to take a heroine whom no one but myself will much like,' declared Jane Austen of Emma, her most spirited and controversial heroine in a comedy of self-deceit and self-discovery.

☐ *Tender is the Night* **F. Scott Fitzgerald** £2.95

Fitzgerald worked on seventeen different versions of this novel, and its obsessions – idealism, beauty, dissipation, alcohol and insanity – were those that consumed his own marriage and his life.

☐ *The Life of Johnson* **James Boswell** £2.95

Full of gusto, imagination, conversation and wit, Boswell's immortal portrait of Johnson is as near a novel as a true biography can be, and still regarded by many as the finest 'life' ever written. This shortened version is based on the 1799 edition.

☐ *A House and its Head* **Ivy Compton-Burnett** £4.95

In a novel 'as trim and tidy as a hand-grenade' (as Pamela Hansford Johnson put it), Ivy Compton-Burnett penetrates the facade of a conventional, upper-class Victorian family to uncover a chasm of violent emotions – jealousy, pain, frustration and sexual passion.

☐ *The Trumpet Major* **Thomas Hardy** £1.50

Although a vein of unhappy unrequited love runs through this novel, Hardy also draws on his warmest sense of humour to portray Wessex village life at the time of the Napoleonic wars.

☐ *The Complete Poems of Hugh MacDiarmid*

☐ Volume One £8.95
☐ Volume Two £8.95

The definitive edition of work by the greatest Scottish poet since Robert Burns, edited by his son Michael Grieve, and W. R. Aitken.

ENGLISH AND AMERICAN
LITERATURE IN PENGUINS

☐ *Main Street* **Sinclair Lewis**   £4.95

The novel that added an immortal chapter to the literature of America's Mid-West, *Main Street* contains the comic essence of Main Streets everywhere.

☐ *The Compleat Angler* **Izaak Walton**   £2.50

A celebration of the countryside, and the superiority of those in 1653, as now, who love *quietnesse, vertue* and, above all, *Angling.* 'No fish, however coarse, could wish for a doughtier champion than Izaak Walton' – Lord Home

☐ *The Portrait of a Lady* **Henry James**   £2.50

'One of the two most brilliant novels in the language', according to F. R. Leavis, James's masterpiece tells the story of a young American heiress, prey to fortune-hunters but not without a will of her own.

☐ *Hangover Square* **Patrick Hamilton**   £3.95

Part love story, part thriller, and set in the publands of London's Earls Court, this novel caught the conversational tone of a whole generation in the uneasy months before the Second World War.

☐ *The Rainbow* **D. H. Lawrence**   £2.50

Written between *Sons and Lovers* and *Women in Love*, *The Rainbow* covers three generations of Brangwens, a yeoman family living on the borders of Nottinghamshire.

☐ *Vindication of the Rights of Woman*
   Mary Wollstonecraft   £2.95

Although Walpole once called her 'a hyena in petticoats', Mary Wollstonecraft's vision was such that modern feminists continue to go back and debate the arguments so powerfully set down here.

CLASSICS IN TRANSLATION
IN PENGUINS

☐ *The Treasure of the City of Ladies*
  Christine de Pisan   £2.95

This practical survival handbook for women (whether royal courtiers or prostitutes) paints a vivid picture of their lives and preoccupations in France, *c.* 1405. First English translation.

☐ *La Regenta* **Leopoldo Alas**   £10.95

This first English translation of this Spanish masterpiece has been acclaimed as 'a major literary event' – *Observer*. 'Among the select band of "world novels" ... outstandingly well translated' – John Bayley in the *Listener*

☐ *Metamorphoses* **Ovid**   £2.95

The whole of Western literature has found inspiration in Ovid's poem, a golden treasury of myths and legends that are linked by the theme of transformation.

☐ *Darkness at Noon* **Arthur Koestler**   £2.50

'Koestler approaches the problem of ends and means, of love and truth and social organization, through the thoughts of an Old Bolshevik, Rubashov, as he awaits death in a G.P.U. prison' – *New Statesman*

☐ *War and Peace* **Leo Tolstoy**   £4.95

'A complete picture of human life;' wrote one critic, 'a complete picture of the Russia of that day; a complete picture of everything in which people place their happiness and greatness, their grief and humiliation.'

☐ *The Divine Comedy: 1 Hell* **Dante**   £2.25

A new translation by Mark Musa, in which the poet is conducted by the spirit of Virgil down through the twenty-four closely described circles of hell.